Sport: Law and Practice

Contributors

Richard Baldwin
David Becker
Alasdair Bell
Stephen Boyd
Caroline Chilvers
Jeff Chue
Max Duthie
Matt Eccles
Charles Flint QC
Paul Goulding QC
Margaret Gray
David Griffith-Jones QC
Paul Harris
Serena Hedley-Dent
Mark Hoskins
Dr Mark James
Satish Khandke
Clive Lawrence
Elizabeth Leggatt
Paul Manning
Richard Moran
Jane Mulcachy
David Pannick QC
Adrian Parkhouse
Parul Patel
Warren Phelops
Dinah Rose
Richard Verow
Karena Vleck
David Walker
Trevor Watkins
Claire Weir

Sport: Law and Practice

Adam Lewis
Jonathan Taylor

Butterworths
LexisNexis™

Members of the LexisNexis Group worldwide

United Kingdom	LexisNexis Butterworths Tolley, a Division of Reed Elsevier (UK) Ltd, Halsbury House, 35 Chancery Lane, LONDON, WC2A 1EL, and 4 Hill Street, EDINBURGH EH2 3JZ
Argentina	LexisNexis Argentina, BUENOS AIRES
Australia	LexisNexis Butterworths, CHATSWOOD, New South Wales
Austria	LexisNexis Verlag ARD Orac GmbH & Co KG, VIENNA
Canada	LexisNexis Butterworths, MARKHAM, Ontario
Chile	LexisNexis Chile Ltda, SANTIAGO DE CHILE
Czech Republic	Nakladatelství Orac sro, PRAGUE
France	Editions du Juris-Classeur SA, PARIS
Hong Kong	LexisNexis Butterworths, HONG KONG
Hungary	HVG-Orac, BUDAPEST
India	LexisNexis Butterworths, NEW DELHI
Ireland	Butterworths (Ireland) Ltd, DUBLIN
Italy	Giuffrè Editore, MILAN
Malaysia	Malayan Law Journal Sdn Bhd, KUALA LUMPUR
New Zealand	LexisNexis Butterworths, WELLINGTON
Poland	Wydawnictwo Prawnicze LexisNexis, WARSAW
Singapore	LexisNexis Butterworths, SINGAPORE
South Africa	LexisNexis Butterworths, DURBAN
Switzerland	Stämpfli Verlag AG, BERNE
USA	LexisNexis, DAYTON, Ohio

A CIP Catalogue record for this book is available from the British Library.

ISBN 0 406 945 926

Typeset by Thomson Litho Ltd, East Kilbride, Scotland.
Printed by and bound in Great Britain by Antony Rowe Ltd, Chippenham, Wilts.

ISBN 0-406-94592-6

9 780406 945921

FOREWORD

Sport has changed. A relatively few years ago the idea that there would be any demand or need for a book devoted exclusively to law and practice in relation to sport would have been regarded as surprising. Those involved in sport would then probably have been of the view that the more limited the interaction between the law and sport the better. The protection and regulation of a sport, and of those engaged in it, could safely be left in the hands of the appropriate governing body, be it a club, county, national or international organisation. However, anyone who had had any exposure to the kind of problems which can arise in relation to sport, and to those engaged in it, would not take that view today.

Why the change? The nature of sport and the place it has in society has changed. While there are still fortunately areas of sporting activity which can organise themselves without the help of lawyers or legal institutions, in virtually every sport there are activities which are no longer amateur, even though amateurs may be engaged in them. These are professional and often highly professional commercial operations. Furthermore, very substantial financial sums can be at stake, both for the sportsmen and women and the organisations to which they belong. There is also a media dimension which must not be ignored, since it can magnify the scale of the issues involved.

Because of these developments the involvement of the law is inevitable. The extremely wide range of issues which can be raised is demonstrated by the contents list of *Sport: Law and Practice*. The variety of subjects with which it has been found necessary to deal took me by surprise. However, each of the subjects contained in the five Parts are of particular concern to those engaged in sport. In addition, I have no doubt that each subject will benefit from a treatment which concentrates on its significance for sport.

Sport and the law is therefore already a subject of considerable importance. Those engaged in the administration of the sport and their advisors will find it enormously helpful to have a book which tackles the subject from their perspective. I am confident that this book will be of great value to them and that that value will increase as time passes. Although the general principles of the law are the same in the field of sport as they are in relation to other activities giving rise to similar problems, the application of those principles to sport does give rise to particular difficulties, especially because of the constraints as to time peculiar to sport.

It is because of the particular constraints that arise in giving effect to the law in the context of sport that this book will be of particular value. I congratulate the editors on producing a new textbook which will no doubt acquire the reputation of being one of the leaders in its field.

The Rt Hon Lord Woolf of Barnes
Lord Chief Justice of England and Wales
November 2002

PREFACE

In the editors' view, the publication of this book signals the maturing of the market for the provision of legal services to those active and involved in the sports sector, be they governing bodies, event organisers, promoters, clubs, broadcasters, sponsors, other commercial partners, agents, sportsmen and women, or others. As Lord Woolf indicates in his Foreword, whereas in the sleepy days of amateurism sport could afford to eschew the law, in the modern age of sport as big business, where the standards are professional and the rewards commensurately large, high quality legal advice is a prerequisite. Furthermore, that advice must necessarily be specialist advice, since (as Lord Woolf also explains), '[a]lthough the general principles of the law are the same in the field of sport as they are in relation to other activities giving rise to similar problems, the application of those principles to sport does give rise to particular difficulties ...'.

This book does *not* seek to address whether there is such a thing as sports law, still less whether there should be, because that is an issue of academic rather than practical interest. Instead, the book consciously avoids consideration of this and some of the other theoretical issues that have occupied certain of its predecessors. It focuses instead on assisting the reader in the provision of realistic and informed advice to clients active in the sports sector, and in particular addressing particular practical problems that have been demonstrated to arise in that sector. Irrespective of whether the principles that are (or may be) applied to those problems are sufficiently developed or homogenous to warrant identifying them as a separate area of law, those problems exist and have to be faced on a day-to-day basis, and those principles have been, and are continually being, adapted to that end. This book is meant to be a tool to assist the reader in solving the problems using those adapted principles.

That said, the editors share the belief of many writers in the field that in at least some areas, for example where international institutions such as the Court of Arbitration for Sport review the decisions of sports governing bodies, a separate and distinct body of law inspired by general principles of law common to all states is in the process of development. This is discussed further in Chapter E4 (The Regulation of Drug Use in Sport). Equally, the extent of the adaptation by the English courts of existing principles of challenge to address the particular circumstances of sports governing bodies' decisions (a process led by the contributor of the Foreword, Lord Woolf, in *Wilander* and *Modahl*, and described in detail in Chapter A3: Challenges in the Courts to the Actions of Sports

Governing Bodies) is well on the way to the construction of a model for review of such decisions analogous to the public law model, where previously there was much greater uncertainty. In addition, the European Commission and Court of Justice have developed specialised concepts in order to distinguish between arrangements of an 'inherently sporting nature' that are outside the ambit of the competition and free movement rules, and arrangements relating to the commercial exploitation of a sport, which are not, a process described in Chapter B2 (The EC and UK Competition Rules and Sport).

Why is this book said to be a mark of the maturity of the market for the provision of legal services to the sports sector? Because it is only in the last decade or so that the commercial value of sport has been properly realised and exploited to its maximum potential, and therefore it is only in that period that the stakes have become high enough for disputes about participation, ownership and control to crystallise and find their way into the courts on a regular basis. During that period, relevant legal authorities and practical guidance have been sparse, scattered and difficult to locate and access.

More recently, as the corpus of relevant materials has grown in size, a number of books have been produced on 'sports law', some of more practical assistance than others, but each addressing only selected topics of particular interest to their authors. This is the first work (to the editors' knowledge) that seeks to provide a comprehensive treatment of the issues that can arise under English law in the sports sector, and that seeks to collect together in one place the various disparate and scattered authorities and materials pertinent to the resolution of those issues.

On the other hand, this book is designed to be more than a mere reference work. It is intended to be a practical resource, helping its readers deal with situations where the law, and how it is applied in practice, affect the organisation, playing and commercial exploitation of sport as a major area of social, recreational and business activity. It seeks to cover the range of relationships and issues that arise between state, governing bodies, clubs, players or other individual participants, and commercial partners. It deals with both contentious and non-contentious aspects of these relationships and issues. Its contributors are all experts in their respective fields as they apply to the sports sector (individual profiles of each author follow this preface), and the reader therefore will receive the benefit of the substantial expertise and experience of leading practitioners working on a daily basis at the cutting edge of the law in this sector. The aim in each chapter, to the extent possible, has been to set down and substantiate practical, reliable and established propositions of law and practice in the context of sport that can form the starting point for advice and argument in particular matters.

The structure of the book is based on the syllabus that has been developed for the one-year, part-time Postgraduate Certificate in Sports Law offered by King's College London. Jonathan Taylor runs that course as Director of Studies in Sports Law at KCL, and both Jonathan and Adam Lewis, as well as several of the other contributors to this book, teach on the course. The KCL course seeks to provide its students with an introduction to the practical legal issues that confront those active in the sports sector. This book builds on that introduction by providing a comprehensive treatment of the issues, for their faster and more efficient practical resolution.

The five separate sections of the book, based again on the structure of the KCL course, have been identified simply as convenient sub-divisions of the area, and there will obviously be a degree of overlap between them. Indeed, in the process of organisation and presentation of the material gathered for this book, the editors have encountered various difficulties of classification, but no apology is made if certain issues are addressed in more than one place in this book, since it is believed that the authors' various comments to be useful in each case. It has also been found to be the case that, notwithstanding the scope of the project, nevertheless various issues have received less consideration than the editors would have liked, or indeed in some cases no consideration at all, but it is hoped to rectify that where appropriate in the future, and in the meantime it is trusted that the reader will find practical guidance and useful references on the core issues that arise most regularly in practice.

The first section of the book, *Part A – Legal Control of the Sports Sector*, lays the foundation for what follows by describing the 'constitutional' landscape of the sports sector, ie the location, hierarchy and limitations of regulatory power exercised within the sector. The limited extent to which the UK government regulates the sector is described, revealing the autonomous self-regulatory role assumed by the voluntary sports movement, in particular by the application of their rules through disciplinary and internal dispute resolution proceedings. The limits on that self-regulation are then examined, and specifically the role of the courts and external arbitral bodies in reviewing the decisions of governing bodies, and the legal bases on which (and the extent to which) they are prepared to interfere with those decisions. In this context the extent to which the Human Rights Act 1998 has influenced the position is also considered.

Part B – European Community Law and Sport, examines the increasing influence of European Community law on decisions in the context of sport, from the promotion of sport as a cultural activity to its regulation under the competition and free movement rules. The section establishes clearly, lest anyone was in any doubt after the seminal 1995 decision of the European Court of Justice in the *Bosman* case, that those acting or advising in the sports sector must be fully aware of the potential impact of EC law on the legality of the decision or course of conduct under consideration.

Part C – Organisational Issues for Sports Entities, deals with the various legal structures available for the organisation of sports entities, as well as matters relating to their taxation, financing and risk management techniques, including insurance. These are the basic building-blocks of legal advice and assistance to such entities.

Part D – The Commercialisation of Sports Events, examines the practical issues that fall to be addressed in the course of developing a commercial programme around a sports event or other property. This entire topic is confronted with the basic threshold problem that English law does not recognise the existence of any proprietary rights per se in a sporting spectacle. Instead, such rights have to be created and protected through control of access to the venue for the event, contractual control over those participating in the event, and use of the protection offered by intellectual property law. That process is examined in Part D, as is the analogous issue of the scope of the right of an individual sportsman or woman under English law to control the commercial use of his or her image or persona (another area of huge practical importance, with several important recent decisions). The section then provides extensive practical guidance in relation to the manner of exploitation of those proprietary rights, in the specific areas of broadcasting and new media, sponsorship and supply agreements, licensing and merchandising, hospitality and representation agreements.

The last section of the book, *Part E – Issues for Individual Sportsmen and Women*, seeks to analyse the key issues confronting individual athletes and their advisors, namely in the context of their contractual relations with clubs and event organisers, player transfers, discrimination, the regulation of drug use, civil and criminal liability for on-field conduct, and tax and financial planning.

Every book has to have a cut-off date for publication, and for this book that date is 1 September 2002. As a result, it has not been possible to address various important developments that have arisen during the proofing stage, including in particular the European Court of Justice's seminal decision issued on 12 November 2002 in *Arsenal Football Club v Reed*, rejecting the High Court's narrow construction of the requirement of trade mark 'use' for infringement purposes, and thereby vindicating the exclusive right of sports trade mark owners to use those marks to underpin sports merchandising programmes.

Notwithstanding the various omissions mandated by limitations of time and space, however, the editors hope that the book proves to be of use. Furthermore, as this book is meant to be a tool to be used in the practical resolution of problems, the editors would welcome any comments, criticism or contributions in the form of experience or accounts or copies of relevant decisions that readers might wish to make available, for inclusion in any supplement or later edition that may be published. The editors' e-mail address for this purpose is **sportlawandpractice@blackstonechambers.com**.

The editors wish to record their enormous gratitude to all of those whose contributions have made this book possible, including Lord Woolf (for his Foreword), each of the author-contributors (listed individually after this preface), Owen Durnin and Ben Johnson at Butterworths, Nicola Brown and the overnight secretaries at Hammonds, Martin Smith and Gary Oliver and the other clerks at Blackstone Chambers, and The Faculty of Law at King's College, London.

Last but certainly not least, the editors wish to apologise for their long absences from, and to dedicate their efforts on this book to, their respective much-loved and cherished (and long-suffering) families, namely Beate, Magnus and Marianne Mjaaland Lewis, and Kate, Sophie and Emily Taylor.

Adam Lewis
Blackstone Chambers
Temple

Jonathan Taylor
Hammonds Solicitors
London

December 2002

AUTHOR PROFILES

EDITORS

Adam Lewis

Adam Lewis is a barrister at Blackstone Chambers, London. He regularly advises national and international governing bodies, clubs and players from a wide range of sports, and businesses involved with those sports. He regularly appears on their behalf before the English courts, the Court of Arbitration for Sport and other arbitral bodies, and the domestic and European regulatory authorities. He lectures on the Postgraduate Certificate in Sports Law course at King's College London and speaks regularly at sports law conferences. His background is as an EC and public law specialist. Between 1991 and 1994 Adam Lewis worked in Brussels, for the EU in the cabinet of the European Commissioner responsible for competition, and for White & Case (Brussels). His practice covers a wide range of contentious sports-related issues, including challenges to the actions and decisions of sports governing bodies, competition and free movement issues, doping and disciplinary proceedings, and disputes between clubs and players. His entry in the Chambers & Partners' Directory for 2002–03 describes him as 'the top junior in the country' for Sports Law.

Jonathan Taylor

Jonathan Taylor is a partner and head of the Sports Law Group at Hammonds Solicitors. He is also Director of Studies in Sports Law at King's College, London, where he runs KCL's annual Postgraduate Certificate in Sports Law (www.kclsportslaw.co.uk), and a board member of the British Association of Sport and the Law. Jonathan has law degrees from Oxford and Virginia and is qualified to practise law in both England and New York State. From 1990 to 1997, Jonathan worked in New York as a commercial litigator for Manhattan-based Schulte Roth & Zabel LLP. In 1997, he joined sports specialists Townleys Solicitors in London. Since then, Jonathan has worked exclusively in the sports sector, advising domestic and international governing bodies, event organisers, commercial agencies, sponsors and broadcasters, clubs and individuals on the full range of sports-related legal issues, including in particular: (1) governance and regulatory matters, including anti-doping and other disciplinary matters; (2) competition law and sport; and (3) dispute resolution and sport. He is recognised as an expert in the field by

Chambers' Guide to the Legal Profession 2002–2003. Townleys merged with Hammonds in 2001.

CONTRIBUTORS

Richard Baldwin

Richard is a senior partner in Deloitte & Touche, based in the London office, leading the firm's team of seven sports tax consultants. Richard has specialised in advising sport for nearly 25 years. He specialises in taxation, providing advice to sports governing bodies, leagues, clubs and sportsmen and sportswomen. He has led discussions with the tax authorities on behalf of sport, eg in relation to the taxation of transfer fees, the availability of tax relief for capital expenditure on sports facilities and clarification of the taxation of National Lottery grants received by sportsmen and sportswomen. His work with sport has enabled him to identify issues common within sport, which can be approached for the benefit of everyone. He has been working closely with the Tax Working Party, which was formed around two years ago by the Department for Culture, Media and Sport to improve tax reliefs for sports clubs. He speaks regularly on the taxation of sport and has written extensively on the subject.

David Becker

David Becker currently practises as an associate solicitor in the Sports Law Group at Hammonds Solicitors. He is internationally qualified and has a Postgraduate Certificate in Sports Law from King's College, London. David is head of the Player Representation, Image Rights and Endorsement Group at Hammonds and specialises in player-related matters, employment and general commercial and corporate sports law. He has advised a number of international football players, world-ranked boxers, World Rally drivers and Premiership football clubs, and has appeared on BBC Breakfast TV and Radio Five Live. David has a keen interest in sport and has completed 27 marathons including the 7-day Marathon de Sables in the Sahara. He is also a motivational speaker and leader in the field of accelerated learning strategies, having competed in the World Memory Championships and Mind Sports Olympiad.

Alasdair Bell

Alasdair Bell is a partner in the EU/competition group at Olswang. He has considerable experience in both EU and UK competition law and practised in Brussels for many years before re-locating to London. He has been involved in many of the most significant cases in recent years concerning the application of EU competition law to sports rules and structures. This experience includes the Bosman case in 1995 and the re-structuring of the international player transfer system in 2001. He has also handled, on behalf of UEFA, a wide variety of competition law questions on issues such as central marketing of television rights, rules on cross-border broadcasting of football, regulations on common ownership of clubs, ticket distribution, 'breakaway' league projects, sponsorship arrangements, merchandising of 'official' equipment, territorial restrictions on ground movement, club licensing systems and salary cap structures. He is recognised as an expert in the field by publications such as 'Chambers Guide to the Legal Profession' and 'The Legal 500'.

Stephen Boyd

Stephen Boyd is a barrister practising from Selborne Chambers at 10 Essex Street, London WC2R 3AA. His practice comprises a broad range of commercial and property litigation. In 2001 he obtained the Postgraduate Certificate in Sports Law at King's College London and was named in Chambers Directory 2001–2002 as one of the leading juniors in the field. He is particularly interested in issues relating to celebrities' image rights and privacy. He is a CEDR-accredited mediator and a member of the Chartered Institute of Arbitrators and in 2002 was appointed to the Mediation Panel of the Sports Dispute Resolution Panel.

Caroline Chilvers

A graduate of York University, Caroline Chilvers trained as a solicitor at sports specialists Townleys, qualifying into Townleys' Dispute Resolution Group in 2001. She joined Hammonds as part of the Townleys merger in August 2001. Throughout her career, Caroline has worked almost exclusively on the resolution of disputes arising in the sports sector, by means of litigation, arbitration and other dispute resolution techniques. Caroline is currently on sabbatical.

Jeff Chue

Jeff Chue is an English solicitor. A Singaporean graduate of the postgraduate sports law programme at King's College, London, Jeff joined the World Sport Group in September 2002 and currently practises sports law in Asia. Prior to that, he practised sports law in London with international law firms Townleys and Hammond Suddards Edge. In the business of sport, Jeff specialises in corporate and commercial matters and has particular experience in the field of corporate governance as applied in the context of sports governance and administration. He has advised international governing bodies of sport (eg netball, water skiing, sailing, bowling, rugby) at strategic levels on organisational and corporate issues, and has also advised on commercial rights programmes in sport (eg golf, football, motor-racing, cricket).

Max Duthie

Max Duthie is a commercial litigator with Freehills in Melbourne, Australia (having worked previously in the UK for Slaughter and May, and sports law specialists Townleys/Hammond Suddards Edge). Max has worked for many years litigating disputes in the sports world, acting for national and international governing bodies, leagues/event organisers, sports marketing companies, clothing and equipment suppliers, sponsors, professional clubs and individual athletes. He has brought and defended cases in the High Court and County Court, the Supreme Court of Victoria, the Australian Federal Court, the International Court of Arbitration, the Court for Arbitration in Sport (CAS), and FIFA's Players' Status Committee, and before a number of sports disciplinary tribunals (including those of the Football Association, the Rugby Football Union, the European Rugby Cup and the National Greyhound Racing Club). Max specialises in disciplinary issues and in all types of contractual disputes (including those relating to broadcast rights, sponsorship rights, player agreements, agency agreements and ticketing). Max is a Cambridge Blue and a former professional rugby union player. He supports Manchester City FC.

Matt Eccles

Matthew works as an in-house solicitor at Octagon CSI. Octagon CSI is a world-leader in the negotiation, production and marketing of international sports for television. Matthew previously worked in the broadcast and new media group at Townleys Sports Lawyers and Hammond Suddards Edge. Matthew's particular area of specialism is the creation, protection and exploitation of sports-related content.

Charles Flint QC

Charles Flint QC is joint head of Blackstone Chambers, practising in commercial and public law. In the field of sports law he has advised and acted both for players and sports organisations, including Rugby Unions, Grand Prix teams, the International Tennis Federation and the British Athletics Federation. He has appeared before a variety of sporting tribunals including the Court of Arbitration for Sport (CAS), the FIA, the IAAF and many national disciplinary bodies. He is a Fellow of the Chartered Institute of Arbitrators, a CEDR registered mediator and on the Sports Dispute Resolution Panel. For further details see www.blackstonechambers.com.

Paul Goulding QC

Paul Goulding QC is a member of Blackstone Chambers. He has acted in many sports law cases across a wide range of sports. In football, he has advised Premier and Nationwide league clubs, players and managers, and has appeared before a number of football tribunals. In Formula One, he has acted for constructors and drivers. In athletics, he appeared for the British Athletics Federation in the proceedings brought by Diane Modahl. He was counsel for the World Snooker Association in the proceedings brought by Stephen Hendry. In rugby, he has advised national rugby bodies as well as clubs and individuals. He is on the Chairmen's Panel of the Sports Dispute Resolution Panel. He is a Vice-President of the Employment Lawyers Association and General Editor of *European Employment Law and the UK*. He is also a qualified football coach and a member of the FA Coaches Association.

Margaret Gray

Margaret Gray is a barrister at Brick Court Chambers and is currently working as a référendaire to Judge Macken at the European Court of Justice. Her areas of practice include EC Law, Competition Law, Public Law, and Human Rights.

David Griffith-Jones QC

David Griffith-Jones QC was called to the Bar in 1975 and took silk in 2000. He is a Fellow of the Chartered Institute of Arbitrators and sits as a Recorder in the Crown and County Courts, as an Assistant Boundary Commissioner and on the Mental Health Review Tribunal. He is a well-known practitioner in sports law, in which he has wide experience, ranging from personal injury and disciplinary/doping cases to employment, commercial and other contractual disputes. He is regularly asked to arbitrate/mediate in sports disputes, is an accredited chairman for both the Sports Dispute Resolution Panel and the Chartered Institute of Arbitrators and has chaired individual Appeal Boards for bodies such as the Football Association and the British Olympic Association. He is also the author of Butterworth's *Law and the Business of Sport* (1997).

Paul Harris

Paul Harris is a barrister at Monckton Chambers, one of the leading commercial sets of Chambers at the Bar. In 2002–2003, under the Sports Law category, *Chambers & Partners* described 'Paul Harris of Monckton Chambers [as] a man most definitely on the rise ... '. *Legal 500* continued to recommend Paul Harris as a leading junior in European and competition law. Paul has an active sports law practice, covering areas such as salary caps, transfers, dominance of governing bodies, national team rights to players, commercial valuation of games, rights to league participation, sports broadcasting, and sports ground advertising. He also acts in sports employment and disciplinary matters. Paul frequently writes and seminars on sports law topics, including, most recently, salary caps and breakaway sports competitions. In 2001, Paul appeared in the House of Lords in *TVDanmark*, concerning the broadcasting of world cup football matches under the EC Directive 'TV Without Frontiers'. Paul is a member of the Bar Sports Law Group and an officer of the British Association for Sport and Law. Sadly, Paul is a Manchester City fan.

Serena Hedley-Dent

Serena Hedley-Dent is a member of the Sports Group at Farrer & Co. She works closely with Karena Vleck and specialises in advising sports bodies and other clients in the sports industry on commercial, disciplinary and constitutional matters. Her particular areas of expertise are sponsorship, broadcasting and merchandising agreements, disciplinary procedures and rules, doping cases, and advice on constitutions both corporate and unincorporated. More generally, Serena advises a variety of clients in relation to commercial and company law, data protection and competition law issues. She is a member of the British Association for Sport and Law, the Association of Regulatory and Disciplinary Lawyers and the Union Internationale des Avocats (UIA).

Mark Hoskins

Mark Hoskins is a barrister at Brick Court Chambers. His areas of practice include Sports Law, EC Law, Competition Law, Public Law, and Human Rights. He has worked as a référendaire at the European Court of Justice and is a current member of the B Panel to the Crown. He is co-author (with Mark Brealey) of *Remedies in EC Law* (2nd edn, Sweet & Maxwell) and has appeared in over 50 cases before the Court of Justice and the Court of First Instance.

Dr Mark James

Mark James is a lecturer in the School of Law at Manchester Metropolitan University where he lectures in Sports Law and Criminal Law. He runs both the

MA (Sport and the Law) and the undergraduate option in Sports Law at MMU. His PhD analysed the role of consent to injuries in contact sports and he has published widely on the legal issues surrounding sports injuries and spectator violence. Mark is a co-author of Cavendish's student textbook 'Sports Law', is the Assistant Editor of the *Sport and the Law Journal* and the Reviews Editor of *Entertainment Law*.

Satish Khandke

Satish joined sports specialists Townleys Solicitors in January 2001 as the Head of its Corporate Department, after spending seven years with the Corporate Department of Baker & McKenzie. Following Townleys' merger with Hammonds, Satish now heads the corporate team within Hammonds' Sports Law Group. Satish advises clients involved in the sports industry sector on corporate matters, including M&A, joint venture, takeover, venture capital and other capital-raising transactions, as well as commercial matters such as sponsorship, agency, event management and the exploitation of media rights. Satish also advises sports governing bodies and commercial entities involved in sport on all aspects of corporate governance and administration.

Clive Lawrence

Clive Lawrence graduated from Downing College, Cambridge in 1990, and received First Class Honours in his Law Society Finals in 1991. He joined McCormicks Solicitors of Leeds that same year, and was appointed as an associate of McCormicks in 1993 and a partner in 1996. McCormicks is a commercial law firm in Leeds and Harrogate recognised as one of the leading practices in the country in the areas of sports law and media law. The firm acts for a broad range of sports clubs, individuals and governing bodies. Clive is a partner in the corporate and commercial department, dealing particularly with all aspects of intellectual property, sports law and media law. Clive was sport and sponsorship editor of 'IP Business' Magazine and is co-author with Peter McCormick of McCormicks and Richard Verow of 'Sport, Business and the Law' (Jordans). He writes and lectures widely in relation to intellectual property law.

Elizabeth Leggatt

Elizabeth Leggatt is a solicitor within the Clarke Willmott & Clarke corporate team with a particular emphasis on transactional work in the sporting environment.

Paul Manning

A graduate of University College, Oxford, Paul attended the Inns of Court School of Law 1996-97, before successfully completing pupillage at the Chambers of Michael Parroy QC. Paul joined Townleys in January 1999, and, following its merger with Hammonds in August 2001, now works in the Dispute Resolution Group of the Sports Law Group at Hammonds. Paul advises on a wide variety of contentious matters for (among others), Bacardi-France, British Lions Limited, the Six Nations Committee, and the International Tennis Federation. Paul specialises in all aspects of dispute resolution, with a particular emphasis on ADR, and the litigious aspects of intellectual property and internet law.

Richard Moran

Richard Moran graduated from the University of Leeds in 1993, and obtained a Post Graduate Diploma in Legal Practice (with distinction) in 1994. He joined McCormicks Solicitors in August 1994, was admitted as a solicitor in 1996 and became a partner in 1999. McCormicks is a commercial law firm in Leeds and Harrogate recognised as one of the leading practices in the country in the areas of sports law and media law. The firm acts for a broad range of sports clubs, individuals and governing bodies. A partner in the corporate and commercial department, Richard deals particularly with commercial contract and corporate matters.

Jane Mulcahy

Jane Mulcahy is a barrister at Blackstone Chambers specialising in sport, employment, human rights and public law. She regularly advises football teams from all the English leagues, and is involved in disputes concerning rugby union and motor racing. She is the case editor of the International Sports Law Review.

David Pannick QC

David Pannick QC practises from Blackstone Chambers in the Temple. He is also a Fellow of All Souls College, Oxford, and contributes a fortnightly column on the law to *The Times* newspaper. He has acted in a number of important sports law cases over the years, including athletics cases involving Diane Modahl and Linford Christie, the disciplinary proceedings against the South African player, Brendon Venter, during the Rugby World Cup in 1999, and Formula One cases for Maclaren. He advised the Premier League in its employment law dispute in 2001 with the Professional Footballers' Association. In 2002, he acted for Wimbledon FC in challenging in arbitration proceedings the refusal of the Football League to allow the club to move to Milton Keynes. He has sat on disciplinary tribunals for the governing bodies of tennis, football and rugby union.

Adrian Parkhouse

Adrian Parkhouse is Head of the Litigation Team at Farrer & Co. His practice is broad, encompassing a wide variety of disputes and modes of resolution. In the area of sports law his advice has been primarily to governing bodies and has included defence of challenges by way of applications for judicial review, constitutional disputes, contract disputes and the conduct of doping cases. He has also advised on disciplinary procedures in governing body constitutions.

Parul Patel

Parul Patel, Sports Marketing Legal Counsel, graduated with a law and business studies (LLB Hons) degree from the University of Birmingham. She qualified as a solicitor in 1998 after two years of training with Eversheds where she began developing her career as a sports lawyer. Upon qualification she moved to a niche law firm in Bristol, specialising in player representation, including the England rugby union team, the Irish rugby team and a number of high profile international rugby players. In 2000 Parul joined Townleys in the Sponsorship and Event Management Department where she expanded her experience in event management and sponsorship contracts whilst continuing the development of her expertise in player issues and in particular the FIFA transfer system. Parul gained much media exposure and became a recognised expert in issues relating to player transfers, player contracts and the business of agents. Parul is currently a lawyer working in-house with a leading global sporting goods company advising on a wide range of sports marketing contracts and commercial and strategic issues affecting the sports marketing industry.

Warren Phelops

Warren is the partner who heads up the Technology Media & Sport Group at Nicholson Graham & Jones. He joined Nicholsons in 1993 from rival City of London law firm Slaughter & May, where he worked as an assistant in one of their corporate and commercial groups, having also trained there. He specialises in business issues relating to sport: in particular rights ownership and exploitation; corporate structuring and strategy; joint ventures; commercial and media. He regularly writes for leading sports industry and legal journals and his opinions are often quoted in the press and on television and radio. He has spoken at a number of domestic and international sports business conferences, is a Director of the Institute of Sports Sponsorship, and sits on the editorial boards of the International Sports Law Review and World Online Gambling Law Report. The clients he has advised cover the full range of businesses operating in the sports industry, including financiers, media companies, domestic and international governing bodies, sponsors, clubs, players, merchandisers/kit manufacturers, event owners, promoters, hospitality and travel companies, and insurers. He has also advised on some of the biggest or most cutting edge deals in sport, particularly football, rugby and cricket. He would like to thank his colleagues at Nicholsons for the tremendous help he received from them in preparing the two chapters on sponsorship and hospitality, particularly Sarah Stone, Mike Sutton, Adam Morallee and Lucy Otterwell.

Dinah Rose

Dinah Rose is a barrister practising at Blackstone Chambers. She specialises in public law, discrimination and employment law, human rights, European law and sports law. Dinah Rose represented Jane Couch in her employment tribunal case against the British Boxing Board of Control, which secured women's right to box professionally, and represented Kenny Dalglish in his claim for wrongful dismissal against Newcastle United FC. She has appeared in many leading discrimination cases, in national courts and before the European Court of Justice. She is married with two children.

Richard Verow

Richard Verow is a senior manager in the in-house legal team at UEFA. He has worked for over ten years in the sports, media and entertainment industries.

Karena Vleck

Karena Vleck is Head of the Sports Group at Farrer & Co. She provides specialist advice for sports governing and representative bodies, individual sports people, sports charities and sponsors. Her areas of practice include sponsorship, broadcasting, merchandising and representation agreements, disciplinary procedures and rules, doping cases, formations and advice on constitutions both corporate and unincorporated, intellectual property, charity and company and commercial law. Her clients include UK Athletics, the British Canoe Union, The Football Association, the British Paralympic Association, the British Olympic Association, Sport England, the Central Council of Physical Recreation, the All England Netball Association and the Lawn Tennis Association. She is a committee member of the British Association for Sport and Law and a member of the Association of Regulatory and Disciplinary Lawyers.

David Walker

David Walker is a solicitor with Clarke Willmott & Clarke, Southampton. He provides sports clients with a range of commercial advice and has a particular interest in the protection, exploitation and enforcement of intellectual property rights. He has a number of high profile clients including Formula One drivers. David is a keen sportsman himself and has an in-depth knowledge of the motor racing industry.

Trevor Watkins

Trevor Watkins is a partner in Clarke Willmott & Clarke, Southampton. He has a thorough understanding of modern sports business, having previously rescued and then run a professional soccer team, AFC Bournemouth. Recognised as a sports law expert by the Legal Experts Directory, he is also recommended as an expert in dispute resolution. Trevor advises many professional sporting teams, sponsors and investors in maximising the potential of their involvement in sport. As a divisional representative to the Football League, he was instrumental in developing their response to the proposed changes to the transfer system. Outside of football, Trevor advises clients in the fields of Formula One, horse racing, rugby and other motor racing competitions. He is also a director of Supporters Direct, the government initiative he helped to found that has taken a key role in helping football address its future.

Claire Weir

Claire Weir is a barrister at Blackstone Chambers, specialising in discrimination and employment law and judicial review. She appeared for Diane Modahl in the House of Lords in her claim arising out of her suspension from athletics following a positive drugs test. She was also instructed (with Dinah Rose) by Kenny Dalgleish in proceedings concerning his departure from Newcastle FC. She has acted for a range of bodies in employment tribunals, including football clubs and even a football commentator. She is a contributor to Sweet and Maxwell's 'Human Rights Practice'.

CONTENTS

PART A

LEGAL CONTROL OF THE SPORTS SECTOR

CHAPTER A1

REGULATION OF THE SPORTS SECTOR

CHAPTER A2

DISCIPLINARY PROCEEDINGS AND INTERNAL DISPUTE RESOLUTION

CHAPTER A3

CHALLENGES IN THE COURTS TO THE ACTIONS OF SPORTS GOVERNING BODIES

CHAPTER A4

THE HUMAN RIGHTS ACT 1998 AND SPORT

CHAPTER A5

ARBITRATION AND ADR IN SPORT

PART B

EUROPEAN COMMUNITY LAW AND SPORT

CHAPTER B1

EUROPEAN COMMUNITY SPORTS POLICY

CHAPTER B2

EC AND UK COMPETITION RULES AND SPORT

CHAPTER B3

EC FREE MOVEMENT RULES AND SPORT

PART C

ORGANISATIONAL ISSUES FOR SPORTS ENTITIES

CHAPTER C1

ORGANISATIONAL STRUCTURES FOR SPORTS ENTITIES

CHAPTER C2

TAXATION OF SPORTS ORGANISATIONS

CHAPTER C3

FINANCING SPORT

CHAPTER C4

RISK MANAGEMENT

PART D

THE COMMERCIALISATION OF SPORTS EVENTS

CHAPTER D1

PROPRIETARY RIGHTS IN SPORTS EVENTS

CHAPTER D2

VENUES

CHAPTER D3

IMAGE RIGHTS

CHAPTER D4

BROADCASTING AND NEW MEDIA

CHAPTER D5

SPORTS SPONSORSHIP

CHAPTER D6

MERCHANDISING AND LICENSING

CHAPTER D7

HOSPITALITY AGREEMENTS

CHAPTER D8

REPRESENTATION AGREEMENTS

PART E

ISSUES FOR INDIVIDUAL SPORTSMEN AND WOMEN

CHAPTER E1

PLAYERS' CONTRACTS WITH CLUBS, TEAMS AND EVENT ORGANISERS

CHAPTER E2

PLAYER TRANSFERS

CHAPTER E3

DISCRIMINATION

CHAPTER E4

THE REGULATION OF DRUG USE IN SPORT

CHAPTER E5

CIVIL LIABILITY FOR ON-FIELD CONDUCT

CHAPTER E6

SPORTS PARTICIPATION AND THE CRIMINAL LAW

CHAPTER E7

TAX AND FINANCIAL PLANNING FOR INDIVIDUALS

TABLE OF STATUTES

[all references are to paragraph number]

TABLE OF STATUTORY INSTRUMENTS

[all references are to paragraph number]

TABLE OF EUROPEAN LEGISLATION

[all references are to paragraph number]

TABLE OF CASES

[all references are to paragraph number]

A

B

D

E

F

G

H

I

J

K

L

M

N

O

P

R

S

T

U

X

Y

Z

Decisions of the European Court of Justice are listed below numerically. These decisions are also included in the preceding alphabetical list.

PART A

LEGAL CONTROL OF THE SPORTS SECTOR

CHAPTER A1

REGULATION OF THE SPORTS SECTOR

Jonathan Taylor (Hammonds) and **Caroline Chilvers** (Hammonds)

Contents

1 INTRODUCTION

A1.1 The aim of this opening chapter is to establish who governs sport in the United Kingdom. It reveals, by providing a basic overview of the role that the state plays in the regulation of the UK sports sector, that the sector is largely governed by the private sports movement in the UK, with the state in a not inactive but still very much secondary role. This establishes the basic constitutional framework of the UK sports sector, which is then developed in the remaining chapters of this first section of the book to provide a foundation for all that follows.

A1.2 In summary, the UK government has traditionally adopted a very non-interventionist approach to the UK sports sector. Sport has historically been regarded as a private affair between its participants, in the administration and regulation of which the government has little or no specific role to play. As the perception of sport as a potent instrument of public policy has developed, along with an appreciation of the 'feel-good' benefits of sporting success at the level of elite international competition, respective governments have slowly become more interested in the field. However, they have defined government sports policy narrowly and have stuck rigidly to the 'arm's length' principle of policy implementation via the Sports Councils, routinely resisting calls for greater and more direct government intervention.

A1.3 The present administration appears to have recognised more than most the potential of sport as an important policy tool, and has put more effort and resources into the development of a 'joined-up' government sports policy than any of its predecessors. However, it retains its predecessors' unwillingness to intervene directly in the sector, preferring to extend the 'arm's length' principle of policy implementation to encompass the private sports movement in partnership with the Sports Councils. The creation of that public-private partnership, fuelled by the flow of significant Lottery funds to sporting causes, has forced the government to seek reform and modernisation of some of the practices of the private sports movement, representing a degree of intervention in the administration of sport that departs significantly from the traditional model. At a fundamental level, however, the government continues to be deeply wary of intervening directly in the sports sector and remains far more comfortable leaving the private sports movement to keep its own house in order.

A1.4 The government's basic non-interventionist approach is outlined below, with an explanation of how it leaves the direct regulation of sport by and large to an autonomous private sports movement[1]. The chapter then discusses the roles and functions of the different governmental and quasi-governmental agencies involved in sport in the UK, before reviewing in brief the few direct legislative interventions into the sector, as well as the current administration's shift towards a public-private partnership, regulating the sector indirectly by conditioning governing body recognition and access to public funding on compliance with government policy objectives in the sector[2]. The chapter concludes by identifying a number of criticisms made of the government's current approach to the regulation of sport in the UK, the response to which will largely shape how the government's role in sport will look in the future[3].

1 See paras A1.5 to A1.30.
2 See paras A1.31 to A1.105.
3 See paras A1.106 to A1.127. It is worth noting that sport, while not specifically designated as a matter of EC competence in the Treaty of Rome, is subject (at least in so far as it constitutes an economic activity) to the Treaty provisions on free movement and competition (see Chapters B1 and B2). In addition, the institutions of the European Community, led by the Sports Unit of the Culture Directorate of the European Commission, are developing an EC sports policy that seeks both to inform the application of the free movement and competition rules in the sports sector and to further EC objectives in areas such as public order, doping and the like. While its work in this field can be queried on grounds of lack of jurisdiction, nevertheless a complete picture of governmental sports policy would not be complete without it, and it is therefore dealt with in some detail in Chapter B3.

2 THE NON-INTERVENTIONIST APPROACH TO THE REGULATION OF SPORT

A Sport as an instrument of public policy

A1.5 It is beyond dispute that sport forms an integral part of popular culture in the UK, capturing the hearts and minds of millions of people from every section of UK society. Millions of people participate in amateur sport as a healthy and comradely pastime. Millions and millions more 'consume' elite sport as an entertainment 'product'. Indeed, certain of the elite sports events are said to 'unite the nation; [to be] a shared point on the national calendar', part of our common heritage and an expression of our national identity[1].

1 Quote taken from appendix to a letter sent by the Department of Culture, Media and Sport in November 1997 to various sports bodies, identifying the criteria for designating events to which public access should be protected under the UK's 'listed events' legislation: see paras A1.80 to A1.92.

A1.6 This enormous public interest in sport gives it 'vast potential … as a policy tool to achieve wider social and political objectives'[1]. As Nelson Mandela once famously said:

> Sport has the power to change the world, the power to inspire, the power to unite people in a way that little else can. Sport can create hope where there was once only despair. It breaks down racial barriers. It laughs in the face of all kinds of discrimination. Sport speaks to people in a language they can understand.

1 Godfrey and Holtham *Sporting Lives: A Vision for Sport in the UK* (1999, IPPR), pp 5, 8. See also (2002) Guardian, 18 March: 'The case for taking sport more seriously rests on its vast untapped possibilities as a source of social cohesion and improved public health'.

A1.7 The European Commission has identified that sport fulfils an education function, a public health function, a social inclusion function, a cultural function and a recreational function, making it 'a particularly effective weapon in the fight against intolerance, racism, violence, alcohol and narcotics abuse'[1]. Similarly, the Central Council for Physical Recreation contends:

> Sport and recreation makes a real contribution to Government policies: improving education both at schools and through lifelong learning; encouraging a healthy lifestyle for all; promoting social inclusion by providing links to employment, reducing crime and promoting social integration; and bringing everyone together to celebrate national success[2].

1 European Commission, The Development and Prospects for Community Action in the Field of Sport (Brussels 1998). See also Labour Party manifesto, 2001: 'Arts and sports are key to our quality of life … [They] should not be seen as peripheral issues … [They] are vital to our identity and enjoyment as a country … Sport is a good health policy, a good crime reduction policy and a good way of building communities'. In its 1998 policy paper, *Using Sport in Europe to Combat Social Exclusion and Regenerate Communities*, the Department of Culture Media and Sport recognised that sport breaks down social barriers and could be 'very effective in regenerating communities and reducing crime. [Sport] should become an integral part of everyday life for as many people as possible'.

2 *Active Britain: A Manifesto for Sport and Recreation* (CCPR, May 2001).

A1.8 These are all seen as 'valid and legitimate reasons to justify government involvement in and funding of sport'[1].

1 Mr Justice Charles Dubin *Report of the Commission of Inquiry into the Use of Drugs and Banned Practices Intended to Increase Athletic Performance* (Ottawa 1990) at pp 517, 525.

B The interventionist model of regulation of the sports sector

A1.9 While references to an 'interventionist' model of sports regulation conjure up images of state-sponsored regimes going to extreme (and often unethical) lengths to use sport to score demagogic points on a world stage[1], in the modern sense it refers to a centralised approach, based on the premise that sport is a public function that the state has the right and the responsibility to deliver, achieved by implementing 'specific legislation on the structure and mandate of a significant part of the [nation's] sports movement'[2].

1 The obvious examples being the former Eastern Bloc countries, China and Cuba. See generally Houlihan 'The World Anti-Doping Agency: Prospects for Success' in *Drugs and Doping in Sport* (2001, Cavendish), pp 125–127.
2 See Chaker *Study on national sports legislation in Europe* (1999, Council of Europe Publishing), p 5.

A1.10 In countries adopting such an approach (for example, many southern and eastern European states), sporting activity is deemed a public good and therefore a social service responsibility of the state, with sports organisations created and existing by virtue of government licence and funding specifically in order to fulfil that responsibility as agents of the state. 'The state has a central role [in sport] in such countries. It endows sports federations with their right to exercise regulatory and disciplinary functions. These are thus public powers which are only delegated to federations as long as they comply with criteria of independence, legality and democracy. The powers can be withdrawn if these criteria are not met or the powers are abused. It is argued that interventionist sports policies produce uniform regulation, better governance, greater public accountability and prevent alternative governing bodies proliferating. Where state intervention is reinforced with state funding, the threat of de-recognition is a powerful tool for the state'[1].

1 Foster 'Can Sport Be Regulated By Europe?: An Analysis of Alternative Models' in Caigner & Gardiner (eds) *Professional Sport in the EU: Regulation and Re-Regulation* (2000, TMC Asser Press) at p 62.

A1.11 In France, for example, the Loi du Sport provides that 'the development of physical activities, sports, and high level sports is incumbent upon the State'[1]. France's Ministry of Sport is responsible for the promotion of sport to all age groups, and for the management and supervision of government grants to sports. The Ministry recognises one national governing body for each sport, and confers on that body the exclusive right to organise events and license participants in its sport in France, under delegated authority from the Ministry. In other words, the recognised sports governing body effectively functions by licence from, and as an organ of, the state. Without such a licence, no body can claim to govern a sport in France.

1 Act no. 84-610, July 16 1984, relating to the organisation and promotion of sport and physical activity, JO of 17 July 1984, Art 1, para 4.

A1.12 This has significant 'constitutional' consequences for those active in the sports sector. For example, as a quasi-public body exercising delegated sovereign powers, a French sports governing body may not recognise and give effect in France to disciplinary sanctions handed down by the international governing body of that sport (even if the French body is a member of that international governing body and has agreed to be bound by its globally applicable rules), if the disciplinary procedures followed by the sanctioning body are deemed to fall short of the standards required of French sports bodies under the Loi du Sport. Any French body that proposes to recognise such sanction can be challenged for acting *ultra vires*, ie beyond the scope of its delegated public powers, and ultimately risks being 'de-recognised', ie stripped of its constitutional authority to govern its sport in France.

C The non-interventionist model

A1.13 In contrast, the UK government, in common with many other northern and western European states, has traditionally taken a far less interventionist approach to sport[1]. Historically, the provision of sport has not been regarded as a public service responsibility of the government. Instead, put at its highest, the UK government's historical attitude has been that sport 'generally presented a complex of problems out of which government was not wholly free to opt'[2]. As a result, no general 'law of sport' has been enacted to regulate activity in the sector. Rather, legislation or other intervention is generally countenanced only as a measure of last resort, in response to a pressing public interest requirement[3].

1 See generally Foster 'How Can Sport Be Regulated?' in Greenfield & Osborn (eds) *Law & Sport in Contemporary Society* (2000, Frank Cass), pp 267–282.
2 Lord Hailsham *The Door Wherein I Went*, p 207, quoted in Grayson *Sport and the Law* (3rd edn, 2000, Butterworths), p 119.
3 See generally paras A1.60 to A1.105.

A1.14 In step with this approach, the idea of the government getting involved in the running of sport has generally been met with horror[1]. In his foreword to the current government's sports strategy paper, *A Sporting Future for All*, the Prime Minister was emphatic: 'The Government does not and should not run sport'[2].

1 As evidenced in the comment of one member of the Committee for Culture, Media and Sport when faced with Tony Banks' suggestion that the Minister for Sport should exercise more executive authority: 'I think the only thing which would be worse than hordes of old buffers [running sport] would be government ministers': Minutes of Evidence before the Committee for Culture, Media and Sport, 1998.
2 *A Sporting Future for All – The Government's Plan for Sport* DCMS PP374 (March 2001).

A1.15 Unlike the French government, then, the UK government does not treat sport as a public service, provision of which is a state responsibility, delegated to one governing body for each sport, recognised and licensed for that purpose. Instead, historically it has left sport almost entirely alone not only to organise and manage itself, but also to regulate the entire conduct of the sport, including fundamental issues of public interest such as child protection[1], corruption[2] and anti-doping[3], through a voluntary and private sports movement consisting of a bewildering array of sports-specific 'governing bodies'[4] that run their sports on an entirely voluntary and consensual basis[5], within the framework of the so-called 'European Model of Sport'[6].

1 See eg Gray 'Swimming and Child Protection: The Story so far' (1999) 2(2) Sports Law Bulletin 8.
2 See eg The FA Premier League Inquiry Into Transfers (particularly illegal 'bung' payments for transfers), 1997; The Condon Report into corruption (particularly match-fixing) in cricket, 2001. See para E6.86 et seq.
3 See para A1.27, and para E4.17.
4 An often-quoted statistic is that for the 112 sports currently recognised by the Sports Councils alone, there are 414 governing bodies (for different home countries, for different disciplines within a sport, for men and for women, and so on).
5 '[V]olunteers contribute more to sport in this country than central government, local authorities and the National Lottery combined': CCPR *Active Britain: A Manifesto for Sport and Recreation* (May 2001), p 3.
6 See paras A1.16 to A1.25.

D The European Model of Sport

A1.16 The European Commission, in its November 1998 consultation paper[1], adopted the term 'The European Model of Sport' to describe the organisational structure that the voluntary sports movement has generally adopted in European sport[2]:

In the Member States sport is traditionally organised in a system of national federations. Only the top federations (usually one per country) are linked together in European and international federations. Basically the structure resembles a pyramid with a hierarchy …

The clubs form the foundation of this pyramid. They offer everyone the possibility of engaging in sport locally, thereby promoting the idea of 'sport for all'. They also foster the development of new generations of sportsmen/women. At this level unpaid participation is particularly important and beneficial to the development of European sport …

Regional federations form the next level; the clubs are usually members of these organisations. Their area of interest is limited to a region in which they are responsible for organising regional championships or co-ordinating sport on a regional level …

The national federations, one for each discipline, represent the next level. Usually all the regional federations are members of the respective national federation. These federations regulate all general matters within their discipline and at the same time represent their branch in the European or International federations. They also organise national championships and act as regulatory bodies.

The top of the pyramid is formed by the European Federations, which are organised along the same lines as the national federations. Every European federation allows only one national federation from each country to be a member. By means of rules, usually involving sanctions for those taking part in championships which have not been recognised or authorised by the international federation, these organisations try to maintain their position.

1 *The European Model of Sport* (Consultation Document of DG X, November 1998), located at www.europa.eu.int/comm/sport/doc/ecom/doe_consult_en.pdf. See para B1.25. See also generally Chapter C1.

2 In fact, this model applies globally, not just in Europe.

A1.17 In fact, the top of the pyramid is formed by the international federation for the sport. For example, the Football Association governs football in England, licensing competition organisers such as The FA Premier League Limited and The Football League Limited to run their competitions; and UEFA governs football in Europe, organising competitions such as the UEFA Champions League and the quadrennial European Championships. However, it is FIFA, as the international governing body of the sport of association football, that organises global competitions such as the FIFA World Cup. FIFA also operates a 'federal' system of regulation, so that issues confined to one region or nation are addressed by the regional or national federation, but issues of global application and importance, such as registration and transfer systems, player release for international matches, and equipment specification[1], are regulated by FIFA, not its regional members and certainly not any of its national members.

1 Each of these FIFA regulations is examined in Chapter B2, in the context of their compatibility with the EC and UK competition rules. FIFA's transfer rules are also examined in Chapters B3 and E2.

A1.18 Recognising this and other limitations, however[1], the Commission's identification of the European Model of Sport still provides a useful analytical tool, particularly in its contrast of the so-called European Model, with its pyramidical hierarchy of power and its spirit of solidarity underpinned by systems of promotion and relegation, with the 'North American Model of Sport', consisting of closed leagues populated by sports 'franchises'.

1 There is no place in the Commission's model, for example, for the various multi-sport organisations that proliferate in the UK and elsewhere. In the UK, the most important of these is perhaps the Central Council for Physical Recreation, which represent aspects of sport on a nationwide basis and whose lobbying efforts are referenced elsewhere in this chapter. Other

examples include the British Olympic Association, and the Commonwealth Games Councils for each of the home countries, who are responsible for the preparation and delivery of their respective international competitions. Internationally, the most important multi-sport association is of course the International Olympic Committee. Others include the General Assembly of International Sports Federations (or GAISF) and the Commonwealth Games Federation.

A1.19 In the UK, the authority of sports governing bodies is not derived from statute or other government mandate. They are not agencies of the state, dependent for their existence and power upon state licence and tolerance. Rather, their authority is entirely consensual, derived from the voluntary contract between themselves and their members and the continuing commitment of those members to submit to their jurisdiction. Having been founded originally in response to the need to codify and standardise the 'rules of the game', the governing body's regulatory remit has expanded to encompass scheduling, discipline, dispute resolution, and regulation of all aspects of development and promotion of the sport, including its commercialisation. Uniform application and enforcement of the regulations is achieved by rules requiring members to participate only in competitions that have received the sanction of the governing body[1].

1 As to which, see further para B2.116 et seq.

A1.20 This is a strength, but also an important constitutional limitation, because the collective only remains powerful while it retains the loyalty of all of its members[1]. This may have been relatively straightforward in the sleepy days of amateurism or quasi-amateurism but is rife with difficulties now that sport is big business and control of sports rights can mean control of significant revenues. The rash of breakaway threats, some of them carried out, is testament to the difficulty that a governing body faces trying to reconcile the long-term interests of all of its constituents, from the mass amateur ranks of the sport to the professional elite at the top of the pile. The resulting warfare is waged largely using the UK and EC competition rules[2].

1 'The role, legitimacy and power of governing bodies depends on the confidence of their stakeholders in their institutional structures, governance arrangements, rules and dispute mechanisms': *The Rules of the Game*, Europe's first conference on the governance of sport (Brussels, February 2001), Advance Conference Paper at p 2. See also Taylor 'Competition Matters' (1999) 6(4) Sports Law Administration and Practice 1.

2 See para B2.116 et seq.

A1.21 The UK government does not have a direct stake in this struggle, because its authority is not at issue, and therefore it feels no compulsion to defend the status quo:

> In the UK at least the governing bodies are autonomous bodies set up and run by their members and it is not for the Government, or [European] community institutions, to decide whether they should be retained, combined with others, or abolished[1].

1 Joint UK Government/Sports Councils' Response to Commission Consultation Paper *The European Model of Sport* (DCMS May 1999).

A1.22 The fact that the legitimacy and authority of a sports governing body under English law is derived entirely from the consent of its members also has other important consequences. First and foremost, because it is a private arrangement between the governing body and its members, those aggrieved by the actions and decisions of a governing body may not invoke the judicial review mechanism that is available to challenge the actions and decisions of public bodies. Instead, a private law cause of action must be identified, and private law remedies apply[1]. Furthermore, the rules issued by the governing body in the exercise of its regulatory authority are not to be construed strictly, as if they were akin to Acts of Parliament; rather, a purposive approach is to be taken to construction of the 'contractual' rule-book, considering the context and the objectives behind the rules[2].

1 See paras A3.60 to A3.65.
2 See *Cowley v Heatley* (1986) Times, 24 July per Browne-Wilkinson V-C. Authority for this proposition also exists in the case law of the Court of Arbitration for Sport. See para E4.82, n 11.

A1.23 On the other hand, because of the social, cultural and economic importance attributed to sport, and the enormous public interest in its conduct, its governing bodies are often seen as trustees of public assets[1]. Combined with their monopoly authority and control over access to the sport, which carries with it enormous power over people's livelihoods, hopes and expectations, this makes the status of sports governing bodies rather more complex. A public-private dichotomy emerges that is reflected in the continuing controversy as to the non-availability of judicial review in relation to the actions and decisions of sports governing bodies, in the application to sports governing bodies of EC free movement rules that are supposedly confined in application to 'state' measures, and in the ongoing debate as to whether sports governing bodies are to be considered 'public authorities' within the scope of the Human Rights Act 1998[2]. It is also reflected in the public law standards that have crept into the English courts' 'private law' analysis of the actions of governing bodies: for example, the courts have accorded a 'margin of appreciation' to governing bodies' actions and decisions, at least where they are carrying out regulatory (as opposed to purely commercial) functions, on the basis that those bodies have expertise and experience that the courts should not second-guess[3].

1 Football, for example, is seen as 'the national game'. Furthermore, there is legislative recognition that certain core events in the UK sports calendar – the 'sporting crown jewels' – are 'public' assets, free access to which must be protected from the vagaries of the sports rights market-place. See discussion of 'listed events' legislation below at paras A1.80 to A1.91.
2 See paras A3.60 to A3.71, A4.14 to A4.27 and B3.8.
3 See paras A3.72 to A3.76.

A1.24 This dichotomy is partly based on the obvious analogy between a sports governing body and a sovereign state: 'the whole structure of a sports federation is that of a small government which, within the limits of what it is trying to do, mainly makes rules and becomes, for that particular area of activity, almost like a sovereign country'[1]. The legislative function of a sports governing body – regulating an activity of broad interest and importance, in the public interest, usually through a council or assembly or other rule-making policy body – is highlighted throughout this book. Not only is it the guardian of the 'laws of the game'. It is also called upon, in the absence of a government regulator, to issue regulations addressing safety, anti-doping, corruption, child protection and a host of other issues of central public interest[2]. A governing body also incorporates an executive function, usually a management committee or executive board, administering the regulations, licensing participation in accordance with those regulations, and monitoring compliance. In addition, the governing body will have to organise a (more or less independent) judicial function, to achieve enforcement of the regulations[3].

1 Max Mosley, President of the Federation Internationale de l'Automobile, speech to *The Rules of the Game,* Europe's first conference on the Governance of Sport (Brussels, February 2001).
2 See further para A1.15.
3 See generally Chapter A2.

A1.25 In each of these functions, however, despite the protestations of the sports movement to the contrary[1], autonomy has its limits. 'Sport is part of society and cannot establish its own political and legal framework'[2]. Rather, it is subject to the rule of law[3]. The law will hopefully be flexible enough to accommodate the 'specificities' of the sports sector[4], but the fact remains that sport must defer to the law, and not the other way around[5].

1 See Foster 'The Discourse of Doping: Law and Regulation in the War Against Drugs' in *Drugs and Doping in Sport* (2001, Cavendish), pp 181, 183 and 184.
2 *The Rules of the Game,* Europe's first conference on the Governance of Sport (Brussels, February 2001), Advance Conference Paper, p 5.
3 See eg M[c]Cutcheon 'The Rule of Law in Sport' (2002) 9(3) Sports Law Administration & Practice 1.
4 See paras B2.54 and B2.55. See also paras B2.56 to B2.61 for a discussion of the 'sporting exception' to the EC and UK competition laws for regulations that are 'inherent in the organisation of sport'.
5 For some of the difficulties that can arise when a governing body is trying to enforce uniform regulations for its sport, across a number of legal jurisdictions, see *Gasser v Stinson* (15 June 1988, unreported) (Scott J), and *Edwards v BAF and IAAF* [1998] 2 CMLR 363 (Lightman J). See also Weatherill 'Do sporting associations make law or are they merely subject to it? (July/August 1998) EBL Rev 217.

E Modern sports policy: a public-private partnership

A1.26 Notwithstanding the traditional approach, it can fairly be argued that the 'non-interventionist' label for UK government sports policy is becoming increasingly misleading, and that the regulatory approach is starting to develop into a more complex public-private mix. The current administration in particular has recognised the importance of sports policy not only as an end in itself but also as a tool for the achievement of a broader social policy agenda. It has therefore used the leverage that comes with control over access to public funding for sport to pursue an increasingly broad agenda in its burgeoning partnership with the private sports movement[1].

1 See generally Houlihan *Dying to Win* (2nd edn, 2002, Council of Europe Publishing), pp 15 to 25.

A1.27 Take drug use in sport as an example. This is an issue with obvious public health implications, as well as ethical implications, and some states have therefore seen fit to intervene, even to the extent of criminalising drug use and supply in sport[1]. In the UK, in contrast, while the government has endorsed the Olympic Movement Anti-Doping Code and is a signatory to the Council of Europe's Anti-Doping Convention 1989 and the International Anti-Doping Arrangement, no specific legislation has been passed to incorporate the provisions of those international instruments into English law, to make them directly applicable to sport in the UK. Still less has the government sought to criminalise the use of drugs in sport in the UK. Instead, it regards the regulation of drug use in sport, and the policing and enforcement of anti-doping rules, as the responsibility primarily of the sports governing bodies themselves. On the other hand, the government's agent, UK Sport, promotes uniform public standards on anti-doping in sport, and offers an independent drug-testing programme for UK sports bodies. Compliance with those standards and use of those services is a condition for access to public funding for sport in the UK. Thus, the policy goals are achieved indirectly, without confusing the message that the governance and regulation of sport is for the private governing bodies, and is not a right or responsibility of the state[2].

1 See para E4.16.
2 See para E4.33 et seq. This approach is reflected well in the following contribution of the current Sports Minister, Richard Caborn, to a recent Parliamentary debate on the regulation of drug use in sport: 'The only practical way of dealing with the use of banned substances is through the action of sport itself. Contravening anti-doping regulations is a case of professional misconduct in sport, and the decision to ban an athlete as a result of a positive drug test is a matter for sport's national governing bodies and international federations. Criminalising what is professional misconduct is not, therefore, an effective option. In the United Kingdom, we favour a non-legislative approach focusing on the standardisation of doping lists, sanctions and procedures within the sporting framework. The national anti-doping policy gives sport a focus to put in place procedures that are consistent, accountable and transparent. Sport itself must continue to own the problem of drug misuse in sport': HC Official Report, 23 April 2002, col 52WH.

A1.28 As set out below, however[1], the scope of this indirect regulation is slowly increasing because of the perception that government sports policy can only be implemented in partnership with the private sports movement, and the recognition that such a partnership, and the increased public funding that comes with it, must be on a professional basis in accordance with normal public standards of transparency, equity and accountability. Thus, recognition as the governing body of a sport, and access to public funds for that sport, is coming to depend on compliance not only with objective standards on public interest issues such as child protection and anti-doping, but also on issues relating to corporate governance and accountability that see the government taking a far more interventionist role (albeit indirectly, through the Sports Councils) not only in developing the strategic policy of sport but also in overseeing the way in which sport is governed and administered on a day-to-day basis.

1 See paras A1.93 to A1.100.

A1.29 The UK government's recognition of the power of sport as an instrument of public policy is shared at the EU-level[1]. Like the UK government, the institutions of the European Community are careful to emphasise that they are not seeking to encroach upon the autonomy of the sports movement[2]. For example, the European Council has stated:

> The European Council stresses its support for the independence of sports organisations and their right to organise themselves through appropriate associative structures. It recognises that, with due regard for national and Community legislation and on the basis of a democratic and transparent method of operation, it is the task of sporting organisations to organise and promote their particular sports, particularly as regards the specifically sporting rules applicable and the make-up of national teams, in the way which they think best reflects their objectives[3].

1 However, the same basic conclusion appears to have been reached there that an alliance needs to be made by the public sector with the private sports movement in an effort to co-ordinate their actions and objectives to the benefit of all[1]. '[A] partnership between public authorities, sports organisations and business is necessary to ensure harmonious and integrated development of sport': Conclusions of the First EU Conference on Sport (European Commission, DG X, August 1999), para 1.1.
2 Thus, the European Commission has concluded that, while the public-private partnership should be developed, 'the integrity and autonomy of sport must be preserved': *The Helsinki Report on Sport*, Communication from the Commission (COM (1999) 644 and /2), p 13.

3 European Council *Declaration on the Specific Characteristics of Sport and Its Social Function in Europe, Of Which Account Should Be Taken In Implementing Common Policies*, Annex IV to Nice Treaty, 7/8 December 2000, para 7. See para B1.27.

A1.30 Once again, however, the fulfilment of a quasi-public function requires compliance with the standards applied to public bodies. Thus, the delegates to a conference on 'The Governance of Sport' commended to sports governing bodies a commitment to its 'Statement of Principles' for sports governance, as a means of keeping the state regulator from the door:

> [S]port is attracting increasing attention from politicians, legislators and courts … [T]his heightened profile also carries risks: calls for legislation or judicial intervention could also undermine the principles of flexible self-regulation which have generated this successful development … [The Council of Europe's support in Nice for the right to autonomy and self-regulation of the sports movement] was conditioned upon the sports bodies observing principles of democracy and transparency, solidarity across the sport and observance of a code of ethics[1].

1 *The Rules of the Game*, Europe's first conference on the Governance of Sport (Brussels, February 2001), post-Conference Papers.

3 UK GOVERNMENT SPORTS POLICY

A The role of central government in the sport sector

(a) Developing a government sports policy

A1.31 Sports policy and direction covers not only immediate sporting issues such as participation, competition and facilities, but also the wider applications of sport in society, including health, education and social exclusion[1]. Emerging sports policy in the nineteenth century pursued 'the maintenance of social stability, the defense [*sic*] of privilege, and paternalism'[2], followed by a desire to create a healthy workforce for the industrial revolution and a fit male population for military service[3]. The Physical Fitness and Training Act 1937 was followed by the Education Act 1944, requiring local authorities to provide facilities for recreation and physical training. In the 1970s, further legislation was passed to promote sport and recreation by encouraging local authorities to provide sports facilities[4].

1 See generally Houlihan 'Sport in the United Kingdom' in *National Sports Policies: An International Handbook* (Chalip, Johnson and Stachura (eds), 1996, Greenwood Press).
2 Houlihan 'Sport in the United Kingdom' in *National Sports Policies: An International Handbook* (Chalip, Johnson and Stachura (eds), 1996, Greenwood Press) at p 379.
3 Chaker *Study on national sports legislation in Europe* (1999, Council of Europe Publishing), p 11.
4 See in particular s 19 of the Local Government (Miscellaneous Provisions) Act 1976, which authorises a local authority to 'provide … such recreational facilities as it thinks fit'.

A1.32 Modern sports policy has its roots in the Wolfenden Report produced by the Central Council of Physical Recreation ('CCPR') in 1960, which recommended (among other things) the creation of a GB Sports Council. That recommendation was eventually implemented in 1965[1]. However, successive governments after that time continued to view sport as a 'minor matter'[2], notwithstanding the 1975 White Paper *Sport and Recreation*, which has been identified as 'one of the few attempts by government to provide a comprehensive philosophy of sport and recreation', portraying sport as part of the welfare state, contributing to the 'physical and mental well-being of the population and to the reduction of hooliganism and delinquency among young people', but also identifying benefits from international sporting success and therefore supporting the funding of elite athletes[3].

1 The GB Sports Council eventually developed into UK Sport and the four Home Country Sports Councils, which are today the primary agents for implementation of government policy on sport in the UK. See paras A1.47 to A1.59.
2 See Grayson *Sport and the Law* (3rd edn, 2000, Butterworths), quoting Lord Hailsham.
3 Houlihan 'Sport in the United Kingdom' in *National Sports Policies: An International Handbook* (Chalip, Johnson and Stachura (eds), 1996, Greenwood Press) at p 380.

A1.33 The National Lottery was introduced in November 1994, pursuant to the National Lottery Act 1993, ushering in a new era of public funding for sport[1]. Nearly 30% of ticket revenues is allocated by the National Lottery Distribution Fund to six 'good causes', including sport[2], which receives 16.667% of funds available for distribution, a percentage that to date has averaged more than £200m a year[3].

1 See generally para C3.34 et seq.
2 Further to s 26 of the National Lottery Act 1993, as amended by the National Lottery Act 1998, the Secretary of State for Culture, Media and Sport issues financial directions that set broad parameters for the permissible application of Lottery funds by the Lottery funding agencies such as UK Sport and the Home Country Sports Councils.
3 Elite Sports Funding Review, Report of the Review Group chaired by Dr Jack Cunningham MP (August 2001).

A1.34 In July 1995, the incumbent Conservative government published a sports policy paper, *Sport, Raising the Game*[1], which led to the reorganisation of the GB Sports Council into UK Sport and Sport England, and UK Sport's eventual designation as a Lottery fund distributor in its own right[2].

1 Department of National Heritage (July 1995).
2 See para A1.47.

A1.35 In April 2000, the Labour government published its strategy for the development of sport over the next decade, *A Sporting Future for All*[1]. In his foreword, Prime Minister Tony Blair wrote:

> The Government does not and should not run sport. Sport is for individuals, striving to succeed – either on their own, or in teams. However those individuals, together or alone, need the help of others – to provide the facilities, the equipment, the opportunities. So there is a key role to play for those who organise and manage sport – local authorities, sports clubs, governing bodies, the Sports Councils and the Government.

Once again, the twin goals were mass participation ('more people of all ages and all social groups taking part in sport') and success at elite level ('more success for our top competitors and teams in international competition'). The perceived obstacles were insufficient opportunities for children and young people, loss of interest after school age, too many obstacles to the attainment of peak performance, and fragmented and unprofessional organisation and management of sport. The document set out both a 'Vision' and an 'Action Plan' to surmount those obstacles.

1 Department for Culture, Media and Sport *A Sporting Future for All* (HMSO 2000).

A1.36 In July 2000, the government announced that, to back its action plan for sport, Exchequer funding for sport would increase[1] from £50m in 2000 to £105m in 2001, £155m in 2002/03 and £225m in 2003/04[2].

1 See www.sportcal.com (19 July 2000). Nevertheless, direct government funding for sport in the UK remains among the lowest in Europe. Direct government funding for sport in the UK currently stands at £1 per head, compared to Norway's £12.10, Germany's £7.90 and France's £5.20. See (2001) Independent, 20 May. Australia spends a massive £67 per head; Sweden spends £18.51 per head: see (2000) Sports Life 4 (Oct).

2 The funding proposals made in July 2000 also included a £750m grant for physical education and sport in schools, through the New Opportunities Fund. This investment in school facilities is combined with Sport England's existing sports lottery allocation for school sports projects, and is administered through the School Sport Alliance, uniting the Department for Education, the Department of Culture, Media and Sport, Sport England, the Youth Sport Trust and the New Opportunities Fund. The Alliance aims to consult with local government authorities to ensure that its proposals for investment in school sport link effectively with local sport and cultural plans and community strategies. See (2000) Sportcal.com, 19 July 2000; Statement by Culture Secretary Chris Smith to Parliament (25 July 2000).

A1.37 The Sports Strategy (A Sporting Future for All) Implementation Group, drawn from leading figures in sport education, local authorities and governing bodies of sport, produced an initial action plan in December 2000[1]. In March 2001, the Department of Culture, Media and Sport published the government's action plan, *A Sporting Future for All – The Government's Plan for Sport*, adopting many of the recommendations of that group[2]. The first annual report, issued in May 2002, noted that some parts of the plan had been delivered and others had not, but concluded that '[w]hat is clear is that sport in education, and sport as a vehicle for delivering social policy, have a higher profile across Government than they did last year'[3].

1 *A Sporting Future for All: Action Plan, Report of the Implementation Group to the DCMS and DfEE* (December 2000), described in the subsequent DCMS publication adopting the plan as 'the most significant sporting manifesto ever seen in the United Kingdom'. *A Sporting Future for All – The Government's Plan for Sport* DCMS PP374 (March 2001, DCMS).

2 DCMS PP374 (March 2001).

3 *A Sporting Future for All – The Government's Plan for Sport*, Annual Report 2001/02.

(b) Central government departments responsible for sport

A1.38 The CCPR claims that seventeen different government departments affect sport and recreation[1].

1 CCPR *Active Britain: A Manifesto for Sport and Recreation* (May 2001), p 4. Grayson counts fourteen. See Grayson *Sport and the Law* (3rd edn, 2000, Butterworths), p 97. Those omitted from the discussion in this text include the Department of Health (health and fitness) and the Department of Trade (health and safety legislation, competition policy).

A1.39 The Department for Culture, Media and Sport ('DCMS') has primary responsibility for sport in the central government, including a co-ordinating role with other central government departments active in the sports sector[1]. Its Parliamentary Under-Secretary is 'Sports Minister'[2], and it has a dedicated Sport & Recreation Division. The aim of the DCMS is 'to improve the quality of life for all through cultural and sporting activities, and to strengthen the creative industries', working to 'bring quality and excellence in the fields, culture, media and sport' and 'mak[ing] these available to the many, not just the few'[3]. The DCMS is responsible, for example, for identifying those sports events that are so much part of the national heritage that public access via free television coverage is protected under 'listed events' legislation[4]. It also receives the bulk of the direct funding for sport allocated by the government in its annual budget of Exchequer funds. However, it does not administer that funding itself. Rather, it takes an 'arm's length' approach to sports delivery[5], delegating its funding, along with its responsibility for implementation of government sports policy, to UK Sport and Sport England, under the terms of formal funding agreements[6].

1 See generally the DCMS website at www.culture.gov.uk. The DCMS's predecessors in this role were (from 1974 to 1991) the Department of the Environment, from 1991 to 1992 the Department of Education and Science, and from 1992 to 1997 the Department of National Heritage. In July 1997, the Department of National Heritage was renamed the Department of Culture, Media and Sport.
2 The role of Minister with responsibility for Sport was created in 1962, at the instigation of Lord Hailsham. The first member of the government to be designated 'Minister for Sport' was Dennis Howell in 1974. Kate Hoey replaced Tony Banks as Parliamentary Under-Secretary of State and Minister for Sport on 29 July 1999 but was herself replaced by Richard Caborn MP (who was given the additional title of Minister of State) in June 2001. See further paras A1.107 to A1.112.
3 Funding Agreement between the English Sports Council and the DCMS for 1999/2002, available at www.culture.gov.uk, p 1.
4 See paras A1.81 to A1.92.
5 Ie Ministers set the financial, administrative, legal and overall policy framework within which funded bodies are expected to operate, but leave operational decisions to those bodies.
6 See eg Funding Agreement between the English Sports Council and the DCMS for 1999/2002, available at www.culture.gov.uk. See also para A1.46.

A1.40 The main other central government departments with significant powers and/or responsibilities impacting upon the sports sector are:

(i) the Home Office;
(ii) the Treasury Department;
(iii) the Department for Education & Skills; and
(iv) the Office of the Deputy Prime Minister.

A1.41 Home Office The Home Office is responsible for enforcement of legislation relating to crowd safety and public order at sports events[1], as well as hunting[2]. It is also responsible for government policy in relation to gambling[3].

1 See paras A1.61 to A1.72.
2 See paras A1.74 and A1.75.
3 See paras A1.76 to A1.79.

A1.42 Treasury The Treasury is responsible for income tax and VAT on sports bodies[1]. Reacting in part to sustained criticism of government fiscal policy with regard to sport[2], the April 2002 budget included tax relief for community amateur sports clubs who cannot or do not wish to apply for charitable status[3].

1 See generally Chapter C2.
2 The CCPR estimates that the government receives approximately four times more money from sport through taxation than it returns through central and local government grants for sport. *Active Britain – A Manifesto for Sport* (May 2001, CCPR). In November 2001, the Rugby Football Union announced that it had estimated it would pay the government £50m in tax over the eight years from March 2001. It pointed out that such a sum could better be used to fund grassroots development of the sport, and noted suggestions that governing bodies committed to the grassroots development of their sports should be tax exempt: 'Profits up but RFU condemns government' www.sportbusiness.com (16 November 2001). UK Sport has stated: 'If the UK wants to be successful in the highly competitive events marketplace, it will need to address the issue of VAT and Corporation Tax levied on sporting bodies. A number of countries including Australia, the Republic of Ireland, Germany and the Netherlands have illustrated the benefits of reducing the tax burden on certain defined major international events': see *A UK Strategy for Sport: Major Events, A 'Blueprint' for Success* (1999, UK Sport).
3 See paras C2.98 and C2.99.

A1.43 Department for Education & Skills The Department for Education & Skills has responsibility for sport in the national curriculum and for sports facilities at schools, colleges and universities. By virtue of the Education Reform Act 1998, physical education is one of the foundation subjects of the national curriculum, and a compulsory subject for pupils aged five to 16 in state-maintained schools in England and Wales[1]. The Department for Education & Skills is a partner in the School Sport Alliance, the grant scheme for school sports launched in 2000[2].

1 The National Curriculum for England states that '[t]he Government believes that two hours of physical activity a week, including the National Curriculum for physical education and extra-curricular activities, should be an aspiration for all schools'. However, a Sport England survey carried out in 1999 revealed that only 33% of school children participate in this amount of sport. The CCPR is lobbying the Government to introduce a compulsory two hours of sport per week for every schoolchild. See www.ccpr.org.uk/campaigns/content/curriculum.
2 See para A1.36, n 2.

A1.44 Office of the Deputy Prime Minister The Office of the Deputy Prime Minister oversees local authorities, county councils and district councils, ie the organs that have traditionally had primary responsibility for providing facilities and opportunities for mass participation in sport in the UK[1]. Section 19 of the Local Government (Miscellaneous Provisions) Act 1976 permits (but does not require) a local authority to provide sports and recreational facilities of any and all types for use by such persons as it sees fit, and/or to contribute to the expenses of any not-for-profit organisations providing recreational or sports facilities. The pressure on local authority revenue caused by the move from domestic rates to poll tax to council tax has led to widespread cuts in spending on non-statutory services such as sport, as well as to sales of capital assets such as sports facilities[2]. However, local authority spending on sport and recreation facilities (admittedly heavily subsidised by Lottery funds) remains one of the most significant sources of public funding for sport in this country: local authorities own and operate the sports centres, swimming pools, playing fields and specialist facilities that facilitate mass participation in sport. Subject to the overriding authority of the Secretary of State, local authorities also have legislative powers and responsibilities in the context of land-use planning that can be relevant to sport[3], including the ability to condition planning consent on the provision of public sports and leisure facilities[4].

1 See *A Sporting Future for All* (DCMS, March 2001) at p 52: 'Local authorities are key providers of sport and recreation and play a central role in the delivery of sport in the community'; Joint UK Government/Sports Councils' Response to the Commission Consultation Paper *The European Model of Sport* (May 1999), para 27: '[T]he promotion of public health through activity, whether sport or less formal physical activity, is essentially a matter which can be dealt with satisfactorily at a lower or national level. Local government in the UK plays a full part in promoting health through sport and leisure, as well as local sports organisations and we certainly believe they are capable of promoting sport for all initiatives'.
2 The Conservative government introduced legislation in 1980 (The Department of Education and Science Regulations 909 and the Local Government Planning and Land Act 1980) that encouraged local authorities to sell off their playing fields to private developers in order to raise finances for investment in educational facilities. It is estimated that between 1981 and 1997 around 5,000 sports fields were sold to developers. See (2002) Independent, 7 March. In 1996 measures were introduced requiring local authorities to consult with Sport England (then the English Sports Council) on receipt of a planning application affecting a playing field. However, Sport England was given no power to prohibit the development. In 1998 new procedures were introduced pursuant to the Town and Country Planning (Playing Fields) Act 1998, empowering the Secretary of State of the Environment to examine applications where the local authority announced its intention to reject the advice of Sport England. In addition, s 77 of the School Standards and Framework Act 1998 required local authorities to obtain the consent of the Secretary of State for the Environment to the disposal of school playing fields. In July 2001 the Department for Education unveiled Guidance

0580/2001 for the Protection of School Playing Fields. Applications for the sale of school playing fields must now be considered by an independent advisory committee called the School Playing Fields Advisory Panel. See generally www.ccpr.org.uk/campaigns/content/plyngfields. See also Ashton 'How a team approach is protecting school fields' (2001) Daily Telegraph, 4 October; (2002) Independent, 7 March.

3 Pursuant to the structure laid down by the Town and Country Planning Act 1990 and the Planning and Compensation Act 1991, a local authority draws up a plan that sets targets for development of housing, industry and transport and designates the approved uses of different sites within the community, such as housing, leisure or industry. Sport and leisure is recommended by the government as a use that should be included in every authority's plan. See generally Planning Policy Guidance Note 17: Planning for Open Space, Sport and Recreation (ODPM, July 2002).

4 See Elson and Payne *Planning obligations for sport and leisure: a guide to negotiation and action* (1993, Sports Council).

A1.45 Responsibility for sport in Scotland, Wales and Northern Ireland has devolved to their respective assemblies. In the Scottish Executive, the Minister for Tourism, Culture and Sport parallels the functions of England's Secretary of State for Culture, Media and Sport. In the National Assembly for Wales, responsibility for sport lies with the Minister for Culture Sport and the Welsh Language. In the Northern Ireland Executive, responsibility for sport lies with the Department of Culture Arts and Leisure (Sports and Recreation Department). Each of those bodies has a funding and policy-implementation relationship with its own country sports council similar to the relationship that exists between the DCMS and UK Sport and Sport England[1].

1 See further paras A1.47 to A1.59.

A1.46 Since 1998, the Ministers with responsibility for sport in England, Scotland, Wales and Northern Ireland have met regularly together as a 'Sports Cabinet', under the chairmanship of the Secretary of State for Culture, Media and Sport, the main purpose being to provide policy guidance for UK Sport.

B Implementing government sports policy: UK Sport and the Home Country Sports Councils

A1.47 Further to its traditional 'arms-length' approach in this area, the UK government delegates the implementation of its sports policy to UK Sport and the home country sports councils.

A1.48 The GB Sports Council was originally set up in 1960s, with responsibility for co-ordinating sports development across the whole of the UK. Following various reorganisations and re-branding exercises, today UK-wide issues are co-ordinated by UK Sport (established by Royal Charter in 1997, fka The United Kingdom Sports Council) and the home country sports councils – Sport England (fka the English Sports Council), the Scottish Sports Council, the Sports Council of Wales and the Sports Council of Northern Ireland – deal with sport in their respective countries[1]. These are publicly funded official government advisory bodies, established by Royal Charter and operating under funding arrangements with the DCMS or its equivalent in Scotland, Wales and Ireland[2]. Their function is to distribute public funding for sport and, by placing conditions on access to that funding, to develop sport in line with government policies on 'sport for all' and international success in elite sport. Their work, along with that of the DCMS, is scrutinised by parliamentary select committees.

1 UK Sport: see www.uksport.gov.uk. Sport England: see www.sportengland.org. Scottish Sports Council: see www.sportscotland.org.uk. Sports Council for Northern Ireland: see www.sportni.org. Sports Council for Wales: see www.sports-council-wales.org.uk.
2 See para A1.39.

A1.49 UK Sport spearheads the development of policy on issues of common interest throughout the UK, such as doping, sports medicine and coaching. UK Sport's primary mission is to develop and support a sports movement system capable of producing a constant flow of world class performers. Related aims include boosting the UK's profile and influence in international sport, and assisting UK sports bodies in bidding to host major international events in the UK[1].

1 See eg UK Sport *Annual Review 2001/02*.

A1.50 UK Sport splits its functions between five directorates. The Performance Services Directorate works with national governing bodies, coaches and athletes to ensure they have the plans and infrastructures in place to encourage and support world class performers who can compete successfully in international competition. The UK Sports Institute Directorate oversees and supports the development by the home country sports councils of a network of facilities and back-up services that the UK's elite athletes need to succeed, including sports science, medicine and coaching expertise and world class training facilities. The International Relations and Major Events Directorate monitors international developments and works to promote the UK and sport overseas. It also works with the Major Events Steering Group to assess applications for bidding for and staging major events in the UK and provides support to national governing bodies and event organisers on staging major sporting events. The Anti-Doping Directorate has specific responsibility for the UK's anti-doping policies and programmes and for co-ordinating with governing bodies over anti-doping, for reviewing anti-doping programmes, for implementing in and out-of-competition testing, monitoring the results of such testing and ensuring a fair process for such testing[1]. Finally, the Corporate Services Directorate is essentially a support team that co-ordinates UK Sport's financial management, human resources, IT and customer care policies.

1 See further para E4.33 et seq.

A1.51 With UK Sport operating on common issues at a UK level, the responsibility for developing sport on a home country basis falls to the respective home country sports councils. Their aim is to increase participation levels in sport, to increase the number of facilities at which sport can be played and ultimately to improve elite sports performance in their respective regions.

A1.52 For example, Sport England's objective is:

> to lead the development of sport in England by influencing and serving the public, private and voluntary sectors. Its aim is more people involved in sport, more places to play sport [and] more medals through higher standards in sport[1].

Sport England works to develop performance and excellence in sport, by providing support to governing bodies of sport, and through the infrastructure of the English Institute of Sport, a network of centres and service providers to World Class programme athletes. In partnership with the Youth Sport Trust and others, it targets resources, through its Active Schools programme, to schemes that support youth sports[2]. Sport England is also a statutory consultee on all planning proposals involving playing fields[3], where it seeks to 'ensure that England's planning system favours the retention of existing opportunities and the development of new facilities – where this is consistent with principles of sustainable development'[4].

1 Funding Agreement between the English Sports Council and the DCMS for 1999/2002, available on www.culture.gov.uk, para 2.7; see also para 2.8: 'The ESC's activities are not principally related to providing specific services direct to the public, although ESC does act as an advocate for English sport. The ESC is dedicated to increasing participation for all groups especially young people and those who are not able to participate in sport because they are in some way excluded. Many community facilities require refurbishment or replacement and there is a shortage of facilities to support performance development. As well as making sure that elite performers have appropriate support there is a need to widen the base from which talented individuals are identified and developed and so that those from disadvantaged groups are not excluded'.

2 See para A1.36, n 2.

3 See para A1.44, n 2.

4 *Sport England* (April 2000, Sport England). See generally *A sporting future for the playing fields of England: policy on planning applications for development on playing fields* (1997, English Sports Council). Sport England also encourages local authorities to draw up strategies for sport and recreation and incorporate them into local plans. See Sport England *Information Sheet 8 – Sport and the Planning System* (February 2000).

A1.53 Both UK Sport and Sport England distribute Exchequer funding[1] and Lottery funding to sport[2].

1 For example, UK Sport currently receives grant-in-aid (or Exchequer) funding of approximately £20m per annum from the DCMS: UK Sport *Annual Review 2001/02*. Sport England was to receive just over £30m a year in grant-in-aid funding between 1999 and 2002. See Funding Agreement between the English Sports Council and the DCMS for 1999-2002, available at www.culture.gov.uk.

2 Currently, sport's share of Lottery funds is shared between the different funding agencies as follows: UK Sport (9.2%), Sport England (75.6%); sportscotland (8.1%); Sports Council for Wales (4.5%); and Sports Council for Northern Ireland (2.6%). See Elite Sports Funding Review, Report of the Review Group chaired by Dr Jack Cunningham MP (August 2001).

A1.54 UK Sport allocates about £12m of its annual Exchequer funding to governing bodies of sport, to support effective management and administration of their sports[1], particularly those with development programmes that fall outside the scope of the World Class Programme.

1 See eg UK Sport *Annual Review 2001/02*. See further para A1.98.

A1.55 With its share of Lottery funding (about £25m per year), and working in combination with Sport England[1], UK Sport funds the World Class Performance Programme. Where a sport has been identified as one likely to produce medal-winners in future major championships, the World Class Performance Programme gives funding:

(a) to the sport's national governing body, to finance long-term training and preparation programmes; and
(b) directly to the UK's most talented athletes in that sport, to enable them to improve their performance and win medals on an international stage[2].

A small portion of UK Sport's Lottery funding is allocated to finance bids by sports bodies in the UK to stage major events in the UK. Further funds finance the UK Sports Institute.

1 See para A1.59.

2 World Class athletes are classified as those falling within the top twenty in the world, and considered current or future medal potential. Performance Programme athletes fall within three categories: Category A (top 3), Category B (top 10), and Category C (top 20). Category A and B athletes currently receive living costs awards of up to £9,800 per year and Category C athletes may receive up to half that figure. Sporting costs awards per year may be up to £12,000 for Category A, £8,000 for Category B, and £4,000 for Category C. These awards take into account each athlete's personal circumstances in an assessment of need.

A1.56 Most of Sport England's Exchequer funding goes towards 'maintaining England's sports infrastructure'[1]. Its Lottery funding is administered by the Sport England Lottery Fund, which since 1994 has distributed over a billion pounds to more than 3,300 projects, sponsored by local authorities, governing bodies, schools, clubs and individuals throughout England.

1 See further para A1.96.

A1.57 After early criticism that the Fund was too reactive (despite initiatives such as the School Community Sport Initiative and the Priority Areas Initiative), revised directions from the Secretary of State for Culture, Media and Sport arising out of the National Lottery Act 1998 allowed Sport England to take a more pro-active approach to funding. Thus, the Sport England Lottery Fund is now split into two core funds: The Community Projects Fund, for community projects, and the World Class Fund, for elite performance.

A1.58 The Community Projects Fund is itself split into three parts: Small Projects – Awards for All (grants of up to £5,000 for schools and voluntary groups, particularly disadvantaged groups, for capital and short-term revenue schemes), Capital Schemes (grants of over £5,000 providing funding for community capital facilities such as sports halls and astroturf pitches) and Revenue Schemes (grants of over £5,000 for programmes tackling social exclusion in sport). Projects funded include the Nottingham Ice Arena, Hampshire County Cricket Club and over 80 facilities for the English Institute of Sport. Funds have also been provided for the new English National Stadium at Wembley[1], various Commonwealth Games facilities for Manchester 2002, and (through the Football Trust) for the improvement of stadia of various Football League clubs (with matching funds provided by the Football Association and the FA Premier League).

1 See para A1.115.

A1.59 The World Class Fund has the aim of achieving international success by providing services (through the English Sports Institute) and grants to individual sportsmen and women, and providing support to bids to bring world events to England. The 'Performance' programme, delivered in partnership with UK Sport[1], focuses on elite athletes with prospects of success in the short term; the 'Potential' and 'Start' programmes concentrate on athletes aiming to meet the performance criteria in the longer term[2].

1 See para A1.55.
2 Further detail about public funding of sport through UK Sport and the home country sports councils can be found in Chapter C3.

C Direct governmental regulation of sport

A1.60 Consistent with the traditional non-interventionist approach taken by successive UK governments in the sports sector, there is no broad legislative programme for the UK sport sector, underpinned by a grand policy design. However, on occasion it has been necessary to legislate specifically and directly on issues relating to the sports sector, not in pursuit of any sports-specific objective[1], but rather to address non-sporting objectives. Limitations of space confine this chapter to a brief overview only of those statutes here[2].

1 The listed events legislation (see paras A1.81 to A1.92) might be seen as an exception to this.
2 Obviously, the sports sector, like any other sector, is subject to the 'law of the land', including the reams of legislation that is not in any way specific to sport. Some of the generic statutes that impact most on the sports sector are addressed elsewhere in this book. See eg Chapter A4, Chapter B2, Chapter C4 (for the Health & Safety at Work Act 1974), Chapter E3 and Chapter E6. This chapter deals only with legislation specific to, or impacting mainly upon, the sports sector.

(a) Public safety

A1.61 Introduced in response to recommendations made after the stand collapse at Ibrox Stadium in 1969 that killed 66 spectators, the Safety of Sports Grounds Act 1975 ('SSGA 1975') established a system of licensing and control of major sports stadia. Section 1 of the SSGA 1975 requires designated sports grounds with capacity for more than 10,000 spectators to apply for a safety certificate from the local authority[1]. Section 2 of the SSGA 1975 gives the local authority a broad discretion to include any conditions in the certificate that it deems necessary to secure spectator safety, and s 10 allows it to cap the number of spectators that may be admitted into the stadium. Section 12 makes it a criminal offence to contravene safety requirements imposed under the licensing scheme.

1 The Safety of Sports Grounds (Accommodation of Spectators) Order 1996 amended the SSGA 1975 to reduce the capacity threshold from 10,000 to 5,000, but only in relation to stadia where Premier League or Football League football is played. The Fire Safety and Safety at Places of Sport Act 1987 also amended the SSGA 1975 by specifying (as a result of the Popplewell reports on the Bradford City fire and Heysel Stadium disasters of 1985) that stands with a capacity of 500 or more at sports grounds not designated under the SSGA 1975 must also obtain a safety certificate from the local authority. The application procedures are set out in the Safety of Places of Sport Regulations 1988, SI 1988/1807.

A1.62 After the Hillsborough disaster of 15 April 1989, the government commissioned Lord Justice Taylor to make further recommendations regarding crowd control and safety at sports events. The Taylor Report, published in 1990[1], found that compliance with existing safety standards were not complied with and were in any event inadequate. It made various recommendations to improve safety standards, the principal one being that major football stadia (specifically, Premier League and Football League Division One grounds) should become all-seater and terracing should be improved at Division Two and Three grounds. The Football Spectators Act 1989 implemented most of the Taylor Report recommendations. Section 10 of the Football Spectators Act 1989 requires that any stadium hosting spectators for a designated football match (currently FA Premier League, Football League and international matches) must be licensed by a new body established by the Football Spectators Act 1989, the Football Licensing Authority. In order to receive a licence from the Football Licensing Authority, the stadium must comply with the safety criteria recommended by the Taylor Report. The Football Spectators Act 1989 also obliges local authorities to comply with directions from the Football Licensing Authority on the issue of licences for such stadia under the SSGA 1975, including imposing conditions as to capacity and seating.

1 *The Hillsborough Stadium Disaster* (Final Report, Cm 962), Taylor LJ.

A1.63 In 1998, with the structural improvement programme for major football grounds recommended by the Taylor Report largely completed, the government concluded that there was no longer a need for the Football Licensing Authority to act as a further regulator of such football grounds, over and above the regulatory role of local authorities under the SSGA 1975. A Culture and Recreation Bill was introduced on 14 December 2000 to reconstitute the Football Licensing Authority as the 'Sports Grounds Safety Authority'. The Bill would repeal the separate licensing function for major football stadia established by the Football Spectators Act 1989 and administered by the Football Licensing Authority. The Sports Grounds Safety Authority would maintain a review function with respect to safety certificates issued by local authorities in relation to such stadia (including the power, via the Secretary of State, to require the inclusion of conditions in such licences), but would also take on an advisory role for central and local government authorities on safety issues associated with all sports that use outdoor sports stadia, including rugby, cricket, athletics, horse racing and dog racing[1]. At the time of writing, the Bill had not been passed into law.

1 See Culture and Recreation Bill [HL], Explanatory Notes, available on www.parliament.the-stationary-office.co.uk/pa/ld200001/ldbills.

(b) Public order

A1.64 The Football Spectators Act 1989 envisaged that the Football Licensing Authority would also have a public order role, controlling access to designated matches via a national football membership scheme. In the event, the government never implemented that broader role. However, other statutes have been enacted to address the serious public order issues associated with football[1].

1 See generally Pearson 'Legislating for the Football Hooligan: A Case for Reform' in Greenfield & Osborn (eds) *Law and Sport in Contemporary Society* (2000, Frank Cass); Greenfield & Osborn *Regulating Football* (2001, Pluto Press), ch 1.

A1.65 On Lord Justice Taylor's recommendation[1], the Football Offences Act 1991 added three football-specific crimes to the statute book specifically to address the 'English disease' of football hooliganism. Therefore, in addition to the generic crimes of assault, criminal damage, riot, affray and so on that apply at sporting events and elsewhere throughout the land, under the Football Offences Act 1991 it is an offence at a regulated sporting event to throw anything at or towards the playing area, its surrounds or any part of the ground where there are spectators[2], to engage in indecent or racial chanting[3] or to go onto the playing area without lawful excuse[4].

1 *The Hillsborough Stadium Disaster* (Final Report, Cm 962), Taylor LJ.
2 See para A1.5 et seq.
3 See para A1.31 et seq.
4 See para A1.106 et seq.

A1.66 Section 1 of the Sporting Events (Control of Alcohol etc) Act 1985 makes it unlawful to carry alcohol or allow alcohol to be carried or consumed on public transport whose primary purpose is to transport spectators to a regulated sporting event (which includes trains and buses running special services to regulated football matches and also any vehicle hired for the purpose of transporting spectators to regulated football matches, ie 'football specials'). Section 2 makes it an offence to be drunk while trying to enter or while in a regulated sports ground, to drink in sight of the pitch or to have in one's possession an article that can be thrown and cause injury to another. In addition, in an effort to ensure segregation of opposing fans, s 166 of the Criminal Justice and Public Order Act 1994 makes the unauthorised offer for sale or sale in a public place of tickets for a regulated match a criminal offence[1].

1 See Greenfield & Osborn 'Criminalising Football Supporters: Tickets, Touts and the Criminal Justice and Public Order Act 1994' [1995] 3 SATLJ 36.

A1.67 Section 14A of the Football Spectators Act 1989, as amended by the Football (Disorder) Act 2000, requires the court to impose a football banning order on anyone convicted of a relevant football-related offence[1] if it 'is satisfied that there are reasonable grounds to believe that making a banning order would help to prevent violence or disorder at or in connection with any regulated football matches'. If it does not impose such an order, it must explain why not.

1 Ie offences that are committed within 24 hours either side of kick-off for a domestic game or up to five days before an international fixture or the start of an international representative tournament abroad. See the Football Spectators Act 1989, ss 1(8) and 14 (5) respectively. A full list of relevant offences is set out in the Football Spectators Act 1989, Sch 1.

A1.68 Section 14B of the Football Spectators Act 1989 allows the police to apply to a magistrate's court to impose a banning order on any person that the police can prove, to the civil standard, ie on the balance of probabilities, 'has at any time caused or contributed to any violence or disorder in the United Kingdom or elsewhere'. There is no requirement that the violence or disorder have been football-related. If the police can make that showing, then provided that the court 'is satisfied that there are reasonable grounds to believe that making a banning order would help to prevent violence or disorder at or in connection with any regulated football matches', it *must* impose a banning order on that person.

A1.69 Section 14B therefore authorises the banning of a person who has not been convicted of any offence, football-related or otherwise. To support applications for a banning order under s 14B, the police usually rely on previous convictions, often in combination with a 'hooligan profile' compiled by the Football Intelligence Unit (as in *Gough*[1]), but previous convictions are not a necessary prerequisite, ie the police may apply based on (for example) a 'hooligan profile' alone.

1 See para A1.71.

A1.70 A person made the subject of a football banning order under the Football Spectators Act 1989 may not attend regulated football matches in England and Wales, nor may he travel abroad when designated football matches are being played abroad; instead he must report to a police station (domestic match) or surrender his passport (overseas match)[1]. The Football Banning Orders Authority determines which matches played abroad trigger the travelling ban in particular cases. These will include any overseas match or tournament involving the England national team, any overseas match involving the team supported by the banned person and any other high-risk match between club sides in an international competition. Where a non-custodial sentence is imposed, the banning order imposed under s 14A of the Football Spectators Act 1989 must be in place for between three and five years following conviction; where a custodial sentence is imposed, the ban must be for between six and ten years. A football banning order imposed under s 14B of the Football Spectators Act 1989 will be for a minimum of two years and maximum of three years.

1 See s 30 of the Public Order Act 1986; the Football Spectators Act 1989; and the Football (Disorder) Act 2000.

A1.71 In *Gough v Chief Constable of Derbyshire*[1], two individuals were each banned for two years under s 14B of the Football Spectators Act 1989 from attending regulated football matches in the UK or from travelling overseas when designated football matches were taking place overseas. They challenged the bans as an infringement of their rights under the European Convention of Human Rights (under Art 6[2], because s 14B makes criminal sanctions applicable simply on a 'reasonable suspicion', proved to the civil standard, which was too low a burden of proof; and under Art 8[3], because s 14B stops people who had not been convicted and imprisoned from leaving the UK) and under Art 49 of the EC Treaty[4] (on the basis that s 14B constitutes an unlawful and disproportionate restriction on the subject's right to give and receive services throughout the EC). The Court of Appeal upheld the Divisional Court's dismissal of these arguments, primarily on the basis that, if the strict showing required by the Football Spectators Act (that the defendant had a propensity for taking part in football hooliganism) was made out, then interference with that individual's rights was necessary for the prevention of disorder. Given the power to allow the subject to travel abroad if he could prove to the Football Banning Orders Authority on the balance of probabilities that the trip was for a purpose other than to attend football matches, the ban from international travel was not disproportionate to that aim. The Court of Appeal did emphasise however that the serious restraints that banning orders involved meant that there had to be individual consideration of each case, and in relation to each case magistrates must be satisfied that the individual has caused or contributed to violence or disorder in the UK or abroad, and that there are strong grounds for believing the individual is likely to become involved in violence or disorder if permitted to attend matches in the future. The Court of Appeal stated that the magistrate should apply an exacting standard of proof to such questions that would in practice be hard to distinguish from the criminal standard.

1 [2002] EWCA Civ 351, [2002] 2 All ER 985, [2002] All ER (D) 308 (Mar).
2 Right to a fair trial: see para A4.36.
3 Respect for private life: see para A4.57.
4 See para B3.23.

A1.72 Under s 14J of the Football Spectators Act 1989, breach of the terms of a banning order is an arrestable offence. A person guilty of an offence under this section is liable on summary conviction to imprisonment for a term not exceeding six months, or a fine not exceeding level 5 on the standard scale, or both. This applies to the failure to report to a police station when required, failure to surrender a passport when required, and the entry into a stadium hosting a regulated football match when the subject of a banning order.

(c) Prohibited sports: combat sports

A1.73 Usually a defendant charged with the crime of intentionally inflicting actual or serious harm on another may not plead that the other consented to that injury; as a matter of public policy, the criminal law does not recognise consent as a defence to the charge[1]. However, boxing and other lawfully constituted combat sports[2] are exempted from that general rule, so that the infliction of injuries in the normal course of such sports will not attract criminal liability. The exemption does not stand on the strongest of footings, either legally or logically[3], and periodically (usually after a high profile fight has resulted in a particularly horrific injury) attempts are made to introduce legislation to repeal the exemption. However, notwithstanding its weak foundations the standing of this exemption in English law remains solid[4] and none of the attempts at a legislative repeal has yet come close to succeeding[5].

1 See para E6.38 et seq.

2 From the case law it is clear that sparring and wrestling would fall within the exemption, but there is no definitive list of what other combat sports fall within the exemption. See para E6.77 et seq.

3 See para E6.78, which explains that no court has specifically held that boxing is exempt from the criminal law; rather, the exemption has been implied from the reasoning of the House of Lords in *R v Coney* (1882) 8 QBD 534, as to why prize fighting is not legal.

4 See *A-G's Reference (No 6 of 1980)* [1981] QB 715 per Lane LCJ: 'nothing which we have said [about fighting outside the context of sport being unlawful] is intended to cast doubt upon the accepted legality of properly conducted sports and games'.

5 For a comprehensive treatment of this subject, including a survey of the public interest arguments for and against an exemption, see Gunn and Ormerod 'Despite the Law: Prize-Fighting and Professional Boxing' in Greenfield & Osborn (eds) *Law and Sport in Contemporary Society* (2000, Frank Cass), pp 21–50. See also Gardiner *Sports Law* (2nd edn, 2001, Cavendish Publishing), pp 114–127.

(d) Prohibited sports: blood sports

A1.74 Whilst boxing survives, it appears that the days of hunting wild mammals with dogs may be numbered. While previous statutes banning animal cruelty[1] always exempted such hunting, significant time has been spent in recent Parliaments debating proposals to ban it outright on the grounds that it involves unnecessary and unacceptable cruelty.

1 See generally Gardiner *Sports Law* (2nd edn, 2001, Cavendish Publishing), pp 129–138.

A1.75 In March 2001, Parliament debated the first ever government bill proposing an outright ban of hunting wild mammals with dogs, all of its predecessors having been private members' bills. On a free vote, the Commons voted by 387 to 174 for a total ban. However, the bill failed in the Lords and ran out of time when the 2001 general election was called. In its manifesto for that election, Labour promised to allow another free vote on the issue, but after its election it stalled, not wishing to alienate rural voters, particularly in the wake of the foot and mouth crisis of 2001. In November 2001 a Parliamentary motion signed by 203 MPs called on the Government to honour its manifesto pledge, particularly in light of the progress (and eventual success) of a Scottish bill to outlaw the sport. The House of Commons voted again on 18 March 2002 for an outright ban on hunting by an overwhelming majority of 386 to 175. The following day, the House of Lords rejected an outright ban, instead voting by a majority of 366 to 59 for restrictions on hunting policed by a licensing scheme. Reluctant to use the Parliament Act to override the House of Lords, the government announced that it would hold six months of consultation before introducing a bill to resolve the dispute[1].

1 'Talks pledge over hunting bill' www.news.bbc.co.uk (21 March 2002). One issue raised in the debate has been the compatibility of an absolute ban with the Human Rights Act 1998, and particularly Art 8 (respect for private life) and Art 1 of Protocol I (right to peaceful enjoyment of property) of that Act. See Burns Report *Report of the Committee of Inquiry into Hunting with Dogs in England and Wales* (2000), quoted at length in Gardiner *Sports Law* (2nd edn, 2001, Cavendish Publishing), pp 134–137. See also Singh and Thomas 'The Human Rights Act implications of a ban on hunting with dogs' [2002] 1 EHRLR 28.

(e) Gambling

A1.76 Gambling and gaming activity in this country is not by any means confined to betting on the outcome or other aspects of sports events. However, a substantial proportion of betting in this country is based on horse-racing and other sports events[1], and gambling is both an important revenue-generator for sport and the source of a corruption risk that many governing bodies have seen fit to introduce regulations of their own to address. Therefore, government legislation on gaming and gambling generally[2] has included various sports-specific provisions, including requirements for approval of horserace courses for betting by the Horserace Betting Levy Board, licensing of on-course bookmakers, and restricting pool betting on horseraces to the Horserace Totaliser Board. Furthermore, by virtue of those two statutory bodies (the Horserace Betting Levy Board and the Horserace Totaliser Board), since the 1960s the government has been directly involved in the determination of funding for the sport of horseracing.

1 According to a 1998 report by the Monopolies and Mergers Commission, 71% of the 1997 turnover of licensed betting offices was on horse racing, 20% on greyhound racing, 5% on other sports, and 4% on numbers betting: *Ladbroke Group plc and the Coral betting business: a report on the merger situation* (Cm 4030, 1998, MMC).

2 Government regulation of gambling currently takes the form of the Betting and Gaming Act 1960, as amended by the Betting, Gaming and Lotteries Act 1963, the Gaming Act 1968, the Lotteries and Amusements Act 1976 and the National Lottery Act 1993. See generally Smith *The Law of Betting, Gaming and the Lotteries* (1987, Butterworths).

A1.77 In March 2000, having 'identified no overriding reason why the assessment, collection and apportion of a levy on horserace betting should be a proper function of the public sector'[1], the Home Office announced the government's decision to abolish the horserace betting levy and the Horserace Betting Levy Board and to sell the Totaliser Board to a consortium of racing interests, thereby seeking 'to bring to an end the Government's direct involvement in the administration and financing of racing, so enabling racing to take responsibility for its own affairs'[2]. In November 2000, the government issued a consultation paper proposing that horseracing's governing body, the British Horseracing Board, succeed the Levy Board as the central funding body for racing, and a new statutory regulator be established to approve and monitor all racecourse betting operations. Implementation has been delayed by a dispute between the British Horseracing Board and the bookmaking industry over the commercial arrangements that should replace the Levy, and the government has said that the Levy may continue to carry out its current responsibilities for another three years or more. Indeed, in March 2002 Culture Secretary Tessa Jowell was forced to fulfil her statutory responsibility to determine the Levy scheme for 2002/03 when the Levy Board members failed to agree a scheme themselves[3]. However, the government remains committed to the eventual abolition of the Levy and a devolution of its functions to the horseracing sector itself[4].

1 Home Office (2000) 'A Consultation Paper on the Proposed Abolition of the Horseracing Betting Levy Board and the Licensing of Racecourse Betting and Pool Betting on Horseracing' quoted in the *Gambling Review Report* (2001, HMSO), para 13.5.

2 *Gambling Review Report* (2001, HMSO), para 4.24.

3 '41st Levy Scheme Finalised', DCMS press release 35/02 (7 March 2002).

4 DCMS press release 71/02 (17 April 2002).

A1.78 In July 2001, the Gambling Review Body, headed by Sir Alan Budd, issued a report recommending a broad liberalisation of UK gambling laws, backed up by stricter regulation of various high risk areas. Specifically, it proposed that all regulation relating to gambling be incorporated into a single Act of Parliament, with regulation and licensing undertaken by a single regulator called the Gambling Commission. In relation to sport-specific issues, it suggested that bookmakers at greyhound tracks should be licensed and regulated in the same way as bookmakers at race courses, as should the privately-owned Tote and pool operators. It also endorsed Home Office proposals for a new legislative framework to deal with corruption, including corruption in sport. However, it was of the firm view that primary responsibility for dealing with corruption in sport should remain with the sports governing bodies[1]. It stated:

> It is clear that corrupt actions to affect the outcome of a sporting event are wholly unfair to the innocent punter and bookmaker. However we believe that the responsibility for preventing such actions lies with the individual sports. They have a strong motive for doing so. Spectators will not attend an event where they believe that the outcome has been fixed in advance … We would mainly expect the punter (and the non-betting spectator) to be protected by rules and disciplinary procedures imposed by the sports themselves[2].

1 The Gambling Review Body noted Jockey Club recommendations that more specific criminal offences be introduced directly relating to criminal behaviour in sport and related betting, such as the doping of a racehorse or greyhound, bribery of sports participants or officials, and corruption in connection with horseracing and other sports events, or in relation to betting on horseracing and other sports events. It did not endorse them, for two reasons: 'We consider that measures to improve the conduct of sportsmen, sporting officials or of punters are outside our remit. We do not think it should be the role of the Gambling Commission to monitor the behaviour of sportsmen … Although we are not unsympathetic to the case that has been put to us, for example that there should be a specific offence of doping a horse, we do not consider that it is properly within our remit to make recommendations relating to such an issue. We have had to concern ourselves with matters that are more directly linked to the actual activity of gambling, although our proposals for the licensing of bookmakers would mean that swift action could be taken against any licensed person who became involved in attempting to influence the outcome of a race in such a way. Secondly, we consider that sports bodies could do more to regulate the participants in their sports, and they should not always look to the criminal law to enforce their regulations. We agree that the law on corruption could be clearer and suggest that the Home Office should consider whether the law could be clarified to meet the concerns we have heard. But overall, we consider that more could be done within the current framework to ensure that betting is fairly conducted. We recommend that the Gambling Commission should work closely with the Jockey Club, and others, to ensure that betting is conducted in a fair manner and that there is not unfair access to information. Areas they may wish jointly to consider might include whether the ban on betting should be extended to more people (for example, trainers)'. *Gambling Review Report* (2001, HMSO), paras 26.33, 26.38 and 26.39.

2 *Gambling Review Report* (2001, HMSO), paras 16.50 and 16.51.

A1.79 In March 2002, the DCMS issued a government white paper[1] that proposed legislative implementation of many of the Gambling Review Body's recommendations.

1 *A Safe Bet for Success – Modernising Britain's Gambling Laws* (26 March 2002, DCMS).

(f) Tobacco sponsorship

A1.80 Like gambling, tobacco advertising and promotion is not confined to sport. However, sponsorship of sports events is a major promotional tool for tobacco brands, and a significant source of income for many sports. The current Labour government made a manifesto commitment in 1997 to ban advertising and promotion of tobacco products (including promotion via sponsorship of sports events), and originally intended to do so by implementing the EC Tobacco Advertising Directive 98/43/EC. However, after that Directive was annulled by the

European Court of Justice for lack of EU competence[1], the government adopted a private member's bill as a government bill, the Tobacco Advertising and Promotion Bill, which at the time of writing is awaiting a third reading. Clause 10 of the Bill would specifically prohibit using a sponsorship arrangement to promote a tobacco product. Under cl 10(2), both parties to such an arrangement (for example, a sports event organiser and a tobacco sponsor) would be guilty of an offence under the Bill[2]. Various sports particularly dependent upon income from tobacco sponsorship (such as snooker and darts) have asked the government for assistance in replacing this key source of income, but with little effect to date[3].

1 *Germany v EU Parliament and Council*, Case-376/98 [2000] ECR I-2247. A new proposed Directive was issued by the European Commission in May 2001. See paras D5.62 and D5.63.
2 See Tobacco Advertising and Promotion Bill [HL], Explanatory Notes, available on www.parliament.the-stationary-office.co.uk/pa/cm200102.
3 See eg 'Task Force signs seven ready to kick tobacco dependency' (1998) 34 Sports Marketing 1.

(g) Listing of events

A1.81 The public interest dimension of broadcasting is expressly recognised in the UK and beyond[1]. The broadcasting of showpiece sports events in particular is deemed to serve as a focal point for the nation, a moment of shared culture and identity[2]. As a result, access to such sports events by their broadcast on free, widely available media is deemed to be not only an important mechanism of 'sport for all', but also an important aspect of the public's (human) right to freedom of information[3].

1 Thus, for example, the European Commission's Communication on Services of General Interest in Europe (COM (96) 443 final) states, under the heading 'Broadcasting', that 'television and radio have a general interest dimension … being linked to moral and democratic values, such as pluralism, information ethics and protection of the individual … '.
2 Witness, for example, the empty streets of the City of London at midday on Friday 7 June 2002, when England played Argentina in Group F of the FIFA World Cup Finals.
3 See EC Directive 89/552/EEC, as amended by EC Directive 97/36/EC, Recitals 15 and 18. See also European Parliament, *Resolution on the broadcasting of sports events*, B4-0326/96, [1996] OJ No C 166/109: '[The European Parliament] considers it essential for all spectators to have a right of access to major sports events, just as they have a right to freedom of information … [and therefore] considers that exclusive broadcasting rights for certain sports events which are of general interest in one or more Member States must be granted to channels which broadcast in non-encrypted form so that these events remain accessible to the population as a whole'. See also Joint UK Government/Sports Councils' Response to the Commission Consultation Paper *The European Model of Sport* (May 1999) at para 21: 'The right to information … Subscription and pay-per-view television is not in itself a threat to sport, so long as it is balanced by requirements to ensure access by a substantial proportion of the public to events of major importance to society without any additional charge being made for reception of these events (ie on free to air television)'.

A1.82 Commercial television (in the form of the ITV Network) first started broadcasting in the 1950s. Legislation has existed in the UK since that time, aimed at securing 'free' public access to sports and other events deemed to be of national importance. The current statute is the Broadcasting Act of 1996 ('BA 1996'), Pt IV of which:

- empowers the Secretary of State to 'list' (ie designate) 'a sporting or other event of national importance', public access to which, through coverage on free-to-air, widely available television, must be protected (s 97);
- distinguishes between category 1 broadcasters (broadcasters whose programming is available without charge to 95% or more of the population, ie currently the BBC, ITV and Channel 4) and category 2 broadcasters (ie all other broadcasters) (s 98); and

- bars a category 2 broadcaster from acquiring exclusive broadcasting rights to a listed event without the consent of the Independent Television Commission ('ITC'), unless those rights have already been offered to category 1 broadcasters on 'fair and reasonable' terms, and no category 1 broadcaster has been willing to acquire them on those terms (s 101).

A1.83 In mid-1997, the Department of National Heritage (now the DCMS) announced that a set of relevant factors would be developed to ensure that the list only includes events 'which we can all, no matter what our personal loyalties, recognise as a quintessential part of our national life and our sense of common identity'. The criteria eventually adopted included as a primary requirement that:

> [t]he event has a special national resonance, not simply a significance to those who ordinarily follow the sport concerned; it is an event which serves to unite the nation; a shared point on the national calendar[1].

1 Appendix to letter sent by the DCMS to various sports bodies in November 1997.

A1.84 An Advisory Group, chaired by Lord Gordon of Strathblane, was appointed to consider (in consultation with sports rights-holders) which events met these criteria and to make recommendations to the Secretary of State. The Advisory Group issued its report on 2 March 1998. It unanimously recommended that certain events (called Group A events) remain protected from exclusive live broadcast by category 2 broadcasters, but that other events (Group B events) be made available for exclusive live broadcast by category 2 broadcasters so long as category 1 broadcasters were offered an opportunity to carry secondary coverage. In June 1998, the Secretary of State announced that he had accepted 'the general principles' of the Advisory Group's report, including the recommendation to distinguish between Group A and Group B events.

A1.85 The protected Group A events are currently the Olympic Games; the FIFA World Cup Finals Tournament; the FA Cup Final; the Scottish FA Cup Final (in Scotland only); the Grand National; the Derby; the Wimbledon Tennis Finals; the UEFA Football Championship Finals Tournament; the Rugby World Cup Final; and the Rugby League Challenge Cup Final. These events cannot be broadcast exclusively live in the UK by Channel 5, BSkyB or other non-'public' broadcasters within the meaning of the Act, unless authorised by the ITC. The ITC publishes a Code on Sports and Other Listed Events that identifies the criteria against which it will decide whether to give such consent, being principally whether or not 'broadcasters have had a genuine opportunity to acquire the rights on fair and reasonable terms', including whether the price sought for the rights was 'fair, reasonable and non-discriminatory as between the two categories of programme service. What is a fair price will depend upon the rights being offered and the value of those rights to the broadcasters'[1].

1 ITC Code on Sports and Other Listed Events, www.itc.org.uk, para 13.

A1.86 The current Group B events are cricket test matches played in England; non-Finals play in the Wimbledon tennis championship; all matches in the Rugby World Cup Finals Tournament prior to the final itself; Six Nations Championship rugby matches involving the four home unions; the Commonwealth Games; the World Athletics Championship; the Cricket World Cup (final, semi-finals and matches involving home nations' teams); the Ryder Cup; and the Open Golf

Championship. These events can be broadcast exclusively live in the UK by Channel 5, BSkyB, etc provided that a 'public' broadcaster (within the meaning of the BA 1996) has been granted the right to show delayed coverage of at least 10% of the scheduled duration of the event, subject to a minimum of 30 minutes for an event lasting an hour or more[1].

1 ITC Code on Sports and other Listed Events, www.itc.org.uk, para 18.

A1.87 The Secretary of State for Culture, Media and Sport can add events to or delete events from the list at any time, subject to a duty to consult with the BBC, the Welsh television authority, the ITC and the rights owners of the events in question[1].

1 A separate voluntary code of conduct has been drawn up by the Major Sports Division of the CCPR and endorsed by the ITC. The purpose of this voluntary code is to encourage rights-holders to make available to public broadcasters (either live, delayed, or in highlights programmes) events of national importance that are not listed for statutory protection by the Secretary of State.

A1.88 In their comments on the ITC Code implementing the provisions of the BA 1996, various UK broadcasters noted that the legislation binds only domestic broadcasters, ie broadcasters within the jurisdiction of the UK government. Therefore, it would not prevent foreign rights-holders from broadcasting coverage of UK listed events on their own channels, broadcast in the UK by satellite/cable platforms, thereby circumventing the protections enshrined in the BA 1996. Similar points were made in other European states that had enacted their own 'listed events' legislation.

A1.89 In response to this concern, in April 1997 the EC Directive known as Television Without Frontiers[1] was amended to add a new Art 3A that establishes a system of mutual recognition and enforcement for member states' lists of designated events. Specifically, Article 3A:

(i) acknowledges the right of member states to take national measures compatible with EC law to ensure public access to broadcasts of key sports and other events;
(ii) requires any member state that wishes to secure extra-territorial effect for its list of events to notify the list to the Commission, for publication (after the Commission, via its Contact Committee, has satisfied itself that the list is compatible with EC law) in the Official Journal; and
(iii) requires every member State to take appropriate steps to ensure that broadcasters within its jurisdiction exercise cross-border rights that they hold to sporting events in a manner that respects the notifying member state's list of events[2].

1 89/552/EEC, amended to insert new Art 3A by 97/36/EC, adopted by the European Parliament and Council on 30 June 1997. See further para B1.49 et seq.
2 Directive 97/36/EC, OJ 30 July 1997 L 202/60. The same provisions are also included in the Council of Europe's European Convention on Transfrontier Television.

A1.90 Article 3A(3) of the 'Television Without Frontiers' Directive was implemented as part of UK domestic law by the Television Broadcasting Regulations 2000. Those regulations confer a power on the ITC to provide information relating to rights to televise UK listed events that it considers appropriate to competent authorities in other EC and EEA states in order to enable those authorities to exercise their obligations under the 'Television Without Frontiers' Directive to prevent broadcasters under their jurisdiction from circumventing the UK listed event rules. They also empower the ITC to prevent a UK-based broadcaster exercising exclusive broadcasting rights in another member state to an event that has been listed for protection in that member state unless such broadcaster is authorised to do so under that state's listed event rules.

A1.91 The UK's listed event rules came up for scrutiny by the House of Lords in the *TV Danmark* case[1]. TV Danmark, the UK-based claimant broadcaster, had acquired exclusive rights to broadcast in Denmark five 'away' qualifying matches played by Denmark in its FIFA 2002 World Cup qualifying group. It sought to exercise those rights by broadcasting coverage of the matches exclusively into Denmark from the UK. However, the matches were included on Denmark's own list of protected events, ie they could only be broadcast by broadcasters reaching at least 90% of the Danish population, and TV Danmark was a subscription-based broadcaster reaching only 60% of Denmark's population. Furthermore, the Danish free-to-air broadcasters that TV Danmark had outbid to acquire the rights still wished to broadcast the same events, and were prepared to pay for the right to do so, just not as much as TV Danmark had bid. The ITC (and the Secretary of State of Culture, Media and Sport, intervening in the House of Lords) argued that consent had to be denied to TV Danmark's proposed broadcast of the matches, because otherwise the Danish public would be denied the right to watch the event on television in Denmark. TV Danmark argued that the ITC had to consent to TV Danmark's exclusive exploitation of the rights, because the public broadcasters had had a fair opportunity (namely, the original tendering process) to acquire the rights but had failed to do so. That was all the ITC Code required for consent to be granted, and the fact that TV Danmark was not prepared, post-acquisition of the rights, to share them with the public broadcasters (as the Danish listed events rules required) did not change the analysis.

1 *R v Independent Television Commission, ex p TVDanmark 1 Ltd* [2001] UKHL 42, [2001] 1 WLR 1604.

A1.92 The Court of Appeals agreed with TV Danmark, stating that the tender auction provided a fair opportunity for public broadcasters to acquire the rights, which vindicated the public's interest in watching the events, and post-acquisition events were irrelevant and could not be taken into consideration by the ITC. The House of Lords overturned that ruling, based on the premise that the purpose of the Directive is 'to prevent the exercise by broadcasters of exclusive rights in such a way that a substantial proportion of the public in another member state is deprived of the possibility of following a designated event'[1]. That right was not vindicated by giving public broadcasters the opportunity to bid for the rights in an open auction. If that was all that was required, then in effect there would be no restriction on free market forces, and therefore no point to the legislation at all. As Lord Hoffman said:

> The argument that the public is given the possibility of watching the event if the public broadcasters are given the possibility of buying the rights at auction is in my opinion wrong. The Directive requires the public to have the possibility of following the event in the sense that a member of the public may watch it if he chooses to switch on his television set[2].

The auction acquisition process is a relevant factor to be taken into account in deciding whether public broadcasters had an opportunity to acquire the rights on 'fair and reasonable terms', but it is not determinative, because 'the clear purpose of Part IV [of the BA 1996] is, if necessary, to protect the public interest in free access to important sporting events against market forces. The ITC is engaged in a delicate balance of the interests of broadcasters, sports organisers and the general public'[3]. Since the auction itself was not determinative, it was appropriate (and could be necessary) to look at subsequent events to determine whether the public broadcasters had been given sufficient opportunity to acquire the rights on fair and reasonable terms, such that consent to exclusive broadcast by non-public broadcasters should be given. Here, the refusal of TV Danmark to give the public broadcasters an opportunity to bid to share the rights with it (a requirement under the Danish law) meant that the pre-condition to consent under the Code (a fair opportunity to acquire the rights on fair and reasonable terms) was not satisfied. The 'right of the European citizen to watch his national football team'[4] was thus resoundingly vindicated.

1 [2001] 1 WLR 1604 at 1613.
2 [2001] 1 WLR 1604 at 1613.
3 [2001] 1 WLR 1604 at 1614.
4 [2001] 1 WLR 1604 at 1606. For comment on the case, see 'Listed Sports Events Protected Against the TV Rights Market' (2001) 4(4) Sports Law Bulletin 1; Harrington 'UK Listed Events Ruling Looks Bad for Kirch' (2001) Sportcal.com, 6 August; Santy 'Listed Events Legislation – Identifying a Rationale' [2001] 8(5) SATLJ 1; Barr Smith 'Listed Events and Sale of World Cup TV Rights' [2001] 9(3) SATLJ 135; Harris 'Transfrontier Broadcasting of World Cup Qualifying Games' [2001] 9(2) SATLJ 100.

D Indirect Regulation of Sport

A1.93 This chapter has already addressed how the Labour government, building on the foundations laid by the Conservatives' 1995 White Paper and in particular the introduction of the National Lottery, has since 1997 pushed sport up the political agenda as a key instrument of public policy[1]. Having done so, however, it has also therefore had to acknowledge the importance of the role of the private national governing bodies in the organisation and promotion of sport in the UK[2], and has used the leverage created by control over access to Lottery funding and increased Exchequer funding to co-opt those bodies as partners in the drive for *A Sporting Future for All*.

1 See paras A1.31 to A1.37.
2 In its landmark April 2000 policy paper for sport, the government stated: 'Many agencies provide funding, support services and programmes for sport. However, delivery at community level is largely driven by three key networks – education, local authority and national governing bodies of sport'. See *A Sporting Future for All* (April 2000), p 51.

A1.94 If government policy is to be implemented by making partners of sports governing bodies, however, then those bodies have to conform to minimum public standards of governance and administration in the running of their sports. In its March 2001 policy statement, *A Sporting Future for All*, the government identified the 'fragmented and too often unprofessional' organisation and management of sport as an obstacle to its goals of mass participation and success at elite levels[1]. It proposed:

a modernising partnership with the governing bodies of sport. The public sector will continue to support sport at its foundations as it has in the past – and give sport greater say over how those funds are spent – but on two conditions:

[1] that commercially successful sports also contribute to the same pot and invest in grassroots facilities; and

[2] that all governing bodies agree to work to a number of clear and agreed targets for the development of their sport[2].

This meant UK Sport and Sport England devolving funding powers to governing bodies, ie allowing those bodies to run their own lottery-funded programmes, but only on the basis that such bodies not only publish clear and realistic plans for broadening participation and identifying talent, but also modernise their management systems and structures so as to be able to demonstrate high standards of corporate governance. The policy statement continued[3]:

> We recognise that a closer partnership with the governing bodies of sport is crucial if we are to deliver our ambitious plans for English sport. We believe that governing bodies must be responsible for setting the strategic vision for their sport and that resources should be put behind these strategies to give them every chance of success. Governing bodies must also take responsibility for demonstrating a high standard of management, and clear, realistic plans for widening participation and developing talent. In return those bodies will be able to secure more control over the distribution of funding to their sport[4].

1 *A Sporting Future for All* (March 2001, DCMS) at p 5.
2 *A Sporting Future for All* (March 2001, DCMS) at p 19.
3 *A Sporting Future for All* (March 2001, DCMS) at p 45. See also *A Sporting Future for All: Action Plan*, Report of the Implementation Group to the DCMS and DfEE (December 2000), Section 9 and App B.
4 *A Sporting Future for All* (March 2001, DCMS) at p 47.

A1.95 Both UK Sport and Sport England play a role in implementing this policy.

A1.96 Sport England 'recognises that the Sport England Lottery Fund will only be truly effective if it is underpinned by a sound sports infrastructure'[1]. Its work in that field includes a quality assurance programme – QUEST for Sports Development – that sets quality service benchmarks for sports development. In addition, it has offered a Running Sport for Governing Bodies programme, including workshops on 'sports equity, child protection and sports development planning. In addition to this, assistance is given to help governing bodies to improve the quality of their planning, corporate governance and financial management'[2].

1 *Sport England* (April 2000, Sport England).
2 *Sport England* (April 2000 Sport England).

A1.97 The 1999 Funding Agreement between the DCMS and Sport England requires Sport England to ensure that 'contractual funding of the CCPR and grant-in-aid to sports Governing Bodies contains measurable outputs for targets that are linked to Government and ESC objectives' and that 'the "modernising" of the CCPR and sports governing bodies takes place. Proposals should include how these bodies intend to address issues relating to equal opportunities and a greater representation of minority groups in formal positions within the organisation'[1]. In December 2000, Sport England announced that, in place of the usual one-year grants, it was going to introduce four-year funding agreements for governing bodies that could demonstrate high standards of governance, management and accountability[2].

1 Funding Agreement between the English Sports Council and the DCMS for 1999/2002, available on www.culture.gov.uk.
2 See eg 'Sport England to extend funding for successful sports' (2001) Sportcal.com, 1 December.

A1.98 Similarly, UK Sport has been given a budget of £7m for the period 2001 to 2004 specifically to pursue the modernisation of national governing bodies, helping them institute structural reform, improve staff and volunteer development, encourage and support the adoption of the highest ethical standards, policies and practices, and enhance communication and income generation[1].

1 *A Sporting Future for All – The Government's Plan for Sport* (Annual Report 2001/02); UK Sport *Annual Review 2001/02*, p 8.

A1.99 Lottery funding is also used to achieve this aim. Thus, World Class Performance funding 'is targeted where there is evidence of medal potential and a commitment to high performance governance, planning, management and implementation'[1]. Similarly, UK Sport's Major Events policy states that applications for assistance will only be considered from governing bodies recognised by UK Sport. Furthermore:

> UK Sport believes that to achieve excellence and be a leader in world sport we must have a sport system which is ethically and morally based, free from allegations of corruption and unacceptable behaviour, particularly when bidding to stage major sports events … UK Sport is currently developing a new policy based on the fundamental principle that grants will not be allocated to any sporting event where officials, representatives or other parties are deemed to have breached acceptable standards of behaviour. Accordingly, UK Sport will need to work closely with organisations tasked with securing events, to ensure adherence to its policy[2].

1 Elite Sports Funding Review, Report of the Review Group chaired by Dr Jack Cunningham MP (August 2001), p 9.
2 *A UK Strategy: Major Events, a 'Blueprint' for Success* (1999, UK Sport).

A1.100 As the next section of this chapter illustrates, the traditional governmental reluctance to take direct responsibility for the running of sport has not fundamentally changed. Without question, however, the introduction of Lottery funding and the increase in Exchequer funding for sport has given the government a leverage over the private sports movement that it never previously had, which it is able to use to improve the standards of governance of private sports bodies, so that they are fitting partners in implementing government policy[1]. The government is still exploring how to strike the balance between on the one hand imposing controls, transparency and accountability on the sports movement and on the other hand respecting the autonomy and expertise of its new-found policy partner.

1 When questioned as to what the government was doing in the face of the perceived incompetence of sports governing bodies, then Sports-Minister Tony Banks pointed out: 'We're discussing a list of priorities with any sports governing body that receives public money and setting them systematic objectives. We'll continue to evaluate their progress'. See 'Banks seeks feel-good factor' (1999) Daily Telegraph, 20 February. Similarly, in his evidence in 1998 to the Select Committee on Culture, Media and Sport, Mr Banks stated: 'In England I think we have spent the last 3½ years through the Lottery some £700m or committed £700m worth of expenditure. That is the nature of it. We are then dealing with organisations that in the past have been arguing around what is the equivalent of a few bob, though it runs into greater sums than that, and I think in many ways the

structures that were in place, with the sort of fairly amateurish way that it was approached, have not moved easily into the area where there are now large amounts of money, never enough of course, as you know, but large amounts of money with sport becoming a bigger and bigger business as we go through. That is changing now in terms of the personnel. Governing bodies are realising that they have to be professional and we require them of course to make themselves very accountable for what is still public monies, because it is not government money that is going through the Lottery, but it is public money, and if anything were to go wrong, the responsibility undoubtedly would be visited back on us here in the House of Commons'.

E The non-interventionist model revisited: the Football Task Force

A1.101 When self-regulating sports bodies get it wrong (and they do, often!), the cry goes out for the government to 'take a controlling influence'[1]. Such calls have been most often focused on football, as the increasing commercialisation of the national game has left supporters and local communities feeling increasingly alienated from their clubs[2]. However, the government has steadfastly resisted assuming a greater regulatory role in football[3], instead insisting on the right and responsibility of football's governing bodies to run the game autonomously.

1 See eg Welch 'Time for real action' (1999) Daily Telegraph, 6 February. The issue raised (usually with more subtlety than in the following quote) is: 'Who are these backward, unwieldy, misguided, greedy, secretive or just plain incompetent organisations answerable to?' Hughes 'Banks seeks feel-good factor' (1999) Daily Telegraph, 20 February. The answer given in that article by Tony Banks, then Minister for Sport, was: 'Sport is just too important for individuals and the country as a whole to be left drifting … There is a central role for government in sport. As enablers, as organisers, as arbitrators at certain times where there is clearly a need for action. We need to modernise our sporting structures'.
2 See eg Conn 'Growing support for fan ownership' (2002) Independent, 3 May.
3 See eg Chris Smith, Secretary of State for Culture, Music and Sport, Soccer Analyst Weekly Bulletin, 29 June 1999 (government regulator for football 'would not be sensible'); Andy Burham, DCMS advisor, The Independent, 9 July 1999 ('The government's preference is for the game to get its own house in order').

A1.102 In 1997, the government established the Football Task Force to look into various issues of general public interest arising out of the growing commercialisation of the national game[1]. Chaired by David Mellor, the Task Force included representatives from football's governing bodies, including the FA Premier League, the Football Association and the Football League, as well as referees' and supporters' organisations, the Local Government Association, the Commission for Racial Equality and Liverpool University (with further members joining a Taskforce Working Group). Over two and a half years, the Task Force submitted recommendations to the government on racism, disabled access, Football in the Community schemes and representation of supporters within clubs[2]. Its final report[3] considered commercial issues such as ticket prices and merchandising, the commercialisation of football and conflicts between shareholders and fans arising from flotations. The report also considered the overall governance of the game, and in particular how to reconcile the conflicting interests of governing bodies, clubs and supporters.

1 See generally Brown 'Taken to Task: The Football Task Force, Government and the Regulation of the People's Game' in Greenfield & Osborn (eds) *Law and Sport in Contemporary Society* (2000, Frank Cass), pp 246–266.
2 Football Task Force reports: *Eliminating Racism* (March 1998); *Improving Disabled Access* (June 1998); and *Investing in the Community* (January 1999).
3 Football Task Force *Commercial Issues* (December 1999).

A1.103 In this last aspect of its final report, the Football Task Force was split. The football authorities protested that they did not have the power to regulate the commercial activities of their member clubs, or to mandate supporter representation at club board level. The majority in response proposed that the Football Association continue to control the playing side of the game, but that an independent outside regulator be created, called the Football Audit Commission, supported by a Football Ombudsman, to monitor compliance by clubs with the recommendations of the Task Force, with sanctioning power in the case of non-compliance. The football authorities refused to sign the majority report, instead producing a report of their own that advocated continued self-regulation with limited accountability to an Independent Scrutiny Panel[1].

1 See eg 'Watchdog to check on soccer' (1999) Guardian, 9 December.

A1.104 The government accepted the first three reports of the Football Task Force in full. On the last report, however, faced with a lack of consensus, rather than intervene in football through the creation of a statutory regulator the government endorsed the football establishment's proposed system of 'improved self-regulation of the sport', with an Independent Football Commission created by the football authorities and charged with reviewing football's improvements in the areas of financial and business matters within its competitions (including ticket prices, accessibility to matches, merchandise and stakeholder involvement), and implementation of the Task Force's recommendations as to customer service[1].

1 Statement of Chris Smith, Response to the Football Task Force, July 2000, available on www.culture.gov.uk. Critics have noted that the Commission is essentially a body without any real power. It is to receive reports from the Football Association and FA Premier League and make its own report on how the football authorities govern the game. It has no teeth to enforce the recommendations of its report. Much controversy was caused over who would be appointed as chairman of the Independent Football Commission. Sir John Smith (former deputy commissioner of the Metropolitan Police and member of the Football Task Force) was proposed, but his appointment was opposed by the Premier League, who threatened to withdraw its support for the Commission if Smith was appointed, since he was an open advocate of increased regulation and supporter involvement. The government was unwilling to stand up to the football authorities, and instead appointed Derek Fraser, vice-chancellor of Teesside University.

A1.105 The strict limits on the government's interest in regulating sport were seen again in March 2002, when it seemed that the loss of broadcasting rights fees caused by ITV Digital's collapse would make many Football League clubs insolvent. Despite public outcry, the government made it clear that it would not intervene in what it saw as a private contractual matter[1]. Sports Minister Richard Caborn offered merely to act as intermediary in negotiations[2].

1 See eg 'Political Football' *Sports Business International* (June 2002), p 54.
2 'Minister offers to act as intermediary in talks with Football League' (2002) Financial Times, 26 March.

4 THE SYSTEM UNDER STRAIN

A1.106 Serious criticisms have been made of the current approach to government policy implementation in the sports sector. Those criticisms have focused on deficiencies in the infrastructure, involving a multiplicity of different actors with varying and sometimes overlapping and conflicting responsibilities, without any clear over-arching framework of reporting and responsibility. This infrastructure is said to hinder a coherent across-the-board approach and to risk allowing important issues to 'fall through the gaps'.

A The role of the Sports Minister

A1.107 One respected commentator has pointed out that no Sports Minister has ever 'been as successful as he or she deserved, or wanted, because the job carries so little power'[1]. The Minister for Sport has traditionally been not a Cabinet Minister with his or her own department, but instead a junior government minister at the level of Parliamentary Under-Secretary, reporting to the Secretary of State for the DCMS. He or she has had no responsibility for setting or executing policy. Instead, all funding and power is devolved to the Sports Councils under the 'arm's length' principle, leaving the Sports Minister with little leverage.

1 Goodbody 'Caborn enters corridor without power' (2001) Times, 13 June.

A1.108 Then Sports Minister Tony Banks, in his 1998 evidence to the Select Committee on Culture, Media and Sport, presented the issue in the following way:

> [I]t is an interesting fact that the budget of my Department for sport is small at about £50 million, and that would not be that bad of course if the £50 million was totally at my disposal, but of course about £49 million of that £50 million goes straight out to other bodies like the English Sports Council and the UK Sports Council, so in terms of money that is available, as it were, to me as a Minister and to our Department directly, it is a very, very small amount and that is why the constant stream of Members who come to me and put great projects to me and ask how we can possibly fund them should realise that, I am afraid, as a Minister, I tend to have to try to influence rather than to take executive action in terms of sports decisions. Lastly, I asked for a list because someone said, 'What does the Sports Minister do?' and it is an exceedingly good question and I think really I would see my function more as an advocate for sport within government because I have been contacting my colleague Ministers who appear to have some element of responsibility for sport within their Departments and so far I have been talking to Education Ministers, Employment, Home Affairs, Defence, the Foreign Office and International Development as all of them have a sport element somewhere within their Department … [I]nfluence rather than executive decision-making is the role of any Sports Minister[1].

1 Minutes of Evidence to the Select Committee on Culture, Media and Sport, 1997. Mr Banks stated that the suggestion that 'the job of the Sports Minister is in some ways, to a large degree, a sham, that it is an enormously publicised post and you get a lot of attention, but actually your effect on British sport is not very great' was 'quite unkind, but probably reasonably accurate'. Similarly, Mr Bank's successor, Kate Hoey, is reported to have said: 'I can try and influence, I can try and persuade, but I have got no real power': (2001) Independent, 15 May.

A1.109 This is perceived as a serious limitation on the ability to get sport high up the political agenda[1]. Calls therefore periodically surface to give the Minister for Sport direct executive power and responsibility, by creating a Department of State with a place for its Minister in the Cabinet, in order to increase his or her influence and accountability, and to achieve access to the wider funding opportunities that exist in separate government departments[2].

1 See eg Houlihan 'Sport in the United Kingdom' in Chalip, Johnson and Stachura (eds) *National Sports Policies: An International Handbook* (1996, Greenwood Press) at p 401: 'The fortuitous combination of a group of senior government members with a clear agenda for sport can evaporate just as rapidly as it emerged, leaving sport at the whim of the next incumbent of number 10 Downing Street'.

2 CCPR *Active Britain: A Manifesto for Sport and Recreation* (May 2001) ('We propose a dedicated British Sports Department with a Cabinet Minister to drive policy across Whitehall Departments in partnership with the devolved administrations'). See also Goodbody 'A Journalist's View' [2001] 9(3) SATLJ 5 (suggesting that the Secretary of State and Minister for Sport should also chair UK Sport and Sport England respectively, thereby assuming executive power and responsibility).

A1.110 In its response to the report of the Committee that heard Mr Banks' evidence quoted above[1], the government stated: 'Ministers do not intend abolishing the arm's length principle, but they do intend that the [DCMS] should give strategic leadership, and should set a clear policy framework within which its bodies can operate', using in particular the policy directions issued by the Secretary of State for the DCMS to Lottery-funded grant bodies under the National Lottery Act 1998[2].

1 See para A1.108.
2 *Objectives and Performance of the DCMS: Government Response to the Fifth Report from the Culture, Media & Sport Committee, Session 1997/98*: available on www.publications.parliament.uk.

A1.111 Starting with Richard Caborn, appointed in June 2001, the Minister for Sport is now at Minister of State level. However, scepticism remains:

> This elevation, however, may be more cosmetic than real. In principle, it means the Government is now giving sport a greater priority. In reality, it will mean little unless Caborn is able to act like a Minister of State. He will be able to do this only if he does what so many of his predecessors have wanted to do, and that is to have executive powers[1].

1 Goodbody 'Caborn enters corridor without power' (2001) Times, 13 June.

A1.112 Mr Caborn wasted no time in imposing himself. He immediately complained about the 'strategic vacuum right across sport', in particular the lack of structure to the pursuit of sports policy objectives of Sport England[1]. He called for decentralisation of funding and resources to the regions, prompting the immediate resignation of Sport England's chief executive, Derek Casey, and his eventual replacement by New Zealander David Moffatt[2].

1 (2001) Times, 25 July.
2 'New UK Minister rings in changes at Sport England' (2001) Sportcal.com, 15 June; 'New broom that promises to make sweeping changes' (2001) Times, 15 June.

B Wembley Stadium and Picketts Lock

A1.113 The report of the Culture Media and Sport Committee Report into the Picketts Lock affair[1], published in November 2001, begins:

> This Report threads its way through the sorry and convoluted way in which a national athletics centre at Picketts Lock was plucked out of the air by the Government and then abruptly dropped. It is a saga of how Government involved itself beyond its scope and powers in conjuring up a project that this Committee judged unviable from the start. It is also a salutary lesson to the Lottery award panels that they are not lucky dips but custodians of public money.

1 *Unpicking the Lock: The World Athletics Championships in the UK*, Report of the Culture, Media and Sport Committee (November 2001): available on www.publications.parliament.uk/pa/cm200102/cmselect.

A1.114 By 1994, it was acknowledged that Wembley Stadium was drawing to the end of its useful life. It was proposed to be replaced by a new national, world-class stadium to accommodate football, rugby and athletics. The combination was important: the government wanted to assist athletics to attract the Olympics and IAAF World Championships to the UK, and knew that a stand-alone athletics stadium of sufficient quality for those purposes was financially unsustainable.

A1.115 In February 1995, Sport England established a Project Steering Group (comprising representatives of Sport England, the Football Association ('FA'), the Football League, the FA Premier League, the Rugby Football League and the British Athletic Federation) to establish a brief for the project. In October 1996, Wembley was chosen to be the site of the new national stadium, and in December 1996 Sport England made a provisional award to the FA of £120m of Lottery funds to acquire the site. The Culture Media & Sport Committee subsequently criticised this grant as 'cavalier', given that planning permission had not yet even been sought, let alone obtained. The English National Stadium Trust was set up to purchase the site and it then leased the site to Wembley National Stadium Limited ('WNSL'), a wholly-owned subsidiary of the FA. Finance was then to be put in place for the construction of the stadium, based on a 20-year commitment by the FA to stage its important events in the new stadium.

A1.116 By December 1999, however, concerns had arisen regarding the provision for athletics in the new stadium. UK Sport commissioned architects to report on the design. The report concluded that the stadium as designed could not provide a suitable venue for the Olympic Games or for any athletics world championships. On 22 December 1999, Chris Smith, the Secretary of State for Culture, Media & Sport announced that whilst Wembley should be the focus of world class football and rugby events, alternative arrangements would have to be made for athletics, and that the FA had therefore agreed to return £20m of the original £120m Sport England grant.

A1.117 The Culture Media and Sport Committee subsequently criticised this decision as 'bizarre, rushed and flawed', failing to consider alternative solutions such as building platforms in and outside the proposed new Wembley stadium to convert it into a suitable athletics venue. It also criticised the agreement made by the government with the FA for the return of £20m from the original £120m Lottery grant as compensation for the dropping of athletics from the project, a figure allegedly 'plucked from the air', not reduced to a formal legal agreement, and made without any consultation with Sport England, the grantor of the funds.

A1.118 The announcement that Wembley could not be used for athletics prompted a search for an alternative athletics site, particularly to stage the 2005 World Athletics Championships that had been awarded to the UK by the IAAF on the basis of plans for a new national stadium in London. On 24 March 2000, UK Athletics announced its preference for a site at Picketts Lock in Lee Valley.

A1.119 In December 2000, WNSL launched a review of the whole Wembley project, including financing requirements, as well as a formal reappraisal of Wembley's suitability to accommodate athletics. However, the Secretary of State wrote to the Lee Valley planning authority to reassure it of the government's view that Picketts Lock remained the best option for hosting the 2005 World Athletics Championships. In February 2001, WNSL was informed by the government that a decision had been made that athletics would not form part of Wembley Stadium and in March 2001 the Secretary of State announced that £60m would be made available from Sport England for the development of a world class athletics stadium at Picketts Lock. Again, the Culture Media and Sport Select Committee subsequently criticised these announcements for ignoring the whole basis of the original concept, namely the recognition that an athletics-only stadium for the largest of events was not economically viable and therefore that a national stadium had to be developed that could stage athletics as well as football and rugby events.

A1.120 The estimated total cost of the Picketts Lock project was £97.3m. Sport England quickly identified serious problems with the project, such as an inadequate transport infrastructure and the lack of possibilities for provision of accommodation for athletes within the vicinity of the stadium site. Nevertheless, UK Athletics announced that the Secretary of State had promised to underwrite the project. The then Minister of Sport, Kate Hoey MP described the underwriting of the project as a 'technicality' that could be performed by UK Sport on the understanding that the government would 'bail them out' if necessary. However, by May 2001, the issues of the funding shortfall and the underwriting of the cost remained unresolved, despite appeals to the Secretary of State for assistance.

A1.121 After the May 2001 general election, Tessa Jowell replaced Chris Smith as Secretary of State for Culture, Media & Sport, and Richard Caborn replaced Kate Hoey as Minister for Sport, and they quickly called for a review of the Picketts Lock project. In June 2001, Sport England and the Lottery Panel agreed to defer the decision on the application for funding of the Picketts Lock project because of, among other things, the funding gap and lack of underwriting of the project, as well as transport and accommodation difficulties. The Select Committee subsequent found that these problems had existed and had been identified from the very beginning, but had been ignored by the government. In October 2001, UK Athletics was informed that the government did not consider Picketts Lock to be a suitable venue for the 2005 World Athletics Championships. Instead, the government proposed that the Championships be held at Sheffield, notwithstanding that the IAAF's acceptance of UK Athletics' bid to stage the event had been premised on London being the venue. The IAAF rejected this offer and reopened the bidding to host the event; UK Athletics immediately announced that it would not be bidding. The Select Committee criticised the government for the damage that the switch caused to the ability to attract major events to the UK in the future[1]. Further, it estimated that more than £6m of public money was spent on the aborted Picketts Lock project.

1 See eg 'IOC members confirm the lasting damage from the Picketts Lock fiasco' (2002) Daily Telegraph, 15 February.

A1.122 Meanwhile, the Wembley project itself had stalled over problems in obtaining the rest of the financing required (£715m) for the construction of the new national stadium. On 1 May 2001, the FA announced that it could not raise the necessary finance from private sources, and could not finance the project itself, so that unless the government underwrote the project it would have to be abandoned. The government declined the invitation and appointed advisor Patrick Carter to examine the options going forward. He concluded that the Wembley project remained the right choice[1], and in December 2001 the DCMS identified five tests to be met by 30 April 2002 in order for the project to continue to receive government support. In March 2002, however, it was announced that, as a result of the uncertainty over the project, London Underground had reallocated the £100m that it had budgeted to improve transport links to the site, creating a further funding gap and putting the grant of planning permission by Brent Council in jeopardy[2]. In April 2002, Richard Caborn announced that Birmingham's original alternative National Stadium bid could be resurrected if the Wembley Stadium team failed to secure that funding by the end of that month (a deadline subsequently extended by the Secretary of State, Tessa Jowell). Caborn described the decision to rebuild Wembley and the subsequent plans for the Picketts Lock athletics stadium as 'knee jerk reaction[s] [taken] without a strategic idea about where we are going as a nation in terms of sport'[3]. Subsequent developments did little to restore public confidence in the project[4]. Financing was secured and demolition work commenced only in October 2002.

1 Carter *English National Stadium Review – Interim Report, December 2001* (TSO, HC 479).
2 'Tube station shortfall stalls Wembley plans' (2002) Daily Telegraph, 12 March.
3 (2002) Birmingham Post, 11 April.
4 See eg '"Explosive" Wembley report reveals a litany of chaos' (2002) Independent, 15 May; 'Dynamite' report threatens Wembley rebuilding plans' (2002) Daily Telegraph, 16 May.

A1.123 The Culture Media and Sport Select Committee concluded that the government must decide, and clearly state, whether it wishes the UK to be the host to world class sporting events, and, if so, whether it is prepared to fund such events at a realistic level. The Committee criticised the government for prevaricating over whether to commit funding to projects, and thus 'holding hostage' major events that have merited Lottery grants but are unsure whether the government's professed commitment is likely to materialise into hard funding. The Committee recommended the appointment of a Minister for Events, who would have clearly identified resources and funding, the authority to commit such resources and the responsibility to drive such projects forward[1].

1 *Unpicking the Lock: The World Athletics Championships in the UK*, Report of the Culture, Media and Sport Committee (November 2001): available on www.publications.parliament.uk/pa/cm200102/cmselect.

A1.124 In response, the government stated that it recognised the need for 'a more effective and robust structure to oversee properly the largest major events from pre-bid evaluation to the organising and staging of the event', and said that it had asked the Cabinet Office's Performance and Innovation Unit to look at the issue as part of a wider sports review[1].

1 Government Response to the First Report from the Culture, Media and Sport Select Committee, February 2002, p 3. With respect to the £120m grant of Lottery funds to the Football Association and the subsequent agreement to return £20m of those funds in recognition of the fact that athletics could not be accommodated at the stadium, the government reiterated that issues relating to conditions on the grant of Lottery funds, variation of original conditions placed on that grant, and repayment of Lottery funds, were 'entirely a matter for Sport England'. As to the review being conducted by the Performance and Innovation Unit, see further para A1.127.

C The Cunningham report

A1.125 A review panel commissioned by the government in October 2000 to consider the future of elite sport in the UK issued a report in September 2001 that concluded: 'all is not well with sport in the UK'. While certain concerns were raised about sport at an amateur level[1], at the elite level it was found that:

> there are some overriding issues which the government must urgently resolve if this report is to herald a new dawn for UK sport:
>
> - The quality of leadership and management in sport at national level must be improved;
> - The opportunity must now be taken to change the style of leadership in Sport England to one which is much more open, inclusive, responsive and sport centred;
> - The complex structure of sport in the UK must be simplified and better understood;
> - Bureaucracy and territorial concerns must take second place to the development of sport itself;
> - There must be clearer responsibility and accountability for decision-making in sport, with proper incentives for delivery;
> - The national governing bodies must be supported to modernise their management systems and performance structures;
> - New investment in high quality club and talent development structures and systems will be required to achieve consistent success at World Class level;
> - There is a need for a radical step change in the way we license, train and employ sports coaches as they are the cornerstone to the development of talented performers;
> - Well co-ordinated, well managed UK wide funding and quality support services and facilities for our top sportsmen and women must be ensured and delivered quickly …
>
> Decisive leadership and a strong commitment from UK Government and the devolved administrations will also be essential if we are to deliver the outcomes and sporting success that everyone wants to see. It will also be crucial for the organisations they support and fund to be given firm direction and responsibility for delivery of the required results and to be held regularly accountable for the progress made. This will be best achieved if there is one lead body – UK Sport – which is given key responsibility for overseeing al the 'World Class' Programmes for Olympic/Paralympic Sports and GB/UK [national governing bodies]. The Sports Cabinet (the collective meeting of Ministers with responsibility for sport in England, Scotland, Wales and Northern Ireland, under the chairmanship of the Secretary of State for Culture, Media and Sport) will also have an essential role to play. This group of Ministers will provide the ideal medium for the collective direction, monitoring, reporting and accountability required to ensure delivery of a sustained programme of support for UK elite athletes[2].

1 For example, it was concluded that club sport was 'less well structured [than school sport] and indeed in some sports barely surviving … We need to ensure that the National Governing Bodies of sport are encouraged to develop clear club and volunteer development strategies and that investment in club sport becomes a greater priority for funding agencies': Elite Sports Funding Review, Report of the Review Group chaired by Dr Jack Cunningham MP (August 2001).

2 Elite Sports Funding Review, Report of the Review Group chaired by Dr Jack Cunningham MP (August 2001). See also Goodbody 'Report calls for cash to boost elite grants' (2001) Times, 12 September.

A1.126 At the Sports Cabinet meeting on 31 October 2001, the Sports Councils accepted and agreed to implement most of the Cunningham Report's recommendations (including a 'one stop shop' for national governing bodies seeking talent development funding), and the DCMS stated that it would consider the remaining recommendations (which require additional funding) in the context of the then-pending Comprehensive Spending Review[1].

1 *A Sporting Future for All – The Government's Plan for Sport*, Annual Report 2001/02.

A1.127 In addition, the Prime Minister announced on 1 February 2002 'the most wide-ranging review of British sport since the White Paper of 1975'[1], a collaboration between the DCMS and the Performance and Innovation Unit of the

Cabinet Office, charged with 'sorting out a new organisation chart for British sport'[2]. At the time of writing, the results of that review were still pending.

1 Trelford 'Watching Brief' (2002) Daily Telegraph, 27 May; *Guardian* leader column, 18 March 2002; *A Sporting Future for All – The Government's Plan for Sport*, Annual Report 2001/02, at 1 (noting that the Performance and Innovation Unit review and the Quinqennial Review of Sport England 'are likely to make recommendations about how the role of sport in delivering the Government's wider agenda should best be organised').

2 Goodbody 'Sporting bodies face top-level review' (2002) Times, 1 February. The article contains the following quote from Tessa Jowell, Culture Secretary: 'Our review is intended to achieve a clear strategy that will deliver sports policy and will take into account the range of different bodies, such as central government and local government, and will address the disparity between regions'.

CHAPTER A2

DISCIPLINARY PROCEEDINGS AND INTERNAL DISPUTE RESOLUTION

Karena Vleck (Farrer & Co), **Serena Hedley-Dent** (Farrer & Co) and **Adam Lewis** (Blackstone Chambers)

Contents

1 INTRODUCTION

A2.1 The governance of sport is all about rules. Without them, and without a mechanism for enforcing them, the sport could not exist. The laws of the 'game' govern how any particular sport is played on the field, and other rules govern how participants arrange their affairs so as to play the game and how they conduct themselves off the field. In relation to each sport the international governing body[1] will generally be the ultimate source of the rules. Each national governing body under the international governing body's jurisdiction will implement those rules in its own set of provisions. The national governing body will also include its own provisions permitting it to discipline internally those that it governs for breach of the rules, and permitting it to resolve internally disputes that arise in other contexts.

The aim of these provisions is, in the first place, to keep these issues within the sport and have them resolved by the relevant governing body itself.

1 The term 'sports governing body' is used to cover the wide range of bodies in different sports which have the common characteristic that they are composite bodies with a membership of others involved in the sport, and they control the organisation of a particular element of the sport or the commercial exploitation of it: see paras A1.16 to A1.24 and A3.3.

A The need to look to the particular rules

A2.2 This chapter deals with the practicalities of when, how and by whom disciplinary rules are enforced and other issues are resolved internally, and the considerations to be borne in mind by governing bodies and by those subject or party to the procedures. There are as many different disciplinary and internal dispute resolution systems as there are sports governing bodies, and therefore this chapter addresses only the common themes. In any particular case where a disciplinary or internal dispute resolution system is being applied, the starting point is the rules[1] of the governing body in question and this chapter should be read together with them.

1 The general rules may be supplemented by more detailed procedural rules, and often different rules of a governing body apply in different contexts. It is important to establish the rules that govern the particular proceedings. Many governing bodies set out their rules on their websites, as well as publishing them in booklet form. There may however be additional rules, and the best approach is to ask the governing body to confirm exactly what rules govern the proceedings.

B The need to comply with the standards set by the courts

A2.3 This chapter should also be read together with the next chapter[1], which addresses, amongst other things, the situation where the approach taken by a governing body in disciplinary or internal dispute resolution proceedings may have been unlawful. The next chapter examines the grounds for challenge before the courts to the approach adopted by the governing body. It is essential for those administering internal proceedings, and those subject to them, to take into account the standards that the courts will require from governing bodies as described in the next chapter. As explained there, the courts regard these matters as best resolved if possible within the sport and are generally reluctant to intervene in the internal regulatory affairs of sports governing bodies[2]. The internal panels charged with disciplining individuals or clubs and with resolving disputes are domestic tribunals, which are not required to act as if they were courts of law: they can follow their own procedures within limits set by the courts. The decisions of sports governing bodies are not (as the law stands) public law decisions capable of being judicially reviewed. However, the courts do operate a private law supervisory jurisdiction over those decisions, which is based on principles analogous to those that apply in the public law context (and which is broadly the same whether or not a contract can be identified between the governing body and the parties to the internal proceedings)[3]. In particular the governing body must arrange and administer internal proceedings in compliance with the governing body's own rules[4]. It must act in a procedurally fair manner in accordance with the rules of natural justice[5]. It must not act unreasonably in the sense of irrationally, arbitrarily or capriciously[6]. It must properly instruct itself as to the facts[7]. It must not act contrary to a legitimate expectation[8]. The parties to the internal proceedings also have an obligation in this context: any criticism that they might have in advance in relation to how the proceedings have been run should generally be made in the first place to the governing body or its internal panel. If a point is allowed to lie, it may be difficult to rely on it subsequently before the courts[9]. It will generally, but not always, be best to exhaust the internal remedies before going to court[10]. A separate consideration is whether the rules or actions of the governing body in the context of disciplinary or internal dispute resolution proceedings are reviewable on the basis that they are in unreasonable restraint of trade[11] or contrary to the competition[12] or free movement rules[13], or conceivably tortious[14].

1 See Chapters A3 and A5. This chapter should also be read together with Chapter A4 which describes the influence of the HRA 1998.

2 See paras A3.70 to A3.77.

3 See paras A3.78 to A3.92. In the absence of a contract the relief available will be different: in particular damages cannot be recovered.

4 See paras A3.93 to A3.98. For example the charge in disciplinary proceedings must be formulated in accordance with the rules and must disclose a breach of them, and the rules must be correctly applied. Any sanction must be within the range permitted by the rules. It would also be possible to argue that rules had not been validly adopted, or that the internal panel had been incorrectly appointed.

5 See Chapter paras A3.99 to A3.106. In particular, the participant must be afforded an adequate opportunity to be heard, and the disciplinary panel must not be tainted by bias and must act in good faith.

6 See paras A3.107 to A3.109. This is hard for a challenger to establish: the disciplinary decision would have to fall outside the range of decisions open to a rational governing body. Sanctions must be related to the severity of the offence.

7 See para A3.110. For example there must be a sufficient factual basis for the disciplinary decision.

8 See para A3.111.

9 See paras A3.50 and A3.173, in particular n 1.

10 See paras A3.48 to A3.50, A3.173 and A3.216 to A3.217.

11 See paras A3.133 to A3.156. There is no reason that such a point could not be taken before the governing body's internal panel itself, as well as in the courts.

12 See paras A3.158 to A3.167 and Chapter B2.

13 See paras A3.168 to A3.172 and Chapter B3.

14 See paras A3.128 to A3.132.

C Issues addressed in this chapter

A2.4 It is essential for a governing body seeking to enforce rules to be able to point to a jurisdictional basis for doing so. The rules of the sport will provide which body is responsible for discipline in what context. Most matters involving individual and club participants will be dealt with by the national sports governing body. However, in some circumstances the international governing body may seek to assume jurisdiction over such individuals or clubs. In other situations the international governing body may institute internal proceedings against the national sports governing body itself. Wherever a particular sports governing body assumes jurisdiction over a particular person and over particular subject matter, it must be possible to identify the arrangements that confer jurisdiction on that governing body. A distinction is to be drawn between the basis for a governing body's jurisdiction to discipline, and the basis for the obligations that it owes once it embarks on such a course. While a governing body may be unable to point to a basis for jurisdiction if it is challenged, it will still owe obligations if it purports to exercise jurisdiction[1].

1 Thus in a particular case, a participant might seek to challenge the jurisdiction of the governing body on the basis that there was no contract between it and the governing body. The absence of such a contract would not however absolve the governing body from the general obligations to which it is subject in the way that it treats others. Equally, the existence of such general obligations does not form a basis for jurisdiction.

A2.5 The range of rules that can give rise to internal proceedings is wide: in effect any of the rules governing a sport might give rise to disagreement which needs to be resolved. However, some rules, by their very nature, generate more disputes than others. In the first place, sports governing bodies have rules that prohibit specified actions, such as doping and misconduct on or off the pitch. In this context the governing body will call a participant before it and a hearing will be held to determine whether there has been a breach of the rules. Secondly, there are rules that contain eligibility criteria and set conditions on participation in the sport at all, or participation at a particular level, or that govern selection, or promotion and relegation. Any proceedings in that context are likely to take the form of an application for internal review of the decision to apply the rules in a particular way. Lastly there are the remaining rules, any of which might give rise to proceedings if a breach is identified (whether by a participant, or by the governing body itself), or if a governing body has refused permission to an applicant to do something under a particular rule, or if two participants are in dispute.

A2.6 The procedure by which sports governing bodies decide matters internally must be carefully structured and applied by the sports governing body. This is because the 'sport' is often perceived as being in the position of prosecutor and judge. This can give rise to accusations of unfairness and prejudice unless procedures are in place to protect the parties to the dispute: accusations which are often particularly stridently made when the party affected is an individual. All sports should therefore have developed and well-structured disciplinary and internal dispute resolution systems in place. The systems will need to be capable of dealing with all the types of dispute that could arise within a particular sport ranging from disciplinary actions about cheating (whether by doping or otherwise) and misconduct, through applications to review decisions of the governing body as to eligibility or selection, to disputes between participants. The system must be rigorously and fairly applied. Apart from disciplinary structures, the sport will need a mechanism to resolve other disputes between participants and the governing body or between participants. That mechanism must also be fairly structured and applied.

A2.7 Equally, the participants subject to the disciplinary structure and amenable to internal dispute resolution must be aware of the approach to take to such hearings.

A2.8 In the light of these considerations, the next section of this chapter addresses the basis on which sports governing bodies have jurisdiction over the various types of participant, whether it be to discipline them, or to deal with their applications to do something. It also addresses the question of the jurisdictional relationship between national governing bodies and international bodies and between different governing bodies at the same level. The third section of this chapter addresses broadly the categories of issue that can arise, from disciplinary proceedings to complaints about actions of the governing body itself. The fourth section addresses the particular question of publication, availability and applicability of the rules under which the disciplinary action is taken or the dispute has arisen, and of the rules containing the disciplinary and dispute resolution procedures. In the fifth section we examine the practical considerations for a governing body in the administration of internal disciplinary and internal dispute resolution proceedings and the practical considerations for those subject or party to them[1].

1 See also generally on disciplinary proceedings: Harris, Carnes and Byrne *The Law and Practice of Disciplinary and Regulatory Proceedings* (2nd edn, 1999, Barry Rose Law Publishers). See also in the specific context of sport Welch and Wearmouth *Getting it right – A guide to sports ethics, disciplinaries and appeals* (1994, Sports Council, ISBN 1-872158-37-4); Bitel 'Disciplinary procedures from the point of view of the individual' [1995] 3(3) SATLJ 7; Parker 'Disciplinary proceedings from the governing bodies' point of view' [1995] 3(3) SATLJ 3; Wearmouth 'No winners on the greasy pole? Ethical and legal frameworks of evaluating disciplinary processes in sport' [1995] 3(3) SATLJ 29; Tim O'Gorman 'A review of the ECB Disciplinary Regulations' [1997] 5(3) SATLJ 30; Popplewell J, David Bean QC, Robert Reid QC, David Griffith-Jones and Susan Cooper 'Sports regulation – a disciplinary hypothetical' [1997] 6(3) SATLJ 49; Simon Gardiner 'The third eye: video adjudication in sport' [1999] 7(1) SATLJ 26; and Beloff [2002] 2 ISLR 35 on the role of the sports disciplinary tribunal in establishing the facts.

2 JURISDICTION

A2.9 In order for a governing body to discipline any person or club, it must have jurisdiction over that person or club[1]. This means first, that the rules must specify that it has such jurisdiction: if the governing body's own rules do not confer jurisdiction there is no basis for it to take it. Secondly it also means that there must be a relationship between the governing body and the person or club that allows the lawful and practical enforcement of that jurisdiction: if there is in fact no basis on which the person or club can be constrained, a claim to jurisdiction is hollow. In short, the person or club must be subject to the rules on some basis and the rules must be practically enforceable against them. The most obvious relationship is a contractual one. However in relation to individuals at least, that relationship often cannot be found in a contract (or at least not in a direct contract) between the governing body and the individual, and may have to be found elsewhere.

1 See paras A2.12 to A2.21.

A2.10 In order for a governing body to be able to exert jurisdiction in relation to a particular matter the sport will need to have rules which provide that the matter is subject to its control[1]. The rules must be clear as to this as they will be construed against the person seeking to rely upon them, in accordance with the 'contra proferentem' principle[2].

1 See paras A2.22 to A2.31.
2 For the principles of construction see paras A3.95 and A3.96.

A2.11 In addition to the questions of jurisdiction over the person and the subject matter, issues may arise as to which of a number of governing bodies have jurisdiction over a particular matter[1]. The most obvious context in which this arises is the allocation of jurisdiction between the national governing body and the international governing body. It may also arise however where there are a number of governing bodies at the same level, whether because the sport is split[2] or because different governing bodies have responsibilities for different areas of the sport[3].

1 See paras A2.32 to A2.36.
2 As in the case of boxing.
3 As in the case of football at the domestic level, with the Football Association, the FA Premier League, and the Football League; or as in the case of rugby union at the international level with (amongst others) the IRB, the European Rugby Cup and the Six Nations Committee.

A Jurisdiction over members

(a) Direct jurisdiction over members

A2.12 In the most straightforward situation, the person or club being disciplined is a member of the disciplining organisation. Members are bound, contractually, by both the disciplining organisation's constitution and any rules derived from it[1]. Clubs are generally (but not always) under the jurisdiction of the national governing body on the basis that they are members of it[2]. This is not necessarily confined to clubs however: where a governing body has a direct membership relationship with its athletes or players, they too fall under the governing body's jurisdiction[3]. Where therefore disciplinary proceedings are taken against a member, it is unlikely that any challenge is possible to jurisdiction.

1 See para A3.116.
2 In each case the specific rules must be examined to identify whether the club is in fact a member.
3 This generally arises where the sport is an individual as opposed to a team sport. But this is not necessarily the case: athletics for example is not so structured, although at first sight an individual sport.

(b) Use of jurisdiction over members to achieve aims in respect of others

A2.13 Where there is no direct membership relationship with individuals, governing bodies may nevertheless be able to exercise jurisdiction over its members and require them in turn to act in a particular way in relation to such individuals. A sports governing body may be made up of its member clubs, and it can control the sport through its control of those clubs. Furthermore, in the context of governing bodies that are made up of other governing bodies, the body at the top of the pyramid structure[1] may be able to require the body below it to exercise jurisdiction over its members, and so on down through to the lowest level of the pyramid with each level being subject to the control of the one above.

1 Discussed in Chapter C1.

(c) The disadvantages of individual membership

A2.14 In terms of the assumption of jurisdiction, the membership mechanism is straightforward and certain. However, there are a number of reasons why a sports governing body (and others) would not want there to be a direct contractual relationship between governing body and individuals by virtue of their being members. First, there is the question of control of the sport. In a sport which is dominated by clubs, the clubs want to be able to exert control through their membership of the governing body. If there was individual membership together with voting rights, this would constitute a fundamental shift in power. Secondly, the administration of a very large membership has logistical and financial implications. Thirdly, the consequence of jurisdiction through a membership contract is the possibility of damages being awarded to an individual member for breach of the contract if a consequent proximate loss is established. This of course applies whether the contract is derived from membership or elsewhere. The existence of a direct contractual membership relationship may provide a neat solution to any question of jurisdiction but is not the only solution.

B Jurisdiction over non-members

(a) The need for a link

A2.15 However, most sports governing bodies do not have the individual participants as members and instead their membership is confined to the sports clubs[1]. If the governing body is not content with control over its members alone, and wants to exercise jurisdiction over individual non-member participants, a different basis must be found for doing so. Where an individual is not a member of the sports governing body there is no presumption that the sports body has jurisdiction. Without something in addition that links the individual to the governing body, jurisdiction will not arise.

1 As can be seen from Chapter C1. As set out above, this is not always the case and the specific rules must be examined.

(b) Direct contractual link

A2.16 First, it is possible for the link between the governing body and the non-member sports person to be established by a direct contractual link outside membership. The contract could be express: for example an entry form for a competition might give rise to a contract between a competitor and the competition organiser to the effect that the competitor will abide by the sports governing body's rules[1]. In some contexts governing bodies contract directly with elite athletes and players. It is also possible that an implied contract might arise on the basis for example of submission to doping control.

1 See paras A3.121 to A3.125.

(c) Link through the pyramid structure

A2.17 Secondly, the link between the governing body and the sportsperson might be achieved through the pyramid structure by the governing body requiring its member clubs to make it a condition of their own contract with players that they submit to the jurisdiction of the governing body. Depending on the facts this could involve two separate contracts and no direct contractual relationship between the individual and the governing body, or it might possibly involve the creation of a direct contract by the club for these purposes acting as agent for either the individual or the governing body. Either way jurisdiction is effectively conferred.

(d) Link through the desire to take part in authorised competition

A2.18 In practical terms, the sports governing body controls the sport and it sanctions or organises competitions and events. However, if individuals for example play football in a park, they are not subject to the jurisdiction of the Football Association. But if they want to play at any developed level they will be seeking to play in competition organised or sanctioned by the Football Association. In this context the governing body can effectively take jurisdiction by setting the criteria for participation in competition organised or sanctioned by it[1]. Put at its simplest, the governing body can say that an individual can only participate in authorised competition if he has not taken drugs, and has not acted violently, and is in compliance with all the other rules that the governing body applies[2]. Jurisdiction arises simply because the governing body provides that any player that it has ruled against will not be able to play: it is up to the player then to decide whether to avail him or herself of the mechanisms provided to prevent or to challenge that ruling. The player or athlete wants to participate in the sport authorised by the governing body and he or she is consequently willing to abide by the sport's rules in order to do so. Whether a contract arises in this context depends on the facts.

1 Even absent any contract. In the context of athletics, the *Modahl* case illustrates the difficulty in establishing a contract between athlete and governing body. Yet the then governing body, BAF, clearly had disciplinary jurisdiction even absent a contract (and so too would UKA today) on the basis of athletes' desire to take part in authorised competition.

2 This goes beyond 'it's my ball, so we'll play the way I want'. The governing body has arrived at rules which reflect a consensus amongst those involved in the sport. It has had to balance the interests of all those involved. The sport will not function without the rules. The governing body is held accountable by the general obligations that it owes.

A2.19 This basis for jurisdiction is reinforced by the standing of the governing body and its control over others. The governing body's position as regulator of the sport in question, its ability to control the sport, its rules and its reputation itself put the governing body in a unique position. The governing body can impose a sanction that will be recognised by its members or other clubs and associations and internationally, and it can effectively withhold access for defined categories or individuals because its members and other individuals will abide by its decisions. In the context of athletics, this approach is employed through rules which even render ineligible individuals who participate in the same events as suspended individuals[1]. The approach is effective to enforce the sanctions that the governing body applies. The validity of the approach and its application may be challenged if they go too far as discussed above, but in general terms it is not improper without more for a governing body to apply proportionate and necessary rules simply on the basis that it does not have a contract with the individual.

1 Known as a 'contamination' rule.

(e) The existence of a contract

A2.20 In practical terms therefore, jurisdiction need not arise out of a direct contractual relationship between individual and governing body, but matters are certainly clearer if such a contract exists. The courts have examined whether such a contract exists in the context of determining the extent of the substantive obligations owed by a sports governing body to individuals when it purports to discipline them, and in the context of examining whether damages are available. This issue is discussed in the next chapter[1].

1 At paras A3.114 to A3.129. See in particular *Modahl v British Athletic Federation Ltd* (28 June 1996, unreported), Popplewell J, CA 28 July 1997, HL 22 July 1998, Douglas Brown J 14 December 2000 and [2002] 1 WLR 1192 , CA, 8 October 2001. Modahl's case was not concerned with whether the British Athletic Federation Limited ('BAF') had jurisdiction to discipline her: she had accepted that it did. Rather the case turned on whether the contractual relationship, which Modahl said existed, had been breached and therefore whether Modahl had a claim for damages. Modahl argued that the BAF had been in breach of an implied term in an implied contract that she would be disciplined fairly. She argued that a member of the BAF disciplinary committee that considered her case had been biased, that this was a breach of the implied term, and that she had suffered loss as a result. At first instance, Douglas Brown J concluded that there was no contract between the BAF and the athlete. He dismissed as untenable Modahl's argument that there was a pre-existing contract by virtue of her membership of Sale Harriers because the BAF's predecessor, the British Amateur Athletic Board, was the governing body for the sport at the time she joined and therefore any indirect contract would be with that separate legal entity. As for a contract based on submission to the BAF's jurisdiction, he said that

Modahl had no choice but to submit to the jurisdiction if she wanted to participate in athletic competition. He found no consideration and no intention to create legal relations. Douglas Brown J concluded that there was therefore no sustainable claim for damages. However, the majority in the Court of Appeal reached a different conclusion. Latham and Mance LJJ concluded that there was a contract incorporating an implied obligation to provide a fair disciplinary process. Parker LJ concluded that there was no contract. Latham LJ made it clear that the BAF's duty to act fairly was not based solely upon the existence of a contract and would arise in any event. The BAF was always under a duty to act fairly because of its role as a governing body. The existence of a contract therefore was only relevant to the remedy sought in the particular case. However Latham LJ held that as the disciplinary process was fair overall, the fact that one of the members of the Disciplinary Committee might have been tainted with bias did not amount to a breach of contract. The judgments, and Parker LJ's dissent, indicate that the issue is far from clear, and a different result may well arise on different facts.

(f) Absence of a link is fatal

A2.21 Where there is no link that provides a basis for the assumption of jurisdiction over a non-member, the institution of disciplinary proceedings can be challenged. In *Roach v Football Association*[1] a football players' agent challenged the jurisdiction of the Football Association ('the FA') to discipline him on the basis of FA rules. The agent was licensed by FIFA, and there was a material difference in that body's rules to the rules under which the FA purported to discipline the agent. A buying club had discharged the player's obligation to pay his agent's fee on his behalf as part of the transfer deal. This practice is common in the industry. Under the FIFA rules there was no case to answer because the relevant rule prohibited an agent acting for more than one party in a transfer, and the agent had not done so. Under the FA rules, an agent acting for a player was prohibited from receiving a payment from a buying club. The FA, on the basis of a strained interpretation of that rule, sought to discipline the agent, even though he had never been in any contractual relationship with the FA (as he was licensed by FIFA, not the FA) and even though the FA rules in question had not been in existence at the time of the relevant transfers. The agent commenced CPR, Pt 8 proceedings for a declaration that the FA had no jurisdiction to discipline him. Shortly afterwards the FA, after initially seeking to defend the claim, acceded to judgment together with costs.

1 *Roach v Football Association* see [2001] 9(3) SATLJ 26. See also *Davis v Carew-Pole* [1956] 2 All ER 524 (unsuccessful attempt to challenge the jurisdiction of the National Hunt Committee to declare an unlicensed livery stable owner a disqualified person for entering a horse when not licensed to do so).

C Subject matter jurisdiction

A2.22 In this context there are two separate issues. First, over what matters has the governing body as a matter of fact assumed jurisdiction? If the rules do not confer subject matter jurisdiction, the governing body may not be able to act. Secondly, on a more general level, over what matters should it or should it not assume jurisdiction? The starting point is, as always, the particular rules. The rules may be set in relatively general terms: for example Football Association Rule G provides that the FA has power to take disciplinary action in respect of any misconduct, and goes on to provide that misconduct is breach of any of the Laws of the Game, the Rules and Regulations of the FA, of FIFA, of UEFA, of any affiliated association, league or competition, and lastly rounding it off, any order requirement or instruction of the FA.

(a) Matters unconnected with the sport

A2.23 The approach of different governing bodies to what they should and should not deal with can be very different. For example the international governing body for skiing and snowboarding (along with many others) does not believe that it is the place of sport to regulate recreational drug use: that is a matter for wider society and sports governing bodies should confine themselves to doping which enhances performance. Other governing bodies do impose rules prohibiting such use, whether on the basis of the possibility that such drugs are harmful or on the basis of a need to keep the sport free of criminality even if it does not affect (or at least does not enhance) performance. Should a sports governing body impose sanctions on players for extra marital affairs or other sexual transgressions? What should be the effect on the entitlement of a player to play that he has been convicted of a criminal act unconnected with the sport? If he has not been imprisoned, and has paid or is paying his debt to society in some other way, should that not be an end to it?

A2.24 At its simplest, the question of subject matter jurisdiction involves examining the rules to see whether the offence in question is caught: do the rules say that this matter is something that the sports governing body can deal with? If the rules are clear (for example if a particular recreational drug is listed) then no point of construction can be taken. However, if the rules are ambiguous, or if the governing body is attempting to shoe-horn a particular matter in under wide words designed to cover other matters, it can be argued that the proper construction of the rules should be confined to matters directly related to the sport. It could be said, for example, that it does not bring the *sport* into disrepute[1] that a player has an extra marital affair, although it does not reflect well on him.

1 Nick Bitel criticises the approach to the charge of 'bringing the game into disrepute' at [1995] 3(3) SATLJ 8, as being nebulous and uncertain. He argues that the charge ought not to be used where a more narrowly drawn rule also applies, and that the charge ought not be used to extend jurisdiction to actions which have previously fallen outside its ambit. The counter argument is of course that the governing body cannot predict and define every action that is inimical to the interests of the sport and has to have some freedom of action. But this cannot be taken too far. It is questionable that if an action is not capable of any closer delineation than that it falls under the general, and possibly subjective, proposition that it brings the game into disrepute, it ought not to be capable of sanction in any event. In practical terms, governing bodies should strive to define as clearly as possible the actions that they prohibit and should take care when using widely drawn provisions, because the courts will, or at least ought, to limit the application of such provisions to matters which clearly do relate to the sport and which those subject to the provisions could reasonably have anticipated would be so covered.

A2.25 Furthermore, even where the rule is clear, if the governing body purports to assume jurisdiction over subject matter which by any reasonable standard is nothing to do with the sport, then the rule or its application in a given context may well fall foul of the restraint of trade doctrine[1], competition law[2], or the free movement rules[3]. In each of those contexts, a rule or its application that is restrictive must be justified by reference to the reasonable and proportionate interests of the sport as represented by the governing body. Stopping a player playing as a result of an unconnected transgression or offence when the state has not attempted to do that risks going beyond what is reasonable. More difficult is the situation where the reaction of the governing body is not to seek to discipline the player in respect of the unconnected event, but rather no longer to select him or her for a particular level of competition. In theory the same challenge could be made, but the action may well become much easier to justify, since it logically should be open to the body to choose who it wants to represent it.

1 See paras A3.135 to A3.158.
2 See paras A3.159 to A3.170 and Chapter B2.
3 See paras A3.171 to A3.175 and Chapter B3.

(b) *Matters already ruled upon*

A2.26 A particular aspect of subject matter jurisdiction is whether a sports governing body has jurisdiction to go behind a decision already made imposing a sanction on a player[1]. The nature of most sports involves the need for officials to be able to impose immediate sanctions when the sport is actually being played. In team sports, fouls are capable of being punished by the referee or umpire by amongst other things a loss of ground, a free kick, a penalty, a warning or 'yellow card', a sin-binning, or a sending off or 'red card'. Each of these involves an immediate sanction that affects the outcome of the match. In some sports the referee or umpire might be able to deduct points from the score in the match. Time penalties might be imposed. In each of these contexts, the official has seen and passed judgment on the actions.

1 See para A3.11 and the cases there cited involving on-pitch offences that have come before the courts, and para A3.16 in relation to challenges to an official's decision or the outcome of an event.

A2.27 A difficult question for a sports governing body is the extent to which it is legitimate for it to go beyond or behind that decision. Again, the question splits into what the rules actually say and how they are to be construed on the one hand, and whether a challenge can be brought to their validity or their application in a particular context on the other hand. The particular circumstances in which sports governing bodies wish to assume subject matter jurisdiction following an official's decision generally fall into three categories.

A2.28 First, an offence on the pitch may have been punished in the context of the game, but it may also warrant a sanction which goes beyond the limited effect that has been achieved by the official over the outcome of the match. For example a particularly violent tackle injuring a player may have resulted in a sending off: that was the most that the referee could impose. But it is clearly legitimate for the governing body to seek to discipline the guilty player further, by for example, imposing a long suspension. The rules will have to state clearly that this can be done, but there is no inherent reason why it is not reasonable and proportionate for the sport to do this. In many sports there is a specific rule which allows disciplinary action for violence on the pitch. More difficult is the situation where the referee has measured an offence and has adjudged that it warranted only a yellow card (which did not carry with it an automatic suspension) Is it then open to the governing body to seek to impose a greater sanction (such as a suspension) when the referee, who was there on the spot, did not even think that a red card was warranted? This question arose in *RFU v Martin Johnson*[1], where the player struck another player contrary to the rules of the game but was awarded only a yellow card. It was held on the proper construction of the particular rules, the governing body had power to discipline a player for any breach of the rules irrespective of the referee having made a decision short of the ultimate sanction. An argument that the governing body should not go behind the decision of the referee was rejected: while the referee was certainly the sole judge of what should happen on the pitch, it was not unfair that a player should also be subject to separate sanction through disciplinary proceedings simply because the referee's view at the time was that the offence only warranted a yellow card. Such disciplinary proceedings could and did not alter the validity of the decision to impose a yellow card, or have any wider ramifications for the outcome of the match, but were rather separate proceedings in relation to the consequences of his actions for the player. While different rules may produce a different result, and it is possible that a different tribunal might take a different view of the need to uphold the sanctity of the referee's decision, it will probably be difficult to prevent a governing body going beyond the decision of a referee not to impose the most onerous sanction that he can, in circumstances where on their face the rules allow it to do so.

1 Internal Appeal under the RFU Rules against a Disciplinary Panel Decision, David Pannick QC (5 March 2002). See also *Six Nations Committee v Perugini*, where the fact that the Italian prop had only been sin-binned for a head butt did not preclude the Disciplinary Committee imposing a suspension.

A2.29 Secondly, the official may not have seen the event in question. Video evidence[1] is now an established part of sport. In the authors' view it is clearly legitimate for properly constructed rules to allow a sports governing body to sanction a player for actions that have not been seen by the referee. The more difficult question is quite what sanction can then be imposed. The correct view is probably that the consequences for the player cannot go beyond what the consequences would have been if the offence had been seen[2]. This involves the disciplinary panel putting itself into the position of the referee and making the decision that he would have made. However, as set out in the preceding paragraph, it is also possible for a disciplinary panel to impose a sanction in addition to that which flows from the referee's decision. There should be separation in this context: first what would the referee have done? Secondly, if he had done that, would it be appropriate for separate disciplinary proceedings to be brought in addition, and what greater sanction should be applied?

1 See Gardiner 'The third eye: video adjudication in sport' (1999) 2(1) Sports Law Bulletin 8.
2 This is the approach adopted by the Football Association in its video evidence rules.

A2.30 Thirdly and more problematically, the sports governing body may want to change the fact that a player has been sanctioned as a result of the referee's decision. This may be because a player has appealed and relies on video evidence. It could be because a club has been adversely affected by the suspension of the player[1]. In our view a distinction is to be drawn between the validity of the decision itself, and the punitive consequences that flow from it. While it is not possible to challenge and overturn decisions on the pitch threatening the validity of the result, there is no reason why it should not be possible to review the consequences for the player. It might for example be the case that the referee had been mistaken as to the identity of the miscreant: should an innocent player then suffer an automatic suspension? On the other hand, it might also be that video evidence revealed that there was genuinely no contact and the 'fouled' player in fact 'dived'. Again should the innocent player be suspended? The complication here is the effect on third parties. If David Beckham had been albeit wrongly sent off and consequently suspended from playing in the FA Cup Final, would it be fair to Manchester United's opponents if he were reinstated[2]? The answer seems to us to be that it would be fair, because the opponents ought not to have the expectation that they could benefit from something that ought not to have happened.

1 For example under the WRU rules clubs that have a certain number of sin-binnings in a season lose points, which can make the difference between promotion and relegation: an issue that arose in *Ynysybwl RFC v WRU* in 2002: see n 2.

2 Or in the case of *Ynysybwl RFC v WRU*, would it be fair to that club if its rivals for promotion, Treherbert RFC, were restored the points that they had lost as a result of having a certain number of sin-binnings in a season, by a player obtaining an extension of time and successfully appealing against his sin-binning and having the consequences of it removed. In that case after a complaint from Ynysybwl the WRU ultimately decided that it was not appropriate in the circumstances to exercise its discretion to extend time for the rival club's player to appeal against the consequences of his sin-binning, with the result that the points remained deducted and Ynysybwl was promoted. Ynysybwl then sought to recover its costs from the WRU. The action was compromised.

(c) Temporal jurisdiction as a part of subject matter jurisdiction

A2.31 The governing body must be able to establish not only that it has jurisdiction under the rules over the type of offence, but also that that jurisdiction existed at the time of the offence in question. This was an aspect of the decision in *Roach* discussed above[1], and it often turns on the question of whether rules have been validly amended and published, as discussed below[2]. The governing principle is that there can be no punishment without a law prohibiting the conduct to be punished. Thus if conduct is not contrary to the rules in force at the applicable time, that conduct cannot be the subject of sanction after the event by virtue of a change in the rules. More difficult is the position where a change in the rules may have been introduced but it has not been brought to the attention of the players involved. In strict contractual terms it may well be questionable that such a term has been imported. Some have even questioned the validity contractually of terms that provide that the parties will be governed by the rules from time to time in force.

1 See para A2.21.
2 See paras A2.56 to A2.59.

D Jurisdictional relationship between international and national bodies

A2.32 Sport is played in an international context. National governing bodies are members of international governing bodies. The sport's international federation or association will retain an overriding jurisdiction over its member federations or associations[1]. The international governing body has direct contractual control over its members, the national governing bodies, but not over the national bodies' members, still less over individuals who are not members of the national bodies. This may not matter, in that a national governing body will usually be obliged, by its membership of the international body, to have in place and to enforce rules which mirror those of the international body. Any basis for direct jurisdiction in the international body over clubs or individual participants would have to be established in one of the ways discussed above.

1 Many of the international bodies provide for appeals against their decisions to be referred to the Court of Arbitration for Sport ('CAS'). CAS has jurisdiction to decide matters by virtue of a rule appointing it or if both parties decide voluntarily to submit to it. See Chapter A5.

A2.33 A situation where an international governing body might want to have direct jurisdiction over clubs or individual participants is where an international federation remains dissatisfied following the determination by a national governing body of an issue in favour of that club or individual. This situation arose in the *Walker*[1] litigation. In that litigation, the athlete Dougie Walker had been cleared of a doping offence by UKA's disciplinary committee and the IAAF (the international governing body of which UKA is a member) sought to take UKA to IAAF arbitration to overturn that decision[2]. Walker brought proceedings in the English courts to stop this happening. Walker took two alternative points. First he contended that since no contract existed between himself and the IAAF, the IAAF had no jurisdiction over him, yet this was in effect what the IAAF was seeking to assume. Secondly, he argued in the alternative that since UKA had had jurisdiction over him and a binding arbitration agreement under the Arbitration Act 1996 arose between them, the arbitral award exonerating him of a doping offence was final and binding on UKA, and it was consequently not open to UKA to abide by any contrary determination of the IAAF. Neither point was decided by the English court because the action was compromised. What happened in fact was that the IAAF arbitration did proceed to reverse UKA's decision, UKA did abide by that determination and the athlete did serve out his suspension. UKA was always subject to the prior contractual obligation to abide by the decision of an IAAF arbitration, and the national disciplinary processes were subject to that constraint.

1 For this case see discussion at paras A3.10, n 7 and A3.124; *Walker v UKA and IAAF* (3 July 2000, unreported) Toulson J, Hallett J 25 July 2000, IAAF Arbitral Award 20 August 2000 reported at [2001] 4 ISLR 264, see also [2000] 2 ISLR 41; and *Korda v ITF Ltd* (1999) Times, 4 February, [1999] All ER (D) 84; revsd [1999] All ER (D) 337, CA.

2 The IAAF has since fallen into line and agreed to refer such disputes to CAS rather than its own arbitral body.

E Jurisdictional relationship between different bodies at the same level

A2.34 In many sports, different aspects of the sport and indeed different events are subject to the control, and disciplinary procedures, of different governing bodies operating at the same level. Thus some aspects of football in England are governed by the Football Association ('the FA') and others by the FA Premier League or the Football League respectively. It is necessary to examine the relevant rules to determine which body has jurisdiction in the particular circumstances. In the context of football, Football Association Rule G provides that misconduct in the form of breach of the Laws of the Game (implicitly within England) shall only be dealt with by the FA or an affiliated association on its behalf, even if it is also a breach of the rules of any affiliated association or competition. Thus the Premier League and the Football League do not involve themselves with disciplinary actions in relation to the actual playing of the sport. However, where the misconduct takes the form of breach of the rules and regulations of the FA, of FIFA, of UEFA or of any affiliated association, league or competition, or of any order requirement or instruction of the FA, the FA has power to discipline, but it may not be an exclusive power. The FA Premier League and the Football League can agree with the FA that they will deal with breaches of their own rules. Breaches of the rules of other competitions fall to be dealt with by those competitions, unless the FA elects to act. FIFA and UEFA have jurisdiction to deal with breaches of their own rules.

A2.35 It may be that the same matters will be dealt with by different bodies depending on the circumstances. To take the example of rugby dealt with above, Martin Johnson was disciplined for misconduct during a club game by the RFU, which was the governing body made up of the clubs involved and which organised the relevant competition[1]. The Italian prop Salvatore Perugini was disciplined by the Six Nations Committee for an offence which occurred during that competition: a simple enough distinction is that in that context the player was playing for his country. But that distinction does not resolve the difficulty: for example if Perugini had been playing for Italy outside the Six Nations Championship, the Committee plainly would not have had jurisdiction. Equally if Martin Johnson had been playing for his club in the European Rugby Cup, he would have been disciplined by that organisation.

1 Equally the players in the *Ynysybwl* case brought their appeal against their sin-binnings in club games before the WRU.

A2.36 It is plain therefore that jurisdiction may arise in different organisations depending on which of them is organising the event. It may also arise in more than one organisation. In the context of the Olympics or the Commonwealth Games, the event organiser (the International Olympic Committee ('IOC') or the Commonwealth Games Federation ('CGF')) will have primary jurisdiction to deal with matters arising at the event itself[1]. Matters arising in other circumstances fall to be dealt with under the applicable international or national governing body's rules. However that governing body may well have a secondary jurisdiction even in respect of matters arising at such events. For example the IOC only disqualifies following disciplinary proceedings at the Olympics. Any wider sanction would generally be left for the relevant sport's governing bodies.

1 Both these organisations submit to the appeal jurisdiction of CAS.

F Jurisdiction in the context of internal dispute resolution

A2.37 The jurisdictional questions are different in the case of internal review of the decisions of a governing body that do not involve disciplinary matters. The questions are also different in the context of internal dispute resolution of disputes between participants.

(a) *Internal review of non-disciplinary governing body decisions*

A2.38 In the first case, it is a club or individual that is seeking to invoke the jurisdiction of the relevant internal body to review a decision of the governing body, for example to refuse permission to do something (such as to move ground as in the *Wimbledon v Football League* case[1]) or not to select an individual for national representation. The rules of the governing body ought to, and generally will, provide for an internal mechanism for reviewing such decisions[2]. It is consequently unlikely, although possible, that the governing body would seek to dispute its own (or its internal body's) jurisdiction. Again, whether an internal challenge is possible by a particular person (locus standi) in relation to particular events (subject matter jurisdiction) will turn primarily on the proper construction of the rules.

1 FA Arbitration (29 January 2002), FA Commission May 2002: see para A3.156 for a discussion of this case.

2 The choice of mechanism will vary: in some contexts (for example rugby) an internal appeal structure will cover both the decisions of any disciplinary committee as to breach of the rules and the decisions of other committees as to the application of the rules in other contexts. The FA chooses to subject any disputes between it and participants to a form of arbitration under Rule K which falls between internal dispute resolution and external arbitration: see para A2.39.

(b) Internal dispute resolution between participants

A2.39 So too in the second case, the rules will determine whether a particular participant can require (through the medium of the rules) another participant to have a dispute between them determined by the governing body. Thus in the context of football, international transfer disputes between clubs are subjected to the jurisdiction of a FIFA committee. At the national level, participants submit to dispute resolution by the FA. In many instances the distinction between internal resolution of disputes between participants and external arbitration[1] are blurred: this is especially the case where the decision making body is not a committee of the governing body as is often the case, but instead an 'independent' appeal panel. For example Rule K of the FA Rules provides for arbitration of 'any dispute between two or more 'participants', which includes the FA itself for these purposes. Rule K goes on to set out the particular rules of the arbitration.

1 As to which see Chapter A5.

(c) Inquiries and Commissions

A2.40 Some sports, such as football, also provide for the institution of Inquiries or Commissions. Under Football Association Rule F, the FA can institute a Commission of Inquiry into any subject. The Football League's rules give its Board power to refer any matter it has power to decide to a Football League internal inquiry committee, or to an FA Commission, for decision in place of the Board.

3 TYPES OF DISCIPLINARY OFFENCES AND INTERNAL DISPUTES

A2.41 The rules of different sports contain a wide variety of rules, breach of which may give rise to disciplinary action, or the application of which may give rise to an internal challenge. It is obviously not possible to deal with them all. The authors summarise below the types of disciplinary offences and internal disputes that can arise and examine some common themes.

A Breach of rules prohibiting specified actions

A2.42 Each sport has rules which prohibit certain actions by those governed, and disciplinary mechanisms to enforce the ban. What those actions are will obviously vary from sport to sport, but there are a number of common aspects which are covered by the rules of almost all sports. First, almost all sports have anti-doping rules banning the use of drugs. Secondly, almost all sports have rules prohibiting misconduct on the pitch and breach of the rules of the game, which fall to be applied where an infringement is sufficiently serious to warrant additional consideration to that given to it by the referee or umpire at the time. Thirdly, there are likely to be rules in relation to misconduct off the pitch, which often includes a general prohibition on 'bringing the sport into disrepute'. Fourthly, there may be other general specific disciplinary rules in relation to players, coaches and members generally.

(a) Doping

A2.43 Each sport has its own rules which regulate how it deals with the situation where a player either admits or is accused of and is ultimately found to have committed a doping offence. This area is addressed in detail in a later chapter[1]. A doping offence is no different, conceptually, from any other disciplinary offence and therefore the same principles apply. Whether an athlete has breached the rules by having a prohibited substance in his or her body, or by punching a fellow player, the same considerations arise as to how that breach of the rules is to be dealt with. That said, the nature of doping is such that it has been the primary area for development of those principles, and certain special aspects have arisen, addressed in that later chapter.

1 See Chapter E4. See also para A3.10 for examples of cases involving doping that have come before the courts.

(b) Misconduct on the pitch and breach of rules of the game

A2.44 Most sports provide for the ability to discipline participants where they breach the rules of the game in such a way as to amount to misconduct on the pitch[1]. Not every breach of the rules of the game, such as being offside, or even an ordinary foul, will trigger disciplinary action. There is likely to be a scale of disciplinary responses to such breaches, often set at international level. The most minor playing breaches have no consequence, other than for example an on-field sanction in the form of a free kick or loss of ground. More serious offences may be dealt with by a yellow card or a red card. Often, as in football, there are automatic disciplinary sanctions that follow a sending off or an accumulated number of yellow cards over time. Those automatic sanctions may escalate if a player is a repeat offender. The rules may allow for internal appeals in defined circumstances against these automatic consequences. For serious on-pitch offences the rules may provide for disciplinary proceedings in addition to the automatic sanctions. The most obvious situation where this arises, for example in football, is where the player has acted violently on the pitch, but other rules, particularly where they are widely drafted, could be relied upon[2]. In the context of violence, sports governing bodies are particularly protective of the referee[3], and indeed the public[4].

1 See para A3.11 for examples of cases involving on-pitch offences that have come before the courts.
2 FA Rule E2 prohibits violent, threatening, abusive, indecent or threatening words or behaviour. Where a player has for example punched another, there is a clear breach of this rule. Other forms of on pitch misconduct might be caught by Rule E3, which prohibits amongst other things racial discrimination. Deliberate cheating on the pitch, for example in order to throw a match or unfairly to win it, might be caught by a number of prohibitions, such as the general prohibition on acting contrary to the best interests of the game, acting improperly or bringing the sport into disrepute (E1) and the more specific rules against taking bribes (E4 to E5) and betting (E7 to E8).
3 See for example Stoner, 'Push and shove, the case of Paolo di Canio' (1998) 5(6) Sports Law Administration and Practice 8. Di Canio's shove sending the referee sprawling earned him an 11-match ban: rugby union international Neil Back received a six-month ban for a similar shove.
4 Eric Cantona's kick at a spectator led to an eight-month ban.

(c) Misconduct off the pitch and bringing the sport into disrepute

A2.45 Most sports governing bodies purport by their rules to control more than just conduct on the pitch[1]. Almost without exception, sports governing bodies' rules contain a provision that prohibits 'bringing the sport into disrepute'. By its very nature this is a 'catch all' provision designed to cover misconduct which is not specifically provided for in more focussed rules[2]. The rule may be drafted more widely to catch any misconduct which 'could' bring the sport into disrepute rather than just that misconduct which 'does' in fact adversely affect a sport's reputation. It will be for the disciplinary committee hearing the case to decide as a question of fact whether the conduct complained of does fall within the phrase actually used. There may be different standards for different sports, and a different level of behaviour may be expected from players in different positions. The rule should be applied consistently. The rule is open to criticism as being too uncertain as to the conduct that it covers.

1 For examples of cases where the courts have reviewed disciplinary decisions in relation to off pitch conduct, see para A3.12.

2 FA Rule E1 is wide in that it covers acting contrary to the best interests of the game, acting improperly or bringing the sport into disrepute, but at least requires the governing body to establish that the conduct actually is contrary to the best interests of the sport or improper, or that it actually does bring it into disrepute. It is not enough on the face of the rule that the conduct could be or could do one of these things.

A2.46 The rules will often include prohibitions on more specific types of off-pitch conduct, such as in particular betting and bribe taking, or the provision of information to bookmakers or others. The FA Rules include a specific prohibition on participants reselling tickets at above face value.

(d) Other disciplinary rules

A2.47 Most sports will have a general disciplinary procedure but may also have procedures which apply specifically to particular participants within the sport, such as coaches. Coaches may commit a variety of offences, such as inappropriate behaviour in respect of the players they coach. Specific sports may well provide for specific offences which are peculiar to the particular sport. Furthermore the rules may also include specific rules in relation to the failure of participants to comply with suspensions or other orders of the governing body, participation by others in an event in which a player who is acting in breach of a suspension or other order is also participating, attempts or agreements to breach the rules, and failure by a club to ensure that those under its control comply with the rules[1]. There may also be provision that conviction of a serious criminal offence can be treated as misconduct.

1 All examples taken from the FA Rules.

B Disputes over governing body decisions on application of the rules

A2.48 The second group of issues differs from the first in that it does not involve disciplinary proceedings, but rather the internal resolution of a dispute that has arisen between the governing body and a participant in relation to the way that the governing body has applied the rules. In other words, it is not a question of the governing body pointing to the rules and alleging that a participant is in breach of them, and then proceeding to institute disciplinary proceedings in order to impose a sanction. Rather it is a question of the governing body having applied the rules in a particular way and the participant objecting and seeking to avail itself of provisions in the rules allowing it to appeal the decision. The range of circumstances that can arise here is even wider than the range of disciplinary offences.

(a) Eligibility

A2.49 The first area of a sports governing body's decision-making that can give rise to conflict is the question of eligibility to compete. Through rules on eligibility the governing body controls access to the sport in the first place, whether it be at all, or to particular competitions. The reasons for refusing access may vary, but will often be based on the perceived lack of fulfillment of entry criteria, which can again cover a wide range from physical fitness, to nationality qualification or payment of a bond[1].

1 See para A3.14 for examples of challenges in the courts to decisions in relation to eligibility.

(b) Selection

A2.50 The governing body may well also have a role in selecting particular participants, for example for national representation[1]. Plainly this is of great importance to the participant, and indeed the public. Some sports set a series of tests for how representatives are to be selected[2], others leave it to the national coach[3] or a selection panel[4]. There are more likely to be such tests where the sport lends itself to objective assessment of ability and form, such as athletics, than in the context of sports where more subjective calculations have to be made, such as team sports. If procedures have been set and not followed, the participant may well have a basis for resort to an internal dispute resolution process, if any is provided for by the rules. However, where selection is discretionary and the procedures have been followed, a sports governing body may choose not to set up an internal appeals system for fear that this would 'open the floodgates' for complaints to be made. A more difficult situation arises where the governing body has incautiously led a player to believe that he or she would be selected for reasons outside the normal guidelines: this may give rise to a legitimate expectation on which the governing body may be unable later to renege[5].

1 See para A3.15 for examples of challenges in the courts to decisions on access to a particular competition or level of competition.
2 For example athletics.
3 For example football.
4 For example cricket.
5 *Watt v Australian Cycling Federation* CAS 96/153 In that case, the cyclist in question was given a 'guarantee' that she would be selected for the team (albeit that the guarantee was subject to certain provisos). The CAS decision (given by Winnecke J) held that an 'expectation' had arisen on the part of the cyclist upon which Watt had placed reliance that she would be a part of the team and that this had to be honoured unless there was a proper justification for its revocation.

(c) Promotion and relegation

A2.51 In the case of team sports based on a multi-divisional league structure, there will be detailed rules dealing with promotion and relegation[1]. These rules may well alter from season to season. They may well contain rules relating to the criteria for a club to play in the next division up, which go beyond the club having finished in the top or some other defined position in the division below. They often, as in the case of football, involve significant financial payments to smooth the transition. Furthermore, with the changes inherent in the modernisation of some previously purely amateur sports, the increased demands of commercial partners and the proliferation of competitions additional to the league in question, there have been attempts by governing bodies to realign the divisional structures. Often this has involved the application of discretionary rules allowing restructuring in the best interests of the sport. A particular example is rugby union in the Celtic nations, where the top division has changed in size and constituents a number of times over the last five or so seasons. As promotion and relegation can often have considerable financial repercussions and because they are emotive issues, they are fertile areas for dispute. Clubs may well seek to challenge the sports governing body's application of the rules to it in this context. In addition, disciplinary sanctions may include docking of points, leading to relegation or a lost opportunity to win promotion.

1 See para A3.27 for examples of challenges in the courts to decisions in relation to promotion and relegation. A prime example is *Stevenage Borough Football Club v Football League Ltd* unreported Carnwath J 23 July 1996, Times 1 August 1996, (1996) 9 Admin LR 109, CA. In the *Stevenage* case the dispute related to the failure of Stevenage to comply with the criteria for entry to the Football League relating to grounds and finances (despite meeting the playing criteria by winning the Vauxhall Conference). Stevenage argued that the rules were an unreasonable restraint of trade and therefore that it ought to be permitted to enter the Football League. The judge found that some of the rules might well be unenforceable as in unreasonable restraint of trade, but declined to grant relief in the light of Stevenage's delay in applying to the court. The Football League's rules as to relegation and promotion were subsequently amended to take into account the judge's criticisms. Note that where a right has vested and an attempt is then made to withdraw it, questions under Article 1 of the First Protocol to the European Convention on Human Rights may arise: see Chapter A4.

(d) Application to be allowed to do something

A2.52 The rules often provide that something can be done by a club or individual but only with the permission of the sports governing body[1]. An example would be an application to move ground, as Wimbledon Football Club recently made successfully to the Football League, or to play abroad, or to transfer from one club to another. Where the governing body decides to refuse the application the decision may be the subject of internal challenge.

1 See paras A3.18 to A3.27 for examples of challenges in the courts to decisions to refuse permission to a player or club to do something.

(e) Challenge to the outcome of an event or an official's decision

A2.53 In some circumstances, the rules of the particular sport may allow for review by the governing body of the outcome of an event or an official's decision[1]. While the courts are very reluctant to intervene when a player or club seeks to make such a challenge, the rules of the sport may allow the governing body a greater degree of freedom.

1 See para A3.16 in relation to challenges in the courts to an official's decision or the outcome of an event.

(f) Disputes arising out of other rules

A2.54 More recently there have been disputes between sports governing bodies and participants about decisions made in relation to the payment of Lottery money under the World Class Performance Plans, where the participants allege that the initial decision was not correct in the light of the merits of their case.

C Disputes between participants

A2.55 The sports governing body may well have procedures in place to resolve disputes between two individuals involved in the sport. This class of dispute is self evidently different from the first two classes, in that the governing body is not directly involved as a party: it rather provides by its rules the mechanism for the internal resolution of disputes. The aim is to avoid airing the matter in public and to save all concerned the cost and time of a court action. Again, such disputes can arise in a wide range of ways. The commonest forms of dispute relate to the transfer of players and the outcome of events. A mediation procedure can be useful in such contexts. As set out above, the FA Rules provide that the participants bound by them agree to have any disputes relating to the application of any of the football governing bodies' rules dealt with by arbitration under Rule K. This therefore covers in effect any dispute between clubs or players in relation to the playing of the game and its organisation pursuant to the rules. It would not cover straight contractual disputes between a player and his club, (which may instead be resolved by the FA Premier League or the Football League as the case may be and failing that in the courts) unless possibly he was seeking to rely on a term of the rules, and it would not cover a non-football related dispute between clubs.

4 PUBLICATION, ALTERATION, AND APPLICABILITY OF THE RULES

A2.56 The basis for the application of rules to a participant is that the rules either form part of a contract to which the participant is a party, or that there is some other link as a result of which the participant is effectively bound by the rules. Consequently the starting point should be that the rule was in force at the relevant time (almost certainly the date of the offence or when the issue arose[1]) and that the participant either knew or was in a position reasonably to have known about the rule. Any substantive rule, or disciplinary procedure or sanction intended to enforce it, must have been clearly set out and available to the persons affected. If it were not the case that a rule had to be in place at the relevant time, a participant could be seriously prejudiced by a retrospective change in the rules. The courts will be very slow to conclude that a purported rule change should be construed as having retrospective effect, or even that the governing body has vires to introduce retrospective rules changes.

1 It is possible that a purely procedural rule could be changed between the date of the offence or dispute arising and the hearing.

A2.57 A conceptual question that arises is whether a change in rules after a participant has become contractually bound, even if it is not retrospective and has been communicated to the participant, can form part of the contract between the sports governing body and the participant. It might for example be said that the contract must stay as it was when the player acceded to it, and that any subsequent change is no more than a purported, and invalid, unilateral variation that is ineffective to incorporate the rule change. It is to be doubted that such an argument could be sustained in most instances. The rules are likely to oblige participants to abide by the rules from time to time in force. This is a valid obligation to impose and to undertake, and it is probable that the principle of certainty is not offended by it, since the rules change would have to be in accordance with the wider constitution of the governing body. The alternative approach would be unworkable, since it holds up the spectre of different participants in the same position being governed by different rules. Furthermore, so long as there is adequate publication of rule changes, the participant will be taken to have affirmed the rule change by not taking any step to withdraw from the contract. Lastly, if the rules can in fact be effectively applied to the participant absent any contract (for the reasons developed above), then a dry contractual analysis such as this will not assist.

A2.58 The rules can only be made in accordance with the sports governing body's constitution and only subsequently altered in accordance with that constitution or with the rules themselves. To this end, it is always vital to set out in the constitution of the governing body how rules can be made and amended and to refer to this in the rules themselves. If the requisite procedures are not followed the rule is ultra vires the governing body and unenforceable.

A2.59 Whenever new rules are adopted or old rules are amended the sports governing body must do what it can to make those who will be subject to them aware of what has been done. They must be available for inspection. It may be impracticable and often impossible to provide every participant with the new rules as soon as they are made. Details should however be provided on request. Further new rules can be posted on a website, as can announcements that new rules are proposed, or have been made. A notice that new rules have been passed could be inserted in the sports governing body's newsletter or in the trade press for that particular sport together with details of from where the rules can be obtained. The rules and any additional contract should expressly provide that participants must comply with the sport's rules as they are amended from time-to-time.

5 PRACTICAL CONSIDERATIONS IN INTERNAL DISCIPLINARY AND INTERNAL DISPUTE RESOLUTION PROCEDURES

A2.60 This section describes how disciplinary and internal dispute resolution procedures operate in practice. It sets out the sequence of events and best practice for governing bodies in that context. It examines the considerations that those that are subject to the procedures should bear in mind.

A Underlying aims of disciplinary and internal dispute resolution procedures

A2.61 There are a number of aims which underlie the procedures, and those aims are common both to governing bodies and to those subject to the procedures. These aims dictate how disciplinary and internal dispute resolution procedures should be structured and applied.

A2.62 First, it is not the intention to create a substitute formal court system. The system remains a domestic tribunal run by the sport for the sport. This means that the formal rules of evidence do not apply. Secondly, the people who decide the issues should have expertise in the sport: they should understand the issues and the background. Thirdly, neither of these two factors detract from the fundamental principle that the system must be fair and just in its structure and in its application. The system must ensure that the standards set by the courts for sports governing bodies, as set out in the next chapter[1] and outlined above[2] are respected. Fourthly, the system should be transparent and understandable to those who are subject to it and there should be consistency in its application: everyone should know what the issue is, what they have to do to establish their case, and what the result will be if they fail to do so. Fifthly the system should be quick and cheap: neither side is assisted by decisions being delayed or by great cost being involved. There may be some tension between some of these aims[3]: the sports governing body must balance them so as to achieve a workable system.

1 See Chapter A3. Note also the influence of the Human Rights Act 1998, described in Chapter A4.
2 See para A2.3.
3 A perceived example is the involvement of lawyers. The preparation and delivery of detailed legal submissions, and cross examination of witnesses doubtless slows down the process and adds to cost. However, the countervailing benefit in ensuring a fair system outweighs these factors. The standards set by the courts as discussed in the next chapter in the authors' view mean that it is in the interests of both the governing body and the club or individual that lawyers are involved, as this very substantially reduces the risk of subsequent challenge in the courts, with the greater expense, delay and uncertainty that that involves. This factor can also militate in favour of the inclusion of a lawyer on the disciplinary panel itself.

(a) *Relationship between express rules and the principles of natural justice*

A2.63 Express rules of a governing body will be construed in accordance with the principles of natural justice described in the next chapter. However in the event of a conflict, the principles of natural justice appear to override contrary express rules. From a contractual point of view, this is arguably counter-intuitive. The rules of natural justice are after all imported into the rules as implied terms, and the general rule is that express terms take precedence over implied terms. Nevertheless the principle appears well established[1]. If a rationale is needed, it can be found in the propositions first, that the rules of natural justice are self standing obligations that exist irrespective of contract[2], and secondly, that governing bodies do not have power to adopt rules which contradict the general principles: rules which do are ultra vires and unenforceable.

1 See para A3.129 and A3.83, n 3. Note that in those contexts the contract was an inferred one. The issue has not yet been considered where express rules, which clearly contractually bind a party, are claimed to contradict a principle of natural justice. The reality may be that if there is clear consent to a rule, the court may be reluctant to regard the principles of natural justice (the ambit of which varies from context to context) as being infringed if the rule is enforced.
2 See para A3.80 to A3.94.

(b) *Formulation of guidelines to reflect the aims*

A2.64 Governing bodies should consider the formulation of guidelines which achieve these aims, dealing with the rules on each of the heads set out below. The guidelines can explain both for the benefit of the disciplinary committee and the defendant, what is expected.

B Sequence of events in disciplinary proceedings and practical considerations for the governing body

A2.65 While all the underlying aims set out above give rise to practical considerations for the governing body, the most immediate is the need to comply with the standards set in this context by the courts. The best practice that we identify below takes into those standards as described in the next chapter, and the matters set out below should be read together with that chapter. The overriding objective is to provide a fair and proper opportunity to be heard before an impartial tribunal. While the standard of fairness may vary from context to context, a governing body will have a broad feel for whether particular restrictive elements in its procedural rules are genuinely necessary and justified. The governing body should also bear in mind that justice must be seen to be done as well as done, and also that prudent acquiescence with essentially non-controversial requests of a defendant in relation to procedure avoid conflict, loss of time and expense.

(a) Investigation and preliminary consideration

A2.66 Whatever the nature of the disciplinary allegation, the first step is the investigation of it. A sports governing body would be unwise to put a matter to a substantive disciplinary hearing without first reviewing if a disciplinary offence has in fact taken place. Unfounded allegations may be made, or there may be a misunderstanding, and the adverse consequences for an individual of his even being charged may be serious, and are not always overcome by a subsequent acquittal. The investigator should talk to everyone involved in the matter and then compile a report. It would be wise to take formal statements.

A2.67 The sports governing body will need to consider the inclusion of provisions to compel other clubs and individuals subject to the rules to assist with a case. If it does, the rules will need to spell out the obligation clearly and what the consequences of non-compliance are. The advantage of such provisions is obviously that it enables the sports governing body to access as much information as possible. The disadvantage is equally obviously that it is likely to be unpopular with those subject to it.

A2.68 After compilation of the report and material, there should then be preliminary consideration, whether by the investigator or by a separate committee, as to whether the report and material disclose sufficient evidence that an offence has been committed to warrant a disciplinary charge being made. This is a preliminary stage, and not an adjudication on the substance, and therefore the standard here should not be whether an offence *has* been committed (on the standard applied at the substantive hearing) but whether the investigator or committee is reasonably satisfied that there is sufficient evidence for the matter to proceed. This can also be expressed as there being 'a case to answer' or 'prima facie' evidence of an offence.

A2.69 The consequence of the determination at this stage may vary from governing body to governing body. If there is a case to answer, the governing body may be obliged, for example by the rules of the international governing body, to proceed to bring charges. It could on the other hand be that under the applicable rules the governing body has a discretion not to bring charges even in these circumstances. The difficulty with such a discretion is more likely to be in its application than in its existence. In particular, where the consequences of bringing or not bringing disciplinary charges may affect a third party (for example in the promotion and relegation context discussed above), great care must be taken. It may be arguable by a third party in such a context, depending on how the rules are structured, that they have an entitlement to see the rules properly enforced.

(b) Formation of the disciplinary panel

A2.70 If the matter is to proceed to a disciplinary committee for substantive decision, the sports governing body's rules will need to provide for how that disciplinary committee is to be established and in particular who is to sit on it. A number of considerations arise. First, the people should be expert in the sport. Secondly, it may be wise to have a lawyer on the panel. Third, great care must be taken that nobody sits on the panel who might be, or who might be perceived to be, biased or interested in the outcome.

A2.71 Expertise and qualifications of the members It is usual for the sports governing body's rules to provide that the sports governing body shall select the disciplinary committee, although increasingly, the rules may provide that an independent dispute resolution tribunal be used instead[1]. The sports governing body should have a standing panel of names so that a disciplinary committee can be selected quickly from people who are likely to be well suited to deal with the matter. Disciplinary committees are usually, but not always, made up of three people: on occasion a much greater number sit. In choosing who should go on the list from which the disciplinary committee will be selected, the governing body has to bear in mind not only that the individuals should be expert in the sport, but also that there are different interest groups within the sport (for example players, clubs and administrators) and that in some circumstances it may be desirable to be able to select committee members who are wholly independent of the governing body and even of the sport itself[2]. Some disputes may involve a conflict with the entire administration of the sport, others may be less divisive. In an ideal world it would be possible to find individuals who were intimate with the issues surrounding a sport, but who were also independent of it. In practice however this may well prove difficult. The governing body should therefore attempt to identify a good cross range of people so that their different strengths can complement one another on the disciplinary committee and so that a suitable committee can be appointed. If complicated legal issues arise, it may well be wise to include a lawyer on the panel, or to have a lawyer advising the panel, as this may well reduce the prospects of the committee straying over the boundaries set by the courts[3]. It may also provide some procedural control over proceedings, saving time and costs. It is also useful where one or other of the parties to the disciplinary proceedings is legally represented. Whether acting as chair or as an adviser, the lawyer should be independent of the body bringing the charges[4]. If the chairman is not legally qualified, he may find it helpful to have regard to a set of guidelines prepared for such chairmen by the sports governing body.

1 See paras A5.43 and A5.44 (discussing FA and RFU provision for appointment of independent people to disciplinary panels); A5.49 (Commonwealth Games Federation provision for referral of first instance dispute to Court of Arbitration for Sport); A5.50 to A5.59 (provision in various governing body rules for referral of appeals to CAS or Sports Dispute Resolution Panel, particularly in anti-doping matters).

2 See para A2.72, n 2.

3 Raj Parker concludes at [1995] 3(3) SATLJ 6 that it is wise to have a lawyer chairing the committee not only because other lawyers may review the decision if a challenge is made, but also because lawyers will find easier to interpret the rule, to ensure natural justice, to deal with evidential points and to manage the situation where there are simultaneous pending proceedings before other tribunals.

4 That said, it might arise that the constituency of the disciplinary committee involved no formal appointment of a lawyer to act as chair or as an adviser, but a member of it happened to be a lawyer. He could then bring that training to bear in the discussions of the committee.

A2.72 Appearance of bias The principles which the courts apply in determining whether there has been bias or an appearance of bias are set out in the next chapter[1], and in the chapter dealing with the Human Rights Act 1998[2]. The crucial thing that is clear from the courts' approach is that the question is only whether a reasonable person might conclude that it appeared from the facts there was a real danger of bias: it is not necessary that actual bias be established, although obviously that would be sufficient. For a governing body forming the panel in advance, the guiding principle must be prudence. From a purely practical point of view, it is better for a member not to sit if there is any possibility of a complaint being made by the club or individual being disciplined, even if by reference to the standards applied by the courts, there is not even an appearance of bias. Accordingly, if an objection is raised to any of the names put forward, the objection should be taken seriously and acted upon. Plainly the objection should not be acted upon if the objection has clearly been made purely for frivolous or vexatious reasons, or as a delaying tactic, but if any doubt arises, the sports governing body should err in favour of acceding to the participant's request.

1 See para A3.105.
2 See Chapter A4, in the section dealing with the right to a fair trial before an independent and impartial tribunal under Art 6. Irrespective of whether the Act strictly applies to the actions of a particular sports governing body, best practice is to adopt the same approach by analogy. It is to be noted that the requirement under Art 6 of the Act that the panel be 'independent', as well as 'impartial', goes some way further than the common law obligation that there should not be an appearance of bias. Application of the requirement that a tribunal be 'independent' would involve its members not be being part of the governing body's apparatus save to the extent of their involvement as a member of the tribunal. It would also impinge on the way in which they were appointed and remunerated. This is dealt with in Chapter A4.

A2.73 An appearance of bias may arise for a number of reasons which are individual to the particular case, and the governing body should assess the position on each occasion. There are however some general propositions. No person involved with the investigation or decision to proceed, or involved in any way with the incident or the individual or club, should serve on the panel. It may be impossible to find someone who does not know of the individual or club alleged to have committed the offence but the panel members should not know personally, or be connected with, the individual or club or have prior knowledge of the incident or the individual. The panel members equally should not be connected with any third party that stands, or themselves stand, to gain from the outcome of the disciplinary proceedings. Care should be taken not to select members who may have expressed a view on the particular subject matter of the disciplinary proceedings, specifically, or even in some circumstances generally[1].

1 As is discussed at paras A3.105, A3.122 to A3.125 and A3.203 Diane Modahl based her claim for damages on an allegation that BAF breached its contract with her to act fairly because there was bias on the part of one of the members of the disciplinary committee. The allegation centred around the proposition that one of the panel had expressed a view that all athletes were potentially guilty of doping until they proved the contrary.

(c) Parties

A2.74 Defendant The defending party in disciplinary proceedings is the individual, club or other participant subject to disciplinary sanction. The identification of this party is not necessarily as simple as identifying who did something wrong. Clubs can only act by individuals, and often a club may be subject to disciplinary sanction in place of or in addition to the individual who acted improperly. For example under the FA rules, a player may be disciplined for violence, but the club may also face disciplinary proceedings consequent upon its players' violent conduct. Clubs may also suffer the consequences of individuals' actions, for example where points are deducted from the club when its players have notched up a particular number of disciplinary offences. Depending on the particular rules, the club's liability may be based simply on the fact that the individual played for it, or it may be based on some systematic failure to regulate its players.

A2.75 Prosecutor The prosecuting party in disciplinary proceedings is the sports governing body, but its identity may be more narrowly defined as the executive of the governing body, or as a specialist investigative officer or committee. It will be for the sports governing body to decide if it would like its internal or external legal representatives to present the case against the participant charged. Much will depend on the severity of the alleged offence and whether the participant charged is legally represented. Whether a legal representative or some other person or body is to present the case, it is essential that they do not advise or discuss the case with the disciplinary committee. This does not however prevent them from liasing with the disciplinary committee in relation to the logistics of the hearing.

(d) Formulation of charge and pre-hearing procedure

A2.76 As explained above, sports governing bodies are not attempting to imitate the courts, and their procedures need not be as formal as those of the courts. Nevertheless it is wise to have rules, or at least guidelines, that describe the way in which the case will be brought on for hearing. While it may be permissible for the disciplinary committee to set its own procedures, it should not, and should not be perceived to be, making up the rules as it goes along. The desire to allow flexibility to cater for the differences in particular cases should not be allowed to eclipse the need to provide certainty and comfort to the defendant that matters are proceeding in a foreseeable and orderly manner. The chairman of the disciplinary committee may have power to give directions as to the pre-hearing conduct of the matter: this usually works well if the chairman is legally qualified, but if he is not, then rules or guidelines are needed to provide the parameters within which such directions can be made. Care needs to be taken in relation to the application of such guidelines if they exist, because if they are not followed, a dissatisfied defendant may use them to argue that something that was or was not done was in breach of the guidelines and therefore unfair. Where guidelines are just that, and not rules, and it is contemplated that the disciplinary committee should be able to step outside them, then they must state clearly that they are provided for the information of the disciplinary committee but are not binding upon them.

A2.77 Notification of the charge The procedure is commenced by the formulation and notification of the charge[1]. The charge should make clear exactly what rule is alleged to have been breached and the facts that disclose that breach. The facts alleged must be capable of disclosing the breach of the rule alleged. In most instances this will be relatively straightforward: a footballer could quite clearly be guilty of using 'violent, threatening, abusive, indecent, or insulting words or behaviour' if the allegation was that he punched the referee at a particular time during a particular match played on a particular day. However where the charge is less clear cut, there may need to be more explanation of why the bare facts disclose the breach of the rule alleged. For example, why exactly has the sport been brought into disrepute? A governing body would be wise to provide further details if requested.

1 See para A3.102, n 2.

A2.78 Interim suspension The governing body's rules will need to set out clearly if an interim suspension can be imposed on the sportsperson. The rules will also have to make it clear if a suspension is imposed automatically[1] or whether the sports governing body retains the right to decide whether to impose a suspension in each individual case[2]. If it does retain such a discretion, then it would have to ensure the discretion is exercised carefully, fairly and consistently as between different defendants.

1 As in the case of a doping charge in athletics.
2 As in the case of the FA Rules.

A2.79 Communication of the evidence in support of the charge The governing body is under an obligation to provide the defendant with a proper opportunity to be heard. Integral to that is the clear identification of the facts and matters to be relied upon by the governing body[1]. The aim should always be to ensure that both sides know exactly what evidence the other will be presenting at the hearing. It is certainly arguable, though not established, that the defendant should be entitled to see all evidence (as opposed to legal advice) that the sports governing body has in relation to the case (even if the sports governing body is not relying upon it). While it may be an interesting debate as to whether disciplinary proceedings are inquisitorial rather than adversarial (and the answer may well vary from sport to sport), it is arguably right that a sports governing body should fall under the same obligation in this particular evidential context as the Crown in criminal cases. At bottom the interests of the sports governing body are only served by the conviction of the guilty, and not by simply winning disciplinary proceedings.

1 See para A3.102, n 3.

A2.80 Setting the hearing date The parties should, as soon as disciplinary procedures commence, endeavour to agree the date for the hearing and the practical timetable for preparation. If they are not able to do this, and probably in any event, it will be necessary for the chairman of the disciplinary committee to rule as to directions. The timing of the hearing is a difficult issue, and often there are a number of competing considerations. The starting point is that defendants are only provided a proper opportunity to be heard if they are afforded sufficient time to prepare their case[1]. On the other hand in many instances a prompt hearing is necessary. For example in some sports the outcome of an event depends on the outcome of the hearing: in racing the stewards may immediately consider an incident, hear from the jockey and rule so that the betting public knows where it stands. In this context, the disciplinary process has to provide for a staged process, so that the adequate opportunity to present a case arises at the second stage. In doping cases, a prompt hearing may be necessary because there might be a disqualification. In other contexts, the player may already have received a sending off, but the question of what additional consequences that should involve remains to be determined. There is not the same urgency as if the result depended upon the outcome, but still the player and club would want to know as soon as possible what will happen. From the point of view of the governing body, there is a greater need for urgency if the perception might arise that a wrong-doer was being allowed to continue competing pending a hearing: from the defendant's point of view there is a greater need for urgency if there has been an interim suspension. The rules must be framed, and applied, so as to balance the competing interests. As stated above, a useful mechanism may be to ensure that promptness is catered for by a first stage of the procedure, and a full opportunity to be heard by a second stage. However, this approach cannot, or ought not[2], to be used to allow for an unfair imposition of a sanction under the first mechanism, and it will not solve all problems in all sports.

1 See para A3.102, n 4.
2 The approach of the courts is that the process should be reviewed as a whole, and that appeals can cure the defects in the earlier stages of the procedure: see para A3.107. Nevertheless this arguably would not justify an arbitrary and restrictive system which prevented a competitor participating in the short to medium term without an opportunity to be heard properly.

A2.81 Exchange of evidence It is helpful in ensuring proper disclosure of the case against a defendant and a proper opportunity to be heard for the system to provide for the exchange of witness statements (including expert reports) and bundles of documents containing the relevant documents well before the hearing so that each side knows what evidence the other intends to bring and can prepare submissions and cross-examination of the other side's witnesses in relation to such evidence. In cases involving complex scientific evidence, it is also helpful if both sides are allowed to prepare and exchange supplemental witness statements to deal with the issues raised by the other side's experts. Expert evidence is often critical and it is important that such evidence is prepared bearing in mind the principles underlying, if not necessarily the letter of, the current practice in court proceedings. Experts are under a duty to be impartial, and to be seen to be impartial. The letter of instruction, and the questions asked of them, should be disclosed. They should identify the discipline in which they are expert, and whether any relevant matters fall outside their expertise. They must identify the factual substratum for their conclusions so that the disciplinary committee can assess if they proceeded on a false premise. They should not hide matters which might put their conclusions into question, but rather deal with them. They should make clear which of their opinions are concluded and which if any contingent, and in the latter case, on what matters they are contingent. Their obligations are continuing ones, and so if they change their minds (if for example the evidence establishing the factual substratum changes), they should report this.

A2.82 Pleadings, legal submissions, bundles and authorities The system may provide for an exchange of pleadings before or at the same time as evidence is exchanged. For example the prosecutor may be required to put in a statement of case and at the same time serve the evidence on which it proposes to rely. The defendant would then put in a defence together with the evidence on which he proposes to rely. In other contexts, legal submissions could be contained in skeleton arguments produced after the exchange of evidence. If the parties exchange skeleton arguments setting out their respective cases together with a list of outstanding issues, time may be cut down at the hearing and the precise matters in issue pinpointed. However, this is by no means compulsory unless the chairman of the disciplinary committee so rules. Bundles should also be produced containing the relevant documents and any authorities relied upon.

A2.83 Treatment of late evidence The obligation on the sports governing body to ensure that the defendant has a fair hearing within the confines of the standards set by the courts, is not an immediately reciprocal obligation. While a sports governing body is clearly compromised in its efforts to uphold the interests of the sport and other athletes if it is treated unfairly in its preparation and presentation of its case, the impact is not as immediate and significant as the impact on an individual if he or she is unfairly treated. Consequently it is generally wise to afford a degree of latitude to defendants if they attempt to serve documents or witness statements late, in particular if they bear significantly on the case. It will often be possible to order an adjournment to mitigate the effects of this.

A2.84 Stay If the police are also investigating the matter and the defendant may be subject to criminal proceedings, there is a real risk that the disciplinary proceedings could compromise them. Equally there may be simultaneous civil proceedings in the courts. In this context, the disciplinary committee should consider staying the disciplinary proceedings until the other proceedings are resolved[1]. Much will depend on the severity of the offence, the precise issue before the other court, and the extent of overlap. If matters do proceed before any criminal proceedings, then the chairman will need to warn the defendant against the risks of self-incrimination.

1 Cf paras A3.219 and A3.220, from the point of view of the courts. See also Parker [1995] 3(3) SATLJ 6.

(e) Hearing

A2.85 Oral hearing or written process The sports governing body's rules should provide for oral hearings, and the body should allow the defendant such a hearing if requested, although it may be that in some circumstances a written procedure will not offend the principles of natural justice[1]. In the context of disciplinary proceedings, as opposed to applications from outsiders, it seems to the authors that an oral hearing is required.

1 See para A3.102, n 7.

A2.86 In public or in private The form of the hearing should be defined in the rules. The hearing is usually held in private, because this is what both the governing body and the defendant would prefer. The governing body is often happy not to have such matters aired in public, and the defendant often wishes to preserve his or her reputation. Equally there may be circumstances where the defendant would prefer to have a hearing in public, and the rules should allow for this to happen if requested[1].

1 Where the Human Rights Act 1998 applies, a person is entitled to a public hearing: see Chapter A4. Irrespective of whether the Act strictly applies to the actions of a particular sports governing body, best practice is to adopt the same approach by analogy.

A2.87 Rules of evidence and procedure As already stated, the disciplinary committee is not amateur court of law, and it is not required to have regard to the legal rules as to evidence or procedure. The disciplinary committee can set the approach at the hearing that it wants so long as that complies with the standards set by the courts.

A2.88 The burden and standard of proof The burden of proving that an offence has been committed should be, and generally is under the applicable rules, on the governing body[1]. However in some situations it is possible to provide that once basic facts are proved, there is a presumption of an offence unless the defendant disproves it. For example in the context of doping, the practicalities of the offence make it legitimate to provide that an offence is committed once the presence in the individual's body of a prohibited substance is established. More difficult is the question of whether it is legitimate to provide that the establishment of that fact is an end to the matter and the defendant is strictly liable, or that the establishment of that fact raises a presumption which the defendant can then disprove. The law in this area is developing: for some drugs, proving the presence of the drug is enough, for others it gives rise to a rebuttable presumption. It is now tolerably clear that while strict liability may operate in certain circumstances to define whether an offence has been committed, it cannot generally be applied so as to result in a mandatory ban from competition: the circumstances must be taken into account in arriving at a proportionate sanction[2]. The governing body's rules should also define the standard of proof, or in other words the degree to which the disciplinary committee should be satisfied that an offence has been committed[3]. Some governing bodies' rules set the standard at the criminal standard of satisfaction beyond all reasonable doubt. In the absence of specific provision, the burden of proof will be the civil standard, satisfaction on the balance of probabilities, but subject to an important caveat. The concept of satisfaction to the civil standard in the context of disciplinary offences involves a sliding scale: the more serious the offence, the greater the degree of satisfaction required[4]. It has been argued that where the disciplinary offence discloses a criminal offence, the standard should be the equivalent of the criminal standard[5], but this may be putting it too high. In the context of doping, the CAS applies a test which appears to be between satisfaction beyond all reasonable doubt and satisfaction on the balance of probabilities, stating that the governing body must establish the offence to the 'comfortable satisfaction' of the disciplinary committee, with what constitutes comfortable satisfaction varying with the gravity of the offence. In these circumstances, the rules of the governing body should seek to define the standard of proof applicable, as this will help to remove uncertainty.

1 See para A3.104.
2 For these propositions see Chapter E4. The authorities there discussed allowing mandatory disqualification from the event and loss of medal (as opposed to a mandatory ban) consequent upon a strict liability offence being proved. It is arguably open to question whether this should always be the case, for example where there can be no question of other contestants having been disadvantaged.
3 See para A3.104.
4 See Chapters E4 and A4. Put another way, the evidence to prove the offence must be all the more weightier: see Beloff [2002] 2 ISLR 4. In the same way, allegations of fraud before the civil courts fall to be determined by reference to the civil standard, but the court must be able to reach a clear conclusion.
5 In reliance on *Re a Solicitor* [1993] QB 69. This authority should be treated with some care: fraud in the civil context may also disclose a crime, but the standard remains the civil one. For the impact of the Human Rights Act 1998 in this context, see Chapter A4.

A2.89 Representation The rules should specify whether the defendant can be represented and whether the representative can be a lawyer. Although the rules of some sports prohibit legal representation, and it is not yet established that this is contrary to the rules of natural justice, in the authors' view best practice is that a defendant accused of a disciplinary offence should be entitled to bring a representative (legally qualified or otherwise) to the hearing[1].

1 See para A3.102, n 8. See also Parker [1995] 3(3) SATLJ 6.

A2.90 Course of the hearing The rules or guidelines should also describe the course of the hearing, while allowing the disciplinary committee to depart from the standard course if appropriate. The prosecuting sports governing body will usually open the hearing by setting out the charge, describing the case against the defendant, and making any submissions on the rules or the law. It may also be desirable for the prosecutor, in agreement with the defendant, to present a list of issues for decision and possibly a list of agreed facts. It will then call the witnesses on which it relies, including expert witnesses. The defendant should have the opportunity to cross-examine those witnesses (although it is not established that the absence of that right is necessarily a breach of natural justice) and the sports governing body should then have the right to re-examine them[1]. The defendant or a representative would then call the defendant's witnesses, who equally should be the subject of cross examination and re-examination if the sports governing body so elects. At this point many rules provide for the prosecutor to close, followed by the defendant. The defendant would presenting the defence, addressing the evidence and making any submissions on the rules and the law. The defendant should be afforded a full opportunity to put his, her or its case, within reason making the points that he wants[2]. If necessary the sports governing body could then reply, but the underlying principle of this order of events is that the defendant should have the last word. This is the normal approach in criminal trials. It might be possible to follow the civil approach with the defendant going after his, her or its evidence, with the prosecutor next, and the defendant having a right of response to genuinely new matters raised for the first time. It would also be possible to introduce an opening statement by the defendant into the process. The rules should allow the disciplinary committee to ask questions of either side's witnesses at any stage. Questions should generally only be asked in response to something said by a witness. Sometimes a member of a disciplinary committee will have knowledge of a particular issue (for example a member of the disciplinary committee who is a scientist may have a view about something that is being said) and may want to address questions to a witness in relation to this. The members of the committee should not give advice or ask leading questions and should avoid making judgmental comments. They should restrict questions to the particular matter before them, and they should act consistently[3]. The sports governing body's rules may also provide for joint experts or for an expert to be appointed by the disciplinary committee to assist it.

1 See para A3.102, n 9.
2 See para A3.102, nn 5 and 6.
3 See Welch and Wearmouth, *Getting it right – A guide to sports ethics, disciplinaries and appeals* (1994, Sports Council, ISBN 1-872158-37-4); Wearmouth, 'No winners on the greasy pole? Ethical and legal frameworks of evaluating disciplinary processes in sport' [1995] 3(3) SATLJ 29.

A2.91 Change of tack A difficult question is whether, and if so the extent to which, either side should be able to change its case in mid-proceedings. The standard for the governing body will be whether by so doing a point is raised on which the defendant has not had a full and fair opportunity to be heard. Generally, the disciplinary committee should be slow to allow the governing body to make substantial alterations to the way it puts its case. The same principles apply in reverse to changes of direction by the defendant: the question is not whether to allow such a change would be procedurally unfair to the governing body, but rather whether to refuse to allow it would be unfair to the defendant. Prudence dictates that within reason, the defendant should be allowed the opportunity to put a new point.

A2.92 Adjournment The disciplinary committee should have power to adjourn if the circumstances require it. If the hearing is likely to go on some time, with breaks, it is best to have separate rooms set aside for the defendant and the sports governing body so that they can retire to discuss matters while the disciplinary committee stays in the hearing room.

A2.93 Third parties The rules may provide for third parties to have the right to make representations at the hearing. If the rules are silent, it will be for the chair to decide if they can and, if so, to regulate the nature of any statements or questioning. The governing body must balance the rights of those that it governs.

A2.94 Record A record should be kept of what happens at the hearing. If there are any preliminary rulings prior to the substantive decision, they should be formally made and recorded.

A2.95 Deciding the facts The first task of the disciplinary committee after hearing the case presented by both sides is to reach a decision on the facts[1]. Whilst at first glance this is the easier of the two tasks facing it, and the one in respect of which it is least likely to be the subject of review[2], it is nevertheless a difficult task. The weight to be attached to evidence is a matter for the disciplinary committee, and the courts are unlikely to intervene, but the disciplinary committee still has to know how to approach the task. The factors which determine what weight should be attached to particular evidence cannot be listed, and in any event are often subjective. Nevertheless a number of points can be articulated. The starting point is to determine which of the witnesses' accounts of disputed facts is preferred. In doing this the committee will take into account the independent evidence disclosed by the documents and any other record such as video evidence. It is useful to ask which account is supported by the external materials. Such external materials are what they are, and are not trammelled by subjective presentation to the committee through an individual before them. They are, prima facie, the safest evidence on which to rely. But care should be taken not to rely on them unthinkingly. Documents may be self serving and their contents could be based on a mistake. A video may fail to tell the whole story. After considering consistency with the external materials, the committee should consider the consistency of the particular witness' evidence with the evidence of other witnesses, the internal consistency of the witness' own evidence, and its consistency with things that he has said before. If there is such consistency, the evidence is stronger. The committee will also take into account the extent to which a witness might be partisan as opposed to independent, or might have 'an axe to grind'. Independent, and in particular independent scientific evidence, is obviously stronger than self serving evidence. However when assessing the evidence of supposedly independent witnesses, such as experts, the committee should ask itself whether the witness has descended into the arena and become an advocate for a particular cause rather than an impartial specialist. In the context of expert evidence, the committee should bear in mind that by its very nature this evidence is opinion evidence, and that often two views can legitimately be taken, although one may be preferable to the other. In the context of witnesses of fact, the committee will assess whether there are particular factors which might put in doubt a witness' recollection, and lead to a conclusion that someone was mistaken. For example it may be useful to ask whether the witness was a long way from the action, or whether his or her view was blocked. It may also be useful to ask whether the events happened a long time ago. The committee will also bear in mind the distinction between direct evidence from a witness on the one hand, and on the other hand, first evidence where the witness reports what others have told him or her (hearsay) and secondly evidence not of facts but of the subjective conclusions that the witness has drawn (opinion). Only at the end of the process do, or should, questions of credibility arise: was a witness lying? In many if not most instances, the dispute of fact can be resolved without a conclusion that somebody is not telling the truth. What is more, it can be very difficult to determine whether somebody is lying without the benefit of material which indicates that this is the case: many truthful witnesses may be nervous, confused and inarticulate, and equally many liars can paint a plausible picture. Having determined which account is preferred, the question is whether the extent of the preference that can be arrived at is sufficient to discharge the standard of proof applicable. If a high standard applies, then it is not enough that on balance the committee thinks that one account was more plausible than another. The committee must ask itself whether the extent to which it was convinced to prefer one account over another has left it sufficiently satisfied that the facts alleged occurred.

1 See also Beloff 'Finding out the facts' [2002] 2 ISLR 35.

2 The substance of a decision on the facts (as opposed to the procedural proprietary of it, and as opposed to a decision on the rules or the law) will only be the subject of review if the decision-maker acts irrationally (for example by ignoring relevant considerations or taking into account irrelevant ones) or if there is no basis in fact for its conclusions: see paras A3.109 and A3.112, n 2. The courts are reluctant to intervene in determinations of fact made by those who are expert in the field: see paras A3.72 to A3.79. Of course the fact that a margin of appreciation is left in this way for the disciplinary committee does not relieve it of its burden of assessing to the requisite standard whether the facts alleged are made out.

A2.96 Deciding on the application of the rules and the law The second stage is to determine what the consequences of the facts so determined are when measured against the rules, and if appropriate, the law. The disciplinary committee will have to consider each side's arguments as to the proper construction of the rules[1], and may have to reach a conclusion in relation to submissions of law advanced. As set out above, the defendant is entitled to take points of law, even if he may ultimately only be preserving the point for a future challenge in the courts.

1 As to which see paras A3.95 to A3.100.

(f) Decision, reasons, sanction and costs

A2.97 When to give the decision When the disciplinary committee should give its decision depends on the degree of urgency involved. If the matter is urgent, for example because it affects whether the defendant can compete in a forthcoming event, the committee may give its decision at the conclusion of the hearing after a short adjournment. Where there is no urgency however it is preferable for the governing body to reserve its decision. This enables it to consider the position in detail and to formulate structured reasons for its decision. The decision should be given to both sides simultaneously.

A2.98 Reasons As a matter of good practice (although not necessarily as a requirement of natural justice), written reasons should be given for a decision[1]. The need to give reasons results in more logical and structured decision making. Reasons allow justice to be seen to be done as well as to be done: they show that thought has gone into the decision and that there is a clear justification for it in the evidence, and they put to rest any speculative allegation that the basis for the decision was flawed. If there is an internal right of appeal[2] reasons are necessary to allow the appeal committee to have the benefit of the disciplinary committee's thinking. Where there is urgency, the decision could be given and the written reasons could follow. The reasons should be as detailed as possible setting out why the disciplinary committee has ruled in the way it has on each issue raised at the hearing.

1 See para A3.103.
2 Where the appeal does not involve a 'de novo' hearing reasons are needed so that the appeal body can consider whether the first instance body erred. Even where the hearing is 'de novo', it may be useful for the appeal body to understand the first instance body's reasoning.

A2.99 Sanction Any sanction imposed must be set out in the rules as being applicable in the circumstances found to have been proved: it must be within the powers of the governing body[1]. A variety of sanctions can often be imposed under the rules, including disqualification, warnings, fines, deduction of points, suspension from competition for defined periods and even expulsion. Some sanctions may be automatic. Further, where there is a discretion in relation to the sanction, it must be exercised fairly and rationally. This means that it will have to be proportionate to the circumstances proven[2], even if it falls within the range of available sanctions for the offence. As well as the circumstances of the offence under consideration, it may be legitimate to take into account the previous disciplinary record of the defendant. The reasons of the disciplinary committee should identify the basis on which the sanction has been set.

1 See para A3.95.
2 See para A3.111.

A2.100 Costs The disciplinary committee may award costs, whether to the defendant or to the governing body, if they are empowered so to do by the rules[1]. If the rules confer no such power then no award can be made.

1 See para A3.108. The Football Association has recently removed the ability of the disciplinary commission to order that an unsuccessful defendant pay the costs of the governing body, apparently over fears that the jurisdiction might preclude the defendant having access to justice. In some circumstances therefore, governing bodies may want to consider limiting the right to award costs, and it would be wise to allow for particular circumstances to be taken into account.

(g) Appeal

A2.101 Sports governing bodies should consider whether to include the possibility of an internal (or external[1]) appeal by the defendant in their rules. The absence of an appeal is not necessarily a breach of natural justice[2]. The advantage of including an appeal is that defects in the initial procedure can often be cured by the availability of an appeal[3]: in the absence of an appeal, the first (and only) stage must be fully compliant with all the requirements set by the courts. The disadvantage is that the addition of an extra stage adds cost and time to the process. A circumstance in which an appeal is indispensable is where the initial decision has to be rapidly taken. A further factor to take into account is the nature of the initial disciplinary committee. If it was a truly independent committee with a legally qualified chairman, it is arguably difficult to see what could be gained by having an appeal to a similarly constituted appeals committee. However, if the original disciplinary committee did not have a legally qualified chairman and was composed of those within the sport's apparatus then the desirability of a right to appeal is all the stronger. Whether the governing body itself can appeal against the decision of its own disciplinary committee is a matter for the proper construction of the rules[4]. Most international governing bodies provide for an appeal to CAS. If this is available to a competitor then the national sports governing body may feel that it does not need its own appeal. A CAS hearing can take place at a time and venue convenient to the parties and the arbitrators.

1 For example to a body like CAS or the Sports Dispute Resolution Panel.
2 See para A3.107, n 1. Nor is it necessarily contrary to the Human Rights Act 1998: see Chapter A4.
3 See para A3.107, n 2.
4 A matter debated at length in *Korda*, referred to at para A2.33, n 1.

A2.102 The nature of the appeal will vary from sport to sport. In some cases there will be a hearing 'de novo', in others a more limited right of appeal exists. FA Rule H confines appeals to disciplinary proceedings other than for breach of the rules of the game, and appeals can only be brought by the party disciplined at the original hearing. The Appeal must be brought within 14 days. The Notice of Appeal must set out the decision appealed against, a statement of facts relied upon, and the grounds of the appeal. If the appellant wishes to adduce new evidence, an application must be made in the Notice. The grounds of appeal are confined to misinterpretation of the rules, the reaching of a decision to which no reasonable body could have come, or the imposition of a penalty which is excessive. Thus the standard imposed by the FA is analogous to the standard of review by the courts, and it is not a 'de novo' hearing.

C Practical considerations for those subject to disciplinary proceedings

A2.103 Just as sports governing bodies should be aware of and comply with the standards set by the courts for the conduct of disciplinary proceedings, so too defendants to those proceedings should bear these requirements in mind and hold the governing body to them. Defendants can and generally should take points (if they arise) on the proper construction of the rules, on procedural propriety and on rationality, before the disciplinary committee or ideally at an earlier stage. If a point is not taken there is a real risk that it might be said to have been waived. Going direct to court might be permissible in some circumstances, but in others it might well be said to be premature[1]. Equally where threatened disciplinary action may infringe other principles, such as the restraint of trade doctrine, the competition rules or the free movement rules, such points can be taken. It is true that doing these things is likely, if the governing body is well advised, to result in the governing body curing defects in its procedures and removing an important basis for challenge in the courts. This may give rise to the perception that to do this is to offer undue assistance to a governing body which is going to reach an adverse conclusion in any event. However, the most that a defendant can secure is a fair and legal hearing. If this can be obtained without going to court, the defendant will save time and incur less costs. Furthermore, in many instances the relief obtained from the court (assuming that it does not regard the points as waived) will not prevent the governing body subsequently changing its procedures and approach and proceeding to discipline the defendant validly and fairly.

1 See paras A3.49 to A3.51 and A3.217 for factors to take into account in making this choice.

A2.104 A difficulty often encountered by those subject to disciplinary proceedings is the potentially shifting nature of the proceedings themselves. Many disciplinary systems, while specifying the basic procedural elements, do not set out in detail how the proceedings are to be conducted: sometimes because governance of the sport is not well developed and sometimes as a deliberate approach to avoid any departure being relied upon to base a claim in the courts based on unfairness. This may have the benefit of protecting the disciplinary body, but unfortunately it can also leave the defendant bereft of detailed guidance.

A2.105 In such circumstances, a defendant would be wise to take steps to define the parameters of the allegation and the procedure at an early stage, and certainly well before the hearing. He, she or it may wish to simply ask for information. Alternatively, the defendant may want the relevant disciplinary committee to make a direction, if it has the power to do so. Ideally it is suggested that the defendant take the following steps.

A2.106 The defendant should seek to ascertain details of how the procedure operates. He, she or it will need to know what all the applicable rules and guidelines are, what the procedural steps are, what the time limits are, what happens at each stage, who has power to deal with each stage, what the levels of privacy and confidentiality required at each stage are, what the position is with regard to witnesses, how the disciplinary proceedings fit in with the rules of other bodies that might have jurisdiction, and whether there is an appeal.

A2.107 The defendant should ensure he, she or it obtains a detailed understanding of the charges made. A simple reference to the rule alleged to have been breached and a nod to the relevant facts is not enough. It is an insufficient basis on which to prepare a defence. Unless he, she or it knows exactly what is alleged, and why, the defendant may plead guilty to a charge which appears much less serious on its face than the allegation that is advanced at the hearing. It is suggested that the defendant ask the disciplinary body for a statement of case, explaining precisely the facts relied on.

A2.108 The defendant should establish the potential penalty, if possible more specifically than by reference to the full range available to the disciplinary committee. Without knowing this the defendant does not know the seriousness with which the disciplinary body views the offence. Arguably the tribunal should supply this information in any event, since not to do so may be a breach of Art 6 of the European Convention on Human Rights[1].

1 See Chapter A4.

A2.109 Once he, she or it knows the extent of the charges, the defendant should consider preparing a fairly detailed defence or statement of mitigation if it is possible to do so. This clarifies the issues and prevents any misunderstanding about the extent of any admissions.

A2.110 In cases where the rules do not specify the standard of proof, or where it is on the civil standard but where the offence sits on the sliding scale is not clear, the defendant should seek to establish the standard of proof. It may be enough to do this through the pleadings, but in other cases it might be wise to discuss this formally with the governing body. If the conduct is to be denied, the defendant must know the standard to be adopted in order to prove the case against him, her or it. And even if the defendant is contemplating pleading guilty the standard should be ascertained as it is an indication of the seriousness of the conduct: if the stated standard is the balance of probabilities, a submission can then be made that the conduct is not so serious as to require the higher standard and the penalty should therefore not be the most serious. Equally it would be wise to establish how the burden of proof and any presumptions are to operate. It might be useful to ask, if a presumption arises, what the defendant must do to rebut it.

A2.111 The defendant should attempt to obtain details (and ideally transcripts) of decisions made in cases where similar charges have been brought. This will help the defendant to ensure that the penalty is consistent and may also give an indication of the penalty he, she or it might face. However, the sports governing body may be prevented from disclosing these on grounds of confidentiality.

A2.112 The defendant should ask for details of the stages of preparation and order of play at the hearing and endeavour to agree the process. The defendant should ensure that the provision of witness statements and documents is on the basis that all the evidence to be relied upon is provided well in advance of the hearing. The defendant should also establish in advance how witness evidence is to be given at the hearing: whether it is to be adduced in chief, whether statements will be taken as read, or whether statements will be read out. It may be useful to ask whether witnesses be available for cross examination. Although this is really a matter for the disciplinary committee at the hearing it may be possible to fix the approach in advance.

A2.113 If necessary, the defendant should request relevant documents not already disclosed. The defendant should ask to see all the documents that constitute the investigation file.

A2.114 In taking these steps and in preparing for the hearing, the defendant should not allow the sports governing body to rush or bully him, her or it. If it is impossible to prepare the defence in the often short time before proceedings then the defendant will no doubt want to consider asking for an adjournment, although a valid reason will clearly have to be shown. The defendant can rely on the proposition that disciplinary proceedings may have a potentially disastrous impact on those against whom charges are brought and that they should be treated with the seriousness they deserve.

D Internal dispute resolution procedures

A2.115 Where the proceedings involve an internal appeal against a decision of a sports governing body as opposed to disciplinary proceedings, the procedure is obviously different. First, the claimant in that situation is the participant as opposed to the governing body. Secondly, the proceedings are not so obviously onerous as where a sanction against the participant is threatened. Nevertheless, the underlying aims are the same, and most of the practical considerations set out above still apply, with minor adaptation. In the context of such an internal appeal, which is essentially the first time that the decision has been subject to review, the standard of review ought not to be the same as on an appeal following disciplinary proceedings, which is the second stage of review. In some sports appeals against the non-disciplinary decisions of the governing body lie to different committees for different matters: in cricket for example appeals against registration decisions lie to the 'Registration and Contracts Appeal Panel'. The arrangements will vary from sport to sport and reference should be made to the particular rules applicable.

A2.116 In some contexts, such as football, the process for resolution of disputes between governing body and a participant does not involve a formal internal appeal process, but rather a form of arbitration (in the context of football under FA Rule K), which is the same procedure that applies to disputes between participants. Rule K sets out in detail the procedure to be applied. Again, many of the same principles apply, but because the tribunal has a greater degree of independence from the governing body some of the difficulties are more easily overcome. The arbitration procedure is essentially analogous to those discussed in a later chapter[1], and reference should be made to that chapter. As also discussed in that chapter, there is room in the sports context for resolution by way of mediation.

1 See Chapter A5.

6 CONCLUSION

A2.117 Sports governing bodies have a difficult task to perform when it comes to disciplinary proceedings and internal dispute resolution. They have to ensure that their rules are clear, comprehensive and fair and yet sufficiently flexible to deal with every circumstance which may arise. The rules must then be applied in accordance with the standards set by the courts. There is therefore no substitute for detailed preparation of rules and guidelines in advance, and adherence to those rules and guidelines and prudence when the system is being administered. Governing bodies should consider the involvement of lawyers as a safeguard against future challenge in the courts. That involvement can usefully take place at the stage of drafting the rules and guidelines, in assisting on whether a particular person should sit on a disciplinary committee, in the formulation of the charge, in the presentation of the case, and in advising on the stance to take should a challenge before the courts be threatened. A different lawyer could usefully be appointed as chair of, or adviser to, the disciplinary committee. Governing bodies may also want to consider the use of external appeal bodies as a way of ensuring that the system overall is fair.

CHAPTER A3

CHALLENGES IN THE COURTS TO THE ACTIONS OF SPORTS GOVERNING BODIES

Adam Lewis (Blackstone Chambers), **Jonathan Taylor** (Hammonds) and **Adrian Parkhouse** (Farrer & Co)

Contents

1 THE DECISION TO CHALLENGE A SPORTS GOVERNING BODY'S ACTIONS IN THE COURTS

A3.1 Sport is important to a very large number of people, for many different reasons. Very many people play or watch a large range of sports for recreation. Some people compete at an amateur level. A few make their living from competing at sport, at least for some years. A very few compete at an elite level, nationally or even internationally. Many other people involve themselves in the organisation of sport, whether as a referee or umpire on the field of play, or as a coach on the side-line, or in an administrative capacity. Some are paid, and some do it voluntarily.

A3.2 Other people, and businesses, make a living from the commercial exploitation of sport. Some of them, such as promoters and event organisers, develop and stage events that the public can attend in return for an entrance fee. They also employ or engage the services of the players to participate in the event, or else contract with clubs to participate in the event, who themselves employ or engage the players. Some make and sell the products, or own and rent out the facilities, necessary to play the sport or stage the event. Others provide broadcasting, webcasting, publishing or other services that allow those not able to attend the event nevertheless to 'consume' the product, in return for some direct or indirect fee. Further people and businesses pay rights fees to the sport in return for the valuable 'spin-off' commercial opportunities that arise in relation to the event, such as the privilege of being associated with the event (ie sponsorship), official supply arrangements, merchandising, publication, travel and ticket arrangements and corporate hospitality.

A3.3 All of these people and businesses are affected by how a sport's governing bodies choose to run the various aspects of the sport. Such bodies have principal responsibility for promoting and encouraging participation and investment in their sports, by preserving and enhancing the features of the sport (a fair and open competition, on a level playing-field, with an uncertain outcome) that make it attractive to its participants, the general public and therefore potential commercial partners. Sports governing bodies take a number of shapes and forms, and the extent of their power and influence varies from sport to sport. In many instances, there will be a number of bodies that have different responsibilities within the same sport, including (in some cases) separate bodies, organised as businesses, who organise and stage events or competitions under the sanction of the governing body[1]. What sports governing bodies have in common, and what this chapter addresses, is that they are composite bodies with a membership of others involved in the sport, and they control the organisation of a particular element of the sport or the commercial exploitation of it. The expression 'sports governing body' is used in this chapter to cover these disparate organisations, but it does not extend to businesses such as clubs, promoters or the owners of facilities[2]. The 'actions' of these sports governing bodies for the purpose of this chapter cover the rules they adopt to govern players and clubs, their decisions applying those rules, and their commercial activities not necessarily covered in the rules but arising out of the competitions they organise and/or sanction. The contexts in which these actions arise cover a very wide spectrum: rules are made by sports governing bodies to cover many different matters, often unique to the particular sport, and their decisions range from disciplinary rulings in relation to conduct on the field of play by an individual amateur, to the sale by an international association to an international broadcaster of broadcasting rights to televise a professional competition, for many millions of pounds.

1 For example, the Fédération Internationale de l'Automobile (FIA) acts as the international governing body of the sport of motor racing, promulgating the rules and sanctioning international competition; the national associations (for example the RAC) govern the sport within their territorial jurisdictions; and commercial organisations (such as Formula One Administration Ltd and Formula One Management Ltd, in the case of the FIA Formula One World Championship) stage the events and exploit the commercial rights, under sanction of the FIA. In English football, the Football Association is the overall governing body of the game, issuing rules and regulations, providing officials, enforcing disciplinary rules and promoting child protection, anti-doping and other policies. It is a member of the regional governing body for football (UEFA) and the worldwide governing body (FIFA). Domestically, it organises the FA Cup and Charity Shield competitions, as well as various amateur competitions. It also sanctions competitions run by separate businesses of member clubs, organised as limited companies, who regulate the conduct of those competitions and exploit the associated commercial rights. Thus, FA Premier League Ltd runs the FA Premier League; The Football League Ltd runs the Nationwide League; and The Football Conference Ltd runs the Nationwide Conference. As a last example, the Rugby Football Union governs rugby union in England. It has entered into a joint venture with its professional clubs and players – England Rugby Ltd – for the running and commercial exploitation of the professional game in England, while retaining direct control over the national representative team and the amateur game and competitions. In addition, the RFU is a shareholder in European Rugby Cup Ltd, which organises and commercially exploits the cross-border rugby union club competitions currently known as the Heineken Cup and the Parker Pen Shield; it is a member of the Six Nations Committee, which organises the Six Nations Championship; and it is a member of the International Rugby Board, which governs the sport worldwide and sanctions the quadrennial Rugby World Cup competition.

2 Nor does it extend to associations representing only one interest within the sport: see *Towcester Racecourse v Racecourse Association Ltd* [2002] EWHC 2141 (Ch) (17 October 2002, unreported) (Patten J), para 23 et seq.

A3.4 The courts[1] provide a number of mechanisms, of varying efficacy, for reviewing the actions of sports governing bodies when they are perceived to have made a wrong, unfair or unlawful decision. Those mechanisms, or causes of action, are the same mechanisms as are used in areas other than sport. There is no general legislation in the UK in relation to sport, such as France's 'Loi du Sport'[2]. There is no single authority to deal with sports disputes. Particular mechanisms and causes of action have been used more readily than others, and the courts have developed principles that can be carried forward to inform the examination of later cases.

1 The English courts and the European Court of Justice.
2 See para A1.11. See also Ponthieu and Rodrigues [2001] 4 International Sports Law Review ('ISLR') 247.

A3.5 Whether this process is sufficiently developed to allow one to describe the courts as applying a law of sport[1], while academically interesting, does not really matter to the practitioner. Equally, it is arid to suggest that the courts' approach to sport should not be addressed as a distinct topic. People and businesses are affected every day by the actions of sports governing bodies; they and their advisers need guidance on the particular ways in which the courts have approached analogous cases in the past, in order to evaluate what steps they should take and whether to challenge the action at issue.

1 See Beloff et al *Sports Law* (1999, Hart Publishing), ch 1; Gardiner *Sports Law* (2nd edn, 2001, Cavendish Publishing), ch 2. The question is of more relevance in the context of the decisions of sports arbitral bodies, in particular international sports arbitral bodies such as the Court of Arbitration for Sport (or 'CAS') in Lausanne, which apply (amongst other things) a developing body of general principles adapted to the sporting context, than it is in the context of English courts, which apply English law: As to this, see paras E4.77 to E4.88 and A3.232 et seq.

A3.6 The first section of this chapter seeks to provide those affected by the actions of a sports governing body with a road map for deciding whether to bring proceedings in the courts. First it considers the broad range of *factual* circumstances in which challenges have arisen. This will allow those evaluating whether to mount a challenge to identify similar situations that have been addressed by the courts, providing a starting point for the evaluation of their own circumstances[1]. The first section then attempts to assist in the identification of an appropriate cause of action. It then addresses the circumstances in which a challenge elsewhere than in the courts is appropriate: resort to the mechanisms described in this chapter by its nature comes after a decision has been made by the sports governing body, and often internal remedies may or ought to have been exhausted first before turning to the courts. In some instances sports governing bodies' rules include arbitration clauses[2].

1 The survey is not exhaustive of court cases in this jurisdiction, still less of cases in other jurisdictions of persuasive authority. The practitioner must always conduct a search in light of the facts of his or her case. Nor can it cover the many disputes that will not have made it to the courts, but rather have been settled or dealt with through some other method of dispute resolution. Furthermore, in some (if not most) cases, a similar situation may not as yet have arisen. However, it may be possible to extrapolate principles derived from situations that have been examined into new situations.
2 See also in this regard Chapter A5.

A3.7 The second section of this chapter touches on whether the decisions of sports governing bodies should be regarded as public or private for the purposes of challenge[1], the applicability of the Human Rights Act 1998[2], and the extension to sports governing bodies of the EU free movement obligations which are generally applicable to the state and not to private bodies[3]. It concludes by warning of the varying degree of review applied by the courts, which have traditionally expressed reluctance in many instances to intervene in the specialist decision-making processes of sports governing bodies, where those bodies have a jurisdiction expressly conferred upon them by the applicable rules.

1 Also addressed in Chapter A4.
2 Also addressed in Chapter A4.
3 Also addressed in Chapter B3.

A3.8 The remaining sections of the chapter deal with the ways in which the courts have adapted particular mechanisms and causes of action in the context of challenges to the actions of sports governing bodies[1], and with procedural aspects before and after litigation in that context is begun. Other chapters in this work address in more detail the content of the substantive legal obligations in particular circumstances, and cross references are given below to the relevant chapters.

1 See also Beloff et al *Sports Law* (1999, Hart Publishing), chs 2, 3 and 8; Gardiner *Sports Law* (2nd edn, 2001, Cavendish Publishing), ch 5; Grayson *Sport and the Law* (3rd edn, 2000, Butterworths), ch 11; Griffith-Jones *Law and the Business of Sport* (1997, Butterworths), ch 2; Moore *Sports Law and Litigation* (2nd edn, 2000, CLT), chs 10 and 11.

A The context of the sports governing body's actions and those affected

(a) Actions of a sports governing body affecting a specific individual participant

A3.9 There are many different individual participants in sport. First and foremost there are players[1], but there are also coaches, trainers, and managers. There are individual owners in sports such as horse and greyhound racing. There are also other individuals, such as agents and promoters, who are not directly involved in the playing of the sport but who nevertheless participate in the sense that they contribute to the structure of an exciting sport capable of generating revenue from the public's interest. The decisions of sports governing bodies can directly relate to and impact upon such individuals.

1 The generic use of the word 'athlete' in the United States and by the IOC to cover all such individuals has not generally been mirrored in the United Kingdom (with the notable exception of Sid Waddell's breathless description of a famous Scots darter: 'Jocky Wilson steps up to the oche … what an athlete'). Instead, in this chapter the word 'player' is used to cover the vast range of names used in different sports for the individuals who actually take to the field (from judoka to paddler and from archer to yachtsman or woman).

A3.10 Drugs The misuse of drugs in sport[1] has given rise to a number of cases in the courts (and very many more before governing bodies' internal tribunals and external arbitration bodies such as the Court of Arbitration for Sport) where individual players, who have been sanctioned by sports governing bodies for the use of performance enhancing or recreational drugs, have sought to challenge the legality of those decisions. There have been challenges both to the validity of a particular doping decision and to the jurisdiction of the sports tribunal to make it. The validity of particular doping decisions has been challenged in the courts on the basis that it was not open to the disciplinary body to conclude that a doping offence had been committed because there had been a failure to follow prescribed procedures in taking, storing or testing the relevant sample[2], or because the governing body had failed for some other reason to prove the presence of a prohibited substance in the sample of the player[3]. Particular doping decisions have been challenged on the basis that the disciplinary body acted in a procedurally unfair manner, or was biased, or reached an unreasonable or disproportionate decision[4]. The rules empowering disciplinary bodies to impose a sanction in doping cases have been challenged on the basis that they are in unreasonable restraint of trade[5] and on the basis that they are contrary to the EC free movement rules and/or competition rules[6]. Jurisdiction has also been challenged on the basis that the wrong sports governing body was attempting to impose the sanction for the doping offence[7]. There have also been challenges in the context of horse and greyhound racing to decisions that the animal was doped and the sanctions imposed on individuals as a consequence[8].

1 See generally Chapter E4.

2 *Gasser v Stinson* (15 June 1988, unreported), QBD (Scott J) (Swiss athlete Sandra Gasser complained that there was no proper proof that she had a prohibited substance in her urine because the sample used was too small and the B test did not exactly confirm the A test, raising the possibility that the two tests related to different samples. Scott J held that the procedural irregularities were insufficient to prevent the IAAF concluding that there was sufficient proof of the presence of a prohibited substance and that the IAAF had not acted outside its powers in so deciding); *Modahl v British Athletics Federation* (28 June 1996, unreported), Popplewell J, CA 28 July 1997, HL 22 July 1998, Douglas Brown J 14 December 2000 and [2002] 1 WLR 1192, CA) 8 October 2001 (On an internal appeal, Diane Modahl had been cleared of a doping offence on the basis that it was possible that her sample had degraded before the B test. Her arguments that she should be cleared because the chain of custody of her sample had not been proven, a non-accredited laboratory had been used, different samples had been tested and the tests were not carried out in accordance with the guidelines, were rejected. Afterwards, she sought to recover damages from the BAF on the bases that in breach of contract her sample had been tested at a non-accredited laboratory and that the original committee that had found her guilty had been tainted by bias. The Court of Appeal struck out the claim that the BAF had acted impermissibly in relying on the tests from an unaccredited laboratory, and this was upheld by the House of Lords. The action proceeded and the second Court of Appeal concluded that although an implied contract had arisen under which the BAF was obliged to operate an anti-doping system that was as a whole fair, there had been no breach of that obligation); *Wilander and Novacek v Tobin and Jude* (19 March 1996, unreported) (Lightman J), (1996) Times, 8 April, CA Lightman J, [1997] 1 Lloyd's Rep 195, CA, [1997] 2 Lloyd's Law Rep 293 (in relation to a case brought under the Anti-Doping Programme of the International Tennis Federation, the players contended that the review board convened to consider the positive tests of their respective samples did not have sufficient material to entitle it to conclude that the A samples had been properly tested (and therefore should not have proceeded to the test of the B sample), because (a) they could not be satisfied of a proper intra-laboratory chain of custody; and (b) there was no information to confirm that the pH and density of the urine tested were within the prescribed limits. In the Court of Appeal, Lord Justice Neill concluded that there was not even an arguable case that the procedures adopted had been so defective that the court ought to intervene); *Bray v NZSDA* [2001] 2 NZLR 160, [2001] 9(2) Sport and the Law Journal ('SATLJ') 79 (swimmer successfully showed that the testing procedures had not been followed and was exonerated). There have been a very large number of such cases before sports governing bodies' appeal bodies and before sports arbitration bodies. A digest of the most important CAS awards has been published, edited by Matthieu Reeb, in two volumes: 1986 to 1998 (1998, Stæmpfli Editions SA Berne) and 1998 to 2000 (2002, Kluwer Law International). Decisions of the IAAF Arbitration Panel on appeals by the IAAF and/or athletes from the anti-doping decisions of national athletics associations' tribunals are described by Tarasti in *Legal Solutions in Doping Cases* (2000).

3 In many CAS and IAAF cases the validity of a finding that a prohibited substance was present in the athlete's sample has been challenged. The result may have been a false positive, or a metabolite may have been found that might have come from something other than a prohibited substance, or the substance found may not be on the list of prohibited substances properly construed and might not fall within a prohibited class (such as anabolic steroids, stimulants, narcotics, masking agents) or be related to a prohibited substance. See generally paras E4.75 to E4.173. A recent example in relation to a British athlete is *Baxter v IOC*, where the skier Alain Baxter challenged the IOC's interpretation of its Code that the word 'methamphetamine' in the list of prohibited substances includes not only methamphetamine, which is a stimulant with the street name 'speed', but also the harmless and non performance enhancing nasal decongestant, levmetamfetamine, contained in a Vicks inhaler. It was held that because levmetamfetamine fell within the prohibited class of 'amphetamines', it was caught: CAS 2002/4/376 (16 October 2002).

4 *Modahl v British Athletics Federation*, see n 2 (the application by the BAF to strike out Diane Modahl's contention that the original disciplinary body that had found her guilty of a doping offence was tainted by bias was rejected, but the contention ultimately failed at trial and before the Court of Appeal). In *Wilander and Novacek v Tobin and Jude* (19 March 1996, unreported), QBD (Lightman J), CA 26 March 1996, the players did not wait for the internal tribunal to reach its decision before asking the courts to intervene. Professional tennis players Mats Wilander and Karel Novacek each gave urine samples at the French Open in June 1995. Each sample tested positive for a metabolite of cocaine. When the tests of B samples confirmed the positive finding, the ITF notified the players, who protested their innocence and appealed to the Appeals Committee. However, in January 1996, just before the hearing before the Appeals Committee was to take place, the players applied to the High Court for an injunction restraining the ITF from taking any further proceedings against them, on three separate grounds: (a) the ITF's Anti-Doping Programme was in unreasonable restraint of trade and therefore void and unenforceable; (b) the ITF's procedure was so defective that the finding of doping violations was unreliable; and (c) the ITF had committed three separate breaches of contract that amounted to a repudiation of its contract with the players on which its disciplinary authority was founded. Those arguments were rejected. In *Baxter v IOC*, see n 3, the athlete also unsuccessfully challenged as disproportionate the imposition of a disqualification (which cost him his Olympic medal) in circumstances where he had acted without fault and the use of a Vicks inhaler was in no way performance enhancing.

5 *Gasser v Stinson*, see n 2 (Gasser's alternative argument was that the doping rules restrained her in her ability to trade and were unreasonable. Scott J held that the doctrine applied but that the rules were reasonable and justified even though they involved strict liability and a mandatory ban); *Wilander and Novacek v Tobin and Jude*, unreported Lightman J 19 March 1996, unreported CA 8 April 1996, Lightman J [1997] 1 Lloyd's Law Rep 195, CA [1997] 2 Lloyd's Law Rep 293 (The players' original allegation that the ITF's doping rules were in unreasonable restraint of trade was struck out); *Robertson v APCC*, unreported, Waddell CJ (NSW) 10 December 1992 (two-year ban overturned as in unreasonable restraint of trade); *Johnson v Athletics Canada and IAAF* (1997) 41 OTC 95 (Ben Johnson's lifetime ban held reasonable). The English approach to strict liability reflected in *Gasser* is not followed in civil law systems, where a mandatory ban is not lawful unless some degree of fault is established: see *Aanes v FILA*, CAS 2001/A/317, award dated 9 July 2001. In that case it was held that a disqualification as opposed to a ban was permissible without fault being established, because if an athlete had a performance-enhancing substance in his body, even innocently, other athletes might have been affected in the relevant competition. (See further paras E4.101 to E4.135). In *Baxter v IOC* (n 3), the skier also unsuccessfully contended that where there was no fault *and* no possibility of performance enhancement, even a disqualification was not permissible. The development in *Aanes* goes only to the consequences of a doping offence being established. The CAS still regards it as possible to establish the offence itself on the basis of strict liability: see for example its decision in *Raducan* CAS Sydney 00/011 (see para E4.125). The question of the law applicable in any given challenge may therefore be of importance. See further paras E4.77 to E4.88.

6 *Wilander,* see n 5 (The players sought leave to amend to allege that the ITF doping rules were contrary to the EC free movement and competition rules. Lightman J granted leave for the free movement amendment, but refused it in the case of the competition amendment. The Court of Appeal refused leave for both amendments); *Edwards v BAF and IAAF* [1998] 2 CMLR 363, [1997] EuLR 721 (Lightman J rejected the shot-putter's contention that the BAF and the IAAF doping rules discriminated against him on grounds of nationality contrary to the free movement rules because the ban for a first offence was a fixed period, or the maximum permissible under local law). In August 2002, the European Commission rejected a challenge based on EC competition law and freedom of movement law by two swimmers against two-year doping bans imposed on them under FINA's anti-doping rules, on the ground that anti-doping rules are necessary for the protection of the integrity of the sport, are proportionate to that aim, and therefore fall within the sporting exception to EC law: see Commission press release IP/02/1211 (August 2002).

7 *Korda v ITF* (1999) Times, 4 February, [1999] All ER (D) 84 (an independent Appeals Committee convened under the terms of the ITF Anti-Doping Programme upheld the finding of an offence, but found that 'exceptional circumstances' existed – namely the player's lack of knowledge of how the substance got into his body – that warranted a waiver of any suspension. The ITF filed an appeal to the CAS against that decision. Lightman J granted the player a declaration that the ITF could not appeal its own decision to the CAS, but his decision was overturned by the Court of Appeal and the ITF was allowed to pursue its appeal to the CAS) (which was eventually successful as well – see paras E4.318 to E4.323); *Walker v UKA and IAAF*, unreported Toulson J 3 July 2000, Hallett J 25 July 2000 (Walker alleged that only UKA – which had cleared him of a doping offence – had jurisdiction to discipline him, and it was not open to the IAAF to seek to overturn that decision. He

sought declaratory relief to that effect and injunctions to prevent the IAAF bringing the UKA decision before an IAAF Arbitration Panel and to prevent UKA abiding by any award of that panel. UKA proposed to defend its decision before the IAAF Arbitral Panel but agreed that the IAAF did have jurisdiction to seek to overturn the acquittal. The IAAF also sought to suspend the athlete pending the IAAF Arbitration being heard. UKA and the athlete objected to that because the rule in question had not been in force at the time of the events in question. The first hearing dealt with the IAAF's opening point, which was that the English court did not have jurisdiction because the IAAF was based in Monaco: Toulson J rejected this argument. At the second hearing, which was of the substantive claim, Hallett J indicated in argument that she would take some persuading that the IAAF could apply the suspension rule retrospectively. Before the hearing concluded the litigation was settled on the basis that the athlete withdrew his complaint that the IAAF did not have jurisdiction to challenge the UKA decision before the Arbitral Panel, and the IAAF agreed that he could compete in the Olympic trials, which were before the Arbitral Panel hearing. In the event the athlete chose not to compete. Subsequently the IAAF Arbitration Panel overturned UKA's decision: IAAF Arbitral Award dated 20 August 2000, mentioned at [2000] 2 ISLR 41 and reported at [2001] 4 ISLR 264. See also para A3.124.

8 *R v Disciplinary Committee of the Jockey Club, ex p Aga Khan* [1993] 1 WLR 909 (The Aga Khan failed to secure judicial review of the Jockey Club's decision to disqualify his horse and fine his trainer for doping); *Pett v Greyhound Racing Association* [1969] 1 QB 125, CA (Challenge to the governing body's decision to suspend the trainer of a doped dog, on the basis that it was procedurally unfair as he had not been represented, held arguable); *Pett v Greyhound Racing Association (No 2)* [1970] 1 QB 46 (Lack of representation held permissible) [1970] 1 QB 67n, CA (Appeal withdrawn following change to rules to allow representation and the promise of a rehearing); *Law v National Greyhound Racing Club* [1983] 3 All ER 300, [1983] 1 WLR 1302, CA (Challenge to the governing body's decision to suspend the trainer of a doped dog, on the basis that it was unfair, contrary to natural justice, unreasonable and in unjustified restraint of trade); *Singer v Jockey Club* (28 June 1990, unreported) (Scott J).

A3.11 Misconduct on the pitch or serious breach of the rules of play A second major area of activity for internal disciplinary bodies involves the improper actions of players while playing the sport[1]. The decisions of internal disciplinary bodies in this context have been challenged in the courts, for example in circumstances where the player alleges that the process has been procedurally unfair, or that the decision is unreasonable or in restraint of trade[2].

1 See Chapter A2.

2 See also the examples in relation to clubs or teams at para A3.23, n 1; *Jones v WRU* unreported Ebsworth J 27 February 1997, (1997) Times, 6 March, unreported Potts J 17 November 1997, unreported CA 19 December 1997, Times 6 January 1998 (Welsh rugby player Mark Jones succeeded before Ebsworth J in obtaining an interim injunction preventing the WRU suspending him for 30 days for stamping and fighting, on the basis that he arguably did not have a proper opportunity to present his case before the internal disciplinary committee. The WRU changed its rules and sought to reach a new decision, but was restrained by Potts J from doing so. The Court of Appeal held that the original interim injunction had been properly granted, but that the WRU could not be prevented from re-opening the matter and dealing with it properly); *Scott Plews v British Ice Hockey Association* unreported Lord Eassie Scottish Court of Session 18 March 1997 (ice hockey player granted interim relief following a ban based on video evidence, which he was not entitled to challenge. He was not informed about the ban). See [1997] 5(1) SATLJ 30; *Re Duncan Ferguson (Ferguson v Scottish Football Association)* (1996) Outer House Cases, Lord Macfadyen 1 February 1996 (SFA on its rules unable to discipline a player not even cautioned at the time by the referee); *Keighley Football Club v Cunningham* (1960) Times, 25 May (action of governing body in disciplining a rugby league player following his sending-off, without giving him notice or an opportunity to be heard held contrary to natural justice); *Davis v Carew-Pole* [1956] 2 All ER 524 (Challenge to National Hunt Committee's decision to disqualify plaintiff for entering a horse when not licensed to do so); *Calvin v Carr* [1980] AC 574, [1979] 2 All ER 440, PC (Challenge to the Australian Jockey Club's decision that a horse had not tried, on grounds of breach of natural justice and unfairness); *Doyle v White City Stadium and the British Boxing Board of Control* [1935] 1 KB 110 (BBBC entitled to withhold purse under its rules after boxer disqualified for hitting below the belt); *Kinane v Turf Club* Irish High Court, (2001) Guardian, 28 July, p S14, (2001) 9(2) SATLJ 92 (interim injunction granted on the basis that the careless riding rules were arguably flawed); *Robert C Allan v Scottish Auto Cycle Union* (1985) Outer House Cases 32 (official punching a competitor and then insulting other officials of the governing body); *Colgan v Kennel Club*,

unreported, Cooke J, 26 October 2001 (disciplinary action following conviction based on inadvertent mistreatment of dogs); *Jackson v Western Australia Basketball Federation* (1990) 21 ALD 283 (no breach of natural justice in disciplinary hearing for punching on court and since the penalty imposed was reasonable there was no unjustified restraint of trade). Another example from overseas would be Hanse Cronje's unsuccessful challenge, on procedural and substantive grounds, to the life-ban from cricketing activities imposed on him by the South African Cricket Board upon his admission that he accepted money from bookmakers to fix the result of a match.

A3.12 Bringing the game into disrepute or breach of rules of conduct

Misconduct is not always on the pitch. Most sports governing bodies have power to discipline players for actions which bring the game into disrepute, or for breaching their specific rules of conduct[1]. Internal decisions sanctioning players for such misconduct off the pitch may be the subject of challenge on similar grounds to decisions in respect of misconduct on it. The type of conduct which falls into this category is obviously wide and ranges from improperly selling Cup Final tickets to physical violence off the pitch. It covers examples such as players refusing to play[2], consultants acting with a conflict of interest[3], and participants disobeying a specific rule of conduct or instruction of the governing body or inappropriately criticising the governing body[4].

1 See further Chapter A2. General rules prohibiting bringing the game into disrepute are open to criticism as being insufficiently certain and governing bodies must take care not to misuse them.

2 *Conteh v Onslow-Fane (for the British Board of Boxing Control)* unreported Walton J May 1975; unreported CA 25 June 1975 (1975) Times, 26 June (successful application by the boxer for an injunction restraining the BBBC from proceeding with disciplinary action pending outcome of litigation between him and his former manager and the fight promoter); *Currie v Barton* unreported Scott J 26 March 1987; unreported CA 28 July 1987 (extension of time) and 11 February 1988, Times, 12 February 1988 (A tennis player, ruled out of selection by his county association for three years for refusing to play in a county match, was also declared ineligible to play for England by the LTA. The player failed in his attempt to challenge the ban and recover damages on the grounds of restraint of trade, breach of contract, natural justice, and an innominate tort).

3 *Bland v Sparkes (for the Amateur Swimming Association)* (1999) Times, 17 December, CA (an ASA independent inquiry found that by taking bribes Hamilton Bland had behaved in a way which tended to bring the association into disrepute and the ASA terminated his engagement as a consultant. The Court of Appeal upheld the finding of the independent inquiry, rejected the argument that it had been procedurally unfair, and held that the contract was properly terminated).

4 *Hughes v Western Australia Cricket Association* (1986) 69 ALR 660 (Governing body's rule disqualifying a cricket player for playing in an unsanctioned match in South Africa held in unreasonable restraint of trade); *Haron bin Mundir v Singapore AAF* [1992] 1 SLR 18 (Athlete unfairly disciplined for abandoning training in Japan). Cf *Russell v Duke of Norfolk* [1949] 1 All ER 109 (Racing governing body's unfettered jurisdiction to withdraw licence for misconduct without any hearing upheld); *Royal Hong Kong Jockey Club v Miers* [1983] 1 WLR 1049 (Privy Council declined jurisdiction to hear appeal of jockey's claim to have been unfairly refused a renewal of his licence because he had no contractual right to a licence and his only claim was to have his application treated fairly, with the result that it did not fall within the financial jurisdictional limit for the Privy Council on appeals from Hong Kong); *Collins v Lane* (22 June 1999, unreported), CA (Member of shooting club successfully challenged expulsion for lack of safety on the range and abusive behaviour, on grounds of breach of natural justice, but was refused an injunction requiring his readmission); and *R v Disciplinary Committee of the Jockey Club, ex p Massingberd-Mundy* [1993] 2 All ER 207 (Local steward failed to secure judicial review of Jockey Club's decision not to put his name on the list of approved local stewards for the following season after he criticised the Senior Stewards' Secretary); *Robert C Allan v Scottish Auto Cycle Union* (1985) Outer House Cases 32 (Official insulting other officials). Another example would be the 2002 fine of Surrey and England cricketer Mark Butcher for calling into question the legality of the action of a Sri Lankan test opponent, which fine he queried but eventually decided not to challenge. Similarly, Dean Ryan of Bristol Rugby Club talked about challenging on human rights (freedom of speech) grounds the £20,000 fine and suspension imposed on him by the RFU in 2001 for criticising a referee, but in the event he brought no challenge.

A3.13 Assumption of exorbitant jurisdiction In most instances any challenge is to the way that a decision in respect of a particular player is taken (for example on grounds of procedural unfairness or unreasonableness), or to the validity of the rules on the basis of which the decision is taken (for example on the grounds of restraint of trade or free movement). In addition, however, there have been challenges to the appropriateness of the particular governing body assuming jurisdiction over the matter at all, on the basis that the matter is properly dealt with by a different body[1]. There have also been challenges to the assumption of jurisdiction by *any* governing body[2].

1 *Roach v FA* (Football players' agent challenged the jurisdiction of the FA to discipline him on the basis of FA rules which were not in place at the time of the conduct in question and when in any event he was a FIFA registered agent subject to different FIFA Rules, and not an FA registered agent. After a CPR, Pt 8 action was commenced by the agent and initially defended, the FA surrendered and acceded to judgment): see [2001] 9(3) SATLJ 26; *Walker v UKA and IAAF*, unreported Toulson J 3 July 2000, Hallett J 25 July 2000, IAAF Arbitral Award dated 20 August 2000, reported at [2001] 4 ISLR 264, see also [2000] 2 ISLR 41 and paras A3.10, n 7, A3.124 and A3.230. See also *Smith v International Triathlon Union* (1999) 20 BLTC 71 (Triathlete cleared by British Triathlon Association of a doping offence in the United States unsuccessfully challenged the jurisdiction of USA Triathlon to appeal that decision to the International Triathlon Union).

2 *Davis v Carew-Pole* [1956] 2 All ER 524 (unsuccessful attempt to challenge the jurisdiction of the National Hunt Committee to declare an unlicensed livery stable owner a disqualified person for entering a horse when not licensed to do so).

A3.14 Denial of access to the sport at all Apart from suspending participants for disciplinary offences, addressed above, sports governing bodies also control access to the sport in the first place. They make decisions which have a fundamental effect on the ability of the player to pursue his recreation, or his business, in the way that he chooses. The decisions are generally made in the context of an application for a licence or other authorisation to take part, and are often based on the perceived lack of fulfilment of entry criteria (such as physical fitness[1], or payment of a bond[2]). Challenges have been mounted in the courts to such decisions on the basis that the refusal of access was in breach of contract, procedurally unfair, discriminatory and/or in unreasonable restraint of trade[3].

1 *Wright v Jockey Club* Sir Haydn Tudor Evans 15 May 1995, QBD, (1995) Times, 16 June (Jockey unsuccessfully challenged refusal of licence on medical grounds. The court rejected on a summary judgment application any implication into the contract between a jockey and the Jockey Club of a duty of care and skill in the carrying out of medical tests, holding that only an obligation to act fairly arose). See also *Hall v Victorian Amateur Football Association* [1999] VCAT AD 30; [1999] 7(2) SATLJ 66 (challenge to exclusion of HIV positive player successfully brought in Australian courts), and *Keefe v McInnes* [1991] 2 VR 235 (paraplegic challenged refusal of permission to participate in motor sport. The decision of the Equal Opportunities Board in his favour was remitted for re-decision).

2 As was required by FIFA of football players' agents. After FIFA changed its rules to delegate the licensing of agents to the national associations and removed the obligation to provide FIFA with a substantial bond and replacing it with compulsory insurance, the European Commission announced that it would no longer pursue complaints that the arrangements were contrary to the competition rules. Commission press release IP/02/585, 18 April 2002. See paras B2.182 to B2.186.

3 *Nagle v Feilden* [1966] 2 QB 633, CA (The Court of Appeal refused to strike out Florence Nagle's action alleging that the Jockey Club had acted unlawfully by refusing to issue her a trainer's licence on the basis that she was a woman, holding that it was arguable that even absent a contract, the Jockey Club was constrained to act fairly, in accordance with natural justice, reasonably and without restraining an individual's ability to pursue her trade); *McInnes v Onslow-Fane* [1978] 1 WLR 1520 (The British Boxing Board of Control was held to be obliged to act fairly and in accordance with natural justice in considering whether to grant a boxing manager a licence); *R v British Basketball Association, ex p Mickan* (17 March 1981, unreported), CA (The Court of Appeal rejected the players' contentions first that on the proper construction of the rules a licence had to be granted whenever a compliant application was received, and secondly that the governing

body had acted capriciously and unreasonably when it refused to licence them to play for a different club than the club which they had originally applied for a licence to play for); *Fisher v National Greyhound Racing Club* (31 July 1985, unreported), CA (Greyhound owner would have been allowed to pursue challenge to refusal to licence his dog on grounds of breach of natural justice and arbitrariness, had he not been deprived of standing as an undischarged bankrupt); *Stinnato v Auckland Boxing Association* [1978] 1 NZLR 1 (Boxer refused declaration that the governing body had acted in breach of natural justice in refusing him a licence without allowing him a hearing, on the grounds that the judge had properly exercised his discretion as to whether relief should be granted. The judge had concluded that even if there had been a hearing there would not have been a different result and the claimant was guilty of delay), [1978] 1 NZLR 609 (leave to appeal to the Privy Council granted in the light of the importance of the matter for the boxer's reputation; the matter does not however appear to have been considered by the Privy Council); *Wright v Jockey Club*, Sir Haydn Tudor Evans, 15 May 1995, QBD, (1995) Times, 16 June (jockey licence refused on medical grounds); *Couch v British Boxing Board of Control*, unreported Employment Tribunal, case no 2304231/97, 31 March 1988 (Female boxer successfully challenged refusal of BBBC to grant her and other women a licence to box against each other). For discussion of the obligation not to discriminate, see Chapter E3. For an early case, see *Russell v Duke of Norfolk* [1949] 1 All ER 109. Most recently in *Phoenix v Fédération International de l'Automobile and Formula One Management* [2002] EWHC 1028 (Ch), unreported Morritt V-C 22 May 2002, a new Formula One team attempted to force its way into the 2002 Championship on the basis that it had acquired rights from the French liquidator of the Prost team not only to enter the competition, but also to benefits under the Concorde Agreement governing the distribution of the revenue from the sport. Its application for an interlocutory injunction allowing it to compete was refused.

A3.15 Denial of access to a particular competition or level of participation

Once a participant in the sport, a player may nevertheless be prevented from taking part in a particular competition or from playing at a particular representative level[1]. The decisions of sports governing bodies in this context may also be susceptible of review, although the courts have been slower to intervene in this context than in others, at least when the decision relates to an evaluation of the player's standard of performance[2]. Where the grounds for exclusion are technical rather than performance-related, the courts are more prepared to intervene[3]. The courts are also prepared to intervene where an improper restriction has been placed on the player for other reasons, for example a requirement that a player only play for a particular team[4], conditions imposed on permission to play outside the governing body's jurisdiction[5], or where a referee has been discriminated against on gender grounds[6]. Further, the courts are likely to be prepared to intervene where the question is essentially contractual (for example if a boxer claims to have the contractual right to make the next challenge to a champion[7]) or possibly where a legitimate expectation of being able to compete has arisen[8].

1 As in rugby union's 'Grannygate' affair, in which, in late 1999, it was discovered that various Antipodeans who had claimed eligibility to play for Wales under the International Rugby Board's 'grandparent' rule did not, contrary to their belief, in fact have any Welsh grandparents. In the fall-out, it transpired that the Scottish Rugby Union had also fielded players whose belief that they had Scottish grandparents was mistaken. The IRB took internal disciplinary proceedings against both the Welsh and the Scottish rugby unions.

2 *Cowley v Heatley* unreported Browne-Wilkinson V-C, 22 July 1986, (1986) Times, 24 July (A swimmer held unable to challenge the refusal to select her for the Commonwealth Games), see also para A3.98, n 2; *Currie v Barton* unreported Scott J 26 March 1987, unreported CA 28 July 1987 (extension of time) and 11 February 1988, Times 12 February 1988 (Tennis player unable to challenge on restraint of trade grounds a decision ruling him out of representative selection for three years); *Sheehy v Judo Federation of Australia*, unreported Bryson J (NSW) 1 December 1995 (injunction requiring reinstatement to team refused); *Deliège v Ligue Francophone de Judo* [2000] ECR I-2549 (A judoka who had not been selected to compete in an event that amounted to an Olympic qualifier was unable to challenge the decision under EC law). The reluctance of the courts to intervene has not been shared by the CAS: see *Watt v Australian Cycling Federation* CAS 96/153, award dated 22 July 1996, *Digest of CAS Awards 1986–1998* (1998, Berne), p 335, in which a cyclist successfully challenged the Australian federation's failure to select her. (A case brought by another cyclist, *Nixon* CAS 96/152, failed on the facts). On eligibility to compete for a

particular nation, see *Perez* CAS Sydney 00/001 and 005, award dated 19 September 2000, *Digest of CAS Awards II 1998–2000* (2002, Kluwer), pp 595, 625, and *Miranda* CAS Sydney 00/008, award dated 24 September 2000, *Digest of CAS Awards II 1998–2000* (2002, Kluwer), p 645 (where opposite conclusions were reached in relation to two former Cubans who wanted to compete for the US and Canada respectively). See also *Ofisa* CAS Sydney 00/002, award dated 12 September 2000, *Digest of CAS Awards II 1998–2000* (2002, Kluwer), p 602 (international governing body's failure to respect national court's overturning of national governing body's suspension); *Kibunde* CAS Sydney 00/004, award dated 18 September 2000, *Digest of CAS Awards II 1998–2000* (2002, Kluwer 2002), p 617 (Boxer's failure to make the weigh-in on time); *Sieracki* CAS Sydney 00/007 (wrestler's challenge to non-selection withdrawn when a national court granted an injunction).

3 *US Swimming v FINA* CAS Atlanta 96/001, award dated 22 July 1996, *Digest of CAS Awards 1986–1998* (1998, Berne), p 377 (CAS rejected US Swimming's argument that Michelle Smith of Ireland should be excluded from the 400 metres freestyle on the basis that her application had been put in out of time); *Andrade v Cape Verde NOC* CAS Atlanta 96/002 and 005, awards dated 27 July 1996 and 1 August 1996, *Digest of CAS Awards 1986–1998* (1998, Berne), pp 389 and 397 (CAS held that a national Olympic committee could not withdraw an athlete's accreditation to compete following a dispute as to who should carry the flag at the opening ceremony without the IOC's permission, and even with permission must give the athlete an opportunity to put his case); both discussed in Beloff, 'CAS at the Olympics' [1996] 4(3) SATLJ 5.

4 *Hall v Victorian Football League* [1982] VR 64 (A rule of the governing body requiring Australian Rules Football players to play for the team in the area where they lived (in the interests of ensuring competitive balance) was declared in unreasonable restraint of trade). See also *Buckley v Tutty* (1971) 125 CLR 353 (where the player was not allowed to transfer outside New South Wales); *R v Adamson, ex p Western Australia National Football League* (1978) 23 ALR 439; *Nobes v Australian Cricket Board*, unreported Marks J 16 December 1991.

5 *Blackler v New Zealand Rugby Football League* [1968] NZLR 547 (New Zealand Court of Appeal held by a majority that a rule under which the NZRFL refused permission to a player to play professionally in Australia was an unreasonable restraint of trade and the player was entitled to a declaration to that effect); *Kemp v New Zealand Rugby Football League* [1989] 3 NZLR 463 (revised NZRFL rule placing modified restrictions on a rugby league player moving from New Zealand to play rugby league abroad again held in unreasonable restraint of trade). See also *Buckley v Tutty* at n 4; *Conteh v Onslow-Fane (No 2)*, Walton J (1975) Times 5 June, (BBBC held unable under its rules to impose conditions on a boxer fighting abroad which were unconnected to the identity of the opponent and the nature of the fight) and see para A3.12 n 2 for other elements of the litigation.

6 *British Judo Association v Petty* [1981] ICR 660 (Governing body found to have discriminated unjustifiably against a referee in its decision that a woman could not referee a men's judo bout). For discussion of the obligation not to discriminate, see Chapter E3.

7 *Lewis v Bruno and WBC,* unreported Rattee J 3 November 1995 (Lewis brought proceedings to restrain the WBC from allowing Bruno to fight Tyson instead of Lewis). The English court declined jurisdiction: see para A3.231.

8 As in *Drummoyne District RFC v NSWRU*, unreported Young J (NSW) 3 December 1993 (expectation of entitlement to compete coupled with unconscionable conduct by the governing body led to an injunction requiring the NSWRU to allow the club to compete).

A3.16 Challenge to the outcome of an event or an official's decision Just as the courts are reluctant to intervene when a player seeks to challenge a decision not to allow him or her to participate at a particular level, they are unlikely to allow a player to challenge the outcome of a particular event, or an official's decision during that event[1]. There may however be circumstances where challenges are possible, in the light of the rules governing the playing of the sport and the ability of the governing body to alter the result by reference to a failure to comply with those rules[2], and it may also be possible to challenge the *consequences* which flow from a particular action of an official, as opposed to the action itself[3]. Fraud by an official may in some circumstances form a basis for challenge[4].

1 *Mendy v IABA* CAS Atlanta 96/006, award dated 1 August 1996, *Digest of CAS Awards 1986–1998* (1998, Berne), p 413 (CAS does have jurisdiction to examine the application of the laws of the game if they are against the law or arbitrary, but will not review the application of purely technical sporting decisions. In that case a boxer sought to use video evidence to challenge the official's

decision that he had hit below the belt), discussed in Beloff 'CAS at the Olympics' [1996] 4(3) SATLJ 5; *Segura v IAAF* CAS Sydney 00/013, award dated 30 September 2000, *Digest of CAS Awards II 1998–2000* (2002, Kluwer), p 680 (CAS declined to intervene in IAAF official's decision that the gold medallist Drace-walker had lifted his feet contrary to the rules of walking); *Machin v Football Association* unreported CA 1983, referred to in Grayson *Sport and the Law* (3rd edn, 2000, Butterworths), p 409 (football referee's decision immune from review); *Birmingham City v Football League* (2001) Daily Mail, 18 May (Birmingham City failed to convince the Football League to disturb the referee's decision that the penalty shoot-out (to decide the play off for promotion) should take place at the Preston fans' end, and to alter the result of the match. Birmingham abandoned any hope of review in the courts).

2 In *Irish and Lithuanian Womens' Hockey Federations v IHF* the CAS examined a case where the referee had misapplied the rules as to how the penalty shoot out should be taken. The Irish team lost the shoot out and complained to the tournament director, who ordered that it be re-taken. The Lithuanian team, which had won, refused to re-take it, and were disqualified. The internal IHF appeal body allowed the Lithuanian appeal, but the CAS restored the tournament director's decision. Although this case involved the referee's decision being overruled, it was in fact an expression of the principle that judicial bodies should not after the event intervene in the decisions at the time, whether they be by the official on the field, or by a second level of authority that could be called upon at the time. It may possibly be easier to make a challenge if the complaint is about the adjudication equipment rather than an official's decision: see *Neykova v FISA and IOC* CAS Sydney 00/012, award dated 29 September 2000, *Digest of CAS Awards II 1998–2000* (2002, Kluwer), p 674 (challenge to accuracy of photo-finish result in the event not upheld). In some circumstances a challenge may be possible where an ineligible player is fielded, or non-compliant equipment is used. In *FFF* [2001] 28 Le Dalloz, p 2241, the French Conseil d'Etat decided that under the governing body's rules match results could not be annulled on grounds of an ineligible player having been fielded, once the result had been ratified by the governing body (thereby raising the possibility of its being overturned under the rules prior to ratification). See also *Mercury Bay Boating Club Inc v San Diego Yacht Club and Royal Perth Yacht Club of Western Australia* 76 NY 2d 256 (Court of Appeals for New York 1990) (Legal challenge to the shape of yachts eligible to compete, there a catamaran, and to the outcome of the event). In a number of other sports, a challenge to the outcome of the event could be mounted before the governing body on the basis that the winner ought to be disqualified. The courts are however likely to be slow to displace the governing body's decision.

3 It is for example possible in circumstances defined in the disciplinary rules of the Football Association to challenge the suspension that flows from a referee's decision to send-off a footballer, and there are many cases of internal appeals in these circumstances. The use of video evidence in these circumstances is now prevalent, and the FA has special rules to deal with this. The corollary is of course that the FA may also seek to discipline players on the basis of video evidence when the referee has not seen an incident. More complex is the situation where the referee has seen an incident, and has for example booked a player, but the governing body wishes to go further and impose a suspension as if the player had in fact been sent off. This may well be contrary to the principle that the quality of the referee's decision cannot be impugned. The FA video rules appear to provide that it is only if the referee states in his report that he did not see the incident, or did not see the whole of the incident, that the governing body can act. Cf reg 16 of the Regulations of the International Rugby Board in relation to subsequent citings for incidents on the field of play even if seen by the match officials. See also Gardiner 'Video adjudication in sport' [1999] 7(1) SATLJ 26.

4 At the 2002 Salt Lake Winter Olympics, Canadian figure skaters were elevated into joint Gold position with the Russian pair following the admission of the French judge that she had marked down the Canadians and marked up the Russians in order to get equivalent support from the Russian judge for French skaters in another event: see Beloff [2002] 2 ISLR 13. The French judge in question, as well as the President of her national federation, who was said to have instructed her to act in this way, were each subsequently banned from participation in the sport for three years. In *Segura*, see n 1, CAS left open the possibility at para 17 that an application of the rules in bad faith could lead to a successful challenge.

(b) *Actions of a sports governing body affecting a class of individual participants*

A3.17 The second way in which the decisions of sports governing bodies affect individual participants is when the sports governing body adopts rules which affect an entire class of individual participants, whether by requiring them to take particular steps, or to have particular qualifications, or by limiting their freedom of action.

A3.18 Transfer rules The paradigm example is transfer rules which control whether, when, and on what terms players can move from one club to another[1]. These rules involve the supplementation (and in some respects circumvention) of national employment law by the operation of a registration system by the governing body. Such systems preclude a player playing for a club unless he or she is registered to it, with the transfer of the registration being subject to conditions, in particular the payment of a fee to the club which currently holds the registration in return for releasing it. This enabled clubs around the world to secure compensation for their development of the player (aiding competitive balance and ensuring clubs were not disincentivised from investing in youth development), but it also prevented players from moving when they wanted to do so, including (at one time) even when they were out of contract. The arrangements have changed over the years as they faced a number of successive challenges in the courts on the basis of restraint of trade, the EC free movement rules and competition law[2]. The challenges have not only been to the validity of the extent of restriction on movement at all, but also to the operation of transfer windows, ie periods outside which no transfers are allowed[3]. Despite attempts by the sports governing bodies and the regulatory authorities to establish a fixed and compliant system, the process of change is still underway[4].

1 See generally Chapter E2. In some countries, notably the US but not the UK, the governing bodies of major sports operate a 'draft' system as part of their rules on player movement. Under this system, new players are not free, at least initially, to select the club of their choice, but are drafted. By giving the least successful clubs earlier choice in the draft than the better clubs, competitive balance is addressed. Such rules have been challenged in the Commonwealth on restraint of trade grounds: see Farrell [1997] 5(1) SATLJ 59; *Adamson v NSW Rugby League* (1991) 100 ALR 479, 27 FCR 535; on appeal 103 ALR 319, 31 FCR 242.

2 *Eastham v Newcastle United and the FA* [1964] Ch 413 (The FA's then transfer rules, which involved the power of a club to retain a player after the end of his contract so long as they paid him a reasonable wage, were held in restraint of trade). Examples of the many Commonwealth cases include *Buckley v Tutty* (1971) 125 CLR 353; *Kemp v NZRFL* [1989] 3 NZLR 463; and *Rugby Union Players' Association v Commerce Commission (No 2)* [1997] 3 NZLR 301. The principal EC case is *Union Royal Belge des Sociétés de Football Association v Bosman* [1995] ECR I-4292 (Transfer rules of national football associations in the EC held to prevent free movement of players to the extent that they prevented cross-border movement out of contract. The Advocate General relied on the competition rules as well as the free movement rules, but the Court of Justice confined itself to the latter). See paras B3.40 to B3.42. See also Farrell 'Transfer Fees and Restraint of Trade' [1996] 4(3) SATLJ 54. Furthermore, the principle has been extended by the courts to players from outside the EU but who come from countries with an equal treatment agreement with the EU. Once playing within the EU, such players are entitled to the same free movement rights as EU players: see *Lilia Malaja v Fédération Française de Basketball* Case No VC 99 NC 00282, Administrative Court of Appeal, Nancy. Malaja was Polish and contracted to play for a French club which had more than the maximum two players from outside the EEA allowed under the FFB's rules. Malaja contended successfully that she was to be treated in the same way as an EEA national under Art 37 of the Association Agreement between Poland and the EU, which provided that workers of Polish nationality lawfully employed in the EU could not be discriminated against on grounds of nationality. See also Auneau [2000] 2 Revue Trimestrielle de Droit Européen, p 389. In *Tibor Balog v Royal Charleroi* C–264/98 the player relied on the competition rules to challenge the post-Bosman transfer system. The Advocate General's opinion, released on 29 March 2001 but withdrawn when the case then settled, held that the then transfer system was contrary to the competition rules to the extent that it allowed a club in the EU/EEA to insist on a transfer fee to sell a non-EU out of contract player to a club either in the EU or EEA or in a third country. See further para B2.159.

3 *Lehtonen v Fédération Royale Belge des Sociétés de Basketball* [2000] ECR I–2681 (transfer windows restricted free movement but were capable of justification. In this instance the difference in the transfer window for players from within Belgium and those from other member states appeared not to be justified, although the decision on justification was for the national court).

4 Agreement has been reached between FIFA, UEFA and the European Commission, following the initiation of a competition investigation, on new transfer rules which are less restrictive of players' ability to move within contract. A challenge was nevertheless brought during the course of 2001 by an individual player, supported by FIFPRO, the players' organisation. Although that action was settled, there remains the possibility of further such challenges. See paras B2.165 to B2.170 and Chapters B3 and E2. See also statement to European Parliament by Viviane Reding, EC Commissioner, on the reform of the FIFA rules governing transfers [2001] 9(1) SATLJ 80; McGrath [2001] 9(2) SATLJ 109; Parker, Lane and Gibson [2001] 2 ISLR 156; Bennett [2001] 9(3) SATLJ 180.

A3.19 Salary caps Sports governing bodies have sought to limit the amount that players can be paid through the introduction of a salary cap, in the hope of holding back spiralling costs and maintaining competitive balance[1].

1 Salary caps are operated in the UK in rugby union, rugby league and basketball, and in European leagues in basketball and ice hockey. See paras B2.187 to B2.190 and E1.84 to E1.88; Harris 'Salary Caps' [2001] 10(1) SATLJ 120; Harris 'What position do team salary caps play in the game of competitive balance?' [1999] 7(3) SATLJ 31; Harris 'The benefits of the team salary cap in English Rugby League' [2000] 8(1) SATLJ 88; Gardiner and Gray 'Will Salary Caps Fit European Professional Football?' (2001) 4(3) Sports Law Bulletin 14; Tsatsas 'Is it time for English football to adopt a salary cap?' [2001] 9(2) SATLJ 126. It was left open in *Adamson v NSWRL* (1991) 100 ALR 479, 27 FCR 535; on appeal 103 ALR 319, 31 FCR 242, whether the salary cap in place in that case was legal.

A3.20 General bans or restrictions on taking part in other competitions Sports governing bodies often attempt to preserve for themselves the sole ability to regulate the sport and to organise events. In order to prevent the development of rival organisations, they have sought to tie players in by prohibiting them from competing in other events, on pain of exclusion from 'official' events, and such rules have been the subject of challenge[1]. Such practices may be more subtle than an express ban: the governing body may require that its permission is sought, or may require that players enter its competition by a certain time, or may accord greater status to its own matches for the purposes of a ranking system[2].

1 *Greig v Insole (for the TCCB)* [1978] 1 WLR 302 (The court held in unreasonable restraint of trade the rules of the TCCB banning any player who wanted to compete under its auspices from taking part in competitions organised by any competing organisation, in that case Kerry Packer's cricket world series); *Wilson v British Darts Organisation Ltd* 95/NJ/1687 (Potts J) (the plantiffs were professional darters who had broken away from the defendant governing body and purported to set up a new governing body for professional darts; the defendant responded by requiring its members only to play in sanctioned events, with any event involving a member of the breakaway WDC being unsanctioned; the case settled during the June 1997 trial); *FIA Formula One Championship* [2001] OJ C 169, p 5 (On a notification of the arrangements for Formula One and a complaint, the European Commission considered that FIA had used the arrangements then in existence 'to block the organisation of races which competed with the events organised or promoted by FIA'. The European Commission accepted amendments to, and then cleared, the FIA Sporting Code, the Concorde Agreement between FIA, FOM and the teams, the FOM contracts with promoters, the FIA/FOM Agreement, and the FOM broadcasting contracts. The amendments were designed to prevent FIA stopping rival competitions arising and sought 'to establish a complete separation of the commercial and regulatory functions in relation to the FIA Formula One World Championship … ; to improve transparency of decision making and appeals procedures … ; to guarantee access to motor sport to any person meeting the relevant safety and fairness criteria; to guarantee access to the international sporting calendar and to modify the duration of free to air broadcasting contracts'. In addition FIA undertook 'to participate in the sporting management and attach FIA's name to a series where the series' organiser wishes to form a partnership with FIA, where an organiser promotes the definitive competition in a particular discipline, where that organiser demonstrably properly manages that competition and where the discipline itself is sufficiently popular and

developed'. Note that FOM was previously called FOA.). See also *McCarthy v Australian Rough Riders Association* unreported Spender J, 3 November 1987.

2 All discussed in *Hendry v World Professional Billiards and Snooker Association* unreported Lloyd J 5 October 2001, [2002] 1 ISLR SLR-1 (Restriction in the WPBSA rules on any member playing in any tournament not under its auspices without its consent held to be an anti-competitive agreement contrary to Art 81 (EC) and s 2 of the Competition Act 1998 and an unjustified abuse of dominant position contrary to Art 82 (EC) and s 18 of the Competition Act 1998. The remaining rules were upheld). In 1998, English First Division Rugby clubs (EFDR) filed a complaint with the Commission against their domestic union, the Rugby Football Union (the 'RFU'), and the international governing body of the sport, the International Rugby Board (the 'IRB'). *EFDR Complaint to the European Commission against the Rugby Football Union and the International Rugby Board* Case No IV/36.994 (March 1998). The RFU implements the rules and regulations of the IRB in England. The clubs complained that RFU and IRB rules and regulations prevented them from organising cross-border competitions themselves and exploiting the commercial rights to those competitions without interference from above. The IRB argued in response that the clubs were complaining not about competition but about control. It asserted that it was in the long-term interests of the sport as a whole for the governing bodies to control the commercial facets of rugby, so as to enforce the collective approach that is vital to the long-term good of the game. The complaint was eventually withdrawn by the clubs without the Commission commencing any formal investigation into the matter. Also in 1998, Media Partners, a commercial enterprise seeking to persuade leading European football clubs to break away from the current regulatory regime for football to form a 'Super-League', complained to the Commission that its initiative was being blocked by strong-arm tactics by UEFA (the regional governing body for football in Europe), threatening sanctions against members who did not rebuff Media Partners' approach. UEFA rejected the complaint as factually and legally flawed, and the Commission shows no signs of making any decision. In *Re an Agreement between the FA Premier League* [2000] EMLR 78, [1999] UKCLR 258 (Restrictive Practices Court July 1999) the proceedings brought before the Restrictive Practices Court in relation to the rules and commercial arrangements of the FA Premier League ('FAPL'), the OFT challenged not only the FAPL's rules on central licensing of broadcasting rights but also its rules limiting member clubs' ability to play in non-Premier League competitions. The court upheld the Premier League rule prohibiting member clubs playing in friendly matches that might clash with a Premier League match, as well as the Premier League rule requiring member clubs to get Premier League consent to play in other competitions. The latter rule was held to be 'necessary to ensure that clubs competing in the league give the league competition a due degree of priority'. Given that the Premier League appeared to give consent to participate in all of the important competitions (including the new World Club Championship), the rule was found not to have an anti-competitive effect in practice. In contrast, the Premier League rule prohibiting member clubs playing matches outside England and Wales without consent was struck out, because here there was some evidence that the rule had been invoked to stifle competition to the Premier League in the form of Media Partners' European SuperLeague. General bans on taking part in unsanctioned matches may also be used to prevent players playing on tours of which the governing body disapproves. See *Hughes v Western Australia Cricket Association* (1986) 69 ALR 660 (Governing body's rule disqualifying a cricket player for playing in an unsanctioned match in South Africa held in unreasonable restraint of trade).

A3.21 Qualification criteria in general As is clear from the challenges that have been brought by players when an individual decision affects them, players have often at the same time challenged the validity of the rules as whole. Just as challenges can be brought to the validity of the doping rules across the board, so too challenges can be brought to the validity of qualification criteria governing access to participate in a sport or at a particular level[1].

1 For example, the rules on the bonds to be posted by football players' agents were criticised as involving prohibitive amounts and as discriminating in favour of companies against individuals. As a result the Commission required FIFA to change the system to one based on insurance policies. Commission press releases IP/99/782 and IP/02/585 (18 April 2002). See paras B2.182 to B2.186. In *Mohammed v FA and FIFA*, unreported Field J, 21 February 2002, a claim by a football players' agent that the introduction of the licensing was itself an interference with existing contractual relations, and contrary to the competition rules, survived an application for summary judgment by the governing bodies, and remains pending. In the context of clubs and teams, see *Stevenage Borough Football Club v Football League Ltd* unreported Carnwath J (1996) Times, 1 August; affd 9 Admin LR 109, CA; and *FIA Formula One Championship* [2001] OJ C 169, p 5 (challenge to admission criteria upon promotion from Conference to League).

(c) A sports governing body's failure to take action in relation to individual participants

A3.22 The third way in which a sports governing body can affect individual participants is by failing to address a particular issue. Where harm to the player has resulted, challenges in the form of claims for damages have been brought[1].

1 *Agar v Hyde* [2000] HCA 41 (Unsuccessful attempt in Australian courts to fix the sports governing body with liability in tort for failing to provide for rules of the game which protected participants against injury); *Watson v BBBC*, Ian Kennedy J 24 September 1999, (1999) 143 Sol Jo LB 235, (1999) Times 12 October, Court of Appeal [2001] QB 1134, CA, 19 December 2000 (Governing body successfully fixed with liability for failing to provide adequate medical resuscitation facilities at the ringside). See para A3.131.

(d) Actions of a sports governing body affecting specific clubs

A3.23 In team sports, the national associations or governing bodies are generally made up of the clubs, and there is a contract between them on the basis of the rules of the association. Action taken by a sports governing body against a specific club may be similar to action taken against individual players[1] and be challenged on the same bases as already discussed above[2], or it may (as addressed below) involve particular aspects specific to clubs that give rise to challenge. Further, there may be proceedings by members against the administrators of the governing body in respect of matters not directly connected with the administration of the sport[3].

1 For example, a club may be sanctioned for misconduct. In July 2001, Wakefield Trinity had points deducted for breach of the Rugby League salary cap. In 2001/02, Agen Rugby Club was fined by an ERC appellate tribunal and banned for one year from European cross-border competition for contriving to lose a game by eight tries so that it would not qualify for the next round of the European Shield and so could concentrate its resources on its challenge for the domestic French championship.

2 See for example *Enderby Town Football Club v FA* [1971] Ch 591, [1970] 3 WLR 1021 (Club challenged before the FA the local association's disciplining of it for perceived financial irregularities. It was held that the FA's prohibition on representation before it was not unfair or contrary to natural justice); *St Johnstone Football Club Ltd v Scottish Football Association* 1965 SLT 171 (Club allowed to pursue a challenge to the SFA's imposition of a fine for the unsanctioned playing of a benefit match on the grounds that the hearing had been procedurally unfair); *Anderlecht v UEFA* CAS 98/185, *Digest of CAS Awards II 1998–2000* (2002, Kluwer), p 469 (alleged bribing of a referee); *Tyrrell Racing Organisation v RAC Motor Sports Association and the Fédération Internationale de L'Automobile*, unreported Hirst J 20 July 1984 (Tyrrell obtained an injunction to require the governing bodies to allow it to compete pending its attempt to overturn a ban imposed for adding fuel improperly during the course of a race. The challenge was put on the footing that the governing body had acted in a procedurally unfair manner by failing to give the team sufficient opportunity to present its case and that a ban should be suspended pending determination of a challenge. Both points were accepted as arguable). With respect to eligibility cases, see *TWR v RAC* (9 October 1985, unreported) (Gibson J), (technical compliance of racing cars); *Stevenage Borough FC v Football League*, Carnwarth J, (1997) Times, 1 August; affd 9 Admin LR 109, CA. As to arrangements in relation to players, see *Dundee United Football Club v Scottish Football Association*, 3 February 1988 (1988) Outer House Cases 1998 SLT 1244n (Club challenged SFA's treatment of it in internal dispute resolution proceedings over the sacking of a player). See also *AEK Basketball v National Basketball Association and Fédération Internationale de Basketball* (7 August 2001, unreported) (R Field QC) (dispute between AEK and the governing bodies as to whether a player was still under contract. The arbitrator had held that he was not, and AEK sought to challenge the validity of the arbitration itself); leave to appeal set aside, CA [2002] Times 13 June.

3 For example, in relation to the application of funds. See *Baker v Jones* [1954] 2 All ER 553.

A3.24 Ban from competition on grounds of ownership Governing bodies may seek to prevent or restrict the common ownership of clubs participating in the same league or tournament[1].

1 *AEK Athens and Slavia Prague v UEFA* CAS arbitration 98/200 interim decision 17 July 1998, final decision 20 August 1999, *Digest of CAS Awards II 1998–2000* (2002, Kluwer), p 38 and in [2001] 1 ISLR 122, (Club failed in its challenge to the application to it of UEFA's Champions League rule prohibiting participation of clubs in common ownership with another participant). See also Broome [2000] 8(2) SATLJ 83 (domestic common ownership) and [2001] 9(1) SATLJ 88 (international common ownership), and [2001] 9(3) SATLJ 171. On 27 June 2002, the European Commission announced that it was not pursuing ENIC's complaint against the UEFA common ownership rule: see Commission press release IP/02/942 dated 27 June 2002. The rule is to all intents and purposes inviolable at this point, subject to any appeal to the European Court of Justice.

A3.25 Refusal of permission to play in a particular country Clubs have also challenged governing bodies' rules which require their member clubs to play their home games within the geographical boundaries of the country of the governing body[1]. Governing bodies in second countries have also sought to stop clubs playing games there pursuant to their involvement in a foreign league[2].

1 *Excelsior Mouscron* decision, IP/99/965, dated 9 December 1999. See Ratliff [1998] 6(3) SATLJ 4; Draft Preliminary Guidelines on the Application of the Competition Rules to Sport, unpublished Commission memorandum, 15 February 1999 (European Commission accepted that the prohibition on the Belgian club playing a home game in a larger alternative stadium just across the border did not contravene the competition rules because the organisation of sport along national geographic lines fell outside the rules).

2 *Newport v Football Association of Wales* interlocutory hearing Jacob J [1995] 2 All ER 87, trial unreported Blackburne J 12 April 1995 (Newport challenged the FAW's actions in preventing it playing in Wales its home games in the English League. It was held that the FAW's actions were in unreasonable restraint of trade). Both Wimbledon and Clydebank football clubs were prohibited by the FA of Ireland from moving their home ground to Dublin in order to play respectively English and Scottish League football in Ireland, which led to the FA and SFA refusing permission out of solidarity. Cf *R v Football Association of Wales, ex p Flint Town* [1991] COD 44 (Flint, a member of the FAW, challenged the FAW's refusal of permission to it to play in a lower league administered by the FA).

A3.26 Refusal of permission to move home ground Some governing bodies restrict the ability of member clubs to move home grounds within the relevant country[1].

1 The homeless Wimbledon Football Club successfully challenged before an FA Arbitration Panel the Football League's refusal of its request to be allowed to establish a home ground in Milton Keynes. The League refused permission on the grounds a club must not move away from the conurbation from which it takes its name and play somewhere else, ostensibly because to do so would involve creating a new club which avoided coming up through the football pyramid. The League perceived this as equivalent to the franchising of clubs, and as running contrary to the underlying principles of the sport in England. However Wimbledon maintained that it was unable to secure a site for a new stadium within its own conurbation, and therefore had no choice but to move outside its conurbation. The club maintained that the League was acting in unreasonable restraint of trade, because the ban was out of proportion to the damage to the club, and that the League had not approached its decision in the right way. It was held by the FA Arbitration Panel (29 January 2002) that the League's decision was flawed on procedural grounds and that the matter should be remitted to it for a new decision, which would have to be proportionate. The League decided to refer the matter to an FA Commission to take a decision in its place. The FA Commission decided in May 2002 that the club's grounds for moving were sound and justified and that it would not be appropriate for the League to restrain the club from moving. See further paras A3.137 and A3.156.

A3.27 Promotion and relegation rules, and docking of points Clubs can be seriously affected by the application to them of the governing body's promotion and relegation rules, or by sanctions which affect promotion and relegation. Challenges may arise in circumstances where rule changes affect a particular club's prospects of staying in the top division, the most notable being reorganisations where the size of the top division is reduced[1], where a club fails additional criteria for promotion set by the sports governing body which go beyond where the club finishes in the table[2], and where relegation may be brought about by deductions of points as a result of a club's breach of the rules[3].

1 Cf *Wayde v New South Wales Rugby League Ltd* (1985) 61 ALR 225 (Reduction in the size of top division held to have been undertaken bona fide in the interests of the sport and not to be oppressive for the purposes of the equivalent of s 459 Companies Act 1985); *South Sydney District Rugby League Football Club v News Ltd* [2000] FCA 1541, [2001] FCA 862; see [2001] 2 ISLR N-20. Cf *Rotherham and English Second Division Rugby Ltd v English First Division Rugby Ltd, English Rugby Partnership Ltd and the RFU*, Ferris J 16 August 1999, [2000] 1 ISLR 33 (Rotherham unable to establish that the arrangements governing promotion between the two divisions had been varied in such a way as to allow it to insist on being one of the two new clubs admitted to the expanded Premier League. Rotherham's travails continued at the end of the 2001–2002 season, when it was unable to meet the non-sport-related criteria for promotion despite finishing top of its division. There was however no legal challenge, Rotherham instead quietly accepting the £750,000 compensation payment provided by the applicable rules). See also Hornsby [2001] 2 ISLR 161.

2 *Stevenage Borough Football Club v Football League Ltd*, Carnwath J, (1996) Times, 1 August; affd 9 Admin LR 109, CA (Stevenage was denied promotion into the League even though it won the Vauxhall conference, because its ground was inadequate. The club challenged the rules on the grounds that they were unreasonably in restraint of trade. The application was dismissed on grounds of delay, but a number of the rules criticised at first instance were subsequently changed); *Rotherham and English Second Division Rugby Ltd v English First Division Rugby Ltd, English Rugby Partnership Ltd and the RFU*, see n 1.

3 *R v Eastern Counties Rugby Union, ex p Basildon Rugby Club*, unreported 10 September 1987 (Basildon not promoted because ECRU disapproved of the way a fixture had been postponed. Judicial review held to be wrong mechanism for challenge). In 1996, Middlesbrough Football Club failed to play a Premier League match against Blackburn Rovers. A Commission established by the FAPL Board found Middlesborough had no good reason for this failure and therefore was in breach of the rules. It fined the club £50,000 and docked it three points, a decision upheld by the Board of Appeal upon challenge by the club. At the end of the season, Middlesborough was relegated when three more points would have saved it. See Stoner, 'The case of Middlesborough Football Club' [1997] 4(4) SLAP 8. As reported there, the same season Brighton was docked two points for failing to control the crowd at its matches, but still avoided relegation by drawing with Hereford United, who were instead relegated to the Conference. In 1990, Swindon Town was demoted from the First Division to the Second Division of the Football League after being found guilty of various financial improprieties.

(e) *Actions of a sports governing body affecting all clubs*

A3.28 In the same way as a class of individual participants can be affected by a sports governing body's actions, a class of clubs may be affected. Again, the effects are often similar, but there are particular types of rules which especially affect clubs and which have been the subject of challenge.

A3.29 Collective selling of commercial rights and other restrictions on the exploitation of commercial rights The collective selling of the rights to broadcast matches may adversely affect particular clubs, although it helps others[1]. The most successful clubs might be able to command a greater price for their home games alone than from their share of the income from the sale of all matches. Equally the individual sale of other commercial rights such as sponsorship, ticket and travel and corporate hospitality (especially in the context of tournaments) might be more lucrative for some clubs than collective sale. While in most contexts clubs have been content to maintain collective selling, some have sought to challenge the approach[2]. The governing body may seek to impose other restrictions on the freedom of the club to exploit its rights, for example in relation to sponsorship or advertising[3].

1 See further Chapter B2.

2 The challenge to collective selling has generally come from the regulatory authorities or from commercial partners that were disadvantaged: see paras A3.37 and A3.41. However in *Williams and Cardiff RFC v Pugh*, later known as *Williams and Cardiff RFC v WRU (IRB intervening)*, interim injunction hearings, unreported Popplewell J, 23 July 1997 and unreported CA, 1 August 1997; application for a stay hearings, unreported Buckley J, 17 March 1998; Eady J, 29 July 1998 [1999] Eu LR 195, the club challenged the validity of the IRB and WRU broadcasting rights collective selling arrangements, but no resolution was reached as a result of the action being stayed. A complaint to the European Commission by English First Division Rugby Clubs Limited challenging the validity of the IRB and RFU collective selling arrangements was subsequently withdrawn. See para A3.20, n 2.

3 It is very common for governing bodies, when acting as event organisers, to preserve the exclusivity granted to companies participating in the central commercial programme by requiring the clubs in the event to provide 'clean stadia' (ie devoid of conflicting commercial messages). For example, a dispute arose in May 2002 between Arsenal and the FA, triggered by Arsenal's disappointment over its share of revenues from the FA Cup Final, but focusing on the FA's requirements that clubs playing home ties in the FA Cup give up the prime stadium advertising space to the FA's sponsors. See further para A3.32, n 4. See *Otakuku Rovers Rugby League Club v Auckland Rugby League* unreported Williams J, New Zealand High Court 12 November 1993 (Governing body required clubs to use Lion Breweries insignia on goal posts, although the particular club was sponsored by Dominion Breweries. The club maintained that the governing body could not sell signage at its ground, but failed). In *Hendry v WPBSA*, unreported, Lloyd J 5 October 2001, [2002] 1 ISLR SLR-1, one of the rules upheld by the court was a rule restricting the number of logos that could be worn by a player: the rule was held to be necessary in the light of broadcasting restrictions.

A3.30 Loyalty arrangements in side agreements Some governing bodies have sought to impose loyalty arrangements in side agreements aimed at keeping clubs in their (and out of another organisation's) competitions for a defined period[1].

1 In *Williams and Cardiff RFC v Pugh*, later known as *Williams and Cardiff RFC v WRU (IRB intervening)*, interim injunction hearings, unreported Popplewell J, 23 July 1997 and unreported CA, 1 August 1997; application for a stay hearings, unreported Buckley J, 17 March 1998; Eady J, 29 July 1998 [1999] Eu LR 195, the club challenged the imposition of a loyalty agreement which obliged it to remain a member of the WRU and to participate in its competitions for 10 years, or else not be nominated by the WRU for participation in cross-border competitions organised by European Rugby Cup Limited. See also the 'Superleague case', *News Ltd v Australian Rugby League* (1996) 135 ALR 33; and *News Ltd v Australian Rugby League (No 2)* (1996) 139 ALR 193; for comment see Rose [1997] 5(3) SATLJ 42 and Veljanovski [1998] 6(1) SATLJ 12. Cf *Scottish Football League v Smith* 1998 SLT 608. Six clubs applied to resign from the SFL. Representatives from the clubs sat on the SFL Management Committee. The SFL sought to restrain those representatives from voting on their own clubs' application to resign. It was held that they could sit. This case may not however translate over to the situation where an individual club is affected by a decision. In the SFL situation, the five remaining rebel club representatives could in each instance have voted on the sixth club's individual application, without voting on a matter which affected their own club. The rules of the International Rugby Board allow representatives from particular unions to vote on a decision which affects their own union, for example in relation to where a Rugby World Cup should be held.

A3.31 Maximum numbers of foreign players, player release, transfers and salary caps Governing bodies impose a variety of rules in relation to what clubs can and cannot do with players. The courts have struck down rules which require clubs to limit themselves to maximum number of foreign players, at least when such a rule prevents players from other EU member states from playing on the same basis as home players[1]. The courts are not on the other hand prepared to interfere with rules as to the composition of a national team[2]. Governing bodies often impose rules on clubs requiring them to release players for international duty, which clubs may perceive to be too onerous and therefore seek to overturn[3]. As set out above[4], governing bodies impose rules on how clubs can transfer players and on how much they can pay their squad.

1 *Union Royal Belge des Sociétés de Football Association v Bosman* [1995] ECR I-4921, n 2 to para A3.18. See Draft Preliminary Guidelines on the Application of the Competition Rules to Sport, unpublished Commission memorandum, 15 February 1999, at 22 (suggesting that nationality quotas, to the extent that they apply not only to EC nationals but also to non-EC nationals that are under contract to a club in a member state, are liable to be caught by EC Art 81). See further para B2.109. A WRU rule requiring a minimum number of players at a club to be eligible to play for Wales was also challenged in *Williams and Cardiff RFC v Pugh*, later known as *Williams and Cardiff RFC v WRU (IRB intervening)*, interim injunction hearings, unreported Popplewell J, 23 July 1997 and unreported CA, 1 August 1997; application for a stay hearings, unreported Buckley J, 17 March 1998; Eady J, 29 July 1998 [1999] Eu LR 195, but this issue was not resolved when the proceedings were stayed as a result of concurrent proceedings before the European Commission and it is not dealt with in the judgments.

2 *Walrave and Koch v Association Union Cycliste Internationale* [1974] ECR 1405 (The governing body was held subject to the free movement rules, but its provision restricting the composition of national teams to citizens of the nation in question was found to be justified).

3 See Chapter E1. In *Williams and Cardiff RFC v Pugh*, later known as *Williams and Cardiff RFC v WRU (IRB intervening)*, interim injunction hearings, unreported Popplewell J, 23 July 1997 and unreported CA, 1 August 1997; application for a stay hearings, unreported Buckley J, 17 March 1998; Eady J, 29 July 1998 [1999] Eu LR 195, the club also challenged rugby union's player release rules, as did the EFDR clubs in their complaint to the European Commission. *EFDR Complaint to the European Commission against the Rugby Football Union and the International Rugby Board* Case No IV/36.994 (March 1998), para A3.20, n 2. Again however the issue is not dealt with in the *Cardiff* judgments, while the EFDR case settled without any decision.

4 See paras A3.18 and A3.19.

(f) Actions of a sports governing body affecting other sports governing bodies

A3.32 The actions of one sports governing body may also affect other sports governing bodies. Disputes can arise between national associations and international associations in circumstances ranging from the international association's perception that the national association wrongly acquitted a player charged with a doping offence[1] or wrongly allowed its clubs to breach international rules[2], to an international association's refusal to admit a national association to membership[3], or decision in relation to where an event should be held[4], or to the provision of a place in an international competition to a club from a particular country[5]. Disputes also arise between different sports governing bodies within a particular country[6]. Disputes between governing bodies are not confined to the playing and organisation of the sport, but extend to disputes in relation to commercial exploitation[7].

1 *IAAF v UKA and Walker* IAAF Arbitral Award 20 August 2000 [2001] 4 ISLR 264 (arbitration proceedings, in which the IAAF challenged UKA's clearing of the athlete and which, before the award, gave rise to the *Walker v UKA and IAAF* litigation, unreported Toulson J 3 July 2000, Hallett J 25 July 2000. See also Beloff [2000] 2 ISLR 41 and paras A3.10, n 7 and A3.124). See also *Smith v International Triathlon Union* (1999) 20 BCTC 71 (triathlete cleared by British Triathlon Association of a doping offence in the United States unsuccessfully challenged jurisdiction of US Triathlon to appeal to the International Triathlon Union).

2 In 1998, the International Rugby Board brought disciplinary proceedings against the RFU and the WRU for failing to stop the EFDR clubs playing 'unofficial' friendlies against the renegade Welsh clubs, Cardiff and Swansea.

3 *Reel v Holder (for IAAF)* [1979] 1 WLR 1252; affd [1981] 1 WLR 1226, CA (the Taiwanese athletics governing body obtained a declaration that the IAAF was not entitled to expel it from membership). See also *Shen Fu Chang v Stellan Mohlin* (5 July 1977, unreported) (Goff J) (Declaration and injunction granted requiring membership of international badminton governing body for Taiwan). A range of sports governing bodies from Gibraltar have challenged the refusal to admit them to membership of the corresponding international sports governing bodies, including UEFA and the IOC. These cases are pending before CAS.

4 The 2003 Rugby World Cup was originally granted to Australia and New Zealand together with Australia as host Union and New Zealand as a sub-host. The NZRFU however failed to conclude a sub-host agreement in the same terms as the ARU's host agreement, because it was not willing to

comply with the requirement that it should not organise any other tournament that would clash with the Rugby World Cup and that it should provide 'clean stadia' so that Rugby World Cup 2003 Ltd's commercial programme could be implemented. The IRB voted in April 2002 to hold the event in Australia alone. The NZRFU did not challenge the decision.

5 The Football League complained to the European Commission about UEFA's removal of a UEFA Cup place for the winner of the League Cup. The spot was restored before the matter progressed: see [1998] 6(1) SATLJ 36.

6 *R v Football Association Ltd, ex p Football League* [1993] 2 All ER 833, [1992] COD 52, 22 August (unsuccessful attempt by the Football League to challenge the decision to establish the Premier League). The Football Conference was for a while in dispute with the Football League over the League's refusal to agree a larger number of promotion and relegation places between the third division and the Conference, and with the FA over the FA's refusal to allow the Conference to change its rules to have play-offs for the one promotion place that then existed, but that dispute was resolved in 2002 with increased promotion and relegation between the Conference and the Third Division of the Football League, underwritten by the FA; *Alwyn Treherne (for the Welsh Amateur Boxing Federation) v Amateur Boxing Association of England*, Garland J 27 February 2001 [2001] 3 ISLR 231, unreported CA 11 March 2002, [2002] EWCA Civ 381, [2002] All ER (D) 144 (Mar) (The WABF, which had been set up as a rival to the Welsh Amateur Boxing Association and which was not recognised internationally, challenged the ABAE's refusal to allow its clubs to affiliate with the ABAE so that former WABF boxers could compete other than with one another. The case turned on whether a binding contract had been entered into that the ABAE would admit the clubs, and it was held that it had not been. Both Garland J and Buxton LJ doubted that even if there had been a contract it would have been appropriate to grant an injunction to force the ABAE to admit the clubs). See also *Auckland Boxing Association v New Zealand Boxing Association* [2001] NZLR 847 (suspension of the Auckland association following its organisation of a 'pro-am' tournament overturned on natural justice grounds).

7 For example, the dispute between the Celtic Unions and the Rugby Football Union as to the value that should be placed, for accounting purposes, on the Five Nations element of the RFU's broadcasting contract with the RFU, which was resolved by expert determination, as required by the terms of the Five Nations Accord. See para A3.37, n 9. See also para A5.14.

(g) *Actions of a sports governing body affecting commercial partners*

A3.33 Commercial partners are affected by the way sports governing bodies exploit the commercial rights that they hold. A number of challenges have arisen to the legality of those commercial choices. In addition sports governing bodies have to take steps to protect the exploitability of the rights that they own, for example where third parties seek to take advantage of the goodwill generated by the sport without compensating the governing body with income for the continued development of the sport[1]. There will plainly also be straightforward contractual disputes as to the extent of the rights granted and failure to comply with specific contractual obligations.

1 For example, as in *PGA v Evans* (25 January 1989, unreported) (Vinelott J) (unofficial corporate hospitality provider using Ryder Cup name).

A3.34 Official endorsement of sports products For manufacturers of sports equipment, official endorsement by the governing body of the sport in a particular country provides an extremely useful advertising tool, suggesting as it does that the people who really know what the product has to do have selected the particular manufacturer's product before those of others[1]. The very usefulness of such an endorsement means that rival manufacturers are likely to be adversely affected, and to object[2], particularly if the endorsement reflects no more than how much the 'official' manufacturer has been prepared to pay. On the other hand, it may be useful for the public to be informed by the sports governing body whether a particular product achieves a particular standard.

1 See further paras B2.191 to B2.211.

2 *Danish Tennis Federation* Case Nos IV/F–1/33.055 and 35.759, OJ, 9/5/96, No C 138/6, Commission press release IP/98/355 (Tennis ball manufacturers adversely affected by the federation's choice of one manufacturer to be named as the official supplier of tennis balls, in that it suggested that the balls of other manufacturers were inadequate, complained to the European Commission which prohibited the practice and set stricter constraints on the degree of recognition that could be given by the sports governing body. The opportunity must be open to all manufacturers to obtain such recognition on the basis of objective criteria); *World Federation of the Sporting Goods Industry v FIFA and ISL*, Case No IV/F–1/35.266, complaint rejected by Commission decision letter dated December 2000 (football manufacturers challenged rule allowing use in official competitions only of 'FIFA-approved' footballs). See further paras B2.202 to B2.206. Approval schemes must be open and transparent and not run for profit.

A3.35 Selected suppliers of sports products Equally manufacturers of sports equipment wish to be selected to supply sports products to governing bodies simply because such contracts are valuable. This is particularly the case where governing bodies seek to require or encourage their member clubs also to buy from that supplier. Selection processes have been the subject of challenge as anti-competitive[1]. Suppliers have also had to challenge the failure of sports governing bodies to approve equipment[2].

1 *Danish Tennis Federation*, Case Nos IV/F–1/33.055 and 35.759, OJ, 9/5/96, No C 138/6, Commission press release IP/98/355 (federation required to allow any supplier that could meet objective criteria to tender for supply contract, with winner obtaining only two-year contract, followed by new tender).

2 See for example *Fisher v NGRC (No 2)* (25 July 1991, unreported), CA (refusal of NGRC to allow racetracks to use jacket designed by claimant led to claim based on restraint of trade, malicious falsehood and inducement of breach of contract). Cf *Australian Olympic Committee* CAS 2000/C/267, advisory opinion dated 1 May 2000, *Digest of CAS Awards II 1998–2000* (2002, Kluwer), p 728 (determining compliance of bodysuits with swimming's equipment rules).

A3.36 Sponsorship and official suppliers of other products A large number of companies, unconnected with the sport, perceive a value in connecting themselves to it, whether through the sponsorship of events, leagues, clubs or individuals, or through being named as official suppliers of anything from timing equipment to soft drinks[1]. Sports governing bodies make dispositive choices which may be the subject of challenge, not only in how they allocate the contracts for the exploitation of the rights that they themselves hold[2], but in the rules that they impose on other participants[3] in relation to such exploitation. Particular problems have arisen in the context of sponsorship of events by tobacco and alcohol producers[4].

1 See further paras B2.306 to B2.317 and Chapter D5.

2 See by way of analogy cases cited at para A3.34, n 1.

3 Such as the steps taken by governing bodies to enforce clean stadia rules or to prohibit players from using equipment from a manufacturer other than the one sponsoring the national team. See para A3.29, n 3. In 1995, Adidas paid the National Football League in France 60m francs in return for the exclusive right to provide equipment to all of the clubs in the first and second divisions of the French football league championship. The League then adopted a rule requiring the clubs in the top two divisions to use equipment as designated by the League. As a result, many clubs cancelled their sponsorship arrangements with Adidas' competitors and signed up with Adidas, so that Adidas soon sponsored 30 or so of the top 42 clubs. The French competition authorities issued interim measures suspending the change in the League's rules. They then held, and subsequently the Court of Appeal in Paris agreed, that the agreement infringed French domestic competition law (which mirror the EC competition rules). The relevant market was said (for reasons that are not clear from the court's judgment) to be the market in France for branded trainers. Adidas' share of that market was almost 50%, allowing the authorities to hold Adidas to be dominant on that market. The arrangements were said to restrict competition appreciably on that market because (a) along with its other sponsorship deals – Adidas was also the exclusive kit supplier and sponsor with respect to the League Cup and French Cup as well as the French national team – the deal with the

League meant that Adidas supplied kit to teams playing in at least 60% of matches broadcast on national television, thereby dominating this particular platform for the promotion of branded trainers; (b) the League held no tendering process for the rights granted to Adidas; (c) the five-year exclusive term of the agreement foreclosed the market to an unacceptable degree; (d) the 'matching rights' renewal clause that Adidas inserted into its contracts with individual clubs protected Adidas further from competition on that market; and (e) the League was not entitled to exercise its regulatory powers to obtain an economic advantage. Adidas was fined €2.4m and the League was fined 800,000 francs. *National Football League/Adidas*, Court of Appeal of Paris, 29/2/2000, [2000] ECLR 10, p N.118/9. See also 'Adidas fined over anti-competitive soccer deal', www.sportcal.com, 2 January 2001. Adidas' 'matching rights' clause was also condemned in *Reebok France v Adidas and Uhlsport*, French Competition Council, 7 October 1997, [1998] ECLR 5, p N–84.

4 Sports such as Formula One motor racing and snooker have relied heavily on tobacco sponsorship. The extent to which sports governing bodies will be able to grant alcohol and tobacco sponsorship deals in the future is in the balance, with the overturning of EC legislation designed severely to limit it (see *Germany v European Parliament* [2000] ECR I-2247, [2000] All ER (EC) 769; Callaghan [2000] 8(1) SATLJ 91). The United Kingdom has said it will go it alone (see para A1.80), but there are difficulties in taking that course, which are highlighted in the case currently pending before the European Court of Justice, *Bacardi v Newcastle* on a reference from the English courts, [2001] Eu LR 45 (Gray J 26 July 2000). In that case Bacardi challenges the validity of the French Loi Evin which amongst other things restricts the broadcast on French TV of certain sports events taking place outside France, where advertising of alcohol or tobacco is displayed at the event venue.

A3.37 Broadcasting Coverage of premium sports events has been used by new platform broadcasters over recent years as a battering ram for new subscriptions. This has led to a massive increase in the sums of money that governing bodies have been able to secure for the rights[1]. However the perceived value can only be realised by the grant of an exclusive contract for a sufficient period to allow the entitlement to be built upon and converted into increased revenue for the broadcaster[2]. The consequences have included a government initiative to try and preserve some 'crown jewel' events for broadcast on terrestrial free to air television[3], and the need for increased vigilance by governing bodies to prevent attempts to circumvent the exclusivity of the arrangements[4]. A wide range of disputes may arise in this context, including challenges to the length and terms of the arrangements granted[5], to the validity of collective selling itself[6], to the validity of the bundling of rights to broadcast on different platforms[7], and to the distribution of the proceeds[8]. Equally, disputes have arisen between governing bodies grouping together to sell rights collectively[9]. Disputes have also arisen as to the ownership of rights in the first place[10]. Governing bodies have had to be astute to ensure that television coverage does not damage the gate receipts of less successful clubs, taking steps which the broadcasters or regulators seek to challenge[11]. Furthermore, the exploitation of these commercial rights has given rise to straight contractual disputes as to the terms of the grant and as to payment[12].

1 See generally Chapter D4. Although the Football League dispute with Granada and Carlton over the failure of their subsidiary ITV Digital to honour its commitment to pay broadcasting rights fees indicates that the figures achievable may be lower in future: see *Carlton Communications plc and Granada Media plc v Football League Ltd* (1 August 2002, unreported), [2002] All ER (D) 1 (Langley J). The dispute in purely legal terms involved whether the broadcasters could be said to have guaranteed the obligations of the subsidiary when they did not sign a formal guarantee. Langley J held that they could not, rejecting the argument advanced by the League that the subsidiary's tender for the rights contained a written statement that the parents guaranteed the subsidiary's liability, which was (a) incorporated by reference into the subsequent contract with the subsidiary and (b) sufficient to satisfy the formal requirements of the Statute of Frauds that a guarantee be in writing.

2 See further paras B2.236 to B2.305 and Chapter D4.

3 See further paras A1.81 to A1.92. In *R v ITC, ex p TVDanmark 1 Ltd* [2001] UKHL 42, [2001] 1 WLR 1604, the House of Lords examined the extent to which the UK regulatory authorities could

and should in any particular case enforce equivalent listing arrangements in another member state against broadcasters that chose to establish themselves in the United Kingdom, but had as their main audience the public in that other member states. See paras A1.91 and A1.92. See also Harris [2001] 9(2) SATLJ 100.

4 Cf *BBC v Talksport* [2001] FSR 53 and *BBC v BSkyB* [1992] Ch 141; para A3.44, n 1, in each of which one broadcaster pursued another.

5 For example *Re an Agreement between the FA Premier League* [2000] EMLR 78, [1999] UKCLR 258 (Restrictive Practices Court July 1999), (consideration of the legality of the English FA Premier League's broadcasting arrangements with BSkyB and the BBC under the UK's predecessor competition legislation). See also [1999] 7(3) SATLJ 18. See further paras B2.236 to B2.305.

6 See n 5.

7 For example the European Commission's statement of objections to UEFA in relation to the bundling of rights to the Champions League (*Commission opens proceedings against UEFA's selling of TV rights to UEFA Champions League*, Commission press release IP/01/1043, dated 20 July 2001), which were resolved to its satisfaction by certain modifications made by UEFA to its programme for the granting of rights (*Commission welcomes UEFA's new policy for selling the media rights to the Champions League*, Commission press release, IP/02/806, dated 3 June 2002).

8 For example the dispute in 2001 between the Professional Footballers Association and the FA Premier League over the PFA's share of the rights fees derived from broadcasting of games in which its members played, and Cardiff RFC's challenge to the collective selling of rights by the WRU: see n 2 to para A3.29.

9 For example, in 1996 the Rugby Football Union sold BSkyB the rights to all its home games, including its home games in the Five Nations Championship (as it then was) without consulting the other Unions in the Championship. The remaining unions refused to play the RFU, and the RFU was forced to sign a September 1996 Accord that recognised the principle of central selling of such rights and sharing of the resulting revenues. Because the deal with BSkyB could not be avoided, the Accord included a requirement that the part of the £65m rights fee paid by BSkyB that was attributable to England's Five Nations matches be pooled by the RFU, the amount to be determined by a valuer if not agreed. In the event, the parties could not agree and an expert determination ensued, leading to a valuation decision in November 1999. See further para A5.14.

10 There remains an issue as to who or what owns what are commonly referred to as 'television rights' or 'broadcast rights'. In *Victoria Park Racing v Taylor* (1937) 58 CLR 479, it was held that these rights were the rights of the owner or controller of land to admit or to refuse to admit a broadcaster onto land in order to film an event. This approach however neglected the contribution of the participants in, and possibly also the organisers of, the event: see Abramson 'Whose rights are they anyway?' [1996] 4(3) SATLJ 100. See also *Anglia TV v Cayton* (1989) Times, 17 February (Hirst J) (dispute over who controlled, and therefore who was rightful grantee, of UK broadcasting rights to Tyson/Bruno fight). See further Chapter D4.

11 Through 'blackout rules' under which matches cannot be broadcast at a time which would make it less likely that spectators would travel to and watch a live match. For example, a host of broadcasters complained to the European Commission (Case Nos IV/C2; 34.319, 33,734, 34.199, 33.145, 34.784, 34,790, 34,948, 35.001, 35.048) about UEFA's blackout rule which banned the broadcast of foreign matches in another country at the same time as that country played its own matches. Originally the ban was over the whole of Saturday and Sunday, with conditional black-outs also during the week, but UEFA was forced to relax this to the 2 hour weekend period when matches were usually actually being played. Commission press release IP/01/583, 20 April 2001. See paras B2.182 to B2.186. In *Scottish FA v Commission* [1994] ECR II-1039, the SFA had set out to prevent Argentinian football being broadcast in Scotland by TESN. The Commission regarded this as contravening the competition rules and addressed a series of questions to the SFA, in a formal decision. The SFA challenged the procedure, but the challenge was rejected.

12 For example *Carlton and Granada v Football League Ltd* (1 August 2002, unreported), [2002] All ER (D) 1 (Langley J), see n 1; and the disputes between Formula One Management and Formula One Administration and various broadcasters such as *MTV v Formula One Management* unreported Harman J 6 March 1998, Carnwath J 1 April 1998, in which the court refused to grant an interim injunction requiring the provision of the feed to the broadcaster because it had not been established to the court's satisfaction that a contractual entitlement had arisen.

A3.38 Intellectual property The increased commercialisation of sport has led to disputes over the use of the governing bodies' intellectual property rights[1], such as their rights in their lists of events and information about the events and those taking part in it[2], their official trade marks[3], their right not to have an unauthorised competition associated with them[4], and even the initials by which the governing body is known[5].

1 See further Chapter D1.
2 *Football League v Littlewoods Pools* [1959] Ch 637 (Unlicensed use by Littlewoods of the League's fixture list held in breach of copyright); *British Horseracing Board and the Jockey Club v William Hill Organisation Ltd* [2001] 2 CMLR 215; revsd [2001] EWCA Civ 1268, [2001] All ER (D) 431 (Jul) (BHB and the Jockey Club successfully enforced their EC Directive 96/9 database rights to prevent the bookmakers using, for their internet business and without paying a licence fee, data derived from the governing bodies' database of meetings, times, runners, and pre-race information), (16 June 2001, unreported) (Ferris J) (permission granted to BHB to hold an emergency board meeting to seek to reach agreement on the terms of permission to use the database). See also Reid [2001] 9(2) SATLJ 105 and also p 29 in the same publication. The Court of Appeal referred the matter to the European Court of Justice [2001] 9(3) SATLJ 85.
3 *RFU and Nike v Cotton Traders* [2002] EWHC 467 (Ch), [2002] All ER (D) 417 (Mar) (RFU and Nike unsuccessfully sought to restrain trader using the red rose symbol on products); *Trebor Bassett Ltd v FA* [1997] FSR 211 (unsuccessful attempt to stop sweet manufacturer giving away cards bearing pictures of footballers wearing the England strip, including the 'Three Lions' symbol). Cf *Rofa Sport Management v DHL Ltd* [1989] 1 WLR 902, para A3.44, n 1, where a governing body's licensee pursued the infringer. Cf *Re Psygnosis Ltd's Trade Mark Application*, unreported, Trade Marks Registry, 30 November 1998 (Refusal of a computer games company's application to register the trademark World Tour Golf, although no governing body ran a world tour). Cf *Arsenal FC v Reed*, Laddie J, [2001] 2 CMLR 481 (action for trademark infringement rejected on grounds, among others, that reproduction of club badge on football shirt is use as a 'badge of allegiance', not as a 'badge of origin'; referred to the European Court of Justice (AG's opinion dated 13 June 2002, Case C-206/01; see also [2001] 9(1) SATLJ 107). See also *PGA v Evans* (25 January 1989, unreported) (Vinelott J), see para A3.39, n 4.
4 *Parish v World Series Cricket Pty Ltd* (1977) 16 ALR 172 (Australian Cricket Board granted injunction against World Series Cricket to restrain it from implying in advertising that its events were authorised by the Board).
5 *World Wide Fund for Nature v World Wrestling Federation* (1 October 2001, unreported) (Jacob J) (World Wide Fund for Nature secured an injunction preventing the World Wrestling Federation from using the initials WWF anywhere outside the United States. The World Wrestling Federation argued unsuccessfully that a contract limiting its ability to use the initials was in restraint of trade and in breach of the competition rules in Art 81(EC) since there was no chance of confusion between their activities and therefore no objective justification for the restriction, but the court held that the risk of injurious association was sufficient to justify it).

A3.39 Corporate hospitality Governing bodies are often also in a position to sell the rights to provide a package of ticket and corporate hospitality at stadia where they have organised an event[1], and in order to extract maximum value they have tended to make exclusive appointments of businesses that they have designated as 'official' providers[2]. In a number of cases, corporate hospitality providers have sought to challenge the selection of particular businesses as official hospitality providers, and the exclusivity of their appointment[3]. Governing bodies have also sought to enforce the exclusivity of appointments[4].

1 See generally Chapter D7.
2 See further paras B2.219, B2.220 and B2.234.
3 For example *Hospitality Group v FA* (24 January 1996, unreported) (Scott V-C) in respect of Euro 96; *Hospitality Group v Australian Rugby Union* [1999] FCA 1136 (interlocutory); [2000] FCA 823 (first instance); [2001] FCA 1040 (on appeal); the complaint to the OFT in respect of *Wimbledon*, OFT Press Release No 20/93, 23 March 1993, and the complaint to the European Commission in *Rugby World Cup 1999*. See paras B2.219, B2.220 and B2.234.
4 For example, in *PGA v Evans* (25 January 1989, unreported) (Vinelott J), in which the PGA and Keith Prowse obtained an interim injunction restraining a rival corporate hospitality provider from passing itself off as having any official connection with the Ryder Cup. The PGA failed to obtain an injunction restraining the defendant from inducing breach of the ticket conditions by ticket holders, but did obtain an injunction that the defendant disclose all those to whom it had sold packages.

A3.40 Ticket and travel The grant of access to match tickets to package with travel and accommodation arrangements, coupled with 'official' designation, is another major source of income for governing bodies organising sports events involving participants from abroad. Again, excluded travel providers have sought to challenge the selection of rivals and the exclusivity granted[1].

1 See generally paras B2.218 and B2.221 to B2.225. For example the complaint that triggered the European Commission decision in *Italia 90* [1992] OJ L 326, p 31; the OFT's commencement of proceedings against the *Rugby Football League*, OFT Press Release 14/98, 26 March 1998 and the complaint to the European Commission in *Rugby World Cup 1999*.

A3.41 Arrangements with promoters and agents Governing bodies often do not have all the resources to organise major events and so contract with the owners of stadia or racecourses and promoters, and employ sports agents, in order to put together an event and/or to develop a commercial programme for the event[1], giving rise to the potential for commercial disputes[2].

1 See further Chapter D8.

2 *R v Jockey Club ex p RAM Racecourses* [1993] 2 All ER 225, DC (Unsuccessful attempt to challenge the Jockey Club's allocation of race dates to racecourses); *Sepoong Engineering Construction Co v Formula One Management (formerly Formula One Administration Ltd)* [2000] 1 Lloyds Rep 602 (dispute over the agreement that a Formula One grand prix should be staged at Sepoong's racecourse in Korea). The arrangements for the FIA Formula One World Championship involve the governing body, Fédération Internationale de l'Automobile, contracting out exploitation of rights to various companies, including FOM and FOA, part owned by Bernie Ecclestone's family's interests and at least at present part-owned by Kirch, which then organise the grand prix and sell on the commercial rights. In the context of football, FIFA licences out the commercial exploitation of the World Cup (see *Rofa Sport Management v DHL International UK* [1989] 1 WLR 902, para A3.44, n 1); the World Cup 2002 was put in peril by the collapse of international sports agents ISL.

(h) Actions of a sports governing body affecting the public

A3.42 The public, in the form of supporters, spectators and viewers, may be affected by the decisions of sports governing bodies. In the main, their interests have been pursued by decisions made by the regulatory authorities[1] or government[2], although those decisions themselves may become the subject of litigation in the courts, either because the sports governing body itself challenges the decision, or because the administrative authority refers a matter to the courts[3]. Smaller groups within the public may however be, or perceive themselves to be, affected by particular matters, and seek to bring actions themselves[4].

1 In particular the wider public interest has been protected by decisions of the competition authorities: for example Albertville and Barcelona unreported, Commission press release IP/92/593; Atlanta, unreported, 1996 Competition Report p. 144 and *France 98* [2000] OJ L 5/55, where the sports governing bodies' systems of ticket sales discriminated against supporters on the basis of nationality; *FIA Formula One Championship* [2001] OJ C 169, p 5; *Italia 90* [1992] OJ L 326, p 31. See also Report of the Mergers & Monopolies Commission on the Proposed BSkyB Merger with Manchester United (1999) (recommending that the Secretary of State block the merger on the grounds that it would be detrimental to the public interest). See generally Chapter B2.

2 For example the listing of events by the government as events which must be available on free to air television. See paras A3.37, n 3 and A1.81 to A1.92.

3 For example *Re an Agreement between the FA Premier League* [2000] EMLR 78, [1999] UKCLR 258 (Restrictive Practices Court July 1999) (consideration of the legality of the English FA Premier League's broadcasting arrangements with BSkyB and the BBC under the UK's predecessor competition legislation).

4 *Finnigan v New Zealand Rugby Football Union (Nos 1, 2 and 3)* [1985] 2 NZLR 159, 181, 190 (NZ HC and CA) (Challenge to the decision by the NZRFU to send a team to South Africa);

Arnolt v Football Association (2 February 1998, unreported) (Unsuccessful action brought by a Middlesbrough supporter against the FA for loss of the opportunity to use his season ticket to watch Premier League football as a result of the club's demotion following the docking of points); *MacDonald v FIFA and SFA* [1999] SCLR 59, [1999] 7(1) SATLJ 33 (Scots Court dismissed a claim made by a fan against the governing bodies consequent upon the cancellation of an international fixture); *Tyrell v FA* (28 April 1997, unreported), Coward [1997] 5(2) SATLJ 5 (action against FA claiming damages for nervous shock caused by bad refereeing decision struck out). Where a governing body organises an event, it may be liable as organiser for injuries sustained by spectators. See for example *Horne and Marlow v RAC Motor Sports Association* (24 May 1989, unreported), CA; and Chapters C4 and E5. There are more examples of actions by the public against clubs or other organisers of events, than against governing bodies: again see Chapter E5 (Civil Liability for On-Field Conduct) for the personal injury cases. There have also been other less usual actions by members of the public against clubs: *Duffy v Newcastle United Football Club* (29 June 2001, unreported), CA, [2002] 2 ISLR SLR-101 (Fans holding debentures unsuccessfully brought proceedings against the club to stop it moving their seats); *Miller v Jackson* [1977] QB 966 (Lord Denning MR's famous judgment (with a remarkable first paragraph) refusing an injunction to a householder complaining of the nuisance caused by a cricket club at the end of his garden); *Prestatyn UDC v Prestatyn Raceway* [1970] 1 WLR 33 (Local authority complained of the nuisance caused by a trotting track); *Goode v Four Ashes Golf Centre* (20 December 2001, unreported), CA (nuisance); *Wheeler v Leicester City Council* [1985] AC 1054 (Local authority held to have unlawfully sanctioned rugby club for failing to condemn tour to South Africa); *R v Secretary of State for the Home Department, ex p Bindel* [2001] Imm AR 1; and *R v Secretary of State for the Home Department and Frank Warren, ex p Rape Crisis Centre* (2000) OHC Lord Clarke 2 June 2000 (attempts to overturn the permission granted to Mike Tyson to enter the UK to box).

(i) Actions of participants affecting other participants

A3.43 The survey set out above does not address the situation where the actions of a participant (in other words a person other than a sports governing body), such as an individual, a club or a promoter, affect another participant. In many instances, these disputes do not involve questions of the regulation of sport, but rather disputes between private parties that happen to arise in a sporting context. In some instances, however, disputes between participants may relate to the way that the sport is played[1] or turn on for example the validity of a standard form contract for use between participants provided for in the rules of the governing body[2]. Where this is not the case, and the governing body is not even involved to this extent, the possible factual scenarios in which disputes are brought to the courts are numerous and outside the scope of this chapter. Many cases involve situations where players, managers or clubs have resort to the courts in disputes arising in relation to their employment or engagement[3]. Particular examples include disputes where promoters, managers or clubs try to hold players or other participants to contracts or sue them for breach (or vice versa)[4], disputes where clubs try to avoid contracts with other clubs and players[5], disputes between clubs or teams for example in respect of attempts to lure away players or other participants[6], disputes between promoters[7], disputes between players or clubs and sponsors or other commercial partners[8], actions for personal injury during the playing of the sport whether by a player[9] or by a spectator[10], actions for damage to vehicles or equipment used in the sport[11], libel actions[12] and even disputes as to the entitlement to describe one's self as holding a particular title[13].

1 For example *Mercury Bay Boating Club Inc v San Diego Yacht Club and Royal Perth Yacht Club of Western Australia* 76 NY 2d 256 (Court of Appeals for New York 1990) (Legal challenge to the shape of yachts eligible to compete, there a catamaran).

2 *Watson v Prager* [1991] 1 WLR 726 (British Board of Boxing Control's standard form boxer-manager contract held in unreasonable restraint of trade); *Barry Silkman v Colchester United Football Club Ltd* (15 June 2001, unreported) (Morland J) (Held that the Football Association's rules on agents not being paid by clubs when they acted for the player were not incorporated into

the contract between the club and the agent in order to give it business efficacy, and therefore that the agent could recover against the club). This decision has considerable relevance to the all too common failure of clubs to comply with Art 30 of the FIFA Transfer Rules, under which the validity of a transfer contract or a player contract cannot be made subject to the successful completion of medical tests or the obtaining of a work permit. According to FIFA these things must be done before the contract is entered into. If the contract was governed by English law, it is arguable on the basis of *Silkman* that Art 30 was not incorporated, and that although the clubs were in breach of Art 30 the contractual position (no liability under the transfer agreement) would remain intact if the player failed his medical. However, such contracts may well not be subject to English law and in any event, it is unlikely that a FIFA arbitral tribunal acting under the transfer rules would take the same view. See further Chapter E2.

3 See further Chapter E1. For discussion of the obligation not to discriminate in this context, see Chapter E3.

4 *Subaru Technica v Burns and Peugeot* (11 December 2001, unreported) (Strauss QC); *Walkinshaw v Diniz* [2001] 1 Lloyd's Rep 632, [2002] EWCA Civ 180, [2002] 2 Lloyd's Rep 165; *Lotus Cars Ltd v Jaguar Cars Ltd*, Nourse J [1982] LS Gaz R 1214; *Nichols Advanced Vehicles Systems v De Angelis and Team Lotus* (21 December 1979, unreported) (Oliver J); *Warren v Mendy* [1989] 1 WLR 853 (court would not enforce negative stipulations in British Board of Boxing Control's standard form boxer-manager contract if to do so would in fact involve forcing an individual into performance of positive obligations); *McLaren v Jaguar* unreported but see [2001] 9(2) SATLJ 88 (Engineer Newey contracted to go to Jaguar from McLaren but changed his mind and decided to stay at McLaren; Jaguar unable to force him to work for them). But cf *Crystal Palace v Bruce* Burton J 22 November 2001 [2002] 2 ISLR SLR 81 (Club successfully enforced garden leave provision to stop manager commencing work for Birmingham); *White v Bristol Rugby Ltd* HHJ Havelock-Allan 17 August 2001, [2002] 1 ISLR SLR-67 (Unsuccessful attempt by prop Julian White to terminate contract to play for Bristol); *Clansman Sporting Club v Robinson* (5 May 1995, unreported) (Johnson J) (Boxing promoter Barry Hearn attempted to enforce a re-match option in a contract entered into with Robinson immediately before Robinson became WBO featherweight champion. Robinson unsuccessfully argued that the WBO rules were incorporated into the contract and they prohibited the option, and that the option was in unjustified restraint of trade); *Warnock v Scarborough Football Club* [1989] ICR 489 (action by club against manager for liquidated damages on his departure, but report deals with procedural matters); *Pulis v Gillingham* (manager dismissed for misconduct, action settled during trial) [2001] 9(2) SATLJ 34; see also [2001] 9(1) SATLJ 23; *Murphy v Southend United Football Club* (18 March 1999, unreported) (Eady J).

5 *Sunderland Football Club v Uruguay Montevideo and Milton Nunes* [2001] 2 All ER (Comm) 828 (Blofeld J) (attempt by Sunderland to avoid transfer contract and player contract on the grounds of misrepresentation and mistake as to the identity of the club transferring the player. Blofeld J held on the hearing of an interim injunction that fraud was not made out; action in relation to innocent misrepresentation and mistake settled before trial).

6 *Nichols Advanced Vehicles Systems v De Angelis and Team Lotus* (21 December 1979, unreported) (Oliver J); *Middlesbrough v Liverpool* FA Arbitration March 2002 and then subsequent court action, (21 May 2002, unreported) (Astill J) (Liverpool alleged to have acted improperly in persuading Christian Ziege to move). In *Bournemouth AFC v Manchester United Football Club* (1980) Times, 22 May, CA, the dispute arose out of a transfer contract which included a higher price if the player scored a certain number of goals; it was held that there was an implied term that the buying club would give the player an opportunity to score by picking him for matches).

7 *Don King Productions v Warren* [1998] 2 Lloyds Rep 176; affd [1999] Ch 291 (dispute between former partners in the field of boxing promotion and broadcasters).

8 *Conchita Martinez v Ellesse Spa* (30 March 1999, unreported), CA. A tennis player sued her sponsor for payment of a bonus; her remuneration was tied to the world standings, and the issue for the court was whether she was the world's number two or lower. It was held that on the proper basis of calculation she was not number two, but the three members of the Court of Appeal were not ad idem as to the proper basis. See also *Bain Budgen Sports v Hollioake* (8 December 1997, unreported) (Pumfrey J); *Gerhard Berger v Mallya and United Breweries* (19 March 1998, unreported) (Tuckey J); *Umbro Europe v McManaman* (20 May 1998, unreported) (Neuberger J); *Mobil Oil New Zealand v Bagnalli* [2001] UKPC 57 unreported Privy Council 11 December 2001; *Bacardi and Cellier des Dauphins v Newcastle United Football Club* [2001] Eu LR 45 (Gray J 26 July 2000) (Club took down Bacardi's adverts for game against French side because under French Loi Evin the game could not be broadcast in France if alcohol was advertised at it); *Leeds Cricket, Football and Athletic Co v Craven Gilpin* (28 January 193, unreported) (contractual dispute over corporate hospitality).

9 See further Chapter E5. There are very many examples of personal injury actions by players, described in that chapter. Players' actions may be against other players (leading examples are

Condon v Basi [1985] 1 WLR 866, footballer injured by foul tackle; and *Caldwell v Maguire and Fitzgerald* 27 June 2001, [2001] EWCA Civ 1054, [2001] 3 ISLR 224, jockey injured by careless riding of others unsuccessfully sued) or against supervisors (a leading example is *Hedley v Cuthbertson* (20 June 1997, unreported) (Dyson J), guide held liable for the decision to use one ice screw instead of two in a mountaineering accident) or referees (*Smolden v Whitworth* [1997] ELR 249, action against a referee following collapse of scrum) or organisers (for example *Morrell v Owen*, Mitchell J, (1993) Times, 14 December and *Stratton v Hughes and RAC* (17 March 1998, unreported), CA. A recent development is an action by a player against his own club for failing to diagnose an injury: *Brady v Sunderland* (17 November 1998, unreported), CA. Cf the question of criminal liability for actions on the pitch: Chapter E5.

10 See further Chapter E5. Again there are very many cases described in that chapter brought by spectators against players (such as *Wooldridge v Sumner* [1963] 2 QB 43, spectator injured at a horse show sued rider unsuccessfully) and against organisers (such as *Horne and Marlow v RAC* (24 May 1989, unreported), CA.

11 *Headcorn Parachute Club v Pond* (11 January 1995, unreported) (Alliott J) (Owners of aircraft sued the parents of a parachutist who died when she collided with the aircraft, damaging it. In this action, as in some of the others set out in nn 8 and 9, the effective defendants were the insurers of the governing body, here the British Parachute Association); *Clarke v Earl of Dunraven, The Satanita* [1897] AC 59 (Action by one yacht owner against another for damage caused by breach of the race rules).

12 Between sportsmen or other participants, such as *Ian Botham v Imran Khan* (1996), Times 15 July, (11 July 1996, unreported), CA, or by sportsmen against newspapers, such as *JPR Williams v Reason* [1988] 1 WLR 96n; *Grobbelaar v News Group* CA 18 January 2001 [2001] EWCA Civ 33, [2001] 2 All ER 437; *Mosley v Focus Magazin* [2001] EWCA Civ 1030; *O'Neill v Guardian Newspapers* (3 December 2001, unreported) (Gray J) or by promoters against sportsmen, such as *Warren v Naseem Hamed* (4 October 2000, unreported).

13 *Serville v Constance* [1954] 1 WLR 487 (Welter-weight champion of Trinidad sued another boxer for falsely describing himself as having the title).

(j) Actions of non participants

A3.44 Lastly, it is plain that sport may be connected with litigation that does not involve participants at all. For example disputes may arise between a commercial partner that has the right to exploit commercial rights in particular sporting events, and a third party that does not[1], or as to which company has the rights in question[2]. There may also be disputes between clubs or players and non-participants[3].

1 For example *Rofa Sport Management v DHL Ltd* [1989] 1 WLR 902 (Exclusive marketing agent for the 1986 FIFA World Cup brought an action to restrain DHL from describing itself as 'the official world wide courier to the FIFA World Cup 1986', when that infringed the rights of Sport Billy Productions); *BBC v BSkyB* [1992] Ch 141 (BBC unsuccessfully sued BSkyB for unauthorised re-transmission of extracts from FIFA World Cup 1990 matches on its news programmes); *BBC v Talksport*, Blackburne J, [2001] FSR 53 (BBC sought an injunction to prevent Talksport broadcasting and describing as live, 'off-tube' radio commentary of Euro 2000 football matches, where a commentator watched the BBC's live broadcast and commentated on what he saw on the screen, to an accompaniment of pre-recorded sound effects).

2 *Anglia TV v Cayton* (1989) Times, 17 February. See Abramson [1996] 4(3) SATLJ 100.

3 *Irvine v Talksport* [2002] EWHC 367 (Ch), [2002] 2 All ER 414 (action for passing off could be based on false suggestion that motor racing driver had endorsed product); *Arsenal Football Club v Reed* [2001] 2 CMLR 481 (continuing litigation in which Arsenal is seeking to restrain a trader using the 'gun' symbol on products, referred to the European Court of Justice (AG's opinion dated 13 June 2002, Case C-206/01, pending before the court; see also [2001] 9(1) SATLJ 107); *Cobra Golf v Rata* [1997] 2 All ER 150; *Victoria Park Racing v Taylor* (1937) 58 CLR 479 (rights to film sports event).

B Identification of a cause of action

A3.45 After first assessing the facts in a given situation against the background of historical review by the courts set out above, the second step[1] in deciding whether to bring proceedings in the courts is to seek to fit the facts into a cause or causes of action. Section 3 and following of this chapter set out the causes of action most commonly raised (although plainly others may be relevant in specific factual circumstances). The discussion reveals that in most instances the courts adopt a supervisory approach to the review of the decisions of sports governing bodies: they examine the way in which the decision at issue was made and the legality of the arrangements against wider public policy considerations[2]. They do not generally re-open the substantive merits of the case.

1 There may be an interim stage in which internal disciplinary proceedings or an internal dispute resolution process produce the decision to be challenged. See paras A3.49 and A3.51.
2 See paras A3.72 to A3.79.

A3.46 The identification of the cause of action in this context can usefully be approached by considering first what it is that the governing body is considered as a matter of fact to have done wrong: does that involve the specific mistreatment of an individual or business, or rather the maintenance of a wider rule which is unfair? If the action involves the specific mistreatment of an individual or business, consideration should turn to whether the action was contrary to the general obligations owed by a sports governing body[1] irrespective of any other cause of action. The general obligations relate (to varying degrees) to how a sports governing body takes a decision. In order to consider whether a decision was taken in accordance with these obligations, the claimant needs to have a copy of the rules of the governing body[2], and should ask the governing body to give its reasons for its decision. Broadly, the governing body cannot take a decision in the purported exercise of a power under its rules:

(i) which is in fact outside its powers as set out in its rules;
(ii) in a manner which is procedurally unfair or contrary to natural justice;
(iii) which is unreasonable (in the sense of irrational), perverse, arbitrary or capricious;
(iv) which is taken without any factual basis; and/or
(v) which is based on improper and/or irrelevant considerations.

As described in more detail below[3], the courts apply a varying degree of review to the different obligations: the question of whether the body has acted outside its rules is hard-edged, whereas the question of whether the action is irrational involves giving the sports governing body a degree of latitude. Importantly, these general obligations may be shown to exist, and to be enforceable by an action for a declaration, even in the absence of a contract. However, where a contract can be shown to exist, it is likely to be easier to establish the obligations contended for (as implied or sometimes express terms) and their extent may be held to be greater than they might in the absence of a contract. In addition, a right to damages only arises if there is a contract[4]. Accordingly, the next thing to do is to consider whether there is a contract between the individual or business affected and the governing body[5]. Such a contract may be contained in the rules, may be a separate written contract, or may arise orally, by conduct or even implicitly. It may impose additional obligations beyond the general obligations owed by all sports governing bodies. Where there is a specific contractual obligation, the courts will evaluate in the normal way whether the sports governing body has been in breach of it, and to this extent the exercise that they undertake is hard-edged, and may well involve more than simply reviewing the way in which the decision was taken. In some contexts it may also be appropriate to give some consideration to whether the facts reveal the commission of a tort[6].

1 See paras A3.80 to A3.113. The possibility of any cause of action under the Human Rights Act 1998 (as to which see paras A3.66 to A3.69 and Chapter A4) also falls for consideration at this point, since the Convention rights likely to be engaged in this context relate to the treatment of specific persons in a way which is not open to the governing body or which is unfair.

2 Many sports governing bodies post their rules on their internet websites. For links to some of them, see www.sportengland.org.uk or www.kelsportslaw.com/resources. However many of the smaller sports have not yet done so, and in addition in many instances what is posted on the website will not be complete, but will concentrate on the principal rules.

3 See paras A3.72 to A3.79.

4 Subject to the existence of a claim under the Human Rights Act 1998, the Competition Act 1998 or some other provision.

5 See paras A3.114 to A3.129.

6 See paras A3.130 to A3.134. In addition to tort, the specific treatment of a club has been characterised (as yet unsuccessfully) by some imaginative practitioners as amounting to the conduct of the affairs of an incorporated sports governing body in a manner which is unfairly prejudicial to the club as a minority shareholder contrary to (in England) s 459 of the Companies Act 1985, as amended by the Companies Act 1989: see para A3.208.

A3.47 Both specific mistreatment and the maintenance of a rule which is unfair may be capable of challenge on the basis of the public policy principles contained in the restraint of trade doctrine[1], the domestic and EC competition rules[2], and the EC free movement rules[3]. Although obviously the detailed constituents of the cause of action vary in each case, the trigger for the application of these principles is very broadly:

(i) does the action significantly restrict the ability of the claimant (or of a class of persons) to earn a living where, and in the way that, he or she would wish to;

(ii) if so, it is open to challenge unless the restriction has been imposed in pursuit of a legitimate aim, and the restriction is proportionate, in other words it goes no further than is necessary to achieve that aim and there is no less restrictive method available[4].

In this context too, therefore, the court does not strictly examine the merits of the underlying decision but rather how it was reached and whether it goes too far[5].

1 See paras A3.135 to A3.158. The doctrine covers decisions or actions as well as rules.

2 See paras A3.159 to A3.170 and Chapter B2.

3 See paras A3.171 to A3.175 and Chapter B3.

4 In some competition law contexts, it is possible that the second stage of the analysis is not reached.

5 See para A3.72 et seq.

C The decision to go to the courts rather than elsewhere

A3.48 Having analysed the facts and considered what causes of action are available, the third step is to consider whether the dispute arising on the facts and the law is best resolved in the courts or elsewhere[1]. The context, in other words not only the identity of the party affected, but also the nature, status and quality of the sports governing body's actions, determines the route of challenge. It is plain from the range of ways in which different individuals or businesses or groups of them can be affected that sports governing bodies' actions can be characterised in a number of ways. They may for example be quasi-legislative, administrative, quasi-judicial or commercial. Sometimes the decision as to which route of challenge to follow is forced upon the claimant; sometimes it can be freely taken.

1 Under English law (and EC law), there is no body with general jurisdiction over challenges to the actions of sports governing bodies. There are specialist arbitral tribunals, but their jurisdiction depends on the consent of the parties, to the dispute. See further Chapter A5.

(a) Internal proceedings and internal dispute resolution

A3.49 In many instances, the actions of the sports governing body at issue involve a decision taken after internal proceedings such as disciplinary proceedings or an internal dispute resolution process[1]. To this extent therefore the choice to pursue those proceedings or that process arises at an earlier stage than the identification of a cause of action. Internal proceedings arise most obviously in the context of disciplinary charges of doping or of misconduct or of other breach of the rules. There may also be internal proceedings in the context of applications under the rules for a licence or for permission to do something[2]. The internal proceedings may involve several stages, for example a first instance hearing and then an internal appeal process (or on occasion appeals to external bodies)[3]. Depending on the rules, it may be that an appeal can be made by the player or participant or by the sports governing body[4], or even by another sports governing body[5].

1 See Chapter A2.
2 An example is Wimbledon FC's ultimately successful application to move to Milton Keynes. The rules of the Football League required it to obtain the permission of the board of the Football League for the move. Permission was originally refused by the Board. FA arbitration proceedings were brought challenging the decision on procedural and substantive grounds. The decision was vacated by an FA Arbitral Panel on procedural grounds in January 2002, and the matter remitted to the Board of the League. The League decided to ask an FA Commission to take the decision in its place. In May 2002, the FA Commission decided in favour of the club and concluded that it should be allowed to move.
3 See further Chapter A5.
4 See *Korda v ITF* (1999) Times, 4 February, [1999] All ER (D) 84; revsd [1999] All ER (D) 337, CA (An independent Appeals Committee convened under the terms of the ITF Anti-Doping Programme upheld the finding of a doping offence, but found that 'exceptional circumstances' existed – namely the player's lack of knowledge of how the substance got into his body – that warranted waiver of any suspension. The ITF filed an appeal to the CAS against that decision. Lightman J granted the player a declaration that the ITF could not appeal its own decision to the CAS, but his decision was overturned by the Court of Appeal and the ITF was allowed to pursue its appeal which was eventually successful: see paras E4.318 to E4.323).
5 See for example *IAAF v UKA and Walker* where the IAAF challenged UKA's acquittal of the athlete before the then IAAF Arbitral Panel, 20 August 2000, reported at [2001] 4 ISLR 264 and see [2000] 2 ISLR 41 and paras A3.10, n 7 and A3.124.

A3.50 Equally, the rules may contemplate other disputes that can (or must) be referred to an internal dispute resolution process after an initial decision is taken by the executive. The mechanism for the internal resolution of disputes may be to refer the matter off to another executive body, or to the governing body in general meeting, or to a specially-convened commission or committee[1]. There are as many systems for internal proceedings or for internal dispute resolution as there are sports governing bodies, and these concepts overlap[2]. Each system will take into account the particular history and circumstances of the sport to which it applies. What they will usually have in common however is that the decision they make is based on the substantive merits of the dispute, as opposed to the exercise undertaken by the court which is to review the way in which the decision is taken, and the legality of the arrangements in the wider context of public policy. Generally, the basis for the applicability of the internal proceedings (whether disciplinary or otherwise) or of any internal dispute resolution system is the existence of some prior relationship between the sports governing body and the player or other affected participant. The latter are susceptible to the process, and equally they are entitled to rely upon it, because they have a contractual relationship with the sports governing body. That relationship arises either out of their membership or out of some other consensual agreement. However, the player or other affected participant may be entitled to rely on a process set out in the rules of the sports governing body even in the absence of a prior contractual relationship, based simply on the fact that the body has made a decision in the course of its administration of the sport which affects the other party, for example because the other party has been refused membership or some sort of licence[3]. More difficult is the situation where it is the governing body that seeks to claim jurisdiction without any contractual basis[4].

1 For example, the Football League's rules allow it to appoint a commission to decide an issue, or to ask the FA to appoint a commission to decide an issue. See para A3.49, n 2.

2 They may also overlap with the concept of external arbitration. See generally Chapter A5.

3 See paras A3.80 to A3.94. The general obligations owed by a governing body apply whether or not there is a contract. Another way of looking at it might be to say that a contract contractual term arises that any application will be dealt with in accordance with the rules: see para A3.125.

4 Cf *Walker v UKA and IAAF* at para A3.124. In that context it can be debatable that jurisdiction strictly exists. In practice, however, such decisions of sports governing bodies can often be put into effect because even if the sports governing body cannot control the player by direct action in the courts, it can generally control access to the sport, through the organisation of competitions and its contracts with, or influence over, others involved in the sport. Therefore, while it might be difficult for the governing body to point to a basis for relief against a player in the absence of a contract, in practice it does not need to do so, because it has other methods of enforcement of its decisions (which are of course subject to the constraints set out above).

A3.51 In most contexts, the first stage of any challenge to the approach of a sports governing body is to fight the disciplinary proceedings, and to exhaust the appeal mechanisms provided for under the rules. Thereafter the resulting decision can be challenged elsewhere if appropriate. To this extent therefore, the question of whether to pursue internal avenues really arises before the identification of the cause of action. It is generally better to pursue internal disciplinary proceedings or an internal dispute resolution process because they will involve a decision which is (or at least ought to be) on the substantive merits of the case. The governing body will be familiar with the sport. The 'prosecuting' executive of the governing body will often have to prove its case to a high standard of proof[1]. As set out above a court will in contrast merely examine the way in which the decision is taken and the legality of the arrangements in the wider context of public policy; it will not take a close look at the merits. It will often be harder to show that the governing body has strayed outside the parameters set for it than to succeed on the underlying merits. In addition, generally the courts will expect the claimant to have exhausted all internal remedies. However, in particular circumstances, the appropriate course may be to challenge the governing body's approach at an earlier stage[2], particularly (a) where the sports governing body is asserting an exorbitant jurisdiction, the validity of which the player or other participant wishes to dispute; or (b) where the process is so procedurally unfair that there is little point in bowing to it. In many instances it will be possible to take such points in front of the internal disciplinary (or dispute resolution) body involved[3]. Equally however it is in the nature of such points that they are unlikely to find favour with the sports governing body's own creature and a challenger may think that his chances on the merits are worse if he takes jurisdictional points. If internal proceedings are continued in these circumstances, care must be taken not to submit to the very jurisdiction that it might be possible to challenge, or to waive any argument about procedural unfairness[4], and in order to avoid doing this it may be necessary for the points to be taken, or at least reserved, before the internal body. Furthermore, if the internal proceedings are pursued, care must be taken by the player not to compound any injustice by his actions, which may preclude later complaint[5]. In these circumstances it may also be possible, and preferable, to bring court proceedings before the matter is dealt with internally[6].

1 See paras A2.88 and A3.104.
2 See *Enderby Football Club v FA* [1971] Ch 591 at 606, [1970] 3 WLR 1021 at 1025.
3 It may depend on the rules in question. However, as a general proposition, it ought to be possible to take points going to the jurisdiction of, or the powers followed by, the internal body. If the points are well-founded the internal body is better off curing the problem as soon as possible, rather than seeing the matter go to court.
4 *Modahl v BAF* (28 July 1997, unreported), CA per Morritt LJ at 40G–42B of the shorthand writers' transcript (waiver of ability to allege appearance of bias); *UCI v A,* CAS 97/175, award dated 15 April 1998, *Digest of CAS Awards II 1998–2000* (2002, Kluwer), pp 158, 166–67; *AEK v NBA and FIB* (7 August 2001, unreported) (R Field QC) (AEK held to have lost chance to object to lawfulness of arbitration by participating in it); *Davis v Carew-Pole* [1956] 2 All ER 524 (stable owner otherwise not governed by National Hunt Committee held to have submitted to its jurisdiction).
5 In *Bland v Sparkes* (1999) Times, 17 December, CA, it was held (at p 9 of the Lexis transcript) that Bland could not complain about the process 'when he refused to cooperate with the enquiry'. While a lack of cooperation probably will not absolve governing bodies from affording natural justice, the lack of cooperation itself may in fact be the cause of the problem.
6 *Enderby*, see n 1. The courts will not insist on futile internal proceedings being pursued. See *Stevenage Borough Football Club v Football League* (1996) 9 Admin LR 109 at 119C, CA. In *Collins v Lane* (22 June 1999, unreported), CA at p 12 of the shorthand writers' transcript, it was held that it would have been better for the claimant to have pursued his appeal but his failure to do so stemmed from the unlawfulness of the initial stages and therefore he was still entitled to relief.

(b) Attempts to oust the jurisdiction of the courts

A3.52 Sports governing bodies cannot by their rules seek to oust the jurisdiction of the courts[1]. Nevertheless in the past many tried to do so[2], and a few may still try to do so today to a greater or lesser extent. A rule stating, for example, that the sports governing body's executive will have the final decision on a particular issue is invalid as contrary to public policy to the extent that it seeks to preclude recourse to the courts to challenge that decision on legal grounds. It is not possible to dress up the clause as one requiring the consent of the executive to any action being brought in the courts: that too is void[3]. Nor generally will it be possible to escape the jurisdiction of the English courts by claiming to be an international governing body not subject to English law or jurisdiction[4].

1 Except through a valid agreement to arbitrate, see para A3.53.
2 *Baker v Jones (for British Amateur Weightlifters' Association)* [1954] 2 All ER 553 at 558. The governing body had power to act as the sole interpreter of rules and its decisions were expressed to be final. It was held that the parties could make an internal body the final arbiter on questions of fact, but could not make it the final arbiter on questions of law. The internal body could rule on such questions, but the court's jurisdiction to review matters of law could not be excluded. See also *Lee v Showman's Guild* [1952] 2 QB 329 (Denning LJ).
3 *Enderby Town Football Club v Football Association* [1971] Ch 591 at 606, [1970] 3 WLR 1021 at 1026F–H, 1028H (FA rule preventing legal proceedings without the consent of the Council was void); *St Johnstone Football Club v Scottish Football Association* 1965 SLT 171 at 175 (SFA rule requiring the consent of the SFA Council to any court action against the SFA was held to be void). Cf *Australian Football League v Carlton Football Club* [1998] 2 VR 546, where it was held that it is for the governing body and not the court to set the penalty if an offence is made out, but always subject to the residual right of the court to intervene to prevent injustice.
4 See para A3.230.

(c) External arbitration

A3.53 The one exception to the rule that the jurisdiction of the courts cannot be ousted is that parties can contractually agree to refer disputes to arbitration[1]. A valid arbitration clause agreed between the parties and covering the dispute in question will be enforced by the courts, which will at the suit of a party to the arbitration agreement almost always stay any action brought in the courts in breach of it[2]. In the sports context, governing bodies often have rules which provide for such arbitration of future disputes. The type of arbitration provided for may be specific to the sport[3], or may be arbitration before a tribunal which specialises in sports arbitration[4], or may be arbitration before one of the major commercial tribunals[5]. Reference to external arbitration generally occurs where a dispute has arisen in respect of a decision is taken by the governing body (whether by its executive or after some sort of internal proceedings) and the arbitral tribunal is substituted for the courts. In many contexts however the last appeal in internal disciplinary proceedings or in an internal dispute resolution system may take the form of reference to an external arbitration[6]. In some contexts the reference to arbitration is not necessarily by the player or participant affected, but by the international governing body in respect of a decision of the national governing body[7]. It is also open to the parties to reach an ad hoc agreement to arbitrate after the dispute has arisen. Whatever the form of the arbitration agreement, if the arbitration is to be held in England, it will be governed by the Arbitration Act 1996.

1 See Chapter A5.
2 But in the absence of suit is unlikely to take the point itself. See para A3.219; *Phoenix v FIA and FOM* [2002] EWHC 1028 (Ch); and *Walkinshaw v Diniz* [2000] 2 All ER (Comm) 237. See also *AEK v NBA and FIB* (7 August 2001, unreported) (R Field QC), leave to appeal set aside, [2002] 3 All ER 897, CA, (2002) Times, 13 June.
3 Such as the arbitration provided for under the Football Association's Rule K.
4 Such as the Court of Arbitration for Sport (CAS), based in Lausanne or the Sports Dispute Resolution Panel (SDRP), based in London. See generally Chapter A5.
5 Such as the London Court of International Arbitration, ICC or UNCITRAL arbitration.
6 See for example *Korda v ITF* (1999) Times, 4 February, [1999] All ER (D) 84 (An independent Appeals Committee convened under the terms of the ITF Anti-Doping Programme upheld the finding of a doping offence, but found that 'exceptional circumstances' existed – namely the player's lack of knowledge of how the substance got into his body – that warranted a waiver of any suspension. The ITF filed an appeal to the CAS against that decision. Lightman J granted the player a declaration that the ITF could not appeal its own decision to the CAS, but his decision was overturned by the Court of Appeal and the ITF was allowed to pursue its appeal to the CAS) (which was eventually successful as well: see paras E4.318 to E4.323).
7 See for example *IAAF v UKA and Walker* IAAF Arbitral Award dated 20 August 2000 reported at [2001] 4 ISLR 264, see also [2000] 2 ISLR 41 and n 7 to para A3.10 and para A3.124 (application of IAAF rules providing for independent arbitration of disputes between the IAAF and the national bodies which are its members, arising out of the national bodies' application of the doping rules to athletes from their country). There are many other examples of such IAAF appeals: for some of them see [2001] 4 ISLR 254 et seq (*Sotomayor*, *Ottey*, *Walker*, *Christie*, *Cadogan*).

A3.54 As set out above, if there is a valid arbitration clause binding on the player or other participant and on which the governing body intends to rely, then the freedom of the player or other participant to choose a different route is very limited. As in the context of internal dispute resolution, difficult questions may arise as to whether the player or other participant, or indeed the governing body, is in fact bound by the arbitration clause[1]. Where a contract exists, then the position is relatively straightforward. Where however there is no contract, the player or other participant might nonetheless be able to rely on an arbitration provision, but it might be more difficult for the governing body to do so[2].

1 See para A3.50. See further Chapter A5. The issue of when an arbitration agreement applies to a non-party was discussed in *Phoenix v FIA and FOM* [2002] EWHC 1028 (Ch).
2 This would be on the basis that when the player or other participant applied to the governing body for some benefit or licence, a collateral contract arose that any dispute as to the application would be determined in accordance with the rules, including the arbitration clause. In *Walker v UKA and IAAF* the athlete disputed that the IAAF could appeal his acquittal by UKA of doping charges to the IAAF Arbitral Panel, because he claimed that there was no contract between him and the IAAF and no contractual submission by him to the jurisdiction of the IAAF Arbitral Panel (unreported Toulson J 3 July 2000, Hallett J 25 July 2000, IAAF Arbitral Award 20 August 2000 reported at [2001] 4 ISLR 264, see also [2000] 2 ISLR 41 and paras A3.10, n 7 and A3.124).

A3.55 Where for whatever reason the player or other participant is able to opt for arbitration or another route, the advantages and disadvantages of arbitration in the specific context have to be weighed in order to make that choice[1]. The principal advantage of arbitration is that the process is generally more flexible than litigation before the courts, or at least more flexible than litigation before the courts in the way that such litigation has traditionally been conducted. The arbitration panel will generally include experts on the particular sport who do not need to be brought up to speed on the background but who can instead proceed directly to the nub of the dispute. The arbitration panel will answer the question referred to it. In many instances, the issues that it will resolve will be the same or at least very similar to the issues that a court would have to resolve, but the parties do have the opportunity to narrow the issues. The arbitration panel will not be constrained by the same rules of evidence and procedure, and again it is open to the parties to agree to limit disclosure and to set constraints on the way that oral evidence and argument is presented. Arbitration may in particular instances represent a cheaper and quicker solution. It is theoretically possible to keep the result of an arbitration confidential.

1 See Chapter A5.

A3.56 There are however drawbacks to arbitration. Arbitration can be less certain: the law and procedure applied by arbitration panels varies from body to body[1]. In addition, under the Arbitration Act 1996, the avenues for appeal of an arbitration decision are extremely limited[2]. Conversely the choice to proceed by way of arbitration may also mean that there is a lack of finality. For example in one case[3], the CAS duly applied EC competition law and determined that there was no breach of Arts 81 or 82 in UEFA's rule-banning ownership of more than one club in the same competition. This certainly resolved the matter under UEFA's rules, but it meant little to the European Commission (which has exclusive jurisdiction to consider applications for exemption of such rules from the application of EC Art 81(1)), which proceeded to consider the matter unconstrained by CAS's determination[4]. It is likely that greater respect would be afforded to a decision of a member state court, but subject always to the Commission's exclusivity with respect to the grant of exemptions. Arbitration panels do not have the same range of sanctions and relief on offer as do the courts. In particular they may not have power to grant the same sort of interim relief as would the courts, or at least as promptly. The problem should not be overstated: the English court can grant relief in support of arbitration proceedings under s 44 of the Arbitration Act 1996 and CAS, for example, does have power to grant interim relief[5], although only once the proceedings are commenced; furthermore, it is often open to a sports governing body to put the application of its decision on hold if a reference is made to arbitration under its rules[6]. Lastly, it may well no longer be the case that arbitration is cheaper and faster than going to court. The parties have to pay the arbitrator, whereas they do not have to pay the court. The courts have become more and more prepared to join with the parties in fashioning a streamlined and efficient approach to the resolution of a particular dispute.

1 For example, Rule 58 of the CAS Code of Sports-Related Arbitration provides: 'The Panel shall decide the dispute according to the applicable regulations and the rules of law chosen by the parties or, in the absence of such choice, according to the law of the country in which the federation, association or sports body which has issued the challenged decision is domiciled'. It is also possible to have the matter decided 'ex aequo et bono' and CAS will apply general principles of law. In relation to cases arising at the Olympic Games, the CAS will apply Swiss principles of private international law to determine the applicable law. See eg Art 7 of the Arbitration Rules of the XXIV Olympic Winter Games at Salt Lake City 2002.

2 See the Arbitration Act 1996. Cf *Angela Raguz v Rebecca Sullivan* [2000] NSWCA 290 (court held that a player could not appeal against the substance of CAS ad hoc decision in relation to which of two judokas should be selected to compete for Australia). See also Beloff [2001] 1 ISLR 105 at 109; and *VZZ v Australian Sports Drug Agency* [2001] FCA 816 (no jurisdiction for court to hear appeal against interim decision of Administrative Appeals Tribunal refusing stay of ASDA proceedings).

3 *AEK Athens and Slavia Prague v UEFA* CAS arbitration 98/200 interim decision 17 July 1998, final decision 20 August 1999, *Digest of CAS Awards II 1998–2000* (2002, Kluwer), p 35, and in [2001] 1 ISLR 122 (Club owned by ENIC failed in their challenge to the application to it of UEFA's Champions League rule prohibiting participation of clubs in common ownership with another participant). See also Broome [2000] 8(2) SATLJ 83 (domestic common ownership) and [2001] 9(1) SATLJ 88 (international common ownership).

4 Commission press release IP/99/965, 9 December 1999. The Commission eventually decided not to pursue ENIC's complaint. See Commission press release IP/02/942, 27 June 2002.

5 CAS Code of Sports-Related Arbitration, Rule 37. See eg *Haga v FIM*, 2000/A/281, award dated 22 December 2000, *Digest of CAS Awards II 1998–2000* (2002, Kluwer), pp 410, 412 (CAS analysed application for interim stay of suspension pending appeal of the decision imposing the suspension in light of likelihood of success on merits, irreparable harm if stay not granted, and balance of convenience); *AEK Athens and Slavia Prague v UEFA* CAS arbitration 98/200 interim decision 17 July 1998, final decision 20 August 1999, *Digest of CAS Awards II 1998–2000* (2002, Kluwer), p35, and in [2001] 1 ISLR 122 (CAS granted interim relief restraining UEFA from applying rule for coming season, pending hearing on merits of challenge to rule; rule subsequently upheld after hearing on merits).

6 The IAAF's attempt to suspend the athlete pending an IAAF arbitration despite his acquittal of doping charges by UKA was criticised by Hallett J during submissions in *Walker v UKA and IAAF*, 25 July 2000, because the rule allowing this to be done was introduced after the events in question. The matter was compromised during the hearing, and the IAAF decided to allow the athlete to compete pending the IAAF arbitration, but he chose not to do so (see n 7 to para A3.10 and para A3.124 for more on this case).

(d) Administrative authorities

A3.57 In particular contexts, the actions of a sports governing body will be contrary to legal rules which are administered, under English domestic legislation or under EC legislation, by specified administrative authorities. The most obvious examples are the Office of Fair Trading and the Competition Directorate of the European Commission. This jurisdiction often applies at the same time as a parallel jurisdiction in the English courts to enforce the same rules (or most of them) in private actions. An alternative to bringing costly court proceedings may therefore be to complain to the administrative authorities, which have the power and obligation to bring an end to serious infringements of the rules. While this approach may cost less, and the arguments involved may be more readily accepted by the regulatory authorities than the courts, it has drawbacks. Once a complaint is made, the matter is effectively out of the control of the complainant. Although in many cases the authorities will not press ahead with a complaint if it is withdrawn or not actively pursued by the complainant, those authorities are able to continue an investigation if appropriate and in serious cases will do so. Equally, the basis of the resolution of any breach (for example by the acceptance of undertakings) is often outside the control or even significant influence of the complainant. The process will often take longer to produce a result than court proceedings, and the complainant cannot force the pace. If the breach of the competition rules involves an agreement to which the complainant is itself a party, there is the theoretical risk that the complainant could also expose itself to sanction. The parameters of the regulatory authorities' investigation cannot be confined quite as easily as the courts: there is a risk that practices that the complainant welcomed (for example collective selling of rights) might be put at risk as well as the particular application of which it complained (for example the sale of the rights to a competitor for too long a period and without a tender process). The last drawback is the corollary of the above: a complaint to the Commission in this context may prove fruitless as a result of the application of the concept of lack of 'Community interest'. The Commission is increasingly unwilling to look at complaints or notifications which it perceives to have little impact on international sport throughout the Community. Furthermore, the Commission is attempting to devolve the responsibility for the application of the competition rules onto the member states[1].

1 See further generally Chapter B2.

(e) Alternative dispute resolution

A3.58 It may be possible in particular cases to resolve the dispute by way of alternative dispute resolution such as mediation. However a difficulty which will often arise is that ADR works on the basis of compromise rather than a finding on a cause of action. Often, sports governing bodies are not in a position to compromise, because the dispute is not of the normal bilateral sort; rather, they are acting in vindication of the interests of all participants and of the public generally in the integrity of the sport: for example if the issue is whether a doping offence has been committed[1].

1 See Chapter A5.

(f) Court

A3.59 The actions of the sports governing body will in any event be subject to general English law. The particular form of the action initiated in the English courts will be determined by the quality of the sports governing body's actions and its effects. The remainder of this chapter addresses the position when the decision is made to go to court.

2 PUBLIC OR PRIVATE?

A3.60 Sports governing bodies take a variety of forms on the spectrum between 'private' and 'public' bodies, and their decisions affect rights which range from the purely private to rights which on any basis have many of the features of a public right. The governing body has responsibility (often sole responsibility) for regulating an area of public activity. It purports to act in the public interest. It is quite possible in many instances that if the governing body did not exist, it would have to be created by government[1]. The governing body often has a particular expertise and experience in making the type of decision involved. Its decisions affect the rights of a range of individuals and businesses, often without there being a contractual relationship between them establishing the right or conferring jurisdiction on the governing body to make decisions affecting those individuals and/or businesses. Even where there is a nominal contractual relationship, arguably it is often not truly consensual or voluntary but rather a constitutional arrangement of rules, regulations and codes of conduct that is deemed to apply to all those who participate in the sport. On the other hand, most governing bodies have their origins some time ago in individuals or groups of individuals forming an unincorporated association to run a sport in which they were involved. They remain characterised by having a membership of private persons, and various committees acting in various areas. To the extent that they have modernised their structure, it has been in the direction of incorporation as private law companies[2]. Their powers are not in the real sense of the word governmental, in that they are at least nominally predicated on a specific consensual or contractual arrangement. Arguably, the rights which their actions affect are also held through the consensus of those involved in the sport. If that consensus disappears, those involved are entitled to walk away and form their own new governing body, in competition with the original. Some sports governing bodies, such as those running leagues in sports where there is a separate regulatory body, have many of the characteristics of a commercial association of commercial businesses.

1 See Chapters A1 and A4.
2 See further Chapter C1.

A3.61 This varying public element has had four consequences of significance to the bringing of a challenge in the courts. First, it has led to debate in the courts and in texts as to whether the decisions of sports governing bodies (or at least some of their decisions) are amenable to judicial review on the basis that their actions affect public rights. Secondly, it has raised the possibility of the application of the Human Rights Act 1998 to the decisions of sports governing bodies. Thirdly it has resulted in the extension to sports governing bodies of EC free movement obligations owed by the state and not by private bodies. Lastly, it has had a fundamental influence on the degree of review to which the courts are prepared to subject different types of decisions. This section looks at the first three consequences[1] and addresses the fourth in more detail[2], all in the context of a challenge to a sports governing body's actions.

1 The first and second matters are also addressed at paras A3.62 to A3.65 and A3.66 to A3.69 respectively and also in Chapter A4. The third matter is addressed in paras A3.70 to A3.71 and in Chapter B2.
2 See paras A3.72 to A3.79.

A Public or private for the purposes of the choice of procedure

(a) The present position

A3.62 On the current authorities, challenges to the actions of sports governing bodies should be brought in private law proceedings and not by way of judicial review. The courts have consistently held[1] (although the opposite view had been argued[2]) that the relationship between a governing body and its members is a private, contractual one and therefore the rights affected by the actions of sports governing bodies are not capable of protection through judicial review.

1 *Law v National Greyhound Racing Club Ltd* [1983] 1 WLR 1302 (The Court of Appeal concluded that there was a contract between the sports governing body and all trainers, which contained the parties' agreement as to when a trainer's licence could be suspended and consequently the decision to suspend such a licence was outside the scope of public law. Here it was the governing body that was attempting to argue that it was subject to judicial review); *R v Eastern Counties Rugby Union, ex p Basildon Rugby Club* (10 September 1987, unreported) (whether Basildon had been wrongly docked points and refused promotion held to be a contractual, not a public, matter); *R v Football Association of Wales, ex p Flint Town* [1991] COD 44 (The Divisional Court concluded that because Flint was a member of the FAW, it was in a contractual relationship with the FAW, and so the court could not judicially review the FAW's decision to stop Flint playing in a lower league); *R v Football Association, ex p Football League Ltd* [1993] 2 All ER 833 (Held that the FA was not susceptible to judicial review at the instance of the League, to which it was contractually bound:

Rose J's analysis was that the FA was not judicially reviewable irrespective of the existence of a contract, because it was not a public body underpinned by statute and there was nothing to suggest the government would step in if it did not exist). In *R v Jockey Club, ex p Massingberd-Mundy* [1993] 2 All ER 207; and *R v Jockey Club, ex p Aga Khan* [1993] 1 WLR 909, it was decided that the actions of the Jockey Club affecting the claimants' various rights were not subject to public law. The rationale was again that the powers of the body were derived from the consent of those governed by it and their rights were derived from the consensus establishing the body and its rules. It was no good to 'try and patch up the remedies available against domestic bodies by dressing them up as organs of the state' (per Hoffmann LJ in *Aga Khan* at 933).

2 In early cases, prior to the decision in *Law v National Greyhound Racing Club Ltd*, the position was not clear. For example in *R v British Basketball Association, ex p Mickan* (17 March 1981, unreported), CA, leave was refused without considering whether the governing body's actions were judicially reviewable. It appears that in 1991 leave was given in *R v Jockey Club Licensing Committee, ex p Wight* [1991] COD 306. After 1987, challengers sought to distinguish *Law* on the basis that the Court of Appeal in that decision had relied on *R v Criminal Injuries Compensation Panel, ex p Lain* [1967] 2 QB 864, in which it was held that private tribunals were outside the scope of the public law remedy of certiorari because the source of their power was not statutory or derived from the royal prerogative, whereas the subsequent case of *R v Panel on Take-overs and Mergers, ex p Datafin* [1987] QB 815 had determined that this 'source of power' test was no longer to be regarded as definitive; rather, other factors relating to an organisation's functions are to be considered. Lord Donaldson MR (at 838) said 'possibly the only essential elements are what can be described as a public element which can take many different forms'. On this basis it was argued that the functions of sports governing bodies may well be public. The argument did not find favour in *R v Football Association Ltd, ex p Football League Ltd* [1993] 2 All ER 833, where Rose J considered the functions of the Football Association but decided that it was a purely private body. There was no evidence that if the FA ceased to exist the state would step in to regulate its former activities. Bearing in mind the apparently close relationship between government and the governors of the national game, this proposition is perhaps surprising; but cf Chapter A1. *Law* was again followed by the Divisional Court in *Massingberd-Mundy* [1993] 2 All ER 207. Roch J considered whether any distinctions could be drawn between the National Greyhound Racing Club and the Jockey Club, such as the fact that the Jockey Club was established by royal charter, but concluded that there was insufficient to warrant a different approach to *Law* (although he appeared to leave the door open in relation to the Jockey Club if different circumstances subsisted). The high water mark for the argument came in *R v Jockey Club, ex p RAM Racecourses* [1993] 2 All ER 225, where the Divisional Court said that in the absence of the authority to the contrary (*Massingberd-Mundy*) it would have regarded the actions of the Jockey Club as governed by public law. Simon Brown J observed (at 247) that if the jurisdictional point had been decisive he would have taken a position of 'limited dissent' from the principles in the earlier cases, on the basis of *Datafin*. Applying the 'function' test, the licensing powers of the Jockey Club were akin to the exercise of a statutory licensing power. In this particular context, RAM was attempting to hold the Jockey Club to a representation made by it that it intended to introduce some 60 new fixtures. The application was dismissed on its merits. It is important to note that there was no contractual relationship between RAM and the Jockey Club, which perhaps explains why the court was so inclined towards a judicial review approach. However, this approach was rejected in *Aga Khan*.

(b) *Is there any exception?*

A3.63 As noted above, the basis for the courts' current approach lies chiefly in the fact that they have often felt able to identify a contractual relationship between a sports governing body and the relevant claimant, which has been regarded as precluding judicial review. There are two bases on which the existence of a contract precludes judicial review, and they have not been clearly distinguished in the authorities. First, it suggests that the rights affected are private law rights as opposed to public law rights. Secondly it means that there is an alternative remedy, which removes the need for a public law avenue for challenge. Although the existence of a contract is the most important factor, it is not the only one[1]. Each case must be assessed in the light of its own particular facts. It is therefore possible that a set of factual circumstances could arise where the sports governing body's decision affected rights in such a way that, even on the current state of the law, the court concluded that judicial review was available: for example if there were no contractual analysis upon which the court could fall back and a plainly injured party would be left without private law recourse. Such a set of circumstances is however unlikely to arise in the light of two factors. First, it is now tolerably clear that sports governing bodies owe broadly the same obligations as a matter of private law as they would if their decisions were susceptible to public law review[2]: certainly it is more likely that a court would hold that the obligations were the same in both contexts than that a sports governing body was susceptible to judicial review. Secondly, the *Modahl* litigation has culminated in a clear demonstration by the courts that they are prepared to find a contract between a governing body and a participant in the sport where they had in the past been unwilling to do so[3].

1 See n 2 to para A3.62; Fordham *Judicial Review* (2001, 3rd edn, Hart Publishing) at pp 545–588; Wade *Administrative Law* (2000, 8th edn, Oxford) at pp 620–635; De Smith *Judicial Review of Administrative Action* (1995, 5th edn (inc supp), Sweet & Maxwell) at pp 155–202; *R v Football Association, ex p Football League Ltd* [1993] 2 All ER 833; *R v Jockey Club, ex p RAM Racecourses* [1993] 2 All ER 225, DC. As set out above, the generally applicable test is set out in *R v City Panel on Take-overs and Mergers, ex p Datafin* [1987] QB 815.

2 See paras A3.80 and A3.91 to A3.94.

3 See paras A3.120 to A3.125.

(c) The contrary view

A3.64 It would therefore be a brave practitioner who advised an applicant to re-open this issue: short of the House of Lords, the approach of the Court of Appeal in *Aga Khan* is likely to be followed in almost all circumstances. There are however a number of judges, commentators and practitioners who have taken a contrary view to the Court of Appeal in that case, and some practitioners may indeed be brave enough to take it further[1]. In addition, it is clear that the contrary view has found favour in other jurisdictions[2], and in analogous contexts[3], and that other developments may bring about a change in approach[4].

1 The argument continues to be made in the texts and articles. See, for example, Beloff, 'Pitch Pool Rink ... Court? Judicial Review in the Sporting World' [1989] PL 95 at 104; Pannick, 'Judicial Review of Sports Governing Bodies' [1997] JR 150; Beloff and Kerr [1996] JR 30; Beloff et al *Sports Law* (1999, Hart Publishing), paras 8.9–8.28; Griffith-Jones *Law and the Business of Sport* (1997, Butterworths), pp 52–57. See also paras A4.14 to A4.31. There remains the support given to the argument by Simon Brown J in *RAM Racecourses*. (See para A3.62, n 2). Furthermore, in *Stevenage Borough Football Club v Football League* (1996) Times, 1 August , Carnwath J appears to have preferred the proposition that sports governing bodies were public bodies (see paras A3.151 to A3.155).

2 Scotland: *Re Duncan Ferguson (Ferguson v Scottish Football Association)* (1996) Outer House Cases, 1 February 1996. New Zealand: *Finnigan v New Zealand Rugby Football Union* [1985] 2 NZLR 159, 181 and 190; see also *New Zealand Trotting Conference v Ryan* [1990] 1 NZLR 143. Australia: *Forbes v New South Wales Trotting Club Ltd* (1979) 143 CLR 242; see also *Justice v South Australian Trotting Control Board* (1989) 50 FAR 613). South Africa: *Jockey Club of South Africa v Forbes* (1993) 1 SA 649. Canada: *Barrieau v US Trotting Association* (1986) 78 NBR (2d) 128, 198 APR 128.

3 Things may also change in the light of the wider test for the application of the Human Rights Act 1998, and under EC law. As discussed in paras A3.66 to A3.71 in this chapter and in Chapter A4, the same governing bodies that are supposedly not susceptible to judicial review are 'emanations of the state' for the purposes of EC law and may be 'public authorities' for the purposes of the Human Rights Act 1998. Some take the view that if sports governing bodies are held to be covered by the Act, the consequence will be that their decisions are also held to be susceptible to judicial review.

(d) Does it matter?

A3.65 As mentioned above, it is now tolerably clear that sports governing bodies owe broadly the same obligations as a matter of private law as they would if their decisions were susceptible to public law review[1]. This means that it is improbable that a claimant would be deprived of relief in private law proceedings that he or she would otherwise be able to obtain on judicial review. Such differences as do exist between private law proceedings and judicial review proceedings (in the latter case three month limitation period, discretionary relief, less likelihood of interim relief, no automatic disclosure, no automatic cross examination, non-availability of damages) would seem to make judicial review a better option for the governing body and a worse option for the claimant. To that extent the inapplicability of judicial review proceedings might well matter to the sports governing body[2].

1 See paras A3.80 and A3.91 to A3.94.
2 Cf *Stevenage Borough Football Club v The Football League* Carnwath J (1996) Times, 1 August.

B The Human Rights Act 1998

A3.66 The Human Rights Act 1998 has introduced new mechanisms for the enforcement in the English courts of the rights protected by the European Convention on Human Rights, explored in the context of sport in the next chapter[1]. In the context of a challenge to a sports governing body's actions, the Act provides, or may provide, the practitioner with two tools: a new cause of action, and a comparative argument.

1 See Chapter A4. See generally Boyes 'Regulating Sport after the Human Rights Act 1998' (2001) 151 NLJ 444; Boyes 'The regulation of sport and the impact of the Human Rights Act 1998' [2000] 6(4) EPL 517; Beloff 'Blood testing, the common law and the Human Rights Act 1998' [2000] 2 ISLR 43; Lask [2000] 2 ISLR 48; Anderson, Mulcahy and Reindorf, 'Independent and impartial? The potential impact of the Human Rights Act 1998 on sports tribunals' [2000] 4 ISLR 65; Cairns [2000] 8(3) SATLJ 60; Lloyd [2000] 8(3) SATLJ 61; Kerr [2000] 8(3) SATLJ 65; Vleck [2000] 8(3) SATLJ 71; Bitel [2000] 8(3) SATLJ 72.

(a) Possible new cause of action against a sports governing body

A3.67 Under s 6 of the Act, 'public authorities' must act in accordance with the Convention rights[1]. The intention behind the legislation is to constrain state action, not to impose obligations on private persons, or indeed on public bodies for 'private acts'. If public authorities act contrary to the Convention rights protected, in pursuit of a public function, the claimant may be entitled to an injunction and damages[2]. Sports governing bodies may in some cases fall within the definition of a public authority and their actions may be public rather than private acts[3]. If that is the case they will be directly bound to act in accordance with the Convention rights, affording a claimant a new cause of action if they fail to do so[4].

1 See paras A4.14 to A4.31.
2 The difficulty in obtaining damages in the absence of a contract means that such relief for a breach of the Act may well be pursued by claimants. Diane Modahl is reported to have considered such an attack following the failure of her damages action based in contract.
3 See paras A4.14 to A4.31 as to the test to be applied and whether it is likely to be met by sports governing bodies. UK Sport's guidance to sports governing bodies presumes the applicability of the Act in some instances. Notably, the then Home Secretary Jack Straw specifically informed Parliament (*Hansard* (20 May 1998), col 1018) that the Jockey Club would be a public authority for the purposes of the Act in respect of the public functions that it exercises. As a consequence the

Jockey Club set about putting its house in order and in February 2001 ([2001] 9(1) SATLJ 2, (2001) Daily Telegraph, 20 February, p 43) announced that its processes complied with the rights protected by the Act. On the other hand, in the light of the *Aga Khan* authority that sports governing bodies are private bodies not susceptible to judicial review (n 1 to para A3.62), the starting point is arguably that sports governing bodies are not caught, and it remains in doubt whether the courts will feel the need to extend the obligations in the Convention to sports governing bodies.

4 Whatever the strength of this cause of action in any given case, it is likely that the uncertainty in this context, and the perceived value in the making of an awkward argument, will give rise to litigation.

(b) As a comparative argument

A3.68 The courts must interpret legislation so far as possible in accordance with the Convention rights, taking into account the decisions of the European Court of Human Rights[1]. Furthermore, when the courts come to review decisions of sports governing bodies, they will have in mind their own obligations as public authorities to respect the rights of the parties, in particular the right to a fair trial protected under Art 6[2], and they will also have in mind the standards that would be required from a public authority in an analogous situation. It is possible that even if a sports governing body is not a public authority for these purposes, these factors may affect the basis on which its decisions are assessed by the courts. Claimants can seek to rely on the position under the Convention in order to inform the debate about the extent of common law protection.

1 See para A4.11.
2 See para A4.36.

(c) The content of the rights

A3.69 The possibility of relying upon the Convention and the Act in the ways set out above[1] is only useful to the extent that the substantive rights protected under the Convention and engaged on the facts afford a greater degree of protection than already exists under the common law or other provisions[2]. The various rights which may be engaged in the sports context, and the extent to which they provide something new, are discussed in detail in the next chapter[3]. It appears likely that the most important rights will be the right to a fair trial under Art 6[4], the right to privacy under Art 8[5], the right to property under Art 1 of the First Protocol[6], and (in combination with another right) the right not to be discriminated against under Art 14. In individual circumstances other rights may be engaged[7].

1 Or at least in the second way set out above: the possibility of the new cause of action as set out above may on occasion be useful even where the substantive rights under the Convention and at common law are similar, if the common law does not afford relief such as damages.

2 The Act implements the European Convention on Human Rights. The rights involved have therefore already been enjoyed by individuals and businesses in the UK for some 50 years. What has changed is the mechanisms available for their enforcement. In many contexts (although not in all), there is little difference between the protection available under the English common law and other provisions and the protection available under the Convention. Most importantly, most of the Convention rights will not be infringed by a proportionate restriction which pursues a legitimate aim. It is arguable that this same test applies to the doctrine of restraint of trade, to breach of the competition rules, and in some contexts at least to the reasonableness standard.

3 See Chapter A4.

4 Article 6 protects due process in the determination of civil rights and obligations: everyone is entitled to a fair and public hearing within a reasonable time by an independent and impartial tribunal. If sports governing bodies' actions are regarded as something more than 'private acts', their internal disciplinary proceedings could be held to be caught. This would mean that challenges

could be made to the validity of decisions taken after such proceedings on the basis (for example) that the disciplinary body was not impartial or independent, or that it took too long to resolve a particular matter. See further paras A4.36 to A4.56.

5 In the context, for example, of dope testing.

6 In the context, for example, of rules depriving clubs of the ability to sell commercial rights other than collectively, or depriving clubs of a place in a higher division.

7 It has been reported that Roy Keane has considered reliance on the protection of freedom of speech as precluding the FA from proceeding against him in respect of his admission in his autobiography of deliberately setting out to injure Alf-Inge Haaland in revenge for a perceived sleight three years previously. See para A4.65.

C The extension to sports governing bodies of EU law free movement obligations owed by the state and not by private bodies

A3.70 Many EU law obligations, such as the free movement rules[1], are ostensibly owed only by member states and their emanations, and not by private bodies. It now appears however that the majority of sports governing bodies will generally be regarded as fulfilling a role which subjects them to at least the free movement rules[2] (as well as the competition rules) and an action can be brought in the English courts on this basis[3].

1 Discussed in paras A3.171 to A3.175 and Chapter B2. The competition rules (discussed in paras A3.159 to A3.170, and Chapter B2) do not fall into the category of rules applicable only against the state because they apply between private parties. Sports governing bodies are subject to the competition rules.

2 On the basis that their rules are aimed at collectively regulating employment and the provision of services in a particular sector. See *Union Royal Belge des Sociétés de Football Association v Bosman* [1995] ECR I-4921, paras 69–87 (Free movement rules held to apply to national football associations, and their transfer systems were struck down as an unjustifiable restriction on freedom of movement); *Walrave and Koch v Association Union Cycliste Internationale* [1974] ECR 1405, paras 12–25 (Governing body held subject to the free movement rules, but its provision limiting the composition of national teams to citizens of the nation in question was not a restriction on free movement); *Donà v Mantero* [1976] ECR 1333 at 1341 (Governing body again caught, but rule confining place in a national team to nationals upheld); *Lehtonen v Fédération Royale Belge des Société de Basketball* [2000] ECR I–2681 (Governing body subject to the free movement rules, but transfer windows held capable of justification); *Deliège v Ligue Francophone de Judo* [2000] ECR I-2549 (Governing body subject to free movement rules but selection criteria for national representation not a restriction on free movement); *Lilia Malaja v Fédération Française de Basketball* Case No VC 99 NC 00282, Administrative Court of Appeal, Nancy. See further Chapter B3. Note another case in relation to the football transfer system which proceeded solely on the basis of the competition rules: *Tibor Balog v Royal Charleroi* C–264/98, Advocate General's opinion of 29 March 2001. The case subsequently settled but the Advocate General concluded that the post *Bosman* transfer system was contrary to the competition rules to the extent that it allowed a club in the EU/EEA to insist on a transfer fee to sell a non-EU out of contract player whether it be to a club in the EU or EEA or in a third country.

3 See *Wilander and Novacek v Tobin and Jude*, unreported Lightman J 19 March 1996, unreported CA 8 April 1996, Lightman J [1997] 1 Lloyd's Law Rep 195; revsd [1997] 2 Lloyd's Law Rep 296, CA (where in the event permission to amend to add the competition and free movement arguments was denied because on the facts a restraint of trade argument, which raised similar questions of proportionality, had already been struck out); *Edwards v British Athletics Federation and the International Amateur Athletics Federation* [1998] 2 CMLR 363, [1997] Eu LR 721 (BAF and the IAAF obliged to respect the free movement rules). Cf *Williams and Cardiff RFC v Pugh,* later known as *Williams and Cardiff RFC v WRU (IRB intervening)*, interim injunction hearings, unreported Popplewell J, 23 July 1997 and unreported CA, 1 August 1997; application for a stay hearings, unreported Buckley J, 17 March 1998; Eady J, 29 July 1998 [1999] Eu LR 195 (WRU rule requiring a minimum number of players at a club to be eligible for Wales challenged on free movement grounds, but issue not resolved because proceedings were stayed).

A3.71 The inconsistency between the courts' approach to the availability of judicial review and the applicability of the free movement rules raises a theoretical problem for the practitioner, since a free movement argument would normally be run as an illegality point in judicial review proceedings. In practice, however, the argument can be run in private proceedings[1] and in view of the courts' reluctance to see form triumph over substance, it is unlikely that any procedural point would succeed.

1 As in *Wilander*, *Edwards*, and *Williams and Cardiff v WRU*, n 3 to para A3.70. Equally the point can be taken in response to an argument that a foreign law precludes compliance with a contractual obligation (see *Bacardi v Newcastle* [2001] Eu LR 45 (26 July 2000) (Gray J) in which Bacardi sued Newcastle for failing to show advertisements at a match against a French club, Newcastle defended on the basis that the match was to be broadcast on French television and therefore the French Loi Evin precluded the adverts being shown, and Bacardi responded by challenging the validity of the Loi Evin under the free movement rules).

D The varying degree of review

(a) Judicial reluctance to intervene

A3.72 In many instances, the expertise and experience of a particular sports governing body makes it best placed to decide how to regulate its own sport and to decide issues arising in the course of its administration of the sport. In addition, many of the decisions taken have a quasi-public or regulatory element to them. In these circumstances, just as a court in public law proceedings will not substitute its view for that of the public body, so too English judges will be reluctant to intervene in the regulatory decisions of sports governing bodies[1]. This principle affords the practitioner representing a sports governing body a useful tool[2], and poses a problem for those representing the player or club challenging the actions of the governing body.

1 At its most marked in *McInnes v Onslow-Fane* [1978] 1 WLR 1520 at 1535F–H; and *Cowley v Heatley* (1986) Times, 24 July (Browne-Wilkinson V-C) ('Sport would be better served if there was not running litigation at repeated intervals by people seeking to challenge the decisions of the regulating bodies'). See also *Wilander v Tobin* [1997] 2 Lloyd's Rep 296 at 301, col 2 per Lord Woolf MR (the court's supervisory role must not be used to make sports governing bodies' non-technical internal disciplinary processes inoperable); *Calvin v Carr* [1980] AC 574 at 597 per Lord Wilberforce; *R v Jockey Club, ex p Aga Khan* [1993] 1 WLR 909 at 930B; *R v Jockey Club, ex p Massingberd-Mundy* [1993] 2 All ER 207 at 220e per Lloyd LJ; *Modahl v BAF* (28 June 1996, unreported) (Popplewell J) at pp 13.3–14.8 of the shorthand writers' transcript and unreported CA 28 July 1997 per Lord Woolf MR at pp 23F–24G of the shorthand writers' transcript; *Stevenage Borough Football Club v Football League Ltd* unreported Carnwath J (1996) Times, 1 August at pp 20, 25 and 26 of the New Law Online transcript and in the Court of Appeal at (1997) 9 Admin LR 109 at p 116; *Gasser v Stinson* (15 June 1988, unreported) (Scott J) at p 40 of the shorthand writers' transcript; *Robert C Allan v Scottish Auto Cycle Union* (1985) Outer House Cases 32 at p 3 of the Lexis transcript; *Currie v Barton* (26 March 1987, unreported) (Scott J), (1988) Times, 12 February, CA per Scott J at p 9 of the Lexis transcript; *Wright v Jockey Club* Sir Haydn Tudor Evans, (1995) Times, 16 June; *Sheehy v Judo Federation of Australia*, unreported Supreme Court of New South Wales, 1 December 1995; *Australian Football League v Carlton Football Club* [1998] 2 VR 546; *Loe v NZRFU* unreported Gallen J New Zealand High Court 10 August 1993 at pp 5 and 14 of the transcript; *Johnson v Athletics Canada and IAAF* (1997) 41 OTC 95 at paras 33–34.

2 Which most cannot resist using, even when the facts do not entirely justify it.

(b) The contexts in which the principle has been applied

A3.73 The origin of this principle of judicial restraint lay not so much in the public law analogy as in the belief that, save in cases of clear breach of obligations (or rank injustice), an association governing an essentially non-commercial activity should be allowed to get on with it without being subjected to time-consuming and costly complaints to the courts about what it was doing. However, with the development of the proposition that sports governing bodies are bound by general obligations of fairness and reasonableness, the principle developed into the expression of the constraint on the extent to which those general obligations can be invoked. Thus, the English courts have been slow to intervene in the governing body's formulation of its rules[1], in its exercise of its discretion as to the grant of licences under the rules[2], in the decisions that it makes as to national representation[3], and in its application of its rules, for example as to doping or access to the sport[4]. The principle extends beyond reluctance to near certain refusal to intervene in the context of challenges to the on-field decisions of referees or umpires applying the 'laws of the game'[5].

1 *Gasser v Stinson* (15 June 1988, unreported) (Scott J) at p 40 of the shorthand writers' transcript.

2 *McInnes v Onslow-Fane* [1978] 1 WLR 1520 at 1535F–H.

3 *Cowley v Heatley* (1986) Times, 24 July 1986 (Browne-Wilkinson V-C). See also para A3.98, n 2.

4 *Modahl v BAF* (28 July 1997, unreported), CA per Lord Woolf MR at pp 23GF–24G of the shorthand writers' transcript; *Wilander v Tobin* [1997] 2 Lloyd's Rep 296 at 301, col 2 per Lord Woolf MR (the court's supervisory role must not be used to make sports governing bodies' non-technical internal disciplinary processes inoperable); *Calvin v Carr* [1980] AC 574 (Procedural defects in a stewards enquiry could be cured by the appeal committee of the Australian Jockey Club); *Enderby Town Football Club v Football Association* [1971] Ch 591, [1971] 1 All ER 215 (court not prepared to hold that *any* party involved in disciplinary proceedings is entitled to legal representation); *R v Jockey Club, ex p Aga Khan* [1993] 1 WLR 909 at 930B; *R v Jockey Club, ex p Massingberd-Mundy* [1993] 2 All ER 207 at 220e per Lloyd LJ; *Wright v Jockey Club* Sir Haydn Tudor Evans 15 May 1995, (1995) Times, 16 June; *Stevenage Borough Football Club v Football League Ltd* (1996) Times, 1 August, 9 Admin LR 109, CA at pp 20, 25 and 26 of the New Law Online transcript; *Sheehy v Judo Federation of Australia* unreported Supreme Court of New South Wales, 1 December 1995.

5 Such decisions are a fortiori examples of where the court is worse placed than the decision maker to reach a conclusion. Furthermore it is integral to the authority of the referee or umpire, to certainty of results and to fairness to players, that the courts and arbitral bodies (and indeed the sports governing body itself) should not intervene in this context. See *Mendy v IABA* CAS (1996) Atlanta Arbitration 006, *Digest of CAS Awards 1986–1998* (1998 Berne), p 413 (CAS does have jurisdiction to examine the application of the laws of the game if they are against the law or arbitrary, but will not review the application of purely technical sporting decisions. In that case a boxer sought to use video evidence to challenge the official's decision that he had hit his opponent below the belt), discussed in Beloff 'CAS at the Olympics' [1996] 4(3) SATLJ 5; *Machin v Football Association* unreported CA 1983, referred to in Grayson *Sport and the Law* (3rd edn, 2000, Butterworths), p 409 (football referee's decision immune from review); *Birmingham City v Football League* Daily Mail 18 May 2001 (Birmingham City failed to convince the Football League to disturb the referee's decision that the penalty shoot-out (to decide the play off for promotion) should take place at the Preston fans end, and to alter the result of the match. Birmingham abandoned any hope of review in the courts). It is extremely unlikely that a court would intervene to disallow a goal or to displace any other technical sporting decision. That said, the courts may increasingly have to review the decisions of governing bodies which have under their rules sought to take disciplinary action notwithstanding the decision, or absence of action, of a referee. The Football Association rules contemplate the use of video evidence to discipline players, but the FA has stated that such evidence will only be used in contexts where the referee did not see the incident in question, and that the punishment to be meted out should be the equivalent of what would have followed if the referee had seen the incident. See also the other cases discussed at para A3.16; *Segura v IAAF* CAS Sydney 00/013, *Digest of CAS Awards II 1998–2000* (2002, Kluwer), p 680; *Neykova v FISA and IOC* CAS Sydney 00/012, *Digest of CAS Awards 1998–2000* (2002, Kluwer), p 674; *FFF* [2001] 28 Le Dalloz, p 2241; Beloff [2002] 2 ISLR 13.

(c) Limitations on the principle

A3.74 Even where it applies, however, this principle does not today mean that an English court will never interfere, but rather that it will apply the quasi-public test in the context of its consideration of implied terms or general obligations of fairness and reasonableness. In other words, the principle of self-regulation is given its rein, but the courts will still exercise a supervisory jurisdiction over the activities of the governing body, and will intervene if the governing body steps outside the boundaries set for it by the quasi-public law test[1]. The governing body will be afforded a margin of appreciation, or latitude, in its decision-making but will still be held to account if it goes too far. As that quasi-public law test becomes more intrusive (as a result of developments in public law), so too the level of judicial reluctance to intervene should decline. Further, the extent of the margin of appreciation, or latitude, will vary from context to context: it will be at its widest where rules confer a discretion on the governing body, where they may be a range of permissible alternatives open to the governing body, whereas where an obligation under the rules is to be interpreted, there may often be only one correct answer. The courts will intervene on a point of law, applying a 'hard edged' test. This supervisory roles of the courts cannot be excluded, however: the rules cannot for example require the sports governing body's consent to any litigation[2]. Further, while the principle applies at the interim stage, the court is then only attempting to ascertain whether an arguable case exists and this may therefore mitigate the effect of the principle[3].

1 But note that the court still retains a discretion whether to grant relief, even where for example it has determined that there has been a breach of natural justice. See the debate in *Stinnato v Auckland Boxing Association* [1978] 1 NZLR 1 at 28 and 12 (where the majority refused relief even though the boxer had been afforded no opportunity to be heard on his application for a licence). See also *Loe v NZRFU* unreported Gallen J, New Zealand High Court 10 August 1993.

2 See *St Johnstone Football Club v Scottish Football Association* 1965 SLT 171 at 175.

3 See *Williams and Cardiff RFC v Pugh* (23 July 1997, unreported) (Popplewell J) at p 5 et seq of the shorthand writers' transcript.

A3.75 The principle does not (or ought not to) extend to the situation where the decision of the governing body is taken in the context of purely private law actions, such as the grant of contractual rights to a commercial partner[1] or a personal injury claim[2]. It should be confined to situations where the decisions of the sports governing body are made pursuant to its regulatory role. Just as an English court will not express reluctance to intervene in the private law activities of a public body, so too it should be prepared to intervene in the non-regulatory actions of a sports governing body. In that context, the courts have an original jurisdiction, as opposed to a supervisory one, and the normal mechanisms will apply.

1 Just as the normal private law rules apply normally when a public body is caught by them: *R v Lord Chancellor, ex p Hibbit and Saunders* ('the shorthandwriters' case') unreported DC, (1993) Times, 12 March.

2 This is evident from *Watson v BBBC*, Ian Kennedy J, (1999) 143 Sol Jo LB 235, (1999) Times, 12 October, [2001] QB 1134, CA, 19 December 2000, where a duty of care was imposed on the governing body to ensure adequate medical assistance at the ringside. In this context, the law of tort may impose its own constraints on the existence of a duty of care however. See Chapter E5.

A3.76 Further, the increased commercialisation of sport has removed one of the underpinnings of judicial reluctance to intervene. As Ebsworth J has put it[1]:

> There are likely to be many people who take the view that the processes of the law have no place in sport and the bodies which run sport should be able to conduct their affairs as they see fit and that by and large they have done so successfully over the years. It is a tempting and attractive view in many ways, particularly to those (and I almost said those of us) who grew up on windy and often half deserted touchlines. However, sport today is

big business. Many people earn their living from it in one way or another. It would, I fear, be naïve to pretend that the modern world of sport can be conducted as it used to be not very many years ago.

It is no longer appropriate to base judicial reluctance to intervene on anything other than the margin of appreciation, or latitude, that should be afforded to a specialist body making a decision within the boundaries of the regulatory function entrusted to it.

1 *Jones v WRU* (1997) Times, 6 March (Ebsworth J). See also *Tyrrell Racing Organisation v RAC Motor Sports Association and the Fédération Internationale de l'Automobile* (20 July 1984, unreported) (Hirst J), where the court took into account that the governing body regulated the claimant's ability to compete in 'a highly remunerative business' in holding that it was arguable that there had been a breach of natural justice in the application of disciplinary proceedings and granting an interim injunction to allow the claimant to compete in the coming grand prix. The court was not impressed by the governing body's submission that the parties had agreed that the governing body should be 'masters of their own procedure in their own hearings'.

(d) Does the principle apply in the context of restraint of trade?

A3.77 An open issue, dealt with below[1], is whether the restraint exhibited by the courts in applying to sports governing bodies contractual and general obligations of fairness and reasonableness is or should be extended by the courts into their application of the private law restraint of trade doctrine. Carnwath J has advanced an argument obiter[2] that it should, and that the courts should apply the public law test when considering the justifiability or reasonableness of a restraint, reversing the burden of proof and elevating the standard to be satisfied by a challenger. On the other hand, the test that has been applied by the courts has in the past been the normal test under the doctrine, and there are a number of arguments (discussed below) why this should continue to be the case.

1 See paras A3.140 and A3.143 to A3.158.
2 *Stevenage Borough Football Club v Football League Ltd*, Carnwath J, (1996) Times 1 August, 9 Admin LR 109, CA.

(e) Should specialist arbitral bodies be so reluctant?

A3.78 Arbitral bodies will prima facie apply the same reluctance to intervene as an English court[1]. The principle is however tempered in the context of arbitrations. The applicable rules[2], or the agreement of the parties[3], may confer an original jurisdiction on the arbitral body to review the merits of the case without restraint. It has been held by CAS that the principle of judicial restraint does not apply with quite the same force where a specialist arbitral tribunal is established under the rules of the governing body[4]:

'7. I am conscious of the caution held out to me by Counsel for the ACF that I should be careful not to readily trespass into the selection process of a professional cycling organisation which processes clearly embrace a wealth of experience and expertise that I cannot hope to share. Counsel referred me to two decisions of the Courts during the course of which the learned judges had expressed such caveats (*Sheehy v Judo Federation of Australia Inc* … and *McInnes v Onslow-Fane* …).

8. Those judgments convey the caution which Courts of law traditionally exercise in interfering with the decisions of domestic bodies. The former judgment also reminds me that decisions made by a domestic body are made, prima facie, in the interests of the body as a whole and not in the interests of any particular individual.

9. I agree with the sentiments so expressed, but there must necessarily be a rider placed upon them in the context of this arbitration. The CAS is not a court of law. It is an arbitral body set up to entertain disputes referred to it (inter alia) by agreement of the parties. It must necessarily, therefore, enter into the procedural affairs of the relevant domestic body if the agreement between the parties requires it to do so. In this case the parties have executed an 'appeal agreement' in which they agree to refer to the exclusive jurisdiction of the CAS any dispute regarding (inter alia) "the nomination of an athlete by the ACF to be a member of the 1996 Olympic Team".

10. By their agreement the parties thus want the selection decision scrutinised by this Tribunal, not in the sense that this Tribunal should set aside the decision simply because it thinks a better one could have been made; but rather to determine whether the decision was arrived at fairly and with due and proper regard, if any was owed, to the interests of the appellant in the peculiar circumstances which existed. Even courts of law will interfere with decisions of domestic bodies made contrary to these principles and will do so by use of injunctive process if necessary (see for example *Sheehy's* case).'

The arbitrators went on to overturn the selection decision.

1 See for example in the context of CAS, *Mendy v IABA* CAS (1996) Atlanta Arbitration 006, *Digest of CAS Awards 1986–1998* (1998 Berne), p 413 (CAS does have jurisdiction to examine the application of the laws of the game if they are against the law or arbitrary, but will not review the application of purely technical sporting decisions), discussed in Beloff 'CAS at the Olympics' [1996] 4(3) SATLJ 5. See also *FIN v FINA*, CAS 96/157, *Digest of CAS Awards 1986–1998* (1998 Berne), p 351.

2 The questions to be answered by arbitral tribunals to which disputes are referred will often be specifically defined in the rules. Thus in *IAAF v UKA and Walker*, reported at [2001] 4 ISLR 264, the question for the IAAF's independent arbitral panel was wide: whether the UKA's disciplinary body 'had misdirected itself' or 'reached an erroneous conclusion' (see n 7 to para A3.10 and para A3.124 for more on this case). In other contexts it may be narrower.

3 The CAS rules allow the parties to agree a full review on the merits. In addition, it claims for itself on appeals 'full power to review the facts and the law', which power it has exercised often to conduct de novo reviews. See CAS Code of Sports-Related Arbitration, Rule 57.

4 *Watt v Australian Cycling Federation* CAS 96/153, *Digest 1986–1998*, at p 340, paras 7–10.

(f) Reluctance to intervene under EU law

A3.79 Under EU law, sport is only subject to the free movement and competition law rules to the extent that it involves an economic activity[1]. A distinction is thus drawn between rules or actions of a sporting nature (which are not susceptible to review under either the free movement or the competition rules) and economic rules or actions (which are). The Commission has recognised the difficulties of drawing this distinction and has identified three classes: the obviously sporting, the obviously commercial, and (in between) rules and actions the objects and effect of which it will assess in their context, and which must if they are to survive be a proportionate response to a legitimate concern[2].

1 See Chapters B2 and B3; n 2 to para A3.160, n 3 to para A3.163 and n 1 to para A3.172; *Walrave and Koch v Union Cycliste Internationale* [1974] ECR 1405, para 4 (Rule requiring support riders to come from the same country upheld as a rule of sporting nature purely); *Donà v Mantero* [1976] ECR 1333 at 1340 (Rule confining place in a national team to nationals upheld as a rule of purely sporting nature); *Union Royale Belge v Bosman* [1995] ECR I-4921 at paras 69–87 (transfer rules outside the sporting exception and court will strike them down to the extent that they are incompatible with the free movement rules); *Jyri Lehtonen v Fédération Royal Belge des Sociétés de Basketball* [2000] ECR I–2681 (Transfer window subject to review but in the event not contrary to free movement rules); *Christine Deliège v Ligue Belge de Judo ASBL* [2000] ECR I–2549 (Confining participation in international event to those selected by national federations not contrary to the free movement rules as a rule of purely sporting nature); *AEK Athens and Slavia Prague v UEFA* CAS arbitration 98/200 interim decision 17 July 1998, final decision 20 August 1999, *Digest of CAS Awards II 1998–2000* (2002, Kluwer), p 36 and [2001] 1 ISLR 122 (Club failed in its

challenge to the application to it of UEFA's Champions League rule prohibiting participation of clubs in common ownership with another participant as justified on the facts). See also Broome [2000] 8(2) SATLJ 83 (domestic common ownership) and [2001] 9(1) SATLJ 88 (international common ownership). The principle has been applied in the English courts: see *Edwards v BAF and the IAAF* [1998] 2 CMLR 363, [1997] Eu LR 721 at 725D–726H (Lightman J held that a rule prohibiting athletes from taking drugs was a rule of a purely sporting nature and did not cease to be so simply because it had economic consequences). Previously, in *Wilander v Tobin* [1997] 2 Lloyd's Law Rep 296, CA Lord Woolf MR was not prepared to accept, at least for the purposes of a strike out application, that a rule suspending tennis players who had tested positively for drugs fell within the ambit of rules of a purely sporting nature.

2 See the European Commission's Draft Preliminary Guidelines on the Application of the Competition Rules to the Sports Sector, unpublished memorandum dated 15 February 1999. The European Commission (and for that matter the OFT) will not investigate the actions of a sports governing body which are related to the underlying sporting activity itself. Rules which are inherent in the sport or necessary for its organisation, and their application, will not be examined. The clearest example of such rules are the rules of the game itself (for example the offside rule or rules about the safety requirements on racing cars). But the principle extends to rules which relate to how sport is organised, such as the rule that representative teams from one country can only field players from that country, or the rule that a club must play in a particular country (*Excelsior Mouscron,* Commission press release IP/99/965, dated 9 December 1999) or rules which define the number of club teams from each country that can participate in an international club competition, or rules on how individuals are selected for representative sides. Furthermore, rules which are necessary, and go no further than is necessary, to ensure uncertainty of results may well escape review. This class is plainly difficult to define. It extends to rules on redistribution of monies coming into the sport, the rules on multi-ownership and even to the basic transfer rules (although not to elements in the transfer rules that go further than is necessary). See further Beloff 'The sporting exception in EC Competition Law' [1999] European Current Law XVI.

3 THE GENERAL OBLIGATIONS OWED BY A SPORTS GOVERNING BODY

A The extent of and basis for the general obligations

(a) Two straightforward propositions

A3.80 There are two straightforward propositions which it ought to be possible to advance in the light of the development of the law in this area over recent years. However it is not yet certain that the propositions are correct or that the previously much less clear-cut state of affairs has been superseded. The first proposition is that although sports governing bodies are not public bodies for the purposes of judicial review, they owe the same general obligations as are owed by public bodies, ie to act lawfully, fairly (in accordance with natural justice) and reasonably (in the sense of rationally and not arbitrarily or capriciously) in all their decision-making pursuant to the regulatory functions contained in their rules[1]. The second proposition is that the content of these general obligations is the same where there is a contract between the sports governing body and the claimant (in which case they are implicit in that contract and enforceable by an action for breach[2]) and where no other legal relationship exists between the sports governing body and the claimant (in which case they are enforceable by an action for a declaration[3]).

1 The range of regulatory functions under the rules to which the general obligations apply may be very wide and will vary from sport to sport. The general obligations will apply in particular to decisions on access to the sport or particular levels of competition, on applications by players or clubs to do something specific such as to move home ground, and on the disciplining of players or clubs. Ostensibly they will not apply to actions which can be characterised as purely commercial, such as a decision as to which commercial partner should be awarded a particular contract. It is not the case that, without more, contractual negotiations have to be pursued by reference to the

principles of natural justice. Care should however be taken, because in some circumstances quite similar obligations may arise, for example under the competition rules: see paras A3.33 to A3.41 and A3.114, A3.115. Nor will the general obligations apply to bodies which are not really governing bodies, but rather associations representing a single interest within the sport: see *Towcester Racecourse v The Racecourse Association Ltd* [2002] EWHC 2141 (Ch), (17 October 2002, unreported) (Patten J).

2 With all the consequent remedies: see paras A3.176 to A3.206.

3 And only a declaration (and possibly an injunction). Damages are not available for breach of the general obligations, absent a contract (and possibly under the HRA 1998). See *Modahl v BAF* (28 June 1996, unreported) (Popplewell J), CA 28 July 1997, HL 22 July 1998, Douglas Brown J 14 December 2000 and [2002] 1 WLR 1192, CA and paras A3.176 to A3.206.

A3.81 The law on the general obligations owed by private law sports governing bodies has seen a steady development over time. The courts have required sports governing bodies to act fairly, lawfully and reasonably (in the sense of rationally), but in some contexts have in the past set relatively restrictive criteria as to when these obligations arise and as to their extent. Under those criteria, not all sports governing bodies are caught in all contexts, and the content of the obligations is not necessarily the same as in the case of a public body. These authorities remain good law and still provide useful arguments for those seeking to limit the applicability or the extent of the obligations owed by a particular sports governing body to a particular claimant in a specific context. In many contexts a claimant will be able to satisfy the criteria in any event, but in cases where this is not possible, it may be necessary to establish that a problematic criterion no longer applies by virtue of developments in the law. The analysis below examines the ways in which the historically-applied criteria are restrictive, and whether the law can be said to have moved on.

(b) The need for there to be monopoly power and an effect on the claimant's ability to earn a living

A3.82 The first restriction relates to the basis for and circumstances in which the general obligations arise for a private law sports governing body to act lawfully, fairly and reasonably (in the sense of rationally). The courts have held that, at least in the absence of a contract, the basis for such obligations is the existence of monopoly power in the hands of the governing body which has an effect on the ability of the claimant to earn a living. If a claimant cannot establish that the governing body in question falls into that category and that its decision has that consequence, the general obligations do not arise. The starting point for the modern law is the Court of Appeal's decision in *Nagle v Feilden*[1]. In that case the Jockey Club refused to issue a trainer's licence to Florence Nagle because she was woman. On the Jockey Club's application to strike out her challenge to its decision, the Court of Appeal held that although there was no contractual relationship between the parties, an arbitrary or capricious decision or one taken by the Jockey Club in a procedurally unfair manner would be subject to review in an action for a declaration[2]. The Court of Appeal took the view that the refusal to issue a licence to a trainer just because she was a woman was indeed arbitrary and capricious. The basis for the obligations on the Jockey Club was that:

> When … authorities exercise a predominant power over the exercise of a trade or profession, the Courts may have jurisdiction to see that it is not abused[3].

On the basis of this authority alone, a claimant would have to show (absent a contract) that the governing body controlled the sport completely and that its decision prevented the claimant earning a living. The general obligations would not apply where for example the claimant was an amateur, or where the sports governing body did not hold monopoly power. The courts have however relaxed this criterion to the extent that it is probably sufficient to show significant control over a significant part of a sport rather than monopoly power[4], and a significant impact on the claimant rather than a complete prevention from earning a living[5]. However (subject to recent developments discussed below) where there is no contract and no impact at all on the claimant's ability to earn a living, the general obligations arguably would not arise[6]: it would arguably not be enough that the claimant is affected in an important aspect of his life[7], or disapproves of a governing body's action on grounds that it does not advance the interests of the sport generally[8].

1 [1966] 2 QB 633.

2 Per Lord Denning MR at 645 and 646 to 647.

3 Per Lord Denning at 647. See also at 646, and per Danckwerts LJ at 650 and per Salmon LJ at 654–655. See also Scott J's description in *Watson v Prager* [1991] 1 WLR 726 at 746–747 of the basis for the decision in *Nagle v Feilden* and Carnwath J's description in *Stevenage Borough Football Club v Football League* (1996) Times, 1 August at p 18 of the New Law Online transcript. In *Stininato v Auckland Boxing Association* [1978] 1 NZLR 1, intervention was put firmly on the basis of restraint of trade through the exercise of monopoly power.

4 *Fisher v National Greyhound Racing Club* (31 July 1985, unreported), CA per Oliver LJ at p 6 of the Lexis transcript; *Pett v Greyhound Racing Association* [1969] 1 QB 125 per Lord Denning MR at 128 where he noted that the governing body did not have monopoly power but exercised important control over a large part of the industry. But it is not enough if the body is just an association representing a single interest: see *Towcester* (para A3.80, n 1).

5 *Fisher v National Greyhound Racing Club* (31 July 1985, unreported) per Oliver LJ at p 6 of the Lexis transcript (the fact that the claimant greyhound-owner had only one dog and could not be deprived of his entire living as a result of a refusal of a licence was no bar to the application of the general obligations). Cf *Enderby Town Football Club v Football Association* [1971] Ch 591, [1971] 1 All ER 215 (The club appealed to the FA against a fine and other sanctions imposed on it by its county association. The fine and sanctions did not prevent the club pursuing its trade. The club brought proceedings when the FA refused to allow it legal representation on the appeal. Denning LJ held that sports governing bodies had to retain a discretion to allow legal representation if and when appropriate but that so long as the discretion was properly exercised an individual refusal of representation was not contrary to the rules of natural justice).

6 *R v British Basketball Association, ex p Mickan* (17 March 1981, unreported), CA at p 4 of the Lexis transcript (In holding that the governing body did not owe an obligation not to act capriciously towards two top amateur players, the Court of Appeal concluded that 'the legal rules imposing duties upon bodies which exercise a monopoly over the opportunities of persons to earn their living do not extend to arrangements for amateur participation in games or other forms of recreation'); *Towcester* (para A3.80, n 1); *Currie v Barton* (1988) Times, 12 February, CA per Scott J at p 10 of the Lexis transcript of his judgment, and per O'Connor LJ at p 8 and Nicholls LJ at p 9 of the Lexis transcript of the CA judgments (A tennis player was not prevented from earning a living by a county association's decision to make him ineligible for selection as a punishment for refusal to play. Consequently the association had no obligation to comply with natural justice in making the decision); *Cowley v Heatley* (1986) Times, 24 July (Browne-Wilkinson V-C), see also para A3.98, n 2.

7 *Currie v Barton* (26 March 1987, unreported) (Scott J) and (1988) Times, 12 February, CA per Nicholls LJ at p 9 of the Lexis transcript of his CA judgment. For the contrary position in New Zealand see *Stininato v Auckland Boxing Association* [1978] 1 NZLR 1 per Woodhouse LJ, dissenting but not on this point, at 12 (Effect on freedom to compete and status held sufficient to impose obligations on a sports governing body with monopoly power), ostensibly accepted by Purchas LJ in *Fisher v National Greyhound Racing Club* (31 July 1985, unreported), CA per Oliver LJ at p 19 of the Lexis transcript.

8 The New Zealand courts held in *Finnigan v NZRFU* [1985] 2 NZLR 159, 181 and 190, that a non-member of the NZRFU could nevertheless challenge the vires of a decision to tour in South Africa. There was no contractual relationship, and the interests of the claimant were not directly affected. This decision is however symptomatic of the willingness of Commonwealth courts to treat sports governing bodies as bodies whose decisions are judicially reviewable under public law.

A3.83 Where on the other hand a contractual relationship exists between the claimant and the sports governing body, it appears to be implicit in that relationship that the sports governing body will act lawfully fairly and reasonably (in the sense of rationally)[1], and it does not appear to be necessary to show monopoly power or an effect on the claimant's ability to earn a living in order to establish and enforce such obligations[2]. Nor can the contract expressly detract from the right to be treated in this way[3].

1 *Wilander and Novacek v Tobin and Jude* [1997] 2 Lloyds 296 at 300, col 1; *R v Jockey Club, ex p Aga Khan* [1993] 1 WLR 909 at 916 per Lord Bingham MR and at 933 per Hoffmann LJ; *Jones v WRU* (27 February 1997, unreported) (Ebsworth J) at p 8 of the Lexis transcript, (1997) Times, 6 March, (19 December 1997, unreported), CA, (1998) Times, 6 January; *R v Football Association, ex p Football League* [1993] 2 All ER 833 at 843a, 851e–h; *Haron bin Mundir v Singapore Amateur Athletic Association* [1992] 1 SLR 18 at 26; *Calvin v Carr* [1980] AC 574, [1979] 2 All ER 440; *Enderby Town Football Club v Football Association* [1971] Ch 591 at 605C–607A, [1970] 3 WLR 1021 at 1025–1026, ; *Lee v Showman's Guild* [1952] 2 QB 329; *Conteh v Onslow-Fane* (1975) Times, 26 June, CA (cf cite in *Wilander* referred to above); *Wright v Jockey Club* Sir Haydn Tudor Evans, (1995) Times, 16 June (QBD), at p 8 of the Lexis transcript; *Davis v Carew-Pole* [1956] 2 All ER 524.

2 As could a player insist on such behaviour from a club, even where it is an amateur club: see *Nolan v Aldwinians Rugby Union Football Club* (MA010173) (10 July 2001, unreported) (James Allen QC) (In which the court regarded natural justice as imposing rigorous requirements on the club which it had failed to meet); *Collins v Lane* (22 June 1999, unreported), CA (Rules of natural justice applied to an amateur shooting club).

3 At least where there is monopoly power. In *Russell v Duke of Norfolk* [1949] 1 All ER 109, it had been held that the express reservation of an absolute or unfettered discretion to withdraw a trainer's licence could not be made subject to the rules of natural justice. The majority of the Court of Appeal rejected a trainer's claim that he was entitled to a hearing when the Jockey Club threatened to withdraw his licence, on the basis that there was a contract which reserved such an unfettered discretion to the Jockey Club to do so. Denning LJ however held that where a person would lose his or her livelihood as a result of a decision of a body which had a 'monopoly in an important field of human activity', natural justice required a hearing at which the person's case could be put. Subsequently, in *Nagle v Feilden* [1966] 2 QB 633 at 647 Denning LJ doubted that natural justice could be excluded by contract and in *Enderby Town Football Club v Football Association* [1971] Ch 591 at 606, [1970] 3 WLR 1021 at 1026 he stated that the contract contained in rules of a sports governing body (which he regarded as a fictional one in any event) could not displace the rules of natural justice.

(c) Application, expectation and forfeiture

A3.84 The second restriction on the general obligations imposed on sports governing bodies relates to the varying extent of the obligations if they arise, depending upon the circumstances. In *McInnes v Onslow-Fane*[1], the British Board of Boxing Control refused the claimant's application for a boxing manager's licence. Again there was no contractual relationship between the parties. Megarry V-C held[2] that a duty to act fairly and in accordance with natural justice arose, based on the analysis involving monopoly power and effect on the ability to earn a living in *Nagle v Feilden*. The intensity of the duty, however, and precisely what would be required under it, varied depending upon whether the case could be described as an 'application' case, an 'expectation' case or a 'forfeiture' case. Forfeiture cases involved the situation where something is to be taken away, and in that context the claimant was entitled to have proper notice of the arguments being made against granting him a licence, an opportunity to make representations orally, and a decision taken without caprice or bias. In that instance there was arguably a pre-existing contractual arrangement. In application cases on the other hand (where there was no pre-existing contractual relationship), the right was confined to having a decision made honestly and without caprice or bias. Expectation cases involved applications for something by a person who has some entitlement to expect that it will be granted[3]. Megarry V-C did not define the ambit of the obligation in that instance[4]. He stated that the courts should be slow to use the obligation to be fair to bring before the courts honest decisions of bodies exercising jurisdiction over sporting activities[5]. He held that since the case before him was an application case, the claimant had no right to know why he was refused a licence or any opportunity to present his case. On the basis of this authority, therefore, the extent of the general obligations on the sports governing body would in many instances be very limited[6].

1 [1978] 1 WLR 1520.
2 [1978] 1 WLR at 1528.
3 Cf *Enfield v Football League* unreported arbitration 1995, chaired by Sir Michael Kerr, cited in *Stevenage Borough Football Club v The Football League Ltd* (1996) Times, 1 August (Carnwath J), p 25 of the New Law Online transcript.
4 For expectation cases, see *Stininato v Auckland Boxing Association* [1978] 1 NZLR 1 (Boxer who had a licence but was refused a renewal was entitled on re-application to be given an adequate opportunity to answer the governing body's reasons for refusal); *Fisher v National Greyhound Racing Club* (31 July 1985, unreported), CA per Oliver LJ at p 8 and Purchas LJ at p 16 of the Lexis transcript. See also *Cowley v Heatley* (1986) Times, 24 July (Browne-Wilkinson V-C), see also para A3.98, n 2.
6 As for example in *Currie v Barton* (26 March 1987, unreported) (Scott J), (1988) Times, 12 February, CA per Scott J at p 11 of the Lexis transcript of his judgment, and per Lloyd LJ at p 8 of the Lexis transcript of the CA judgments (If natural justice applied, it would not extend to requiring a hearing).

(d) No obligation to accept a claimant as a member

A3.85 The decisions in both *Nagle v Feilden* and *Onslow-Fane* reflect the traditional approach of English law that a private sports governing body cannot be forced to accept as a member someone with whom it has no pre-existing contractual relationship[1] (although in neither case was the claimant seeking to become a member as such). Under the traditional approach, sports governing bodies can sometimes be constrained to act fairly in their decision-making but the court will not force them to admit a club or person as a member, because to do that would be to force them into a contract.

1 *Lee v Showmen's Guild* [1952] 2 QB 329 per Denning LJ at 342; *Faramus v Film Artistes' Association* [1964] AC 925 at 941 to 942 per Lord Evershed; *Collins v Lane* (22 June 1999, unreported), CA (Member of amateur shooting club unable to regain membership even if expelled in breach of natural justice). The principle is analogous to the principle that a contract of employment will not be specifically enforced: see the cases referred to at para A3.43, n 4 and E1.68 to E1.71.
2 See *Stevenage Borough Football Club v Football League Ltd*, Carnwath J, (1996) Times, 1 August, at p 23 of the New Law Online transcript. In that case the question was not decided, as the club's application was refused on the grounds of delay (as to which see also the Court of Appeal [1997] 9 Admin LR 109).

(e) Attempts to make sports governing bodies subject to judicial review

A3.86 As discussed above[1], there have been a number of unsuccessful attempts to seek the public law remedy of judicial review of the actions of sports governing bodies. Although the courts have held that the actions of sports governing bodies are not judicially reviewable as a matter of public law, and that claimants may be left without an effective remedy if they cannot establish a contract, they have arguably not expressly stated that the underlying substantive standards against which the actions of a private law sports governing body are to be measured are different to those that would be applied to a public body[2].

1 See paras A3.62 to A3.65.
2 *Law v National Greyhound Racing Club Ltd* [1983] 1 WLR 1302 (Relief available in private law); *R v Football Association of Wales, ex p Flint Town* [1991] COD 44 (where the Divisional Court held that judicial review was not available but then went on to examine whether the club had been given a fair opportunity to put its case on why it should be allowed to play outside Wales. The Divisional Court held that it was open to the FAW to take the decision it did in the light of its re-organised league. The club did not subsequently commence private law proceedings, presumably because it felt that the issues had already been examined); *R v Jockey Club, ex p Massingberd-Mundy* [1993] 2 All ER 207 per Roch J at 223 (A claimant who could not establish a contract might be left without an effective remedy); *R v Jockey Club, ex p RAM Racecourses* [1993] 2 All ER 225 (The court examined the substance of the claimant's case that the Jockey Club had given it a legitimate expectation that new races would be assigned to its new course, before addressing whether it had jurisdiction under Order 53. Stuart Smith LJ said at 243j '… it appears to me that in an appropriate case, very similar relief could be obtained by a writ action, to that which is sought by the applicant in this case …'. See also Simon Brown J at 247h–j); *R v Football Association, ex p Football League Ltd* [1993] 2 All ER 833 per Rose J at 843a–b ('… public bodies must comply with the requirements of natural justice, but so, in many cases, must private bodies …' but at 849c '… to apply to the governing body of football, on the basis that it is a public body, principles honed for the control of abuse of power by government … would involve … a quantum leap.' But this does not necessarily suggest that the same underlying substantive standards do not apply to the governing body of football, as a private body, as would apply if it were a public body. Certainly the procedures for challenge and the remedies available might be different, but not necessarily the standards against which conduct is measured); *R v Jockey Club, ex p Aga Khan* [1993] 1 WLR 909 per Bingham MR at 924 and Farquharson LJ at 930 (Claimant had effective remedies in private law) and per Hoffmann LJ at 932 to 933 (Control of the sports governing body was to be found in the law of contract, the doctrine of restraint of trade, the competition rules, and 'all the other instruments available in law for curbing the excesses of private power'. Hoffmann LJ went on to state that the possibility that there might be 'gaps in the private law' had led the courts to consider (in *R v Jockey Club, ex p RAM Racecourses* [1993] 2 All ER 225) the possibility of extending judicial review to sports governing bodies, but that he did not think that the courts should 'try to patch up the remedies available against domestic bodies by pretending that they are organs of government'. Again, it is arguable that the gaps perceived were in the remedies available, as opposed to in the underlying standard to be applied).

(f) A less restrictive approach?

A3.87 Since 1996 there have been signs that the English courts may be prepared to adopt a less restrictive approach both to the circumstances in which sports governing bodies will be held to owe the general obligations to act lawfully, fairly and reasonably (in the sense of rationally) and in relation to the content of the obligations[1]. In *Stevenage v Football League*[2] (a case in which there was no contract), Carnwath J held that the exercise of discretion by bodies such as the Football League, which exercise regulatory power in the public interest, fell to be reviewed by reference to the same tests as are applied to bodies subject to judicial review. He however then went on to follow the approach in *McInnes v Onslow-Fane*, which arguably does not impose the same tests[3]. In *Jones v WRU*[4], Ebsworth J (later supported by the Court of Appeal[5]) concluded that it was arguable for the purposes of interim relief that the WRU owed obligations as a matter of natural justice to allow a player appealing against his sending off not only to have an oral hearing, but also to be represented (although not necessarily by a lawyer), to question witnesses, and to comment on the video-tape recording of the incident as the disciplinary body watched it[6]. She stressed the greater financial significance of sports governing bodies' decisions today[7], and doubted the validity in modern circumstances of the courts' traditional reluctance to intervene[8]. She went on to suspend the ban imposed on the player until after the trial of the action[9]. The WRU changed its rules to meet Ebsworth J's concerns[10].

1 See Dawn Oliver 'Common values in public and private law' [1997] PL 630 for an analysis of the rationale behind a less restrictive approach.
2 *Stevenage Borough Football Club v Football League Ltd*, Carnwath J, (1996) Times, 1 August.
3 (24 July 1996, unreported), (1996) Times, 1 August 1996, at p 25 of the New Law Online transcript (see (1996) Times, 1 August 1996 for the judgment at first instance and Times 9 August 1996 and (1997) 9 Admin LR 109 for the judgment on appeal); see paras A3.151 to A3.155 for a full discussion; see also Stewart [1996] 4(3) SATLJ 110 (and Alderson at p 110 in the same publication) and Stewart [1998] 6(3) SATLJ 41).
4 (27 February 1997, unreported) (Ebsworth J), (1997) Times, 6 March, (17 November 1997, unreported) (Potts J), (19 December 19978, unreported), CA, (1998) Times, 6 January. See also Rose [1997] 5(1) SATLJ 20.
5 Albeit still in the context of interim relief.
6 At p 9 of the Lexis transcript of Ebsworth J's judgment.
7 At pp 2 and 9 of the Lexis transcript.
8 At p 9 of the Lexis transcript.
9 At p 10 of the Lexis transcript. She approached the grant of interim relief on the basis that if it was arguable that there had been a breach of natural justice, the relief should be granted. She was not impressed by the WRU's argument that because the outcome, namely a three week suspension, fell within the range of responses reasonably open to the WRU, no injunction should be granted.
10 The WRU then held a further hearing, which the player was invited to attend. He refused to do so and the WRU imposed a new ban. Potts J (17 November 1997, unreported) restrained the WRU from taking new disciplinary proceedings against the player on the basis of the new altered rules. The Court of Appeal upheld Ebsworth J's original decision in favour of the player, but also allowed the WRU's appeal against the decision of Potts J. The Court of Appeal held that a sports governing body could re-take a decision in a fair manner.

A3.88 In *Wilander and Novacek v Tobin and Jude*[1], two tennis players challenged the validity of rule 53 of the ITF Anti-Doping Programme, which banned tennis players found to have committed a doping offence. Lord Woolf MR concluded[2] that even if the ITF's disciplinary body was not judicially reviewable it still owed the same general obligations to act lawfully, fairly and reasonably (in the sense of rationally):

> Assuming, but not deciding, that the appeals committee is not subject to judicial review because it is not a public body, this does not mean that it escapes the supervision of the High Court. The proceedings out of which this appeal arises are part of that supervision. The Appeals Committee's jurisdiction over the plaintiffs arises out of a contract. That contract has an implied requirement that the procedure provided for in rule 53 is to be conducted fairly (*Lee v Showmen's Guild* [1952] 2 QB 329 and *Conteh v Onslow-Fane* (1975) Times, 26 June, CA]). If the Appeals Committee does not act fairly or if it misdirects itself in law and fails to take into account relevant considerations or takes into account irrelevant considerations, the High Court can intervene. It can also intervene if there is no evidential basis for its decision.

While it is true that the facts of this case satisfied the criteria in the earlier cases[3] (it involved the contractually binding rules of a governing body with monopoly power, and a decision which affected the claimant's livelihood by withdrawing something that he already had), Lord Woolf MR chose to express the obligations on the governing body in a much broader way, as being directly equivalent to the obligations owed in public law.

1 [1997] 2 Lloyd's Rep 296.
2 [1997] 2 Lloyd's Rep 296 at 300, col 1.
3 See para A3.82.

A3.89 Lord Woolf MR also considered the question in *Modahl v British Athletic Federation*[1], in which Diane Modahl, having been banned for a doping violation by an internal BAF tribunal but subsequently exonerated by a BAF appeal tribunal, sued the BAF for damages for breach of the implied contractual duty in its anti-doping programme to apply that programme fairly, including avoiding manning its internal tribunals with biased members. When the BAF's application to strike out came before the Court of Appeal, Lord Woolf MR held[2] that the normal judicial review standard of fairness applied to the review of private body disciplinary decisions:

> Mr Pollock suggested that Mr Pannick was in error in seeking to rely on what he referred to as an administrative law approach in the different field of contract. There are distinctions between an action which is brought for breach of contract and proceedings for judicial review but Mr Pollock is wrong in suggesting that the approach of the Courts in public law on applications for judicial review have no relevance in domestic disciplinary proceedings of this sort. The question of whether a complaint about the conduct of a disciplinary committee gives rise to a remedy in public law or in private law is often difficult to determine. However, the complaint in both cases would be based on an allegation of unfairness. While in some situations public and private law principles can differ, I can see no reason why there should be any difference as to what constitutes unfairness or why the standard of fairness required by an implied term should differ from that required of the same tribunal under public law ... Indeed in areas such as this, the approach of the Courts should be to assimilate the applicable principles. There would however remain the procedural differences and differences as to the remedies which are available.

In the House of Lords, the issue did not arise. At the substantive hearing, Douglas Brown J investigated the content of the putative implied term (which he held could not exist as no contract existed) on the basis of the content of public law obligations[3]. When the matter came before the Court of Appeal again, it was held that there was indeed a contract between the athlete and the BAF. In so holding the court displayed a greater preparedness to infer an implied contract out of the circumstances of a governing body/member relationship than it had displayed previously[4].

1 The *Modahl* case has now been before the High Court and the Court of Appeal twice, first on the strike out application ((28 June 1996, unreported) (Popplewell J), (28 June 1996, unreported); (28 July 1997, unreported), CA) and then on the substantive hearing ([2002] 1 WLR 1192). The case went to the House of Lords on the strike out appeal (22 July 1999, unreported). For a commentary before the final Court of Appeal hearing, see Farrell [2001] 9(1) SATLJ 110. For a summary of Douglas Brown's decision, see [2001] 2 ISLR 193.

2 At (28 July 1997, unreported), CA at pp 20F–21G of the shorthand writers' transcript.

3 See, for example, p 12 of the shorthand writers' transcript.

4 See paras A3.121 to A3.125 on contract. See also *Sheehy v Judo Federation of Australia* unreported Bryson J (NSW) 1 December 1995, where the court was prepared to infer a contract to act fairly and rationally beween a governing body and a judoka being considered for selection; *Haron bin Mundir v Singapore Amateur Athletic Association* [1992] 1 SLR 18; and *Australian Football League v Carlton Football Club* [1998] 2 VR 546.

A3.90 When *Modahl* came before the Court of Appeal on the second occasion[1], Latham LJ stated in relation to the content of the obligation to act fairly:

> It does not seem to me that the nature or extent of the obligation to act fairly depends upon the existence or otherwise of a contract. In other words the answer to the question whether or not the respondent did act fairly should be the same whether or not a contract exists. I can see no justification for implying into the contract any further or different obligation from that which would be considered the appropriate test in considering the exercise of the Courts' supervisory jurisdiction whether or not the proceedings were fair.

In other words, how the obligation arose is irrelevant to its content. It may however be that this statement must be read as being that on the facts in *Modahl* no distinction could be drawn.

1 [2002] 1 WLR 1192 at 1209, para 54.

(g) Are the two straightforward propositions correct yet?

A3.91 The *Wilander* and *Modahl* cases make it tolerably clear that where there is a contract, a sports governing body owes the same general obligations as those owed by public bodies, to act lawfully, fairly (in accordance with natural justice) and reasonably (in the sense of rationally) in all of its decision-making pursuant to its regulatory functions under the rules. Where the existing relationship can be characterised as contractual, the obligations appear to apply whatever the level at which the sport is played by the claimant, whatever the sport and whatever the degree of power and influence the sports governing body has. Where there is no contract on the other hand, the position appears to remain that something else in the circumstances has to be found to justify the imposition of the same standards as apply in the public law context. In the authors' view, that something else should be no more than that the sports governing body exercises control through a set of rules over a significant aspect of the player's or other participant's life, whether the player is an amateur or a professional, whether the sport is football or tug of war and whether the sports governing body has complete or only partial control over the sport[1]. If general obligations of lawfulness, fairness and rationality arise in these circumstances because a contract is identified, often artificially, then there is little reason that they should not also arise in circumstances which are identical save for the fact that the artificial contract cannot be identified. The decision is the same in both instances and its effects are the same in both instances. This appears to have been Latham LJ's approach in Modahl[2]. As can be seen from the debate in *Modahl*, a contract that some regard as implied others regard as stretching the concept of contract too far[3].

1 In 'Common values in public and private law' [1997] PL 630 at 638, Dawn Oliver puts it in this way: '… the foundation for the exercise of this supervisory jurisdiction independent of contract is a developing common law right of those seriously affected by decisions taken by powerful bodies, to have the effects of a decision upon them considered fairly and rationally before the decision is made …' Oliver goes on to discuss criteria for the imposition of such a duty. As set out in n 1 to para A3.80, the duty does not apply to *all* the actions of private law sports governing bodies, only those carried out in the exercise of the body's regulatory functions, and the principle does not extend to organisations which are not governing bodies but rather represent a single interest within the sport. Competition law and other principles (see for example as discussed at n 2 to para A3.115) provide the appropriate level of constraint on the commercial activities of the sport governing body. Care should however be taken, since those principles may provide similar protection.
2 See para A3.90.
3 See paras A3.121 to A3.125.

A3.92 Equally and for the same reasons, the *content* of the obligations should, in our view, be the same whether or not there is a contract. Again this appears to have been Latham LJ's approach in *Modahl*[1]. It will of course always be the case that the precise content of the obligation to act consistently with natural justice and in a procedurally fair manner varies from case to case[2]: that is the public law position. Much of what is said in *Onslow-Fane* would therefore still apply[3]. It is however probable that where the standard of natural justice and fairness set out in *Onslow-Fane* would offer less protection than would be the case in a public law context involving the same type of application or disciplinary proceedings, the court would now insist on the greater degree of protection. If that greater degree of protection applies where there is a contract, then so too it should apply where one cannot be identified. This is the case irrespective of the advent of the Human Rights Act 1998 and in particular Art 6 of the Convention, protecting the right to a fair trial. However, whether or not the sports governing body in question is in fact a public authority for the purposes of the Human Rights Act, the nature and extent of its common law obligations will be informed by the substantial movement in the law in relation to the right to a fair trial under Art 6[4].

1 See para A3.90.
2 And only applies to decisions which relate to the exercise of regulatory power as opposed to purely commercial decisions: see n 1 to para A3.80 and n 1 to para A3.91.
3 See para A3.84.
4 See Chapter A4 and paras A3.66 to A3.69. In addition arguments based on other rights may be brought in to support substantive entitlements, such as the entitlement to be promoted when a division or league is won.

A3.93 Less clear is whether the law has developed sufficiently to cast doubt on the principle that a sports governing body cannot be forced to take a person or body as a member. In the authors' view, if it is right that sports governing bodies owe the same obligations as public law bodies, then there is less justification for an argument that they cannot be forced to accept a member on the grounds that this would amount to forcing them to enter into a contract. As was made clear in *Nagle v Feilden*[1], the contract that the sports governing body would be forced into is an artificial construct in a context where the reality is that the sports governing body controls access to the sport and being excluded from membership prevents the claimant from participating in the sport. Membership in this context is something very different from membership of a private club[2]. One way to test this is to ask what Carnwath J would have gone on to do had he not dismissed Stevenage's case on grounds of delay. If he had decided that Stevenage had been unlawfully excluded from promotion by reason of the imposition of unjustifiably restrictive criteria, would he have gone on to say that the court was powerless to order the League to promote the club? That seems to the authors to be unlikely. Instead he would in the authors' view have forced the League to take Stevenage as a member. That said, it is clear that the courts are still reluctant to force membership even in the presence of a contractual entitlement[3].

1 [1966] 2 QB 633, and see para A3.82.
2 As in *Collins v Lane* (22 June 1999, unreported), CA.
3 See *Alwyn Treherne (for the Welsh Amateur Boxing Federation) v Amateur Boxing Association of England*, Garland J 27 February 2001 [2001] 3 ISLR 231, [2002] EWCA Civ 381, [2002] All ER (D) 144 (Mar) (The WABF, which had been set up as a rival to the Welsh Amateur Boxing Association and which was not recognised internationally, challenged the ABAE's refusal to allow its clubs to affiliate with the ABAE so that former WABF boxers could compete other than with one another. The case turned on whether a binding contract had been entered into that the ABAE would admit the clubs, and it was held that it had not been. Both Garland J and Buxton LJ felt that, even if there had been a contract, it would not have been appropriate to grant an injunction to force the ABAE to admit the clubs).

A3.94 In our view, therefore, the two straightforward propositions are probably already largely correct. But nevertheless it remains better to establish a contract if it is possible to do so, both to make it easier to show that the sports governing body owes the general obligations to act lawfully, fairly and reasonably (in the sense of rationally) and to make it easier to show that the obligations apply with their full force. Establishing a contract is also preferable for the not inconsequential reason that it sets up a right to damages[1].

1 See paras A3.199 to A3.203.

B The obligation to act lawfully in accordance with the sports governing body's rules

(a) *Acting within the rules*

A3.95 The first general obligation on a sports governing body is to follow its rules and not to step outside them. As explained above[1], the content of the obligation is the same as that owed by a public body. Reliance can be placed on the principles developed by the courts in that context[2]. The sports governing body is obliged properly to instruct itself as to its rules and to act lawfully in accordance with them. It must not act for an improper purpose[3]. This is not only a negative obligation prohibiting breach of the rules, but also a positive obligation to do what the rules require[4]. In disciplinary proceedings, for example, the allegation made must be one that can be made under the rules and it must be formulated in accordance with the rules. Any sanction must be permissible under the rules. If the rules provide for a discretion, then the discretion must be exercised and not ignored by applying an inflexible criterion[5]. Put at its simplest, the question for the practitioner is essentially whether or not the rules say that what has happened can happen, or that something should have happened that has not happened. The advantage of a lawfulness argument is that it is broadly either right or wrong, and the court ought not to decline to intervene on the basis that it is a matter for the sports governing body[6]. Consequently, many challenges to the actions of sports governing bodies involve a lawfulness argument, whether alone or coupled with other arguments.

1 See paras A3.80 to A3.94.

2 For a detailed description of those principles, see Fordham *Judicial Review* (3rd edn, 2001, Hart Publishing) at pp 185, 703–727; Wade *Administrative Law* (8th edn, 2000, Oxford) at pp 219–314; De Smith *Judicial Review of Administrative Action* (5th edn 1995, (inc supp), Sweet & Maxwell) at pp 295–374.

3 *Auckland Boxing Association v New Zealand Boxing Association* [2001] NZLR 847 (improper use of suspension as punitive measure).

4 The club or player has the right to have a rule properly applied: see *Stevenage Borough Football Club v Football League Ltd*, Carnwath J, (1996) Times, 1 August, 9 Admin LR 109, CA; *Wimbledon v Football League* unreported FA arbitration 29 January 2002; *R v British Basketball Association, ex p Mickan* (17 March 1981, unreported), CA (whether the rules contemplated that any applicant who satisfied the eligibility criteria was automatically entitled to a licence); *TWR v RAC* (9 October 1985, unreported) (Gibson J) (whether the rules included power to order an unsuccessful party in internal proceedings to pay costs). See also *JWC v New Zealand Sports Drug Agency* [1996] DCR 939 (compliance with details of drug testing regime is required); *Fox v New Zealand Sports Drug Agency* [1999] DCR 1165 (failure of official to comply with regime justified claimant in refusing to provide a sample); *Bray v New Zealand Sports Drug Agency* [2001] 2 NZLR 160, CA (on their proper construction, the rules required delivery of the sample to the laboratory within a particular time, and not simply that they be sent within that time).

5 The construction of rules is a matter for the court: *Modahl v BAF* (28 June 1996, unreported) (Popplewell J) at pp 13.3–14.8 of the shorthand writers' transcript; *Tyrrell Racing Organisation v RAC Motor Sports Association and the Fédération Internationale du Sport Automobile* (20 July 1984, unreported) (Hirst J) at p 11 of Lexis transcript; *Enderby Town Football Club v Football Association* [1971] Ch 591 at 605; *Reel v Holder* [1981] 1 WLR 1226 per Lord Denning MR at 1230 to 1231 (On the proper construction of the IAAF Rules, which was for the court, the Taiwanese athletic association could not be expelled); *Lee v Showmen's Guild* [1952] 2 QB 329 at 354. In Fordham's terminology, it is a hard-edged basis for challenge (see Fordham *Judicial Review* (3rd edn, 2001, Hart Publishing), pp 257–269). But for an arguably contrary view, see *Cowley v Heatley* (1986) Times, 24 July (Browne-Wilkinson V-C) and para A3.98, n 2. It is arguable that the court there allowed the concept of judicial reluctance to intervene to affect its decision on the purely legal question of what the rules meant: see pp 4–6 of the Lexis transcript. See also Beloff 'Pitch Pool Rink … Court? Judicial Review in the Sporting World' [1989] PL 95 at 96–97. The rules cannot oust the jurisdiction of the court: see para A3.52.

A3.96 That said, the courts will not interpret the rules of a sport's governing body as if they were a statute, or even a technical legal document such as a conveyance. The courts accept that often they have not been drafted by lawyers and should not be given an unduly legalistic interpretation[1]. They will be interpreted so as to give effect to their purpose, and so as not to conflict with the obligations of procedural fairness and natural justice[2].

1 *Cowley v Heatley* (1986) Times, 24 July (Browne-Wilkinson V-C), p 4 of the Lexis transcript, see also para A3.98, n 2. Cf *Gasser v Stinson* (15 June 1988, unreported) (Scott J) at p 29 of the shorthand writers' transcript (failure to comply with technical elements of the guidelines could not invalidate doping result); *Widnes RFC v Rugby Football League* (26 May 1995, unreported) (Parker J); *Smith v FINA* CAS (1996) Atlanta 001, *Digest of CAS Awards 1986–1998* (1998, Berne), p 377 (CAS held that the entry time limit rules ought not to be applied over-restrictively).

2 *Modahl v BAF* (28 June 1996, unreported) (Popplewell J) at pp 18.7–21.7 of the shorthand writers' transcript, citing *Lee v Showmen's Guild* [1952] 2 QB 329, CA per Somervell LJ at 341, Denning LJ at 342 and Romer LJ at 351; *Modahl v BAF* (28 July 1997, unreported), CA per Lord Woolf MR at pp 16F–17B, where Lord Woolf MR also pointed out that national governing body rules should be interpreted in the light of international governing body rules, with which they must be consistent; *R v BBA, ex p Mickan* (17 March 1981, unreported), CA at p 5 of the Lexis transcript (rules to be construed so as to give effect to their purpose, and in the light of their context). The normal canons of construction of contracts may well be relevant. Rules will generally be construed: (a) purposively; (b) in favour of the athlete or club and against the body imposing the rules (the contra proferentem principle); (c) where they give rise to penal sanctions, narrowly; (d) consistently; (e) so that they accord with natural justice and fairness; and (f) if possible in a way that does not put the governing body in breach of its other obligations. See also para A3.232, in relation to the general principles of law which are often applied by bodies such as the CAS and which will be of increasing relevance even in the English courts. In some instances, the courts have been prepared to go a long way in interpretation in order to ensure that arrangements are fair: see *Stewart v Judicial Committee of the Auckland Racing Club* [1992] 3 NZLR 693 (appeals construed as involving a full re-hearing in order to provide a fair procedure overall in the light of the fact that the first hearing was peremptory); cf *Naden v Judicial Committee of the Auckland Racing Club* [1995] 1 NZLR 307 (where it was held that the grant of a right of appeal precluded the appeal body being limited in its ability to overturn the original decision to circumstances where the original decision was 'manifestly wrong': the appeal body was to make up its own mind and had a discretion to admit new evidence). See *Martinez v Ellesse Spa* (30 March 1999, unreported), CA for the principles of construction of a commercial contract.

A3.97 There ought to be no difference in approach depending upon whether or not the rules constitute a contract between the sports governing body and the claimant. Where they do constitute such a contract, the obligation on the governing body to act in accordance with its rules is an obligation to comply with its contractual obligations[1], enforceable in the normal way through injunction, declaration or damages. Where there is no contract, and no other cause of action, a player or other participant can nevertheless seek a declaration that the governing body has not acted in compliance with its rules[2].

1 See paras A3.116 to A3.125.

2 See *Gasser v Stinson* (15 June 1988, unreported) (Scott J) at p 24H of the shorthand writers' transcript; *Korda v ITF* (1999) Times, 4 February, [1999] All ER (D) 84; *Davis v Carew-Pole* [1956] 2 All ER 524 (where the court found that a contract arose but held that even if there was no contract a declaration would still lie where a sports governing body went outside its rules).

A3.98 The most common circumstances where a challenge is made to a wrongful interpretation of rules which do not constitute a contract between the claimant and the sports governing body[1] are:

(i) where the claimant is seeking access to the sport or to a particular level of competition[2]; and
(ii) where a governing body has found there to be a doping offence[3].

1 Although there may be a contract in these contexts also.

2 See for example *Cowley v Heatley* (1986) Times, 24 July (Browne-Wilkinson V-C). In that case a swimmer sought to challenge the decision of the Commonwealth Games Federation, with which she had no contract, to declare her ineligible to appear for England at the Games. The Federation had construed the word 'domicile' in its rules in a particular way. Cowley tried to persuade the court that the Federation had construed it incorrectly. She made 'no allegation of lack of good faith, or breach of the rules of natural justice or any other procedural impropriety against the Federation. What she [raised was] a pure question of law' (p 3 of the Lexis transcript). Browne-Wilkinson V-C left open the question of whether a player who was not in a contractual relationship with the governing body could seek a declaration that it had acted outside its rules, holding that even if it was assumed that a declaration could be granted and even if Cowley had won on the merits he would not have granted a declaration (p 7 of the Lexis transcript). In the event he held that on its proper construction in its context the word 'domicile' had the non-technical meaning attributed to it by the sports governing body. He went on to hold that the way the sports governing body then applied that test to the facts was a matter for it, with which the court would be slow to interfere, and there was nothing to suggest that the sports governing body had acted unreasonably in the Wednesbury sense (ie irrationally). He then held that even if the stricter legal test of domicile applied it still was not satisfied.

3 See *Modahl v British Athletics Federation* unreported, Popplewell J 28 June 1996, CA 28 July 1997, HL 22 July 1998, Douglas Brown J 14 December 2000 and [2002] 1 WLR 1192, CA 8 October 2001; *Gasser v Stinson* (15 June 1988, unreported) (Scott J); *Walker v UKA and IAAF* unreported Toulson J 3 July 2000, Hallett J 25 July 2000, IAAF Arbitral Award 20 August 2000 reported at [2001] 4 ISLR 264, see also [2000] 2 ISLR 41 and n 7 to para A3.10 and para A3.124. After the second Court of Appeal decision in *Modahl,* the courts will be much more prepared to hold that there was a contract between a governing body and someone participating in the sport, even in the absence of a membership application, entry form or other written contract. See para A3.125. In the context of doping, the challenge is often based on what test is to be applied under the rules, specifically whether deliberate ingestion has to be established: see paras E4.75 to E4.173, and (for example) *USA Shooting and Quigley v Union Internationale de Tir* CAS 94/129, *Digest of CAS Awards 1986–1998* (1998, Berne), p 187; *Lehtinen v FINA* CAS 95/142, *Digest of CAS Awards 1986–1998* (1998, Berne), p 225; *National Wheelchair Basketball Association v International Paralympic Committee* CAS 95/122, *Digest of CAS Awards 1986–1998* (1998, Berne), p 173 (which also addressed whether on the wording of the rules the whole team could be disqualified following one member's offence); *Chagnaud v FINA* CAS 95/141, *Digest of CAS Awards 1986–1998* (1998, Berne), p 215; *Volkers v FINA* CAS 95/150, *Digest of CAS Awards 1986–1998* (1998, Berne), p 265; *Smith de Bruin v FINA* CAS 98/211, *Digest of CAS Awards II 1998–2000* (2002, Kluwer), p 255.

A3.99 The range of circumstances in which a lawfulness argument can arise on the proper construction of the rules (whether or not there is a contract) is however as wide as the variety of rules that exist. Cases that have arisen include disputes over end of season promotion rights under the rules[1], the extent of a contractual right to stay in an association or league[2], the contractual right to play pending the outcome of proceedings based on a breach of the rules[3], the allocation of functions between internal organs of the sports governing body[4], the constituents of an offence and availability of opportunity to impose a further sanction[5], criteria for selection[6], the existence of a right to appeal for the sports governing body against a decision of its own disciplinary body[7], the existence of a power to award costs[8], and whether or not the rights of a competitor can be assigned to another competitor[9].

1 Whether a champion of a second division had the right under the rules and agreements to form part of an expanded first division operated by the same sports governing body: *Rotherham and English Second Division Rugby Ltd v English First Division Rugby Ltd and the RFU*, Ferris J, 16 August 1999 [2000] 1 ISLR 33.

2 For example *Reel v Holder* [1981] 1 WLR 1226 per Lord Denning MR at 1230 to 1231 (On the proper construction of the IAAF Rules, the Taiwanese athletic association could not be expelled). Whether a club has the right under the rules to continue to play in a particular division: *Widnes v Rugby Football League* (26 May 1995, unreported) (Parker J) (Widnes contended that it had a contractual right to participate in a new league being established by the Rugby Football League with support from Rupert Murdoch. The new league was to be smaller than the former top division, with the result that the clubs that finished lowest would not make it into the new league. Widnes

failed to establish on a proper construction of the rules that the governing body was unable to re-organise the league in this way). Cf the Australian Rugby League Superleague case: *News Ltd v Australian Rugby Football League Ltd* (1996) 135 ALR 33, *(No 2)* 139 ALR 193 (At issue, amongst other things, was whether clubs had breached contractual obligations to the League when they were tempted away to join the new superleague); and *South Sydney District Rugby League Football Club v News Ltd* [2000] FCA 1541, [2001] FCA 862.

3 Whether on the proper construction of the rules a sanction has to be suspended pending the hearing of an appeal: *Tyrrell Racing Organisation v RAC Motor Sports Association and the Fédération Internationale du Sport Automobile* (20 July 1984, unreported) (Hirst J) at p 10 of the Lexis transcript. The issue was also raised in *Walker v UKA and IAAF* unreported Toulson J 3 July 2000, Hallett J 25 July 2000, IAAF Arbitral Award 20 August 2000 reported at [2001] 4 ISLR 264, see also [2000] 2 ISLR 41 and n 7 to para A3.10 and para A3.124.

4 How under the rules jurisdiction is to be allocated between the governing body's committees and tribunals and the effect on earlier rulings of subsequent decisions: *Robert C Allan v Scottish Auto Cycle Union* (1985) Outer House Cases 32 and see also *Anderlecht v UEFA, CAS 98/185, Digest of CAS Awards II 1998–2000* (2002, Kluwer), p 469 (decision taken by the wrong UEFA body).

5 What the rules provide the elements of different offences are: *Jockey Club of South Africa v Forbes* (1993) (1) SA 649 (The sports governing body was entitled under its rules to convict an individual of having been a trainer of a horse in respect of which there had been a positive drug test. It could also convict of the more serious offence of being party to the administration of a drug to a horse, but only if the drug was actually proved to have been administered. The sports governing body was not entitled under its rules to convict of the more serious offence on the basis of there having been a positive drug test). Whether a further sanction can be imposed: *Re Duncan Ferguson (Ferguson v Scottish Football Association)* (1996) Outer House Cases Lord Macfadyen 1 February 1996 (SFA unable on proper construction of the rules to impose an additional penalty on a player who had not been cautioned by the referee).

6 What criteria for selection are provided by the rules: *Cowley v Heatley* (1986) Times, 24 July (Browne-Wilkinson V-C), and para A3.98, n 2. See also *Nixon v Australian Cycling Federation* CAS 96/152; and *Watt v Australian Cycling Federation* CAS 96/153, *Digest of CAS Awards II 1998–2000* (2002, Kluwer), p 335.

7 In *Korda v ITF* (1999) Times, 4 February, [1999] All ER (D) 84, an independent Appeals Committee convened under the terms of the ITF Anti-Doping Programme upheld the finding of an offence, but found that 'exceptional circumstances' existed – namely the player's lack of knowledge of how the substance got into his body – that warranted a waiver of any suspension. The ITF filed an appeal to the CAS against that decision. Lightman J granted the player a declaration that the ITF could not appeal its own decision to the CAS, but his decision was overturned by the Court of Appeal and the ITF was allowed to pursue its appeal to the CAS) (which was eventually successful as well: see paras E4.318 to E4.323).

8 *TWR v RAC* (1985) Times, 12 October (where there was power to award costs).

9 *Phoenix v Fédération International de l'Automobile, Formula One Management and Formula One Administration* [2002] EWHC 1028 (Ch) (Morritt V-C). Phoenix sought an interim injunction requiring FIA and FOM to allow it to participate in the 2002 Formula One Championship. Phoenix claimed to have acquired the right to entry and the entitlement to financial benefits of the defunct Prost team under the Concorde Agreement. The Concorde Agreement contained an arbitration clause, and Phoenix's claim was 'under or through' Prost, a party to that arbitration agreement, for the purposes of s 82 of the Arbitration Act 1996. Phoenix's action was accordingly stayed pursuant to s 9 of the Arbitration Act 1996. Its application for interlocutory relief under s 44 of that Act was refused on the basis that it had not made out an arguable case that it had acquired a right that was capable of assignment, and that in any event on the balance of convenience an injunction should not be granted.

(b) The validity of the rules

A3.100 A lawfulness argument may also arise on the basis that the particular rule that the sports governing body is seeking to apply is unlawful. It could be unlawful as being in unreasonable restraint of trade[1], or as being contrary to the competition rules[2] or the free movement rules[3], or on public policy grounds if it ran directly contrary to the obligation to act fairly and in accordance with natural justice[4]. A particular rule could also be unlawful because it was 'unconstitutional', ie the sports governing body did not have the power to adopt it[5], or because it was adopted in the wrong way[6].

1 See paras A3.135 to A3.158 and E2.32 to E2.36.
2 See paras A3.159 to A3.170 and Chapter B2.
3 See paras A3.171 to A3.175 and Chapter B3.
4 See paras A3.101 to A3.108; *Nagle v Feilden* [1966] 2 QB 633 at 647 per Denning LJ (Doubting that natural justice could be excluded by contract); *Enderby Town Football Club v Football Association* [1971] Ch 591 at 606, [1970] 3 WLR 1021 at 1026 per Lord Denning (Stating that the contract contained in rules of a sports governing body could not displace the rules of natural justice). Cf *Russell v Duke of Norfolk* [1949] 1 All ER 109 (The express reservation of an absolute or unfettered discretion to withdraw a trainer's licence could not be made subject to the rules of natural justice, but see the conclusions of Denning LJ and his subsequent decisions).
5 For example because it was outside its objects: *Baker v Jones (for British Amateur Weightlifters Association)* [1954] 2 All ER 553. See also *AEK Athens and Slavia Prague v UEFA* CAS arbitration 98/200 interim decision 17 July 1998, final decision 20 August 1999, *Digest of CAS Awards II 1998–2000* (2002, Kluwer) p36 and in [2001] 1 ISLR 122 (ENIC owned both clubs. Prague and then Athens qualified for the Champions' League. CAS ordered at the interim stage that UEFA could not deprive AEK Athens of its place in the Champions' League on the basis of a rule introduced after Athens qualified which purported to exclude retrospectively the qualification of two clubs in the same ownership. However, on the final hearing the validity of the rule 'as opposed to its retrospective application' was upheld). In *Walker v UKA and IAAF* (unreported Toulson J 3 July 2000, Hallett J 25 July 2000, IAAF Arbitral Award 20 August 2000 reported at [2001] 4 ISLR 264, see also [2000] 2 ISLR 41 and n 7 to para A3.10 and para A3.124), the IAAF purported to rely on an ex post facto change in its rules which had the effect of suspending athletes already cleared by their national associations and whose cases had already been referred to arbitration by the IAAF. UKA objected to this treatment of the athlete on the basis that in the absence of an express power to adopt retrospective rules changes, and in the absence of the rule not expressing itself to be retrospective, it should not be construed as capable of retrospective application. After an indication from Hallett J, the case was compromised inter alia on the basis that the IAAF undertook to let the athlete compete pending the IAAF arbitration hearing. The IAAF Arbitration Panel eventually overturned UKA's decision, but since the athlete had chosen not to compete despite the permission to do so, he had served out his ban without competing and was able to go back into competition soon afterwards. In *Gibraltar Football Association v UEFA*, pending before CAS, the GFA challenges the ability of UEFA to change its rules to preclude the GFA's already pending (and compliant) application for membership.
6 In *FFSA v FISA*, CAS 97/168, *Digest of CAS Awards 1986–98* (1998, Berne), the FFSA challenged the adoption by an Extraordinary Congress of the FISA of a new bye-law relating to 'Commercial Publicity, Sponsorship and Advertising'. The CAS rejected the FFSA's arguments that the Extraordinary Congress did not have jurisdiction to make such a decision, but accepted that the procedure followed in adopting the amendment without allowing for a considered discussion of this important change to the bye-laws was in breach of FISA's Statutes, and accordingly the adoption was declared void.

C The obligation to act fairly in a procedural sense, or 'natural justice'

(a) General points

A3.101 Sports governing bodies are generally obliged to afford minimum standards[1] of procedural protection to the individual, club or other constituent affected by their actions, and to act fairly[2]. That obligation cannot be excluded by contract[3]. As already stated[4], the content of the obligation to act fairly in a procedural sense is, at least in most situations[5], the same as that owed by a public body. Reliance can be placed on the principles developed by the courts in that context[6]. The extent of the obligation to act fairly in a procedural sense varies from case to case, in the light of all the circumstances[7]. Sports governing bodies, and the disciplinary bodies or committees that they establish, are not courts of law. They are not bound by the same evidential and procedural constraints. Nevertheless some general principles are discernible in the cases involving sports governing bodies, which are dealt with below by reference to the various types of protection which the courts are likely to expect them to offer to their constituents. It is however clear that the law on procedural fairness is fluid, and the extent of protection which the courts are prepared to offer is steadily increasing across the board. This process will be encouraged by the increasing number of cases under the Human Rights Act 1998 in relation to the right to a fair trial protected in Art 6 of the European Convention on Human Rights[8]. Even if a claim cannot be made under the Act, the courts will be informed by Art 6 considerations and precedents when determining the level of behaviour expected of sports governing bodies by the courts. Consequently the categories of protection dealt with below are not exhaustive, and the current position on the authorities is not definitive. At bottom, if the court thinks that a player's treatment has been unfair, it will say so. The question for the practitioner is therefore first and foremost whether what has happened has really been unfair in the ordinary sense of the word. The disadvantage of an argument based on procedural unfairness is that it impugns only the particular decision: the sports governing body can often legitimately go back and make a decision which is procedurally fair[9], but which is to the same effect as the original decision[10]. Indeed, a court might even refuse to remit a procedurally flawed decision for reconsideration, for example because of delay or (more questionably) on the basis that procedurally lawful treatment would have made no difference to the outcome[11].

1 Their rules can expressly provide for a greater degree of protection, but there is a floor that will apply in any event. The obligation is categorically not an obligation to reach the right conclusion, only an obligation to apply a fair process: see *Colgan v Kennel Club* (26 October 2001, unreported) (Cooke J).

2 *Modahl v BAF* (28 July 1997, unreported), CA per Lord Woolf MR at pp 20–26 Morritt LJ at pp 36 to 39 and Pill LJ at pp 43 to 44 of the shorthand writers' transcript; *R v Jockey Club, ex p Aga Khan* [1993] 2 All ER 853 at 876b, [1993] 1 WLR 909 at 933; *Enderby Town Football Club v Football Association* [1971] Ch 591 at 605C–607A, [1970] 3 WLR 1021 at 1025–1026; *R v Football Association, ex p Football League* [1993] 2 All ER 833 at 843a, 851e–h; *Haron Bin Mundir v Singapore AAA* [1992] 1 SLR 18 at 26B; *Russell v Duke of Norfolk* [1949] 1 All ER 109 at 118 per Tucker LJ; *Jones v WRU* (27 February 1997, unreported) (Ebsworth J), (1997) Times, 6 March, unreported Potts J 17 November 1997, unreported CA 19 December 1997, (1998) Times, 6 January; *Tyrrell Racing Organisation v RAC Motor Sports Association and the Fédération Internationale de l'Automobile* (20 July 1984, unreported) (Hirst J) p 11 of the Lexis transcript. For a case where the obligation was curtailed, see *Currie v Barton* (26 March 1987, unreported) (Scott J) and unreported CA 11 February 1988 (Scott J held that a selection committee should not be subject to the rules of natural justice). For the questions that a sports governing body should ask itself, see Morton-Hooper 'The right to a fair hearing' [2001] 9(3) SATLJ 155. For the Australian position, see *Australian Football League v Carlton Football Club* [1998] 2 VR 546, [2001] 9(3) SATLJ 67; Carmichael 'No vires to be ultra' in the Australian publication, *Law Institute Journal* (August 2000), p 81; Parpworth 'Sports governing bodies and the principles of natural justice, an Australian perspective' [1996] 4(2) SATLJ 5. In the context of the CAS, see *Andrade v Cape Verde NOC* CAS OG 1996/002 and 005, *Digest of CAS Awards 1986–1998* (1998, Berne), pp 389 and 397 (CAS held that a national Olympic committee could not withdraw an athlete's accreditation to compete following a dispute as to who should carry the flag at the opening ceremony without the IOC's permission, and even with permission must give the athlete an opportunity to put his case), discussed in Beloff 'CAS at the Olympics' [1996] 4(3) SATLJ 5.

3 See paras A3.83, n 3 and A3.129; *Nagle v Feilden* [1966] 2 QB 633 at 647; *Enderby Town Football Club v Football Association* [1971] Ch 591 at 606, [1970] 3 WLR 1021 at 1026. Cf *Russell v Duke of Norfolk* [1949] 1 All ER 109.

4 See paras A3.80 to A3.94.

5 A problematic situation might be where there is no contract and the claimant's challenge falls into the category of an 'application' case for the purposes of the test in *McInnes v Onslow-Fane* (see para A3.84) and where there is no monopoly power or restraint of trade (see para A3.82).

6 For a detailed description of those principles, see Fordham *Judicial Review* (3rd edn, 2001, Hart Publishing) at pp 186, 821–901; Wade *Administrative Law* (8th edn, 2000, Oxford) at pp 435–550; De Smith *Judicial Review of Administrative Action* (5th edn, 1995 (inc supp), Sweet & Maxwell) at pp 375–548.

7 See *Russell v Duke of Norfolk* [1949] 1 All ER 109 at 118 per Tucker LJ; *McInnes v Onslow-Fane* [1978] 1 WLR 1520; para A3.84; *Justice v South Australian Trotting Control Board* (1989) 50 SASR 613 (Sports governing bodies retain discretion to set the procedure for their disciplinary actions). Several of the courts' indications of reluctance to intervene have arisen in cases where a breach of natural justice is alleged: see para A3.72.

8 See Chapter A4 and paras A3.66 to A3.69. The common law and Art 6 often confer the same degree of protection. However if Art 6 applies, there is much less room for the dilution of the obligations by reference to the circumstances of the case.

9 As in *Jones v WRU*, at n 2 (Ebsworth J held that Jones arguably did not have a proper opportunity to present his case before an internal disciplinary committee. The WRU changed its rules to meet the problems identified, and sought to reach a new decision, but was restrained by Potts J from doing so. The Court of Appeal held that the original interim injunction had been properly granted, but that the WRU could not be prevented from re-opening the matter and dealing with it properly). See also Fordham *Judicial Review* (3rd edn, 2001, Hart Publishing), pp 69–72.

10 There will be cases where this is not the case, for example where the decision-making panel was biased and cannot be reconstituted with people who are unaffected.

11 See A3.190 to A3.191; *Stinnato v Auckland Boxing Association* [1978] 1 NZLR 1 at 28, where delay and the belief that a proper hearing would have made no difference, amongst other factors, were held to justify a refusal of relief. See also *Loe v NZRFU* unreported Gallen J, New Zealand High Court 10 August 1993. Cf however *Jones v Welsh Rugby Union* (27 February 1997, unreported) (Ebsworth J), (1997) Times, 6 March, (12 November 1997, unreported) (Potts J), (19 December 1997, unreported), CA, (1998) Times, 6 January, where a similar argument that the absence of the procedural flaw would have made no difference did not find favour with Ebsworth J. The preferable view is that a procedurally flawed decision should be remitted to test whether it would make a difference: see the dissenting judgment of Woodhouse J in *Stinnato* at 12.

(b) Proper opportunity to be heard

A3.102 Sports governing bodies must afford the player, club or other participant a fair opportunity to put his, her or its case[1]. What this means will vary from case to case, depending amongst other things on the nature of the dispute and the severity of the consequences, and on whether the sports governing body is considering an application by the player, club or other participant to exercise its regulatory powers in some way, or is rather pursuing disciplinary proceedings against the player, club or other participant. The starting point is however that in order to have a proper opportunity to be heard, the player, club or other participant must actually be informed[2] that the matter is to be considered, and when. The case put against the player, club or other participant must be fully disclosed[3]: the respondent to disciplinary proceedings must know the details of the charge, and the applicant for a licence must know the objections, if any, to its being granted. Sufficient time must be given to allow the sports governing body's case to be considered and the player, club or other participant to prepare his, her or its case[4]. The player, club or other participant must have an adequate opportunity to convey his, her or its case to the decision-making body[5]. Within reason, the player, club or other participant should not be prevented from making points which he, she or it believes to be pertinent to the issue[6]. While it is possible that in some instances written submissions may be sufficient, the preferable view is that the player, club or other participant should have the option of a full oral hearing at which to present evidence and arguments[7]. Whether representation must be allowed will vary from case to case, as will whether *legal* representation must be allowed[8]. Whether the player, club or other participant must be permitted to call witnesses or to cross-examine the sports governing body's witnesses[9], and whether submissions must be allowed to take the particular form that the player, club or other participant wishes[10], will also depend on the circumstances. The obligation on the governing body probably does not extend to conducting further investigations at the request of the player, club or other participant[11]. It is to be borne in mind that under Art 6 of the European Convention on Human Rights, some of the elements of procedural protection set out above are mandatory[12].

1 For the generally applicable position, see Fordham *Judicial Review* (3rd edn, 2001, Hart Publishing) at pp 826–863; Wade *Administrative Law* (8th edn, 2000, Oxford) at pp 469–550;

De Smith *Judicial Review of Administrative Action* (5th edn (inc supp), 1995, Sweet & Maxwell) at pp 431–454.

2 *Keighley Football Club v Cunningham* (1960) Times, 25 May (Contrary to natural justice to impose suspension on player without any notice); *St Johnstone Football Club Ltd v Scottish Football Association* 1965 SLT 171 (Contrary to natural justice to censure and fine without advance warning); *Collins v Lane* (22 June 1999, unreported), CA at p 11 of the shorthand writers' transcript (Club member must be informed of intention to consider complaints against him).

3 *Stinnato v Auckland Boxing Association* [1978] 1 NZLR 1 (where it was held that even though no proper notice had been given to the boxer of consideration of his application and he was afforded no opportunity to be heard, it was open to the court to refuse discretionary relief on the basis that a hearing would have made no difference and the boxer had been given full hearings in the past. This proposition must be treated with great care. If a decision is procedurally flawed, the proper course is to remit for reconsideration in a procedurally lawful way: see Woodhouse J, dissenting, at 12; see also n 11 to para A3.101); *Tyrrell Racing Organisation v RAC Motor Sports Association and the Fédération Internationale de l'Automobile* (20 July 1984, unreported) (Hirst J) at p 11 of the Lexis transcript (Claimant arrived at disciplinary hearing without full knowledge of charges, and there was no evidence to suggest that if he had asked for an adjournment it would have been granted. Furthermore, some of the documents provided to him for the first time at the hearing were not in English); *Wright v Jockey Club* (1995) Times, 16 June (QBD) at p 9 of the Lexis transcript (where the jockey was held to have had a full and proper opportunity to question the medical evidence that suggested he was unfit to ride, and to put forward contrary evidence from other doctors). Cf *P v FEI* CAS 98/184, *Digest of CAS Awards 1986–1998* (1998, Berne), p 197 (the governing body must make full disclosure of material which might assist the individual to establish there was no liability. In that instance a negative blood test was not communicated to the owner of the horse when a doping charge was based on a positive urine test. If the owner had known, he would have sought a confirmatory analysis which might have exonerated him). In *Loe v NZRFU* unreported Gallen J, New Zealand High Court 10 August 1993, the court rejected complaints that no 'brief' of the case against the player had been provided, and that the videotape of the on-field incident had not been made available until the morning of the hearing. See also *Auckland Boxing Association v New Zealand Boxing Association* [2001] NZLR 847 (scope of concerns and possible consequences of decision must be communicated); *Freedman v Petty and Greyhound Racing Control Board* [1981] VR 1001.

4 See *Tyrrell Racing Organisation v RAC Motor Sports Association and the Fédération Internationale de l'Automobile*, n 3 at p 11 of the Lexis transcript; *Stewart v Judicial Committee of the Auckland Racing Club Inc* [1992] 3 NZLR 693 (hearing immediately after a race did not afford sufficient time for case to be considered and response prepared, but the availability of an appeal saved the process). The deadlines set must be reasonable: In *G v International Equestrian Federation* CAS 91/53, *Digest of CAS Awards 1986–1998* (1998, Berne), p 79 at paras 10–12, the CAS held that the rider had to be allowed to see the results of a second drug test on his horse before deciding whether to submit an explanation and evidence. Cf the approach in *Currie v Barton* (26 March 1987, unreported) (Scott J), (11 February 1988, unreported), CA, (1988) Times, 12 February (no need for charges to be formulated before hearing). In *Loe v NZRFU*, at n 3, the court rejected a complaint that there had been insufficient time to prepare because it had before it no affidavit stating what additional evidence was kept out as a result.

5 See *Angus v British Judo Association* (1984) Times, 15 June (no opportunity given to a judoka to explain positive drug test); *Collins v Lane*, see n 2; *Scott Plews v British Ice Hockey Association* unreported, Lord Eassie Scottish Court of Session 18 March 1997 (interim relief granted to ice hockey player who was banned based on video evidence which he was not entitled to challenge. He was not informed about the ban); *Andrade v Cape Verde NOC* CAS OG 1996/005, *Digest of CAS Awards 1986–1998* (1998, Berne), p 397 (withdrawal of accreditation by a governing body not possible without an opportunity to answer charge). It is possible that in some instances there may not be a right to make further representations: see *Ray v Professional Golfers' Association* (15 April 1997, unreported) (Judge Dyer QC); (Ray was refused permission to step up to a different level of membership because he failed the examinations on which that level of membership depended. He was not entitled to make further representations as to why he should be allowed to step up, as he had had his chance in the examinations).

6 *Stewart v Judicial Committee of the Auckland Racing Club Inc*, see n 4 (failure to consider affidavits obtained). In *Angus v British Judo Association*, above, the judoka was not allowed to explain why his prescription from a Canadian doctor was for a bona fide asthmatic condition. In *Loe v NZRFU*, n 3, the judge rejected a complaint that no opportunity to call character evidence had been given because no adjournment was sought and such material was available on the appeal hearing. See also *Freedman v Greyhound Racing Control Board,* n 3.

7 Based on *McInnes v Onslow-Fane* [1978] 1 WLR 1520, it appears that an oral hearing would be required in forfeiture and legitimate expectation cases, but not application cases. The need for an oral hearing was implicit in *Jones v WRU* (27 February 1997, unreported) (Ebsworth J), (1997) Times, 6 March, (17 November 1997, unreported) (Potts J), (19 December 1997, unreported), CA, (1998) Times, 6 January. In *Currie v Barton* (26 March 1987, unreported) (Scott J), (11 February 1988, unreported), CA, (1988) Times, 12 February, the absence of an oral hearing was held on the facts not to amount to a breach of natural justice. See also *Colgan v Kennel Club* (26 October 2001, unreported) (Cooke J) (lack of oral hearing not unfair but there in circumstances where there had already been a criminal conviction). In *USA Shooting and Quigley v Union Internationale de Tir*, CAS 94/129, *Digest of CAS Awards 1986–1998* (1998, Berne), p 187, it was suggested that an oral hearing was not required. In our view, however, things have moved on and in almost all cases the requirements of natural justice extend to requiring an oral hearing.

8 If the rules provide for representation, they must of course be followed. If they do not, the circumstances may dictate that representation, and even legal representation, should be allowed. Sports governing bodies are not required always to allow such representation, but they must not rule out the possibility of doing so altogether. In *Pett v Greyhound Racing Association* [1969] 1 QB 125, Lord Denning MR concluded that the rules of natural justice required a trainer facing disciplinary charges before a tribunal governing greyhound racing to have a fair opportunity of meeting the charge he faced, and that the claimant had an arguable case that he was entitled to legal representation in order to provide him with such an opportunity because the charge he faced might affect his livelihood and his reputation. When the matter came on for trial in *Pett v Greyhound Racing Association (No 2)* [1970] 1 QB 46; on appeal [1970] 1 QB 67n, CA, Lyell J decided that even though the hearing could affect the claimant's livelihood and reputation, the rules of natural justice did not require legal representation in the circumstances of the case. The appeal against Lyell J's decision was withdrawn when the governing body allowed the claimant to be legally represented. In *Enderby Town Football Club v Football Association* [1971] Ch 591, [1971] 1 All ER 215, the FA refused the club permission to have legal representation on an appeal and the club sought an injunction. The Court of Appeal rejected the application on the basis that it was not a breach of natural justice to refuse representation in the particular circumstances. Lord Denning however referred to *Pett v Greyhound Racing Association* and stated (at 605) that in his view the correct analysis was that sports governing bodies had to retain a discretion to allow legal representation if and when appropriate but that so long as the discretion was properly exercised an individual refusal of representation was not contrary to the rules of natural justice. In *Jones v WRU* (27 February 1997, unreported) (Ebsworth J), (1997) Times, 6 March, (17 November 1997, unreported) (Potts J), (19 December 1997, unreported), CA, (1998) Times, 6 January, Ebsworth J appears (at p 5 of the Lexis transcript) to endorse Lord Denning's conclusion in *Enderby*. See also [1997] 5(1) SATLJ 20. For another case where there was held to be no right to legal representation, see *Wright v Jockey Club* Sir Haydn Tudor Evans, (1995) Times, 16 June (QBD), at p 11–12 of the Lexis transcript. See also *Colgan v Kennel Club*, n 7; and *Freedman v Petty and Greyhound Racing Control Board* [1981] VR 1001.

9 See *Jones v WRU*, n 7 (On an interlocutory hearing, Ebsworth J held, at p 9 of the Lexis transcript, that it was arguable that preventing the player calling evidence or questioning witnesses in the context of disciplinary proceedings in a professional sport was contrary to natural justice. The Court of Appeal upheld this interlocutory conclusion: see Potter LJ at p 17 of the transcript, where he said that the requirements of natural justice in the context of professional sport may well need further development. However the WRU changed its rules so as to deal with the problem before it was tested at trial whether the obligations went so far). In *Stewart v Judicial Committee of the Auckland Racing Club*, n 4, failing to allow cross-examination was held to be a breach of natural justice. Cf *Justice v South Australian Trotting Control Board* (1989) 50 SASR 613 (Lack of availability of stewards for cross-examination not a breach of natural justice); *Loe v NZRFU*, n 3 (Judge rejected a complaint that governing body witnesses had not been made available for cross-examination, because the material would not have been of significance in reaching a conclusion).

10 See *Jones v WRU*, nn 7 and 9 (Ebsworth J held, at pp 7 and 9 of the Lexis transcript that it was arguable that refusing Jones permission to make submissions on the content of a video of the incident while the video was being played was contrary to natural justice. Again the WRU changed its rules to meet the problem before it was tested at trial).

11 See *Wright v Jockey Club* Sir Haydn Tudor Evans, (1995) Times, 16 June (QBD), at p 11 of the Lexis transcript.

12 See paras A4.36 to A4.56.

(c) Reasons

A3.103 It is not yet established that there is an obligation on sports governing bodies and their tribunals to give reasons for their decisions[1]. That said it is generally likely to be wiser for a sports governing body to provide the reasons for its decisions, particularly if there is an appeal process that involves something other than a complete re-hearing[2]. Again the influence of Art 6 of the European Convention on Human Rights may lead to the imposition of more rigorous standards[3].

1 For the generally applicable position, see Fordham *Judicial Review* (3rd edn, 2001, Hart Publishing) at pp 874–901; Wade *Administrative Law* (8th edn, 2000, Oxford) at pp 516–520; De Smith *Judicial Review of Administrative Action* (5th edn (inc supp), 1995, Sweet & Maxwell) at pp 457–474. See also *McInnes v Onslow-Fane* [1978] 1 WLR 1520 (No obligation to give reasons in an application case); *Fisher v National Greyhound Racing Club* (31 July 1985, unreported), CA per Oliver LJ at pp 8–9 of the Lexis transcript (Arguable that a right to reasons arises on an *Onslow-Fane* expectation case); *Naden v Judicial Committee of the Auckland Racing Club* [1995] 1 NZLR 307 (where additional reasons are given in an informal publication after the original decision, natural justice requires that the party affected can point to those additional reasons in its argument on an appeal. Arguably, this suggests an entitlement to adequate reasons).

2 In *Dundee United Football Club v Scottish Football Association*, 3 February 1988 (1988) Outer House Cases, 1998 SLT 1244, it was held that on the facts the failure to give reasons did not amount to a denial of natural justice, but that in general where there is a right of appeal reasons should be given. See also [1998] 10(1) SATLJ 54.

3 See paras A4.36 to A4.56.

(d) Burden of proof and strict liability offences

A3.104 An unfair burden of proof must not be placed on the player, club or other participant, for example that he, she or it must prove innocence beyond all reasonable doubt. This does not mean that the onus must be on the sporting body to establish guilt beyond all reasonable doubt, although this is often the standard set by the rules[1]. In the normal course, in the absence of specific provision, the standard of proof will be the 'civil' standard of balance of probabilities, although within that measure there should be a sliding scale of satisfaction depending on the gravity of the allegation[2]. Nor does it mean that it is not open to sports governing bodies to provide for presumptions in their rules if the circumstances dictate. For example, it is legitimate to include a presumption that a doping offence has been committed if a particular concentration of a particular banned substance or its metabolite is found in the athlete's sample[3]. It may also be legitimate for the rules to impose a strict liability offence, at least in the context of doping and at least in relation to the commission of the offence as opposed to the sanction, so long as the rules are properly constructed[4]. Again the influence of Art 6 of the European Convention on Human Rights may lead to the imposition of more rigorous standards[5].

1 See for example as to the standards of proof required in doping cases, paras E4.248 to E4.252.

2 *Johnson v New Zealand Racing Conference* (16 July 1996, unreported), NZCA at p 10 of the transcript; *Korneev*, CAS OG 1996/003–4, award dated 4 August 1996 (Standard of satisfaction must reflect the nature of the offence and evidence must be sufficient; the governing body must prove its case to the 'comfortable satisfaction' of the tribunal), discussed in Beloff [1996] 4(3) SATLJ 5. See further paras E4.248 to E4.252; *N J, Y and W v FINA* CAS 98/208, *Digest of CAS Awards II 1998–2000* (2002, Kluwer), p 234, para 13

3 See paras E4.75 to E4.135. The justification for this in the doping context is first that an advantage is conferred however a prohibited substance comes to be ingested, and secondly that the process would be unwieldy and impractical if the sports governing body had to prove deliberate ingestion on every occasion. See *Gasser v Stinson* (15 June 1988, unreported) (Scott J), *Wilander and Novacek v Tobin and Jude* (19 March 1996, unreported) (Lightman J), (8 April 1996, unreported), CA (Lightman J), [1997] 1 Lloyd's Law Rep 195; revsd [1997] 2 Lloyd's Law Rep 296, CA.

4 While the approach of the English courts has been to uphold strict liability, there is a considerable movement to limit its ambit in the CAS jurisprudence at least in so far as the ability of the governing body to ban without showing fault is concerned: see paras E4.130 to E4.134 and A3.10, and in particular *Aanes v FILA,* CAS 2001/A/317A, award dated 9 July 2001. *Raducan* CAS Sydney 00/011 is a good example of the CAS still applying strict liability to the question of whether an offence has been committed: see para E4.125. It may be that the approach in the earlier English cases would not be followed today. It is arguable that strict liability should be confined to whether an offence is committed, with all consequences of such an offence (whether they be disqualification, expulsion from event, fine or a ban or suspension) being in the discretion of the governing body, rather than automatic.

5 See paras A4.36 to A4.56.

(e) Bias, prejudging the issue and good faith

A3.105 The committee, panel or tribunal of the sports governing body that is to take the decision must approach the matter with an open mind[1]. It must make the decision for the right reasons as opposed to for some ulterior and improper motive, and must act in good faith[2]. It must exercise its discretion in light of the circumstances of the case before it, and cannot simply apply an over-rigid policy[3]. It must not be actually biased, and must not have the appearance of being biased, against the player, club or other participant[4]. The test is whether there is a real danger of bias arising from the facts[5]. The panel must be free from any interest, such as a financial interest[6], in the outcome. An appearance of bias can arise if the decision-making body includes individuals who have previously been connected with the dispute to be decided upon (for example if they have participated in an anterior decision to make the charges or to refuse an application)[7] or who have made a statement as to what the outcome should be[8]. Any statements to the press should come from people who will not take part in the decision-making process. Lastly in this context, there should be a separation between the roles of prosecutor and judge[9]. Again the influence of Art 6 of the European Convention on Human Rights may lead to the imposition of more rigorous standards[10].

1 For the generally applicable position, see Fordham *Judicial Review* (3rd edn, 2001, Hart Publishing) at pp 741–750; Wade *Administrative Law* (8th edn, 2000, Oxford) at pp 328–333, 526–528; De Smith *Judicial Review of Administrative Action* (5th edn (inc supp), 1995, Sweet & Maxwell) at pp 505–520.

2 For the generally applicable position, see Fordham at pp 751–759; Wade at pp 410–416; De Smith at pp 330–346; *Wright v Jockey Club* Sir Haydn Tudor Evans, (1995) Times, 16 June (QBD), at p 9 of the Lexis transcript; *Haron bin Mundir v Singapore AAA* [1992] 1 SLR 18. A sports governing body cannot go back on a policy it has adopted for entry deadlines for a competition: *US Swimming v FINA* CAS OG 1996/001, *Digest of CAS Awards 1986–1998* (1998, Berne), p 377; nor can it go back on the selection of an athlete. *Watts v Australian Cycling Federation* CAS 96/153, *Digest of CAS Awards 1986–1998* (1998, Berne), p 335.

3 *Blackler v NZRFL* [1968] NZLR 547 at 552 (player argued that the league had no power to prevent him playing abroad, alternatively that the rule was in unreasonable restraint of trade, alternatively that the league had not addressed its mind to his particular case but had simply applied a rigid policy. In the event the case succeeded on restraint of trade grounds and the court did not deal with the last argument). In *Wimbledon Football Club v Football League*, FA Arbitration Panel decision dated 29 January 2002, on the other hand, the panel preferred to remit the matter to the League on the basis that the League's decision had been procedurally flawed because it applied an over-rigid policy without considering in detail the particular facts of the club's application to move ground or the restraint of trade argument advanced. The League referred the matter to an FA Commission to make the decision, and it was decided that the club should be allowed to move.

4 For the generally applicable position, see Fordham at pp 864–873; Wade at pp 445–468; and De Smith at pp 521–548.

5 *Modahl v BAF* [2002] 1 WLR 1192, CA at para 63. See also *Freedman v Petty and Greyhound Racing Control Board* [1981] VR 1001.

6 *Barnard v Jockey Club of South Africa* (1984) 2 SALR 35 (Member of panel was a partner in the firm of lawyers representing the Jockey Club).

7 In *Collins v Lane* (22 June 1999, unreported), CA at p 11 of the shorthand writers' transcript, the principle was regarded as infringed where the official who made the complaint against the shooter also participated in the disciplinary decision. See also *Colgan v Kennel Club* (26 October 2001, unreported) (Cooke J), where the judge pointed to the fact that this was not the case in respect of Mrs Colgan's disciplinary proceedings. Cf *Jackson v Western Australian Basketball Federation* 21 ALD 283 (1990), where it was held that there was no absolute rule that natural justice is denied when the person laying charges adjudicates, nor is there a rule of law that a committee that has adjudicated guilt on issues cannot afford natural justice on a second hearing of the same issues. See also *Riley v Racing Appeals Tribunal*, unreported Balmford J (Victoria) 1 August 2001 (chairman of tribunal also a member of the governing body whose decision was being challenged: held not to amount to apparent bias).

8 *Modahl v BAF* [2002] 1 WLR 1192, CA at para 68 (Panel member alleged to have said that all athletes are guilty of doping until they have proved their innocence); *Revie v Football Association*, Cantley J, (1979) Times, 14 December (FA tribunal members had expressed a view on the merits of an action against Don Review before hearing the charges).

9 *Freedman v Petty and Greyhound Racing Control Board* [1981] VR 1001 (Contrary to natural justice for the Board to act as both prosecutor and judge).

10 See paras A4.136 to A4.156.

(f) Delay

A3.106 Justice delayed is justice denied. The case must come on within a reasonable time[1]. This is a specific requirement of Art 6 of the Human Rights Act[2].

1 For the generally applicable position, see Fordham *Judicial Review* (3rd edn, 2001, Hart Publishing) at pp 626–628; Wade *Administrative Law* (8th edn, 2000, Oxford) at pp 408–410. For a case in the sports context, see *Barrieau v US Trotting Association* (1986) 78 NBR (2d) 128, 198 APR 128.

2 See para A4.48.

(g) Possibility of appeal and fairness of the process as a whole

A3.107 It is not yet established that procedural fairness requires that there be a right to appeal against the decision of a sports governing body[1]. On the other hand the great benefit for a sports governing body of providing for a right of appeal is that a properly carried out appeal can cure defects in earlier stages of the process (because it is the fairness of the process as a whole that will be assessed[2]).

1 For the generally applicable position, see Wade *Administrative Law* (8th edn, 2000, Oxford) at pp 520–523; *Jones v WRU* (27 February 1997, unreported) (Ebsworth J), (1997) Times, 6 March (absence of an appeal not a ground of unfairness, citing *Ward v Bradford Corpn* (1971) 70 LGR 27).

2 See *Modahl v BAF* (28 July 1997, unreported), CA per Lord Woolf MR at pp 20–26, Morritt LJ at pp 36 to 39 and Pill LJ at pp 43 to 44 of the shorthand writers' transcript; *Calvin v Carr* [1980] AC 574, PC; *Lloyd v McMahon* [1987] AC 625, HL; *Colgan v Kennel Club* (26 October 2001, unreported) (Cooke J). See also *Stewart v Judicial Committee of the Auckland Racing Club* [1992] 3 NZLR 693 (appeals construed as involving a full re-hearing in order to provide a fair procedure overall in the light of the fact that the first hearing was peremptory); *Naden v Judicial Committee* [1995] 1 NZLR 307. But cf *Collins v Lane* (22 June 1999, unreported), CA at pp 11–12 of the shorthand writers' transcript, where the absence of a right to make representations before a disciplinary decision was made could not be saved by the possibility of an appeal. CAS's position is that where a de novo hearing before CAS is allowed, this cures any procedural defect in the original process: see eg *USA Shooting and Quigley v Union Internationale de Tir*, CAS 94/129, *Digest of CAS Awards 1986–1998* (1998, Berne), p 187.

(h) Costs

A3.108 Fairness does not require costs to be awarded to a player, club or other participant if he she or it succeeds in an action. It may be required under Art 6 however[1].

1 See paras A4.36 to A4.56.

D The obligation not to act unreasonably, arbitrarily or capriciously

(a) Reasonableness of the substantive decision

A3.109 Sports governing bodies must act reasonably (in the sense of rationally). They must not act irrationally, arbitrarily or capriciously[1]. The test of unreasonableness in this context[2] has traditionally been regarded as a high one for a challenger to overcome. The courts will not substitute their view of the merits for that of the expert decision-maker; instead, they will only overturn a decision on this ground if it was one which no sports governing body properly instructing itself as to the facts and the law could have made[3]. That said, there are a number of circumstances that are indicative of an unreasonable decision which may not be quite so difficult to establish. For example, the sports governing body must take into account relevant considerations and must not take into account irrelevant considerations[4]. Sports governing bodies must not treat like situations differently or unlike situations the same[5].

1 For the generally applicable position, see Fordham *Judicial Review* (3rd edn, 2001, Hart Publishing) at pp 188, 770–820; Wade *Administrative Law* (8th edn, 2000, Oxford) at pp 315–434; De Smith *Judicial Review of Administrative Action* (5th edn (inc supp), 1995, Sweet & Maxwell) at pp 549 to 608. See also *Nagle v Feilden* [1966] 2 QB 633 at 646; *Wilander and Novacek v Tobin and Jude* [1997] 2 Lloyd's Rep 296 at 300 col 1; and the cases cited in n 1 to para A3.83.

2 Often referred to as Wednesbury unreasonableness (after *Associated Provinical Picture Houses v Wednesbury Corpn* [1948] 1 KB 223). In Fordham's terminology, the ground for review is a 'soft' one: see Fordham *Judicial Review* (3rd edn, 2001, Hart Publishing), pp 222–256.

3 *Le Roux v NZRFU* unreported, Eichelbaum CJ, New Zealand High Court, 14 March 1995, at p 3 of the transcript.

4 *Wilander and Novacek v Tobin and Jude* [1997] 2 Lloyd's Rep 296 at 300, col 1; *Le Roux v NZRFU*, n 3, at pp 3 to 10 of the transcript. The argument was rejected because the claimant was in reality complaining about the weight attached to the factors rather than whether they should or not have been taken into account.

5 *Nagle v Feilden* [1966] 2 QB 633.

(b) Proportionality as an element of reasonableness

A3.110 For some time a distinction has been drawn for public law purposes between reasonableness and proportionality. Whereas reasonableness has been seen as a test to be applied in the fulfilment of a purely supervisory jurisdiction, proportionality has been characterised as a test that (while supervisory) trespasses to a greater degree on the merits. Proportionality involves balancing the legitimate aim pursued against the impact of the action chosen. To be proportionate, the action must go no further than is reasonably necessary in the pursuit of the legitimate aim. If the adverse consequences are out of proportion to the benefit gained, or if a less onerous course could have been adopted with the same results, the action will be disproportionate. In fact, the proportionality test allows a margin of appreciation, or latitude, to the decision-maker just as does the reasonableness test[1]. It too is a flexible concept, and the extent of the margin of appreciation will vary from context to context. Developments in the public law test for review make it arguable that proportionality is a part of the public law test in this context[2]. The logic of the *Modahl*[3] and *Wilander*[4] decisions is that as the public law test develops, so too does the test to be applied to sports governing bodies. Accordingly, if it is correct that proportionality falls to be considered in the review of public bodies' actions, so too it falls to be considered in the review of the decisions of sports governing bodies. Arguably, it would be inappropriate to limit the test in the sports context to traditional interpretations of arbitrariness and capriciousness, when those interpretations have been left behind in the public law context[5].

1 See *R v Chief Constable of Sussex, ex p International Trader's Ferry* [1999] 2 AC 418, HL per Lord Slynn. See also *Le Roux v NZRFU* unreported, Eichelbaum CJ, New Zealand High Court at p 14 of the transcript ('unreasonable, unreasonable in the Wednesbury sense, inconsistent, disproportionate, altogether excessive and out of proportion, or irrational, whichever formulation is used makes little difference. All are aspects, criteria, or different formulations of unreasonableness. Has the decision gone beyond the limits within which a reasonable appeals committee could exercise its discretion? And in considering the possible breach of the discretion weight should be given to the fact that the decisions under consideration are those of domestic tribunals consisting in part or whole of persons chosen for their background in the particular field of activity – here the playing and administration of rugby').

2 See *R (Alconbury) v Secretary of State for the Environment* [2001] UKHL 23, [2001] 2 WLR 1389 per Lord Slynn at 1406–1407 paras 50–52; *R v Secretary of State for the Home Department, ex p Daly* [2001] UKHL 26, [2001] 2 WLR 1622 at 1634H–1635B, para 27. See Fordham 'Common law proportionality' [2002] JR 110.

3 *Modahl v British Athletics Federation* (28 June 1996, unreported) (Popplewell J), (28 July 1997, unreported), CA, (22 July 1998, unreported), HL, [2002] 1 WLR 1192, CA.

4 *Wilander and Novacek v Tobin and Jude* (19 March 1996, unreported) (Lightman J), 8 April 1996, unreported), CA (Lightman J), [1997] 1 Lloyd's Rep 195; revsd [1997] 2 Lloyd's Rep 296.

5 In *Wimbledon Football Club v Football League*, 29 January 2002, an FA Arbitration Panel decided as much: see para A3.156.

(c) Availability and proportionality of sanctions

A3.111 A sports governing body may not impose sanctions that are out of proportion to the gravity of the offence involved[1].

1 *Colgan v Kennel Club* (26 October 2001, unreported) (Cooke J); *R v General Medical Council, ex p Colman* (1989) 1 Admin LR 469 at 489; *R v Barnsley Metropolitan Borough Council, ex p Hook* [1976] 1 WLR 1052. See also *Edwards v BAF and IAAF* [1998] 2 CMLR 363, [1997] Eu LR 721 (The IAAF's mandatory ban of four years for a first doping offence had been ruled disproportionate in Germany with the result that athletes there had been reinstated. Edwards, a shot putter who had been banned by the BAF for four years, sought to challenge the BAF's and the IAAF's continued insistence on four years in the UK when it could not be sustained in other countries, on the grounds that this approach amounted to discrimination on grounds of nationality. The action failed, but the IAAF subsequently reduced its ban from four to two years). For a more restrictive approach, see *Re Duncan Ferguson (Ferguson v SFA)* (1996) Outer House Cases 1 February 1996. The same principle is applied by the CAS: *Tzagaev* CAS Sydney 00/010, *Digest of CAS Awards II 1998–2000* (2002, Kluver), p 658 (held that the IWF could not ban the entire wrestling team following the failure of three of them to pass a drugs test). Cf *National Wheelchair Basketball Association v International Paralympic Committee* CAS 95/122, *Digest of CAS Awards 1986–1998* (1998, Berne), p 173 (CAS held it was proportionate for entire team to lose gold medals as a result of doping offence by one member). See also *Chagnaud v FINA* CAS 95/141 (2 year ban reduced because inter alia another swimmer had simply received a strong warning in a parallel case and because the swimmer had a generally good reputation for compliance); *Cullwick v FINA* CAS 96/149, *Digest of CAS Awards 1986–1998* (1998, Berne), p 251 (a case where there was a technical offence without knowledge and no additional sanction was imposed beyond the finding of guilt). See also *Australian Football League v Carlton Football Club* [1998] 2 VR 546. In *Loe v NZRFU*, unreported Gallen J, New Zealand High Court, 10 August 1993, the court regarded six months for eye-gouging by a rugby player to be fair. The court also indicated that penalties should not generally be deferred to start at a later date, but in that instance it was fair so that the penalty actually applied while rugby was being played. In the first stage of his challenges against his treatment following a positive doping result consequent upon the use of a Vicks nasal inhaler, the skier Alain Baxter succeeded in convincing CAS that the International Ski Federation could not split up his minimum three month ban so that parts of it applied at different times over the coming season: *Baxter v FIS*, CAS (August 2000). In *Le Roux v NZRFU*, unreported Eichelbaum CJ, New Zealand High Court, 15 March 1995, the court regarded 19 months for ear-biting by a rugby player to be legitimate, after listing the factors to be taken into account.

E The obligation on a sports governing body to instruct itself properly as to the facts

A3.112 A sports governing body cannot make a decision for which there is no evidential basis, and it must instruct itself properly as to the facts before reaching a decision[1].

1 For the generally applicable position, see Fordham *Judicial Review* (3rd edn, 2001, Hart Publishing) at pp 728–740; Wade *Administrative Law* (8th edn, 2000, Oxford) at pp 278–285; *Wilander and Novacek v Tobin and Jude* [1997] 2 Lloyd's Rep 296 at 300, col 1; *Wright v Jockey Club* Sir Haydn Tudor Evans, (1995) Times, 16 June (QBD), at p 11 of the Lexis transcript.

F The obligation not to act contrary to a legitimate expectation

A3.113 Traditionally, the extent of a legitimate expectation protected by the courts has been the right to be consulted before a policy is changed for the future[1], or to be given a fair opportunity to explain why a particular state of affairs, such as the licensed status of a participant, should not be altered[2]. In other words, the obligation has been essentially procedural. There has however been movement in the law generally, raising the possibility that in certain circumstances the courts will protect a substantive legitimate expectation of a particular outcome, as opposed to simply of a fair opportunity to make a case before something happens. It is now possible that a sports governing body may be unable to depart from a previously stated policy giving rise to a substantive legitimate expectation[3].

1 For the generally applicable position, see Fordham *Judicial Review* (3rd edn, 2001, Hart Publishing) at pp 760–769; Wade *Administrative Law* (8th edn, 2000, Oxford) at pp 370–373, 494–500; De Smith *Judicial Review of Administrative Action* (5th edn (inc supp), 1995, Sweet & Maxwell) at pp 401–430; *R v Jockey Club, ex p RAM Racecourses* [1993] 2 All ER 225, DC.

2 As in *McInnes v Onslow-Fane* [1978] 1 WLR 1520.

3 *R v North and East Devon Health Authority, ex p Coughlan* [2001] QB 213. See also *R v Jockey Club, ex p RAM Racecourses* [1993] 2 All ER 225, DC at 243f. Cf *US Swimming v FINA* CAS OG 96/001, *Digest of CAS Awards 1986–1998* (1998, Berne), p 377; *Watts v Australian Cycling Federation* CAS 96/153, *Digest of CAS Awards 1986–1998* (1998, Berne), p 335. Cf also the Australian approach in *Drummoyne District RFC v NSWRU* (3 December 1993, unreported) (Young J) (an expectation of participation coupled with unconscionable conduct by the governing body led to an injunction compelling the governing body to allow the club to participate).

4 CONTRACT

A3.114 As set out above, it remains the case that the most effective way to challenge the actions of a sports governing body in pursuit of its regulatory powers[1] is to establish the existence of a contract to which it is a party, and of which it is in breach[2]. The source for such a contract, and its contents, varies as much in the sports sector as in any other. Contract of course also forms the basis for other legal actions involving the purely commercial actions of sports governing bodies, and indeed for most other legal actions in the sports sector not involving sports governing bodies, for example as between players[3], clubs[4], other participants[5] and commercial partners[6].

1 The regulatory powers will vary from sport to sport, but in particular include control over eligibility criteria and access to the sport, control over requests to do something specific (for example, relocate a club) and disciplinary control over doping and other offences.

2 A sports governing body can only be a party to a contract in its own name if it has legal personality: see Chapter C1.

3 Players are generally in a contractual relationship with their club (or its members), whether it be a contract based on membership of the club or a contract of employment. See generally Chapter E1. Note that where a club (such as a swimming pool or gymnasium) is no more than a provider of facilities to individuals in return for a fee (even one described as a membership fee), the relationship may not truly be one of membership of a club and there is probably no contractual relationship between members. See *Chitty on Contracts* (28th edn, 1999, Sweet & Maxwell), para 9-085.

4 There may be an implied contract between the competitors in the same event to comply with the rules: *Clarke v Earl of Dunraven, The Satanita* [1897] AC 59, HL (Contractual obligation on a yacht owner to comply with the rules of racing, such that a breach of that obligation gave rise to an action by a competitor in damages), but see *Chitty* at para 2-101 for criticism of this analysis.

5 For example contracts involving the right to mount the next challenge to a boxing champion, as in *Lewis v WBC and Bruno* (3 November 1995, unreported) (Rattee J) (failed attempt to prevent WBC bout between Bruno and Tyson on basis of an alleged contractual entitlement of Lewis to fight Bruno first).

6 Broadcasting, sponsorship, merchandising, corporate hospitality and other forms of commercial exploitation. See Chapters D4 to D7.

A The sources of contracts to which sports governing bodies are party

(a) *Written contracts between sports governing bodies and commercial partners*

A3.115 The most obvious contracts to which a sports governing body is party are the straightforward contracts (generally written or at least evidenced in writing) that it enters into with commercial partners[1]. Breaches of these arrangements can obviously be the subject of legal action in the normal way, and subject to the normal defences. Ostensibly the contractual obligations owed by sports governing bodies in the context of a purely commercial contract (as opposed to the exercise of some regulatory function) do not include the general obligations of fairness and nationality dealt with above[2].

1 Assuming that it has legal personality. Otherwise representatives will have to contract on behalf of the membership.

2 When a sports governing body is contracting for the purchase of half-time oranges, it does not have to observe the principles of natural justice. This statement should however be taken with some care, since even in the purely commercial context analogous obligations may arise as a matter of contract. See *Blackpool and Fylde Aero Club v Blackpool Borough Council* [1990] 1 WLR 1195 (A private company inviting tenders is under a collateral contractual obligation to tenderers to consider the tenders submitted in accordance with the invitation); *Harmon CFEM Façades (UK) Ltd v Corporate Officer of the House of Commons* [1999] All ER (D) 1178 at para 217 (where the implied terms held to exist in the collateral contract arising on a tender extended to an obligation to deal with tenderers equally and fairly). It might be arguable that a disappointed tenderer had a recourse based on a collateral contract if a project or particular commercial rights were granted in breach of a sports governing body's own rules, or if the tenderer were prompted to tender when it had no prospect of success. Further, competition law and the free movement rules may impose an obligation to afford an equal opportunity to companies to tender on transparent terms and not to discriminate in the selection of the successful tenderer, and conceivably not to select a tender that was not the economically most advantageous one.

(b) *The sports governing body's rules as a contract between members and the sports governing body*

A3.116 It is a well-established proposition that the rules of a sports governing body constitute a contract between the members of the sports governing body, and between each member and the sports governing body itself[1]. For example the International Rugby Board is made up of the rugby unions of each rugby-playing nation, each of which is bound by the IRB Constitution[2]. In turn the individual unions are made up of the individual rugby clubs in each nation, each of which is bound by its union's rules. The union may have incorporated, but there remains a contract between the members, which may now have become shareholders, on the basis of the rules. Perceived breaches of those rules can therefore be the subject of legal action in the normal way. Actions have been brought on the basis of breach of a sports governing body's rules as a contract in a wide range of circumstances[3].

1 See s 14 of the Companies Act 1985; *Chitty on Contracts* (28th edn, 1999, Sweet & Maxwell), paras 9–029, 9–079 to 9–080. Where the association is unincorporated, each of the members enters into a contract with the other members when it joins (it may be expressly or by conduct) on the terms of the rules of the association. Where the association is incorporated, for example as a limited company, there is a contract on the terms of the memorandum and articles of association and the rules produced pursuant to them, between all the members and between each member and the association itself. The rules can be changed periodically in accordance with defined procedures and the parties continue in a contractual relationship on the basis of the changed rules. Departure from the procedures may however preclude the incorporation of the change into the rules. The members may be constituted as shareholders and as such they can enter into their own shareholder agreements and they have available to them shareholders' remedies against the company as a matter of company law. See generally Chapter C1.

2 See IRB Bye-Law 7: Membership of the Board by a Union or Association shall be effective as an agreement binding such Union or Association (which agreement requires such Union or Association to similarly by agreement bind its affiliated membership which such Union or Association undertakes to do) to abide by the Bye-Laws, Regulations and Laws of the Game and to accept and enforce all the Board's decisions (unless and until revoked or set aside by the Council) in respect of the playing and/or administration of the Game throughout the country or countries within the jurisdiction of such Union or Association.

3 See paras A3.95 to A3.100, in relation to actions based on breach of the sports governing body's rules.

(c) Side contracts between a sports governing body and its members

A3.117 There may also be side contracts between specific clubs and the sports governing body. Since the European Model of Sport remains pyramidical in structure, with every level from the top to the bottom linked by the possibility of promotion and relegation[1], sports governing bodies regulate a diverse group, ranging from amateur sides playing in the park to professional clubs turning over many millions of pounds. The interests, expectations and entitlements of these completely different clubs are wholly different, in particular in terms of the funds to be received from the central selling of broadcasting and other rights that are derived solely from the activities of the elite clubs. Side contracts have been used by sports governing bodies to define specific obligations and rights that apply between the sports governing body and only some of the clubs that are members of it. That may well often be entirely legitimate, but on occasions clubs have sought to challenge the imposition of side contracts, or of terms in them, regarding them as attempts by the sports governing body to prevent them breaking away and keeping the broadcasting revenue to themselves[2].

1 See paras A1.16 to A1.25.

2 *Williams and Cardiff RFC v Pugh*, later known as *Williams and Cardiff RFC v WRU (IRB intervening)*, interim injunction hearings (23 July 1997, unreported) (Popplewell J), (1 August 1997, unreported), CA; application for a stay hearings (17 March 1998, unreported) (Buckley J), [1999] Eu LR 195. The litigation, brought by Cardiff Rugby Club against the WRU, was aimed at challenging some of the terms which the WRU sought to impose in a side contract with its elite clubs, principally their length and the arrangements for the distribution of income from the broadcasting contract negotiated by the WRU. Cf *News Ltd v Australian Rugby Football League Ltd* (1996) 135 ALR 33, *(No 2)* (1997) 139 ALR 193 (News Limited intended to set up a superleague of rugby league teams. In order to stop this happening the ARFL introduced a side contract between itself and a number of clubs. Under the side contract the clubs were bound to stay

in ARFL's league for five years and not to play in any other competition not approved by ARFL. News Limited contended that the arrangements were contrary to competition law and started setting up a superleague, inviting clubs contracted to the ARFL, and their players, to join it. ARFL alleged that News Limited was thereby inducing a breach of contract. The final decision was that part of what the ARFL had done had gone too far, but equally some of the contractual obligations (specifically in relation to the current season) had been valid and News Limited had consequently induced a breach of contract).

(d) The contractual relationship between the rules of international sports governing bodies and national sports governing bodies

A3.118 In the same way that the clubs that are the members of a national sports governing body are in a contractual relationship with it and with each other, the national bodies are likely to be members of an international sports governing body, and in a contractual relationship with it and with each other[1]. That relationship can be enforced by action in the courts[2] or before an arbitral tribunal[3]. It is through this international contract that the national sports governing bodies maintain the structure of the sport along national lines: a national sports governing body in one country can cause a national sports governing body in another country to act in a particular way towards a member of the latter[4].

1 As set out above, the IRB is made up of the national rugby unions which are in turn made up of the clubs in each country. See n 2 to para A3.116. In football broadly the same arrangements apply, although each national association is a member not only of the international governing body, FIFA, but also of a regional association, such as (in Europe) UEFA. Contracts between national governing bodies may also arise outside the international governing body's rules. See *Alwyn Treherne v ABAE* (27 February 2001, unreported) (Garland J), [2001] 3 ISLR 231, (11 March 2002, unreported), CA, [2002] EWCA Civ 381, [2002] All ER (D) 144 (Mar).

2 See in relation to membership, *Reel v Holder (for IAAF)* [1979] 1 WLR 1252; affd [1981] 1 WLR 1226, CA (the Taiwanese athletics governing body obtained a declaration that the IAAF was not entitled to expel it from membership). In *Walker v UKA and IAAF* (3 July 2000, unreported) (Toulson J), (25 July 2000, unreported) (Hallett J), the athlete challenged the ability of the IAAF to take UKA to arbitration under UKA's contract of membership of the IAAF, over UKA's acquittal of the athlete on a doping charge. See also paras A3.10, n 7 and A3.124.

3 For the hearing of the IAAF's challenge to UKA's acquittal of Walker, see *IAAF v UKA and Walker*, IAAF Arbitration Panel Award 20 August 2000 reported at [2001] 4 ISLR 264, see also [2000] 2 ISLR 41.

4 See *Newport v Football Association of Wales* interlocutory hearing Jacob J [1995] 2 All ER 87, trial unreported, (12 April 1995) (Blackburne J) (Football Association of Wales persuaded the FA not to allow the Welsh clubs to play their home games in the English league at their grounds in Wales).

A3.119 The issue may arise as to the nature of the relationship between a club and the international governing body, given that the club is a member of the relevant national body but not of the international body. Often the international body's rules are expressly incorporated by reference into the rules of the national body: the international body's rules may require the national body to do this[1]. This allows such rules of the international body to be enforced by the national body against the clubs that are its members (and vice versa), but ostensibly it does not give rise to a contract between the members of the national body and the international body capable of enforcement by either of them against the other[2]. Such a contract would have to be found elsewhere in the same way as a contract between a national sports governing body and a non-member player or participant[3].

1 Such as the IRB's rules. See n 2 to para A3.116. See *Williams and Cardiff RFC v Pugh*, later known as *Williams and Cardiff RFC v WRU (IRB intervening)*, interim injunction hearings (23 July 1997, unreported) (Popplewell J), (1 August 1997, unreported), CA; application for a stay hearings (17 March 1998, unreported (Buckley J), [1999] EuLR 195.

2 Still less is there a direct contract on that basis between the international association and an individual participant who is not even a member of the national association. In *Walker v UKA and IAAF* (3 July 2000, unreported) (Toulson J), (25 July 2000, unreported) (Hallett J), IAAF Arbitral Award 20 August 2000 reported at [2001] 4 ISLR 264, see also [2000] 2 ISLR 41 and paras A3.10, n 7 and A3.124, one issue was whether the IAAF had a contractual entitlement to sanction the athlete for a doping offence after he had been cleared by UKA. See also *Drummoyne District RFC v NWS Rugby Union* (18 November 1993, unreported) (Young J) (no privity of contract between district club and state controlling body. Drummoyne was a member of Sydney Rugby Union which was a member of the NSWRU).

3 See paras A3.120 to A3.125. The possibilities include that the club enters into a separate written, or an implied, contract with the international body (for example when it applies for something or when it enters a competition), or that the national body could be characterised as acting as agent for its members when it undertook to be bound by the rules, or that an implied contract arises by conduct. It is also possible that an argument might arise under the Contracts (Rights of Third Parties) Act 1999, if the requirements of that legislation are met.

(e) *Express contracts between individual participants and sports governing bodies*

A3.120 One of the more difficult areas of contract law in the context of sport over recent years has been the question of when individual players and participants have a contract with the sports governing body[1]. In many instances, the answer is relatively straightforward because an express contract can be identified. First, in some sports the player or participant is actually a member of the sports governing body and consequently in a contractual relationship on the basis of the rules and able to sue and be sued on the basis of them[2]. In other instances the player or other participant is not a member but enters into a direct written contract with the sports governing body[3]. A written contract sometimes arises when players or other participants complete event entry forms[4]. A written contract may also arise in relation to compliance with a drugs testing regime[5]. In some cases a contract may arise out of previous participation[6]. In other cases, the player may be bound by the rules of the sports governing body because his or her contract with the club includes a requirement to comply with the rules[7]. Again however that does not necessarily give rise to a contract between the player and the sports governing body.

1 Which has found particular expression in the *Modahl* litigation. See paras A3.121 to A3.125. The same questions would also arise in relation to whether a club had a contractual relationship with an international governing body, or (as in *Walker v UKA and IAAF* whether a player has a contract with the international governing body: (3 July 2000, unreported) (Toulson J), (25 July 2000, unreported) (Hallett J) IAAF Arbitration Award 20 August 2000 reported at [2001] 4 ISLR 264, see also [2000] 2 ISLR 41 and paras A3.10, n 7 and A3.124.

2 This is obviously more likely to be the case in the context of individual sports. For example, darters become members of the British Darts Organisation, and are in a contractual relationship with that organisation, the content of which may be determined by referenced to the rules and regulations of the British Darts Organisation.

3 For example, the national rugby unions often contract direct with players that are likely to be in the national squad. The IAAF contracts directly with elite athletes.

4 *Earl of Ellesmere v Wallace* [1929] 2 Ch 1, CA (each entrant to a race regarded as having a contract with the Jockey Club and not each other). Cf *Clarke v Dunraven, The Satanita* [1897] AC 59, HL (each entrant regarded as having a contract with all of the other entrants).

5 By the player similarly signing a form. See for example *Korda v ITF Ltd* [1999] All ER (D) 337.

6 See *Lewis v WBC and Bruno* (3 November 1995, unreported) (Rattee J) (WBC rules provided for the next title contender to be the winner of an elimination bout, and Lewis argued that the WBC had wrongly applied the rule in putting Tyson ahead of him to fight Bruno. Although Lewis was not a member of the WBC and had no ostensible contract with it, he argued that he had a contractual right to be the next contender by virtue of his participation and victory in the elimination bout. The court did not resolve the issue but instead held that England was not the proper forum for the dispute).

7 For example, the standard FA Premier League/Football League player contract requires football players to abide by the FA's rules. See para E1.21.

(f) Implied contracts between individual participants and sports governing bodies

A3.121 A more difficult situation arises where there is no express contract and the parties have instead sought to argue that an implied contract arises out of the circumstances and the conduct of the parties. In that context the traditional approach has been that it is not for the courts to invent fictitious contracts[1]. Recently, however, as explained below, the courts have shown a greater willingness to find a contractual relationship in order to confer effective rights on players and participants who have been supposedly badly treated at the hands of a sports governing body.

1 Note however that in *Clarke v Dunraven, The Satanita* [1897] AC 59, HL, a contract was held to arise between each of the entrants to a yacht race and all of the other entrants that they would race in accordance with the rules. See also *Sheehy v Judo Federation of Australia* (1 December 1995, unreported) (Bryson J) (NSW), where the court was prepared to infer a contract to act fairly and rationally between a governing body and a judoka in relation to selection for national representation.

A3.122 At the trial of *Modahl v BAF*[1], Douglas Brown J reiterated the traditional approach to the implication of a contract between sports governing bodies and non-member players by stating that the court should not invent a fictitious contract where the standard essentials of a bargain (intent to create legal relations, offer and acceptance of terms, and consideration) were not proven. Diane Modahl had tested positive for testosterone at an event in Portugal in a test organised by the Portuguese Athletic Federation, and had been convicted of a doping offence by the BAF's first instance body. On appeal she was acquitted by the BAF's appeal body. In the meantime she had been unable to run, and had suffered loss as a result. She chose to bring proceedings against the BAF on the basis that there was a contract between her and the BAF, which the BAF had breached by its procedurally unfair first instance hearing, giving rise to a right to damages. The athlete alleged that the first instance body had been biased and that in breach of the BAF's own rules the sample had been provided to an unaccredited laboratory. The BAF sought to strike out the action, and that application went to the Court of Appeal[2] and then on to the House of Lords[3]. On those occasions the argument was conducted on the basis that the athlete was correct in her allegation that she had a contract with the BAF: the BAF sought to satisfy the court that even if there was a contract it could not include the terms alleged. After the strike out applications, one alleged term was left to go forward to trial: a supposed obligation to act fairly (and therefore without bias) at each stage of the disciplinary process (as opposed to in the process overall). Douglas Brown J conducted a review of the earlier cases[4]. He pointed to exhortations from Lord Denning MR in *Nagle v Feilden*[5] and Scott J in *Gasser v Stinson*[6] not to create fictitious contracts, and concluded that it was quite artificial to identify a contract as arising between the athlete and the BAF out of either her membership of Sale Harriers, her participation in other meetings organised by the governing bodies or her submission to doping control at an international event abroad run by a different organisation[7]. He identified that she was not without any remedy at all, because the free-standing general obligations applied, but that only by establishing a contract could she set up a right to damages. He then went on to hold that in any event, even if there had been a contract, the term would only extend to an obligation to provide a disciplinary process that was fair overall[8], and in any event there was no breach because the first instance body was not and did not appear to be biased[9], and Diane Modahl had had a fair disciplinary process overall.

1 (14 December 2000, unreported) (Douglas Brown J).
2 (28 July 1997, unreported), CA.
3 (22 July 1998, unreported), HL.
4 At pp 4 to 11 of the shorthand-writers' transcript of 14 December 2000.
5 *Nagle v Feilden* [1966] 2 QB 633 at 644 to 646 (646 in particular). See also per Lord Salmon at 652. He could also have pointed to Lord Denning's reiteration of the point in *Enderby Town Football Club v Football Association* [1971] Ch 591 at 606, [1970] 3 WLR 1021 at 1026.
6 *Gasser v Stinson* (15 June 1988, unreported) (Scott J) at p 24 of the shorthand-writers' transcript.
7 At pp 8 and 11 of the shorthand-writers' transcript of 14 December 2000.
8 At p 13 of the shorthand-writers' transcript of 14 December 2000.
9 At pp 17, 19, 21 and 23 of the shorthand-writers' transcript of 14 December 2000.

A3.123 In reaching this conclusion in *Modahl*, Douglas Brown J rejected the relevance of a number of earlier authorities where the courts had been prepared to infer a contract on a number of different bases. The courts had been prepared to infer a contract where participants had submitted to the disciplinary jurisdiction of the sports governing body, because in return for agreeing to abide by the result they were implicitly promised a fair and proper hearing[1]. In *Korda v ITF*[2], it was held that there was a contract in relation to doping control on the basis of the player's participation in the event, in the general knowledge that there were anti-doping rules, and his submission to doping control. In circumstances where a player takes steps to compete in the knowledge that the sport is subject to rules, and the sports governing body that administers the rules facilitates his or her so competing, it is a relatively small step to conclude that he or she implicitly agrees by so doing to abide by the rules in return for (amongst other things) the commitment of the governing body to administer the rules properly and fairly. It is also possible that in some circumstances the national body could be characterised as acting not only in its own capacity when contracting with the international body, but also as agent for all its members[3]. Furthermore, a contractual arrangement may even arise where the issue is whether a party could gain access to the sport in the first place. An example would be where someone wishes to set up as a player agent, manager or as a trainer, and the sports governing body controls access to these activities. Although in *Nagle v Feilden*[4] and *McInnes v Onslow-Fane*[5] no contract was regarded as arising in this context, it remains arguable that sports governing bodies invite applications for licences (in the same way as a business might invite tenders) and that when they receive such applications they become contractually bound to consider them fairly and in accordance with the general law[6].

1 *Davis v Carew-Pole* [1956] 2 All ER 524 at 539 (Contract held to have arisen when a livery stable keeper submitted to the jurisdiction of the National Hunt Committee); *Haron Bin Mundir v Singapore AAA* [1992] 1 SLR 18 at 25 (Contract held to have arisen out of acceptance of offer to go on a training trip and out of submission to the jurisdiction). Douglas Brown J concluded that these cases were distinguishable because the event at which Diane Modahl had been tested was not an event organised by the BAF but by another organisation, and the BAF was not responsible for doping control at that event. See also *Law v National Greyhound Racing Club* [1983] 3 All ER 300, CA, where a contract was also held to exist on the basis of submission to the jurisdiction.
2 (29 January 1999, unreported) (Lightman J), [1999] All ER (D) 84; (25 March 1999, unreported), CA. Douglas Brown J concluded in Modahl that this case was distinguishable because Diane Modahl's participation did not reveal any intention to conclude contractual relations or any consideration passing.
3 Toulson J envisaged this as a possibility in *Walker v UKA and IAAF*, together with the additional proposition that the club acted as agent for its individual members (3 July 2000, unreported (Toulson J)). It is also possible that an argument might arise under the Contracts (Rights of Third Parties) Act 1999, if the requirements of that legislation are met.
4 [1966] 2 QB 633.
5 [1978] 1 WLR 1520.
6 See cases cited at para A3.115, n 2. See also *Forbes v Australian Yachting Federation*, unreported, Santour J (NSW) 4 April 1996 (contention rejected that published selection criteria gave rise to a contract on application including terms as to how selection would be carried out).

A3.124 The problem of whether a contract could be inferred between an athlete and a sports governing body arose in a slightly different way in *Walker v UKA and IAAF*[1]. In that case Walker had been acquitted of a doping offence by the UKA disciplinary body. The IAAF disagreed with the verdict and sought to bring disciplinary proceedings before an IAAF arbitral panel against UKA, with the aim of having a ban imposed on the athlete. The athlete sought a declaration in High Court proceedings that he was subject only to the jurisdiction of UKA and not the IAAF and seeking to enjoin UKA from submitting to arbitration or enforcing any decision against him. UKA argued that it had been right to acquit, but equally that the IAAF was entitled to bring arbitration proceedings against that acquittal before the IAAF Arbitration Panel, the decision of which UKA had a right and a duty to enforce. The IAAF first unsuccessfully challenged the jurisdiction of the court[2]. The IAAF then introduced a new rule to the effect that even if an athlete had been acquitted by his or her national association, the IAAF could require an interim ban to be imposed pending the hearing of the IAAF's action against the national association[3]. The IAAF sought to apply this rule retrospectively to Walker. UKA argued that the IAAF could not impose such a ban. During the hearing of the application[4], Hallett J indicated her dissatisfaction with such a retrospective change. It was agreed that the athlete would not be banned pending the hearing of the IAAF arbitration, but that he would abide by the result of it. In the event he was found guilty, but because he had chosen not to compete until the issue was resolved completely, he had very little time still to serve. This was the right result. UKA and the IAAF based the contention that the athlete was subject to the IAAF arbitration on two grounds. First, irrespective of whether there was any contract between the IAAF and Walker, the IAAF could require UKA as a result of its contractual relationship with the IAAF to act so as to prevent his being eligible to compete. The IAAF was in control of its own eligibility criteria, one of which was that a player should not have been guilty of a doping offence. If the IAAF held Walker to have been guilty of a doping offence, then he was simply ineligible, and that ineligibility would have to be respected by all members of the IAAF, and indeed as a result of the IAAF's 'contamination rule' (which bans any player who competes in the same event as a player who has already been banned) by fellow athletes as well. Putting it in more general terms, a sports governing body (or an international governing body) can by its contractual authority over a club (or a national governing body) insist on the latter's enforcing the former's own contractual rights further down the chain. In the contract between player and club there may be an obligation on the player to submit to the jurisdiction of the sports governing body. Alternatively, a sports governing body can simply refuse to accept the entry into any event of a player which it has disciplined, on the basis that eligibility to entry is determined by reference to the rules, whether or not they contractually bind the player, and force clubs and other governing bodies to do the same. Secondly, it was argued that there was a contract between the athlete and the IAAF on the basis of the consent given by the athlete to doping control. The athlete, in contrast to Modahl, argued that no contract arose. Neither ground was in the event determined.

1 *Walker v UKA and IAAF* (3 July 2000, unreported) (Toulson J), (25 July 2000, unreported) (Hallett J), IAAF Arbitral Award 20 August 2000 reported at [2001] 4 ISLR 264, see also [2000] 2 ISLR 41 and para A3.10, n 7.
2 Before Toulson J, 3 July 2000.
3 See para E4.235 et seq for interim suspensions.
4 Hallett J, 25 July 2000.

A3.125 The second Court of Appeal decision in *Modahl*[1] represents a move away from the traditional approach in the cases relied upon by Douglas Brown J at the trial. Latham LJ[2] identified three different bases on which Diane Modahl might have been said to have entered into a contract with the BAF. First, the club acts as agent for its members from time to time in contracting with the governing body (the 'club' basis). Secondly, a contract arises out of repeated participation in events organised by the governing body (the 'participation' basis). Thirdly, a contract arises when a player provides a sample and relies on the appeal process (the 'submission basis'). Latham LJ concluded[3] that the court should consider all the surrounding circumstances to see whether a contract could be implied. He held that the basic structure for a contract was readily identifiable in the fact that the athlete had participated in events under the auspices of the BAF or the IAAF and subject to their rules, and that the governing bodies had accepted responsibility to administer those rules. Contractual intention could be found in the athlete entering those events, even if no entry form was actually completed. Latham LJ went on to conclude[4] that the fairness obligation contemplated the provision of a fair process as a whole, and that the fact that one member of the first instance body might have been tainted by apparent bias was irrelevant[5]. Mance LJ agreed, albeit tentatively in the light of the paucity of the evidence[6], that a contract arose on a combination of the three bases identified by Latham LJ. Mance LJ reached similar conclusions to Latham LJ on the content of the implied obligation of fairness[7], and bias[8]. Jonathan Parker LJ on the other hand was not convinced that a contract arose[9]. He took the view that the BAF's only obligation was to set up the first instance body and that the BAF had no contractual obligation in respect of how the first instance body carried out its functions thereafter[10].

1 [2002] 1 WLR 1192, CA.
2 [2002] 1 WLR 1192, para 25.
3 At paras 49 to 52.
4 At paras 61 and 67, in reliance on *Calvin v Carr* [1980] AC 574, PC.
5 At para 67.
6 At para 91 and 103 to 111.
7 At paras 112 to 122.
8 At paras 123 to 131.
9 At paras 72 to 83.
10 At para 87.

B Express contractual obligations

A3.126 The enforcement of express obligations contained in the rules or in commercial contracts is relatively straightforward. The express obligation is there and must be construed and enforced[1]. The limits of a sports governing body's jurisdiction can be interpreted and set by the courts. The court will ask whether the rules confer the power on the sports governing body that it is purporting to exercise. It may of course also be possible to challenge the existence or validity of the relevant contractual obligation, for example if it has not been correctly adopted or if it is contrary to other pre-existing rules, or on grounds of restraint of trade, competition law or the free movement rules[2].

1 See para A3.96 for the principles of construction of rules, and *Martinez v Ellesse SPA* (30 March 1999, unreported), CA for the principles of construction of a commercial contract.
2 See paras A3.135 to A3.158, A3.159 to A3.170 and A3.171 to A3.175.

C Implied contractual obligations

(a) The implication of the general obligations

A3.127 As described above, it is now tolerably clear that where a contract does arise between the player, club or other participant and the sports governing body, that contract will include implied obligations, which mirror the grounds for judicial review in public law cases, and which can be said to arise irrespective of contract, as general obligations[1]. Specifically, the sports governing body must instruct itself properly as to the meaning of its rules and act within them[2]. The sports governing body must comply with the principles of natural justice by acting fairly and by affording minimum standards of procedural protection to the player, club or other participant affected[3] (which includes a fair opportunity to put his, her or its case, a fair burden and standard of proof, and an unbiased and open minded decision-maker acting in good faith). The sports governing body must act rationally, and not arbitrarily or capriciously[4] (which includes obligations to take into account relevant considerations and to exclude irrelevant considerations, to treat like situations alike and different situations differently, and possibly to act proportionately and not to depart from a previously stated policy giving rise to a legitimate expectation). The sports governing body must not reach a decision for which there is no factual basis in the evidence[5].

1 See para A3.80 to A3.94. See *Wilander v Tobin* [1997] 2 Lloyd's Rep 296, Lord Woolf MR at 300, col 1.
2 See para A3.95 to A3.100. See *Korda v ITF* (1999) Times, 4 February, [1999] All ER (D) 84, (25 March 1999, unreported), CA.
3 See paras A3.101 to A3.108. See *Modahl v BAF* (28 July 1997, unreported), CA per Lord Woolf MR at pp 20–26 Morritt LJ at pp 36 to 39 and Pill LJ at pp 43 to 44 of the shorthand writers' transcript; *Wilander v Tobin* [1997] 2 Lloyd's Rep 296, Lord Woolf MR at 300, col 1.
4 See paras A3.109 to A3.111. See *Wilander v Tobin* [1997] 2 Lloyd's Rep 296, Lord Woolf MR at 300, col 1.
5 See para A3.112. See *Wilander v Tobin* [1997] 2 Lloyd's Rep 293, Lord Woolf MR at 300, col 1.

(b) The implication of other terms

A3.128 As in any other context, other terms may be implicit in the arrangements if the circumstances of the contract so dictate[1]. The normal rules on the implication of terms apply[2]. It is *not* an implied term of a sports governing body's rules that it will not act in unreasonable restraint of trade[3].

1 In *News Ltd v Australian Rugby League* (1996) 135 ALR 33, *(No 2)* (1997) 139 ALR 193 (the 'Superleague' case) it was held that there was an implied term each season that the clubs and the League would do everything reasonably necessary to make the season's competition run smoothly. It was breach of this implied term by the clubs that the rival Superleague organisers were held to have induced. However, the restrictions imposed that went beyond that season (loyalty arrangements) were in restraint of trade and void. See also *Australian Rugby League v Cross* (1997) 39 IPR 111 (implied term that a competition would be organised of sufficient size to provide players with a proper opportunity to earn a living and that players would have the opportunity to be selected on merit).
2 See para A3.115, n 2 for the implication of terms in the context of commercial tendering.
3 *Newport Town Football Club v Football Association of Wales* (12 April 1995, unreported) (Blackburne J), p 45 of the New Law Online transcript. This precludes the recovery of damages based on the restraint of trade doctrine and preserves that doctrine's status as a defence only (or basis for a declaration of invalidity).

D The relationship between express and implied contractual obligations

A3.129 In a normal contractual context, express terms take precedence over implied terms, subject to legislative interference. This will be the case in the context of sport when it comes to straightforward implied terms. The situation is more complex however where the implied term is one of the general obligations. It is now apparent that the general obligations cannot be excluded: a sports governing body cannot for example exclude the obligation to comply with the principle of natural justice by refusing to inform a player, club or other participant of the disciplinary charges against him, her or it[1]. Equally however, it is likely that the content of the rules, which were entered into consensually (at least nominally), will strongly influence the court's evaluation of what amounts to adequate procedural protection and fair treatment in a given context[2].

1 At least where there is monopoly power. In *Russell v Duke of Norfolk* [1949] 1 All ER 109, it had been held that the express reservation of an absolute or unfettered discretion to withdraw a trainer's licence could not be made subject to the rules of natural justice. The majority of the Court of Appeal rejected a trainer's claim that he was entitled to a hearing when the Jockey Club threatened to withdraw his licence, on the basis that there was a contract which reserved such an unfettered discretion to the Jockey Club to do so. Denning LJ however held that where a person would lose their livelihood as a result of a decision of a body that had a 'monopoly in an important field of human activity', natural justice required a hearing at which the person's case could be put. In *Nagle v Feilden* [1966] 2 QB 633 at 647, Denning LJ doubted that natural justice could be excluded by contract and in *Enderby Town Football Club v Football Association* [1971] Ch 591 at 606, [1970] 3 WLR 1021 at 1026, Lord Denning stated that the fictional contract contained in rules of a sports governing body could not displace the rules of natural justice. In that these obligations are implied terms in contracts, they are implied terms of a special type, which are apparently not capable of being overridden by express terms. The reality is of course that it is nowadays unlikely that a sports governing body would seek expressly to exclude the basic obligation to act fairly.

2 However express terms imposing some limitations will be taken into account in deciding what the content of the obligation is in any given case. See *Modahl v BAF* (28 July 1997, unreported), CA per Lord Woolf MR at pp 20–26.

5 TORT

A3.130 The law of tort has been used by practitioners in the context of sport not so much to mount challenges to the actions of governing bodies, but rather (not surprisingly) in relation to personal injury negligence actions brought by players or spectators against other players or the organisers of events[1]. The tort of inducing breach of contract or unlawful interference with contractual relations has also been put to use in disputes between clubs when players have been enticed away[2]. The few tort actions that have been brought against governing bodies have arisen in similar contexts.

1 See Chapter E5 and the examples set out in nn 9 and 10 to para A3.43. There have also been actions for damage to equipment (footnote 11 to that para) and in nuisance (n 4 to para A3.42).

2 See Chapter E1 and the examples set out in n 6 to para A3.43.

A Actions in negligence against sports governing bodies

A3.131 Players injured while participating in a sport have brought actions against another player who for example tackled them illegally, or the referee who for example failed to prevent repeated scrum collapses. An alternative defendant for them is the governing body of the sport concerned, on the basis that that body owed a duty of care to ensure that the rules of the sport were safe and that it was safely organised throughout its jurisdiction. The limits of the responsibility of governing bodies in this context are uncertain and developing. Where a sports governing body actually organises an event itself, it may well be liable on normal principles to spectators for collapsing stands or flying wheels, or in one case to a participant for placing an archery contest too close to the discus throwers[1]. More difficult is the situation where what is being impugned is not the sports governing body's own actions, but the quality of its control through its rules over the actions of others. In *Agar v Hyde*[2], two injured rugby players argued that the governing body, there the International Rugby Board, owed a duty 'to take reasonable care in monitoring the operation of the rules of the game to avoid the risk of unnecessary harm to players' and 'to take reasonable care to ensure that the rules did not provide for circumstances where risks of serious injury were taken unnecessarily'. It was held that the sports governing body did not owe such duties of care to the many thousands of people who participated in the sport; indeed it was held to be unarguable that such duties of care existed[3]. In contrast, in *Watson v British Boxing Board of Control*[4] the governing body was held to owe a licensed boxer a duty of care to ensure that rules were in place providing for adequate ring-side medical assistance, and (what is more) was also held to be in breach of that duty. The duty of care arose out of the particular circumstances of the sport, and in particular the fact that the BBBC licensed a relatively small number of boxers. There was sufficient proximity to give rise to a duty of care, and it was fair and just to impose such a duty. The governing body set out by its rules, directions and guidance to make comprehensive provision for the services to be provided to safeguard the health of professional boxers taking part in the sport, the object of the sport was to inflict physical injury, and all those involved in a boxing contest were obliged to accept and comply with the board's requirements. The BBBC was a governing body with specialist knowledge giving advice to a defined class of persons in the knowledge that that class would rely upon that advice in boxing contests, and the boxer in fact relied on the board to exercise skill and care in ensuring his safety during a fight. The boxer belonged to a class of persons within the contemplation of the governing body, which was itself involved in an activity which gave it complete control over and a responsibility for a boxing contest that would be liable to result in injury to the claimant if reasonable care were not exercised by the governing body. The BBBC was held to be in breach for failing to make it a requirement that ringside resuscitation be available. Accordingly it is possible that in particularly strong and clear circumstances, a sports governing body may owe a duty of care in relation to what it provides in its rules. There is no doubt that *Watson* provides a sound foundation for such arguments. In many instances, however, it is unlikely that a duty of care will arise, because, as in *Agar v Hyde*, there is not the same clear proximate relationship between the governing body and a limited, defined class of participants, nor does the governing body have such a clear ability to control and address the risks[5]. That said it is plain that governing bodies would be wise to take advice regularly as to the best ways of avoiding injuries in their sport and should insure themselves against a challenge such as that brought against the BBBC. Consideration should also be given to whether it is possible to define the respective responsibilities of contestant, organiser and governing body, as the International Ski Federation has sought to do through its 'Athlete's Declaration'[6].

1 *Morrell v Owen* (1 December 1993, unreported) (Mitchell J), (1993) Times, 14 December. See also *Horne and Marlow v RAC Motor Sports Association* (24 May 1989, unreported), CA; *Stratton v Hughes and RAC* (17 March 1998, unreported), CA; and Chapter E5.

2 (2000) 201 CLR 552, [2000] HCA 41, 173 ALR 665. See also Chapter E5; [2001] 9(3) SATLJ 50. For another case where an action against a governing body (there on the basis of a referee's decision) was struck out, see *Tyrell v FA* (28 April 1997, unreported) (claim by fan for nervous shock as a result of a poor refereeing decision struck out, no duty of care being owed by a referee or his governing body to a spectator in these circumstances).

3 Gleeson CJ concluded at the end of his judgment: 'I am unable to accept that the circumstances of life in this community are such that the conception of legal responsibility should be applied to the relation which existed between the appellants and all people who played the game of rugby football and were, on that account, affected by their action or inaction in relation to the rules of the game. Undertaking the function of participating in a process of making and altering the rules according to which adult people, for their own enjoyment, may choose to engage in a hazardous sporting contest, does not, of itself, carry with it potential legal liability for injury sustained in such a contest'.

4 (1999) 143 Sol Jo LB 235, (1999) Times, 12 October, [2001] QB 1134, CA. See also Chapter E5; Mackay [2000] 1 ISLR 2. See also *Fox v Ministry of Defence* [2002] EWCA Civ 435, (6 March 2002, unreported), CA, for the responsibility of organisers for the actions of their doctor at boxing match.

5 For further discussion, see Manning 'Michael Watson v British Boxing Board of Control' [2000] 7(1) Sports Law Administration and Practice; Manning and Taylor 'Liability of sports governing bodies for injuries to players – Agar v. Hyde' [2000] 7(6) Sports Law Administration and Practice; Manning 'The implications for other sports of the Court of Appeal's Michael Watson Judgment' [2001] 7(7) Sports Law Administration & Practice; Block [2001] 2 ISLR 168 and 201; Thompson [2000] 8(1) SATLJ 4 and Chapter E5.

6 See [2001] 3 ISLR 219.

A3.132 In *Wright v Jockey Club*[1], the jockey alleged that the Jockey Club owed him a duty of care and skill in carrying out the medical tests that would ascertain whether he was fit to ride. The claim in tort was withdrawn in argument and the court rejected the implication of a term that the Jockey Club owed such a duty. The Jockey Club's duty was held simply to be to act fairly. At the very outset in *Modahl*, consideration was given to alleging a general duty of care in negligence in the taking of a drugs test to ensure that it is properly taken and dealt with and not mixed up or mistreated[2]. In the event, however, such a claim was not pursued. Outside the sports context, it has been held that claims do not lie for negligent prosecution of disciplinary charges[3], or even for malicious prosecution of disciplinary charges[4]. Rather, the only claim in such circumstances would be for defamation[5]. In the sports context, more general attempts to impose a duty of care in how the sport is administered have not been successful[6].

1 (15 May 1995, unreported) (Sir Haydn Tudor Evans), QBD, (1995) Times, 16 June, at p 8 of the Lexis transcript.

2 Cf [2002] 1 WLR 1192, CA per Latham LJ para 4.

3 See *Calveley v Chief Constable of the Merseyside Police* [1989] AC 1228, HL (no claim lies against police force for bringing disciplinary proceedings negligently).

4 In *Gregory v Portsmouth City Council* [2000] 1 AC 419, a claim against a Council for bringing disciplinary charges maliciously was rejected. The court ruled that the recourse, if any, must be found in the tort of defamation, which (through the qualified privilege doctrine) reflects the balance struck by the common law between the need to ensure disciplinary proceedings are brought without fear where appropriate, and the need to protect the rights of the individual. See Taylor 'Disciplinary charges brought maliciously and without reasonable basis; What are the remedies?' [2000] 7(2) Sports Law Administration and Practice. Cf *Currie v Barton* (26 March 1987, unreported) (Scott J), (11 February 1988, unreported), CA, (1988) Times, 12 February.

5 See n 4.

6 See *MacDonald v FIFA and SFA* [1999] 7(1) SATLJ 33 (Scottish court dismissed a claim made by a fan against the governing bodies on the basis that they owed a duty of care to fans to ensure that an international match would not be cancelled).

B Inducing breach of contract and the economic torts

A3.133 The tort of inducing breach of contract or unlawful interference with contractual relations[1] has been included in actions brought against sports governing bodies, particularly where there has been a battle over control of the sport. In *Greig v Insole*[2], a number of Test cricket players decided to sign up for Kerry Packer's alternative tournament, which challenged the ICC's established control over the sport. In a defensive response, the ICC and the TCCB made a number of changes to their rules that effectively banned players that played for Kerry Packer from playing not only in tests for their country, but also from playing first class cricket. Importantly, the changes were introduced after players had already concluded contracts with Kerry Packer and were applied retrospectively. The court concluded that the rule changes constituted inducement of the players to breach their contracts and unlawful interference with contractual relations[3]. The argument is not however confined to battles for control. In *Walker v UKA and IAAF*[4], the athlete accused the IAAF of seeking to induce UKA to breach UKA's contract with the athlete by requiring UKA to participate in an arbitration brought by the IAAF to review the validity of UKA's own decision. UKA was said to owe a contractual obligation to treat its disciplinary process as final. The argument there was flawed because not only was there no breach of any contract between UKA and the athlete, but also because the IAAF rules which it sought to enforce were pre-existing rules (in contrast to the position in *Greig v Insole)*. In *Mohammed v The FA and FIFA*, an action alleging that the introduction of the player-agent licensing system was an unlawful interference with existing contractual relations between players and agents, and in breach of the competition rules, survived a summary judgment application by the governing bodies, at least in part, and remains pending[5]. In other contexts less well established, economic torts have been valiantly argued, but to little effect[6].

1 For the ingredients of the torts, see *Clerk & Lindsell* (18th edn, 2000), ch 24, paras 1–64 and 88–115.

2 [1978] 1 WLR 302. See also para A3.145 in relation to restraint of trade.

3 Cf *News Ltd v Australian Rugby Football League Ltd* (1996) 135 ALR 33, *(No 2)* (1997) 139 ALR 193 (News Limited intended to set up a superleague of rugby league teams. In order to stop this happening, the ARFL introduced a side contract between itself and a number of clubs. Under the side contract the clubs were bound to stay in ARFL's league for five years and not to play in any other competition not approved by ARFL. News Limited contended that the arrangements were contrary to competition law and started setting up a superleague, inviting clubs contracted to the ARFL, and their players, to join it. ARFL alleged that News Limited was thereby inducing a breach of contract. The final decision was that part of what the ARFL had done had gone too far, but equally some of the contractual obligations imposed had been valid and News Limited had consequently induced a breach of contract). See also *Fisher v NGRC (No 2)* (25 July 1991, unreported), CA (Fisher alleged that NGRC induced racetracks to breach their contracts with Fisher to use a racing jacket that he had designed); *Australian Rugby League v Cross* (1997) 39 IPR 111 (Superleague induced player to breach loyalty agreement).

4 *Walker v UKA and IAAF* (3 July 2000, unreported) (Toulson J), (25 July 2000, unreported) (Hallett J), IAAF Arbitration Award 20 August 2000 reported at [2001] 4 ISLR 264, see also [2000] 2 ISLR 41 and paras A3.10, n 7 and A3.124.

5 *Mohammed v FA and FIFA* (21 February 2002, unreported) (Field J).

6 See for example *Currie v Barton* (26 March 1987, unreported) (Scott J), (11 February 1988, unreported), CA, (1988) Times, 12 February (Tennis player was banned by his county association for three years for refusing to play in a county match and was consequently ruled ineligible to play for England by the LTA. Among other things the player relied on a tort of interference by unlawful means with his profession of tennis player and coach, but the argument was rejected: see p 12 of the Lexis transcript of Scott J's judgment).

C Actions against sports governing bodies based on other torts?

A3.134 There is obviously the possibility of proceedings being brought against sports governing bodies based on other torts. The range of actions by sports governing bodies is wide and may therefore throw up particular factual circumstances revealing the commission of a variety of torts. At least hypothetically there could be cases ranging from defamation[1] of individuals or goods to nuisance.

1 The authorities suggest that defamation would be the most suitable cause of action in the event that disciplinary charges are brought against an athlete without basis. See Taylor 'Disciplinary charges brought maliciously and without reasonable basis; What are the remedies?' [2000] 7(2) Sports Law Administration and Practice.

6 COMMON LAW RESTRAINT OF TRADE

A3.135 The common law doctrine of restraint of trade[1] has provided a useful mechanism for challenging the actions of sports governing bodies, principally where access has been refused to a sport, where the governing body has refused a particular request of a player, club or other participant, where disciplinary action has been taken on the basis of a rule that is restrictive, and where restrictive rules such as transfer rules have been challenged in their entirety. The doctrine has also been used in the context of challenges by players to the contractual constraints imposed upon them by the clubs employing them. That topic falls outside the scope of this chapter and is dealt with elsewhere[2]. The doctrine of restraint of trade is a defensive mechanism: if a rule or action restrains trade without justification, it is void and unenforceable. The doctrine does not give rise to any action for damages, although an action can be brought for a declaration that a particular rule or term or decision is void[3].

1 See *Chitty on Contracts* (28th edn, 1999, Sweet & Maxwell), paras 17-075 to 17-139; Mehigan and Kamerling *Restraint of Trade and Business Secrets* (4th edn, 2002, Sweet & Maxwell).
2 For a general analysis of the application of the doctrine to sport, see Stewart [1996] 6(3) SATLJ 41.
3 Nor is it possible to circumvent this position by arguing that an implied obligation arises not to act in restraint of trade: see *Newport v FAW* (12 April 1995, unreported) (Blackburne J), p 45 of the New Law Online transcript.

A The basis for and extent of the doctrine

(a) The basis for the doctrine

A3.136 The basis for the doctrine of restraint of trade is that as a matter of public policy a person should not be restricted in his or her ability to earn a living by an obligation that goes beyond what is necessary to achieve some legitimate and desirable aim[1]. It is in the interests of the individual or companies involved, and the public, that the individual should be free to be as productive as possible, so long as that does not prevent some equally worthwhile benefit being achieved. The doctrine is therefore based on a similar premise to the competition rules[2], and it is likely that the two approaches will produce the same result in many instances. If an individual term falls foul of the doctrine, it is unenforceable[3]. If the offending clause cannot be 'severed' in such a way as to leave a legal contract that is not so substantially removed from the bargain originally reached that the commercial benefit intended has been lost, then the whole contract will be unenforceable[4]. It is generally not illegal to perform a contract in restraint of trade if both parties choose to abide by it, but either party to the contract, or a third party injured by the operation of the agreement, can seek a declaration that it is unenforceable[5].

1 See *Chitty on Contracts* (28th edn, 1999, Sweet & Maxwell), paras 17-075 to 17-100; *Herbert Morris v Saxelby* [1916] 1 AC 688; *Esso Petroleum v Harper's Garage* [1968] AC 269.
2 See generally Chapter B2.
3 See *Chitty on Contracts* (28th edn, 1999, Sweet & Maxwell), para 17-075.
4 See n 3.
5 See *Chitty on Contracts* (28th edn, 1999, Sweet & Maxwell), para 17-075; *Eastham v Newcastle United* [1964] Ch 413; *Greig v Insole* [1978] 1 WLR 302; and *Nagle v Feilden* [1966] 2 QB 633, as discussed further below at para A3.144.

(b) The stages in the analysis

A3.137 The constituents of the restraint of trade argument, in its conventional form, are set out in *Nordenfelt v Maxim Nordenfelt Guns*[1]. The starting point is that all restraints of trade are void unless justified. In the first stage of the analysis, the onus falls on the party advancing the argument (here the player, club or other participant) to prove that there is a restraint of trade, in other words that an obligation has been imposed on the player that prevents him from earning, or limits him in his ability to earn, a living at his chosen occupation. Governing bodies have often argued that their rules and actions are not in restraint of trade in the first place, on the basis that the obligation does not affect the complainant's ability to earn a living at his occupation to a sufficiently substantial extent[2], or on the basis that what the obligation affects is not the ability to earn a living, but to pursue a particular recreational activity, such as an amateur sport[3], or on the basis that rules essential to the creation of a competitive sport should not be regarded as a restraint of trade but rather as encouraging trade[4], or on the basis that the doctrine cannot apply to the rules of an international governing body regulating participants from around the world, who would not be subject to the doctrine in their home countries[5], or on the basis that the restraint does not operate on trade within the geographic jurisdiction of the court[6].

1 [1894] AC 535. Other leading cases include *Herbert Morris v Saxelby* [1916] 1 AC 688; and *Esso Petroleum v Harper's Garage* [1968] AC 269, HL.
2 See *Chitty on Contracts* (28th edn, 1999, Sweet & Maxwell) paras 17-071 to 17-085; and see para A3.82. The restraint need not be absolute, but can be partial. For example it is clear from *Stevenage Borough Football Club v Football League Ltd* (1996) Times, 1 August; affd 9 Admin LR 109, CA (see paras A3.151 to A3.155) that a partial restraint on a club's ability to play in a higher division contained in an entry qualification is a restraint for these purposes. Equally in *Newport v Football Association of Wales* interlocutory hearing Jacob J [1995] 2 All ER 87, trial unreported Blackburne J 12 April 1995 (see para A3.148 and A3.149), a restriction on a club's ability to play in the League of its choice was caught, and in *Greig v Insole* [1978] 1 WLR 302 (see para A3.145), a ban on playing in particular matches was covered. In *Buckley v Tutty* (1971) 125 CLR 353, the court held a transfer system to be a restraint whether the players affected were full or part time, and although it did not stop them playing. See also *Stinnato v Auckland Boxing Association* [1978] 1 NZLR 1 at 8. So too *Eastham v Newcastle United Football Club and the FA* [1964] Ch 413 where the transfer system was held to be a restraint. In *Wimbledon v Football League* (FA Arbitration 29 January 2002), the FA Arbitration Panel held that a decision that the club could not move to Milton Keynes was a restraint. In each of these instances, the participants were not stopped from playing the sport, but stopped from playing it as they would want. See also *Fisher v National Greyhound Racing Club* (31 July 1985, unreported), CA (sufficient if governing body controls only part of the sport); see also *Pett v Greyhound Racing Association* [1969] 1 QB 125 at 128. There must come a point, obviously, where a player or club cannot do everything that they would want, and stopping them from doing it would not be a restraint. An example would be the qualification of only some players or clubs to qualify for a particular tournament, following for

example a knock-out stage. Cf *Currie v Barton* (26 March 1987, unreported) (Scott J), (11 February 1988, unreported), CA, (1988) Times, 12 February (where it was held that banning a tennis player from representative selection did not affect his ability to earn his living as a player or a coach, and therefore did not give rise to a restraint of trade).

3 *Gasser v Stinson* (15 June 1988, unreported) (Scott J) at p 37D–G of the shorthand-writers' transcript. Scott J also concluded that it was not enough that the player was seeking to build up his career to a level where he could earn money from it. For the contrary view, see *Hall v Victorian Football League* [1982] VR 64. Cf *Blackler v NZRFU* [1968] NZLR 547 at 554 (where the league imposing the restraint was amateur but the player wanted to play professionally abroad, the doctrine did apply. Woodhouse LJ at 12 took into account questions of reputation as well as livelihood). See also *Ray v Professional Golfers' Association* (15 April 1997, unreported) (Judge Dyer QC) (Rule requiring a golfer to pass an exam in order to qualify did not restrain him in the exercise of his trade as he was still training and not trading – possibly a surprising decision); *R v BBA, ex p Mickan* (17 March 1981, unreported), CA at p 4 of the Lexis transcript; *Johnson v Athletics Canada and IAAF* (1997) 41 OTC 95; *Fisher v NGRC* (see n 2) at p 6 of the court transcript (sufficient that an individual who wanted to be licensed to own one greyhound would be deprived of only part of his living).

4 An approach which is analogous to the 'rule of reason' or 'ancillary restraint' doctrines in competition law: see paras A3.163 and B2.62 to B2.75. The approach was rejected in *Buckley v Tutty* (1971) 125 CLR 353. In *Wimbledon v Football League* (FA Arbitration 29 January 2002) the League contended that its rule requiring a club to have permission to move outside the conurbation from which it takes its name, and the League's exercise of its discretion in applying that rule, were essential to maintain the pyramidical structure of the sport, and therefore not a restraint on the club's ability to pursue its trade. The arbitrators rejected this approach, holding that the decision was a restraint, and therefore the legitimate need to preserve the pyramidical structure of the sport had to be weighed against the harm to the club if it was not allowed to move. Ultimately the FA Commission in May 2002 held that the club's need to move outweighed the possibility of damage to the pyramid.

5 Rejected in *Gasser v Stinson* (15 June 1988, unreported) (Scott J) at p 35F to 36H of the shorthand-writers' transcript.

6 Rejected in *Blackler v NZRFL* (see n 3) at 555 and 571.

A3.138 If a restraint of trade is established, then in the second stage of the analysis (at least in the conventional form of the doctrine[1]) the onus switches to the party resisting the argument and seeking to uphold the obligation, here the governing body, to show that the restraint is reasonable and justified in the interests of the parties. This is the first limb of the *Nordenfelt v Maxim Nordenfelt* reasonableness test[2]. To be reasonable and justified in the interests of the parties, the restraint must (a) pursue a legitimate aim which is worthy of protection and (b) do so in a reasonable and proportionate manner. To be proportionate the restraint must not only be necessary to achieve the governing body's legitimate aim, but it must also go no further than is reasonably necessary to achieve that aim[3]: the governing body must show that there is no less onerous alternative course of action available to it to achieve its legitimate aim. Furthermore, the harm caused to the player, club, or other participant by the imposition of the obligation must not be out of proportion to the benefit secured by the governing body. Accordingly the quality of the legitimate aim must be assessed and balanced against the effect of the obligation. If the aim is actually not that important, or even if it is important but it would not be substantially undermined if the restriction were not applied, it will not justify a substantial detriment to the player, club or other participant. In the sports context, the principal justifications offered by sports governing bodies for restrictions have included: the need to maintain competitive balance between clubs and thus public interest in the sport[4], the need to encourage new entrants (whether players or clubs)[5], the need to generate revenue for re-investment in the sport at grass roots level[6], the need to maintain the integrity of the pyramidical and geographic structure of the sport[7], the need to have a workable and deterrent system of doping control[8], the need to improve the quality of the domestic league in order to improve the quality of the players from which the national team can be selected[9], the need to have a commercially viable competition[10], and the need to satisfy and respond to the demands of media companies, support from which is crucial to the particular sport's survival[11].

1 As explained at para A3.140, there is authority that in the context of a challenge on restraint of trade grounds to the rules of a sports governing body, the doctrine is adapted so that the second stage of the analysis is effectively omitted, leaving the challenger to establish both that there is a restraint, and that it does not operate reasonably in the interests of the public.

2 [1894] AC 535 at 565.

3 Cf *Esso Petroleum v Harper's Garage* [1968] AC 269, HL.

4 See *Buckler v Tutty* (1971) 125 CLR 353 at para 17. Cf *Blackler v NZRFL* [1968] NZLR 547; *Kemp v NZRFL* [1989] 3 NZLR 463 (restriction on players moving abroad in order to maintain quality of players in a particular country); *Hall v Victoria Football League* [1982] VR 64 (restriction on players moving outside particular local areas); *Adamson v NSWRL* (1991) 100 ALR 479; on appeal 103 ALR 319, 31 FCR 242 (draft arrangement) (1991) 27 FCR 535 on appeal. This is the chief justification offered in respect of restrictions on the ability of players to move and in respect of rules requiring transfer fees, drafts and salary caps.

5 See *Adamson v NSWRL* at n 4.

6 See for example *Rugby World Cup 1999*: Pugh and Martin 'How the Rugby World Cup Plays by the Rules' *Sportvision* (Autumn 1999), p 72; and Whitehead 'Anatomy of a Tournament' (1999) 6(3) Sports Law Administration & Practice 1 (Rugby World Cup 1999).

7 See *Wimbledon Football Club v Football League* unreported FA Arbitration Panel decision dated 29 January 2002, FA Commission May 2002.

8 See *Gasser v Stinson* (15 June 1988, unreported) (Scott J); *Johnson v Athletics Canada and IAAF* (1997) 41 OTC 95 (where it was also held reasonable as necessary to protect Ben Johnson from himself).

9 See *Williams and Cardiff RFC v Pugh* (23 July 1997, unreported) (Popplewell J) and (1 August 1997, unreported), CA; subsequently known as *Williams and Cardiff RFC v WRU (IRB intervening)* (17 March 1998, unreported) (Buckley J), [1999] Eu LR 195.

10 See *South Sydney District Rugby League Football Club v News Ltd* [2000] FCA 1541, [2001] FCA 862.

11 See *South Sydney District Rugby League Football Club v News Ltd* n 10; *Williams and Cardiff RFC v Pugh* (23 July 1997, unreported) (Popplewell J) and (1 August 1997, unreported), CA; subsequently known as *Williams and Cardiff RFC v WRU (IRB intervening)* (17 March 1998, unreported) (Buckley J), [1999] Eu LR 195.

A3.139 If the governing body establishes that the restraint is reasonable and justified in the interests of the parties, in the third stage of the analysis (again in the conventional form of the doctrine[1]) the party seeking to challenge the imposition of the obligation has a last chance. The doctrine requires restraints to be reasonable not only in the interests of the parties but also in the interests of the public. The onus of proving that an obligation is not reasonable in the interests of the public lies on the party challenging the obligation, here the player, club or other participant. This is the second limb of the *Nordenfelt v Maxim Nordenfelt* reasonableness test[2].

1 See n 1 to para A3.138, and para A3.140.

2 [1894] AC 535 at 565.

(c) Questions raised

A3.140 The particular circumstances of sport have meant that some of the cases applying the doctrine in that context have introduced additional elements to the standard restraint of trade analysis as set out above. In particular, the debate as to whether sports governing bodies are in reality public bodies, or at least quasi-public, and the development in the general obligations owed by governing bodies has led to the suggestion being made by Carnwath J[1] that the three-stage analysis set out above should be adapted. He has suggested that if a rule or decision of a sports governing body is established to be in restraint of trade, the first limb of the *Nordenfelt v Maxim Nordenfelt* reasonableness test (whether the restraint is in the interests of the parties) should be omitted, leaving the court to apply only the second limb, ie shifting the onus onto the player, club or other participant to prove why the restraint is not in the public interest. As part of the same analysis, Carnwath J concluded that the standard of unreasonableness to be shown by the challenger should be the public law standard, in other words Wednesbury unreasonableness, or irrationality. This approach constituted a marked departure from the previous approach in most sports law cases, under which the full *Nordenfelt v Maxim Nordenfelt* test was applied without adaptation[2]. This is addressed below in the discussion of the application of the doctrine in the sports sector the arguments in favour and against each approach. First, though, two threshold questions are addressed:

(i) does the doctrine apply to rules of governing bodies that do not have contractual force in a particular instance? and
(ii) does the doctrine apply to governing bodies' decisions as well as to their rules?

1 Technically obiter, in *Stevenage Borough Football Club v Football League Ltd*, Carnwath J (1996) Times, 1 August. For the Court of Appeal, see (1997) 9 Admin LR 109, CA.
2 Notably and relatively recently by Blackburne J at trial in *Newport v Football Association of Wales* (12 April 1995, unreported).

(d) The restraint need not be imposed by contract

A3.141 Although in the normal course the restraint of trade doctrine is applied to render specific contractual clauses unenforceable[1], the doctrine does have wider applicability. Even where there is no contractual relationship, a specific rule of a body with power to affect the ability of a person to trade can be declared incompatible with the doctrine[2]. In the sports context this means that even where no contract arises between a governing body and an individual player, rules of the governing body that affect the player will nevertheless be subject to the doctrine.

1 See also the way the questions for decision are put in *Gasser v Stinson* (15 June 1988, unreported) (Scott J) at 25D–F of the shorthand writers' transcript.
2 *Pharmaceutical Society of Great Britain v Dickson* [1970] AC 403, HL per Lord Wilberforce at 440C; *Eastham v Newcastle United Football Club and the FA* [1964] Ch 413 at 443; *Greig v Insole (for the TCCB)* [1978] 1 WLR 302; *Buckley v Tutty* (1971) 125 CLR 353.

(e) The doctrine applies to the decisions, as well as the rules, of sports governing bodies

A3.142 Nor does the obligation, or the restraint, have to arise out of a sports governing body's rules. It may arise out of a particular decision of the sports governing body to apply in an unjustifiably restrictive way rules that in themselves are valid. For example, it may be perfectly appropriate to have a rule affording a sports governing body a discretion, but if the body seeks to exercise that discretion in an unreasonable way which restricts the ability of a person or company to trade, that decision is reviewable on the basis of restraint of trade[1]. If this were not the case, any contractual exercise of power on the basis of a discretion would escape review by reference to the doctrine. Nor does the fact that a discretion exists to disapply a rule save a rule that is prima facie a restraint, since the party affected cannot be expected to rely on the favourable application of that discretion[2].

1 *Newport v FAW* [1995] 2 All ER 87 at 97g–h per Jacob J (interlocutory); unreported, Blackburne J, 12 April 1995 (trial) at 24, 33–35 and 45 of the New Law Online transcript. See also *Stinnato v Auckland Boxing Association* [1978] 1 NZLR 1 (decision to refuse a licence capable of being a restraint of trade).
2 *Buckley v Tutty* (1971) 125 CLR 353.

B The application of the doctrine to the rules and actions of sports governing bodies

A3.143 The starting point in relation to the application of the restraint of trade doctrine to the rules and actions of sports governing bodies is *Eastham v Newcastle United Football Club and the Football Association*[1]. At issue in that case was (inter alia) the validity of the Football League's then transfer and retention rules. The rules allowed a club to retain a player's registration, notwithstanding that his contract with the club had expired, until a transfer fee was paid by a new club. Wilberforce J held[2] that:

> the two systems when combined were in restraint of trade and, since [the League] had not discharged the onus on them of showing that the restraints were no more than was reasonable to protect their interests, were in unjustifiable restraint of trade, and … as such they were ultra vires.

The burden was therefore regarded as being on the governing body to show that the restraint was reasonably necessary in the interests of the parties[3]. The test applied was the first limb of the *Nordenfelt v Maxim Nordenfelt* reasonableness test, and Wilberforce J did not go on to the second limb. No doubt, however, if the governing body had established the reasonableness of the transfer rules as between the parties, the question would have moved on to whether the player could establish that the rules were not reasonably necessary in the public interest. The rules were held to be in restraint of trade because notwithstanding that the governing body and the clubs supported them, and notwithstanding that they had some benefits, the value of the benefit was wholly outweighed by the detriment to players, and the restraint went further than was necessary to protect the governing body's legitimate interests. The case is also authority for the proposition that the rules of a governing body should where possible be construed so as not to give rise to a restraint of trade[4].

1 [1964] Ch 413. The application of the *Nordenfelt v Maxim Nordenfelt* test in *Eastham* has been followed in the Commonwealth: see the cases in n 2 to para A3.151 (in particular, *Blackler v New Zealand Rugby Football League* [1968] NZLR 547; and *Buckley v Tutty* (1971) 125 CLR 353. In *Buckley* the New South Wales Rugby Football League attempted by its rules to prevent a player transferring outside NSW and imposed a transfer system. It was held that the restraint of trade doctrine applies to full or part time professionals; that it was not possible to argue that the rules fostered trade rather than restrained it (on the basis that it was essential to the organisation of the sport, and players could not take the benefits without the corollary restraint); that the doctrine applies even in the absence of a contractual relationship; that applying the *Nordenfelt v Maxim Nordenfelt* test, with the onus on the governing body, the prevention of transfer outside NSW and the transfer system went further than was necessary; and that the fact that the governing body had a discretion to disapply the rule did not make it valid. The court arguably went further than Wilberforce J had in *Eastham*. The League subsequently adopted a replacement transfer system which is similar to that agreed by FIFA and the European Commission some 30 years later). A similar issue arose in *Cooke v Football Association*, Foster J, [1972] CLY 516 (The player sought to transfer from Sligo Rovers in Ireland to Wigan, but was prevented from doing so by the Football Association of Ireland rules (which were equivalent to those struck down in *Eastham*, but which FIFA had continued to apply). The FA, under contract to FIFA, was obliged not to register the player. Foster J held that the FIFA rules were in unreasonable restraint of trade and consequently the player could be registered.
2 See the headnote.
3 See pp 431 and 439.
4 See p 440.

A3.144 Carnwath J's analysis in *Stevenage* has its origins in *Nagle v Feilden*[1]. That case involved a decision by the Jockey Club in the application of its rules. It had a discretion whether to grant trainers' licences. It refused the applicant a trainer's licence. The applicant's case was that the Jockey Club reached that decision only because she was a woman, and that such an approach was contrary to natural justice. The Jockey Club applied to strike out the action, and the Court of Appeal had to decide whether the action was arguable. The Court of Appeal used the broad concept of restraint of trade as the foundation for the proposition that it was arguable that a sports governing body owes general obligations to act fairly and reasonably when it takes a decision, and that the Jockey Club was in breach of such obligations. The court had to resort to this analysis because there was no contract on which to hang the obligations. The Court of Appeal couched the obligation to act reasonably in terms of an obligation not to act arbitrarily or capriciously[2]. The case arguably did not involve the application of the doctrine of restraint of trade doctrine as such[3], but rather defined the minimum standards of conduct to be expected from a body carrying out a quasi-public role in a context where an individual's livelihood was at stake.

1 [1966] 2 QB 633; see para A3.82. See p 18 of the New Law Online transcript of Carnwath J's decision in *Stevenage*.

2 See Lord Denning at 647; Danckwerts LJ at 649–651; Salmon LJ at 653–654. Salmon LJ arguably went on (at 655) to put the test on the classic footing of *Nordenfelt v Maxim Nordenfelt*, although he does refer to capriciousness after citing that case. The burden was not addressed.

3 See *R v Jockey Club, ex p RAM Racecourses* [1993] 2 All ER 225 at 247h to 248b; *R v Jockey Club, ex p Aga Khan* [1993] 1 WLR 909 at 933. For the contrary view, see (in addition to Carnwath J in *Stevenage* at p 20 of the New Law Online transcript), Scott J's statement in *Watson v Prager* [1991] 1 WLR 726 at 747 (a case involving a dispute between a boxer and his manager) that '*Nagle v Feilden* established in my judgment that where the rules or regulations of a body with power to control professional sport are restrictive of the ability of professionals within that sport to earn their living from the sport, the doctrine of restraint of trade applies. The restrictive rules or regulations must be franked by passing through the reasonableness gateway'. However the reasonableness test applied by Scott J in the *Watson v Prager* case (at 747 et seq) was the conventional test: he examined the interests of the boxer and the sport as a whole by reference to whether the restrictions were 'fair' and not by a quasi-public law standard. Although the case involved a contract between a boxer and manager, the agreement was the standard form imposed by the governing body. In Stewart's view however (at [1996] 4(3) SATLJ, p 110), Scott J nevertheless applied the normal restraint of trade reasonableness test.

A3.145 In *Greig v Insole*[1], the ICC and the TCCB changed their rules relating to qualification to play in test matches and county cricket. The new rules provided that any player who played in a match that had been disapproved by the ICC or TCCB would be ineligible to play in any test match or county cricket match without the consent of the ICC or TCCB, such consent only to be given on the application of the player's national governing body. The ICC and TCCB then passed resolutions disapproving the World Series matches organised by Kerry Packer. The players thereby rendered ineligible for ICC and TCCB matches brought a challenge. That challenge was to rules, albeit rules introduced in specific response to the players' desire to do something that they had not previously done. This reveals the artificiality on occasion of any distinction being drawn for the purposes of restraint of trade between a rule and a decision: in this context, the challenges were just as much against the resolutions in relation to Kerry Packer's matches, which were necessary to achieve the bans as against the rule which gave power to withhold consent to allow a player to play in a test match after he had played in a disapproved match. The court held that the ICC and TCCB had legitimate interests in the proper administration of cricket, but that they had failed to discharge the burden on them of showing that the new rules were reasonable in the circumstances. The test applied was the *Nordenfelt v Maxim Nordenfelt* reasonableness test[2]. The judgment analyses the justifiability of the combination of the new rules and the resolutions disapproving the Kerry Packer World Series matches.

1 [1978] 1 WLR 302.
2 [1978] 1 WLR 302 at 345.

A3.146 In *Gasser v Stinson*[1] the court concluded that the drugs rules applied to Ms Gasser were certainly a restraint of trade (although she was nominally amateur), but that they were proportionate and reasonable in the interests not only of the parties but also the public. Scott J concluded that although the relevant IAAF rules imposed a strict liability offence, that was justified in the particular circumstances of the threat to sport posed by drug-taking and the difficulties in detecting and proving an offence. Scott J examined simultaneously the reasonableness of the rules in the interests of the public and in the interests of athletes, and introduced the concept of judicial reluctance to intervene into the restraint of trade analysis[2].

1 (15 June 1988, unreported) (Scott J). See also *Wilander v Tobin* (19 March 1996, unreported) (Lightman J), (8 April 1996, unreported), CA, where an argument that the anti-doping rules were in restraint of trade was struck out as unarguable. For later developments on the legality of strict liability in the context of doping, see paras E4.75 to E4.135.
2 See pp 37H to 40E of the shorthand writers' transcript. Although *Gasser v Stinson* case was not cited by Carnwath J in *Stevenage*, it provides some support for his analysis in *Stevenage*, in particular Scott J's reliance on *McInnes v Onslow-Fane*, on which Carnwath J also placed reliance. That said, Scott J did not suggest that he was departing from the conventional approach to restraint of trade. See also Scott J's analysis in *Currie v Barton* (26 March 1987, unreported) (Scott J) (which involved collateral reliance on the restraint of trade doctrine in order to support a natural justice argument, as in *Nagle v Feilden*), and his statement in *Watson v Prager* [1991] 1 WLR 726 set out at para A3.144, n 3.

A3.147 In *R v Jockey Club, ex p RAM Racecourses*[1], a prospective racecourse developer sought judicial review of a decision by the Jockey Club not to allocate any racing dates to the proposed racecourse. The court stated that were it not for authority to the contrary (which authority was subsequently upheld in *Aga Khan*[2]) it would have held that the Jockey Club was amenable to judicial review. On the facts however it was decided that the developer could not have had a legitimate expectation of being granted any races. The court did however conclude obiter that it could have interfered if the exercise of power had been unlawful, even though the action ought to have been a private one. Stuart Smith LJ said[3]:

> [The Jockey Club] accepted that in an appropriate case where a body enjoys a monopoly position such that it can prevent a person from earning his living by not admitting him or from conducting a legitimate business, in restraint of trade, it will be amenable to a declaratory judgment in an action begun by writ, if it has acted in an arbitrary and capricious way in refusing to permit the applicant's activities: see *Eastham* [1964] Ch 413 at 446, [1963] 3 All ER 139 at 157; *Greig v Insole* [1978] 3 All ER 449 at 495, [1978] 1 WLR 302 at 345 and *Nagle v Feilden* [1966] 2 QB 633, [1966] 1 All ER 689. Thus, in my opinion, if the Jockey Club, enjoying the monopoly power that it does, had given a clear and unambiguous statement to anyone seeking to open a new racecourse that they would be allotted a certain number of fixtures, that being in accordance with their declared policy, it would prima facie be unlawful and in restraint of trade to refuse such an application. And equally, if a licence to operate a racecourse depends, as it appears to do, on the allocation of fixtures (all other necessary conditions being satisfied), it would prima facie be in restraint of trade and unlawful if the Jockey Club refused a licence on the

grounds that they had not allocated the necessary fixtures to the applicant contrary to their declared policy and clear representation. The significance of the declared policy and representation in these circumstances would be that it would be virtually impossible for the Jockey Club to contend that the restraint of trade was reasonable.

Implicit in this is the proposition that the onus was on the Jockey Club to show that the restraint was reasonable. However, the test (at least on the basis of the Jockey Club's concession) involved arbitrariness and caprice, albeit that the conclusion of the passage quoted seems to refer back to a *Nordenfelt v Maxim Nordenfelt* approach. Again however, as in *Nagle v Feilden*, the decision was arguably not an application of the restraint of trade doctrine itself.

1 [1993] 2 All ER 225, DC.
2 See para A3.62; *R v Jockey Club, ex p Aga Khan* [1993] 1 WLR 909. The earlier authority upheld was *R v Jockey Club, ex p Massingberd-Mundy* [1993] 2 All ER 207.
3 At 243f.

A3.148 In *Newport v Football Association of Wales*, the issue was whether the Football Association of Wales (FAW) could stop ex-members playing home games in Wales in a competition not controlled by the FAW. There were two hearings, at each of which the clubs succeeded. At the interlocutory hearing[1], Jacob J granted an interim injunction in support of an action for a declaration alone. He also held that there was a serious issue to be tried, namely whether the FAW had by its decisions fettered the free choice of Welsh clubs as to where to play[2]. Jacob J proceeded on the basis that unreasonable 'arrangements' as well as contracts could fall foul of the restraint of trade doctrine. He also pointed out that making the clubs play away from home reduced their income to the point at which they would collapse imminently. The source of the problem was a resolution of the FAW that no Welsh clubs would henceforth be sanctioned under Rule 57 of the FAW Rules to play home games in Wales as part of the English league pyramid (excepting those clubs already playing in the Football League itself). In essence the decision was to refuse consent to the non-league Welsh clubs that wished to continue to play in the English pyramid to play their home games in Wales. There were appeals against that resolution. One of the appeals was even successful (that of Merthyr Tydfil, which was in the Conference). The appeals of Newport, Caernafon, Colwyn Bay and others were unsuccessful. They then resigned and joined up with the FA. The FAW responded with sanctions, causing the FA to ban the three clubs from playing their home English league games in Wales. The three clubs then challenged the decisions of the FAW to exclude them from playing at home as being in restraint of trade. Jacob J was not impressed with an argument that the three clubs ought to have sued the FA not the FAW. He took the view that the FA's decision was at the behest of the FAW, and that the FAW was the operator of the restraint. Jacob J held[3] that the doctrine of restraint of trade is not technical and looks to substance not form. He asked himself whether the decisions involved restrained trade, and held that it was arguable that they did[4]. Jacob J held that the test for reasonableness (by which he measured whether there was a serious issue to be tried) was the *Nordenfelt v Maxim Nordenfelt* test[5].

1 [1995] 2 All ER 87.
2 In that instance whether they could play home games within the English pyramid non-league system (ie below the Football League) in Wales.
3 At 95f.
4 At 97 g–h.
5 At 97j–98d.

A3.149 The trial in *Newport v FAW* was before Blackburne J[1], who held that the FAW resolution was in restraint of trade, and that it was not reasonably necessary for protecting the FAW's legitimate interests. In so doing he examined the compatibility of a decision, not a rule, against the doctrine[2], and he specifically stated that this was what he was doing[3]. He applied the *Nordenfelt v Maxim Nordenfelt* reasonableness test[4]. He examined whether the FAW had discharged the burden of justifying the restraint[5]. He rejected an argument from the FAW that the very nature of the organisation of football within the UK, split into England, Wales, Scotland and Northern Ireland, gave rise to the restriction on the ability of clubs in one country to play home games for the league of another country[6].

1 (12 April 1995, unreported).
2 See pp 24 and 33–35 of the New Law Online transcript.
3 At p 45.
4 At p 36.
5 See pp 36 and 39.
6 See pp 35–36.

A3.150 Soon after the decision in *Newport*, Lightman J and the Court of Appeal had to consider in *Wilander v Tobin*[1] whether it was arguable that the anti-doping rules of the International Tennis Federation were in restraint of trade. Lightman J followed Scott J's approach in *Gasser v Stinson*[2]. In the Court of Appeal, Neill LJ upheld Lightman J's decision, asking simply whether the rules in question were reasonable[3]. Subsequently the players attempted, ultimately unsuccessfully, to amend to add arguments based on the free movement and the competition law rules[4]. In the Court of Appeal on the second occasion, Lord Woolf MR reached the conclusion, dealt with above, that it is implicit in the contract between players and a governing body contained in its rules that the governing body will abide by general obligations which mirror those of a public body[5]. It is arguable that in so concluding, Lord Woolf MR was setting the *upper*, as opposed to (or as well as) the *lower* limits, on a sports governing body's liability. In other words, if it is right that the quasi-public law test should apply, then arguably that involves protecting the governing body from over-intrusive review just as much as ensuring a minimum level of review to claimants, and it ought not to be possible to circumvent this protection for the governing body by the application of a more intrusive test under the restraint of trade doctrine. Lord Woolf MR went on to say[6], in assessing whether the free movement argument should be allowed in after the restraint of trade argument had been struck out, that:

> The requirement of proportionality [for the purposes of the free movement rules] may not be identical … with reasonableness or natural justice but it is certainly close to these concepts.

This leaves open the question of whether the test under the restraint of trade doctrine is the same as the quasi-public law test. If the reference to reasonableness here was a reference to reasonableness under the restraint of trade doctrine, Lord Woolf MR appears to have been equating it with the 'natural justice' test. On the other hand, he also appears to have contemplated that proportionality under the free movement rules is close to the appropriate test for the purposes of restraint of trade. At least until recently, the proportionality test under the free movement rules was not regarded as being the same as the traditional form of public law reasonableness: proportionality under the free movement rules is a more intrusive test than arbitrariness or capriciousness. It is possible that Lord Woolf MR was foreshadowing more recent developments that treat the reasonableness and proportionality tests as involving broadly similar considerations in a flexible and variable way dependent on the particular circumstances[7].

1 (19 March 1996, unreported) (Lightman J), (8 April 1996, unreported), CA.
2 See p 20 of the New Law Online transcript of Lightman J's judgment.
3 See Lexis transcript of Neill LJ's judgment.
4 The action came back before Lightman J, [1997] 1 Lloyd's Law Rep 195, who gave leave to amend to add the free movement argument but refused leave to add the competition law argument on the basis that it was insufficiently particularised. The Court of Appeal refused leave to amend to add either argument. [1997] 2 Lloyd's Law Rep 296. The second Court of Appeal decision (December 1996) came after the decision in *Stevenage* (July 1996).
5 [1997] 2 Lloyd's Law Rep 296 per Lord Woolf MR at 300, col 1. Shortly thereafter (July 1997), Lord Woolf MR gave judgment in *Modahl v BAF*, where he held that that the normal judicial review standard of fairness applied to the review of private body disciplinary decisions. See para A3.89.
6 Per Lord Woolf MR at [1997] 2 Lloyd's Law Rep 301, col 1.
7 See para A3.110.

A3.151 The position on the authorities following the *Newport* decision, and following the first round of *Wilander* decisions but before the judgment of Lord Woolf MR described above[1], was that if a challenger established that a rule or decision of a sports governing body restricted his ability to earn a living at his chosen profession, the governing body would have to satisfy the first limb of the *Nordenfelt v Maxim Nordenfelt* reasonableness test by establishing that the restriction was necessary to achieve a legitimate aim of the governing body and that it was proportionate[2]. It is against this background that Carnwath J's analysis in *Stevenage Borough Football Club v Football League Ltd*[3] is to be measured. In that case Carnwath J had inter alia to examine whether entry criteria for the club winning the Conference to gain promotion to the League were in unjustifiable restraint of trade. He decided the case on the basis that the club had delayed too long before making an application and that in its discretion the court should refuse relief since third party rights were affected[4]. He was upheld on this point by the Court of Appeal[5]. He also held obiter that a number of the criteria were in unreasonable restraint of trade[6], and the consequence was that the League changed the rules that he had criticised. Although it is not certain, it appears that Carnwath J applied an adapted version of the restraint of trade doctrine in reaching this conclusion. Earlier in his judgment he suggested, technically obiter, that the test to be applied by the courts when considering whether a sports governing body is acting in restraint of trade was a rather different test to that used by the courts that had applied the doctrine in sports cases previously. It is arguable that Carnwath J did not reach a firm conclusion in relation to the test and how it applied in practice. The Court of Appeal[7] noted that in the context of one of the rules Carnwath J said that he 'would return later to consider whether this was the correct test', but that 'in the event, however, he did not do so' and instead dismissed the action on grounds of delay. The Court of Appeal appeared[8] to regard Carnwath J as evaluating whether the League had discharged the burden of showing that the restraints were necessary to protect its legitimate interests[9].

1 The second Court of Appeal decision in *Wilander*, described above (at para A3.150), came after the *Stevenage* decision.
2 The same position applied in the Commonwealth. For the leading cases on the use of restraint of trade to challenge the rules and decisions of sports governing bodies in Australia, see *Buckley v Tutty* (1971) 125 CLR 353 at para 15 (described at para A3.143, n 1); and following *Buckley v Tutty: Hall v Victorian Football League* [1982] VR 64; *Foschini v Victorian Football League*, unreported Crockett J (Victoria) 15 April 1983; *Hughes v Western Australia Cricket Association*

(1986) 69 ALR 660; *Barnard v Australian Soccer Federation* (1988) 81 ALR 51; *Adamson v NSW Rugby League* (1991) 100 ALR 479, 27 FCR 535; on appeal 103 ALR 319, 31 FCR 242; *Nobes v Australian Cricket Board*, unreported Marks J (Victoria) 16 December 1991; *Robertson v Australian Professional Cycling Council*, unreported Waddell CJ (NSW) 10 December 1992; *Australian Rugby League v Cross* (1997) 39 IPR 111; *News Ltd v Australian Rugby League* (1996) 135 ALR 33, *(No 2)* (1997) 139 ALR 193; *Wickham v Canberra District RLFC and Canberra District Junior Rugby League* [1998] SCACT 95; *South Sydney District Rugby League Football Club v News Ltd* [2000] FCA 1541, 3 November 2000, Finn J [2001] FCA 862; see also [2001] 2 ISLR N-20 and Farrell, 'The draft system and restraint of trade in Australian Rugby League [1997] 5(1) SATLJ 59. Cf the position in Australia where the action is brought by a commercial partner: *Hospitality Group v Australian Rugby Union* [1999] FCA 1136 (interlocutory); [2000] FCA 823 (first instance); [2001] FCA 1040 (on appeal). In relation to New Zealand, see *Blackler v New Zealand Rugby Football League* [1968] NZLR 547 at 555 and 568; *Stinnato v Auckland Boxing Association* [1978] 1 NZLR 1 at 26 per Cooke J; *Kemp v New Zealand Rugby Football League* [1989] 3 NZLR 463, applying the same approach as in *Blackler*, and *Rugby Union Players' Association Inc v Commerce Commission (No 2)* [1997] 3 NZLR 301. In relation to Canada, see *Johnson v Athletics Canada* (1997) 41 OTC 95 at paras 23 to 29; *Yashin v NHL* [2000] OTC 681. In relation to South Africa, see *Coetzee v Comitis* [2001] 4 BCLR 323.

3 *Stevenage Borough Football Club v Football League Ltd* (1996) Times, 1 August; affd 9 Admin LR 109, CA.

4 At pp 34 to 35 of the New Law Online transcript.

5 At (1997) 9 Admin LR 109 at 117 to 121 per Millet LJ, at 122 to 123 per Hobhouse LJ.

6 At pp 26 to 33 of the New Law Online transcript. In the earlier FA arbitration, *Enfield v Football League*, the Panel had rejected a restraint of trade challenge to entry criteria. See Carnwath J at pp 31 to 32 of the New Law Online transcript.

7 (1997) 9 Admin LR 109 at 117E.

8 At 117D.

9 The Court of Appeal's decision in *Stevenage* focuses on the question of delay, and specifically did not address the test for restraint of trade. See for example Hobhouse LJ at 121F–H.

A3.152 Carnwath J suggested[1] that because sports governing bodies (and specifically the League) act in pursuance of a quasi-public role, the appropriate test of justifiability is whether the restraint is justified in the *public* interest (the second as opposed to the first limb in the *Nordenfelt v Maxim Nordenfelt* reasonableness test), putting the burden on to the challenger to show why the restraint operated against the public interest, rather than on the governing body to show why it was justified in the interests of the parties. He regarded the test applied in *Greig* and in *Newport* (the first limb of the *Nordenfelt v Maxim Nordenfelt* reasonableness test) as misleading[2]. He also held[3] that the standard of unreasonableness for these purposes was the public law standard. In so doing he drew on the references to the words 'arbitrary or capricious' in *Nagle v Feilden* and in *McInnes v Onslow-Fane*. Carnwath J did however state after examining the law that it was 'not the time to attempt a reconciliation of these various strands of authority'. This does not however in the authors' view undercut the status of his discussion of the doctrine[4], to which weight should still be attached.

1 At p 25 of the New Law Online transcript.

2 At p 24 of the New Law Online transcript.

3 At pp 22 and 25–26 of the New Law Online transcript

4 At pp 17–24 of the New Law Online transcript.

A3.153 There has been academic support for Carnwath J's analysis from writers who believe that sports governing bodies fulfil a public role and ought to be subject to judicial review rather than dealt with in private law proceedings[1]. That position is lent some support by Carnwath J's approach, which is at bottom to characterise sports governing bodies as public authorities and then to apply a quasi-judicial review test not only to the general obligations of fairness and reasonableness, but also to the separate doctrine of restraint of trade itself. Further, as set out above[2],

Carnwath J's analysis is consistent with an approach that defines the ambit of the implied terms and general obligations of sports governing bodies by reference to public law obligations even though their decisions are not subject to judicial review. If restraint of trade could be used to impose a different, more easily satisfied, test for the review of the rules and decisions of sports governing bodies, it is arguable that the purpose behind defining their obligations by reference to a quasi-public law test would be defeated. Carnwath J's analysis is useful to sports governing bodies seeking to defend actions brought against them on the basis of restraint of trade[3].

1 Beloff et al *Sports Law* (1999, Hart Publishing) at para 3.44. The authors conclude that 'the upshot … is that it is not always clear (1) where the burden of proof lies in a restraint of trade case involving a sporting body, nor (2) precisely how the applicable standard of reasonableness should be formulated'.

2 See paras A3.64, n 1 and A3.87.

3 Although, as appears below (para A3.156), Carnwath J's analysis has not as yet been followed in any court decision on the merits, it was certainly argued by the governing bodies, first in *Williams and Cardiff RFC v Pugh*, later known as *Williams and Cardiff RFC v WRU (IRB intervening)*, interim injunction hearings (23 July 1997, unreported) (Popplewell J), (1 August 1997, unreported), CA; application for a stay hearings (17 March 198, unreported) (Buckley J), [1999] Eu LR 195, secondly in *Hendry v World Professional Billiards and Snooker Association Ltd*, Lloyd J 5 October 2001 [2002] 1 ISLR SLR-1 and thirdly in *Wimbledon v Football League* unreported FA Arbitration Panel 29 January 2002, in none of which was the issue decided.

A3.154 On the other hand an equally arguable analysis open to challengers is that the *Nordenfelt v Maxim Nordenfelt* reasonableness test continues to apply in full to the rules and decisions of sports governing bodies[1]. The courts have now categorically held[2] that the decisions of sports governing bodies in situations such as this are not amenable to judicial review. Until that position is overturned, it would be argued, the analysis in *Stevenage* starts from the wrong premise. It is also plain that the courts can legitimately draw, and have drawn, on public law considerations in identifying general obligations implied as contractual terms or enforceable by an action for a declaration; these are implicit, quasi-public obligations to which the court is endeavouring to set parameters. It could however be argued that the fact that the courts can draw and have drawn on the public law analogy to *impose* obligations on sports governing bodies, even though they are not subject to judicial review, does not mean that it is appropriate for the courts also to *limit* the obligations owed by such bodies as a function of their private law nature by adapting the established doctrine of restraint of trade. Arguably, the doctrine of restraint of trade applies precisely because the rules of a sports governing body, and their application, involve the domestic private law administration of a trade by those involved in it[3]. It does not appear to be the position that the restraint of trade test is applied differently in cases involving the rules of other trade organisations fulfilling a similar role to that of a sports governing body albeit in a different sector[4].

1 The argument would be put on the basis of *Eastham v Newcastle United* [1964] Ch 413, and *Newport v FAW* (at trial, unreported Blackburne J 12 April 1995, interlocutory hearing reported at [1995] 2 All ER 87), and the analysis in *Stevenage* would be refuted on the basis set out in this para and the following paras. The decision in *Stevenage* has been criticised. See Stewart [1996] 4(3) SATLJ 110; see also Alderson at p 107 in the same publication and Stewart [1998] 6(3) SATLJ 41. See also Dawn Oliver [1997] PL 630). Stewart argues, amongst other things, that Carnwath J relied on the absence of any contract in order to adapt the doctrine, yet there was no contract in *Newport* and that did not lead to the doctrine being adapted by Jacob J or Blackburne J; that Carnwath J was wrong to characterise the Football League as a sports governing body because

that role is fulfilled by the FA, and the Football League is simply a group of commercial football clubs organising a competition; that Carnwath J was wrong to conclude that the earlier cases did not take into account the quasi-public role of governing bodies; that the analysis in *Stevenage* was complicated by the fact that the club was technically applying for membership, which has always been treated more restrictively by the courts; and that arguably Carnwath J did not formally decide the issue.

2 In *R v Jockey Club, ex p Aga Khan* [1993] 1 WLR 909; and *R v Football Association, ex p Football League* [1993] 2 All ER 833; see paras A3.62 to A3.65. In *Aga Khan* at 932H to 933A, Hoffmann LJ's test arguably presumes the full application of private law remedies such as the restraint of trade doctrine.

3 At bottom the decisions of many sports governing bodies are the decisions of a collection of commercial concerns in relation to how one particular commercial concern can act, which is precisely the area where the restraint of trade doctrine should be given full effect. There is arguably no proper basis for limiting interference in that context. This approach has the benefit of subjecting potentially highly restrictive rules to the full rigours of the proportionality test, rather than see them survive by virtue of the difficulty in establishing arbitrariness or caprice.

4 See *Pharmaceutical Society of Great Britain v Dickson* [1970] AC 403, HL, where the majority so held: Lord Morris at 426G to 427H, Lord Hodson at 430F to 431E, Lord Upjohn at 436A to 437D, Lord Wilberforce at 440B to 441F; but see also Lord Reid at 421B–D.

A3.155 Any challenger pursuing this analysis would argue that Carnwath J's analysis wrongly elides the question of restraint of trade and the question of breach of the general obligations governing the way in which decisions are made. It would be argued that these are two separate conceptual areas. The first involves competition law analysis, albeit blunt. The second involves questions of due process and rationality that are separate from restraint of trade. It would be said that it is not the case, where for example a competition law issue arises in a public law context, that the court ignores the proportionality test applicable under the competition rules and applies a different, harder to satisfy, judicial review test. Nor arguably is there any reason for it to do so when both issues arise in private law proceedings through the traditional common law doctrine of restraint of trade. Carnwath J stated[1] that concentration on the second limb of the *Nordenfelt v Maxim Nordenfelt* reasonableness test (necessary in the public interest) is more significant in the context of cases which do not involve a contract, as there it is harder to see where the general obligation enforceable by an action for a declaration comes from. It would be said that this is again to elide the two separate bases for challenge. On this basis, the proper way of explaining the overlap between the bases for challenge in *Nagle v Feilden* and *Onslow-Fane* is that in those cases the courts were endeavouring to find a basis for the general obligations that they needed to imply to do justice, and they resorted to an ad hoc invocation of elements of the established doctrine of restraint of trade. They did not actually apply that doctrine, but rather pointed to the degree of influence that the sports governing body had over the player, club or other participant involved, in order to set up the general obligations of fairness and reasonableness. The fact that they did so is not however, it would be said, a basis for whittling away the restraint of trade doctrine in the sports context, which is one private law context out of many. The doctrine falls to be applied in full as it would be in any other analogous private law context.

1 At p 18 and 20 of the New Law Online transcript.

A3.156 Subsequent cases have not significantly clarified the position. In *Ray v PGA*[1], the doctrine was held, perhaps surprisingly, not to apply because the restriction did not relate to the golfer's trade but to training. The court concluded that if the doctrine applied, a restraint requiring golf-related examination qualifications as a prerequisite of entry into specified events was justified. In the litigation between Cardiff RFC and the Welsh Rugby Union, Cardiff challenged (amongst other things) the WRU's attempt to introduce a rule under which a club that wished to play in the WRU's competitions was obliged to agree to do so for a fixed period of time[2]. The argument was put in contract, in restraint of trade and in competition law. At the hearing before Popplewell J, the WRU argued that the test on restraint of trade was whether the decision was arbitrary or capricious[3] and that the court should be slow to intervene, and that therefore the court could be satisfied that Cardiff did not have an arguable case sufficient to found an entitlement to an interim injunction. Popplewell J quickly dismissed the proposition that Cardiff did not have an arguable case, but did not specifically decide the test. Ultimately the WRU and International Rugby Board successfully applied to have the action stayed on the basis that the issue of compliance with the EC competition rules was pending before the European Commission as a result of notification by the governing bodies, and there was consequently a risk of conflicting decisions. In that context, Eady J approached the restraint of trade issue as being so analogous to the EC competition law issue that it was not safe to stay only that part of the action that related to EC competition law[4]. The conclusion that the doctrine of restraint of trade and the competition rules are two sides of the same coin, involving the same premise and the same public policy rationale, arguably goes against the application of a narrower, quasi-public law test to assess when rules and decisions fall foul of the restraint of trade doctrine. Lloyd J took a similar approach in *Hendry v World Professional Billiards and Snooker Association*[5]. Having assessed in detail the arguments based on the competition rules, he appears to have considered there to be little room for a different conclusion under the restraint of trade doctrine, and he declined to decide whether the *Stevenage* case had altered the test to be applied[6]. Lloyd J examined whether the WPBSA's rule A5 (requiring players to have its permission to play in any snooker tournament, except in specified circumstances) was reasonably justified. The vice was of course that it enabled WPBSA to limit the growth of rival organisations. Lloyd J held that Rule A5 was contrary to the competition rules and that 'even absent the constraints of competition law as such, WPBSA cannot justify this restriction as being no more than is reasonably required for the protection of its own legitimate interests'[7]. Other rules that had been challenged were upheld both as a matter of the competition rules and the restraint of trade doctrine[8]. In *Wimbledon Football Club v Football League*[9], the Football League argued that the appropriate test was whether the club could establish first, that the Football League's decision to refuse permission for it to move to Milton Keynes was a restraint, and secondly that it was not reasonable in the interests of the public, applying a high standard (in other words Carnwath J's test in *Stevenage)*. The club contended that once a restraint was established, the onus was on the League to justify its restrictive decision as being proportionate and in the reasonable interests of the parties (in other words the traditional test). In the event the FA Arbitration Panel ruled that the League's decision had been procedurally flawed, and remitted the matter to the League to consider again[10]. The Panel went on to say however [11] that a decision to refuse the club permission to move was a restraint, and that the League had to satisfy the court that preventing the club moving was proportionate, in the sense of no more than was reasonably necessary to protect the interests of the efficient organisation, administration and promotion of football as a whole [12]. Because the matter had been remitted on procedural grounds, the Arbitration Panel did not consider whether the League's refusal was proportionate.

1 Judge Dyer QC 15 April 1997.

2 *Williams and Cardiff RFC v Pugh*, later known as *Williams and Cardiff RFC v WRU (IRB intervening)*, interim injunction hearings (23 July 1997, unreported) (Popplewell J), (1 August 1997, unreported), CA; application for a stay hearings (17 March 1998, unreported) (Buckley J), [1999] Eu LR 195.
3 See shorthand-writers' transcript p 8 line 29.
4 At 200.
5 Lloyd J 5 October 2001 [2002] 1 ISLR SLR-1. There is also an unreported judgment of the Court of Appeal on a procedural matter dated 11 July 2001.
6 At paras 114 to 116, 128 and 138.
7 A phrase which is plainly more similar to the test in *Maxim Nordenfelt* than the test advanced by Carnwath J in *Stevenage*. Lloyd J not only appears to have contemplated the burden being on the WPBSA, but also addressed the issue from the point of view that the question was whether the WPBSA's interests, as opposed to the public's, were engaged. This is possibly a reflection of the fact that the WPBSA arguably has less of the hallmarks of a quasi-public body pursuing public functions than do some other governing bodies.
8 See para A3.170, n 6.
9 (29 January 2002, unreported), FA Arbitration Panel. The club had also pleaded a competition law argument, but reserved its position in relation to it at the hearing before the FA Arbitration Panel.
10 The League subsequently decided in April 2002 to refer the question to an FA Commission for de novo consideration in its place. The FA Commission decided in May 2002 that the club should be allowed to move, because the damage to it as a result of not moving outweighed any perceived damage to the football pyramid, as advanced by the Football League as a reason for refusing permission.
11 Following Blackburne J in *Newport v FAW* (12 April 1995, unreported).
12 In so doing, the Arbitration Panel proceeded on the basis that in any event the doctrine of proportionality now forms part of domestic administrative law (cf Lord Slynn in *R (Alconbury) v Secretary of State for the Environment* [2001] UKHL 23, [2001] 2 All ER 929), that the proportionality test is as described by Lord Steyn in *R v Secretary of State for the Home Department, ex p Daly* [2001] UKHL 26, [2001] 2 AC 532, and that developments in administrative law are to be carried over into the content of the general obligations owed by sports governing bodies by virtue of the analysis of the Court of Appeal in *Modahl* and *Wilander*.

A3.157 As things stand, there is a basis for both arguments, and sports governing bodies and claimants will no doubt continue to advance whichever suits their respective positions. The relevance of the debate is however dependent upon the public law test continuing to involve a higher standard than that which applies under the restraint of trade doctrine in its conventional form. If it is correct that the standard of review in the public law context can include the principle of proportionality, and if it is correct that it does so when that standard of review is translated across into the general obligations owed by sports governing bodies, then it may well be that there is no real distinction between that test and the test under the conventional restraint of trade doctrine. The difference might come down to where the burden lies.

A3.158 Either way, practitioners mounting a challenge on these grounds will clearly be well advised to plead in full why the restraint is not justified. As sports governing bodies become increasingly aware of the need to avoid significant and unjustified restrictions in their rules, it will become less likely that rules will be struck down on this basis. Equally it is well arguable that the approach to be taken should be to measure rules against a proper proportionality test, rather than to suppress substantive review. On this view, the proportionality test affords sufficient protection to the freedom of action of a sports governing body while still protecting the rights of those affected by its actions.

7 EC AND DOMESTIC COMPETITION LAW

A3.159 The EC competition rules and their domestic equivalent are an important element of the legal control of the sports sector, particularly in the context of challenges to the rules and decisions of sports governing bodies. The substantive competition law rules and their application in the sector are dealt with at length in another chapter[1]. Most of the application of the rules in the sports sector is conducted by the regulatory authorities: the European Commission Competition Directorate and the UK Office of Fair Trading. On occasion the issue has arisen before the European Court of Justice[2]. Arguments based on the competition rules can however be made in the English courts, and on occasion parties challenging the actions of sports governing bodies in those courts have sought to base their attack, or at least part of their attack, on competition law grounds. Until recently this has not proved successful, but there are now grounds for believing that the argument may prove more fruitful in the future[3]. This section of this chapter simply draws the reader's attention to the availability of the argument in English proceedings, briefly mentions the substantive rules which are dealt with in detail later, explains the extent to which, and the manner in which, they can be applied by the English courts, and then outlines the limited application of the rules that there has been in the English courts in the sports sector.

1 See Chapter B2. Two leading competition law texts are Bellamy and Child *Common Market Law of Competition* (5th edn, 2001, Sweet & Maxwell); and Coleman and Grenfell *The Competition Act 1998 Law and Practice* (1999, Oxford).

2 Although, perhaps surprisingly, not that often: see para A3.166.

3 In particular in the light of the decision in *Hendry v World Professional Billiards and Snooker Association*, Lloyd J 5 October 2001 [2002] 1 ISLR SLR-1, see para A3.170; and also the decision in *AEK Athens and Slavia Prague v UEFA* CAS arbitration 98/200 interim decision 17 July 1998, final decision 20 August 1999, reported in *Digest of CAS Awards II 1998–2000* (2002, Kluwer), p 36 and in [2001] 1 ISLR 122 (Club failed in its challenge to the application to it of UEFA's Champions League rule prohibiting participation of clubs in common ownership with another participant). See also Broome [2000] 8(2) SATLJ 83 (domestic common ownership) and [2001] 9(1) SATLJ 88 (international common ownership). Although the latter is a CAS decision, it demonstrates that the application of the complex EC competition law rules can be undertaken by bodies other than the regulatory authorities.

A The competition rules in brief, and how the English courts can apply them

(a) Article 81/the Chapter I prohibition

A3.160 The English courts have jurisdiction to decide whether a sports governing body is in breach of Art 81 (ex 85) of the EC Treaty[1]. Article 81 prohibits agreements between undertakings, or decisions of associations of undertakings, which have the object or effect of appreciably restricting competition within the common market and affecting trade between member states[2]. The English courts also have jurisdiction to decide whether there is a breach of the equivalent domestic prohibition under the Competition Act 1998 ('the Chapter I prohibition'), which replaced the Restrictive Trade Practices Act 1976[3].

1 See para B2.16 et seq. For the extent to which the EC competition rules can be applied by the English courts, see Bellamy and Child *Common Market Law of Competition* (5th edn, 2001, Sweet & Maxwell), ch 10.

2 See para B2.16. It is fundamental tenet of the application of the competition law rules to the sporting context that those rules apply only to the rules and decisions of sports governing bodies that relate to the commercial aspects of sport; they do not apply to the rules and decisions of sports governing bodies that relate to the way the sport is played, or its essential organisation: see paras A3.163 and B2.56 to B2.75. This is an approach that has been developed by the European Court of Justice and the European Commission, but its logic extends to the domestic competition rules as well.

3 See para B2.17.

A3.161 For these purposes, the rules of a sports governing body are an agreement, and its decisions are decisions of an association of undertakings[1]. Side contracts with clubs and the normal commercial contracts entered into by governing bodies are caught as agreements between undertakings. If a rule or decision or agreement is contrary to the prohibition[2], and has not been notified as required to the relevant regulatory authority, it is void (subject to severance) and cannot be relied upon and there is a right to a declaration, an injunction and damages[3].

1 See paras B2.19 and B2.20.
2 See para B2.21. In order to refute the argument, the sports governing body need only show that there is no effect on trade between member states, or that the agreement does not restrict competition, or that any effect or restriction is de minimis (or negligible). The claimant on the other hand must jump over all the hurdles.
3 See para A3.205; Bellamy and Child *Common Market Law of Competition* (5th edn, 2001, Sweet & Maxwell), paras 10-029 to 10-060.

A3.162 If the rule or decision has been notified to the relevant regulatory authorities and has been formally exempted, the English court will not hold it to be in breach of the competition rules. It is also unlikely to do so if it has been the subject of a negative clearance (which is a decision that the competition rules do not apply in the first place)[1]. The situation is more complex where although the rule or decision has been notified there has been no formal response from the regulatory authority[2]. Exemption is based, broadly, on whether the restriction is justified[3]. Justification will take into account the transparency, objectivity, equality and proportionality of the restriction[4]. Exemption is currently a matter for the regulatory authorities alone; the English court cannot absolve a rule or a decision or an agreement that is caught by Art 81 by granting an exemption or theorising that an exemption would be granted[5].

1 See para B2.90; paras A3.221 to A3.227; Bellamy and Child *Common Market Law of Competition* (5th edn, 2001, Sweet & Maxwell), paras 10-017, 10-024 to 10-027. Where an exemption has been granted, there is formally no jurisdiction in the English court to proceed. Where a complaint has been rejected by the Commission, and the complainant has participated in the procedure, it will not be allowed as a matter of English domestic law to reopen the issue before the English courts. Where the Commission has issued a negative clearance, litigation by a third party in the English courts is not technically precluded, but the practical reality is that a court is very unlikely to go behind a decision of the Commission without good grounds. Where the EC Commission has decided that there *was* a breach of the competition rules, that is effectively binding before an English court on the party found to have acted in breach.
2 See paras A3.221 to A3.227, in relation to procedural aspects. It is likely that there will be a stay of the English proceedings. Where a 'comfort letter' has been issued, the position is that it is not technically binding but the English court is likely to afford it considerable weight.
3 See paras B2.22 and B.23.
4 As in the context of restraint of trade (para A3.138), the justification offered by sports governing bodies centres around the need to ensure competitive balance between clubs, the need to encourage new entrants (whether players or clubs), the need to generate revenue for re-investment in the sport at grass roots level, the need to maintain the integrity of the pyramidical and geographic structure of the sport, the need to have a workable and deterrent system of doping control, and the need to tackle the black market in tickets.
5 See paras B2.23 and A3.221 to A3.227. The English courts can apply the block exemptions, but cannot grant individual exemption.

A3.163 However it may be (particularly in the sports context) that the question of the justifiability of, in the sense of the rationale for, a particular rule or decision or agreement arises at the anterior stage of deciding whether Art 81 is engaged at all. This the English court *can* consider. The rationale behind a rule, decision or agreement may be relevant at this stage on the basis (sometimes called the 'rule of reason' or the 'ancillary restraint doctrine') that a restrictive provision should be regarded as falling outside Art 81 if it is a necessary building block in the achievement of a pro-competitive structure overall[1]. In practical terms this involves the English court considering substantially the same questions of legitimate objective, necessity and proportionality as it would consider in the context of restraint of trade. Some doubt has recently been thrown on the applicability of this principle[2]. If it is not open to sports governing bodies to make such an argument, then claimants are in a much stronger position, at least where the sports governing body has failed to notify. It is nevertheless clear that in the sports context the competition rules do not apply to rules that do not relate to the commercial exploitation of sport, but to the way that the sport itself is played and organised. Purely sporting rules are not caught. The difficulty in a particular context may however be whether the rule is properly so described[3].

1 See paras B2.62 to B2.75. See also *Hendry v WPBSA*, Lloyd J 5 October 2001 [2002] 1 ISLR SLR-1; para A3.170.
2 See paras B2.62 to B2.75.
3 See paras B2.56 to B2.61. The English courts can and will consider whether the impugned rule or decision falls outside Art 81 (and the Chapter I prohibition) in the first place on the basis that it relates not to the commercial exploitation of sport but rather to how the sport is played. The issue has not yet arisen. In *Hendry* (at n 1) the rules did not relate to how the sport is played. Although Lightman J did not need to take this point when striking out the competition law claim in *Wilander v Tobin* [1997] 1 Lloyd's Rep 195, he did follow the approach in relation to the analogous free movement rules: see *Edwards v British Athletics Federation and the International Amateur Athletics Federation* [1998] 2 CMLR 363, [1997] Eu LR 721. Cf *AEK Athens and Slavia Prague v UEFA* CAS arbitration 98/200 interim decision 17 July 1998, final decision 20 August 1999, reported in *Digest of CAS Awards II 1998–2000*, p 36, and in [2001] 1 ISLR 122 (Club failed in its challenge to the application to it of UEFA's Champions League rule prohibiting participation of clubs in common ownership with another participant). See also Broome [2000] 8(2) SATLJ 83 (domestic common ownership) and [2001] 9(1) SATLJ 88 (international common ownership). The European Commission announced on 27 June 2002 that it was not pursuing a complaint into UEFA's common ownership rule, because it was a sporting rule. See Commission press release IP/02/942 dated 27 June 2002. In August 2002, it rejected an attack on FINA's anti-doping rules on the same grounds. See Commission press release IP/02/942 dated 9 August 2002.

(b) Article 82/the Chapter II prohibition

A3.164 The English courts have the power to decide whether a sports governing body is in breach of Art 82 (ex 86) of the EC Treaty. Article 82 prohibits the abuse of a dominant position affecting trade between member states[1]. The English courts also have jurisdiction to decide whether there is a breach of the equivalent domestic prohibition under the Competition Act 1998 ('the Chapter II prohibition')[2].

1 See paras B2.29 to B2.33.
2 See para B2.30.

A3.165 Whether a sports governing body holds a dominant position depends on the definition of the relevant market in the particular context[1]. Where the governing body is acting to regulate the particular sport, and is controlling access to it for players and clubs, it is likely to be held to be in a dominant position, as it has a de facto monopoly on the market for access to competition in the particular sport. If on the other hand the governing body is for example granting a corporate hospitality contract, it is unlikely to have a dominant position on the market for access to tickets to sports events to re-sell in corporate hospitality packages, because corporate hospitality companies can use a variety of sports (or indeed other events) to carry on their business. Matters are more uncertain where the governing body is operating on the market for the sale of broadcasting rights, or the sale of tickets to the public for a particular event that it has organised. In this instance, it is not clear that the market can be confined to the individual sport, because the television company, or the spectator could equally choose to broadcast or to attend another sport. It is possible that, with the exception of 'must have' sports such as football, the broadcasting rights market is wider than the individual sport. In the case of the market for tickets on the other hand, it is likely that most spectators would not regard other sports as substitutable for their favourite sport, and so the governing body is more likely to be in a dominant position[2]. Where a governing body is in a dominant position it must take care to ensure that it does not abuse that position by acting on the market in such a way as to restrict competition without justification[3]. In this context, the English courts are permitted to assess whether there has been an abuse, and this involves it assessing whether the conduct impugned is justified[4].

1 See paras B2.76 to B2.88.
2 See paras B2.212 to B2.235.
3 See para B2.33.
4 See para B2.33. The 'sporting exception' described above (at para A3.163) in favour of rules and decisions which relate to the way the sport is played as opposed to its commercial exploitation will also operate in this context.

(c) *When the issue is likely to arise*

A3.166 There is a wide range of factual circumstances when a competition law argument may arise, described in detail in Chapter B2[1]. Indeed, in many contexts, the most important controlling factor on a sports governing body's activities is the competition rules. This is particularly the case:

(i) where a sports governing body enters into commercial arrangements to exploit economically the rights in the sport, and some providers are chosen as commercial partners in preference to others[2];
(ii) where a sports governing body promulgates and enforces rules aimed at preserving its predominant position as the regulator of the sport and principal organiser of tournaments, competitions and events[3];
(iii) where a sports governing body promulgates and enforces rules which set restrictions on the way that participants organise themselves and take part in the sport[4].

Attempts have been made to persuade the English courts to extend the competition rules to less obvious contexts, such as the application to a club of entry or qualification criteria in order to secure promotion[5], and the validity of the anti-doping rules[6]. The reader is referred to Chapter B2 for a comprehensive review of the issues in this context.

1 See Chapter B2.
2 See for example in the English courts, para A3.168; *Hospitality Group v Football Association* Scott V-C 24 January 1996 (Hospitality Group sought to injunct the FA from selecting only one corporate hospitality provider for Euro 96, without a tender process). See also *Rugby World Cup 1999*, where a number of complaints were made, none successful, about the commercial programme on the basis that some providers were unfairly excluded from the opportunity to link their products to the event. The grant of broadcasting rights has in particular been an area of commercial exploitation where the competition rules have been brought into play. The decision in *Re an Agreement between the FA Premier League* [2000] EMLR 78, [1999] UKCLR 258 (Restrictive Practices Court July 1999) related to the legitimacy of the Premier League's sale of television rights to BSkyB, albeit under predecessor legislation. The European Commission has taken a long look at the same area in various cases, culminating in its June 2002 decision on the broadcasting arrangements for the UEFA Champions League, Commission press release IP/02/806,

dated 3 June 2002. See para B2.278. In relation to the distribution and sale of tickets for major sports events, including the sale of tickets packaged with other products, the key cases are *Italia 90* [1992] OJ L 326, p 31, and *France 98* [2000] OJ L 5/55. See paras B2.212 to B2.235. In relation to sponsorship, in the *Danish Tennis Federation* case [1996] OJ C 138, p 6 9 May 1996, 1998 EC Competition Policy Newsletter No 2, p 54, the Commission held that a governing body could not grant 'official' status to particular sports equipment if that artificially suggested that one brand was better than another. See paras B2.191 to B2.211.

3 See for example in the English courts, para A3.168, *Williams and Cardiff RFC v Pugh*, later known as *Williams and Cardiff RFC v WRU (IRB intervening)*, interim injunction hearings (23 July 1997, unreported) (Popplewell J), (1 August 1997, unreported), CA; application for a stay hearings (17 March 1998, unreported) (Buckley J), [1999] Eu LR 195; *Wilson v British Darts Organisation*, 95/NJ/1687 (QBD) (see para A3.20, n 1); *Hendry v WPBSA*, Lloyd J 5 October 2001 [2002] 1 ISLR SLR-1; *Greig v Insole (for the TCCB)* [1978] 1 WLR 302. In 1998, English First Division Rugby clubs (EFDR) filed a complaint with the Commission against their domestic union, the Rugby Football Union (the 'RFU'), and the international governing body of the sport, the International Rugby Board (IRB). *EFDR Complaint to the European Commission against the Rugby Football Union and the International Rugby Board* Case No IV/36.994 (March 1998). The RFU implements the rules and regulations of the IRB in England. The clubs complained that RFU and IRB rules and regulations prevented them from organising cross-border competitions themselves and exploiting the commercial rights to those competitions without interference from above. The IRB argued in response that the clubs were complaining not about competition but about control. It asserted that it was in the long-term interests of the sport as a whole for the governing bodies to control the commercial facets of rugby, so as to enforce the collective approach that is vital to the long-term good of the game. The complaint was eventually withdrawn by the clubs without the Commission commencing any formal investigation into the matter. Also in 1998, Media Partners, a commercial enterprise seeking to persuade leading European football clubs to break away from the current regulatory regime for football to form a 'Super-League', complained to the Commission that its initiative was being blocked by strong-arm tactics by UEFA (the regional governing body for football in Europe), threatening sanctions against members who did not rebuff Media Partners' approach. UEFA rejected the complaint as factually and legally flawed, and the Commission shows no signs of making any decision. For an indication of the Commission's approach when it does decide to act, see *FIA Formula One Championship* [2001] OJ C 169, p 5. Sports governing bodies regularly rely on the proposition that in order to make an association work the members of the association can legitimately be prevented from belonging to other competing associations (citing *Gøttrup Klim* [1994] ECR I-5641, there an agricultural co-operative), but the Commission is astute to prevent rules and practices which might prevent rival competitions growing up. See generally paras B2.116 to B2.141.

4 Such as the imposition of transfer rules. Although the invalidation of the then transfer rules in the *Bosman* case turned in the European Court of Justice on the application of the free movement rules (see paras A3.171 to A3.175, Chapters B3 and E2), the Advocate General stated that the same result would be achieved under the competition rules. In Case C–264/98 *Tibor Balog v Royal Charleroi Sporting Club*, the Advocate General reached a similar conclusion (Opinion 29 March 2001), only for her Opinion to be withdrawn when the case was immediately settled by the football governing bodies. See para B2.159. The Commission's competition rules have recently brought about a change in the FIFA policy requiring players agents to lodge a substantial bond in order to practise: now it is sufficient if satisfactory insurance is obtained (for the initiation of proceedings, Commission press release, IP/99/782; for the resolution, Commission press release, IP/02/585, 18 April 2002). Cf in contrast *Excelsior Mouscron v UEFA* (Belgian club Mouscron wanted to play its UEFA Cup home game against FC Metz over the border in a larger stadium in Lille. UEFA maintained that home games had to be played in the relevant home country. The European Commission rejected the complaint on the basis that sporting organisation along national lines fell outside the competition rules. See Ratliff [1998] 6(3) SATLJ 4. Cf Wimbledon's and Clydebank's failed attempts to move to Dublin. The CAS in *AEK Athens v UEFA* CAS 98/200 upheld the UEFA rule that no club in common ownership could compete in the same competition and rejected the competition arguments made by ENIC which owned two clubs: interim decision 17 July 1998, final decision 20 August 1999, reported in *Digest of CAS Awards II 1998–2000* (2002, Kluwer), p 36, and in [2001] 1 ISLR 122. The Commission has rejected ENIC's complaint about the common ownership rule which the Commission entertained despite the CAS decision: see Commission press release IP/02/942, dated 27 June 2002. See generally paras B2.145 to B2.151.

5 See for example in the English courts para A3.168, *Stevenage Borough Football Club v Football League Ltd* (1996) Times, 1 August; affd 9 Admin LR 109, CA, where Art 81 was argued but the court took the view that it was fanciful to suppose that trade between member states was affected because Stevenage, which was seeking access to the lowest division of the League, might qualify for European football. This was before the Competition Act Chapter I prohibition came into force.

6 See for example in the English courts para A3.168; *Wilander v Tobin* [1997] 1 Lloyd's Law Rep 195; revsd [1997] 2 Lloyd's Law Rep 296, CA. For the European Commission's position, see Commission press release IP/02/1211, dated 9 August 2002.

(d) State aid

A3.167 It is possible that unlawful state aid may be granted in the sports sector[1]. Where state aid in the form of financial assistance confers an economic advantage directly or indirectly through state resources on selected recipients only, in a context where it distorts or threatens to distort competition in the market properly defined and the advantage has a potential or actual effect on trade between member states, that aid must be notified (so long as it is new aid or an alteration to existing aid). If it is not notified then it cannot be implemented and the English courts will order its repayment by the recipient. If it is notified, it can be cleared on a number of grounds, but only by the Commission. Although the situations where the issue has arisen in the sports context are so far few and narrow[2], it is possible that the issue could arise in other situations, in particular where there is tax-advantageous treatment of or other assistance to sports clubs or governing bodies, lottery funding or the purchase of sports rights by publicly funded broadcasters such as the BBC. It is also possible (although probably unlikely) that grants from certain sports governing bodies themselves could be regarded as state aid. It would be a substantial development if the actions of sports governing bodies could be challenged on state aid grounds.

1 See paras B2.34, B2.35 and B2.326 to B2.333.
2 *Salomon SA v EC Commission* [1999] ECR II-2925; [1997] OJ L 025, p 26, 28 January 1997 (no unlawful aid on the facts where a sports equipment manufacturer in financial difficulties was assisted); *Public grants to professional clubs*, Aid N118/00 – France, [2001] OJ C 333, pp 6, 28 November 2001, decision of 25 April 2001, IP/01/599 (assistance to professional clubs for training alone not an unlawful state aid); *Ladbroke Racing v EC Commission* [1998] ECR II-1, on appeal *France v EC Commission* [2000] ECR I-3271; *Tiercé Ladbroke v EC Commission* [1997] ECR II-923 (arrangements in respect of betting in France). See 'The financing of professional football and EC competition law: is the Zidane deal in an off-side position?' [2001] 3 SATLJ 159.

B Application of the competition rules by the English courts in the context of sport

A3.168 With two exceptions[1], consideration by the English courts of competition law principles in the sports context has occurred at an interim stage and has consequently been cursory or of peripheral relevance. In *Hospitality Group v Football Association*[2], the Hospitality Group sought to injunct the FA from selecting only one corporate hospitality provider for Euro 96 without a tender process. The Hospitality Group argued that the FA was in a dominant position on the market for the provision of tickets to Euro 96 for inclusion in corporate hospitality packages, and had abused that position by excluding all the competitors of the chosen partner from the market. Scott V-C recognised the force in the argument, but so too had the FA: by altering the arrangements when the action was commenced and notifying the new arrangements immediately to the Commission, the FA gave Scott V-C little choice but to stay the English action in order to avoid the risk of inconsistent decisions in England and in Brussels[3]. In *Stevenage Borough Football Club v Football League*[4], the club advanced a competition law argument in addition to its restraint of trade argument. Because the action pre-dated the Competition Act 1998, that argument had to be based on the EC rules. Carnwath J dealt with it in short order, stating that it was not established that there could be any effect on trade between member states. In *Wilander v Tobin*[5], Lightman J and the Court of Appeal had decided that the claimant tennis player did not have an arguable case that the ITF's anti-doping rules were in unreasonable restraint of trade and had refused to grant an interlocutory injunction. The plaintiffs then sought to amend to plead that the rules were contrary to the EC free movement and competition rules. Lightman J allowed the amendments in relation to free movement but refused permission to amend to add the case under the competition rules, ostensibly because the case was inadequately particularised, but also because he was not convinced that there was any basis for contending that the anti-doping rules restricted competition. The Court of Appeal did not allow either amendment. In *Williams and Cardiff RFC v WRU*[6], the club challenged a wide range of actions including a requirement that a club that wished to play in the WRU's competitions was obliged to agree to do so for ten years; the requirement in the IRB and WRU rules that a club should not sell the broadcasting rights to its matches absent governing body consent; the IRB and WRU rules requiring release of players by clubs for international matches; and the WRU rule requiring a minimum number of players at a club to be eligible for Wales. When the action commenced and was first heard by Popplewell J, the challenge was focused on the requirement that the clubs should commit to playing in the WRU's leagues and tournaments for ten years. Popplewell J held that it was arguable that this requirement was contrary to the competition rules, granted an injunction limited to the current season prohibiting the WRU from expelling the club for failing to enter into the ten year commitment, and ordered a speedy trial. The pleadings were subsequently amended to add the other challenges. Before these matters could be determined, the action was stayed to avoid the risk of inconsistent decisions because the IRB and the WRU intended to notify the rules in question to the Commission. In *Mohammed v FA and FIFA*, a claim that the introduction of the player-agent licensing system was an interference with existing contractual relations and in breach of the competition rules survived an application for summary judgment by the governing bodies[7].

1 The two exceptions are *Re an Agreement between the FA Premier League* [2000] EMLR 78, [1999] UKCLR 258 (Restrictive Practices Court July 1999) (the then Restrictive Practice Court's consideration of the legality of the English Football FA Premier League's broadcasting arrangements with BSkyB and the BBC under the UK's predecessor competition legislation); and *Hendry v WPBSA*, Lloyd J 5 October 2001 [2002] 1 ISLR 'SLR-1'; both discussed below and in Chapter B2. A case of peripheral relevance is *World Wide Fund for Nature v World Wrestling Federation Entertainment Inc* (1 October 2001, unreported) (Jacob J); affd [2002] EWCA Civ 196, [2002] NLJR 363 (the World Wide Fund for Nature sought to restrain the World Wrestling Federation from using the initials WWF more than it was allowed to do under the terms of an agreement between the two of them. The defence was that the agreement was in restraint of trade and contrary to the competition rules. Jacob J gave summary judgment for the Fund, and was upheld on appeal).

2 (24 January 1996, unreported) (Scott V-C).

3 For the availability of a stay, see paras A3.221 to A3.226. In *Hospitality Group v Football Association* the stay effectively ended the issue in the light of the proximity of the event. The Commission did not reach any formal decision on the notification, but it appears that the Commission was satisfied that the relevant market could not be confined to tickets to the single event, or even to football events. Corporate hospitality providers could use a variety of other events as the vehicle for their add-on packages. A similar conclusion was reached by the Australian Courts in *Hospitality Group v Australian Rugby Union* [1999] FCA 1136 (interlocutory); [2000] FCA 823 (first instance); [2001] FCA 1040 (on appeal) and by the OFT in relation to *Wimbledon* (OFT press release no 20/93, 23 March 1993). See paras B2.219 and B2.220.

4 (1996) Times, 1 August. See also *Wimbledon v Football League*, where the governing body refused the club's application to establish a home ground in Milton Keynes. A competition law argument was available and was pleaded, but was reserved at the hearing before the Football Association Arbitration Panel.

5 In relation to restraint of trade: (19 March 1996, unreported) (Lightman J), (8 April 1996, unreported), CA. In relation to the competition rules: [1997] 1 Lloyd's Law Rep 195; revsd [1997] 2 Lloyd's Law Rep 296, CA.

6 *Williams and Cardiff RFC v Pugh* (23 July 1997, unreported) (Popplewell J), (1 August 1997, unreported), CA; subsequently known as *Williams and Cardiff RFC v WRU (IRB intervening)* (17 March 1998, unreported) (Buckley J), [1999] Eu LR 195. This was another action stayed. As in the *Hospitality Group* case, the approach was extremely effective to block disruptive English proceedings taking an EC competition law point. In the event matters moved on faster than the Commission's procedures, and the WRU and its clubs re-ordered their arrangements, a process which is still continuing as of the time of writing.

7 *Mohammed v Football Association and FIFA* (21 February 2002, unreported) (Field J).

A3.169 In *Re an Agreement between the FA Premier League*[1], the then Restrictive Practices Court considered at great length the legality of the Premier League's broadcasting arrangements with BSkyB and the BBC under the UK's predecessor competition legislation, the Restrictive Trade Practices Act 1976. Although that Act was notoriously difficult to apply and its mechanistic test was very different from the current competition rules, the issues before the Restrictive Practices Court extended to basic competition law concepts including whether the arrangements restricted competition and whether they were justified in the public interest. The court's conclusions in that context consequently retain great relevance. The case is dealt with in more detail elsewhere[2]. In summary for these purposes, the court held that the Premier League's rule that its permission was required for any broadcast (which allowed collective selling) and the exclusivity granted to the broadcasters each restricted competition between broadcasters on the market for football broadcasting rights, but that those restrictions were justified in the public interest. The court did however rule illegal the incumbent broadcaster's right to match the best offer received from elsewhere in the context of negotiation of the next contract.

1 *Re an Agreement between the FA Premier League* [2000] EMLR 78, [1999] UKCLR 258 (Restrictive Practices Court July 1999).

2 See paras B2.236 to B2.305.

A3.170 In *Hendry v World Professional Billiards and Snooker Association Ltd*[1], Lloyd J for the first time in a trial before an English court applied the current competition rules to the rules and practices of a sports governing body, finding one rule illegal. Although the EC rules and the common law doctrine of restraint of trade were also in issue, Lloyd J concentrated on the Chapter I prohibition and the Chapter II prohibition under the Competition Act 1998. He appears to have approached both prohibitions on the basis that he could take into account the justification offered for any restrictions in the rules or practices of the sports governing body[2]. He carried out a detailed assessment of what the relevant market was, and decided that it was the market for the supply of services between snooker players and the organisers of snooker tournaments[3]. The WPBSA was such an organiser, although it was also a governing body; it was irrelevant that the money made by the WPBSA was re-invested in the sport. The WPBSA was dominant on the market: even though others could come in to rival it, they could not do so in the short or even medium term[4]. The WPBSA had abused that dominant position by the adoption of Rule A5, which required the players (all of whom were members of the WPBSA) to obtain its permission to play in snooker matches, with some specific exceptions. The rule effectively allowed the WPBSA to restrict the ability of any rival organisation to gain a foot-hold and it could not be justified on the basis that it was necessary in order to support the broadcasting and sponsorship revenue of the

WPBSA for reinvestment in the sport, or to ensure that events were properly organised[5]. The rule was also held contrary to the Chapter I prohibition, to Arts 81 and 82, and to the common law doctrine of restraint of trade. Other rules and practices were held valid[6].

1 Lloyd J 5 October 2001 [2002] 1 ISLR SLR-1. There was also an unreported Court of Appeal judgment dated 11 July 2001 upholding the judge's decision during the course of the trial to exclude the calling of new evidence.
2 See para 27 of the judgment of Lloyd J.
3 See para 89.
4 See paras 98.
5 See para 110.
6 Rule P limiting the number of logos that could be worn by a player and requiring the WPBSA's approval was restrictive of competition but was justified because of broadcasting restrictions: para 128. Rule S requiring players to assist in the promotion of tournaments was not restrictive of competition and was not a restraint of trade: para 138. The criticism advanced of the WPBSA's ranking system, namely that it did not take into account results in competitions organised by other promoters (and thereby made it harder for them to compete) was held not to be established on the facts: para 141. The WPBSA's imposition of a deadline for the submission of entry forms for its competitions was also criticised as making it harder for rival organisers to compete. Lloyd J held that the imposition of the deadline was reasonable and justified and was not an abuse: para 154.

8 THE EC FREE MOVEMENT RULES

A3.171 The EC free movement rules are also of importance for the legal control of the actions of sports governing bodies. Again the substantive principles are discussed in a later chapter[1]. There have been a number of cases in the European Court of Justice in relation to the application of the rules in the sports sector, most notably the *Bosman* case itself. Again this section simply draws attention to the availability of the rules as a basis for challenge, briefly sets out the rules and how they can be applied in the English courts and touches on the limited occasions that they have actually been applied by the English courts.

1 See Chapter B3.

A The free movement rules in brief, and how the English court can apply them

A3.172 The EC free movement rules contained in Arts 39 (ex 48), 43 (ex 52 and 49 (ex 59) prohibit restrictions on the ability of workers to move from one member state to another, on the ability of persons to establish a business in another member state, and on the ability of persons from one member state to provide services in another. The EC free movement rules apply in the context of sport, but only to the extent that a commercial activity is affected[1]. Nominally the rules are addressed to member states, but they extend to public authorities and sports governing bodies have been held to be included[2]. Most sporting bodies are sufficiently public for these purposes to be governed by the rules, although it is possible that many may not be. The dividing line may be whether the sport actually involves any commercial activity at all. If it is such a marginal interest sport that there is no real economic activity associated with it, it may not be regarded as caught by the rules.

1 See paras B3.10 to B3.23. The European Court of Justice decisions in the context of sport are *Walrave and Koch v Association Union Cycliste Internationale* [1974] ECR 1405 (Governing body held subject to the free movement rules, but its provision limiting the composition of national

teams, there support riders, to citizens of the nation in question was not a restriction on free movement because it was a purely sporting rule and not a rule in relation to the commercial exploitation of the sport); *Donà v Mantero* [1976] ECR 1333 at 1340 (rule confining places in national football team to nationals held not caught by free movement rules); *Union Royal Belge des Sociétés de Football Association v Bosman* [1995] ECR I-4921, paras 69 to 87 (Free movement rules held to apply to the transfer systems imposed by national football associations. The system was not protected by the sporting exception and was disproportionate and unjustified); *Deliège v Ligue Francophone de Judo* [2000] ECR I-2549 (Governing body subject to free movement rules but selection criteria for national representation not a restriction on free movement as within the sporting exception); and *Lehtonen v Fédération Royale Belge des Sociétés de Basketball* [2000] ECR I–2681 (Governing body subject to the free movement rules and transfer windows outside the sporting exception, but held capable of justification). See also the French decision *Lilia Malaja v Fédération Française de Basketball* Case No VC 99 NC 00282, Administrative Court of Appeal, Nancy (national from third country which has an association agreement with the EU and who is legally working in the EU/EEA must be treated in the same way as if they were an EU/EEA national). See also the CAS decisions *AEK Athens v UEFA* CAS 98/200 interim decision 17 July 1998, final decision 20 August 1999, reported in *Digest of CAS Awards II 1998–2000* (2002, Kluwer), p 38 and in [2001] 1 ISLR 122 (UEFA rule against common ownership of teams in the same competition not necessarily within the sporting exception, but in any event capable of justification); and *Celtic v UEFA* CAS 98/201, *Digest of CAS Awards II 1998–2000* (2002, Kluwer), p 106 (the *Bosman* ruling applies where the transfer is to a club (Monaco FC) outside the EU but playing in an EU member state league (the French). Monaco rightly maintained that it did not have to pay Celtic a transfer fee for an out of contract player registered at Celtic to move to Monaco). The Gibraltar Football Association also relies amongst other things on the free movement rules in its challenge before the CAS to UEFA's failure to consider its application for membership when it was made or by reference to the rules in force when it was made, in which circumstances the application would have been successful. Instead, UEFA delayed and changed the admission rules in such a way as to preclude the GFA's application succeeding, the case is pending before CAS.

2 See paras A3.70 to A3.71.

A3.173 The free movement rules can be relied upon before the English courts. Indeed the lack of any procedural regulation equivalent to that which applies to the competition rules means that the European Commission is less able itself to tackle breaches of the free movement rules by individual governing bodies, still less by international associations[1]. It would have to bring proceedings against the relevant member state.

1 It is for this reason that the Commission's investigation of the football transfer rules was under the competition rules. See Chapters B2, B3 and E2.

A3.174 As in the context of the competition rules, a restriction on the free movement of players, whether as employees or in order to provide services, may be justified and therefore permissible if it pursues a legitimate aim[1] and is proportionate in the sense that it goes no further than is necessary to achieve that aim[2]. Again therefore, the exercise is similar to that carried out under the restraint of trade doctrine and under the competition rules. Indeed the Advocate General in *Bosman*[3] expressed the view that the entire analysis could equally well be put on the basis of the competition rules as the free movement rules, and Lord Woolf MR suggested in *Wilander*[4] that the proportionality test under the free movement rules was equivalent to the reasonableness test under the domestic doctrine of restraint of trade and the implied quasi public obligations owed by sports governing bodies.

1 The legitimate aims available are arguably more limited than in the context of the competition rules. The party seeking to justify its actions must bring its motivation within the specific aims listed in the relevant Treaty Articles in respect of each freedom. It is however clear from the *Bosman* case that the justifications which would generally be advanced by sports governing bodies can be raised in the context of the free movement rules, albeit in that case they were insufficient to sustain the previous transfer system. Accordingly the grounds of justification set out at para A3.162, n 4 are likely to be relied upon. See further paras B3.48 to B3.59.

2 See paras A3.110 and A3.138 for the proportionality test in the contexts of public law and restraint of trade respectively.
3 At para 262 et seq. Although this point was not developed by the court in *Bosman*, the Commission's subsequent investigation into the transfer rules was based on the competition rules, as opposed to the free movement rules, as set out above. Furthermore, the issue arose subsequently in case C–264/98 *Tibor Balog v Royal Charleroi*. In that case a Hungarian player challenged on competition law grounds the validity of the post-*Bosman* rules which required the payment of a transfer fee for a non-EU/EEA national who was out of contract. The Advocate General's opinion (29 March 2001) was released and then withdrawn the same day when the action was settled. She had held that the then transfer system was contrary to the competition rules to the extent that it allowed a club in the EU/EEA to insist on a transfer fee to sell a non-EU out of contract player whether it be to a club in the EU or EEA or in a third country.
4 At [1997] 2 Lloyd's Rep 296 at 301, col 1; para A3.150.

B Application of the free movement rules by the English courts in the context of sport

A3.175 As with the competition rules, the English courts' consideration of the free movement rules in the sports context has been largely at the interim stage of proceedings and therefore at best relatively cursory. In *Williams and Cardiff v WRU*[1], the club included in its pleadings a challenge on free movement grounds to the WRU rule requiring a minimum number of players at a club to be eligible for Wales. The issue was never resolved because the proceedings as a whole were stayed for fear that there would be inconsistent decisions on the competition law aspects, and the judgments do not address the issue of free movement. In *Wilander v Tobin*[2], an amendment to add an argument that the ITF's anti-doping rules were contrary to the free movement rules was allowed by Lightman J, only to be disallowed by the Court of Appeal. Lord Woolf MR took the view that the test of proportionality under the free movement rules was sufficiently similar to 'reasonableness or natural justice', on the basis of which the player had previously advanced an unsuccessful case, to allow the court to conclude that the new amendment was also unarguable[3]. He was not however prepared to hold that the anti-doping rules were necessarily within the sporting exception, although he saw 'considerable force' in the submission[4]. In *Edwards v BAF and IAAF*[5], the athlete complained that he had been unfairly discriminated against on grounds of nationality and had been unlawfully prevented from exercising his free movement rights, since the BAF enforced the IAAF's requirement of a mandatory four year ban for a first doping offence, but other national associations were allowed not to do so by the IAAF if their local laws regarded such a ban as illegal. Lightman J held that the BAF and IAAF anti-doping rules fell within the sporting exception, as rules that related to how the sport was played and not to its commercial exploitation. Lightman J went on to hold that the anti-doping provisions were in any event proportionate and necessary to stop cheating. He also held that there was no discrimination on grounds of nationality: the rule was that the ban should be four years, but that if the law of a particular state made this unlawful, the last two years would be remitted. Lightman J held that the vice arose in the difference in national laws, not in any discrimination by the sports governing bodies. In *Bacardi v Newcastle*[6], the English courts were prepared to grant an Art 234 reference in relation to whether the French 'Loi Evin', by restricting the provision of cross-border broadcasting services by restricting French broadcasters from showing coverage on French television of sports events played outside France in venues with alcohol advertising in them, was contrary to the free movement rules.

1 *Williams and Cardiff RFC v Pugh* (23 July 1997, unreported) (Popplewell J), (1 August 1997, unreported), CA; subsequently known as *Williams and Cardiff RFC v WRU (IRB intervening)* (17 March 1998, unreported) (Buckley J), [1999] Eu LR 195.
2 *Wilander and Novacek v Tobin and Jude*, in relation to restraint of trade (19 March 1996, unreported) (Lightman J), (8 April 1996, unreported), CA; in relation to the competition and free movement rules [1997] 1 Lloyd's Rep 195; revsd [1997] 2 Lloyd's Rep 296, CA.
3 [1997] 2 Lloyd's Rep 296 at 301 col 1 per Lord Woolf MR where he said that the concept of proportionality for the purposes of the free movement and competition rules was not identical with reasonableness or natural justice but it was certainly close to these concepts. The court proceeded on the basis that the ITF was bound by the free movement rules.
4 [1997] 2 Lloyd's Rep 296 at 300, col 2.
5 *Edwards v British Athletics Federation and the International Amateur Athletics Federation* [1998] 2 CMLR 363, [1997] Eu LR 721. Again, the court proceeded on the basis that the BAF and the IAAF were bound by the free movement rules (although those rules did not apply in Lightman J's view to the doping system).
6 *Bacardi-Martini SAS and Cellier des Dauphins v Newcastle United Football Club* [2001] Eu LR 45 (Gray J 26 July 2000). Newcastle had removed Bacardi's advertising for a game against a French side, because the French broadcasters took the position that they could not broadcast matches into France if there was alcohol advertising visible at the venue. Bacardi alleged that in so doing, Newcastle had induced the marketing company, with which Bacardi had a contract for the advertising, to breach that contract. The validity of the Loi Evin was regarded as critical to the outcome of the proceedings, even if not necessarily determinative. The reference was made before trial. Much of the reason for the court's approach appears to have been that it was not felt appropriate that an English court should consider the validity of a French law when the European Court of Justice was available to do this instead.

9 REMEDIES

A3.176 The preceding sections of this chapter describe the causes of action most commonly used to challenge the actions of sports governing bodies before the courts. This section addresses the procedural means by which the courts enforce the obligations of sports governing bodies, or give remedies to challengers for the infringement of those obligations. The discussion is limited to the remedies available in the courts and does not address remedies that may be available under any internal processes of the sports governing body or as a consequence of a referral to any external arbitral body[1]. The possibility of such remedies through internal mechanisms or effective arbitration agreements may however be relevant to the point at which an application to the court can be made and the issues that the court may be asked, or will be willing, to consider. While it is too absolute a statement to say that the courts will not intervene if an internal dispute resolution process is in place that has not been exhausted, intervention in such circumstances will require the claimant to show a real risk of prejudice if he is confined to his domestic remedies or that pursuing those remedies would be futile[2]. Where there is an arbitration agreement, if the defendant sports governing body insists that that process be followed it will almost always succeed in obtaining a stay of any litigation[3].

1 See further Chapters A2 and A5.
2 See paras A3.219 and A3.220; *Enderby Town Football Club v Football Association* [1971] Ch 591, where Lord Denning MR suggested (at 605) that a party could bring an action either before or after disciplinary proceedings, and would not be disadvantaged either way; *Modahl v BAF* (28 July 1997, unreported), CA per Morritt LJ at 39A–C; *Stevenage Borough Football Club v Football League Ltd* (1997) 9 Admin LR 109 at 119C, CA; *Collins v Lane* (22 June 1999, unreported), CA at p 12 of the shorthand-writers' transcript. That said, a claimant must take care not to waive any objections that he might have to, for example, the procedural fairness of the internal process. See *Modahl v BAF* (28 July 1997, unreported), CA per Lord Woolf MR at 28A–G (if all that a party relies upon is matters known before the internal hearing and they are not raised then, there may be a

waiver of ability to raise the point subsequently). See also *AEK v NBA and FIB* (7 August 2001, unreported) (R Field QC), leave to appeal set aside (2002) Times 13 June, CA; and *Smith v International Triathlon Union* (1999) 20 BCTC 71 ('… there are many reasons for waiting to review any legal issues arising from the decision of the appeals board rather than anticipating them and answering them pre-emptively'). See further n 4 to para A3.51.

3 See para A3.220.

A3.177 The same private law remedies are available on the causes of action referred to above in the context of challenges to the actions of sports governing bodies as in any other context, and the discussion in this section is limited to the particular issues that arise in the sports context where what is challenged is the exercise of a regulatory function by the sports governing body. The discussion does not deal with the remedies available in the normal course in respect of the commercial, non-regulatory activities of sports governing bodies, where the normal principles apply. The remedies available are the private law remedies because, as described above, the courts at present refuse to treat the actions of sports governing bodies as susceptible to public law challenge by way of judicial review[1]. Those that criticise this approach suggest that one of its consequences is the unnecessary limitation of the remedies available. In judicial review proceedings challenging the actions of public bodies, claimants may seek orders quashing decisions and orders prohibiting or requiring specific action. While there may be some nominal differences in terminology, it is to be doubted that any practical difference arises in the courts' ability to enforce the relevant obligations.

1 See paras A3.62 to A3.65.

A3.178 The available private law remedies include in particular the grant of an injunction[1], either in mandatory form (requiring a positive action to be taken) or in prohibitory form (stopping an action from being taken), the grant of a declaration as to the parties' rights and obligations[2], and the award of damages[3]. Where appropriate there may be orders for specific performance or restitution, as in other contexts, and the remedies available under the Human Rights Act 1998[4] are adapted to that particular context. In particular instances of regulatory action, other specialised remedies may of course be available. For example, sports governing bodies that are companies may be the subject of the forms of relief available under the Companies Acts[5]. In respect of non-regulatory actions, still other remedies may on particular occasions be appropriate. For example, a sports governing body is as susceptible as any other occupier of land to an order for possession. Furthermore, as in other contexts, some relief may be available at an interim stage pending a final resolution of the dispute[6].

1 See paras A3.182 to A3.192.
2 See paras A3.193 to A3.198.
3 See paras A3.199 to A3.206.
4 See para A3.207.
5 See para A3.208 and Chapter C1.
6 See paras A3.182 et seq and A3.193 et seq.

A The concerns of those challenging the actions of sports governing bodies

A3.179 While challenges to the actions of sports governing bodies in the non-regulatory contexts in which those bodies on occasion operate may centre around claims for damages or some other form of financial relief, it is relatively rare for actions brought by players or clubs in respect of regulatory action to have the predominant motive of recovering damages, or other financial relief[1]. There have been some actions of this type, such as the unsuccessful action by Diane Modahl against the British Athletic Federation in which she sought compensation for loss of earnings in the period between her initial conviction by BAF on a doping charge and her subsequent acquittal, together with the wasted expenditure incurred in relation to defending her position[2]. It is also the case that in some challenges in respect of regulatory actions a claim for damages might be included for completeness or as a tactical device.

1 Plainly where a sports governing body has entered into a commercial contract, the action might well be for damages. An example would be the proceedings brought against the Welsh Rugby Union by its sponsor, Scottish Life. See 'WRU court case puts sponsorship on trial' *Marketing Week* (6 August 1998), p 19. This is much less likely where one of those governed by the body is challenging its exercise of its regulatory functions.

2 *Modahl v British Athletics Federation*, unreported, Popplewell J 28 June 1996, CA 28 July 1997, HL 22 July 1998, Douglas Brown J 14 December 2000 and [2002] 1 WLR 1192, CA 8 October 2001. Other examples of where damages were claimed are *Williams and Cardiff RFC v Pugh* (23 July 1997, unreported) (Popplewell J), (1 August 1997, unreported), CA; subsequently known as *Williams and Cardiff RFC v WRU (IRB intervening)* (17 March 1998, unreported) (Buckley J), [1999] Eu LR 195 (damages for breach of EC competition law, action stayed before the point was resolved); *Phoenix v FIA and FOM* (22 May 2002, unreported) (Morritt V-C) (Damages sought for breach of contract in excluding alleged assignee of Prost's right to participate in Formula One 2002 championship, action stayed on the basis of arbitration agreement). See also *Currie v Barton* (26 March 1987, unreported) (Scott J), (11 February 1988, unreported), CA, (1988) Times, 12 February (A tennis player, banned by his county association for three years for refusing to play in a county match was ruled ineligible to play for England by the LTA. The player unsuccessfully challenged the ban and sought damages, including exemplary damages, on the grounds of breach of contract, breach of natural justice, and an innominate tort).

A3.180 Rather, the principal concern of those challenging most actions of sports governing bodies is usually to stop or reverse regulatory action. This is best achieved by an injunction, but a declaration may be sufficient because a sports governing body is unlikely to act inconsistently with it. However the concern of claimants is not only to stop or reverse action, but to do so as quickly as possible. The expression 'justice delayed is justice denied' is particularly apt in the context of sporting competition. Indeed, even waiting for the normal amount of time to prepare for and argue a full trial may have irreversible and irremediable consequences for the challenger[1]. This could be because, first, the challenge relates to a specific event that is taking place imminently: if the individual or club is to participate, an immediate answer is required or it is too late. Secondly it could be because the individual or club is being kept out of competition until the decision is reached, for example because a suspension applies following the governing body's decision that is to be reviewed. The period during which many individuals can compete at the highest level is often limited. Any interruption in that period may have very severe consequences for them. They often need to obtain a speedy solution that will allow them to resume competition or to train or to clear their name (whether for purely private reasons or to protect public funding or commercial sponsorship). This is not confined to individuals: clubs too may be kept out of competitions and the effect may be long-lasting[2]. Consequently challengers would argue that damages would not be an adequate remedy for the loss of the ability to participate. The English law of damages, in any event, takes a narrow approach to assessing a value on non-financial loss, making damages even less attractive an alternative to resolution. Further, there may be cases based on the causes of action commonly used in the sports context where damages are actually not available in respect of the wrong alleged[3]. That said, there may equally be circumstances where the *only* remedy is damages, unless the sports governing body voluntarily reconsiders its position[4].

1 It may also be that it is the sports governing body that requires some sort of certainty in the meantime. The consequences for a sports governing body of a decision coming some time after the challenge was initiated are often much more problematic than if there had been a prompt decision. There may be a greater number of analogous cases to deal with. Further decisions may have flowed from the first, making it harder to unravel the position.

2 For example where a club is wrongly denied promotion, the absence of immediate protection would be likely to lead to the club missing out on promotion and possibly not being eligible the following season. Cf *Rotherham and English Second Division Rugby Ltd v English First Division Rugby Ltd, English Rugby Partnership Ltd and the RFU*, Ferris J 16 August 1999, [2000] 1 ISLR 33.

3 See paras A3.200 to A3.202. For example, damages are not available for unreasonable restraint of trade, and no contractual term will be implied that a sports governing body will not act in restraint of trade: see para A3.135. In these circumstances the challenger is confined to seeking other relief.

4 See para A3.192. For example, the English courts will not force an association to take a new member against its will and will not specifically enforce contracts involving mutual trust and confidence.

A3.181 Accordingly, speed is often of the essence and while a claim form and particulars of claim may seek a final injunction or declaration and damages, the real issue will often be whether the claimant can obtain interim relief in the form of either an interim injunction or possibly now an interim declaration[1].

1 Under CPR, Pt 25.1(1)(b). See paras A3.193 to A3.195.

B Injunctions

(a) *interim injunctions*

A3.182 The primary form of interim relief is the interim injunction, which either prevents a party doing something or requires him to do something in the period leading up to the final resolution of the dispute. The basis on which the court will grant an interim injunction and the procedure for applying for one are well established, and are not addressed in detail here[1]. The claimant must show that there is an arguable case on the merits (including an entitlement to the relief ultimately sought[2]) and that the balance of convenience, or 'the balance of justice'[3], lies in favour of the grant of an injunction. The court then has a discretion[4]. In considering the claimant's case, and whether it is arguable, the court will address the basis for the cause of action as discussed in the preceding sections of this chapter, and will take into account the principle that the courts should be slow to interfere in the exercise of discretion by the sports governing body in the regulatory areas entrusted to it. In considering the balance of convenience, the court will examine whether damages will or will not provide an adequate remedy for either party, as well as all other relevant circumstances. The overall aim is where possible to ensure that a claimant is not deprived of the fruits of a putative victory, whilst still ensuring that a defendant is not unfairly prevented from doing something that it might ultimately prove to be entitled to have done. The threshold may be regarded as relatively low, and is certainly lower than the threshold to be achieved at trial[5]. In specific instances, however, the court may raise the threshold. First, although the way in which the test is expressed involves little difference dependent upon whether the relief sought is prohibitory or mandatory[6], the balance of convenience may well be affected in practice if the governing body is to be required actively to do something, rather than not to do something. Certainly it is something to be taken into account, and there is an inclination to maintain the status quo. Secondly, it is also possible to argue in some instances that the court should be satisfied that the claimant's case is rather better than arguable, for example where the interim relief sought is in effect dispositive of the action[7]. This would arise where for instance[8] interim relief is sought to allow the claimant to do something in the short term, which once done cannot be undone subsequently even if there were a trial[9].

1 See the Supreme Court Act 1981, s 37; CPR, Pt 25.0 to 25.4; and *American Cyanamid v Ethicon* [1975] AC 396. The availability of injunctions generally, including on an interim basis, is dealt with in *Spry on Equitable Remedies* (5th edn, 1997, Sweet & Maxwell). The relief can even be sought before an action is begun, and in respect of a threatened event just as in respect of an event that has taken place. For an explanation of the test in the sports context, see *Williams and Cardiff RFC v Pugh* (23 July 1997, unreported) (Popplewell J) at p 6 of the shorthand writers' transcript.

2 See paras A3.189 to A3.192. A temporary injunction will not be granted in circumstances where a final injunction could not be granted even if the challenger were to succeed at trial, for example in the light of the principle that the courts will not force an association to accept a member.

3 *Tyrrell Racing Organisation v RAC Motor Sports Association and Fédération Internationale de l' Automobile* (20 July 1984, unreported) (Hirst J).

4 The Court of Appeal is generally slow to overturn the first instance judge's exercise of his discretion as to whether or not to grant interim relief.

5 If the expectation is that there will be a full trial, the test often militates in favour of the applicant and against the sports governing body, because the standard is lower. See for example *Jones v WRU* (27 February 1997, unreported) (Ebsworth J), (1997) Times, 6 March, (17 November 1997, unreported) (Potts J), (19 December 1997, unreported), CA, (1998) Times, 6 January, where the implementation of a four week ban for stamping was suspended pending trial when an action was brought alleging that the disciplinary process suffered from procedural defects. If in the event there is no trial, the issue may effectively have been determined on the basis only that the claimant's case was arguable.

6 *Zockoll v Mercury* [1998] FSR 354, CA. It is wise if possible to couch the relief sought in negative terms if possible. Cf *Jones v WRU* (27 February 1997, unreported) (Ebsworth J), (1997) Times, 6 March, (17 November 1997, unreported) (Potts J), (19 December 1997, unreported), CA, (1998) Times, 6 January for a case where the distinction between whether the relief was mandatory or prohibitory was blurred.

7 *Tyrrell Racing Organisation v RAC Motor Sports Association and Fédération Internationale de l' Automobile* (20 July 1984, unreported) (Hirst J). The hearing of the application for an interim injunction is in many cases in effect the end of the case. The grant of the injunction is enough to enable the parties to resolve the remaining issues. In these circumstances it may be appropriate to apply a higher standard. See eg *West Harbour RFC v NSWRU* (16 August 2001, unreported) (Young CJ) (NSW) ('The result of granting an order … will be that the first plaintiff will play in the semi-finals, taking the place of the tenth defendant … Thus the making of the interlocutory order will, to a great degree, deal with the major subject matter of the suit for all practical purposes, through not for legal purposes. In such a situation the court pays particular attention to the strength of the plaintiff's case. Ordinarily on an interlocutory application one merely looks to see whether there is an arguable case, but where the interlocutory injunction will solve for practical purposes the dispute between the parties one looks a little deeper'). On occasions the court may even decide to treat the hearing of the interim injunction as the trial of the action. Equally, the court may take the view that it is unwilling to grant an interim injunction, but will instead order a speedy trial, as to which see para A3.216. A middle way adopted by Popplewell J in *Williams and Cardiff RFC v Pugh* (23 July 1997, unreported) was to grant an interim injunction for a limited period and to order a speedy trial (see pp 14–15 of the shorthand writers' transcript).

8 A higher standard would also be required if for example fraud is alleged. See *Sunderland Association Football Club Ltd v Uruguay Montevideo FC* [2001] 2 All ER (Comm) 828.

9 Thus in *Walker v UKA and IAAF*, Hallett J ensured (by extracting undertakings) that the athlete was able to attempt to qualify for the Olympics at an event which would take place before the final resolution of whether he had been properly convicted of a doping offence. If he had raced (and in the event he chose not to do so) it would not have been possible to undo the fact of his having done so (3 July 2000, unreported) (Toulson J), Hallett J 25 July 2000, IAAF Arbitral Award 20 August 2000 reported at [2001] 4 ISLR 264, see also [2000] 2 ISLR 41 and paras A3.10, n 7 and A3.124).

A3.183 Cross-undertaking in damages The price of obtaining the relief is that the court will almost always[1] require the claimant to provide a cross-undertaking to pay any loss or damage incurred by the defendant or by any third party as a consequence of the grant of the injunction should it appear to the court at full trial that the injunction should not have been granted. The claimant must produce evidence of its ability to meet the cost of this undertaking being called upon, and may be required to put up security. In the context of sport this hurdle may be difficult for the claimant to jump[2].

1 But not always. See for example *Barnard v Australian Soccer Federation and FIFA* (1988) 81 ALR 51.

2 Inadequacy of the cross-undertaking offered was one of the reasons that relief was refused in *Phoenix v FIA and FOM* [2002] EWHC 1028 (Ch), (22 May 202, unreported) (Morritt V-C). Phoenix sought an interim injunction requiring FIA and FOM to allow it to participate in the 2002 Formula One Championship. Phoenix claimed to have acquired the entry and the entitlement to financial benefits of the defunct Prost team under the Concorde Agreement. The Concorde Agreement contained an arbitration clause, and Phoenix's claim was 'through or under' Prost, a party to that arbitration agreement, for the purposes of s 82 of the Arbitration Act 1996. Phoenix's action was accordingly stayed pursuant to s 9 of the Arbitration Act 1996. Its application for interlocutory relief under s 44 was refused on the basis that it had not made out an arguable case that it had acquired a right that was capable of assignment, and that in any event on the balance of convenience an injunction should not be granted. At para 67 Morritt V-C concluded that the accounts of Phoenix suggested that it was unable to pay on a cross undertaking and that the limited security of £250,000 offered was 'inadequate in the circumstances of such an expensive activity as Formula One racing'.

A3.184 Factors in favour of interim relief in the sports context As mentioned above, a number of factors are in favour of a claimant seeking an interim injunction in the sports context[1]. First it is generally impossible to assess the loss likely to be suffered consequent upon the actions of sports governing body. For example if a player or a club is excluded from the opportunity of competing, what quantifiable financial loss has he, she or it suffered? Damages are therefore unlikely to be an adequate remedy[2]. Secondly, individual participants may have a relatively short time at the top of their sport. Any delay may affect them disproportionately. Thirdly, the specific effect on an individual or club of its ability to compete on a given occasion may well be wider than the immediate effects of being excluded on that occasion[3]. Fourthly it has on a number of occasions been contended that the absence of interim relief would actually lead to a club going out of business: finances are often on a knife edge[4].

1 For a complete analysis of factors to be taken into account in favour of the grant of an interim injunction, see *Spry on Equitable Remedies* (5th edn, 1997, Sweet & Maxwell), pp 446 to 510.

2 As in *Phoenix v FIA and FOM* [2002] EWHC 1028 (Ch), (22 May 2002, unreported) (Morritt V-C) at paras 65 to 66; *Williams and Cardiff RFC v Pugh* (23 July 1997, unreported) (Popplewell J) at p 10 of the shorthand writers' transcript; *Jones v WRU* (27 February 1997, unreported) (Ebsworth J), (1997) Times, 6 March, (17 November 1997, unreported) (Potts J), (19 December 1997, unreported), CA, (1998) Times, 6 January, p 9 of the Lexis transcript of Ebsworth J's judgment.

3 As in *Phoenix v FIA and FOM* [2002] EWHC 1028 (Ch), (22 May 2002, unreported) (Morritt V-C) at paras 65 to 66. In that case the entitlement to benefits the following season was based on performance in the previous season. If Phoenix was kept out of competing in 2002, it would not be entitled to benefits the following season if it was ultimately allowed to participate. See too *Tyrrell v RAC and FISA* (20 July 1984, unreported) (Hirst J), for a catalogue of consequences that were cumulatively regarded as sufficient to warrant an injunction being granted.

4 Accepted in *Newport v WFA* [1995] 2 All ER 87, rejected in *Williams and Cardiff RFC v Pugh* (23 July 1997, unreported) (Popplewell J).

A3.185 Factors against interim relief in the sports context While the relatively low threshold on an application for an interim injunction may militate against the defendant sports governing body, other factors may incline the court against the grant of the remedy in the sports context[1]. Two major, and connected, factors (which may also prevent the grant of a final injunction[2]) are delay in making the application[3] and the effect on third parties of the relief sought[4]. Both of these factors are material to the exercise of the court's discretion as to whether to grant interim relief. It is in the nature of the sports sector that the regulatory actions of sports governing bodies are likely to affect one way or another not only the challenger but also the other individuals or clubs with which the challenger is in sporting competition. An obvious example is that if one club is denied promotion, another either stays up or goes up in its stead. The longer that a challenger delays in making an application, the more likely that third parties will have acted on the basis that the unchallenged state of affairs will continue. A third factor in the sports context is that the inclination of the courts to maintain the status quo is informed by the distinction in *McInnes v Onslow-Fane* between forfeiture, application and expectation cases. If a player or club already has a right which is being taken away, the inclination will be to prevent that in the interim; if on the other hand the challenger is seeking to gain a right in the interim, the courts will be much harder to convince[5]. Fourthly, the inadequacy of damages of course cuts both ways in the sports sector: in many if not most instances, damages will not be an adequate remedy for a sports governing body if it sees its careful regulation of the sport temporarily and wrongly upset[6].

1 For a complete analysis of factors to be taken into account against the grant of an interim injunction, see *Spry on Equitable Remedies* (5th edn, 1997, Sweet & Maxwell), pp 446 to 510. Other factors include whether there is a sufficient threat of the action to be injuncted, whether a sufficient injury would arise to warrant the injunction, whether grant of the injunction would cause undue hardship, whether it would be impossible to police or enforce the injunction, whether the claimant had clean hands, and whether the claimant had acquiesced in the action to be injuncted.

2 See paras A3.189 to A3.192.

3 Compare *Stevenage Borough Football Club v Football League Ltd* (1996) Times, 1 August; affd 9 Admin LR 109, CA where delay precluded relief (see para A3.190), and *Newport v FAW* [1995] 2 All ER 87 where a very substantial delay did not preclude interim relief in the light of the other powerful factors in favour of relief.

4 See para A3.191. *Stevenage Borough Football Club v The Football League Ltd* (1996) Times, 1 August; affd 9 Admin LR 109, CA; *Phoenix v FIA and FOM* [2002] EWHC 1028 (Ch), (22 May 2002, (22 May 2002, unreported) (Morritt V-C), para 67: Morritt V-C considered that allowing Phoenix to compete on an interim basis was not possible because although the points (if any) that they took away from other competitors could be restored if the team failed at trial, it would not be possible to take away the effect of other factors such as the team securing a better grid position at the start than other teams, or a Phoenix car shunting another car off the track. It is to be noted that Morritt V-C felt (paras 68 and 70) that it would not be appropriate to force the other Formula One teams to accept Phoenix as an *interim* participant against their will, even assuming the court's ability or willingness to do so after a trial in the light of the principles that the courts will not enforce a contract based on mutual trust and confidence and will not force parties to accept a new party as a participant in an association (see para A3.192).

5 Compare *Tyrrell Racing Organisation v RAC Motor Sports Association and the Fédération Internationale de l' Automobile* (20 July 1984, unreported) (Hirst J), where an existing team was allowed to compete in an event pending the challenge to its suspension, and *Phoenix v FIA and FOM* [2002] EWHC 1028 (Ch), (22 May 2002, unreported) (Morritt V-C), para 71: 'Finally there is the all important consideration of the status quo. Phoenix has not hitherto competed in any Formula One event. It would require a strong case on the merits to justify disturbing that position in anticipation of a trial'.

6 *Phoenix v FIA and FOM* [2002] EWHC 1028 (Ch), (22 May 2002, unreported) (Morritt V-C), para 65, where Morritt V-C concluded that damages would not be an adequate remedy for either the team or the sports governing body. This was a proposition that, perhaps wrongly, did not cut much ice in *Jones v WRU* (27 February 1997, unreported) (Ebsworth J), (1997) Times, 6 March, (17 November 1997, unreported) (Potts J), (19 December 1997, unreported), CA, (1998) Times, 6 January, where Ebsworth J concluded that the WRU would suffer neither financially nor in its reputation if an interim injunction were granted against it. See para A3.186.

A3.186 Dealing with an interim injunction As set out above, it may be that an interim injunction is obtained on the basis only that the challenge is arguable. In these circumstances, the sports governing body has to decide how to deal with the situation. It can accept the position as ordered at the interim stage and settle the action, or it can fight the action at trial, which may be some time later. On occasion there is however a third approach, which is for the governing body to take its own steps to cure the vice identified, and spike the guns of the challenger. This approach was successfully pursued by the WRU in *Jones v WRU*[1]. The international player Mark Jones and his club sought an interim injunction preventing the WRU implementing a four week ban for fighting. The ban had been imposed following the completion of the WRU's internal disciplinary procedure. The player complained that the process had been flawed in various respects[2]. An interim injunction was sought and granted on the basis that it was arguable that the procedure was flawed and because the player and his club had satisfied the court that damages were an inadequate remedy if the player was unavailable for selection[3]. Rather than leave the injunction in place and see the case proceed to trial at the normal pace of litigation, the WRU decided instead to amend its procedures and to reconvene the disciplinary committee to hear the case in a manner that cured the alleged defects. It invited the player to participate but he declined. In his absence at the next hearing he was again suspended for four weeks. A further injunction was sought by the player and obtained[4]. On this occasion the WRU appealed. The Court of Appeal held[5] that the original interim injunction had been properly granted, but that the WRU could not be prevented from re-opening the matter and dealing with it properly. It found no basis for criticising the later disciplinary process. The second ban was therefore properly imposed. The court noted that had the ban been served immediately after the date of the first injunction hearing, then because of inclement weather it would have been served by the player without a game having been played or missed by him, which is a salutary lesson that obtaining interim relief may not necessarily be in the player's best interests[6].

1 *Jones v WRU* (27 February 1997, unreported) (Ebsworth J), (1997) Times, 6 March, (17 November 1997, unreported) (Potts J), (19 December 1997, unreported), CA, (1998) Times, 6 January.
2 In particular that the player had not had the opportunity to make submissions in relation to the video evidence while it was watched by the disciplinary committee.
3 Ebsworth J said 'there is … an air of unreality about a court sitting down to decide whether a player would have made a difference between his team winning or losing a particular match or whether or not he would have been selected for a particular game. It would also be difficult, if not impossible, for a court to calculate the cause of any demotion of the club if there were a suspension and whether, and if so what, loss flowed from that'.
4 (17 November 1997, unreported) (Potts J).
5 (19 December 1997, unreported), CA, (1998) Times, 6 January.
6 Cf *Walker v UKA and IAAF* where although the athlete secured the ability to compete while a challenge to his suspension for doping was pending before the IAAF arbitral body, he chose not to do so because his ban was nearly served and if he had competed and the supsension had subsequently been re-imposed, he would have had to have served a longer time out of competition (unreported Toulson J 3 July 2000, Hallett J 25 July 2000, IAAF Arbitral Award 20 August 2000 reported at [2001] 4 ISLR 264, see also [2000] 2 ISLR 41 and n 7 to para A3.10 and para A3.124).

A3.187 Interim injunction in support of sports arbitration In many instances in the sports context, the substantive dispute falls to be decided by an arbitral body, which may have its seat in or outside the jurisdiction[1]. Although such arbitral bodies generally have jurisdiction to grant interim relief themselves[2], in some instances the body may not have yet been convened and the matter may be too urgent to wait. The English courts have jurisdiction in these circumstances to grant interim relief in support of the arbitration[3].

1 See generally Chapter A5.
2 And the ability and willingness to use it. The CAS has power under Rule 37 to order provisional measures, but only after the arbitration is submitted to it. See for example *AEK Athens and Slavia Prague v UEFA*, CAS 98/2000 award on provisional relief application 17 July 1998, the full award, 20 August 1999, is at *Digest of CAS Awards II 1998–2000* (2002, Kluwer), p 38. The CAS applies a test which has largely the same outcome as would the application of the English law test. See eg *Haga v FIM*, 2000/A/281, award dated 22 December 2000, *Digest of CAS Awards II 1998–2000* (2002, Kluwer), pp 410, 412 (CAS analysed application for interim stay of suspension pending appeal of the decision imposing the suspension in light of likelihood of success on merits, irreparable harm if stay not granted, and balance of convenience). In *AEK*, CAS restrained UEFA from applying a new rule excluding two clubs in common ownership from playing in the same competition, on the grounds that the new rule was introduced too late to be capable of application in good faith to the clubs involved, which already had a legitimate expectation of being allowed to compete, having satisfied the published entry criteria.
2 See the Arbitration Act 1996, ss 44 and 2; *Phoenix v FIA and FOM* [2002] EWHC 1028 (Ch), (22 May 2002, unreported) (Morritt V-C).

A3.188 Interim injunction when the action is for a declaration in respect of the general obligations In *Newport v FAW*[1], there was no contract; rather, the claim was simply for a final declaration, and was based solely on the general obligations owed by a sports governing body and restraint of trade[2]. Jacob J had to deal with the question of whether an interim injunction could be granted in such circumstances. He granted the injunction on the basis that if he could grant a declaration at trial than he must be able to protect that position pending trial[3], a sensible and practical conclusion.

1 [1995] 2 All ER 87.
2 See para A3.80 et seq.
3 At 92 b–e. Jacob J went on to distinguish *The Siskina* [1979] AC 210 where it was held that the grant of an interim injunction is dependent upon there being a pre-existing cause of action for breach of an invasion, actual or threatened, of a legal or equitable right. It had been argued that where a party can only hope to obtain a declaration in relation to the general obligations at trial, that party does not have a legal or equitable right. Jacob J regarded Wilberforce J's judgment in *Eastham v Newcastle United Football Club* [1964] Ch 413 at 440 as categorising the right to obtain a declaration in respect of the general obligations as a cause of action in respect of a right. Jacob J's approach, as well as being necessary to do justice, is supported by Commonwealth authority (see for example *Buckley v Tutty* (1971) 125 CLR 353 at paras 21 to 24, where the court held that it could grant a player an injunction preventing the enforcement of the sports governing body's transfer system and a declaratiom that that system was illegal as in restraint of trade, although the player was not a member of the governing body and had no contractual relationship with it), and arguably by Carnwath J in *Stevenage Borough Football Club v Football League Ltd* (1996) Times, 1 August. A similar approach was followed in *Re S* [1995] Fam 26. Notwithstanding, the contrary may remain arguable: Hoffmann LJ in *R v Jockey Club, ex p Aga Khan* [1993] 1 WLR 909 had previously stated (at 933) that the ability to grant an injunction in the circumstances of *Nagle v Feilden* had 'probably not survived' *The Siskina*.

(b) Final injunctions

A3.189 Plainly, in order to secure a final injunction the challenge must actually have succeeded on the merits. To that extent a final injunction is harder to obtain than interim relief. On the other hand, some of the factors that preclude interim relief will have fallen by the wayside once a final hearing is reached. The 'balance of justice' as between the parties at least has been determined by the determination of the merits. If for example the case is made out, there can obviously be no question of maintaining an incorrect status quo. Equally it will probably make little difference whether the order is mandatory or prohibitory. That said the remedy remains discretionary. Although final injunctions are an effective method of ensuring that sports governing bodies alter existing approaches and comply with their obligations in the future, there are limits to the availability of the remedy[1].

1 For a complete analysis of factors to be taken into account in the grant of a final injunction, see *Spry on Equitable Remedies* (5th edn, 1997, & Maxwell), pp 382 to 444. Other factors include whether damages would be a perfectly appropriate remedy, whether there is a sufficient threat of the action to be injuncted, whether a sufficient injury would arise to warrant the injunction, whether it would cause undue hardship, whether it would be impossible to police or enforce the injunction, whether the claimant had clean hands, and whether the claimant had acquiesced in the action to be injuncted. A court may be unwilling to injunct an international sports governing body outside the jurisdiction and made up of associations from many foreign countries. Cf the unwillingness to grant a declaration in these circumstances in *Cowley v Heatley* (1986) Times, 24 July; see also para A3.98, n 2 (an injunction requiring the governing body to accept her entry was also sought by the athlete, but not addressed by the court).

A3.190 Delay and retrospective effect As mentioned above, delay in the making of a challenge may even preclude final relief. In the *Stevenage* case[1], the claimant football club succeeded in showing that a number of the League's entry criteria on promotion were in unreasonable restraint of trade, but Carnwath J nevertheless refused a final injunction following a speedy trial, primarily on the basis that the club could have challenged the criteria earlier, instead of leaving it to the eleventh hour after it had won the Conference and was eligible for promotion. The Court of Appeal agreed with Carnwath J and stated[2] the principle in terms of the undesirability of granting relief which would have retrospective effect:

> What was in issue was the validity of the rules for promotion and relegation to and from the League, not merely whether Stevenage should be promoted to the League. In such a case the Court is concerned with three questions: (i) whether any and if so which of the rules is invalid; (ii) if so, whether it should grant a declaration to that effect; and (iii) if so, whether it should make an order (whether by way of injunction or declaration) giving effect to the rules as modified by the excision of those which it finds to be invalid. Even where it is satisfied that each of these questions requires an affirmative answer, it would be an exceptional case in which it would be right to give retrospective effect to the modified rules.
>
> In the present case Stevenage has known of the position since at least August 1994. It had sixteen months in which to bring its ground up to the required standard if it wished to be considered for promotion to the League in time for the 1996–7 season. It did not do so. By November 1995 Mr Green knew that Stevenage could not meet the criteria by the deadline of 31st December 1995 and that the League would not grant an extension of time. He knew that Stevenage would not qualify for promotion in 1996–7 unless it won the Conference championship and succeeded in challenging the criteria. He decided to mount a legal challenge but only if Stevenage won the championship and to conceal his intentions in the meantime. The inevitable consequence was that he was compelled to ask the Court, not merely to declare the parties' 'rights' for the future, but retrospectively to upset the basis upon which the previous season's competitions had been held. In my judgment the Court should be extremely slow to accede to such an invitation.'

In the context of final injunctions, however, a delay which does not involve the court in effectively granting retrospective relief ought not to matter. If the effect of the order is only as to the future, and there is a good basis for it, then it ought to be made.

1 *Stevenage Borough Football Club v Football League Ltd* (1986) Times, 1 August. See also *Stinnato v Auckland Boxing Association* [1978] 1 NZLR 1 at 29; and *Ray v Professional Golfers' Association* (15 April 1997, unreported) (Judge Dyer QC) for other cases where delay was a reason not to grant an interim injunction.

2 (1997) 9 Admin LR 109, CA.

A3.191 Adverse effect on third parties Also as mentioned above, an adverse effect on third parties may lead a court to refuse final relief. In the *Stevenage* case this was again a major factor in the refusal of Carnwath J and the Court of Appeal to grant a final injunction. As Carnwath J put it[1]:

> The position of Torquay is of special relevance. They are the club which will be relegated if Stevenage is promoted. Although they could not complain of that, provided they were given adequate notice, the scheme of the rules of both the League and Conference entitle them to be notified of that shortly after the end of the season, so that they can make their arrangements. The change from the League to the Conference necessarily affects sponsorship, players' contracts and the planning of the season. It is unfair to them that they should be left in uncertainty until very shortly before the new season. The mere fact that they were made aware at an early stage of this litigation, and indeed even made parties to it at one stage, did not give them any certainty as to the outcome. Mr Bateson, chairman of Torquay, gave evidence of the arrangements which have been made, including negotiations with the 18 members of the first team who have been signed to play third division football, the pricing of season tickets, and contracts of commercial sponsorship including the catering franchise.

1 *Stevenage Borough Football Club v Football League Ltd* (1996) Times, 1 August.

A3.192 Injunction not available to force membership or participation It is well established that as a matter of English law[1] the courts will not force a person to work for an employer or an employer to employ an employee and will not force parties into a contractual relationship of membership against their will[2]. There are two parallel principles at work here: first that a contract involving mutual trust and confidence will not be specifically enforced, and secondly that parties will not be forced into a contractual relationship that did not previously exist with a new member. In the sports context these principles have been repeatedly applied in disputes between an employee player and an employing club[3], between a self-employed driver and a team[4], and between an amateur member and a sporting club[5]. It is less clear nowadays that the principle should necessarily extend to a dispute as to a club's or an individual's membership of a league or association, or even to an association's membership of an association. However, as discussed above[6], it remains the case (despite the new approach to review of sports governing bodies' actions as reflected in the *Modahl* litigation) that there has not been an English case where a sports association was forced by the courts to accept a new member. As Carnwath J put it in the *Stevenage* case[7], where the club ultimately unsuccessfully sought to force its way into the League (and where, on the *McInnes v Onslow-Fane* classification, the case was an application case):

> Even if a case in principle is established, the question of remedies poses difficulties in an application case. No case has been cited in which the Court has forced a private organisation to admit a member against its will, even where the organisation controls the member's right to work …

Carnwath J did not decide the point. However, if he had not dismissed the case on grounds of the lateness of the application, it is to be doubted that he would have balked at forcing Stevenage's admission. It seems likely that the courts would enforce an individual's or a club's right to compete, but would not grant a governing body an injunction requiring the individual or club to compete. Be that as it may, the most recent case suggests (albeit obiter) that the principle still applies even in a context where there is a contractual entitlement and the issue is not as stark as in the *Stevenage* case. In *Alwyn Treherne v Amateur Boxing Association of England*[8], Garland J suggested that even if he had found that a contractual arrangement had existed, he would not have granted an injunction forcing two 'non commercial bodies concerned with the organisation and regulation of amateur sport' to stay in a contractual relationship to which one of them objected. He saw the position as being analogous to forcing a club to accept or reinstate a member whom it found unacceptable. Buxton LJ in the Court of Appeal made a similar comment. It may be the case that the circumstances that existed in that action may now arise only rarely.

1 Though not notably of most civil law systems.
2 *Lee v Showmen's Guild* [1952] 2 QB 329 per Denning LJ at 342; *Faramus v Film Artistes' Association* [1964] AC 925 at 941 per Lord Evershed. The decisions in both *Nagle v Feilden* and *Onslow-Fane* reflect the traditional approach of English law that a private sports governing body cannot be forced to accept someone with whom it has no pre-existing contractual relationship as a member (although in neither case was the claimant seeking to become a member as such). Under the traditional approach, sports governing bodies can sometimes be constrained to act fairly in their decision making but the court will not force them to admit a club or person as a member, because to do that would be to force them into a contract.
3 See Chapter E1 and the examples referred to in n 4 to para A3.43.
4 See n 3.
5 *Collins v Lane* (22 June 1999, unreported), CA (Member of amateur shooting club unable to regain membership even if treated in breach of natural justice).
6 See paras A3.85 and A3.93.
7 *Stevenage Borough Football Club v Football League Ltd* (1996) Times, 1 August, at p 23 of the New Law Online transcript. In that case the question was not decided, as the club's application was refused on the grounds of delay (as to which see also the Court of Appeal (1997) 9 Admin LR 109).
8 *Alwyn Treherne (for the Welsh Amateur Boxing Federation) v Amateur Boxing Association of England*, Garland J 27 February 2001 [2001] 3 ISLR 231, [2002] EWCA Civ 381, [2002] All ER (D) 144 (Mar) (The WABF, which had been set up as a rival to the Welsh Amateur Boxing Association and which was not recognised internationally, challenged the ABAE's refusal to allow its clubs to affiliate with the ABAE so that former WABF boxers could compete other than with one another. The case turned on whether a binding contract had been entered into that the ABAE would admit the clubs, and it was held that it had not been. As noted above, however, both Garland J and Buxton LJ doubted that even if there had been a contract it would have been appropriate to grant an injunction to force the ABAE to admit the clubs).

C Declarations

(a) Interim declarations

A3.193 A new jurisdiction? In *Newport v FAW*[1], Jacob J held that the submission that 'an interlocutory declaration cannot be granted because it is a juridical nonsense … you cannot have a provisional determination of the final rights of the parties' was 'manifestly right'. The opposite view had long been taken by Lord Woolf MR[2], and the CPR introduced an express power to grant an interim declaration[3]. However the notes to the White Book[4] state that 'it may be doubted whether jurisdiction to grant interlocutory declaratory relief can be conferred by a rule of Court'[5].

1 *Newport Association Football Club v Football Association of Wales* [1995] 2 All ER 87 at 92a and 93e. There is also Court of Appeal authority to the effect that an interim declaration is 'a creature unknown to English law': *Riverside Mental Health NHS Trust v Fox* [1994] 1 FLR 614.
2 In the leading text on declaratory relief: Zamir and Woolf *The Declaratory Judgment* (3rd edn, 2002, Sweet & Maxwell) at paras 3.094 to 3.099 and 9.05. Lord Woolf feels that this jurisdiction is advantageous because it gives the courts greater flexibility.
3 Under CPR, Pt 25.1(1)(b).
4 CPR, Pt 25.1(3).
5 Cf Lord Woolf, Zamir and Woolf *The Declaratory Judgment* (3rd edn, 2002, Sweet & Maxwell), para 3.097.

A3.194 It would therefore be wise not to confine any interim relief application to an application for interim declaratory relief. It is in fact difficult to conceive of many instances in which interim declaratory relief would be necessary or of particular use. This is especially the case if Jacob J's approach in *Newport v FAW*[1] of filling the gap by granting an interim injunction is valid. If there is an interim injunction there is generally little need for an interim declaration. The possibility of the relief can therefore only be useful in circumstances where for some reason an interim injunction might not be available or sufficient. Examples of this situation in the sports context might include where a party is seeking membership of an association without any contractual right, where a cross-undertaking in damages cannot be substantiated, where a court is unwilling to injunct an international sports governing body, where an effect on a wider audience than the other party is desirable, or where the court is unwilling to grant an injunction in the light of the difficulties of enforcement.

1 *Newport v Football Association of Wales* [1995] 2 All ER 87 at 92b–e; see para A3.188.

A3.195 When an interim declaration is available An interim declaration, like an interim injunction, can only be made if a prima facie case is established and if the balance of convenience justifies granting the relief[1]. Declarations, like injunctions, are discretionary remedies and many of the same factors will apply[2]. The relief has rarely been granted[3].

1 Zamir and Woolf *The Declaratory Judgment* (3rd edn, 2002, Sweet & Maxwell), para 3.097.
2 See paras A3.184 and A3.185.
3 The one sports-related instance of an interim declaration being granted was in *R v ITC, ex p TVDanmark 1 Ltd* [2001] UKHL 42, [2001] 1 WLR 1604.

(b) Final declarations

A3.196 A final declaration granted by the court after a matter is resolved on the merits affords the parties certainty as to their respective relevant rights. The declaration can be positive or negative. The claimant must take great care in drafting the declaration sought to ensure that it corresponds with the ruling that the court is likely to be able to make, while at the same time providing the certainty required. An important aspect of the remedy is that it is available not only in cases where the claimant has a contractual right (where the declaration is as to the existence, extent and ambit of those rights)[1], but also where there is no contract and the claim is based on the doctrine of restraint of trade as a free-standing principle[2] or on the general obligations owed by sports governing bodies in the absence of a contract[3] (where the declaration may be less specific). Declarations are also available in the context of other causes of action, such as breach of the competition or free movement rules[4].

1 A declaration can arise in the situation where the existence of the contract is in question or where a difficult point of construction needs to be resolved. See for example *Reel v Holder (for IAAF)* [1979] 1 WLR 1252; affd [1981] 1 WLR 1226, CA (Declaration that on the proper construction of the IAAF Rules, the Taiwanese athletics governing body was entitled to membership). It could also arise in a contractual context where one party sought a declaration that a term in his contract with the other party was invalid, for example as being in restraint of trade, for instance as in *Watson v Prager* [1991] 1 WLR 726 (Declaration that a standard term in the British Boxing Board of Control contract was in unreasonable restraint of trade).
2 Under the doctrine of restraint of trade, a declaration is available against a person or body who does not stand in a contractual relationship with the claimant. For example as in *Eastham v Newcastle and the FA* [1964] Ch 413; *Blackler v NZRFL* [1968] NZLR 547; *Buckley v Tutty* (1971) 125 CLR

353; and *Kemp v NZRFL* [1989] 3 NZLR 463 (Declarations that the respective rules on transfers or permission to play outside the governing body's jurisdiction were in unreasonable restraint of trade); *Greig v Insole (for the TCCB)* [1978] 1 WLR 302 (Declaration that a rule prohibiting players playing for a rival organiser was in unreasonable restraint of trade); *Newport v Football Association of Wales* interlocutory hearing Jacob J [1995] 2 All ER 87, trial unreported Blackburne J 12 April 1995 (Declaration that the FAW's actions in preventing the club playing its home games in the English League, in Wales were in unreasonable restraint of trade).

3 A declaration may also be sought for breach of the general obligations. See for example the discussion in *Modahl v British Athletics Federation* [2002] 1 WLR 1192, CA 8 October 2001 at paras 36 to 48; *Nagle v Feilden* [1966] 2 QB 633, where the court was prepared to consider making a declaration that the defendants' action was unlawful (in that case discriminatory on the grounds of gender) and harmful to the Claimant notwithstanding the absence of any direct contractual relationship. See also *McInnes v Onslow-Fane* [1978] 1 WLR 1520 at 1528; *Gasser v Stinson* 15 June 1988 at p 24 F of the shorthand writers' transcript; *R v Jockey Club, ex p RAM Racecourses* [1993] 2 All ER 225, DC at 242. *Stevenage Borough Football Club v Football League Ltd* (1996) Times, 1 August; affd 9 Admin LR 109, CA, at pp 24 to 26 of the New Law Online transcript.

4 See *Hendry v WPBSA*, Lloyd J 5 October 2001 [2002] 1 ISLR SLR-1, and para A3.198. In *Bacardi-Martini SAS and Cellier des Dauphins v Newcastle United FC* 2001 Eu LR 45, QBD, the claimants seek a declaration that (in effect) the Loi Evin is incompatible with the EC freedom of movement rules.

A3.197 Because the remedy is discretionary, many of the considerations that defeat a claim for a final injunction may also defeat a claim for a final declaration[1]. Thus in the *Stevenage* case a final declaration was not available in the light of the delay and adverse effect on third parties[2], notwithstanding that the court determined that at least some of the League's rules were void. A declaration will only be granted if it serves some practical purpose to grant it. If some other remedy is appropriate, that may be preferred to the granting of a declaration.

1 See Zamir and Woolf *The Declaratory Judgment* (3rd edn, 2002, Sweet & Maxwell), ch 4 for an analysis of when a final declaration will be granted. See paras A3.189 to A3.192.

2 *Stevenage Borough Football Club v Football League Ltd* (1996) Times, 1 August; affd 9 Admin LR 109, CA at 117 to 121, at pp 34–35 of the New Law Online transcript.

A3.198 A declaration without a judgment explaining it may be inadequate. In *Hendry v WPBSA*[1], the WPBSA made a tactical retreat and withdrew its Rule A5 which it regarded as being the most vulnerable of the rules challenged, and which in the event was the only one overturned. The WPBSA stated that it would accede to a declaration of invalidity in respect of that rule alone, and that the trial should not continue in respect of it. Lloyd J however held that the claimant was entitled to know the reasons why Rule A5 was void, as it was only against such reasons that future conduct could be measured. A declaration alone would not be adequate. Lloyd J eventually granted a declaration that Rule A5, as in force between specified dates, was void under Arts 81 and 82 and ss 2 and 18 of the Competition Act 1998. His judgment explained the reasons why it was void[2].

1 Lloyd J 5 October 2001 [2002] 1 ISLR SLR-1.

2 See paras B2.131 to B2.141.

D Damages

A3.199 As set out above, generally the player's or club's concern is not to recover damages in respect of regulatory action but rather to stop or undo that action. It is however relatively common for athletes and clubs to include claims for damages in their pleadings. The losses generally claimed focus on the loss of sponsorship and advertising opportunities, as well as the loss of a chance to win prize money. The practical ability to recover such damages is however limited for a number of reasons.

(a) Compensation only available where there is a cause of action that sounds in damages

A3.200 Damages compensating a claimant for loss[1] will only be available for breach of an obligation that gives a right to damages. Most obviously this is breach of contract, but it could also be negligence or some other tortious cause of action, and damages are available for breach of the competition rules. This is of particular importance in the sports context, because two of the major bases for challenge in that context do not sound in damages.

1 Damages other then for compensation are unlikely to be available. For an example of an (unsuccessful) attempt by a player to claim exemplary damages as opposed to compensatory damages following a ban, see *Currie v Barton* (26 March 1987, unreported) (Scott J), (11 February 1988, unreported), CA, (1988) Times, 12 February. In *Stinnato v Auckland Boxing Association* [1978] 1 NZLR 1 at 22, the boxer sought damages in lieu of an injunction under the 1858 Chancery Amendment Act. The claim, which had been added late, was dealt with on the basis that no injunction was claimed so that there was no question of damages in lieu.

(b) No damages for breach of the general obligations in the absence of a contract

A3.201 Damages are not available for breach of the general obligations owed by sports governing bodies if those obligations do not become implied terms of a contract between the claimant and the sports governing body. Accordingly the trainer in *Nagle v Feilden* could not have recovered damages. She was confined to a declaration. It was this problem that confronted Diane Modahl[1]. In the initial stages of the litigation, which proceeded to the House of Lords, it was assumed for the purposes of the strike out application that a contract had arisen between the athlete and the sports governing bodies. When the case came on for trial, the sports governing bodies accepted that they owed limited general obligations that could give rise to a declaration, but contended that there was no contract that was capable of giving rise to a right to damages. It was decided at first instance that there was no contract, but on appeal it was held that a contract did arise that included the general obligations as implied terms. However a breach was not established on the facts, and in any event there would have been causation problems that stood in the way of recovery.

1 *Modahl v British Athletics Federation* (28 June 1996, unreported) (Popplewell J), (28 July 1997, unreported), CA, (22 July 1998, unreported), HL, [2002] 1 WLR 1192, CA.

(c) Damages are not available under the restraint of trade doctrine

A3.202 It is well established that the restraint of trade doctrine does not sound in damages[1]. Nor can this principle be avoided by seeking to identify a breach of an implied term. In the *Newport* case, Blackburne J rejected the proposition that there is an implied term that a party will not act in restraint of trade, thereby heading off the attempt to circumvent the principle[2].

1 *Eastham v Newcastle and the FA* [1964] Ch 413 at 452.
2 *Newport v Football Association of Wales*, trial unreported Blackburne J 12 April 1995, p 45 of the New Law Online transcript.

(d) Damages are available for breach of contract

A3.203 The *Modahl* case[1] proceeded on the obvious basis that damages are recoverable if a breach of contract leading directly to a financial loss is established[2]. If the general obligations are included in an implied contractual term, damages are recoverable for breach of them[3].

1 *Modahl v British Athletics Federation* (28 June 1996, unreported) (Popplewell J), (28 July 1997, unreported), CA, (22 July 1998, unreported), HL, [2002] 1 WLR 1192, CA.
2 [2002] 1 WLR 1192 at para 25.
3 But, as explained in *Colgan v Kennel Club* (26 October 2001, unreported) (Cooke J), damages are not available in this context purely because a governing body made the wrong decision. It must be shown to have departed from the general obligations in such a way as to cause damage.

(e) Damages are available in tort

A3.204 In *Watson v BBBC*[1], the sports governing body was held liable in damages for its negligent failure to ensure adequate medical facilities were available at the ringside.

1 *Watson v BBBC* (1999) 143 Sol Jo LB 235, (1999) Times, 12 October, Court of Appeal [2001] QB 1134, CA, 19 December 2000. The damages were so great that the existence of the BBBC, which did not insure itself, was threatened.

(f) Damages for breach of the competition rules

A3.205 If a rule or decision or agreement is contrary to a relevant prohibition[1], and has not been notified as required to the relevant regulatory authority, it is void (subject to severance) and cannot be relied upon and there is a right to damages as well as to a declaration and an injunction[2]. An individual or company that is party to the rule or decision or agreement challenged may find it harder to recover damages than third parties, but theoretically can do so in circumstances where the rule or decision has been forced on the party challenging it[3].

1 See paras A3.159 to A3.167 and Chapter B2.
2 See Bellamy and Child *Common Market Law of Competition* (5th edn, 2001, Sweet & Maxwell), paras 10-029 to 10-060.
3 See Bellamy and Child *Common Market Law of Competition* (5th edn, 2001, Sweet & Maxwell), para 10-058. See also *Hendry v WPBSA*, Lloyd J 5 October 2001 [2002] 1 ISLR SLR-1 at para 159. In *Courage Ltd v Crehan,* C-453/99, [2001] All ER (EC) 886, [2001] ECR I-6297, it was held that Art 81 of the Treaty precludes a rule of national law under which a party to a contract liable to restrict or distort competition within the meaning of that provision is barred from claiming damages for loss caused by performance of that contract on the sole ground that the claimant is a party to that contract; but that Community law does not preclude a rule of national law barring a party to a contract liable to restrict or distort competition from relying on his own unlawful actions to obtain damages where it is established that the party bears significant responsibility for the distortion of the competition. It is likely that this approach would be followed in the context of the Competition Act 1998 as well.

(g) Assessment of damages and the particular problem of causation

A3.206 The normal principles of assessment of damages apply in the sports context as in other contexts, and they are not set out here[1]. The usual limitations, such as the requirement of establishing causation, will also apply. So, for example, it would not be enough for the claimant to establish simply that there was a breach of contract; it must also be shown that that breach of contract caused the loss for which the claimant seeks compensation. In the *Modahl* case, both the judge at first instance and the Court of Appeal[2] decided that a finding of apparent bias in one member of the initial tribunal did not cause any loss. First the remaining members of the initial tribunal were unaffected by his attitude and the decision was unanimous. The reason that the initial tribunal's decision was overturned was that fresh material was subsequently presented, not that its decision was flawed in the light of what it had seen. Secondly, even if there had been a breach of contract when the initial tribunal sat that nullified its decision, the effect of that would have been to have left the suspension in force and the athlete would still have been unable to compete. The loss was therefore the loss of the chance that a properly constituted initial tribunal would have found in her favour, but the fact that the second tribunal found as it did only because of fresh material not available before the initial tribunal suggested that this would not have been much of a chance. Thirdly, the only finding had been one of *apparent* bias by one member: he had not been actually biased. Accordingly his decision itself would not have been different. The same problem of causation would arise in the context of tortious claims, in respect of which there may also be other limitations on the recovery of compensation for loss. In the context of amateur sport, there is a real risk that nothing more than nominal damages will be recoverable even if a player is successful in his action[3].

1 See *McGregor on Damages* (16th edn, 1997, Sweet and Maxwell).
2 (14 December 2000, unreported) (Douglas Brown J), [2002] 1 WLR 1192, CA per Latham LJ at para 68 and Mance LJ at paras 132 to 135.
3 See *Collins v Lane* (22 June 1999, unreported), CA at pp 12–14 of the shorthand writers' transcript where £250 was awarded for wrongful expulsion from a shooting club. Membership would not be re-imposed.

E Remedies under the Human Rights Act 1998

A3.207 The remedies available under the Human Rights Act 1998 are adapted to the particular circumstances of that legislation[1]. Where there is a breach of a Convention right, the court has a discretion under s 8 of the Act to grant such relief as falls within its powers and as it considers just and appropriate in order to afford 'just satisfaction' to the victim. This may be damages, or it may be confined to a finding that there has been a violation.

1 See paras A4.78 to A4.80.

F Unfair prejudice petitions under s 459 of the Companies Act

A3.208 Section 459 of the Companies Act 1985[1] provides a mechanism by which a member of a company can object if the company is being operated in a way that is unfairly prejudicial to its interests. The member can petition the court to secure suitable relief. Many sports governing bodies are companies of which each of the clubs under their jurisdiction is a member[2]. In an Australian case, *Wayde v New South Wales Rugby League*[3], the claimant unsuccessfully relied on the equivalent of s 459 in the relevant legislation when the sports governing body decided to reduce the size of the top division, depriving the claimant of its place. The claim was unsuccessful because the measure of unfairness for the purposes of the section was equivalent to the measure applicable under the general obligation on a sports governing body not to act unreasonably in its handling of issues relating to the governance of the sport. It is accordingly unlikely that resort to the particular mechanisms of the Companies Act will achieve a different result to that which could be achieved in any event on the basis of the general obligations. The court will feel the same constraints in relation to intervention in the actions of a sport governing body in both contexts. This has not stopped imaginative practitioners seeking to use the mechanism in England against sports governing bodies, in reliance on the proposition that the English courts are not restrictive in general when considering what is 'unfair' under s 459. No attempt has proceeded beyond the stage of posturing, however.

1 As amended by the 1989 Act. See *Tolley's Company Law* (2001), para 54026 et seq.
2 See Chapter C1.
3 (1985) 61 ALR 225.

10 PROCEDURAL ASPECTS

A3.209 A claim challenging the actions and rules of a sports governing body involves the same procedural considerations as any other action, and this section does not address all of those considerations, since they will be obvious to the practitioner. This section is confined to addressing specific aspects of the courts' procedure which may prove to be of specific use to those making, or resisting, a claim brought against a sports governing body. It concentrates on those aspects of procedure that may enable the parties to obtain a speedy resolution of the matter in issue by the courts or in contrast to take the matter away from the courts.

A Obtaining a quicker resolution of the issue

A3.210 As set out above in the discussion of interim remedies, in the specific context of challenges to sports governing bodies' actions, the remedies of damages, declaration or final injunction, are often not really adequate. A faster solution is often required by the challenger and indeed on occasion by the sports governing body[1]. The usual process of litigation involves exchange of statements of case setting out the parties' respective legal positions, the exchange of evidence in the form of relevant documents, written statements of the oral evidence that will be given at trial by witnesses of fact and by experts, for a trial in which the evidence will be given orally and subject to cross-examination. In any case of reasonable substance, this process inevitably may take several months even without taking account of the pressure on the court's time. A practitioner seeking to speed matters up must find procedural mechanisms to circumvent these delays. The following are offered as suggestions as to how this might be achieved.

1 Those that argue that sports governing bodies should be subject to judicial review contend that the process on paper which is used in judicial review cases and which can lead to speedier less complex pleadings would suit claims involving sporting bodies. However, as noted above (paras A3.62 to A3.65), judicial review is not available. Nonetheless there are a number of procedures that can truncate the lengthy process of private law litigation.

(a) Interim relief

A3.211 The first, and most obvious method is to seek interim relief, as described above. While the test on an application for interim relief is not the same as at trial, it offers the claimant the prospect of some protection should he ultimately succeed.

Equally, it allows a sports governing body to gain a fair understanding of the attitude of the court to its actions, which it can then reappraise on a more informed basis. The hearing can be brought on very quickly, even without pleadings, and the evidence is contained in statements on which there will generally be no cross-examination. In procedural terms the courts are prepared and able to show great flexibility in the manner in which applications may be heard and dealt with. At one end of the scale, the conventional manner of application would be by way of a notice of application served on the other party giving at least two clear days notice of the hearing and serving witness statements containing the relevant evidence and exhibiting the relevant documentation. The first hearing date would then be an opportunity to give directions for the service of evidence by the defendant and any evidence in reply before the matter comes for hearing. This process would take several weeks. At the other end of the scale however, where urgency is essential, an order could be sought on immediate application to a judge, if necessary by telephone and without notice to the defendant. In such cases if the order is granted the claimant must give undertakings to take steps as soon as practical to issue proceedings and to 'paper' the process retrospectively. Where orders are made without notice to the other side, the court will stipulate a return date when the matter will be heard again and the defendant given an opportunity to put its case. In practical terms however, the challenger would have been provided with protection in very short order. It should also be noted that the Court of Appeal is more disposed to deal quickly with appeals from interim decisions[1].

1 In the *Stevenage* case, (1996) Times, 1 August; affd 9 Admin LR 109, CA, the Court of Appeal considered the issue within a week of the hearing before the first instance judge, during the course of the August vacation.

(b) *Agreeing that an interim hearing disposes of the matter*

A3.212 Taking this consideration a step further, it is possible for the parties, with the consent of the court, to agree that the interim hearing actually disposes of the matter. This has obvious costs advantages, but equally it has obvious risks for the sports governing body and indeed the challenger. It is a mechanism that it is likely would only be of much use where the case turns on a point of law (such as construction of the rules) that the court would in effect decide the same way whether the hearing was an interim hearing or a final hearing. Any agreement should be made on the basis that the test that the court will apply will be the balance of probabilities rather than the lower test (arguable case) applicable on an interim hearing.

(c) *Summary judgment and striking out*

A3.213 A more aggressive approach for a sports governing body to take would be to apply immediately for summary judgment or to strike out the claim. Either party may seek summary judgment under CPR, Pt 24 on the grounds that the other has no 'real prospect of succeeding' on a claim or an issue where there is no other compelling reason why the case should be disposed of at trial. The party may also apply to strike out an opponent's claim or defence if it discloses no reasonable grounds for bringing or defending the claim under CPR, Pt 3.4. Many cases falling within Pt 3.4 are also the subject of applications under Pt 24. An application under CPR, Pt 24 may not be made by a claimant until after a defendant has acknowledged service or served a defence. However, this is subject to the court giving permission and in cases of urgency permission can be sought from the court at the time that the claim is originally issued. If necessary this can be coupled with an application that will truncate the usual time scales for acknowledgment of service and service of evidence under Pt 24. It may be possible, therefore, to commence a Claim and have an application for summary judgment heard within days or a few weeks. Equally a strike out claim can be brought on quickly[1].

1 In *Modahl v British Athletics Federation* (28 June 1996, unreported) (Popplewell J), (28 July 1997, unreported), CA, (22 July 1998, unreported), HL, [2002] 1 WLR 1192, CA, however, the sports governing body attempted to strike out the action in the hope of securing a speedy resolution, only to fail ultimately in striking out the whole action after the matter went all the way up to the House of Lords, several years after the action was begun (although in that case there was no urgency as the issue was the recoverability of damages). Equally in *Wilander and Novacek v Tobin and Jude* (19 March 1996, unreported) (Lightman J), (8 April 1996, unreported), CA (Lightman J) [1997] 1 Lloyd's Law Rep 195; revsd [1997] 2 Lloyd's Law Rep 296, CA there was a series of interim applications and appeals, and the whole process took a year.

(d) Preliminary issues

A3.214 It may be possible to identify an issue or issues in a claim that if determined would effectively dispose of the whole case. In such circumstances, it may be possible to obtain an order from the court that these issues be dealt with in advance of the remainder of the claim. If these issues do not involve contested facts, this may speed up the process.

(e) CPR, Pt 8

A3.215 CPR, Pt 8 provides an 'alternative procedure for claims' which is most appropriate where there is unlikely to be a substantial dispute as to fact. The evidence is filed at the same time as the claim is issued and defence served. Since the relevant evidence is limited, it may be possible for the matter to come to hearing relatively quickly. It is particularly appropriate where an issue such as the interpretation of a contract or of rules is raised[1].

1 This approach was successfully adopted by a players' agent in *Roach v Football Federation*, see [2001] 9(3) SATLJ 26. The mechanism was used in order to determine as speedily as possible whether the FA, as opposed to FIFA, had jurisdiction to discipline him. The agent was licensed by FIFA, and there was a material difference in that body's rules to the rules under which the FA purported to discipline the agent. A buying club had discharged the player's obligation to pay his agent's fee on his behalf as part of the transfer deal. This practice was prevalent in the industry. Under the FIFA rules there was no case to answer because the relevant rule prohibited an agent acting for more than one party in a transfer, and the agent had not done so. Under the FA rules, an agent acting for a player was prohibited from receiving a payment from a buying club. The FA, on the basis of a strict interpretation of that rule, sought to discipline the agent, even though he had never been in any contractual relationship with the FA (as he was licensed by FIFA, not the FA) and even though the FA rules in question had not been in existence at the time of the relevant transfers. The agent commenced Pt 8 proceedings for a declaration that the FA had no jurisdiction to discipline him. Shortly afterwards the FA, after initially seeking to defend the claim, acceded to judgment together with costs. If an action had been commenced under the normal procedure, it is unlikely that it would have been brought to such a rapid conclusion.

(f) Speedy trial

A3.216 Where there is an obvious need for urgency, the court may be asked to order that there be a speedy trial[1]. In that case there will usually be directions for the exchange of evidence that take account of the date for which the trial is fixed. Other orders may be sought which may for example limit the issues on which evidence is required or limit the extent of the evidence needed on any issue. For example it may be helpful to consider and specifically limit the extent of disclosure of documents on any issue. In seeking a speedy trial the parties will want to have in mind that there is a 'trade-off' between the advantage of speed and the disadvantage of hurried preparation. Many judgments delivered following a speedy trial, while expressly commending the parties for the speed with which matters were brought together, note that unfortunately specific points were not fully dealt with in the evidence.

1 *Korda v ITF* Times 4 February 1999, [1999] All ER (D) 84, (25 March 1999, unreported), CA (An independent Appeals Committee convened under the terms of the ITF Anti-Doping Programme upheld the finding of an offence, but found that 'exceptional circumstances' existed – namely the player's lack of knowledge of how the substance got into his body – that warranted a waiver of any suspension. The ITF filed an appeal to the CAS against that decision. On an expedited trial, Lightman J granted the player a declaration that the ITF could not appeal its own decision to the CAS, but his decision was overturned by the Court of Appeal, also on an expedited basis, and the ITF was allowed to pursue its appeal to the CAS) (which was eventually successful as well – see paras E4.318 to E4.323). A speedy trial was also ordered in *Williams and Cardiff RFC v Pugh* (23 July 1997, unreported) (Popplewell J) at p 14–15 of the shorthand writers' transcript, although it did not take place because the governing bodies successfully applied for a stay (see paras A3.221 to A3.227). An order was also made for a speedy trial of the dispute between the Football League's and Granada and Carlton as to whether they had guaranteed the payment of rights fees promised by ITV Digital to the Football League in return for the broadcasting rights to League and Worthington Cup matches: *Carlton Communictions plc and Granada Media plc v Football League* (1 August 2002, unreported), [2002] All ER (D) 1 (Langley J). In *Gasser v Stinson* (15 June 1998, unreported) (Scott J) at p 2B of the shorthand writers' transcript, Scott J said that the procedure to produce a speedy trial adopted in that case had been the model of what was possible.

(g) Limiting evidence

A3.217 Other directions relating to evidence may be given in any case. For example it is possible to order that matters are dealt with on the basis of witness statements alone (analogous to CPR, Pt 8 proceedings or judicial review) where the parties or the court can be satisfied that those issues will not be dealt with any more clearly through cross-examination.

(h) Arbitration or alternative dispute resolution

A3.218 Although this chapter is concerned with challenges in the courts rather than alternative forms of dispute resolution, the two are not exclusive. The CPR includes specific provisions that encourage the use of mediation and other ADR techniques even during the course of litigation[1]. Furthermore, as described above, interim relief is available from arbitral bodies with jurisdiction over the substantive case, and arbitration may often prove quicker than the courts[2].

1 See Chapter A5.
2 See para A3.187.

B Stay in the light of an arbitration clause or internal proceedings

(a) Arbitration clause

A3.219 The most obvious method by which a sports governing body can seek to take a matter away from the courts is where there is a valid arbitration clause in an agreement between the challenger and the governing body. The same principles apply to the grant of such a stay in the sports context as in other contexts[1]. The courts will be slow to review the legality of the arbitration once it has happened[2].

1 See Mustill and Boyd *Commercial Arbitration* (2nd edn, 1989, Butterworths), ch 30 and 2001 Companion Volume in relation to the 1996 Arbitration Act at pp 268 to 273; Merkin *Arbitration Law* (LLP), ch 6. A stay was sought and obtained by the sports governing bodies in *Phoenix v Fédération Internationale de l'Automobile, Formula One Management and Formula One Administration* [2002] EWHC 1028 (Ch), (22 May 2002, unreported) (Morritt V-C), where Phoenix alleged that it had acquired from the liquidator the insolvent Prost team's right to entry to the 2002 Formula One Championship and entitlement to benefits under the Concorde Agreement between the teams, the FIA and FOM. Phoenix sought an interim injunction requiring FIA and FOM to allow it to compete. FIA and FOM sought in turn a stay of the English proceedings under s 9 of the Arbitration Act 1996, on the basis that the Concorde Agreement, under which Phoenix purported to claim as an assignee of Prost's rights, contained an arbitration clause. It was held that the action should be stayed. Whether to grant a stay was also in issue in *Walkinshaw v Diniz* [2000] 2 All ER (Comm) 237 (on the true construction of the Concorde Agreement and the Arrows contract, the reference of disputes to arbitration by the Board was limited to disputes concerning contracts between drivers and teams, which did not cover the issue on the proceedings, and so a stay was refused).

2 See *AEK Basketball v NBA and FIBA* (7 August 2001, unreported) (R Field QC) (AEK sought to establish that a player acquired by the Phoenix Suns was still under contract to AEK. Under the rules such issues were to be resolved by arbitration. AEK challenged the legality of the arbitration, but was held to have waived the ability to do so by participating in it), leave to appeal set aside CA (2002) Times, 13 June.

(b) Internal proceedings

A3.220 Whether the courts will intervene in internal proceedings, or suspend their own proceedings in the light of them, will turn on the individual facts of the case. The courts will be slow to stop on-going internal proceedings, in the absence of the claimant showing real prejudice[1]. This is because the sports governing body has a wider responsibility to all involved in the sport to enforce the rules as they are set down, and it is in the best position to enforce those rules[2].

1 *Modahl v BAF* (28 July 1997, unreported), CA per Morritt LJ at 39A–C. The claimant must take care to safeguard any points at the internal hearing that he may want to take later. If a point is available but is not taken, the claimant may have waived the right to take it. See n 4 to para A3.51.

2 In *Enderby Town Football Club v Football Association* [1971] Ch 591, [1971] 1 All ER 215, the claimant's application to the court for an injunction restraining the FA from hearing the club's own appeal to the FA from an FA Commission without the club being allowed legal representation was refused, as the rules did not provide for such representation and the claimant had chosen to take the route that it did. An injunction restraining anti-doping proceedings was also refused in *Wilander and Novacek v Tobin and Jude* (19 March 1996, unreported) (Lightman J), (8 April 1996, unreported), CA (Lightman J), [1997] 1 Lloyd's Law Rep 195; revsd [1997] 2 Lloyd's Law Rep 296, CA. In contrast in *Conteh v Onslow-Fane* (25 June 1975, unreported), CA, [1975] Times 26 June, the court was prepared to intervene where BBBC disciplinary proceedings were pending at the same time as an action in the courts for a declaration because in the 'special circumstances' of the case 'the interests of justice so demanded'. The special circumstances were that there was already pending High Court litigation on exactly the same issues and therefore the risk of real prejudice in the form of inconsistent decisions. In *Tom Walkinshaw Racing v RAC* (1985) Times, 12 October, an action was brought to restrain internal proceedings but then settled at trial on terms that the internal proceedings should go ahead. TWR lost the internal proceedings and costs were awarded against it. TWR returned to court to challenge the jurisdiction to award costs. The court held that costs could be awarded by the internal tribunal.

C Stay in the light of parallel regulatory competition proceedings

A3.221 A stay is not only available where there is an arbitration agreement. In addition in contexts where a complaint or notification has been (or is about to be) made to the administrative or regulatory authorities at the same time as an action in the English courts, an application may be made to stay the English proceedings. Furthermore, the decisions of regulatory bodies may have disposed of an issue. The effect of such parallel regulatory proceedings depends upon the stage reached. The discussion below relates principally to proceedings before the European Commission.

(a) *The jurisdiction of the English court where the European Commission is also, or may also become, involved*

A3.222 The jurisdiction of an English court to apply the EC competition rules effectively ceases if the European Commission has reached a formal decision in relation to the matter in question. If following notification the Commission has formally exempted an agreement under Art 81(3), or if it has made a formal decision rejecting a complaint and probably in effect if it has granted negative clearance (in other words a decision that the matter in question does not breach the competition rules in the first place), then the English court will not in practice go on to examine the matter[1]. If on the other hand the European Commission has not yet made a formal decision, then the English court technically still has jurisdiction even if the agreement or conduct has been notified and even if the Commission has initiated a procedure[2]. Three problems arise for the English courts however. First, since only the Commission can grant an individual exemption under Art 81(3), there is a risk of inconsistent decisions if the English court examines the matter by reference to Art 81(1) alone. Arguably there is also a risk of inconsistent decisions even if the question is likely to be confined to the applicability of the rules in the first place. Secondly, the English court is not in the same position as the Commission to know what approach is likely to be taken by the Commission. Thirdly, in the light of the weight of notifications and complaints made to the Commission, it often adopts the procedural expedient of not reaching a formal decision (or even initiating a procedure), by either issuing a non-binding 'comfort letter' stating that there does not appear to be a breach, or by not pursuing a complaint. In these circumstances the question arises whether an English court should proceed to examine the matter. In addition, the situation provides sports governing bodies that wish to block domestic court proceedings with a mechanism for doing so.

1 See Bellamy and Child *Common Market Law of Competition* (5th edn, 2001, Sweet & Maxwell), para 10-17. Where an exemption has been granted, there is formally no jurisdiction in the English court to proceed, because it must give effect to the active decision of the Commission: see *Whitbread plc v Falla* (16 November 2000, unreported). Where a complaint has been rejected by the Commission, and the complainant has participated in the procedure, it will not be allowed as a matter of English domestic law to reopen the issue before the English courts (although as a matter of EC law it may technically be possible): see Bellamy and Child *Common Market Law of Competition* (5th edn, 2001, Sweet & Maxwell), paras 10-024 and 10-027; *Coal Authority v HJ Banks* [1997] Eu LR 610, (31 July 1998, unreported), CA. The position remains less clear where the Commission has issued a negative clearance: see Bellamy and Child *Common Market Law of Competition* (5th edn, 2001, Sweet & Maxwell), para 10-024. While technically a negative clearance does not preclude litigation by a third party in the English courts, the practical reality is that a court is very unlikely to go behind a decision of the Commission without good grounds. The difference is that the third party may not have participated in the proceedings before the Commission. Plainly in each instance, the exemption or decision must be in relation to the same subject matter as the English proceedings. For completeness, where the EC Commission has decided that there *was* a breach of the competition rules, that is effectively binding before an English court on the party found to have acted in breach: see Bellamy and Child *Common Market Law of Competition* (5th edn, 2001, Sweet & Maxwell), paras 10-025 to 10-026.

2 See Bellamy and Child *Common Market Law of Competition* (5th edn, 2001, Sweet & Maxwell), para 10-006. Although the initiation of a procedure does not prevent the English courts examining the matters, it does prevent the national competition authorities, in this case the OFT, from doing so.

(b) *Stay of domestic proceedings where the matter is also, or may also be, pending before the Commission*

A3.223 The European Commission has produced a Notice on Co-operation between National courts and the Commission[1] to deal with the situation where a matter is pending before the Commission (or may become pending[2]) but is also the subject of action in the domestic courts. Broadly the position is that first, if the English court decides that the competition rules (either Arts 81 or 82) are clearly not engaged, and that there is no real risk that the Commission will reach a different conclusion, then the court can proceed to judgment. Secondly, if the court decides that there clearly is a breach of the competition rules (either Arts 81 or 82), which in the light of the practice of the Commission could not possibly benefit from individual exemption by the Commission under Art 81(3), then again the court can proceed to judgment. If however the English court is in any doubt either as to what view the Commission would take as to the application of Arts 81 or 82 in the first place, or as to the availability of individual exemption, the English court should consider staying the proceedings before it in order to avoid the possibility of inconsistent decisions. The English court could also grant interim relief if such a stay were granted. The decision whether or not to stay should be taken in the light of all the circumstances, including the availability of guidance from previously published decisions as to the Commission's likely approach to the particular issue, whether there has been a notification or complaint, the stage of the proceedings before the Commission and the nature of the relief sought.

1 See Bellamy and Child *Common Market Law of Competition* (5th edn, 2001, Sweet & Maxwell), para 10-014 et seq.

2 The jurisdiction to stay arises even if nothing is yet pending before the Commission: see *Williams and Cardiff RFC v WRU (IRB intervening)* [1999] Eu LR 195 at 199H to 200B. In that instance the rugby governing bodies informed the court that they would notify the matter.

A3.224 The English courts have granted a stay where the matters complained of in the action before it are already the subject of a complaint or notification[1], or may become so. In the context of sport the first use of the mechanism was by the Football Association to block an action by a corporate hospitality provider complaining about the anti-competitive way in which the FA granted hospitality rights for the Euro 96 football championship[2]. The FA amended its agreement with the successful provider, notified it to the Commission and applied successfully for a stay. Subsequently the WRU faced a challenge in English proceedings to the validity of its attempt to introduce a rule under which a club that wished to play in the WRU's competitions was obliged to agree to do so for a fixed period of time[3]. The WRU and the IRB (which intervened because the validity of its rules was also impugned) informed the court that they intended to notify their arrangements to the Commission and applied successfully for a stay. Eady J accepted the governing body's submission that the stay should extend not only to the EC competition law elements of the club's challenge, but also to the domestic competition law and restraint of trade arguments that the club ran, because the same issues would arise and there was an equal risk of an inconsistent decision as there would be if the English court looked at the EC competition law issues.

1 See Bellamy and Child *Common Market Law of Competition* (5th edn, 2001, Sweet & Maxwell), paras 10-019 to 10-020 for a detailed analysis of the English courts' approach. *MTV Europe v BMG Records* [1995] CMLR 437; affd [1997] 1 CMLR 867, [1997] Eu LR 100, CA (English proceedings by satellite TV company seeking damages for breach of Arts 81 and 82 stayed in the light of already pending complaint and a notification made after the proceedings were commenced.

The Commission had expressed a preliminary view that although Art 81 applied there were probably good grounds for an exemption. Evans-Lombe J, upheld later by the Court of Appeal, ordered that the action could proceed up until the date of setting down, but should then be stayed pending the Commission's decision). Cf *Iberian UK v BPB* [1996] 2 CMLR 601, [1997] Eu LR 1.

2 *Hospitality Group v FA* (24 January 1996, unreported) (Scott V-C). See para A3.168. The stay was complete pending the decision of the Commission and no interim relief was granted. Because the application was made six months before Euro 96 was due to begin, the stay was effective to block the utility of the English proceedings.

3 *Williams and Cardiff RFC v WRU (IRB intervening)* (17 March 1998, unreported) (Buckley J), [1999] Eu LR 195 (formerly known as *Williams and Cardiff RFC v Pugh* (23 July 1997, unreported) (Popplewell J), (1 August 1997, unreported), CA. Again, no interim relief was granted. As in the *Hospitality Group* case, the approach was extremely effective to block disruptive English proceedings taking an EC competition law point. In the event matters moved on faster than the Commission's procedures, and the WRU and its clubs re-ordered their arrangements: a process which is still continuing today.

(c) *Assistance from the Commission*

A3.225 Under the Notice on Co-Operation, the English court can seek assistance from the Commission. It can ask the Commission for details of the procedural status of proceedings before the Commission. It can ask for guidance on a point of law (without reference to the particular case). It can ask for general factual data, such as market data in relation to a particular sector. The Commission has now suggested that it will be willing to offer preliminary guidance on whether an individual exemption is a realistic possibility[2]. It is not entirely clear what status the answers to such requests have, but it is plain that the English court will take them into account and in all likelihood will afford them some considerable weight.

1 See Bellamy and Child *Common Market Law of Competition* (5th edn, 2001, Sweet & Maxwell), paras 10-021 to 10-022.

2 See Bellamy and Child *Common Market Law of Competition* (5th edn, 2001, Sweet & Maxwell) at para 10-021, n 85.

(d) *The status of Commission comfort letters*

A3.226 In the light of the weight of notifications and complaints made to the Commission, the Commission has announced in the Notice on Co-operation that it will confine itself to taking formal decisions on matters of particular importance[1]. Most matters are dealt with by either issuing a non-binding 'comfort letter' stating that there does not appear to be a breach, or by not pursuing a complaint. The English courts are not bound by a comfort letter, but they will take it into account in determining whether there has been a breach of the rules, and in all likelihood it will be an important factor. The absence of any action is however much less probative[2].

1 See Bellamy and Child *Common Market Law of Competition* (5th edn, 2001, Sweet & Maxwell), para 10-028.

2 See Bellamy and Child *Common Market Law of Competition* (5th edn, 2001, Sweet & Maxwell) at para 10-028, n 26.

(e) *The position under the Competition Act 1998*

A3.227 The position under the Competition Act 1998 is likely to mirror the position in relation to pending EC proceedings[1]. Under s 58 of the Competition Act 1998, a decision by the Director General of Fair Trading is binding as to the facts in subsequent private proceedings if it has not been appealed, 'unless the Court directs otherwise'[2]. Thus a prior OFT exemption, finding of infringement, or negative clearance is likely to be followed by the courts. As with EC Commission comfort letters, administrative letters from the OFT or other guidance would not be binding but would in all likelihood be followed[3]. Where proceedings are pending before the OFT but not yet determined, it is again likely that the court proceedings will be stayed[4].

1 See Coleman and Grenfell *The Competition Act 1998 Law and Practice* (1999, Oxford), 2002 Supplement at para 10.87. See generally paras 10.85 to 10.94.
2 There are a number of other exceptions in particular factual situations. See Coleman and Grenfell *The Competition Act 1998 Law and Practice* (1999, Oxford) at para 10.90(i) to (iii).
3 See Coleman and Grenfell *The Competition Act 1998 Law and Practice* (1999, Oxford) at para 10.90(iv) and (v).
4 See Coleman and Grenfell *The Competition Act 1998 Law and Practice* (1999, Oxford) at para 10.91; *Synstar Computer Services v ICL* [2002] ICR 112 (Lightman J.).

D Article 234 reference to the European Court of Justice

A3.228 Courts will refer to the European Court of Justice broadly any question of EC law which they do not feel confident of dealing with themselves and which is necessary to their decision. It is possible that such questions will arise in the course of challenges to the legitimacy of a sports governing body's actions. It is generally more likely that such issues would arise in the context of the free movement rules[1] than in the context of the competition rules[2]. Liability under the competition rules generally turns on the facts rather than on questions of legal principle so complex that an English court would regard it as necessary to seek the assistance of the European Court of Justice. The EC rules on intellectual property in the sports context have been the subject of references[3].

1 In the context of English proceedings, as in *Bacardi-Martini SAS and Cellier des Dauphins v Newcastle United FC* [2001] Eu LR 45 (Gray J 26 July 2000). Newcastle had removed Bacardi's advertising for a game against a French side, because the French broadcasters took the position that they would not be able to broadcast into France if alcohol advertising was present in the stadium. Bacardi alleged that in so doing, Newcastle had induced the marketing company, with which Bacardi had a contract for the advertising, to breach that contract. Newcastle sought to justify that inducement by reference to the need to comply with the Loi Evin. Bacardi responded that the Loi Evin could not justify anything because it was incompatible with the EC free movement rules. The validity of the Loi Evin was regarded as critical to the outcome of the proceedings, even if not necessarily determinative. The reference was made before trial. Much of the reason for the court's approach appears to have been that it was not felt appropriate that an English court should consider the validity of a French law when the European Court of Justice was available to do this instead.
2 Although this is plainly possible (the Belgian court made a reference in *Tibor Balog v Royal Charleroi* C–264/98, Advocate General's opinion of 29 March 2001). It is to be noted that there could even be a reference under Art 234 by an English court considering whether there was a breach of the Chapter I or Chapter II prohibitions in the Competition Act 1998, since those prohibitions are based on and must be interpreted in the light of Arts 81 and 82. See Coleman and Grenfell *The Competition Act 1998 Law and Practice* (1999, Oxford), para 10.94.
3 *British Horseracing Board v William Hill* [2001] RPC 612 (Laddie J, 9 February 2001), [2001] EWCA Civ 1268, [2001] All ER (D) 431 (Jul). See [2001] 9(3) SATLJ 85; *Arsenal Football Club v Reed* [2001] RPC 46 (Laddie J, 6 April 2001), AG's opinion dated 13 June 2002, Case C–206/01.

E Jurisdiction and applicable law

A3.229 As in any other context involving contracts between parties based in different jurisdictions and subject to different legal systems, issues can arise as to which courts have jurisdiction to hear a particular matter, and as to which law should be applied. As sport becomes increasingly better organised, the role of international federations and associations is becoming pivotal. Again, as is the case in respect of the other procedural aspects addressed above, the general principles governing jurisdiction and applicable law in the sports context are the same as in other contexts, and they are not dealt with in detail here[1].

1 See Dicey and Morris *Conflict of Laws* (13th edn, 1999, Sweet & Maxwell).

(a) Avoiding the jurisdiction and English law

A3.230 International federations and associations have on occasion attempted to avoid the jurisdiction of the English courts and the application of English law. The IAAF is a good example of this approach[1]. In *Reel v Holder*[2], proceedings could be brought in England because the defendants actually sued were IAAF officers based in England. The court applied English law to the construction of the IAAF rules. Lord Denning MR's basis[3] for assuming jurisdiction and applying English law was that:

> We are simply concerned with the interpretation of the rules of the federation. The rules are in English. The head office of the federation is in England. It is right that, if the rules need to be construed, the matter should come to the English Courts to be decided.

In *Gasser v Stinson*[4] the IAAF was again sued through its officers present in the jurisdiction. English law was held to apply, chiefly on the basis that the organisation was based in England. The IAAF did not dispute that English law applied to the construction of the rules. The IAAF did however contend that English public policy rules such as the doctrine of restraint of trade could not apply to the IAAF because it was an association of foreign sports governing bodies. Scott J rejected this contention on the basis that English restraint of trade principles had been applied in *Greig v Insole* to the rules of the ICC, and that in order to prevent the IAAF escaping the rule of law, the full force of English law should apply to it. The IAAF subsequently moved to Monaco and took on Monegasque personality. The IAAF opens all litigation with which it is involved in England with a challenge to the jurisdiction, or at least with a reservation as to its ability to challenge the jurisdiction. However a substantial problem that it faces in this approach is that the IAAF is often joined as a second defendant after the English governing body. If the English governing body is properly sued in this country, the international governing body will have difficulty in showing that it is not properly joined as a co-defendant. In *Edwards v BAF and IAAF*[5], the IAAF reserved its position and fought the case on the merits. In *Walker v UKA and IAAF*[6] the IAAF sought to challenge the jurisdiction, but that challenge failed before Toulson J on 3 July 2000 on the basis inter alia that UKA had been validly sued and the IAAF was a proper party to be joined. Further in that case, the IAAF's case was that it was entitled to take proceedings against the national governing body in respect of the governing body's acquittal of an athlete under its jurisdiction. In the United States, in *Reynolds v IAAF*[7], the IAAF maintained throughout protracted litigation that the US courts did not have jurisdiction over it. The IAAF was ultimately successful on the issue before the Federal Court of Appeal. Before the CAS, the IAAF was less successful in disputing the jurisdiction in *Baumann*[8], a case at the Olympic Games, and the IAAF has since decided to provide for CAS jurisdiction in all its cases[9].

1 See also *Tyrrell Racing Organisation v RAC Motor Sports Association and the Fédération Internationale de l' Automobile* (20 July 1984, unreported) (Hirst J) at p 10 of Lexis transcript. The FIA argued that the English court ought not to exercise jurisdiction to review an international governing body's decision. The FIA relied (see p 9 of the Lexis transcript) on *Fitipaldi Automotive Ltd v FISA* unreported Lloyd J in 1980, in which leave to serve process on FISA (FIA's former name) outside of the jurisdiction was refused. Hirst J held that the RAC had been properly served and the FIA had been joined as a proper party, and distinguished the *Fitipaldi* decision which had been an action by constructors against FISA, and which had not involved the RAC. In *Phoenix v FIA and FOM* [2002] EWHC 1028 (Ch), (22 May 2002, unreported) (Morritt V-C), FIA initially challenged the jurisdiction on the grounds that it ought to have been sued in France where it was based, but then withdrew the application and concentrated on the application for a stay on the basis that Phoenix's claim was subject to an arbitration clause.

2 *Reel v Holder (for IAAF)* [1979] 1 WLR 1252; affd [1981] 1 WLR 1226, CA (the Taiwanese athletics governing body obtained a declaration that the IAAF was not entitled to expel it from membership).

3 At p 1230. The assumption of jurisdiction on this basis in *Reel v Holder* was followed in *Cowley v Heatley* (22 July 1986, unreported) (Browne-Wilkinson V-C), (1986) Times, 24 July at p 4 of the lexis transcript; see also para A3.98, n 2.

4 (15 June 1988, unreported) (Scott J). For a similar absence of any reluctance to apply the English restraint of trade rules to international bodies to that exhibited in *Gasser v Stinson* and *Greig v Insole* ([1978] 1 WLR 302), see *Cooke v Football Association* [1972] CLY 516 where the court applied the doctrine to the FIFA rules.

5 *Edwards v BAF and IAAF* [1998] 2 CMLR 363, [1997] Eu LR 721 (Lightman J rejected the shotputter's contention that the BAF and the IAAF doping rules discriminated against him on grounds of nationality contrary to the free movement rules because the ban for a first offence was a fixed period, or the maximum permissible under local law).

6 *Walker v UKA and IAAF* (3 July 2000, unreported) (Toulson J), (25 July 2000, unreported) (Hallett J), IAAF Arbitral Award 20 August 2000 reported at [2001] 4 ISLR 264, see also [2000] 2 ISLR 41 and paras A3.10, n 7and A3.124.

7 935 F 2d 270 (1991); on appeal 968 F 2d 1216; 112 S.Ct 2512 (1992); on appeal 23 F 3d 1110; 115 S.Ct 423 (1994).

8 In *Baumann* CAS Sydney 00/006, *Digest of CAS Awards II 1998–2000* (Kluwer 2002), p 633, the German national governing body acquitted the athlete on a drugs charge. The IOC consequently accredited the athlete for the Olympics. The IAAF took the decision of the national governing body to the then IAAF Arbitral Panel. A two year suspension was imposed. The IOC removed the accreditation. Baumann appealed to the CAS. The IAAF disputed the CAS's jurisdiction on the basis that there was no submission of IAAF decisions to CAS arbitration. The CAS rejected this argument holding both the IOC and the IAAF to be bound by its ad hoc jurisdiction at the Olympics.

9 Reeb [2001] 4 ISLR 246.

A3.231 Equally, however, in an appropriate case, such as where the rules expressly provide for the courts of another country to have jurisdiction, the English courts are likely to decline jurisdiction. In *Lennox Lewis v World Boxing Council and Frank Bruno*[1], permission to serve out on the World Boxing Council (based in Mexico) was originally given on the basis that it was a necessary and proper party to the action brought by Lewis against Bruno to restrain him from accepting a challenge from Tyson in place of Lewis. Rattee J however concluded that the substance of the action was against the WBC, and that Bruno had only been joined in order to form a basis for the action against the WBC in England[2]. Rattee J enforced an exclusive jurisdiction clause in the WBC Rules in favour of Texas. It should however be remembered that even where the courts may not have jurisdiction over the substantive matter, in some circumstances they can grant interim relief[3].

1 (3 November 1995, unreported) (Rattee J).

2 Cf *MacDonald v FIFA and SFA* (1998) Outer House Cases, McEwan QC, 2 December 1988 [1999] SCLR 59, where it was held that dismissal of the action against the defendant domiciled in the jurisdiction did not remove jurisdiction against the remaining defendant domiciled in Switzerland.

3 In *SPI v National Football Museum and FIFA* (9 January 1998, unreported) (Lloyd J), it was noted that even though the court did not have jurisdiction to grant substantive relief against FIFA in the light of pending proceedings in Switzerland, interim relief could be granted under s 25 of the Civil Jurisdiction and Judgments Act 1982.

(b) Applicable law

A3.232 As the involvement of international organisations becomes increasingly important, so too does the question of which law applies to challenges against their actions and rules. Again the normal principles apply[1]. Where a governing body is made up of national governing bodies from around the world, it may be difficult in the absence of an express choice of law clause in the relevant rules to ascertain which law applies, and it appears that recourse can only be had to where the body is based[2]. As a result, the majority of international governing bodies specify the law that governs their rules. As set out above[3], the international nature of such bodies also raises the issue, addressed in *Gasser v Stinson*, of whether some of the specific public policy doctrines of a particular legal system should also be applied to such bodies. In the English courts, the answer appears to be that they should. A second, related issue arising out of the international nature of such governing bodies is the willingness of international arbitral bodies such as the CAS to apply 'general principles of law' which draw on the legal systems of all nations[4]. It may be that English courts will in the future have to consider whether such principles should be applied by them; the principles are already applied by the European Court of Justice. These general principles already largely find expression in English public law principles[5]. Further, the international nature of these governing bodies may affect the approach taken by the court to the construction of the rules. In *Cowley v Heatley*[6], the court concluded that because the federation was made up of associations from so many different countries, it would be wrong to apply a particular legalistic meaning from one particular legal system to a word in the rules, and that instead a normal everyday meaning should be attributed. As a result, the word 'domicile' was construed according to its ordinary non-technical meaning, and not in accordance with the precise legal meaning that the word bore under English law[7].

1 See Dicey and Morris *Conflict of Laws* (13th edn, 1999, Sweet & Maxwell).

2 See para A3.230; *Reel v Holder (for IAAF)* [1979] 1 WLR 1252; affd [1981] 1 WLR 1226, CA; *Cowley v Heatley* (22 July 1986, unreported) (Browne-Wilkinson V-C), (1986) Times, 24 July; *Gasser v Stinson* unreported, Scott J 15 June 1988, at p 3B of the shorthand writers' transcript. In addition, as set out at para A3.230, there may be particular rules of a particular system (such as the English restraint of trade doctrine) which it would arguably not be appropriate to extend to international governing bodies.

3 See para A3.230.

4 See *AEK Athens and Slavia Prague v UEFA* CAS 98/2000, interim decision 17 July 1998, final decision 20 August 1999 at paras 155–158, reported in Reeb, *Digest of CAS Awards II 1998–2000*, p 38 and in [2001] 1 ISLR 122. These general principles in the context of sports law have been referred to by a number of Latin tags such as the lex sportiva and the lex ludica. They are of particular importance in the context of doping disputes: see paras E4.77 to E4.88.

5 The general principles are discussed at para E4.81. They include the principles of: (a) Legality: rules must be construed and applied consistently with their own terms and on the basis that there can be no sanction without a law or rule providing for it; (b) Legal certainty and retrospective application: the rules and how they can be applied must be clear and capable of being predicted at the time of the events in question. In general, rules cannot be construed as allowing retrospective application, or be applied retrospectively; (c) Legitimate expectation and acquisition of rights: rules must be construed and applied in a way which respects the legitimate expectations and acquired rights of those affected; (d) Good faith: rules must be construed and applied openly and honestly, and not in bad faith, arbitrarily or capriciously; (e) Fairness: the sports governing body must act in a procedurally fair manner; (f) Non-discrimination: like situations must be treated alike and different

situations differently; (g) Proportionality: rules must be construed and applied in a way which goes no further than is reasonably necessary to pursue a legitimate aim. The benefit supposedly achieved by an approach must not be out of proportion to the detriment suffered by the applicant; (h) Fundamental rights: rules must be construed and applied in accordance with the fundamental rights protected under the European Convention on Human Rights; (i) Construction: rules must be purposively construed, in favour of the athlete or club and against the body imposing the rules (the contra proferentem principle); where they give rise to penal sanctions, rules must be construed narrowly, in the sense that a sanction can only be imposed which is clearly provided for by the provision. They must be construed consistently so that force is given (if possible) to each provision in the material part of the code, and no such provision is rendered useless.

6 (22 July 1986, unreported) (Browne-Wilkinson V-C), (1986) Times, 24 July.

7 At pp 4–5 of the Lexis transcript.

11 CONCLUSIONS

A3.233 The law applicable to challenges to a sports governing body's actions is developing along with the increasing commercialisation of sport. That development has not yet reached the stage where a single method of challenging a sports governing body's actions, such as judicial review or automatic arbitration, applies.

A3.234 Instead, the practitioner has to choose the appropriate procedural route for challenge in the particular circumstances of the case. It might be appropriate to pursue an internal dispute resolution process. It might be appropriate to go to arbitration. It might be appropriate to complain to the administrative authorities. It might be appropriate to go to the English courts.

A3.235 A sports governing body's actions have to be challenged by reference to private law rights. The most commonly used bases are breach of the general obligations owed by sports governing bodies irrespective of any other cause of action, breach of contract, tort, restraint of trade, breach of EC or domestic competition law, and breach of the EC free movement rules.

A3.236 Whichever of these routes and bases for challenge is chosen, however, the conceptual analysis is likely always to be based on two fundamental factors. First, the reviewing authority will be slow to step into a role that is best carried out by the sports governing body. Whether this principle is couched in terms of the standard of review, or in terms of whether the rule is necessary for the underlying sport, or in terms of the margin of appreciation, the basic approach is essentially the same. Secondly, a reviewing authority will be unlikely to overturn a sports governing body's actions that pursue a legitimate aim proportionately.

CHAPTER A4

THE HUMAN RIGHTS ACT 1998 AND SPORT

David Pannick QC (Blackstone Chambers) and **Jane Mulcahy** (Blackstone Chambers)

Contents

1 INTRODUCTION

A4.1 This chapter considers the possible effect of the Human Rights Act 1998 ('HRA 1998') in the context of sport[1]. It is very likely that the HRA 1998, which came into force on 2 October 2000, will provide a new route[2] by which to challenge the actions of sporting bodies[3]. This clearly has ramifications both for the bodies themselves and for those seeking to mount such challenges.

1 In attempting this exercise in a specialist work such as this, it is impossible to give an in-depth account of the HRA 1998 and the European Convention on Human Rights. There are, however, many works entirely devoted to human rights which do so, for example Lester & Pannick *Human Rights Law and Practice* (1999, Butterworths); Clayton & Tomlinson *The Law of Human Rights* (2000, Oxford); Grosz et al *Human Rights: The 1998 Act and the Convention* (2000, Sweet & Maxwell); Simor & Emmerson *Human Rights Practice* (2001, Sweet & Maxwell).

2 In order to mount a human rights challenge under para 7(1) of the HRA 1998 (see para A4.74): (i) the person bringing the challenge must be a victim (see para A4.75); (ii) the body under challenge must be a public authority for the purposes of s 6 (paras A4.14 to A4.31) and the action being challenged must arguably be incompatible with a Convention right (see paras A4.32 to A4.73). In the case of Arts 8 to 11 of the Convention (see paras A4.57 to A4.69) this means that, arguably, not only is there an infringement with the right in question, but also such infringement cannot be justified under the express exceptions listed in the Articles (para A4.61). A claim must be brought before the end of one year beginning with the date on which the act complained of took place (see para A4.77). Most of those mounting a human rights challenge will no doubt be seeking damages (see para A4.79). But in many cases, where the interpretation of legislation is involved, the primary remedy is a declaration of incompatibility under s 4 (para A4.013). It is to be noted that such declarations leave the individual complainant without any other remedy if the public authority in question could not have acted differently, since in such circumstances the authority acted lawfully (s 6(2) of the HRA 1998).

3 The phrase 'sporting bodies' is used throughout this chapter, but refers in the main to sports governing bodies. In relation to other organisations, such as event organisers, promoters and agencies, and professional teams, it is very unlikely that they would be considered to be public authorities susceptible to a human rights challenge.

A The Human Rights Act 1998

A4.2 The HRA 1998 ensures that the rights protected by the European Convention on Human Rights ('the Convention') are enforced in the English courts to a far greater extent than previously[1]. The long title of the HRA 1998 states that it is designed 'to give further effect to rights and freedoms guaranteed under the [Convention]'[2]. Prior to the coming into force of the HRA 1998, the Convention – as an international treaty – had only a limited effect in domestic law[3].

1 See paras A3.66 to A3.68.
2 The Lord Chancellor, Lord Irvine of Lairg, explained during the committee stage of the Bill in the House of Lords (see 583 HL Official Report (5th series) col 478 (18 November 1997)) that 'the reason the long title uses the word 'further' is that our courts already apply the Convention in many different circumstances'. This is a reference to the Convention being considered in specific circumstances *prior* to the coming into force of the HRA 1998, for example, as an aid to the construction of legislation in cases of ambiguity: *R v Secretary of State for the Home Department, ex p Brind* [1991] 1 AC 696 at 760. Clearly, such prior usage throws no light on the provisions of the HRA 1998 itself, for example, whether it applies to sporting bodies (see paras A4.14 to A4.31).
3 See para A4.6.

A4.3 The HRA 1998 aims to 'bring rights home'[1] by imposing various duties on the courts:

(i) so far as it is possible to do so, primary and subordinate legislation must be read and given effect in a way compatible with Convention rights[2];
(ii) where not possible to read legislation compatibly, the court may make a declaration of incompatibility[3]; and
(iii) 'public authorities' within the meaning of the HRA 1998, which includes courts and tribunals, must not act in a way which is incompatible with Convention rights[4].

1 *Rights brought home: the Human Rights Bill* (Cm 3782).
2 Section 3 of the HRA 1998. See also paras A4.11 to A4.012. Subordinate legislation will be struck down if incompatible with the HRA 1998 unless the interference with Convention rights is required by the relevant primary legislation: s 3(2)(c).
3 Section 4 of the HRA 1998. See also para A4.13.
4 Section 6 of the HRA 1998. See also para A4.14 to A4.15.

A4.4 The HRA 1998 thereby gives considerable further effect to the Convention in domestic law, while at the same time maintaining Parliamentary sovereignty. This means the HRA 1998 is no ordinary law. Rather it is a legally enforceable charter of human rights and freedoms.

B The European Convention on Human Rights

A4.5 International human rights law developed in the aftermath of the Second World War[1]. The United Nations Charter was signed on 26 June 1945 and resulted in the establishment of a Commission on Human Rights. The Commission took responsibility for drafting the Universal Declaration of Human Rights, adopted by the 48 members of the General Assembly on 10 December 1948. Subsequently the Council of Europe began to frame a human rights charter for Europe, based on the Declaration. This resulted in the Convention, which was opened for signature in November 1950. The United Kingdom was the first state to ratify the Convention.

1 Clayton & Tomlinson *The Law of Human Rights* (2000, Oxford), p 3.

A4.6 Prior to the coming into the force of the HRA 1998, the Convention had a limited, although important, effect in English law[1]:

(1) courts were required to interpret ambiguous legislation consistently with the Convention;
(2) the Convention informed the application of the common law where it was uncertain, unclear or incomplete;
(3) judicial discretion was exercised consistently with the Convention, where relevant;
(4) the human rights context was relevant to whether a Minister or other public authority had acted reasonably (although there was no duty to exercise powers consistently with the Convention); and
(5) where a dispute concerned directly effective EC law, the courts took account of the Convention because EC law includes the principles recognised by the Convention.

The Articles of the Convention now have a much greater impact by virtue of the HRA 1998[2].

1 Lester & Pannick *Human Rights Law and Practice* (1999, Butterworths), para 2.03. The general principle of United Kingdom law is that 'a treaty is not part of [domestic] law unless and until it has been incorporated into the law by legislation': *J H Rayner (Mincing Lane) Ltd v Department of Trade and Industry* [1990] 2 AC 418 at 500C per Lord Oliver of Aylmerton.
2 See para A4.3.

C Possible impact on sporting bodies

A4.7 Historically, sporting bodies[1] have not been subject to public law challenges[2]. The HRA 1998 is likely to alter this position since it provides for human rights challenges against 'public authorities'[3]. The prevailing opinion – with which the authors agree – is that the majority of sporting bodies will satisfy this criterion, at least in relation to some of their functions[4].

1 See para A4.1, n 3.
2 See paras A3.60 to A3.63, and at paras A4.19 to A4.21. This is because they were seen as creations of private law with their authority dependent on contract rather than the state.
3 See s 6(1) of the HRA 1998, and paras A4.14 to A4.31. Although sporting bodies have traditionally been protected from challenge in judicial review proceedings, they are likely to be susceptible to a human rights claim by virtue of the wide definition of 'public authority' in the HRA 1998. Further, once found to be amenable to human rights challenges, it will be more difficult for sporting bodies to continue to fend off judicial review: why should they be a public body for one purpose but not for the other?
4 Anderson, Mulcahy and Reindorf 'Independent and impartial? The potential impact of the Human Rights Act 1998 on sports tribunals' [2000] 2 ISLR 65; Boyes 'Regulating Sport after the Human Rights Act 1998' (2001) 151 NLJ 444; Boyes 'The regulation of sport and the impact of the Human Rights Act 1998' [2000] 6(4) EPL 517; Vleck 'The Human Rights Act – The Impact on Sports Governing Bodies' [2000] 8(3) SATLJ 71; Bitel 'Human Rights Act' [2000] 8(3) SATLJ 72; Lloyd 'Sports Disciplinary Proceedings and the Human Rights Act' [2000] 8(2) SATLJ 61; Bray *Legal Week*, 2 November 2000, p 32; Haines (2000) Sol Jo 1054. For the Articles of the Convention most relevant to sport, see para A4.33 and onwards.

2 THE HRA 1998

A4.8 The HRA 1998 was given royal assent on 9 November 1998, but most of its important provisions came into force on 2 October 2000. The Convention rights which apply by virtue of the HRA 1998 are set out at Sch 1.

A The Convention rights (section 1)

A4.9 Section 1 specifies which Convention rights are to be given effect in domestic law by virtue of the HRA 1998[1]. The rights do not include Art 1 of the Convention, which provides that the contracting states 'shall secure to everyone within their jurisdiction' the rights and freedoms guaranteed under the Convention. This is because the HRA 1998 itself gives effect to those rights and freedoms[2]. Nor does the HRA 1998 include Art 13 of the Convention, which requires an 'effective remedy before a national authority'. Again, this is because the HRA 1998 itself establishes a scheme under which Convention rights can be relied upon before the domestic courts[3].

1 Section 1:
'(1) In this Act 'the Convention rights' means the rights and fundamental freedoms set out in–
(a) Arts 2 to 12 and 14 of the Convention,
(b) Arts 1 to 3 of the First Protocol,
(c) Arts 1 and 2 of the Sixth Protocol, as read with Arts 16 to 18 of the Convention … '.
The Articles are considered in detail at paras A4.34 to A4.73.

2 Lester & Pannick *Human Rights Law and Practice* (1999, Butterworths), para 2.1.2.

3 See n 2.

B Interpretation of Convention rights (section 2)

A4.10 Section 2 requires United Kingdom courts and tribunals to 'take into account' relevant jurisprudence of the Convention institutions when determining a question that has arisen in connection with a Convention right[1]. This obligation is an important one[2], although the jurisprudence is not binding[3].

1 Section 2 states:
'(1) A court or tribunal determining a question which has arisen in connection with a Convention right must take into account any–
(a) judgment, decision, declaration or advisory opinion of the European Court of Human Rights,
(b) opinion of the Commission given in a report adopted under Art 31 of the Convention,
(c) decision of the Commission in connection with Art 26 or 27(2) of the Convention [decisions on the admissibility of complaints], or
(d) decision of the Committee of Ministers taken under Art 46 of the Convention, whenever made or given, so far as, in the opinion of the court or tribunal, it is relevant to the proceedings in which that question has arisen.'

2 'In the absence of some special circumstances … the Court should follow any clear and constant jurisprudence of the European Court of Human Rights': *R (Alconbury) v Secretary of State for the Environment, Transport and the Regions* [2001] UKHL 23, [2001] 2 WLR 1389 per Lord Slynn at para 26, 1399C. In the light of this courts are expected to follow Strasbourg decisions whenever possible.

3 Lord Irvine of Lairg, committee stage in the House of Lords, 583 HL Official Report (5th series), cols 514–515 (18 November 1997).

C Interpretation of legislation (section 3)

A4.11 Section 3 requires courts and tribunals to interpret and apply primary and subordinate legislation consistently with Convention rights, so far as possible[1]. All courts and tribunals are required to interpret and apply legislation in this way where it is relevant to any case before them, whether or not a public authority is a party to the proceedings[2].

1 Section 3 states:
'(1) So far as it is possible to do so, primary legislation and subordinate legislation must be read and given effect in a way which is compatible with the Convention rights.
(2) This section–
(a) applies to primary legislation and subordinate legislation whenever enacted; ...'

2 Lester & Pannick *Human Rights Law and Practice* (1999, Butterworths), para 2.3.1.

A4.12 The interpretative obligation is a strong one[1]. If necessary courts must read down provisions that would otherwise breach Convention rights, limiting their scope, or read in necessary safeguards to protect those rights[2]. The court's role is to find the meaning which best accords with the Convention[3].

1 'This [obligation] goes far beyond the present rule which enables the courts to take the Convention into account in resolving any ambiguity in a legislative provision. The courts will be required to interpret legislation so as to uphold the Convention rights unless the legislation itself is so clearly incompatible with the Convention that it is impossible to do so': Rights Brought Home (Cm 3782, 1997), para 2.7.

2 'In accordance with the will of Parliament as reflected in section 3 it will sometimes be necessary to adopt an interpretation which linguistically may appear strained. The techniques to be used will not only involve the reading down of express language in a statute but also the implication of provisions. A declaration of incompatibility is a measure of last resort. It must be avoided unless it is plainly impossible to do so': *R v A (No 2)* [2001] UKHL 25, [2001] 2 WLR 1546 per Lord Steyn at para 45.

3 Lester & Pannick *Human Rights Law and Practice* (1999, Butterworths), para 2.3.2.

D Compatibility and incompatibility (section 4)

A4.13 Section 4 comes into play only if it is impossible to read and give effect to primary legislation in a manner compatible with the Convention, and any provision of subordinate legislation cannot be 'cured' because of the terms of the relevant primary legislation[1]. Under s 4, courts may make a 'declaration of incompatibility' to draw the perceived flaw in the legislation to the attention of the Government and Parliament[2]. Section 4 also specifies which courts have the power to make declarations[3], and indicates the effect of such declarations[4]. Declarations of incompatibility have already been made in various cases[5].

1 See paras A4.11 to A4.12.

2 Section 4 states: '... (2) If the court is satisfied that the provision is incompatible with a Convention right, it may make a declaration of that incompatibility ...'

3 Section 4(5). The courts are the House of Lords, Judicial Committee of the Privy Council, the Courts-Martial Appeal Court, the High Court of Judiciary in Scotland (sitting otherwise than as a trial court of Court of Session), the High Court and Court of Appeal (in England and Wales, or Northern Ireland).

4 Section 4(6). A declaration of incompatibility does not affect the validity, continuing operation or enforcement of the provision in respect of which it is given, and is not binding on the parties to the proceedings in which it is made. The legislation will therefore continue to have force and effect until such time as it is amended. (Section 10 of the HRA 1998 deals with the power to take remedial action.)

5 For example, *Alconbury* at first instance, although overturned on appeal to the House of Lords, *R (Alconbury) v Secretary of State for the Environment, Transport and the Regions* [2001] UKHL 23, [2001] 2 WLR 1389; *Wilson v First County Trust (No 2)* [2001] EWCA Civ 633, [2002] QB 74; *International Transport Roth GmbH v Secretary of State for the Home Department* [2002] EWCA Civ 158, [2002] 3 WLR 344 (Sullivan J); *Matthews v Ministry of Defence* [2002] EWHC 13 (QB), subsequently overturned by the Court of Appeal.

E What is a 'public authority' (section 6)

A4.14 This section is of central importance for sporting bodies[1]. If they are covered by s 6 (in any of the ways mentioned at para A4.17) then the HRA 1998 and Convention rights apply to them and their actions and decisions are open to challenge on human rights grounds[2]. If not, then potential litigants are constrained to use traditional routes[3].

1 See para A4.1, n 3. Section 6 states:
'(1) It is unlawful for a public authority to act in a way which is incompatible with a Convention right …
(3) In this section 'public authority' includes–
(a) a court or tribunal, and
(b) any person certain of whose functions are functions of a public nature …'
2 See para A4.7.
3 See Chapter A3.

A4.15 Both the Jockey Club[1] and the Football Association[2] apparently expect that they will fall within the 'public authority' definition, since they have changed their disciplinary systems to satisfy Convention rights. UK Sport has suggested that sporting organisations amend their procedures to comply with Convention rights on the basis that they may be considered to be public authorities[3]. We consider this is a sensible approach.

1 During the committee stage of the Bill, on 20 May 1998, the Home Secretary, Jack Straw MP, stated that the Jockey Club carries out public functions and so would fall within s 6 in relation to those functions (312 HC Official Report (6th series) col 1018). As a result, the Jockey Club has reformed its disciplinary procedures, adding a new independent appeal board: (2001) Daily Telegraph, 20 February, p 43. This is good evidence that sporting bodies will be covered by the HRA 1998, although the courts have not necessarily followed the wider approach advocated by the Government during the stages of the Bill when deciding what constitutes a public authority (see para A4.26).
2 Michael Gerrard 'Life is sweet at the FA' *Legal Week* (2 November 2000), p 29.
3 UK Sport *Human Rights Act – Implications for Sport* v3 14/12/2000. A separate UK Sport publication also considered the implications of the HRA 1998 for anti-doping procedures. UK Sport *Human Rights Act – Implications on Anti-Doping* v3 14/12/2000.

(a) The 'definition' in the HRA 1998

A4.16 The HRA 1998 states that 'public authority' includes a court or tribunal and any person 'certain of whose functions are functions of a public nature'[1]. Beyond this it does not define 'public authority'; however the concept is intended to be a broad one[2].

1 See n 1 to para A4.14. See also Lester & Pannick *Human Rights Law and Practice* (1999, Butterworths), para 2.6.3 for a detailed consideration of the definition.
2 The principle is deliberately broad 'because we want to provide as much protection as possible for the rights of individuals against the misuse of power by the state …': Lord Irvine of Lairg (583 HL Official Report (5th series) col 808, 24 November 1997). 'State' is referred to in the widest sense, hence Jack Straw's comment about the Jockey Club (para A4.15). Definite contenders are central government (including executive agencies), local government, the police, immigration officers, prisons, courts and tribunals, and, to the extent that they are exercising public functions, companies responsible for areas of activity previously within the public sector, such as the privatised utilities: *Rights Brought Home* (Cm 3782), para 2.2.

A4.17 Because of the way the HRA 1998 is drafted, there are effectively three reasons why a sporting body may have to take account of Convention rights. First, it may be a 'public authority' as broadly defined and carry out functions of a public nature. Secondly, an aspect of its disciplinary procedure may constitute a 'tribunal' for the purposes of s 6. Or, thirdly, the court as a public authority hearing a case involving a sporting body may have to take account of certain Convention rights even between private parties. In any of these circumstances, the Articles of the Convention come into play.

(b) Functions of a public nature

A4.18 The government indicated, during debates on the Bill, that in deciding whether an organisation was carrying out functions of a public nature, the courts should look to two separate sources: domestic judicial review and the Strasbourg jurisprudence. The Home Secretary envisaged that the courts would use domestic judicial review jurisprudence as a starting point in coming to a flexible and dynamic definition of what constitutes a 'public authority'[1]. He also stressed that the category of bodies susceptible to challenge must not be narrower than that envisaged by Strasbourg. This would ensure that the purpose of 'bringing rights home' was achieved[2].

1 'The most valuable asset that we have to hand' was jurisprudence relating to judicial review: 314 HC Official Report (6th series) col 409.

2 'The principle of bringing rights home suggested that liability in domestic proceedings should lie with bodies in respect of whose actions the United Kingdom Government were answerable in Strasbourg. The idea was that if someone could get a remedy in Strasbourg, he or she should be able to get a remedy at home. That point was crucial to the Bill's construction': 314 HC Official Report (6th series) cols 406, 432–433 (17 June 1998).

A4.19 Judicial review and sporting bodies Judicial review jurisprudence is an obvious source for a definition of what is a 'public authority' since, like the Convention, it deals exclusively with the effect on individuals of the abuse and misuse of power by the state. Clearly sporting bodies[1] do not fall into the category of the 'state' as narrowly defined (for example, central government or the police). They are private institutions and relationships between them and their members are usually created and governed by contract. Traditionally that has been the decisive factor for English courts in deciding that sporting bodies are not susceptible to judicial review[2].

1 See para A4.1, n 3.

2 See paras A3.62 to A3.64.

A4.20 However, as with Convention jurisprudence, the notion of the 'public sphere' for the purposes of judicial review has been expanded in recent years[1]. The continuing exclusion of sporting bodies[2] from this broad category is a matter of some surprise to commentators[3].

1 This means that it is possible to argue that a sporting body should be covered by the HRA 1998, notwithstanding past authority protecting it from judicial review, on the basis that the concept of a public body has moved on and sporting bodies should now be included. Alternatively, an argument could be made that a sporting body is not amenable to human rights challenge for the same reason as it is not amenable to judicial review. (To some extent amenability to judicial review has become an academic issue, since the modern approach is to subject sporting bodies to the same substantive tests in private law: see para A3.65).

2 See para A3.62.

3 See, for example, Pannick 'Judicial Review of Sports Bodies' *Judicial Review* (September 1997), p 150; Beloff et al *Sports Law* (1999, Hart Publishing), pp 224–232; Griffith-Jones *Law and the Business of Sport* (1997, Butterworths), pp 52–57.

A4.21 In the light of the Home Secretary's comments on the Jockey Club and its susceptibility to a human rights challenge[1], the preferable approach is that of Simon Brown J in *RAM Racecourses*[2]: by applying *Datafin* and concentrating on functions such as the quasi-statutory licensing powers of sporting bodies[3], their monopolistic powers, whether government would be likely to instigate a statutory regime in their absence, and the extent to which their decisions affect members of the public (such as fans), many sporting bodies should be susceptible to judicial review.

1 See para A4.15.
2 *R v Jockey Club, ex p RAM Racecourses Ltd* [1993] 2 All ER 225.
3 See para A4.14.

A4.22 'State responsibility' in Strasbourg Even if an English court decides that a particular body is not amenable to a human rights challenge, that does not mean that the European Court in Strasbourg will agree[1]. Convention terms are autonomous so as to ensure that rights are secured on a practical and effective basis. Accordingly, Strasbourg's understanding of the circumstances in which 'state responsibility' is engaged in respect of the actions of a private body differs in material respects from the criteria applied in domestic courts[2].

1 As yet the European Court has not had to consider whether a sporting body comes within the ambit of state responsibility, although the Commission considered a case involving a football transfer in the early 1980s: Application 9322/81, *X v Netherlands* 32 DR 180 (1983); Gardiner *Sports Law* (2nd edn, 2001, Cavendish Publishing), p 238.
2 If a claimaint failed to persuade the English courts that a sporting body was amenable to a human rights challenge, and exhausted his remedies in doing so, then he could still apply to Strasbourg in the usual way.

A4.23 The doctrine of state responsibility encompasses a number of separate principles. Two are of particular relevance here:

(1) states cannot absolve themselves from responsibility by delegating their obligations to private bodies or individuals[1]; and
(2) state responsibility attaches to the acts of private individuals if the state has facilitated or colluded in those acts[2].

1 In *Costello-Roberts v United Kingdom* (1993) 19 EHRR 112, corporal punishment by the headmaster of an independent school was held to be capable of constituting a violation of Convention rights for which the state was responsible. The Strasbourg Court emphasised that it had 'consistently held that the responsibility of a state is engaged if a violation of one of the rights and freedoms defined in the Convention is the result of non-observance by that state of its obligation under Article 1 to secure those rights and freedoms in its domestic law to everyone within its jurisdiction … the state cannot absolve itself from responsibility by delegating its obligations to private bodies or individuals' (paras 26 and 27).
2 See *Lopez-Ostra v Spain* (1994) 20 EHRR 277, in which the state was responsible for pollution caused by a private treatment plant because it had subsidised the plant and had granted it planning permission.

A4.24 In Convention proceedings under Art 6, the right to a fair trial in the determination of civil rights and obligations may be claimed regardless of the 'character of the authority which has jurisdiction in the matter'[1]. Proceedings are regularly brought in respect of the decisions of professional disciplinary tribunals, particularly in the medical and legal fields[2]. In these cases, the fact that the outcome of the disciplinary proceedings is capable of affecting an individual's pecuniary interests is sufficient to characterise the complaint as one concerning the determination of civil rights, thereby engaging state responsibility. It is difficult to see how the decisions of sporting disciplinary tribunals could be excluded from this formulation.

1 *Stran Greek Refineries and Statis Andreadis v Greece* (1994) 19 EHRR 319, para 39.
2 *Le Compte, Van Leuven and De Meyer v Belgium* (1981) 4 EHRR 1; *H v Belgium* (1987) 10 EHRR 339.

A4.25 Under the HRA 1998, the English courts will have to take relevant Convention jurisprudence into consideration (although they will not be bound by it)[1], and will be expected to ensure that the minimum level of protection afforded to individuals under the HRA 1998 is equal to that provided at Strasbourg. Because of the wide and dynamic approach indicated by the Convention jurisprudence there is a strong argument that the domestic courts will conclude that sporting bodies[2] fall to be defined as public authorities for these purposes, at least in respect of some of their functions[3].

1 Section 2 of the HRA 1998. See also para A4.10.
2 See para A4.1, n 3.
3 Although government does not regulate sport in this country, this is only because it delegates the responsibility it would otherwise have to sporting bodies. (Imagine there was no Football Association. Would the Government really allow football to fade away for lack of regulation?). See para A1.5 et seq. The close relationship between the Government and sporting bodies is further illustrated by the provision of funding by the former for the latter, not least from lottery money. See para A1.53 et seq.

A4.26 'Public authority' as defined by the courts What constitutes a public authority under the HRA 1998 was considered in *Poplar Housing and Regeneration Community Association Ltd v Donoghue*[1]. The defendant argued that an order for possession would contravene her right to respect for her private and family life contract to Art 8 of the Convention. However, before she could rely on her Convention right, she first had to persuade the court that the Association was a public authority for the purposes of the HRA 1998. The Court of Appeal considered the case was borderline, but that, on the facts, the Association was 'a functional public authority' (para 66). The nature of the function[2] was all important[3].

1 [2001] EWCA Civ 595, [2002] QB 48. *Heather v Leonard Cheshire Foundation* [2001] EWHC Admin 429, [2001] All ER (D) 156 (Jun), upheld in the Court of Appeal ([2002] 2 All ER 936) distinguished *Poplar*: the Foundation was not a public authority. (The claimants in this case were long stay patients in a home run by the Foundation. They wanted to rely on Art 8 and their right to a private life in relation to the closure of the home. However, they could not do so. Although the duty on the local authority to house the claimants was statutory, the services for the publicly funded residents was the same as those for private and the Foundation was not standing in the shoes of the local authority.) A parish council was held to be a public authority in *Parochial Church Council of Aston Cantlow and Wilmcote v Wallbank* [2001] EWCA Civ 713, [2002] Ch 51.
2 For example, a sporting body as employer is unlikely to be considered a public authority. Contrast this with its role as regulator of the sport.
3 The Court of Appeal (para 58) agreed that:
'the definition of who is a public authority, and what is a public function, for the purposes of section 6, should be given a generous interpretation. However … [t]he fact that a body performs an activity which otherwise a public body would be under a duty to perform, cannot mean that such performance is necessarily a public function. A public body in order to perform its public duties can use the services of a private body. Section 6 should not be applied so that if a private body provides such services, the nature of the functions are inevitably public … Section 6(3) means that hybrid bodies, who have functions of a public and private nature, are public authorities; but not in relation to acts which are of a private nature. The renting out of accommodation can certainly be of a private nature. The fact that through the act of renting by a private body a public authority may be fulfilling its public duty, does not automatically change into a public act what would otherwise be a private act.'

For a critique of the courts' approach so far to determining what is a public authority see the discussion paper 'What is public power? The courts' approach to the public authority definition under the Human Rights Act', by Kate Markus, Doughty Street Chambers, to be published in a forthcoming book for Justice. The critique suggests the courts are too concerned with a judicial review-type test, and not sufficiently open to the Government's intentions to include organisations such as charities or companies 'acting in the shoes of the state': paras 49 to 71; *Hansard* HC, 17 June 1998, cols 409 and 410; *Hansard* HL, 24 November 1997, col 800.

A4.27 Sporting bodies as 'emanations of the state' Many EC law obligations, such as the free movement rules, are owed only by member states and 'emanations' of those states, and not by private bodies. It now appears that the majority of sporting bodies[1] will generally be regarded as constituting such emanations, at least in regard to the free movement rules[2]. It would be curious if a body was considered to be an emanation of the state in EC law, yet did not constitute a public authority for the purposes of the HRA 1998.

1 See para A4.1, n 3.
2 See paras A3.68 and B3.8.

(c) *Are aspects of sporting bodies 'tribunals'?*

A4.28 The HRA 1998 applies to tribunals as well as courts[1], the former defined as 'any tribunal in which legal proceedings may be brought'[2]. From statements made in Parliament by the Home Secretary, it does not appear that the government envisaged that non-statutory tribunals would fall within the definition[3]. Nevertheless, no such distinction is drawn in the HRA 1998 itself, many sports tribunals do 'adjudicate upon a citizen's legal rights'[4] and Convention decisions have expressly imposed Art 6 obligations upon private tribunals[5]. It may therefore be that the disciplinary tribunals of sporting bodies[6] qualify as tribunals for the purposes of the HRA 1998.

1 Section 6(3)(a).
2 Section 21(1).
3 In response to a proposed amendment removing the category of tribunal from Section 6 altogether, the Home Secretary said:
'I do not know why the amendment was tabled. We think that tribunals should be public authorities, at least in so far as they are bodies in which legal proceedings may be brought. If they were not, there would be a significant gap in the protection of human rights offered by the Bill. 'Tribunals' include industrial tribunals, the employment appeals tribunal, immigration adjudicators and the immigration appeals tribunal. If those bodies are not required to comply with convention rights, it is hard to think of bodies that should be. If the employment appeals tribunal were deemed not to be a public body, the cases would go straight to the court in Strasbourg': *Hansard*, HC, Vol 314, col 414.
4 On the application of s 6(3)(a) to religious courts and tribunals, Lord Hardie, the Lord Advocate, explained during the third reading of the Bill in the House of Lords, that the government did not regard courts of the Church of Scotland as within the scope of the sub-section because they 'do not, as a matter either of their constitution or practice, carry out any judicial functions on behalf of the state. Nor do they adjudicate upon a citizen's legal rights or obligations, either common law or statutory … ': 585 HL Official Report (5th series) col 794, 5 February 1998.
5 See para A4.39.
6 See para A4.1, n 3.

A4.29 The distinction is not academic, since inclusion as a 'tribunal' avoids consideration of how far a body's functions are 'functions of a public nature'. Further, s 6(5) of the HRA 1998 provides that bodies falling under s 6(3)(b) will not incur liability in respect of actions which are of a private nature. Courts and tribunals, on the other hand, will be liable in respect of *all* of their actions. This may include employment and commercial functions.

(d) Positive obligation on the courts

A4.30 In any event, the Convention is relevant in private law actions. The inclusion of 'courts and tribunals' in s 6(3)(a) means that all courts and tribunals in all proceedings will be under a duty to act in a way which is compatible with Convention rights. The extent of this obligation is considered below[1].

1 See para A4.31.

A4.31 Courts hearing private law actions will be obliged, for instance, to provide the parties with a fair trial in accordance with Art 6 of the Convention. But the obligation extends further than this. Section 6(3)(a) creates a 'horizontal' effect in that, even in cases between private individuals, the courts must ensure that human rights are protected as between the parties by developing and applying the law in such a way that Convention rights are not violated. (Quite how far the courts will go in this respect is still a matter of debate, although there is every indication that they will protect rights that should be positively secured by the state, for example privacy[1].) So, in addition to the s 3 duty to interpret legislation in a way which is compatible with Convention rights, courts are under a similar duty in relation to developing the common law in some areas. Certainly, this appears to have been the intention of the Government when the Bill was drafted[2].

1 *Douglas v Hello! Ltd* [2001] QB 967. See also para A4.59, n 6. Courts have been happy to consider the competing interests of privacy (Art 8) and freedom of expression (Art 10) in cases involving newspapers (by no stretch of the imagination public authorities for the purposes of the HRA 1998): *Theakston v MGN Ltd* [2002] EWHC 137 (QB), [2002] EMLR 398; *A v B, sub nom Garry Flitcroft v Mirror Group Newspapers Ltd* [2002] EWCA Civ 337, [2002] 2 All ER 545; *Campbell v Mirror Group Newspapers* [2002] EMLR 30.

2 The Lord Chancellor said that: 'We also believe that it is right as a matter of principle for the courts to have the duty of acting compatibly with the Convention not only in cases involving other public authorities but also in developing the common law in deciding cases between individuals. Why should they not? In preparing this Bill, we have taken the view that it is the other course, that of excluding Convention considerations altogether from cases between individuals which would have to be justified. The courts already bring Convention considerations to bear and I have no doubt that they will continue to do so in developing the common law' HL Debs col 783, 24 November 1997. See also Starmer *European Human Rights Law* (1999), pp 74 and 75. There has been considerable debate in relation to the 'horizontal effect' between private parties. For a detailed consideration see Lester & Pannick *Human Rights Law and Practice* (1999, Butterworths), para 2.6.3, at nn 3 and 4; Boyes 'Regulating sport after the Human Rights Act 1998' in Gardiner *Sports Law* (2nd edn, 2001, Cavendish Publishing), pp 236–238.

3 THE CONVENTION

A4.32 The Articles of the Convention which constitute 'Convention rights' for the purpose of s 1 of the HRA 1998 are Arts 2 to 12 and 14 of the Convention, Arts 1 to 3 of the First Protocol, and Arts 1 and 2 of the Sixth Protocol (as read with Arts 16 to 18 of the Convention)[1]. These Articles are set out in Schedule 1 to the HRA 1998.

1 See para A4.9.

A Articles relevant to sport

A4.33 Many of the Articles have some relevance in the sporting context, some more directly than others[1]. For example, Art 4, prohibition of slavery and forced labour, was relied on in a football transfer case[2]. Art 6, the right to a fair trial, is central to the activities of sports disciplinary bodies. Art 8, the right to a private life, has implications in relation to confidential information about competitors. Article 14, the prohibition on discrimination, prevents competitors being treated differently from one another on one of the grounds listed in the Article (but only in the context of another Convention right). An important concept in relation to Arts 8 to 11 is that of justification[3].

1 As stated above at para A4.1, it is impossible in the context of a work such as this to provide a detailed account of each of the Convention Articles. Rather, the following paragraphs attempt to give a flavour of the content of the rights and to suggest possible ways in which they might be relevant in a sporting context. In undertaking this exercise, it is of course necessary to take as read that the HRA 1998 applies to sporting bodies. A full consideration of this issue is set out at paras A4.14 to A4.31.
2 See para A4.34.
3 See para A4.61.

(a) Article 4, prohibition of slavery and forced labour

A4.34 Article 4 prohibits slavery and forced labour[1]. At first glance, it is difficult to see how this might apply in the sporting context. However, that did not prevent the matter of 'forced labour'[2] being relied on in a Dutch case concerning the football transfer system[3]. A player complained that an obligation in his contract with his club which prevented him playing for another club (because he was still registered with the first) was a breach of Art 4. Strasbourg dismissed the claim on the basis that it was manifestly ill-founded. The player had freely entered into the contract with the first club, knowing he would be effectively prevented from leaving should he choose to do so before the end of the agreement without approval[4]. This was not 'oppressive' or 'unavoidable hardship'[5].

1 Article 4 states: '1. No one shall be held in slavery or servitude. 2. No one shall be required to perform forced or compulsory labour …'
2 Strasbourg has adopted the definition of 'forced labour' derived from the International Labour Organisation: 'First that the work or service is performed by the worker against his will and, secondly, that the requirement that the work or service be performed is unjust or oppressive or the work or service involves avoidable hardship' (Application 4653/70, *X v Germany* (1974) 17 Yearbook 148, 172).
3 Application 9322/81, *X v Netherlands* 32 DR 180 (1983); S. Boyes, 'The regulation of sport and the impact of the Human Rights Act 1998' [2000] 6(4) EPL 517, pp 525–528.
4 The player was not so much complaining about having to play for the first club, but about being prevented from playing for the second in restraint of trade. The doctrine of restraint of trade as it applies to sport is dealt with at para A3.135 et seq, and particularly in the context of player contracts at paras E1.32 to E1.36.
5 Query whether Bosman, who was out of contract would have been more successful in bringing this claim. See paras B2.154 et seq, B3.40 et seq and E2.37 et seq.

A4.35 Even where work does not otherwise fall under the definition of 'forced labour', it may still be possible to raise an issue under the Convention by reference to Art 14 and the prohibition against discrimination[1]. This is because 'work or labour that is itself normal may be rendered abnormal if the choice of the groups or individuals bound to perform it is governed by discriminatory factors'[2]. The Strasbourg Court found such a violation where men, but not women, were required to serve as local firefighters or pay a service levy in lieu[3]. Since there were in fact no vacancies, in practice the only obligation was to pay the levy. The court found that the sex discrimination in relation to the imposition of the financial burden could not be justified.

1 See para A4.70.
2 *Van Der Mussele v Belgium*, para 93 of the Commission's Report Series B: judgment is at (1983) 6 EHRR 163.
3 *Schmidt v Germany* (1994) 18 EHRR 513.

(b) Article 6, right to a fair trial

A4.36 Article 6 provides for the right to a fair trial in both civil and criminal contexts[1]. The fundamental right to a fair procedure has long been recognised in the law of the United Kingdom[2]. The importance of Art 6 is such that it is to be given a broad and purposive interpretation[3], although it is accepted that parties entering into *voluntary* arbitration agreements fall outside its scope[4]. Corporations have rights under Art 6 in the same way as individuals[5].

1 Article 6 is set out as follows:
'1. In the determination of his civil rights and obligations or of any criminal charge against him, everyone is entitled to a fair and public hearing within a reasonable time by an independent and impartial tribunal established by law. Judgment shall be pronounced publicly but the press and public may be excluded from all or part of the trial in the interests of morals, public order or national security in a democratic society, where the interests of juveniles or the protection of the private life of the parties so require, or to the extent strictly necessary in the opinion of the court in special circumstances where publicity would prejudice the interests of justice.
2. Everyone charged with a criminal offence shall be presumed innocent until proved guilty according to law.
3. Everyone charged with a criminal offence has the following minimum rights:
a. to be informed promptly, in a language which he understands and in detail, of the nature and cause of the accusation against him;
b. to have adequate time and facilities for the preparation of his defence;
c. to defend himself in person or through legal assistance of his own choosing or, if he has not sufficient means to pay for legal assistance, to be given it free when the interests of justice so require;
d. to examine or have examined witnesses against him and to obtain the attendance and examination of witnesses on his behalf under the same conditions as witnesses against him;
e. to have the free assistance of an interpreter if he cannot understand or speak the language used in court.'
2 The Magna Carta, in 1215, compelled the King to pledge that '[t]o no one we will sell, to no one will we deny or delay right or justice'. Sporting bodies have long been obliged to act fairly in a procedural sense. See, for example, *Jones v Welsh Rugby Union* Ebsworth J, 27 February 1997, The Times, 6 March 1997, and CA, The Times, 6 January 1998: Jones complained of the disciplinary sanctions placed on him by his disciplinary body. An injunction was granted allowing him to continue playing rugby pending his appeal against the ban. See para A3.102, nn 7, 9 and 10.
3 *Delcourt v Belgium* (1970) 1 EHRR 355, para 25; *Moreira de Azevedo v Portugal* (1990) 13 EHRR 721, para 66.
4 'However, a waiver [of Art 6 rights] will only be effective if it is clear and unequivocal, made in the absence of constraint and made in the full knowledge of the nature and extent of the right. It is therefore arguable that an arbitration clause will not be effective if, for example, the applicant was effectively compelled to agree an arbitration clause or where the arbitration clause was not expressly agreed': Clayton & Tomlinson *The Law of Human Rights* (2000, Oxford) at para 11.317B. See also para A4.41, n 3. This leaves it open for a sports person to argue that he did not enter into any arbitration voluntarily and therefore Art 6 still applies, although the sporting body will obviously argue the contrary.
5 See, for example, *Air Canada v United Kingdom* (1995) 20 EHRR 150.

A4.37 Article 6 is probably the most important in the sporting context as it encompasses all disciplinary hearings and procedures which determine someone's civil rights and obligations. Although the right to a fair procedure has always been a cornerstone of United Kingdom law[1], Art 6 is likely to have a profound impact on the *content* of the duty of fairness[2]. As a result, many sporting bodies[3] have adapted their procedures to comply with Art 6. For example, UK Sport's Statement of

Anti-Doping Policy was written to incorporate the fundamental requirements of the Article[4]; the Jockey Club set up an independent and impartial appeal board[5]; and the Football Association has changed its disciplinary system[6].

1 See para A4.36.
2 Beloff et al *Sports Law* (1999, Hart Publishing), para 7.84. See, for example, *International Transport Roth GmbH v Secretary of State for the Environment, Transport and the Regions* [2002] EWCA Civ 158, [2002] 3 WLR 344, where the general fairness of a system which entailed hauliers paying £2,000 per head per clandestine entrant was considered under Art 6.
3 See para A4.1, n 3.
4 *Human Rights Act – Implications for Sport* v3 14/12/2000.
5 'Club act on Rights' (2001) Daily Telegraph, 20 February (Sport Section), p 3.
6 'Life is sweet at the FA' *Legal Week* (2 November 2000), p 29.

A4.38 In the determination of civil rights and obligations For Art 6 to apply, there must be a dispute over civil rights and obligations which are, at least arguably, recognised under domestic law[1]. The dispute must be of a 'genuine and serious nature'[2]. It must also be decisive of civil rights and obligations[3] (rather than failing to determine them).

1 *H v Belgium* (1987) 10 EHRR 339, para 40; *Georgiadis v Greece* (1997) 24 EHRR 606, para 30.
2 *Le Compte, Van Leuven and De Meyere and Belgium* (1981) 4 EHRR 1, para 49.
3 *Ringeisen v Austria* (1971) 1 EHRR 455, para 94.

A4.39 Civil right The concept of a civil right is an autonomous one, ie it has been for the European Court in Strasbourg to determine whether or not a particular 'right' is a civil right for the purposes of the Convention. Consequently, there is much authority on the subject. However, this is simplified in the sporting context since Art 6 'covers proceedings before a plethora of statutory or non-statutory bodies exercising punitive or regulatory jurisdiction'[1]. It is therefore tolerably clear that Strasbourg would consider that the hearing of sporting bodies'[2] need to comply with Art 6.

1 Beloff et al *Sports Law* (1999, Hart Publishing) at 7.83; *H v Belgium* (1987) 10 EHRR 339 (lawyers); *Albert and Le Compte v Belgium* (1982) 5 EHRR 533 (doctors); *König v Germany* (1978) 2 EHRR 170 (doctor); *Le Compte, Van Leuven and De Meyere v Belgium* (1981) 4 EHRR 1 (doctors); *Kraska v Switzerland* (1993) 18 EHRR 188 (doctor); *Diennet v France* (1995) 21 EHRR 554 (doctor); *Philis v Greece (No 2)* (1997) 25 EHRR 417 (engineer); *De Moor v Belgium* (1994) 18 EHRR 372 (barrister).
2 See para A4.1, n 3.

A4.40 Civil/criminal Like the concept of 'civil right', the concept of 'criminal' is an autonomous one under the Strasbourg jurisprudence. Various attempts have therefore been made to designate disciplinary proceedings, which can have a wide-ranging impact on an individual's ability to earn a living, as criminal rather than civil for the purpose of Art 6. (In sport, such proceedings may result in fines and/or suspension, for up to life, and can ruin reputations, for example doping cases.) The Strasbourg Court has declined to rule on whether serious disciplinary charges should be classified as civil or criminal[1]. Rather, if the allegation is grave and the consequences sufficiently far-reaching, the court will treat the proceedings as analogous to criminal proceedings, such that guarantees similar to those under Art 6(2) and 6(3) (the criminal protections) will be held to apply[2]. The English courts have followed the same route[3]. As a result the following paragraphs deal briefly with the most important substantive criminal protections as well as those under Art 6(1).

1 *Albert and Le Compte v Belgium* (1982) 5 EHRR 533.
2 Simor & Emmerson *Human Rights Practice* (2001, Sweet & Maxwell), para 6.020; *Albert and Le Compte* (see n 1); *H v Belgium* (1987) 10 EHRR 339; *Ginikanwa v United Kingdom*, App. No. 12502/86, 55 DR 251. A different approach was taken by the Arbitration Court of the Norwegian Confederation of Sport ('the Confederation') after a hearing on doping at which Athlete A was excluded from competition and training for life: [2001] 2 ISLR N-23. The finding was upheld on appeal even though the athlete was acquitted in the Oslo criminal courts. The Arbitration Court considered the Confederation's charge to be criminal and therefore the presumption of innocence applied. As a result of the acquittal in the criminal courts the Confederation's finding against the athlete should not have been upheld. It seems the Arbitration Court agreed with the Confederation that the athlete in question would not have been able to lodge a complaint with Strasbourg because only States can be responsible for breaches. This is surprising since the concept of state responsibility has been held to encompass the regulation of various professions (see para A4.39).
3 *Official Receiver v Stern* [2000] 1 WLR 2230; *R v Securities and Futures Authority, ex p Fleurose* [2001] EWCA Civ 2015, [2002] IRLR 297.

A4.41 Substantive protections *Right of access to a court* There is no express guarantee of the right of access to a court in Art 6 but the European Court of Human Rights has determined that the right is inherent in Art 6[1]. The right can be waived, for example by means of an arbitration agreement[2], but such waiver will be subjected to 'particularly careful review' to make sure a party was not subject to constraint[3]. The Article does not guarantee a right of appeal. However, if such a right is provided, Art 6 will apply to the appeal procedures[4]. And if an appeal is provided for some, it must be provided for all lest it fall foul of Art 14's prohibition of discrimination[5].

1 *Golder v United Kingdom* (1975) 1 EHRR 524.
2 See para A4.36, n 4. See generally Chapter A5.
3 Lester & Pannick *Human Rights Law and Practice* (1999, Butterworths), para 4.6.20; *Deweer v Belgium* (1980) 2 EHRR 439, para 49.
4 Lester & Pannick *Human Rights Law and Practice* (1999, Butterworths), para 4.6.22.
5 *Belgian Linguistic Case (No 2)* (1968) 1 EHRR 252, para 8. See para A4.70.

A4.42 Where a decision determinative of civil rights and obligations is taken by a body *not* complying with Art 6(1), Art 6 requires that the state provide a right to challenge the decision before a judicial body with full jurisdiction[1]. This raises the question in relation to a non-compliant sports organisation: what judicial body? If it remains impossible to proceed by way of judicial review (which may not be sufficient in any event) and the body is not considered to be a public authority for the purpose of proceedings under the HRA 1998, then the victim may have to apply to Strasbourg (unless there is a contractual route available)[2].

1 *Albert and Le Compte v Belgium* (1982) 5 EHRR 533, para 29.
2 See generally Chapter A3.

A4.43 *Fair hearing* In determining whether there has been a breach of the right to a fair hearing, the proceedings may be considered as a whole as well as by reference to the individual deficiencies in order to determine whether the cumulative effect is unfair[1].

1 *Barberà, Messegue and Jabardo v Spain* (1988) 11 EHRR 360, paras 68 and 69.

A4.44 *Oral hearing* A general right to an oral hearing derives from the guarantee of a public hearing in Art 6(1)[1]. A right to a hearing in one's presence is extended to cases which involve an assessment of a party's personal conduct[2]. A party may waive his right to be present at an oral hearing provided such a waiver is unequivocal and attended by minimum safeguards commensurate to its importance[3].

1 See para A4.47. Lester & Pannick *Human Rights Law and Practice* (1999, Butterworths), para 4.6.28.
2 *Muyldermans v Belgium* (1991) 15 EHRR 204, para 64.
3 *Poitrimol v France* (1993) 18 EHRR 130, para 31.

A4.45 *Equality of arms* Everyone who is a party to proceedings must have a reasonable opportunity of presenting his case under conditions which do not place him at a disadvantage as regards his opponent. This principle of equality of arms involves striking a fair balance between the parties[1].

1 *Neumeister v Austria* (1968) 1 EHRR 91, para 22; *Delcourt v Belgium* (1970) 1 EHRR 355, para 28; *Dombo Beheer v Netherlands* (1993) 18 EHRR 213, para 33; *De Haes and Gijsels v Belgium* (1997) 25 EHRR 1, para 53.

A4.46 *Freedom from self-incrimination* The right to a fair trial in a criminal case includes 'the right of anyone charged with a criminal … offence to remain silent and not to contribute to incriminating himself'[1]. The right was violated in *Saunders v United Kingdom* because evidence admitted at the criminal trial was obtained when the applicant was under a duty to answer questions which was enforceable by criminal proceedings for contempt[2]. The right is also relevant in relation to disciplinary proceedings where serious charges are determined[3] (by virtue of the quasi-criminal nature of the charges).

1 *Funke v France* (1993) 16 EHRR 297.
2 (1996) 23 EHRR 313. Such information can be used in the actual proceedings for which it is obtained, but not subsequently: *R v Kearns* [2002] EWCA Crim 748, [2002] All ER (D) 363 (Mar).
3 *Official Receiver v Stern* [2000] 1 WLR 2230, CA; *R v Securities and Futures Authority v Fleurose* [2001] EWCA Civ 2015, [2002] IRLR 297.

A4.47 *Public hearing* This right implies the right to an oral hearing unless there are exceptional circumstances. The purpose of this fundamental guarantee is to protect litigants from 'the administration of justice in secret'[1]. Nevertheless, the right is subject to the express exceptions in the text of the Article and private hearings have been found to be justified in the context of disciplinary proceedings[2]. The Convention does not require a public hearing if a party has waived his right to such a hearing, provided that the waiver is unequivocal and there is no important public interest which requires the hearing to be in public[3]. It is permissible to have a practice that hearings are heard in private subject to application by a party for a public hearing: failure to request a public hearing will be a waiver[4]. The right to public pronouncement of judgment is satisfied by the judgment being made available in some form[5].

1 See para A4.44; and *Pretto v Italy* (1983) 6 EHRR 182, para 21.
2 See para A4.36; and Application 15561/89 *Imberechts v Belgium* 69 DR 312 (1991), European Commission.
3 *Hakansson v Sweden* (1990) 13 EHRR 1, para 66.
4 *Schüler-Zgraggen v Switzerland* (1993) 16 EHRR 405, para 58.
5 Lester & Pannick *Human Rights Law and Practice* (1999, Butterworths), para 4.6.44.

A4.48 *Hearing within a reasonable time* In civil cases, time usually begins to run from the initiation of proceedings[1]. In criminal cases, the reasonable time guarantee runs from charge[2] (as in the official notification of an offence[3]). What constitutes a 'reasonable time' depends on the circumstances of the case. Factors include the complexity of the issues; the conduct of the parties; and what is at stake[4].

1 *Guincho v Portugal* (1984) 7 EHRR 223, para 29; *Ausiello v Italy* (1996) 24 EHRR 568, para 18.
2 *Wemhoff v Germany* (1968) 1 EHRR 55, para 19; *Neumeister v Austria* (1968) 1 EHRR 91, para 18; *A-G's Reference (No 2 of 2001)* [2001] UKHRR 1265.
3 *Eckle v Germany* (1982) 5 EHRR 1, para 73.
4 *Eckle v Germany* (above), para 80; *Buchholz v Germany* (1981) 3 EHRR 597, para 49; Grosz et al *Human Rights: The 1998 Act and the Convention* (2000, Sweet & Maxwell), C6-73; *Dyer v Watson, K v Lord Advocate* [2002] 4 All ER 1.

A4.49 *'Tribunal'* The tribunal for the purposes of Art 6 (either the original disciplinary body or on appeal):

(a) must have jurisdiction to examine all questions of fact and law relevant to the dispute[1];
(b) must give decisions which are legally binding rather than merely advisory[2]; and
(c) may be composed of people who are not professional judges[3].

The fact that a body also carries out non-judicial functions (eg administrative) does not prevent it being a tribunal[4].

1 *Terra Woningen v Netherlands* (1996) 24 EHRR 456, para 52.
2 *Belilos v Switzerland* (1988) 10 EHRR 466, para 64; *Benthem v Netherlands* (1985) 8 EHRR 1, para 40; *Van de Hurk v Netherlands* (1994) 18 EHRR 481, para 52.
3 *Ettl v Austria* (1987) 10 EHRR 255, para 38.
4 *Campbell and Fell v United Kingdom* (1984) 7 EHRR 165, para 81.

A4.50 *'Independent'* The European Court has regard[1] to:

(a) the manner of appointment of a tribunal's members, and their term of office;
(b) the existence of guarantees against outside pressures; and
(c) whether the body presents an appearance of independence[2].

The latter entails an objective test, bearing in mind the importance of justice not only being done, but being seen to be done.

1 *Bryan v United Kingdom* (1995) 21 EHRR 342, para 37. See also Anderson, Mulcahy and Reindorf 'Independent and Impartial? The Potential Impact of the Human Rights Act 1998 on Sports Tribunals' [2000] 2 ISLR 65–73.
2 Planning inspector not independent, *Bryan* (above); inquiry independent if set up by Secretary of State but no more, *R v Secretary of State for Health, ex p Wagstaff* [2001] 1 WLR 292; legislative role of bailiff of Guernsey imperilled independence (and impartiality), *McGonnell v United Kingdom* (2000) 30 EHRR 289; deputy sheriffs lacking security of tenure not independent, *Starrs v Procurator Fiscal, Linlithgow* [2000] HRLR 191; court not independent when it accepted Foreign Office advice on the meaning of a treaty, *Beaumartin v France* (1994) 19 EHRR 485, para 38; convening officer in UK courts-martial undermined independence of the system because members subordinate to his rank, *Findlay v United Kingdom* (1997) 24 EHRR 221.

A4.51 *'Impartial'* For the purposes of the Convention this means the absence of prejudice or bias[1]. Regard must be had not only to the personal conviction of a particular judge in a given case (the subjective approach) but also to whether there were sufficient guarantees to exclude any legitimate doubt in this respect (the objective approach)[2]. Personal impartiality is to be presumed unless there is proof to the contrary[3]. A party's belief that a tribunal is not impartial is important but not conclusive. The question is whether the doubt can be objectively justified[4]. A judge must withdraw from the case if there is legitimate doubt as to his impartiality[5]. It is unclear whether the requirement of impartiality may be waived[6].

1 *Piersack v Belgium* (1982) 5 EHRR 169, para 30.
2 *Bulut v Austria* (1996) 24 EHRR 84, para 31; *Thomann v Switzerland* (1996) 24 EHRR 553, para 30.
3 *Debled v Belgium* (1994) 19 EHRR 506, para 37.
4 *Ferrantelli and Santangelo v Italy* (1996) 23 EHRR 288, para 58.
5 *Hauschilt v Denmark* (1989) 12 EHRR 266, para 48.
6 *Oberschlick v Austria* (1991) 19 EHRR 389, para 51: waiver must be established in unequivocal manner; *Bulut v Austria* (n 2), whether or not waiver made out, Strasbourg had to determine the question of impartiality.

A4.52 Article 6 was violated where a judge:

(a) was previously a prosecutor and commenced proceedings against the complainant[1];
(b) previously acted as investigating judge[2];
(c) voiced his suspicions on a bail application prior to trying the case[3];
(d) had a financial or personal interest in the subject matter of the case[4].

Article 6 was also held to be violated where a court carried out both advisory and judicial functions[5], and the distinction between a court and the state became blurred[6]. A doctor's disciplinary tribunal was not impartial because of a 'worrying connection' with the competitors of the applicants' organisation[7]. (However, there was no bias on the part of a judge where one side's solicitors acted for him in connection with his will[8]).

1 *Piersack v Belgium* (1982) 5 EHRR 169, para 30(d).
2 *De Cubber v Belgium* (1984) 7 EHRR 236, paras 26 to 30.
3 *Hauschildt v Denmark* (1989) 12 EHRR 266, para 50.
4 *Demicoli v Malta* (1991) 14 EHRR 47, paras 36 to 42; *Langborger v Sweden* (1989) 12 EHRR 416, para 35.
5 *Procola v Luxembourg* (1995) 22 EHRR 193, paras 44 and 45.
6 *Lobo Machoda v Portugal* (1996) 23 EHRR 79, para 31.
7 *Gautrin v France* (1998) 28 EHRR 196, paras 57 to 60.
8 *Taylor v Lawrence* [2001] EWCA Civ 90, [2002] 2 All ER 353.

A4.53 The English law bias test, post the HRA 1998, was outlined in the Court of Appeal in *Re Medicaments and Related Classes of Goods (No 2)*, and approved in the House of Lord in *Porter v Magill*[1]. According to these two cases, the test of apparent bias in *Gough*[2] should be reconciled with the jurisprudence of Strasbourg as follows:

(a) the court should ascertain all the circumstances which have a bearing on the suggestion that a judge or tribunal is biased;
(b) the court should ask whether those circumstances would lead a fair-minded and informed observer to conclude there was a real possibility or real danger that the tribunal was biased.

The court did not have to rule on any explanation advanced by the judge or tribunal as to his/its conduct, but the explanation was a matter to be taken into account from the viewpoint of the fair-minded observer.

1 [2001] 1 WLR 700 and [2002] 1 All ER 465 respectively.
2 [1993] AC 646.

A4.54 *Established by law* A court or tribunal must be established by law for the purposes of Art 6. The requirement aims to ensure a measure of parliamentary control over the organisations of courts[1]. However, in interpreting the words as meaning 'in accordance with national law' Strasbourg retained the competence to review the legality of an Art 6(1) tribunal in relation to its compliance with domestic law[2] (although this is exercised with caution). The requirement will be infringed if a tribunal does not function in accordance with its governing rules[3].

1 Grosz et al *Human Rights: The 1998 Act and the Convention* (2000, Sweet & Maxwell), C6-61.
2 *Oberschlick v Austria* (1991) 19 EHRR 389; *Pfeifer and Plank v Austria* (1992) 14 EHRR 692.
3 Lester & Pannick *Human Rights Law and Practice* (1999, Butterworths), para 4.6.58.

A4.55 *Presumption of innocence* Article 6(2) guarantees the presumption of innocence in criminal proceedings. It does not prohibit rules that transfer the burden of proof to the accused, but – if the overall burden of proving guilt does not remain with the prosecution – any such rule must be confined within reasonable limits[1]. Offences of strict liability do not violate Art 6(2) providing the prosecution retains the burden of showing that the offence was committed[2]. Adverse comment by officials runs the risk of violating the presumption of innocence if the statements carry the implication that an alleged wrongdoer is in fact guilty[3] (as does the refusal to award costs because of a suspicion that the accused was in fact guilty[4]).

1 *Salabiaku v France* (1988) 13 EHRR 379, para 28; *Hoang v France* (1992) 16 EHRR 53; *L v DPP* [2001] EWHC Admin 882, [2002] 2 All ER 854; *R v Lambert* [2001] UKHL 37, [2001] 3 All ER 577 (where s 3 of the HRA 1998 was used to interpret legislation). For an analysis of statutory reverse onus provisions see *R v DPP, ex p Kebilene* [2000] 2 AC 326, per Lord Hope at 378 to 380.
2 *Salabiaku* (above); *Bates v United Kingdom* [1996] EHRLR 312, EComHR (Dangerous Dogs Act 1991).
3 *Allenet de Ribemont v France* (1995) 20 EHRR 557.
4 *Minelli v Switzerland* (1983) 5 EHRR 554.

A4.56 *Article 6(3) rights* These (which are listed at n 1 to para A4.36) have relevance to disciplinary proceedings only if the allegation is so serious as to render the proceedings akin to criminal, for example doping.

1 See para A4.40.

(c) *Article 8, right to respect for private and family life*

A4.57 Article 8 guarantees the right to respect for private and family life, home and correspondence[1]. In the sporting context, this imposes a duty to keep personal information on competitors protected and confidential[2]. Issues also arise out of the taking of urine and blood samples as part of anti-doping policies[3].

1 Article 8 states:
'1. Everyone has the right to respect for his private and family life, his home and his correspondence.
2. There shall be no interference by a public authority with the exercise of this right except such as is in accordance with the law and is necessary in a democratic society in the interests of national security, public safety or the economic well-being of the country, for the prevention of disorder or crime, for the protection of health or morals, or for the protection of the rights and freedoms of others.'
2 UK Sport *Human Rights Act – Implications for Sport* v3 14/12/2000. In addition, competitors might argue that their names and images are part of their private life and should be protected. See Moore *Sports Law and Litigation* (2nd edn, 2000, CLT), p 40, and para A4.59. See also paras D3.57 to D3.64.

3 See generally para A4.173 et seq. A blood sample (taken in connection with determining the amount of alcohol in the bloodstream for the purposes of road traffic legislation) did not contravene Art 8 as the interference was justified by the need to protect the rights of others: *X v Netherlands* 16 DR 184, 189 (1979), European Commission. A blood sample taken for a paternity suit was justified on similar grounds: *Application 8278/78, X v Austria* 18 DR 155, 157 (1980). For an analysis of the position in the United States, and the Fourth Amendment right to privacy, see Gardiner *Sports Law* (2nd edn, 2001, Cavendish Publishing), p 240. See also Beloff M and Beloff R 'Blood Sports – Blood testing, the common law and the Human Rights Act' [2000] 2 ISLR 43.

A4.58 Article 8 covers a broad range of interests, as set out in its first paragraph. However, the second paragraph of Art 8 encompasses specific and express qualifications to the right set out in the first. The obligation in Art 8 is primarily negative, ie the right should not be interfered with save as provided for by the qualifications. However, Art 8 also imposes a positive obligation on the state to secure the right to a private life[1].

1 Lester & Pannick *Human Rights Law and Practice* (1999, Butterworths), para 4.8.3.

A4.59 Private life A person has the right to protect his physical and moral integrity which are important aspects of private life. Individuals have the right not to be subjected to compulsory physical interventions (but see the cases on samples at para A4.57, n 3[1]). Where hazardous activities might have hidden adverse consequences for the health of those involved, then there should be an effective procedure to help people seek the relevant information[2]. The right to an identity is part of private life: this encompasses the right to use a name[3] and the right to choose a mode of dress and appearance[4]. Sexual relations and orientation are also included[5] as is the question of the extent to which the state must go to provide remedies to prevent revelations about an individual's private life[6]. (There are inevitable tensions in the latter case with the right to freedom of expression under Art 10[7]).

1 See also *Peters v Netherlands* 77-A DR 75 (1994), European Commission: complaint concerning compulsory random drug testing by urine sample in prisons manifestly ill-founded because within Art 8(2).
2 *McGinley and Egan v United Kingdom* (1998) 27 EHRR 1, paras 96 to 98, 101.
3 *Burghartz and Burghartz v Switzerland* (1994) 18 EHRR 101; *Sterjna v Finland* (1994) 24 EHRR 195.
4 Application 8317/78 *McFeeley v United Kingdom* 20 DR 44 at 91 (1980); Application 8209/78 *Sutter v Switzerland* 16 DR 166 (1979).
5 See, for example, *Dudgeon v United Kingdom* (1981) 4 EHRR 149; *Smith and Grady v United Kingdom* (1999) 29 EHRR 493, paras 71 to 112; *Lustig-Prean and Beckett v United Kingdom* (1999) 29 EHRR 548, paras 64 to 105.
6 *Theakston v MGN Ltd* [2002] EWHC 137, [2002] EMLR 30; *A v B* [2002] EWCA Civ 337, [2002] 2 All ER 545; *Campbell v Mirror Group Newspapers* [2002] EWHC 499 (QB). See also *Douglas v Hello! Ltd* [2001] QB 967; Application 10871/84 *Winer v United Kingdom* 48 DR 154 (QB), [2002] EMLR 398 (1986), European Commission; Application 28851/95 *Earl Spencer and Countess Spencer v United Kingdom* (1998) 25 EHRR CD 105.
7 See paras A4.65 to A4.67.

A4.60 Correspondence, communications and confidential data Examples of cases where breaches under this head of Art 8 have been alleged include:

(a) the collection of private details in a security check[1];
(b) tapping a telephone[2];
(c) checking, intercepting or stopping mail[3]; and
(d) maintaining medical records[4].

1 *Hilton v United Kingdom* 57 DR 108 (1988) at 117.
2 *Malone v United Kingdom* (1984) 7 EHRR 14; *Klass v Germany* (1978) 2 EHRR 214, para 49; *Valenzuela Contreras v Spain* (1998) 28 EHRR 483, para 47.
3 *Hewitt and Harman v United Kingdom* (1992) 14 EHRR 657; *Campbell v United Kingdom* (1992) 15 EHRR 137; *Foxley v United Kingdom* (2000) 31 EHRR 637.
4 Application 14461/88 *Chare (nee Jullien) v France* 71 DR 141 (1991), European Commission.

A4.61 Justification Justification is a concept which applies to the rights protected by Arts 8 to 11 (private life, freedom of religion, expression and assembly) and Art 1 of the First Protocol (property). Interference with the right in issue does not alone constitute a breach of the relevant Article – unless such interference cannot be justified, in this case under Art 8(2). The public authority must first demonstrate that the interference is 'in accordance with the law'[1], ie the relevant domestic law[2]. It must also show that the interference is 'necessary in a democratic society' and comes under one of the express exceptions in Art 8(2). The test of necessity involves deciding whether there is a 'pressing social need' for the interference and whether the means employed are proportionate to the legitimate aim pursued. The nature, context and importance of the right asserted and the extent of the interference must be balanced against the nature, context and importance of the claimed public interest[3].

1 See the wording of Art 8(2) at para A4.57.
2 It is rare to argue a complete absence of domestic law (ie. that no law exists which sanctions the conduct in issue) but it has been done, eg *Halford v United Kingdom* (1997) 24 EHRR 523, paras 61 to 63.
3 Lester & Pannick *Human Rights Law and Practice* (1999, Butterworths), paras 3.15 and 3.16; *Sunday Times v United Kingdom* (1979) 2 EHRR 245 at 275, para 59; *Handyside v United Kingdom* (1976) 1 EHRR 737 at 753 to 754, para 48.

(d) Article 9, freedom of thought, conscience and religion

A4.62 Article 9 guarantees freedom of thought, conscience and religion[1]. This 'precious asset'[2] is crucial in a democratic society, although its impact in the sporting context is limited. Nevertheless, it does, for example, mean that sporting bodies should have an awareness of holy days when scheduling sporting events[3]. Perhaps the most famous example of a sportsman refusing to perform on such a day is that of Eric Liddell, the Scottish runner portrayed in the 1981 film 'Chariots of Fire' who refused to enter the 100m metres heats in the 1924 Olympic Games because they were held on a Sunday. (He won the gold medal in the 400m). No sportsman should be discriminated against on the grounds of his beliefs[4].

1 Article 9 states:
'1. Everyone has the right to freedom of thought, conscience and religion; this right includes freedom to change his religion or belief and freedom, either alone or in community with others and in public or private, to manifest his religion or belief, in worship, teaching, practice and observance.
2. Freedom to manifest one's religion or beliefs shall be subject only to such limitations as are prescribed by law and are necessary in a democratic society in the interests of public safety, for the protection of public order, health or morals, or for the protection of the rights and freedoms of others.'
2 *Kokkinakis v Greece* (1993) 17 EHRR 397, para 31.
3 UK Sport *Human Rights Act – Implications for Sport* v3 14/12/2000.
4 See Art 14 and paras A4.70 and A4.71. Arguably Liddell would have had a claim on this ground.

A4.63 The general freedoms in Art 9(1) are absolute rights[1]. It is only the manifestation of beliefs that is qualified by Art 9(2). The rights are essentially personal: they cannot be enjoyed by corporations[2], nor are associations capable of exercising the right to freedom of conscience[3]. They can however be enjoyed by an organisation such as a church, which is simply a collection of people[4].

1 *Kokkinakis v Greece* (1994) 17 EHRR 397, para 33 (Jehovah's Witnesses had right to proselytise as long as not improper).
2 Application 3798/68 *Church of X v United Kingdom* 12 YB 306 (1969), European Commission; Application 7865/77 *Company X v Switzerland* 16 DR 85 (1981), European Commission.
3 Application 11308/84 *Vereniging Rechtswinkels Utrecht v Netherlands* 46 DR 200 (1986), European Commission; Application 11921/86 *Kontakt-Information-Therapie and Hagen v Austria* 57 DR 81 (1988), European Commission.
4 Application 7805/77 *X and Church of Scientology v Sweden* 16 DR 68 (1979), European Commission; Application 45701/99 *Metropolitan Church of Bessarabia v Moldova* (13 December 2001, unreported).

A4.64 The notions of religion and belief have been given a wide interpretation by the European Commission and have been held to include non-religious beliefs[1]. Pacifism, for example, is a 'philosophy' and falls within the ambit of the right to freedom of thought and conscience[2].

1 *Kokkinakis v Greece* (1993) 17 EHRR 397, para 31.
2 Application 7050/75 *Arrowsmith v United Kingdom* 19 DR 5 (1980), European Commission.

(e) Article 10, freedom of expression

A4.65 Article 10 guarantees the right to freedom of expression[1]. This right is one of the essential foundations of a democratic society[2]. In the sporting world, arguments about freedom of expression may arise in various contexts, for example:

(a) attire: the imposition of a dress code may interfere with participants' ability to express themselves[3];
(b) efforts to prevent players, managers and officials from talking to the press[4]; and
(c) coverage by the press of off-field activities[5].

1 Article 10 states:
'1. Everyone has the right to freedom of expression. This right shall include freedom to hold opinions and to receive and impart information and ideas without interference by public authority and regardless of frontiers. This Article shall not prevent States from requiring the licensing of broadcasting, television or cinema enterprises.
2. The exercise of these freedoms, since it carries with it duties and responsibilities, may be subject to such formalities, conditions, restrictions or penalties as are prescribed by law and are necessary in a democratic society, in the interests of national security, territorial integrity or public safety, for the prevention of disorder or crime, for the protection of health or morals, for the protection of the reputation or rights of others, for preventing the disclosure of information received in confidence, or for maintaining the authority and impartiality of the judiciary.'
2 *Handyside v United Kingdom* (1976) 1 EHRR 737.
3 UK Sport *Human Rights Act – Implications for Sport* v3 14/12/2000. Dress constitutes expression, Application 11674/85 *Stevens v United Kingdom* 46 DR 245 (1986), European Commission.
4 Gardiner *Sports Law* (2nd edn, 2001, Cavendish Publishing), p 240, and 'Human Rights Act saves Tyson' *The Guardian*, 23 August 2000. But note that the European Commission has held that there will be no interference where an individual has agreed to limit his freedom of expression: Application 11308 *Vereiging Rechtswinkels Utrecht v Netherlands* 46 DR 200 (1986). So, managers who agree not to bring the game into disrepute may not be able to rely on Art 10 if they speak out against referees and in the process do just that. Similarly, football players agree not to bring the game into disrepute, but may 'contribute to the public media in a responsible manner': cl 13 of the Premier League contract. Roy Keane, of Manchester United, was reported as preparing to run an Art 10 defence in disciplinary proceedings relating to comments made in his autobiography regarding a tackle on Manchester City's Alf-Inge Haaland: (2002) Independent, 10 September, (2002) Times, 11 September.
5 *A v B, sub nom Garry Flitcroft v Mirror Group Newspapers Ltd* [2002] EWCA Civ 337, [2002] 2 All ER 545.

A4.66 The range of expression protected by Art 10 is extensive and includes expression which would be regarded as offensive[1]. Article 10 also protects the form in which the ideas or information is conveyed. The freedom is not limited to words written or spoken but includes artistic works[2], images[3] and dress[4]. Nevertheless, while a range of expression is protected, interference with political speech will be less easily tolerated than commercial and artistic speech[5].

1 *Oberschlick v Austria (No 2)* (1998) 25 EHRR 357.
2 *Müller v Switzerland* (1988) 13 EHRR 212.
3 *Chorherr v Austria* (1993) 17 EHRR 358.
4 See para A4.065, n 3.
5 *Wingrove v United Kingdom* (1996) 24 EHRR 1, 30, para 58.

A4.67 As with Art 8[1] any interference with freedom of expression must be prescribed by law and necessary in a democratic society in the interests of a legitimate aim. The specific qualifications to the right are set out in Art 10(2).

1 See para A4.61.

(f) Article 11, right to freedom of peaceful assembly and association

A4.68 Article 11 guarantees the right of peaceful assembly and association[1]. It may be relevant in the sporting context in relation to 'association' (or, indeed, the right *not* to associate[2]). The European Court has stated that the fact that 'citizens should be able to form a legal entity in order to act collectively in a field of mutual interest is one of the most important aspects of the right'[3]. A professional association established under private law which also performs some public law functions is not precluded from being an association for the purposes of Art 11 if its predominant function is to promote the interests of its members[4]. The freedom to form and join a trade union does not guarantee any particular treatment of the union or its members: there is no right to strike or to be consulted[5].

1 Article 11 states:
'1. Everyone has the right to freedom of peaceful assembly and to freedom of association with others, including the right to form and to join trade unions for the protection of his interests.
2. No restrictions shall be placed on the exercise of these rights other than such as are prescribed by law and are necessary in a democratic society in the interests of national security or public safety, for the prevention of disorder or crime, for the protection of health and morals or for the protection of the rights and freedoms of others. This Article shall not prevent the imposition of lawful restrictions on the exercise of these rights by members of the armed forces, of the police or of the administration of the State.'
2 *Sigurjonsson v Ireland* (1993) 16 EHRR 462. A law which made membership of an automobile association a prerequisite for the acquisition of a taxi driver's licence violated Art 11. Query whether clubs could make the same argument about forced membership of national or international associations. Staff members of sporting organisations must be allowed to form associations with unions or any other mutually beneficial group: UK Sport, 'Human Rights – Implications for Sport'.
3 *Sidiropoulos v Greece* (1998) 27 EHRR 633.
4 *Sigurjonsson v Ireland* (1993) 16 EHRR 462. However, the requirement to be a member of Ordre de Medecins to practise law in Belgium did not breach Art 11 because the public nature of the professional body meant it did not qualify as an 'association': *Le Compte, Van Leuven and De Meyere v Belgium* (1981) 4 EHRR 1.
5 *National Union of Belgian Police v Belgium* (1975) 1 EHRR 578.

A4.69 The general principles concerning justification are as stated above[1]. The European Commission has held that the banning of unions at GCHQ was an interference with Art 11, but was justified bearing in mind the activities carried out there[2]. However, only convincing and compelling reasons can justify any restriction on a party's freedom of association concerning a political party[3].

1 See para A4.61, in relation to Art 8.
2 *Council of Civil Service Unions v United Kingdom*, Application 11603/85 50 DR 228 (1987).
3 *United Communist Party of Turkey v Turkey* (1998) 25 EHRR 121, paras 45 to 46.

(g) Article 14, freedom from discrimination in respect of Convention rights

A4.70 Article 14 guarantees freedom from discrimination[1] only in so far as the discrimination touches on another Convention right. The Article does not, however, presuppose a breach of another provision. A measure which in itself conforms with another Article may violate Art 14 because it is discriminatory in nature[2]. So, a sporting body must ensure that there is equality of treatment in any area which is within the ambit of a Convention right to avoid a breach of Art 14 (and any relevant UK and EC legislation)[3]. If a state chooses to guarantee an aspect of a right when it has no obligation to do so (for example providing a right to appeal under Art 6), there will be a violation of Art 14 if discrimination occurs, notwithstanding the voluntary nature of the state's action[4].

1 Article 14 states: 'The enjoyment of the rights and freedoms set forth in this Convention shall be secured without discrimination on any ground such as sex, race, colour, language, religion, political or other opinion, national or social origin, association with a national minority, property, birth or other status.'
2 *Belgian Linguistics Case (No 2)* (1968) 1 EHRR 252, para 9. See the Eric Liddell case, para A4.62.
3 UK Sport suggests that equal opportunity policies must be followed within organisations, and that team selection practices must be clear and adhered to: 'Human Rights Act – Implications for Sport'. See generally Chapter E3.
4 Lester & Pannick *Human Rights Law and Practice* (1999, Butterworths), para 4.14.5.

A4.71 The list of prohibited grounds of discrimination is set out in the Article itself but is not exhaustive because of the inclusion of 'other status' as the last category[1]. A claim of discrimination contrary to Art 14 will succeed if a claimant shows that he has, within the ambit of a Convention right, been treated differently on a prohibited ground from people in a similar, or analogous, situation[2] and that treatment cannot be justified[3]. Justification will be shown where the difference in treatment pursues a legitimate aim and there is a 'reasonable relationship of proportionality between the means employed and the aim sought to be realised'[4]. The difference in treatment should 'strike a fair balance between the protection of the interests of the community and respect for the rights and freedoms safeguarded by the Convention'[5]. Very weighty reasons have to be advanced for some types of discrimination, for example on the grounds of sex[6] and nationality[7].

1 This includes sexual orientation, Application 33290/96 *Salgueiro da Silva Mouta v Portugal* [2001] 1 FCR 653 and professional status, *Van der Mussele v Belgium* (1983) 6 EHRR 163.
2 The burden is on the claimant to show less favourable treatment in comparable circumstances, and that the basis of the treatment was a prohibited ground: *Selcuk and Asker v Turkey* (1998) 26 EHRR 477, para 102; *Larissis v Greece* (1999) 27 EHRR 329, para 68. If the situation is not comparable, there will be no discrimination: *Stubbings v United Kingdom* (1996) 23 EHRR 213, paras 68 to 71.
3 *Belgian Linguistic Case (No 2)* (1968) 1 EHRR 252.
4 *Darby v Sweden* (1990) 13 EHRR 774, para 31.
5 See n 3.
6 *Abdulaziz, Cabales and Balkandali v United Kingdom* (1985) 7 EHRR 471, para 82.
7 *Gaygusuz v Austria* (1996) 23 EHRR 365, para 42.

(h) Article 1 of the First Protocol, right to property

A4.72 Article 1 of the First Protocol ('A1P1')[1] in substance guarantees the right to property[2]. A wide range of economic interests are protected, including the economic interests connected with running a business (including licences)[3] and the right to exercise a profession[4]. Sporting organisations would therefore be wise to adhere to clear policies in relation to granting licenses, equipment and merchandise and to ensure that terms and conditions of any licences granted are similarly clear[5].

1 A1P1 states: 'Every natural or legal person is entitled to the peaceful enjoyment of his possessions. No one shall be deprived of his possessions except in the public interest and subject to the conditions provided for by law and by the general principles of international law. The preceding provisions shall not, however, in any way impair the right of a state to enforce such laws as it deems necessary to control the use of property in accordance with the general interest or to secure the payment of taxes or other contributions or penalties.'

2 *Marckx v Belgium* (1979) 2 EHRR 330, para 63. The classic example of property is land. It was argued in football disciplinary proceedings, where a team was potentially to be demoted, that such demotion was a breach of Art 1 since the team had a right to play in the higher league.

3 *Tre Traktörer Aktiebolag v Sweden* (1989) 13 EHRR 309, para 53; *Fredin v Sweden* (1991) 13 EHRR 784, para 39; *Catscratch Ltd and Lettuce Holdings Ltd v City of Glasgow Licensing Board* [2001] UKHRR 1309, Ct of Session (licence for bar may be property).

4 *Van Marle v Netherlands* (1986) 8 EHRR 483, paras 41 to 42. See paras D3.62 to D3.64 for a discussion of the possible use of this case to support a sportsman's claim to image rights.

5 UK Sport *Human Rights Act – Implications for Sport* v3 14/12/2000.

A4.73 If domestic law does not recognise a particular interest, Strasbourg may do so (the concept of 'possession' is autonomous[1]). Corporate bodies are protected where they are victims of a violation[2]. There are three rules in A1P1:

(a) the first sentence, which sets out the peaceful enjoyment of property;
(b) the second sentence, which covers deprivation of possessions; and
(c) the third sentence, which deals with control of use[3].

If there is an interference with any part of A1P1, this can be justified only if it is in the public interest[4], although the authorities should be given a wide margin of discretion in making this judgment[5]. Nevertheless, there must still be a reasonably proportionate relationship between the means employed and the aim of the measure, ie there must be a fair balance (which, in any event, is inherent in the whole Convention[6]). Compensation is generally required where there has been a deprivation of property[7].

1 *Tre Traktörer Aktiebolag v Sweden* (1989) 13 EHRR 309, para 53.
2 *Application 9266/81 Yarrow v United Kingdom* 30 DR 155 (1983), European Commission.
3 *Sporrong and Lönnroth v Sweden* (1982) 5 EHRR 35, para 61.
4 *Sporrong* (n 3), paras 69 and 73 (first rule); *Scollo v Italy* (1995) 22 EHRR 514, para 32.
5 *James v United Kingdom* (1986) 8 EHRR 123, para 46.
6 *Sporrong* (n 3), paras 69 and 73.
7 *James v United Kingdom* (1986) 8 EHRR 123, para 54.

4 THE HRA 1998 IN PRACTICE

A The claim

A4.74 This section aims to give a brief overview of what is required in bringing a claim (or making good a defence incorporating a human rights point). A person who claims that a public authority has acted (or proposes to act) in a way which is unlawful under the HRA 1998 may:

(a) bring proceedings against the authority; or
(b) rely on the Convention right or rights concerned in any legal proceedings, but only if he is, or would be, a victim of the unlawful act[1].

This gives a party that qualifies as a 'victim' a new cause of action (and defence) based on the HRA 1998[2].

1 Section 7(1)(a) and (b). Under s 7(1)(b) a victim can rely on a Convention right in any 'legal proceedings'. These are defined as including proceedings brought by or at the instigation of a public authority, and an appeal against the decision of a court or tribunal.
2 For helpful guidance on how to plead a human rights claim or defence, see Leigh-Ann Mulcahy *Human Rights and Civil Practice* (2001, Sweet & Maxwell), paras 8.44 to 8.48.

(a) The victim requirement

A4.75 A person is a 'victim' of an unlawful act only if he would be a victim for the purposes of Art 34[1] of the Convention[2]. The victim test applies even where Convention rights are relied on in judicial review proceedings[3]. The requirement of victim status is narrower than the 'sufficient interest' test in judicial review[4]. For example, it is likely to exclude pressure groups which have standing to bring public interest challenges by way of judicial review. (This does not, of course, prevent them from supporting an individual who is a victim of a breach of human rights.) There is no right to bring proceedings about the law in the abstract[5]. However, it may be possible to be a victim where someone else (such as a close relative) has been affected in certain circumstances[6]. Someone living in a non-Convention country can rely on his Convention rights in certain circumstances[7].

1 Formerly Art 25, it states: 'The Court may receive applications from any person, non-governmental organisation or group of individuals claiming to be the victim of a violation by one of the High Contracting Parties of the rights set forth in the Convention of the protocols thereto. The High Contracting Parties undertake not to hinder in any way the effective exercise of this right.' Governmental organisations can therefore never be victims.
2 Section 7(7).
3 Section 7(3).
4 Grosz et al *Human Rights: The 1998 Act and the Convention* (2000, Sweet & Maxwell), para 4–25.
5 *F v Switzerland* (1988) 10 EHRR 411.
6 Parents of a child had standing to bring a claim under s 7: *R (Holub) v Secretary of State for the Home Department* [2001] 1 WLR 1359, CA at 1364H. But the father of a child who had been murdered did not have standing to challenge the minimum sentences fixed for the killers: *R v Secretary of State for the Home Department, ex p Bulger* [2001] EWHC Admin 119, [2001] 3 All ER 449.
7 For example, where he wishes to exercise his right to freedom of expression in a Convention country: *R (Farrakhan) v Secretary of State for the Home Department* [2002] EWCA Civ 606, [2002] 4 All ER 289.

(b) Forum

A4.76 Proceedings may be brought only in the 'appropriate court or tribunal'[1]. The CPR 1998 provide that a claim under s 7(1)(a) in respect of a 'judicial act' may be brought only in the High Court[2]. Otherwise claims can be brought by way of judicial review[3] or in the County Court or High Court (including by way of counterclaim).

1 Sections 7(1)(a) and 7(2).
2 CPR 1998, Pt 7.11.
3 This is true in relation to sporting bodies only if they are found at some point to be susceptible to review.

(c) *Time limit*

A4.77 Proceedings must be brought before the end of one year beginning with the date on which the act complained of took place[1]. The court has a discretion to extend time if it considers it equitable to do so having regard to all the circumstances[2]. However, if a rule imposes a stricter time limit in relation to a particular procedure, then that stricter time limit applies (for example, the three months or less for judicial review)[3].

1 Section 7(5)(a).
2 Section 7(5)(b).
3 Section 7(5).

B Remedies

A4.78 Where an unlawful act has been committed, the court may grant any relief or remedy within its powers as it considers just and appropriate[1]. But damages may be awarded only by a court which has the power to award damages, or to award compensation, in civil proceedings[2]. No award of damages may be made unless, in all the circumstances of the case, the court is satisfied that the award made is necessary to afford 'just satisfaction' to the victim[3]. The court must take into account the principles applied under Art 41 of the Convention[4].

1 Section 8(1). This includes injunctive relief.
2 Section 8(2).
3 Section 8(3).
4 Section 8(4). Art 41 states: 'If the Court finds that there has been a violation of the Convention or the protocols thereto, and if the internal law of the High Contracting Party concerned allows only partial reparation to be made, the Court shall, if necessary, afford just satisfaction to the injured party.'

(a) *Just satisfaction*

A4.79 The European Court of Human Rights has a discretion whether or not to award damages[1]. It frequently decides that a finding of a violation of a Convention right is sufficient to provide just satisfaction[2]. Damages can, however, be awarded both for pecuniary loss (eg. loss of earnings[3]) and non-pecuniary loss (eg. injury to feelings and distress[4]). The principles in relation to the grant of pecuniary damages are that:

(a) the applicant should be restored as far as possible to the position he was in before the breach;
(b) the inherently uncertain nature of the damage resulting from a breach may prevent a precise calculation; and
(c) the level of damages depends on what is equitable[5].

Awards for pecuniary loss tend to be highest in relation to Art 1 of the First Protocol[6]. Most awards for non-pecuniary damage are not high, with few exceeding £15,000[7].

1 *Guzzardi v Italy* (1980) 3 EHRR 333.
2 See, for example, *Saunders v United Kingdom* (1996) 23 EHRR 313.
3 *Lustig-Prean and Beckett v United Kingdom* (2001) 31 EHRR 601.
4 *Halford v United Kingdom* (1997) 24 EHRR 523.
5 *Lustig-Prean*, see above.

6 IR£1.2m in *Pine Valley Developments Ltd v Ireland* (1993) 16 EHRR 379.

7 Mulcahy *Human Rights and Civil Practice* (2001, Sweet & Maxwell), para 8.54. See also para A3.199 et seq for a more detailed exposition on damages and Simor & Emmerson *Human Rights Practice* (2001, Sweet & Maxwell), App 9.

(b) Judicial acts

A4.80 Under the HRA 1998, damages may not be awarded in respect of a judicial act[1] done in good faith, other than to compensate a person to the extent required by Art 5(5) of the Convention[2].

1 A judicial act means a judicial act of a court or tribunal and includes an act done on the instructions, or on behalf, of a judge: s 9(5).

2 Section 9(3). Article 5(5) provides that: 'Everyone who has been the victim of arrest or detention in contravention of the provisions of this article shall have an enforceable right to compensation.'

CHAPTER A5

ARBITRATION AND ADR IN SPORT

Paul Manning (Hammonds) and **Max Duthie** (Freehills)

Contents

1 INTRODUCTION

A5.1 Chapter A3 of this book identifies the broad range and scope of issues that can arise between participants in the sports sector, and explains how those disputes can be resolved by litigation in the courts, by arbitration or other alternative dispute resolution mechanism, or even (in specific circumstances) by reference to administrative authorities such as the European Commission and the Office of Fair Trading.

A5.2 This chapter focuses on the second of these routes, ie the use of arbitration and other alternative dispute resolution (ADR) mechanisms to resolve disputes in the sports sector[1], broadly defined to encompass any and all 'methods of resolving disputes otherwise than through the normal trial process'[2]. First, it identifies the main types of ADR used in the sports sector. Then it surveys some of the advantages (both general and sports-specific), as well as the disadvantages, of using ADR mechanisms rather than litigation to resolve disputes. Next it considers the routes to ADR in the sports sector, including the provision made for ADR in the rules and regulations of governing bodies and event organisers, and in the contracts underpinning sports-related commercial programmes, as well as ad hoc ADR agreements made after a dispute has arisen. It then describes the main sports-specific ADR providers. Finally, it highlights some of the practical issues that should be addressed when drafting ADR clauses for use in the sports sector.

1 Practice varies as to whether arbitration is considered to be distinct from, or simply one species of, ADR. This is because, as a binding, adjudicative mechanism, arbitration is closer in many ways to litigation than to the non-binding facilitative ADR methods such as mediation and conciliation. In this chapter, however, arbitration is treated as simply one form of ADR, and references to ADR should be deemed to encompass arbitration.
2 See definition of ADR in the Glossary to the Civil Procedure Rules (2002).

2 TYPES OF ADR USED IN SPORT

A Arbitration

A5.3 Arbitration is the adjudication of disputes by an independent third party or parties. The process is adversarial and can be very similar to litigation, with the parties presenting their respective cases to the arbitrator(s) in the form of legal submissions as well as documentary evidence and (where appropriate) witness testimony, and the arbitrator(s) then making binding rulings on the issues of law and fact in dispute, set out in an award that is enforceable in much the same way as a court judgment. The main difference from traditional litigation is that the parties can choose the arbitration forum, the identity of the arbitrator(s), and the specific rules and procedures that are to be followed. In addition, unlike litigation the arbitration proceedings are private.

A5.4 Any bilateral dispute arising between participants in a sport, or between a sports party and its commercial partner, may be resolved by arbitration before a specialist arbitration forum such as the Court of Arbitration for Sport[1] or the Sports Dispute Resolution Panel[2]. There have been a series of high profile disputes resolved in this manner, such as the recent dispute between ENIC and UEFA over the application of UEFA's multiple ownership rule[3], and the various doping decisions made by the Ad Hoc Division of CAS sitting at recent Olympic Games in Salt Lake[4].

1 See paras A5.84 to A5.123.
2 See paras A5.124 to A5.134.
3 See paras A5.182 and A5.183.
4 See para A5.122, n 1.

A5.5 In addition, the proceedings in which disciplinary charges are heard, vindicating the collective interests of the participants in a sport in the application and enforcement of the rules and regulations of that sport, will often effectively take the form of arbitration proceedings[1].

1 See further paras A5.142 to A5.146. See generally Chapter A2.

B Mediation

A5.6 Mediation involves the submission of a dispute to an impartial third party who tries to assist the parties in negotiating a settlement of the dispute. Generally, all mediation discussions are confidential and 'without prejudice'. The mediator does not usually hear arguments or consider evidence. Rather he holds informal joint and private meetings with the parties, and seeks to facilitate the settlement of the dispute by finding common ground and focusing on common interests rather than areas of contention.

A5.7 One of the key features of mediation is that it is non-binding: the mediator is not adjudicating on the issues in dispute between the parties, and cannot impose a solution on them. Rather, it is for the parties to adopt a proposed solution and enter into a binding settlement agreement.

A5.8 The profile of mediation in the sports sector has increased considerably with the successful Richie Woodhall/Frank Warren and George Graham/Tottenham Hotspur mediations[1]. The former in particular illustrates some of the advantages of ADR in general and mediation in particular over litigation. Mr Woodhall was a boxer who had signed management and promotion agreements with Mr Warren pursuant to which Mr Warren would exclusively represent Mr Woodhall, and Mr Woodhall would fight exclusively in Mr Warren's promotions. In April 1999, Mr Woodhall purported to terminate those agreements on the grounds that (1) Mr Warren was in breach of those agreements and in any event (2) the agreements were unenforceable. Mr Woodhall had apparently fought his last bout in the Warren "stable" and began to sound out alternative manager/promoters. However, Mr Warren denied any breach of the agreements, and sought to hold Mr Woodhall to what he regarded as a valid and binding agreement. Mr Woodhall issued proceedings in June 1999 for a declaration that he was not bound by the contracts, but time was against him as he was compelled under World Boxing Organisation (WBO) rules to defend his WBO world title within the three months that followed, ie by September 1999. In addition, the agreements contained clauses referring disputes to arbitration by the British Boxing Board of Control.

1 Blackshaw 'Resolving sports disputes the modern way – by mediation' [2000] 1 SATLJ 18; Newark 'Is mediation effective for resolving sports disputes?' [2000] 5(6) ISLJ 37. See also generally Blackshaw 'Sporting Settlements' 145(27) Sol Jo, 13 July 2001; Blackshaw 'Mediating Sports Disputes' (2002) 5(4) Sports Law Bulletin 12; Blackshaw *Mediating Sports Disputes: National and International Perspectives* (2002, TMC Asser Press); Carroll and Mackie *International Mediation – The Art of Business Diplomacy* (1999, Kluwer Law International); Slate *The Growth of Mediation and Mediation in Sports Disputes in the US* (2000), Paper presented at the CAS Symposium on Mediation (Lausanne, 4 November 2000).

A5.9 A lengthy and expensive dispute loomed, but that would have served the interests of neither party. In particular, it would not have been practical for Mr Woodhall to defend his WBO title with the ongoing legal battle unresolved. This shared interest proved the catalyst for the parties to agree to seek a resolution of the matter by mediation before Mr Warren had even served his defence to the claim.

A5.10 The mediation was conducted at short notice by the Centre for Effective Dispute Resolution. Within less than 72 hours, the dispute was resolved, with Mr Woodhall signing a new contract with Mr Warren. The matter remained private (the details of the settlement remain confidential), and the parties were able to preserve and restore their relationship instead of moving to the entrenchment of views and estrangement that almost inevitably results from litigation[1].

1 See Gibb 'How to settle disputes without a legal punch up' (1999) Times, 3 August. Another good example of the use of mediation in sport relates to the dispute between Ellery Hanley and the directors of his club Leeds arising from his public comments about them. Leeds could not realistically sack him because he was too popular with the club's fans, but after a full day of mediation/negotiation, the club accepted a public apology from Hanley and he accepted a 10-day suspension. The value of mediation when the true objective of one of the parties is to get an apology from the other party was emphasised by the Court of Appeal in the *Dunnett* case, discussed below at para A5.80.

C Other forms of ADR

A5.11 The other main forms of ADR are fact-finding/expert determination, early neutral evaluation and mini-trial.

A5.12 Fact-finding/expert determination is the process by which an appropriately qualified impartial third party is asked to determine certain facts in dispute. The process is adjudicative and usually binding, and as such can be similar to arbitration, save that there are usually no issues of law to be resolved, only factual issues, and the procedure (which the parties are completely free to fashion as they see fit) is likely to tend towards the inquisitorial rather than the adversarial[1].

1 See generally, Kendall *Expert Determinations* (3rd edn, 2001, Sweet & Maxwell).

A5.13 Expert determination may be particularly appropriate and useful in the context of sponsorship agreements or similar arrangements involving the granting and delivery of a package of commercial rights relating to a sports property. In the case of long-term agreements, the contracting parties may not be able, or may not wish, to predict at the time of entering into the contract the value of the rights in the future. One option is to refer the matter for expert determination at the appropriate time. Alternatively, where part of the package of rights is not delivered – for example, in a title sponsorship agreement some perimeter boards were not placed, or were placed wrongly, or were obscured – rather than have a claim for damages for breach the parties may agree instead to refer the matter to an expert to place a value on the rights not delivered in order to fix the level of compensation required.

A5.14 The most high-profile use of this procedure in the sports context in recent times was the expert determination of the value of the television rights to England's home matches in the Five (now Six) Nations Championship rugby union tournament. The dispute arose when the RFU unilaterally departed from the collective selling arrangement that the four home unions had previously operated in relation to the television rights to their home matches in the Championship. The RFU sold to BSkyB for £65m the worldwide broadcasting rights to a package of matches under the RFU's control, most significantly the rights to all of the national team's home matches, both in the Five Nations Championship and against incoming touring teams. The resulting dispute was settled by an Accord, with the parties agreeing that the proportion of the rights fee paid by BSkyB to the RFU that was attributable to the Five Nations Championship matches would be pooled with the revenue from the sale of broadcasting rights to the Celtic Unions' home Five Nations matches for division between the four home unions according to an agreed formula.

A5.15 However, BSkyB had paid one global rights fee for the whole package of rights granted by the RFU, without allocating a value to the different component parts. The greater the value of the Five Nations games, the more the RFU would have to pay into the central pot. Therefore, it was no surprise when the parties could not agree on the value, with the Celtic Unions saying that most of the £65m rights fee was attributable to the Five Nations element of the rights package, and the RFU insisting that only a small portion of it should be attributed to the Five Nations matches. Under the terms of the Accord, the dispute was referred for determination by an expert appointed by the President of the Law Society. Although the resulting procedure took over a year, and involved voluminous documentary and witness evidence, as well as submissions on legal and accounting issues, this was in all likelihood quicker than court proceedings would have been, and there was a great deal of flexibility over the procedures followed, adapting as the matter proceeded to the circumstances of the case. Moreover, the highly sensitive result was kept secret.

A5.16 Early neutral valuation is where the parties refer an issue in dispute to an independent third party, such as a Queen's Counsel, for a non-binding evaluation of the merits, which can help to bring realism to the parties' negotiating positions. Mini-trial is where the parties agree to an expedited adjudicative process before a forum other than the court, the scope of which is usually narrowed (for example, no live testimony, restricted documentary evidence) and the result of which may or may not be binding. Neither method is widely used at present in the sports sector.

3 WHY USE ADR?

A5.17 ADR mechanisms are perceived to have various advantages over litigation as a means of dispute resolution, some of them generally applicable and others specific to sport[1]. In some circumstances, however, there may be disadvantages to using ADR rather than issuing proceedings.

1 See generally Paulsson 'Arbitration of International Sports Disputes' [1993] *Arbitration International* Vol. 9, p 359; *Using Alternative Dispute Resolution to Settle Sports Disputes* (1995, American Arbitration Association); Perry G 'Dispute resolution in sport: new challenges new options' [2001] 1 ISLR 92; Blackshaw I 'Settling Sports Scores' www.sportbusiness.com (20 May 2002); Blackshaw I 'Sporting Settlements' 145(27) Sol Jo, 13 July 2001; Lazic V 'Conference on ADR in Sports Disputes' (2000) International Sports Law Journal 35; Richbell D 'Don't hesitate – mediate' *Sport Business* (December 1999).

A Advantages of ADR

(a) A unitary system of dispute resolution

A5.18 One of the main reasons why governing bodies use ADR is the desire for a unitary system of dispute resolution in sport applying, in so far as is possible, a uniform set of principles in a consistent way. Just as participants expect the same on-field playing rules to apply wherever in the world they take part in their sport, they can also justifiably expect to be subject to broadly the same non-playing rules and principles applied in the same way wherever in the world they are. In other words, the desire for a level playing-field extends beyond the content and application of the 'laws of the game' to such matters as disciplinary proceedings, anti-doping, selection/eligibility and transfers.

A5.19 The danger is that if the resolution of such disputes is left to the courts, then different courts in different nations may reach conflicting decisions on the same issues, leading to inequality and unfairness as between participants in different countries. In contrast, ADR bodies have more flexibility to develop and apply general principles and rules uniformly and across the board, throughout the whole of the sport.

A5.20 Consequently, many sports require participants to submit their disputes to ADR, and specifically to one unitary system of ADR[1]. Local disputes may be resolved by reference to a local ADR mechanism, but usually there will be provision for appeal to one universally applicable international ADR mechanism, either internal or external to the sport, so that ultimately the same body construes and applies the rules of the sport in every case.

1 For example, in the field of anti-doping. See paras A5.53 to A5.58.

(b) Speed

A5.21 Litigation through the courts leads to delay, which can often render the result of the dispute meaningless, particularly in a sporting context. For example, for an athlete in a dispute over his or her eligibility to participate in particular event, delay in the case coming to trial until after that event would make any victory a pyrrhic one. It would also undermine the integrity of the event itself to find out in retrospect that the athlete who was forced to sit out the event should have been allowed to participate.

A5.22 While courts are able to act quickly when the occasion demands[1], they would be hard-put to match, for example, the Ad Hoc Division of CAS, which sits on site at major events such as the Olympics and the Commonwealth Games, and aims where necessary to resolve disputes in a matter of hours[2].

1 For example, in the aftermath of the collapse of ITV Digital, on 17 May 2002, the effect on Football League clubs of the failure of ITV Digital to pay the rights fees due under the Football League broadcasting contract was predicted to be disastrous, and a number of clubs were threatened with insolvency. Therefore, it was vitally important to have the Football League's claim that ITV Digital's parent companies (Carlton and Granada) had guaranteed those payments resolved expeditiously. Consequently, the High Court set the matter down for trial in July 2002, only two months after proceedings were issued.

2 See para A5.92 and A5.106

(c) Expertise

A5.23 Parties appreciate having disputes resolved by people who understand the field in which the dispute has arisen. This is as true in the sporting context as in any other area. The arbitrator or mediator, for example, is more likely to enjoy the confidence of the disputing parties if he or she knows one end of a tennis racket from the other. The confidence in the decision-making process is further increased by the fact that the party may be entitled under the applicable rules to choose (or at least influence the choice of) an arbitrator or mediator.

A5.24 Sports disputes can involve certain concepts that are largely peculiar to sport, such as the concepts of 'bringing a sport into disrepute'[1], or 'just sporting cause'[2]. In addition, some of the remedies available – eg suspension from participation, docking of points, promotion or relegation – will be very unfamiliar to courts, and consequently difficult for them to apply with any confidence that the decision will be fair in the context of the specific event or sport.

1 See para A2.45.
2 As to which see para E1.63 et seq.

A5.25 When faced with such alien concepts, it is highly likely that different courts will arrive at different, and often unusual and unexpected, interpretations and decisions. Sports ADR bodies, on the other hand, can construe and apply such concepts from a background of knowledge and expertise in the field that will inspire confidence in their decision-making abilities.

A5.26 In sum, the practical benefits of having an independent third party involved in the resolution of the dispute who has this particular expertise include:

(1) greater efficiency, with associated costs savings;
(2) a greater understanding of, and familiarity with, the range of sporting sanctions available and the appropriateness of their use in the particular circumstances of the case; and
(3) the result therefore being realistic, well-reasoned and informed.

(d) Cost

A5.27 It is often said that ADR is a cheaper alternative to litigation. This can be overstated, particularly in arbitrations, where much of the process is very similar to litigation, and where (in contrast to the courts) the parties have to pay the arbitrators for their services. However, even in arbitrations the choice that the parties have in relation to the procedures to be followed can cut down on process and therefore cost, while the other forms of ADR can be far narrower in nature and scope and therefore should allow for genuine cost savings if successful in bringing about a resolution of the dispute.

(e) Finality

A5.28 Arbitral awards are open to challenge in the courts on only limited grounds[1]. Therefore, parties to an arbitration proceeding can reasonably expect to resolve the dispute once and for all, thereby ensuring that all affected parties know exactly where they stand, which can be very important to minimise the inevitable disruption when the dispute impinges in some way on an ongoing competition or event.

1 See paras A5.173 to A5.180.

(f) Enforceability

A5.29 120 nations are party to the New York Convention[1], which governs the international recognition and enforcement of arbitral awards. In contrast, outside Europe there are few multi-lateral conventions for the enforcement of court judgments. Consequently, arbitral awards are more readily enforceable on a global basis then court judgments[2].

1 The New York Convention for the Recognition and Enforcement of Foreign Arbitral Awards (June 1958).
2 See *Russell on Arbitration* (21st edn, 1997, Sweet & Maxwell) at para 1-017.

(g) Privacy

A5.30 Trials are conducted in public, while as a rule ADR is conducted in private. This can be particularly important in commercial sports disputes where, for example, neither the rights-holder nor its commercial partner wants the value of the rights sold, or the dispute that has arisen in relation to those rights, to become public knowledge.

(h) Preservation of goodwill

A5.31 As the Woodhall/Warren case noted above illustrates[1], at least in the case of mediation or negotiation, it may be possible to protect to some degree the relationship between the parties and perhaps enable the relationship to continue in the future without the animosity that litigation or arbitration can often generate.

1 See paras A5.8 and A5.9.

A5.32 The sports business is often very small and close-knit, so that it serves everyone in that community to maintain their relationships with each other, especially with player/manager, player/sponsor and board/executive disputes. Litigation is inherently adversarial and uncooperative, and can drive an irreconcilable wedge between the parties. Mediation focuses on the shared interests of the parties and therefore serves to bring those parties together and to reopen lines of communication that would have been severed permanently by litigation. Mediation is forward-looking and avoids the winner-loser attitudes and outcomes of litigation, making win-win outcomes a possibility. Even if win-win results are not possible, the 'pain' may be shared between the parties.

(i) Negotiation compromise

A5.33 ADR can offer a useful compromise when negotiating a jurisdiction clause in a contract, particularly in the international context, where contracting parties from different nations may each seek to insist that their national courts have exclusive jurisdiction over disputes arising under the contract.

(j) Avoiding court sanction

A5.34 After a dispute has arisen, even if there is no express obligation in any applicable contract or rules to refer the matter to ADR, there is an obligation on litigants before the English courts to assist the courts in furthering the overriding objective of dealing with cases justly and efficiently[1], which is being construed to mean (among other things) taking very seriously the possibility of resolving the dispute by ADR, without recourse to the courts, on pain of sanction in case of default[2].

1 See Pt 1.1 of the CPR 1998.
2 See further paras A5.78 to A5.81.

B Disadvantages of ADR

A5.35 Arbitral procedures are potentially subject to delay while disputes are resolved as to the validity, scope and applicability of the alleged agreement to arbitrate[1]. Under the Arbitration Act 1998, disputes as to the jurisdiction of the arbitrator may be resolved by the arbitrator him or herself, and it is also possible for an arbitrator to defer resolution of that question until after he or she has heard all of the evidence on the merits of a case, which can be inefficient if the eventual conclusion is that he or she has no jurisdiction[2].

1 See paras A5.147 to A5.172.
2 See s 30 of the Arbitration Act 1996, and *Caltex*, cited at para A5.160, n 1.

A5.36 Similarly, if mediation does not lead to a resolution of the dispute, the time and costs invested will have been wasted[1].

1 When the RFU and the then English First Division Rugby (EFDR) clubs were in conflict, the chief executive of the EFDR clubs was quoted as saying 'It wouldn't make any difference if they brought the Queen in to arbitrate': (2000) Guardian, 20 October. This sort of entrenched position would make mediation difficult.

A5.37 There will also be certain cases when the relief sought by the disputing party (for example, emergency interim relief in the form of an injunction) simply is not available from the ADR body, and so court proceedings are unavoidable. Even if such a remedy is available under the rules of the ADR forum chosen by the parties, (1) an injunction from the court is backed up by the court's powers of enforcement, whereas the sanctions that an ADR tribunal may impose on a party that breaches an injunction imposed by that tribunal may be limited; and (2) arbitral tribunals, unlike the courts, may be unable to compel a third party to comply with the terms of an injunction.

A5.38 While mediation may be appropriate for the resolution of purely bilateral disputes, it can be inappropriate where there are broader interests at stake. For example, when a breach of the rules and regulations of the sport is alleged, there is a collective interest in enforcing those rules and thereby upholding the integrity of the sport. An obvious example would be an allegation of use during competition of a prohibited doping substance or method. With other disciplinary offences too, the governing body is often faced with certain conduct that must be stamped out so as to ensure the safety of participants (such as spear tackles in rugby) or to maintain the reputation of sport with the public (such as match-fixing). Mediation would appear inappropriate in relation to such disputes because of the need to vindicate the rights of those who are not directly parties to the dispute[1].

1 This is implicitly acknowledged by the CAS rules restricting the disputes that may be referred to its mediation service to those that would otherwise be brought under the Ordinary Arbitration Procedure, excluding disputes that would be brought before the Appeals Arbitration Division: 'CAS mediation is provided solely for the resolution of disputes related to the CAS ordinary procedure. A decision passed by the organ of a sports organization cannot be the subject of mediation proceedings before the CAS. All disputes related to disciplinary matters, as well as doping issues, are expressly excluded from CAS mediation': Art 1, CAS Mediation Rules.

4 ROUTES TO ADR

A5.39 This section addresses first the use by governing bodies and event organisers of ADR in their rules and regulations, then the provision for ADR in contacts with commercial partners, before considering the ad hoc use of ADR in relation to existing disputes, the motivation for which should be much stronger now that the Civil Procedure Rules require litigating parties to consider ADR seriously, on pain of costs sanctions if they fail to do so.

A Governing body rules and regulations

A5.40 Governing bodies make use of ADR in various ways and at different stages of disputes. For example, most governing bodies will exercise a disciplinary function in relation to enforcement of the rules of the game and other regulations. Traditionally, this has involved the referral of charges to be heard by disciplinary tribunals that follow arbitral or quasi-arbitral procedures. This type of mechanism, which is examined in some detail in Chapter A2, was traditionally a purely internal affair, with disciplinary personnel drawn from within the sport itself (indeed, often from within the governing body itself). However, in order to comply with developing standards of procedural fairness, the recent trend has been to incorporate external elements into the disciplinary process, so that the disciplinary panels are manned by personnel who are independent of the governing body or event organiser itself and/or there is provision for reference to an external body such as CAS or the SDRP, either at first instance or on appeal.

A5.41 In addition, where disputes arise between participants in a sport outside the disciplinary context, then the rules and regulations of the governing body of the sport may require them to keep that dispute 'within the game' by submitting it to some form of ADR.

(a) Use of ADR in relation to disciplinary charges

A5.42 Where a governing body brings disciplinary charges against a participant for breach of the rules and regulations of the sport, it may refer those charges to a disciplinary panel that it itself has convened from suitably experienced people within the sport. A good example of this is the International Rugby Board, which provides that breaches of the Laws of the Game and/or of the Regulations Relating to the Game, as well as 'any conduct [by a Union or Association] which may be prejudicial to the interests of the Board or of the Game [of rugby union]' shall be referred to a 'Judicial Committee' for adjudication, subject to appeal to an 'Appeal Committee'[1]. Such committees are selected from a panel of individuals appointed on two-year terms by the IRB Council, which individuals may (in the case of Judicial Committees but not Appeal Committees) include Council members themselves. The only requirements for such individuals are that (if they are to serve on Appeal Committees) they be '(a) senior legal practitioners with previous experience of judicial proceedings in rugby ...; (b) [e]minent rugby administrators, rugby players, coaches and officials with previous experience of judicial proceedings in rugby; [or] (c) [s]uch other individuals as the Council may consider appropriate'[2].

1 See IRB Constitution, Bye-Law 7 and reg 17 of the Regulations Relating to the Game (2002).
2 Regulation 17.3.2 of the IRB Regulations Relating to the Game (2002).

A5.43 Under the Rules of the Football Association (FA Rules), disciplinary charges against a 'Participant'[1] for breach of the FA Rules are normally heard by a Disciplinary Commission, comprising not less than three members of the FA Council. However, the Disciplinary Commission may also include an independent individual 'who is a Barrister or Solicitor of seven or more years standing and whose appointment has been approved by the FA Board'[2].

1 Defined in Rule A2 of the FA Rules as an 'Affiliated Association, Competition, Club, Club Official, Player, Official, Match Official and all such persons who are from time to time participating in any activity sanctioned either directly or indirectly by the [FA]'.

2 FA Rule G9.

A5.44 Similarly, under the Rules and Procedures of the Rugby Football Union (RFU), disciplinary charges instituted by the RFU's Disciplinary Officer may be heard either by a disciplinary panel convened from people within the game *or* by an independent arbitrator. The RFU Council decides who should determine the case, while the Disciplinary Officer has a limited role of ensuring that the panel appointed by the RFU Council has the necessary expertise[1].

1 See paras 2.2 of the Delegation of Powers Regulations, and para 17.1(iii) of the 'Instructions for the guidance and assistance at Disciplinary Committees on the Procedure and Conduct at Disciplinary Hearings' (RFU Disciplinary Rules). In the recent hearings arising from Leicester Tigers, England and British Lions captain Martin Johnson punching Saracens player Robbie Russell during the Leicester/Saracens fixture on 9 February 2002, decided at first instance by a panel chaired by Richard Smith QC (22 February 2002) and on appeal by David Pannick QC (5 March 2002), Mr Johnson's counsel suggested that under the RFU rules it was for the Disciplinary Officer to bring the charges and appoint the Panel, which was in breach of the rules of natural justice (not being a judge in one's own cause). However, David Pannick QC rejected this interpretation of the RFU Rules and Procedures in favour of the Disciplinary Officer having the more limited role of supervising the suitability of the potential panel members.

A5.45 Having the option in the rules and regulations to use an independent panel/panelist can be particularly useful in high-profile cases like that of Martin Johnson[1], where there is a lot riding on a decision and the likelihood of a challenge to an adverse award is high.

1 See para A5.44, n 1.

(b) Use of ADR in relation to other disputes

A5.46 Disputes may arise outside the disciplinary context, for example in relation to an interpretation of the rules and regulations of the sport, or the application of those rules to a particular situation, such as selection for a representative team. Such disputes may arise between participants in the sport, or between a participant and the governing body itself. Many governing body rules and regulations provide for the referral of such disputes to an ADR forum, which may be internal or external.

A5.47 For example, FA Rule K provides that disputes between 'Participants'[1], or between a Participant and the FA itself, 'including but not limited to a dispute arising out of or in connection with (including any question regarding the existence or validity of):

(i) the Rules and Regulations of the Association;
(ii) the rules and regulations of an Affiliated Association or Competition;
(iii) the Statutes and Regulations of FIFA and UEFA; or
(iv) the Laws of the Game shall be referred to and finally resolved by arbitration under these Rules'[2].

The parties each nominate an arbitrator and agree on a third arbitrator to act as chair. In the absence of agreement, a chair is nominated by the Chairman of the FA (or, if the FA is a party to the dispute, by the President of the Chartered Institute of Arbitrators)[3]. The arbitrators must be 'impartial and independent of all of the parties to the arbitration at all times'[4]. However, except in cases involving the FA the arbitrators do not necessarily have to be independent of the FA[5].

1 See para A5.43, n 1.
2 FA Rule K(1)(a). FA Rule K(1)(b) provides that the arbitration agreement 'shall not apply to any dispute or difference which fails [sic] to be resolved pursuant to any rules from time to time in force of any Affiliated Association or Competition'.
3 FA Rules K2(a)(IV), K2(c)(IV), K3 (c)(iii). FA Rule K3 also provides for the appointment of the panel in the event that one of the disputing Participants fails to nominate an arbitrator.
4 Rule K3(C)(D) of the FA Rules.
5 So, for example, Wimbledon FC's challenge in 2001 to the refusal of the board of the Football League to grant permission for the club to relocate to Milton Keynes was heard by a three-person arbitration panel convened under FA Rule K, consisting of a nominee of the club, a nominee of the League and a QC appointed by the FA to act as chair. See para A3.26, n 1.

A5.48 Similarly, the Football League (FL) recently instituted a new arbitration panel, The Football Disciplinary Commission (FDC), to determine 'all complaints and charges made under [the Regulations of the Football League Limited]'. The FDC will sit in three member panels, consisting of a chairperson, who will be a solicitor or barrister of at least five years post-qualification experience, and one member nominated by each of the Complainant and the Respondent[2].

1 Regulation 72 of the Regulations of the Football League Limited (2002/2003). The FDC was approved at the FL's annual meeting in June 2002, and it will operate with the assistance of the Chartered Institute of Arbitrators, which will, among other things, appoint an independent chairperson when a complaint is made to the FDC against the FL itself: Regulations 72.5 and 75.9 of the Regulations of the Football League Limited.

The FDC was called into action on 23 August 2002 when it had to decide the claim brought by Dennis Wise against Leicester City FC for unfair dismissal arising from the incident in pre-season training that resulted in Mr Wise's team-mate, Callum Davidson, suffering a fractured cheekbone. The FDC panel of Sir Philip Otton, the retired Court of Appeal judge (chair), Robbie Earle, the former Wimbledon player, and Frank Clark, the former Nottingham Forest manager, allowed Mr Wise's claim and ordered Leicester City FC to re-instate him.

However, on 18 September 2002 that decision was overturned on appeal by an FA Commission consisting of Sir Robert Reid QC, Andy Williamson of the FL, ex-player John Bramhall and Keith Burkinshaw, the former Tottenham Hotspur manager. See further para E1.19, n 6.

A5.49 In contrast, other governing bodies refer such disputes to CAS for resolution. For example, the Commonwealth Games Federation (CGF) provides in its rules that '[a]ny dispute or difference arising under or concerning the interpretation of [the CGF] Constitution, or the Games Management Protocol, or the Regulations shall, if not able to be resolved by agreement whether by mediation or otherwise, be settled by arbitration' before the CAS[1].

1 Article 30 of the CGF Constitution. The Games Management Protocol and the Regulations govern, among other things, the logistical, technical and administrative details for hosting the Commonwealth Games.

(c) Use of ADR on appeal

A5.50 A number of governing bodies and event organisers provide for appeals from the first instance decisions of internal tribunals to be resolved by arbitration.

A5.51 The RFU once again takes a combined approach. Under para 2 of the RFU's Delegation of Powers regulations, and para 17.1 of the RFU's Disciplinary Rules, an appeal against a first instance disciplinary decision may be heard by either:

(i) an independent arbitrator;
(ii) an Appeal Panel of between three and five members of the RFU Council, or
(iii) an Appeal Panel chaired by an independent person, ie not a member of the RFU Council, and consisting of two to four other panellists who may be RFU Council members.

A5.52 Similarly, Rule H6 of the FA Rules provides that the FA's Appeal Board, ordinarily comprising three members of the FA Council, may instead be chaired by 'a Barrister or Solicitor of seven or more years standing and whose appointment has been approved by the [FA] Board', but who need not be a Member of the FA Council[1].

1 This provision mirrors the use of independent third parties to chair FA Disciplinary Committees, under FA Rule 69, noted at para A5.43.

A5.53 More usually, however, the rules simply provide for appeal to an external arbitral forum, in particular CAS[1].

1 See eg Art 64 of the General Bye-Laws of the International Basketball Federation; Art 059 of the Statutes of the International Equestrian Federation; Art C20 of the Constitution of the International Amateur Swimming Federation; and Art 13.8 of the Constitution and r C1 of the Competition Rules of the International Triathlon Union, all of which provide for appeal to the CAS.

A5.54 The best example of this, and a mechanism that best exemplifies the use of ADR to establish a unitary dispute resolution system ensuring uniform and consistent enforcement of globally applicable sporting rules, is the provision in the IOC Anti-Doping Code and now the draft World Anti-Doping Code for a right of appeal from the decisions of anti-doping tribunals of international federations to the CAS.

A5.55 So, for example, the IOC Anti-Doping Code provides: 'Any Participant affected by a decision rendered in application of this Code by the IOC, an [International Federation], an [National Olympic Committee] or other body may appeal from that decision to the Court of Arbitration for Sport, in accordance with the provisions applicable before such court'[1]. The IOC Code states:

> Participants shall accept the individual or joint obligation to submit disputes concerning the application of this Code to the Court of Arbitration for Sport. Such acceptance is presumed by the very fact of participation by the Participants in the Olympic Movement. Any de facto refusal of such acceptance shall result in the Participants being considered as having excluded themselves from the Olympic Movement[2].

1 Olympic Movement Anti-Doping Code (Lausanne 2001), Ch Three, Art One.
2 Olympic Movement Anti-Doping Code (Lausanne 2001), Ch Three, Art Six. 'Participants' is defined in Chapter One, Article One as '... any athlete, coach, trainer, official, medical or para-medical personnel working with or treating athletes participating in or preparing for sports competitions of the Olympic Games, those competitions to which the IOC grants its patronage or support and all competitions organised under the authority, whether direct or delegated, of an IF or NOC.'

A5.56 Similarly, the current draft of the World Anti-Doping Code that is to replace the IOC Code in 2004[1] designates CAS as the exclusive appeal body against 'decisions rendered in the application of the [Code], or in the application of the anti-doping policies or rules of any *anti-doping agency* which has accepted the [Code] and which affect any *person's* competitive status or opportunity to participate in sport' (emphasis in the original)[2].

1 See para E4.45.
2 Draft WADA Code, E-Version 1.0, issued 10 June 2002. Interestingly, the draft Code also notes, without further explanation, that 'various issues still need to be resolved with CAS before it is designated as the exclusive appellate body under the Code'. The draft Code also provides that not only the athlete, the athlete's National Olympic Committee, national federation and national anti-doping organisation but also any anti-doping agency involved in the proceedings, the international federation, the IOC and WADA may appeal a decision (Draft Code, para 8.9.2), and that 'CAS decisions shall be subject to judicial review as provided by Swiss law' (Draft Code, para 8.9.3).

A5.57 It is hardly surprising, given the threat of exclusion from the Olympic Movement, that many governing bodies and event organisers have altered their rules and regulations to provide for appeal to the CAS in anti-doping matters[1]. As a result, the CAS has been able to make a significant contribution to the development of globally applicable principles in this vital area of sports law[2].

1 However, not all governing bodies have yet done so: the world governing bodies of football (FIFA) and rugby union (the International Rugby Board) do not use the CAS. Moreover, the IAAF had its own internal arbitral appeals board until it resolved in 2001 to adopt the OMADC and refer its doping appeals to the CAS. See Reeb 'The IAAF to recognise the jurisdiction of the Court of Arbitration for Sport' [2001] 4 ISLR 246.
2 See detailed discussion at paras E4.77 to E4.82.

A5.58 For example, under the Anti-Doping Programme of the International Tennis Federation (ITF), challenges to a Review Board's determination of a doping violation are heard by the Anti-Doping Tribunal[1]. The Anti-Doping Tribunal is appointed by the ITF Executive Director, Medical, or his or her designee, and is formed of three experts with medical, legal and technical knowledge of anti-doping procedures, with the panellist with legal expertise acting as chairman. Both the player and the ITF[2] are entitled to appeal decisions of the Anti-Doping Tribunal to the CAS.

1 Section (E)(4)(A) of the ITF Anti-Doping Programme 2002. This is the successor to the Appeals Committee mentioned at paras A5.150 to A5.155, in relation to the *Korda* case.
2 See paras A5.150 to A5.155.

A5.59 Similarly, UK Sport's Statement of Anti-Doping Policy (with which governing bodies seeking recognition and access to public funds for sport must comply[1]) encourages the appointment of independent persons (such as from the list of arbitrators held by the Sports Dispute Resolution Panel) to first instance anti-doping tribunals (who must have a legally qualified chair drawn from a panel of persons who have not represented or advised the governing body in any capacity[2]). It also provides:

> Where the decision of the Disciplinary Committee is disputed by either party then (subject to any appeal requirement by the relevant International Federation under its rules) the dispute may be referred to an independent Appeal Panel formed by the governing body, or by agreement between the parties to an independent body such as the Sports Dispute Resolution Panel or Court of Arbitration for Sport[3].

1 See para E4.36.
2 The Guidelines to Annex A to the SADP.
3 UK Sport Statement of Anti-Doping Policy (2002), Annex A, para 32.

(d) Use of ADR in football

A5.60 Football has the highest profile transfer system of any sport, and its governing bodies make provision for the use of ADR to resolve disputes that arise from player transfers.

A5.61 For example, domestic transfer disputes involving Football League clubs and FA Premier League clubs are determined by the Football League Appeals Committee (FLAC)[1]. Its 'Independent Chairman' is the Chairman of the Professional Football Negotiating and Consultative Committee, and he is accompanied by a nominee of the Board of Directors of the Football League Limited when Football League clubs are involved, a nominee of the Professional Footballers' Association, a nominee of the Institute of Football Management and Administration, and a nominee of the FA Premier League when its member clubs are involved.

1 Regulation 64 of the Regulations of the Football League Limited, 2001/2002 (FL Regulations).

A5.62 The FLAC decides disputes arising from, among other things, the inability of the clubs to agree the compensation fee payable upon transfer of a player[1]. Moreover, where the Football League's board has made a decision relating to a transfer (for example, in relation to the payment of signing-on fees[2]), the FLAC will hear any appeal from such decision. The decisions of the FLAC are expressed to be 'final and binding on all parties'[3].

1 Regulations 58.3.1 and 59.5 of the FL Regulations.
2 Regulation 55.13 of the FL Regulations.
3 Regulation 64.8 of FL Regulations.

A5.63 Disputes in relation to international transfers fall under the jurisdiction of the FIFA Player Status Committee[1]. This is dealt with in detail below[2].

1 FIFA Article 34(e).
2 See para A5.138.

(e) Use of other forms of ADR

A5.64 Although arbitration is the most common form of ADR used by sports governing bodies, other mechanisms are sometimes used. For example, under the FA Rules the Chief Executive of the FA may appoint a Commission of Inquiry to monitor compliance by each 'Participant' with the FA Rules[1]. Under Rule F6 of the FA Rules, that Commission 'may consist of such persons and have such terms of reference as are considered appropriate.' This broad discretion clearly allows the selection of independent third parties to sit on the Commission.

1 FA Rule F.

A5.65 An FA Commission may also consider matters referred to it under the rules of competitions sanctioned by the FA. For example, in May 2002, after an FA Rule K arbitration panel had ordered the board of the Football League to reconsider Wimbledon FC's application for permission to relocate to Milton Keynes[1], the League board referred that application to an FA Commission. Under the League's rules, the FA Commission therefore stood in the place of the League's board with the right and responsibility to consider whether the discretion conferred under the

League's rules should be exercised in favour of the applicant club. It also had a broad discretion as to the procedure that should be followed in its inquiry. On 29 May 2002, after conducting hearings that included considering written submissions and live testimony from witnesses and submissions from lawyers for various parties, the FA Commission granted Wimbledon permission to move.

1 See paras A3.26, n 1 and A5.47.

A5.66 The World Boxing Council (WBC) provides in its Rules and Regulations that any claim against the WBC or any 'controversy or dispute' concerning the WBC Constitution or the Rules and Regulations must be referred first to the President or Board of Directors of the WBC. If that reference does not settle the dispute, then it must be submitted to mediation[1].

1 Rule 5.3 of the Rules and Regulations of the WBC.

A5.67 FIFA is to put in place conciliation facilities for the resolution of disputes arising from the new Regulations for the Status and Transfer of Players[1]. Similarly, provision exists in the regulations of the International Rugby Board for its Chief Executive to mediate disputes between member Unions, if all parties to the dispute agree[2].

1 Article 42(2) of the Regulations for the Status and Transfer of Players.
2 Regulation 18 of the IRB Regulations Relating to the Game (2002).

A5.68 Under the rules of the Amateur Swimming Association, the District Judicial Tribunal (DJT) hears complaints on various issues, such as the actions of clubs and individuals (Complaints), and also appeals against decisions of referees or juries of appeal arising from protests that the 'ASA Laws, Technical Rules or the promoters conditions' have not been complied with or have been misinterpreted (Protests)[1]. The members of the DJT must not be ASA Committee members or District Executive Committee members, and the Chairman may appoint individuals with specialist skills to serve on a particular panel[2]. However, the Chairman may also direct that any Protest (but not any Complaint) be referred for consideration by 'an informal mediator without resort to the formal judicial procedure'[3]. The Chairman may act a mediator or may nominate another DJT panel member to mediate, with the parties having the right to object to his nominee[4]. If the mediator fails to facilitate a settlement within 28 days, the dispute is then resolved using the adjudicative procedure before the DJT[5].

1 ASA Judicial Laws 102 and 105.
2 ASA Judicial Law 103.
3 ASA Judicial Law 109.1.
4 ASA Judicial Law 109.2 to 109.4.
5 ASA Judicial Law 109.6.

B Use of ADR in event organiser rules and regulations

A5.69 Event organisers also provide for the use of ADR in the rules and regulations governing their events. Their key objective is to ensure that disputes arising in relation to the conduct of the event are resolved quickly and definitively, so as to maintain the smooth running and sporting integrity of the event.

A5.70 For example, if there is a dispute as to the right of an athlete to be selected to compete in the first place, or as to his or her continuing eligibility in light of an alleged disciplinary offence (for example a doping offence), then a speedy and unambiguous resolution is vital if participation rights are not to be undermined.

A5.71 The use of the Ad Hoc Division of the CAS at the Olympic Games and the Commonwealth Games[1] is the best example of the use by event organisers of expedited ADR to resolve disputes that arise during competition. The Ad Hoc Division of the CAS sits on site at the Games venue and can hear cases at very short notice and outside normal business hours. Its workings are addressed in detail below[2].

1 Article 28(7) of the Constitution of the Commonwealth Games Federation (CGF), available on the CGF's website at www.thecgf.com/about/constitution.
2 Addressed in detail at paras A5.92, A5.106 and A5.109.

C Use of ADR by commercial partners

A5.72 Any event will involve a network of commercial contracts, with the owner of the venue at which the event will be staged, with suppliers of services required to stage the event (for example, catering, ticketing, hospitality), and (where the demand exists) with broadcasters, sponsor, licensees and other commercial partners. As with any commercial contract, disputes may arise relating to a broad range of issues, and it is appropriate here, as elsewhere, to consider the inclusion of a clause that requires the parties not to litigate but rather to submit such disputes to arbitration or other ADR mechanism.

A5.73 In the commercial context, there is of course no overriding regulation (such as the IOC Code) that compels the parties to waive their right to recourse to the courts in favour of arbitration or other ADR. Instead, their decision as to whether to use ADR will be driven by numerous factors, including their views of the advantages and disadvantages of ADR as compared to litigation[1], general commercial habit and practice, personal preference and compromise during the negotiation of the contract.

1 See paras A5.18 to A5.38.

A5.74 The specific ADR route chosen will depend on the nature of the issues that are likely to arise. For example, if the contract involves the grant to a sponsor of a package of rights associated with the event, for example, title credit, pitch branding, perimeter boards, tickets and hospitality, a dispute may arise as to whether or not the entire package has been delivered and, if not, what the value is of the undelivered part of the package. In such cases, as noted above[1], the best option may be a provision for referral of the issue to an expert, who can use his or her experience and expertise in sports commercial programmes and the objectives and needs of sponsors to determine the value of the rights not delivered and therefore the level of compensation required to be paid.

1 See para A5.13.

A5.75 In contrast, a contract for (say) the supply of catering services at the event is unlikely to raise any sport-specific issues, and therefore the contract may provide for reference of any dispute not to a sport-specific ADR provider but rather to one of the established commercial ADR service providers[1].

1 For example, the International Chamber of Commerce's International Court of Arbitration (www.iccwbo.com), the London Court of International Arbitration (LCIA) (www.cia-arbitration.com); the Centre for Effective Dispute Resolution (CEDR) (www.cedr.co.uk); and the ADR group (www.adrgroup.com). For useful internet material on the commercial ADR providers, see the Lovells arbitration pages, www.lovells.com/Arbitration, and the Linklaters arbitration pages (www.linklaters.com/disputetoolkit).

D Ad hoc references to ADR

A5.76 Even if there is not a pre-existing binding provision to refer disputes to ADR, either in governing body or event organiser rules or in a commercial contract, the parties to a dispute are perfectly entitled to agree ad hoc, after the dispute has arisen, that it is in their mutual interests to refer the matter to ADR rather than have recourse to the courts.

A5.77 For example, there was no provision for mediation of disputes in the Woodhall/Warren or Graham/Spurs contracts, but in each case the parties agreed ad hoc, after the dispute had arisen, to use mediation to try to resolve the dispute quickly and efficiently[1].

1 See paras A5.6 to A5.10.

A5.78 The introduction in 1999 of reformed procedures governing litigation in the English courts, in the form of the Civil Procedure Rules (CPR), has added further impetus to the move towards ADR of sports (and other) disputes. This is because the CPR place an obligation on parties in England and Wales to consider seriously at every stage, even after proceedings have been issued, whether or not to submit to ADR of the dispute.

A5.79 This duty on the parties derives from the overriding objective of the CPR. Under the relevant rules of the CPR[1], the overriding objective is to deal with cases as fairly, efficiently and expeditiously as possible. One of the ways in which the court must give effect to the overriding objective is by encouraging the use of ADR rather than the courts to resolve disputes. The parties are required to help the court to further the overriding objective and therefore are under a duty to consider ADR for their own disputes[2].

1 Rules 1.1 and 1.3 of the CPR.
2 Lord Woolf's Final Report on Access to Justice was more straightforward. At pp 4 and 5 of the Final Report, Lord Woolf boldly stated 'Litigation will be avoided wherever possible', and 'The court will encourage the use of ADR at case management conferences and pre-trial reviews, and will take into account whether the parties have unreasonably refused to try ADR or behaved unreasonably in the course of ADR.'

A5.80 Until recently, the exact ambit of this obligation was unclear, and many parties did not feel any great compulsion to consider ADR of their disputes. However, the Court of Appeal has recently clarified the ADR-related requirements imposed on parties by the overriding objective. It has established its own mediation service, and has handed down two decisions – in the cases of *Dunnett v Railtrack*[1] and *R (Cowl) v Plymouth City Council*[2] – that provide clear warning of the risks of failing to take ADR seriously. In *Dunnett*, the Court of Appeal refused to award the successful party its costs because it had failed to consider mediation in spite of the court's recommendation that ADR should be explored, thereby missing an opportunity to avoid incurring the costs in the first place. In *Cowl*, Lord Woolf and the Court of Appeal rejected an application for judicial review, again because of a failure to explore ADR and in particular mediation[3].

1 [2002] EWCA Civ 303, [2002] 2 All ER 850.
2 [2001] EWCA Civ 1935, [2002] 1 WLR 803.
3 In *Cowl*, Lord Woolf stated: 'We do not single out either side's lawyers for particular criticism. What followed was due to the unfortunate culture in litigation of this nature of over-judicialising the processes which are involved. It is indeed unfortunate that, that process having started, instead of the parties focussing on the future they insisted on arguing about what had occurred in the past ... the parties should have been able to come to a sensible conclusion as to how to dispose of the issues which divided them. If they could not do this without help, then an independent mediator should have been asked to assist. That would have been a far cheaper course to adopt. Today sufficient should be known about ADR to make the failure to adopt it, in particular when public money is involved, indefensible.'

A5.81 Therefore, the old problem of convincing clients of the advisability of at the very least considering ADR, and possibly suggesting it to the opposition, has changed. The advice now must be something along the lines of 'either you explore the possibility of ADR or you risk not recovering your costs even if you win the court proceedings.' Tactically, proposing ADR may now be considered as an aggressive option, rather than one betraying a lack of confidence in the client's case.

A5.82 In any event, what is clear is that, even if there is no pre-existing agreement to submit a dispute to arbitration or other ADR, and one of the parties files proceedings in the court, nevertheless both parties must seriously consider the possibility of an ad hoc agreement to refer the matter to ADR.

5 ADR FORA

A5.83 There are numerous commercial ADR organisations, among the most prominent being the International Chamber of Commerce's International Court of Arbitration, and the London Court of International Arbitration, each of which has dealt with disputes arising in the sports sector. However, one of the main reasons for opting for ADR is the ability to choose a forum with particular knowledge of and expertise in the sector in which the dispute arises and procedures suited to that context. This is a particular advantage in sport, which has various unique features and concepts. An arbitrator or mediator conversant with, for example, the sports broadcasting rights market, is likely to inspire the confidence of the parties and to come to a decision that reflects the realities of that market[2].

1 See paras A5.23 to A5.26.

A The CAS[1]

A5.84 The pre-eminent position of the Court of Arbitration for Sport in field of sports-specific ADR is based on the quality of its work in the two decades since its inception, and has been confirmed and consolidated by the provision in the IOC

Anti-Doping Code and the draft World Anti-Doping Code for a right of appeal against the decisions of sports' anti-doping tribunals to CAS[2]. The recent decision of the International Association of Athletics Federations (IAAF) to make the CAS the appeal tribunal for its and its member federations' anti-doping decisions[3] means that the only major international federations that do not provide for last resort recourse to CAS in doping matters are FIFA and the International Rugby Board. In fact, as set out below, in most cases the scope of CAS's jurisdiction extends far beyond doping issues to encompass a broad range of sporting disputes.

1 The CAS website is www.tas-cas.org. By way of general background to the CAS, see 'Court of Arbitration for Sport – Guide to Arbitration', available on the website. See also Reeb M 'The Court of Arbitration for Sport' (2000) 3 Sports Law Bulletin 10; Gearhart S 'Sporting Ambition and the International Olympic Committee Court of Arbitration for Sport' (1989) 6 Journal of International Arbitration; Polvino A 'Arbitration as preventative medicine for Olympic ailments: the International Olympic Committee Court of Arbitration for Sport' (1994) 8 Emory International Law Review 347.

2 See paras A5.54 to A5.57.

3 Up until this amendment, all doping appeals were referred to the IAAF Arbitration Panel as the tribunal of last instance. Now doping cases under IAAF doping regulations will first be decided by an anti-doping tribunal of the IAAF (for IAAF competitions) or of the national federation (for domestic events), with any party (and the IAAF, if it is not a party to the original proceedings) able to appeal the decision to the CAS. See Reeb M 'The IAAF to recognise the jurisdiction of the Court of Arbitration for Sport' [2001] 4 ISLJ 246; 'IAAF set to scrap arbitration panel' *Sport Business* (29 November 2000).

(a) Background

A5.85 The CAS was created in 1983, under the auspices of the Olympic Movement, its principal aim being to 'secure the settlement of sports-related disputes', but with a longer term objective of harmonising the procedural rules of national and international sports governing bodies.

A5.86 In 1994, the executive and judicial functions of the CAS were separated by the creation of the International Council of Arbitration for Sport (ICAS), which assumed the administrative and financing roles, leaving the CAS to concentrate on its judicial function as a semi-autonomous body[1].

1 A list of the ICAS functions can be found at S6 of the Statutes of the CAS. This development was in response to the comments made by the Swiss Federal Tribunal in the appeal from CAS decision 92/63 brought by Elmar Gundel. The Swiss court's judgment was published in the *Recueil Official des Arrêts duTribunal Fédéral* 119 II 271. The decision is discussed in detail below at paras A5.95 and A5.96.

A5.87 The ICAS is composed of 20 members, headed up by a President, currently H.E. Judge Kéba Mbaye. all of whom are high-level jurists with particular experience or expertise in sport. Four members are appointed by each of the International Olympic Committee (IOC), the International Sports Federations (IFs) and the Association of National Olympic Committees (ANOC). Those 12 then appoint four more members to safeguard the interests of athletes. Those sixteen then appoint the remaining four members, who shall be independent of the IOC, Ifs and ANOC. The ICAS members elect the President, two Vice-Presidents, together with the Presidents of the two divisions of the CAS and their deputies.

A5.88 One of the functions of the ICAS is the appointment of the CAS arbitrators, each for a renewable period of four years. Thirty arbitrators are chosen by each of the IOC, the IFs and the National Olympic Committees (NOCs). Thirty are selected with a view to protecting the interests of athletes, and the final thirty arbitrators are chosen from persons independent of the bodies responsible for selecting the other arbitrators.

A5.89 The CAS is based in Lausanne, Switzerland, but there are also administrative offices for the Oceania region in Sydney, and for North America in New York (formerly Denver). Moreover, after consultation with the parties, the president of the arbitral panel or the President of the particular Division of the CAS (see below) may decide to hold the hearing elsewhere than Lausanne[1].

1 Rule 28 of the Procedural Rules of the 'Code of Sports-Related Arbitration' (Code).

A5.90 However, wherever the hearing physically takes place, the juridical seat of the CAS is always Lausanne, so as to ensure, among other things, consistency in the procedural regime governing CAS proceedings and equal treatment for all parties who appear before the CAS, wherever it sits[1].

1 See further paras A5.97 to A5.102.

A5.91 Proceedings before CAS are usually arbitration proceedings. Like other forms of ADR, disputes can be referred to the CAS on the basis of a prior agreement or ex post facto agreement. The CAS has two arbitration procedures: the 'ordinary arbitration procedure', which is a tribunal of first instance; and the 'appeals arbitration procedure', which deals with appeals from the last instance decisions of disciplinary and other tribunals internal to the sports governing body. As noted above, the latter procedure is more commonly found in governing body regulations than the former.

A5.92 In addition, as noted above, there is the Ad Hoc Division of the CAS, which is now a fixture at Olympic Games and certain other major events, providing speedy, on-site resolution of disputes. The Ad Hoc Division of the CAS has sat at the Summer Olympics in Atlanta and Sydney, the Winter Olympics at Nagano and Salt Lake City, the Commonwealth Games in Kuala Lumpur and Manchester, and the European Football Championships in Belgium and the Netherlands.

A5.93 However, although the main focus of the CAS is on its arbitration procedures, it also offers mediation services and an advisory opinion mechanism. The procedures and key features of the services offered by the CAS are discussed in the following paragraphs.

A5.94 Two court decisions relating to the status and jurisdiction of CAS have been key to its emergence as the pre-eminent ADR provider in the sports sector.

A5.95 Elmar Gundel In 1992, the CAS was a single entity, combining its judicial functions with its executive and fund-raising functions. The International Equestrian Foundation (FEI), Mr Gundel's governing body, was also a benefactor of, and contributed members to the CAS ruling board. After a decision of the CAS went against him, Mr Gundel alleged that the CAS did not meet the conditions of independence and impartiality needed for it to be accepted as an arbitration court under Swiss law, because of this failure to separate the different functions of the CAS.

A5.96 In its judgment, the Swiss Federal Court rejected the appeal and ruled that the CAS was a true court of arbitration, thereby rejecting the charge of partiality and lack of independence in this case. The CAS was not an organ of the FEI, it did not receive instructions from the FEI and the FEI only provided three out of then 60 members of the CAS. However, the court noted that there may have been an issue if the IOC was a party to a dispute before the CAS, because the CAS was financed almost exclusively by the IOC, the IOC was competent to modify the CAS Statute, and considerable power was given to the IOC and its President to appoint members to the CAS[1].

1 As noted above (at para A5.86), it was as a result of this judgment that the ICAS was set up to take care of the running and financing of the CAS, leaving the CAS to focus exclusively on its judicial function.

A5.97 **Raguz v Sullivan** Shortly before the Sydney Olympics, in the case of *Raguz v Sullivan* the Court of Appeal of New South Wales gave a vital ruling on the effect of the provision in Rule 40.3 of the Code of Sports-Related Arbitration that the seat of each and every CAS arbitration is deemed to be Lausanne[1].

1 *Angela Raguz v Rebecca Sullivan* [2000] NSWCA 240, reproduced in full in Kaufmann-Kohler *Arbitration at the Olympics* and *Digest of CAS Awards 1986–1998*.

A5.98 The dispute concerned the selection procedure for the Australian women's judo squad for the Sydney Olympics. At the end of the Judo Federation of Australia Inc's (JFA) slightly convoluted selection process, Ms Raguz was nominated for the team. Ms Sullivan complained that the JFA had misapplied its selection criteria and that she, not Ms Raguz, was entitled to be selected for the team. Ms Sullivan appealed to the JFA's Appeal Tribunal, which ruled in Ms Raguz's favour. In accordance with the JFA's Selection Agreement, Ms Sullivan then appealed to the CAS via its Oceania registry in Sydney. An Order of Procedure was issued by the panel following a preliminary conference, stating that the seat of the arbitration was Lausanne (as stated in Section 1 and Rule 28 of the Code), but that the substantive law of the dispute would the law of New South Wales. The hearing took place in Sydney, and the panel decided in Ms Sullivan's favour, ruling that the JFA had incorrectly applied its nomination criteria and requiring the JFA to nominate her for selection by the Australian Olympic Committee.

A5.99 Ms Raguz applied to the New South Wales Supreme Court for leave to appeal against the CAS's decision. The threshold question for the Court was whether it had jurisdiction to hear the application under the Australian Commercial Arbitration Act 1984 (CAA), and particularly whether the CAS proceedings took place pursuant to a 'domestic arbitration agreement' under s 40 of the CAA.

A5.100 The Court of Appeal undertook a comprehensive review of Section 1 and Rule 28 of the Code in light of, among other things, the applicable case law,[1] and, in the absence of a relevant provision in the CAA, s 3 of the Arbitration Act 1996, Art 20 of the UNCITRAL Model Law on International Arbitration, and the legislative history of the CAA. The Court of Appeal also referred to an article by the then President of the ad hoc CAS, Professor Gabrielle Kaufmann-Kohler, in which she set out the reasons for the choice of a sole seat of arbitration, regardless of where the arbitration actually takes place[2].

1 See, for example, *Naviera Amazonica Peruana SA v Bompania Internacional de Seguros del Peru* [1988] 1 Lloyds Rep 116, and the Australian case of *American Diagnostica Inc v Gradipore Ltd* (1998) 44 NSWLR 312.

2 Kaufmann-Kohler 'Identifying and Applying the Law Governing the Arbitration Procedure – The Role of the Law of the Place of Arbitration', International Council for Commercial Arbitration, Congress Series no 9 (1998, Paris).

A5.101 The Court of Appeal held that the 'seat' of an arbitration was a legal concept and recognised that there was a 'vital distinction between the so-called place (or seat) of arbitration and the place or places where the arbitrators may hold hearings, consultations or other meetings.' Accordingly, the Court decided that the CAS proceedings fell outside the jurisdiction of New South Wales courts:

> The unqualified choice of Lausanne as the 'seat' of all CAS arbitrations within the scope of the arbitration agreement means that that agreement *did* provide for arbitration in a country other than Australia. Accordingly, this was not a 'domestic arbitration agreement'.

A5.102 As a consequence, if this decision is followed by other courts around the world, the sole forum for an appeal against a CAS award, whether the full CAS or the Ad Hoc Division, is the Swiss Supreme Court, regardless of where the CAS proceedings have taken place[1].

1 This is exactly what happened in the *Raducan* case, in which a 16 year-old Romanian gymnast was stripped of her gold medal having taken a cold and flu remedy. The CAS upheld the IOC's decision: *Raducan v IOC*, award of 28 September 2000. Ms Raducan unsuccessfully appealed the case to the Swiss Supreme Court: *Raducan v Comité International Olympique,* judgment of 4 December 2000, not officially reported, but reproduced in full in Kaufmann-Kohler 'Arbitration at the Olympics'.

(b) Procedure in brief

A5.103 'Ordinary arbitration' proceedings are commenced by filing with the CAS a written application, and the court office fee[1]. That application is sent to the opposing party, which is given a deadline to respond to the arbitration application. The panel is then agreed or, in the absence of agreement, appointed. The procedure before the panel consists of a written phase and an oral phase. The written phase consists of one or two exchanges of pleadings; the oral phase consists of a hearing at which witness evidence may be given.

1 At the time of writing, SFr. 500.

A5.104 'Appeals arbitration' proceedings are commenced by the submission of a statement of appeal, together with the requisite court fee[1]. The main purpose of this document is to invoke the jurisdiction of CAS inside the time limit set for appeal from the governing body's decision. If the federation's regulations do not set a time limit for the appeal, then the CAS time limit of 21 days from the appealed decision applies. The appellant has only 10 days from the expiry of the time limit for appeals in which to file a pleading setting out his factual and legal arguments, together with the evidence in support. The respondent has 20 days in which to submit its answer to the statement of appeal. In principle, these are the only submissions that the parties are entitled to make.

1 As with the ordinary procedure, the court fee for appeals is currently SFr. 500. The statement must contain: (1) a copy of the decision appealed against; (2) a statement of the relief sought by the appellant; (3) notice of the appellant's nominated arbitrator (with the other two in the usual run of things to be nominated by the respondent, and selected by the two nominated arbitrators, respectively), unless the parties have agreed on a sole arbitrator; (4) if applicable, an application to stay the execution of the decision appealed from; and (5) evidence of CAS's jurisdiction over the dispute, such as a copy of the agreement or the governing body regulations containing a provision to that effect.

A5.105 One word of warning: if the respondent wishes to argue that the CAS has no jurisdiction to decide the issue referred to it, then it would be safer to raise this immediately, and not when the respondent makes its arguments on the merits in response to the appeal notice. Otherwise, the CAS takes the position, notwithstanding a suggestion in its rules to the contrary[1], that the respondent will have submitted to its jurisdiction.

1 Rule 39 of the Procedural Rules of the Code.

A5.106 Because of its very aims and nature, the procedure before the Ad Hoc Division of the CAS is radically different from that before the ordinary and appeals divisions. For the Salt Lake City Winter Games, the complainants filed an application with the Ad Hoc court office (pro formas were available), and the President of the Ad Hoc Division then appointed from the list of arbitrators for the Games a three-member panel to hear the dispute. The aim of the Ad Hoc Division is for the decision of the panel to be rendered within 24 hours of the lodging of the application[1]. However, in appropriate cases, the Ad Hoc Division may refer all or part of a dispute for resolution under the regular CAS procedures[2].

1 Article 18 of the Arbitration Rules for the XVII Commonwealth Games in Manchester.
2 Article 20(a) of the Arbitration Rules for the XVII Commonwealth Games in Manchester.

(c) Choice of law

A5.107 The parties are free to choose the law that will govern the merits, but in the absence of a choice of law, there is a difference between the provisions relating to the Ordinary Arbitration Division and the Appeals Division.

A5.108 Rule 45 of the Code of Sports-Related Arbitration states that in relation to ordinary arbitration proceedings, Swiss law will apply if the parties do not chose the law applicable to the merits. However, as to Appeals Arbitration proceedings, if the parties do not specify the choice of law, the dispute will be decided according to 'the law of the country in which the federation, association or sports body is domiciled'[1].

1 In CAS 96/161, *International Triathlon Union (ITU) v Pacific Sports Corpn Inc (PSC)*, award of 4 August 1999, an Ordinary Arbitration Division proceeding, it was argued by PSC that in the absence of or choice of law by the parties, Art 187 of Chapter 12 of the Swiss Federal Code on Private International law should apply. PSC argued that this would mean that the Panel should apply the law with which the action was most closely connected, in this case, PSC contended, Ohio law. The CAS panel rejected these arguments and applied Rule 45 of the Code of Sports-Related Arbitration, and, therefore, Swiss law. However, the digest of the case records that 'the Panel has not been directed to any aspect of Swiss law that would have created any prejudice to the parties', suggesting that if such prejudice could be demonstrated, then Rule 45 and Swiss law may not be applied.

A5.109 By contrast, the Ad Hoc Division at the Olympic Games determines cases according to '... the Olympic Charter, the applicable regulations, general principles of law and the rules of law, the application of which it deems appropriate'[1].

1 See Art 17 of the Arbitration Rules for the XIX Olympic Winter Games in Salt Lake City. Article 17 of the Arbitration Rules for the XVII Commonwealth Games in Manchester substitutes the Commonwealth Games Federation's Constitution for the Olympic Charter.

A5.110 In fact, in keeping with CAS's status as a unitary dispute resolution system for sport, even where a particular national law is said to apply to the substance of a dispute the Panel is likely to import into the analysis 'general principles of law' derived from general sports law jurisprudence and from basic norms followed by most jurisdictions[1].

1 For a detailed discussion of the content and application of said 'general principles of law', see paras E4.77 to E4.82.

(d) Jurisdiction and remedies

A5.111 There is no express power in the Code of Sports-Related Arbitration or the Guide to Arbitration for the Ordinary Arbitration Division to award damages or impose any other remedies on final hearing. However, the CAS has (among other remedies) awarded damages[1], declared the decision of a governing body void[2], and ordered a stay of the application of a governing body decision[3].

1 CAS 96/161, *ITU v PSC* (at para A5.108). The Panel also decided in that case that punitive damages may only be awarded if the parties had agreed that CAS should have that power, or if the contractual breach was 'of such a malicious nature as to give rise to a separate tort.' The Panel also confirmed that the objective in assessing contractual damages was the familiar common law restitution principle of putting the innocent party in the position it would have been in but for the breach.

2 CAS 97/168, *Fédération Française des Sociétés d'Aviron (FFSA) v International Rowing Federation (FISA)*, award of 29 August 1997.

3 CAS 98/200, *AEK Athens and SK Salvia Prague v Union of European Football Associations (UEFA)*, award of 20 August 1999 (Enic), *Digest of CAS Awards II 1998–2000* (2002, Kluwer), p 36. See paras A5.182 and A5.183.

A5.112 Moreover, under Rule 37 of the Code of Sports-Related Arbitration, once the request for arbitration or statement of appeal has been filed, the parties may seek interim provisional or conservatory measures[1]. The same provision also applies to Appeals Arbitration proceedings.

1 So, for example, in *Enic*, an interim stay of the application of the UEFA rule on multiple ownership of clubs was granted pending the full hearing.

A5.113 Rule 57 of the Code of Sports-Related Arbitration provides with respect to appeals that '[t]he Panel shall have full power to review the facts and the law ...' In other words, the Panel can review all or part of the decision being appealed *de novo*. It might uphold all or part of the decision, vacate all or part of it, or even increase a sanction[1].

1 See eg para E4.133.

(e) Costs

A5.114 The procedural rules for ordinary arbitration proceedings provide that, at the end of the proceedings, the CAS court office shall determine the final amount of the cost of arbitration, including the CAS's fees, the arbitrators' costs, a contribution to the CAS's expenses and the costs of the witnesses, experts and interpreters. The Panel includes in its award a costs order as to which costs shall be paid by which party or parties, employing the general rule that 'the award shall grant the prevailing party a contribution towards its legal fees and other expenses ... When granting such contribution, the Panel shall take account of the outcome of the proceedings, as well as the conduct and financial resources of the parties'[1].

1 Rule 64 of the CAS Code of Sports-Related Arbitration.

A5.115 Apart from the fee payable upon filing the notice of appeal, Appeals Arbitration proceedings are stated to be free, ie CAS pays the arbitrators' fees and costs, in keeping with the objective of ensuring access to this last instance appeal institution[1]. However, Rule 65.3 of the Code of Sports-Related Arbitration gives the Panel the power to shift all or part of the costs incurred by the parties in conducting the arbitration between the parties as it sees fit, 'taking into account the outcome of the proceedings, as well as the conduct and financial resources of the parties'.

1 Rule 65.1 of the CAS Code. But see CAS 2000/A/264.G, *Federazione Italiana Sport Equestri*, order of 23 October 2000 for an example of the CAS ordering the parties to pay the costs of the CAS in Appeals Arbitration proceedings. In that case, the parties settled the dispute prior to the hearing before the CAS, but only informed the CAS on the day of the hearing, with the result that the panellists had unnecessarily attended at the CAS.

(f) Rights of appeal

A5.116 Awards handed down by the CAS are final and binding, but there is a right of challenge to the Swiss Federal Tribunal, albeit on limited natural justice and/or public policy grounds[1].

1 See para A5.176.

A5.117 The decision of the Ad Hoc Division of CAS is expressed to be 'enforceable immediately and may not be appealed against or otherwise challenged'[1]. This again is subject to any rules of applicable law limiting the power of the parties to oust the jurisdiction of the courts[2].

1 Article 21 of the Arbitration Rules for the XVII Commonwealth Games in Manchester.
2 See paras A5.173 to A5.180.

(g) CAS mediation

A5.118 As noted above, the CAS also provides a mediation service. The ICAS appoints a list of mediators drawn from the list of CAS arbitrators. The CAS has also provided a model mediation agreement[1]. A party wishing to initiate the mediation should submit a request with the CAS, setting out, among other things, a description of the dispute. If the parties fail to agree on the mediator, selected from the list appointed by the ICAS, the mediator is designated by the President of the CAS. The procedure for the mediation may also be agreed by the parties, but in the absence of agreement, the mediator will determine how the mediation will proceed. If the parties reach a settlement, such agreement is drafted by the mediator and signed by the parties. If the parties fail to settle the dispute, they are free to institute arbitration proceedings. The costs of the mediation, unless the parties agree otherwise, are borne equally by the parties.

1 'Any dispute, any controversy or claim arising under, out of or relating to this contract and any subsequent amendments of or in relation to this contract, including, but not limited to, its formation, validity, binding effect, interpretation, performance, breach or termination, as well as non-contractual claims, shall be submitted to mediation in accordance with the CAS Mediation Rules.'

In addition, the CAS provides an additional clause in the absence of settlement of the dispute: 'If, and to the extent that, any such dispute has not been settled within 90 days of the commencement of the mediation, or if, before the expiration of the said period, either party fails to participate or continue to participate in the mediation, the dispute shall, upon the filing of a Request for Arbitration by either party, be referred to and finally settled by CAS arbitration pursuant to the Code of Sports-related Arbitration. When the circumstances so require, the mediator may, at his own discretion or at the request of a party, seek an extension of the time limited from the CAS President.'

A5.119 The main limitation of the CAS mediation service is that it is available only for cases that would be suitable for resolution under the ordinary arbitration procedure. In other words, it is not possible to refer appeals from decisions of governing bodies to the mediation procedure.

(h) CAS advisory opinions

A5.120 The final service offered by the CAS is the provision of advisory opinions through the consultation procedure. This service is available to the IOC, the international federations, the National Olympic Committees, the associations recognised by the IOC, and the Olympic Games Organising Committees, who may ask the CAS for an advisory opinion about 'any legal issue with respect to the practice or development of sports or any activity related to sports.' The request for an opinion is considered by the CAS President, who will determine if the issue is a suitable one for the provision of an opinion. The request is liable to be declined if (for example) the question addressed to the CAS concerns an existing dispute likely to be brought to the CAS for arbitration. If the question is deemed to be suitable, the CAS President will appoint either a one or three-member panel from the CAS list of arbitrators to review the issue and draft the opinion. Advisory opinions are not binding arbitral awards[1].

1 See Rules 60 to 62 of the Code of Sports-Related Arbitration.

A5.121 The consultation procedure has not been frequently used. Indeed, between 1995 and 2000 only 11 advisory opinions were provided. Opinions have been given in relation to the waiting period required for a change of nationality, the direct affiliation of professional cycling teams to the international federation, and the compatibility of swimsuits with the international federation rules.

(i) CAS jurisprudence

A5.122 The CAS is building up a considerable jurisprudence[1]. It has considered a wide range of issues, including a contractual dispute involving the organisation of a sport's world championships[2], the equivalent of judicial review proceedings against the decision of a governing body[3], what amounted to a request for a mandatory injunction in the context of the football transfer system[4], and a broad range of anti-doping cases that it considers as a result of the incorporation of the CAS within the ICO Anti-Doping Code[5].

1 For the jurisprudence of the CAS, see the *Digest of CAS Awards 1986–1998* (1998), and in the *Digest of CAS Awards II 1998–2000* (2002), both edited by Matthew Reeb, formerly counsel to the CAS and now Secretary General. The Digests contain certain of the awards of the Ordinary and Appeals Arbitration Divisions, together with the awards of the Ad Hoc CAS at the Olympics and advisory opinions issued by the CAS. The decisions of the Ad Hoc CAS from the Salt Lake City Winter Olympics may be found on the CAS website at www.tas-cas.org. See also Ditchen 'The Court of Arbitration's Appellate Doping Cases: Analysis and Evaluation' (2002) 5(2) Sports Law Bulletin 8; Oschütz 'Harmonization of Anti-Doping Code through Arbitration: the Case Law of the Court of Arbitration for Sport' [2002] 12(2) Marquette Sports Law Review 675; and Oschütz 'The Jurisprudence of the CAS in Doping Cases' (2001) 2(7) ISLJ 22.

2 CAS 96/161, *International Triathlon Union v Pacific Sports Corpn* at para A5.108.

3 CAS 97/168, *FFSA v FISA* at para A5.111. The FFSA challenged the adoption by an Extraordinary Congress of the FISA to adopt a new By-law relating to 'Commercial Publicity, Sponsorship and Advertising.' The CAS rejected the FFSA's arguments that the Extraodinary Congress did not have jurisdiction to make such a decision, but accepted that the procedure followed in adopting the amendment without allowing for a considered discussion of an important change to the By-laws was in breach of FISA's Statutes, and accordingly the decision was declared void.

4 CAS 98/201, *Celtic plc v UEFA, Digest of CAS Awards II 1998–2000* (Kluwer 2002), p 106. The dispute concerned Celtic and Scotland player John Collins signing to play for AS Monaco in 1996. Collins' contract with Celtic expired on 1 July 1996. On 27 June 1996, he entered into a contract with AS Monaco effective as of 1 July 1996. Celtic claimed compensation from AS Monaco, who pointed to the then recently decided *Bosman* case (Case C-415/93 *Union Royale Belge de Sociétés de Football v Jean-Marc Bosman* [1995] ECR I-4921) and refused to pay a compensation fee because Collins had been out of contract. Celtic demanded that the relevant UEFA board determine the fee, but UEFA referred the matter to the FIFA Player Status Committee, which found in favour of AS Monaco, as did the FIFA Executive Committee on appeal under the old FIFA procedures. Celtic asked the CAS to order the relevant UEFA board to (1) decide the fee and (2) order AS Monaco to pay the fee. In the event, the CAS decided that UEFA had been right to refer the dispute to FIFA, but did not question its ability to give the award sought by Celtic.

5 One of the most significant cases decided by the CAS in terms of its ability to decide certain issues relating to fundamental rights and freedoms is the *Enic* case, considered at paras A5.182 and A5.183.

A5.123 These decisions of the full CAS have been supplemented by the awards of the Ad Hoc Division of the CAS at recent Olympic Games[1] in disputes relating to the jurisdiction of the CAS[2], national eligibility rules[3], the validity of suspensions imposed by the IOC or the international federations[4], non-interference with 'on-field' sporting decisions[5], and commercial advertising at the Olympics[6].

1 See Kaufmann-Kohler *Arbitration at the Olympics* (2001); McLaren 'A New Order: Athletes' Rights and the Court of Arbitration at the Olympic Games' *Olympika: The International Journal of Olympic Studies* (1998), pp 1 to 24; McLaren 'Introducing the Court of Arbitration for Sport: the Ad Hoc Division at the Olympic Games' [2001] 12(1) Marquette Sports Law Review 515; Beloff 'The CAS Ad Hoc Division at the Sydney Olympic Games' [2001] 1 ISLJ 105; Fitzgerald 'The Court of Arbitration for Sport, Doping and Due Process During the Olympics' [2000] Sports Lawyer Journal 213; 'A Brief Worth Its Salt' Law Society Gazette (21 February 2002).

2 For example, *Dieter Baumann v IOC, National Committee of Germany and IAAF*, 22 September 2000 at the Sydney Olympics, in which the panel decided that it did have jurisdiction to determine an appeal brought by Baumann against the IAAF Arbitral Panels's decision to suspend him from competition for two years for a doping offence, in spite of the fact that, at that time, the IAAF did not recognise the jurisdiction of the CAS. It held that it had jurisdiction over the athlete by virtue of his signing the Olympic entry form, and it held that both the IOC and the IAAF had consented to the jurisdiction of the Ad Hoc Division of the CAS by virtue of Article 74 of the Olympic Charter.

3 See the awards in *Arturo Miranda, Canadian Olympic Association and the Canadian Amateur Diving Association v IOC*, 13 September and 24 September 2000 (*Miranda I and II*), and *United States Olympic Committee and USA Canoe/Kayak v IOC*, 13 September 2000, *Angel Perez v IOC*, 19 September 2000, and *Angel Perez*, 25 September 2000 (*Perez I, II and III*) at the Sydney Games, which raised issues relating to the interpretation of Article 46 of the Olympic Charter, requiring an athlete to have been a national of a country for three years in order to eligible to compete for that country at the Olympics.

4 For example, *Rebagliati v IOC*, 12 February 1998 at the Nagano Games, in which the panel overturned the IOC's decision to rescind the Canadian snowboarder's gold medal on the basis that he had tested positive for marijuana metabolites.

5 For example, *Mendy v International Amateur Boxing Association*, 1 August 1996, at the Atlanta Games, in which the French boxers appeal against his disqualification for punching below the belt was dismissed.

6 For example, *Fédération Française de Gymnastique v Sydney Organising Committee for the Olympic Games*, 30 September 2000, concerning the size of a logo on a French gymnast's leotard.

B The Sports Dispute Resolution Panel (SDRP)

A5.124 Whereas the CAS is an international, cross-jurisdictional sports dispute resolution mechanism, the SDRP aims to replicate CAS's functions on a UK-wide basis.

(a) Background

A5.125 The SDRP was founded by (among others) the British Olympic Association, the Central Council of Physical Recreation and the Welsh, Scottish and Northern Irish sports associations.

A5.126 Its main aim is to 'provide a simple, independent and effective mechanism for parties in dispute to resolve their differences fairly, speedily and cost effectively'[1]. Therefore, the SDRP's core services are arbitration, mediation, the appointment of independent panellists/panels to act under sport-specific disciplinary rules, and the provision of advisory opinions.

1 SDRP 'Outline Review of Operations: April 2001/September 2001'. See also Siddall 'The UK Sports Dispute Resolution Panel – Report on the First Two Years' (2002) 5(4) Sports Law Bulletin 15.

A5.127 However, the SDRP also aims to fulfil a more proactive and wide-ranging role than that of a simple alternative to the courts. Indeed, the SDRP's other principal objective is to 'promote best practice within the field of sports dispute resolution'. The breadth of the SDRP's objectives is clear from the following extract from the SDRP's 'Outline Review of Operations: April 2001 – September 2001':

> SDRP's Mission put simply is **'Just Sport'** for every individual or organisation involved in sport – ***Just Sport*** in terms of the ability to compete or participate free from the unwelcome and costly distraction of unresolved disputes and litigation and ***Just Sport*** in the sense of achieving fairness in sport
>
> SDRP seeks to fulfil its role as 'The Dispute Resolution Service For Sport in the UK' by working on Sport's behalf and by providing a service that is dedicated to meeting the needs of Sport at all levels and in all forms of dispute resolution. It does this by acting as reference point, agency, service provider, facilitator, educator, advocate of best practice, moderniser and co-ordinator.

A5.128 In its first 18 months in operation, up to 30 September 2001, 33 matters from 14 different sports were referred to the SDRP: eight arbitrations, four mediations, one advisory opinion, one investigation/inquiry, and 19 appointments of an independent chair or panel ranging from intellectual property disputes to an enquiry into child protection issues. All of the referrals have led to the disputes being resolved without recourse to the courts[1].

1 In July 2002, the SDRP played a role in the process that resulted in England's finest shot-putting prospect since Geoff Capes, Carl Myerscrough, being cleared to appear in the Commonwealth Games 2002 in Manchester. Myerscrough had been suspended for two years for failing a drug test, and had served his ban, which expired in February 2002. However, while eligible for all other competition, under the Commonwealth Games Council of England rules, this drug ban prevented him from taking part in the Manchester Games. On appeal, the SDRP cast doubt on the validity of the ban, and opened the way to Myerscrough's participation in the Games: (2002) Times, 22 June.

A5.129 Of the 33 referrals, only one arose as a result of provision in a governing body's procedures for referral to the SDRP[1]. However, provision is increasingly being made in such rules for recourse to the SDRP. For example, the British Darts Organisation Code of Conduct No 3 (Disciplinary Proceedings) provides for appeal against disciplinary proceedings to the SDRP. Perhaps most significant to the prospects for the future development of the SDRP is the reference to it in UK Sport's Statement of Anti-Doping Policy and the threat of withdrawal of public funding from governing bodies that fail to provide for a right of appeal against anti-doping decisions to an independent body such as the SDRP[2].

1 Although a number of the appointments were made under the terms of a standing arrangement with another governing body.
2 See para A5.59; see further Chapter E4.

(b) Procedure

A5.130 Arbitration proceedings are commenced by a party serving a written request for arbitration on the respondent and submitting the request and the applicable fee to the SDRP. The general rule is that the respondent has 14 days from receipt of the claim by the SDRP in which to send a reply to the request for arbitration. In the normal case, the parties each nominate an arbitrator from the SDRP list with the nominated panellists agreeing on a third person to act as chairman of the panel. The rules envisage a procedure consisting of the exchange of two sets of statement of case per party and an oral hearing, but the panel retains a discretion to amend that procedure if requested by the parties, to fit with the circumstances of the particular case.

A5.131 The Panel has a complete discretion as to awards of costs.

A5.132 The rules are silent as to the finality of an SDRP award. Under the Arbitration Act 1996, however, a challenge to the award will lie only on standard, very limited grounds that there was serious irregularity affecting the tribunal, the proceedings or the award, or that the tribunal had no substantive jurisdiction over the dispute, or for error of law[1].

1 See paras A5.178 to A5.180.

A5.133 In mediation proceedings, the parties choose a mediator. In the absence of agreement, the Director of the SDRP selects one. The mediator, the parties and the SDRP then enter into a mediation agreement. At least two weeks before the mediation, each party submits to the mediator a summary of its case, together with supporting documentation. Any settlement reached in the mediation will only be binding once it is in writing and signed by the parties. Unless otherwise agreed, the SDRP's fees are paid equally by the parties, and each side will bear its own costs.

A5.134 Advisory Opinions are non-binding, and the request for such an opinion may be made by either or both parties in the SDRP's standard form. The party/parties can select the panellists, or failing that the Chairman of the SDRP will perform that task. The costs of the advisory opinion must be given before the opinion is released.

C Arbitration Tribunal for Football (TAF)

A5.135 FIFA has set up the TAF as part of the root and branch reform of its transfer regulations.[1] Its role is defined in article 63 of the FIFA Statutes:

> 63.2 Only TAF is authorised to settle any disputes involving FIFA, the confederations, national associations, leagues, clubs, players, officials and licensed agents for which the value involved in the litigation is the same as or more than a specified value fixed from time to time by the Congress[2].

TAF is also responsible for settling disputes arising between a third party and any of the foregoing entities or persons provided they are covered by an arbitration agreement.

63.3 TAF is responsible for dealing with appeals against decisions of the last instance, after all previous stages of appeal provided for a FIFA, confederation, national, league or club level have been exhausted. TAF does not, however, hear appeals on:

– violations of the Laws of the Game
– suspensions of up to four matches.

1 See Blackshaw 'FIFA Approves the Creation of an Independent Arbitration Tribunal' (2001) 4(5) Sports Law Bulletin 18.
2 At the time of writing it is US $5,500.

A5.136 The TAF is expected to be closely modelled on the CAS. Indeed, as the ICAS was set up to take on the financial and executive functions from the CAS, and thereby eliminate any suggestions of a lack of independence if the IOC was involved in a dispute before the CAS, so the International Chamber for Football Arbitration has been set up to ensure the independence of the TAF. However, at the time of writing, the TAF regulations still had not been drawn up.

A5.137 The impetus for the creation of the TAF was the introduction of the new transfer system, and indeed part of the responsibility of the TAF will be to determine disputes arising under the new 'FIFA Regulations for the Status and Transfer of Players'. The new regulations include a dispute resolution procedure[1]. The procedure is expressed to be without prejudice to the right of parties to pursue remedies before their national courts, making it an essentially voluntary ADR scheme.

1 Article 42 of the FIFA Regulations for the Status and Transfer of Players.

A5.138 Disputes as to whether a contract was breached, with or without just cause, or 'sporting just cause', or as to training compensation fees are first determined by the Dispute Resolution Chamber of FIFA's Players Status Committee, which has the power to impose sporting sanctions in appropriate cases. Players may also seek the advice of the Dispute Resolution Chamber as to whether they are entitled to terminate their contract with their club on the basis of just cause or sporting just cause. The Player Status Committee also has the power to discipline national associations for failure to implement the Code of Conduct for the Protection of Minors in the EU, or for a failure to implement the ban on transfers and first registration of players under the age of 18[1]. Appeal from the decisions of the Dispute Resolution Chamber lies with the TAF[2].

1 Chapter II, Arts 3 and 4 of the Regulations governing the Application of the Regulations for the Status and Transfer of Players.
2 Article 42(c) of FIFA's Regulations for the Status and Transfer of Players. See also Arts 3(8) and 4(6) of the Regulations governing the Application of the Regulations for the Status and Transfer of Players.

D Other ADR organisations of specific relevance to sport

A5.139 Disputes concerning intellectual property rights often arise in sport. Therefore, the World Intellectual Property Organisation's Arbitration and Mediation Center (WAMC) deserves specific mention. As its name suggests, the WAMC provides both arbitration and mediation services. Although not expressly limited to IP disputes, the WIPO's expertise in this area is obvious. For a guide to the WAMC and for the arbitration and mediation rules, see the WIPO website www.arbiter.wipo.int/center/index.

A5.140 Specific mention should also be given to the Internet Corporation for Assigned Names and Numbers (ICANN) and its Uniform Domain Name Dispute Resolution Policy (UDRP), a papers-only arbitration service for dealing with domain name cyber-squatting disputes. This has already had a significant impact for rights-owners and brand management in the sporting context. By way of example, see the transfer to FIFA of numerous domain names connected with the FIFA World Cup in WIPO case no D.2001-0097, the transfer to Fulham FC of the www.fulhamfc.com domain name in D.2001-0335, and the transfer of www.jaapstam.com to the Dutch defender Jaap Stam[1].

1 See also 'Protecting Your "SportsEvent.com": Athletic Organisations and the Uniform Domain Name Dispute Resolution Policy' by Patrick L Jones at www.wvu.edu/~wvjolt/Arch/Jones/Jones.htm.

6 ISSUES IN ADR

A5.141 Considered below are certain of the critical issues that must be addressed when a dispute arises in a situation where there is provision in a contract or in applicable rules and regulations for the referral of the dispute to resolution by arbitration or other ADR.

A Does the Arbitration Act 1996 apply?

A5.142 The Arbitration Act 1996 applies to all written arbitration agreements that have their legal seat in England or Wales[1]. 'Arbitration Agreement' is defined as 'an agreement to submit to arbitration present or future disputes'[2].

1 Sections 2 and 5(1) of the Arbitration Act 1996. Obviously, this will be of great significance in cases where it is doubtful whether there is a contract between the participant and the governing body, for example. See para A5.159.

2 Section 6(1) of the Arbitration Act 1996.

A5.143 The next and crucial question is what constitutes an 'arbitration'. Unfortunately, the Act does not give a definition of 'arbitration', or even any firm guidance on this issue, although s 1 does provide a steer as to one of the factors when it states that 'the object of arbitration is to obtain a fair resolution of disputes by an impartial tribunal'. One definition of 'arbitration' is as follows:

> ... the process by which a dispute or difference between two or more parties as to their mutual legal rights and liabilities is referred to and determined judicially and with binding effect by the application of law by one or more persons (the arbitral tribunal) instead of by a court of law[1].

1 Arbitration, *Halsbury's Laws*, Vol 2 (4th edn Reissue), para 601. The subsequent paras go on to consider in more detail the elements of this definition, namely 'dispute or difference', 'mutual legal rights and liabilities', determined by one or more persons', 'determined judicially', 'the application of law' and 'binding effect'.

A5.144 Mustill and Boyd set out a list of the factors which must be present for a process to categorised as an arbitration as follows:

(i) the agreement pursuant to which the process is, or is to be, carried on (Procedural Agreement) must contemplate that the tribunal that carries on the process will make a decision that is binding on the parties to the procedural agreement;

(ii) the Procedural Agreement must contemplate that the process will be carried on between those persons whose substantive rights are determined by the tribunal;

(iii) the jurisdiction of the tribunal to carry on the process and to decide the rights of the parties must derive either from the consent of the parties, or from an order of the court or from a statute the terms of which make it clear that the process is to be an arbitration;

(iv) the tribunal must be chosen, either by the parties or by a method to which they have consented;

(v) the Procedural Agreement must contemplate that the tribunal will determine the rights of the parties in an impartial manner, with the tribunal owing an equal obligation of fairness towards both sides;

(vi) the agreement of the parties to refer their disputes to the decision of the tribunal must be intended to be enforceable in law;

(vii) the Procedural Agreement must contemplate a process whereby the tribunal will make a decision upon a dispute that is already formulated at the time when the tribunal is appointed[1].

1 Mustill and Boyd *Commercial Arbitrations* (2nd edn, 1989, Butterworths), p 41. Although the book pre-dates the 1996 Arbitration Act, as noted above the Act provides no definition of 'arbitration'. Therefore, Mustill and Boyd's discussion is still relevant. The authors go on to consider other attributes that are relevant in determining whether a process is an arbitration, namely: (i) whether the Procedural Agreement contemplates that the tribunal will receive evidence and contentions, or at least give the parties the opportunity to put them forward; (ii) whether the wording of the agreement is consistent or inconsistent with the view that the process was intended to be an arbitration; (iii) whether the identity of the chosen tribunal, or the method prescribed for choosing the tribunal, shows that the process was intended to be an arbitration; and (iv) whether the procedural agreement requires the tribunal to decide the dispute according to law.

A5.145 It will be clear from the foregoing that while there will be clear examples of what is and what is not an 'arbitration', there will be some procedures in the sports context, as elsewhere, where there may be no obvious answer to the question of whether the given procedure is an 'arbitration'[1].

1 While not necessarily conclusive, it is certainly helpful if the parties stipulate that the particular dispute resolution mechanism is an arbitration governed by the Arbitration Act 1996.

A5.146 The practical consequence of deciding whether a process is an 'arbitration' is that if it is, and the Arbitration Act 1996 applies, then the process becomes subject to the procedures, rights and remedies set out in the Act, some of which are considered below[1].

1 For example, paras A5.178 to A5.180.

B Does the clause cover the dispute in question?

A5.147 The scope of the obligation to arbitrate will depend on the wording of the arbitration agreement, and under English law at least such wording is interpreted in light of its language and the circumstances in which the agreement was made[1]. For example, the International Hockey Federation provides for arbitration before the CAS of any dispute that falls outside the jurisdiction of one of its 'jurisdictional bodies'[2]. As the 'jurisdictional bodies' determine eligibility disputes, alleged doping offences, breaches of the Statutes, bye-laws, Rules or Regulations and acts of 'misconduct on or off the field', it is difficult to see what category of disputes the CAS would decide at first instance, other than (perhaps) straight commercial disputes[3].

1 *Heyman v Darwins Ltd* [1942] AC 356.
2 Namely, the Congress, the Executive Board and the Disciplinary Commission. (Article 20 of the Statutes of the International Hockey Federation).
3 In addition, the CAS has exclusive jurisdiction over appeals from decisions of 'jurisdictional bodies'. There is no internal appeal mechanism. See Art 21.3 of the Statutes of the International Hockey Federation.

A5.148 One particular problem for governing bodies when their regulations are being interpreted is the operation of the principle of *in dubio contra proferentem.* The effect of this principle is that when one party has drafted a contract and the other party merely adheres to its terms, as with participants adhering to governing body rules and regulations, including dispute resolution provisions, any doubt as to the interpretation of the terms is resolved in favour of the adhering rather than the drafting party[1].

1 *Chitty on Contracts* (28th edn, 1999, Sweet & Maxwell), para 12-045.

A5.149 There is extensive case-law on the meanings of certain common forms of words such as 'arising out of the contract', in connection with' etc, that appear in arbitration clauses[1].

1 See *Mustill and Boyd*, pp 119–121; and *Russell on Arbitration* at paras 2–067 to 2–072.

A5.150 The importance of the interpretation of arbitration clauses is best illustrated in the sporting context by the case of *Petr Korda v International Tennis Federation*[1] The central issue of the case was the construction of Section (V)3 of the International Tennis Federation's Anti-Doping Programme, which stated:

> Any dispute arising out of any decision made by the Anti-Doping Appeals Committee shall be submitted to the Appeals Arbitration Division of the Court of Arbitration for Sport which shall resolve the dispute in accordance with the Code of Sports Related Arbitration.

1 [1999] All ER (D) 337, CA. See further para E4.317 et seq.

A5.151 Mr Korda tested positive for the prohibited substance nandrolone. He was held by the (ITF) Review Board to have violated the ITF's anti-doping policy, and the mandatory sanction of a one year ban was imposed on him. However, the Anti-Doping Appeals Committee held that Mr Korda had established 'exceptional circumstances' under the anti-doping policy, and accordingly withdrew the mandatory one-year suspension from competition, because it found that Mr Korda did not know how the banned substance had entered his system[1]. The ITF appealed to the CAS under Section (V)3, alleging misinterpretation of the 'exceptional circumstances' test.

1 21 December 1998.

A5.152 In response, Mr Korda cited Section (L)8 of the Anti-Doping Programme, which stated that the decision of the Appeals Committee would be the 'full, final and complete disposition of the appeal and will be binding on all parties.' He contended that cl (V)3 therefore gave the ITF only a limited right of appeal to CAS, basically confined to issues relating to the validity, enforceability or construction of a decision of the Appeals Committee.

A5.153 At first instance, Mr Justice Lightman decided in favour of Mr Korda. In his view, the limited interpretation proposed by Mr Korda was correct looking at Section (V)3 both in isolation and also as part of the Anti-Doping Programme as a whole. In Mr Justice Lightman's opinion, the need for certainty and the expeditious determination of doping disputes pointed to such a limited right of appeal. This was emphasised by Section (L)8 of the Anti-Doping Programme, which Mr Justice Lightman held to be inconsistent with the existence of any further broad right of appeal[1].

1 Citing *Jones v Sherwood Computer Services plc* [1992] 2 All ER 170.

A5.154 The Court of Appeal overturned Mr Justice Lightman's decision[1]. Lord Justice Clarke noted that the expression 'arising out of' should ordinarily be given a wide meaning[2] and would include a full rehearing on the merits. He saw no reason within the clause itself for the narrower meaning contended for by Mr Korda. However, it was generally agreed that the appeal boiled down to how to interpret Section (V)3 in conjunction with Section (L)8. Lord Justice Clarke, with whom the other Lord Justices agreed, held that the two sections should be read together so as to mean that the Appeals Committee's decision is a 'full, final and complete disposition of the appeal and binding on the parties subject to a reference to the Appeals Division of the CAS of any dispute arising out of any decision of the Appeals Committee as expressly provided for in Section (V)3'. Policy arguments such as the need for doping cases to be resolved quickly could not alter the ordinary and natural meaning of Section (V)3. Accordingly, the ITF was permitted to take the matter to the CAS (which upheld its appeal[3]).

1 *Korda v ITF Ltd* [1999] All ER (D) 337, CA.
2 Referring to *Mustill and Boyd*, p 120, the cases cited therein, and *Harbour Assurance Co (UK) Ltd v Kansa General International Insurance Co Ltd* [1993] QB 701.
3 See para E4.323.

A5.155 *Korda* demonstrates that not only must close consideration be given to the use of such phrases as 'full, final and binding', 'arising out of', and 'in connection with', but great care must be taken to avoid what Lord Justice Auld referred to as 'internal inconsistencies' within rules and regulations. Moreover, where a specific arbitral body is referred to, and if that body suggests model arbitration clauses, such clauses should be ordinarily adopted, but consideration must be given to how they sit with the structure and content of the relevant rules and regulations as a whole.

C Is the clause valid and enforceable?

(a) Relationship between the validity of the primary contract and the validity of the arbitration clause

A5.156 When the dispute results from a commercial contract, in the sports context as generally it will often be concerned with the vitiation of the contract (for example, by frustration), or the wrongful termination of that contract. However, in such circumstances, if the contract is vitiated, then is the arbitration clause necessarily also vitiated so that the parties are no longer contractually bound to use arbitration to determine their dispute? Similarly, if the contract is terminated, does this not also mean that the arbitration clause was terminated, and a contracting party may, if it wishes, issue proceedings in the courts for wrongful termination in relation to that contract?

A5.157 Under English law at least the answer is generally no. The arbitration clause has long been held to constitute an agreement between the parties that is separate to and severable from the other rights and obligations of the contract in which the arbitration clause appears. This is now codified in s 7 of the Arbitration Act 1996:

> Unless otherwise agreed by the parties, an arbitration agreement which forms or was intended to form part of another agreement (whether or not in writing) shall not be regarded as invalid, non-existent or ineffective because that other agreement is invalid, or did not come into existence or has become ineffective, and it shall for that purpose be treated as a distinct agreement.

A5.158 Consequently, arbitration agreements have been held to survive not only contracts that have been discharged by breach or frustration, but also contracts that have been rendered void ab initio because, for example, of mistake as to person or illegality[1]. As a result, arbitral tribunals are able to rule on the validity, existence or effectiveness of the primary contract notwithstanding its alleged discharge.

1 See *Westacre Investments Inc v Jugoimport-SDRP Holding Co Ltd* [1999] QB 740; *Harbour Assurance Co (UK) Ltd v Kansa General International Insurance Co Ltd* [1993] 1 Lloyd's Rep 455. However, as to contracts that are void ab initio because they are illegal, whether the form of illegality will render both the primary contract and the arbitration agreement void depends on the nature of the illegality: *Harbour Assurance* at p 461 per Ralph Gibson LJ. As Lord Hoffman pointed out: '... it is particularly necessary to have regard to the purpose and policy of the rule which invalidates the contract and to ask ... whether the rule strikes down the arbitration as well. There may be cases in which the policy of the rule is such that it would be liable to be defeated by allowing the issue to be determined by a tribunal chosen by the parties': *Harbour Assurance* at p 469. See also *Soleimany v Soleimany* [1998] 3 WLR 811 at 821 per Waller LJ.

It was on the basis of this reasoning that the Court of Appeal held in *O'Callaghan v Coral Racing Ltd* (1998) Times, 26 November, that a clause in a wagering contract referring unresolved disputes to the editor of The Sporting Life for arbitration did not survive the illegality of the wagering contract under s 18 of the Gaming Act 1845.

A5.159 The *Modahl* case[1] shows that it is not always obvious that there is a contract between a participant and a governing body. If a dispute arose as to the existence of a contract between the participant and a governing body, and the governing body rules required disputing parties to refer such cases to an independent arbitral panel, how would such arbitral tribunal approach the issues of validity of the primary participant/governing body contract and its own substantive jurisdiction?

1 See para A3.121 et seq.

A5.160 It is clear that the tribunal must first be satisfied that there is a valid arbitration agreement in place, and so the first question would be whether the issue as to the validity of the primary contract also goes to the validity of the arbitration clause. This is a matter for the arbitral tribunal to determine, either before or after hearing the case on the merits, but its decision as to whether the arbitration clause is valid, and hence whether it has jurisdiction to determine the broader dispute on the primary contract, is open to challenge in the courts[1].

1 [2001] EWCA Civ 788. See paras A5.178 to A5.180. See also the case of *LG Caltex Gas Co Ltd v China National Petroleum Corpn* [2001] 1 WLR 1892 for an example of the arbitral tribunal postponing its ruling on its substantive jurisdiction until it had considered all of the evidence, as the argument on the merits of the dispute was essentially that there was no enforceable contract, which argument also applied to the validity of the arbitration agreement.

(b) Duress vitiating the arbitration agreement

A5.161 A participant may also consider a challenge to the validity of the arbitration clause, or the contract containing such clause, on the basis that the participant had no option but to consent to the contract containing such provision for arbitration.

A5.162 For example, it can be artificial to argue that the rules and regulations that are said to form the terms and conditions of participation in a sport are the product of a freely negotiated bargain between the sports governing body and the participating entities. Looking at football, FIFA requires those participating in its association football to submit disputes to arbitration. Article 63(1) of the FIFA Statutes states:

> National associations, clubs or club members shall not be permitted to refer disputes with the Federation or other associations, clubs or club members to a court of law and they shall agree to submit each one of such disputes to an arbitration tribunal appointed by common consent.

A5.163 This obligation is backed up by Art 63(3), which states:

> Even if the law of a country allows clubs or club members to contest at a civil court any decisions pronounced by sports bodies, clubs or club members shall refrain from doing so until all the possibilities of sports jurisdiction within, or under the responsibility of, their national association have been exhausted.

A5.164 By Art 63(2), the national associations are required to insert into their own national rules and regulations provisions to give effect to Art 63(1). If sports bodies clubs or club members do not comply with this obligation, they will be liable to sanction by FIFA[1]. Such sanctions include, for clubs, suspension from all international/cross-border matches.

1 Article 63(6) of the FIFA Statutes.

A5.165 The reality is that a club is unlikely to challenge FIFA's authority by arguing that it did not freely consent to and therefore is not bound by this arbitration clause.

A5.166 What about an individual athlete? The entry form for participation in the Sydney Olympic Games stated, among other things:

> I agree that any dispute in connection with the Olympic Games ... shall be submitted exclusively to the Court of Arbitration for Sport (CAS) for final and binding arbitration in accordance with the Arbitration Rules for the Olympic Games in Sydney, which form part of the Code of Sports-Related Arbitration ...
>
> I hereby surrender any right I may have to commence proceedings in a court in relation to any such dispute or to file any appeal, review or recourse to any state court or other judicial authority from any tribunal award, decision or ruling issued by the CAS.

A5.167 Quite apart from the question of whether the jurisdiction of the courts can be excluded completely in this way[1], there was such a strong element of compulsion in the presentation of this clause to prospective participants (because if an athlete did not agree to the clause, he or she would not be allowed to compete in the Olympic Games) that an argument would seem to be available that consent to the arbitration clause was vitiated[2].

1 See paras A5.173 to A5.180.
2 At Appendix I of its Guide to Arbitration, the CAS provides two model clauses to be signed by participants, one of which grants the CAS jurisdiction over disputes 'excluding all recourse to ordinary courts'. However, it is noted that: '[t]he validity of the clause excluding recourse to ordinary courts is not recognized by all national legal systems.'

A5.168 The IOC has an absolute monopoly over the terms of entry to the Olympic Games. Of course, the same could be said for the rules and regulations of most sports governing bodies and participation agreements of most event organisers; essentially, the position is that if you want to participate in this sport or this event, you have to abide by these rules. If you do not, then you do not participate. However, the coercive force of the undertaking presented to athletes before the Olympic Games was all the greater because of the very nature of the Olympic Games. It happens once every four years, and for many athletes, there may only one opportunity in a lifetime to become an Olympian.

A5.169 So is the compulsion enough to vitiate the agreement to arbitrate? The validity, effect and interpretation of an arbitration agreement are determined by the law governing the arbitration agreement. There is no uniform international practice by reference to which the governing law of the arbitration agreement may be decided[1]. Moreover, the English courts have not considered this question in any detail.

1 See Dicey & Morris *The Conflict of Laws* (13th edn), Rule 57(1) at para 16-012.

A5.170 However, the entry form for the Olympic Games specifically refers to 'arbitration in accordance with the Arbitration Rules for the Olympic Games in Sydney.' Article 7 of these rules states that the 'arbitration is governed by Chapter 12 of the Swiss Act on Private International Law.' While this is not strictly the same as the law governing the 'arbitration agreement', it is likely that with the juridical seat of the CAS also being in Switzerland, a decision as to the validity, effect and interpretation of the Olympic entry form would fall to be considered under Swiss law.

A5.171 Under English law, a party seeking to raise such a challenge would have to resort to the doctrine of duress. Unfortunately, it is not clear whether the insistence that participants agree to use ADR or face exclusion from a sport or particular competition, which would be considered to be a threat not to contract, would constitute duress such as to vitiate the contract. However Commonwealth case-law suggests that as the governing body/event organiser is under no duty to enter into a contract with participants, it should be free to set its own terms, even where the participant has little choice to comply[1].

1 See *Smith v William Charlick Ltd* (1924) 34 CLR 38; and *Morton Construction Ltd v City of Hamilton* (1961) 31 DLR (2d) 323.
By contrast Art 8.1 of the Constitution of Greece stipulates that: 'No person shall against his will be deprived of the judge assigned to him by law.' As the Athletes Union of Constantinople (AEK)

argued in the arbitration that gave rise to the case of *Athletics Union of Constantinople v (1) National Basketball Association (2) Phoenix Suns (3) Fédération Internationale de Basketball EV* [2002] 1 Lloyd's Rep 305, this provision of the Greek constitution rendered invalid any compulsory or coercive arbitration. Specifically, AEK argued that 'any coercive form of arbitration, lacking the *free* consensus of the parties (or one of them) does not fall within the constitutional permissible meaning of arbitration and it is therefore non existent as a genuine meaning of arbitration agreement, unconstitutional, illegal, null and void.' Therefore, it seems likely that the validity of the reference if disputes to the CAS under the Olympic entry form would be at questionable under Greek law. With the 2004 Summer Olympics, and in spite of what is said above in relation to the law that would govern the arbitration agreement itself, it would not be surprising to see the validity of the provision for arbitration in the Olympic entry form challenged under Greek law. The Court of Appeal dismissed AEK's appeal on 28 May 2002, unreported.

(c) Dispute resolution clause infringing competition law

A5.172 The European Commission had indicated that the rules of the governing bodies that prevent participants from referring disputes to the ordinary courts, requiring them instead to use arbitration, may infringe Art 81(1) (then Art 85(1)) of the EC Treaty to the extent that it concerned the application of rules of that governing body that may be anti-competitive. This is because the effect of such dispute resolution provisions could be that such anti-competitive provisions may be enforced more effectively, as the parties would be deprived of the right to seek redress in the courts[1].

1 The European Commission made these comments in an unpublished memorandum *Draft Preliminary Guidelines on the Application of the Competition Rules to Sport* (15 February 1999) in the context of FIFA Art 59 (as it then was, now Art 63) and certain aspects of the old FIFA transfer system in particular. However, such comments could equally be applied to UEFA Art 59, pursuant to which the CAS decided the *ENIC* case, which is discussed both below at paras A5.182 and A5.183, and at paras B2.148 to B2.151.

D Finality of arbitration awards

A5.173 As noted above, one of the attractions of ADR over traditional litigation is finality. For example, by Art 58(2) of its Statutes, UEFA purports to oust completely the jurisdiction of the courts:

> The decisions of the Organs for the Administration of Justice[1] shall be final and binding. There shall be no recourse to legal action in the ordinary courts of law in relation to such matters.

1 The Control and Disciplinary Body, which deals with disciplinary cases arising from the UEFA Statutes, regulations and decisions taken by UEFA that do not fall within the competence of another committee or body, and the Appeals Body, which hears appeals from the Control and Disciplinary Body.

A5.174 This provision is repeated at Art 59(2) in the context of decisions of the CAS under the UEFA Statute, and the exclusion of the courts is repeated again at Art 60(4).

A5.175 However, while it may be possible to limit review of factual decisions of such tribunals, it may not be possible to prevent review of their interpretation and application of the law or the procedures they have followed in reaching the award.

A5.176 For example, under Swiss law, which governs the UEFA Statutes, arbitral awards are subject to the court's supervisory jurisdiction. Awards can be overturned on the basis of irregular constitution of the tribunal, jurisdictional error, failure to rule on a claim/ruling on a claim not submitted to it, breach of the right to equality of treatment or the right to be heard, and on public policy grounds[1].

1 Article 190 of the Swiss Federal Code on Private International Law of 18 December 1987. The application of this provision to awards rendered by the CAS is considered below.

A5.177 The English common law rule[1] is that an attempt to oust the jurisdiction of the English court completely is unenforceable, and the corollary of that rule is that the courts retain a supervisory jurisdiction over an arbitration.

1 *Thompson v Charnock* (1799) 8 Term Rep 139; *Scott v Avery* (1856) 5 HL Cas 811. As Scrutton LJ commented in *Czarnikow v Roth, Schmidt & Co* [1922] 2 KB 478: 'There must be no Alsatia in England where the King's writ does not run'.
In the sporting context, note the case of *Baker v Jones* [1954] 2 All ER 553, which concerned a clause in the constitution of the British Amateur Weightlifters' Association (BAWLA) that stated that '[t]he decision of the central council of the BAWLA] in all cases, and under all circumstances, shall be final.' As Lynskey J noted at p 558: 'Although parties in a contract may, in general, make any contract they like, there are certain limitation imposed by public policy, an done of those limitation may be that parties cannot, by contract, oust the ordinary courts from their jurisdiction ... The parties can, of course, make a tribunal or council the final arbiter on questions of fact. They can leave questions of law to the decision of a tribunal, but they cannot make it the final arbiter on questions of law. They cannot prevent its decisions being examined by the courts.'

A5.178 The statutory position is similar. The Arbitration Act 1996 gives parties the right to challenge in the courts:

(1) the arbitral panel's exercise of jurisdiction; or
(2) its final award.

Section 30 of the Arbitration Act 1996 empowers an arbitrator to rule on a jurisdictional objection, and the arbitrator may reserve his decision until his award on the merits. However, under s 32, the court is empowered to rule on the 'substantive jurisdiction' of the arbitration, ie:

(1) whether there is a valid arbitration agreement;
(2) whether the tribunal is properly constituted; and
(3) what matters have been submitted to arbitration in accordance with the arbitration agreement.[1]

However, such an application may only be made with the permission of the arbitrator or of the other party, which, needless to say, severely restricts its usefulness.

1 See s 30 of the Arbitration Act 1996.

A5.179 Under s 67 of the Arbitration Act 1996, parties may:

(1) challenge the tribunal's award as to its substantive jurisdiction (s 67(1)(a)); or
(2) the party may apply to have an award declared invalid because the tribunal did not have substantive jurisdiction (s 67(1)(b))[1].

Section 67(1)(a) is appropriate to challenge an arbitrator's interim award on jurisdiction, whereas s 67(1)(b) may be used to appeal a jurisdictional decision made at the same time as the final award on the merits. It would also appear from the wording of the two sections that s 67(1)(a) envisages challenges to the decision of an arbitrator to deny, as well as to accept, jurisdiction, whereas s 67(1)(b) appears to be limited to cases where the arbitrator has exceeded his jurisdiction[2]. Parties wishing to challenge the arbitrator's jurisdiction should make their objections as early as possible: if the objecting party fails to do so, and takes part, or continues to take part in the arbitration proceedings, he may lose his entitlement to challenge the arbitrator's jurisdiction under s 67[3].

1 Section 67 states:
'(1) A party to arbitral proceedings may (upon notice to the other parties and to the tribunal) apply to the court–
(a) challenging any award of the arbitral tribunal as to its substantive justification; or
(b) for an older declaring an award made by the tribunal on the merits to be of no effect, in whole or in part because the tribunal did not have substantive jurisdiction.'

2 See I.N. Duncan Wallace QC 'Arbitration: No Contract, No Jurisdiction?' (2002) 118 LQR, p 175.

3 Section 73 of the Arbitration Act 1996. As I.N. Duncan Wallace QC points out, s 73 only applies to a contentious assumption rather than a contentious denial or jurisdiction. Similarly, in the context of objections made to the tribunal itself, rather than to the tribunal and the courts, as is the case with s 73, s 31(1) states that an objection to the tribunal's substantive jurisdiction must be raised by the party 'no later than the time he takes the first step in the proceedings to contest the merits of any matter in relation to which he challenges the tribunal's jurisdiction.' Section 31(3) gives the tribunal a discretion to permit later objections if it considers the delay 'justified'.

A5.180 Challenges to the final award made by the arbitral tribunal may be made under ss 68 and 69 of the Arbitration Act 1996:

(1) under s 68 on the grounds of 'serious irregularity', including, among numerous other things, breach of the 'General duty of the tribunal', set out at s 33, which broadly means the principles of natural justice; and
(2) under s 69 on a question of law[1].

1 However, it should be noted that the parties may agree to exclude appeals under s 69. Moreover, while s 68 is 'mandatory' and therefore cannot be excluded by the agreement of the parties, it is possible to lose the right to appeal under this section as a result of unjustified delay, and it is also subject to the restrictions set out in ss 70(2) (exhaustion of remedies) and 70(3) (28-day limitation period from the date of the award or of the date of notification of the award, depending on the procedure followed).

E Issues that may be the subject of arbitration

A5.181 Whether a particular dispute is arbitrable will usually depend on whether it falls within the scope of the arbitration agreement in question.

A5.182 However, there are certain areas of the law that are so fundamental to the legal system of which they are part that to allow an arbitral body to make binding decisions on the rights of parties in relation to such areas is either inconceivable or permissible only with a guaranteed right of appeal to the courts of law. Examples are human rights or the fundamental freedoms (of movement, competition, establishment etc) enshrined in the EC Treaty. A key case here is the decision of the CAS in the *Enic* case in which AEK Athens and Slavia Prague challenged the UEFA rule that prohibited clubs in common ownership from competing in the same UEFA sanctioned competition (the Contested Rule), on various grounds including infringement of both Swiss and EC competition law[1].

1 CAS/98/200 *AEK Athens and Slavia Prague v UEFA*. See paras B2.148 to B2.151.

A5.183 The dispute fell to be decided by the CAS[1]. After an extensive analysis of the legal and factual background, the Panel held that the Contested Rule was a proportionate response to the legitimate goal of preventing conflicts of interest. Moreover, the Panel held that the Contested Rule did not constitute an abuse of a dominant position under Art 82 (formerly 86) of the EC Treaty[2].

1 Although Art 56 (now Art 59) of the UEFA statutes appeared to cover this dispute, being a '*civil law* dispute (of a *pecuniary nature*) relating to UEFA matters which arise *between UEFA and* Member Associations, *clubs*, players or officials, and between themselves' (emphasis added), and was therefore a dispute that should have been automatically referred to the CAS, UEFA and the clubs nonetheless agreed separately to refer the dispute to the CAS. The parties also agreed that EC competition law would apply to this case. However, even if they had not, the panel noted that, in spite of the fact that the governing law of both the UEFA Statutes and, in the absence of contrary agreement, proceedings before the CAS was Swiss law, and that Switzerland is not a member of the European Union, the CAS would have been bound to apply EC competition law by Art 19 of the Swiss Federal Code on Private International Law. (See paras 39–42 of the *Enic* judgment.)

2 The other grounds alleged in support of the claim that the Contested Rule should be declared void were also rejected.

A5.184 However, only the European Commission has the power to grant an exemption to agreements or rules that would otherwise fall foul of Art 81(1) EC, and on that basis it would not feel itself bound in any way by the decision of a body such as the CAS. Indeed, the European Commission did go ahead and consider the compatibility of the Contested Rule with the EC competition rules, eventually deciding that it is a rule of sporting conduct that can be justified by the need to guarantee the integrity of competitions[1].

1 European Commission press release IP/02/942, dated 27 June 2002. See further Chapter B2.

A5.185 What is the position when an arbitral tribunal is faced with an issue of EC competition law or EC law on the fundamental freedoms of movement, establishment etc, and the arbitral tribunal reaches a decision incompatible with EC law and which the party wishes to challenge? These issues were considered by the European Court of Justice in the case *Eco Swiss China Time Ltd v Benetton International NV*[1]. Benetton applied to the Dutch District Court to annul the awards made by the Netherlands Institute of Arbitrators, under Netherlands law. Benetton argued that the awards were contrary to public policy by virtue of the fact that the licensing agreement, from which the dispute arose, was null and void under Art 81 EC. However, neither the parties nor the arbitrators had considered breach of EC competition law.

1 Case C-126/97, [1999] ECR I-3055.

A5.186 One difficulty faced by Benetton was the fact that, not unusually, the rules of Netherlands procedural law allowed for the review of arbitral decisions on only a limited number of grounds. One of the grounds for challenge was breach of public policy, but this was not taken to include competition law.

A5.187 However, while acknowledging the need for only limited bases for reviewing arbitral awards, the ECJ emphasised the central importance of EC competition law:

> [A]ccording to Article 3(g) of the EC Treaty (now after amendment, Article 3(1)(g)), Article 81 EC (ex Article 86) constitutes a fundamental provision which is essential for the accomplishment of the tasks entrusted to the Community and, in particular, for the

functioning of the internal market. The importance of such provision led the framers of the Treaty to provide expressly, in Article 81(2) EC (ex Article 85(2)), that any agreements or decisions prohibited pursuant to that article are to be automatically void[1].

1 Case C-126/97 *Eco Swiss China Time Ltd v Benetton International NV* [1999] ECR I-3055, para 36.

A5.188 Indeed, the ECJ held that such is the importance of EC competition law that 'where its domestic rules of procedure require a national court to grant an application for annulment of an arbitration award where such an application is founded on failure to observe national rules of public policy, it must also grant such an application where it is founded on failure to comply with the prohibition laid down in Article 81(1) EC'[1]. The ECJ held that the provisions of Art 81 EC are to be regarded as a matter of public policy within the meaning of the New York Convention on the Recognition and Enforcement of Foreign Arbitral Awards, and therefore qualifies as one of the limited number of grounds on which recognition and enforcement can be denied under that instrument[2].

1 Case C-126/97 *Eco Swiss China Time Ltd v Benetton International NV* [1999] ECR I-3055, para 37.

2 Case C-126/97 *Eco Swiss China Time Ltd v Benetton International NV* [1999] ECR I-3055, para 38.

A5.189 Fundamentally, the importance of the uniform interpretation of Community law required that national courts must allow appeals against arbitral awards on the basis of breach of EC law *irrespective of the circumstances in which it is to be applied*[1]. Indeed, Advocate General Saggio stated that '[n]ational procedural rules which allow judicial review of the compatibility of arbitration awards with Community law only in highly exceptional cases should therefore be disapplied'[2]

1 Case C-126/97 *Eco Swiss China Time Ltd v Benetton International NV* [1999] ECR I-3055, para 40, and see Case C-88/91 *Federconsorzi* [1992] ECR I-4035, para 7.

2 See para 33 of the Opinion of Advocate General Saggio in *Eco Swiss China Time Ltd v Benetton International NV*, dated 25 February 1999.

A5.190 The combination of the fact that an arbitral tribunal cannot refer questions to the ECJ for a preliminary ruling under Art 177 EC[1], and a finding that there would be no conflict with public policy if the award is contrary to Art 81 EC would result in serious undermining of the rights safeguarded under EC law. As the ECJ stated in *Almelo:*

> [I]t follows from the principles of the primacy of Community law and of its uniform application, in conjunction with Article 5 of the Treaty, that a court of a Member State to which an appeal against an arbitration award is made pursuant to national law must, even where it gives judgment having regard to fairness, observe the rule of Community law, in particular those relating to competition[2].

1 An arbitration tribunal constituted pursuant to an agreement between the parties is not a 'court or tribunal of a Member State' within the meaning of Art 234. See Case C-102/81, *Nordsee* [1982] ECR 1095 at paras 10 to 12.

2 See para 23 of case C-393/92 *Almelo* [1994] ECR I-1477.

A5.191 Therefore, in answer to the question posed by the Netherlands court, the ECJ ruled:

> [A] national court to which application is made for annulment of an arbitration award must grant that application if it considers that the award in question is in fact contrary to Article 81 EC (ex Article 85), where its domestic rules of procedure require it to grant an application for annulment founded on failure to observe national rule of public policy.

A5.192 Under the Arbitration Act 1996, the grounds for review of arbitral decisions set out in ss 68 and 69 of the Act do not include such broad public policy grounds. However, it would be possible to bring an appeal on a point of law under s 69 on the basis that the arbitral body's interpretation of EC law was incorrect. The parties, however, may agree inter se exclude the right to appeal on this ground. Even if they have not done this, if the parties do not agree to an appeal on such a point of law, the court's permission must be obtained before bringing such a challenge, and the appellant must satisfy the criteria set out in s 69(3). If *Eco Swiss China Time* had been decided in the context of the Arbitration Act 1996, the decision of the tribunal would not have been subject to review on the grounds of error of law under s 69 because the question of the compatibility of the licence agreement with EC competition law in that case was not one 'which the tribunal was asked to determine'. It is difficult to see what grounds an English court could have granted permission to appeal against the tribunal's decision on facts such as those in *Eco Swiss China Time*.

A5.193 Moreover, while the CAS in *Enic* held that it was bound by Art 19 of the Swiss Federal Code of Private International Law to apply EC competition law, the fact remains that Switzerland is not a member state of the EU, and so it must at least be doubtful whether the Swiss Federal Court would allow an appeal against a decision of an arbitral body on the basis of either (1) a mistake in the interpretation of, or (2) the public policy in the consistent interpretation of, EC law, when Switzerland is not itself bound by such law. Even if the Swiss Federal Court permitted a challenge on the basis that the award breached the fundamental rights integral to the operation of the EU, Switzerland is not a member state, and so, the Swiss Federal Court would not be able to refer the case for a preliminary ruling under Art 234 EC.

A5.194 Consequently, it remains possible that we may in the future see further cases such as *ENIC* in which an arbitral body has ruled on a fundamental freedom or right, and a dispute arises as to whether that award is open to challenge in the courts.

7 DRAFTING ADR CLAUSES

A5.195 Interlocutory disputes as to the validity, effect and interpretation of ADR clauses or agreements can make the resolution of the primary dispute considerably more expensive and time-consuming, often defeating the object of agreeing to ADR in the first place. Careful drafting may overcome or at least limit the scope for, such disputes.

A5.196 Similarly, disputing parties may often want to restrict the ad hoc use of ADR to the resolution of a particular dispute, while reserving their positions in relation to other potential causes of action arising in the same fact situation. Again, careful drafting is required.

A5.197 Many of the ADR bodies provide model clauses/agreements[1]. While these are a useful starting-point, there remain certain issues that must be carefully considered when drafting ADR clauses in general and arbitration/expert determination clauses in particular.

1 The CAS arbitration clause reads as follows:
'*The CAS Ordinary Arbitration proceedings*
Any dispute arising from or related to the present contract will be submitted exclusively to the Court of Arbitration for Sport in Lausanne, Switzerland, and resolved definitively in accordance with the Code of Sports-related Arbitration.
The CAS Appeals Arbitration proceedings
Any decision made by ... [insert name of the disciplinary tribunal or similar court of the sports federation, association or sports body which constitutes the highest internal tribunal] may be submitted exclusively by way of appeal to the Court of Arbitration for Sport in Lausanne, Switzerland, which will resolve the dispute definitively in accordance with the Code of Sports-related Arbitration. The time limit for appeal is twenty-one days after the reception of the decision concerning the appeal.'

A Pre-dispute clauses

A5.198 The objective will usually be to draft a clause in the widest possible terms so as to ensure that all possible disputes arising under the contract will be caught by the clause[1]. The safest formula proposed is that used by the parties in the case of *Government of Gibraltar v Kenney*:

> Any dispute or difference which arises or occurs between the parties in relation to any thing or matter arising out of or under this agreement[2].

1 *Russell on Arbitration* (21st edn, 1997, Sweet & Maxwell) at para 2-077.
2 [1956] 2 QB 410.

B Multi-stage/multi-tier ADR

A5.199 One option that parties may wish to consider is a multi-stage or multi-tier approach to dispute resolution. Parties may wish to use one method of ADR to resolve certain types of disputes under the contract, and another method of ADR to resolve other types of disputes. Alternatively, parties may wish first to use one type of ADR to resolve all disputes under the contract, but, if that fails, to use another form of ADR. Typically, this would be mediation followed by arbitration. There is no magic to drafting such clauses, but care must be taken in, for example, defining the types of dispute that are to be decided by a certain method of ADR, or as to how long the period of mediation is to continue before the parties may refer the dispute to arbitration.

C Choice of law

A5.200 This is a crucial aspect of the ADR clause, mainly relevant to adjudicative forms of ADR, such as arbitration and expert determination. The choice of law will radically affect the parties' procedural rights and can be determinative of the outcome of the dispute itself.

A5.201 As noted in passing above, it is possible for a number of different laws to apply in arbitrations:

(1) the law regulating the arbitration agreement itself;
(2) the law governing the substantive rights of the parties in the dispute (often called the 'Proper law'); and
(3) the law governing the disputing parties' procedural rights.

A5.202 Again, as noted above, the procedural law will be that of the juridical seat of the arbitration, which may, as with the CAS, be specified in the ADR bodies' rules, or which the parties may have to chose. The most important thing to remember is that the juridical seat of the arbitration, and hence the procedural regime governing the arbitration, is not necessarily that of the nation where the proceedings themselves are held.

A5.203 The parties must also seek to agree the substantive law governing the arbitration and the arbitration agreement itself[1].

1 In the absence of agreement, choice of law will fall to be decided according to usual principles: see Rule 57 of Dicey and Morris *The Conflict of Laws* (13th edn, 2000, Sweet & Maxwell).

D Privacy and confidentiality

A5.204 Under English law, it is an implied term of arbitration agreements that the proceedings are private and confidential. However, the scope of this term is not certain. Therefore, parties should make express provision if they want the award itself, and/or the reasons behind the award, to remain private and confidential.

E Miscellaneous: the ADR body to be used, location of the ADR

A5.205 Generally, it is easier to reach agreement with another party before the dispute has arisen. After the dispute, every choice gives rise to a potential argument, and thus the potential for expense or cost. Consequently, the ADR clause should be as specific as possible, including the choice of ADR forum. As noted above, there can be very real advantages in selecting a sports-specific ADR provider. The agreement should also stipulate how many panellists will sit on the tribunal and who will appoint the arbitral, unless such matters are already dealt with in the rules of the particular ADR provider.

A5.206 Moreover, a key, practical consideration often overlooked in the case of international ADR is the choice of language for the ADR process, and the place where the process will take place.

PART B

EUROPEAN COMMUNITY LAW AND SPORT

CHAPTER B1

EUROPEAN COMMUNITY SPORTS POLICY

Max Duthie (Freehills)

Contents

1 INTRODUCTION

B1.1 This chapter does not review the substantive provisions of European Community ('EC') law that impact on sport, since these are covered in other chapters of the book, in particular in Chapters B2 and B3. Rather, this chapter looks at the other legal and non-legal impact (if any) that the various EC institutions (and some institutions that are not strictly part of the EC[1]) have, or seek to have, in the sport sector. It considers briefly the general roles that are played by each of the institutions and then considers what those institutions say and/or do in the field of sport. It tries to unearth the EC's policy on sport and considers some specific areas in which the EC is particularly visible.

1 Those being the European Council and the Council of Europe. See para B1.7.

B1.2 In summary, aside from the areas of competition law and freedom of movement, where the activities of the EC's institutions (specifically, the European Court of Justice and the European Commission) impact directly (and heavily) on aspects of sport (even if not specifically targeted at sport), the EC institutions' activity in the sport sector is limited. The principal reason for this is that the EC institutions simply do not have a blanket legal authority to act in any area (such as sport), but rather can only act:

(a) in the areas for which the EC has been given exclusive competence under the various enabling treaties (which include, for example, competition[1], but which do not include sport); or
(b) in areas where the member states could not achieve what the EC would like to achieve, and only then *to the extent* that the member states could not so achieve.

These principles of 'subsidiarity' define the limits of the legislative competence of the EC[2].

1 Under Arts 3 and 85–94 (as was) of the EEC Treaty (Rome) 1957. See generally Chapter B2.
2 Attempts by the EC institutions to legislate outside their area of competence will be struck out by the European Court of Justice. For example, the Parliament and Council's 1998 Directive outlawing almost all tobacco advertising and sponsorship (Directive 98/43/EC), which would have had a significant effect on a number of major sports events, was adopted as a measure of preserving the internal market. But when challenged before the European Court of Justice, the Directive was annulled since parts of it did not advance the interests of the internal market but rather had other objectives such as protecting public health. See Case C-376/98, *Germany v EC Parliament* [2000] ECR I-2247, available at http://curia.eu.int.

B1.3 It is universally accepted by all the EC institutions that sport is generally a 'good thing' for a number of reasons, including its effects on social cohesion, national and cultural identity, health and fitness, discipline, youth development, and job creation, and in particular as a means of making EC nationals feel part of one cohesive body. It is also universally recognised by those same bodies that sport has some significant problems, including doping, over-commercialisation, and the potential for mistreatment of young elite athletes. However, aside from identifying these and other issues that relate to sport, and discussing them at length in various committees, conferences and discussion groups, the EC institutions rarely consider themselves to be in a position to act on (rather than discuss) an issue relating to sport. The European institutions recognise that they have no 'direct powers in this area'[1] and that 'as Community powers currently stand, there can be no question of a large-scale intervention or support programmes or even of the implementation of a Community sports policy'[2]. That said, when the EC institutions act in areas where they do have competence, their legislative measures or judicial decisions are as likely to impact on sport as on any other sector, and they frequently have a fundamental impact on sport. There are also exceptions to the general rule, where pro-active sport-specific steps are taken, most notably in the fight against doping. But generally in the field of sport the EC institutions recognise that the member states and the individual federations have the regulatory prerogative. As the Commission states in its publication *Europe on the Move*, 'the Commission's *main interest* in sport is in constructing an active and permanent dialogue with all those involved on issues of common interest'[3]. This is quite typical of how the EC institutions view their respective roles in sport. Whatever the restrictions imposed by the principle of subsidiarity on the institutions' ability to regulate sport, this is not the language of interventionist ambition.

1 European Council *Nice Declaration*: see para B1.27.
2 European Commission *Helsinki Report on Sport*: see para B1.25, n 2.
3 Available from the European Commission's website: http://europa.eu.int/comm (emphasis added).

2 THE EC INSTITUTIONS – THEIR RESPECTIVE ROLES AND SPORTS-SPECIFIC BODIES AND INSTRUMENTS[1]

B1.4 Of the various EC institutions established under the various treaties, this chapter considers the Council of the European Union, the European Commission and the European Parliament. The work of the Court of Justice is discussed elsewhere[2], and the Court of Auditors is left aside as its role in sport is minimal.

1 See generally Wyatt & Dashwood *European Union Law* (Sweet & Maxwell), and information available at http://europa.eu.int.

2 Chapters B2 and B3 consider in some detail the case law emanating from the European Court of Justice ('ECJ') and the Court of First Instance that is relevant to sport. A few words about the general structure and role of the ECJ: it was established under the 1957 Convention on Certain Institutions Common to the European Communities, and sits in Luxembourg. Its members (the 15 judges and eight advocates general) are appointed not by any institution or a single member state but 'by common accord of the Governments of the Member States' (Art 167 EEC) and sit for a renewable period of six years. The ECJ's jurisdiction includes actions brought by the Commission against member states for failure to comply with EC law, actions brought against the Council or Commission seeking annulment of an act or decision, and references from national courts for preliminary rulings on points of EC law. In 1989, the ECJ's work was supplemented by the establishment of the Court of First Instance. The CFI also sits in Luxembourg but has a more limited jurisdiction. It was established to reduce the case-load of the ECJ and to improve the administration of justice in the Community by engaging in more detailed investigations of factual matters.

A The Council of the European Union

B1.5 The Council of the European Union ('the Council') is one of the legislative bodies in the EC, although it shares its legislative role on many issues with the Parliament. The Council's other functions include co-ordinating member states' economic policies and concluding international treaties on behalf of the EC.

B1.6 The Council is made up of representatives from the governments of each member state. It is in fact a series of councils, each made up of different representatives, that meet from as frequently as once a month (as with Foreign Ministers under the General Affairs Council) to once a year (as with Chancellors/ Finance Ministers under the Budget Council). The Council's presidency rotates around the member states, with each holding it for a six-month stretch.

B1.7 It should be made clear what is meant here by the 'Council'. This is the EC institution called the Council of the European Union. It is not (1) the 'European Council', which is not strictly speaking an EC institution but is the collection of the heads of state or government of the 15 member states along with the President of the European Commission. The 'European Council' meets at least twice a year and its role is to provide impetus for the EC's development and to give guidance on policy to the EC. Nor is it (2) the 'Council of Europe', an international organisation separate from the EC, with 43 member states (including the 15 EC member states plus others such as Albania, Azerbaijan, Romania, Turkey and the Former Yugoslav Republic of Macedonia). The 'Council of Europe' has as its aims the protection of human rights (it drew up and administers the European Convention on Human Rights, which itself established the European Court of Human Rights), the development of cultural identity, and the maintenance of democratic stability. It is based in Strasbourg, has a permanent staff of 1300 people, and has an annual budget (paid for by its member states) of around €169m (£105m). These two bodies will be referred to specifically as the 'European Council' and 'Council of Europe', respectively, so as to distinguish them from each other and from the Council of the European Union (or 'Council'). In addition to the comments made below in respect of the Council, reference will be made to the work in sport that is carried out by the European Council and Council of Europe, notwithstanding that they are not EC institutions.

B1.8 There is no particular council (of the Council) where ministers in charge of sports meet regularly. No particular council (of the Council) is given the subject of sport to the exclusion of others and so it may fall upon foreign ministers, education ministers, health ministers or any other ministers to represent their respective countries on sporting issues discussed in Council. The *General Affairs Council*, for example, has dealt with sporting issues in the past – as it did when it adopted a 'declaration on sport' in December 2000[1]. The UK representatives at the Council on that occasion were then Foreign Secretary and horseracing fan, Robin Cook, and then Foreign Office Minister, Keith Vaz. Similarly, the *Council on Youth issues* met in November 1999 and resolved to invite the European Commission to devise a coherent approach to exploit the educational potential of sporting activities. The UK representative at that meeting was Education and Employment Under-Secretary of State, Malcolm Wicks. In May 1999, the Council (on which the UK representatives were Robin Cook, again, and Foreign Office Minister, Joyce Quin) called on European sports organisations (especially UEFA) effectively to sever sporting ties with the Former Republic of Yugoslavia. And back in 1991 the Council and the Health Ministers of the member states made a declaration on the use of doping in sport (calling for sports bodies to take all steps to ensure drug-free sport and calling for athletes to compete without drugs).

1 This became (when endorsed by the European Council in Nice) the 'Nice Declaration', as to which see para B1.27 and B2.55.

B1.9 As of February 2002, the Council listed 85 representatives of the UK government who regularly take part in Council meetings. Apart from Messrs Blair, Brown, Prescott et al, these included the Culture Media and Sport Secretary, Tessa Jowell, and Sports Minister, Richard Caborn.

B1.10 However, despite no particular council having exclusive jurisdiction over sporting issues, there are informal meetings of the sports ministers of the 15 EC member states, the most recent of which was held in Brussels in November 2001. And these can have an impact of sorts: it was at three of these meetings in 1999 (in Bonn, Paderborn and Vierumaki) that the sports ministers resolved to press ahead with EC support for the World Anti-Doping Agency[1].

1 See paras B1.44 and B1.45 and E4.42 et seq.

B1.11 The European Council similarly has no set structure that is preoccupied with sport. However, it does appear to venture into the realms of sports policy a little more than the Council, and it has made various (admittedly often fairly bland) recommendations, requests, comments or invitations to the Commission, the Council and others following many of its recent meetings, including those in Vienna in 1998, Cologne and Helsinki in 1999, and Santa Maria da Feira and Nice in 2000[1].

1 See paras B1.24 to B1.27.

B1.12 In fact, of the three 'councils', it is the Council of Europe (ie the one that is most clearly separate from the EC) that considers sporting issues with the most precision. The Council of Europe has since 1975 held nine conferences of European Ministers Responsible For Sport. Its most recent such conference was held in Bratislava in May 2000 (attended on the UK's behalf by then Sports Minister and George Best fan, Kate Hoey, and then British Ambassador to the Slovak Republic, David Lyscom)[1]. In addition, the Council of Europe's Committee of Ministers[2] has in recent years made a number of decisions, recommendations and statements on specific sporting issues, such as the development of an Anti-Doping Convention[3], the development and revision of a European Sports Charter and a Code of Sports Ethics (for governments and sports federations to follow), a policy of Sport for All, sport and television, the disabled and sport, racism in sport, physical fitness, and sport and the aged. In addition to the Committee of Ministers, there is also a Steering Committee for the Development of Sports, which meets annually and discusses a broad range of issues including doping, youth and sport, sexual harassment in sport, child abuse in sport, and racism in sport. The UK representatives at the meeting held in March 2001 in Strasbourg, were UK Sport's Chief Executive, Richard Caldicott, UK Sport's International Relations Director, John Scott, and Alan Grosset from the Confederation of British Sport.

1 The next conference was scheduled to take place in Warsaw, Poland, in September 2002.
2 The Committee of Ministers is made up of the Foreign Secretary of each member state, plus one permanent representative of each member state.
2 Established 16 November 1989, and available at the following address: http://conventions.coe.int/Treaty/en/Treaties/Html/135.htm. See also para B1.42 and E4.17. n 3.

B The European Commission

B1.13 The European Commission ('the Commission') is effectively the executive organ of the EC but it also has the power to present legislative proposals to the Council and the Parliament. The Commission also has a responsibility as guardian of the EC treaties. It is in this role that it may bring legal action against the member states for failing to act in accordance with EC law as set down in the treaties.

B1.14 The Commission's members (the 20 Commissioners) are not elected but are appointed by the member states and are usually former holders of high political office domestically. The Commissioners are supposed to be completely independent of the member states that appoint them, and of anyone and anything else. The Commission is divided into a number of directorate-generals (DGs), dealing with set subject matters such as competition, agriculture, energy and transport, fisheries, and justice and home affairs.

B1.15 The directorate-general that has direct responsibility for sport is DG Education and Culture, currently headed by Luxembourg journalist and politician, Viviane Reding. It has a dedicated Sports Unit, currently headed by Spaniard, Jaime Andreu. The Sports Unit is responsible for co-operating on sporting issues with:

(a) the other directorates-general when their activities touch on sport (which means in practice especially DG Competition and DG Internal Market);
(b) the other EC institutions (effectively on the Commission's behalf); and
(c) national and international sports federations.

B1.16 By late 1998, the Commission had become aware of a number of developments in sport: its rapid growth, its increasing commercialisation, a growing number of sports-related complaints being made to DG Competition, and a gap appearing between sport and the mechanisms designed to regulate it. Wanting to try to assist those involved in sport in dealing with those developments, and responding to the European Council's request that the Commission produce a report on the protection of sport's structures and social function[1], the Commission began a grand consultation exercise with those involved in sport (which was exactly what had been envisaged a year earlier when the conference of member states that agreed the Amsterdam Treaty declared therein that 'the bodies of the European Union [should] listen to sports associations when important questions affecting sport are at issue'[2]). And so this important task fell to the Sports Unit – it organised a Europe-wide consultation process that began with the publication of the document 'The European Model of Sport'[3] and then saw the EC Conference on Sport held in Olympia in May 1999, and concluded with the Commission's Helsinki Report to the Council in December 1999[4]. This was a significant step, or at least appeared to be, as it was a specific and defined attempt by the Commission to see what those involved in sport had to say about (among other things) what the European institutions should be doing about sport (if anything) in the future[5].

1 Section XII of the Vienna European Council Presidency Conclusions. See para B1.24.
2 Declaration 29 ('Declaration on Sport') annexed to the Amsterdam Treaty (ISBN 92-828-1652-4) and reproduced in full at para B1.23.
3 Available from the European Commission's website: http://europa.eu.int/comm.
4 Brussels (10.12.1999) COM (1999) 644 final. See para B1.25.
5 See further para B1.25.

B1.17 In addition to this process, since 1991, in conjunction with the member state holding the Council's presidency during the second six-month semester of each year, the Commission has organised regular European Sports Forums at which member states' ministers, EC representatives and people involved in the running of European sport get together to discuss various issues pertaining to sport. This process was set up following the Commission's communication to the Council and Parliament in July 1991[1]. The most recently held European Sports Forums were held in Brussels in October 2001 and Lille in October 2000 and the next is scheduled for Copenhagen in November 2002.

1 SEC (91) 1438 final of 31.07.1991.

C The European Parliament

B1.18 The European Parliament ('the Parliament') is made up of 626 democratically-elected members, representing over 375m people in the 15 member states. Following the treaties made in Maastricht (1992) and Amsterdam (1997), it now shares legislative power in many fields with the Council, and this means that many directives (such as the Television Without Frontiers Directive[1]) need to be passed by a 'co-decision' of the Council and the Parliament. The Parliament also has significant power in terms of finances; it sets the budget for the EC and determines what is spent in various initiatives and projects. Geographically, the Parliament is a moving target. The secretariat is based in Luxembourg, but the politicians meet in their various committees for two weeks a month in Brussels, and then they all move to Strasbourg for one week a month for a full sitting.

1 See para B1.49 et seq.

B1.19 The Parliament has a Committee on Culture, Education, Youth, the Media and Sport, on which 52 MEPs currently sit, including (from the UK) Barbara O'Toole, Christopher Beazley, Roy Perry, Eurig Wyn, Phillip Whitehead and the Earl of Stockton. The committee meets monthly.

B1.20 In addition, in late 2001 the Sports Intergroup was resurrected after having been dormant for a year or more. The Sports Intergroup is an all-party non-partisan group of 20 or so MEPs that meet in Strasbourg every two months to discuss issues that relate to sport in the European member states (such as racism, doping, disability, child protection and television broadcast rights). The Intergroup's current president and secretary are UK MEPs Glyn Ford and Chris Heaton-Harris, respectively, and one of its current members is Spanish MEP and double Olympic gold medallist, Theresa Zabell. The Intergroup has no official lines of reporting, but rather generates discussion that may lead the member MEPs to pursue issues outside the Intergroup. Notably, unlike a number of other Intergroups that are officially recognised and financed by the EC (such as those on health and disability), the Sports Intergroup is unofficial and not financed[1].

1 There are other less formal methods adopted by MEPs when seeking to have some influence over sport, such as the informal meetings held in June 2001 between a selection of MEPs and representatives of UEFA, various national football leagues and various television companies on the subject of the central selling of television broadcast rights.

3 A RECENT HISTORY OF EC SPORTS POLICY

B1.21 Set out briefly below is the chronology of how those European institutions considered in the foregoing section have come in recent years to examine sporting issues.

B1.22 It was the 'intervention' into sport by the ECJ in the *Bosman* case[1] in 1995 that sparked the most recent trail of sports-related activity among the European institutions (and the European Council and Council of Europe). Although *Bosman* might be characterised as a simple confirmation of the application of European freedom of movement rules to one sphere of activity (football), and despite the fact that the application of European law to sport had been confirmed by the courts at least twenty years previously[2], it was nevertheless considered by many in sport to be a significant invasion by European law into an area in which it did not belong. The sports world mobilised its forces and applied political pressure on the EC institutions to understand and take account of the specific nature of sport, as a social and sometimes commercial activity.

1 *Union Royale Belge de Sociétés de Football v Jean-Marc Bosman* [1995] ECR I-4921. See paras A3.172, n 1, B2.153 to B2.156, B3.40 et seq and E2.40 et seq.
2 *Walrave and Koch v Union Cycliste International* [1974] ECR 1405; *Donà v Mantero* [1976] ECR 1333. See paras B3.17 and B3.18.

B1.23 In October 1997, the post-*Bosman* sports lobbying achieved a degree of success when a declaration on the subject of sport was annexed to the Amsterdam Treaty[1]. That declaration (the Amsterdam declaration) reads as follows:

> The Conference emphasises the social significance of sport, in particular its role in forging identity and bringing people together. The Conference therefore calls on the bodies of the European Union to listen to sports associations when important questions affecting sport are at issue. In this connection, special consideration should be given to the particular characteristics of amateur sport[2].

1 A treaty that dealt with issues no less weighty than workers' fundamental social rights, the implementation of a common foreign and security policy across the member states, and the amendments to the EC and EU Treaties necessitated thereby.
2 (ISBN 92-828-1652-4); text reproduced from the European Commission's website: http://europa.eu.int/comm.

B1.24 The momentum was carried on a year later by the European Council (although not strictly an EC institution[1]) when the following request to the Commission was set out in the Presidency conclusions from the European Council's Vienna conference in December 1998:

> Recalling the Declaration on Sport attached to the Treaty of Amsterdam and recognising the social role of sport, the European Council invites the Commission to submit a report to the Helsinki European Council with a view to safeguarding current sports structures and maintaining the social function of sport within the Community framework.
>
> The European Council underlines its concern at the extent and seriousness of doping in sports, which undermines the sporting ethic and endangers public health. It emphasises the need for mobilisation at European Union level and invites the Member States to examine jointly with the Commission and international sports bodies possible measures to intensify the fight against this danger, in particular through better co-ordination of existing national measures[2].

1 See para B1.7.
2 Paragraphs 95 and 96 of Section XII of the Vienna European Council Presidency Conclusions; text reproduced from the European Commission's website: http://europa.eu.int/comm.

B1.25 So, prompted by the Amsterdam declaration, and the request of the European Council in Vienna, the Commission published *The European Model of Sport* document[1] and embarked on a consultation exercise with sports federations, clubs, agencies and others, before publishing its conclusions in its report to the European Council in December 1999 (the Helsinki Report on Sport)[2]. The *European Model of Sport* document invited views on three broad issues: the organisation of sport in Europe, sport and television broadcasting, and sport and social policy. It may have had its flaws (for example, it focused heavily on certain commercially elite sports like football and Formula One motor racing) but it was essentially well-meaning and something of a breakthrough as a consultative exercise. The Commission received over 100 responses to the document and over 300 delegates attended the subsequent EC Conference on Sport in Olympia in May 1999. Those delegates presented the views of (among others) national, European and international governing bodies; national Olympic committees; and national governments of member states. The Helsinki Report that followed contained a number of conclusions, ranging from the general:

> the European Union recognises the eminent role played by sport in European society and attaches the greatest importance to the maintenance of its functions of promoting social integration and education and making a contribution to public health …

to the specific:

> the system of promotion and relegation is one of the characteristics of European sport[3].

1 Available from the Commission's website: http://europa.eu.int/comm. In fact, this document had been preceded by a 'Staff Working Paper' produced on 29 September 1998 by DG X (as it was then) that was entitled 'The Development and Prospects for Community Action in the Field of Sport'. This identified the three major challenges for sport in Europe as being: (1) excessive commercialisation; (2) the health risks for young sports people; and (3) doping.

2 Brussels, 10.12.1999 COM (1999) 644 final. The initial conclusions of the consultation exercise (produced after the Commission's conference on sport held in Olympia in 1999) were published in May 1999. Both documents are available from the Commission's website: http://europa.eu.int/comm.

3 See n 2 above.

B1.26 The European Council's response to the Commission's Helsinki Report on Sport was to include the following statement in the Presidency conclusions from its Santa Maria da Feira conference in June 2000:

> The European Council requests the Commission and the Council to take account of the specific characteristics of sport in Europe and its social function in managing common policies[1].

1 Part IV(D), para 50; available from the Commission's website: http://europa.eu.int/comm. And do the Commission and the Council take account of the specific characteristics of sport in Europe and its social function in managing common policies? One example of where that has happened is in football and in particular in the protracted discussions that took place throughout 2001 between the Commission and UEFA and FIFA on football transfers. The details of the transfer regulations that came out of those discussions are dealt with elsewhere in this book (see paras B2.164 et seq, E1.63, E1.64 and E2.66 et seq and passim). But it is interesting to note the role played by the Commission: following a lengthy period of issues having been identified but never resolved, the Commission entered into talks with UEFA and FIFA to try to establish a system of international transfers that was appropriate for the sport of football but that was also in compliance with the basic principles of Community law. As it does in similar cases outside of sport, the Commission sought dialogue rather than proceeding with a more heavy-handed approach, and talks began between Commissioners Viviane Reding, Mario Monti and Anna Diamantopoulou and representatives from FIFA and UEFA, including Joseph Blatter, Michel Zen-Ruffinen, Lennart Johansson, Gerhard Aigner and Chairman of the football transfers task force, Per Omdahl. In March 2001, agreement was reached between all parties, FIFA and UEFA went off to amend their respective regulations and the Commission's interventionist approach effectively ended its formal investigative procedure against FIFA. See paras B2.158 et seq, B3.66 et seq and E2.66 et seq.

B1.27 The Council (specifically the General Affairs Council) then came to the following conclusion at its meeting in Brussels in December 2000:

> The Council adopted a declaration on the specific characteristics of sport and its social function in Europe, account of which should be taken in implementing common policies. This declaration will be forwarded to the European Council in Nice for endorsement, with the suggestion that it be annexed to the conclusions[1]

And so at its next meeting (five days later in December 2000 in Nice) the European Council did then endorse the Council's declaration and annexed it to the Presidency conclusions from the Nice meeting[2]. The terms of the Nice declaration are as follows:

DECLARATION ON THE SPECIFIC CHARACTERISTICS OF SPORT AND ITS SOCIAL FUNCTION IN EUROPE, OF WHICH ACCOUNT SHOULD BE TAKEN IN IMPLEMENTING COMMON POLICIES

1. The European Council has noted the report on sport submitted to it by the European Commission in Helsinki in December 1999 with a view to safeguarding current sports structures and maintaining the social function of sport within the European Union. Sporting organisations and the Member States have a primary responsibility in the conduct of sporting affairs. Even though not having any direct powers in this area, the Community must, in its action under the various Treaty provisions, take account of the social, educational and cultural functions inherent in sport and making it special, in order that the code of ethics and the solidarity essential to the preservation of its social role may be respected and nurtured.

2. The European Council hopes in particular that the cohesion and ties of solidarity binding the practice of sports at every level, fair competition and both the moral and material interests and the physical integrity of those involved in the practice of sport, especially minors, may be preserved.

Amateur sport and sport for all

3. Sport is a human activity resting on fundamental social, educational and cultural values. It is a factor making for integration, involvement in social life, tolerance, acceptance of differences and playing by the rules.
4. Sporting activity should be accessible to every man and woman, with due regard for individual aspirations and abilities, throughout the whole gamut of organised or individual competitive or recreational sports.
5. For the physically or mentally disabled, the practice of physical and sporting activities provides a particularly favourable opening for the development of individual talent, rehabilitation, social integration and solidarity and, as such, should be encouraged. In this connection, the European Council welcomes the valuable and exemplary contribution made by the Paralympic Games in Sydney.
6. The Member States encourage voluntary services in sport, by means of measures providing appropriate protection for and acknowledging the economic and social role of volunteers, with the support, where necessary, of the Community in the framework of its powers in this area.

Role of sports federations

7. The European Council stresses its support for the independence of sports organisations and their right to organise themselves through appropriate associative structures. It recognises that, with due regard for national and Community legislation and on the basis of a democratic and transparent method of operation, it is the task of sporting organisations to organise and promote their particular sports, particularly as regards the specifically sporting rules applicable and the make-up of national teams, in the way which they think best reflects their objectives.
8. It notes that sports federations have a central role in ensuring the essential solidarity between the various levels of sporting practice, from recreational to top-level sport, which co-exist there; they provide the possibility of access to sports for the public at large, human and financial support for amateur sports, promotion of equal access to every level of sporting activity for men and women alike, youth training, health protection and measures to combat doping, acts of violence and racist or xenophobic occurrences.
9. These social functions entail special responsibilities for federations and provide the basis for the recognition of their competence in organising competitions.
10. While taking account of developments in the world of sport, federations must continue to be the key feature of a form of organisation providing a guarantee of sporting cohesion and participatory democracy.

Preservation of sports training policies

11. Training policies for young sportsmen and -women are the life blood of sport, national teams and top-level involvement in sport and must be encouraged. Sports federations, where appropriate in tandem with the public authorities, are justified in taking the action needed to preserve the training capacity of clubs affiliated to them and to ensure the quality of such training, with due regard for national and Community legislation and practices.

Protection of young sportsmen and -women

12. The European Council underlines the benefits of sport for young people and urges the need for special heed to be paid, in particular by sporting organisations, to the education and vocational training of top young sportsmen and -women, in order that their vocational integration is not jeopardised because of their sporting careers, to their psychological balance and family ties and to their health, in particular the prevention of

doping. It appreciates the contribution of associations and organisations which minister to these requirements in their training work and thus make a valuable contribution socially.

13. The European Council expresses concern about commercial transactions targeting minors in sport, including those from third countries, inasmuch as they do not comply with existing labour legislation or endanger the health and welfare of young sportsmen and -women. It calls on sporting organisations and the Member States to investigate and monitor such practices and, where necessary, to consider appropriate measures.

Economic context of sport and solidarity

14. In the view of the European Council, single ownership or financial control of more than one sports club entering the same competition in the same sport may jeopardise fair competition. Where necessary, sports federations are encouraged to introduce arrangements for overseeing the management of clubs.
15. The sale of television broadcasting rights is one of the greatest sources of income today for certain sports. The European Council thinks that moves to encourage the mutualisation of part of the revenue from such sales, at the appropriate levels, are beneficial to the principle of solidarity between all levels and areas of sport.

Transfers

16. The European Council is keenly supportive of dialogue on the transfer system between the sports movement, in particular the football authorities, organisations representing professional sportsmen and -women, the Community and the Member States, with due regard for the specific requirements of sport, subject to compliance with Community law.

* * * * * *

17. The Community institutions and the Member States are requested to continue examining their policies, in compliance with the Treaty and in accordance with their respective powers, in the light of these general principles.

1 Available at http://europa.eu.int. The General Affairs Council also came to a series of conclusions on doping, which are reproduced at para B1.41.

2 Paragraph 54 of and Annex IV to the Nice European Council Presidency Conclusions, available on the Commission's website: http://europa.eu.int/comm.

4 SPECIFIC EC SPORTS POLICIES

B1.28 It is clear, then, that the subject of sport has been much discussed in the corridors, chambers and meeting rooms of the EC institutions in recent years. But, whether because of the breadth of the subject matter, or because of the number and variety of interested entities within the EC, it is not easy to identify a cogent and consistent policy on sporting issues that underlies the sports-related activities of the EC institutions. Sport is certainly not exempt from other elements of community law. Sports federations may desire the introduction of such an article, in particular if it was to grant them exemption from community laws on competition and freedom of movement, but it does not appear that it is going to happen, at least not in the near future[1]. Indeed, Commissioner Reding has said that she is 'against a solution which would exempt sport from the Community rules' and that 'so far, no such exemption has been made, and rightly so'[2]. That is why there has been a need to ensure an application of Community rules to the sector in a 'sport-sensitive' manner, sport is not afforded a specific article in the treaties that would give the European institutions competence to legislate directly in the area. Instead, the principle of subsidiarity[3] means that the institutions have little or no competence to act directly in sport and so many of their activities will inevitably be toothless. Furthermore, no EC funds are allocated specifically to the development of sport in the member states (save for in doping) and so sports initiatives must compete with all other initiatives when vying for funding under the various educational and cultural programmes[4].

1 See paras B2.11 and B2.12.
2 Address by Commissioner Reding at the 9th Sports Forum of the Konrad Adenauer Foundation (May 2001).
3 See para B1.2.
4 Answer given by Commissioner Reding on 21 December 2001 to the written question of Chris Heaton-Harris MEP, OJ C 134 E, 6 June 2002 (p 216).

B1.29 In addition to the lack of specific legislative competence and targeted funding, the EC institutions have not managed to co-ordinate their sports-related activities to the extent of producing a joint sports policy document. However, it is possible to trawl through the various publications, minutes of meetings, declarations, press releases and other documents to try to piece together themes in sport that are to an extent universally acknowledged among the European institutions. Set out below are the generally-held positions on the following issues: sport and social cohesion, the role of amateur sport, sport and the disabled, sport and the young, and doping in sport. Later in the chapter there are set out some of the few examples of where specific action is taken by the institutions to supplement the rhetoric. As a general matter, however, it is easy to get the impression that sport is little more than a fine subject for discussion in the EC's talking shops, and an excellent topic on which to make well-meaning but ultimately banal recommendations to be passed from institution to institution[1].

1 What follows is not a comprehensive list of all of the EC institutions' activities that have had an impact in sporting circles but rather edited highlights of some of the things that have been done. The majority of the 'activity' in question is in fact simply the publication of very broad policy statements. As to whether these statements have any practical impact, see para B1.67.
Further information (including some additional examples of the EC institutions' limited activity in the sports sector) can be found in *The Impact of European Union Activities on Sport*, a study carried out in 1995 by Coopers & Lybrand for DG X (as it was) of the Commission, and in *Sport and the EU*, a report published in 1996 by the EC Committee of the Danish National Olympic Committee and the Danish Sports Confederation.

A Sport and social cohesion

B1.30 The European Council, the Parliament and the Commission all recognise the significance and function of sport in bringing people together, particularly people from different cultures, and the Commission in particular has noted the threat that is posed to this function of social cohesion by other aspects of sport, such as crowd violence, doping, and increasing over-commercialisation.

B1.31 The declaration annexed to the Amsterdam Treaty in October 1997 was clear on sport's function of social cohesion[1]. The European Council's position, as set out in the Presidency conclusions from Vienna in December 1998[2] and Nice in December 2000[3], is that sport is important in 'forging identity', and that 'the social function of sport' should be maintained. In its Helsinki Report on Sport[4], the Commission recognised the importance of sport in bringing 'together the citizens of the European Union', and warned of the effects on this function of new phenomena such as doping, crowd violence and 'the search for quick profits'. The Commission urged the European Community to use sport to combat 'exclusion, inequalities, racism and xenophobia' and the Parliament reiterated this in its July 2000 report on the Helsinki Report by Pietro-Paulo Mennea, legendary Italian Olympic sprinter and now an MEP and member of the Committee on Culture, Education, Youth, the Media and Sport[5]. That report at least recognises the limits to the Parliament's ability to safeguard sport and its social function, but asks for a new approach to questions of sport based on harmony among the EC institutions, member states, and sports federations, and mutual respect for common principles (recognition of sport's importance, preservation of sport's integrity, maintaining promotion and relegation, continuation of the fight against doping, and insistence on vocational training for young elite sportsmen and women).

1 See para B1.23.
2 See para B1.24.
3 See para B1.27.
4 See para B1.25.
5 A5-0208/2000 (18 July 2000).

B1.32 Of course, as with a lot of the statements made by the various EC institutions, the response may be 'so what?' While the EC may in some instances act in support of its policies[1], in many cases it does not. For the Commission or the Parliament to recognise, say, the necessity of having sporting leagues with promotion and relegation, or to insist on young sportsmen having vocational training, may be rather useless unless the sentiments are backed up with legislation or other forms of regulation, which (as a result of the EC's constitutional limitations) is very unlikely to happen.

1 See para B1.39 et seq.

B Amateur sport

B1.33 The European Council and the Parliament have noted the differences between professional and amateur sport, but have stressed the importance of the latter to huge numbers of people, and have urged those involved in the professional sector to support those in the amateur sector (and vice versa).

B1.34 The Amsterdam declaration stated that 'special consideration should be given to the particular characteristics of amateur sport'[1], and the European Council went slightly further in the Nice declaration, stressing that sport is not the preserve of the elite professional athlete but 'should be accessible to every man and woman, with due regard for individual aspirations and abilities, throughout the whole gamut of organised or individual competitive or recreational sports'[2]. The Parliament went into more detail in its Mennea Report[3], calling for mutual support to be provided by professional and amateur sport, since 'one cannot do without the other', and warning of the major differences that may emerge between the professional part of a sport and the amateur part[4].

1 See para B1.23.
2 See para B1.27.
3 See para B1.31, n 5.
4 See also para B1.47 for details of an EC-funded study into doping among amateur sportsmen and women.

C Sport and the disabled

B1.35 The EC institutions recognise the importance of sport for the disabled and therefore encourage all those involved with sport to promote the participation of the disabled community.

B1.36 The European Council stressed in the Nice declaration[1] the value of sport in developing 'individual talent, rehabilitation, social integration and solidarity' for the physically and/or mentally disabled, of which there are 37m in Europe[2]. In the Mennea report for the Parliament, member states were urged to establish specific sporting federations for the disabled, and to give particular attention to the 'development, funding and promotion of sport for disabled people'[3]. Barbara O'Toole's Parliamentary report in 2001 stated that the right of disabled people to engage in sports activities is 'fundamental'[4]. The Council of Europe adopted a similar line; at its most recent Conference of Ministers Responsible for Sport, it called on governments to adapt sports facilities so that they can be used by the disabled and to establish projects promoting sports to disabled people; it also asked sports bodies to co-operate with disabled sports bodies in moving towards greater integration[5]. The conclusions of the Commission's first European Conference on Sport included the suggestion that some of the profits made by sports' elite should be ploughed back into disabled sports[6].

1 See para B1.27.
2 According to the Commission's report from the first European Conference on Sport in Olympia in 1999. See para B1.25.
3 See para B1.31.
4 PE 286.761 (23 March 2001).
5 Available at http://www.coe.int.
6 Available at http://europa.eu.int/comm. See also para B1.47 for details of the EC's funding for the campaign against doping in disabled sport.

D Sport and the young

B1.37 The basic theme of the European institutions' various 'policy' statements in relation to sport and the young is an acknowledgement that sport is good for young people and that efforts should be made to continue to train young athletes. But there is also a warning that young talented sportsmen and women should not be deprived of continuing education while they undergo their athletic training, and there is also concern about the commercial trade of minors within sport.

B1.38 The European Council stated in the Nice declaration that '[t]raining policies for young sportsmen and women are the life blood of sport, national teams and top-level involvement in sport and must be encouraged' but also emphasised 'the need for special heed to be paid, in particular by sporting organisations, to the education and vocational training of top young sportsmen and women in order that their vocational integration is not jeopardised because of their sporting careers, to their psychological balance and family ties and to their health, in particular the prevention of doping'[1]. The Commission's position (as set out in the Helsinki Report and in the European Model of Sport document) is similar: it has made much of sport's importance in the development of young people, enhancing their physical well-being and teaching them about competitiveness, tenacity, determination and fair play[2]. In the Mennea report[3], the Parliament calls on sports federations to ensure young athletes receive an education and vocational training as well as their sports training, and also demands that a study be carried out by the member states and the federations into the trade of professional athletes who are under 18. The Council of Europe, in its 1996 parliamentary assembly's recommendations on young people in high-level sport[4], expressed fears about the over-training of young people and called on federations and national governments to consider setting age limits for competing children, particularly in sports where competition level can be reached at an early age (such as tennis, gymnastics and swimming) or where there is inherent danger (such as boxing).

1 See para B1.27.
2 See para B1.25.
3 See para B1.31, n 5.
4 Available at http://www.coe.int.

E Doping in sport

B1.39 All of the European institutions appear to be intent on harnessing their own powers (such as they are) and those of the member states and the sports federations in doing what they can to keep up the fight against doping.

B1.40 In its Vienna Presidency Conclusions, the European Council made special mention of 'its concern at the extent and seriousness of doping in sports', in particular because doping 'undermines the sporting ethic and endangers public health'[1]. It called upon the Commission, the member states and sporting federations to 'examine … possible measures to intensify the fight against doping'[2]. In its Helsinki Report, the Commission stated that it had taken certain of such 'measures', focused on:

(1) referring the issue of doping to the European Group on Ethics, who suggested a number of processes that could be adopted by the member states and federations;
(2) co-operating with the Olympic community to create and fund the World Anti-Doping Agency ('WADA')[3]; and
(3) mobilising community instruments to support member states' work in research and education, and in co-ordinating legislation[4].

Interestingly, the Commission makes certain comments in the Helsinki Report about the causes of doping (including 'the overloading of sporting calendars'), and the Parliamentary Committee on Legal Affairs and the Internal Market made some rather controversial remarks in its report on the Commission's Helsinki Report, including the comments of the draftsman (Klaus-Heiner Lehne) that 'he regards the criminalisation of persons who freely decide to take [rather than peddle] performance enhancing drugs as inappropriate' because, he says '[e]ach individual is responsible for his or her own health' and '[m]oralising statements about sportsmen and women who freely take performance-enhancing drugs must be rejected'[5].

1 See para B1.24, n 2.
2 See para B1.24, n 2.
3 See para B1.41 et seq.
4 See para B1.25, n 2.
5 PE 286.005 (13 April 2000).

B1.41 The General Affairs Council of the Council reached the following conclusions on doping at its meeting in Brussels in December 2000[1]:

THE COUNCIL OF THE EUROPEAN UNION AND THE REPRESENTATIVES OF THE GOVERNMENTS OF THE MEMBER STATES, MEETING WITHIN THE COUNCIL, IN AGREEMENT WITH THE COMMISSION

(1) EMPHASISE the importance of measures to combat doping in sport, as acknowledged by the European Union in the conclusions of the European Council in Vienna on 11 and 12 December 1998. The European Council's conclusions underlined 'its concern at the extent and seriousness of doping in sport, which undermines the sporting ethic and endangers public health. It emphasises the need for mobilisation at European Union level and invites the Member States to examine jointly with the Commission and international sports bodies possible measures to intensify the fight against this danger …

(2) NOTE the recent developments in this area and the creation of the World Anti-Doping Agency (WADA), and WADA's intention to become an international body based on public international law, and consider that arrangements should be made for the Member States' and the European Union's roles in that body in order to ensure that they are suitably represented on its Foundation Board[2].

(3) AGREE that the European Community and its Member States will be represented by the President-in-Office of the Council and a member of the Commission. Within a reasonable period of time before each meeting, co-ordination will take place under the responsibility of the Presidency. The Commission member will be able to speak on matters within the Community's sphere of competence in accordance with the Treaty and the case-law of the Court of Justice (given that there is no direct Community competence in the area of sport). The content of the statements made by the Commission member will be approved in accordance with the principles referred to above and following the customary procedures. Where appropriate, the Commission member may speak on matters which are not within the Community's sphere of competence, along the lines approved by a consensus of the Member States and in addition to the Presidency.

(4) NOTE that any Community expenditure on activities of WADA involving measures within the Community's sphere of competence will be decided in accordance with the Inter-institutional Agreement on budgetary discipline. In particular, any significant Community expenditure will require the adoption, following a proposal from the Commission, of a measure with an appropriate legal basis.

(5) CONSIDER that the Member States should encourage co-operation between the competent authorities at national level on efforts to combat doping in sport.

1 Ref: 13999/00 (Presse 465), available at http://europa.eu.int/comm.

2 For more information on WADA, see paras B1.44 and B1.45, as well as para E4.42 et seq.

B1.42 Doping is one of the relatively few issues where the EC can boast that it is actually doing something rather than merely suggesting that others do something. Aside from the universal condemnation of doping in sport, the EC institutions, the European Council and the Council of Europe have actually taken specific steps to combat what the European Council has called the 'scourge' of doping. As far back as the 1960s, the Council of Europe was active in the fight against doping. Its 1967 resolution was instrumental in bringing about the first round of testing at the 1968 Grenoble Winter Olympics[1]. In the 1980s, it drafted and promoted the Anti-Doping Convention[2], which obliges signatory nations to adopt certain legislative, educational and financial measures to combat trafficking, raise awareness, strengthen testing and ensure the effectiveness of bans and other penalties. It also established a Monitoring Group to ensure compliance with the Convention and to report to the Committee of Ministers of the Council of Europe. The Anti-Doping Convention is currently binding on over 30 states worldwide.

1 Resolution 67/12, and available at http://www.coe.int.
2 See para B1.12, n 3.

B1.43 The President of the Commission told the Parliament in July 1999 that doping is 'an issue where decisive, co-ordinated transnational action is clearly needed'. The European Council had already called for 'mobilisation at European Union level' the year before. This, along with the conclusions of the member states' 15 sports ministers, led to the EC's support for the International Olympic Committee's initiative in establishing WADA.

B1.44 Late in 1999, the EC institutions (represented by Viviane Reding and Finnish Sports Minster, Suvi Linden) reached agreement with the International Olympic Committee on the establishment of WADA, although even in the early stages, the role to be played by the EC within WADA was not substantial, and it was to become even less so. Nevertheless, it was agreed that WADA would establish a list of banned substances, harmonise testing procedures, organise the accreditation of testing laboratories, undertake or organise research into aspects of doping, organise education programmes on doping, and co-ordinate out-of-competition testing with sports federations[1]. WADA is funded on a case by case basis by the Commission (including €2m [£1.2m] provided for WADA's pilot projects such as the development of athletes' health certificates), but in the latter part of 2001, it was announced that the Commission would not agree to provide funding for the ongoing operating budget of WADA (estimated at about US $18 to 25m [£12.5 to 17.5m] per annum over the next few years) unless and until WADA agreed to the financial criteria set down by the European Council and the EC budget rules, including the provision of clear and transparent budget estimates and a particular degree of control. To date, WADA has not agreed to meet the criteria, and individual governments of the EC member states have been asked to contribute directly to the operating budget of WADA. In February 2002, WADA raised fears that it would collapse without the funding from the EC institutions. To add to the EC's frustration at the limits on its influence at WADA, WADA decided to make its permanent home outside of the EC, in Montreal, despite the other four bidding cities (Lausanne, Bonn, Vienna and Stockholm) all being in Europe and the latter three having the unequivocal support of Commissioner Reding and others.

1 See further para E4.42 et seq.

B1.45 Europe has been represented on the Foundation Board of WADA, with seats for representatives of the EC member states, Viviane Reding and Bert Anciaux (government minister of Flanders), and two seats for representatives of the Council of Europe, George Walker (Head of Sport) and Alain Garnier (Chairman of the Anti-Doping Convention Monitoring Group). And in February 2002, in a show of solidarity between the EC and WADA, Commissioner Reding and WADA's chairman, Dick Pound, unveiled the WADA anti-doping passport. This is a voluntary scheme for athletes each to have a 'passport' style document (also available on the WADA website[1]) that lists his/her history of doping tests as well as personal data on his/her blood levels, testosterone levels etc. WADA hopes the passport will become compulsory for all athletes by the 2004 Summer Olympics in Athens. However, in May 2002 the Commission announced that

WADA had not agreed to the Commission's pre-conditions for continued funding and therefore Viviane Reding would be withdrawing from her position as observer on WADA's board and the funding would not be provided[2].

1 http://www.wada-ama.org.
2 COM (2002) 220 from the Commission to the Council concerning the Commission's participation in WADA and its funding (6 May 2002).

B1.46 Outside of WADA, the Commission funds a number of anti-doping projects throughout the EC (it spent €2.9m [£1.8m] in 2001). These include an educational project in Italy called (rather clumsily) 'Dracula doesn't drink doping', a research project in Germany on the harmonisation of doping knowledge on food supplements and recreational drugs, and a Portuguese project to create a computer database of doping issues and controls to assist the harmonisation of testing in Europe. In December 2001, the Commission signed a convention with the International Basketball Federation, FIBA, setting up a campaign to raise awareness among players and spectators of the dangers of doping, and the penalties imposed for using banned substances. The Commission provided €84,000 (£50,000) to support this project.

B1.47 Aside from its other activities in doping, the Commission is also active in technical research on doping issues, in particular in improving detection and assessing the damage to health from certain substances, and in seeking ways to harmonise the approach to doping across Europe and the rest of the world[1]. For example, it gave €180,000 (£110,000) of funding (through the Research Directorate-General) to the Hardop Project, which researched the measures necessary for combating doping in sport. There are a number of other doping research projects that receive funding from the Commission through the Research Directorate-General, including the 'Isotrace' project that is developing new Isotope Ratio Mass Spectrometry technology to detect the specific isotope content of prohibited synthetic hormones; the 'SGLC/MS' project that is developing methods for synthesising Anabolic Androgenic Steroids (to make testing for them easier) and establishing new Liquid Chromatography/Mass Spectrometry techniques for their rapid detection; and the 'Aladin 2002' project that is developing a proficiency-testing programme for implementation among IOC-accredited doping laboratories located in Europe. In total, the Commission spent €3.5m (£2.1m) on anti-doping research projects in 2001. The Commission also funds the European Paralympic Committee's 'Doping Disables' project, which leads the fight against doping in disabled sport. And in addition, a May 2002 study of doping among amateur sports persons (conducted at fitness centres in Belgium, Germany, Italy and Portugal) was funded by the EC[2].

1 For more information, see http://europa.eu.int/comm/dgs/research.
2 See Commission press release reference IP/02/709, available at http://europa.eu.int. Over 5% of fitness centre users in the four member states admitted to taking performance-enhancing drugs on a regular basis.

B1.48 The EC institutions assert that they have jurisdiction to act on doping issues. They base this claim principally (and perhaps rather dubiously) on Art 152.1 of the EC Treaty, which provides that a 'high level of human health protection shall be ensured in the definition and implementation of all Community policies and activities', on Art 39, since differences between member states' respective anti-doping legislation may constitute a barrier to the free movement of athletes, and also on Art 29, which provides that:

the Union's objective shall be to provide citizens with a high level of safety within an area of freedom, security and justice … That objective shall be achieved by preventing and combating crime … in particular … illicit drug trafficking …

There is also support for the authority to act in doping in the directive on the protection of youth and the directive on the health and safety of workers[1].

1 Council Directives 94/33/EC of 22 June 1994, and 89/391/EEC of 12 June 1989, respectively.

F Free-to-air televising of sports

B1.49 Another area of EC activity in sport is in the televising of sport. Then President of the Parliament's Committee on Culture, Youth, Education and the Media, Luciana Castellina, said in 1996 that 'watching a football match on TV is a human right' and that 'it is obviously not desirable for major sporting events to be encrypted'. This may be an overstatement worthy of Liverpool FC's Bill Shankly, but it is this sense of the fundamental importance of sporting and other events that gave rise to the 1997 amendment to the Television Without Frontiers Directive (Council Directive of 3 October 1989, 89/552/EEC[1]) to add Art 3A (Directive 97/36/EC[2]), which allows each member state to draw up a list of sports events that must be available on free-to-air television (or at least which may not be broadcast exclusively on pay-television) in its territory[3].

1 OJ L 298/23, 17.10.1989.
2 OJ L 202/60, 30.07.1997.
3 In fact, the provisions in Art 3A of the EC's Television Without Frontiers Directive are very similar to the provisions in Art 9 *bis* of the Council of Europe's European Convention on Transfrontier Television (ETS 132, as amended by the Protocol ETS 171, both available on http://conventions.coe.int). This convention has been ratified by 24 countries, including the UK and six other EC member states.

B1.50 Recital 18 to the amending directive[1] reads:

> Whereas it is essential that Member States should be able to take measures to protect the right to information and to ensure wide access by the public to television coverage of national or non-national events of major importance for society, such as the Olympic games, the football World Cup and European football championship; whereas to this end Member States retain the right to take measures compatible with Community law aimed at regulating the exercise by broadcasters under their jurisdiction of exclusive broadcasting rights to such events.

1 Directive 97/36/EC, OJ L202/60, 30.07.1997.

B1.51 Article 3A states as follows:

1. Each Member State may take measures in accordance with Community law to ensure that broadcasters under its jurisdiction do not broadcast on an exclusive basis events which are regarded by that Member State as being of major importance for society in such a way as to deprive a substantial proportion of the public in the Member State of the possibility of following such events via live coverage or deferred coverage on free television. If it does so, the Member State concerned shall draw up a list of designated events, national or non-national, which it considers to be of major importance for society. It shall do so in a clear and transparent manner in due and effective time. In so doing the Member State concerned shall also determine whether these events should be available via whole or partial live coverage, or where necessary or appropriate for objective reasons in the public interest, whole or partial deferred coverage.

2. Member States shall immediately notify to the Commission any measures taken or to be taken pursuant to paragraph 1. Within a period of three months from the notification, the Commission shall verify that such measures are compatible with Community law and communicate them to the other Member States. It shall seek the opinion of the Committee established pursuant to Article 23a [the contact committee]. It shall forthwith publish the measures taken in the Official Journal of the European Communities and at least once a year the consolidated list of measures taken by Member States.
3. Member States shall ensure, by appropriate means, within the framework of their legislation that broadcasters under their jurisdiction do not exercise the exclusive rights purchased by those broadcasters following the date of publication of this Directive in such a way that a substantial proportion of the public in another Member State is deprived of the possibility of following events which are designated by that other Member State in accordance with the preceding paragraphs via whole or partial live coverage or, where necessary or appropriate for objective reasons in the public interest, whole or partial deferred coverage on free television as determined by that other Member State in accordance with paragraph 1.

B1.52 The Council has thus taken the significant step of allowing each member state to decide what sports (and other) events it regards as important enough to have their coverage on free-to-air television guaranteed. And it has also compelled each member state to ensure that broadcasters from that state do not prevent the guaranteed coverage in another member state of sports events that the other member state has deemed to be so important. Indeed, it is this latter element (Art 3A(3)) that is the principal justification for the involvement of the EC. It is necessary to have cross-border legislation, rather than leaving the matter to the legislative bodies in the member states, since without the compulsion on member states to ensure citizen's respect for other member states' protected lists, this would purely be a matter of each state deciding to take domestic measures to protect its 'crown jewels' which would have limited extra territorial effect. With a growing number of transfrontier broadcasters (setting up in one member state to make programmes and broadcast them to one or more other member states), extra-territorial legislation was required[1].

1 See further para A1.88.

B1.53 According to the Commission's third report on the application of the directive[1], by 24 October 2000, only the UK, Germany, Italy and Denmark had taken measures under the directive to protect their respective 'crown jewels'[2]. The relevant legislation in the UK, the Broadcasting Act 1996[3], provides that (1) there is to be full live coverage on free-to-air (and fully available) television[4] of certain sports events (including the Olympic Games, the FIFA World Cup finals tournament and the FA Cup Final), and (2) other events (including test cricket matches played in England, matches involving England, Scotland, Ireland or Wales in the Six Nations rugby tournament, and the Ryder Cup) may be covered live and exclusive on pay-television so long as there are satisfactory arrangements for delayed or highlights coverage on free-to-air (and fully available) television[5].

1 COM (2001) 9 final, Brussels, 15.1.2001.
2 Although since then Austria has notified the Commission of its protected events (see n 5 below) and Belgium, the Netherlands and France have indicated that they intend to do so in the future.
3 See further para A1.82 et seq.
4 This is limited to the BBC, ITV and Channel Four. Channel Five is not included because of its limited coverage, ie it is below the UK threshold of 95%. This is not a threshold set out in the Directive, and other states have lower thresholds (eg 90% in Italy, 67% in Germany).

5 In comparison, Italy's protected events include the Olympics, the major football events (including the semis and final of the UEFA Champions League/UEFA Cup when an Italian team is playing), the Formula One Italian Grand Prix, cycling's Giro d'Italia, and the San Remo Italian music festival. Germany's protected events are limited to the Olympics and football. The Danes listed the Olympics, certain football events and also the World and European Handball Championships. Interestingly, despite a lengthy legal battle in the English courts concerning the effect of the Danish legislation under the Directive and the continuing 'protection' of free-to-air coverage of the sporting events listed in that legislation (see para A1.91 et seq), the Danish government then decided in early 2002 to scrap its listed events legislation and allow any broadcaster to screen its football, handball and other 'crown jewels'. Austria has recently (January 2002) notified the Commission that it has passed domestic legislation listing certain events to be protected, which events included not just sporting events such as the Olympic Games, the Austrian (football) Cup final, the World Alpine and World Nordic Skiing Championships, but also non-sporting events like the Vienna Philharmonic Orchestra's New Year Concert and the Vienna Opera Ball.

G Training and education

B1.54 There are a number of programmes that are set up and funded by the EC institutions to promote vocational training, education and general youth policies. The Leonardo da Vinci, Socrates and Youth programmes are perhaps the best examples, all of which are administered by the Education and Culture Directorate-General. The Leonardo da Vinci programme was set up in 1995 to implement a community-wide vocational training policy. It allowed bodies within member states to submit proposals for projects that improved vocational training (which would include those of a sporting nature, such as coaching), and these would, if successful, receive funding. The second phase of this programme has now begun (as has that of the Socrates programme – aimed at education – and the Youth programme)[1].

1 See further para C3.73 et seq.

B1.55 One sport-specific programme is that set up in 2001 to promote the Olympic ideals in schools in Europe. It is a joint venture of the Commission and the International Olympic Committee and is aimed at spreading the ethical values of sport among European school children, through individual projects financed out of the programme budget, which in 2001 was €750,000 (£450,000). For 2001/02 the programme was restricted to French, Italian and Dutch projects but it was intended that it would be open to all member states for 2003 and 2004.

B1.56 Perhaps most significant of all, certainly in terms of budget, is the Commission's proposal that the Parliament declare 2004 the European Year of Education through Sport[1]. Aimed at coinciding with the Athens Olympics, there would be a budget of €11.5m (£7m) to finance projects that (for example) encourage those in education and those in sports to work together to exploit the educational value of sport, promote voluntary activities within sports, combat discrimination and social exclusion through sport and education, or find solutions to the problems of young elite athletes whose education is affected by their sporting careers.

1 See, for example, the draft report by Doris Pack of the Parliament's Committee on Culture, Youth, Education, the Media and Sport, dated 12 March 2002, PE 312.520, and available at http://europa.eu.int/comm.

B1.57 Linked with the EC institutions' action in respect of training and education is the Commission's willingness to take action against member states where they fail to recognise professional qualifications of nationals of other member states, in breach of Art 226 of the EC Treaty and Directive 92/51/EEC. This applies across all industries, and action has been taken by the Commission against many states for their domestic restrictions in certain sectors, including Austria (in dentistry and the paramedic professions), France (in teaching), and Spain (in air traffic control). However, the Commission has also acted to protect the rights of sports coaches to ply their trade across the community, most recently (2001) and notably against Italy in failing to take all necessary steps to recognise the education and training of professional coaches, technical directors and trainers[1].

1 For more information, see the internal market section of the Commission's website, and particularly http://europa.eu.int/comm/internal_market/en/qualifications/01-1129.htm.

H Football violence

B1.58 The European institutions have long mounted a campaign against hooliganism in sport, particularly in football. And their efforts have not always been confined to the usual rounds of meetings, studies, acknowledgements, recognitions and toothless recommendations.

B1.59 The European Convention on Spectator Violence and Misbehaviour at Sports Events and in particular at Football Matches, a treaty of the Council of Europe, was established in 1985 and has been ratified by 33 countries, including the UK, Belgium, France, Italy, the Netherlands and Turkey (but not Germany).

B1.60 Under the convention, the ratifying states undertake to co-operate between themselves to prevent violence and control the problem of violence and misbehaviour by spectators at sports events. Similarly, public authorities and independent sports organisations are encouraged to co-operate. To this end, the convention sets out a number of measures that the ratifying states must adopt, including close co-operation between police forces; the prosecution of offenders and application of appropriate penalties; the strict control of ticket sales; restrictions on the sale of alcoholic drinks; the effective segregation of groups of rival supporters; and the appropriate design and physical fabric of stadia to prevent violence and allow effective crowd control and crowd safety.

B1.61 Throughout the 1990s, the Council made a series of resolutions aimed at defining the responsibilities owed by sports event organisers and encouraging the active co-operation and exchange of information between sports federations, police forces, member states and other interested parties in the running battle against hooliganism. In 1999, the Council resolved to develop a handbook on football violence issues for police organisations to use, with particular emphasis on the need for an exchange of information[1]. This handbook was updated in December 2001[2] following lessons learned at the 2000 European Championships in Belgium and the Netherlands. In brief, the handbook recommends:

- that each member state establish a permanent national police information unit (through which international co-operation and information is directed);
- that each member state shall be able to legislate so as to ensure that such a unit can perform appropriately within the national law of that state;

- that each unit maintains a 'risk analysis' report in respect of its relevant national team and leading clubs (for the benefit of the units in other countries);
- that each unit administers data on 'risk supporters';
- that prior to a cross-border match/tournament, the unit of the host country liaises with the unit(s) of the visiting country/countries and exchanges information on the organisers, the relevant police authorities, the teams, their fans (separated if necessary into 'normal' and 'risk'), the likely movements of the fans, police spotters, and ticket availability and sales. For example, the type of information to be exchanged on 'risk' fans includes their likely number, their meeting places, their average age, their usual 'outfits' (including any special logos or tattoos), their travel details, their supposed political persuasions, their links with criminal circles, their usual behaviour towards police and stewards, their usual consumption of alcohol, their usual reaction to unfavourable decisions by the match officials, their usual reaction to their team losing, the nature of their violence, and what weapons they use;
- that each member state should, when hosting a football event of an international nature, request the assistance of the police forces of visiting states where this can add value in terms of intelligence gathering, reconnaissance, 'spotting', and crowd control;
- that each member state take whatever steps it may use in accordance with its national law to prevent 'risk' supporters travelling abroad (the UK government chose to amend its national law so that draconian measures could be used to prevent certain fans travelling abroad, including fans that had never been convicted of an offence); and
- that event organisers take all necessary steps to maintain public order in and around the relevant stadia, before during and after the event(s).

1 OJ 1999 C196, 13.7.99, p 1.
2 OJ 2002 C22/01, 24.1.02.

5 WHO THE EC INSTITUTIONS THINK SHOULD BE ACTING ON SPORTING ISSUES

B1.62 If the EC institutions, the European Council and the Council of Europe are not able and/or prepared to take action in sport (except in exceptional cases like doping and free-to-air broadcasting), then who, one might ask, do they think ought to be taking action? The general view appears to be that, no matter how much they like to discuss sports and various issues that are related thereto, they ought to leave the decision-making and actions to the member states and/or the international and national sports federations themselves. In short, the institutions are happy for sport to govern itself, with a little help from the member states, so long as that assisted self-governance does not infringe Community law.

B1.63 The Amsterdam declaration called on the EC institutions to 'listen to sports associations when important questions affecting sports are at issue'[1], and the European Council in the Nice declaration said that '[s]porting organisations and the Member States have a primary responsibility in the conduct of sporting affairs' and that 'it is the task of sporting organisations to organise and promote their particular sports, particularly as regards the specifically sporting rules applicable and the make-up of national teams'[2]. It further recognised that the functions of the sports federations include 'ensuring the essential solidarity between the various levels of sporting practice … [providing] the possibility of access to sports for the public at large, human and financial support for amateur sports, promotion of equal access to every level of sporting activity for men and women alike, youth training, health protection and measures to combine doping, acts of violence and racist or xenophobic occurrences' and that the sports federations 'must continue to be the key feature of a form of organisation providing a guarantee of sporting cohesion and participatory democracy'[3].

1 See para B1.23.
2 See para para B1.27, n 2.
3 See para B1.27, n 2. See further para A1.29.

B1.64 The Commission has echoed the European Council's sentiments on the important roles of sports federations and the member states. In fact it has gone further: in the Helsinki Report, the Commission warned of the dangers of breakaway leagues/federations to the traditional structure of sport and praised the use of 'one umbrella organisation' for each sport[1]. In the same document, the Commission stressed the need for each member state to find a place in its education system for physical and sporting activities, and also commented on the ability of member states to affect the commercial dynamics of sport in Europe by having different tax systems and adopting different legislative measures in respect of sport and commerce. Interestingly, the Commission suggested that one way of safeguarding national sports federations (and so the current structure and functions of sport in Europe) would be for the member states to take action to recognise such federations as having specific legal status (as is the case, for example, in France).

1 See para B1.25, n 2.

B1.65 The Parliament has been more specific in its assessment of the roles of the member states and sports federations, or certainly it was in the Mennea report. It not only recognised the autonomy and competence of national and international federations, but also called on those bodies to 'revitalise their internal democracy and take account of the different needs and management methods of professional and amateur sport, by setting up the appropriate representative structures'[1]. As for the member states, the Parliament called on them to take action and/or legislate on the issues of football violence, the encouragement of private investment in sport, sport for disabled, and the availability of important sporting events on free-to-air television.

1 See para B1.31, n 5.

B1.66 All of this leaves little for the European institutions themselves to do, even if they could. However, the Commission noted that if the sporting landscape changes as it believes it should (with traditional values being maintained but at the same time a new economic and legal environment being assimilated), then the EC (whether as a collection of member states acting separately or through the EC organs) would 'have an essential part to play in implementing the new approach'[1]. A new era of involvement by the institutions is also suggested by the Parliament calling in the Mennea report[2] for an express reference to sport in the EC Treaty.

1 Helsinki Report on Sport: see para B1.25, n 2.
2 See para B1.31, n 5.

B1.67 At the time of writing, that still looks very unlikely and, many would argue, quite unattractive. So in the near future at least, the institutions in Europe will take a great deal of interest in sport, but not a great deal of action. And if any action *is* taken by the institutions, then the legal competence for such action ought reasonably to be closely examined, since the principle of subsidiarity effectively dictates that the circumstances must be exceptional. However, it may just be the case that the rhetoric of the institutions does have an indirect impact and so when the courts and the Commission decide on, say, competition law cases involving sport, or when the Council and the Parliament legislate on issues involving sport, a slightly different result may be achieved because the 'specificities of sport', that have been formally identified since *Bosman*, have been taken into account.

CHAPTER B2

EC AND UK COMPETITION RULES AND SPORT

Alasdair Bell (Olswang), **Adam Lewis** (Blackstone Chambers) and **Jonathan Taylor** (Hammonds)

Contents

1 INTRODUCTION

B2.1 Sport in Europe has historically been more of a social, cultural and educational activity than an economic pursuit. It was traditionally perceived as a leisure-time activity rather than as an entertainment 'product'.

B2.2 The position has changed dramatically, however, as deregulation of the television industry has allowed in new entrants who have identified elite sports programming as an effective means to win audiences and advertisers. For pay-TV operators in particular, capturing the exclusive rights to top sporting events has been regarded as a crucial means to attract new subscribers. No doubt it is for this reason that Rupert Murdoch famously remarked that premium sport was the '*battering ram*' to bring pay-TV into peoples' homes.

B2.3 At the same time, advertising and sponsorship revenues have soared as corporate brands have identified association with elite sports not only as an efficient means of communicating with target demographic groups but also as a way of tapping into the unique loyalty of the sports fan to his or her chosen sporting 'brand'.

B2.4 Consequently, sport in Europe is now big business and along with this evolution towards greater commercialism has come a change in the legal landscape as well. In particular, sports bodies, clubs, and players have found that being involved in the 'business' of sport also means that they are subject to the general laws that govern the conduct of 'business'. Of these general business laws, the competition rules have a very important part to play, vindicating the perceived public interest in free and unrestricted competition in all relevant markets. The purpose of this chapter is to explain how competition law impacts on the organisation, structure and commercial exploitation of sport.

B2.5 The traditional arrangements for the governance and commercial exploitation of sport (usually involving centralised decision-making and marketing by the 'governing body') are generally analysed as a contract between the governing body and the clubs and/or individuals who constitute the membership of the governing body[1]. Where an objective is to challenge these contractual arrangements, a possible route offered by the law is a claim that the contract 'restricts competition'. The common law offered the doctrine of restraint of trade to advance such arguments[2]; the EC Treaty and the Competition Act 1998 have now added to the armoury of possible competition law claims.

1 See paras A1.19 to A1.22 and A3.116.
2 See paras A3.135 to A3.158.

B2.6 When considering a competition law claim, an important preliminary question to address is the forum in which the claim should be pursued. In practice, the choice tends to be between the regulatory authorities (such as the European Commission or Office of Fair Trading) or the civil courts. However, a further possibility to consider might be the Court of Arbitration for Sport ('CAS') in Lausanne, since many sports governing bodies have recognised the jurisdiction of the CAS and the panel of CAS arbitrators compromises members with both significant legal experience and also specialist knowledge of sport[1]. Each course of action has its advantages and disadvantages, as explained in detail elsewhere in this work[2].

1 See generally para A5.84 et seq. For example, the claim brought in the CAS by AEK Athens and Slavia Prague against UEFA centred on the compatibility of the UEFA rule on common ownership of clubs with EU competition law. See *AEK Athens and Slavia Prague v UEFA*, CAS 98/2000, award dated 20 August 1999, *Digest of CAS Awards II 1998–2000* (2002, Kluwer), p 38, also reported in [2001] 1 ISLR 122. For a discussion of the decision, see paras B2.145 et seq and para A3.24.
2 See paras A3.159 to A3.170.

B2.7 Perhaps largely as a consequence of the famous *Bosman* ruling[1], the European Commission found that in the second half of the 1990s it was frequently called on by parties to investigate different aspects of professional sport and in particular to examine the compatibility of sports rules and structures with the competition provisions of the EC Treaty. Thus, in 1999, the Commission reported that it had received more than 60 complaints relating to the sports sector based on the competition rules of the EC Treaty[2].

1 See paras A3.172, n 1, B2.153 to B2.156, B3.40 et seq and E2.40 et seq.
2 Pons *Sport and European Competition Policy* (October 1999) at 2.

B2.8 However, it is not only the European competition authority that has been called upon to investigate sports-related issues; domestic regulators have been involved as well. For example, it was a procedure launched by the Office of Fair Trading in the UK that resulted in the FA Premier League spending most of 1999 in the Restrictive Practices Court, defending its broadcasting arrangements from competition law challenge[1].

1 *Re an Agreement between the FA Premier League* [2000] EMLR 78, [1999] UKCLR 258 (Restrictive Practices Court 1999). See para B2.264 et seq.

B2.9 Direct recourse to national courts (as opposed to the competition authorities) is also possible. Indeed, 2001 saw the first judgment by an English court upholding a claim that a sports governing body's exercise of its regulatory powers amounted to an abuse of a dominant position in breach of the competition rules[1].

1 *Hendry v World Professional Billiards and Snooker Association Ltd* [2002] UKCLR 5, [2002] ECC 8, [2001] Eu LR 770, [2002] 1 ISLR 'SLR-1' (Lloyd J, 5 October 2001). See para B2.131 et seq.

B2.10 Against this background, no sports regulator or rights-holder can afford to ignore competition law when making decisions either as to the exercise of regulatory powers or as to the exploitation of commercial rights.

B2.11 Moreover, the suggestions periodically made that sport should somehow be 'exempt' from the application of competition law[1] have little force[2]. As mentioned[3], the acquisition and exploitation of commercial sports rights is, for example, a very important factor in the development of competition in broadcasting markets. It is not plausible to argue that such commercial arrangements should be immune from scrutiny under competition law[4]. Nevertheless, the application of competition law in the sports area does require an analysis that takes account of the specific structural characteristics of sport and (in particular the structural characteristics that make sport such a unique and vibrant proposition), and that is sufficiently attuned to help preserve those characteristics.

1 See eg 'Sport should be exempt from competition law, says UK' (1999) *TV Sports Markets* (23 April).
2 See eg Weatherill 'Do sporting associations make "law" or are they merely subject to it?' (July/August 1998) EBL Rev 217.
3 See para B2.2.
4 See para B2.12, n 1.

B2.12 The Commission has stated its view that an exemption for sport from EC law is 'unnecessary, undesirable and unjustified'[1]. Rather, the Commission is clearly of the view that there is sufficient flexibility in the competition rules to reflect the specific characteristics and requirements of sport as a social, cultural and economic product[2]. Thus, the European Court of Justice and the Commission have each recognised that competitive team sports have unique characteristics that require on-field competitors to co-operate with each other off the field in a manner that would be suspect in other contexts[3]. The European Court of Justice and the

Commission have also recognised that those unique characteristics should inform and temper the application of competition law in this sector[4].

1 Director-General Schaub 'EC Competition Policy and Its Implications for the Sports Sector', speech to the World Sports Forum, 8 March 1998. See also 'Reaction of Commissioners Flynn and Van Miert to press reports regarding FIFA's proposal to exclude sport from the scope of competition law', Commission press release dated 7 January 1998, IP/98/8 ('There can be no question of professional sports being exempted from the Treaty provisions or of attempting to side-step rulings from the Court of Justice'); 'Commission debates application of competition rules to sports', Commission press release dated 24 February 1999, IP/99/133; Reding 'The European Community and European Sport', speech dated 3 May 2001.

2 See eg Commissioner Monti *Competition and Sport: the Rules of the Game* (DN Speech/01/84, Brussels 26 April 2001): 'It is my belief that, from the moment sporting federations accept the rule of law and realise the limits the law imposes on their practices, it is a question of time to find the appropriate solution however complicated the issues may be. The Commission has proved more than once its flexibility and its willingness to work for the good of sport in Europe'. See also Director-General Schaub *EC Competition Policy and Its Implications for the Sports Sector*, speech to the World Sports Forum, 8 March 1998: 'We believe that the competition rules are flexible enough to come up with solutions which respect not only Community competition law but also the particularities of the sports sector'.

3 See paras B2.72 to B2.75.

4 See para B2.95.

B2.13 After setting out in outline the legal and institutional framework of the EC and UK competition rules[1], this chapter considers the special features of applying those rules to the sports sector[2], and then surveys the case law and regulatory decisions in this area[3].

1 See para B2.14 et seq.

2 See para B2.54 et seq.

3 See para B2.102 et seq.

2 THE LEGAL AND INSTITUTIONAL FRAMEWORK OF THE EC AND UK COMPETITION RULES

B2.14 The member states of the European Community operate a federal system of competition regulation broadly akin to that of the US system. Anti-competitive conduct that affects trade between member states falls within the jurisdiction of the Competition Directorate of the European Commission in Brussels, applying the competition provisions (Arts 81 and 82) of the Treaty of Rome. Anti-competitive conduct that is confined to the territory of a single member state falls within the jurisdiction of the domestic competition authority of the state concerned, applying domestic competition law. For example, in the UK the principal competition law is the Competition Act 1998, which is enforced by the Office of Fair Trading (the 'OFT')[1].

1 Where there is a potential overlap in jurisdiction, the regulators' competing claims are resolved by determining whether the matter in question has an impact primarily felt in one member state or else has broader repercussions. In the former case, the Commission may leave the domestic regulators to apply not only domestic competition law but also the competition provisions of the Treaty of Rome. However, the Commission currently retains exclusive authority to grant exemptions to individual arrangements from the EC competition rules. See para B2.23.

B2.15 Generally speaking, the domestic competition laws of the EC member states track the competition rules of the Treaty of Rome. For example, the core prohibitions of the UK's Competition Act 1998 are almost a mirror image of EC

Arts 81 and 82[1], and the Competition Act 1998 also includes a provision obliging the English courts and the OFT to interpret and apply the Act, insofar as possible, in accordance with the provisions and the jurisprudence of the EC Treaty[2]. However, an important practical distinction is that the Competition Act 1998 does not require (as EC competition law does) a showing that the conduct in question impacts on trade between member states[3].

1 See paras B2.17 and B2.30.
2 Section 60 of the Competition Act 1998. This does not mean complete convergence. For example, the EC Treaty provisions are interpreted and applied in light of the mandate for a single internal market in Europe, which is not a concern of domestic regulators. However, s 60 does mean that administrators and lawyers working on a national level will have to take EC jurisprudence and practice squarely into account in their analysis. This chapter proceeds on that basis.
3 For any claim based on EC law, however, this is a threshold jurisdictional issue. See further Bellamy & Child *European Community Law of Competition* (5th edn, 2001), para 2-128 et seq.

A The substantive rules[1]

(a) The prohibition of anti-competitive agreements, decisions of associations and concerted practices: Art 81 of the EC Treaty and Chapter I of the Competition Act 1998

B2.16 Article 81(1) (ex 85(1)) of the EC Treaty prohibits 'all agreements between undertakings, decisions by associations of undertakings and concerted practices which may affect trade between member states and which have as their object or effect the prevention, restriction or distortion of competition within the common market …'.

1 This chapter cannot provide anything more than a broad overview of competition law as a whole. For an exhaustive treatment, see eg Bellamy & Child *European Community Law of Competition* (5th edn, 2001); Coleman and Grenfell *The Competition Act 1998* (1999).

B2.17 Similarly, s 2 of Chapter I of the Competition Act 1998 prohibits 'agreements between undertakings, decisions by associations of undertakings or concerted practices which may effect trade within the UK; and which have as their object or effect the prevention, restriction or distortion of competition within the UK' (the 'Chapter I prohibition').

B2.18 Each of Art 81 and the Chapter I prohibition lists the following specific examples of infringing agreements: agreements that fix prices, limit production, share markets, apply dissimilar conditions to equivalent transactions with other trading parties, and/or tie unrelated obligations together[1].

1 See Bellamy & Child *European Community Law of Competition* (5th edn, 2001), para 2-001.

B2.19 The reference to agreements between undertakings, decisions by associations of undertakings and concerted practices clearly covers bilateral commercial agreements in the sports sector, such as broadcasting agreements, sponsorship arrangements and the like. There is little doubt, for example, that a television contract between the FA Premier League and BSkyB is an 'agreement between undertakings' for the purposes of competition law.

B2.20 It is not so apparent, however, whether the institutional framework of sport, ie the rules, constitutions and statutes of a governing body regulating the organisation and conduct of a sport, also fall within the scope of EC Art 81 and/or the Chapter I prohibition. The answer seems to be that such rules constitute 'decisions by associations of undertakings' or possibly 'agreements between undertakings' and, as a result, potentially fall within the ambit of the Art 81 (or Chapter I) prohibition[1].

1 See *Pauwels Travel Bvba v FIFA Local Organising Committee Italia 1990*, OJ 1992 L326/31, [1994] 5 CMLR 253, paras 47–53; Opinion of Advocate-General Lenz, *Union Royale Belge des Sociétés de Football ASBL v Bosman*, C-415/93, [1996] 1 CMLR 645, para 255 et seq. See also Commission decision of 27 June 2002, rejecting ENIC complaint against UEFA multiple ownership rule, Case COMP/37.806, at paras 25, 26.

B2.21 Where an agreement is caught by EC Art 81 or the Chapter I prohibition, it will be void and unenforceable as between the parties to it. It is important to note, however, that if the English law conditions for severance are satisfied, then the anti-competitive provisions may be severed and the rest of the arrangement may still be enforced[1].

1 Bellamy & Child *European Community Law of Competition* (5th edn, 2001), para 2.120.

B2.22 Furthermore, an agreement that falls within the scope of Art 81 may be exempted if it satisfies the conditions set out in Art 81(3), ie if it:

> contributes to improving the production or distribution of goods or to promoting technical or economic progress, while allowing consumers a fair share of the resulting benefit, and … does not (a) impose on the undertakings concerned restrictions which are not indispensable to the attainment of these objectives; [or] (b) afford such undertakings the possibility of eliminating competition in respect of a substantial part of the products in question.

Similarly, s 4 of the Competition Act 1998 provides that agreements may qualify for exemption from the Chapter I prohibition, provided they satisfy the same substantive conditions[1].

1 See further paras B2.89 to B2.94.

B2.23 Only the European Commission may grant an exemption from Art 81(1) pursuant to Art 81(3)[1]. Similarly, in the United Kingdom, only the Director-General of Fair Trading may grant an exemption from the Chapter I prohibition of the Competition Act (but the grant of an Art 81(3) exemption by the Commission will trigger an automatic exemption from the Chapter I prohibition[2]). In each case, a necessary pre-condition is for the parties concerned to notify their agreements to the relevant regulatory authority[3].

1 Bellamy & Child *European Community Law of Competition* (5th edn, 2001), para 3-002. The intention is that the application of Act 81(3) be devolved from the European Commission and that this Treaty provision should become directly applicable before national courts: Proposal COM (2000) 582, 27 September 2000. See Commission press release dated 27 September 2000, IP/00/1064.
2 Section 10(1)(b) of the Competition Act 1998.
3 See generally Bellamy & Child *European Community Law of Competition* (5th edn, 2001), ch 11; Coleman and Grenfell *The Competition Act 1998* (1999), ch 12.

B2.24 As noted below[1], the competition regulators have the power to impose substantial fines for competition law violations. A notification seeking an exemption provides the parties concerned with immunity from such fines, at least from the date of notification[2]. In practical terms, however, that particular benefit may be largely theoretical, since fines are mostly imposed for 'hard core' anti-competitive practices, such as price fixing, market sharing, or abusive or predatory conduct. Few experienced competition lawyers would advise notification of the kind of agreement liable to result in the imposition of a fine.

1 See para B2.44.

2 Bellamy & Child *European Community Law of Competition* (5th edn, 2001), para 11.011; Coleman and Grenfell *The Competition Act 1998* (1999), para 10.69.

B2.25 Notification of an agreement to the competition authorities may also have important practical consequences with regard to the enforceability of certain clauses or provisions, and in particular as regards the willingness of domestic courts to intervene on competition law grounds. In practice, where a notification for an exemption is pending before the Commission, the English courts are likely to stay proceedings, to avoid the risk of inconsistent rulings.

B2.26 In this connection, the Notice on Co-operation with National Courts[1] establishes a policy of co-operation between national courts and the Commission, with the aim of ensuring a 'seamless' competition system. National courts are supposed to avoid taking decisions that might possibly conflict with those taken or envisaged by the Commission. To this end, para 18 of the Notice provides that '[national courts] must take account of the Commission's powers in order to avoid decisions which could conflict with those taken or envisaged by the Commission'[2].

1 OJ C 313, 15/10/97, p 3.

2 See n 1. See further paras A3.221 to A3.226.

B2.27 The European Court of Justice stressed the importance of avoiding conflicting decisions in the *Delimitis* case[1] (which actually led to the adoption of the Notice referred to in the preceding paragraph). The court stated that:

> Account should here be taken of the risk of national courts taking decisions which conflict with those taken or envisaged by the Commission in the implementation of Articles 8[1](1) and 8[2], and also of Article 8[1](3). Such conflicting decisions would be contrary to the general principle of legal certainty and must, therefore, be avoided when national courts give decisions on agreements or practices which may subsequently be the subject of a decision by the Commission[2].

The court went on to say[3] that:

> [a] stay of proceedings or the adoption of interim measures should also be envisaged where there is a risk of conflicting decisions in the context of the application of Articles 8[1](1) and 8[2].

1 Case C-234/89, *Stergios Delimitis v Henninger Bräu AG* [1991] ECR I-935, para 47.

2 [1991] ECR I-935, para 47.

3 [1991] ECR I-935, para 52.

B2.28 Thus, when an agreement or set of rules has been notified to Brussels it is unlikely that a domestic court will intervene and find the agreement or rules contrary to EC competition law (since the matter is essentially *sub judice* before the Commission). A discussion of cases arising in the sports sector where a stay has been granted of English court proceedings to avoid the risk of inconsistency with decisions to be taken by the Commission appears elsewhere in this work[1].

1 See para A3.224.

(b) Abuse of a dominant position: Art 82 of the EC Treaty and Chapter Two of the Competition Act 1998

B2.29 Whereas EC Art 81 is aimed at collusive conduct by two or more undertakings, EC Art 82 (ex 86) addresses monopolistic behaviour and prohibits 'any abuse by one or more undertakings of a dominant position within the common market or in a substantial part of it …'.

B2.30 Chapter II of the Competition Act 1998 mirrors Art 82, prohibiting any conduct on the part of one or more undertakings that amounts to the abuse of a dominant position in a UK market that may affect trade in the UK (the 'Chapter II prohibition').

B2.31 Examples of certain types of abusive conduct are listed in both Art 82 and the Chapter II prohibition, and include the imposition of unfair trading conditions, limiting production to the prejudice of consumers, applying dissimilar conditions to equivalent transactions with other trading parties, and tying unrelated obligations together[1].

1 See Bellamy & Child *European Community Law of Competition* (5th edn, 2001), para 9.065 et seq.

B2.32 Since sport is generally organised in a kind of 'pyramid' structure[1], with a single governing body controlling most regulatory and commercial aspects of each sport, the governing body appears to be de facto 'dominant' and therefore claims relating to the abuse of monopoly power may be relatively easy to make. However, simply *having* a dominant position is not, in itself, problematic. Rather it is the *abuse* of a dominant position that infringes Art 82. As the Commission has said:

> [I]t is not the power to regulate a given sporting activity as such which might constitute an abuse but rather the way in which a given sporting organisation exercises such power[2].

1 See paras A1.16 and A1.17. A useful reference document is the consultation paper, *The European Model of Sport*, published by DG X of the European Commission in November 1998, which can be located at www.europa.eu.int/comm/sport/doc/ecom/doc_consult_en.pdf.

2 'Commission debates application of competition rules to sport', Commission press release dated 24 February 1999, IP/99/133.

B2.33 Unsurprisingly, it is not possible (under either the EC Treaty or the UK Competition Act) to grant an exemption for conduct that constitutes an abuse of a dominant position. Nevertheless, the factors considered relevant to the grant of an exemption under Art 81(3)[1] may be relied upon to demonstrate that conduct alleged to be abusive is in fact compatible with EU competition law.

1 See paras B2.22 and B2.89 to B2.94.

(c) State aid

B2.34 EC competition law also includes the rules in the EC Treaty on state aid[1]. The state aid rules prohibit member states from granting to undertakings, without the clearance of the Commission, 'aid' that distorts or threatens to distort competition and trade between member states. In other words, in very broad terms, where the state confers an advantage on only selected businesses active in a particular sector, it puts them in a better position to compete with their rivals, which are correspondingly disadvantaged. If the advantage has not been conferred in return for anything (for example in contrast to where the state pays a business to do some work) and the Commission has not been told about it, then it may well be illegal as a state aid, and its repayment could be sought by the disadvantaged business or businesses. The Commission may however clear the aid as compatible with the common market on a number of specific bases[2].

1 EC Arts 87 to 89 (ex 92 to 94).
2 For a full analysis, see Bellamy and Child *Common Market Law of Competition* (5th edn, 2001), ch 19; Hancher, Ottervanger and Slot *EC State Aids* (2nd edn, 1999).

B2.35 To date these rules have not had a significant impact on the sports sector, but their application in this context should not be discounted completely[1].

1 See further paras B2.326 to B2.333.

(d) Merger control

B2.36 To complete the overview of EC and UK competition rules, brief mention must be made of the merger control provisions.

B2.37 Both EC and English competition law contain specific provisions[1] allowing the regulatory authorities to control mergers, acquisitions and other 'concentrations' of businesses that threaten to create or reinforce a dominant position on the relevant market[2]. This section summarises the provisions; a subsequent section[3] describes the circumstances in which they have been, or may be, applied in the sports context.

1 In addition to the normal anti-trust rules (Arts 81 and 82 and the Competition Act 1998, Chapter I and II prohibitions): see Bellamy and Child *European Community Law of Competition* (5th edn, 2001), paras 6-269 to 6-280.
2 For a full analysis, see Bellamy and Child *European Community Law of Competition* (5th edn, 2001) ch 6; Verloop *Merger Control in the EU: a survey of European Competition Laws* (3rd edn, 1999); Cook and Kerse *EC Merger Control* (3rd edn, 2000); and Finbow & Parr *UK Merger Control: Law and Practice* (1999).
3 See paras B2.334 to B2.342.

B2.38 **The EC Merger Regulation** Under the EC Merger Regulation[1] and its Implementing Regulation[2], where a 'concentration' arises that has a 'community dimension' it must be notified to the European Commission, which has exclusive jurisdiction to review it. A concentration arises where two or more previously independent undertakings merge, or where one or more undertakings acquire direct or indirect control over the whole or part of one or more other undertakings[3]. Control is a broad concept involving mixed questions of fact and law: the issue is whether in all the circumstances the undertaking or undertakings involved can exercise decisive influence over the decisions of another undertaking, whether through ownership, contractual rights, or other means[4]. In order to have a community dimension[5] the undertakings involved must have a combined worldwide turnover of more than €5,000m and at least two of them must each have a turnover within the Community in excess of €250m (provided that there must be no single member state in which all the undertakings involved achieve two thirds or more of their turnover in the Community)[6]. The sheer size of these figures means that it will be rare that the EC Merger Regulation applies to mergers and acquisitions in the sports context: the involvement of sport in EC merger cases is likely to be tangential to the substantive issues.

1 Council Regulation 4064/89 [1989] OJ L 395, p 1 and [1990] OJ L 257, p 14, as amended by Council Regulation 1310/97 [1997] OJ L 180, p 1, corrected by [1998] OJ L 3, p 16 and [1998] OJ L 40, p 17.
2 Commission Regulation 447/98 [1998] OJ L 61, p 1. The Commission has also published a number of guidelines that set out how the provisions will be interpreted. In addition further guidance is contained in decided cases and interpretative notes.
3 See Bellamy and Child *European Community Law of Competition* (5th edn, 2001), paras 6-022 to 6-028. Some 'joint ventures' may fall within the definition.
4 See Bellamy and Child *European Community Law of Competition* (5th edn, 2001), paras 6-029 to 6-068.
5 The above states the general position. A community dimension may also arise where the worldwide turnover of each of the undertakings concerned is more than €2,500m, and the combined turnover of all of them in at least three member states is more than €100m, and in at least three of those member states two of the undertakings each achieve a turnover of more than €25m and the community wide turnover of each of at least two of the undertakings is more than €100m.
6 See Bellamy and Child *European Community Law of Competition* (5th edn, 2001), paras 6-069 to 6-092.

B2.39 Under Art 2 of the EC Merger Regulation, the question for the Commission when it reviews such a concentration is whether it creates or strengthens a dominant position as a result of which, effective competition would be impeded in the common market or a substantial part of it. If it does not do so, the concentration will be declared compatible[1]. As always, therefore, one of the crucial questions is the proper definition of the relevant market, as is described below[2]. It is to be noted, however, that the test under the EC Merger Regulation is not equivalent to asking (as under Art 82) whether the concentration would result in the abuse of a dominant position. Rather, the test is structural and the question is whether the concentration will result in a position of market strength that might impede effective competition[3].

1 See Bellamy and Child *European Community Law of Competition* (5th edn, 2001), paras 6-093, 6-135 to 6-183.
2 See para B2.76 to B2.88.
3 Bellamy and Child *European Community Law of Competition* (5th edn, 2001), paras 6-093 to 6-134.

B2.40 Notification of concentrations falling within the EC Merger Regulation criteria is compulsory before implementation. Once a potential concentration is notified, there is an accelerated procedure for the Commission's Merger Task Force to review it[1]. The Commission can also initiate proceedings on its own initiative. The Commission may refer a matter to the competition authorities of a particular member state, or a particular member state may seek to intervene, in circumstances where the merger has a particular effect in that member state[2].

1 See Bellamy and Child *European Community Law of Competition* (5th edn, 2001), paras 6-184 to 6-224.
2 See Bellamy and Child *European Community Law of Competition* (5th edn, 2001), paras 6-225 to 6-268.

B2.41 Merger control under English law The English merger control provisions may apply where a merger or other concentration impacting the UK does not fall under the EC Merger Regulation. Under the Fair Trading Act 1973 as amended by the Competition Act 1998, a concentration (or 'merger situation') arises where two or more businesses, at least one of which carries on business in the UK, are brought under common ownership or control[1]. The jurisdictional threshold is either that the gross value of the worldwide assets being acquired exceeds £70m, or that a combined market share in excess of 25% is achieved or further increased in the UK or a substantial part of it[2]. Plainly these thresholds are very substantially lower than those that apply under the EC Merger Regulation, and it is quite possible that they might be met in the sports context[3]. A concentration may be voluntarily notified to the OFT, or may be the subject of independent investigation. If the OFT considers that a concentration might operate against the public interest, then it may make a reference to the English Competition Commission (previously the Monopolies and Mergers Commission). The Competition Commission then considers whether the concentration does indeed operate contrary to the public interest, and reports to the Secretary of State, who may or may not accept the report and implement the recommendations of the Competition Commission.

1 See Finbow & Parr *UK Merger Control: Law and Practice* (1995), para 1.007.
2 See n 1.
3 See eg MMC Report into the Proposed Merger between BSkyB Group plc and Manchester United Football Club plc (Cm 4305, 1999). See further paras B2.336 to B2.338.

B Enforcement

B2.42 The parties to an anti-competitive agreement, and/or third parties who have been injured as a consequence of an anti-competitive agreement, may bring a private cause of action in the English courts for breach of the Competition Act 1998 and/or of Arts 81 and/or 82 of the EC Treaty (which have direct effect in the UK[1]), seeking a declaration, an injunction, or possibly damages[2].

1 *Garden Cottage Foods Ltd v Milk Marketing Board* [1984] AC 130; *Cutsforth v Mansfield Inns Ltd* [1986] 1 WLR 558.
2 Bellamy & Child *European Community Law of Competition* (5th edn, 2001), para 10.054 et seq. See generally Good and Hudson 'Competition disputes: bringing a competition action in the English courts' PLC (May 1999) p 19. See also para A3.205.

B2.43 An alternative course is to file a complaint with the European Commission under the EC competition rules and/or the Office of Fair Trading under the Competition Act. It is also possible, though it does not happen that often in practice, that the regulatory authorities may initiate an investigation of their own accord.

B2.44 In cases where infringements of the competition rules are established, the Commission has the authority to fine the parties involved up to 10% of group worldwide turnover[1]. Similarly, the OFT has the power to impose fines of up to 10% of UK turnover for each year of the infringement, up to a three year maximum[2]. In the sports sector, the power to impose fines has not been exercised meaningfully to date[3], which is not surprising given the complexity of applying the competition rules in this sector. However, the power to fine is a significant tool in the hands of the regulator.

1 See Council Regulation 17/62.
2 Section 36 Competition Act 1998.
3 In *Italia '90* (see para B2.222), the Commission decided that, in light of the fact that the case was the first to involve the arrangements relating to tickets to a sports event, and the safety issues presented 'undoubted complicating factors', a fine would not be imposed. In *France '98* (see para B2.227), notwithstanding that again the infringing practices related to ticketing arrangements for the FIFA World Cup, the Commission imposed a 'symbolic' fine of only €1,000.

B2.45 The European Commission has a duty to investigate complaints made to it under the EC competition rules. Its usual practice, upon receiving a complaint, is to send a copy of the document to the party that is the subject of the complaint. The Commission typically allows that party a period of about one to two months to respond to the legal and factual accusations made in the complaint. If the Commission has particular questions deriving from the complaint it may also send out 'Article 11' letters (requests for information), asking the parties to clarify specific issues[1].

1 The process is similar with respect to the OFT under the Competition Act 1998. See eg 'Premier clubs stand accused of operating cartel' (2002) The Times, 4 October.

B2.46 There is no standard time-frame for the Commission to deal with complaints and it is not unknown for cases to drag on for years or more. In practice, and particularly if the complainant considers that it has a good case, it may seek to keep the pressure up on the Commission by providing further evidence of the damage it has (allegedly) suffered as a consequence of the supposedly infringing conduct. In urgent cases, where there is risk of serious and irreparable harm as a consequence of anti-competitive conduct, a party may also ask the Commission to take 'interim measures'[1]. In practice, however, it is rare for the Commission to award interim measures and given the complexity of most sports-related cases it is perhaps not surprising that there are few (if any) examples of interim measures awards in this area[2].

1 Case 792/79R *Camera Care v Commission* [1980] ECR 119, [1980] 1 CMLR 334.
2 For an example of a grant of interim measures in the competition law context by the Court of Arbitration for Sport, see *AEK Athens and Slava Prague v UEFA*, CAS 98/2000 award on provisional relief application 17 July 1998, full award 20 August 1999, *Digest of CAS Awards II 1998–2000* (2002, Kluwer), p 38, discussed at para B2.148.

B2.47 One practical result that the Commission occasionally favours is the informal settlement of a case between the complainant and the party being complained against. From the perspective of the Commission, settlement has the attraction of the complaint usually being withdrawn and (as a result) there being no obligation on the Commission to take a formal decision that might subsequently be challenged[1]. However, this practice does not help the development of legal certainty in the field[2].

1 See eg para B2.169 on the outcome of the Commission's investigation into FIFA's transfer rules.
2 See Kinsella and Daly 'European Competition Law and Sports' (2001) 4(6) Sports Law Bulletin 7, 12, 13.

B2.48 If the Commission believes that a complaint raises a serious case to answer, it can issue a 'statement of objections'. A statement of objections does not constitute a 'decision' capable of review by the courts. It is, however, an important procedural step and must comply with certain formal requirements and, in particular, provide the party being 'charged' with the full factual and legal case presented against it.

B2.49 Sending a statement of objections discharges the Commission's obligation to state its case to the undertakings concerned. That obligation is set out in Regulation 2842/98[1], which provides (at Art 3) that '[t]he Commission shall inform the parties in writing of the objections raised against them'. The Court of Justice has described the importance of the statement of objections in a number of cases. For example, in *Dyestuffs*[2] it stated:

> In order to protect the rights of the defence during the course of the administrative procedure … undertakings should be informed of the essential elements of fact on which the objections are based.

1 Regulation 2842/98 of 22 December 1998 on the hearing of parties in certain proceedings under Arts 85 and 86 of the EC Treaty, OJ L 354, 30/12/1998, p 18; see also Art 19(1), Regulation 17: First Regulation implementing Arts 85 and 86 of the Treaty, OJ 013, 21/02/1962, p 204.

2 Case 48-69, *Imperial Chemical Industries Ltd v Commission* [1972] ECR 619, para 22. See also Joined Cases 56 and 58-64, *Etablissements Consten S.à.R.L. and Grundig-Verkaufs-GmbH v Commission* [1966] ECR 299 at 338.

B2.50 The statement of objections must clearly and comprehensively set out the facts and legal arguments on the basis of which the Commission alleges there to be an infringement of the competition rules[1]. Any final decision taken by the Commission must be based on the objections set out in the statement of objections[2]. Thus, Art 2 of Regulation 2842/98 provides that '[t]he Commission shall in its decisions deal only with objections in respect of which the parties have been afforded the opportunity of making their views known'. This key principle has also been affirmed by the European Court of Justice[3]. The Commission may not, therefore, in a final decision, materially deviate from the factual and legal assessment as set out in the statements of objections. To do so would be contrary to the rights of the defence[4].

1 Case C-62/86, *AKZO v Commission* [1991] ECR I-3359, para 29; see also Cases T-10-12, 15/92R, *Cimenteries v Commission* [1992] ECR II-1571, para 33 and Cases C-89/85 etc, *A. Ahlström v Commission* [1993] ECR I-1307, paras 40–54, 148–154.

2 Cases C-89/85 etc, *A. Ahlström v Commission* [1993] ECR I-1307, paras 40–54, 148–154.

3 For example, in Joined Cases 142 and 156/84, *British American Tobacco Co Ltd and R.J Reynolds Industries Inc v Commission*, Order of the Court of 18 June 1986, [1986] ECR 1899, para 13, the court stated that the statement of objections 'delimits the scope of the administrative procedure initiated and thereby prevents the Commission from relying in its decision on other objections …'. See also Cases C-89/85 etc, *A. Ahlström v Commission* [1993] ECR I-1307, paras 40–53 and Joined Cases T–39/92 and T–40/92, where the Court annulled parts of a Commission decision on the grounds that it introduced new elements that had not been set out in the statement of objections, on the ground that such a tactic was contrary to the rights of the defence.

4 See n 3.

B2.51 Consequently, before the Commission may proceed to a formal decision establishing an infringement of Art 81 or 82 or imposing a fine, it must issue a statement of objections to the party (or parties) concerned. This does not necessarily mean, however, that a formal decision follows in every case where a statement of objections has been issued. Indeed, the Commission may send a statement of objections as a means of indicating the seriousness with which it views a case. And it is possible that, having received a formal statement of objections, parties may feel more inclined to alter their behaviour or amend some rule or practice objected to by the Commission. The Commission often issues a press announcement when it delivers a statement of objections and this may also send a message out to the market that certain activities or rules are questionable from a legal point of view. Thus, receiving a statement of objections can provide parties with quite an incentive to 'negotiate' with the Commission.

B2.52 Even when a party considers that a statement of objections contains serious legal or economic errors, it may still face a difficult strategic choice in deciding whether or not to 'fight' the Commission on the matter. If no compromise solution can be found, and if the Commission is minded to proceed to a formal condemnation decision, parties must be aware of the risks they run. Apart from the power that the Commission enjoys to fine parties for anti-competitive behaviour[1], a formal Commission decision condemning a rule or practice under Art 81 or 82 means that the rule or practice is outlawed[2]. National courts cannot give effect to any agreement that has been formally condemned by the Commission under EU competition rules. Subject to the doctrine of severance[3], parties have no obligation to observe contracts that contain provisions in violation of the competition rules. Indeed, third parties may seek to obtain damages if they can prove that they have been injured by the anti-competitive agreement or practice and if they can quantify their resultant losses[4].

1 See para B2.44.
2 See para B2.21.
3 See para B2.21.
4 See para B2.42.

B2.53 Although a party can ask the European Court of First Instance for a judicial review of a condemnation decision by the Commission under the EC competition rules, it is an unfortunate fact that such cases can take two or three years or more to resolve. Furthermore, appeals to the court will not suspend the effect of a Commission decision and whilst it is possible for the court to make an interim order suspending the operative effect of a Commission decision it is only in rare circumstances that it has done so. Operating in a legal void whilst waiting for a judgment from the European Court of First Instance may not, from a practical perspective, be an attractive proposition[1]. Consequently, whilst the Commission's legal analysis should always be examined with a critical eye, there are often fairly powerful commercial and practical incentives to reach solutions that do not involve resort to the courts.

1 For example, it may well frighten off potential investors in the sport. See eg 'Warburg spurns F1 bond issue' (1998) Independent, 25 November (citing uncertainty over future TV income as a result of Commission investigation as a reason for declining to invest in Formula One).

3 APPLYING THE COMPETITION RULES IN THE SPORTS SECTOR

B2.54 The competition rules of the EC Treaty were drafted with more orthodox industries in mind than sport. Concepts such as 'undertakings', 'cartels' and 'the single market' do not translate easily when applied to the sports sector. Therefore, the question is whether or not the rules are sufficiently flexible in their application to take account of the specificites of the sports sector. Whether the argument is framed in terms of respecting the 'unique characteristics' of sport, or applying the 'sporting exception' to the competition rules, essentially the same appeal is being made, ie that the specific nature and unique economic features of sport be properly appreciated in any competition law assessment. The institutions of the European Community have each expressed a willingness and desire to adopt such an approach, and it does arguably seem to be (more or less) reflected in the emerging jurisprudence in this area.

B2.55 Significantly, and largely in response to the growing number of cases that the European Commission was being requested to investigate in the post-*Bosman* era, the member states of the European Union considered it necessary to include some 'soft' language in the EU Treaty, indicating (in broad terms) a political desire to see the application of classical competition law principles tempered somewhat in the sports sector. In 1997, the member states' governments agreed to annex a Declaration on Sport to the Treaty of Amsterdam, emphasising the social importance of sport in Europe and calling on the EU institutions to listen to sports associations before taking any decisions in this area[1]. This was followed by a more detailed Declaration, annexed to the Treaty of Nice in 2000[2]. The Nice Declaration addresses, among other things, some more practical issues, including the desirability of protecting solidarity structures in sport and support for measures that are designed to protect the integrity of competition[3]. Whilst these Declarations have no binding legal effect, they are nevertheless of both political and legal significance. For example, the European Commission would not lightly embark on a course of conduct that contradicted the spirit of a Treaty Declaration. And the European Court of Justice has itself considered it appropriate to refer to these Declarations when examining sports-related cases[4]. The Declarations annexed to the Amsterdam and Nice Treaties therefore constitute important first steps toward recognising that sport has certain unique defining characteristics that should be taken into account when the competition rules (and other Treaty rules) are applied to this area[5].

1 See further para B1.23.
2 Declaration on the specific characteristics of sport and its social function in Europe, of which account should be taken in implementing common policies, Annex IV to the Presidency Conclusions, Nice, 7-9 December 2000. See para B1.27.
3 See further para B1.27.
4 See eg *Deliege*, para B2.176, n 1, and *Lehtonen*, para B2.172, n 1. See generally Bell and Turner-Kerr 'The Place of Sport within the Rules of Community Law: Clarification from the ECJ? The Deliege and Lehtonen Cases' [2002] 5 ECLR 256.
5 See further Kinsella and Daly 'European Competition Law and Sports' (2001) 4(6) Sports Law Bulletin 7, 8.

A The sporting exception to the competition rules[1]

B2.56 The European Court of Justice has emphasised several times that 'the practice of sport is subject to Community law to the extent that it constitutes an economic activity'[2]. This principle is easy to state but less easy to apply in practice. It implies that rules that are inherent to the nature and/or necessary for the organisation of sport itself, as opposed to how it is exploited commercially, fall outside the scope of the EC Treaty, even if they have an incidental economic impact. This is subject to the limitation that the rules be applied in an objective, transparent and non-discriminatory way[3] and that they be 'proportionate', ie that they go no further than necessary to achieve their (legitimate) objective[4].

1 See generally Beloff 'The Sporting Exception in EC Competition Law' [1999] European Current Law lvi.
2 See eg Case 36/74 *Walrave and Koch v Union Cycliste Internationale* [1974] ECR 1405; Case 13/76 *Donà v Mantero* [1976] ECR 1333; in Case 222/86 *Heylens* [1986] ECR 4097; Case 415/93 *Union Royale Belge des Sociétés de Football ABSL v Bosman* [1996] 1 CMLR 645; Case C-176/96 *Lehtonen* [2000] ECR I-2681; Joined Cases C-51/96 and C-191/97 *Deliège* [2000] ECR I-2549.
3 Mario Monti, European Commissioner for Competition Policy, *Sport and Competition*, speech to a Commission-organised conference on sports (Brussels, 17 April 2000); and DN: SPEECH/01/84, 26 February 2001.
4 See eg *Deliège v Ligue Francophone de Judo et al*, Joined Cases C-51/96 and C-191/97, [2000] ECR I-2459, para 43. See further Mario Monti, European Commissioner for Competition Policy, Commission press release dated 9 August 2002, IP/02/1211: '[R]ules drawn up by sporting organisations to ensure in a proportionate manner the integrity of sporting events … fall outside the scope of Community competition rules'.

B2.57 However, many rules that are characterised as mere 'rules of sporting conduct' have undeniable and often fairly direct economic effects, making the distinction set out in the preceding paragraph hard to draw[1]. A difficult balance has to be struck between allowing sports governing bodies freedom to regulate the sport itself and the need to prevent anti-competitive conduct in the way the sport is commercially exploited.

1 See eg para B2.100. See also Bell and Turner-Kerr 'The Place of Sport within the Rules of Community Law: Clarification from the ECJ? The Deliege and Lehtonen Cases' [2002] 5 ECLR 256, 257 ('whether a rule is "non-economic" in nature or of "sporting interest only" is rather a vexed question…. For the court to continue with this test may make it a hazardous task to draw the line between legitimate sporting rules (which fall outside the scope of the Treaty) and non-sporting rules (which fall under the provisions of the Treaty)'); Kinsella and Daly 'European Competition Law and Sports' (2001) 4(6) Sports Law Bulletin 7, 8.

B2.58 The European Commission has expressed the distinction as follows:

> [S]port comprises two levels of activity: on the one hand the sporting activity strictly speaking, which fulfils a social, integrating and cultural role that must be preserved and to which in theory the competition rules of the EC Treaty do not apply. On the other hand a series of economic activities generated by the sporting activity, to which the competition rules of the EC Treaty apply, albeit taking into account the specific requirements of this sector[1].

The Commission itself has acknowledged, however, that 'the interdependence and indeed the overlap between these two levels render the application of competition rules more complex'[2]. Most sports regulations have as their object the preservation of one or more aspects of sport that make it such a popular 'product' for consumers. Similarly, many of the perceived restrictions on the commercialisation of sport are reflections of the same regulatory objectives. For example, the 'collective selling' rules and 'black-out' rules that restrict the manner of exploitation of broadcasting rights to elite football events derive from regulatory concerns to preserve and broaden the competitive playing base of the sport[3].

1 'Commission debates application of its competition rules to sports', Commission press release dated 24 February 1999, IP/99/133.

2 'Commission debates application of its competition rules to sports', Commission press release dated 24 February 1999, IP/99/133. See also Reding 'Commission's investigation into FIFA's transfer rules; Statement to European Parliament' (7 September 2000, DN: Speech/00/290): 'The Commission recognises the autonomy of the sports movement to establish the 'rules of the game' that are inherently necessary. The Commission accepts the specificity of sport in that the game requires a certain degree of competitive equality between players and clubs in order to ensure the uncertainty of results that is its essence. The Commission investigates only cases that have a Community and an economic dimension'.

3 See paras B2.262 to B2.263 and B2.301 to B2.303 respectively.

B2.59 To take a further example, the essential object of anti-doping regulations is the preservation of the integrity of the sporting contest[1]. As such, they are an inherent part of sport, essential to the creation and organisation of the sport in the first place. On the other hand, their provisions, including lengthy suspensions from participation in the sport for transgressors, are by definition restrictive and can have an enormous economic impact on individual athletes. Are they therefore to be treated as outside the scope of the competition rules? Or should they be deemed within the scope of those rules, so that the restrictions they encompass must be justified? While the English courts have regarded such rules as falling within the 'sporting exception'[2], other civil law jurisdictions, and the Court of Arbitration for

Sport[3], have not. In August 2002, the European Commission agreed with the English courts, rejecting a competition law challenge to a two-year doping ban on the basis that 'rules drawn up by sporting organisations to ensure in a proportionate manner the integrity of sporting events by providing for effective control of doping fall outside the scope of Community rules'; and that 'the anti-doping rules in question are closely linked to the smooth functioning of competition in sport, that they are necessary for the fight against doping to be effective and that their restrictive effects do not go beyond what is necessary to achieve this objective. Accordingly, they are not caught by the prohibition under Articles 81 and 82 of the EC Treaty'[4].

1 See para E4.8.
2 *Edwards v BAF and IAAF* [1998] 2 CMLR 363, [1997] Eu LR 721. Cf *Wilander v Tobin* [1997] 2 CMLR 346, CA.
3 *Aanes v FILA*, CAS 2001/A/317, award dated 9 July 2001. On the other hand, the Court of Arbitration for Sport assisted in defining the scope of the 'sporting exception' to the competition rules in the *ENIC* case: see para B2.145 et seq.
4 'Commission rejects complaint against International Olympic Committee by swimmers banned from competitions for doping', Commission press release dated 9 August 2002, IP/02/1211.

B2.60 Similarly, a transfer 'deadline' has clear sporting objectives, namely preserving the regularity and proper functioning of competition by avoiding changes to playing squads late in the season that would distort the course of a championship. On the other hand, such a deadline clearly restricts the ability of clubs to compete with each other, as well as freezing temporarily the market for the services of players. Nevertheless, the European Court of Justice has indicated that transfer deadlines are necessary for the proper functioning of sport and do not offend either free movement or competition principles, provided they remain 'proportionate' to their legitimate sporting objectives[1].

1 Case C-176/96, *Jyri Lehtonen and Castors Canada Dry Namur-Braine ASBL v Fédération Royale Belge des Sociétés de Basket-ball ASBL (FRBSB)* [2000] ECR I-2681. See paras B2.171 to B2.175.

B2.61 Various other sporting rules and practices have also been identified as falling within the 'sporting exception' to Community law[1]. However, notwithstanding the growing list of examples, it remains difficult to draw the distinction in practice.

1 See para B2.96. See also Beloff 'The Sporting Exception in EC Competition Law' [1999] European Current Law lvi at lx.

B The 'rule of reason' and the unique competitive dynamics in the sports sector

B2.62 Where a rule or practice cannot be categorised as a 'rule of sporting conduct', and so as falling within the 'sporting exception' to the competition rules, it still does not automatically follow that the rule or practice infringes Art 81(1) and/or the Chapter I prohibition.

B2.63 If a literal approach was taken to the interpretation of Art 81(1) and the Chapter I prohibition, then almost all contractual arrangements containing prima facie restrictive clauses would fall within the scope of these provisions and consequently be rendered void and unenforceable. Nevertheless, certain arrangements that appear on their face to be restrictive may actually turn out, when considered in the broader context, to be pro-competitive and/or to improve the quality of the 'product' made available[1]. Such arrangements do not infringe the competition rules[2].

1 See eg Commission Decision of 27 June 2002, rejecting ENIC's complaint against UEFA multiple ownership rule, Case COMP/37.806, para 27: 'In order to assess whether an agreement is caught by the prohibition contained in Article 81(1) of the Treaty, it is necessary to consider whether, taking account of the economic context in which it is to be applied, its *object* or *effect* is to restrict or distort in an appreciable manner competition within the common market …' (emphasis in original). Cf Case T-112/99 *Métropole Television v Commission* [2001] ECR II-2459, CFI (rejecting existence of rule of reason inherent in Art 81(1)). But see contra *Wouters v Algemane Raed*, Case C-309/99, ECJ [2002] All ER (EC) 193, points 97 and 110.

2 See generally Beloff 'The Sporting Exception in EC Competition Law' [1999] European Current Law vi. The same analysis applies in the context of allegations of breach of Art 82. See *Gottrup-Klim v Dansk Landburgs Grovvareselskab,* Case C-250/92, [1994] ECR I-5641, paras 31–34 (discussed at para B2.121).

B2.64 This principle, sometimes referred to as the 'rule of reason', was explained by Advocate-General Lenz in the *Bosman* case[1] as follows:

> If a rule which at first sight appears to contain a restriction of competition is necessary in order to make that competition possible in the first place, it must indeed be assumed that such a rule does not infringe Article 85(1) [now 81(1)].

1 Opinion of Advocate General Lenz, *Union Royale Belge des Sociétés de Football Association ASBL v Bosman* Case 415/93, (1996) 1 CMLR 645 at para 265.

B2.65 In the sports context, the 'rule of reason' doctrine is often confused with the 'sporting exception' to the competition rules[1]. However, it is indeed distinct[2], providing an important potential defence to a competition law challenge to a provision that has too significant an economic object and/or effect to be characterised as a mere sporting rule[3]. Indeed, it can be argued that the doctrine has particular resonance in the sports sector, where it is accepted that certain forms of co-ordination or restraint between 'competitors' are necessary for the sporting 'product' to be created in the first place[4].

1 Discussed at paras B2.56 to B2.61. For an example of the failure to distinguish clearly between the two, see para B2.96, n 2.

2 See eg Beloff 'The Sporting Exception in EC Competition Law' [1999] European Current Law lvi, lx.

3 See 'Commission debates application of its competition rules to sport', Commission press release dated 24 February 1999, IP/99/133: 'Sports also have features, in particular the interdependence of competitors and the need to guarantee the uncertainty of results in competitions, which could justify that sporting organisations implement a specific framework, in particular on the markets for the production and the sale of sports events'. See also Competition Commissioner Marco Monti *Competition and Sport: the Rules of the Game* (DN Speech/01/84: Brussels, 26 February 2001): 'arrangements that provide for a redistribution of financial resources to – for example – amateur levels of sport may be justified, if they are necessary to preserve sport's essential social and cultural benefits'); Reding 'Commission's investigation into FIFA's transfer rules; Statement to European Parliament' (7 September 2000, DN: Speech/00/290): 'The Commission recognises the autonomy of the sports movement to establish the 'rules of the game' that are inherently necessary. The Commission accepts the specificity of sport in that the game requires a certain degree of competitive equality between players and clubs in order to ensure the uncertainty of results that is its essence. The Commission investigates only cases that have a Community and an economic dimension'. See further para B2.75, n 3.

4 See paras B2.66 to B2.75.

B2.66 A competitive sports league requires a significant degree of off-field cooperation and solidarity (ie 'equality of arms') between the teams for an interesting and exciting product to be made available to the public. Fundamentally, this is because sporting competition is necessarily a *joint* product. It is clear enough that no single team can ever create the product that is of interest to television, sponsors, the newspapers, the public, or anyone else. A single team is essentially incapable of producing anything of independent value because without its competitors it would have no product at all. As an American antitrust court colourfully put it: '[A] league with one team would be like one hand clapping ...'[1]. Thus, sports teams are not engaged in a series of individual business ventures. Rather, the venture is necessarily a collective one: they must agree among themselves on a host of issues in order to create and define the product itself. Put more simply, competition on the field is dependent upon co-operation off it. Such restraints on off-field competition are essential in order for the product (the athletic contest) to exist at all.

1 *Chicago Professional Sports LP v NBA* 95 F 3d 593, 598–99 (7th Cir 1996).

B2.67 Similarly, sports teams playing each other on a haphazard, 'friendly' basis produce a different, lesser product from teams that are competing with each other to win a league or other competition. Matches of the latter kind have an additional ingredient that is very attractive to the spectator: it is part of a broader competition, a 'quest for the championship'[1]. In this case, it has been argued that it is not the individual club or clubs but the league or other event organiser that is the relevant business unit: the league or other competition is the minimum form of economic activity required in order to produce and market the product[2].

1 See eg Veljanovski 'Is Sports Broadcasting a Public Utility?' (Paper to IEA Seminar, 18 October 2000).

2 See Roberts 'The Antitrust Status of Sports Leagues Revisited' 60 Tulane Law Review 562, 569, n 21 (1986): 'Only in this wholly integrated structure can the league product be produced and be a distinct and far more attractive product than any team or two teams could make acting alone'. See also Carne 'The FA is not offside over TV rights' (1999) Times, 9 February: 'you cannot separate the matches from the tournament without destroying the economic value of the matches'.

B2.68 On this analysis, a sport's operating rules, practices and decisions should not be viewed in the same way as agreements among horizontal business competitors in a more traditionally structured industry. Rather, the 'firm', in this context, may be regarded as the league or competition organiser, responsible for creating the product that is of value to broadcasters, sponsors, and the public. 'Because the league's existence and operation are essential to the production of the entertainment product that no single team can produce alone, it [the league] by definition exists and operates to enhance efficiency and promote consumer welfare'[1].

1 Roberts 'The Antitrust Status of Sports Leagues Revisited' 60 Tulane Law Review 562, 591 (1986). 'A venture occurs that might not otherwise be possible and thus its internal controls are pro-competitive': Weistart 'League Control of Market Opportunities: A Perspective on Competition' (1984) Duke Law Journal 1031, 1041.

B2.69 This 'single entity' theory has received little judicial endorsement in the United States[1], and European competition regulators also view with scepticism the claim that there is no co-operation between competitors in this context[2]. Nevertheless, the interdependence between the clubs in a league has been recognised, for example, in the landmark case of *OFT v FAPL*[3], where the

Restrictive Practices Court remarked that it was 'facile' to speak of clubs having 'individual' television rights because they clearly depended on the existence of their fellow clubs for the possibility meaningfully to exploit these rights.

1 See Weiler and Roberts *Sports and the Law* (1998, West), ch 7.
2 See para B2.274.
2 *Re an Agreement between the FA Premier League and BSkyB* [2000] EMLR 78, [1999] UKCLR 258 (Restrictive Practices Court, 28 July 1999). See paras A3.169 and B2.265 et seq.

B2.70 The 'rule of reason' analysis does not stop there. It is not enough to have another team to play against, or even a league of other teams. Rather, the opposing teams must be *worthy* competitors. Sport is of interest to the public, and therefore to broadcasters and sponsors, only because of the excitement and drama generated by uncertainty of outcome. Uncertainty of outcome in turn requires competitive balance. If there is a great disparity in the ability and resources of individual clubs, then the outcome of the contest will be predictable and public interest in the league will decline[1]. Conversely, the more uncertain the outcome, the greater the interest will be in the league[2].

1 See eg *'Predictable' FA Cup is losing interest of fans*, (2001) Sportcal.com, 19 February. See also Veljanovski 'Is Sports Broadcasting a Public Utility?' (Paper to IEA Seminar, 18 October 2000): 'The appropriate analogy is handicapping in horse racing, where the natural advantages of better horses are evened out in order to increase the uncertainty of outcome and make the race more of a gamble'.
2 See *Re an Agreement between the FA Premier League and BSkyB* [2000] EMLR 78, [1999] UKCLR 258 (Restrictive Practices Court, 28 July 1999), judgment at 98: 'an important element in the maintenance of the quality of the Premier League competition is competitive balance, that is to say the unpredictability of the outcome of a high proportion of the matches played within the competition and thus uncertainty about which club will win the championship'.

B2.71 Thus, whereas economic actors in other sectors benefit from the failures of their competitors, sport clubs have a vested interest in creating an environment in which their competitors are able to present effective (and therefore exciting) opposition[1]. Put differently, the fundamental economic principle that the public interest is best served by unrestrained competition in a completely free market environment simply *does not apply* in the sports sector[2].

1 See eg *Re an Agreement between the FA Premier League and BSkyB* [2000] EMLR 78, [1999] UKCLR 258 (Restrictive Practices Court, 28 July 1999), judgment at 99: 'an increase in financial inequality will tend to result in a reduction in competitive balance'. See also *United States v National Football League* 116 F Supp 319, 323-24 (E.D Pa 1953): 'Professional teams in a league, however, must not compete too well with each other, in a business way. On the playing field, of course, they must compete as hard as they can all the time. But it is not necessary and indeed it is unwise for all the teams to compete as hard as they can against each other in a business way. If all the teams should compete as hard as they can in a business way, the stronger teams would be likely to drive the weaker ones into financial failure. If this should happen not only would the weaker teams fail, but eventually the whole league, both the weaker and the stronger teams, would fail, because without a league no team can operate profitably … The net effects of allowing unrestricted competition among the clubs are likely to be, first, the creation of greater and greater, inequalities in the strength of the teams; second, the weaker teams being driven out of business; and, third, the destruction of the entire League'.
2 See Kinsella and Daly 'European Competition Law and Sports' (2001) 4(6) Sports Law Bulletin 7 ('For this reason, complete regulatory and sporting rules exist to try to make the sporting and, to a degree, economic playing field as level as possible').

B2.72 As a result, if a 'restrictive' sports rule or practice is necessary to preserve competitive balance between clubs, and does not go further than is necessary to achieve that balance, then on a 'rule of reason' analysis it may be considered to be pro-competitive and not to infringe EC Art 81 or the Chapter I prohibition.

B2.73 The European Court of Justice recognised the essential role of competitive balance in the context of professional team sports, in the famous *Bosman* case:

> In view of the considerable social importance of social activities and in particular football in the Community, the aims of maintaining a balance between clubs by preserving a certain degree of equality and uncertainty as to results and of encouraging the recruitment and training of young players must be accepted as legitimate[1].

1 *Union Royale Belge des Sociétés de Football ASBL v Bosman*, C-415/93, [1996] 1 CMLR 645, para 106. 'Encouraging the recruitment and training of young players' expands the size and competence of the playing base of a sport, and thereby also encourages competitive balance.

B2.74 In his opinion in *Bosman*, Advocate-General Lenz considered that restrictions agreed under the auspices of a sports governing body are lawful if they are necessary 'to ensure by means of specific measures that a certain balance is preserved between the clubs'[1]. He accepted that 'a professional league can flourish only if there is no too glaring imbalance between the clubs taking part. If the league is clearly dominated by one team, the necessary tension is absent and the interest of the spectators will thus probably lapse within a foreseeable period'[2]. He concluded by agreeing 'entirely' with the view 'that it is of fundamental importance to share income out between the clubs in a reasonable manner'[3].

1 Opinion of Advocate-General Lenz, *Union Royale Belge des Sociétés de Football ASBL v Bosman*, C-415/93, [1996] 1 CMLR 645, 734.
2 Opinion of Advocate-General Lenz, *Union Royale Belge des Sociétés de Football ASBL v Bosman*, C-415/93, [1996] 1 CMLR 645, para 219.
3 Opinion of Advocate-General Lenz, *Union Royale Belge des Sociétés de Football ASBL v Bosman*, C-415/93, [1996] 1 CMLR 645, para 223.

B2.75 The same fundamental principles have now been accepted by the UK competition authorities[1] and courts[2]. They have also been accepted by the European Commission, for which the then-Commissioner in charge of competition policy described the position in the following terms:

> Whatever type it may be, one aspect is common to all sports: in order to ensure a quality event which interests the spectator, there must be an element of uncertainty concerning the results of the competition. For this reason, a balance of forces between the adversaries, ie the competitive equality of opportunities, is essential. This is why, for example, certain individual sports such as golf have introduced a handicap system. In team sports, teams are divided into divisions or leagues for the duration of each sporting season. The economic aspect of sport is linked to this peculiarity, which stems from the fact that the production of a sporting event is not possible with just one team or player (the sporting event is a product which results from competition between teams, or at least between two players). This interdependence between competitors, most pronounced in team sports, is a characteristic which is unique to sport and distinguishes it from other industrial or service sectors. In effect, in industry or service sectors, the competition between businesses aims to remove inefficient companies from the market, so that only those companies which are efficient and viable remain. On the other hand, in the sports sector, clubs have a direct interest not only in the continued existence of other clubs, but also in their economic viability as competitors, with a view to maximising the spectator's interest and as a consequence, the income from sale of the sporting event. The need to guarantee the uncertainty of the results of competitions and the interdependence between competing clubs are therefore aspects which are completely peculiar to sport which justify the restrictions on competition, but which do not exclude the existence of competition between clubs. This competition is, in any case, both singular and paradoxical because each club aims to end the season with the best score, but at the same time, each club has a

> direct interest that the success of other clubs of the same standard should also continue. A club cannot aim simply to maximise its financial benefits and to remove competitors from the market. The maximisation of success without any regard to the financial aspects is no more desirable either. The objective should be more that of obtaining the best results in the competitions, and thus the prestige, on condition of making a minimum profit. The profitability varies with success, and success depends essentially on the quality of the players and the synergy within the team, and all of this in a context of interdependency between clubs and the guarantee of the uncertainty of the results. In this logic of global interest, the market is unstable by nature as long as there is a financial imbalance between the clubs. This imbalance must therefore be rectified ...[3]

As a result, anyone considering the apparently 'restrictive' nature of a sports rule must clearly address the question of whether the rule, when considered in its broader context, is necessary in order (for example) to preserve competitive balance among those participating in the sport, and therefore can be said to be not anti-competitive but rather pro-competitive in overall effect. If so, then that rule will fall outside the scope of the competition rules and any attack based on such rules should fail[4].

1 See eg *MMC Report into the Proposed Merger between BSkyB Group plc and Manchester United plc* (Cm 4305, 1999). See para B2.336.

2 See *Re an Agreement between the FA Premier League* [2000] EMLR 78, [1999] UKCLR 258 (Restrictive Practices Court, 28 July 1999), judgment at 110.

3 Competition Commissioner Karel Van Miert, Speech to the European Sports Forum, Luxembourg, 27 November 1997. See also 'Commission debates application of competition rules to sports', Commission press release dated 24 February 1999, IP/99/133: 'Sports also have features, in particular the interdependence of competitors and the need to guarantee the uncertainty of results in competitions, which could justify that sporting organisations implement a specific framework, in particular on the markets for the production and the sale of sports events'; Reding 'Commission's investigation into FIFA's transfer rules; statement to European Parliament' (7 September 2000, DN Speech/00/290): 'The Commission accepts the specificity of sport in that the game requires a certain degree of competitive equality between players and clubs in order to ensure uncertainty of results that is its essence'; Monti, DN: Speech/01/84, 26 February 2001 ('The interdependence between competing adversaries and the need to maintain a balance between them are features specific to sport').

4 For examples of this type of analysis in action, see eg paras B2.121 and B2.262 et seq.

C Market definition in the sports sector

B2.76 Even if a rule or practice under challenge cannot be shown to fall outside the scope of Art 81 or the Chapter I prohibition as a rule of sporting conduct or a pro-competitive 'restraint', that still does not necessarily mean that Art 81 and/or Chapter I are infringed. To establish a breach of Art 81 or of the Chapter I prohibition, it is necessary to show not simply that the rule or practice in question is restrictive (for example, as between the parties to the dispute at hand) but also that the rule or practice has an *appreciable* effect on competition on a relevant market[2]. Similarly, to establish a breach of Art 82 or the Chapter II prohibition, it is necessary to show that an undertaking occupies a *dominant* position on a relevant market. Therefore, a key element in any competition law analysis is defining the relevant market: a broad definition of the relevant market may lead to the conclusion that the rule or practice under scrutiny has no appreciable impact on competition and/or that the defendant has no dominant position, which brings the case to an end.

1 See generally Brinckman and Vollebregt 'The Marketing of Sport and Its Relation to EC Competition Law' (1998) 5 ECLR 281.

2 See para B2.77.

B2.77 The requirement of an 'appreciable' effect on competition was confirmed by the European Court of Justice as early as 1969 in *Völk v Vervaecke*[1], and was clarified by the European Commission in its Notice on Agreements of Minor Importance in 1970. The current version of this Notice dates from 2001[2], and indicates, with reference to market share thresholds, that certain restrictions on competition are not considered 'appreciable' and so do not fall within the prohibition of Art 81 of the EC Treaty. For agreements between non-competitors (ie vertical agreements), the Notice indicates that where market shares of parties to the agreement are less than 15% it may generally be assumed that there is no appreciable effect on competition (subject to certain exceptions[3]). For agreements between competitors (ie horizontal agreements), the figure is 10%. Under UK competition law, restrictions on competition are generally considered *de minimis* where the parties' combined share of the relevant market does not exceed 25% (although there will be circumstances in which this is not the case)[4].

1 Case 5/69, [1969] ECR 295, [1969] CMLR 273.
2 Commission Notice on agreements of minor importance which do not appreciably restrict competition under Art 81(1) of the Treaty establishing the European Community (de minimis), OJ C 368, 22.12.2001, p 13.
3 Such as where an agreement contains a 'hard core' restriction, for example, price fixing, output limitation or market allocation.
4 OFT Guidelines on the Chapter I Prohibition.

B2.78 To apply the relevant threshold – 10%, 15% or 25% as the case may be – it is of course necessary to identify the market that is being measured in the first place (ie to define the relevant market). In 1997, the Commission issued a Notice on the Definition of the Relevant Market[1] to provide guidance as to how it applies the concepts of relevant product and relevant geographic markets in its enforcement of Community competition law.

1 Commission Notice on the definition of the relevant market for the purposes of Community competition law, OJ C 372, 9/12/1997.

B2.79 The relevant *product* market is defined in the Notice as follows:

> A relevant product market comprises all those products and/or services which are regarded as interchangeable or substitutable by the consumer, by reason of the products' characteristics, their prices and their intended use[1].

1 Commission Notice on the definition of the relevant market for the purposes of Community competition law, OJ C 372, 9/12/1997.

B2.80 The relevant *geographic* market is defined as follows:

> The relevant geographic market comprises the area in which the undertakings concerned are involved in the supply and demand of products or services, in which the conditions of competition are sufficiently homogeneous and which can be distinguished from neighbouring areas because the conditions of competition are appreciably different in those areas[1].

1 Commission Notice on the definition of the relevant market for the purposes of Community competition law, OJ C 372, 9/12/1997.

B2.81 The Notice explains how the Commission determines the scope of the relevant markets for competition law purposes[1]. The methodology used by the Commission depends mainly on the application of 'demand-side substitutability'.

In appropriate cases, however, the Commission will also consider 'supply-side substitutability'.

1 Commission Notice on the definition of the relevant market for the purposes of Community competition law, OJ C 372, 9/12/1997.

B2.82 In essence, demand-side substitution consists of identifying effective alternative sources of supply for the *customers* of the undertakings involved, in terms of both products/services offered and geographic location of suppliers. This basically involves identifying the range of products that are viewed as substitutes by the consumer. For this purpose, the Commission uses the 'hypothetical monopolist' or 'SSNIP' test[1], which involves establishing whether customers would switch their preferences elsewhere in response to a hypothetical small (in the range 5%–10%) price increase. If substitution would be enough to make the price increase unprofitable because of the resulting loss of sales, the alternative products are included in the relevant market[2].

1 SSNIP stands for 'a small but significant non-transitory increase in price'.
2 To take a theoretical example, if a 5–10% increase in the price of a ticket to watch an FA Premier League match would prompt consumers to go and watch a Zurich Premiership match instead, then professional rugby union and professional football are competing for the same consumer spend, ie they are in the same market. In such a theoretical case, therefore, someone who is (for example) the sole supplier of tickets to FA Premier League matches does *not* have a monopoly, because the market in which FA Premier League tickets are sold, properly defined, also encompasses Zurich Premiership tickets. For a similar example from the case law, see para B2.219.

B2.83 In general, the competitive constraints arising from supply-side substitutability are less immediate. An analysis of supply-side substitution involves consideration of whether alternative suppliers could fairly easily switch production in response to small change in relative prices. If they could, then the additional production that would be released on to the market would have a disciplinary effect on the ability of companies to raise prices. In practice, supply-side substitution has been of limited relevance in sports-related cases, which is not surprising given the structure of the sports 'business'.

B2.84 On the demand side, the European Commission has developed some theories concerning the substitutability of sports television rights from the perspective of broadcasters. This is not surprising, given the importance of sport to television and, in particular, pay-television. Thus, in the *UEFA Broadcasting Regulations* case[1], the Commission observed that there might be:

> a separate market for the acquisition of broadcasting rights to football events played regularly throughout every year and which would in practice mainly involve national first and second league and cup events as well as the UEFA Champions League and UEFA Cup[2].

This was largely on the basis that football was considered important for the 'brand image' of television stations and had an ability to attract a particular kind of audience that was of interest to television advertisers[3].

1 Commission Decision of 19 April 2001, Case 37.576 *UEFA Broadcasting Regulations*, OJ L171, 26/06/2001, p 12. See paras B2.276 et seq.
2 Commission Decision of 19 April 2001, Case 37.576, *UEFA Broadcasting Regulations*, OJ L171, 26/06/2001, para 42.
3 For further discussion of market definition in sports broadcasting cases, see paras B2.238 to B2.247.

B2.85 Similarly, the Court of Arbitration for Sport found that UEFA's multiple ownership rule[1] operated on the 'market for ownership of football clubs capable of taking part in UEFA competitions'[2], not on a broader market for ownership of clubs from various sports, holding that: 'because of the peculiarities of the football sector, investment in football clubs does not appear to be interchangeable with investments in other businesses, or even in other leisure businesses'[3]. In other cases, however, it is clear that the relevant product market may be wider than any particular sport, or even sport as a whole. For example, in the *Wimbledon* case[4], the OFT rejected a complaint from a corporate hospitality provider about the exclusive appointment of two operators to supply hospitality packages including Wimbledon tickets. The OFT determined that providers of corporate hospitality were clearly not confined to Wimbledon tickets. They could equally well use tickets to other high profile sports events, or even non-sports events, for the purposes of selling corporate hospitality packages. Provided the event with which the hospitality was packaged was sufficiently prestigious, the purchaser would probably regard the various options as interchangeable. As a result, giving one hospitality supplier exclusive access to tickets to any particular event would not create a monopoly or otherwise restrict competition on the market properly defined[5].

1 See paras B2.145 to B2.151.
2 *AEK Athens and Slavia Prague v UEFA*, CAS 98/2000, award dated 20 August 1999, *Digest of CAS Awards II 1998-2000* (2002, Kluwer), at 133.
3 *AEK Athens and Slavia Prague v UEFA*, CAS 98/2000, award dated 20 August 1999, *Digest of CAS Awards II 1998-2000* (2002, Kluwer), at 135.
4 OFT press release no 20/93, dated 3 March 1993, announcing DG FT decision of March 1993. See further para B2.219.
5 The same approach was taken in the European Commission's investigations of the hospitality arrangements at UEFA's 1996 European Championships and the 1999 Rugby World Cup. See para B2.220.

B2.86 As previously mentioned[1], the relevant geographic market is an area where 'the conditions of competition are relatively homogeneous'. This test also presents interesting questions in relation to sports cases because it is clear that sporting preferences (and, therefore, markets) are by no means identical in each member state. Thus, one commentator has observed that:

> sport is far from being a global market. Even when fans are interested in the same sporting event, such as the Olympics, coverage differs dramatically from one country to another. Is it really imaginable that any country covered the rowing events as intensively as the British in Sydney?[2]

1 See para B2.80.
2 Szymanski 'Sport and Broadcasting' (Paper presented at the IEA on 18 October 2000).

B2.87 There is indeed little doubt that different sports tend to achieve varying degrees of popularity in the different members states of the European Union. It is well-known, for example, that cricket is not exactly a major draw in Europe outside the UK (or even England). On the other hand, basketball, which is popular in countries such as Italy, Spain and Greece, only achieves modest success in northern European countries. Across Europe as a whole it is really only football (and possibly Formula One motor racing) that has managed to achieve almost uniformly high levels of popularity.

B2.88 These national preferences have an impact on competition law analysis because they reflect different levels of demand (and, therefore, demand substitutability) for sporting events. For example, if an Italian broadcaster was ever minded to conclude a 10-year exclusive contract for the television broadcasting rights in Italy to the Cricket World Cup and other elite cricket competitions, it is hard to see how that contract would have any impact on competition in the Italian broadcasting market. The same conclusion could not be reached in England, where an exclusive contract of such duration would most likely be frowned upon, or at least considered thoroughly, by the competition authorities[1].

1 See further para B2.281 et seq.

D Seeking an individual exemption from the competition rules

B2.89 If no clear get-out is provided by either the 'sporting exception' to the competition rules[1], or the 'rule of reason' doctrine[2], or a rigorous approach to market definition[3], then the rule or practice in question may well be considered to constitute an appreciable restriction on competition within the meaning of Art 81(1) and/or the Chapter I prohibition. Still, however, all is not lost: if the criteria are satisfied[4] then it is possible to notify the provision to the relevant regulatory authority (the European Commission in the case of Art 81 or the OFT in the case of the Chapter I prohibition), seeking an individual exemption from the competition rules for the rule or practice in question.

1 See paras B2.56 to B2.61.
2 See paras B2.62 to B.2.75.
3 See paras B2.76 to B2.88.
4 See para B2.22.

B2.90 In fact, when filing a notification, it is usual to do two things:

(1) to argue for a 'negative clearance', which is a decision confirming that the provision in question does not fall foul of Art 81(1) (because it falls within the 'sporting exception' to the competition rules, and/or it is a pro-competitive ancillary restraint, and/or it does not have an appreciable affect on competition on the market properly defined); *and*
(2) to argue that in any event the rule qualifies for an 'exemption' under Art 81(3) or of the EC Treaty or s 4 of the Competition Act 1998, as the case may be.

B2.91 The criteria that must be satisfied for the grant of an exemption have already been set out at para B2.022. A significant jurisprudence has already developed as regards the type of arrangements that may benefit from an exemption under the competition rules[1]. As regards the sports sector, however, although various arrangements have been notified[2], there have been relatively few decisions to date[3].

1 See generally Bellamy & Child *European Community Law of Competition* (5th edn 2001), ch 3.
2 For example, in 1999 UEFA notified the ticketing arrangements for the 2000 European Championships to the European Commission. See 'Commission examines ticketing arrangements for next year's European Football Championships', Commission press release dated 5 May 1999, IP/99/304. In August 2000 the British Horseracing Board and the Jockey Club notified their constitutional arrangements and certain commercial arrangements to the OFT. See 'UK industry seeks anti-cartel exemption' (2000) Sports Business 9 August; 'Competition Authority "Unlikely to Rule against Racing"' (2000) Sportcal.com, 10 August.
3 See eg paras B2.295 to B2.298 for a discussion of the exemptions granted by the Commission to the system of joint purchasing of sports broadcasting rights administered through the European Broadcasting Union.

B2.92 The Commission has attempted to develop some kind of analytical framework for assessing sports-related arrangements notified for negative clearance and/or an exemption, and has set out its views in a number of policy papers and public statements. For example, a DG Competition Paper published in May 1998, on the subject of 'Broadcasting of Sports Events and Competition Law', stated as follows:

> The special characteristics of the sport in question have to be taken into account. These could include, for example, the need to ensure 'solidarity' between weaker and stronger participants, or the training of young players, which could only be achieved through redistribution of revenue from the sale of broadcasting rights. Such aims would have to be a genuine and material part of the objectives and ones which could not be achievable under less restrictive arrangements[1].

1 Wachtmeister, Chef d'Unité IV/C2, 'Broadcasting of sports events and competition law' *Competition Policy Newsletter* (June 1998, No 2).

B2.93 In April 2000, the Commissioner in charge of Competition (Mr. Mario Monti) commented that the aim of the Declaration on Sport annexed to the Treaty of Amsterdam was to:

> emphasise the social significance of sport and in particular its role in 'forging identity and bringing people together'. The Commission's Helsinki Report on Sport reaffirmed this view. The Commission therefore considers it appropriate to apply the competition rules in a way which preserves sport's essential social and cultural benefits. Therefore, exemption from the competition rules of arrangements which provide for a redistribution of financial resources to (for example) amateur levels of sport may be justified if necessary to retain those benefits[1].

1 Competition Commissioner Mario Monti, 'Sport and Competition', speech given at a Commission-organised conference on sports (Brussels, 17 April 2000).

B2.94 It seems, therefore, that when applying the competition rules of the EC Treaty to the sports sector the Commission is willing to take a rather different set of criteria into account than would be the case in relation to more conventional industries or service sectors. There is no reference in Art 81(3) of the Treaty to the need to preserve 'social and cultural benefits'. Nor is it immediately obvious that ensuring 'financial solidarity' between competitors is a benefit within the meaning of Art 81(3). It is submitted that what the Commission is trying to achieve here is a kind of *sui generis* framework for analysing and assessing sports rules and structures against the background of Community competition law[1].

1 See further para B2.097.

E The analytical framework developed by the European Commission in sports-related cases

B2.95 In February 1999, the Commission published 'preliminary conclusions' on the application of the competition rules to sport[1]. It set out the view that the competition rules should be applied to sport in light of its specific features, accepting practices that are necessary and essential to the pursuit and organisation of sport, and taking action against practices and abuses that go beyond what is necessary. The Commission suggested that it would place sports rules or practices into one of four categories.

1 'Commission debates application of its competition rules to sports', Commission press release dated 24 February 1999, IP/99/133. See generally *Draft/Preliminary Guidelines on the Application of the Competition Rules to Sport*, unpublished Commission memorandum (15 February 1999) at 29 et seq. These followed on from initial guidelines published in 1994: Preliminary Guidelines on the Application of Competition Rules to the Sports Sector, Comm (February 1994). See also Commission, The Helsinki Report on Sport, COM(1999) 644 and 121.

B2.96 The first category is practices that are not caught by Art 81(1), namely 'rules [that] are inherent in sport and/or necessary for its organisation'[1]. Acknowledging that it is not always easy to identify the intrinsic sporting nature of certain rules (because such rules may also have economic effects), the Commission nevertheless identified some examples of rules or practices that would not infringe Art 81, namely: the 'rules of the game'; nationality clauses in competitions between teams representing countries; quotas limiting the number of competitors per country in European and international competitions; transfer deadlines; rules for organising sport on a geographical basis; and rules needed to ensure uncertainty as to results[3]. So long as the rules of this nature are proportionate, the Commission will not intervene[4].

1 'Commission debates application of its competition rules to sports', Commission press release dated 24 February 1999, IP/99/133; 'Limits to application of Treaty competition rules to sport: Commission gives clear signal', Commission press release, dated 9 December 1999, IP/99/965. See also Competition Commissioner Monti, DN: Speech/D1/84, 26 February 2001.

2 'Draft/Preliminary Guidelines on the Application of the Competition Rules to Sport', unpublished Commission memorandum (15 February 1999) at p 29. The inclusion of 'rules needed to ensure uncertainty as to results' seems to indicate that the Commission is contemplating here not only provisions that fall outside Art 81(1) because they are rules of sporting conduct, but also provisions that do not fall within this 'sporting exception' and yet still fall outside Art 81(1) because, on a rule of reason analysis, they are pro-competitive as opposed to restrictive of competition. See para B2.65.

3 See para B2.56, n 3.

B2.97 The second category is practices that fall within Art 81(1) but may be exempted under Art 81(3)[1]. The European Court of Justice in its *Bosman* judgment accepted as legitimate the aims of maintaining competitive balance and of encouraging the recruitment and training of young players[2]. As such, the Commission has indicated that these principles provide a framework for exempting practices that otherwise might infringe Art 81(1). Consequently, a transfer system where fees are calculated on the basis of training/development costs incurred, or the sale of exclusive broadcasting rights for a limited period, or certain sports quality certification schemes, might all be capable of being exempted under Art 81(3)[3].

1 See para B2.96, n 1.

2 See para B2.073.

3 'Commission debates application of its competition rules to sports', Commission press release dated 24 February 1999, IP/99/133. See also *EC Competition Policy Newsletter* (June 1998) at 26; European Commission, *Helsinki Report on Sport*, COM (1999) 644 and /2, para 4.2.1.3: 'The *Bosman* judgment mentioned above recognised as legitimate the objectives designed to maintain a balance between clubs, while preserving a degree of equality of opportunity and the uncertainty of the result, and to encourage the recruitment and training of young players. Consequently, it is likely that agreements between professional clubs or decisions by their associations that are really designed to achieve these two objectives would be exempted. The same would be true of a system of transfers or standard contracts based on objectively calculated payments that are related to the costs of training, or of an exclusive right, limited in duration and scope, to broadcast sporting events. It goes without saying that the other provisions of the treaty must also be complied with in this area, especially those that guarantee freedom of movement for professional sportsmen and women.'

B2.98 The third category is practices that are caught by Art 81(1) and cannot be granted an exemption under Art 81(3)[1]. In this category, the Commission provided the following examples: impeding parallel imports of sports goods; ticket sales arrangements that discriminate between nationals of different member states; sponsorship arrangements that foreclose markets by barring other suppliers without any objective reason; transfer systems based on arbitrarily calculated fees that bear no relation to training/development costs; nationality clauses limiting the number of nationals of other member states that may play in a team or in a particular competition; and grants of exclusive broadcasting rights for a period sufficiently long to foreclose the market. As discussed in detail in the next section of this chapter, such practices are prohibited under the EC competition rules.

1 See para B2.96, n 1.

B2.99 The fourth category is practices caught by Art 82. The Commission noted that governing bodies generally have a 'monopoly' regulatory power over their sports and on that basis might be considered to be prima facie 'dominant'. However, the Commission made clear that it is not the power as such of the regulator of a sporting activity that can constitute an abuse but rather the manner in which, in real situations, sporting organisations exercise such power[1].

1 'Commission debates application of competition rules to sport', Commission press release dated 24 February 1999, IP/99/133. See also *Draft/Preliminary Guidelines on the Application of the Competition Rules to Sport*, unpublished Commission memorandum, at 33.

B2.100 In December 1999, the Commission issued the following statement:

> (i) the Commission recognises the regulatory powers of sports organisations as regards the non-economic aspects linked to the specific nature of the sport;
> (ii) the rules of sports organisations that are necessary to ensure equality between clubs, uncertainty as to results, and the integrity and proper functioning of competitions are not, in principle, caught by the Treaty's competition rules;
> (iii) the Commission investigates only cases that have a Community dimension and significantly affect trade between Member States[1].

This statement perhaps reflects more clearly the three possible defensive arguments to a competition law challenge to a sports rule or practice, ie:

(i) sporting exception;
(ii) 'rule of reason' analysis; and
(iii) definition of relevant market[2].

1 'Limits to application of Treaty competition rules to sport: Commission gives clear signal', Commission press release dated 9 December 1999. See also Competition Commissioner Monti, DN: Speech/01/84, 26 February 2001.
2 See para B2.89. Cf para B2.96, n 2.

B2.101 The Commission has stated its hope that '[t]his guideline for applying the competition rules to sport will make it possible to create a framework that provides the world of sport with the legal certainty which it quite legitimately seeks'[1]. Explaining the overall rationale for its approach, a senior Commission official[2] commented that:

> The Commission will try to put a stop to the restrictive practices of sport organisations, which have significant economic impact and which are unjustified in the light of the goal of improving the production and distribution of sport events or with regard to the specific

objectives of a sport. The Commission will, however, accept those practices of sport organisations which do not give rise to problems in the light of the competition rules of the Treaty either because they are inherent in the sport or necessary for its organisation or because they are justified in terms of the positive objectives referred to above.

It is not always easy to identify the intrinsic sporting nature of certain rules, either because they have significant economic consequences or because the rule, originally established for purely sporting reasons, has taken on more of an economic character as a result of the development of the economic activities associated with the sport. It may also be difficult to establish whether a rule is necessary to the organisation of sport or to the organisation of competitions. For these reasons it is only gradually on a case-by-case basis that the Commission and/or the Court of Justice on the basis of preliminary questions presented by national courts will be able to clarify what must be regarded as a rule inherent in sport or a rule necessary for the organisation of sport or sporting competitions.

It is to the case law of the European Commission and the Court of Justice in the sports sector (as well as the decisions of the OFT and the English courts) that this chapter now turns.

1 'Limits to application of Treaty competition rules to sport: Commission gives clear signal', Commission press release dated 9 December 1999, IP/99/965. For a searching analysis of whether this has yet been achieved, see Kinsella and Daly 'EC Competition Law and Sports (2001) 4(6) Sports Law Bulletin 7, 8-9 ('the greatest difficulty faced by all parties that might be subject to Community competition law is that it is very often unclear what the law actually is … [A] stark lack of guidance exists in the area of sport and competition law… Rather than publishing decision and thus forming precedents, the Commission has largely relied on a series of press releases, non-binding notices, reports and summaries in its annual reviews. As a result, in none of those instances can the Commission be held to any particular principle or point. No approval is available as none of these measures are "formal". Although these do give some useful indications, they are unreliable, because addressees do not have any legal protection in the event that the Commission changes its mind or in the event that different interpretations of a particular statement are possible. Such "soft law" options are not, and should not be, substitutes for clear "black letter" law').

Nevertheless, the Commission congratulated itself on the success of its work in this area in June 2002. See 'The application of the EU's competition rules to sport' 5 June 2002, DN: MEMO/02/127: 'The Court of Justice has ruled on several occasions that the sport, in its economic aspect is subject to Community law, but again recognising at the same time certain special characteristics of the sector. Commissioners Monti and Reding in particular have engaged in constructive discussions with sporting organisations over the last two years to put those principles into practice. As a result, the sporting organisations have put into effect very important changes to bring their rules into line with their legal obligations, bringing about better legal security to sport as a basis for future economic and sporting development, and a better deal for fans and consumers'.

2 Jean-Francois Pons, Deputy Director General, Competition Directorate, *International Antitrust Law & Policy*, (Paper delivered to the Twenty-Sixth Annual Conference of the Fordham Corporate Law Institute, October 1999).

4 COMPETITION LAW JURISPRUDENCE IN THE SPORTS SECTOR

A The European Model of Sport

B2.102 Broadly speaking, sports in Europe are organised on a 'pyramid' model, with individuals joining teams or clubs that are members of local or regional governing bodies, who in turn are members of national governing bodies, presided over by one international governing body with ultimate regulatory authority over the sport. Importantly, the organisation of the sport is usually 'seamless'. Not only are all forms of a sport, professional and amateur, usually accommodated within one governance structure. In addition, through the mechanism of promotion and relegation, the lowliest club can rise through the ranks to compete with the professional elite. Theoretically, at least, this is reflected in the division of the spoils generated by the sport, by means of redistribution mechanisms pursuing not just 'horizontal' solidarity (between professional teams competing on the same level) but also 'vertical' solidarity (between the professional elite and the amateur grass roots)[1].

1 See The European Model of Sport, Consultation Document of DG X, November 1998: www.europa.eu.int/comm/sport/doc/ecom/doc_consult_en.pdf.

B2.103 Several aspects of this model of sports governance have come under intense scrutiny in recent years, and their compatibility with the competition rules has been questioned.

(a) *The organisation of sport on a geographical basis*

B2.104 Within Europe, sport is organised on a national basis. Teams from one country play each other in domestic leagues. Those successful in domestic competition then qualify as that country's entrants to cross-border competitions, where they are seen as 'representing' their country in matches against clubs from other countries[1]. The best players are then picked to represent their country directly in competitions between national representative sides, such as (in football) UEFA's European Championships and FIFA's World Cup.

1 The best examples are football's UEFA Champions League and UEFA Cup, and (on a lesser scale) rugby union's European Rugby Cup and European Challenge Cup and Shield.

B2.105 The traditional organisation of sport on a geographical basis sits uncomfortably with the Community imperative towards economic integration within a single market. The Commission has accepted, however, that the competition rules should not be applied to create a single market for any sport[1]. There is no economic need for such unification. Instead, 'unification' would act to remove the role sport plays in expressing and preserving national identity. Thus, the Commission has observed that:

> The organisation of football on a national or regional geographic basis seems to be part of the nature of the sport and allows international championships to be held between club teams. Accordingly the regulations of sports organisations laying down rules along these lines or decisions applying such rules in an objective and non-discriminatory manner are not in principle caught by Article 81 or 82 of the Treaty[2].

In other words, rules underpinning the organisation of football on a national or regional basis are deemed to be purely 'sporting' rules, falling within the 'sporting exception' to the EC competition rules[3].

1 *Draft/Preliminary Guidelines on the Application of the Competition Rules to Sport*, unpublished Commission memorandum (15 February 1999) at 12.
2 *Draft/Preliminary Guidelines on the Application of the Competition Rules to Sport*, unpublished Commission memorandum (15 February 1999) at 14.
3 See para B2.96.

B2.106 Ground movement The observation noted in the preceding paragraph was made, it is believed, as a result of the *Mouscron* case[1], where the Commission was asked to consider a UEFA rule requiring clubs to play two-legged ties first in one club's country and then in the other club's country (the 'home and away' rule). Excelsior Mouscron, a Belgian club, got an attractive tie and sought to exploit demand for tickets for the home leg by staging it at the stadium of Communaute Urbaine de Lille, a nearby French club. UEFA refused permission because of the 'home and away' rule and was accused of abusing its dominant position. The Commission rejected the *Mouscron* complaint, holding that UEFA's rule was a rule of sporting conduct that fell *within* the scope of UEFA's regulatory power over the sport of football in Europe, and *outside* the scope of the competition rules of the EC Treaty. The Commission stated that the case had to:

> be assessed within the context of the national geographic organisation of football in Europe, which is not called into question by Community law[2].

1 'Limits to application of Treaty competition rules of sport: Commission gives clear signal', Commission press release dated 9 December 1999, IP/99/965.
2 See n 1.

B2.107 In similar vein, the rules of most sports governing bodies prohibit clubs located in the jurisdiction of one national association playing in competitions organised by a national association in another jurisdiction. The objectives may include preserving the integrity of the national league structure and protecting an emerging domestic league from having to compete for popular support with a neighbour playing in a far stronger 'foreign' league.

B2.108 For example, the Commission received a complaint from Clydebank to the effect that a league rule prohibiting cross-border movement of the club violated Art 43 of the EC Treaty, which guarantees freedom of establishment throughout the Community. In this case, Clydebank wished to move to Dublin while continuing to play in the Scottish league. Although it did not issue a final decision, the Commission stated, in response to a question in the European Parliament:

> It seems at first sight that the organisation of national football leagues on a territorial basis is not related to the economic issues in this sport but to the very nature of the sport in question[1].

As leading teams in smaller domestic leagues consider breaking away to join (or create) stronger competitions[2], these precedents do not provide them with much encouragement[3].

1 [1996] OJ C217/87, 12 April 1996. See also 'EU: Football – Wimbledon FC complains over block on Dublin move' (1998) European Reports, 7 February.
2 See eg 'Celtic could complain to Brussels over Euro league' (2001) Sportcal.com, 23 July; 'Old Firm favour Premier switch' (2001) Guardian, 13 July; 'Atlantic League back on the agenda', www.bbc.co.uk (1 August 2001).
3 As with the situation described in relation to the international movement of clubs, some domestic governing bodies may restrict ground movement within their own territories. For example, the rules of the English Football League provide that no club may relocate to a conurbation other than the one from which it takes its name or with which it is traditionally associated without the consent of the League's Board of Directors. In August 2001, the Board refused Wimbledon FC permission to relocate from Selhurst Park (a ground it shared with Crystal Palace FC) to a new stadium in Milton Keynes. Wimbledon brought FA arbitration proceedings challenging that decision on grounds of procedural unfairness, breach of contract and restraint of trade. The League argued that the restriction was needed to protect certain fundamental sporting imperatives in British football (including the relationship between communities and clubs and the fundamental principle of promotion and relegation). It argued that because a club was struggling in one community, that was not a reason to allow it to reinvent itself and move to a new community whilst retaining its place in the 'pyramid' structure of the English game. Such a move, it argued, would usher in US-style 'franchise' system that might radically alter the nature of the game in the UK. Wimbledon did not take issue with the arguments of principle put forward by the League but instead concentrated on its

own particular circumstances, arguing that prohibition of the desired move was disproportionate by reference to those circumstances. The club argued that its case was 'unique' since it was sharing a ground with another club and was unable to find a site to build a stadium in Wimbledon at anything like a reasonable cost. The club contended that its unique circumstances meant that allowing it to move would not set a damaging precedent, so that the Board's veto was a disproportionate exercise of its powers. The arbitration panel found that the Board's initial decision was procedurally flawed since the Board had applied a blanket prohibition and had not considered the particular position of the club. The Board was ordered to reconsider Wimbledon's application afresh. It subsequently referred the matter to an FA Commission, which accepted Wimbledon's arguments and allowed the move. See further paras A3.26, n 1, A3.137, n 4 and A3.156.

B2.109 Nationality rules On the other side of the line, however, are those sports rules that have purported to limit the freedom of professional sportsmen and women to offer their services across national borders within the European Community. Thus, in *Bosman*[1], the European Court of Justice ruled that rules limiting the number of foreigners that could play in club competitions constituted an unjustifiable restriction on the free movement of workers. In the circumstances of the case, the court found it unnecessary to rule on the compatibility of these 'nationality quotas' with competition law. Notably, however, Advocate-General Lenz considered the quotas to be also contrary to competition law[2], and the Commission has taken a similar view[3].

1 *Union Royale Belge des Sociétés de Football ASBL v Bosman*, C-415/93, [1996] 1 CMLR 645. See paras A3.172, n 1, B2.153 to B2.156, B3.40 et seq and E2.40 et seq.

2 Opinion of Advocate General Lenz, *Union Royale Belge des Sociétés de Football ASBL v Bosman*, C-415/93, [1996] 1 CMLR 645 at para 262.

3 *Draft/Preliminary Guidelines on the Application of the Competition Rules to Sport*, unpublished Commission memorandum (15 February 1999) at 22 (suggesting that nationality quotas, to the extent that they apply not only to EC nationals but also to non-EC nationals that are under contract to a club in a member state, are liable to be caught by EC Art 81).

B2.110 However, the court in *Bosman* made it clear that it was not in any way attacking the practice of limiting participation in national representative teams to 'nationals' of the state concerned[1]. Thus the Commission has stated:

> the Treaty provisions concerning freedom of movement for persons do not prevent the adoption of rules or practices excluding foreign players from certain matches for reasons which are not of an economic nature, which relate to the particular nature and context of such matches and are thus of sporting interest only, such as, for example, matches between national teams from different countries[2].

It may be inferred that a rule that provides that (for example) the German national team in the European Championships may only consist of German nationals will not offend EU law principles[3].

1 [1995] ECR I-4921, [1996] CMLR 645, 767, and AG Lenz at 695 et seq. See also the ECJ's judgment in *Walrave* [1974] ECR 1405, [1975] CMLR 320, at 331: 'This prohibition however does not affect the composition of sports teams, in particular national teams, the formation of which is a question of purely sporting interest …'; and *Donà v Mantero* [1976] ECR 1333, [1976] 2 CMLR 578, 583 (same).

2 *Draft/Preliminary Guidelines on the Application of the Competition Rules to Sport*, unpublished Commission memorandum (15 February 1999) at 12. See Forrester *Sport and EC Law* (Paper presented at the Third Annual Conference on Sports Marketing Law, Tax & Finance: Lausanne, September 1994) at p 18: 'in the case of sport, far from imposing arbitrary partitioning of the market, the organization of sport on national lines in fact forms a basic aspect of its attraction. Reaching national superiority through sporting effort is the very essence of the activity'.

3 Ie again such rules fall within the 'sporting exception' to EC competition law. See para B2.96.

B2.111 A similar principle was upheld by the European Court of Justice in the *Deliege* case[1], where the court confirmed that selection rules applied by a federation to govern participation in an international competition inevitably limit the number of participants in the competition, but such a limit is inherent in the organisation of the event and therefore falls outside the scope of the EC free movement (and competition rules).

1 *Deliège v Ligue Francophone de Judo et al*, Joined Cases C-51/96 and C-191/97 [2000] ECR I-2549. See further paras B2.176 et seq.

B2.112 Whilst the wording of the judgment of the *Deliège* court is not clear and comprehensive (it refers to matches between national teams only as one example of a 'sporting rule'), the European Commission has stated its clear view that *club* sides may not limit the number of EC nationals in their teams, even when these clubs play against each other in a national representative capacity (ie in *international* club competitions)[1]. Consequently, so far as club competition is concerned, it seems that either direct or indirect limitations on the number of EC nationals in a team will almost inevitably be legally problematic.

1 See eg 'Door kept open for foreign players – Brussels backs freedom of movement as sacred principle' (1999) Guardian, 30 November; 'Brussels protects players' rights' (1999) Times, 2 December.

B2.113 Player release rules Where a sport includes competitions between national representative teams as well as competitions between club teams, there needs to be a mechanism to address the release of players by their clubs to play for the national representative side. For example, both the International Rugby Board ('IRB'), the international governing body of rugby union, and the Fédération Internationale de Football Association ('FIFA'), the international governing body of association football, have rules governing release of players for international competitions[1].

1 See Regulation 9 of the IRB Regulations Relating to the Game, www.irb.ie; Arts 36 to 41 of the FIFA Regulations for the Status and Transfer of Players, www.fifa.com. See further para E1.89.

B2.114 This situation can lead to certain frictions, not least because that it is typically the club (rather than the national team) that pays the wages of the player. There may be a reluctance of clubs to release players for national team fixtures, particularly when these fixtures (especially 'friendly' matches) are perceived as unnecessary by club coaches[1].

1 See eg 'Rugby Union Clubs Wage £400,000 War' (1999) The Mirror, 26 November (Welsh ruby clubs seeking compensation from WRU for non-availability of players during RWC 1999; compensation block by IRB); 'Club v Country War' (2000) Daily Mail, 16 February (leading soccer clubs objecting to FIFA allowing countries to play three over-age players in Sydney Olympics event).

B2.115 In 1998, the leading English professional rugby clubs complained to the European Commission that the IRB's player release rules constituted an illegal agreement between the IRB and its member unions to suppress club rugby and thus limit the possibility for club rugby to compete commercially with national representative rugby[1]. The IRB responded that its player release rules had no anti-competitive effect and were necessary to ensure that developing rugby nations did not have their progress undermined (and therefore a broader competitive playing base threatened) by the recruitment of their players by professional rugby clubs in other nations. The case was eventually settled and the English clubs withdrew their complaint. Nevertheless, as club/country competition for player services continues (and with increasing physical and commercial demands on players) it may be expected that these issues will not go away. Interestingly enough, in early 2002 the G14 pressure group of leading football clubs repeated previous suggestions that national teams ought to compensate clubs for the use of their players in national team matches[3].

1 See further paras B2.119, n 2 and A3.31, n 3.
2 See eg Glendinning 'G14 Calls for Compensation' (2002) Sports Business, 15 March. See also 'G14 Call for more Control' (1999) Soccer Analyst Weekly, 7 June; (1994) Daily Telegraph, 8 June.

(b) Restrictions on the market for the organisation of new events

B2.116 The traditional model of sport in Europe is that there be one national, and one international, governing body for each sport. This system is underpinned by rules that require teams and individuals not to join other organisations or to play in other competitions that have not been sanctioned by the 'official' governing body.

B2.117 The monopoly regulatory control over a sport that the sanctioning system confers on the 'official' governing body allows it to achieve various important and uncontroversial regulatory objectives, such as enforcing uniform 'rules of the game' and disciplinary and anti-doping regulations, and protecting players through insurance and other risk management mechanisms[1]. However, it also gives a governing body (at least one that has genuine control over the sport) a more controversial ability, namely the ability to be active in the market for the organisation of new events in the sport, protecting the primacy of its own competitions and/or imposing conditions on promoters wishing to introduce new competitions.

1 It also serves an important public good by enabling the public to identify the 'world champion' of the sport. See eg Neale 'The Peculiar Economics of Professional Sports' (1994)1 Quarterly Journal of Economics ('[O]nly a single league can produce that most useful of joint products, the World Champion'). Indeed, a former Competition Commissioner (Van Miert) stated that 'it is generally acknowledged that the most effective institutional structure for promoting sport is the creation of a single federation in each Member State and a single international federation for each sport'; [1996] OJ C217/87, 12 April 1996.

B2.118 Tensions caused by the increasing commercialisation of sport have led to 'breakaway' conflicts in certain sports that follow a familiar pattern. Typically, the professional elite claims that the governing body is failing to exploit the full commercial value of the sport and/or that the income deriving from commercial exploitation is not properly distributed (ie the professional elite the 'drivers' of commercial income, are not getting their proper share). The amateur ranks, already believing their share of the spoils is inadequate, accuse the professional elite of disloyalty and of damaging the grass roots. Threats and counter-threats of breakaway and expulsion arise. Usually these matters are resolved within the relevant organs of the sport itself. However, in recent years, competition law has also been used as a means to exert pressure and influence the decision-making process in this sphere.

B2.119 For example, in 1998, a complaint was filed with the European Commission against UEFA by an organisation known as Media Partners, which aimed to set up a 'Super League' in European football. The basis of the complaint seems to have been that UEFA enjoyed a regulatory monopoly over football in Europe that restricted the possibility for an organisation such as Media Partners to establish a rival league that could compete with the events organised by UEFA. Little appears to have come of the complaint, but in the meantime the structure of European club competitions has been altered in a way that probably results in more income being generated for the leading clubs who would have been involved in the 'Super League' proposal[1]. Similarly, in rugby, a complaint filed with the Commission by the English First Division Rugby clubs against their domestic union, the Rugby Football Union, and the International Rugby Board[2] ended in a compromise that included changes to the way that European rugby competitions were organised[3].

1 See van den Brink 'EC Competition Law and the Regulation of Football: Part One' [2000] ECLR 359, 364–65.

2 *EFDR Complaint to the European Commission against the Rugby Football Union and the International Rugby Board,* Case No IV/36.994 (March 1998). The RFU implements the rules and regulations of the IRB in England. The clubs complained that RFU and IRB rules and regulations prevented them from organising cross-border competitions themselves and exploiting the commercial rights to those competitions without interference from above. The IRB argued in response that the clubs were complaining not about competition but about control. It asserted that it was in the long-term interests of the sport as a whole for the governing bodies to control the commercial facets of rugby, so as to enforce the collective approach that is vital to the long-term good of the game. The complaint was eventually withdrawn by the clubs without the Commission commencing any formal investigation into the matter. The complaint itself followed on from a similar challenge made by Cardiff RFC to the regulations of the Welsh Rugby Union (and, by incorporation, the IRB), as to which, see further para A3.29, n 2.

3 In a document known as the Paris Accord. In England, the Rugby Football Union has since set up a joint venture with its elite clubs and players to run the professional side of the game at club level, while the RFU itself remains in charge of the international representative team and retains responsibility for the amateur ranks. See para C1.24. A similar move is mooted from time to time for football in England. See eg 'Premier League plan FA takeover' (1999) Observer, 4 April.

B2.120 The leading authorities on the issue of governing body control over the emergence of new sports events are set out below.

B2.121 Gottrup-Klim In *Gottrup-Klim e.a. Grovvareforeninger v Dansk Landbrugs Grovvareselskab AmbA*[1], the claimant argued that the rules of an agricultural co-operative purchasing association that prohibited members from participating in competing co-operatives breached EC Arts 81 and 82. The European Court of Justice adopted a rule of reason approach[2], holding that:

(1) co-operation between purchasers creates collective strength that, by forcing suppliers to drop their prices, may be pro-competitive;

(2) members of the co-operative who also join another co-operative 'make each association less capable of pursuing its objectives for the benefit of the rest of its members'; and therefore

(3) a prohibition on dual membership does not necessarily constitute a restriction on competition within the meaning of the competition rules; in fact, such a rule may be pro-competitive, *provided that*:

 (a) the restrictions are 'limited to what is necessary to ensure that the co-operative functions properly and maintains its contractual power in relation to producers'; and

(b) the minimum membership period is reasonable and penalties for non-compliance are proportionate.

1 Case C-250/92 [1994] ECR I-5641.
2 See para B2.63.

B2.122 Sports leagues too are essentially a form of co-operative, their strength arising from the collective efforts of their individual constituents[1]. There would therefore appear to be a fairly clear analogy from *Gottrup-Klim* to the standard sporting rule that a club wishing to participate in one league may not play in other competitions without the permission of the league's organisers[2]. Putting the matter more directly, clubs cannot, on the basis of competition law, claim that they are legally entitled to 'pick and choose' between the events in which they participate. For example, a Liverpool or Arsenal might be free to join a 'Super League' of the top European clubs, but it could not at the same time insist on being allowed to retain its place in the FA Premier League and/or the UEFA Champions League.

1 See para B2.66 to B2.68.
2 In 'The Sporting Exception in EC Competition Law' [1999] European Current Law lvi at lx, Beloff quotes a Commission document stating that *Gottrup-Klim* 'appears to be capable of application in the field of sport'.

B2.123 Greig v Insole In *Greig v Insole*[1], the English High Court (Slade J) applied the common law doctrine of restraint of trade to similar restrictions imposed in a sports context. The 34 first class cricket players who had signed to play in Kerry Packer's unsanctioned tour were banned indefinitely by the ICC and TCCB from playing in official competitions. The court held that it was legitimate for the ICC and TCCB to try to protect the public interest in the proper organisation and administration of cricket, and in particular the status of the test calendar as the principal source of revenue for the sport as a whole, but ruled that imposing a total and retrospective ban from first class cricket on players who had contracted to play for an unsanctioned series was not reasonable and justifiable in the circumstances of the case. Importantly, however, Mr Justice Slade expressed disapproval of the 'free-riding' efforts of Mr Packer, and noted that a *prospective* prohibition from competing in both sanctioned and unsanctioned events might well have been justified:

> If cricketing authorities employ a player to go on a tour or indeed perhaps even if they employ him to play in one or more test matches at home, it may be open to them, as a matter of fair negotiation, to demand from him, as a price for the privileges which he himself will derive from participating in the match, a limited covenant precluding him from playing for competitors. If such covenant represents no more than is reasonably required for the authorities' protection, in terms of duration, place and otherwise and is reasonable in the interest of the public, it may perhaps be enforceable according to its terms[2].

1 [1978] 3 All ER 449 (Ch D 1977).
2 [1978] 3 All ER at 464.

B2.124 OFT v FAPL In the proceedings brought before the Restrictive Practices Court in 1999 in relation to the rules and commercial arrangements of the FA Premier League ('FAPL')[1], the OFT challenged not only the FAPL's rules on central licensing of broadcasting rights[2] but also its rules limiting member clubs' ability to play in non-Premier League competitions. The court upheld the rule prohibiting Premier League clubs from playing in 'friendly' matches that might clash with Premier League fixtures, as well as a rule requiring member clubs to obtain Premier League consent to play in other competitions. These provisions were considered to be 'necessary to ensure that clubs competing in the league give the league competition a due degree of priority'[3].

1 *Re an Agreement between the FA Premier League and BSkyB* [2000] EMLR 78, [1999] UKCLR 258 (Restrictive Practices Court, 20 July 1999). See discussion at para A3.169.
2 See para B2.265 et seq.
3 *Re an Agreement between the FA Premier League and BSkyB* [2000] EMLR 78, [1999] UKCLR 258 (Restrictive Practices Court, 20 July 1999), judgment at 191.

B2.125 In fact, the legality of this kind of rule will largely depend on how it is applied in practice[1], and in particular whether it goes further than is necessary to protect the legitimate interests of the league or other governing body that seeks to rely on it[2].

1 For example, the Restrictive Practices Court did strike out an FAPL rule requiring clubs to obtain FAPL consent before playing certain games outside England and Wales, because of evidence that this rule had been used to prevent Premier League clubs pursuing Media Partners' Super League proposals. See *Re an Agreement between the FA Premier League and BSkyB* [2000] EMLR 78, [1999] UKCLR 258 (Restrictive Practices Court, 20 July 1999), judgment at 191. As to those proposals, see para B2.119.
2 See especially the *Hendry* case, discussed at para B2.131 et seq.

B2.126 The Formula One case Similar issues were considered by the European Commission in the context of a controversial case relating to the Federation Internationale de l'Automobile ('FIA'), the governing body of motor sport. The FIA has a de facto regulatory monopoly in the motor-racing field. Its sanction is required for all official motor-racing events, including by far the most commercially valuable motor-racing event, the FIA Formula One World Championship. The popularity of the FIA Formula One World Championship allowed the FIA to impose conditions of participation on manufacturers, teams, and circuits that required them to be loyal to the FIA as against any rival promoter. Consequently, any 'independent' organiser of a motor-racing event had to join the FIA or obtain its sanction in order to attract participants to rival events. Against this background, a complaint was made to the European Commission alleging that the FIA had refused to authorise a rival championship in order to ensure that events that FIA itself organised continued to be a commercial success.

B2.127 In June 1999, the Commission sent the FIA and two related commercial companies a statement of objections, claiming that the FIA was 'abusing a dominant position' in the market for the organisation of motor sports events. Essentially, what the Commission objected to was the FIA using its regulatory power to protect the FIA Formula One World Championship from any competing series. Thus, participants in FIA events had to make certain exclusive commitments precluding them from participating in non-FIA events; the FIA only sanctioned new events on condition that the broadcasting rights to those events were ceded to the FIA; and the FIA had (allegedly) used its regulatory monopoly to force a competing series (the GTR organisation) out of the market. Broadcasters were also given incentives not to support any motor sports event that might constitute competition to Formula One[1].

1 Commission press release dated 30 June 1999, IP/99/434. For example, certain broadcasters of the FIA Formula One World Championship were offered a 33% 'discount' from the rights fee otherwise payable provided that they did not broadcast any 'open wheeler' racing other than Formula One.

B2.128 In response to the criticisms made by the Commission, FIA agreed to separate its regulatory functions from the commercial exploitation of the FIA Formula One World Championship. This was supposed to remedy the perceived conflict of interest identified by the Commission. What this 'separation of functions' seems to have involved, however, was the transfer of the commercial rights to the FIA Formula One World Championship for a 100-year period by the FIA to a company controlled by a vice-president of the FIA (Mr. Bernie Ecclestone). It might have been thought that, in normal circumstances, the assignment of such commercially valuable rights for a 100-year period would have been an issue that would arouse the suspicion of the competition authorities. In the Formula One case, however, this century-long assignment appears to have been part of the solution approved by Brussels[1].

1 For good measure, it seems that FIA did accept that conditions of access to motor sport should be justified on objective grounds relating to the secure, equitable and orderly conduct of the sport. The FIA also accepted that it could not require event organisers and promoters to cede their broadcasting rights to FIA as a condition of regulatory sanction, although it has to be said that this hardly represents a significant concession to reach agreement with a competition authority.

B2.129 In June 2001, the Commission published an Art 19(3) Notice[1] in which it suggested that the modifications would mean that FIA should no longer be tempted to exercise its regulatory powers to promote its own commercial interests over those of potential competitors. The Commission stated that:

> FIA will have neither the commercial incentive nor the regulatory power to limit the type and number of events it authorises, other than on the basis of objective criteria.

It closed the case in October 2001[2].

1 Notice published pursuant to Art 19(3) of Council Regulation No 17 concerning Cases COMP/35.163, OJ C 169/5, 13 June 2001.
2 'Commission closes its investigation into Formula One and other four-wheel motor sports', Commission press release dated 30 October 2001, IP/01/1523.

B2.130 Although the FIA case with the Commission was a high profile matter, it remains difficult to divine any clear legal principle from the settlement of the case. Citing the case, the Commission has remarked that: 'where regulation and organisation being vested in a single body leads to significant commercial conflicts of interest, the Commission will look carefully at whether another scenario should be required'[1]. However, no formal decision was ever taken by the Commission on the matter (perhaps to the relief of the Commission's own Legal Service) and the Notice published under Art 19(3) of Regulation 17 is hardly a model of legal clarity. Interestingly enough, the Commission had originally contended that the FIA had acted 'abusively' by appropriating the commercial rights to Formula One motor-racing. Nevertheless, as noted above[2], a key part of the settlement was the Commission approval of a 100-year assignment of rights by the entity that had abusively acquired the rights (the FIA) to an entity controlled by an individual with strong links to the governing body itself. Legally, therefore, the case appears to represent something of a mystery.

1 Commission Monti *Competition and Sport: the Rules of the Game* (DN Speech/01/84: Brussels, 26 February 2001). But see Cartlidge, 'Commission unlikely to treat other sports like Formula One' (2001) Sportcal.com, 30 July.
2 See para B2.128.

B2.131 Hendry v WPBSA Of clearer precedent value was the decision of the English High Court in late 2001 in the *Hendry* case[1]. That case primarily concerned a rule of the World Professional Billiards and Snooker Association (WPBSA) prohibiting its members from playing in any tournament that was not organised or sanctioned by the WPBSA[2].

1 *Hendry v World Professional Billiards & Snooker Association Ltd* [2002] UKCLR 5, [2002] ECC 8, [2001] Eu LR 770 (Lloyd J, 5 October 2001). For case comment, see eg Stoner 'Competition matters: the rules of snooker under scrutiny in English courts' (2002) 9(3) Sports Law Administration & Practice 8; Harris 'Abusive sports bodies' [2002] 10(1) SATLJ 122.
2 For discussion of that and other aspects of the case, see para A3.170.

B2.132 The WPBSA is the world governing body for snooker. As well as exercising regulatory and disciplinary functions in the sport, it also organises and promotes professional snooker tournaments (the 'WPBSA tour') and enters into agreements with broadcasters and sponsors for some of these events. The WPBSA is, in effect, a players' association – virtually all professional snooker players in the world are members. Its main object is to promote, encourage and popularise snooker and billiards.

B2.133 Two leading snooker players and The Sportsmasters Network Ltd ('TSN') challenged the WPBSA rule preventing its members from participating in professional snooker tournaments other than those organised or sanctioned by the WPBSA. TSN was a private company wishing to set up a rival snooker tour to the WPBSA tour. It wanted to run tournaments open only to the top 64 snooker players in the world.

B2.134 It was argued by the claimants that the WPBSA rule was contrary to both EC and UK competition law rules and the English common law doctrine of restraint of trade[1]. It was also argued that the rule was contrary to Art 49 of the EC Treaty in that it restricted the freedom of players based in one member state to provide their services by playing tournaments organised by promoters in other member states[2]. Finally, it was argued that the WPBSA had 'abused its dominant position' to stifle TSN's competing tour by bringing forward a 'deadline' for players to submit their application forms for entry to the 2001/2002 WPBSA tour.

1 As to which, see paras A3.135 to A3.158.
2 As to which, see Chapter B3.

B2.135 Lloyd J observed that in commercial terms there was a market for organising and promoting snooker tournaments. That market comprised two aspects: the acquisition of 'raw materials' and the sale of the 'product'. The tournament organiser acted as a 'buyer' in relation to securing the services of players as participants in the events, and a 'seller' in relation to the marketing of the events to broadcasters, sponsors, advertisers and the paying public.

B2.136 Lloyd J held that the market on which the WPBSA acted as 'buyer' – ie the market for the supply of services by professional snooker players and organisers and promoters of professional snooker tournaments – was a separate relevant market on its own. This was largely on the basis that, so far as snooker players were concerned, there was no substitute for the services of tournament organisers. On the other hand, as regards the market on which the tournament organiser acted as 'seller' (ie to broadcasters and sponsors), there was a wide range of alternative 'products' open to broadcasters and sponsors and so snooker could not be considered as 'non-substitutable' for television or sponsorship purposes.

B2.137 Lloyd J held that the WPBSA was 'dominant' on the market for the organisation of professional snooker tournaments, based on the following facts:

(1) the WPBSA members accounted for almost 100% of all professional snooker players in the world;
(2) snooker tournaments involving WPBSA members could not take place without WPBSA consent;
(3) any promoter/organiser of a rival event had to disclose a substantial amount of information when applying for WPBSA to 'sanction' the event;
(4) WPBSA events were the most important in terms of participation, ranking, prestige and prize money; and
(5) as promoter *and* regulator, and with major broadcast and sponsorship contracts in place, the WPBSA was in a position of great advantage vis-à-vis other tournament promoters or organisers in competing in the 'market' for the services of snooker players.

B2.138 Lloyd J went on to hold that, in all the circumstances, the WPBSA rule and policy on sanctioning amounted to an abuse of that dominant position. He also held the rule to constitute an anti-competitive agreement, an unjustifiable restraint of trade, and an infringement of the freedom to provide services. It seems that Lloyd J considered that the WPBSA had attempted to entrench its dominant position by using its power as a regulatory body to deter players from participating in rival events. This was designed to ensure that the WPBSA continued to have the best players and therefore good television coverage (which also limited the opportunity for any rival tournament organiser to emerge).

B2.139 Again, no suggestion was made that the combination of regulatory and commercial authority was per se illegal. Rather, it was the manner in which the WPBSA has exercised its powers that was problematic. The court held that the fact that the WPBSA was the regulator was not, in itself, restrictive of competition. Nor was it a problem that nearly all snooker players were members of the WPBSA or that this body had major contracts with broadcasters and sponsors. The potentially restrictive 'barrier to entry' really depended on the manner in which the WPBSA's regulatory power was exercised and, in particular, whether that power was used in a manner designed to protect the position of the WPBSA and ensure that it continued to have the major broadcast contracts in future.

B2.140 Whilst the ruling may be understandable as a matter of conventional competition law theory, it does not contain any real analysis of how a professional sport is supposed to operate with 'rival' tours. Lloyd J himself recognised that the existence of a second regulatory body would be unsatisfactory with the result of a 'split sport'. He also recognised that the WPBSA had certain overarching policy objectives that gave it a legitimate interest in protecting its commercial income. For example, the court referred to the support which the WPBSA gave to a wider group of players than the 'top' players in which TSN was interested. In this connection, Lloyd J stated:

> As a general proposition, WPBSA must be concerned about the sport as a whole, including its future players, which might well lead to a course of conduct inconsistent with the view taken by some current players of what would be in their best interests[1].

1 *Hendry v WSPBA Ltd* [2002] UKCLR 5, [2002] ECC 8, [2001] Eu LR 770.

B2.141 Lloyd J also referred to the WPBSA policy of spreading prize money more widely that would have been the case for the TSN rival tour. However, despite this, Lloyd J was not convinced that the legitimate interests of the WPBSA could only be protected by the 'sanctioning' rule and, in the final analysis, the judgment seems to have been that the rule (or its operation) was disproportionate to the legitimate objectives that the WPBSA sought to secure[1].

1 See further paras A3.170. In a similar vein, in May 2002, it was reported that the OFT was considering whether the British Horseracing Board's centralised control over the fixture lists of the 59 British racecourses was in breach of the Competition Act 1998. See 'OFT to put racing under starters orders' (2002) Daily Telegraph, 9 May. By September 2002, the newspapers were speculating (see eg (2002) Times, 23 September) that the OFT was going to rule such centralised control illegal under the Competition Act 1998.

(c) Promotion/relegation

B2.142 Promotion and relegation are considered by many to be a fundamental aspect of European sport, an essential mechanism for ensuring not only competitive balance but also a collective approach based on solidarity throughout all levels of the game. The alternative US model of 'closed' leagues, admitting no new members, is regarded as inconsistent with those fundamental principles[1]. However, the 'closed league' model is sometimes mooted by those seeking to attract new capital into a sport, on the grounds that relegation from the elite, with its financially disastrous consequences, is an unacceptable investment risk.

1 See eg The European Model of Sport Consultation Document of DG-X, November 1998, para B2.102, n 1.

B2.143 There are not many examples of such 'closed' league structures in Europe[1]. However, a proposed European 'Super League' in football, first promoted by an organisation known as Media Partners, would have been modelled along these lines. The suggested marketing arrangements for the commercial rights to this competition were notified to the European Commission in 1999. In terms of structure, the 'Super League' would have given founder members clubs three years' guaranteed participation, with others having to qualify[2].

1 The leading professional rugby clubs in England have sought to restrict relegation in various ways, usually challenged by the clubs in the Second Division. See para B2.144, n 4. Similarly, Europe's leading football clubs have explored various ways of guaranteeing their own entries to UEFA's Champions League. And many would argue that the increasing financial chasm between Premier League clubs and Football League clubs is creating on effective 'closed league' at the top of the English pyramid.

2 *European Football League notification* [1999] OJ C70/07, Case IV D3/3700.

B2.144 One of the key justifications for allowing central marketing of television rights to football is the fact that it facilitates equitable re-distribution of revenues (ie financial solidarity)[1]. It might be supposed that this important ingredient would be missing from the 'Super League' model: in this scheme, the members of the 'closed' league would share the collectively-generated revenue between themselves, with little (if any) of the money finding its way back to the 'grass roots' of the sport. Furthermore, it might possibly be argued that an essentially arbitrary 'closed' league structure may be difficult to reconcile with EU competition principles that require that entrance criteria to (trade) associations be based on fair and non-discriminatory rules[2]. The European Commission has yet to give any indication of how it views this project and, at the time of writing, the closed 'Super League' remains a hypothetical construct[3]. Some clarification of the relevant principles may come, however, from the Office of Fair Trading, which is currently investigating the latest in a long line of complaints made by English second-tier rugby union clubs about perceived restrictions on promotion and relegation imposed by rugby's Premiership clubs[4].

1 See para B2.262 et seq.
2 See eg Joined Cases T-528, T-542/93 and T-546/93, [1996] ECR II-649 the *Eurovision* judgment. See also Hornsby, 'Closed Leagues': A Prime Candidate for the 'Sporting Exception' in European Competition Law?', (2001) 2 ISLR 161 ('if there is to be a valid economic objection to closed leagues, what counts is not the denial of access to a particular club, but rather the denial of the opportunities to organise other leagues for that particular sport').
3 For a review of court cases on aspects of promotion and relegation, see para A3.27.
4 See 'Premiership clubs stand accused of operating cartel' (2002) Times, 4 October. See also 'Top clubs to defend promotion rules against legal threat' (2000) Sportcal.com, 28 September; 'Second Division Clubs Launch Legal Action' (2000) The Independent, 8 November; 'Rotherham case reopened by OFT' (2002) The Observer, 19 May (OFT investigating 'whether a ring-fenced Premiership is an illegal cartel').

B Common ownership of competing clubs

B2.145 Sports regulators have long recognised that common ownership of competing clubs undermines the prerequisite feature of any successful sport: public confidence in the integrity and authenticity of the contest and the uncertainty of the outcome. In any match, both sides must be able, and be perceived to be able, to compete to their best of their abilities to win the match, free of any external constraints. Putting the matter differently, it seems legitimate that sports governing bodies may take such measures as are reasonable and necessary (ie 'proportionate') to prevent any conflict of interest occurring, where such a conflict may lead to the manipulation of sporting results and/or public perception that the results of a sporting contest may be influenced by any factor other than the efforts and sporting skills of the teams or athletes concerned.

B2.146 Sports governing bodies in both Europe and the United States have adopted rules and regulations to prevent such conflicts occurring. One example would be the FA Premier League's Rule U(3), which provides that 'no person, by himself or with one or more Associates, may directly or indirectly hold or acquire any interest in more than 10 per cent of the issued share capital of a Club … while he or any Associate is a director of, or directly or indirectly holds any interest in the share capital of, any other Club …'. The rule explains why the media companies that have invested in a number of FAPL clubs[1] have confined their investments to 9.9% of the shares of those clubs.

1 See para C3.173.

B2.147 Of course, it might be argued that such rules theoretically 'restrict competition' in the sense that they preclude the same person or corporate entity from investing in (and therefore having influence or control over) more than one team participating in the same sporting competition. Indeed, as the commercial opportunities presented by the ownership and operation of sports teams become more apparent, the rules of governing bodies to avoid such conflicts of interest have also been subject to legal challenge.

B2.148 In 1997, an investment vehicle called ENIC started buying stakes in clubs around Europe (including Slavia Prague, Glasgow Rangers, Vincenza and AEK Athens). There was a risk (which in fact materialised) that two or more clubs controlled by ENIC might qualify for the same UEFA club competition. Therefore, in 1998, UEFA introduced a rule prohibiting clubs under common control from playing in the same UEFA club competition[1]. As a consequence of this rule, AEK Athens was excluded from the 1998 UEFA Cup (since Slavia Prague had qualified for this competition as well). Following this exclusion, the claimant clubs made an emergency application to the Court of Arbitration for Sport and managed to obtain an interim injunction prohibiting UEFA from applying the rule for the 1998/99 season. However, this interim ruling was based essentially on procedural grounds, with the CAS being critical of the fact that insufficient warning of the rule change had been given to the clubs concerned so that consequently they had a 'legitimate expectation' of being allowed to compete[2].

1 Annexe VI to the Regulations of the UEFA Champions League (and the UEFA Cup, and the UEFA Intertoto Cup), Regulations concerning the Integrity of the UEFA Club Competitions – Independence of Clubs.
2 *AEK PAE and SK Slavia Praha v UEFA* CAS 98/2000, award dated 20 August 1999, *Digest of CAS Awards II 1998–2000* (2002, Kluwer), p 36.

B2.149 Some months later, the CAS proceeded to a full hearing on the substantive merits of the case, and in particular the allegation made by the clubs that the UEFA rule was anti-competitive. The CAS found[1] that the purpose of the UEFA rule was to maintain the integrity of the sport, and not to restrict competition. It also found that the rule was a proportionate measure, necessary to prevent match-rigging, either actual or perceived. It held that the rule did not fall within any 'sporting exception' to competition law, given its economic nature. However, insofar as the rule affected competition on a 'market for ownership interests in football clubs', it actually served to enhance, rather than restrict, competition. The CAS considered that the contested rule might discourage the merger of football clubs between existing owners but, at the same time, this left the field open for a greater number of potential investors in football clubs. On that basis, the CAS held that the rule:

> appears to have the effect of preserving competition between club owners and between football clubs rather than appreciably restricting competition on the relevant market or on other football markets[2].

In other words, the rule did not qualify for the 'sporting exception' to the EC competition rules[3] but still fell outside the scope of Art 81(1) on a 'rule of reason' analysis[4].

1 *AEK PAE and SK Slavia Praha v UEFA* CAS 98/2000, award dated 20 August 1999, *Digest of CAS Awards II 1998–2000* (2002, Kluwer), p 36.
2 *AEK PAE and SK Slavia Praha v UEFA*, CAS 98/2000, award dated 20 August 1999, *Digest of CAS Awards II 1998–2000* (2002, Kluwer), p 36, paras 150–151.
3 See para B2.56.
4 See para B2.62.

B2.150

The ruling of the CAS on this matter was in no way binding on the European Commission. Nevertheless, the Commission had the opportunity to take a position on the subject when ENIC, having lost before the CAS, filed a complaint with the Brussels authorities about the same UEFA rule. On 27 June 2002, the Commission rejected ENIC's complaint. In a relatively lengthy and detailed decision letter[1], the Commission noted that:

(a) an agreement is only caught by the Art 81(1) prohibition if, considered in the economic context in which it is to be applied, its object or effect is to restrict or distort competition on the market to an appreciable effect;
(b) the object of the UEFA multiple ownership rule is not to distort competition but rather to protect the integrity of UEFA tournaments by avoiding any perception that the outcome of a match is not uncertain;
(c) while the contested rule does incidentally restrict the freedom of action of football club and investors, that restriction is inherent in achieving the objective of clean competition that is essential to the very existence of credible sporting competition[2];
(d) there appears to be no viable less restrictive means of achieving the same objective;
(e) 'the limitation on the freedom to act therefore merely constitutes the effect of the application of a rule which is deemed necessary and proportionate to the need to maintain the public's confidence in the fairness and authenticity of the game, the absence of which would have the effect of rendering, in the long term, any competition impossible'.

1 Decision letter of 27 June 2002 from Commissioner Mario Monti to ENIC, Case COMP/37.806, available on www.europa.eu. For background, see Commission answer dated 3 September 1998 to written question from the European Parliament, OJ 22 February 1999 C50/143; Commission press release dated 9 December 1999, IP/99/965.

2 The decision letter (n 1) states: 'without the UEFA rule, the proper functioning of the market where the clubs develop their economic activities would be under threat, since the public's perception that the underlying sporting competition is fair and honest is an essential precondition to keep its interest and marketability'.

B2.151 In a concurrent press release, the Commission stated that the decision:

> makes clear that a rule may fall outside the scope of competition rules despite possible negative business effects, provided that it does not go beyond what is necessary to ensure its legitimate aim and that it is applied in a non-discriminatory way[1].

1 Commission press release dated 27 June 2002, IP/02/942.

C Movement of players

(a) Transfer regulations

B2.152 Many sports operate a system of player registration and clearance that allows them to regulate the movement of players from club to club within the sport. These regulations operate over and above the contractual arrangements entered into between clubs and players[1]. One sporting imperative behind this regulatory system is the need to ensure that the result of a competition played over the course of a season is not distorted by the indiscriminate movement of players from one team to another. In addition, it is appropriate that clubs have the incentive (including the financial incentive) to develop young players. Furthermore, payment of transfer fees can act as an important revenue redistribution mechanism. Nevertheless, to the extent that such transfer regulations might restrict player movement, and specifically restrict competition on the 'market' for the services of players, they may be subject to challenge not only under the free movement rules of the EC Treaty[1], but also under the competition rules[2].

1 See generally Chapter E2.
2 See Chapter B3.
2 Under English and Commonwealth law, there may also of course be a restraint of trade claim. See paras A3.135 to A3.158 and paras E2.32 et seq.

B2.153 FIFA's original player registration system permitted a club to retain the registration of a player (and thus obtain a fee for him from any other club that desired his services) even after his contract had come to an end. In other words, even out-of-contract players could only move from one club to another if a transfer fee was paid. This aspect of the player transfer system was famously challenged by Belgian footballer Jean-Marc Bosman on the basis that it infringed the free movement rules and/or the competition rules of the EC Treaty.

B2.154 In its 1995 judgment in the *Bosman* case[1], the European Court of Justice upheld Mr Bosman's challenge, finding that the transfer rules preventing a player from being employed by another club unless an agreed transfer fee was paid, even when the player's contract with his current club had expired, contravened the free movement rules of the Treaty. The court accepted that there were arguments in favour of transfer fees, specifically, that they could constitute a means of maintaining financial and competitive balance between clubs and could support the training efforts of clubs. Nevertheless, the Court of Justice essentially found that these legitimate aims could be achieved by other means that did not entail adverse consequences for the free movement of workers. The Court of Justice, and in particular the Advocate-General Lenz (in the opinion he provided for the guidance of the Court of Justice), considered that it would be more appropriate to have a more direct system of redistribution of income between large and small clubs[2].

1 *Union Royale Belge des Sociétés de Football Association ASBL v Bosman*, Case 415/93, [1996] 1 CMLR 645. For case comment, see eg Ulhoorn 'The Bosman case: Freedom of Movement for sports players and its implications' [1998] 10 Euro C.L. lvi; Weatherill 'Do sporting associations make "law" or are they merely subject to it?' EBL Rev 217 (July/August 1998); Hornsby 'Sport in the EU: Has self-regulation a future in the light of the Bosman case?' [1995] 5 Int. TLR 181. For further discussion of the case from a free movement perspective, see paras B3.40 et seq and E2.40 et seq.

2 See further para B2.263.

B2.155 Since the European Court of Justice found that the transfer rules infringed Art 48 of the EC Treaty (ie free movement of workers), it did not find it necessary to decide whether the rules also infringed Art 81 of the Treaty. In his opinion, however, Advocate-General Lens did state the view that the transfer rules did contravene EC Art 81:

> … those [transfer] rules replace the normal system of supply and demand by a uniform machinery which leads to the existing competition situation being preserved and the clubs being deprived of the possibility of making use of the chances, with respect to the engagement of players, which would be available to them under normal competitive conditions. If the obligation to pay transfer fees did not exist, a player could transfer freely after the expiry of his contract and choose the club which offered him the best terms … The current transfer system … means that even after the contract has expired the player remains assigned to his former club for the time being. Since a transfer takes place only if a transfer fee is paid, the tendency to maintain the existing competition situation is inherent in the system[1].

1 Opinion of Advocate-General Lens, *Union Royale Belge des Sociétés de Football Association ASBL v Bosman*, Case 415/93, [1996] 1 CMLR 645 at para 262.

B2.156 Having reached this conclusion, however, Advocate-General Lens did not rule out the possibility of a transfer system in all cases:

> That does not mean, however, that a demand for a transfer fee for a player would, following the view I have put forward, have to be regarded as unlawful in every case. The

> argument that a club should be compensated for the training work it has done, and that the big, rich clubs should not be able to enjoy the fruits of that work without making any contribution of their own, does indeed in my opinion have some weight. For that reason it might be considered whether *appropriate* transfer rules for professional footballers might not be acceptable ... Such rules would in my opinion have to comply with two requirements. First, the transfer fee would actually have to be limited to the amount expended by the previous club (or previous clubs) for the player's training. Second, a transfer fee would come into question only in the case of a first change of clubs where the previous club had trained the player. Analogous to the transfer rules in force in France, that transfer fee would in addition have to be after having been trained, since during that period the training club will have had an opportunity to benefit from its investment in the player[1].

1 Opinion of Advocate-General Lens, *Union Royale Belge des Sociétés de Football Association ASBL v Bosman*, Case 415/93, [1996] 1 CMLR 645 at para 239.

B2.157 Ever since the *Bosman* ruling, sports governing bodies and clubs have complained about its detrimental effects, in particular the prohibition on transfer fees for out-of-contract players. It has been suggested that money that was previously paid to clubs to 'compensate' them for player development is instead now paid to the players themselves, in the form of signing-on fees and increased salaries, and thereafter is lost to the game[1]. Furthermore, depriving smaller clubs of compensation when an out-of-contract players moves on has, it is argued, served only to exacerbate the wealth gap that exists between the elite clubs and the rest[2]. Nevertheless, the European Commission has consistently expressed scepticism about these arguments and has preferred instead to point to the comments of the European Court of Justice and the Advocate General in *Bosman* that the same legitimate objectives – development of young players and maintenance of competitive balance between clubs – could be achieved by other, less restrictive, means[3].

1 This is the so-called 'prune juice' effect.
2 See eg Deloitte & Touche *Annual Report of Football Finances 1996–2001*, passim.
3 See para B2.154.

B2.158 After the *Bosman* ruling, FIFA amended its regulations to abolish the payment of transfer fees for players who were EU or EEA nationals and who moved cross-border in the territory of the EEA on expiry of their contracts. This, however, left a whole raft of situations remaining in which transfer fees *did* still have to be paid for out-of-contract players, including domestic transfers (ie transfers within the territory of a single member state); transfers from a club in a member state to a club in a non-member state (and the other way round); and even cross-border transfers within the EEA of non-EEA nationals. None of these situations were covered by Art 48 of the EC Treaty. It remained possible, however, that one or more of these situations might be caught by Art 81 of the Treaty.

B2.159 Some of these questions (at least in relation to transfers involving non-EEA nationals) might have been answered had the European Court of Justice ever given a ruling in the *Tibor Balog* case, which started (almost inevitably) in the Belgian domestic courts before being referred to the European Court of Justice in 1998[1]. The case concerned a Hungarian footballer (Mr. Balog) who challenged the transfer rules restricting his ability to move at the end of his contract from Charleroi in Belgium to Nancy in France. The case was settled on 29 March 2001, the day that the Advocate-General issued her opinion[2]. Since the case related to a player at the end of his contract, there was no reason why the European Court should have addressed the legality of the FIFA rules concerning transfer of in-contract players. However, largely because of a contemporaneous dispute it was having with FIFA on precisely this subject[3], the Commission tried to encourage the court to opine on the legality of the rules governing the transfer of players under contract as well. In the event, the court was probably relieved that it did not have to deal with the case at all.

1 *Tibor Balog v Royal Charleroi Sporting Club ASBL*, Case C-264/98, opinion dated 29 March 2001. Advocate-General Stix-Hackl's opinion was that the restriction was incompatible with EC Art 81(c).
2 As to which, see para E2.062.
3 See para B2.160.

B2.160 In December 1998, following receipt of various complaints, the Commission sent FIFA a statement of objections in which it took issue with the remaining aspects of the international transfer system noted at para B2.158. More controversially, however, the Commission also expressed the view that the transfer rules relating to players who were still under contract were contrary to Art 81 of the Treaty as well. Essentially, there were two main objections raised by the Commission, relating to the FIFA rules concerning:

(1) unilateral breach of contract; and
(2) 'agreed' transfers.

B2.161 Firstly, under the FIFA rules 'unilateral' termination of contract was effectively prohibited. In practice, this meant that if a player broke his contract with his club, *and* even if he paid whatever damages were due for the breach of contract under national law, he still could not be registered to play with a new club in another country. Thus, if 'unilateral' breach of contract occurred, no international clearance certificate would be issued and the player would not be able to play with a new club. The Commission claimed this rule was both anti-competitive and contrary to the free movement rules of the Treaty.

B2.162 Secondly, under the FIFA rules, all three parties ('buying' club, 'selling' club, and player) were free to agree 'amicably' on a transfer fee but that fee did not have to bear any relation to the actual costs that the 'selling' club had invested in training or developing the player. In the view of the Commission, this system (combined with the ban on unilateral breach of contract) could lead to 'excessive' transfer fees being charged. The Commission claimed that transfer fees that bore no relation to investment or training costs were again anti-competitive and liable to impede freedom of movement[1].

1 This is an echo of Advocate General Lenz's remarks in *Bosman*: see para B2.156.

B2.163 There were also two further objections that the Commission made to the FIFA regime, relating to:

(1) the rule that obliged national associations to organise their domestic transfer regimes according to the principles set out in the FIFA international system; and
(2) the provision contained in the FIFA Statutes that prohibited clubs and players from taking transfer disputes to civil courts.

B2.164 Following months of negotiations involving FIFA, UEFA, and (initially at least) FIFPRO (the international players' union)[1], the Commission announced in March 2001[2] that it was satisfied with a new set of principles proposed by FIFA for the international transfer of players[3]. The immediate effect of reaching agreement on these principles was that it brought the competition proceedings against FIFA to an end[4].

1 Reding *Commission's Investigation into FIFA's transfer rules – Statement to European Parliament* (DN: Speech/00/290, dated 7 September 2000); *Football transfers: Commission underlines the prospect of future progress*, Commission press release dated 6 December 2000, IP/00/1412.
2 'Outcome of discussions between the Commission and FIFA/UEFA on FIFA Regulations on international football transfers', Commission press release dated 6 March 2001, IP/01/314.
3 'Principles for the amendment of FIFA rules regarding international transfers (new basic rules)' dated 5 March 2001.
4 See Egger and Stix-Hackl 'Sports and Competition Law: A Never-Ending Story?' [2002] 2 ECLR 81; Mcauley 'They think its all over … it might just be now: unravelling the ramifications of the European football transfer system post-Bosman' [2002] 7 ECLR 331.

B2.165 By then, however, FIFPRO had withdrawn from the negotiations over the revised international transfer system and was not a party to the agreement reached between FIFA and the European Commission. Having been unable to shape the outcome of these discussions with the Commission, FIFPRO launched a challenge to the legality of the agreed principles in May 2001, by suing both FIFA and the Belgian FA in a Brussels court[1]. As the new system had not even entered into effect when this court action was commenced, it remains doubtful whether this hypothetical claim would have got anywhere. Nevertheless, the commencement of the action appears to have served some purpose in that, a few months later, FIFA and FIFPRO announced that they had reached an agreement on how the new international transfer system would be applied and the action before the Brussels court was formally withdrawn[2].

1 See (2001) 4(3) Sports Law Bulletin 16.
2 See www.fifa.com.

B2.166 The new rules were adopted at FIFA's July 2001 Congress in Buenos Aires[1]. Full details of them are provided elsewhere in this work[2]. However, from the point of view of those seeking to understand what kind of restrictions on competition and free movement will be considered justified by the Commission on sporting grounds, the most important provisions are those relating to stability of contract and compensation for breach of contract.

1 FIFA Circular No 769 (24 August 2001). See [2001] 9(3) SATLJ 185.
2 See paras A5.135 to A5.138, B2.164 et seq, E1.63, E1.64 and E2.66 et seq and passim.

B2.167 To protect the 'regularity and proper functioning of sporting competition', it was agreed that players may only be registered (which means, in practice, transferred) during two defined registration periods per season. Furthermore, should there be a breach of contract (by either the player or the club), 'sporting sanctions' may be applied. These sanctions could, in certain cases, disqualify the player from playing for up to six months as from the commencement of the next sporting season. As regards a breach committed by the club, it might be prohibited from registering any new players for up to 12 months. In addition to these provisions regarding breach of contract, rules were also introduced for the calculation of 'compensation' for the transfer of a player[1]. This would be based largely (though not exclusively) on the relevant national employment law. Finally, the system even provided for compensation to be paid to clubs that lost players at the end of their contract, provided this was restricted to the real costs incurred in training the player, along the lines suggested by Advocate-General Lenz in the *Bosman* case[2].

1 See paras E2.92 et seq.
2 See para B2.156.

B2.168 Interestingly, the agreed principles provide that national football associations are obliged to organise their domestic transfer regimes according to these new norms. Consequently, in future it seems that domestic transfer regimes will also follow these principles endorsed by the European Commission. The new FIFA rules also provide for a dispute resolution and arbitration system, although it is expressly stated that this is 'without prejudice to the right of any player or club to seek redress before a civil court'[1].

1 See further paras A5.135 to A5.138.

B2.169 The principles agreed with the Commission do not take the form of an exemption decision within the meaning of Art 81(3) of the Treaty. Essentially, what the Commission has done is to discontinue the previous competition case against FIFA rather than give formal legal approval to the new arrangements[1]. It remains the case, therefore, that some interested party (player, club, agent) may still challenge one or other aspect of the new transfer rules. It seems unlikely, however, that a national court (or the European Court of Justice) would feel disposed to interfere with the content of this agreement given the Commission's implicit (if not explicit) approval of the system.

1 See 'Commission closes investigation into FIFA regulations on international transfers', press release dated 5 June 2002, IP/02/824.

B2.170 The fact that the international players' union (FIFPRO) has now given its support to the agreement would, in practice, probably constitute an additional disincentive for any judge to rule against the system. Putting the matter differently, it could be argued that the new transfer system now has some elements of a genuine 'collective bargaining' type arrangement. Interestingly, such 'collective bargaining' agreements are outside the reach of anti-trust law in the United States on the basis of what is called the 'labour exemption'[1]. Whilst there is no identical 'exemption' in the EU, it would nevertheless be unusual if a court did not at least take account of the position of the 'workers' on such a regulatory system before opining on the legality of it.

1 See eg Weiler and Roberts *Sports and the Law* (1998, West), p 188 et seq.

(b) Transfer deadlines

B2.171 Many sports have rules that prevent clubs from registering new players after a certain point in the season. Such rules might be portrayed as restricting competition between clubs on the market for the services of players. Nevertheless, the purpose of such rules is to preserve the integrity of the competition and to prevent the distortion of results by ensuring that teams do not buy in talent at critical points in the season, if (for example) they appear to have a better than anticipated chance of winning a championship or a promotion.

B2.172 In the *Lehtonen* case[1], the European Court of Justice was asked to determine the compatibility of such transfer deadlines with both the competition rules and the rules on free movement of workers. The deadline in question prevented basketball clubs from fielding in national championships any player who had already played in another country in the same 'zone', unless the player was transferred before the relevant deadline.

1 Case C-176/96, *Jyri Lehtonen and Castors Canada Dry Namur-Braine ASBL v Fédération Royale Belge des Sociétés de Basket-ball ASBL (FRBSB)* [2000] ECR I-2681.

B2.173 In fact, the European Court of Justice declined to pronounce on the compatibility of such transfer deadlines with competition law (on the basis that it had not been provided with sufficient information by the national court that referred the question). However, it did address the question under the free movement provisions of the Treaty. It held that the transfer deadlines constituted a *de facto* obstacle to freedom of movement of workers since they were liable to restrict the free movement of players by preventing clubs in one member state from fielding players from other member states if they were engaged after a specified date. Nevertheless, it considered that the rules might be justifiable on 'non-economic grounds concerning only sport as such', since the setting of such deadlines may meet the objective of 'ensuring the regularity of sporting competitions'. Late transfers could substantially alter the sporting strength of one or other team in the course of the championship, thus calling into question the 'proper functioning' of sporting competition. Having said this, to be lawful such measures also had to satisfy the 'proportionality' test, ie they could not go beyond what was necessary for achieving the aim pursued[1].

1 Case C-176/96, *Jyri Lehtonen and Castors Canada Dry Namur-Braine ASBL v Fédération Royale Belge des Sociétés de Basket-ball ASBL (FRBSB)* [2000] ECR I-2681.

B2.174 In this connection, the Court of Justice observed that players from a federation *outside* the European zone were subject to a transfer deadline of 31 March, whereas players *inside* the European zone were subject to a transfer deadline of 28 February. On this basis, the Court of Justice thought, at first sight, that the rule 'must be regarded as going beyond what was necessary' as no evidence was presented to show why the transfer of a player between 28 February and 31 March from a federation *inside* the European zone would jeopardise the course of the championship more than a transfer in the same period of a player from a federation *outside* the European zone. However, this was ultimately a question for the national court to determine[1].

1 Case C-176/96, *Jyri Lehtonen and Castors Canada Dry Namur-Braine ASBL v Fédération Royale Belge des Sociétés de Basket-ball ASBL (FRBSB)* [2000] ECR I-2681.

B2.175 Following on from that judgment, the Commission made it clear in its discussions with FIFA over football's transfer rules that 'in order to avoid disruption of championships, the Commission would be prepared to accept rules which require transfer to take place within the specified period only'[1]. And as noted above[2], the rules eventually agreed included two transfer 'windows' per season, outside which transfers may not take place, the justification being the need to protect the 'regularity and proper functioning of sporting competition'[3].

1 Reding *'Commission's investigation into FIFA's transfer rules; statement to European Parliament'* (DN: Speech/00/290, 7 September 2000, para 4).

2 See para B2.166.

3 Subsequently, however, the Football League sought and eventually obtained from FIFA an exemption for its members from the pre-Christmas transfer embargo on the ground that such embargo would have a devastating effect on its member clubs' finances. See eg 'English soccer hits out at FIFA's new transfer system' (2002) Sportcal.com, 16 May. See also 'FIFA lifts transfer window for unemployed players' (2002) Sportcal.com, 13 September.

(c) *Selection of national teams*

B2.176 The European Court of Justice has even been asked to consider whether rules relating to the selection of athletes to represent their national team may infringe one or other provision of the EC Treaty (including the competition provisions). This was the subject of discussion in the *Deliège* case[1], a matter which concerned national selection rules in the sport of judo.

1 Joined Cases C-51/96 and C-191/97, *Christelle Deliège v Ligue Francophone de Judo et Disciplines Associées ASBL, Deliège and Ligue Belge de Judo ASBL, Union Européenne de Judo; Christelle Deliège v Ligue Francophone de Judo et Disciplines Associées ASBL, Ligue Belge de Judo ASBL, François Pacquée* [2000] ECR I-2549. This was not a challenge to the rule restricting eligibility for national representative teams to nationals of the country in question. (See para B2.110). Deliege was Belgian. Rather, the challenge was to the way that Belgian judokas were selected to compete for their national side.

B2.177 It goes without saying that only a limited number of players can participate in any given sporting event. However, in this case, Deliège (a highly accomplished judoka) claimed that the Belgian judo federation had improperly frustrated her career by failing to select her for the national team, thus encroaching on her right to 'provide services' and on her professional freedom. The case may be seen as perhaps the high-water mark of ridiculous sports-related legal disputes emanating from the Belgian courts.

B2.178 In any event, the European Court of Justice considered that although the selection rules had the effect of limiting the number of participants in a tournament, that limitation was inherent in the conduct of an international high-level sports event, which necessarily involved certain selection rules (and limits on the number of participants). Such rules could not, in themselves, constitute a restriction on the freedom to provide services prohibited by Art 49 of the Treaty.

1 Joined Cases C-51/96 and C-191/97, *Christelle Deliège v Ligue Francophone de Judo et Disciplines Associées ASBL, Deliège and Ligue Belge de Judo ASBL, Union Européenne de Judo; Christelle Deliège v Ligue Francophone de Judo et Disciplines Associées ASBL, Ligue Belge de Judo ASBL, François Pacquée* [2000] ECR I-2549.

B2.179 The court also accepted that the selection system for an international sports tournament must be based on a large number of considerations unconnected with the personal situation of any athlete, such as the nature of, or organisation and financing of, the sport concerned. Although a selection system may prove more favourable to one category of athletes than another, it could not be inferred from that fact alone that the adoption of such a system constituted a restriction on the freedom to provide services[1].

1 Joined Cases C-51/96 and C-191/97, *Christelle Deliège v Ligue Francophone de Judo et Disciplines Associées ASBL, Deliège and Ligue Belge de Judo ASBL, Union Européenne de Judo; Christelle Deliège v Ligue Francophone de Judo et Disciplines Associées ASBL, Ligue Belge de Judo ASBL, François Pacquée* [2000] ECR I-2549.

B2.180 Finally, the court stated that it was for the sports federations and organisers of tournaments to lay down appropriate rules and make selections accordingly, and that 'the delegation of such a task to the national federations, which normally have the necessary knowledge and experience, is the arrangement adopted in most sporting disciplines, which is based in principle on the existence of a federation in each country'[1].

1 Joined Cases C-51/96 and C-191/97, *Christelle Deliège v Ligue Francophone de Judo et Disciplines Associées ASBL, Deliège and Ligue Belge de Judo ASBL, Union Européenne de Judo; Christelle Deliège v Ligue Francophone de Judo et Disciplines Associées ASBL, Ligue Belge de Judo ASBL, François Pacquée* [2000] ECR I-2549.

B2.181 In sum, therefore, the court held that a selection rule that derives from a need inherent in the organisation of sporting competition could not, in itself, constitute a restriction on the freedom to provide services prohibited by Art 49 of the Treaty. Furthermore, sports bodies enjoyed a degree of discretion in deciding what these selection rules should be. Once again, although not expressed in such terms, this is the 'sporting exception' to the competition rules[1] at work.

1 See paras B2.56 to B2.61, and B2.95.

(d) Player-agent regulations

B2.182 In the modern era of professional sport, with an increasing number of opportunities for players to exploit their talents commercially, it is not surprising that the role of the agent has come to the fore. Often resented by team coaches, agents may nevertheless perform a valuable service to their player clients. However, it is also a fact that many agents probably stand to generate their largest commission when a player transfers from one team to another, and so they may have a vested interest in provoking a move. Many sports governing bodies have therefore identified a need to regulate the activities of those who act as agents for individual players, in order to establish uniform professional and ethical standards and safeguard the wider interests of the sport. However, it is not possible for a sports governing body to lay down arbitrary or unduly 'restrictive' criteria for regulating the activities of agents. An important precedent in this respect may be found in the case which the Commission brought against FIFA concerning its rules on agents.

B2.183 The FIFA rules banned players and clubs from using the services of agents who were not licensed by FIFA and prohibited companies (as opposed to individuals) from applying to be licensed. The grant of a licence was also conditional on the provision of a non-returnable, non-interest-bearing bank guarantee of CHF 200,000.

B2.184 In response to a number of complaints, the Commission began an investigation and, in October 1999, issued a statement of objections in which it asserted that the FIFA player-agent rules contravened Art 81(1) of the Treaty by limiting access to the player-agent market, especially by requiring payment of what was considered to be an overly large deposit. The Commission thought the benefits of the regulatory system could be achieved by less restrictive means and were not sufficient grounds to offset the anti-competitive nature of the rules:

> The rules prevent or restrict natural or legal persons with the necessary vocational skills from having access to the job. The Commission recognises that there must be checks on access to the profession and that some rules are necessary in order to ensure smooth operation and to prevent any deterioration in the ethical values in sport. However, the rules must be in proportion to the objective pursued. There are clearly other rules which could ensure professionalism on the part of agents without being unduly restrictive[1].

1 Commission press release dated 21 October 1999, IP/99/782.

B2.185 In response to the Commission's pressure, FIFA revised its rules to dispense with the requirement that agents post a CHF 200,000 guarantee to get a licence. Instead, the revised rules allowed player-agents to obtain professional liability insurance to cover any claims for compensation arising from their activities. It was set out that player-agents also had to pass an exam and sign a Code of Professional Conduct containing principles of professional integrity, transparency, honesty and fair management of interests. They were also required to keep accurate accounts of their business transactions.

B2.186 In April 2002, the Commission announced that it was satisfied that these revisions removed the 'most restrictive provisions' of the FIFA rules[1]. The Commission acknowledged the right of FIFA 'to regulate the profession in an attempt to promote good practice, as long as access remains open and non-discriminatory'. The Commission also stated that any remaining restrictions in the system were justified by the legitimate interest of FIFA in extending good practice and protecting the sport from the practice of unscrupulous agents. It therefore, announced its closure of the case, with the following caveat:

> [S]hould it later emerge that these objectives can be achieved without the FIFA rules because, for example, member states regulate the profession or because players' agents are able to introduce self-regulation while ensuring a high level of professionalism and integrity, the Commission could review the rules[2].

1 Commission press release dated 18 April 2002, IP/02/585.
2 See n 1.

(e) Salary caps

B2.187 Many sources blame professional football's current financial woes on the massive escalation in player wages. For example, most FA Premier League clubs spend a seemingly unsustainable proportion of their turnover on player wages[1]. The wage inflation is driven by a desire to compete not only on the domestic stage but also in UEFA cross-border competitions against elite foreign clubs. The biggest clubs, driven to capture the riches of European competition, are paying players millions of pounds a year.

1 Deloitte & Touche *Annual Report on Football Finances, 1996/2002*.

B2.188 One apparent solution would be a restriction in the rules on the amount of money that each club can pay on player wages, ie a salary cap[1]. Salary caps already exist in rugby league, rugby union and basketball in England, as well as in European ice hockey and basketball leagues. They are also of course a central feature of the big four professional sports in the United States (baseball, basketball, grid-iron football and ice-hockey). In May 2001, UEFA indicated it wished to generate a debate about the pros and cons of introducing salary caps to European football[2]; and in May 2002 the G-14 clubs announced their support[3].

1 See eg Boon 'A time for salary caps – the financial case' [2002] 10(1) SATLJ 118. See further para E1.84 et seq.
2 Gardiner and Gray 'Will Salary Caps Fit European Professional Football?' (2001) 4(3) Sports Law Bulletin 14. See also 'UEFA tells EU: Salary Caps would Guarantee Equality' (2002) Sportcal.com, 19 April.
3 'G14 soccer clubs in favour of salary caps' (2002) Sportcal.com, 16 May (claiming EC Culture Commissioner Viviene Reding had offered to help draft the proposals).

B2.189 Obviously salary caps restrict the ability of clubs to compete with each other for the services of players, and would therefore appear to be anti-competitive. The argument in response would be that salary caps:

(a) maintain the economic viability of teams competing in the league; and
(b) preserve competitive balance between clubs[1].

The latter is very difficult on a pan-European basis. Any system would have to apply to *all* clubs throughout Europe, or indeed throughout the world[2].

1 *Johnson v Cliftonville Football and Athletic Club* [1984] 1 NI 9, 21, Ch D. See also Cleary (2000) Telegraph, 23 August: *Evans welcome wage-capping* (Harlequins chief executive claims salary cap has saved professional rugby union in England); Gardiner and Gray 'Will Salary Caps Fit European Professional Football?' (2001) 4(3) Sports Law Bulletin 14. See also 'UEFA tells EU: Salary Caps Would Guarantee Equality' (2002) Sportcal.com, 19 April. Salary caps in US professional sports have survived antitrust attack because they are deemed to be restrictions agreed as part of a collective bargaining arrangement and therefore to be covered by the labour exemption to the antitrust laws. See Weiler and Roberts *Sports and the Law* (1998, West), p 188 et seq.
2 See Harris 'Salary Caps' [2002] 10(1) SATLJ 120; Bishop 'Controlling the Wage Spiral' (NERA 1999), p 3; Glendinning 'Does the Cap Fit?' (June 2002) Football Business International p 8; (2002) Times, 23 September (reporting that the European Rugby Clubs Association is considering whether to bring in a European-wide salary cap). Other difficulties with a salary cap system include evasion (and the policing necessary to limit it), the differences in exchange rates, taxation and cost of living in different countries, and the difficulty of splitting (for example) image rights income from playing income.

B2.190 To withstand a challenge, it would be absolutely necessary to have buy-in from the players' unions, eg the PFA and/or FIFPRO[1]. Even then, it is difficult to see how such a system could be said to be the least restrictive means of achieving the objectives of preserving competitive balance and maintaining economic viability[2]. Tellingly, the Commission was quick to fire a warning shot across the bows of the G-14 members' May 2002 salary cap proposal[3].

1 See para B2.170. See also Gardiner and Gray 'Will Salary Caps Fit European Professional Football?' (2001) 4(3) Sports Law Bulletin 14.
2 See generally Harris 'Salary Caps' [2002] 10(1) SATLJ 120; Harris 'The Benefits of The Team Salary Cap in English Rugby League' [1999] 7(3) SATLJ 88; Gardiner and Gray 'Will Salary Caps Fit European Professional Football?' (2001) 4(3) Sports Law Bulletin 14; Tsatsas 'Is it time for English football to adopt a salary cap?' [2001] 2 SATLJ 126; Farrell 'Salary Caps and Restraint of Trade' [1997] 5 (1) SATLJ 53; Buti 'Salary caps in professional team sports: an unreasonable restraint of trade' (1999) 14 Journal of Contract Law 130 (examining salary caps in relation to Australian professional team sports). It was left open in *Adamson v NSWRL* (1991) 100 ALR 479, (1991) 27 FCR 535, on appeal (1991) 103 ALR 319, (1991) 31 FCR 242, whether the salary cap in place in Australian rugby league was legal. See also *Johnson v Cliftonville Football and Athletic Club* [1984] 1 NI 9, Ch D.
3 Frost 'Commission could call "foul" on soccer deal' (2002) European Voice (30 May).

D Sports equipment

B2.191 The role that equipment plays in sport varies greatly from one sport to the next. At one end of the spectrum, sports like motor-racing and sailing are very 'equipment-intensive'. At the other end of the spectrum are sports like swimming, where one would have thought that equipment would play a minimal role. Even in the latter case, however, technological developments have greatly increased the significance of equipment in the sporting contest.

B2.192 The development of sports equipment presents governing bodies with both challenges and opportunities. It presents challenges, in that technological developments can threaten the character, integrity, fairness and/or safety of sporting competition, all of which it is the governing body's responsibility to safeguard. It also presents opportunities, however, in that manufacturers/suppliers may be willing to pay significant fees to secure their position in the sports equipment market.

B2.193 Competition law issues are raised by:

(1) the regulation of the use of equipment on 'sporting' grounds, for example to safeguard the integrity of the competition; and
(2) commercial arrangements made by governing bodies/event organisers with one or more suppliers of sports equipment.

(a) Regulating the use of equipment on 'sporting' grounds

B2.194 Most sports bodies have rules that regulate on 'sporting' grounds the type of equipment that can be used in competitions that they organise. This may be to improve the sport as a spectacle, to safeguard the character of the sport as a test of human skill, or to ensure the safety and enjoyment of participants. Above all, these regulations may be aimed to ensure that the playing-field is level, so that uncertainty of outcome is preserved.

B2.195 Two examples of the equipment regulatory function hit the headlines in 2000. In March 2000, golf equipment manufacturer Callaway launched a new driver, the 'ERC Forged Titanium Driver'. It claimed that, as a result of improvements in design and technology, the club hit the ball a lot further. The US governing body, the USGA, banned use of the club in its competitions, on the ground that it infringed the USGA's long-established 'spring-like effect' standard. The Canadian governing body, the RCGA, promptly adopted the USGA's ban, on the basis that Canadian players also participate extensively in USGA competitions, and so any discrepancy in authorised equipment between USGA and RCGA events was undesirable[1]. The European governing body, the R&A (whose rules govern golf played outside North America) was more circumspect, announcing that, while it also believed that developments allowing golfers to hit the ball further simply by use of technology rather than individual skill were 'not in the best long-term interests of the game', it would not make any rulings on specific equipment until a test protocol had been established and the comments of manufacturers received and considered. Subsequently, it accepted the USGA's test protocol and adopted the same ban on use of the driver at the professional level[2].

1 On 8 May 2000, Callaway filed suit against the RCGA in US federal court, claiming (among other things) that the RCGA's simple adoption of the USGA's ban amounted to an unfair and arbitrary abuse of the RCGA's regulatory powers.
2 'Tour outlaws "trampoline" drivers' (2002) Independent, 10 May.

B2.196 The second example comes from swimming. Rule 10.7 of the Rules of Swimming of FINA, the international governing body of swimming, provides that: '[n]o swimmer shall be permitted to use or wear any device that may aid his speed, buoyancy or endurance during a competition (such as webbed gloves, flippers, fins etc)'. In October 1999, each of Speedo and Adidas made presentations to FINA about a new bodysuit it was developing using technological advancements (in Speedo's case, a design intended to mimic shark skin) to enhance performance by increasing speed and reducing drag. Subsequently, FINA declared that such bodysuits were not 'technical equipment', to which Rule 10.7 applied, but rather 'costumes', which fall outside the scope of Rule 10.7, and so could be used in official competitions[1].

1 Perhaps unsurprisingly, an attempt was made to challenge that decision. The Australian Olympic Committee, concerned about complaints by swimmers who lost out in Olympic trials or the Olympics themselves to competitors wearing such bodysuits, asked the Court of Arbitration for Sport for an advisory opinion on the merits of FINA's ruling. The CAS refused to intervene, holding that none of the limited grounds on which it might interfere with a governing body's decision were present in this case. CAS Advisory Opinion, TAS 2000/C/267, award dated 1 May 2000, *Digest of CAS Awards II 1998–2000* (2002, Kluwer), p 725.

B2.197 What limits does competition law place, then, on the ability of governing bodies to regulate equipment use on sporting grounds? The starting point here seems to be that the rules in favour of free competition apply to the distribution of sports goods in the same way as they apply to the distribution of any other product. As the ultimate regulatory authority for the sport worldwide, with the power to set conditions for access to/participation in the sport, including conditions regarding the equipment that can be used, it might be argued that the governing body is in a 'dominant position' and is able to use (or abuse) that dominance to restrict competition on a market for sports equipment. A rule laying down conditions for equipment to be used in official competitions may create a 'barrier to entry' to an equipment market and might, therefore, possibly restrict competition.

B2.198 Probably the key issue for the governing body here is that, whenever it regulates this area, it must be able to justify its decisions on an objective basis, and demonstrate that it has not discharged its regulatory powers in a manner that is disproportionate, arbitrary or discriminatory. Provided it can satisfy these legal tests, the regulatory decisions of a sports governing body should not be 'second-guessed' by a competition authority.

B2.199 This position finds support in comments made by the European Commission. For example, a Commission policy document dating from 1999 states:

> Problems may arise in respect of competition law … in the context of rules and standards laid down to govern the specification of sports goods. Such standards may be considered necessary, for example:
>
> – in order to improve sporting performance or spectator appeal;
> – to ensure that similar equipment is used by all competitors in the interests of fairness;
> – or for reasons of safety.
>
> As long as these rules remain objective, and as long as there is no difficulty in demonstrating that goods comply with the appropriate standards, there is no reason for the Commission to intervene on competition policy grounds. Nevertheless, where there appear to be arbitrary or discriminatory practices on the part of governing bodies in sport, or by tournament organisers, the rules on competition may be applicable and official action by national authorities or the Commission may become necessary.

> [O]ne of the abuses regularly banned under Article 86 [now 81] is the restriction of production, markets or technical development to the detriment of consumers. Consequently, a sports organisation would probably be committing an infringement of Article 86 [now 81] if it used its regulatory power to exclude from the market, without an objective reason, any competing organiser or any economic operator who, even if he met the justified quality or safety standards, was not able to obtain a quality or safety certificate for his products from the organisation or if, in order to obtain it, he had to satisfy non-objective conditions that were not related to such a certification system[1].

1 *Draft Preliminary Guidelines on the Application of the Competition Rules to Sport*, unpublished Commission memorandum (15 February 1999). Much of the substance of this draft memorandum has also appeared in public Commission documents. See eg Pons *Sport and European Competition Policy* (October 1999); Commission press release dated 24 February 1999, IP/99/133; Schaub *EC Competition Policy and its Implications for the Sports Sector* (8 March 1998) (quality requirements 'must be reasonable. They must not be a disguised means of pushing customers to prefer the products of one or other manufacturer; moreover, the quality certification system itself must be fair, open and transparent').

B2.200 In its 1995 study on sport and the EU[1], Coopers & Lybrand referred to the Commission's decision on a complaint by Tretorn regarding the Lawn Tennis Association's rule requiring the use in LTA-sanctioned competitions of pressurised balls:

> Tretorn happens to be the only large manufacturer which does not make pressurised balls (although it does made grade 1 balls) and therefore feels it is being arbitrarily discriminated against. The UK federation said it preferred pressurised balls because they respond faster. The Commission has told Tretorn that as long as the UK federation has technical reasons for its decision, it has no cause to act. The only exception is if Tretorn can prove that the rule has been set up with a view to excluding Tretorn, a situation which would be extremely difficult to prove[2].

1 Coopers & Lybrand *The Impact of EU Activities on Sport* (1995).
2 Coopers & Lybrand *The Impact of EU Activities on Sport* (1995), para 4074.

(b) Regulating the use of equipment for commercial purposes

B2.201 One example of a 'non-objective' criterion that is likely to be frowned on would be a requirement that manufacturers pay a governing body or event organiser a royalty fee over and above the costs of any quality approval scheme in order to gain access to the sport. Here it might be argued that products that have been made to the appropriate specifications are nevertheless excluded simply because a manufacturer refuses to pay a fee for obtaining approval. In this type of situation, governing bodies must be careful not to use regulatory powers in an unfair manner to derive commercial benefit from equipment manufacturers. When governing bodies and event organisers move into this commercial sphere, the degree of deference afforded to their decisions by competition regulators will decrease considerably.

B2.202 A good example of a controversial case in this area related to the so-called FIFA 'Denominations' Scheme. Prior to 1995, the FIFA Laws of the Game laid down only limited technical criteria for footballs, relating to shape, weight and size, but without reference to other specifications such as bounce, water absorption, or pressure. In order to provide uniform standards in the interests of the sport[1], FIFA adopted its 'Denominations Programme' in March 1995. This was a testing, certification and licensing scheme for footballs, incorporating:

(a) the adoption of a common technical standard for match quality footballs;
(b) a FIFA rule specifying that only footballs meeting the standard could be used in certain FIFA-governed matches; and
(c) the implementation of a certification procedure pursuant to which an independent agency certifies the balls as meeting the technical standard.

The scheme involved stamping a ball either 'FIFA Approved' or 'FIFA Inspected' or 'International Matchball Standard'. A licence fee was payable for one of the FIFA designations. However, there was no licence fee payable for the 'International Matchball Standard' designation.

1 Other objectives identified by FIFA included making policing easier for referees, controlling use of the FIFA mark (and thereby protecting consumers from being misled into buying poor quality products), and promoting ethical standards in the manufacture of footballs.

B2.203 Under the FIFA Laws of the Game:

(1) in competitions organised by FIFA or one of its regional confederations, a ball bearing one of the three designations has to be used; and
(2) in domestic competitions, a national association may (but does not have to) require the use of a FIFA-marked ball. However, if it does so require, it also has to allow the use of the 'International Matchball Standard' as an alternative.

B2.204 The Commission started an investigation in 1996 with the aim of establishing whether or not this Denominations scheme was operating in the manner claimed, ie to determine whether manufacturers had a real choice and could market their products without paying the FIFA royalty, by obtaining the 'International Matchball Standard' designation. This investigation was apparently prompted by a complaint filed by a trade body representing sports equipment manufacturers, the World Federation of the Sporting Goods Industry[1]. The Commission went so far as to conduct 'dawn raids' at the offices of the English, Danish and French football associations to collect evidence for their investigation.

1 Case No IV/F-1/35.266 (FIFA).

B2.205 The outcome seems to have been a determination by the Commission that manufacturers whose footballs met the objective criteria did have an option:

(a) they could pay the royalty, and obtain the benefit of the FIFA stamp of approval[1]; or
(b) if they do not wish to pay the royalty, they can still access the market by obtaining 'International Matchball Standard' designation.

The technical criteria were found to be uniform, objective and necessary for the guarantee of high standards in footballs for official matches. As such they did not pose any competition law concerns. The Commission therefore rejected the complaint which had been filed by the World Federation of the Sporting Goods Industry in relation to the Denominations Programme[2].

1 FIFA has advertised its scheme to the sports industry using the slogan: 'Score more business with FIFA's new marking scheme.' And manufacturers who pay extra for the FIFA hallmark also get the benefit of a FIFA marketing support programme directed at all domestic football authorities, the sports goods trade and consumers.
2 Commission decision letter dated December 2000, Case No IV/F-1/35.266 (FIFA).

B2.206 It may be inferred that this case that if, as a result of a regulatory provision, a manufacturer has no option other than to pay a fee to the governing body that includes a royalty element in order to access the market, the governing body may be in danger of a finding of abuse of dominant position. On the other hand, if there is a genuine option to gain access to the market without paying such a royalty, the governing body would be entitled to charge an additional fee for the right to use its stamp of approval as an additional marketing device.

B2.207 Another case in this domain was the decision taken by the Commission in 1998, in the Danish Tennis Federation ('DTF') case, relating to the use of 'official' balls[1]. The DTF had granted certain manufacturers the right to attach labels to their tennis balls bearing the DTF logo and identifying the balls as 'official' balls that had been approved by the DTF. The DTF then required that only such 'official' balls be used in competitions that it organised, as well as in competitions falling within its jurisdiction.

1 Case Nos IV/F-1/33.055 and 35.759, [1996] 4 CMLR 885.

B2.208 This was not an equipment approval scheme per se and seems to have had little (if anything) to do with safety or technical considerations. Instead, it was more of a commercial arrangement under which the DTF secured a rights fee from the supplier in return for the right to use the logo and the 'official' designation, as well as the exclusive right to supply the balls for certain competitions. There were also measures taken to prevent parallel imports of the balls, and to punish (by forfeiture of matches) those who used other balls in official competitions.

B2.209 Various manufacturers complained that these arrangements infringed EC competition law and the Commission agreed, sending a statement of objections to the DTF on this basis. It also criticised the 'official' denomination on the basis that its use could 'mislead consumers into believing that the products which benefit [from the denomination] are technically superior to or of better quality than others, which is not always the case'[1].

1 'The Commission conditionally approves sponsorship contracts between the Danish Tennis Federation and its tennis ball suppliers', Commission press release dated 15 April 1998, IP/98/355.

B2.210 Consequently, the DTF revised its arrangements in various ways. Any manufacturer whose balls met minimum objective criteria could join a 'pool' of manufacturers entitled to use the DTF logo, even if they did not supply the federation directly. Manufacturers in the ball pool could compete in a regular tender to be appointed to supply balls for DTF tournaments. To avoid the risk of consumer confusion identified by the Commission, the manufacturer that won the contract to supply the federation could not call itself 'official supplier', or state that its products were 'official balls'. Instead, it would call itself 'sponsor of the DTF'. The Commission approved these amended arrangements[1].

1 1998 Competition Report, p 160. See 'The Commission conditionally approves sponsorship contracts between the Danish Tennis Federation and its tennis ball suppliers', Commission press release dated 15 April 1998, IP/98/355. A similar arrangement was reached with respect to tennis balls in the UK, whereby sponsors who had previously been given the title 'official supplier' became instead 'members of a tennis ball sponsoring group': Coopers & Lybrand *The Impact of EU Activities on Sport* (1995) at para 4065.

B2.211 The case confirms that sports bodies have the right to require that equipment used in their competitions meets certain quality standards. They cannot, however, use their 'official' stamp of approval to give a chosen manufacturer an edge over its competitors that is not justified on the basis of technical quality. The case also suggests that sports bodies would be well advised to ensure that the appointment process for suppliers of equipment is fair and open and does not unreasonably shut out certain companies from the market[1]. The word 'official' (when it is used) should be to clearly denote a relationship of sponsorship, rather than be suggestive of quality superior to that of rival manufacturers[2].

1 See para B2.316.
2 See para B2.317.

E Ticketing

(a) The regulatory and commercial objectives

B2.212 The core revenue stream for many sports comes from the sale of admission tickets allowing purchasers to attend the event. For the top sports events, demand for such tickets usually far outstrips supply.

B2.213 This may sound like good news for the event organiser, but it can raise several regulatory concerns. First, it may be seen as important to ensure that a certain number of tickets go to reward volunteers whose efforts support the grass roots of the game. Secondly, to 'advertise' the sport and fuel its future growth it is important to keep the event 'affordable' and so accessible to the general public. On the other hand, it is important to raise funds to plough back into the game. One way to do so may be to create official hospitality programmes, appointing commercial partners who pay a premium in return for a supply of tickets. These corporate customers may generate revenues for the sport, and effectively subsidise the 'ordinary' fan, but the balance needs to be struck carefully to ensure that the atmosphere and character of the event is not undermined. Likewise, in international events it is important to ensure fans from all of the participating nations have access, to reflect the global nature of the event and of the sport. In sports afflicted by hooliganism, the need to segregate supporters may be important.

B2.214 Achievement of these objectives depends on the ability to keep tickets to the distribution channels to which they have been allocated. Otherwise, a secondary ('black') market will likely develop in which tickets are sold at substantial margins by opportunistic third parties. This allows unauthorised (and non-quality-controlled) operators to exploit for their own benefit the goodwill that the organisers have built up in the event.

B2.215 Therefore, many event organisers work out sophisticated distribution plans for tickets, involving a number of different distribution channels, to different categories of consumer, including specific allocations to 'official' hospitality providers and tour and travel providers, backed up and enforced by means of non-transferability conditions incorporated into the conditions of sale of the tickets themselves[1]. Such arrangements have periodically come under competition law challenge, particularly from unauthorised entities who would like to compete in the market for admission tickets, packaged with other services or otherwise, to such events.

1 See paras D1.129 and D1.130.

(b) Market definition in ticketing cases

B2.216 Notwithstanding the regulatory objectives that may underlie ticketing arrangements, their central economic function means they cannot be said to fall within the 'sporting exception'[1] to the EC competition rules[2]. However, as with all competition cases, an important preliminary question to address when analysing a competition law challenge to ticketing arrangements is the definition of the relevant market on which the arrangements operate[3]. As mentioned above, this issue normally involves analysing issues of 'demand substitution'[4]. However, whether or not a ticket to a sports event is 'substitutable' (ie a ticket to another event may be an adequate substitute and therefore the tickets to the two events are in the same market) may depend on the category of purchaser being considered.

1 See paras B2.56 to B2.61.
2 The analogy would be to the rule restricting common ownership, which has a clear regulatory objective but has too direct an economic effect (at least in the view of the Court of Arbitration for Sport) to fall within the exception. See para B2.149.
3 See paras B2.76 to B2.88.
4 See para B2.82.

B2.217 The supply of a ticket direct to the individual who will attend the event may be materially different (in terms of characteristics, price and intended use) to the supply of tickets to businesses that intend to package them up for resale together with other products or services. The individual wants to see a particular match; the business wants access to any attraction around which to build a package through which it can sell its own products, whether they be travel and accommodation arrangements or corporate hospitality. Moving on to the next level of supply, the demand for corporate hospitality packages comes from those in charge of marketing budgets at large corporations, who are simply looking for a high quality event at which to entertain their clients, and (provided the requisite level of quality and prestige is present) could be said to be indifferent to whether the particular event is the Cup Final or Royal Ascot or the Lord's Test, or indeed a non-sporting event (such as a private viewing of a Matisse exhibition at the National Gallery).

B2.218 Past decisions of the European Commission in this area are of limited value. For example, in its only published full decision on the sale of tickets to sports events, *Italia '90*[1], the Commission did not even attempt to analyse the relevant market in detail, but appears simply to have worked on the basis that tickets to the 1990 FIFA World Cup Finals formed a distinct market at all levels of supply[2]. Nor does it appear that any detailed market definition was attempted in the various *Olympics* cases[3]. Instead, again, it appears to have assumed that tickets to the Olympics formed a distinct market at all levels of supply.

1 *Re World Cup 1990 Package Tours: Pauwels Travel Bvba v FIFA Local Organising Committee Italia '90*, Commission decision of 27 October 1992, OJ L 326, 12/11/92, p 31, [1994] 5 CMLR 253. See para B2.222.
2 It may well be that, had the Commission undertaken an analysis of the relevant market in *Italia '90*, it would have concluded (as instead it simply assumed) that tickets to the Football World Cup are non-substitutable (ie its attraction is such that tickets to no other event are an adequate substitutable) at any level of supply. This appears likely given the Commission's approach to defining the relevant market in the broadcasting context, which is that elite football is in a market of its own. See para B2.243. It can be argued that the appointment of (for example) one tour operator in relation to any *other* event, however, does not have an appreciable effect because the market properly defined is not confined (as in *Italia '90*) to the supply to tour operators of tickets to the particular tournament to be included in ticket and travel packages. If the market properly analysed is the market for the supply to tour operators of tickets to any

major sporting event for packaging together with travel arrangements, then one event organiser's share of the market will be small. The implicit approach in *Italia '90* is however that the market is confined to the individual event.

3 *Albertville*, *Barcelona* unreported, Commission press release dated 16 July 1992, IP/92/593; *Atlanta*, unreported, 1996 Competition Report, p 144.

B2.219 A more instructive decision on market definition in ticketing cases can be found in the analysis of the Office of Fair Trading in the *Wimbledon* case[1]. In that case, an 'unofficial' hospitality provider complained about the exclusive appointment by the organisers of the Wimbledon tournament of two official agents to provide hospitality packaged with tickets at the event. The conditions printed on tickets issued for admission to the tournament prohibited the resale or other commercial use of tickets. It was alleged that the exclusive appointment and supply of tickets to the official agents, backed up by the non-transferability condition of sale of tickets to the general public, restricted competition in the market to supply packages of hospitality services and admission tickets to the Wimbledon championship. The OFT rejected the complaint on the grounds, inter alia, that the relevant market in which the restriction has to be assessed was much broader than the market to supply corporate hospitality at Wimbledon alone:

> The market for corporate hospitality is huge. Demand for corporate hospitality comes from companies wishing to entertain clients and may be satisfied at a great number of sporting events. The requirement is for prestigious occasions, involving famous personalities and accompanying hospitality of a high standard. Race meetings, golf tournaments, rugby and football matches may all provide substitutes for Wimbledon tennis in this market, though the Club is clearly aware that its event is a very strong competitor, and the complainant is well aware of that too. The corporate hospitality market is a discrete market but it is likely that the ability of a company providing Wimbledon tickets within that market to raise its prices at will is very seriously constrained by the availability of other sporting fixtures and of other corporate hospitality events. The conclusion therefore is that there is no effective sub-market for corporate hospitality for Wimbledon.

On the basis of that market definition, the OFT concluded that the organisers did not have sufficient market power to restrict competition to an appreciable extent. This is an excellent example of how careful market definition can stop a competition law challenge in its tracks.

1 OFT press release no 20/93, dated 23 March 1993, announcing full decision of the DG FT of March 1993. Although the issues were discussed in that case in the context of the Fair Trading Act 1973, nevertheless the process of market definition under that Act is exactly the same as under the Competition Act 1998 and Arts 81 and 82 of the EC Treaty.

B2.220 Similarly, an unofficial hospitality provider brought proceedings in England alleging a breach of the competition rules as a result of the FA's exclusive appointment of two official hospitality providers in relation to its hosting of UEFA's 1996 European Championships. The English action was stayed when the FA amended its arrangements and notified them to the European Commission. Although no formal decision was published, it appears that the Commission accepted that, in that context, the market was not confined to the provision of hospitality at the particular event, even though the sport was football, but rather extended to hospitality at least at other major sports events within the temporal vicinity of the 1996 European Championships. The Commission apparently decided not to pursue the matter because the arrangements were considered not to have an appreciable effect on competition in such a market[1].

1 *Hospitality Group Ltd v Football Association Ltd* (24 January 1996, unreported) (Scott V-C). The English proceedings were not pursued thereafter because by that time the event had taken place. See further para A3.224.

A similar complaint was made to the European Commission in relation to the appointment of a single consortium of providers to provide official hospitality packages in relation to the Rugby World Cup 1999. As in the *Euro '96* case, so in relation to RWC 1999 the Commission took a broad view of the relevant market on which the arrangements operated, and the complaint was not acted upon.

For an example of a similar approach taken in an Australian competition law case, see *Australian Rugby Union v Hospitality Group Pty Ltd* [1992] FCA 1136 (Sackville J) ('The corporate hospitality market has grown rapidly in Australia over a short period of time and encompasses many different kinds of sporting and entertainment events in major population centres. Hospitality providers … offer packages to many different events and the evidence … suggests that there is a strong degree of substitutability among the various events'), upheld on appeal [2001] FCA 1040 (FCA 3 August 2001) para 60 ('It is obvious that there is plainly substitutability between hospitality packages for elite (or international) rugby matches and other events including, for that matter, opera or ballet, whether or not it is the case that some primary consumers might not be inclined to buy hospitality packages for other sports or cultural events. The fact that some purchasers in the market might only purchase hospitality packages for international rugby union matches does not prove the existence of a separate market in hospitality packages for such matches. It would be necessary to show that this was the case for a quite substantial number of purchasers of packages').

(c) General principles

B2.221 Exclusive appointments Event organisers are charged with the responsibility of raising funds for the sport and one way to do this is through the grant of exclusive rights. Typically, it is through exclusivity that a commercial partner is able to derive most value, and historically therefore event organisers have often granted exclusive ticket rights to 'official' tour operators and hospitality providers.

B2.222 Such arrangements may give rise to certain competition concerns, as seen in the *Italia '90* case[1]. On that occasion, the organisers of the 1990 Football World Cup in Italy appointed a single 'tour operator' as the sole supplier of tour and travel packages including tickets to the World Cup. This operator appointed travel agents in different member states to sell the packages. The Commission found that this arrangement restricted competition between tour operators (others could only provide travel to fans without an assured ticket) and also restricted competition between travel agents as they had no choice of tour operators with whom to bargain. FIFA made an (admittedly limp) attempt to justify the arrangements on grounds of crowd safety but this was rejected by the Commission.

1 *Re World Cup 1990 Package Tours: Pauwels Travel Bvba v FIFA Local Organising Committee Italia '90*, Commission decision of 27 October 1992, OJ L 326, 12/11/92, p 31, [1994] 5 CMLR 253.

B2.223 It would appear that, following the *Italia '90* decision, the organisers of the Barcelona and Albertville Olympic games amended their arrangements to withdraw exclusivity from their appointed tour operators by allowing nationals of EC member states also to buy tickets direct from the organisers or from travel agents distributing them in other member states[1]. The organisers of the 1999 Rugby World Cup, the 2000 UEFA Championships and the 2002 FIFA World Cup also avoided appointing tour operators with exclusive rights in Europe.

1 Commission press release dated 16 July 1992, IP/92/593.

B2.224 The *Italia '90* decision does not itself give an indication of how many tour operators or other ticket resellers ought to be appointed for any given sports event but it seems unlikely that the Commission would try to be prescriptive of this issue. Common sense suggests that the practicalities of organising a major sports dictate that there can only be a limited number. The answer probably is that there is no competition law objection to appointing a limited number of resellers, provided there is an open tendering process to determine who is appointed as a re-seller. Notably, in the case of the Atlanta Olympics, the Commission was prepared to accept the appointment of a limited number of undertakings selling tickets throughout the Community, so long as the appointments were made on the basis of a competitive tendering process, applying 'objective and non-discriminatory' selection criteria[1]. It also did not object to a similar approach in relation to Rugby World Cup 1999.

1 See 1996 Competition Report at p 144.

B2.225 Exclusive national sales territories In *Italia '90* and in the various Olympic Games cases, event organisers sought to limit resellers to selling tickets within their own national territories. The Commission has repeatedly taken the position that such arrangements are unlawful because they divide what is supposed to be a single market and they restrict competition between resellers in different member states. For example, the Commission intervened in the arrangements for distribution of tickets to the Atlanta Olympics to require the organisers to permit appointed European distributors to sell tickets anywhere within the Community, without discrimination[1]. Similar action was taken with respect to tickets for the Barcelona and Albertville Olympics[2].

1 1996 Competition Report at p 144.
2 Commission press release dated 16 July 1992, IP/92/593. See also 'Commission examines ticketing arrangements for next year's European Football Championships' Commission press release dated 5 May 1999, IP/99/304: 'The Commission is assessing UEFA's proposals [for the sale of match tickets to Euro 2000] with a view to ensuring that tickets are offered to European consumers under fair and, to the extent that is reasonable, non-discriminatory arrangements'.

B2.226 Segmentation of sales territories along national lines may be viewed more sympathetically in the case of football than might be the case in relation to other sports events. This is because there are concerns in football about security and the need to segregate rival supporters. These considerations do not really exist for other sporting events, such as the Olympic Games. Nevertheless, even in football, if territorial segmentation of ticket distribution goes over the top, this will also result in legal problems.

B2.227 In the *France '98* decision[1], the Commission concluded that ticket distribution arrangements that *in practice* discriminate in favour of residents of one member state (in this case the country hosting the event) may contravene the competition rules of the Treaty. In the case in question, it appears that the organisers only paid lip-service to the principle of 'non-discrimination' and failed to articulate security-based reasons for the arrangements that had been put into place. In practice, the organisers:

(a) required delivery of tickets to an address in France;
(b) provided French residents with a quicker purchasing system not available to non-residents; and
(c) took no real steps to inform non-residents that they could purchase tickets.

This practical discrimination was considered to be an abuse of the organisers' dominant position of the type proscribed by EC Art 82, and the organisers were fined €1,000[2].

1 See Commission press release dated 20 July 1999, IP/99/541, announcing 00/12/EC: Commission decision of 20 July 1999, [2000] OJ L 005, 8 January 2000, pp 55-74. For case comment, see Weatherill 'Fining the Organisers of the 1998 Football World Cup' [2000] 6 ECLR 275.
2 See para B2.44, n 3.

B2.228 Tying arrangements As a matter of general principle, tying arrangements are frowned on by the competition authorities. Basically, they regard them as a tactic often employed by a dominant undertaking to force a customer into buying a product that he does not want (for example an airline ticket) as a condition for obtaining a product he does want (for example a ticket to an important sporting event).

B2.229 The Commission held in relation to the ticketing arrangements for the Atlantic Olympic Games that organisers could not supply tickets to resellers on terms that required them to be 'packaged' and prevented them from being sold alone:

> … The Commission's intervention enabled a solution to be found which was compatible with the competition rules. In particular … the distribution of tickets complied with certain non-discriminatory rules set out in the standard contract between the various national organising committees and the Atlanta Games organiser, including the 'first come, first served' rule and the impossibility of making the sale of tickets conditional on buying transport or accommodation services …[1]

1 Unreported, Competition Report 1996, p 144.

B2.230 The Commission has reported that in the context of packaging tickets with other services, it has 'always insisted that tour operators should compete to sell tickets and should be free to combine the sale of tickets with other services, but the Commission would not accept organisers obliging them to do so'[1].

1 Commission Working Paper (29 September 1998), para 4.1.2.

B2.231 In specific circumstances, however, it might be possible to show that tying the match ticket sale to the airline ticket sale is necessary to achieve a legitimate aim (for example, keeping the tickets off the black market), and therefore is justified and not contrary to the competition rules. However, it would have to be shown that the measure is proportionate, ie it goes no further than is necessary to achieve the legitimate objective. Therefore, for example, it would be difficult, on these grounds, to justify tying the match ticket sale to the sale of an air ticket issued by a *particular* airline, as opposed to by any airline serving the required route.

B2.232 Non-transferability conditions Complaints have on occasion been made to both the Commission and the OFT about the inclusion of a 'non-transferability' clause in match ticket conditions[1]. The arguments made are that:

(a) someone who purchases a ticket should be entitled to do whatever they want with it, including selling it on for a profit if they so wish;
(b) 'artificial' restraints such as non-transferability clauses should not be used to subvert the 'laws of supply and demand'; and

(c) the condition is really an attempt to restrict the development of a secondary market for tickets and to protect the exclusivity granted to 'official' tour operators and corporate hospitality providers.

1 See paras D1.129 and D1.130.

B2.233 To date, neither the European Commission nor the OFT has shown any enthusiasm for pursuing this argument, which seems to have little legal merit. It is hardly the job of a competition authority to improve the business environment for operators on the black market.

B2.234 In the *Wimbledon* case[1], the OFT concluded that non-transferability clauses were intended to protect the organisers' judgment of the proper balance between ordinary fans and corporate hospitality by ensuring that tickets allocated to one distribution channel (ordinary fans) stayed in that channel and were not diverted to another distribution channel (corporate hospitality). Unsurprisingly, the OFT did not accept that policies intended to ensure access to the event at prices below what might have been achieved on a free market could be deemed to be abusive or otherwise against the public interest[2].

1 OFT press release no 20/93, dated 23 March 1993, announcing decision of the DG FT dated Match 1993.
2 A similar argument made by an unofficial corporate hospitality provides in relation to Rugby World Cup 1999 was not pursued by the Commission. See also *Hospitality Group Pty Ltd v Australian Rugby Union* [1992] FCA 1136 (Sackville J) ('The Court is not equipped to judge whether keeping a competitor out of a particular aspect of commerce is against the public interest when set against organising a successful and profitable test match series, with tickets for followers kept at a reasonable level, and with profits distributed to help the sport'), on appeal [2001] FCA 1040 (FCA 3 August 2001).

B2.235 In conclusion, therefore, it seems that regulators treat with suspicion arguments that a black market for tickets to sports events is in fact a genuine 'secondary market' that ought to be encouraged by use of competition law.

F Broadcasting

B2.236 It is probably in the area of television broadcasting[1] that the competition authorities have most frequently been involved in the 'business' of sport. At root, this is largely because of the great importance of sport (especially elite sport) as a driver for television and especially pay-television[2]. Further technological innovations, such as interactive television, 3G mobile telephony and internet streaming, may also be dependent on (or at least largely influenced by) the exploitation of top sporting content, particularly on an exclusive basis, to achieve market penetration. Concerned to ensure that competition remains strong and innovations are encouraged, the regulators (the OFT as well as the Commission) have closely scrutinised arrangements that appear to restrict competition in the market for the acquisition of premium sports content.

1 See generally Chapter D4.
2 See eg Oliver 'Dawn of pay-TV kicks off new soccer battle' (1999) Sunday Business, 28 February: 'Sport, especially soccer, is the battering ram of pay-TV … As digital TV lowers the costs of market entry in TV and most technical barriers to new competition are removed, the need to obtain key assets such as sports rights has become even more important'.

B2.237 In recent years, however, it would appear that courts and competition authorities alike have started to appreciate that there is a peculiar economic dynamic in sport that justifies a different, sui generis, application of the competition rules in the sports broadcasting context[1]. Significant jurisprudence has emerged in the sports broadcasting sphere seeking to reconcile this recognition with the desire for free competition in the broadcasting markets.

1 See paras B2.65 to B2.75 and B2.262 et seq.

(a) Market definition in broadcasting cases

B2.238 Proper market definition forms an important part of the evaluation of the competition law implications of a particular broadcasting arrangement or television contract[1]. Once again, it is the substitutability test that is used, ie whether one type of programming is an adequate substitute for another from the purchaser's point of view[2].

1 See para B2.76 et seq.
2 See para B2.82.

B2.239 It is important to note that different broadcasters, when acting as purchasers of content, may analyse potential purchases differently. In particular, in the case of *MSG Media Service*[1], the Commission observed that:

> Pay-TV constitutes a relevant product market that is separate from commercial advertising-financed television and from public television financed through fees and partly through advertising. While in the case of advertising-financed television, there is a trade relationship only between the programme supplier and the advertising industry, in the case of pay-TV there is a trade relationship only between the programme supplier and the viewer as subscriber. The conditions of competition are accordingly different for the two types of commercial television. Whereas in the case of advertising-financed television the audience share and the advertising rates are the key parameters, in the case of pay-TV the key factors are the shaping of programmes to meet the interests of the target groups and the level of subscriber prices …

Similarly, in the case of *Vivendi/BSkyB*, the UK Competition Commission stated:

> In our view, the focus of pay-TV, with its particular emphasis on film and sport, is significantly different to that of free-to-air TV; it is funded differently, since finance comes primarily from subscriptions; the prices it charges to customers for all but some very limited bundles of programmes are significantly higher and have increased over time; and its subscription income puts it in a considerably stronger market position than free-to-air TV to bid for the most significant rights. Only a pay-TV channel is in a position to finance the acquisition of the most expensive rights or to broadcast sport and films so extensively. Hence, we believe pay-TV can be regarded as a market separate from that of free-to-air TV[2].

1 Case IV/M.469 *MSG Media Service*, OJ L 364/1, December 31, 1994, para 32.
2 Competition Commission Report on the Vivendi SA and BSkyB Group plc merger, April 2000: http://www.competition-commission.org.uk/reports/440vivendi.htm#full at para 4.40.

B2.240 Other national antitrust authorities have come to similar conclusions. Thus, in the case of *Stream/Telepiu*[1], the Italian competition authority stated:

> The pay-TV market is a separate market to that of free-TV, by virtue of the different methods of financing (payment by subscribers in the first case, advertising revenue and television licence fees for public television channels in the second case), which imply different commercial policies and conditions of competition.

1 Provvedimento n. 6999 (A274), *Stream/Telepiù, L'Autorita' Garante Della Concorrenza E Del Mercato Bollettino n.* 12/1999, 26/03/1999. The above is an unofficial translation. The Italian text states as follows:
'9. … Il mercato della pay-TV è un mercato distinto dalla TV in chiaro, in virtù delle diverse modalità di finanziamento (pagamenti degli abbonati nel primo caso, entrate pubblicitarie e canone di abbonamento per le TV pubbliche nel secondo caso), che implicano politiche commerciali e condizioni concorrenziali diverse.'

B2.241 The German competition authority has also indicated that free-to-air and pay-TV are to be regarded as distinct markets. That was, for example, the conclusion in the *Premiere* case[1].

1 *BKartA, BeschluBvom* 1.10.1998, B6-92201-U-72/98 – *Premiere.* See also *AEK PAE and SK Slavia Praha v UEFA* CAS 98/2000, award dated 20 August 1999, *Digest of CAS Awards II 1998–2000* (2002, Kluwer), p 36: 'With regard to the television broadcasting market, there appears to be a growing consensus among competition authorities that pay (including pay-per-view) television and free-to-air television are separate product markets (see MMC Report, paras 2.36 and 2.39; Office of Fair Trading, The Director General's review of BSkyB's position in the wholesale pay TV market, London, December 1996, paras 2.3 and 2.6; 'Autorita garante della concorrenza e del mercatora, that is the Italian competition authority, Decision no 6999 of 26 March 1999, Stream/Telepiu, in Bollettino 12/1999, para 9).'

B2.242 Whilst sports programming is important for generalist, 'free', television stations, it does appear to have a particular significance for pay-television. Pay-television needs to have exclusive rights to truly compelling content to persuade the public to subscribe to watch pay-television rather than view the alternatives available for free on the other channels. For example, in its consideration of a proposed joint venture between BT, BSkyB, Midland Bank and Matsushita to provide digital interactive TV services in the UK[1], the Commission stated as follows:

> Retail pay-TV operators' demand for programming reflects subscriber demand for particular types of programmes. For retail pay-TV operators, the fact that some sports and films programmes achieve very high viewing rates is crucial as it is a reflection of viewers' willingness to pay for sports and film channels which is higher than [their] willingness to pay for other channels. The fact that films and sports channels are not substitutable for other forms of channels for a retail pay-TV operator is also borne out by the relative cost to wholesalers of acquiring these forms of rights as compared to other programming. Sports and films rights are by far the most expensive.

1 Case No IV/36.539, *BiB*, [1999] OJ C322, 21 October 1998. See also *Bertelsmann/Kirch/Premiere*, Case No IV/M.999, [1999] OJ L364/1, paras 34 and 48.

B2.243 In considering these issues, however, it should be recognised that it is really only *premium* sports content that confers substantial competitive advantages on the broadcaster who purchases it. Generally speaking, most sports in the UK would command the attention of committed followers but not necessarily huge numbers of viewers. Consequently, these sports would not represent 'must have' content for a pay-television service and would be readily substitutable for a wide range of other sporting (or non-sporting) programme material[1]. Thus, a long-term contract for a 'minority' interest sport would be most unlikely to have an appreciable effect on competition in broadcast markets. For example a grant of seven years' exclusive rights to broadcast British squash or badminton is unlikely to give the regulators any cause for concern.

1 See generally Commission Report *Broadcasting of Sports Events and Competition Law* (June 1998), Section I. See also para B2.136 (similar finding of Lloyd J in the *Hendry* case).

B2.244 In contrast, an analysis of viewing figures and rights fees paid suggests that there is a limited number of sports that are 'must see' sports that are of very considerable importance to broadcasters (and thus potentially require closer regulatory scrutiny). In Europe, it seems that the sports that probably fall into this category are football and Formula One motor racing[1].

1 Commission Report *Broadcasting of Sports Events and Competition Law* (June 1998), Section I: 'there may well be a difference between big sports, such as football and Formula One which may constitute markets in themselves, and minor sports'.

B2.245 For example, in the *FA Premier League* case before the Restrictive Practices Court[1], the OFT took the position that football was 'non-substitutable' for other sports programming. Indeed, it suggested that any broadcaster trying to compete on the UK pay-TV market would have to have exclusive rights to at least some Premier League matches to do so. Similarly, in a 'Background Note' which accompanied a statement of objections sent to UEFA regarding the arrangements for the sale of broadcasting rights to the UEFA Champions League[2], the Commission stated that:

> football is in most countries the driving force not only for the development of pay-TV services but it is also an essential programme item for free TV broadcasters[3].

1 *Re an Agreement between the FA Premier League and BSkyB* [2000] EMLR 78, [1999] UKCLR 258 (Restrictive Practices Court July 1999), judgment at para 128. See para B2.273.
2 See para B2.276.
3 European Commission, MEMO/01/271 (20 July 2001).

B2.246 However, even within football itself, it is probably only the elite competitions that are of significant value to broadcasters[1]. This fact was illustrated by the debacle of ITV Digital in the UK, which acquired the exclusive rights to broadcast Nationwide First Division football in 2000, but was only able to attract a small number of subscribers with the material, prompting its subsequent default and bankruptcy in 2002[2].

1 As the Commission itself has suggested in the UEFA Champions League case: see para B2.84.
2 See para D4.5.

B2.247 Indeed, the propensity of pay-television stations to acquire the most attractive sports events even resulted in a piece of EU legislation (Art 3A of the Television Without Frontiers Directive) that was explicitly designed to rig the market in favour of free TV stations by allowing member states to 'list' certain sporting events that could not, once listed, be acquired and exploited on an exclusive basis by pay-television[1].

1 See para B2.300. See also paras A1.81 to A1.92 and B1.49 to B1.53.

(b) Territorial licensing of sports broadcasting rights

B2.248 Broadcasting rights to sports events are usually sold on a territorial basis, usually country by country (or, in the EC, member state by member state)[1]. While this would appear to cut across the principle of a 'single' market, the Commission has accepted that there are distinct geographical markets for broadcasting, including sports broadcasting[2]. There are various cultural, linguistic and regulatory differences in Europe that justify the territorial licensing of television rights and, as such, licensing on a national basis does not create any *artificial* barrier to trade[3]. In addition, sport is a 'nationalistic' business and consumer preferences vary greatly from one country to the next.

1 See generally paras D4.30, D4.35 and D4.36.
2 In its *Eurovision* decision, the Commission noted the practice – 'Television rights to sports events are normally granted for a given territory, usually country by country, on an exclusive basis' – without objection. Joined Cases T-528, T-542/93 and T-546/93, [1996] ECR II-649 the *Eurovision* judgment, June 1993 at para 21.
3 *Case 262/81, Coditel SA v Ciné-Vog Films SA* [1982] ECR 3381, para 20 (exclusive territorial licences allowed provided that they do not create 'artificial or unjustifiable' barriers to trade).

(c) Central selling of broadcasting rights

B2.249 Television rights to sports are often sold on a 'central' or 'collective' basis. In other words, the governing body or the league may sell the television rights on behalf of its member clubs and often the statutes or regulations of the governing body or league will have provisions that explicitly envisage this[1].

1 See eg para D4.29.

B2.250 Both the Commission and the OFT have at times suggested that such 'collective' deals limit competition and could amount to cartel-type behaviour. It has sometimes been suggested that it would be better for competition (and for the consumer) if clubs sold 'their' television rights to their respective 'home' matches on an individual basis. A concern of the regulator has been that if rights to premium content are concentrated in the hands of one central body (ie the event organiser) and that body then concludes an exclusive contract with a broadcaster, this may limit competition in television markets to the detriment of the consumer. There is, it is alleged, a 'horizontal' restriction on competition (joint selling by the league) coupled with a 'vertical' restriction on competition (exclusive TV deal with a broadcaster) and the combination of these 'horizontal' and 'vertical' restrictions is anti-competitive. The situation is viewed as especially problematic since premium sports content is an important driver of various broadcast technologies[1].

1 See para B2.236.

B2.251 In the words of the Commission:

> The rights holders for popular sports events are in a strong position. The concentration of the rights in the hands of certain sports federations reduces the number of rights available, and these are reduced even further if contracts are concluded on an exclusive basis for a long duration, or covering a large number of events. The Commission is particularly concerned about the impact on the structure of the TV market, with the risk of development of oligopolistic market structures[1].

1 Competition Commissioner Mario Monti *Sport and Competition* (Speech 00/152 delivered to Commission-organised conference on sport: Brussels, 17 April 2000). See also OFT press release, May 1999: FAPL collective deal with Sky means 'a lack of access to rights which will impede the development of competition in the pay-TV market in which premium sports programming is the main driver … There is also less chance for new and exciting forms of broadcasting to develop such as new regionally or locally focused programmes or channels covering matches of the local clubs'. See Szymanski *Collective selling of broadcast rights to sports events* (Paper presented to the European Parliament, 31 May 2001): 'If collective selling is a mechanism that can lead to foreclosure of broadcast markets, then any benefits to the sport concerned may be outweighed by the loss of competition in wider broadcast markets'.

B2.252 There are various arguments in response to the allegation that 'collective' selling is anti-competitive. The first is that the entity selling the rights (the event organiser) cannot be readily compared to a simple 'sales cartel'. The event organiser will typically have invested a significant amount of creative and organisational effort in putting together the competition framework in which the 'individual' events take place. This may justify the event organiser being regarded as the owner (or at least 'co-owner') of the commercial rights. If this analysis is applied, clubs would be unable to conduct 'individual' sales in any event since they would need the consent of the co-owner (ie the league) to effect a sale in the first place.

B2.253 Another way of looking at this issue is to recognise that the 'product' that is of interest to the broadcaster (and the public) is not the individual match but rather the match *within the framework of the competition*[1]. Consequently, there would, in effect, be no pooling or collective sale of individual products because what is being put on the market is essentially a league product[2].

1 See further para B2.68.
2 See further para B2.256 et seq.

B2.254 However, even if it were accepted that broadcasters are interested in acquiring 'individual' matches (as opposed to matches taking place within the competition) there are still various arguments in favour of 'central' or 'collective' selling. For example, a single (ie central) deal is economically efficient because it minimises the transaction costs for a broadcaster (ie it is not necessary for the broadcaster to conduct multiple 'individual' deals with clubs in order to obtain coverage of a sporting event)[2].

1 In relation to the FIA Formula One World Championship, the Commission has acknowledged that 'it is impossible to market in individual rights of each team participating in the race. As FIA, FOA, the teams, the drivers, the manufacturers and the local organiser or promoter may all have rights in the event, some arrangement between all of them for the sale of rights, especially the broadcasting rights, appears to be indispensable. The Concorde Agreement provides for FOA to be the commercial rights holder for the FIA Formula One World Championship and to negotiate on behalf of the teams and FIA the organisation of the races with the local promoters and the sale of broadcasting rights with broadcasters'. Notification published pursuant to Art 19(3) of Council Regulation 17 concerning Cases COMP/35.163, OJ C169/5, 13 June 2001.

B2.255 Moreover, from the perspective of the sport, central licensing also facilitates certain fundamental economic imperatives: namely the maintenance of financial (and, therefore, sporting) balance within the league structure. A system of 'individual' selling is more likely to exacerbate financial imbalance between clubs, with the result being that the sports product (ie a contest between competitively balanced contestants that is therefore of uncertain outcome) is less interesting to broadcasters and consumers alike. Thus, where a substantial proportion of the income generated is redistributed within the sport, this may be seen as ultimately pro-competitive, even if it might restrict the opportunities for clubs to sell commercial rights on an individual basis[1].

1 See further para B2.262 et seq.

B2.256 Collective selling is a misnomer There is some debate concerning which entity actually 'owns' the television rights to a football match. Is it the organiser of the competition? Is it the 'home' club (ie the club controlling access to the ground where the match is played)? Or is it both clubs that play on the pitch (ie the 'home' club and the 'away' club)? Whatever the correct answer may be, the question cannot be answered by Community law. Article 295 (ex 222) of the EC Treaty states that the Treaty shall not prejudice the rules of any member state governing the system of property ownership in its territory. Consequently, the ownership issue falls to be determined according to relevant national law.

B2.257 This question of ownership has come up in various cases where domestic competition regulators (and courts) have been called on to examine the broadcasting arrangements for professional football.

B2.258 In the Netherlands, the courts have suggested that it is the 'home' club that takes the economic risk in staging the match and therefore that club should be regarded as the owner and supplier of the 'product'. Against this background, it has been held that rules requiring individual clubs to engage in collective deals are anti-competitive and void[1].

1 See *KNVB/Sport 7*, Case IV/36.033, [1996] OJ C228/4; *Feyenord/KNVB*, Hof Amsterdam, 8 November 1996, RvdW/KG 1996, No 448.

B2.259 In Germany, the domestic competition authorities followed a similar reasoning and ruled that collective selling, through the DFB (the German equivalent of the FAPL), of the broadcast rights to the home matches played by German teams in the UEFA Cup and Cup-Winners Cup was unlawful[1]. However, the case was unusual in that the DFB sought to market (on behalf of German clubs) rights to competitions that the DFB played no part (or, at least very little part) in organising. The German Federal Supreme Court subsequently recognised that the entity that creates and organises the competition in which the matches are played may also be regarded as at least a co-owner of the commercial rights to these matches[2]. Consequently, if joint selling is conducted by the entity that actually creates and organises the competition there will be less of a problem (and perhaps no problem at all) under German competition law.

1 Order of 2 September 1994, B6-747000-A105/92, Wu W/E BkartA 2682, upheld by German federal court, December 1997.

2 *Deutscher-Fussball-Bund v Bundeskartellant* (Federal Antitrust Authority), Federal Supreme Court, 11 December 1997. Accord *AE TV Corpn GmbH v Federation Internationale de l'Automobile*, Higher Regional Court Frankfurt Am Main, 15 December 1998.

B2.260 In Italy, domestic regulators have suggested that the national football federation, the Lega Calcio, did not bear any of the economic risk involved in staging Series A and B matches and so should not be considered as the owner of these rights. Collective selling of the rights has been permitted only to a limited extent (for highlights and Cup matches)[1].

1 See Rumphorts 'Collective selling of sports television rights', paper delivered at London Conference on Sports Broadcasting Rights and EC Competition Law, 12 October 1999.

B2.261 English law does not recognise the concept of broadcasting rights in sports events per se; instead, such rights are derived from a mixture of real property rights, contractual rights and intellectual property rights, based on control over access to the venue where the match is to take place[1]. Theoretically, therefore, the entity controlling access to the venue where the match is played would also 'own' the television rights to the match being played there. Such an interpretation would, however, ignore the economic realities surrounding the creation of the sports 'product'[2]. The Restrictive Practices Court in the *FA Premier League* case clearly preferred an economically realistic approach. It stated, for example, that:

> the product which has value is the Premier League championship as a whole, rather than the individual matches played in the course of the championship[3]

It went on to say[4]:

> Secondly we regard it as somewhat facile to speak of individual selling in a way which assumes that each club, or the home club in each match, is entitled to sell the television rights to the matches in which it participates. We know of no principle which, in the absence of a special rule, gives a club such a right. It is true, of course, that the home club, as the owner or controller of the ground at which a match is to be played, can prevent a broadcaster having access to that ground for the purpose of making a broadcast or recording of the match. But this is a mere power of veto. It does not enable the home club to sell the television rights to a match without the concurrence of the visiting club …
>
> In practice, therefore, 'individual selling' can only be achieved by a series of trilateral deals between home and visiting clubs and particular broadcasters, such deals being limited to matches played between the clubs in question …

In summary, therefore, the Restrictive Practices Court was plainly unimpressed with the arguments put forward in support of individual selling of television rights to the Premier League and preferred the view that the Premier League clubs were engaged in the production of a joint product, which was the Premier League championship itself.

1 See paras D1.17 to D1.21 and D4.8 to D4.28.
2 See paras B2.66 to B2.68.
3 *Re an Agreement between the FA Premier League and BSkyB* [2000] EMLR 78, [1999] UKCLR 258 (Restrictive Practices Court July 1999), judgment at 95.
4 *Re an Agreement between the FA Premier League and BSkyB* [2000] EMLR 78, [1999] UKCLR 258 (Restrictive Practices Court July 1999), judgment at 101.

B2.262 Are central licensing deals pro-competitive? A strong argument exists that it is appropriate to follow a 'rule of reason' approach in the analysis of central selling arrangements to sporting events, examining whether the arrangements, when examined overall, have a net pro-competitive effect[1]. Indeed, there has been legislative recognition of these principles in the United States and in Germany[2].

1 See paras B2.66 to B2.75. See also Competition Commissioner Monti *Sport and Competition* (Speech 00/152 to a Commission-organised conference on sports: Brussels, 17 April 2000): 'The effect [of central broadcasting deals] has to be evaluated in its economic and legal context, taking into account, for example, the feasibility of participants selling rights individually'.
2 The Sports Broadcasting Act, 15 USCA ss 1291–1294 (2000), permits the central selling of television rights by the four major league sports in the USA, as a means of ensuring competitive balance through an equitable distribution of the revenues. See eg Senate Report No 1087, 87th Cong, 1st Sess (1961); House Report No 1178, 87th Cong, 1st Sess (1961) ('The antitrust laws … shall not apply to any joint agreement by or among persons engaging in [a professional football, baseball, basketball or hockey league], by which any league … sells or otherwise transfers all or any part of the rights of such league's member clubs in the sponsored telecasting of [its games] …'). Germany adopted a similar statute in May 1998. See Section 31 GWB, BR-Dr, 852/2/97 (exempting from its competition statute 'the collective sale of television broadcasting rights to sports competitions organised under the authority and pursuant to the regulations of sports federations which, in compliance with their socio-political responsibility, are committed to the promotion of youth and amateur sports and fulfil this responsibility by means of a reasonable participation in the revenues generated by the collective marketing of television rights').

B2.263 In his opinion in the *Bosman* case, Advocate-General Lenz acknowledged the need to preserve competitive balance in sport and suggested that 'an appropriate and reasonable alternative' to the player transfer system would be the collective sale and redistribution of a proportion of television income[1]. He cited with approval UEFA's distribution of income generated by the marketing of television and commercial rights to the UEFA Champions League, not only to the participating clubs but also to national member associations, with a proportion reserved to be invested for the benefit of football[2].

1 Opinion of Advocate General Lenz, *Union Royale Belge des Sociétés de Football Association ASBL v Bosman*, Case 415/93, [1996] 1 CMLR 645 at para 230.
2 See n 1 at para 231.

B2.264 The issue of 'collective' selling was perhaps given its most comprehensive judicial examination by the Restrictive Practices Court ('RPC') in the *FA Premier League* case[1].

1 *Re an Agreement between the FA Premier League and BSkyB* [2000] EMLR 78, [1999] UKCLR 258 (Restrictive Practices Court 1999).

B2.265 Since its inception in 1992, the Premier League has sold live television rights on a central basis to BSkyB. When the contract was renewed in 1999 and BSkyB again obtained exclusive Premier League rights for a further four years (1997/98 to 2000/01), the OFT referred the matter to the Restrictive Practices Court.

B2.266 Under the relevant UK law (the Restrictive Trade Practices Act 1976 [RTPA], now replaced by the Competition Act 1998), the burden was on the FA Premier League, BSkyB and the BBC (which obtained highlights) to establish that the restrictions were not contrary to the public interest[1]. Although the public interest test is not the same as the criteria for the grant of an exemption under Art 81(3) of the EC Treaty (or s 4 of the Competition Act 1998), many of the principles underlying the judgment of the Restrictive Practices Court would also hold good under the Competition Act and the EC competition rules. The essential task for the RPC was to weigh the alleged anti-competitive effects of the collective licensing arrangements against any benefits accruing to the public as a result of those benefits. And the conclusion, although framed in the arcane language of the RTPA, 'was nonetheless in its practical application extremely similar to the exercise which the Commission undertakes under Art 81(1) EC'[2].

1 Specifically, the test applied was as follows. Every restriction was to be deemed to be contrary to the public interest unless the court was satisfied that: (i) it passed through one of the statutory 'gateways' (the statutory gateway primarily relied on was 'gateway b', ie that removing the restriction would deny to the public 'specific and substantial benefits or advantages'); (ii) it was not unreasonable, having regard to the balance between the circumstances that enable it to pass through the gateway and any detriments to the public that result from acceptance of the restriction.
2 Nicholas Green QC *Sports Broadcasting and EC Competition Law* (Paper given at BASL Annual Conference, October 1999), p 8. Cf Szymanski *Broadcasting and Sport* (Paper presented at the IEA, 18 October 2000), who points out that the RPC confined itself to comparing the FAPL arrangements to a completely unrestricted market, whereas the EC rules and new Competition Act require consideration of whether there are less restrictive ways of achieving the same result; Robertson 'The Implications of the Restrictive Practices Court's Decision in the Premier League/BSkyB Case' (2000) 1 ISLR 23 (decision turned on RTPA provisions; Premier League deals still face scrutiny under EC and new UK competition rules). See also Ross & Sqymanski 'Necessary Restraints and Inefficient Monopoly Sports Leagues' (2001) 1 ISLR 27; Szymanski 'Collective Selling of Broadcasting Rights' (2002) 1 ISLR 3. For further case comment, see Bishop and Oldale 'Sports Rights: The UK Premier League Football Case' [2000] 21(3) ECLR 185.

B2.267 The OFT argued that the Premier League clubs were independent economic operators that should compete with each other for the sale of broadcasting rights to their home matches but that were instead acting as a classic sales cartel, combining the rights into a single bundle in order to restrict output and raise prices. The OFT pointed to the fact that only 60 out of 320 matches were shown live each season on BSkyB. It argued that the long exclusivity periods of the contracts enabled BSkyB and the BBC to obtain an unfair competitive advantage over other UK broadcasters. The OFT contended that it would be more appropriate for Sky to be granted live and exclusive rights to the 60 matches but for the clubs to sell the other matches individually. On the other hand, the Premier League argued (among other things) that individual selling would harm competitive balance, cause scheduling chaos, reduce match attendance and limit the amount of money paid overall for Premier League broadcasting rights.

B2.268 After a trial that took over four months and involved about sixty witnesses, the RPC concluded that if the Premier League provisions on central selling were struck down the public would be denied the following benefits, which outweighed any incidental disadvantages:

(1) The Premier League would no longer be able to sell the product that the broadcasters and their viewers want, namely the Premier League championship as a whole.
(2) Less money would be generated by the sale of broadcasting rights in Premier League matches, so clubs would be less able to improve their stadia and other facilities, as well as their playing squads and football academies. Furthermore, the ability of the Premier League to confer benefits on clubs outside the League would also be threatened[1].
(3) The Premier League's ability to achieve competitive balance through an equitable distribution of television revenues (financial solidarity) would be threatened.

1 The Restrictive Practices Court noted that the Premier League currently makes payments to the Football League, the Football Trust, and the PFA, among others, which it might not be able to continue without control of television revenues.

B2.269 In relation to the last factor, the Restrictive Practices Court noted:

> the significant point is … whether competitive balance is something which makes a football competition more attractive … [I]t seems to us to be manifest that this is the case … There can, in our view, be no doubt that the sharing between clubs of a major source of revenue such as the proceeds of the sale of television rights is one way in which to promote a degree of financial equality.

It went on to state that:

> The existence of a scheme for redistribution of television income is, in our view, an extremely important factor, in the creation and preservation of competitive balance, which, for reasons we have already indicated, is a vital factor in maintaining the quality and interest of Premier League football[1].

1 *Re an Agreement between the FA Premier League and BSkyB* [2000] EMLR 78, [1999] UKCLR 258 (Restrictive Practices Court July 1999), judgment at 110.

B2.270 The Restrictive Practices Court stated that it considered that the provisions in the Premier League rules for the sharing of television income (50% equally, 25% based on results, and 25% based on actual appearances on television):

> have a real and substantial effect, in that the less successful and less popular clubs receive a greater share of the aggregate income from the broadcasting of Premier League matches on television than they would be likely to receive if the present system for the distribution of such income became inoperative and was not replaced by a new system which is equally effective. If the aggregate income were diminished by the abolition of collective selling, the adverse effect on the finances of smaller and weaker clubs would, in the absence of a new system for redistribution, be serious[1].

1 *Re an Agreement between the FA Premier League and BSkyB* [2000] EMLR 78, [1999] UKCLR 258 (Restrictive Practices Court July 1999), judgment at 110.

B2.271 The court did not accept the OFT's arguments that alternative methods of redistribution could be found: 'suggestions such as a levy on the gate receipts of member clubs or a levy on their total income [a]ll … present quite serious practical problems. Thus a levy on gate receipts operates as a disincentive to the making of improvements which increase ground capacity or enable higher prices to be charged, although these improvements themselves provide benefits to the public … We are satisfied that it would be difficult to devise a system of redistribution as effective and straightforward as that achieved by' the current Premier League rules[1]

1 *Re an Agreement between the FA Premier League and BSkyB* [2000] EMLR 78, [1999] UKCLR 258 (Restrictive Practices Court July 1999), judgment at 152. The Commission, however, has kept this issue alive as an important step in the analysis. Se eg Competition Commissioner Monti, DN: Speech/0184, 26 February 2001: 'the possibility for less restrictive models for collective selling also has to be examined'.

B2.272 The Restrictive Practices Court rejected the suggestion that the same beneficial effect could be achieved by individual clubs cross-subsidising their competitors by paying part of their individual licensing fees into a solidarity pool. Evidence taken from club directors suggested that this just would not happen:

> They would recognise the need to support the League as a whole and the need for competitive balance. But their primary duty would be to do what they consider to be in the interests of their club. We think they would be likely to find it much more difficult to agree to part with considerable sums out of their own club's income than they find it to continue to participate in the present arrangement under which what is distributed is money which never belongs to an individual club until the distribution is made[1].

1 *Re an Agreement between the FA Premier League and BSkyB* [2000] EMLR 78, [1999] UKCLR 258 (RPC 1999), judgment at para 155.

B2.273 With regard to the impact on the broadcasting market, the Restrictive Practices Court held that joint selling by the Premier League on an exclusive basis could, on balance, be regarded as pro-competitive. Specifically, the court pointed out that the removal of exclusivity would mean that the rights would no longer be available to a new entrant for use as a driver of subscriptions and a provider of a differentiated product:

> If it be the case … that it is impossible to establish a new premium sports channel without exclusive Premier League rights, then the establishment of a new premium sports channel will become more difficult, if not impossible, as a result of exclusivity not being available[1].

1 *Re an Agreement between the FA Premier League and BSkyB* [2000] EMLR 78, [1999] UKCLR 258 (RPC 1999), judgment at para 128.

B2.274 Interestingly enough, the European Commission responded to the judgment of the Restrictive Practices Court by calling on the Premier League to notify its new broadcast arrangements so that the Commission could assess their compatibility with EU law[1]. Subsequently, however, the Commission itself also started to make noises that demonstrated a more sympathetic approach to central selling arrangements[2].

1 On 5 August 1999 just one week after the Restrictive Practices Court's judgment, the Commission sent 'Article 11' questionnaires to the Premier League and each of its member clubs, seeking information about the new deal and requesting its notification as soon as possible: (1999) Sunday Telegraph, 19 September. The Commission subsequently confirmed that it had started a formal investigation into the new deal: (2001) Reuters, 29 October. See 'Premier League to face EU fine over TV rights' (2001) www.sportbusiness.com, 31 October (reporting that the Commission had started a preliminary investigation into the FAPL's renewal of its broadcasting agreement with BSkyB).

2 See eg (1999) Guardian, 2 December, quoting Culture Commissioner Viviene Reding as saying central deals could be cleared or exempted if more of the money was used to fund the training and development of young players.

B2.275 The current position appears to be that the Commission remains concerned that central or collective selling restricts output (ie limits the number of matches available to the public) and also leads to further media concentration, restricting opportunities for smaller broadcasters[1]. It has therefore taken the view that such deals do restrict competition within the meaning of Art 81(1) and so must qualify for an exemption under Art 81(3) to be enforceable[2]. One of the criteria which has to be satisfied for the grant of an exemption is that the restrictions are 'indispensable' and, consequently, that the positive results of deriving from joint selling cannot be achieved by 'less restrictive' means[3]. The Commission has stated that:

> It has to be determined to what extent the collective selling of rights by a sports association, combined with a balanced distribution of the income in a spirit of solidarity towards smaller clubs, can be deemed necessary and may be justified for the purpose of promoting sporting activities among the general public and popular sporting competitions[4].

1 See eg Competition Commissioner Monti, DN: Speech/01/84, 26 February 2001. See para B2.250.

2 See paras B2.97 and B2.98.

3 See para B2.22.

4 Draft/Preliminary Guidelines on the Application of the Competition Rules to Sport, unpublished Commission memorandum (15 February 1999) at 26.

B2.276 In a 'Background Note' that accompanied a statement of objections sent in July 2001 to UEFA concerning the arrangements for the sale of broadcasting rights to the UEFA Champions League competition, the Commission was careful to state that it was not objecting to the collective selling of football rights per se:

> while joint selling arrangements clearly fall within the scope of Art 8(1), the Commission considers that in certain circumstances, joint selling may be an efficient way to organise the selling of TV rights for international sports events. However, the manner in which the TV rights are sold may not be so restrictive as to outweigh the benefits provided[1].

1 European Commission, MEMO/01/271 (20 July 2001).

B2.277 The Commission also stated that it:

> fully endorses the specificity of sport as expressed in the declaration of the European Council in Nice in December 2000, where the Council encourages a redistribution of part of the revenue from the sales of TV rights at the appropriate levels, as beneficial to the principle of solidarity between all levels and areas of sport. The statement of objections sent by the Commission does not put this principle into question[1].

1 European Commission, MEMO/01/271 (20 July 2001).

B2.278 After several months of negotiations, the European Commission agreed to a modified central marketing structure for the UEFA Champions League[1]. The resolution of the case foresees that the core live rights to UEFA Champions League continue to be sold on a central basis but certain categories of rights (including delayed television rights and some new media rights) may be commercialised by the clubs on an individual basis[2]. The Commissioner in charge of Competition (Mr. Mario Monti) stated that:

> … the UEFA settlement proposal represents good news for clubs, broadcasters and fans. It is a clear example of the Commission's ability to achieve a balanced solution in sports related cases with the existing legal instruments and allows both sport and competition to flourish, to the benefit of the European consumer[3].

1 Commission press release dated 3 June 2002, IP/02/806.
2 See para B2.279, n 1.
3 See n 1.

B2.279 It may be assumed that the regulatory solution that the Commission has adopted in the UEFA Champions League case[1] will also inform its handling of other cases involving national league football. At the time of writing it would seem that both the German Bundesliga and the English FA Premier League have notified their respective television arrangements to the Commission[2].

1 See 'Joint selling of the media rights of the UEFA Champions League on an exclusive basis', Art 19(3) Notice concerning Case COMP/C.2/37.398, [2002] OJ C 196/03.
2 As to the FAPL notification, see para B2.274.

B2.280 Finally, it should be noted that when central or collective arrangements are provided for the sale of sports television rights it is important that the governing body conducts the sales process in a manner which affords all interested bidders a fair opportunity to tender for the rights. The Commission has stated that:

> it is important to note that the collective selling of broadcasting rights by an association must be carried out in a transparent manner and that the award should respect objective and non-discriminatory criteria[1].

1 *Draft/Preliminary Guidelines on the Application of the Competition Rules to Sport*, unpublished Commission memorandum (15 February 1999).

(d) *Exclusive licensing of broadcasting rights*[1]

B2.281 The grant of exclusive rights is not, per se , contrary to EC competition law[2]. This is particularly the case in relation to the audio-visual industry, where both the European Court of Justice and the European Commission have recognised that exclusivity may, in fact, have fundamentally pro-competitive effects. Without obtaining exclusivity, broadcasters are less likely to invest money and develop production techniques (for example better presenters, better set, more coverage, more incentive to promote upcoming coverage). The fact that broadcasters are willing to undertake such tasks if they obtain exclusivity in return translates into better services being offered to the end consumer.

1 See generally Fleming 'Exclusive Rights to Broadcast Sporting Events in Europe' [1999] 3 ECLR 143.

2 See generally Case 56/65, *Société Technique Minière v Maschinenbau Ulm* [1966] ECR 235; Case 258/78, *Nungesser v Commission* [1982] ECR 2015.

B2.282 Thus, in *Coditel II*[1], the European Court of Justice held that exclusive licences of performing rights could *not* be presumed to infringe Art 81(1):

> … a contract whereby the owner of the copyright in a film grants an exclusive right to exhibit that film for a specific period in the territory of a Member State is not, as such, subject to the prohibitions contained in Article 85 [now 81] of the Treaty.

1 Case 262/81, *Coditel SA, Compagnie générale pour la diffusion de la télévision v Ciné-Vog Films SA* [1982] ECR 3381, para 20.

B2.283 In the specific context of sports broadcasting, the Commission has stated that it 'does not believe that exclusive broadcasting rights are anti-competitive per se'[1]. In a 1998 policy paper, the Commission stated that 'the sale of exclusive broadcasting rights for sports events is established and accepted commercial practice'[2]. The Commissioner responsible for competition policy (Mr. Mario Monti) has made similar remarks in various speeches[3]. Most clearly, the Commission has observed:

> Exclusivity is an accepted commercial practice in the broadcasting sector. It guarantees the value of a programme, and is particularly important in the case of sports, as a broadcast of a sports event is valuable for only a very short time. Exclusivity for limited periods should not in itself raise competition concerns …
>
> [F]or the broadcaster … exclusivity represents … the only way to guarantee the value of a given sports programme … for pay-TV channels, exclusivity of rights to very popular sports events is fundamental in order to attract new subscribers; this is especially true for sports theme channels[4].

1 The European Model of Sport, Consultation Document of DG X, November 1998: www.europa.eu.int/comm/sport/doc/ecom/doc_consult_en.pdf.

2 Commission Staff Working Paper *The Development and Prospects for Community Action in the Field of Sport* (Brussels, 29 September 1998).

3 See eg Mario Monti, European Commissioner for Competition, Conference on 'Governance in Sport' (Brussels – 26 February 2001, SPEECH/01/84).

4 Wachtmeister, 'Broadcasting of Sports Events and Competition Law' *EC Competition Policy Newsletter* (1998 No 2, June). See also European Parliament's Resolution on the broadcasting of sports events, B4-0326/96, 22 May 1996 [1996] OJ C166/109, 10/6/96: 'exclusive broadcasting rights are a necessary part of the normal functioning of the highly competitive broadcasting market and are seen as a central driving force in the generation of revenue for both sports organisation and television broadcasters; whereas the exclusivity has led to an increase in both the amount of sport broadcast and the number of different sports televised, particularly with the rise of televised minority sports'.

B2.284 A question arises, however, as to the degree of exclusivity that it is permissible to grant without falling foul of the competition rules. The regulatory authorities will examine the duration of exclusive contracts carefully, especially when the contract is for so-called 'premium' sports content, to determine whether the length of the exclusivity granted effectively 'forecloses' the market for premium sports broadcasting rights. The Commission has said that 'any exclusivity which, because of its time-span or its scope, would foreclose the market is probably prohibited'[1].

1 *Draft/Preliminary Guidelines on the Application of the Competition Rules to Sport*, unpublished Commission memorandum (15 February 1999) at 32. See para B2.98.

B2.285 Thus, the Commission has noted that 'exclusive contracts for a sporting event or for one season in a given competition do not normally pose any competition problem'[1]. Such a grant, if deemed to fall within Art 81(1), would likely be exempted[2]. However, one season is not a very long period of time for a broadcaster to develop audience loyalty or build a brand identity for its programming.

1 Competition Commissioner Mario Monti *Sport and Competition* (Speech 00/152 to Commission-organised conference on sport: Brussels 17 April 2000).

2 See para B2.97. See also *Draft/Preliminary Guidelines on the Application of the Competition Rules to Sport*, unpublished Commission memorandum (15 February 1999) at 29.

B2.286 The Commission has also recognised that a longer period of exclusivity can be justified in particular circumstances, for example, where an operator seeks to enter a new market or introduce a new technology requiring significant up-front investment and risk. Such was the case in 1988, when the Football Association sold Sky and the BBC exclusive broadcasting rights to all FA Cup and Charity Shield matches and all England international matches for five years (1988–1993). In July 1993, the Commission announced its view that the grant of exclusive rights to BSkyB and the BBC was caught by EC Art 85(1) (now 81(1)), and that in general the exclusivity of such attractive rights should be limited to no more than one year, to give competitors the chance to compete for those rights. Nevertheless, the Commission issued a 'comfort letter'[1] on the grounds that the purchase of the rights facilitated the launch of a pay-TV direct-to-home satellite channel, and the period of exclusivity was needed to justify the investment made and the risks being taken[2]. In a similar case involving Audiovisual Sport in Spain, the Commission indicated that a three-year exclusivity period for Spanish football would be acceptable for the same reasons[3].

1 As to the nature of which, see para A3.226.

2 European Commission, 1993 Completion Report at p 459. The Commission stated that its decision was 'without prejudice to the view the commission may take on any future contracts to be concluded by the parties'.

3 *Audiovisual Sport*, Case IV/36.438, [1997] OJ C120/5.

B2.287 In a newspaper interview[1], the then-European Commissioner in charge of competition (Mr Karel van Miert) stated as follows:

> There is no general rule. The unique nature of each competition must be taken into account. The IOC, for example, has sold its European TV rights to the EBU for five Olympic Games. This sounds like a long time. But the Olympic Games are different from a football competition. We cannot oppose it. Even more so if all conditions are satisfied. The IOC was satisfied with receiving less money in order to ensure the broadcasting of the Games on the maximum number of terrestrial televisions. However, with regard to football championships, the period should be shortened. This also applies to pay-per-view. When BSkyB acquired the rights to the English championship, the exclusivity period was fixed for five years. At the time this was a new concept and we did not know what was going to happen. Looking back on it, BSkyB have made a good investment. We have learned since then, and we believe that the length of contracts of exclusivity should be shortened.

1 (1998) Le Monde, 27 October.

B2.288 Perhaps unsurprisingly, then, the Commission expressed disapproval of a seven-year exclusive term for the rights to Dutch football[1]. The content would have to be very substitutable in the marketplace for such a long period of exclusivity to be cleared[2].

1 *KNVB/Sport 7*, Case IV/36.033, [1996] OJ C-228/4.
2 See eg paras B2.88 and B2.243.

B2.289 In between these extremes, a grant of exclusive rights that is limited in time, scope or effect may be exempted[1]. The analysis applied would involve consideration of issues such as the length of time required to obtain a return on the investment; and the 'foreclosure' effect of granting exclusivity, including the position of actual or potential competitors to the grantee of the rights. As the Commission has stated:

> … it is difficult to determine an ideal time-span for exclusivity agreements, since each agreement has its own specific characteristics. The criteria laid down in Article 81(1) of the EC Treaty that would justify exemption for an agreement must be examined case by case[2].

1 See para B2.97. See also *Draft/Preliminary Guidelines on the Application of the Competition Rules to Sport*, unpublished Commission memorandum (15 February 1999) at 32.
2 *Draft/Preliminary Guidelines on the Application of the Competition Rules to Sport*, unpublished Commission memorandum (15 February 1999) at 32.

B2.290 In the authors' view, contracts of up to three years (even for premium content) should not pose regulatory concerns. The breadth of material available in the market (which may extend to non-sporting as well as sporting material) is such that it is difficult to argue that a particular sporting event is a 'must have' or 'non-substitutable' item for a broadcaster and should therefore be put on the market on an annual basis. Indeed, even as regards the FIA Formula One World Championship, the broadcasting rights to which are viewed as largely non-substitutable[1], the Commission in 2001 expressed the view that the grant of exclusive terrestrial rights for five years to host broadcasters and three years to licensed broadcasters did 'not exceed what seems reasonable in view of the nature of the rights and the obligations and investments undertaken by the broadcasters, given the specific features of the sport'[2].

1 See para B2.244.
2 Notice pursuant to Art 19(3) of Council Regulation 17 concerning cases COMP/35.163, OJ C169/5, 13 June 2001; Commission press release dated 30 October 2001, IP/01/1523.

B2.291 The Commission reached a similar view with respect to broadcasting rights to the UEFA Champions League, which again it appears to view as 'must have' programming from the broadcasters' perspective[1]. When the Commission published a Notice[1] and Background Note[2], announcing that it had issued a statement of objections in relation to the broadcast arrangements for the UEFA Champions League, it suggested that the 'commercial policy of selling all the free and pay-TV rights on an exclusive basis to a single broadcaster per territory for a period lasting several years may be incompatible with EC competition law'. However, in 2002 the Commission announced that it was satisfied by various amendments made by UEFA that maintained the practice of selling the rights for a term of three years, albeit in an 'unbundled' form that foresees a greater number of rights packages being put on the market[3].

1 See para B2.84.
2 Commission press release dated 20 July 2001, IP/01/1043.
3 MEMO/01/271 (20 July 2001).
4 See 'Joint selling of the media rights of the UEFA Champions League on an exclusive basis', Art 19(3) notice concerning Case COMP/C.2/37.398, [2002] OJ C 196/03.

B2.292 In the *FA Premier League* case, the OFT challenged not only the collective sale of television rights but also the exclusive grant of those rights for a four-year period. However, the focus of the OFT argument was on the subject of 'broad exclusivity', that is to say, the right of the grantee (in this case BSkyB) to show 60 matches live and exclusive with no other broadcaster having any live rights to Premier League matches. The OFT would have preferred a solution whereby BSkyB could have obtained 60 live matches but the other matches would have been sold by the participating clubs themselves. Nevertheless, this argument did not impress the Restrictive Practices Court, which pointed out that competition between broadcasters was largely dependent on their ability to obtain exclusive rights as this enabled them to differentiate their programming from that of their competitors. Such competition would be impeded, not encouraged, if 'broad exclusivity' was not available[1].

1 See para B2.273.

B2.293 Finally, it should be noted that the Commission has suggested that the potential anti-competitive effects of exclusive arrangements may be mitigated by the operation of a sub-licensing regime[1]. This was the kind of solution that the Commission adopted in the *EBU/Eurovision* decision in 1993, a case which related to the collective purchase, rather than the collective sale, of exclusive sports rights[2]. In practice, however, sub-licensing arrangements can be difficult to enforce effectively and there is always the issue (difficult for a competition authority to address) of what is the appropriate fee for the grant of a sub-licence. Interestingly, in the Notice that the Commission issued upon sending a statement of objections to UEFA concerning the UEFA Champions League[3], it criticised the sub-licensing arrangements that had been put in place for allowing only one other broadcaster per member state to broadcast coverage of UEFA Champions League matches[4]. The Commission subsequently indicated that it intended to approve modifications to those arrangements by UEFA that contemplated broader sub-licensing arrangements with respect to delayed highlights rights and certain new media rights[5].

1 Wachtmeister 'Broadcasting of Sports Events and Competition Law' EC Competition Policy Newsletter (1998 No 2, June); Draft/Preliminary Guidelines on the Application of the Competition Rules to Sport, unpublished Commission memorandum, 15 February 1999, at 32.
2 See para B2.294 et seq. Similarly, Spanish pay-TV broadcasters Sogecable and Telefonica avoided being fined by the Commission for jointly acquiring exclusive rights to the Primera Liga for 11 years by promising to sub-license some of the rights to their competitors. See www.sportcal.com (1 December 2000).
3 See para B2.291, n 1. See also EP Culture Committee secretariat, Background Note, 27 March 2002 (NT\465\465312EN): 'If pay-TV rights and free-TV rights were sold separately, or for shorter periods, more broadcasters (smaller or regional channels, for example) could realistically bid for them'.
4 See para B2.278.
5 See 'Joint selling of media rights of the UEFA Champions League on an exclusive basis', Art 19(3) Notice concerning Case COMP/C.2/37.398, [2002] OJ C 196/03.

(e) Collective purchasing of broadcasting rights

B2.294 In addition to collective selling[1], sports rights may also be purchased on a 'collective' basis. Such collective purchasing arrangements may be analysed on the basis of standard competition law principles. Broadcasters who 'pool' their resources to engage in joint purchasing arrangements are 'eliminating or restricting competition' between themselves. Moreover, unlike sports teams, these joint purchasers *are* in horizontal competition with each other and they have no interest in ensuring their competitors' competitiveness. As a result, their co-operation in the sphere of acquiring sports rights does require some form of justification. The usual justification, in circumstances where the pooling arrangements allow members of the buying group to bid for rights that would be beyond their individual reach, is that this enhances rather than restricts competition[2].

1 See para B2.249 et seq.
2 See *Gottrup-Klim v Dansk Landburgs Grovvareselskab,* Case C-250/92, [1994] ECR I-5641. See also Jaime Andreo, DG-X, 'The application of competition rules to sport: the media' (November 1999): 'Such agreements should not pose a competition problem in the cases of a regrouping of operators who, individually, would not have the financial resources to acquire the rights. In such a situation, a joint purchase could even prove pro-competitive'; Commissioner Mario Monti, *Sport and Competition* (speech 00/152 to Commission-organised conference on sports: Brussels, 17 April 2000) (same) and DN: Speech/01/84, 26 February 2001 (same).

B2.295 An important case on the legality of joint purchasing of sports rights concerned the European Broadcasting Union ('EBU'), an association of public service broadcasters in Europe. Members of the EBU are required to provide a service of national character, covering at least 98% of television households, and containing varied and balanced programming for all sections of the population[1]. The 'Eurovision system' was an agreement that involved, among other things:

(a) the joint acquisition of exclusive television rights to international sports events;
(b) the sharing of those rights between members who operate in the same market;
(c) the provision by a member acting as a host broadcaster of a free signal to members, on a reciprocal basis; and
(d) (after the intervention of the Commission described below[2]) access to the programming for non-members through a system of sub-licensing.

1 The EBU members are mainly public broadcasters such as VRT/RTBF (Belgium), France 2 (France); ZDF, ARD (Germany), RTVE (Spain); BBC (UK) etc. However, a few private broadcasters such as TF1 and Canal+ (both French) have been accepted into the EBU.
2 See para B2.296.

B2.296 Following a complaint from a non-EBU member, the Commission started proceedings against the EBU with regard to its members' joint acquisition of sports rights. The outcome of these proceedings was that joint acquisition within the framework of the Eurovision system could only be allowed if the EBU accepted an obligation to grant non-members sub-licences in relation to the rights acquired (such sub-licences to be granted on reasonable terms). An exemption was granted on that basis under Art 81(3)[1].

1 Decision of 11 June 1993, 93/403/EEC (IV/32.150, OJ 1993 L 179, p 23).

B2.297 Notwithstanding the existence of this sub-licensing obligation, however, the conclusion of the Commission procedure proved unpopular with several non-EBU members and they challenged the exemption decision before the European Court of First Instance ('CFI')[1]. The CFI went on to annul the decision on the grounds (among others) that the Commission had not examined whether the rules on EBU membership were objective and sufficiently definite to be applied uniformly and in a non-discriminatory manner. The CFI did not, however, rule out the possibility that the conditions for an exemption might be fulfilled[2].

1 Joined case T-528/93 *Métropole Télévision SA*, T-542/93 *Reti Televisive Italiane SpA*, T-543/93 *Gestevisión Telecinco*, T-546/93 *Antena 3 de Television* [1996] ECR II-649.
2 *Métrople Télévision SA, Reti Televisive Italiane SpA and Gestevisión Telecino v European Commission* [1996] ECR II-649 CFI.

B2.298 Subsequently, the Commission issued a new exemption decision intended to address the criticisms that had been made by the CFI. This time, the Eurovision system was granted an exemption on the following basis:

- Joint acquisition reduced the transaction costs that would be associated with a multitude of separate negotiations and, as a result, more sports events could be broadcast by a larger number of broadcasters. The improved coverage extended to both popular sports and minority sports (improvements in distribution, more consumer choice).
- Joint acquisition of rights was indispensable: the success of the joint negotiations would be put in jeopardy if individual members simultaneously engaged in separate negotiations. Furthermore, the joint buying, rights sharing and exchange of the television signal were interdependent matters, all based on the principle of solidarity and reciprocity between EBU members.
- There was no elimination of competition. In particular, a set of sub-licensing rules was introduced aimed to ensure that all non-EBU members could have access to Eurovision sports rights on reasonable terms[1].

1 Commission Decision of 10 May 2000, Case IV/32.150.

B2.299 Outside the context of the EBU, but staying with collective purchasing, it was reported in August 2001 that Kirch Sport, the holder of the broadcasting rights to the 2002 and 2006 FIFA World Cup Finals, had complained to the OFT about the decision of the BBC and ITV not to bid against each other for the UK rights but rather to submit a joint bid[1]. Subsequently, however, Kirch accepted an improved joint bid and the complaint was apparently quietly dropped[2].

1 'Kirch complains to regulator over ITV-BBC World Cup cartel' (2001) Sportcal.com, 14 August.
2 The Commission has considered the joint acquisition by three Spanish broadcasters of broadcasting rights to eleven seasons of Spanish Premier League football matches, which also included a sub-licensing system to competitors. See Commission press release dated 23 November 2000, IP/00/1352. See also 'Serie A clubs go to Brussels over pay-TV "collusion"' (2002) TV Sports Markets, 2 August (Italian clubs accuse Telepiu and Stream of colluding over bids for clubs' TV rights).

(f) Modality of transmission

B2.300 Without question, the sale of broadcasting rights to the highest bidder has meant that much of elite sport is now accessible only on pay-TV, which has greatly reduced public access to broadcast sport. The Commission has stated that competition law is neutral with respect to whether broadcasting rights should be granted either to free or pay-television[1]. However, Art 3A of EC Directive *Television without Frontiers*[2] gives member states the possibility, at national level, to 'list' events that must be made available to the public on an unencrypted (ie 'free') basis[3]. It follows, therefore, that Community law contains a legislative bias allowing member states the possibility to favour free television at the expense of pay-TV. The only qualification is that the listed event should be 'of major importance to society'. In practice, however, it seems rather unlikely that the Commission would interfere with the judgment of a national government regarding which events, sporting or otherwise, are of interest and importance to people in their own country.

1 See eg Commission Report, *Broadcasting of Sports Events and Competition Law* (June 1998) at Section VI. See also Joined Cases T-528, T542/93 and T-546/93, the *Eurovision* judgment [1996] ECR II-649.

2 Council Directive 89/552/EEC, as amended by Directive 97/36/EC of the European Parliament and Council of 30 June 1997 on the co-ordination of certain provisions laid down by law, regulation or administrative action in member states concerning the pursuit of television broadcasting activities.

3 See paras A1.81 to A1.92.

(g) Black-out rules

B2.301 It is an important regulatory objective of most sports governing bodies to encourage participation in amateur events and paying attendance at professional events. Nevertheless, there are many competing attractions in today's sport and leisure market, not least the coverage of events from other countries and/or other sports. In particular, in the post-*Bosman* era, sports events from neighbouring European countries are of more interest than ever, owing to the international flavour of competitions in which many 'foreign' stars are present.

B2.302 In European football, the leading attractions are probably the top national league competitions in England, Germany, Italy and Spain. For example, many Irish football fans are avid fans of FA Premier League football, and would probably watch it in preference to their own domestic football. The same may apply in various Scandinavian countries.

B2.303 UEFA, the governing body of European football, operates a regulatory system that is intended to give football associations some degree of 'protection', allowing them to schedule their domestic fixtures at times when they will not be likely to be disrupted by the contemporaneous broadcast of football by restricting the sale of broadcasting rights to football matches into their territories during those periods. Nevertheless, such a regulatory regime does involve a limited restriction on broadcasting freedom and the UEFA system initially attracted the hostility of several television stations, who complained about it to the European Commission[1]. It was alleged that the effect of the regime (contained in Art 44 (ex 14) of the UEFA Statutes) was to restrict the exploitation of broadcast rights to football, limiting the ability of broadcaster to compete with each other and reducing the choice of programmes available to the consumer. In July 1998, the Commission issued a statement of objections asserting that the black-out rules infringed Art 81(1) and were not eligible for an exemption under Art 81(3).

1 Case Nos IV/C2; 34.319; 33.734; 34.199; 33.145; 34.784; 34.790; 34.948; 35.001; 35.048.

B2.304 Following the issuance of this statement of objections, UEFA modified its broadcasting regulations and narrowed the scope of the 'black-out' rules significantly[1]. Under the revised rules, a national association may only prevent the broadcasting of football within its territory for two and a half hours either on a

Saturday or a Sunday, at hours corresponding to its main domestic football schedule. So, for example, the English FA has blocked foreign football programming between 14.45 and 17.15 on a Saturday afternoon, which corresponds to the traditional time of the main domestic matches in England.

1 See Art 19(3) Notice concerning Case 37.576 (UEFA's broadcasting rules), OJ 29 April 2000, C121/14.

B2.305 In April 2001, the Commission announced that it considered the revised rules to have no appreciable effect on competition. This was because the black-out possibilities are now so limited in scope that they do not interfere, or do not interfere to any appreciable extent, with the operation of the broadcast market. In light of this finding, no exemption was needed since the UEFA rules were deemed not to fall within Art 81(1) in the first place. On adoption of the decision[1], Commissioner Monti stated:

> The present decision reflects the Commission's respect of the specific characteristics of sport and of its cultural and social function in Europe in trying to play the role of an impartial referee between the different interests of broadcasters and football clubs[2].

1 Commission Decision of 19 April 2001 in Case 37.576 (UEFA's broadcasting regulations'), OJ 26 June 2001, L171/12.

2 'Commission clears UEFA's new Broadcasting Regulations', Commission press release dated 20 April 2001, IP/01/583.

G Sponsorship and supply agreements

B2.306 Sponsorship is a prominent and valuable component of a sport's commercial programme[1]. Nevertheless, competition law issues are relatively few, largely because the vast array of alternative promotional platforms for sponsors makes the market a very broad one. In this scenario, there is much less concern regarding 'foreclosure' of markets.

1 See Chapter D5.

(a) Market definition in sponsorship cases

B2.307 Sponsorship is a form of advertising and as such competes with an almost limitless number of methods for promoting the brand, product or service at issue. Companies seeking to promote particular products or services, or their 'brand' generally, have a wide range of platforms from which to choose, including television advertising and programme sponsorship, advertising in the print media, billboard advertising, sponsorship of cultural events, and so on. Even assuming the sponsor is only a UK brand (thus limiting the geographic market to the UK), the range of promotional opportunities delivering the same exposure is huge.

B2.308 Even if a sponsor insists on a sports-related platform, the range of 'substitutable' possibilities is still enormous. There are endorsement deals with individual sportsmen or women (such as David Beckham's endorsement of Police sunglasses), advertising at sports venues (such as on perimeter boards, in match programmes, on big screens etc), and sponsorship of a vast range of different events (such as the Embassy World Professional Darts Championship), clubs (such as NEC Harlequins) and/or sports programming (such as Coca Cola's sponsorship of ITV's 'Premiership' programme).

B2.309 If a marketing department insists on a football-related platform rather than any other sport, there would *still* be a very wide range of promotional opportunities, each of which is broadly substitutable for the other. Even ignoring traditional advertising around football events (such as match programme advertising, perimeter boards at football stadia, and so on), it is possible to sponsor a broad range of different teams (such as Carlsberg's sponsorship of Liverpool) and events (such as the FA Barclaycard Premiership, the Nationwide League, the Axa FA Cup), or even to create events of one's own (such as Nike Park). It is also possible to obtain the endorsement of a range of individual 'superstar' footballers.

B2.310 As a result of this broad range of market opportunities, an 'exclusive' agreement of a breadth and length that would set alarm bells ringing in the broadcasting market is likely to raise little concern in the sponsorship market. Even if, for example, the FA Premier League extended its current title sponsorship deal with Barclaycard for a further five years, the huge array of substitutable opportunities left for Barclaycard's competitors to promote themselves makes it difficult to suggest that the grant of rights by the FA Premier League has any appreciable effect on competition on the market on which that agreement operates.

(b) Central marketing of sponsorship rights

B2.311 As previously discussed[1], several top sports forbid the sale of television rights by individual clubs, instead packaging the rights into a single package that is then sold centrally by the league organiser with the revenue being distributed according to pre-set rules. This arrangement also reflects the fact that the championship matches of interest to a broadcaster are necessarily a 'joint' product, which no club on its own would be capable of producing[2].

1 See para B2.249.
2 See para B2.66.

B2.312 In contrast, however, sponsorship arrangements involve the grant of a right to be associated with the particular brand of the grantor. A club's 'brand' identity is not perceived to be a joint product[1] and, as a result, rather than the event organiser granting one entity the right to sponsor each participating team (or the right to supply branded kit to each participating team), the accepted practice is for each club to retain the right to license the intellectual property rights in its name, badge and other marks to a sponsor or kit manufacturer of its own choosing[2].

1 In North America, where the professional elite play exclusively in one closed league, it is easier to argue that the value of the individual club brand 'derives almost entirely from the fact that the team is a member of the league'. See Roberts 'The Legality of the Exclusive Collective Sale of Intellectual Property Rights by Sports Leagues' *Virginia Journal of Sports and the Law*, Vol 3:1 (Spring 2001), p 53. In Europe, however, where clubs play in many different tournaments, run by different tournament organisers – eg the Premier League (run by The FA Premier League Ltd), the FA Cup (run by The Football Association, the League Cup (run by The Football League) and the UEFA Champions League (run by UEFA) – the position is different. Roberts (above) at 55.
2 See generally Chapter D6. Typically, the various manufacturers of football kit enter into licensing arrangements with individual clubs, for example Umbro/Manchester Utd (at least until season 2002/03), Nike/Leeds, Reebok/Liverpool, Adidas/Spurs. The manufacturer supplies the clubs with shirts for use by the club's own teams. The club also licenses the manufacturer to produce replica kit adorned with the club regalia for retail sale, in exchange for payment by the manufacturer to the club of a royalty on each kit sold. If the club has also done a deal with a separate shirt sponsor, then the kit manufacturer is required to reproduce that sponsor's name or logo on the shirt as well.

B2.313 It is, therefore, currently a moot point as to whether a central sponsorship or supply deal covering all the clubs in (say) the FA Premier League would raise any competition law issues. Such an arrangement between Adidas and the French National League was struck down on competition grounds[1], but based on a very narrow (and not properly explained or substantiated) definition of the relevant market[2].

1 Prior to 1995, the applicable league rules allowed clubs to enter into individual licensing deals. Under this system, Adidas sponsored less than 10 of the top 42 French professional football clubs; its competitors (including Reebok, Nike and Asics) sponsored many of the others. In 1995, Adidas paid the National Football League in France 60m francs in return for the exclusive right to provide equipment to all of the clubs in the first and second divisions of the French football league championship. The League then adopted a rule requiring the clubs in the top two divisions to use equipment as designated by the League. As a result, many clubs cancelled their sponsorship arrangements with Adidas' competitors and signed up with Adidas, so that Adidas soon sponsored 30 or so of the top 42 clubs. Upon complaint by Adidas' competitors, the French competition authorities issued interim measures suspending the change in the League's rules. They then held, and subsequently the Court of Appeal in Paris agreed, that the agreement infringed French domestic competition law (which mirrors the EC competition rules). *National Football League/Adidas*, Court of Appeal of Paris, 29/2/2000, [2000] 10 ECLR, p N.118/9. See 'Adidas fined over anti-competitive soccer deal' (2001) Sportcal.com, 2 January. See also Sheppard and Reid 'Rights holder shouldn't panic over Adidas fine' (2001) Sportcal.com, 5 January.

2 The relevant market was said (for reasons that are not clear from the court's judgment) to be the market in France for branded trainers. Adidas' share of that market was almost 50%, allowing the authorities to call it dominant on that market. The arrangements were said to restrict competition appreciably on that market because: (a) along with its other sponsorship deals – Adidas was also the exclusive kit supplier and sponsor with respect to the League Cup and French Cup as well as the French national team – the deal with the League meant that Adidas supplied kit to teams playing in at least 60% of matches broadcast on national television, thereby dominating this particular platform for the promotion of branded trainers; (b) the League held no tendering process for the rights granted to Adidas; (c) the five-year exclusive term of the agreement foreclosed the market to an unacceptable degree; (d) the 'matching rights' renewal clause that Adidas inserted into its contracts with individual clubs protected Adidas further from competition on that market; and (e) the League was not entitled to exercise its regulatory powers to obtain an economic advantage. Adidas was fined €2.4m and the League was fined 800,000 francs. *National Football League/Adidas*, Court of Appeal of Paris, 29/2/2000, [2000] 10 ECLR, p N.118/9. See 'Adidas fined over anti-competitive soccer deal' (2001) Sportcal.com, 2 January. See also Sheppard and Reid 'Rights holder shouldn't panic over Adidas fine' (2001) Sportcal.com, 5 January. Adidas' 'matching rights' clause was also condemned in *Reebok France v Adidas and Uhlsport*, French Competition Council, 7 October 1997, [1998] 5 ECLR, p N-84.

B2.314 When event organisers enter into sponsorship arrangements, these are typically grants of 'title' rights, ie the right to associate the name of the sponsor with the event, such as the FA Barclaycard Premiership and the Nationwide League (in football), the Zurich Premiership (in rugby union), and the Embassy World Professional Darts Championship (darts). Such deals are not properly analysed as 'central' or 'collective' arrangements at all. The product being sold to the title sponsor is name association with the competition as a whole, not with individual teams within the competition. As a result, it is by definition only the competition organiser, and not any individual club, that could grant such rights. It remains possible, however, that issues might conceivably arise if, for example, the event organiser sought to restrict individual clubs with regard to their own sponsorship deals with third parties competing in the same sector as the title sponsor[1].

1 See eg Schaub (Director-General of Competition) 'EC Competition Policy and its Implications for the Sports Sector', speech to World Sports Forum, March 1998: 'Requirements imposed by sports associations to the effect that only equipment of a certain manufacturer may be employed during competitions will be examined with care'. Cf *Otakuku Rovers Rugby League Club v Auckland Rugby League* unreported, Williams J, New Zealand High Court 12 November 1993 (governing body required clubs to use Lion Breweries insignia on goal posts, but plaintiff club was sponsored by Dominion Breweries; club claimed unsuccessfully that the governing body did not have the right to sell signage space at its ground).

(c) The Danish Tennis Federation case again

B2.315 If a market is defined narrowly enough it is possible that a sponsorship arrangement may be deemed capable, in certain cases, of having an appreciable effect on competition[1]. Should that be the case, the Commission will try to ensure that arrangements do not foreclose competition on the market. Typically, it will consider the length and scope of the exclusivity granted, and look for evidence that the sales process for the grant of the sponsorship rights was fair and open to all competitors. This was the approach taken in the *Danish Tennis Federation* ('DTF') case[2].

1 See eg *National Football League/Adidas*, Court of Appeal of Paris, 29/2/2000, [2000] ECLR 10, p N118/9; para B2.313, nn 1 and 2.
2 Case Nos IV/F-1/33.055 and 35.759, [1996] 4 CMLR 885. See para B2.207 et seq.

B2.316 The DTF granted Slazenger and Tretorn the exclusive right to supply tennis balls for use in all official tennis tournaments in Denmark for a three-year period. Slazenger and Tretorn got the right to use the DTF logo and the denomination 'DTF official balls' on their packaging, in a manner that effectively allowed them to prevent parallel imports. They were also allowed to say the balls were 'selected by' or 'approved by' the DTF. Various manufacturers complained that this restricted their ability to compete and the Commission agreed, sending the DTF a statement of objections. The DTF subsequently revised its arrangements, setting up a competitive tendering process for the appointment of manufacturers or distributors as suppliers of equipment to the competitions that it organised. Any manufacturer meeting objective quality criteria was entitled to join a 'ball pool' and to participate in the tender to be appointed to supply balls to the DTF. The successful company was appointed for a maximum of two years. All those who qualified for the ball pool were entitled to use the ball pool logo[1]. The Commission noted that such sponsorship and supply arrangements 'can contribute considerably to the promotion of sport without threatening competition, provided that certain criteria for openness and transparency are met'[2].

1 1998 Competition Report, p 160.
2 'The Commission conditionally approves sponsorship contracts between the Danish Tennis Federation and its tennis ball suppliers', Commission press release dated 15 April 1998, IP 98/355. See also Commissioner Mario Monti *Sport and Competition* (speech given at a Commission-organised conference on sports: Brussels 17 April 2000 and in DN: Speech/01/84 26 February 2001): 'Sponsorship arrangements should be organised in an objective and transparent manner. In particular, exclusive rights should only be granted according to objective selection criteria'.

B2.317 Furthermore, under the amended rules of the DTF the successful bidder was only allowed to use the designation 'sponsor of the DTF'. It could not label itself as 'official supplier', or state that its products were 'official balls', because that would have run the risk of confusing consumers into thinking that its products were technically superior to those of its competitors[1]. This last concern arises whenever a sponsor is a manufacturer of equipment used in the sport (and when the governing body is effectively a 'monopolist' with regard to the organisation of sports competitions). The same concern would not appear to arise, for example, where the product or service of the sponsor is not linked to the sport. So, whilst it may be problematic to call 'Slazenger' balls the official ball of the DTF, it would not be a problem (say) to call IBM the official IT supplier of the DTF.

1 'The Commission conditionally approves sponsorship contracts between the Danish Tennis Federation and its tennis ball suppliers', Commission press release dated 15 April 1998, IP/98/355.

H Merchandising

B2.318 Aspects of the widespread commercial practice developing lines of merchandise around sports-related brands[1] have also attracted the attention of the competition regulators.

1 See generally Chapter D6.

B2.319 For example, in *Dunlop Slazenger*[1] and *Tretorn*[2], the Commission confirmed that the distribution of sports goods is subject to the same rules as any other goods and so a system of exclusive distribution cannot be used to prevent parallel imports. In the cases referred to, the firms involved were fined for prohibiting exports of their products in order to protect their exclusive distribution networks, and enforcing this prohibition in respect of tennis balls, squash balls, tennis rackets and golf equipment by means of refusals to supply, marking and follow-up of exported products and discriminatory use of official labels[3]. These are serious violations of EC competition law.

1 92/261/EEC: Commission decision dated 18 March 1992, OJ 1992 L 131/32 *Dunlop-Slazenger v European Commission* Case T-43/92, [1994] ECR II-441, CFI.
2 Commission decision 94/987/EEC, [1994] OJ L378/45 31 December 1994; [1997] 4 CMLR 860.
3 Dunlop Slazenger affixed 'approved' stickers to balls sent to its exclusive distribution network in Belgium and the Netherlands. Balls shipped back into the UK at lower prices than offered by Dunlop Slazenger in the UK did not have such stickers, and were easily noticed, allowing the supplier to be traced.

B2.320 As another example, in January 1997 the OFT launched a campaign against resale price maintenance in markets for the supply of sporting goods. Retailers complained that manufacturers of replica football shirts were 'punishing' them for undercutting minimum resale price levels. Subsequently, the OFT obtained assurances from various manufacturers of the official and replica kit of various professional clubs (as well as from other manufacturers of various different sporting goods) that they would not enforce minimum resale prices[1].

1 See eg OFT press release no 19/98 dated 21 April 1998, 'Supplier of football shirts gives price promise'.

B2.321 During the investigation, the OFT apparently uncovered evidence that certain football clubs had put pressure on manufacturers or distributors to withhold supplies from retailers which had sold replica kit at a discount. In August 1999, the OFT announced that the FA and the Scottish FA (licensors of English and Scottish national shirts respectively), as well as the FA Premier League clubs, had each agreed to include provisions in their licensing contracts forbidding manufacturers to take punitive action against retailers who sold replica kit at a discount[1]. Nevertheless, in May 2002, it was reported that the OFT had uncovered further evidence of such practices in relation to (among other items) Manchester Utd kit and England kit manufactured by Umbro[2].

1 OFT press release no PN 30/99, 6 August 1999, 'Football kit price fixing ended'; OFT Fair Trading News, October 1999. See [1999] 7(3) SATLJ 18.
2 'OFT proposes to find that replica football kit prices have been fixed', OFT press release dated 17 May 2002; 'Manchester Utd and FA face fines in 'price fixing' inquiry' (2002) www.sportcal.com, 17 May; 'A fair price for the shirt on your back' (2002) Times 28 May.

I Data Agreements

B2.322 There has always been a demand, from the news media and the betting industry, for standard sports data in the form of fixtures and results. Now, however, as a result of the proliferation of sports websites, the development of interactive television and the emergence of spread betting, a significant demand has developed for more sophisticated data relating to sporting events. Largely because of gambling interest, the demand is for 'official' data. Commercialisation of such data is developing, based on copyright in fixture lists and database rights in compilations of match data[1]. For example, the British Horseracing Board ('BHB') spends significant sums each year compiling and maintaining comprehensive information about the thousands of races, horses, owners and trainers active in the UK each year, and then licenses the use of that data by the news media and by the betting industry[2]. Once again, competition law issues can arise.

1 See paras D1.45 and D1.47.
2 See para D1.68 et seq.

B2.323 In *Magill*[1], an Irish company sought to publish a comprehensive television guide containing the listings from all available programme guides. The television broadcasters produced their own listings. However, they neither produced themselves nor would they license anyone else to produce combined listings from all stations. The broadcasters sued Magill for breach of copyright in their respective listings and Magill complained to the European Commission that the broadcasters' refusal to license their intellectual property rights to Magill constituted an abuse of a dominant position. The Commission and the Court of First Instance upheld the complaint, as did the European Court of Justice, which held that a refusal to license intellectual property rights could 'in exceptional circumstances' amount to an abuse of dominant position[2].

1 Joined Cases C-241/91 P and C-242/91 P, *RTE and ITP v EC Commission* [1995] 4 CMLR 718.
2 See n 1.

B2.324 *Magill* was distinguished in *Tierce Ladbroke SA v EC Commission*[1], a case concerning access to pictures of horse races for bookmaking purposes. Ladbroke complained that the holders of the rights to television images and sound commentaries of French horse-racing had refused to license the rights to Ladbrokes in Belgium. The Commission, and subsequently the Court of First Instance, rejected the complaint, observing that the relevant market was Belgium and the respondents were not active in the Belgian gaming market. Ladbrokes was, in fact, the main player on that market and whilst the pictures were an attractive add-on service for punters they were not – in contrast to the TV listings in *Magill* – 'indispensable' to the activity in question (ie the taking of bets). In the circumstances, the respondents had not reserved any market for themselves and so the fact that Ladbrokes was willing to pay a reasonable fee for a licence was irrelevant.

1 Case T-504/93 [1997] OJ C252/24; [1995] ECR II-2537 (CFI), affirmed [1997] ECR I-7007 (ECJ).

B2.325 In June 2001, William Hill filed a complaint with the OFT alleging that the BHB was abusing its dominant position in relation to prices charged for the supply of pre-race information for use on William Hill's web-site[1]. The complaint was bound up with another dispute over William Hill's unlicensed use on the

Internet of information from BHB's database[2]. It was alleged that the BHB's demand for a percentage of its total turnover from betting on horseracing in return for the grant of a licence was excessive, as well as discriminatory. The OFT announced that, on the basis of its preliminary inquiries, it considered that the matter should be investigated for evidence of abuse under Chapter II of the Competition Act 1998[3]. Nevertheless, the complaint was subsequently withdrawn as part of a global deal that saw William Hill and the other four big UK bookmakers agree to pay the BHB 10% of their gross profits as a licence fee for the use in their betting shops as well as in their telephone and internet operations of pre-race information from the BHB's database[4].

1 See Hammon 'William Hill's pre-race data claims could be hard to prove' (2001) Sportcal.com, 18 June.
2 See para D1.68 et seq.
3 See 'OFT investigates horserace board' (2001) Financial Times, 22 October.
4 BHB press release (17 April 2002).

J State aid

B2.326 The state aid rules of the EC Treaty[1] have seen limited application to date in the sports sector.

1 See paras B2.034 to B2.037.

(a) Manufacturers of sports equipment

B2.327 The most obvious sports-related context in which the issue of state aid might arise is in fact the only context in which the issue has gone to the European Court of Justice. In *Salomon SA v EC Commission*[1], the government made financial injections to restore the fortunes of Head, a ski equipment manufacturer that was in financial difficulty. The aid rescued the company. Its competitors, including Salomon, complained to the Commission that the injections had not been notified to the Commission and were unlawful and incompatible state aid. The Commission cleared the aid, subject to Head giving certain undertakings[2]. Salomon brought proceedings against the Commission on the basis of its refusal to act on its complaint, but the European Court of Justice refused to overturn the Commission's approach.

1 [1999] ECR II-2925.
2 [1997] OJ L 025, p 26 (28 January 1997).

(b) Grants to clubs

B2.328 In *Public grants to professional clubs*[1], the French government introduced and notified measures aimed at improving 'the organisation and promotion of physical and sporting activities' in France. The measures involved the public subsidisation through local authorities of professional football, basketball, rugby and volleyball clubs of up to €2.3m per year per club. The Commission concluded that the measures did not involve state aid because the local authorities were confined to making grants to professional clubs with state-approved youth training centres. The encouragement of those centres was aimed at providing young people with an education allowing them to reach the best sporting level and to reconcile sports training with a thorough education and so enable them to find a job either in the sports field or outside it. The scheme also achieved the provision of community facilities and helped to reduce violence in particular areas. Consequently the funding constituted an educational or comparable scheme. The Commission insisted however that the French authorities undertake to avoid any overcompensation for the net costs of school and sports training, and therefore cross-subsidisation. The authorities were required to monitor the use of grants received by insisting on separate accounts for training activities and economic activities, and to ensure the repayment of any funds used for purposes other than those explicitly provided for[2].

1 Aid N118/00 – France, [2001] OJ C 333, p 6 (28 November 2001), decision of 25 April 2001, IP/01/599. See [2001] 1 ISLR 8.

2 It is worth noting that, in the European Parliament's Resolution on the role of the European Union in the field of sport, [1997] OJ C 200, p 252 of 30 June 1997, it called 'in particular on the Commission … (b) since it has failed to refer to sport in its White Paper on Education and Training, to rectify that omission, on the basis of Article 126 of the Treaty, in the activities to be carried out on the basis of that White Paper, to encourage the Member States to reverse the trend to reduce the time devoted to sport in schools and to encourage the establishment of closer links between schools and sports clubs … (f) to examine whether the various schemes for state aid to professional clubs applied in the Member States and the current disparities relating to social security and tax burdens have an effect on the fairness of European competitions and whether the transparency of the financial situation of the various professional clubs in the Community should be guaranteed'.

(c) *Other situations*

B2.329 The application of the state aid provisions in the sports context is only in its infancy. It is possible that the issue will be raised in a number of other sports-related situations, particularly as the amount of money involved in sport increases, as many clubs find it difficult to survive with spiralling costs and as the desire to improve national team performance leads to similar subsidisation to that embarked upon in France[1].

1 See para B2.328.

B2.330 First, any state measures (such as grants or tax breaks or assistance with infrastructure such as stadiums) offering favourable treatment to particular clubs, which do not benefit from the block exemptions, may be caught by the prohibition and if not notified could be the subject of successful action in the English courts[1]. The state for these purposes covers local authorities as well as central government. Further, even where one sport as a whole is granted assistance ahead of others, the assistance may be caught if an argument can be made that they compete for the same public attention and participation. It is also theoretically possible that the advantaged business might be an individual player.

1 Cf Montana-Mora 'Financing of Professional Football and EC Competition Law' [2001] 3 SATLJ 159 (state aid analysis of Real Madrid's acquisition of Zinedine Zidane).

B2.331 Secondly, it may well be that the payment of grants by Sport England or UK Sport out of lottery funding[1] could be caught. These grants by their nature favour particular bodies and clubs. Although the Commission operates a threshold that would not be met by most such grants, the threshold does not have any status before the English courts (although they may conclude that grants below the threshold do not affect competition at all).

1 See paras A1.53 and C3.34 et seq.

B2.332 Thirdly, in the broadcasting sector competitors of such publicly-funded broadcasters as the BBC may seek to challenge the BBC's use of licence fee funding for the purchase of sports rights. Although the budget of the BBC has not allowed it recently to compete for major rights with commercial television and in particular BSkyB, there is an increasing likelihood that the readiness of such broadcasters to pay over the odds will decrease rapidly as either their new platforms become well-established (as in the case of BSkyB) or they collapse as a result of unwise investment (as in the case of ITV Digital). In these circumstances, the prospect of more competition at a lower price level becomes likely. At that level, the price to be paid for rights will increasingly be referable to the anticipated advertising revenue (or possibly pay-per-view revenue) to be derived from the rights. Under these conditions the BBC may enjoy a considerable advantage by virtue of the breadth of its public funding, and be able to pay more than its commercial counterparts. Furthermore, the BBC is also in a strong position in relation to minor, lower-priced rights, and vis-a-vis smaller broadcasters. Disappointed tenderers for rights might therefore raise a challenge[1]. Indeed, one already has[2], albeit to the OFT.

1 The disappointed tenderer would have to go on to show more, in particular that there had not been any notification of the relevant use of the licence fee and that there was an effect on trade between member states.

2 'Talksport/BBC feud continues' (July 2001) Sports Marketing 3 (Talksport reported to have complained to the OFT about the BBC using licence fee money to outbid commercial stations, paying 'inflated prices' for radio rights to sports events).

B2.333 The fourth and more speculative situation is where a sports governing body itself grants assistance, such as the parachute payments made to relegated football clubs by the football authorities. While these payments are ostensibly justified by the need to maintain competitive balance and to produce the exciting competition that the public want to watch, there is little doubt that they provide an advantage to clubs not enjoyed by those with whom they are in direct competition. If the analysis in *Bosman* of sports governing bodies as state actors[1] could be extended to characterise such bodies as providing funding out of state resources, and the payments had not been notified, then again action in the English courts might well be mounted. That said, the preferable analysis may well be that the basis on which the football authorities were elevated in to the position of quasi-state bodies in *Bosman* is confined to the particular circumstances of the free movement rules.

1 See paras A3.70, A3.71, B3.8 and B3.9.

K Mergers

B2.334 The application of the merger rules in the sports sector has also been limited to date.

(a) UK merger regulations[1]

B2.335 Sports governing bodies have sought, for reasons of sporting integrity, to prevent the same party owning more than one club in the same competition[2]. However, if there is no issue of multiple ownership, then generally there is no limitation as to what type of individual or company may acquire a club. For example, no sports governing body has thought it important, from a sporting perspective, to prevent a media company acquiring an interest in a club. Thus,

Canal Plus owes Paris St Germain in France; Mediaset owns AC Milan in Italy; and in the United States various basketball and hockey teams are owned by media groups.

1 See para B2.41.
2 See para B2.145 et seq.

B2.336 When it was announced in late 1998, however, that BSkyB proposed to acquire Manchester United FC, concerns were raised in particular about the impact this might have on competition on the market for broadcasting rights to the FA Premier League. The Secretary of State referred the proposed acquisition to the Monopoly and Mergers Commission ('MMC') which, after a wide-ranging inquiry, issued a report recommending that the Secretary of State block the merger[1], and that is exactly what happened.

1 MMC *Report into the Proposed Merger between BSkyB Group plc and Manchester United plc* (Cm 4305, 1999).

B2.337 The main reason for the MMC's recommendation was its concern that the proposed acquisition would impact adversely on competition for the broadcasting rights to FA Premier League matches. In particular, notwithstanding the offer of various undertakings by BSkyB, including the proposed creation of various 'firewalls', the MMC remained concerned that BSkyB would still sit on both sides of the table in future Premier League rights negotiations and that would undermine fair competition for the rights. There was a risk that BSkyB would obtain access to confidential information about other bids and this would serve to entrench its dominant position as provider of premium sports channels in the UK. It would, in short, make it even more difficult for any competitor to enter that market.

B2.338 However, the MMC was not only concerned about the impact of the merger on the market for broadcasting rights. It also considered that allowing the acquisition would widen the gap between rich and poor clubs and thus undermine competitive balance in the league. Indeed, it even expressed a concern about the FA Premier League having its pursuit of sporting imperatives compromised by BSkyB's purely commercial objectives[1].

1 For commentary on the MMC's decision, see Welsh [1999] 7(3) SATLJ 44; Harbord and Binmore 'Toeholds, takeovers and football' [2000] 21(2) ECLR 142; Usher 'Can broadcasters buy UK football clubs?' The Commercial Lawyer, June 1999.

B2.339 Another recent sports-related transaction considered in the context of the UK merger regulations was Octagon Motorsport Ltd's proposed acquisition of certain assets of British Racing Drivers Club Ltd, including the Silverstone racing circuit. In May 2001, the UK's Competition Commission (the successor to the MMC) announced that the Secretary of State had asked it to examine that proposed acquisition under the merger provisions of the Fair Trading Act 1973. The Commission noted claims that the acquisition was essential to ensure that the UK continued to host one of the FIA Formula One World Championship grands prix, but sought views on whether it would have any appreciable anti-competitive effects on any relevant market[1]. In its subsequent report dated 6 September 2001[2], the Commission concluded that the merger would not have adverse effects and therefore was not against the public interest, but it proposed that the operation of the relevant markets be reviewed again after five years.

1 See 'Regulator Examines Silverstone Merger Issues and Remedies' (2001) Sportcal.com, 25 May.
2 Available on www.competition-commission.org.uk.

(b) EC merger regulations

B2.340 The EC Merger Regulation[1] only applies to mergers or acquisitions where various turnover thresholds are met. In light of the high threshold tests that need to be satisfied before the Regulation applies[2], it will in practice be rather uncommon for this to have any application as regards sports clubs.

1 See paras B2.38 to B2.40.
2 See para B2.38.

B2.341 Clearly, however, mergers and acquisitions of media groups may have an incidental impact on the sports business, owing to various cross-holdings and other business links. One merger notified in September 2001 to the European Commission in the sports rights sector was the proposed acquisition by Canal+ and Luxembourg-based RTL Group of the French sports rights agency Groupe Jean-Claude Darmon SA (and the resulting merger of the newly acquired agency with their own sports rights agencies, Sport+ and UFA Sports). This was, in other words, a concentration of buying power in the sports rights market. The Commission granted clearance to the transaction on the basis that it would result in only insignificant 'horizontal' overlaps, ie in the market for the acquisition and resale of sports broadcasting rights, and would not appreciably affect the markets for downstream television broadcasting. This was amongst other reasons, because KirchMedia was a strong pay-TV competitor to Canal+ and the EBU was a strong competitor to free-to-air RTL[1].

1 Case No COMP/M.2483-Group Canal+/RTL/GJCD/JV. See Commission press release dated 14 November 2001, IP/01/1579; [2001] 3 SATLJ 83.

B2.342 In 2000, BSkyB acquired 24% of Kirch Pay TV from the Kirch Group. The acquisition resulted in Kirch's sole control over Kirch Pay TV being transformed into joint control with BSkyB, which consequently amounted to a concentration for the purposes of the Merger Regulation. The concentration had a community dimension. One of the relevant markets on which both BSkyB and Kirch Pay TV operated was the market for the acquisition of rights to sports events. As noted above[1], sports rights are one of the 'drivers' of pay TV, leading to increased subscription and advertising revenue. Kirch Pay TV held many rights to broadcast major sports in Germany, including the Bundesliga, Formula One, boxing, tennis, ice hockey, golf, handball, athletics, American sports and wrestling, and held a dominant position on the market in Germany. It also held a number of important pan-European rights. BSkyB held a dominant position on the market in the UK, holding in particular the rights to Premier League football as well as many other sports. It had been found to be dominant on the market by the OFT in December 1996. It also held a number of pan-European rights. One of the concerns was that the concentration would allow them to bid jointly for pan-European sports rights where they had previously competed, and that they would preferentially sell territorial rights to each other, making it more difficult for competitors to secure access to key sports rights. However the Commission concluded that the fact of the concentration did not make this more likely: it could happen in any event, and therefore there was a lack of causation for the purposes of the Merger Regulation. The Commission was concerned about the effect on other markets, but secured commitments from the parties that satisfied it[2].

1 See para B2.236.
2 *BSkyB/Kirch Pay TV* Case COMP/JV.37 (21 March 2000): the Commission reached a non-opposition decision in relation to a joint venture between the two broadcasters and notified by them.

CHAPTER B3

EC FREE MOVEMENT RULES AND SPORT

Mark Hoskins (Brick Court Chambers) and **Margaret Gray** (Brick Court Chambers)

Contents

1 INTRODUCTION: THE STATUS OF SPORT UNDER THE EC TREATY

B3.1 The EC Treaty does not contain any special exemption for sport or sporting rules. The closest that the European Communities have come to recognising a special status for sport is to be found in the Declaration on Sport (Declaration 29) annexed to the final act of the Conference which adopted the text of the Amsterdam Treaty, which states:

> The Conference emphasises the social significance of sport, in particular its role in forging identity and bringing people together. The Conference therefore calls on the bodies of the European Union to listen to sports associations when important questions affecting sport are at issue. In this connection, special consideration should be given to the particular characteristics of amateur sport.

As is clear from its terms, Declaration 29 is an expression of political desire, rather than a legally binding instrument. However, it does give some indication as to the source of the difficulties in this area. Sport does have particular attributes. This is because, unlike other economic activities, sporting activities did not start out as a means to make money. They began as a recreational past-time, and then developed into an important social and political activity, with great significance at local, national and international levels.

B3.2 The problem for the people and organisations participating in and organising sport is that, as sport becomes increasingly commercialised, they can no longer plead for special treatment. Sport has become a business like any other, the people who participate in and organise it have become businessmen and women, and this increased commercialisation has resulted in sport coming under increased legal scrutiny.

B3.3 Therefore, it is not surprising that the Court of Justice has not shown itself to be particularly sympathetic to arguments based upon the special position which applies to sport and has generally applied the full rigours of the free movement rules to sport.

2 THE FREE MOVEMENT RULES ESTABLISHED BY THE EC TREATY

B3.4 In the context of sport, the most relevant Treaty free movement rules are Art 39 EC (ex Art 48) (free movement of workers), Art 43 EC (ex Art 52) (freedom of establishment) and Art 49 EC (ex Art 59) (freedom to provide services)[1].

1 In this chapter, references to Treaty articles generally will be given as references to the renumbered articles of the Treaty establishing the European Community (EC), brought about by the Treaty of Amsterdam. For example, Art 39 EC denotes the article of that Treaty as it stands after 1 May 1999. The corresponding provision of the same Treaty as it stood before 1 May 1999 may be given in brackets, eg (ex Art 48). However, where reference is made to, or a passage is cited from, a judgment of the Court of Justice, reference is made to the Article as it was numbered at the time of the judgment, with the corresponding provision of the same Treaty as it stands after 1 May 1999 given in brackets, eg (now Art 39 EC).

B3.5 Article 39 EC, which governs the free movement of workers, provides that:

> 1. Freedom of movement for workers shall be secured within the Community.
>
> 2. Such freedom of movement shall entail the abolition of any discrimination based on nationality between workers of the Member States as regards employment, remuneration and other conditions of work and employment.
>
> 3. It shall entail the right, subject to limitations justified on grounds of public policy, public security or public health:
>
> (a) to accept offers of employment actually made;
> (b) to move freely within the territory of Member States for this purpose;
> (c) to stay in a Member State for the purpose of employment in accordance with the provisions governing the employment of nationals of that State laid down by law, regulation or administrative action;
> (d) to remain in the territory of a Member State after having been employed in that State, subject to conditions which shall be embodied in implementing regulations to be drawn up by the Commission.
>
> 4. The provisions of this Article shall not apply to employment in the public service.

B3.6 Article 43 EC, which governs the freedom of establishment, provides that:

> Within the framework of the provisions set out below, restrictions on the freedom of establishment of nationals of a Member State in the territory of another Member State shall be prohibited. Such prohibition shall also apply to restrictions on the setting-up of agencies, branches or subsidiaries by nationals of any Member State established in the territory of any Member State.
>
> Freedom of establishment shall include the right to take up and pursue activities as self-employed persons and to set up and manage undertakings, in particular companies or firms within the meaning of the second paragraph of Article 48, under the conditions laid down for its own nationals by the law of the country where such establishment is effected, subject to the provisions of the Chapter relating to capital.

B3.7 Article 49 EC, which governs the freedom to provide services, provides that:

> Within the framework of the provision set out below, restrictions on freedom to provide services within the Community shall be prohibited in respect of nationals of Member States who are established in a State of the Community other than that of the person for whom the services are intended.
>
> The Council may, acting by a qualified majority on a proposal from the Commission, extend the provisions of this Chapter to nationals of a third country who provide services and who are established within the Community.

3 SCOPE OF APPLICATION OF THE FREE MOVEMENT RULES

A State measures and sporting bodies

B3.8 A party may rely on the free movement rules established in the EC Treaty in order to set aside contrary national laws[1]. Further, the scope of application of the free movement rules is not restricted to State measures, as has been made clear by the Court of Justice in Case 36/74 *Walrave and Koch v Union Cycliste Internationale*[2] and Case C-415/93 *Union Royale Belge des Sociétés de Football Association ASBL v Jean-Marc Bosman*[3]. These cases concerned rules that had been drawn up by international sports governing bodies (for cycling and football respectively), which were neither State nor public bodies. In *Walrave*[4], the Court of Justice held that the prohibitions on the restriction of free movement should apply to the rules of such bodies on the following basis:

> Prohibition of such discrimination does not only apply to the action of public authorities but extends likewise to rules of any other nature aimed at regulating in a collective manner gainful employment and the provision of services …
>
> Since, moreover, working conditions in the various Member States are governed sometimes by means of provisions laid down by law or regulations and sometimes by agreements and other acts concluded or adopted by private persons, to limit the prohibitions in question to acts of a public authority would risk creating inequality in their application.

1 For example, see Case 167/73 *Commission v France* [1974] ECR 359.
2 [1974] ECR 1405.
3 [1995] ECR I-4921.
4 [1974] ECR 1405 at paras 17 to 19.

B3.9 Therefore the free movement rules may affect sport and may be applied to sporting issues in a large number of ways. They have been held to apply to the rules of the International Cycling Federation[1], the Italian Football Federation[2], the Belgian Football Association, incorporating the rules of FIFA and UEFA[3], the Francophone and Belgian Judo Leagues[4], and the Belgian Basketball Federation and International Basketball Federation[5].

1 Case 36/74 *Walrave v Union Cycliste Internationale* [1974] ECR 1405.
2 Case C-13/76 *Donà v Mantero* [1976] ECR 1333.
3 Case C-415/93 *Union Royale Belge des Sociétés de Football Association ASBL v Jean-Marc Bosman* [1995] ECR I-4921
4 Joined Cases C-51/96 and C-191/97 *Deliège v Ligue Francophone de Judo et Disciplines Associées ASBL* [2000] ECR I-2549.
5 Case C-176/96 *Lehtonen v FRBSB* [2000] ECR I-2681.

B Economic activities

B3.10 The Court of Justice has held that 'sport is subject to Community law only in so far as it constitutes an economic activity'[1]. This means that sports may be affected by Community law in a number of ways, as discussed below. The greater the level of commercialisation of a particular sport, the greater the impact that Community law will have.

1 *Walrave* at para 4; *Donà v Mantero* at para 12; *Bosman* at para 73.

(a) Participants

B3.11 If the participants in a sporting activity are remunerated for taking part, they will be entitled to rely on Art 39 EC (if they are employees) or Art 49 EC (if they are providing a remunerated service). For example, professional or semi-professional footballers will be entitled to rely on the free movement rules contained in the EC Treaty[1].

1 *Donà v Mantero* at para 12; *Bosman* at para 73.

B3.12 However, the application of the free movement rules is not limited to participants who receive direct remuneration in return for their sporting activities. In Joined Cases C-51/96 and C-191/97 *Deliège v Ligue Francophone de Judo et Disciplines Associées ASBL*[1], the Court of Justice considered whether Ms Deliège, a Belgian Judoka, fell within the scope of Art 59 of the EC Treaty (now Art 49 EC). Whilst noting that it was for the national court to apply Community law to the facts of the particular case, the court observed that Ms Deliège had received grants by reason of her sporting achievements and had been sponsored by a banking institution and a motor-car manufacturer. It also stated:

> 56. … sporting activities and, in particular, a high-ranking athlete's participation in an international competition are capable of involving the provision of a number of separate, but closely related, services which may fall within the scope of Article 59 of the Treaty *even if some of those services are not paid for by those for whom they are performed*…
>
> 57. For example, an organiser of such a competition may offer athletes an opportunity of engaging in their sporting activity in competition with others and, at the same time, the athletes, by participating in the competition, enable the organiser to put on a sports event which the public may attend, which television broadcasters may retransmit and which may be of interest to advertisers and sponsors. Moreover, the athletes provide their sponsors with publicity the basis for which is the sporting activity itself' [Emphasis added].

1 [2000] ECR I-2549.

B3.13 *Deliège* is an example of the potentially very far-reaching scope of the free movement rules in the context of sport. The court's example suggests that, even where a particular sports person does not receive any direct financial benefit from participation in a competition, but is able to attract sponsorship by virtue of participation in such an event, that sports person will fall within the scope of, and be able to rely on, the free movement rules. It leaves open the question of the status of a wholly amateur sports person who participates in an event which generates the provision of services, for example, because it is televised and/or attracts sponsors or advertisers.

(b) Transfer fees

B3.14 The legality of transfer fees in association football was considered by the Court of Justice in *Bosman*[1]. The Court of Justice held that the application of rules laid down by sporting associations, under which a professional footballer who was a Community national could not, on the expiry of his contract with one club, be employed by a club in another member state unless the latter club had paid to the former club a transfer, training or development fee, was precluded by Art 39 EC (ex Art 48)[2].

1 Case C-415/93 *Union Royale Belge des Sociétés de Football Association ASBL v Jean-Marc Bosman* [1995] ECR I-4921.
2 *Bosman* at para 114. See further paras A3.172, n 1, B3.40 et seq, B2.153 to B2.156 and E2.40 et seq.

(c) Transfer deadlines

B3.15 In *Lehtonen*[1], the Court of Justice considered a rule laid down by the Belgian basketball federation, the FRBSB, which prohibited clubs from fielding players registered after a certain date for the remainder of the championship season. Players could be transferred after that date, but could not play until the following season. The Court of Justice, whilst recognising that transfer deadlines may be acceptable in order to preserve the integrity of sporting competitions, held that the particular rules applied by the Belgian Federation to players coming from federations in the European zone could not be justified in circumstances where a later deadline was applied to players coming from outside the European zone. The rule that applied to players coming from the European zone was therefore precluded by Art 48 (now Art 39 EC).

1 Case C-176/96 *Lehtonen v FRBSB* [2000] ECR I-2681. See further para B2.172 et seq.

(d) Joint ownership rules

B3.16 EC free movement rules may be relied upon to challenge rules which prevent clubs under the same ownership from participating in the same competition. This was the position in the case that AEK Athens and Slavia Prague brought before the Court of Arbitration for Sport[1]. The clubs, which were both under the control of ENIC, argued, inter alia, that the UEFA rule that prevented clubs under common ownership from participating in the UEFA Cup were contrary to the EC rules on freedom of establishment and free movement of capital. The court held that, even assuming that the contested rule restricted the right of establishment or the free movement of capital, it was justified by the need to preserve 'the authenticity and uncertainty of results'.

1 Arbitration CAS 98/200, *AEK Athens and SK Slavia Prague/Union of European Football Associations (UEFA)*, award of 20 August 1999. See further paras A3.24, n 1, and B2.145 et seq.

(e) Nationality requirements

B3.17 In some cases, the prohibition on discrimination based on nationality contained in Arts 12 EC (ex Art 6), 39 EC and 49 EC may apply to rules regarding the composition of teams or the conditions to be fulfilled by persons wishing to participate in certain sporting activities or competitions. In an early case, *Walrave*[1], two Dutch nationals who acted as remunerated motorcycle pacemakers in bicycle races brought an action against the Union Cycliste Internationale, whose rules provided that, for the purposes of the medium-distance World championships behind motorcycles, the pacemaker had to have the same nationality as the stayer. The Court of Justice held that the prohibition on discrimination based on nationality does not affect the composition of sport teams, in particular national teams, the formation of which is a question of purely sporting interest and as such has nothing to do with economic activity. It was for the national court to determine the nature of the activity in question and to decide whether the pacemaker and stayer did or did not constitute a team[2].

1 Case 36/74 *Walrave v Union Cycliste Internationale* [1974] ECR 1405.
2 The legality of restrictions on participation in national teams is considered further in the section below on discriminatory restrictions (see paras B3.37 to B3.39).

B3.18 In *Donà v Mantero*[1] the Court of Justice had to consider the compatibility with Art 6 (now Art 12 EC), Arts 48 and 59 (now Arts 39 and 49 EC) of certain provisions of the rules of the Italian Football Federation. The provisions in question stipulated that only players affiliated to that federation could take part in matches as professional or semi-professional players, and that affiliation was, in principle, only open to players of Italian nationality. The court held that rules or national practices, even adopted by a sporting organisation, which limit the right to take part in football matches as professional or semi-professional players solely to the nationals of the state in question, are incompatible with Art 6 (now Art 12 EC), Arts 48 and 59 (now Arts 39 and 49 EC). It continued, however, that such provisions do not prevent the adoption of rules or of a practice excluding foreign players from participation in certain matches for reasons which are not of an economic nature, which relate to the particular nature and context of such matches and are thus of sporting interest only, such as, for example, matches between national teams from different countries[2].

1 Case C-13/76 *Donà v Mantero* [1976] ECR 1333 at para 19.
2 See [1976] ECR 1333 at para 14. This issue is considered further at paras B3.37 to B3.39.

B3.19 In *Bosman*[1], the Court of Justice held that Art 48 (now Art 39 EC) precludes the application of rules laid down by sporting associations under which, in matches in competitions which they organise, football clubs may field only a limited number of professional players who are nationals of other member states.

1 Case C-415/93 *Union Royale Belge des Sociétés de Football Association ASBL v Jean-Marc Bosman* [1995] ECR I-4921.

(f) Restrictions on advertising at sporting events

B3.20 In Case C-318/00 *Bacardi-Martini v Newcastle United Football Club*[1], the Court of Justice has been asked to rule on the legality of a French law that makes it unlawful to show alcohol advertisements on television. The law, 'the Loi Evin', has been interpreted and applied so as to apply to advertisements that are visible at televised sporting events, eg pitch-side hoardings. Bacardi is arguing that the French law is in breach of Art 59 of the EC Treaty (now Art 49 EC) as it has the practical effect of preventing or restricting the advertising of alcoholic drinks at sporting events (eg on pitch-side hoardings) taking place in member states other than France when the events are to be televised in France.

1 [2001] Eu LR 45.

(g) Restrictions on broadcasting sporting events

B3.21 It is well-established that restrictions on television broadcasters and broadcasts may fall within the scope of the EC free movement rules[1].

1 See Case C-23/93 *TV10* [1994] ECR I-4795.

(h) Disciplinary sanctions

B3.22 In *Wilander and Novaceck v Tobin and Jude*[1], the English Court of Appeal assumed (for the purposes of an appeal on a procedural matter) that it was arguable that the International Tennis Federation ('ITF') rule 53, which contained the ITF code on drug testing and provided for the suspension of players who contravened the code, constituted a restriction on the freedom to provide services pursuant to Art 59 (now Art 49 EC). In a subsequent case in the English courts, *Edwards v British Athletic Federation*[2], Lightman J considered the International Amateur Athletics Federation ('IAAF') Rules, pursuant to which the plaintiff athlete had been banned from competitions after he tested positive for anabolic steroids. The plaintiff contended that the refusal of his application for reinstatement before the expiry of the ban under the 'exceptional circumstances' provision constituted discrimination in breach of Art 59 of the EC Treaty. The court held that the IAAF Rules were of sporting interest only and did not constitute an economic activity and accordingly, Art 59 of the EC Treaty did not apply. Lightman J held[3]:

> As it appears to me, rr 55 to 61 merely regulate the sporting conduct of participants in athletics. They are designed to ban cheating by taking drugs and thus secure a level playing-field for all participants in the sport. The imposition of penalties for cheating is essential if cheats are to be kept out of the sport and the rules against cheating are to be effective. It is common ground that the four-year period of ineligibility is reasonable, justified and proportional. Necessarily the imposition of the sanction may have serious economic consequences for those who breach the rules, and the IAAF and all concerned must obviously at all times have appreciated this. But this is a mere incidental and inevitable by-product of having the rule against cheating. A rule designed to regulate the sporting conduct of participants does not cease to be such a rule because it does not allow those who break it to earn remuneration by participating in the sport for what is (by common consent) an appropriate period[4].

1 [1997] Eu LR 265.
2 [1997] Eu LR 721.
3 [1997] Eu LR 721 at 726F.
4 Compare the position adopted by the Court of Justice in *Deliège*, discussed at para B3.12.

(i) Restrictions on spectators

B3.23 In *Gough v Chief Constable of the Derbyshire Constabulary*[1], the Divisional Court considered the compatibility with EC free movement rules of 'banning orders' made pursuant to s 14B of the Football Spectators Act 1989, which:

(a) in relation to regulated football matches in England and Wales, prohibited the person subject to the order from entering any premises for the purpose of attending such matches; and
(b) in relation to such matches outside England and Wales, required that person to report to a police station in the United Kingdom on the day of the match and to surrender his passport.

The Divisional Court held that, whilst such orders were capable of imposing restrictions on an individual's right to travel to another member state to provide or receive services under Art 49 EC, they were justified and proportionate, and were therefore lawful. The Divisional Court's judgment was subsequently upheld by the Court of Appeal[2].

1 [2001] EWHC Admin 554, [2002] QB 459, [2001] 4 All ER 289 per Laws LJ at para 46.
2 (2002) Times, 10 April.

C Non-EU nationals and third countries

(a) Non-EU nationals

B3.24 The rules on free movement within the EC Treaty may only be relied upon by Community nationals[1].

1 Case C-230/97 *Criminal proceedings against Ibiyinka Awoyemi* [1998] ECR I-6781.

B3.25 Non-EU nationals may only benefit from similar rights where:

- the Community has entered into an international agreement with a third country which includes rights of free movement within the EU; and
- the free movement provisions of that agreement have direct effect.

B3.26 If a provision is said to have direct effect, this means that it can be relied on in proceedings before the national courts. Under Community law, a provision of an international agreement will have direct effect when, having regard to the wording, purpose and nature of the agreement, the provision contains a clear and precise obligation which is not dependent on the adoption of any subsequent measure[1].

1 See pp 77 and 78 of Brealey and Hoskins *Remedies in EC Law* (2nd edn, 1998, Sweet & Maxwell).

B3.27 The European Economic Area (EEA) Agreement (which applies between the member states, Norway, Iceland and Liechtenstein) has free movement provisions[1] and is capable of having direct effect as a matter of Community law[2].

1 Articles 28 to 39.
2 Case T-115/94 *Opel Austria v Council* [1997] ECR II-39 at paras 100–102.

B3.28 In addition, the Community has entered into Association or Co-operation Agreements with a fairly large number of other countries (eg Cyprus, Turkey, Algeria, Morocco, and the former Soviet Block countries, such as Hungary, the Czech Republic and Poland).

B3.29 The Court of Justice has been willing to find that such agreements have direct effect, but, in each case, it will be necessary to ascertain whether the relevant provision contains a clear and precise obligation which is not dependent on the adoption of any subsequent measure[1].

1 See Case 12/86 *Demirel v Stadt Schwäbisch Gmünd* [1987] ECR 3719 at para 14; Case C-18/90 *ONEM v Kziber* [1991] ECR I-199 at para 15; Case C-277/94 *Taflan-Met* [1996] ECR I-4085 at para 24.

B3.30 In the case of *Malaja*, the Administrative Court of Appeal of Nancy, France, was called upon to consider the situation of Lilia Malaja, a professional basketball player with Polish nationality. Ms Malaja had signed a contract to play for Racing Club de Strasbourg in the 1998-1999 season. However, the rules of the French Basketball Federation stated that a club was only allowed to play a maximum of two non-EEA nationals in each match. Racing Club already had a Croatian and a Bulgarian on their books. Ms Malaja and Racing Club argued that this rule was contrary to Art 37, para 1 of the Association Agreement between the European Community and Poland, which provided that Polish workers should not be discriminated against because of their nationality. These arguments were accepted by the Administrative Appeal Court in Nancy[1].

1 Case No99NC00282, judgment of 3 February 2000.

B3.31 A provision in an international agreement will generally not be unconditional where it establishes a 'programme' for the creation of substantive rights which are therefore dependent upon the adoption of further measures. For example, Art 55(1) of the EC-Hungary Europe Agreement provides that:

> The Parties undertake in accordance with the provisions of this Chapter to take the necessary steps to allow progressively the supply of services by Community or Hungarian companies or nationals who are established in a Party other than that of the person for whom the services are intended taking into account the development of the services sector in the Parties.

B3.32 The necessary further measures are usually adopted by an 'Association Council' established pursuant to the relevant agreement. Decisions adopted by such Association Councils are themselves capable of having direct effect[1].

1 Case C-192/89 *Sevince v Staatsecretaris* [1990] ECR I-3461.

(b) Third countries

B3.33 The position of an EU national who wishes to move to a third country with which the Community has entered into an agreement will depend upon the nature of any free movement provisions in that agreement, and the status accorded to that agreement in the national law of the third country concerned.

4 SUBSTANTIVE APPLICATION OF THE FREE MOVEMENT RULES

B3.34 The Court of Justice has tended to take the view that there is no practical difference between the conditions which must be satisfied for the application of Art 39 EC (ex Art 48), Art 43 EC (ex Art 52) or Art 49 EC (ex Art 59)[1].

1 For example, see Case 48/75 *Royer* [1976] ECR 497 at para 12.

B3.35 In order to establish whether there has been a breach of the free movement rules, it is necessary to ask the following questions:

(a) Is there a restriction on free movement?
(b) If so, is its existence justified on the basis of a legitimate objective?
(c) If so, are the restrictions imposed proportionate?[1]

1 For an example of the approach to be adopted, see Case C-384/93 *Alpine Investments* [1995] ECR I-1141.

A The existence of restrictions

B3.36 Restrictions on free movement may arise due to:

(a) a rule which discriminates on the grounds of nationality (directly or indirectly discriminatory); or
(b) a rule which, even though it is applicable without discrimination on grounds of nationality, is liable to hamper or to render less attractive the exercise of fundamental freedoms guaranteed by the Treaty (non-discriminatory).

(a) Discriminatory restrictions

B3.37 In sport, the most obvious example of a discriminatory measure is a rule which imposes nationality restrictions on participation in a particular team or competition. For example:

- Until the mid-1970s, the rules of the Italian football federation provided that only players who were affiliated to that federation could take part in matches as professional or semi-professional players, and affiliation was, in principle, only open to players who were Italian nationals. These rules were effectively declared to be illegal by the Court of Justice in *Donà v Mantero*[1].
- Rules which limited the number of players from other member states that a football club could field at any one time were declared to be unlawful in *Bosman*[2].

1 [1976] ECR 1333.
2 [1995] ECR I-4921.

B3.38 As regards national teams, the rules for selection are clearly discriminatory as selection for a particular national team is restricted to the nationals of that country. However, in 1974 in Case 36/74 *Walrave v Union Cycliste Internationale*[1], the Court of Justice stated that the prohibition on discrimination:

> does not affect the composition of sport teams, in particular national teams, the formation of which is a question of purely sporting interest and as such has nothing to do with economic activity.

1 [1974] ECR 1405.

B3.39 Whilst this view of international competition as having 'nothing to do with economic activity' may have been tenable in 1974, it has subsequently become more questionable. In some sports, such as rugby and cricket, certain internationals have entered into contracts with their national associations in respect of their appearance for the national team. In addition, competitions involving national teams generate the provision of services by and to spectators, television companies, sponsors and advertisers. The increasing commercialisation of international events inevitably increases the likelihood that the EC free movement rules may be applied to such events. Furthermore, certain sports, such as rugby, have adopted a broad notion of 'nationality'. The more liberal the approach that sporting governing bodies take to the question of eligibility for national teams, the greater the risk that they will find that the matter is taken out of their hands by the application of EC law.

(b) Non-discriminatory restrictions

B3.40 The issue of non-discriminatory rules is more difficult. The leading case is Case C-415/93 *Union Royale Belge des Sociétés de Football Association ASBL v Jean-Marc Bosman*[1], which concerned transfer fees for out of contract football players. Mr Bosman, a professional footballer of Belgian nationality, was employed from 1988 by RC Liège, under a contract expiring 30 June 1990, and was subject to the rules of the Belgian national football association, the URBSFA, which incorporated the UEFA and FIFA regulations by reference. Before the expiry of his contract, RC Liège offered Mr Bosman a new contract, which Mr Bosman refused to sign, and he was put on the transfer list. An offer from a French club, UC Dunkerque, fell through and on 31 July 1990, RC Liège, pursuant to the relevant rules, suspended him, thereby preventing him from playing for the entire season. The Court of Justice held that a rule which enabled a football club to demand a transfer fee from another club in respect of the transfer of a player whose contract had expired was capable of constituting a restriction for the purposes of Art 48 of the EC Treaty (now Art 39 EC).

1 [1995] ECR I-4921.

B3.41 In reaching that conclusion in *Bosman*, the Court of Justice reasoned as follows:

- Provisions which preclude or deter a national of a member state from leaving his country of origin in order to exercise his right to freedom of movement constitute an obstacle to that freedom even if they apply without regard to the nationality of the workers concerned[1].
- Since the transfer rules provide that a professional footballer may not pursue his activity with a new club established in another member state unless it has paid his former club a transfer fee agreed upon between the two clubs or determined in accordance with the regulations of the sporting association, those rules constitute an obstacle to freedom of movement for workers[2].
- Further, although the rules apply also to transfers between clubs belonging to different national associations within the same member state and are similar to those governing transfers between clubs belonging to the same national association, they still directly affect players' access to the employment market in other member states and are thus capable of impeding freedom of movement for workers[3].

1 [1995] ECR I-4921 at para 96.
2 See n 1 at para 100.
3 See n 1 at para 103.

B3.42 This constitutes a very broad approach to the definition of a restriction on free movement of workers as the effect of the obligation to pay a transfer fee was wholly neutral when viewed in terms of free movement[1]. The existence of the transfer rule did not make it more difficult to move between clubs in different member states than between clubs in the same State. In effect, all regulatory rules or contractual obligations are capable of being 'restrictions' on economic activity, eg a notice period in a contract of employment. The obligation to give notice makes it more difficult to move jobs. However, the obstacle that it imposes applies to the same extent regardless of whether a person wishes to move jobs whilst remaining in the same country or wishes to re-locate to another member state.

1 See generally Craig & de Búrca *EC Law* (2nd edn, 1998, Oxford) at pp 671 and 672.

B3.43 The Court of Justice adopted a more 'sports-sensitive' approach in its later judgment in Joined Cases C-51/96 and C-191/97 *Deliège v Ligue Francophone de Judo et Disciplines Associées ASBL*[1]. In this case, Ms Deliège complained of the fact that she had been prevented from competing in an important international competition as participation was only open to those selected by their national federations, and Ms Deliège had not been selected. In considering whether the relevant selection rules constituted a restriction on the freedom to provide services, the court held that:

- Although selection rules inevitably have the effect of limiting the number of participants in a tournament, such a limitation is inherent in the conduct of an international high-level sports event. Such rules may not therefore in themselves be regarded as constituting a restriction on the freedom to provide services.
- It naturally falls to the bodies concerned, such as organisers of tournaments, sports federations or professional athletes' associations, to lay down appropriate rules and to make their selections in accordance with them. Delegation of such a task to the national federations, which normally have the necessary knowledge and experience, is the arrangement adopted in most sporting disciplines, which is based on the existence of a federation in each country.
- Moreover, the selection rules at issue in the main proceedings apply both to competitions organised within the Community and to those taking place outside it and involve both nationals of member states and those of non-member countries.

1 [2000] ECR I-2549. See further para B2.176 et seq.

B3.44 The approach adopted by the Court of Justice in this case was somewhat unorthodox. The court did not address the matter according to the three-stage approach outlined above at para B3.35. It did not analyse the effect of the selection rules in practice in order to determine whether as a matter of fact they constituted an obstacle to free movement. Rather it held that the selection rules did not constitute an obstacle to free movement as they were justified by objective factors[1]. The question of justification would normally arise as a separate issue only after the court had found the existence of a restriction. The court therefore adopted a 'rule of reason' approach under which not all of those rules which create obstacles as a matter of fact are treated as restrictions in law within the scope of the free movement rules.

1 [2000] ECR I-2549 at para 64: '[a]lthough selection rules like those at issue in the main proceedings inevitably have the effect of limiting the number of participants in a tournament, such a limitation is inherent in the conduct of an international high-level sports event, which necessarily involves certain selection rules or criteria being adopted. Such rules may not therefore in themselves be regarded as constituting a restriction on the freedom to provide services prohibited by Article 59 of the Treaty [now Article 49 EC]'.

B3.45 There are two further aspects to note here:

- First, the court relied on the fact that selection rules are neutral in terms of the effect on free movement. This can be contrasted with the approach adopted in *Bosman*[1].
- Secondly, the court recognised that it was better to leave sporting issues to sporting bodies who had expertise in such matters. Again, this can be contrasted with *Bosman*[2].

1 See paras B3.40 to B3.42.
2 See paras B3.57 to B3.59 and B3.60 to B3.63.

B3.46 The court reverted to a more orthodox analytical approach by adopting the three-stage test, rather than a 'rule of reason' approach, in Case C-176/96 *Lehtonen v FRBSB*[1], which was decided only two days after *Deliège*. This case concerned a transfer-deadline rule laid down by the Belgian Basketball Federation which prohibited clubs from fielding players registered after a certain date for the remainder of that championship season. The court held that, because this rule restricted the ability of professional players to participate in championship matches, it constituted an obstacle to the free movement of workers. Having established the existence of a restriction, the Court of Justice then went on to consider whether the rule in question was justified and proportionate[2].

1 [2000] ECR I-2681.
2 See paras B3.15 and B2.171 et seq.

B3.47 In summary, as regards non-discriminatory rules, the Court of Justice has not always adopted a consistent approach to the question of whether a sporting rule or regulation constitutes an obstacle to free movement. It has applied both the orthodox analytical three-stage test, and also the 'rule of reason' (which is more 'sports sensitive'). It is unclear how the jurisprudence in this field will develop.

B Objective justification

B3.48 Discriminatory rules are contrary to the fundamental principles of Community law in particular those regarding free movement. They are closely scrutinised by the Court of Justice and any possible exceptions are narrowly defined[1]. The only exceptions permitted are those based on public policy, public security or public health[2].

1 For a discussion of the issue of the differences between discriminatory and non-discriminatory rules, in particular, as regards justification, see Craig & de Búrca *EC Law* (2nd edn, 1998, Oxford) at pp 627–630.
2 See Art 39(3) EC (ex Art 48(3)) (workers) and Art 46 EC (ex Art 56) which applies both Art 43 (ex Art 52) (right of establishment) and to Art 49 EC (ex Art 59) (services) pursuant to Art 55 EC (ex Art 66).

B3.49 By contrast, it is a well-established principle of Community law that non-discriminatory obstacles may be justified by 'imperative requirements' or 'mandatory requirements'[1]. The rationale for this is that some rules which regulate trade and are capable of restricting trade may, in fact, serve objectively justifiable purposes, and it may be inappropriate to render such rules unlawful per se[2]. There is no exhaustive list of mandatory requirements[3].

1 See, for example Case 120/78 *Rewe-Zentrale AG v Bundesmonopolverwaltung für Branntwein (Cassis de Dijon)* [1979] ECR 649, Case 788/79 *Italy v Gilli and Andres* [1980] ECR 2071 at para 6, and Case 113/80 *Commission v Ireland* [1981] ECR 1625 at paras 5–8.
2 For a general discussion of the principle, see Craig & de Búrca *EC Law* (2nd edn, 1998, Oxford) at pp 627–637.
3 The case law on mandatory requirements is most fully developed in the context of Art 28 EC (ex Art 30). Justifications have been based, for example, upon consumer protection, fairness of commercial transactions, public health and the protection of the environment.

B3.50 In *Bosman*[1], the Court of Justice recognised that, in view of the considerable social importance of sporting activities and in particular, of football, restrictions on free movement were capable of being justified by:

- the need to maintain a balance between clubs by preserving a certain degree of equality and uncertainty as to results[2]; and
- the need to encourage the recruitment and training of young players[3].

1 [1995] ECR I-4921.
2 See n 1 at para 106.
3 See n 2.

B3.51 This indicated that the particular attributes of sport may be taken into account in justifying restrictions.

B3.52 This sport-specific approach was confirmed in *Lehtonen*[1] where the Court of Justice, having first found that the transfer deadline rules constituted an obstacle to free movement, held as follows:

> 53. On this point, it must be acknowledged that the setting of deadlines for transfers of players may meet the objective of ensuring the regularity of sporting competitions.
>
> 54. Late transfers might be liable to change substantially the sporting strength of one or other team in the course of the championship, thus calling into question the comparability of results between the teams taking part in that championship, and consequently the proper functioning of the championship as a whole.
>
> 55. The risk of that happening is especially clear in the case of a sporting competition which follows the rules of the Belgian first division national basketball championship. The teams taking part in the play-offs for the title or for relegation could benefit from late transfers to strengthen their squads for the final stage of the championship, or even for a single decisive match.

1 [2000] ECR I-2681.

B3.53 In summary, a number of justifications particular to sporting activities have been identified by the Court of Justice as objectives which may justify the imposition of prima facie restrictions on free movement. As the jurisprudence develops, and the Court of Justice is asked to adjudicate on further cases concerning sport, it is likely that this list of sport-specific possible justifications will be added to incrementally.

B3.54 A further example is provided by the decision of the Court of Arbitration for Sport in a case concerning a UEFA rule that prevented clubs under common ownership from participating in the UEFA Cup[1]. The court held that, even assuming that the contested rule restricted the right of establishment, it was justified by the need to preserve 'the authenticity and uncertainty of results'.

1 Arbitration CAS 98/200, *AEK Athens and SK Slavia Prague/Union of European Football Associations (UEFA)*, award of 20 August 1999. See further paras A3.24, n 1 and B2.145 et seq.

C Proportionality

B3.55 Proportionality is an established general principle of Community law and is expressly recognised in Art 5 EC (ex Art 3b)[1]. The Court of Justice has defined the proportionality principle as follows:

> By virtue of that principle, the lawfulness of the prohibition of an economic activity is subject to the condition that the prohibitory measures are appropriate and necessary in

order to achieve the objectives legitimately pursued by the legislation in question; when there is a choice between several appropriate measures recourse must be had to the least onerous, and the disadvantages caused must not be disproportionate to the aims pursued[2].

1 For a discussion of the general principle see Craig & de Búrca *EC Law* (2nd edn, 1998, Oxford) at pp 349–357, Brealey and Hoskins *Remedies in EC Law* (2nd edn, 1998, Sweet & Maxwell) at pp 27–37; and Wyatt & Dashwood's *European Union Law* (4th edn, 2000, Sweet & Maxwell) at pp 135–137.

2 See C-331/88 *R v MAFF, ex p Fedesa* [1990] ECR I-4023 at para 13; Joined Cases T-466/93 and others *O'Dwyer v Council* [1995] ECR II-2071 at para 107; Joined Cases C-254/94 and others *Fattoria Autonoma Tabacchi* [1996] ECR I-4235 at para 55. The principle at para 13 of *Ex p Fedesa* was cited by Bingham LCJ in *R v Secretary of State for Health, ex p Eastside Cheese Co* [1999] Eu LR 968 at para 41.

B3.56 When examining the legality of restrictions on free movement, it is necessary to consider whether they are proportionate to the specific objective pursued. As the quotation in the preceding paragraph indicates, in determining whether a restriction is proportionate, the court will ask the following questions:

- Is the restriction an appropriate method for the attainment of a legitimate objective?
- Are the means employed limited to what is necessary for the attainment of the legitimate objective?
- Are the disadvantages caused or restrictions imposed unacceptable given the objective pursued?

B3.57 The decision in *Bosman* was based upon the application of the proportionality principle. In *Bosman* the Court of Justice held that the transfer rules were not proportionate as:

(a) they were not an adequate means of achieving the objectives pursued (namely, maintaining a balance between clubs and encouraging the recruitment and training of young players)[1];
(b) the same aims could be achieved at least as efficiently by other means which did not impede freedom of movement for workers[2];
(c) they were not necessary either to safeguard the worldwide organization of football[3], or to compensate clubs for the expenses which they have had to incur in paying fees on recruiting their players[4].

1 [1995] ECR I-4921 at para 109.
2 See n 1 at para 110.
3 See n 1 at para 112.
4 See n 1 at para 113.

B3.58 In reaching its conclusion, the Court of Justice expressly relied on the Opinion of Advocate-General Lenz in which he stated that the redistribution of income between clubs would provide a less restrictive means of achieving the objectives pursued than the system of transfer fees. The Advocate-General justified his idea of redistribution of income in the following terms:

> 227. It can scarcely be doubted that such a redistribution of income appears sensible and legitimate *from an economic point of view*. UEFA itself has rightly observed that football is characterized by the mutual economic dependence of the clubs. Football is played by two teams meeting each other and testing their strength against each other. Each club thus needs the other one in order to be successful. For that reason each club has an interest in the health of the other clubs. The clubs in a professional league thus do not have the aim of excluding their competitors from the market. Therein lies…a significant

difference from the competitive relationship between undertakings in other markets. It is likewise correct that the economic success of a league depends not least on the existence of a certain balance between its clubs. If the league is dominated by one overmighty club, experience shows that lack of interest will spread …

It therefore is indeed necessary, in my opinion, to ensure by means of specific measures that a certain balance is preserved between clubs. One possibility is the system of transfer payments currently in force. Another possibility is the redistribution of a proportion of income …

233. Finally, it must be observed that a redistribution of a part of income appears substantially more suitable for attaining the desired purpose than the current system of transfer fees. It permits the clubs concerned to budget on a considerably more reliable basis. If a club can reckon with a certain basic amount which it will receive in any case, then solidarity between clubs is better served than by the possibility of receiving a large sum of money for one of the club's own players. As Mr Bosman has rightly submitted, the discovery of a gifted player who can be transferred to a big club for good money is very often largely a matter of chance. Yet the prosperity of football depends not only on the welfare of such a club, but also on all the other small clubs being able to survive. That, however, is not guaranteed by the present rules on transfers.

234. In so far as the rules on transfers pursue the objective of ensuring the economic and sporting equilibrium of the clubs, there is thus at least one alternative by means of which that objective can be pursued just as well and which does not adversely affect players freedom of movement. The transfer rules are thus not indispensable for attaining that objective, and thus do not comply with the principle of proportionality.

B3.59 It was optimistic (to say the least) to imagine that the individual football clubs, whose prime objective is the creation of maximum profits for themselves and their shareholders, would join together altruistically for the good of the sport. The problem with the approach of the Advocate-General and the Court of Justice in *Bosman* is that they presumed that they were best placed to decide what is best for football, when in that case, as in many other cases, such decisions are often best left to the relevant sports regulatory bodies.

D Conclusion

B3.60 As indicated at the outset, the Court of Justice has not shown itself to be particularly sympathetic to arguments based upon the special position that applies to sport.

B3.61 However, regardless of how commercialised sport becomes, it should be recognised that it does have special characteristics. It is not like all other businesses. Clearly, whilst sporting bodies should not be allowed to overstep the mark and must be subject to judicial control, the crucial question is 'How much control?' Rigorous application of economic legal principles is liable to lead to grave problems in sport. One has only to think of the situation that *Bosman* has created. Whereas money used to circulate within the game, it now goes into the pockets of players and players' agents. If one adopts a pessimistic, but not wholly unrealistic view, the abolition of the transfer system, without the adoption of a meaningful 'solidarity fund' of the sort envisaged by the Court of Justice in *Bosman*, will lead to smaller clubs going out of business. The irony is that, if small clubs go bust, then, whilst *Bosman* may have improved the situation for a limited number of top-class players, there will in fact be less professional players able to benefit from the fruits of *Bosman*. Rather than liberalising the employment market for professional footballers, *Bosman* will have made it harder for journeyman footballers to find employment.

B3.62 *Bosman* shows the dangers of mixing law and sport without taking account of the particular characteristics of sport. Sport *is* special and the courts should recognise this by allowing regulatory bodies a certain degree of latitude in deciding what is best for their sport as a whole. There is a clear analogy with judicial review, under both domestic and Community law, where the courts recognise that public bodies are best placed to take policy decisions and therefore will only interfere if a decision is irrational or manifestly wrong. This more measured approach appears to be reflected, to a certain extent, in *Deliège*[1]. However, it is significant that that case concerned judo, a sport in which the level of commercialisation is still relatively low.

1 [2000] ECR I-2549.

B3.63 However, one cannot simply blame the courts for failing to recognise the particular characteristics of sport. The greater the degree of commercialisation of a particular sport, the less those involved can complain if they are treated like a business. In *Bosman*, the Court of Justice was clearly heavily influenced by the fact that Mr Bosman had been very badly treated by his club and the football authorities. The bottom-line is that perhaps football simply got what it deserved.

5 ENFORCEMENT

A Judicial proceedings

B3.64 Article 39 EC (ex Art 48), Art 49 EC (ex Art 59) and Art 43 EC (ex Art 52) are directly effective, and therefore may be relied on by individuals or undertakings in proceedings before the national courts[1].

1 For example, see Case 167/73 *Commission v France* [1974] ECR 359 (Art 48, now Art 39 EC).

B3.65 Indeed, in most cases, sporting issues that concern the free movement rules will be raised initially in proceedings before a national court or tribunal. A national court or tribunal is entitled to refer questions of Community law to the Court of Justice for a preliminary ruling pursuant to Art 234 EC (ex Art 177)[1]. Pursuant to this procedure, the Court of Justice receives written observations from the parties before the national court, the Commission of the European Communities and any member states which apply to intervene. It will then normally hold an oral hearing, and, having received the Opinion of the Advocate General, deliver its judgment. The Court of Justice does not give a decision on the facts or merits of the case referred to it. Its jurisdiction under Art 234 EC extends only to the interpretation of Community law and the validity of Community acts. It is the task of the national court to apply the ruling of the Court of Justice to the facts of the particular case in order to come to a decision.

1 For further discussion, see Anderson and Demetriou *References to the European Court* (2nd edn, Sweet & Maxwell) and ch 11 of Brealey and Hoskins *Remedies in EC Law* (2nd edn, Sweet & Maxwell).

B The role of the European Commission

B3.66 Following the decision in *Bosman*, the Commission entered into negotiations with FIFA and UEFA in relation to the transfer rules which applied whilst a player was still under contract to a particular club. At the outset it was reported that the negotiations were being conducted in the context of the competition rules. Over time it appeared that the talks were substantially concerned with the free movement rules. This is reflected in the content of the 'agreement' which was reached between FIFA and UEFA on the one hand, and the Commission on the other hand at a congress in Buenos Aires on 5 July 2001, and the FIFA regulations which were adopted[1]. Initially, FIFPro, the European players union, did not support the agreement, but after negotiation with FIFA, it was agreed that FIFPro would have increased participation in the implementation of the regulations.

1 The full text of the FIFA regulations can be found at the FIFA website (www.fifa.com). See further paras B2.164 et seq, E1.63, E1.64 and E2.66 et seq and passim.

B3.67 The regulations consist of a set of substantive employment rules for the football industry. Article 4 provides that contracts will have a minimum duration of one year and a maximum of five years. Article 5 allows transfers to be made during one of two registration periods per year, with a limit of one transfer of registration per player in the same sports season in a period of 12 months. Articles 21 to 24 provide for the maintenance of contractual stability and permit players to break contracts without punishment after a 'protected period', which is three years if the player is aged between 23 and 28, and 2 years if the player is over 28. Players face bans of four months if they breach their contract during the 'protected period'. Article 25 creates a solidarity mechanism to redistribute transfer income to clubs involved in the training and education of transferred players.

B3.68 There are a number of points to note about the 'agreement':

- Whilst the Commission can bring legal proceedings before the Court of Justice against the member states for breach of the free movement rules under Art 226 EC, it has no competence to commence legal proceedings against private law bodies such as sports governing bodies. There was therefore no legal obligation on FIFA/UEFA to negotiate with the Commission in respect of the free movement rules.
- Whilst the Commission has jurisdiction to deal with breaches of the competition rules in the EC Treaty pursuant to Arts 81 (ex Art 85), 82 (ex Art 86) and 85 (ex Art 89) EC, it has no competence to adopt binding legal measures in the context of the free movement rules. The 'agreement' therefore has no legal status as a matter of Community law. The rules adopted by FIFA/UEFA pursuant to the 'agreement' will remain open to challenge before national courts, eg by individual players. The obvious advantage of the agreement is that, if the matter comes before the Court of Justice on a preliminary reference, the Commission will presumably intervene in support of FIFA/UEFA. However, the 'agreement' provides no guarantee that the new transfer system will be immune from challenge[1].

1 See Editorial in (2001) E L Rev 99 on the 'spectre' remaining that the Court of Justice may have to arbitrate on whether the FIFA Regulations are compatible with the EC Treaty.

PART C

ORGANISATIONAL ISSUES FOR SPORTS ENTITIES

CHAPTER C1

ORGANISATIONAL STRUCTURES FOR SPORTS ENTITIES

Karena Vleck (Farrer & Co) and **Serena Hedley-Dent** (Farrer & Co)

Contents

1 INTRODUCTION

C1.1 It is essential for any practitioner to understand the legal framework within which the sport with which he or she is dealing operates. Sports organisations are essentially private undertakings although they may undertake many public or quasi-public functions[1]. Sport at a national or lower (ie county or club) level fits within an international framework for that sport which cannot be ignored. Most sports operate within a pyramid structure. The international federations sit at the top. The national federations are members of the international federations. There may be area associations which are also members of the international federations and which also have the national federations in their respective areas as members. Beneath the national federations are regional associations or federations, and beneath those, district associations or counties. Beneath those are clubs or community associations and beneath the clubs, the individual participants. Each sport will be structured in a slightly different way within this framework.

1 See para A1.19 et seq.

C1.2 At a national level, there is a plethora of organisations involved in any sport ranging from those regulating the sport, those participating in the sport and representative organisations for the different interest groups. For example in horseracing in the UK, the Jockey Club is the governing body which sets the Rules of Racing. The British Horseracing Board is responsible for the promotion and financing of racing and deals with rights exploitation. The representative organisations include the Racecourses Association which represents 59 racecourses, the Super 12 which represents and is responsible for the commercial exploitation of the 12 'premier' racecourses, the Racehorse Owners' Association, the Jockeys' Association, the Federation of Bloodstock Agents, the National Trainers' Federation and the Stable Lads' Association.

C1.3 There is no common form of organisation for these different bodies. Some, which are unincorporated associations, are not even legal entities in their own right whereas others will be private companies, others public companies or perhaps Industrial and Provident Societies (IPSs) or Royal Charter bodies.

C1.4 This chapter explains the pyramid structure and the interrelationship between sports bodies at an international and national level. It will set out the constitutional structures which are typically used for UK sports organisations within the different elements of the pyramid framework. It will describe how these traditional structures are having to change to reflect the increasing need for efficiency in administrative operation as well as the move to greater professionalism in sport and observance of the principles of corporate governance[1]. Finally, it will deal with charitable status and Community Amateur Sports Clubs.

1 See also paras A1.93 to A1.100.

2 THE INTERNATIONAL SCHEME

C1.5 Each sport is organised in a different way, largely as a result of its own development over time (for example the split of Rugby League (or the Northern Union) from the RFU in the late nineteenth century). There is no template which can be used to provide the perfect structure for a sport. However, there are common features between sports. Each sport usually has an international (or world-wide) federation. The names of international federations are well known, FIFA (football), IAAF (athletics), FIBA (basketball), FINA (swimming), ICC (cricket) and IRB (rugby union) being a few. These international federations are responsible for promoting the sport, setting rules relating to the sport and for regulating the sport at an international level. They will make rules regulating the staging of international competitions. They will be responsible for, and make rules governing the relationship between, the international federation and the national federations, the relationship between national and other affiliated federations. To some degree they will regulate the relationship between a national federation and its own constituent members.

C1.6 It can sometimes be difficult to see exactly how all the elements of the pyramid work together. The relationships can be fairly loose. There will be a series of rights and obligations on different sides. Although the relationship between the different elements will usually be contractual, it will all depend on the facts of each individual case[1].

1 See discussion of the *Modahl* case at para A3.122 et seq.

C1.7 The international federation is the association of all the national federations. It exists to provide a set of uniform rules for the sport and to ensure these are enforced[1]. It provides the means whereby international competitions may be regulated and may help channel funds to reduce the differences between the sport in rich and poor nations.

1 The rules of the game for certain sports (golf and cricket) are set not by the relevant international federation but rather by the Royal & Ancient Club and the Marylebone Cricket Club respectively.

C1.8 International federations come in a variety of guises. Some will be legal entities in their own right recognised in the country where they were established. Others will not be legal entities and the laws governing them will be those where their headquarters are based from time to time. It will be necessary to examine the laws of the country having jurisdiction over the international federation to see how it is recognised[1].

1 It is beyond the scope of this work to examine the legal structure of different international federations.

C1.9 There is usually, but not always, a relationship of membership between the national federation and the international federation. The national federation is bound by virtue of its membership to abide by the constitution of the international federation and its rules. In certain cases the governing body responsible at a national level will not be a member of the international federation but will be 'recognised' by it. In such a case, a condition of recognition will be that the national body must abide by the international body's rules[1]. Whether the relationship is one of membership or recognition, there is normally a contractual relationship between the two bodies. The IAAF for example is a membership organisation and each national governing body for athletics is a member of the IAAF and thereby bound by its rules. By contrast, the members of the International Olympic Committee (IOC) are individuals from each country, as opposed to the National Olympic Committees (which are 'recognised by the IOC').

1 For example, the IOC Charter requires National Olympic Committees (which are recognised and not members) to adhere to and comply with the Olympic Charter. The Olympic Charter itself is fairly specific as to who the members of a National Olympic Committee are. See Olympic Charter (Lausanne, 29 July 2001).

C1.10 In well-developed sports there will be a layer of area associations. The national federations within a particular geographic area will also be members of the area association for that particular area. The area associations will be responsible for representing the national federations in the particular area and for organising competitions within a particular geographic area for their sport. For example, UEFA and EAA are 'governing bodies' for football and athletics respectively at a European level and responsible for pan-European competitions in those sports. It is likely that there will always be one or two area associations within a particular sport which are more powerful than the other area associations. There can also be tensions, usually of a political nature, between the individuals on the executive committee representing the interests of their continent and country over and above the interests of the sport as a whole.

C1.11 Throughout the different sports therefore there will be a chain of interlocking associations/organisations responsible for the sport's governance at each level. This can lead to tensions between national, area and international federations particularly where national law and the international federation's rules are in conflict. The European Commission's statement of objections to FIFA's rules governing the international transfer of players (raised in light of the *Bosman* ruling) on the basis that the rules breached Community law[1] is a good example of the sort of conflict that can arise. Another example of the conflict between national law and the rules of an international federation was in the case of Katrine Krabbe who was reinstated half way through her four-year ban from athletic competition. This was on the basis that a four-year ban would have been void in Germany on public policy grounds as an unreasonable restraint of trade. The IAAF therefore in turn had to reduce the ban it imposed for serious doping offences from four to two years[2].

1 See further paras B2.160 et seq, B3.66 et seq and E2.66 et seq.
2 See further paras E4.151, n 1 and E4.335, n 2.

C1.12 Within the different sports there may be players' associations which are usually outside the pyramid structure but nevertheless can play an important role within the sport. The negotiations between the European Commission, FIFA, UEFA and FIFpro in respect of FIFA's transfer rules also demonstrated the importance of international players' organisations and the increased voice that such organisations have[1].

1 See paras B2.164 to B2.170 and B3.66 et seq.

C1.13 As well as the international federations for each sport there are various other sporting bodies of an international nature. The IOC is the ultimate governing body for the sports that participate in the Olympic Games and as a result those sports need to ensure that their rules and regulations comply with those of the IOC. The Commonwealth Games Federation is responsible for the Commonwealth Games and each Commonwealth country has its own Commonwealth Games Council. The World Anti-Doping Agency (a Swiss foundation under the Swiss Civil Code entered on the Lausanne Trade Register) and the Court of Arbitration for Sport are other important international sporting organisations dealt with elsewhere in this book[1].

1 In relation to the World Anti-Doping Agency, see para E4.42 et seq. In relation to the Court of Arbitration for Sport, see para A5.84 et seq.

3 THE NATIONAL SCHEME

C1.14 This chapter describes the legal structures commonly used by sports organisations in the UK. In order to understand why different structures are used, it is necessary to understand the different roles the various types of organisation play within the UK and how the national federation sits within the modern-day sporting framework.

A Regulation of sport

C1.15 In the UK, each sport generally has its own recognisable national governing body responsible for its regulation within the UK[1]. Such regulation would involve rule making, rule enforcement, regulating relations between clubs and between competitors, and regulating competitions. Some sports may have joint governing bodies such as The British Ski and Snowboard Federation. Some governing bodies may govern a variety of sports such as the Royal Yachting Association, which includes windsurfing as well as yachting.

1 See para A1.16 et seq.

C1.16 Typically, the national governing body will have responsibility for all regulatory matters at a UK level with functions delegated to area or county associations to administer at a lower level (such as management of the sport generally and discipline other than for doping offences). Many governing bodies will be responsible for organising national championships and other national competitions although these may be delegated to organising committees.

C1.17 Each sport will have a different competition structure. Team sports are likely to have a very different competition structure to individual sports. Individual sports are more likely to have global tours with a centralised ranking system whereas team sports will usually compete on a league basis. The national federation will usually want to ensure that competitions where a GB or England team is competing have precedence over domestic competitions or international competitions where the competitor or team competes as an individual. This can lead to tensions between individual and country and between club and country.

C1.18 The national federation will not necessarily be responsible for all competitions for the sport within the UK. Indeed there is no rule of English law which would prevent individuals setting up a competition not under the auspices of the national federation[1]. The national federation may well find itself in difficulties on restraint of trade grounds if it tried to ban competitors or clubs from competing in a non-authorised event[2]. This may not apply if the competitors were employed by the national federation which could thereby direct what they did or if they or the clubs were in a direct contractual relationship with the national federation which dealt specifically with such matters.

1 See further paras A1.19 and A1.20.
2 See further para B2.116 et seq.

C1.19 There may also be governing bodies for the home countries (Scotland, England, Wales and Northern Ireland). Football is peculiar as there is no UK governing body for the sport (and hence no men's UK Olympic football team). Each home country has its own football association and The Football Association is only responsible for the game in England.

C1.20 The national federation is part of the international pyramid but it is also the top of the national pyramid for the sport. It is important to ensure that each level of the pyramid is bound by, and operating by, the same rules and procedures (which ultimately emanate from the international federation). Some UK governing bodies (such as the Lawn Tennis Association) have the county and other affiliated associations as their members, which in turn have the clubs as their members. Other governing bodies have the individual athletes as members (such as the British Canoe Union).

C1.21 It is important to remember that the national governing body governs both amateur and professional sport within the country and there may be conflicts between those two arms of a sport. In some sports and particularly in football, the professional sports organisations (clubs) are able to exploit their assets commercially more easily than the governing body. The result is that many of the individual clubs (eg Manchester United plc) have far greater resources than the governing body. However for many others and in particular rugby and cricket, where it is the England team which counts, the national federation is more likely to be on a firmer financial footing than the clubs[1].

1 See paras C1.23 to C1.27 for a discussion as to the dichotomy between professional and amateur sport.

C1.22 How a UK governing body is structured will probably have a great deal more to do with the history of the sport's development than with what is necessarily the most sensible option from a governance and administration point of view.

B Competitions – professional sport and amateur sport

C1.23 The tension between the amateur and the professional (elite) game is increasingly an issue for all sports. The governing bodies are required to invest in the 'grass roots' development of the sport and yet the success of the sport is judged by the success of the elite competitors and clubs. Lottery money under the World Class Performance Plans has done little to ease this tension as governing bodies enjoy greatly increased funds but they must be spent on specific elite activities[1].

1 See further paras A1.53 et seq and C3.34 et seq.

C1.24 In rugby union, the split between the amateur and elite came to a head in the early 1990s, which led to the game becoming professional in 1995. It is fair to say that it has taken some time for the sport to adapt to the change, as the recent overhaul to the structure of the professional game demonstrates. The RFU (governing body) and Premier Rugby Limited (a private company existing to promote the Zurich Premiership and represent the clubs in the Premiership, the players and staff involved) have formed a joint venture company known as England Rugby Limited. England Rugby Limited is responsible for a number of governance issues, in particular managing international and elite professional club rugby, regulations governing the Premiership, structure and regulation of national competitions, negotiation of TV and commercial rights, reviewing the salary cap and managing the elite player squad[1]. The RFU remains responsible for the rest of the game in England.

1 Premier Rugby Annual Report 2000/2001.

C1.25 In football, the professional competitions are managed by companies set up for that purpose. The creation of The FA Premier League Limited and The Football League Limited as separate companies demonstrated the need for the professional football leagues to be administered separately from the amateur game. The Football Association, as the national governing body, has been able to retain particular rights in relation to the leagues by means of a preference share (with voting rights only in relation to particular matters).

C1.26 As a result of the creation of the Premier League in football, some of the member clubs floated on the stock exchange and became public companies (such as Manchester United plc, Newcastle United plc and Chelsea Village plc)[1]. These clubs have become major commercial businesses in their own right.

1 See further para C3.175 et seq.

C The role of representative bodies

C1.27 The different interests in a particular sport may well be served by a collective voice. During the late 1990s the popularity of supporters' organisations was demonstrated in football. The purposes of these organisations (which are usually IPSs[1]) are to forge closer links between the supporters and the club, to acquire shares in the particular club which are then held by the IPS for the benefit of its members and to involve supporters in the club's administration by securing election of supporters to the board of the club.

1 See paras C1.50 to C1.56.

C1.28 There are representative bodies not only for supporters but also for sportsmen. In the UK the Professional Footballers' Association is well known. Other organisations representing the interests of players include the BOA Athletes Commission, the Professional Golfers' Association, the Professional Rugby Players' Association and UK Competitors. Most of these organisations are private companies limited by guarantee[1].

1 See paras C1.43 and C1.4.

4 TYPICAL CONSTITUTIONAL STRUCTURES FOR NATIONAL GOVERNING BODIES AND OTHER SPORTS ORGANISATIONS IN THE UK

C1.29 This section sets out various general principles relating to the types of organisation which are used for sports bodies. It is not intended to be exhaustive and when dealing with any particular type of legal structure the reader should refer to a specialist work on that type of organisation (for example, Gore-Brown or Palmer on Companies).

A Unincorporated associations

C1.30 Traditionally, an unincorporated association is probably the most common form of structure for sports bodies as it is the simplest way to establish an organisation. Such organisations typify the non-profit-distributing, amateur organisations that the governing bodies, sports clubs and other sports organisations were, prior to the increased commercialisation of sport. The British Olympic Association remained an unincorporated association until 1981. Increasingly, as governing bodies become professional entities handling large sums of money, employing people, owning or leasing their own premises, the problems of this type of organisation outweigh the benefits and many governing bodies are changing their legal status to become limited companies. In fact, the government agencies involved in sport in the UK[1] are keen to ensure that governing bodies are corporate entities, to protect the individuals running them.

1 See para A1.47 et seq.

C1.31 Unincorporated associations are essentially groups of individuals coming together to carry out a mutual purpose other than to distribute profit. They are members' organisations and have no legal personality distinct from the individuals who comprise their membership. This structure is therefore suitable for grassroots clubs, county associations or other sports bodies which do not hold property, employ staff and whose liabilities can be easily covered by having in place appropriate insurance policies.

C1.32 The rules regulate the relationship between the members and will usually give authority to a committee to run the affairs of the unincorporated association. The relationship between the members is a contractual one based on the provisions of the rules.

C1.33 There will usually be a series of secondary regulations taking the form of bye-laws dealing with technical and practical aspects of the sport. Usually the rules of the unincorporated association can only be amended by a specified majority of the members of the association at a general meeting. If the power is given to a committee of the association to make bye-laws, this can give flexibility in relation to those types of regulations which may need to be changed more frequently.

C1.34 The rules of an unincorporated association must be carefully drafted to ensure that the practicalities of how it is run are set out as there is little general law to be relied upon where the rules are silent. They are entirely private organisations and as such the rules are not a matter of public record.

C1.35 It is worth noting that the Lawn Tennis Association, the Amateur Swimming Association and the MCC, three large sports organisations, remain unincorporated. This is no doubt for particular reasons affecting each such organisation but if they were being established today they would probably be established as corporate entities.

C1.36 The lack of separate legal identity is not without dangers for unincorporated associations. The power to run and the responsibility for running the association will usually be delegated to a committee. The members of such a committee are usually volunteers who are not remunerated. However, the committee members will be personally liable for any liability of the club beyond its assets. Potentially the members may also be liable depending upon what the rules provide. The relative informality of the rules may not be adequate to cover what the organisation is doing.

C1.37 The constitution must include rules dealing with the following matters: name, objects, membership, fees and subscriptions, expulsion, composition of committee and committee responsibilities, appointment of trustees (or other mechanism for the holding of property), general meetings, alteration of rules, power to make regulations, bye-laws and standing orders, finance and accounting, borrowing, property, indemnity and dissolution. The power to make separate regulations, bye-laws and standing orders is particularly important as it ensures that the constitution is not cluttered with administrative matters such as expenses policies and the rules for the club cup competition.

C1.38 The rules will need to take account of any particular requirements that an organisation may need. For example, if it is to be licensed under the Licensing Act 1964 for the sale of alcohol, there are various constitutional matters for which provision must be made. The VAT exemption on sports supplies can only be claimed if an organisation's constitution is compliant with the Value Added Tax (Sport, Sports Competitions and Physical Education) Order 1999[1]. In order to claim mutual trading status for the purposes of corporation tax the association must have a rule which provides that any surplus on a winding up must revert to the members.

1 SI 1999/1994. See para C2.39 et seq.

B Companies or other corporate bodies

C1.39 Increased commercialisation and the onus on sport to become more accountable means that a company structure lends itself well to sports bodies. Corporate governance principles aim to strike a balance between democratic process and administrative efficiency and accountability. There are various types of company that can be used and the most appropriate for different types of sports bodies are set out below. Again, the reader should refer to a specialist publication in relation to the detail of company law.

C1.40 The real benefit of incorporation as a limited company is that the liability of the members is limited either to the price paid for the share in the company (company limited by shares) or to a nominal figure in the event of the company being dissolved (company limited by guarantee). This contrasts with the position of the members of an unincorporated association. It is the committee members of the unincorporated association who are primarily liable and therefore who have most to gain if the association incorporates. However, there are other benefits such as the ability to hold property in the association's own right and the ability to sue and be sued in its own name rather than in the name of certain individuals.

C1.41 The constitutional documents for a company are its memorandum and articles of association. These are public documents and can be viewed by anyone (by obtaining them from Companies House). There are annual filing requirements in respect of the annual return and the directors' report and accounts which means increased administration costs compared to an unincorporated association (whose rules and accounts are private documents).

C1.42 The directors of the company have to abide by company law and must have regard to their responsibilities to the company.

(a) Private companies limited by guarantee

C1.43 A company limited by guarantee can only be a private company as opposed to a public company[1]. A company limited by guarantee is very flexible. Its memorandum and articles of association will be tailored to the purposes of the particular sports organisation. It is likely to be non-profit-distributing and the guarantee (which the members are liable to pay in the event of the company being wound up) is limited to a nominal sum (usually £1 or £10). Only guarantee companies can benefit from mutual trading status for the purposes of corporation tax and the VAT exemption. This makes them particularly suitable for sports bodies which have members.

1 See para C1.45.

C1.44 Such companies are usually used for non-profit-distributing organisations, membership organisations and smaller clubs and governing bodies. Non-profit-distributing does not mean non-profit-generating. Sports organisations should aim to make a profit but most will not want to distribute it to their members. Examples of sporting organisations incorporated as companies limited by guarantee include the British Olympic Association, the British Paralympic Association, UK Athletics Limited, the British Canoe Union Limited, the All England Netball Association Limited, the Ski Club of Great Britain, the Amateur Boxing Association Limited and the Amateur Rowing Association Limited.

(b) *Private or public companies limited by shares*

C1.45 The authors do not know of any national governing body which is a plc but some are companies limited by shares rather than by guarantee (eg The Football Association Limited, incorporated 23 June 1903). However, many other sports organisations are constituted as either public or private share companies, such as Manchester United plc, Newcastle United plc, Arsenal Football Club plc, The Football Association Premier League Limited and England Rugby Limited.

C1.46 Companies limited by shares do connote commercial organisations run to make profits for the shareholders. If the shares in any company are not to be freely transferable, the articles will need to contain restrictions on transfers. There may be other specific articles which will need to be inserted. For example, the articles of The FA Premier League contain provision for one preference share, which is held by The Football Association (FA) and which entitles the FA to repayment of capital on a winding up in preference to the other classes of share. The other shareholders in The FA Premier League are the football clubs in the Premiership from time to time.

C1.47 The memorandum of association of a sports organisation is likely to need to be tailored to the particular functions which the organisation carries out. The directors will need power to make rules and regulations under the articles. If these are to bind all the members, the articles would need to give the directors (or perhaps even a separate council) power to provide for what is envisaged. Where shareholders are to have particular agreements amongst themselves (perhaps as to voting or profit share) which are not matters to be included within the articles, a shareholders' agreement may be required. Since such an agreement is private, it does not need to be filed at Companies House.

(c) *Royal charter body*

C1.48 Royal charter bodies are created either by royal charter of incorporation from the Crown or by statute making provision for the creation of a corporation by grant of royal charter. As a result such bodies are the exception rather than the rule for sports organisations. Examples include the Jockey Club and the Sports Councils[1]. Generally, a royal charter is granted for an organisation where the body has the support of a government organisation which will petition the Privy Council.

1 See para A1.47 et seq.

C1.49 When a practitioner is advising in relation to a charter body, it will be important to check the terms of the charter carefully to make sure that all of the powers that the organisation is likely to need are included within the charter (and particularly the ability to make subordinate rules). The charter is the 'governing document' or constitution for the particular organisation and seeking amendments to the charter is not as easy as amending a company's articles and so forth. Charter bodies are corporations for legal purposes.

(d) Industrial and Provident Societies ('IPSs')

C1.50 There are several Industrial and Provident Society Acts namely 1965, 1967, 1975 and 1978. A bill relating to IPSs is, at the time of writing, before Parliament. The 1965 Act is the principal statute governing IPSs.

C1.51 An IPS is traditionally an organisation conducting an industry, business or trade either as a co-operative or for the benefit of the community. It is a mutual organisation and any profits are ploughed back into the organisation for the benefit of the IPS. Democracy is paramount and different classes of member are not permitted. For this reason, many trade unions are established as IPSs.

C1.52 Establishment of a sports organisation as an IPS is usually on the basis that it is a co-operative organisation. A few sports organisations are structured as IPSs, notably the Rugby Football Union and certain rugby, cricket and golf clubs. More recently, many of the football club supporters' organisations[1] have been constituted as IPSs on the recommendation of Supporters Direct (a company which assists supporters to establish such organisations).

1 See para C1.27.

C1.53 Like a company, an IPS is a legal entity in its own right and can therefore hold property and sue and be sued in its own name. The structure also affords limited liability to its members. Under the new financial services regime, the Financial Services Authority ('FSA') has become responsible for the maintenance of the public registers for IPSs.

C1.54 An application to register an organisation as an IPS needs to be made to the FSA[1]. The FSA will scrutinise the proposed rules (on registration) and also any proposed changes to the rules to ensure compliance with the requirements of the legislation governing an IPS. Annual returns and annual accounts are also required to be lodged with the FSA. Changes to registered office, name and amendments also need to be undertaken in accordance with the correct procedures and relevant forms completed.

1 Mutual Societies Registration, Financial Services Authority, 25 The North Colonnade, Canary Wharf, London E14 5HS (Tel: 020-7676-9850).

C1.55 The fees currently payable in respect of registration, rule changes and annual returns are significantly greater than those of registering a company. The filing fees are also greater. It is anticipated that the fees may be reduced in the near future.

C1.56 Most sports organisations will choose to incorporate as companies rather than IPSs. This is because companies are simpler to administer and (perhaps more importantly) because most practitioners are more familiar with companies than

IPSs. However, there may be stamp duty issues which would lead a sports organisation choosing to incorporate as an IPS rather than a company[1].

1 See para C1.63.

C Changing legal structure

C1.57 From time to time and for a variety of reasons, sports organisations want to change their legal structure. For example, a small unincorporated club may incorporate as a company limited by guarantee or by shares or as an IPS. The entity chosen will depend on what is the most suitable for the association. A private company may become a public company and float on the stock market[1].

1 See para C3.175 et seq.

C1.58 Where such a change in legal status is envisaged, it is important for the body involved to take appropriate professional advice to ensure that its existing constitution is adhered to in making the change and that any necessary statutory or other regulatory procedures are followed.

C1.59 The incorporation as a company of an unincorporated association is complicated. Below is set out a brief summary of the steps which will need to be taken:

- It will be necessary to ensure that the unincorporated association has power to dissolve and is also able to pass its assets by way of a scheme of reconstruction to a separate entity before a resolution to transfer the assets and undertaking to that entity is proposed. This may necessitate a change in the existing rules at the same time.
- A company will need to be established with an appropriate constitution to which the unincorporated association's assets and undertakings can be transferred. The memorandum and articles are likely to need a considerable amount of work before they reflect the association's current structure and include any changes to its structure for the future. Incorporation can provide the opportunity to streamline the way the unincorporated association is governed and administered.
- The company will need to be incorporated and all the necessary Companies House forms (such as notice of new directors, change of accounting reference date, change in registered office etc) completed in readiness.
- The transfer resolution will need to be prepared. This must identify all the assets to be transferred and set out the date on which the transfer will take place (which should be some time after the date of the meeting at which the transfer resolution is proposed to allow for administrative matters to be dealt with). It will usually also provide that the unincorporated association will be dissolved after the transfer.
- The relevant tax clearances will need to be obtained from the Inland Revenue and Customs and Excise. The association may need to re-register for PAYE.
- The transfer resolution will need to be put to a general meeting of the members and will be effected if passed by the appropriate majority.
- If the transfer resolution is passed all the pre-completion matters will need to be attended to. The members of the unincorporated association will have to apply to be members of the new company before the effective date of the

transfer. The various Companies House documents will need to be filed. The employees will (having been consulted beforehand about the change) need to be informed of their new employer as TUPE will apply. All the unincorporated association's contracts will need to be novated in favour of the new company. The documents to transfer any property, or assign any lease, or transfer any investments will need to be completed. The association's bank will need to be informed and a new mandate completed. The association will need to re-register at the Information Commission. New stationery and other documents for the new company will have to be ordered.

- After completion, the unincorporated association will usually dissolve.

C1.60 Care will need to be taken to ensure that the unincorporated association is not dissolved if legacies are expected. There may be certain assets of the unincorporated association which are particularly valuable and which will need protecting either by being retained in the unincorporated association or by being kept in a separate company to the newly incorporated company.

C1.61 Incorporation as a company limited by guarantee can be structured so that it is tax neutral for capital gains tax if it is a 'scheme of reconstruction' under s 139 of the Taxation of Chargeable Gains Act 1992. Any mutual status of the association should be preserved if a guarantee company (as opposed to a company limited by shares) is used. The transfer may fall within one of the exceptions for stamp duty provided the association's property is not charged with a mortgage in excess of the stamp duty threshold.

C1.62 Where an unincorporated sports organisation wants to become an IPS, it will be necessary to ensure that new rules are adopted or the existing rules changed by a resolution of the members so that the rules comply with the requirements of the Industrial and Provident Societies Act 1965. This should enable the organisation to be registered with the FSA. Before putting the resolution to the members, it is advisable to consult with the FSA to ensure that it will register the organisation if the new rules are adopted and to bear in mind any changes suggested by the FSA.

C1.63 If stamp duty will be an issue on the transfer, incorporation as an IPS should be considered. This is because (in simple terms) the association 'becomes' the IPS rather than having to transfer its assets to a new entity.

C1.64 Where a private company (limited by shares) changes to a public company, there will need to be compliance with the Companies Act 1985 requirements and any applicable Stock Exchange regulations[1]. A summary of this process is beyond the scope of this book and reference should be had to a specialist work.

1 See para C3.175 et seq.

D Charitable status and Community Amateur Sports Clubs

C1.65 The promotion of sport is not, in itself, a charitable purpose. This means that an organisation set up to promote sport will not be charitable. However, sport can be a means to achieving another charitable purpose, for example, where it is part of the education of young people or for people with a disability. Organisations providing certain multi-sports facilities may be charities under the Recreational Charities Act 1958 if the facilities are provided in the interests of social welfare and the public benefit test (set out in s 1(1) of that Act) is met.

C1.66 There are hundreds of 'sports charities' in existence. These range from the benevolent funds of county football associations, which make payments to players injured in the course of the game and memorial funds such as The Ron Pickering Memorial Fund which assists young athletes in full time education and disabled athletes to the larger, well known sports charities such as The Football Foundation and The Football Association Youth Trust. As relief of a disability is charitable in its own right, many of the sports organisations which run sport for disabled people are charities including the British Paralympic Association, British Disabled Water Ski Association, British Blind Sport and Riding for the Disabled to name a few.

C1.67 The question of whether sport should be charitable has been much debated particularly in relation to the consideration by the Charity Commissioners as to whether the North Tawton RFC should be registered as a charity (under the Recreational Charities Act)[1]. In 2001 both HM Treasury and the Charity Commission looked at the question of amateur sports clubs. The driving force for this consideration was the repeated call for such sports clubs to be treated as if they were charities with respect to taxation, rate relief and donations. The Charity Commission subsequently issued guidance on charitable status and sport.

1 Decisions of the Charity Commissioners Vol 5, pp 7–13.

C1.68 The guidance from the Charity Commission published in November 2001[1] has confirmed that the Charity Commission will now recognise as charitable an organisation set up for:

> the promotion of community participation in healthy recreation by the provision of facilities for playing particular sports

provided that two conditions are fulfilled, namely:

(i) the sport in question must be capable of promoting health and fitness; and
(ii) the club's (or organisation's) facilities must be genuinely available to all members of the public who wish to use them.

1 Charity Commission *Charitable Status and Sport* (November 2001) (www.charity-commission.gov.uk).

C1.69 The Charity Commission's decision to recognise organisations promoting community participation in healthy recreation by the provision of facilities for playing particular sports as charitable needs to be considered in context. Most sports clubs have been set up to promote the sport itself (as was found in the *North Tawton* case) rather than community participation in healthy recreation. In order to be registered as charities, many clubs would need to change their objects in order to satisfy the Charity Commission that they fall within the accepted charitable purpose.

C1.70 Many clubs will not want to go through the constitutional change required to become a charity and adhere to the increased reporting standards required. Annual reports and accounts have to be provided to the Charity Commission. Those persons running the club may not want to become charity trustees and therefore bound by the standards imposed on them by the Charities Act 1992. Any sports club with a social element (such as the running of a bar) would need to establish a trading company subsidiary to run that activity as it will not be charitable. Any property owned by the sports club would become charitable property. These 'burdens' of charitable status will have to be weighed against the financial advantages of charitable status.

C1.71 To justify the change to charitable status, the benefits from the charity tax regime would need to be substantial. Certain clubs, which have significant legacies in sight may be justified in making the change but others will not be, particularly since clubs are often afforded favourable tax status as a result of being mutual organisations and getting some rate relief.

C1.72 The Charity Commission Guidance[1] also stated that it would now recognise as charitable:

> the advancement of the physical education of young people not undergoing formal education.

The Charity Commission views this particular addition as an extension of the existing position and a natural progression from the judgments given in the House of Lords in *IRC v McMullen*[2].

1 See para C1.68, n 1.
2 [1981] AC 1, [1980] 1 All ER 884, HL.

C1.73 Charities are usually constituted as trusts, unincorporated associations, companies limited by guarantee or bodies incorporated by royal charter[1].

1 See further paras C1.29 to C1.56. The Charity Commission has produced basic template constitutions for charitable trusts, unincorporated associations and companies limited by guarantee. These may be appropriate for use by sports charities which do not require complex structures.

C1.74 If an association has exclusively charitable objects, it will be a charity and must (if it has an income over £1,000 a year) register with the Charity Commission. If the association does not want the burden of being a charity, it must ensure that its objects are not exclusively charitable.

C1.75 In the March 2001 Budget, the Chancellor announced that there would be a new scheme of tax treatment for 'community amateur sports clubs' ('CASCs'). The Treasury proposals were to encourage donations and legacies to CASCs by the creation of a gift aid scheme for CASCs and an inheritance tax exemption and provide relief from Capital Gains Tax and Corporation Tax in certain (limited) circumstances. However, in order to qualify for these benefits the sports club would need to meet certain criteria as to membership and other constitutional matters.

C1.76 In light of the Charity Commission's guidance on charitable status and sport, HM Treasury consulted within sport as to whether its proposals were still necessary. Following consultation, in the March 2002 Budget, a package of tax reliefs to support CASCs was announced. This means that a sports club has two options open to it if it is wanting to obtain tax relief on the basis of its 'community' status. Either it can apply to the Inland Revenue for the tax reliefs or it can apply to the Charity Commission to register its charitable status.

C1.77 The main tax reliefs available for CASCs from April 2002 are:

(i) up to £15,000 of trading income is exempt from Corporation Tax;
(ii) interest on bank balances is also exempt from Corporation Tax;
(iii) up to £10,000 of rental income is exempt from tax;
(iv) disposals of assets are exempt from Capital Gains Tax;
(v) donations to a CASC will attract the 'Gift Aid' relief;
(vi) gifts will attract Inheritance Tax relief;
(vii) gifts of assets will be taken to be on a no-gain, no-loss basis for Capital Gains Tax for both individuals and businesses; and
(viii) gifts of trading stock will attract business relief[1].

1 The details of the tax reliefs available to CASCs will need to be checked by practitioners when claiming them as these are due to change. See further para C2.98.

C1.78 In order to qualify as a CASC, the sports club's constitution must reflect the three criteria set out in the Finance Bill 2002, which are as follows:

(i) the club must be open to the whole community;
(ii) the club must be organised on an amateur basis; and
(iii) the club must provide facilities for and promote participation in one or more eligible sports (ie those recognised by the national Sports Councils).

C1.79 Many sports clubs may not currently reflect these criteria in their constitutions as they will have been established as private members' clubs and may well include (for mutual trading purposes) a clause which provides for surpluses on a dissolution to be paid to the members. Such a clause would no longer be permitted[1]. The change to CASC status will therefore involve a shift of emphasis from a club established to benefit the members and one established to benefit the community. This is a question which each club considering CASC status will itself need to determine.

1 See para 3(1)(c) of Sch 18 to the Finance Bill.

C1.80 Schedule 18 of the Finance Bill 2002 sets out the details on the criteria for qualification as a CASC. Membership can be divided into different classes (as set out in the Bill) but must be open to all without discrimination. Membership fees must not pose an obstacle to membership.

C1.81 For a club to be organised on an amateur basis, it must not be profit-distributing either during the life of the club or on dissolution (although CASC to CASC donations are permitted). It may only provide members with the 'ordinary benefits of an amateur sports club', which are defined in Sch 18, para 3(3) of the Finance Bill. The ordinary benefits are fairly limited and do not include payment to players for playing. The sale/supply of food and drink is permitted only as a social adjunct to the sporting purposes.

C1.82 A club can register as a CASC with effect from 1 April 2002 or any other date prior to enactment of the Finance Bill. The exemptions would take effect from 1 April 2002. Before registering as a CASC, clubs will need to:

(i) review their constitution and structure to see if they qualify;
(ii) make any necessary changes to their constitutions;
(iii) consider whether the benefits of CASC status really outweigh their current tax treatment.

C1.83 Such a club may also want to consider whether its interests would be better served by registering as a charity. It is worth pointing out that the criteria for CASCs are less strict than those set down in the Charity Commission's guidance[1] and do recognise that the purpose of a particular CASC is participation in that particular sport.

1 See para C1.68, n 1.

5 CONCLUSION

C1.84 There are various forms of organisation that a sports body can take. Some sports bodies may be structured as unincorporated associations for historical reasons. The increased commercialisation of sport and the concessions in relation to the tax regime for CASCs means that sports bodies must review, from time to time, whether their constitutional structure adequately protects them from liability and affords them all the available tax benefits.

CHAPTER C2

TAXATION OF SPORTS ORGANISATIONS

Richard Baldwin (Deloitte & Touche)

Contents

1 WHY TAX IS IMPORTANT

C2.1 Officers and management, whether paid or voluntary, of sports organisations should be aware that tax can have an important impact on finances. Sports organisations, whether non-profit distributing clubs, associations, leagues, governing bodies or commercial entities, generally enjoy no special exemptions from tax. Often, in practice, unexpected tax liabilities arise and opportunities to minimise tax are lost.

C2.2 Sport in general is very visible through the media. Inspectors of taxes in the Inland Revenue and Customs and Excise are often keen on sport. In addition to their personal interest in sport, tax authorities have formalised their approach to dealing with it. Thus, for example, a special unit in the Inland Revenue Special Compliance Office in Solihull deals with professional sport. The tax authorities have come under increased pressure to become cost-effective. Sport is a happy hunting ground yielding significant amounts of additional tax from tax investigations.

C2.3 Club officers could find themselves personally liable for tax liabilities and should consider restructuring the organisation's activities through a limited company to obtain protection[1].

1 See further paras C1.36 and C1.40.

C2.4 Tax is an issue for professional and amateur clubs. If sources of income are within the tax statutes, whether for corporation tax or VAT purposes, they will be taxable no matter how the organisation is run or the income is applied. Even relatively casual fund-raising, such as dinner dances, beer and jazz festivals run to raise funds for the club can be subject to tax. Exceptions to this rule are where the organisation is a charity or community amateur sports club for which tax exemptions are available.

2 THE TYPES OF ENTITY AND THE TAXES THEY FACE

C2.5 Corporation tax applies not only to companies but also to unincorporated associations. At the top of sport, professional clubs are likely to be incorporated, but at local league level, clubs usually exist as unincorporated associations.

C2.6 Clubs have to deal with:

- corporation tax on income and capital gains
- PAYE withholding and National Insurance contributions
- value added tax.

Other taxes, such as stamp duty and uniform business rates, also impinge on their activities. This chapter is, however, concerned only with the three major taxes.

3 CORPORATION TAX

A Liability

C2.7 All sports entities prima facie are liable to corporation tax. Even though many are loss-making, corporation tax compliance and planning can be relevant.

C2.8 A sports club pays tax on taxable income and gains within the taxing schedules. Typical sources include:

- trading income, eg gate receipts and central distributions from sponsorship, television and other commercial income;
- fund-raising income;
- income from lotteries, raffles and prize draws;

- sponsorship income or licence fees;
- investment income, whether interest or income from investments or from property;
- profits on the sale of capital assets, including land.

C2.9 Not all income is taxable since member clubs are likely to be able to take advantage of the mutual trading exemption. This applies if income is derived from members (usually from subscriptions) and surpluses are applied for the benefit of the members with distributions and surplus assets on winding up going to the members. No taxable profit can arise since members cannot make a profit out of themselves.

B Taxable profits

C2.10 Profits are computed by reference to each income source after deductible expenses. As a general rule, losses from one source cannot be offset against profits from another.

C2.11 Sports clubs are likely to have taxable trading income (subject to the mutual trading exemption above) comprising gate receipts, sponsorship income, catering and hospitality income.

C2.12 Certain income may fall outside the tax net altogether, for example, UK dividends and donations from unconnected third parties. Unsolicited donations should be tax-free. If something is provided in return, for example, advertising rights, the 'donations' will constitute taxable trading income.

C2.13 Gains from capital transactions, such as the sale of land and buildings, are taxable, computed under the capital gains rules. Such gains may be deferred under the rollover relief provisions[1].

1 See para C2.27.

C2.14 Tax deductions are available for two different types of expenses in arriving at taxable profits; expenses deductible when incurred against a particular source of income and charges on income deductible against total profits when paid. Sports clubs carrying on a trade can deduct expenditure incurred wholly and exclusively for the purposes of that trade. There are exeptions such as business entertaining and expenditure of a capital nature. Generally, a club will have difficulty in deducting development expenditure if it cannot be shown to benefit the club's trade.

C2.15 Charges on income include payments to charity under the Gift Aid rules. It is no longer necessary to deduct income tax at source from such payments, which are allowable for tax purposes when paid.

C Capital expenditure

C2.16 Tax relief is not generally available on capital expenditure unless the items purchased qualify as plant and machinery, eg furniture, computer and sports equipment, tractors and mowers. Relief is given against trading income via a writing-down allowance of 25% per annum on a reducing balance basis. Small or medium-sized companies qualify for a plant and machinery first year allowance of 40%, with a 25% writing-down allowance on the balance in subsequent years. The writing-down allowance on a car is limited to £3,000 in any year.

C2.17 Expenditure on buildings will not normally qualify for relief, and clubs building sports facilities therefore face repayment of any borrowing out of after-tax income.

D Self-assessment returns

C2.18 Sports organisations have to make self-assessments of their corporation tax liability as part of the tax return. It is not necessary for the Inland Revenue to instigate the filing of the return. It is the organisation's responsibility to file within 12 months of the end of the accounting period. Failure will result in late filing penalties. The tax return form CT600 must be submitted with the accounts for the period covered by the return and any tax computation indicating how the entries disclosed on the form have been calculated.

C2.19 An accompanying corporation tax computation is unnecessary where there is only investment income to report. The return would normally be signed by the club's secretary, treasurer or finance director. The return must be completed correctly or it is likely to be rejected by the Inland Revenue. Once the return is filed, the Inland Revenue has to power to inquire into it within 12 months of the filing date and to obtain access to all records.

E Corporation tax rates

C2.20 The starting rate of corporation tax of 10% for companies in the band between £nil and £10,000 has been in effect from 1 April 2000 (nil from 1 April 2002). Profits falling in the band between £10,001 and £50,000 will be charged at a marginal rate of 22.5% (23.75% from 1 April 2002).

C2.21 Many clubs will find that they pay tax at a rate of 20% (19% from 1 April 2002), since their profits are lower than the small companies lower profit limit, which currently stands at £300,000.

C2.22 Profits which fall in the band between £300,000 and £1,500,000 (the upper limit for 'large' companies) are taxable at the marginal rate of 32.5% (32.75% from 1 April 2002). Profits over the upper limit are taxed at 30%.

C2.23 The lower and upper limits for small companies rate will be reduced if there are other bodies which are connected to the club.

F Payment dates

C2.24 A quarterly instalment payment regime affects 'large' companies. Most sports clubs will not be within this and will pay their tax nine months after their year-end. Clubs should keep up-to-date with their tax affairs and complete their computations and return promptly. Interest is payable/re-payable on any under/overpayment.

G Key issues

(a) *Tax planning*

C2.25 Corporation tax planning is relevant because:

- With increased income and expendidture, budgets of income and expenditure should incorporate adequate provision for corporation tax.
- Increased revenues from broacasting sponsorship and merchandising means that many loss-making clubs may now be making profits, resulting in corporation tax liabilites.
- Even where there are losses, they may be used elsewhere, enhancing cash flow.
- A sports club financed by individuals may be able to benefit from structuring their investment through a profit-making company owned by each individual. The losses of the club can be used against such companies' profits in return for a payment under the consortium provisions.
- Trading losses can be offset against other profits, including capital gains arising in the year in which the losses are incurred. Unrelieved trading losses can be carried back against income and gains of the previous year.

C2.26 Sports clubs should minimise taxable income and maximise taxable expenditure, thus reducing taxable profits or increasing taxable losses which are available for use elsewhere.

(b) *Particular types of income and gains*

C2.27 Particular attention needs to be given to:

- Sponsorship income which is generally taxable whether received in cash or in kind. Clothing, equipment or other products received from sponsors should be recorded at market value in the accounts and taxed accordingly, usually subject to a deduction for the cost of using the product, equipment etc.
- Many sports clubs run prize draws, raffles and lotteries to generate much needed income. The legality of such lotteries under the Lotteries and Amusements Act 1976 needs to be carefully considered, and registration with the Gaming Board or local authority needs to be effected. Prime facie, this income is subject to corporation tax and should be reported as taxable income. However, where a lottery is run by an organising body outside the club for whose benefits the proceeds accrue, it is possible that part of the proceeds from the lottery may be exempt from tax.
- Fees, distributions or prize monies in respect of participation in sports competitions organised by a sports governing body is generally taxable since it is generated from the sports clubs' trade, notwithstanding that the funds are designated for either youth or facilities development. Full relief may not be available in the year the money is spent, eg if it is on a capital project that does not qualify in full for plant and machinery allowances[1].

- Taxable profits will also arise on the sale of a club's capital assets such as land and buildings. Often the tax effects are not taken into account, which can give rise to problems where the proceeds are spent and an unexpected tax bill arrives. The capital gains rules are complex, and if a capital disposal is contemplated, professional advice should also be taken. Gains from assets used for the purposes of the club's trade can be deferred if the proceeds are fully or partly reinvested in other qualifying assets within a period of one year before the sale of the old asset and three years afterwards. To obtain full deferral, sales proceeds must be reinvested in their entirety. Typically, a club would reinvest in the following types of qualifying assets:
  - land or buildings, provided they are used for the purposes of the club's activities;
  - fixed plant and machinery;
  - goodwill (special rules apply after 1 April 2002).

1 See para C2.16.

(c) Particular expenses

C2.28 Clubs should carefully scrutinise:

- Capital projects which can cause a significant additional strain on resources if tax relief is not maximised. This involves not only evaluating the tax relief for the expenditure itself, but the availability of tax relief for any finance used to fund the project, including grants.
- The normal capital allowance reliefs[1] are available for certain safety work in spectator sports incurred in meeting the safety requirements of a local authority under the Safety of Sports Grounds Act 1975[2]. It is certainly worth getting advice from a capital allowances consultant so that the maximum possible can be claimed for items qualifying for tax relief.
- Grants can reduce tax relief for expenditure incurred by the club whether they are either capital or revenue in nature. Revenue grants towards running expenses, eg the cost of staging a competition, are normally treated as a subsidy towards the cost it is helping to meet and are thus taxable. A capital grant contributes towards capital expenditure and its tax treatment depends on the precise nature of the grant. If the grant is towards expenditure qualifying as plant, the club's right to claim capital allowances may be restricted. If, however, the asset does not qualify for capital allowances, the tax position is not prejudiced since no capital allowances will be foregone.

1 See para C2.16.
2 See para A1.61.

H Planning opportunities

C2.29 Clubs should consider the following opportunities for tax planning.

(a) Charitable status

C2.30 Some sports clubs can obtain charitable status for part of their activities, eg community work. Generally the clubs themselves would not satisfy the public benefit requirement to be eligible for charitable status. Recently, the Charity

Commission has relaxed its requirements for sports clubs to register as charities. Community amateur sports clubs, which exist for the benefit of the community and have as their object the participation by the public in healthy sport and recreation, can be charitable[2]. Before registering, great care should be taken; this will not be a suitable route for the club to follow where it has substantial sources of commercial income and exists to excel in competitions rather than to provide healthy sports recreation. However, where a club establishes community sports schemes for youngsters, or generally makes sporting facilities available to the general public, a separate charity can carry on such activities. The tax and other related benefits, include:

- tax relief for payments to the charity under gift aid;
- exemption from tax on income and gains applied for charitable purposes;
- 80% mandatory business rate relief and discretionary relief for the balance of 20%.

1 See further para C1.65 et seq.
2 See para C2.98.

(b) *Player registrations*

C2.31 In professional sports such as rugby and football, payments for player registrations can be an important part of the club's tax planning. Under FRS10, goodwill and intangibles, which apply for accounting periods on or after 23 March 1999, the cost of acquiring a player's registration must be capitalised in the balance sheet. This cost will be amortised over the period of the player's contract and tax relief will be given in accordance with the write-off. Difficulties can arise where a club sells a player for a significant sum, realising a profit (after deducting un-amortised transfer costs) which will be taxable in full in the year the player is transferred. Under a recent change in the tax law effective from 1 April 2002, it is now possible for the tax on a gain from the sale of a player signed after that date to be deferred if it is reinvested in new players. This is welcome relief for sports clubs which sell players they have developed and reinvest the proceeds in strengthening their squads.

(c) *Tax effective funding*

C2.32

- Often, sports club directors who are the major shareholders provide funds for the club, either themselves or through their companies. Such finance can be provided tax effectively by way of share subscription, loans, or guaranteeing loans made by third parties, eg the banks. The funding method should be carefully considered; there are potential tax savings.
- On making the investment, Enterprise Investment Scheme (EIS) relief may provide income tax relief at 20% on an investment of up to £150,000 per tax year. Under EIS, any capital gain made by the individual can be deferred by reinvesting in new ordinary shares of professional sports clubs provided the qualifying conditions are met. Share capital can also benefit individuals by using taper relief on ultimate disposal of the shares bringing the effective capital gains tax rate down to 10%. These are all technical matters and require detailed consideration but can, nevertheless, create tax savings.

- Where investment is through a company or group of companies carrying on the directors' other business activities, advantage may be taken of the group and consortium relief provisions. The former apply if 75% of the sports club's ordinary share capital is owned by another company (subject to certain other tests being met). If the group relief tests are met, the sports club's losses can be surrendered and used by the other company or group of companies on a current year basis in their entirety even though the club is only a 75% subsidiary. The club can then receive payment of an amount up to the amount of the loss surrendered, and this payment will be ignored for tax purposes. The group company benefits, since it will not have to pay the tax covered by the surrender of the losses from the sports club.
- A consortium exists where all of the club's ordinary share capital is owned by twenty or fewer companies. This test may be difficult to satisfy where the sports club shares are owned widely. Consortium relief will be available when the club is a 90% subsidiary of a holding company which is itself owned by a consortium. The club's losses can be offset on a current basis against the profits of the various consortium members in proportion to their interest. Again, if payment is made for the losses offset, this can provide valuable finance to the club.

4 DEALING WITH VALUE ADDED TAX

A Registration

C2.33 When the taxable standard, reduced rate or zero-rated turnover of a club exceeds certain limits, it must apply for VAT registration. This is separate from any notification required for PAYE or corporation tax purposes. Sports clubs generally have taxable turnover for VAT purposes even if they do not make a profit and are not organised on commercial lines. Certain income is exempt, which may mean that clubs are not required to be registered. Failure to register for VAT exposes the club to significant penalties and interest.

C2.34 VAT registration is compulsory when taxable turnover in the preceding 12 months (or expected turnover in the next 30 days) exceeds the VAT registration threshold, which is currently £55,000 with effect from 25 April 2002. Customs & Excise must be notified in writing. A sports club may voluntarily register for VAT even if taxable income is less than the threshold. This may suit the sports club if the VAT it incurs on its expenditure is significant. The disadvantage of applying for voluntary registration is that the club will have to charge VAT on all standard rated supplies made and file VAT returns. Once registered for VAT, pricing policies may need to alter to enable the sports club to charge VAT where necessary; cash flow is also likely to be affected.

C2.35 VAT registration is applied for by completing form VAT1 and submitting this to the VAT authorities. Businesses with a London post code send their applications to the central VAT registration unit at Newry. Other businesses send their VAT applications to the local VAT offices. Normally, 7 to 10 days elapse for an application to be processed, and once approved, a Certificate of Registration (form VAT4) is issued showing the VAT registration number and the VAT return periods allocated to the business.

B Taxable supplies

C2.36 Registered sports clubs charge VAT on their standard rated supplies at the current rate of 17.5% and are entitled to recovery of VAT charged on supplies to them, resulting in net payments to or repayments from Customs & Excise. Small sports clubs may wish to take advantage of the flat rate, annual and cash VAT accounting schemes.

C2.37 The following types of supply determine the amount of VAT due on supplies and recoverable on related expenditure:

- zero rate supplies, where VAT is chargeable at 0% with full recovery on connected expenditure;
- reduced rate supplies where VAT is chargeable at 5% and full recovery on connected expenditure;
- standard rate supplies where VAT is chargeable at 17.5% and full recovery on connected expenditure;
- exempt supplies where no VAT is chargeable on the supply but VAT on related costs cannot be recovered, subject to de minimis limits[1];
- outside the scope income is entirely outside the scope of VAT so no VAT is chargeable. This income is not taken into account in considering whether the sports club needs to be registered for VAT.

1 See para C2.50.

C2.38 Appendix 1 contains guidance on the VAT liabilities of the main sources of income that a sports club is likely to have. Specific rules and exceptions apply to each item and must be looked at carefully.

C Exemptions for fees and subscriptions

C2.39 VAT exemption was introduced on 1 April 1994 for 'services closely linked and essential to sport and physical education', which affects many VAT registered sports clubs which are 'non-profit making'. Membership fees and subscriptions charged to members who take part in sport will be exempt.

C2.40 A non-profit making body includes members clubs run for their benefit and which cannot distribute profits to members. Organisations run commercially for the benefit of owners who can take dividends will not qualify. The exemption applies principally to local sports clubs who principally rely on membership subscriptions and match fees for financial survival.

C2.41 To be treated as members, individuals must be granted membership for a period of three months or more. Non-playing and social subscriptions, where the persons are not taking part in sport, are excluded from the exemption and remain standard rated.

C2.42 Customs have drawn up a list of recognised sports which determine which sports and recreational facilities benefit from exemption, having regard to those sports officially recognised by the Sports Councils.

C2.43 Exemption is not always to a club's advantage since, by creating exempt income, VAT on expenditure incurred to generate that income will not be recoverable. Further, the subscriptions are not always fully exempt and it may be necessary to apportion subscription fees between exempt and taxable elements when part of it is for a subsidy, for example, a bar. Different elements of the subscription may attract different rates, although if part of the subscription is for a zero-rated supply, eg a publication, book or magazine for members, this may help the sports club's overall VAT recovery position.

C2.44 This is a complex area of tax law, particularly for the level of sports club at which it is aimed. There are anti-avoidance provisions and a hidden cost, eg capital expenditure programmes may suffer irrecoverable VAT if subscriptions are exempt.

D Recovery of VAT on expenditure

(a) Non-recoverable VAT

C2.45 VAT registered sports clubs receiving taxable income can reclaim the VAT charged on most of their expenditure. VAT on expenditure is called 'input tax' but recovery of input tax on certain purchases is not allowed:

- purchase of a motor car unless wholly used for business purposes;
- business entertainment where no onward charge is made;
- business gifts costing more than £50.

(b) Partially exempt income

C2.46 Where a VAT registered sports club receives exempt income, for example rent, as well as taxable income, it will not be allowed to recover all of its input tax. VAT on costs incurred on taxable activities can be reclaimed, but VAT on costs incurred in connection with VAT exempt income, if those costs exceed certain de minimis limits, cannot. For example, as income from lotteries is exempt, potentially the VAT on goods, purchases, prizes or on printing the tickets cannot be recovered. VAT on costs connected with exempt income is called exempt input tax.

C2.47 Some exempt input tax will be clearly identifiable but frequently input tax incurred on expenses relates to both exempt and taxable income, eg telephone bills, club overheads. This is known as residual input tax. If it exceeds certain limits, VAT on those expenses will have to be apportioned between exempt input tax and taxable input tax.

(c) Partial exemption

C2.48 Partially exempt sports clubs generally use the standard method of apportioning residual or 'mixed use' input tax by reclaiming a percentage of it. The percentage is calculated by taking taxable income as a proportion of total income excluding some outside the scope income. If this does not give a fair and reasonable result, it is possible to apply to use another method to establish the recoverable element of mixed use input tax. For example:

- values of taxable and exempt inputs (purchases);
- staff time spent on taxable and exempt activities; or
- floor space for various use for taxable and exempt activities.

C2.49 Customs approval must be obtained prior to using any method that is not the standard method. The method should be carefully chosen, particularly where substantial VAT costs will arise on improved or new buildings and facilities.

C2.50 Under the de minimis rules, if exempt input tax, including the VAT on the relevant portion of overheads, is less than £625 per month on average and less than 50% of all input tax for the period, it can be reclaimed in full. With effect from 18 April 2002, if the standard method is used, there is an override calculation if residual input tax exceeds £50,000 or 50% or more of the value of residual input tax but not less than £25,000. This is unlikely to impact on sports clubs.

C2.51 Recoverable VAT for partially exempt sports clubs is calculated on a provisional basis for the periodic monthly or quarterly VAT return figures. At the end of the year, usually March, April or May, the figures must be recalculated for the whole year. This will show whether or not the exempt input tax incurred falls below the de minimis limits on average. Any difference between the annual calculation and the amounts previously claimed should be declared on the next VAT return (whether the amount is due to or from Customs).

(d) Non-business income

C2.52 A sports club incurring expenditure related to a non-business activity, is not entitled to recover VAT on these costs. Unlike the partial exemption calculations, there is no threshold before the non-business restriction applies.

E Records, accounts and returns

(a) Records

C2.53 Records should be maintained to enable visiting VAT officers to check the make-up of the figures on VAT returns. All invoices received and issued should be kept as evidence in support of claims for input tax and declaration of output tax. For smaller sports clubs, an analysed cash book system with VAT columns may be sufficient, although receipts could usefully be categorised, eg gate receipts, bar takings, game and machine receipts and sundry sales and purchases analysed in detail.

(b) Accounting

C2.54 VAT should be separately identified in the club's accounting records, not just by entering the gross income figures. In particular, clubs should not record only the 'profit' element of an event, eg catering receipts less cost of foods, as the VAT due would be understated. Cash payments from the till should be included in the till total takings figure before cashing up.

(c) Returns

C2.55 Output tax, ie VAT on sales, normally has to be recorded on the VAT return either in the period when an invoice is issued or when a payment is received, whichever happens first. Deposits or instalments are generally treated as advance payments, and VAT must be accounted for on receipt. A sports club is entitled to a refund of VAT accounted for on bad debts if certain criteria are met.

C2.56 VAT registered businesses have to submit VAT returns and payments to the VAT central unit in Southend. This will normally be quarterly, although there are exceptions such as annual accounting and monthly returns, which are usually for those businesses that receive regular repayments of VAT. Certain large payers of VAT are required to make payments on account, although this is unlikely to apply to the average sports club.

C2.57 VAT returns are made on form VAT100 issued by Customs to businesses in advance of their becoming due. If a sports club does not receive a return form, it is important to let the VAT office know as soon as possible so that duplicates can be issued. Customs will not accept non-receipt of a VAT form as an excuse for late payment, and automatic penalties for late submission of payment or returns will be due.

C2.58 VAT returns and payments should be received by Customs by the last day of the month following the end of the return period. For example, a VAT return form for the quarter ended June must be received by Customs with payment before 31 July. Special rules apply where VAT returns do not cover standard monthly or quarterly periods. The due date for payment can be extended by up to seven days by the use of a credit transfer system, but this requires Customs approval.

(d) Interest and penalties

C2.59 The reporting regime for VAT is tough; in addition to interest being chargeable on late payment of tax, there is a whole series of penalties, which include the following:

- A late registration penalty for failing to register for VAT on time. Penalties are calculated as a percentage of the VAT due to Customs from the date when registration should have taken place to when Customs were actually notified.
- A default surcharge is raised if a VAT payment is received late by Customs. Customs issue a surcharge liability notice after the first default and, as the defaults continue, the penalty increases. This penalty is calculated on the net tax due on the late VAT returns.
- A 15% mis-declaration penalty is triggered when a VAT return has under-declared the VAT due or overstated the amount of VAT recoverable, subject to certain limits.
- A repeated mis-declaration penalty applies to persistent errors. A penalty liability notice is issued if a material error is discovered within five return periods of it occurring.

C2.60 It is possible to appeal against the above penalties if a sports club has a reasonable excuse, for example, but this is an area to avoid.

C2.61 Interest may be charged when the sports club has paid an assessment which later turns out to be too low or when it has underpaid or over-claimed VAT. However, where a repayment of tax is due and payment is unnecessarily delayed by Customs, a repayment supplement could be due to the club.

F Key issues

C2.62 The following is a series of key issues for planning the sports club's VAT affairs:

- Business entertainment includes the provision of food and drink, hotel accommodation and entry to sporting or similar events to persons other than employees. An exception to the general entertainment disallowance is where a sports club provides hotel accommodation to a visiting team under a reciprocal agreement, and in that case, input VAT can be recovered on the associated expenditure.
- Governing bodies and leagues may have rulings from Customs & Excise regarding income received centrally from sponsorship, broadcasting and other commercial agreements. Such income on distributions to sports clubs may be outside the scope of VAT. Governing bodies and leagues should be able to advise sports clubs on the VAT treatment of such distributions.
- Sports clubs enter into contracts which involve the granting of intellectual property rights, eg the sale of rights to use the club's logo or name. Supplies under such contracts are treated as being made in the country where they are received. Therefore, where a club sells the rights to a business in the UK, VAT has to be charged. Great care needs to be taken where supplies are made to businesses outside the UK or, indeed, to private individuals or other non-business entities in the EU since UK VAT may have to be charged in some cases.
- Sponsorship income is normally received in the expectation of doing something in return, eg advertising, hospitality etc. In those instances VAT should be charged by the club to UK supplies of sponsorship. However, where sponsors belong outside the UK, the supply may be VAT free. Sponsorship may include an element of business entertainment, eg hospitality. In such circumstances the VAT incurred by the sponsor will not be recoverable as business entertainment. Goods or services may be provided free of charge under a value-in-kind agreement, ie the club receives goods or services in return rather than payment. For VAT purposes, this arrangement results in both parties making supplies, and VAT must be accounted for on the full value of those supplies by both parties as a general rule. This is often overlooked by sports clubs and sponsors alike.
- Sports clubs may incur overseas VAT costs, eg travel and accommodation as a result of tours, European or international matches. It may be possible to recover such VAT under special refund procedures known as the 8th and 13th Directive procedures. Subject to certain conditions, VAT incurred in other countries can be refunded periodically, provided the sports club is not registered or liable to be registered for VAT in those countries.
- The retail sale of goods, including shirts, scarves and badges, would generally be standard rated unless they qualified for zero-rating as children's clothing or footwear, or as relevant publications. Zero rating applies to articles designed as children's clothing, and in practice this means clothing or footwear suitable for children up to 13 years as determined by the BSI.

G Planning opportunities

C2.63 Generally, for VAT registered sports clubs, VAT incurred on expenditure should not represent a cost. However, VAT may be minimised by any of the following means:

- Avoiding a VAT liability on supplies by analysing supplies into their component parts and taking full advantage of zero rating.

- Taking full advantage of the available exemptions identified in Appendix 1.
- Making the most of partial exemption by negotiating the best method of recovering input tax with Customs & Excise or reducing exempt input tax below the de minimis limit of £625 per month.
- Timing output VAT liability, eg there will be a longer VAT cash flow benefit for an invoice issued at the beginning of a VAT quarter rather than at the end.
- In the case of sponsorship, carefully analysing what is provided, particularly if the sponsor is partly exempt, eg a bank, building society or an insurance company. If part of the sponsorship receipt is not subject to VAT or is exempt from VAT, then this may result in more net cash for the club but watch partial exemption.
- Ensuring that VAT is charged when it is due, since if it is not, recovery from the customer may be difficult. Any exchange of letters or agreement or contract should make the VAT position clear in relation to payments under it.

5 PAYE AND NIC

A Inland Revenue interest

(a) Clubs

C2.64 The Inland Revenue regularly collects unpaid PAYE and NIC from sports organisations which have not complied with their obligations. Sport has attracted detailed Inland Revenue interest and has generally tightened up both the rules and its practice in this area. Major spectator sports, such as football and rugby union, have suffered co-ordinated efforts by the Inland Revenue to collect PAYE and NIC which the Revenue believes is due from their major professional sports clubs. Other governing bodies, eg cricket, have been visited to discuss particular areas of potential tax leakage.

C2.65 Inland Revenue Special Compliance Offices started to investigate football at the beginning of the 1990s. At the time, two Special Compliance Offices were identified to deal with professional and semi-professional clubs respectively. Solihull Special Compliance Office commenced its activities by requesting the top professional clubs in England to prepare detailed reports dealing with PAYE compliance. Unpaid tax was collected from this process from certain clubs and, generally, procedures were tightened. The Solihull unit continues its work today, having particular interest in transfers of players from overseas but also covers other sports. The Inland Revenue also reviewed semi-professional football, particularly non-contract players. At its suggestion, guidelines were produced in May 1995, highlighting the unacceptable practices. Although the Special Compliance Office is no longer actively monitoring the semi-professional game, PAYE audit teams continue to review semi-professional clubs to ensure compliance. All sports clubs making payments to players and other employees should ensure that their PAYE and NIC affairs are in order to avoid substantial and often unexpected costs.

(b) Governing bodies

C2.66 Governing bodies of sport have a role to play in this process educating clubs in the pitfalls that can arise; thus the Football Association has issued brochures dealing with the collection of PAYE and NIC. Governing bodies will often be approached by the Inland Revenue if a particular tax abuse is perceived. They are in a position to negotiate and agree a satisfactory treatment within their sport and issue guidelines to improve compliance.

B Responsibilities

C2.67 Sports clubs are treated the same as any other employer but, because of the nature of the sports industry and sports' own regulations, certain areas can give rise to particular tax problems. The club's responsibilities for employees (including people not automatically regarded as employees, such as stewards, gatemen, bar staff etc) are to:

- collect and account for PAYE and NIC on all payments to 'employees'; and
- fill in forms and returns in relation to PAYE and NIC and expenses paid and benefits provided to employees.

C2.68 The club needs, therefore, to:

- keep adequate records;
- deduct the correct amounts of PAYE and NIC and pay them over on time; and
- send in the appropriate forms and returns completed accurately and on a timely basis.

C2.69 Sports club staff are not experts in this complex and administratively time-consuming area of tax. Clubs should establish procedures covering these responsibilities and periodically review their effective operation. Failure to do this will mean tax charges and penalties arising, eg after an investigation by the Inland Revenue.

C2.70 There are time limits for the payment of tax and the submission of returns and forms; all employers incur automatic penalties for failure to meet these since they are strictly enforced. Details of the time limits for each tax year, together with penalties for non-compliance, are included at Appendix 2 below. As well as penalties for not sending forms in on time, interest will be charged on any unpaid PAYE and NIC.

C Problem areas – PAYE and NIC

(a) General

C2.71 The largest potential exposure is payments to players; significant time may be spent on devising tax effective remuneration packages. Even here, PAYE remains a risk since often if a tax planning strategy does not work, the burden falls on the club under PAYE rather than the player. Even small to medium sized sports clubs are paying their players and therefore will be at risk in the PAYE and NIC area. Typically, the following PAYE problems will exist.

(b) Gross payments

C2.72 Gross cash payments made without deduction of PAYE or NIC are sometimes made to players, managers etc, outside their normal responsibilities and additional to their normal salary. Tax often should have been deducted and the Inland Revenue will seek to treat the actual cash paid as a net sum after the deduction of tax and NIC, ie it would seek to gross up the payments and charge tax and NIC on the gross amount. Petty cash payments in particular are at risk from the Revenue since they usually provide an easy target in an investigation. Distributions from players' pools, eg out of sponsorship and appearance money, can also create difficulties and need to be dealt with carefully.

(c) Round sum allowances

C2.73 Round sum allowances are often not expenses at all but disguised salary from the Revenue's perspective. They are regarded as salary on which PAYE and NIC should be paid. Genuine expenses need to be reimbursed specifically, and if paid by way of a round sum estimate, need to be cleared in advance with the local Inspector of Taxes. Any sports club paying round sum allowances without the necessary support and clearance should review its policy as a matter of urgency. Travel and subsistence are most at risk.

(d) For the love of the game

C2.74 Many individuals help out at clubs and, indeed, players can play 'for the love of the game'. Expense payments are made to cover genuine travel and other expenses, and the Inland Revenue may agree that individuals play 'for the love of the game'. In this event the Revenue will not regard them as employees because no money is made out of their participation. Football has agreed this approach with the Inland Revenue in relation to non-contract players in semi-professional football. However, this will only succeed where there is no contract of employment with the player concerned and the payments do no more than reimburse actual costs computed on a reasonable basis. Clearance from the local PAYE Inspector is recommended in advance and detailed records need to be kept.

(e) Second employments

C2.75 Contracted players will often have a second employment; these individuals will be subject to PAYE by the second employer in most instances. In this event the player is likely to be treated as taxable at the basic rate on his income from the sports club, since his personal allowance will be allocated against his income from his main employment. He will be likely to pay the maximum National Insurance contributions from that employment and can apply to have any wages from the sports club paid without deduction of NIC.

(f) Testimonials and benefits

C2.76 Players may be granted testimonial or benefit matches, receiving the proceeds personally. These may be free of tax in the player's hands provided a number of conditions are met. In particular, there must be no contractual entitlement, written or oral, to the benefit and no custom must exist in respect of it. The danger for the sports club is that it is involved in the organisation or has agreed to provide the benefit, in which event the Inland Revenue may, again, look to the sports club for the tax that would be due. There are guidelines in football and cricket for the organisation of such benefits providing assurance that, if appropriately organised, the proceeds will be tax-free and the club should have no exposure.

(g) Training gear

C2.77 Players may be reimbursed for equipment such as footwear, training gear etc. If this is to be tax-free, the sports club must keep documentary evidence of the actual expenses. Reimbursement must be no more that the actual costs incurred. If round sum allowances are paid in excess of these costs[1], the entire amount will be subject to tax under PAYE, giving rise to costs for the sports club.

1 See para C2.73.

(h) Non-playing staff

C2.78 Whilst the main exposure is usually with players, other individuals receiving payments may also be at risk in relation to PAYE and NIC. Particular areas of weakness are:

- Treatment as self-employed whereas under the tax law there is an employment giving rise to PAYE and NIC. Each tax district has a nominated status inspector whose role is to review the relationship between individuals and the business to determine whether they are in fact employees or self-employed consultants. The tax status of these individuals does not depend on what labels the club puts on a relationship, since all the facts and circumstances will be reviewed. A self-employed individual needs to be genuinely in business on his own account. In particular, casual workers will also be within the PAYE net and will not be exempt. These could include match day and bar staff, consultants and others helping out at the club.
- Committee members and unpaid officers are often awarded honoraria in recognition of their services. Extreme care should be taken with such awards since often they are taxable as ordinary earnings. Sports clubs should not pay such honoraria without accounting for PAYE and NIC before confirming that no PAYE is due with Inland Revenue.

D Expenses and benefits

(a) Forms P11D

C2.79 Expenses and benefits provided to directors and employees earning over £8,500 per annum are reportable on forms P11D. These include non-taxable business expenses unless, to prevent unnecessary reporting of business-related travel and expenses, a dispensation is obtained from the Inspector of Taxes. Expenses and benefit forms may need to be completed for unpaid directors receiving benefits. The rules are difficult and should be confirmed with Inland Revenue after taking professional advice if there is doubt. If the forms P11D are not completed correctly, a penalty can be levied. This can lead the Revenue to seek to collect outstanding tax from the club rather than from employees. Often clubs settle this tax to keep its employees happy, although there is no legal obligation to do so. The Revenue benefits from having to collect one cheque from the club rather than from individual employees.

(b) Travel expenses

C2.80 Travel expenses are reportable on forms P11D unless a dispensation is in force. Reimbursement or payment of travel from the player's home to the ground or to the training ground can be difficult. Where players are classed as employees, reimbursement of these travel costs is taxable. However, reimbursement of travel costs in respect of journeys from home to an away ground would typically not be taxable. The rules are complex, and a permanent place of work needs to be established for all categories of employees to ensure that the correct treatment of travel expenses for PAYE and NIC purposes. Inland Revenue agreement to the reimbursement policy should save time and expense.

(c) Telephone expenses

C2.81 Employees or other club officials sometimes conduct club business using their home or mobile telephone. In these cases, the cost of business calls may be reimbursed. However, rental charges are taxable if reimbursed. Supporting documentation, eg telephone bills, should be kept showing itemised business calls and a dispensation should be sought to cover such expenses.

(d) Complimentary tickets

C2.82 Larger professional sports clubs often provide complimentary tickets to a wide variety of people, including players, employees and relatives of employees. The Revenue is generally aware of this and may very well seek to tax the benefits of providing tickets to employees and their family members. Generally, this will not be an issue at matches organised by the sports club, but where tickets are bought for other events, eg Cup Finals, not within their control, taxable benefits may arise. The Revenue will argue that the cost for benefit-in-kind purposes will be the cost of the tickets to the club.

(e) Overseas tours

C2.83 Taxable benefit issues may arise where the sports club organises a tour, which it pays for wholly or in part for the players. The Inland Revenue will usually seek to satisfy itself that the tour is justifiable and not a holiday for the players. The latter might be the case for an end of season tour. Sports clubs should be able to demonstrate that tours have a legitimate business objective in order to avoid a taxable benefit.

(f) Healthcare

C2.84 Health insurance premiums, eg BUPA, are likely to be taxable even though the cost significantly exceeds that payable in other occupations. Where no health insurance is provided, it may be possible to argue that a player's medical expenses in respect of an actual injury sustained while playing or training are not taxable.

E PAYE settlement agreements

C2.85 Reporting expenses and benefits often causes taxable benefits or expense to result, eg staff entertaining, which is taxable on the employee receiving the benefit. The old practice of disallowing staff entertaining costs for corporation tax purposes as a quid pro quo for not seeking income tax can no longer be used. In such circumstances, a PAYE settlement agreement may help; this is an agreement between the sports club and the Revenue to settle tax due on behalf of employees. However, as well as the benefit being grossed up to take account of the clubs settling the individual's own liability, NIC is also due on the tax paid by the club.

F Dealing with an investigation

C2.86 Clubs should review procedures now, as protection against an investigation by the tax authorities, ie prevention is better than cure. However, if the Revenue makes contact before this review has been carried out, professional advice should be taken before meeting the Revenue or providing any documents.

C2.87 There are many reasons why the Inland Revenue launches investigations. In sport, that reason may be that it is targeted because of tax issues which are found elsewhere within sports clubs. They might wish to check, for example, that professional sports clubs generally have not adopted practices which create tax leakages. Alternatively, the Revenue may select a particular sports club as a target because of information in its possession which leads it to believe there is under-assessed tax. This is the most dangerous position and often arises because of publicity in the national or local press about the club.

C2.88 Where the Revenue decides to investigate, it is well worth considering delaying the inquiry until the sports club has carried out the review itself. Particularly if there are problems, any settlement is likely to be easier if more of the detailed work and information is provided by the sports clubs itself. This also provides the club with the opportunity of evaluating the extent of its exposure. Professional advice will put the club in a position to identify areas of difficulty, investigate the problems and determine a strategy for dealing with the Revenue's visit. Such an approach also gives more control to the club over the way in which the investigation proceeds. The Revenue will often ask for information which strictly it is not entitled to, and restricting the scope of the information that is provided to the Inspector is an essential part of dealing with an investigation. The amounts involved can be significant since the Inland Revenue is likely to go back for six years if it finds a problem. This, together with potential interest and penalties, makes a settlement even on relatively small individual items but which are repeated, very expensive.

6 SPECIAL TYPES OF SPORTS ORGANISATIONS

A Governing bodies and leagues

(a) Basis of taxation

C2.89 Governing bodies and leagues exploiting their sport at the highest level to maximise commercial income and reinvest in grass roots do not escape taxation[1]. They face all the taxes that sports clubs themselves meet, ie corporation tax, PAYE and NIC and value added tax. Indeed, their affairs are typically more complex and they are taxed more harshly than commercial companies. There are wide variations in the way they are taxed in practice and there is considerable scope for tax planning. However, tax planning is often carried out in the full blaze of publicity, since their affairs make good news stories.

1 See further para A1.42, n 2.

C2.90 Often special bases of taxation have been agreed historically with the Inland Revenue, which may be favourable or unfavourable. Generally, the objects of the sports body may hinder tax planning, since usually they relate to the promotion and regulation of a particular sport or competition as well as to commercial objectives. Unfortunately, large sums of sponsorship and broadcasting income are subject to tax in the sports governing body's hands. Very often full tax relief is not available for expenditure, with the result that a governing body that breaks even for accounting purposes, may end up with a substantial deficit because of the corporation tax bill which it faces.

(b) Areas of difficulty

C2.91 Two particular areas of expenditure create difficulty:

- Tax relief for the costs of running the sport and developing its grass roots. The Inland Revenue often argues that such expenditure is not deductible because it is not incurred wholly and exclusively for the purposes of the governing body's trade.
- Payments to members, made out of sponsorship and television monies or the proceeds from matches can raise additional tax questions. Although historically the Inland Revenue has accepted that such payments to members are generally tax deductible and members pay tax on the income they receive, this is not always the case since they may be viewed as non-deductible distributions. Tax is then paid by the governing body on commercial income without relief for the payments out to members for whom the receipts are tax-free. Since member clubs often have tax losses, there is a tax leakage, since the members' losses cannot be used effectively against the governing bodies' income.

C2.92 Tax planning can help avoid such problems; thus governing bodies have established charitable trusts to carry on grass roots development activities. Such trusts, which are generally established for youngsters and the provision of facilities to grass roots sports, are tax exempt. The governing body can make tax deductible gifts under the Gift Aid provisions to the charity, thus allowing the charity to make payments to grass roots development on a tax-free basis. Such charities cannot, however, support elite or international sport but can contribute towards grass roots capital expenditure when the use of the facility is wide.

C2.93 Distributions can be avoided by clear documentation of the nature of the payment to members. In many cases, these payments will be in the nature of fees for services or rights provided, and provided that the relevant agreements specify the true nature of the payments, they may be tax deductible to the governing body and taxable as trading income in the sports clubs' hands.

B Charities

C2.94 Some sports organisations may be able to register as charities[1]. The savings available can be substantial and include both tax and business rate relief[2].

1 See para C1.65 et seq.
2 See para C2.30.

C2.95 Charities, whether sporting or not, often assume that their status will mean exemption from tax. This is not automatically the case: income and gains have to be applied for charitable purposes in order to be exempt. Further, most trading activities carried on within a charity will still fall to be taxed and will not be exempt. However, it is possible to run trading activities through a wholly-owned subsidiary entity and effectively gain tax exemption for any profits earned.

C2.96 In order to be eligible to register, a sports organisation must be providing facilities for recreation or leisure available to the public or it must assist the development of physical education of youngsters. It is now also possible for community amateur sports clubs to register as charities[1].

1 See para C2.98.

C2.97 Most reasonably sized clubs, particularly those providing spectator sport, are unlikely to be able to register as a charity, although some of their activities, eg their youth development activities in the community could be registered.

C Community Amateur Sports Clubs (CASCs)

C2.98 In 2001 the Government acknowledged the contribution that community amateur sports clubs make to local communities, together with the valuable work that volunteers undertake running CASCs. The benefits brought by CASCs include health, community building and crime reduction. The Government consulted on the best means of providing encouragement through the tax system for CASCs to help develop and enhance their contribution to community life. The consultation document that was issued in November 2001 discussed how such tax relief should be given. Following on from that process, further consultation with the Charity Commission and the Finance Act 2002, CASCs can obtain tax relief either by:

- registering as a charity; or
- qualifying under the special tax relief package for CASCs.

C2.99 The tax benefits under each of these routes are different, being more generous under the former. However, the latter involves less administration. Clubs may choose which route to follow and should do so with care. However, qualification is open to the whole community and organised on an amateur basis with generally no restrictions or membership.

APPENDIX 1 – VAT TREATMENT OF DIFFERENT TYPES OF INCOME

Standard rated

- Season ticket income
- Gate receipts

- Sponsorship
- Advertising
- Royalties
- Merchandising
- Player transfer fees (UK)
- Hire of equipment
- Corporate events
- Catering
- Sales of goods (but see under 'zero rated')
- Vending machine income
- Bar sales
- Telephone income
- Gaming machine income
- Sales of assets/equipment
- Fees for sports 'summer schools'
- Memorabilia sales
- Stadium tour income
- Fan club membership
- Team/player appearance fees
- Subscriptions (but see para C2.39).

Zero rated

- Books, magazines and handbooks
- Programmes and fixture cards
- Overseas tours (although these may crystallise VAT issues in the countries where the tours take place)
- Cold take-away food (not including soft drinks, ices etc)
- Exports

Exempt

- Perimeter advertising (unless taxation option taken up)
- Hire of facilities (unless taxation option taken up)
- Lotteries and raffles
- Other lettings (unless taxation option taken up)
- Competition fees (where all returned as prizes or when provided by non-profit distributing bodies)
- Interest and insurance commission
- Affinity card commissions
- Subscriptions (but see para C2.39).

Outside the scope

- Donations
- Grants
- Insurance settlements
- Compensation payments

APPENDIX 2 – PAYE RETURNS: TIME LIMITS AND PENALTIES

Deadlines

Forms	*Date*		*Penalty provisions*
P14, P35, P38	19 May following tax year	Income Tax (Employments) Regulations 1993 (S1 1993/744), reg 43	TMA 1970, s 98A
P9D, P1lD, P11D(b)	6 July following tax year	Income Tax (Employments) Regulations 1993 (S1 1993/744), reg 46	TMA 1970, s 98

Penalties that may be imposed for late returns

Forms	*Initial*	*Continuing*	*Delay exceeds 12 months*
P14, P35, P38, P11D(b)	£100 per 50 employees	£100 monthly per 50 employees	Penalty not exceeding 100% of the tax or NICs payable for the year of assessment but not paid by 19 April following the end of the year of assessment
P9D, P11D	£300 per return	£60 per day, per return	

Penalties that may be imposed for incorrect returns

Forms	*Provision*	*Penalty*
P14, P35, P38	TMA 1970, s 98A	Maximum of 100% of tax underpaid (s 98A(4))
P9D, P11D	TMA 1970, s 98	Maximum penalty £3,000 (s 98(2))

Interest on unpaid PAYE/NIC

Interest Rate	*Date*	*Statutory provision*
Interest Rate of 6.5% (as at 6 November 2001)	Accrues from 19 April following end of tax year	TMA 1970, s 86

CHAPTER C3

FINANCING SPORT

Satish Khandke (Hammonds) and **Jeff Chue** (World Sport Group)

Contents

1 THE NEED TO RAISE FINANCE AND POSSIBLE SOURCES

C3.1 Although sport is fundamentally a recreational activity engaged in by participants for their personal enjoyment, at virtually every level more serious than a kick-about in the back garden, sport requires funding to enable it to take place. Even at a basic level, individuals and teams need to purchase clothing and equipment and facilities must be paid for or maintained. Further, as sports face increasing competition for the attention of participants and spectators, with newer and more innovative sports and other leisure interests increasing in popularity, sports clubs, associations and organisations are under increasing pressure to generate interest in their sport if they are to survive and thrive. At the grassroots level, sports clubs organise open days, coaching sessions and other events to attract interest from new participants, and such efforts inevitably involve expenditure. At the other end of the scale in professional sport, clubs and governing bodies must pay players and officials and fund other costs of participation, such as the costs of building and maintaining stadia and staging events[1]. The need to obtain finance is therefore a constant at virtually every level in sport.

1 At the uppermost end of the scale, the published accounts of FIFA, the world football governing body, indicate that its expenditure in the four year period leading up to the 2002 World Cup was approximately £1.24 billion, and accounts published by the organising committee of the 2002 Sydney Olympic Games indicated that the cost of staging the Games exceeded US $1 billion.

C3.2 This chapter will focus on the methods of raising of finance available to sports clubs, teams or governing bodies that are either responsible for the organisation and staging of sporting events or which participate in those events. (Such organisations will be referred to generically as 'sports entities')[1]. The authors aim to provide a first point of reference to any such sports entity or its advisers on the ways in which it can finance its activities.

1 Financing of the activities of individual sportsmen and women, or commercial entities such as broadcasters, sports rights agencies or sponsors whose involvement in sport is indirect, arising through their exploitation of the commercial rights belonging to the entities that directly participate in sport, is beyond the scope of this chapter.

C3.3 At the elite level of certain sports, sufficient demand exists from 'consumers' of the sporting spectacle to allow the sports entities involved to generate sufficient revenues to meet their costs solely by exploiting commercial opportunities arising from participation in the sport, for example by charging spectators to enter their venue to watch the event (and perhaps enjoy hospitality), selling food and drink to spectators (or selling the right to do so to a third party)[1], selling sponsorship or advertising at the venue or on its team's kit[2], selling the right to broadcast the event[3] or selling merchandise relating to its team or event[4]. Such 'commercial' or 'operational' means of generating income (ie income which is essentially derived from the sporting event itself by the sale of tangible or intangible products connected with it, whether it be food, merchandise or the right to view, sponsor or broadcast the event) and commercial programmes designed to extract the most revenue from these sources are dealt with in detail in Part D of this book. However, many sports or the participants in them do not enjoy such popular appeal and therefore, in order to finance participation in such sports, such sports entities need to rely substantially on other means of finance to supplement any revenue which they can raise commercially.

1 For a discussion of issues relating to hospitality income, see Chapter D7.
2 For a commentary on sponsorship, see Chapter D5.
3 For a commentary on broadcasting and new media, see Chapter D4.
4 For a commentary on licensing and merchandising, see Chapter D6.

C3.4 Even a sports entity that is able to generate significant commercial income may find that such income is irregular[1] and will inevitably be subject to fluctuations due to events that are outside its direct control or cannot necessarily be anticipated or planned for. This is a particular problem for sports entities because the popularity of sport is founded on its unpredictability and the uncertainty of outcome[2]. For example, matchday and merchandising income will usually fall if a club becomes less successful on the field. If such lack of success is ongoing, sponsorship and other revenues may also fall[3]. The effect of sporting failure on commercial revenues can be most pronounced in sports or leagues that operate a promotion and relegation system as commercial revenues can suffer dramatically after relegation[4]. Some sports entities may be able to hedge somewhat against such downturns in revenues by selling their income-generating commercial rights to agencies (which hope to exploit them for a profit) in exchange for a lump sum or minimum guaranteed payment[5]. However, such commercial agencies' valuation of such commercial rights will obviously take into account the prospect of relegation or other factors that may cause a reduction in their value. Even sources of commercial income for a sports entity which are seemingly stable and predictable can become unreliable[6]. Therefore, perhaps even more so than businesses operating in other industry sectors, a sports entity whose commercial or operational income will almost certainly be seasonal or erratic will need to augment or perhaps replace such income with more predictable and stable sources of finance in order to smooth the operation of its business and to enable it to satisfy financial obligations which arise on a more regular basis than its operational income[7].

1 For example, most professional sports clubs will generate much of their income from season-ticket sales prior to the season and the bulk of merchandising revenue may be received immediately after the launch of a new kit and in the Christmas period.

2 The possibility of last season's Premier League champions being relegated this season, however remote, makes the competition more interesting to spectators.

3 This effect may be exacerbated in sports in which participants allow an event organiser or governing body to exploit certain of their commercial opportunities collectively with those of other participants and then distribute the resulting revenues according to factors including sporting success.

4 An obvious example of this is relegation from football's FA Premier League. Notwithstanding 'parachute' payments from the League designed to cushion this effect, clubs relegated at the end of the 1999/2000 season suffered a fall in their income in the following season of £5–7m: Deloitte & Touche Sport's *Annual Review of Football Finance Incorporating England's Premier Clubs* (June 2002).

5 See further paras D8.54 to D8.56.

6 A point illustrated by the inability of ITV Digital to meet its contractual obligations under its collective broadcast rights agreement with the Football League in 2002, which resulted in Football League member clubs' projected income for the remainder of the anticipated term of the agreement being reduced very significantly. See further para D4.5.

7 For example, players' salaries will need to be paid on a regular basis and will not usually automatically fall in proportion to a fall in the income of a sports entity should it suffer sporting failure or relegation (although clubs are increasingly looking to build such an automatic reduction into player contracts).

C3.5 Additionally, many sports entities' ultimate aim is to progress to a higher level, and perhaps ultimately to the elite, of sporting competition. Whilst it would hope that greater sporting success would also deliver a commensurate rise in commercial income, such a sports entity will often have to make a significant up-front speculative investment to try to achieve its goal. In most cases, such significant additional expenditure cannot be financed solely by the sports entity's commercial income (whether it be commercial income derived from an existing sports entity's current operations, or commercial income such as sponsorship that may be received by a new sports entity in advance of its participation) and so will have to be supplemented by other sources of finance[1].

1 For example, Fulham Football Club's published accounts for the year to 30 June 2001 show that in successfully pushing to gain promotion to the FA Premier League in the 2000/2001 season, it recorded losses of £24m (increasing its total debts to £61.7m) and the salaries it paid to its players rose from approximately £10m to £19m, partially funded by an increase in borrowings of over £18m: Deloitte & Touche Sport's *Annual Review of Football Finance Incorporating England's Premier Clubs* (June 2002) and its *Annual Review of Football Finance* (August 2001).

C3.6 For these reasons, most sports entities need to secure some finance to supplement any commercial income that they are fortunate enough to be able to generate. The remainder of this Chapter looks at the possible sources of such 'non-commercial' finance and the means of securing it[1]. These sources can be broken down into five main categories:

(a) membership subscriptions[2];
(b) specific fund-raising appeals[3];
(c) grant financing[4];
(d) debt financing[5]; and
(e) equity financing[6].

1 References in the remainder of this Chapter to 'finance' or 'funding' refer only to funding from such non-commercial sources. However, any sports entity seeking such non-commercial finance should not lose sight of the fact that its ability to generate commercial income will almost certainly have a strong influence, at least to some extent, on its ability to raise finance from other sources. For example, the difficulty experienced by Wembley National Stadium Limited and its parent, the Football Association, in securing the requisite debt financing for the proposed rebuilding of Wembley Stadium was in part due to potential lenders' misgivings about the ability of the project to generate sufficient commercial income to fund the capital investment required in addition to the debt (eg through advance sales of 'premium' seating and catering and pourage rights) and the estimated annual debt service payments.
2 See para C3.16 et seq.
3 See para C3.22 et seq.
4 See para C3.29 et seq.
5 See paras C3.79 et seq and C3.98 et seq.
6 See paras C3.79 et seq and C3.158 et seq.

C3.7 Some of the key considerations which may influence a sports entity's decision to seek financing from one or more of these sources are set out below.

C3.8 The purpose for which the finance is sought Different sources of finance will be available for different purposes. For example, if the sports entity is seeking finance to improve safety at its stadium, it may be eligible to receive public grant finance. Conversely, grants and fund-raising appeals are unlikely to generate funds required for increases in player salaries.

C3.9 The amount of finance being sought Sufficient funds may simply not be available from a particular source (such as membership subscriptions) if the cost of a particular project for which a sports entity is seeking finance is too great. Some projects are so large that they are impossible to finance using one source and so a combination of financing mechanisms must be utilised[1]. Conversely, the method of raising finance should be economical in the context of the sums required, so that the costs of securing the finance do not eat too deeply into the funds raised. For example, a relatively inexpensive project is likely to be more economically financed by an appeal to supporters rather than a debenture scheme involving substantial set-up costs.

1 See also paras C3.61 to C3.64. Examples include the proposed rebuilding of Wembley Stadium, the projected £757m cost of which, it is planned, will be financed by a combination of grant finance from Sport England and The London Development Agency, equity finance from the Football Association, and senior and subordinated debt finance from banks. (See HC479 – Return to an Address of the Honourable the House of Commons dated 19 December 2001 for the English National Stadium Review, Interim Report, December 2001 and HC1179 – Return to an Address of the Honourable The House of Commons dated 16 October 2002 for the English National Stadium Review, Final Report, October 2002).

C3.10 The likely profitability of the sports entity or project for which finance is required Sports entities or projects which are unlikely to generate significant or any profit are likely to find the pursuit of finance from investors seeking to make a commercial return on their investment (ie lenders or subscribers for shares) to be fruitless.

C3.11 The sports entity's ability to satisfy conditions to the provision of the finance For example, a sports entity will have to satisfy certain conditions before being provided with grant finance. Equally, in order to maximise the prospect of making a profit on their investment, potential subscribers for shares in, or lenders to, a sports entity are likely to require it to have a particular capital structure, asset portfolio, level of other borrowings and/or track record of creditworthiness. Such conditions may also limit the ability of the sports entity to raise further finance from other sources (for example, a lender will impose restrictions on the ability of a sports entity to borrow funds from other lenders in order to reduce the risk of default on its loan[1]).

1 An example of a condition imposed for other reasons is the condition imposed by Sport England under its Lottery Funding Agreement with WNSL (see para A1.115) precluding naming rights to the redeveloped Wembley Stadium being sold.

C3.12 Tax issues The different methods of raising finance are likely to have different tax implications for the sports entity. Tax advantages associated with it may make one source more suitable than another[1].

1 See further para C2.32.

C3.13 Regulatory restrictions Regulatory restrictions which bind the sports entity (whether imposed by the relevant sport's governing body or otherwise) may preclude it from accessing certain sources of finance[1].

1 For example, a rule imposed by UEFA (the governing body of European football) which prevents a company or individual from having a controlling shareholding in more than one club participating in UEFA competitions (and which has recently been upheld by the European Commission) means that a European club cannot receive significant equity finance from an investor which already has an ownership interest in one of its competitors. Similarly, the rules of The FA Premier League and The Football League prevent any person or company from owning more than 10 per cent of the share capital of more than one of its clubs. See further para C3.158 et seq. Further, UEFA and governing bodies in other sports are considering introducing controls (such as licensing requirements) to prevent their members for undertaking excessive borrowing. See para B2.145 et seq.

C3.14 Other factors Other considerations, such as the perception of the sports entity's fans, may dictate the ways in which a sports entity raises finance.

C3.15 It is important that a sports entity considers these factors when deciding from which source or sources to seek finance, in order to determine which will be available to it and best suited to its requirements. Otherwise, it could spend significant time and money in pursuing a source of finance that will ultimately be unavailable or unsuitable. Equally, if a sports entity commences a project before the finance required to complete it has been secured, additional expenditure may be incurred[1]. In the remainder of this Chapter, we describe the various methods of raising finance that may be available to a sports entity.

1 For example, in addition to the adverse publicity generated by the prolonged process of raising finance for the rebuilding of Wembley Stadium, it is estimated that the cost of security at the stadium and associated fees since its closure in October 2000 are reported to have amounted to £300,000 per month.

2 MEMBERSHIP SUBSCRIPTIONS

C3.16 From community sports clubs to international sports governing bodies, the majority of sports entities around the world are constituted as private members' associations which are managed and operated by volunteers[1]. In most cases, such a sport entity will require its members to pay subscriptions or fees to it periodically and such income will often constitute its most easily accessible and perhaps most vital source of finance[2].

1 See para A1.13 et seq.

2 This is particularly so if the sporting entity or the sport in which it participates does not have sufficient appeal to raise significant revenue by way of the commercial exploitation of its sports events and associated rights.

C3.17 Under the typical hierarchical model of sport, individual athletes (being at the bottom of the hierarchy) are responsible for the payment of membership subscriptions to the sports club of which they are members. Typically, the sports club then pays a proportion of the fees it receives to the regional federation of which it is a member (retaining the remainder for its own operational requirements) and the regional federation in turn pays a proportion of what it receives from its member clubs to the national federation to which it is affiliated, and so on. The regional, national and international federations receiving funds from lower down the hierarchy may then redistribute such funds received back down the structure, often to fund the development of the sport in under-funded regions. Such distribution of subscription fees within each level of the sporting hierarchy is the financial lifeblood of many sports.

C3.18 The obligation of each participant in a sport (whether it be an individual athlete or a club or governing body) to pay a subscription to the club or body higher up the sporting structure of which it is a member is usually a contractual one which is embodied in the constitution or rules of the recipient club or body and by which its members agree to abide. For its part, the recipient will be bound to use the funds collected only in accordance with such constitution or rules[1]. To ensure the proper operation of this method of funding, the power of the sports entity to collect subscriptions, the obligation of each of its members to pay them and the consequences of non-payment should be unambiguously set out in its constitution or rules (and this will be particularly important where subscriptions are a vital source of finance for the sports entity). The sports entity's constitutional documents should therefore deal with the following issues.

1 The constitution or rules of a sports entity should specify the purpose for which funds raised from members' subscriptions may be used. Typically, an executive committee of the sports entity (being charged with management and operational responsibilities) should be authorised to use such funds for any bona fide purpose which furthers the aims and objectives of the sports entity. The use of funds beyond these purposes can lead to liability on the part of the recipient or its individual officers to account to its members for such misused funds. See further para C3.22 et seq.

C3.19 Date of Payment Membership subscriptions are usually paid on an annual basis although it is not uncommon for payments to be made more frequently. A sports entity's rules should specify the date on or before which payment by each member of the applicable subscription is to be received.

C3.20 Method of Payment The sports entity should specify its preferred method of receiving payment from its members (eg by cheque or telegraphic transfer to its bank account). If payment of the subscription is made by way of cheque, it should be made out in the name of the sports entity (as opposed to one of its officers). The constitution or rules of the sports entity should also specify that payment of the subscription must be received in cleared funds before a member is regarded as having properly discharged its payment obligations.

C3.21 Late Payment and Suspension of Membership Rights Prompt payment of subscriptions will be particularly important to a sports entity's cashflow if such subscriptions are a vital source of funding. Prompt payment is most easily encouraged by making the exercise of a member's rights (for example, its right to participate in official tournaments and events or to attend and vote at members' meetings) conditional upon the timely payment of its subscriptions. The consequences of a failure or delay in the payment of subscriptions should be set out in detail in the sports entity's constitution. Ordinarily, such non-payment should lead to the suspension of membership rights, including a member's right to participate in the sport or vote at meetings, during any period in which a member's subscription is in arrears. It should be specified if such suspension is automatic, or is dependant on positive action by the sports entity (for example, by members' resolution in general meeting). The duration of any such suspension should also be specified[1]

1 It may be considered desirable for membership rights to be automatically reinstated upon the settlement of any arrears of subscriptions. If this is to be the case, the constitution or rules should expressly provide for this. However, this may encourage members to defer payment until immediately before or at an event or meeting in which he or it wishes to compete or participate, which can cause cash-flow problems for the recipient. This may be regarded as undesirable and, if there is to be a period of continued suspension after payment of arrears, this should be specified in the constitution or rules.

3 FUND-RAISING APPEALS

C3.22 Aside from collecting subscriptions from its members, probably the most direct and least complex method of raising finance available to a sports entity is to launch an appeal for funds directly to the general public or its own supporters. However, the public will ordinarily only be receptive to such appeals for 'worthwhile' causes (eg raising money for a school to build a swimming pool rather than for a professional sports club to pay its players higher wages). Even supporters of a sports club are only likely to be receptive to appeals for finance made by the club as a last resort in circumstances where its financial predicament is such that its future is in doubt (ie it is on the verge of insolvency)[1]. Therefore fund-raising appeals are unlikely to feature in any sports entity's long-term financing strategy. Nevertheless, if a sports entity is undertaking a 'worthy' project, or finds itself in a financial predicament such that an appeal to the generosity of the public or its supporters is one of its only possible sources (or perhaps the only possible source) of the finance that it needs to survive, it will nevertheless need to observe certain laws and regulations governing the conduct of such an appeal.

1 Even in such circumstances, the supporters may place conditions on the donation of funds. For example, when Northampton Town Football Club appealed to its fans for funds to save it from bankruptcy in 1992, they formed a Supporters Trust which collected funds from supporters itself and then used such funds to subscribe for 7% of the club's share capital on condition that this gave representatives of the Supporters' Trust a seat on the Board. (See the Report from the Football Governance Research Centre, Birkbeck, University of London for Supporters Direct entitled *Fresh Players, New Tactics: Lessons from the Northampton Town Supporters' Trust* (Phil Frampton Jonathan Michie and Andy Walsh))

C3.23 Donations received by a sports entity as a result of a fund-raising appeal will normally be categorised in law as a gift by the donor to the sports entity for it to apply for its own benefit. However, a sports entity seeking to raise funds by such an appeal should beware when stating the purposes for which it intends to use the funds raised when drafting its appeal publicity materials. Otherwise, any subsequent use of the appeal funds for purposes other than those stated in such materials, could constitute fraud, or the offence of obtaining property by deception[1], on the part of the sports entity or its officers. Therefore, care should be taken in drafting any statements specifying how any funds raised will be used, and all individuals involved in collecting donations should be carefully briefed, to ensure that the aims of the appeal are not misstated. Thought should also be given to how the funds raised will be used if they are insufficient to achieve the stated purpose (eg if only half of the funds required to build a swimming pool are raised, the club might want to use the funds that are raised for something other than building a half-size swimming pool). Similarly, if the funds raised exceed what is required to pay for the stated purpose of the appeal, the sports entity is likely to want to use the surplus funds for other purposes. However, in the absence of a statement to the contrary, the donations received could be construed as having been made by the donors on condition that they be used only for the expressly stated purposes of the appeal. In such event the sports entity could be required to return any funds raised which it does not use for those purposes to the donors[2]. Therefore, it is advisable for the club to state that such sums raised which cannot be used for the primary purpose of the appeal (because they are either insufficient for, or exceed, what is required for such purpose) will be used to fund some other specified activities of the sports entity, or its general expenses.

1 Theft Act 1968, s 15.
2 Although if the sums raised are received from a wide variety of anonymous donors each contributing a relatively small amount, it is less likely that such donations would be construed as having been made by the donors on the expectation that they would ever be returned. However, even if the donations are not construed as having been made conditionally in this way, this will not be a defence to fraud or obtaining property by deception if the donee did not intend to use the funds raised for the stated purposes when it solicited them.

C3.24 In some circumstances, donations made in a fund-raising appeal launched for the benefit of a sports entity cannot take effect as a gift by the donor to the sports entity itself. This will be the case if the funds are raised for use by an unincorporated sports club because such an unincorporated entity has no separate legal personality and therefore cannot hold any property, including money, in its own right[1]. Consequently, donations to such a sports entity may give rise to a trust, of which particular officers of the club will be trustees, for the funds held therein to used in accordance with the stated aims of the appeal. This gives rise to a potential problem under the 'beneficiary principle' of trust law, which provides that any trust, other than one which is charitable[2] (or which falls within other limited exceptions, none of which are likely to be available in the context of a sports entity) which is established for particular *purposes*, rather than for the benefit of identifiable legal persons, will be void (on the basis that a trust must have a beneficiary with capacity to enforce its terms). Therefore, a trust that arises from an appeal for funds which are intended to be used for the purpose of financing an unincorporated sports club's activities could potentially be declared void under the beneficiary principle. However, it has been held that, notwithstanding the fact that a trust is expressed to be for a *purpose* benefiting an unincorporated association, it can instead be properly construed as having actually been established for the direct benefit of the individual members of the sports club from time to time[3], and therefore valid[4]. Nevertheless, it may be that this potential problem can be avoided altogether by the sports entity specifying in its constitution or rules that any property received for the benefit of the sports entity will be held in accordance with such constitution or rules, which will apply as a contract amongst its members, rather than under any trust arrangement. If this is the case, materials published by the sports entity in its appeal for funds should also state that sums received will be held and applied in accordance with its rules, rather than under any trust. Nonetheless, the issues relating to use (or misuse) of any funds raised for an incorporated sports entity which were discussed at para C3.23 will apply equally to unincorporated sports entities. As with funds raised for incorporated sports entities, if funds raised for an unincorporated sports entity cannot be used for the purposes for which they were stated to be solicited and no alternative use was specified, they could be construed as having been donated on condition that they be used for the stated purposes only, in which event such funds could be required to be returned to the donors (unless the recipient entity is a charitable trust, in which case they may be applied for similar charitable purposes)[5]. Further, even if it is concluded that such donations were not made on such condition, the trustees of a recipient trust would still not be free to apply them for such other purposes as they saw fit. Instead, such funds would pass under the rule of 'bona vacantia' to the Crown. Therefore, in order to ensure that the funds raised can be applied for the benefit of the sports entity for which they were raised (whether incorporated or not) care should be taken to state the purposes of any appeal for funds sufficiently broadly.

1 See further para C1.30 et seq.
2 See paras C3.25 to C3.27.
3 As a result of the Perpetuities and Accumulations Act 1964, even if the gift is construed as being made for the benefit of future as well as present members of the club, it will not infringe what is known as the rule against perpetuities under trust law.
4 As in the case of *Re Lipinski's Will Trusts* [1976] Ch 235.
5 As in the case of *Re Gillingham Bus Disaster Fund* [1959] Ch 62. See further para C3.25.

C3.25 As indicated in the preceding paragraph, an appeal which has charitable status benefits from an exception to the beneficiary principle. Such trusts can also benefit from the rule of 'cy-près' under which any sums collected which cannot, for whatever reason, be applied for the stated purposes can be applied under for charitable purposes similar to those stated in the appeal (rather than passing to the Crown). Additionally, a trust which is charitable can thereby benefit from the advantageous tax regime afforded to charities[1]. Although there is no statutory definition of what constitutes a charity, it has been held[2] that in order for a trust to be deemed charitable its purposes must fall entirely within one or more of four accepted categories, only two of which are potentially relevant in this context, being:

(i) the advancement of education; and
(ii) other charitable purposes which are beneficial to the community[3].

1 It is worth noting that certain tax advantages similar to those from which charities benefit have been made available in the 2002 Budget to community amateur sports clubs, even if they are not registered as charities, provided that they satisfy certain other requirements. For further guidance see the document *Support for Community Amateur Sports Clubs* on the Inland Revenue website at http://www.inlandrevenue.gov.uk/budget2002. See also paras C1.75 to C1.83, C2.98 and C2.99.
2 *Income Tax Special Purposes Comrs v Pemsel* [1891] AC 531.
3 See further Picarda *Law and Practice Relating to Charities* (3rd edn, 1999, Butterworths).

C3.26 Although it has also been held that the promotion of competitive sport in itself is not charitable if it does not also serve one of the charitable purpose specified above (ie it is also educational or of benefit to the community)[1] doubts over whether the provision of sports facilities could be a charitable purpose were alleviated somewhat by the Recreational Charities Act 1958 which provided that 'the provision of facilities for recreation or other leisure time occupation, if the facilities are provided in the interests of social welfare' is a charitable purpose[2]. On this basis, trusts for the provision of playing fields, recreation grounds, sports centres and swimming pools have all been recognised as being charitable. However, until recently the Charity Commission would not register a sports club as a charity if it existed for the promotion of a particular competitive sport (rather than the promotion of physical education and health generally), or if it was for the exclusive benefit of its members rather than the public as a whole. A change in the Commission's interpretation of the law has occurred recently however, as it has announced that it will recognise 'the promotion of community participation in healthy recreation by providing facilities for playing particular sports' as being a charitable purpose. The provision of 'facilities' can encompass the provision of organisational services as well as land, buildings and equipment[3]. This relaxation of the Charity Commission's requirements is stated to be aimed at 'community amateur sports clubs' or 'CASCs', and appears to enable such CASCs to qualify for charitable status even though their facilities relate to a particular sport and are made available only to members (rather than to the public at large or the disadvantaged) provided that its aims are to promote 'community participation in healthy recreation'. To demonstrate such aims, the sport which a CASC promotes must be 'healthy'[4] and its membership must be genuinely available to anyone wishing to participate (meaning that membership fees must be affordable and the facilities must be available to people of all skill levels, although some membership restrictions will be acceptable if they are justified in the context of the operation of the CASC and are not based on the proficiency of the applicant)[5]. However, the Commission has reiterated that 'the promotion of sport (for its own sake and as an end in itself) continues not to be charitable' but that the change in its interpretation is a recognition that the promotion of sport can be charitable if the ultimate aim is the promotion of health in the community. It seems that the absence of selection or elitism and the provision of the facilities irrespective of the proficiency of participants is the key to this distinction[6]. Consequently, CASCs which are able to satisfy these eligibility criteria may now be able to take advantage of the benefits afforded by charitable status, as described at para C3.25.

1 *Re Nottage* [1895] 2 Ch 649.
2 However, in order to be 'in the interests of social welfare', the facilities have to be provided with the object of improving the conditions of life for those at whom they are aimed, and aimed at the 'public at large' or people needing them by reason of youth, disability, age, infirmity, poverty etc.
3 See the documents *Charitable Status and Sport* and *Charities Status & Sport – FAQs* on its website at http://www.charity-commission.gov.uk/registered charities/sport. The Commission has also recognised that sport can fall within the charitable category of the education of young people even if it is not part of their formal education.
4 The Commission has not provided a definition of what is 'healthy' recreation but has stated that healthy recreation should tend to make the participant 'fitter and less susceptible to disease'. On the margins, medical evidence may be relevant and dangerous sports are unlikely to qualify. Specific examples of sports which the Commission does not consider to satisfy the requirements are included in its guidance.
5 See the documents referred to in the previous footnote for further guidance.
6 The Commission has suggested in its guidance that any CASC wishing to register as a charity should actually amend its stated purposes (eg in its governing documents) to expressly state that it exists 'for the promotion of community participation in healthy recreation in particular by the provision of facilities for the playing of particular sports'.

C3.27 A sports entity, whether charitable or not, may choose to raise funds by making collections within its own venue or in the street or other public places. If so, it must comply with any regulations which control such collections which the relevant local authority has the power to make[1]. Such regulations ordinarily require the organiser of the collection to apply for a licence, which would be granted on condition that the collection meets the local authority's requirements. These requirements may cover the manner in which collecting is carried out, the method of counting the sums collected and the publication of accounts. Additionally, further legislative controls[2] must be observed if a sports entity wishes to raise funds by collecting from house to house or by visiting business premises such as pubs[3].

1 For example, under the Police, Factories etc (Miscellaneous Provisions) Act 1916.
2 For example, under the House to House Collections Act 1939. Generally speaking, licences are less likely to be granted if the collection is not for a charitable purpose or only a small proportion of the funds raised will be applied for a charitable purpose.
3 It was intended that the current regimes would eventually be superseded and simplified, at least in part, by the coming into force of Pt III of the Charities Act 1992, although the regime thereunder would effectively consolidate and be of broadly similar effect to the current legislation and apply to public appeals the proceeds of which will be applied for charitable, benevolent or philanthropic purposes. However, ten years after the enactment of the Act itself, Pt III is yet to be brought into force. In any event, a sports entity contemplating making a collection in a public place rather than at its own venue or on other private premises (eg a venue which it has hired for such purpose) is advised to consult with the relevant local authority to ensure compliance with the applicable regulations.

C3.28 Another method that a sports entity may employ to raise funds directly from its supporters or the public is to sell tickets for a prize draw or lottery. In organising any such lottery, the sports entity must take care to ensure that it complies with the requirements of the applicable legislation, primarily the Lotteries and Amusements Act 1976 as amended by the National Lottery etc Act 1993. Such requirements are beyond the scope of this Chapter, but sports entities contemplating organising such a lottery can obtain guidance on complying with the law from the Gaming Board for Great Britain[1].

1 See *Lotteries and the Law* – GBL6 Publication (Oct 97), available on its website at http://www.gbgb.org.uk.

4 GRANT FINANCE

A Introduction

C3.29 Although membership subscriptions and appeals to the public (or particular Sections thereof) for funds, as described in the preceding Sections of this Chapter, can be very important sources of finance for many sports entities (particularly those operating at the community level) a sports entity planning to undertake any significant project (eg a major improvement to its facilities) or requiring a significant injection of funding for any other purpose may be unable to raise sufficient funds from its members and from the public. Even if sufficient funds could be raised from a sports entity may prefer to reduce the burden on them, and perhaps raise the necessary finance more rapidly and predictably, by securing grants which may be available from private or public sources.

C3.30 Although substantial funding can be obtained by a sports entity by accessing private grant funding, public sources of grant funding (ie from the government or other state-funded organisations) have provided the majority of grant funding received by sports entities in the UK. State funding of sport is provided primarily by way of the National Lottery and annual Treasury budgeted allocations. Provided that a particular sport is officially recognised by the appropriate authorities, participants in it may be eligible for grant funding from one or both of these sources. Currently, the relevant authorities (the four national Sports Councils[1] and their umbrella organisation, UK Sport) officially recognise 112 sports and activities[2]. If a sports entity intends to seek grant funding for an as yet unrecognised sport or activity, it should consult with the appropriate Sports Council and submit a formal request for official recognition[3].

1 Sport England (formerly English Sports Council), Sport Scotland, Sports Council for Northern Ireland, and Sports Council for Wales. See further para A1.47 et seq.
2 Details of the recognised sports and activities may be found on www.sportengland.org/gateway/recognised_activities.htm.
3 The Sports Councils (including UK Sport), however, do not determine whether a particular activity is or is not a 'sport', and neither do they attempt to define the term 'sport'. Instead, a recognition procedure is jointly operated by the Sports Councils with which new sports and activities deserving official association and support (both financial and otherwise) are identified.

C3.31 In order for a new sport or activity to be recognised by the Sports Councils and therefore become eligible for government funding, the sport or activity must generally involve physical skills, physical effort and physical challenge. It will help if the new sport or activity is unique, accessible to the public, has established rules and organised events and competitions, includes skill and tactics as elements for success, and has at least 5,000 regular participants in the UK[1].

1 See www.sportengland.org/about/policy_briefing_notes/recog_act_gov_bodies_3.htm.

C3.32 Even if it is participating in a recognised sport, a sports entity may often find that it is not eligible for state funding if it is not a non profit-distributing organisation[1]. Further, funding from some government-funded programmes is available only to sports governing bodies[2]. Whilst sports entities that do not qualify for state-provided grant funding may be able to obtain grant (or quasi-grant) funding from other sources[3], such funding is beyond the scope of this Chapter, which will focus on state grant funding available to non profit-distributing sports clubs, associations and organisations.

1 The phrase 'non profit-distributing' does not mean that the sports entity, organisation or association cannot generate any profit whatsoever from its activities. Instead, 'non profit-distributing' means that any profit or surplus which is generated must be applied *solely* for the purpose for which the sports entity is established, rather than being distributed in any way to its members as profit or for commercial purposes. Many sports entities seek to generate profit or surplus and will still qualify as non profit-distributing organisations provided that all such profit or surplus is used solely for the purpose of the provision of its services (See, for example, *Kennemer Golf and Country Club v Staatssecretaris Financiën* [2002] All ER (EC) 480, ECJ.
2 In order to qualify as a 'sports governing body' a sports entity should: (a) be acknowledged as the sole governing and administrative authority of that sport in the relevant region; (b) be comprised of a membership representing a reasonable proportion of all the participants in that sport or activity; (c) have a structured governance and regulatory framework (including a written constitution) that provides for democratic representation of the sport's participants in its national and/or regional administration; (d) be financially self-sufficient in terms of its core administrative processes; (e) be accessible to members of the public in relation to membership and services; and (f) have been in operation for at least three years.
3 Sport-specific grant making trusts normally provide such funding to commercial sports entities. Examples include The Football Trust (grant funding is provided by the FA Premier League to professional football clubs for the purpose of, for example, improving stadia facilities and safety); The Cricket Foundation and The RAC British Motor Sports Training Trust. The ability of a sports entity to obtain grant funding from one of these trusts will obviously depend on the eligibility criteria applied by that particular trust, a subject which is beyond the scope of this Chapter.

C3.33 It will not be possible to cover each and every programme or initiative through which state funding is made available to sports entities in the UK. Instead, this Chapter will give a broad overview of the programmes which are most relevant to sports entities seeking grant funding. Any sports entity, whether a national sports governing body or a local/community sports club, before deciding to apply for funding under any particular grant programme, should appraise itself fully of all of the options that are available to it[1]. A community sports clubs may find that advice is available from the regional or national sports governing body to which its is affiliated. In turn, such regional or national sports governing bodies seeking grant funding should consult the appropriate Sports Council for information and guidance on which the sources of grant funding are available to it and the requirements and procedures to be satisfied and completed in order to access them.

1 A sports entity may find that it is eligible to receive grant funding under a number of programmes. For example, UK Athletics has received significant funding under a number of the programmes described below.

B Lottery funding

C3.34 Lotteries are a key source of funding for sport in Europe generally[1]. Most lottery schemes are established by virtue of state legislation. In the UK, the National Lottery was established in 1994, with sport as one of the six 'good causes' to benefit. Since its inception, over £1.6 billion of lottery money has been distributed with the objectives of creating greater access to and participation in sport, and/or assisting in the training and development of talented athletes[2].

1 See André-Noël Chaker *Study on National Sports Legislation in Europe* (1999, Council of Europe), ch 2.7; Wladimir Andreff *Les Enjeux Economiques du Sport en Europe* (1994, Council of Europe). Wholly or partially state-operated lotteries and pools that provide key funding to sports have been established in the following European countries: Austria (state lottery and football pools); Belgium (public national lottery); Cyprus (*Lotto-Proto, Pro-po*); Czech Republic (*Sazka*); Denmark (national lottery); Finland (*Oy Veikkaus Ab*); France (*Loto Sportif, Pari Mutuel Urbain*); Germany (*Glocks-spirale*); Hungary (national lottery); Iceland (*Lottó*); Italy (CONI); Luxembourg (state lottery); Portugal; Romania; Slovenia (National Lottery); Spain (*Pari-mutuel*); Switzerland (*Sport-Toto Society*).

2 Up to the first quarter of 2002, Sport England had distributed over £1.29 billion of lottery funding to over 12,000 sports-related projects. The figures for the other Sports Councils are as follows: Sport Scotland (3517 projects, £118m); Sports Council for Northern Ireland (621 projects; £42m); Sports Council for Wales (653 projects; £68m); UK Sport (918 projects; £94.7m). See further para A1.56 et seq.

C3.35 The government is not directly responsible for the distribution of lottery proceeds to sport. Instead, this function has been delegated by the Department of Culture, Media and Sport to the four Sports Councils and the umbrella organisation, UK Sport. Each of the four Sports Councils is responsible for the promotion and development of all aspects of sport within its geographically designated area, whilst UK Sport focuses on sport at a national level with the objective of developing sporting excellence on the world stage[1]. A sports entity should therefore consult with the appropriate Sports Council and/or UK Sport in relation to any plans it may have for lottery funding applications.

1 See further para A1.48 et seq.

C3.36 There are numerous lottery-funded programmes operated by each of the lottery distributing bodies[1]. This Chapter will focus on the programmes which are of relevance to local/community sports entities and which should constitute the first ports of call for any such sports entity seeking financial assistance *via* lottery-funded programmes.

1 For example, Sport England operates (either on its own or in partnership with others) the English Institute of Sport, the Football Foundation and the Outdoor Basketball Initiative.

C3.37 A sports entity should first consider the nature (both in legal terms and within the sporting framework) of its organisational structure prior to considering which lottery-funded programme is best suited to its requirements. As with most other state grant funding, only non profit-distributing organisations will qualify for lottery funding and it is therefore important to ensure from the outset that a sports entity is so eligible[1]. Moreover, different lottery-funded programmes cater to different types of sports entities. For example, funding from the World Class Programmes described below is available only to recognised sports governing bodies in sports likely to produce elite-level success. In contrast, most types of sports entities (including sports clubs, associations and governing bodies) will be eligible to apply for lottery funding from the government-sponsored Sportsmatch scheme described below. Sports entities should therefore shortlist the programmes under which it will be eligible before considering which programmes are best suited to the purpose for which it is seeking funding.

1 See para C3.32. Commercial sports entities or professional sports clubs are generally ineligible unless their projects are for the public benefit and not for their commercial gain.

(a) *World Class Programmes*

C3.38 The World Class series of programmes is operated by Sport England and UK Sport and is established to develop a comprehensive system of identifying, nurturing and training talented sportsmen in order to achieve consistent British sporting success at international level[1]. As sports governing bodies (both national and regional) will have the best idea as to how their respective athletes can be developed, they will have the responsibility of putting together an application for World Class lottery funding. Participation in World Class programmes is open only to sports governing bodies (both national and regional)[2]. An eligible sports entity may therefore consider applying for lottery funding from any of the following programmes.

1 See further paras A1.55 and A1.59.
2 See para C3.32, n 2. Individual athletes cannot apply directly for lottery funding under these programmes. In order to receive financial support, an individual athlete must be identified in a sports governing body's application for grant funding.

C3.39 World Class Performance, Potential and Start Programmes These programmes provide lottery funding generally to develop and support sports governing bodies' training programmes for elite, talented and young athletes who have the potential to excel in international competitions and events (for example, the Olympics) within a four to eight year period[1]. National and regional sports governing bodies[2] seeking financial assistance to develop and implement comprehensive athlete training programmes, employ training directors, coaches and other support staff, and to establish training support for, and research in, sports medicine, sports sciences and personal development policies, should look to any or all of these programmes for support. To apply, a sports entity should present a 'World Class Plan' setting out an athlete development model or strategy and the relevant athlete training/development programme(s) for which it is seeking funding, as well as providing details of the sporting discipline in relation to which funding is sought, including identifying the individual participating athletes. It is usually the case that up to 90% of the cost of the World Class Plan will be funded under these programmes. However, sports entities need to raise at least 10% of such costs, either from its own resources, or from other sources[3].

1 For example, the British Taekwondo Council received a grant of £360,000 under the World Class Performance Programme to provide customised support programmes to players considered to have a realistic chance of winning medals at the 2004 Olympic Games. UK Athletics also receives £3m annually under the programme.

2 Funding for national governing bodies is provided by UK Sport; funding for regional governing bodies is provided by the regional sports councils.

3 This contribution does not need to be made entirely in cash; it may include benefits in kind such as goods and services contributed by third party supporters.

C3.40 Moreover, Athlete Personal Awards, which supplement an athlete's living and sporting costs, are available to athletes participating in a World Class Participation programme. These awards are not salaries but are paid to athletes to supplement subsistence and living costs so that they may dedicate as much of their time as possible towards training and competition[1]. Applications by sports governing bodies for such awards are assessed by reference to three criteria, namely:

(1) the athlete's financial circumstances;
(2) the athlete's age; and
(3) the athlete's competitive performance level and world ranking.

1 Specifically, the awards are a contribution towards basic living costs, personal training and the cost of sports equipment. In certain circumstances, applications for contribution towards education costs may also be made.

C3.41 Commonwealth Games Programme Regional and national sports governing bodies which have athlete training programmes targeted at achieving Commonwealth Games success may apply to the relevant Sports Council pursuant to the Commonwealth Games Programme for lottery funding to develop and support such training programmes. The applicant will have to demonstrate the potential for an athlete participating in such training programme to win a medal. Although at the time of writing, the Commonwealth Games Programme was specifically aimed only at improving the medal chances at the 2002 Commonwealth Games in Manchester, it is expected that the programme will continue in relation to future Commonwealth Games.

C3.42 World Class Events Programme UK Sport distributes lottery money under this programme to national and regional governing bodies for the purpose of attracting and staging major sporting events to the UK. Generally speaking, funding under this programme is granted in relation to sports events that are held in the UK on a 'one-off' basis, as opposed to recurring events, although certain exceptions apply. Since its inception, the World Class Events Programme has contributed over £1.6m of lottery money to the staging of various international sports events in the UK[1].

1 Examples include the 1999 World Judo Championships (£295,000); the 2000 Pre-Olympic & European Amateur Boxing Championships (£65,000); and the 2001 European Top Twelve Table Tennis Championships (£3,100). Additionally, UK Sport has pledged £1.15m to the Amateur Rowing Association should it be successful in its bid to host the 2006 World Rowing Championships in England.

C3.43 A sports entity seeking funding under this programme should first determine whether the event in question meets the eligibility requirements set out by UK Sport for a World Class Event[1], ie:

- participants (whether teams and/or individuals) competing in the event represent different nations;
- the event is of significant public interest both inside and outside the UK; and
- the event is of international significance to the sport concerned and features prominently on its international calendar.

1 See http://www.uksport.gov.uk. There are currently four broad categories of major events recognised by UK Sport: Mega Events (eg Summer Olympics; IAAF World Championships); Calendar Events (eg British Open Golf Championship; Wimbledon Tennis Championships); One-off Events (eg Rugby World Cup; ICC Cricket World Cup); and Showcase Events (eg IJF Judo Championships, FEI European Show Jumping Championships).

C3.44 Prior to the submission of any application for funding, or indeed the commissioning of any preparations for such application, it is imperative that a sport entity notifies, and consults with, UK Sport's Major Events Team about its plans to stage a major sporting event. Following this consultation process, the sports entity will be required to submit a pre-application form. This pre-application process determines whether the subject event satisfies the criteria for funding so as to avoid (as far as possible) the sports entity wasting its resources by undertaking considerable planning and preparations for an application which is unlikely to be approved. Following a successful pre-application process, there are strict timeframes within which the sports entity will have to submit its full application to UK Sport[1]. It is therefore strongly recommended that a sports entity seeking World Class Event funding notify UK Sport of its plans as early as possible.

1 These timeframes vary depending on whether the sports entity is looking to bid for and stage the event, bid for the event only, or stage the event only.

C3.45 If the event does not meet UK Sport's criteria for funding, the pre-application will instead be considered by the relevant Sports Council, which will again usually follow a pre-application screening process. If the application passes the pre-application process, the sports entity will be invited to submit a full application, including a detailed business plan for the bidding and/or staging of the event.

(b) *Community Capital Funding Programme*

C3.46 The Community Capital Funding programme, administered by each of the four Sports Councils, is by far the largest lottery-funding programme; for example, Sport England has distributed over £1.2 billion pursuant to this programme between 1994 and January 2002. Funding under this programme is available to cover the construction or upgrade of community-based sports facilities, the purchase of land or permanently based equipment with a cost of £5,000 or more. Not only governing bodies but also clubs, associations, local authorities and others qualify for lottery funding under this programme.

C3.47 Under the programme managed by Sport England, up to 65% of the cost of such projects and schemes may be financed by way of lottery money. Sports entities seeking capital funding for the construction of club houses, ice rinks, tennis courts or other facilities, or the purchase of permanent equipment such as club boats, or wheelchairs for a basketball team, should seek assistance under this programme. For a project to be eligible for lottery funding under the programme administered by Sport England, the sports entity must ensure[1] that:

(i) the proposed project or scheme is originated by a *bona fide* organisation (if not the sports entity itself) that has exhausted all other avenues of finance;

(ii) the proposed project or scheme relates to a recognised sport[2];

(iii) the cost of the proposed project or scheme is more than £5,000[3];

(iv) at least 35% of the total cost of the project or scheme is from non-lottery sources of finance; and

(v) the proposed project or scheme leads to a significant increase in sporting participation or a measurable improvement in sporting standards.

1 See www.sportengland.org/lottery/funding/comm_capital.htm. The eligibility requirements for such programmes operated by the other Sports Councils differ slightly.

2 See para C3.31 for a discussion of recognised sports.

3 Where the cost of the project is more than £5m, the applicant should contact the Facilities Development Unit. See para C3.52.

C3.48 It is strongly recommended that sports entities consult with their appropriate regional Sports Council in relation to preparing and developing an application by submitting an Intent to Apply Form[1]. Thereafter, the sports entity should proceed with stage one of the application process. This involves the sports entity making a business case for an award. The sports entity will need to demonstrate (among other things) how the proposed project will complement the policies and priorities of the lottery funding strategy. If successful, either an award is granted at stage one, or a decision is made for the application to proceed to stage two of the application process[2]. A stage two decision means that although the overall principles of the project appear to comply with the funding strategy, further development is required before a final decision is made. An Action Plan will be drawn up and Sports Council Development Managers will provide guidance to the sports entity to further develop the project. A stage two approved application will receive funding which is likely to be subject to a series of terms and conditions.

1 The sports entity should also familiarise itself with the Application Pack which contains useful guidance on preparing an application. Application Packs are available from the Sports Councils.

2 Decisions are normally given within 16 weeks of the Sports Council receiving the application. It is usual for very small projects such as the purchase of equipment to be granted an award in stage one of the application process.

C3.49 Further, Sport England also operates, as part of this programme, the Priority Areas Initiative (PAI) which, subject to eligibility requirements, provides enhanced lottery funding of up to 90% of the cost of facilities projects. To be eligible, not only must the usual criteria for capital funding be met, but the sports entity must also demonstrate that its project will substantially benefit residents of a Priority Area or other people experiencing social and economic deprivation. Sport England has designated numerous local authority wards with Priority Area status and a sports entity seeking capital funding should therefore determine whether its project would so qualify for enhanced funding under this initiative.

(c) Community Revenue Programme

C3.50 This programme supports the Community Capital Funding Programme as well as other programmes such as the Athlete Personal Awards under the World Class Programmes and the series of Active Programmes[1].

1 The Active Programmes essentially comprise of the Active Communities Programme, the Active Sports Programme and the Active Schools Programme, of which only the Active Communities Programme can truly be said to be a source of grant finance for sports entities.

C3.51 Active Communities Development Fund The fund supports projects that have the objective of increasing sports participation and development within the following priority groups: black and ethnic communities, disabled people, women and girls, and people on low incomes[1]. In order to be eligible, a sports entity must have a proper written constitution and qualify as a non profit-distributing organisation[2]. In relation to the project in question, it must be working in partnership with at least one other organisation. The project should deal with any of the priority groups and seek to link sport to any one of a number of specified themes[3]. Applications may be made for funding of between £5,000 and £30,000 per annum and awards can be made for up to five years.

1 Up to £9m will be awarded in 2002/2003 and £15m in later years.
2 See further para C3.32, n 1.
3 These include education, health, employment and economic growth. Specifically, awards may be made to fund a community sports worker, to provide for a sports development fund operated by a sports entity, and/or to provide for the establishment by a sports entity of education/training schemes.

C3.52 Active Communities Programme This programme establishes a sporting framework which, in partnership with other organisations and agencies, funds the development of sport and sporting participation in areas of social, economic and recreational deprivation[1]. As part of this programme, lottery money funds numerous initiatives including the Facilities Development Unit (FDU), workshops on (for example) sports club administration and management for the benefit of local sports bodies and administrators, the Positive Futures projects[2], the Showcase projects as well as the Ethnic Minorities Communities projects. The FDU is established to assist national governing bodies of sport devise strategies for identifying and prioritising the development of sports facilities. Eligible sports entities may therefore apply for lottery funding under this programme to finance the production of such strategies, whether in conjunction with the FDU, private consultants or otherwise[3].

1 The framework comprises the following objectives: (1) promoting social justice; (2) increasing participation in sport; (3) developing community sports programmes and facilities; (4) planning for sport and recreation; and (5) developing community sports leaders.
2 These are joint efforts between Sport England, the United Kingdom Anti-drugs Co-ordination Unit and the Youth Justice Board with the objective of using sport to reduce crime and drug-abuse amongst juveniles. There are currently 24 such projects in operation throughout the UK.
3 The sports currently receiving financial assistance under the FDU's auspices include athletics, basketball, canoeing, cycling, rowing, squash and table tennis.

C3.53 Active Sports Programme This is a relatively new national programme established to develop structured access to sport for children and young people. The programme involves Sport England partnering with sports clubs, associations and governing bodies, to increase participation, competition and skills improvement opportunities for young people in sport. There are currently 45 such lottery-funded partnerships, working in ten[1] selected sports.

1 Athletics, basketball, cricket, girls' football, netball, hockey, rugby league, rugby union, swimming, and tennis.

(d) Awards for All Scheme

C3.54 The Awards for All scheme provides grants of between £500 and £5,000 to smaller organisations with a community focus for the purpose of developing new or existing projects[1]. The scheme is of particular relevance to local voluntary sports clubs and associations as it is targeted at smaller sports entities. Each of the four Sports Councils currently administers an Awards for All scheme which grants lottery funding to projects that develop and support community activity, and which aim generally to improve sporting access and opportunity for all. The scheme is open only to non profit-distributing organisations with a written constitution and funding priority is given to sports entities that have an annual income of less than £20,000. Most local or community level sports entities will therefore qualify to apply for lottery funding under this scheme. Examples of projects for which an eligible sports entity may seek funding for include the organising of a sports event such as a community sports day, the purchase of sports equipment, start-up costs for new activities and teams, transport costs and the hire of sports facilities[2]. Unlike most other programmes, the scheme has the benefit of a streamlined application process with minimal funding criteria[3]. Nevertheless, funding under the scheme is subject to funding conditions and for the reasons previously discussed, sports entities should still be alert to the legal implications of the funding agreement.

1 The English scheme is jointly administered by Sport England, the Arts Council of England, the Community Fund, the Heritage Lottery Fund and the New Opportunities Fund.

2 By way of further example, a local netball club received £2,128 from the scheme administered in London to run a series of taster days for children from local schools – offering them professional coaching and the opportunity to join the club if they decided they liked the sport.

3 Eligible applicants need only complete and submit a 10-page application form to the appropriate regional Awards for All office. The application form is available for download on www.awardsforall.org.uk/england/application_form.html.

C Direct state/government funding

(a) Central government funding

C3.55 Article 12 of The European Sports Charter provides:

> Appropriate support and resources from public funds (at central, regional and local levels) shall be made available for the fulfilment of the aims and purposes of this charter. Mixed public and private financial support for sport should be encouraged, including the generation by the sports sector itself of resources necessary for its further development.

C3.56 In the UK, the Department for Culture, Media and Sport (DCMS) is the central government department responsible for sport and its development[1]. Part of its annual Exchequer funding is specifically allocated to sport. This Exchequer funding, like lottery funding, is distributed to sport through the Sports Councils and UK Sport, which act as the developmental and funding agencies for sport in the UK. Exchequer funding is available primarily[2] to complement the lottery funding programmes by assisting sports governing bodies modernise and develop existing governance and regulatory frameworks based on the principles of good corporate governance[3].

1 See para A1.39.
2 In addition, Exchequer funding is also available to partner organisations such as the National Sports Medicine Institute and the British Paralympic Association to support projects, schemes and courses designed to improve access to, for example, sports sciences and sports medicine.
3 See further para A1.93 et seq. The Treasury has specifically allocated £19m to UK Sport's modernisation programme for sports bodies and organisations.

C3.57 Under the modernisation programme, sports governing bodies may apply to their appropriate regional Sports Council or to UK Sport for Exchequer funding to:

(i) improve and modernise governance, regulatory and administrative frameworks;
(ii) support sports-related programmes that are not funded by the National Lottery; and
(iii) develop training and coaching programmes.

C3.58 An applicant must submit a four-year business proposal indicating its 'vision' for its sport in general. This includes a detailed one-year operational plan highlighting the sports governing body's proposed activities and projected costs of achieving its targets and objectives. Thereafter, the application process may be summarised as follows:

(i) the applicant presents its proposal to the appropriate regional Sports Council for assessment and consideration;
(ii) if approved by the regional Sports Council, the proposal is put to a meeting of the four Sports Councils for joint assessment and consideration;
(iii) following joint approval, the proposal is presented to the Awards Panel of UK Sport;
(iv) the Awards Panel assesses the proposal and submits its recommendations to the full Council of UK Sport;
(v) UK Sport's full Council considers the proposal and either approves, amends, or rejects the recommendations of the Awards Panel. If the recommendations are approved or amended, an offer of Exchequer funding is made to the applicant; and
(vi) at the end of the four-year period, the applicant submits a report to the regional Sports Council/UK Sport on the successes and failures of the business proposal.

C3.59 For the period between April 2000 to March 2001, a total of £5,834,896[1] was granted to over 45 national sports governing bodies[2].

1 See http://www.uksport.gov.uk. This is an increase from the previous year's funding by over £1m.
2 Sports governing bodies that have received Exchequer funding include the Grand National Archery Society (£38,000), British Bobsleigh Association (£117,500) and the British Judo Association (£160,000).

(b) Local government funding

C3.60 Although the role of local authorities as supporters of sport has declined in importance due to competition for resources from other sectors such as community development and housing[1], financial assistance in the form of both capital and revenue projects may be available to local/voluntary sports associations.

1 See further para A1.44. Although local authorities' expenditure on sport amounted to almost £1 billion at the end of the nineties, budgets for sports and recreational facilities fell by approximately 7.5% (around £40m) between 1991/92 and 1996/97. See Eastwood *The Sports Funding Guide* (1999, The Directory of Social Change).

(c) *Public Private Partnerships (PPP) and Private Finance Initiatives (PFI)*

C3.61 PPP is a term generally used to describe any collaboration between the public and private sector it essentially involves the use of private sector finance and expertise in the provision of public infrastructure and services, through the investment of such private sector finance alongside public money to fund a particular project using structures that require the private investors to share some of the financial risk of a project for the provision of public services in return for a profit on their investment. PFI is a variant of PPP in which private companies agree to build large-scale capital projects (such as hospitals and schools) and lease them back to the public sector over a period of time (often 30 years or more). Design, Build, Finance, Operate or 'DBFO' schemes are the most common form of PFI and involve the private company builder of a capital project also being involved in its day-to-day running after building has been completed.

C3.62 Such mechanisms are aimed at providing a mechanism through which the public sector can improve value for money by partnering with the private sector on such projects. As they are concerned with the provision of public services, in the sporting context PPP/PFI has been predominantly relevant in connection with financing the provision and construction of local authority leisure facilities, which is beyond the scope of this chapter. However, structures exhibiting some of the characteristics of PPP are increasingly being used in the building of sporting infrastructure which is partly funded by grant finance and partly by private money. An example of this is the Wembley Stadium redevelopment project, which will involve a combination of grants from Sport England, infrastructure development funding from the London Development Agency, private finance from the Football Association and other commercial entities and additional debt finance from banks. Whilst the ongoing commercial operations of the stadium will be run entirely by, and for the commercial benefit of, the private financiers (and the stadium does constitute a service that the government is obligated to provide to the public) the commitment of quasi-governmental (ie lottery) funds alongside private finance means that the Department of Culture, Media and Sport is taking, and will continue to take, an interest in the project to ensure that such funds are not wasted. This ongoing involvement of the DCMS in the process is seen by some as making it a quasi-PPP project, but one which is being run outside the formal constraints of an 'official' PPP project.

C3.63 Similarly, the proposed Kings Waterfront Development project includes the building of a new stadium for Everton Football Club alongside a housing and leisure complex. Whilst there is not space in this Chapter to give a full description of the financing structure, it essentially involves the funding of the project using a combination of equity finance from the football club (including money raised from the sale of its old stadium) and commercial entities (which will also exploit commercial opportunities arising from the development) and from local, regional and central government[1]. European grant funding[2] and debt is also to be raised. The equity funders (including the public authorities) will each have a stake in a group of companies established to develop and run the development and share in the profits generated by it.

1 Ie from Liverpool City Council, the North West Regional Development Agency and English Partnerships.
2 See para C3.73 et seq.

C3.64 Also, project structures replicating some of the principles of PPP/PFI to finance projects using a combination of different sources of private sector investment, without any involvement of public grant funding, have also been developed and these are described further at para C3.98 et seq.

D Sportsmatch

C3.65 Launched in 1992, the Business Sponsorship Incentive Scheme for Sport, otherwise known as Sportsmatch, has since generated over £35m for grass-roots sporting and physical recreation, events and activities in the UK. Essentially, Sportsmatch is aimed at encouraging existing commercial sponsors of major sporting events to extend their involvement with sport into the grass-roots level by matching any contribution made by commercial sponsors with an equivalent amount from Sportsmatch funds (up to a limit of £50,000).

C3.66 In England, the Sportsmatch scheme is administered by the Institute of Sports Sponsorship (ISS)[1] using approximately £3.5m per annum to operate the scheme. Such funding is derived from the Treasury and is provided via the Department of Culture, Media and Sport as grant aid from Sport England[2]. Up to February 2002, over £28m of Sportsmatch funding has been granted to more than 3,000 projects in over 70 different sports. Projects that have been granted Sportsmatch funding include Kenwood Electronic's sponsorship of Saracens Football Club and Asda's sponsorship of Northamptonshire County Cricket Board[3].

1 The ISS is a national non profit-making organisation representing commercial sponsors of sport. See www.sports-sponsorship.co.uk.
2 In Scotland and Wales, the scheme is funded and managed by the Scottish and Welsh Sports Councils.
3 On a smaller scale, Hull Ionians Rugby Club received £20,000 from local sponsors to develop local talent under its Ionians Mini Juniors scheme aimed at developing home grown talent which was matched under the Sportsmatch programme, allowing the scheme to be expanded significantly.

C3.67 Sportsmatch publishes a document detailing eligibility requirements and conditions of funding[1]. Sports entities seeking Sportsmatch funding should consult this document carefully. In short, however, in order to qualify for Sportsmatch funding, the sports entity must:

(i) be a non profit-distributing organisation[2];
(ii) have an organisational framework with a written constitution that provides for sufficient legal and financial accountability;
(iii) operate mainly within the UK; and
(iv) have attracted potential commercial sponsorship for its activities.

1 This can be downloaded from www.sportsmatch.co.uk/how_to_apply.htm.
2 See para C3.32.

C3.68 In addition, the sponsored event or activity for which funding is sought must relate to a recognised sport. Moreover, the sports entity will have to demonstrate that the sponsored event or activity encourages increased participation and/or improved performance at grass-roots level, and should be open to participation by members of the public in general[1]. A commercially sponsored project should therefore qualify for Sportsmatch funding if it:

(i) increases sporting participation or skills at the grass roots level; and/or
(ii) promotes new sporting activities or extends/enhances existing ones; and/or
(iii) develops links with, and creates long term benefits for, the local community.

1 If the sponsored event or activity benefits any one or more of the Priority Groups, particularly favourable consideration will be given to such application. The Priority Groups are young people, disabled people, schools and school-related projects, ethnic minorities, and recreationally deprived areas.

C3.69 Importantly, the value of the commercial sponsorship for the activity or event must be at least £1,000. The sponsor must be a commercial organisation sponsoring grass-roots sport for the first time, or increasing the amount of existing sponsorship.

C3.70 Applications should be jointly prepared by the sports entity and the sponsor, and submitted to the appropriate Sportsmatch office[1]. Applications will be considered and assessed by the Sportsmatch awards panel. It is imperative that sponsorship of the event or activity is not formally concluded prior to assessment of the application by the awards panel. If commercial sponsorship monies are handed over to the sports entity before assessment of the application by the awards panel, the application for Sportsmatch funding will not be considered.

1 Application forms can be downloaded from www.sportsmatch.co.uk/how_to_apply.htm.

E The Foundation for Sport and the Arts

C3.71 Sports entities may also seek financial assistance from grant-making trusts[1]. In most cases, grant-making trusts are charities and may therefore only be able to fund projects which are of a charitable, benevolent or philanthropic nature[2]. However, the Foundation for Sport and the Arts ('FSA') is not a registered charity and supports a wide spectrum of sports. It was established in 1991 and remains one of the most important sources of grant finance in sport for smaller sports clubs and associations. Sports entities may apply for grant finance in relation to capital and revenue projects. Most awards are between £1,000 and £50,000 although grants of up to £75,000 can be made[3].

1 Examples include The Football Trust, Cliff Richard Tennis Development Trust, Women's Squash Trust.
2 See para C3.22 et seq and Chapter C1 for a discussion on how sport may be considered 'charitable'.
3 Examples include £2,500 to an archery club for a new building, £12,500 to a sailing club for new dinghies, £20,000 to a tennis club for the resurfacing of three tennis courts.

C3.72 The FSA usually grants funding to applications made by regional and local sports entities in relation to projects that benefit the general community as a whole. The FSA, in considering the application, will address issues relating to the project, including what the benefits are to the community, whether children and young people will benefit, whether the project is conducted efficiently etc. To apply, a sports entity should first notify the FSA of its intentions, giving an overview of the project and the amount of funding sought. If the project appears at first sight to be supportable by the FSA, a questionnaire will be sent to the sports entity requesting detailed information[1]. Following submission of the questionnaire and provision of the requested details the application will be assessed and a decision made in relation to funding.

1 This process avoids the sports entity having to waste resources on preparing a complete application in relation to a project which may not ultimately be supported by the FSA.

F European funding

C3.73 The four European Structural Funds[1] are aimed at focussing resources on developing the poorest regions in Europe and helping reduce the stark differences in social and economic conditions found in the member states. The Funds account for over a third of the EU budget and the UK's allocation from the Funds for the period 2000 to 2006 amounts to €15.5 billion (approximately £10 billion). Spending by the Funds is targeted at three objective areas. Of the three, Objective One is the highest priority designation for European financial aid and is targeted at areas where prosperity, measured in Gross Domestic Product per head of population, is 75% or less of the European average. Objective One funding currently amounts to around £300m of which 60.4% is provided by the European Regional Development Fund ('ERDF') and 20.3% by the European Social Fund.

1 These funds, which are essentially four European Community budgets, are the European Regional Development Fund (ERDF), the European Social Fund (ESF), the European Agricultural Guidance and Guarantee Fund (EAGGF), and the Financial Instrument for Fisheries Guidance (FIFG). Between 1989 and 1993, the UK received financing of around £3.8 billion from these Structural Funds.

C3.74 Although the Department of Trade and Industry co-ordinates overall government policy on these Funds, implementation and administration thereof is devolved to regional government and administrative offices. Of relevance to sport are the two main Funds, the European Regional Development Fund ('ERDF') and the European Social Fund ('ESF'). The ERDF primarily funds capital projects and investments in socially and economically deprived regions which, for example, create employment opportunities, develop small and medium sized enterprises and generally promote social and economic cohesion within the EU. The ESF on the other hand deals with employment issues and provides funding for training, human resources and equal opportunities schemes (with particular focus on disabled groups) to encourage the employability of residents in Objective One areas. There are no restrictions on eligibility for funding and although these Funds are not specifically directed at granting financial assistance to sports-related projects, all sports entities (whether non-profit-distributing or otherwise) may, at least in theory, apply for such European funding. Importantly, Objective One funding applies in the UK only to eligible projects within West Wales, Merseyside, Cornwall and Isles of Scilly (all of which are designated Objective One status).

C3.75 In the UK, Objective One projects receive funding for up to a maximum of 50% of the project costs and it is normally the responsibility of the applicant to obtain the remainder from other sources of funding to match the contribution from the Structural Funds. Previous sports-related projects that have received financial assistance from the Funds include the Parkside Community Centre in County Durham[1], and more recently, the much publicised £300m Kings Waterfront Development project in Liverpool involving the building of new stadium for Everton Football Club[2].

1 The project is expected to have created 200 new jobs and funding was granted to provide, inter alia, for the construction of leisure facilities including an all-weather sports pitch.
2 The Kings Waterfront Development comprises two aspects – a leisure complex and Everton FC's new stadium. The cost of the new stadium itself has been estimated at £155m, of which approximately £35m is to be financed by way of an ERDF Objective One grant. See further para C3.63.

C3.76 Such Structural Funds available for sports-related projects, although sizeable, are thoroughly bureaucratic and accessing them requires significant planning, application and execution. Even more so than when contemplating other sources of grant finance, sports entities considering applying for European funding should therefore seek professional advice in relation thereto. Generally however, applications for funding from the ESF should be made directly to the appropriate regional government office in England, or devolved administrative offices of the other home countries. Normally, invitations for the submission of project funding applications are publicised by these government offices and sports entities should seek guidance from them. Basically, the applicant sports entity must be a legally constituted organisation (ie a body corporate) and must be able to secure an equivalent level of funding for the project in question from other sources. The sports entity should ensure that the project will lead to increased employability of participants by, for example, offering training opportunities that lead to vocational qualifications. There have been a number of previous projects with elements of sports-related training, including coaches' training and outdoor pursuits training, that have benefited from ESF funding.

C3.77 The application process for ERDF funding is similar to that under the ESF. Sports entities should, in their application, identify the specific economic benefits that will accrue as a result of the project, and should be prepared to demonstrate in detail and quantify such economic benefits[1].

1 For example, applications in relation to the funding of a sports event or facility should be supported by data on the number of visitors attracted, number of full/part time jobs created etc.

G Receipt and use of grant funding

C3.78 As with other funding it receives, any sports entity which successfully applies for any form of grant finance must put in place such additional measures (such as setting up a separate bank account for its receipt and amending bank mandates appropriately) as are necessary to control the expenditure of such finance. Such a sports entity will usually be required to observe stringent conditions in relation to any grant which it receives[1], and any breach of such conditions could trigger a repayment obligation. In the case of a sports entity organised as an unincorporated members' club, such repayment obligation could fall jointly and severally on each individual member personally. Therefore, in addition to tightly controlling access to such funds and the uses for which they are applied, it is also advisable that a sports entity seeks expert legal advice before taking any action which may be considered to be in breach of any conditions attaching to grant funding which it has received.

1 For instance, a sports entity will not normally be permitted to dispose of any equipment or assets acquired with state-granted funds without first obtaining the prior written approval of the appropriate funding authorities.

5 DEBT AND EQUITY FINANCE

A The need for investment finance

C3.79 Notwithstanding the ability of a sports entity to attract funding (perhaps to supplement revenues generated by commercial activities) from subscriptions, fund-raising appeals and grants, as described above, funding from those sources may not be available to a particular sports entity, or may not be sufficient to meet its requirements, particularly if it is seeking to progress to, or simply remain competitive within, the elite of its sport. Therefore, a sports entity may need to attract further funding from other sources. However, once a sports entity has exhausted the funding potential of subscriptions, donations and grants, such further funding is unlikely to be forthcoming from parties willing to provide it simply because sport is an interesting, worthy or socially beneficial activity deserving of financial support. Although there will always be some who are willing to provide a sports entity with significant funding for 'emotional' rather than financial reasons[1], such further funding is usually available from those who will only provide it in the anticipation that they will make a profit on their investment. Therefore, in order to secure funding from such sources, a sports entity will have to convince such potential financiers that it is likely to provide them with the desired return on their investment, and that the risk of it not doing so is acceptable. Generally speaking, the sources of such 'investment' finance to a sports entity can be broken down into those willing to lend funds to it (debt finance) and those willing to buy shares issued by it (equity finance)[2].

1 For example, wealthy supporters of sports clubs: see further para C3.158 et seq.

2 In this chapter, the term 'equity' finance is used to describe the issue of shares of any class by a company, although the term 'equity' or 'risk' capital it is sometimes used to refer only to ordinary shares carrying basic rights relating to voting, dividends and distributions of capital rather than shares with enhanced rights. See further para C3.158 et seq. Also, by definition, an unincorporated sports entity without share capital cannot issue of shares and so must incorporate as a company limited by shares if it wishes to raise equity finance. A company limited by guarantee cannot raise finance in this way as its members are required to provide funds to it upon the winding up of the company.

B Debt and equity – essential characteristics and differences

C3.80 The remainder of this chapter will describe a variety of methods of raising 'investment' finance, focusing on those particularly suited to sports entities, and highlighting particular issues that arise when these methods are used in the sports sector. Inevitably, as football is the most commercially developed sport in the UK, generating the largest revenue and costs, to date use of the more complex methods of financing described below has been confined largely to football clubs. However, there is no reason why they should not also be available in other sports, provided that they can meet the relevant commercial criteria applied by the investor in making its decision on whether to invest. In any event, a sports entity considering raising additional finance by way of debt or equity finance will first have to consider the fundamental characteristics of each and determine whether one is more suitable than the other, or whether a combination is appropriate. The fundamental factors to be considered are described below.

(a) Leverage

C3.81 In basic terms, debt financing involves a lender entering into an arm's length relationship with the sports entity by providing funds which the entity is obliged to repay, normally over a specified time, together with interest at a specified rate. The lender's financial interest in the sports entity will comprise of its right to repayment of the principal amount of the debt together with interest on that amount. From the sports entity's standpoint, whilst it has a definite obligation to repay the amount borrowed from its creditors with interest, these obligations are finite.

C3.82 By contrast, an investor acquiring shares in the capital of a sports entity will ordinarily have a right to share in any distributions of profit that the sports entity makes by paying dividends to its shareholders (their relative shares of such profit ordinarily being proportional to the stake in the company that they have acquired in return for their investment). If the sports entity is financially successful and is therefore able to distribute significant profits, equity investors will thereby receive significant returns on their investment. (Further, the capital value of their shares may also increase dramatically allowing equity investors to realise a profit on the resale of their shares). Such returns are not fixed (unlike the return the sports entity must provide on a debt) and so the 'upside' for the shareholder is unlimited. However, by issuing more shares in its capital to new investors, the company thereby dilutes its existing shareholders' entitlement to profits that it distributes, as such profits now have to be shared with such additional shareholders. There is theoretically no limit on the amount of distributed profits which existing shareholders could cede to incoming equity investors in this way in the event that the company is successful. However, unlike raising debt finance, raising equity finance does not necessarily place the sports entity under a contractual obligation to provide the investor with a return on its investment whether or not the entity is doing well[1].

1 Even the holders of cumulative preference shares which are stated to carry a fixed percentage dividend per year payable in preference to the other shareholders of the company and which accumulates if such dividend is unpaid in any year can only ever receive such accumulated unpaid dividends if the company has accumulated sufficient profits available for distribution to enable it to pay such a dividend.

C3.83 The ability of the company to increase its profits using finance which entitles the investors to receive only a finite return (leaving the remaining profit to be distributed amongst its equity investors) is known as 'leverage'. Most businesses will take the opportunity to take advantage of some leverage. However, in doing so a borrower should be confident that it will generate additional profit using the funds borrowed, and that such profit will exceed the amount it has to pay to meet its fixed obligations to repay the debt and interest on it.

C3.84 Whilst no borrowers in any sector of the economy can make this assessment with any certainty, it can be a particularly difficult one in the sporting sector. Whilst debt funding is often sought with the intention of improving performance on the field of play, spending is by no means a *guarantee* of success. Further, a club which competes in a league which operates a promotion and relegation system can suffer a very significant downturn in its revenue if sporting failure results in relegation[1]. However, whilst its revenues decrease, the relegated club's debt obligations will not necessarily be reduced by a corresponding amount[2]. Therefore, in order to meet its debt service obligations from diminished revenue, the club can either use reserves or additional funding from other sources such as equity to meet its costs, or reduce its expenditure accordingly. However, relegation and the prospect of declining revenues is unlikely to attract equity investments into the club. A relegated club may therefore find that it needs to reduce expenditure and that the only expenditure that it can reduce quickly will be its wage bill, and selling highly-paid players can also be a source of additional revenue to offset the decline in other revenues. However, this will usually reduce the quality of the club's playing staff and consequently reduce its chances of regaining its former status and income levels via promotion, thereby prolonging the reduction in its income levels and potentially condemning the club to an extended period of sporting failure[3].

1 As mentioned at para C3.4, n 4, clubs relegated from football's FA Premier League at the end of the 1999/2000 season suffered a fall in their income in the following season of between £5 and 7m.

2 Indeed, it is understood that Leicester City FC's relegation from the FA Premier League at the end of the 2001/02 season actually triggered an increase in its debt repayment obligations.

3 Leicester City FC has sought to avoid this situation by requesting its current playing staff to accept a reduction in their salaries in exchange for a bonus payable in the event that the club achieves promotion.

C3.85 The alternative reaction to relegation is for the club to gamble on regaining its former status quickly via immediate promotion by not reducing costs immediately but retaining the quality of its playing staff or even enhancing it by signing new players. However, if this strategy can only be funded by increasing debt, a gamble on swift promotion, particularly by a club which is already highly leveraged, can be a costly one if it does not pay off (and spending is by no means a guarantee of promotion)[1]. If the club is not promoted quickly, it can find itself increasingly unable to service its debt obligations with revenues that diminish through continued failure on the field and the need to then cut back costs can become even more pressing. In a worst-case scenario, the club's debts can increase to a point where it is no longer able to meet its repayment obligations, in which event its creditors could petition for its winding-up[2].

1 As Wolverhampton Wanderers FC discovered in the 1990s.

2 This effect has been exacerbated in English Football's second tier, the Football League, by the collapse of revenues expected under the League's broadcast deal with ITV Digital, leading to estimates that a consequent inability to pay creditors could lead to as many as thirty of 70 clubs going out of business. Similarly, an inability to service high levels of debt ($27m) run up in the search for sporting success led to the bankruptcy of the Prost Formula One motor racing team in 2001.

C3.86 In order to protect their clubs from the possibility of such financial 'meltdown' and extinction, some leagues and governing bodies operate 'closed' leagues from which relegation is not a possibility[1]. As a result, clubs can take on debt safe in the knowledge that their income is unlikely to fall below a particular level, even if they suffer a period of sustained sporting failure (as they will continue to receive a minimum share of revenue from centrally exploited rights and will continue to play games against the top teams). However, the absence of the possibility of new clubs entering the league and other clubs falling a long way can make the sport too predictable and less exciting for spectators, and consequently less able to generate revenue as a whole. Also, closing the top league not only prevents lower teams from reaching the elite, it also deprives them of money-spinning games against 'big' teams which have fallen to their level. Consequently, whilst closed leagues can make financial sense for the elite, it can be detrimental to a sport as a whole.

1 This system is prevalent in North American professional sports. It is also increasingly put forward as a possibility in European elite sport. For example, in 2000, proposals were put forward that the First Division in English rugby be 'ring-fenced' for a period to allow clubs to attract investment, at the outset of professionalism in the sport, in an atmosphere of financial stability rather than, as the owner of one of the clubs put it, 'allowing two clubs to be relegated and effectively going bankrupt every year'. See further paras B2.142 to B2.144.

(b) *Control*

C3.87 Assuming there is no default on the repayment of its debt[1], the contractual arrangements between a borrowing sports entity and a lender will provide the latter with only limited control over the conduct of the sports entity's underlying business[2]. By contrast, an investor acquiring equity in the capital of a sports entity will ordinarily acquire more wide-ranging rights in relation to the running of the company itself, which will be embodied in the company's constitutional documents and by the extensive laws governing a company's relationship with its shareholders. The size of its shareholding and the rights attaching to its shares will determine the degree of control that an investor in shares has over the sports entity, which can be considerable and may be enhanced by further contractual controls if the size of the investment gives the 'incoming' investor sufficient bargaining power in relation to existing shareholders[3].

1 In the case of default, the terms of the loan will often provide remedies to the lender, such as the entire debt becoming repayable immediately and/or the lender being able to enforce any security provided by the borrower, such as a charge over its property, so that the lender can then sell the property and use the proceeds to satisfy the debt owed to it.
2 Most significant lending arrangements include specific restrictions on how the borrower's business is conducted in order to safeguard the lender's interests (eg if the borrower borrows further funds or changes the nature of its business fundamentally without the lender's consent, the loan may become immediately repayable in full).
3 See further para C3.158 et seq.

C3.88 Perhaps more so in this sector than others, the degree of control over a sports entity that its existing owners have to cede to new investors may be of more concern than how big a share of any financial 'upside' that the sports entity may generate they have to give up. This may be the case if the owners of a sports entity feel some emotional attachment to it or duty to ensure its continuing well-being and/or adherence to its traditional sporting values (although this may be becoming increasingly rare). Such desire to retain control to ensure the safeguarding of traditions may be particularly strong amongst a sports entity's owners if they are its founders or their descendants, or otherwise have a long-standing association with the entity. For example, again in the football context, some club owners have sold off equity stakes to newcomers or led their clubs to flotations in which many new shareholders have acquired a significant proportion of the club's share capital, but nevertheless retain a controlling interest[1]. Nevertheless, it is inherently more difficult for existing owners of a sporting entity to retain control if it issues equity to new investors rather than debt[2].

1 For example, even after issuing a strategic 9.9% stake to Granada in 1999, David Moores of the Moores family which had a long-held controlling interest in the club retained a 51% shareholding. Similarly, after Newcastle United floated on the Stock Exchange in 1997, Sir John Hall's interest remained at over 50% and, if fully subscribed, the 2002 public share offering by Norwich City will dilute the interests of the current controlling shareholders to 51%. Indeed, the rules of the Stock Exchange generally require only 25% of shares in a listed company to be distributed to the public, allowing the scope for a controlling interest to be maintained.

2 This effect can however be mitigated to a certain degree by creating classes of shares for such existing owners which give them special voting rights on particular issues of concern. See further para C3.158 et seq. However, issuing shares publicly to a large number of outsiders can mean that a third party is able to make an offer to purchase the entity's shares which a large number of such outsiders may accept, thereby giving such third party control of the sports entity. See further the Chapter 'Takeovers' by Mark Pinder and Nicola Green in *Tolley's Company Law* (Tolleys).

(c) Availability

C3.89 Market conditions and perceptions of the return that can be delivered by an investment in the sports sector, or in the particular sport in which a sporting entity looking to raise finance operates, or the financial prospects of that entity, will dictate to a large degree whether it can raise equity or debt finance, or either. As a sporting entity receiving an equity investment is not ordinarily contractually obligated to deliver any return on it, providing equity finance is by its nature more speculative than debt and it may therefore be harder to raise in the quantities required by a sports entity, particularly if market conditions dictate against such speculation. For example, the poor performance of shares in football clubs which have been floated on the UK stock markets[1] has meant that football clubs now find it increasingly difficult to raise 'genuine' equity finance (being equity investment received other than from 'emotional' investors[2]). This poor performance of football club shares has coloured investors' view of not only football but of sport in general, with the result that most sports entities looking to raise significant equity finance have to overcome negative assumptions about their ability to generate a financial return for investors.

1 At the time of writing, shares in all of the UK football clubs that have been floated are trading below their issue price, with many having lost more than 80% of their value over a five-year period. The football investment fund launched by merchant bank Singer & Friedlander in 1997 at the peak of football club flotation activity, and which focused on the football shares most likely to generate a return, lost over half of its value and sought investors approval to focus on other sectors in March 2002. Similarly, ENIC plc, a sports and leisure investment company which has taken significant stakes in UK and overseas football clubs, has seen the value of those stakes fall significantly.

2 See further para C3.158 et seq.

(d) Cost, Purposes and Flexibility

C3.90 The initial costs involved in raising debt may be lower than those involved in raising equity finance because, given the less speculative nature of the transaction, a lender will usually require less information about the sports entity seeking finance than a potential shareholder considering investing an equivalent sum would. An equity investor will be interested in the future earnings potential of the sports entity in which it is hoping to share as well as current earnings, whereas a lender will focus more on the sports entity's current level of earnings and liabilities and whether the surplus is sufficient to service the loan (although this distinction may be less clear-cut if long-term debt finance is being sought[1]). However, as well as charging interest during the term of a loan, a lender may also charge up-front fees upon providing the loan and further charges during its term.

1 See further para C3.98 et seq.

C3.91 If a sports entity needs to raise finance quickly, or to meet only its short-term requirements, debt finance may be more appropriate than equity as it can usually be raised more quickly and with fewer procedural obstacles[1]. If the sports entity in question is unincorporated, raising equity finance will obviously require it to first go through the process of incorporation as a company limited by shares (although this will be a one-off process which will not have to be repeated to make future issues of equity)[2]. In contrast, incorporation is not required for a sports entity to access some basic forms of debt finance, and debt can also be more easily structured to provide finance required in the short term only to meet short-term requirements. Debt may also offer the sports entity more flexibility to meet its requirements than equity[3].

1 Most companies' articles of association will permit directors to borrow up to a certain amount without requiring shareholder approval, whereas the issue of shares will always require shareholder approval (although a general authority to issue shares of up to a certain limit can usually be obtained in advance: s 80 of the Companies Act 1985).

2 For example, the operations of Hampshire County Cricket Club were transferred into an Industrial and Provident Society in 2000 and subsequently reorganised in 2002 into a group structure with Rose Bowl plc at its head in order to raise £5,000,000 by a private placing of shares to finance the completion of development of the Rose Bowl cricket ground (including the repayment of £1.4m of bank debt). It is anticipated that this is a precursor to the flotation of the plc on the Alternative Investment Market.

3 A sports entity needing money to finance a short-term requirement can borrow money and then repay it when the loan is no longer needed. A debt facility can provide a pool of funding which need not all be drawn down at once or at all. Interest will only accrue on sums after they have been 'draw-down'. In this way, such a facility can be used when required to supplement the sports entity's other income. By contrast, continually seeking additional rounds of equity funding to meet funding requirements as they arise is not usually practicable, but a company may not want to raise more funds that it needs by the issue of equity as this will dilute the interests of its existing shareholders. Although shares can be issued as redeemable and therefore redeemed at the option of the company, the procedural requirements for redemption will be more onerous than for the early repayment of a loan.

C3.92 The ongoing cost of debt (ie the interest payable) is more certain than the cost of equity (ie dividends that may be paid) but can be reduced in a variety of ways[1], usually involving reduction of the risk to the lender that the borrower will not fulfil its repayment obligations. The most common means of achieving this is by the borrower granting security to the lender in the form of a charge over its assets which the lender can enforce to satisfy the debt in the event of non-payment by the borrower (ie by taking possession of and selling the asset over which security has been granted and satisfying its debt from the proceeds). Clearly, the greater the value of the asset over which it obtains security, the less the risk to the lender that it will not recoup its investment should the borrower default (which should consequently reduce the interest rate payable by the borrower), and the more the lender will be prepared to lend to the sports entity. For the majority of sports entities, the most valuable asset over which it can grant security, and therefore against which it can borrow the most funds, will be its stadium[2]. However, a sports entity may be surprised to learn how little it can actually borrow against the value of its stadium. Whilst the value of the stadium to the sports entity itself (as its principal revenue generating asset without which it would struggle to exist) is clearly significant, a lender will be more concerned with the value that *it* could generate from the stadium were it to enforce its security in the event of default by the borrower and take possession of the stadium (hopefully including the freehold of the land on which it is built) to satisfy its debt. It is highly unlikely that the lender would be able to use the stadium as a sports stadium (most probably by leasing it to another sports entity, as the lender will not have its own team to install as the 'home' team). However, the likelihood of another sports entity buying it are also small as there are unlikely to be such other entities, close enough geographically to avoid protests to the move from their fans, which do not already have a suitable stadium of their own. Therefore, the lender will have to focus on the 'alternative use' value that will determine how much the lender will receive in a sale of the stadium for other purposes. This alternative use value may be much lower than its value to the borrower sports entity, particularly if it is not possible to redevelop the stadium for retail or residential use (eg because it is either in an unsuitable or undesirable area or the necessary planning consents to change its use cannot be obtained). Consequently, many sports entities are pursuing alternative methods of giving lenders security that their debt will be repaid. Some of these are discussed further at para C3.98 et seq.

1 See further para C3.79 et seq.

2 Using football as an example again, even if a high proportion of the value of a club's assets on its balance sheet is represented by player values, these 'assets' may not be viewed as a lender as suitable security as it would have difficulty in enforcing such security by taking over the player's contract and registration and selling them to another club against his will. The *Bosman* ruling, (meaning players can leave the club at the end of their contract without the club receiving a transfer fee) also means that the value of such 'assets' depreciates rapidly over the term of the players' contracts which may be much shorter than the term of the lending. Nevertheless, reports have suggested that some clubs are basically mortgaging their players by borrowing from banks against player values. (See further player sale and leaseback arrangements as described at para C3.98 et seq.)

(e) Tax Treatment

C3.93 In basic terms, payments of interest on loans received by the sports entity will be deductible expenses of the sports company in the calculation of its corporation tax liability, whereas dividend payments that it makes on equity investments will not[1].

1 See further para C2.32.

(f) Power to Borrow

C3.94 Whilst most businesses recognise that some leverage is beneficial, a business that is too highly leveraged will be too susceptible to short-term setbacks in its business and cashflow. A company that is too highly leveraged or 'geared' risks defaulting on its debt servicing and repayment obligations, which will be both relatively high and contractually obligated (unlike its obligations on equity), particularly if it is involved in a volatile industry such as sport in which its income can suffer a relatively sudden drop as a result of sporting factors which can be, by their nature, unexpected[1]. A failure by a sports entity to meet its debt repayment obligations can have serious immediate consequences for it if the creditor decides to enforce its rights in such event of default. Even if the borrower manages to come to arrangement with the lender to avoid such consequences, it is likely to suffer in the future by having to pay a higher rate on any future debt financing it seeks as a result of a fall in its creditworthiness. In an effort to avoid such situations, a company's gearing may be limited by its constitutional documents (usually specified as a percentage or multiple of the company's paid up share capital plus its reserves) so that its board of directors cannot cause the company to borrow in excess of a such limits without the approval of its shareholders. Additionally, the terms of its existing loans may limit the ability of a company to incur further debt (to protect against the company overburdening itself with debt and defaulting on such existing loans). If a sports entity has reached and cannot increase its gearing limit, any additional investment finance it needs will have to be sought through the issue of shares[2].

1 For example, the published accounts of Leeds Sporting plc showed that Leeds United's relatively unexpected failure to qualify for the UEFA Champions' League in 2001 led directly to a fall in revenues of £4m.

2 However, a loan to a company which has exceeded its borrowing limits may still be enforced unless the lender was acting in bad faith in making the loan – s 35A (1) of the Companies Act 1985. Also, 'quasi-lending' arrangements can be structured to avoid falling foul of gearing limits. See further para C3.98 et seq.

(g) Sport-Specific Factors

C3.95 Aside from being influenced by the characteristics of debt and equity that apply in all industry sectors, sports entities may find that other factors, perhaps particular to their sport or individual circumstances, can determine which of these funding sources it is able to access. The rules of a governing body by which it may be bound may be a limiting factor. For example, until relatively recently the Football Association's Rule 34 prevented football clubs from paying dividends in excess of 15% of the nominal value of its shares to their shareholders[1]. The purpose of this Rule was precisely to discourage investors who might be seeking to make an equity investment in a football club with a view to realising a commercial return on such investment by extracting dividend payments from the club. It was thought that such money should remain within football club, thereby protecting its value to the local community and its supporters. Similarly, Rule 34 also prohibited the payment of salaries to the directors of clubs (which could otherwise be used to circumvent the purpose of the Rule) and required the assets of any club on a winding up to be distributed for use for other sporting purposes, rather than to its shareholders (effectively preventing 'asset stripping' by shareholders)[2].

1 This limit was increased from 5% in 1981.

2 However, the FA allowed Rule 34 to be circumvented by Tottenham Hotspur in 1983 when the assets of the club were transferred to a holding company, which was expressly stated not to be subject to the FA Rules and then floated on the Stock Exchange. The flotation clearly would not have attracted investors had there been a limit on the profits that could be distributed to them and this restructuring allowed the purpose of Rule 34 to be defeated by enabling such distributions of significant profits of the holding company (which were expected to be generated, at least in part, by the club assets). The FA's failure to enforce the spirit of Rule 34 may have been motivated by the reasoning that, whilst allowing significant amounts of money to be paid out of football in the way of dividends, flotations also allowed significant funds to be raised by football clubs. Other clubs subsequently used the same mechanism to avoid Rule 34 and the FA eventually dropped this limb of the Rule in 1998 (along with the complementary rule preventing the payment of salaries to directors).

C3.96 A restriction on European football clubs' ability to attract equity investment is also applied by UEFA, whose rules provide that 'no person or company may control more than one club participating in the same UEFA competition', on the basis that competition between clubs could be hindered by such common ownership. This will obviously hinder a European club seeking significant equity finance from an investor which already has a significant shareholding in another European club[1]. This principle behind this rule is also reflected in the more stringent rules of The FA Premier League and The Football League which prevent any person or company from owning more than 10% of the share capital of more than one of its clubs[2]. In addition to these limitations on raising equity finance (which are motivated mainly by a desire to maintain the integrity of its sporting competitions), some sports governing bodies such as UEFA are also considering introducing controls (such as licensing requirements to be met by clubs taking part in their competitions) aimed at preventing their members from taking on excessive debt in pursuit of sporting success (which are motivated more by a desire to prevent such excessive debt eventually leading to the bankruptcy of sporting entities).

1 This rule has recently been challenged but upheld by the European Commission in response to a complaint lodged by ENIC plc, which at the time of writing holds stakes ranging from 25.1% to 99.9% in six European clubs. (Case No 37.632 – UEFA rule on 'integrity of the UEFA club competitions: independence of clubs'). See paras B2.145 to B2.151.

2 Rule U.4 of the Rules of The Football Association Premier League and Regulation 84.5 of the Regulations of The Football League Limited respectively.

C Hybrid funding

C3.97 Whilst the differences between 'pure' debt and 'pure' equity funding can be significant, the lines can be blurred as some shares exhibit characteristics more akin to debt and vice versa. The ability to raise finance which combines suitable aspects of debt and equity can allow a sports entity to structure the investment which it receives to best suit its requirements. Such mechanisms are described in more detail in the remainder of this chapter.

6 DEBT FINANCE

A Types of debt and characteristics

C3.98 As stated in the preceding section of this chapter, most companies operating in any industry sector finance their operations at least in part through debt in order to achieve some leverage. There are a number of forms of debt potentially available to companies wishing to raise finance. Whilst a detailed description the characteristics of various debt structures and instruments is beyond the scope of this chapter, those most likely to be utilised by sports entities are described below.

(a) Overdrafts and Term Loans

C3.99 The most simple form of debt finance that will be available to most sports entities will be an overdraft facility offered by a bank. Such facilities are inexpensive to set up because complex structuring is not required (although an arrangement fee may be payable) and they offer the sports entity the flexibility to deal quickly with short-term or unexpected mismatches between its income and expenditure (ie a sports entity can draw funds under its overdraft facility almost instantaneously to meet payment obligations when other funds are not available). If a sports entity is incurring relatively occasional and low levels of borrowing (perhaps because its other income is ordinarily sufficient to meet its outgoings) an overdraft facility should be sufficient to cover its borrowing requirements. However, the financial limits applicable to most such facilities[1] mean that their simplicity is matched by their inability to meet any significant financing requirements a sports entity may have. Additionally, the rate of interest charged will normally be higher than with other sources of debt, particularly if the overdraft is unsecured, to reflect the risk of default taken on by the lender and so an overdraft facility will not be the most economic way of financing a sports entity's long-term borrowing requirements. Further, unless an agreement is entered into with the lending bank specifying a repayment date, repayment of an overdraft can be demanded at any time by the lender. Therefore, rather than risk the bank calling for repayment at an inopportune time which could lead to default on this or other obligations, it is preferable for the an agreement governing repayment terms and interest terms to be entered into.

1 The degree of risk taken on by the lender, particularly if the debt is unsecured, means that most lenders will not be prepared to lend as much under an overdraft facility as they would under more structured and secure lending arrangements.

C3.100 Larger sums can usually be borrowed by a sports entity at lower rates of interest under term loans than under overdraft facilities. Term loans are taken out for specific periods of time and may be repayable in one lump sum at the end of the term or in accordance with a schedule of repayments. Unlike overdrafts, they are ordinarily governed by agreements between the borrower and the lender specifying terms such as the amount of the loan and the interest payable. They may also include restrictions on the purposes for which the borrower can use the borrowed funds and security in the form of a charge over some or all of the borrower's assets[1]. Such additional protection against the borrower's default will usually mean that the interest rates payable on such term loans are lower than on overdraft facilities, although some flexibility to avoid paying unnecessary interest on funds can be retained if the borrower utilises a loan facility which allows it to 'draw down' parts of the total amount made available as and when it requires them. Guarantees given by individuals with an interest in the sports entity (such as its directors or shareholders) can also provide the lender with additional protection against default and thereby reduce the interest payable. If a substantial sum is being borrowed, the lender may seek to syndicate the loan by either directly involving other lenders to advance part of the total amount to be borrowed to the sporting entity or remaining as the sole lender to the sporting entity but entering into collateral agreements with other lenders itself[2]. Loans of up to five years' duration are commonly structured as term loans. However, longer term borrowings required by sports entities will more ordinarily be structured via the issue of bonds, loan stock or debentures.

1 However, see para C3.92 with regard to the value of the security that a sports entity may be able to offer.

2 For example, at the time of writing it is proposed that the principal lender to the Wembley Stadium redevelopment project, Westdeutsche Landesbank Girozentrale, may eventually syndicate the lending of approximately £400m of its lending in relation to the project.

(b) Loan Notes and Bonds

C3.101 These are essentially debt instruments issued by a company which amount to a promise to the holder of the note or bond to pay the amount specified in the note (ie the sum loaned to the company in exchange for the note) on the date that the instrument matures (bonds generally evidence longer-term debt than notes although the term are often used interchangeably), together with interest at a specified rate (either fixed or variable). Notes or bonds are usually transferable so that the original lender is free to sell them and the person entitled to repayment of the loan upon maturity will be the holder of the note or bond at that time.

Transferability of the notes or bonds makes them more attractive to lenders who may want the flexibility to realise the value of their investment before maturity of the note.

(c) Convertible Debt

C3.102 A sports entity that wishes to raise debt rather than equity funding, but which needs to give an added incentive to lenders, can issue debt which is convertible into shares at a later date at the option of the lender. The right of conversion will mean that the interest payable on the loan will be less than the interest rate that would otherwise be payable (perhaps reducing it to an affordable level), as it is anticipated that the lender will be able to convert the debt into shares at a time when the conversion price is lower than the market price of shares thereby providing it with an additional financial return[1]. Another reason for issuing convertible debt might be if the borrower would prefer to raise finance by issuing shares for reasons described earlier in this chapter, but the market price for its shares at the time is too low (resulting in excessive dilution for existing shareholders were it to issue sufficient shares to raise the required finance at such price) or conditions for equity issues are otherwise unfavourable[2]. The debt is normally convertible into shares at a fixed price which is determined by reference to the market price of the borrower's shares at the time of issue of the convertible debt (enabling the lender to benefit from an immediate capital gain if the market price of the shares increases above the conversion price before it exercises its rights of conversion)[3]. If the option is not exercised by the lender, the loan simply becomes repayable with any unpaid interest upon its maturity. However, if the loan is converted the consequent reduction in the company's borrowings and increase in its share capital will have a twofold effect in reducing the company's gearing[4].

1 This additional benefit is known as an 'equity kicker'.

2 This may have been a factor behind such an issue of £25m of convertible loan notes in 1999 by Newcastle United plc to a subsidiary of Ntl Incorporated, simultaneously with its purchase of shares from existing shareholders which gave Ntl an aggregate shareholding of 9.8% in Newcastle. The loan notes were interest free (although commercial rights were granted to Ntl in exchange) and convertible after five years into a further 9.99% of the share capital of the company at a price per share of approximately 155p (compared with the market price at the time of issue of 81p). However, the loan notes were instead converted into deferred shares in 2002 as part of a restructuring of the arrangements between Ntl and the club, including the sale by Ntl of its shareholding (see further para C3.158 et seq).

3 However, the issuing company may seek to limit this potential upside to the lender by triggering automatic conversion of the debt if the market price of its shares reaches a specified level.

4 See para C3.81.

(d) Subordinated and Limited-Recourse Debt

C3.103 Very briefly, there are further sub-classifications of the types of debt financing that a sports entity could raise, such as subordinated or 'mezzanine' debt. A subordinated lender agrees that it will not be repaid until lenders to whom it is subordinated have been repaid. Such debt is also known as 'mezzanine' debt because it occupies territory between 'true' equity and debt in that a subordinated lender ranks behind unsubordinated lenders on a liquidation but ahead of shareholders. Other forms of debt can be structured so that repayment relies only on the revenue generated by particular assets of the borrower (often those to be acquired or constructed using the sum borrowed), rather than the whole of the borrower's business, and security is often granted only over those particular assets.

Such 'limited recourse' debt is often used to finance high-risk projects to ensure that a failure of the project does not give the lender rights against the whole of the borrower's business. This limitation of the lender's recourse in the event of default by the borrower will mean that the interest rates on such lending are high. However, an adaptation of limited recourse lending has been used in sport to allow sports entities to borrow against their *low risk* assets, isolating them from the more risky aspects of the sports entity's business that could otherwise act as a drain on them, thereby *reducing* the risk for the lender of default and allowing the sports entity to borrow more and at lower rates than would otherwise be possible. These mechanisms are described further below.

B Particular methods of debt finance in sport

(a) Debenture Schemes

C3.104 Whilst the term 'debenture' does not have a precise legal meaning, in the sporting context, it is usually associated with schemes implemented by sports entities to raise funding by offering supporters rights in relation to seats in their stadia. These schemes, which are also sometimes called 'bond schemes', are usually launched to finance the building or redevelopment of stadia or stands in which such seats will be housed, although the finance raised does not necessarily have to be used in this way.

C3.105 The basic structure of a debenture schemes involves the relevant sports entity raising debt finance from potential spectators. These loans are governed by the terms of the debenture scheme and evidenced by debenture certificates issued to the lenders. They are usually unsecured and no interest is payable on them. Instead, the debenture holders ordinarily receive the right to purchase tickets for events which take place at the borrower's stadium during the term of the loan[1]. Such schemes differ from the sale of season tickets therefore, as the payment by the supporters under a 'true' debenture scheme entitles them only to a *right* to purchase tickets in the future, and they will nevertheless have to pay for any tickets that they purchase in exercise of such right[2]. The basic premise of the scheme therefore is that the right to buy tickets has sufficient value in itself to entice potential spectators to lend the sports entity money to secure this right. (The value of the right should approximate to the value of the interest that the lender could obtain if it were to lend the same sum to another borrower otherwise on the same terms). Such right to purchase tickets will normally only have a value if demand for the tickets exceeds their supply, such that spectators wishing to attend an event cannot be sure that they can simply buy tickets for any event they wish to see. Consequently, the more difficult it is for supporters to obtain tickets, the more valuable a guaranteed right to buy tickets will be and the more the sports entity should be able to raise by offering such rights in lieu of interest on the sums borrowed[3] (thereby utilising the 'asset' of scarcity to generate additional funding, rather than allowing touts and other resellers of tickets to utilise this 'asset' exclusively). Paradoxically, use of the funds to increase the capacity of the sports entity's stadium increases the supply of tickets and can therefore makes the debenture rights less valuable.

1 Ancillary benefits, such as exclusive bars and car parking facilities are often also granted to debenture holders attending events.

2 However, the price of such tickets may be discounted or protected from future rises under such schemes.

3 For example, a series of debenture issues by the Scottish Rugby Union plc to raise funding for the redevelopment of Murrayfield Stadium in the early 1990's gave holders the right to purchase tickets for certain matches for a minimum of 50 years and were issued at up to £9,900 each. Over £35m was raised by such issue. Debentures issued by The All England Lawn Tennis Ground plc which entitled each holder to a (very much in demand) Centre Court ticket for each day of Wimbledon for 5 years from 2001 were issued at a price of £23,150. However, these differ from 'true' debentures as debenture holders receive their tickets *automatically* within that price, rather than simply having the *right* to purchase tickets. A bond scheme introduced by Newcastle United Football Club in 1994 followed the more usual structure as fans were offered a £500 'bond' which guaranteed them the right to buy a season ticket for the next 10 seasons. This scheme raised approximately £4.5m in total.

C3.106 The loans advanced by the debenture holders will normally have a fixed term (commonly between five and 99 years)[1], over which period the lender receives its rights in lieu of monetary interest payments. At the end of the fixed term the debentures will be redeemed by the issuer by repayment of the loan. As with any loan, the effects of inflation should gradually diminish the financial impact on the issuer of its repayment obligations in real terms, perhaps reducing it to a negligible burden by the time redemption of a long-term debenture actually becomes due (although it should be remembered that this effect will be countered by the cost of providing the benefits to the debenture holders over such a lengthy term).

1 However, the terms of the scheme might provide for the loan to have a minimum term and to thereafter be repayable at any time at the option of the sports entity.

C3.107 As stated above[1], the scarcity of tickets, plus the value of any ancillary benefits to which the debenture holders are entitled, will determine whether followers of a sport or club consider a debenture to be worth the financial outlay. The following features may also affect the attractiveness of debentures to potential subscribers (and therefore the price at which they can be offered).

1 See para C3.105.

C3.108 Transferability Even loyal supporters may not wish to attend every event for which a debenture enables them to purchase tickets, and so may look to the scheme to allow debenture holders to allow other persons to use tickets purchased by the debenture holder. Further, supporters may even envisage a situation in which they will need to recover some or all of their expenditure on the debenture (or maybe more) before the end of the loan period. Debentures which are transferable permanently will allow them to do so if another person is willing to purchase the debenture from them[1]. Liquidity of debentures can be enhanced by facilitating their resale (for example, provision was made by the Scottish Rugby Union plc for its 1992 debentures to be traded on a 'matched bargain' basis under Rule 535.2 of the London Stock Exchange). Conversely, whilst a debenture holder's right to purchase tickets will ordinarily relate to a particular seat allocated to them upon the issue of the debenture, a sports entity implementing such a scheme may wish to retain the flexibility to allocate a different seat to a debenture holder in specified circumstances or at its discretion. However, this may reduce the value of the benefits to the debenture holder[2].

1 For example, debentures issued by The All England Lawn Tennis Ground plc are transferable temporarily (ie for particular days) and permanently, and often trade at above their issue price, even after the initial Championships to which they relate have taken place.

2 For example, if certain areas of the sports entity's stadium in which debenture holders sit must be given over to 'away' fans for particular games, it should reserve the right to relocate those debenture holders temporarily. Further, it seems that, if the scheme is appropriately worded, the

sports entity can also reserve the right to relocate debenture holders' seats permanently if it so wishes. It was decided by Mr Justice Blackburne in the High Court in March 2000 that, whilst many thought cl 9(b) of Newcastle United Football Club's bond scheme allowed it to *temporarily* relocate debenture holders, who had paid £500 to the club for the right to purchase a season ticket for each of the following 10 seasons, for various reasons (such as that described above or in the event of rebuilding work etc) it in fact also allowed the club to permanently relocate such debenture holders and sell the seats that they had previously occupied for corporate hospitality at a higher price. Although the debenture holders were given leave to appeal the decision on the question of whether the club had misrepresented to them in promotional material issued by the club in connection with the bond scheme that their right related to a particular seat they had chosen, the decision was not appealed due to costs (unreported – see the report by Ian Herbert in (2000) Independent, 3 March).

C3.109 Timescales In the case of debenture schemes used to finance the building or development of stadia, debenture holders will seek assurances that the seat to which their debenture relates will be available to them within a certain timescale, in default of which their loan will be returned (preferably with interest as they will have received no benefits in lieu of interest).

C3.110 Events A debenture holder will look for assurance that there will be a minimum number of events (perhaps involving the specified 'home' team) taking place at the stadium in each season during the term of the loan for which it can exercise its right to purchase tickets. However, whilst the issuing sports entity may be able to guarantee a minimum number of events, it may wish to exclude certain events from the debenture holders' rights. For example, it may plan to provide its stadium to third parties (such as the governing body of a sport) to host events such as a cup final or international matches, perhaps in return for a significant fee[1]. Such event organisers will usually seek to control the sale of tickets and the receipt of ticket revenues in relation to such events, and if the stadium owner has previously granted debenture holders the right to a seat for the event (eg if it has granted rights to *all* events held at the stadium) such seats cannot then be made available to the event organiser for sale. If it considers such erosion of its ability to sell seats to be too great, the event organiser may seek an alternative venue at which it can sell a larger proportion of the seating and the debenture issuer will thereby lose out on the fee and/or prestige associated with hosting the event. Therefore, sports entities implementing debenture schemes must strike a balance between granting rights which are sufficient to attract the requisite funding from debenture holders without thereby reducing too greatly the rights which it can thereafter make available to third party event organisers[2].

1 In addition to any fee it receives, a sports entity hosting an event organised by a third party at its stadium can also benefit financially from the right to sell merchandise or exploit other commercial opportunities (such as catering) at the event if it does not cede these rights to the event organiser.

2 For example, the debentures issued by the Scottish Rugby Union plc in 1999 gave holders the right to buy a ticket for each of Scotland's games played at Murrayfield in what was then the Five Nations Championship, but only an opportunity to gain priority, but not guaranteed, to buy tickets for games in the 1999 Rugby World Cup held at the stadium, allowing the distribution of all tickets for such games to be controlled by the event organiser, Rugby World Cup Ltd.

C3.111 Premium Sports entities may seek to reduce the cost of raising funds via a debenture scheme by issuing debentures at a premium over their nominal value, so that the issuer has to repay only the nominal value but not the premium upon redemption[1]. However, this benefit to the sports entity will clearly be a disadvantage that the debenture holder would prefer not to suffer. Further, whilst any premium element will reduce the sports entity's eventual repayment obligations, the amount of funding that it will receive initially could be reduced (when compared with what it would receive if there were no premium element to the debenture and its entire value were repayable) because the premium received might therefore be treated not as a loan but as a payment to the club in exchange for the grant by it of a right (or for the tickets themselves if these are received automatically, as in the case of the debentures issued in relation to the Wimbledon tennis championships[2]). Consequently VAT may be payable by the sports entity on the premium element[3]. However, if the scheme does not actually involve any indebtedness and is simply involves the payment of a fee for rights, the sports entity can avoid having to comply with some of the regulatory requirements that apply to the issue of debt instruments by companies which are described later in this Section.

1 For example, debentures issued by the Scottish Rugby Union plc in relation to Murrayfield in 1999 were of £1 nominal value but were issued at premiums ranging from £999 to £1,999.

2 See para C3.105.

3 Some schemes involve no repayment at all and the entirety of the sum received by the sports entity amounts to a fee. Such schemes are not 'true' debenture schemes as they involve no debt and although less complicated than debenture schemes to establish, the entirety of the fee is likely to attract VAT.

C3.112 Early redemption Whilst a potential debenture holder can assess whether the value of the benefits that it will receive over the term of the debenture provide it with sufficient return on the sum it advances to the issuing sports entity, the risk that such return will not be sufficient will increase if the debenture can be redeemed by the issuer prior to the specified redemption date (for example, if the sports entity moves to another ground). This risk factor will be particularly important if the debenture is issued at a significant premium which is not returnable upon such early redemption (meaning that the debenture holder would not receive the entirety of the benefits for which it had paid this 'fee' element).

C3.113 Debenture schemes have proved to be a very useful and significant means for some sports entities to raise finance over the years. A form of debenture has been issued by The All England Lawn Tennis Ground plc[1] since the 1920s. That initial issue raised £75,000. The three issues covering the Championships from 1986 to 2000 raised an aggregate of over £80m and the issue covering the 2001 to 2005 Championships raised approximately £46m[2]. In UK football, one of the first such schemes was launched by Arsenal in the early nineties and raised approximately £10m for the club. However, a sports entity considering launching a debenture scheme must pitch the benefits granted to debenture holders at the appropriate level if a scheme is to raise the funding sought. For example, also in the early nineties, insufficient numbers of fans of West Ham United Football Club were enticed to pay almost £1,000 for a guaranteed right to buy a season ticket for life at a 10% discount and the scheme had to be abandoned.

1 A company jointly owned by The All England Lawn Tennis Club and The Lawn Tennis Association which was established as a private limited company to administer the facilities at Wimbledon, registering as a public company in 1996.

2 See the Wimbledon Championships official website at www.wimbledon.org/about/debentures_history.html.

C3.114 In addition to considering the pricing and benefits of debentures which it is planning to issue, a sports entity (or its advisers) must also consider the legal implications of launching such a scheme. If they involve some element of debt and are not simply structured as a fee to be paid for a right to purchase tickets which has no element of repayment, the debentures issued by a sports entity are likely to be considered 'securities' and 'debentures' within the meaning of the Companies Act 1985[1] and other applicable legislation and must therefore be issued in compliance with the requirements of such legislation. The most likely of these to affect a sports entity planning to implement a debenture scheme are discussed in the remainder of this Section.

1 For example, s 744 of the Companies Act 1985. For a full discussion of the effects of issuing securities, see *Tolley's Company Law* (Tolleys).

C3.115 The first obstacle that a sports entity may encounter when considering implementing a debenture scheme is that a private company may not offer debentures to the public (or issue any debentures privately but with a view to them being subsequently offered to the public)[1]. To do so would be an offence under s 81 of the Companies Act 1985 causing the company and each of its officers to be liable to a fine of up to the statutory maximum[2]. For the purposes of s 81, an offer is made to 'the public' includes an offer to 'any Section of the public however selected'[3]. Consequently, even if a sports entity proposes to issue debentures only to selected supporters (eg existing season ticket holders) rather than to its supporters generally or to the general public, this is likely to be considered to be an offer to the public for the purposes of the relevant legislation and the sports entity will therefore have to re-register as a public company in order to make such an offer[4]. It therefore must consider whether the finance that it could raise under such a debenture scheme would justify the expense of re-registration and submitting to the stricter regulatory regime to which public companies are subject[5].

1 For the purposes of this chapter, we are assuming that the sports entity considering raising a significant amount of funding in this way has already taken the decision to incorporate as a company limited by shares, rather than being unincorporated or limited by guarantee without a share capital.
2 Currently £5,000.
3 See s 742A of the Companies Act 1985, which replaced s 59 pursuant to the Financial Services and Markets Act 2000 (Consequential Amendments and Repeals) Order 2001 from 1 December 2001.
4 Section 742A of the Companies Act 1985 does specify certain circumstances in which an offer will not be regarded as being an offer to the public, for example if it is made only to: (i) existing members or employees of the company; or (ii) existing holders of debentures. However, a sports entity is unlikely to generate significant finance from a debenture scheme which fall within these exceptions.
5 See also para C3.176.

C3.116 Another consequence of issuing securities such as debentures to the public is that in most cases[1] the issuing sports entity will have to comply with the Public Offer of Securities Regulations 1995 (the 'POS Regs')[2]. In essence, the POS Regs require the issuer of the debentures[3] to the public to publish a prospectus containing specified information[4]. These requirements are designed to ensure that potential purchasers of the debentures are provided with sufficient and accurate information on which to base their decision on whether or not to invest. The preparation of such a prospectus can be an onerous task and so a sports entity considering issuing debentures might look into ways of avoiding the application of the Regulations. This is most commonly done by structuring the issue so that it is not an 'offer to the public' for the purposes of the Regulations. The test of whether an offer of debentures by a sports entity is one that is made 'to the public' for the purposes of the POS Regs is very similar to that set out in the Companies Act as described above, in that an offer made to any section of the public is to be regarded as being made to the public. Again, it is likely that an offer by a sports entity to a particular group, for example its season ticket holders, will nevertheless be an issue to the public under this test unless it falls within one of the exceptions that are set out Regulation 7 of the POS Regs. Many of these cover the same ground as the exceptions from s 81 described above[5]. However, the scope of the exemptions from the POS Regs is broader, as there are over 20 categories of exemption set out in reg 7. However, those most likely to apply to an offer of debentures by a sports entity are the following:

- the offer is made to no more than 50 people;
- the offer is made only to the members of a club or association who can reasonably be regarded as having a common interest with each other and with the club or association in the affairs of the club or association and in what is to be done with the proceeds of the offer (although it should be noted that the offerees must actually be 'members' of the club in some sense, rather than just supporters of it);
- certain financial thresholds relating to the debentures are not exceeded;
- the issuing entity is a charity, an industrial and provident society[6] or other non-profit making entity; or
- the debentures are not transferable (although this will affect their attractiveness to investors, as described above).

However, as with the exceptions to s 81, a debenture scheme implemented by a sports entity that falls within one of these exceptions is less likely to generate significant finance than one that does not.

1 Unless the debentures are being listed on the Official List maintained by the Financial Services Authority (which was the Official List of the London Stock Exchange until May 2000), in which case they will be subject to a separate and more stringent regime applicable to securities listed in that way. See further para C3.117.
2 SI 1995/1537.
3 Regulation 3 specifically includes 'instruments creating or acknowledging indebtedness' within the ambit of the Regulations.
4 These requirements are detailed and beyond the scope of this chapter. For a full description, see Gleeson 'Prospectuses and Public Issues' in *Tolleys Company Law* (Tolleys).
5 See para C3.115.
6 Ie it is registered under the Industrial and Provident Societies Act 1965. See further para C1.50 et seq.

C3.117 As stated above[1], increasing the transferability of debentures issued by a sports entity is likely to increase their attractiveness to potential investors and will therefore enhance their value. Such liquidity of the debentures will be especially enhanced if they can be traded on an accessible market. Therefore, an issuing sports entity may seek to have its debentures listed for trading on one of a variety of exchanges in order to enhance their attractiveness to potential lenders. If it does so it will need to comply with both the rules of the exchange and the POS Regs, unless the debentures are to be traded on the Official List maintained by the Financial Services Authority ('FSA')[2]. The Official List is the most high-profile and highly regulated exchange on which a sports entity could list its debentures and would give the debenture holders the most liquidity and assurance regarding the issuer, thereby enhancing the attractiveness of the debentures to them and consequently their value. As such, the Official List is governed by a separate regime from other exchanges, and issues of debentures and other securities which are to be listed on it will be regulated by the listing rules published by the FSA and the Financial Services and Markets Act 2000 (the 'FSMA 2000')[3], rather than the POS Regs.

These impose even more stringent requirements on the issuer in terms of the information regarding the debentures that must be provided to potential purchasers (in the form of a prospectus or listing particulars) and ongoing requirements. The administrative burden of complying with these requirements will in most cases make a listing of its debentures on the Official List impractical for a sports entity. Therefore this chapter will not go into any detail on these requirements[4]. However, if a sports entity does choose to have securities admitted to the Official List (as with the compliance with the POS Regs) the officers and advisers of the company should ensure that these requirements are complied with as they could otherwise be liable to compensate acquirers of the debentures for any loss that they may suffer as a result of such non-compliance.

1 At para C3.108.
2 Which took over as the UK Listing Authority from the London Stock Exchange in May 2000.
3 Which superseded Pt IV of the Financial Services Act 1986.
4 For a full description, see the Chapter 'Prospectuses and Public Issues' (Simon Gleeson) in *Tolley's Company Law* (Tolley).

C3.118 Whether or not a sports entity issuing debentures is subject to the POS Regs or will be admitted to the Official List, any materials which it issues to attract people to acquire such debentures will nonetheless be subject to the requirements of s 21 of the FSMA 2000 which governs what is termed 'financial promotion', being essentially an invitation or inducement to engage in investment activity (such as acquiring debentures). Basically, this legislation prohibits the such invitations or inducements being made (by any means of communication) unless issued by, or approved by, a person authorised to do so under the FSMA 2000 (such as an investment bank). Therefore, a sports entity which launches a debenture scheme falling within this regime must take great care to ensure that all such 'financial promotion' conducted in connection with the scheme is engaged in or approved by a person authorised for such purposes under the FSMA 2000.

(b) Securitisation

C3.119 As described above[1], limited-recourse debt generally involves borrowing to finance the acquisition or creation of specific assets which will then generate the income required to repay the debt and interest on it. Only the revenue produced by those specific assets will be available to generate the revenue required to meet the borrower's payment obligations and the lender will commonly take security over those assets (ie its recourse against the borrower is limited to those assets). Such limited-recourse debt has been used to finance particularly large or expensive projects which are relatively high risk but, if successful, are expected to generate significant future revenue. In the event that such a project does not perform as expected the borrower avoids such failure resulting in its insolvency. This limitation of the lender's recourse in the event of default by the borrower will ordinarily mean that the interest rates on such lending are higher than would otherwise be the case. However, a lending structure known as securitisation has been developed, and used in sport, to allow borrowers to isolate their relatively low risk financial assets from the more risky aspects of their business and use them to secure debt finance. By confining the lender's interest to the performance of these low risk/high performing assets by isolating them from the effects of less certain aspects of its business, the sports entity can reduce the lender's risk and can consequently borrow more and at lower rates than would otherwise be possible.

1 See para C3.29 et seq.

C3.120 The profile of some elite sports entities in the UK, and particularly football clubs, is that they have relatively high and stable income streams in the form of gate receipts (particularly season ticket sales) or contractually obligated income (such as sponsorship revenues) when compared to the value of their fixed assets, the most valuable of which is likely to be their stadium[1]. However, other aspects of the club's business (such as player transfer income or prize money from European competition) can be relatively unpredictable, certainly in the long term. Consequently, the securitisation of such predictable and stable income streams is increasingly being used to raise finance for football clubs. A number of such schemes have already been implemented, which will be described in more detail below. However, it is necessary to give a basic description of the 'traditional' securitisation structure first, before describing the modifications required to adapt its application to the sporting sector, and football in particular.

1 See para C3.92.

C3.121 'Traditional' Securitisation Structure Securitisation is a relatively new means of raising finance, but insofar as there is a traditional model, it essentially involves the entity seeking the finance (the 'originator') 'securitising' receivables (eg trade receivables or other debt owed to it by third parties under contract) by assigning them to a company specially formed for the purpose of receiving them (a 'special purpose vehicle' or 'SPV' which can but need not be a subsidiary or sister company of the originator) in exchange for an immediate payment for those receivables (and the originator thereby raises finance by converting its income stream into a lump sum payment from the SPV).The funds used by the SPV to buy the receivables from the originator are raised by procuring loans from third party investors by the issue of notes or bonds to them which evidence and set out the terms of such loans (such notes or bonds are securities, the issue of which thereby 'securitise' the receivables which the originator has transferred to the SPV). The SPV then meets its repayment obligations under the notes using the income from the receivables which it has purchased (using the proceeds of the issue of the notes) from the originator (although such receivables may still be managed and collected by the originator on behalf of the SPV). The notes created by the SPV can be offered publicly[1] or 'privately placed' with institutional lenders[2] and will usually be listed on an exchange.

1 Although note the implications of a public issue of securities as described in at para C3.29 et seq.
2 In the sporting context, the notes issued in connection with the UK football club securitisations that have been implemented to date (by Newcastle United, Leeds United, Southampton, Ipswich Town, Leicester City and Everton) were all privately placed with institutional lenders. See further para C3.29 et seq.

C3.122 Reasons for Securitisation Securitisation is at first sight a similar concept to the factoring of debts, whereby receivables owed to an entity are sold to a third party in exchange for a discounted lump sum payment. However, securitisation is essentially different in that the lump sum payment is made by an SPV which is established purely for the purpose of the structure and for the benefit of the originator (although it may be legally structured to be 'orphaned' from the originator's group). Rather than the lump sum payment, the 'real' finance raising is achieved by the issue of the notes by the SPV, which enables the originator to access debt funding provided by financial institutions and/or the public which, for reasons described below, might not otherwise be prepared to lend to the originator. Such debt finance is also usually provided for longer terms and at more favourable fixed rates than lending that the originator could otherwise access. Consequently, as the debt finance is cheaper and can be repaid over a longer term, securitisation can be used to raise more substantial levels of funding for the originator than other debt structures. The fixed rate of return over a long term also means that inflation will work to the borrower's advantage if the value its revenue streams increase as a result of inflation throughout the life of the notes, whilst its debt service obligations will remain static.

C3.123 The reason that the SPV is able to issue notes to lenders that would otherwise not be prepared to lend to the originator lies in the isolation of the receivables which will be used to meet its repayment obligations under the notes. As stated above, by securing the repayment obligations under the notes on relatively certain income streams (ie receivables which are owed under contract) and preventing them from being used instead to pay other creditors of the borrower's business, the risk to the lender of default on the notes can be reduced to a level which is acceptable to institutional investors seeking low-risk investments. This separation of the SPV and the predictable income stream purchased by it from the remainder of the originator's business and its creditors mean the SPV is 'insolvency remote'. In a 'classic' securitisation structure, the receivables purchased by the SPV would have been owed to the originator under contracts then assigned to the SPV in a 'true sale' for value. As such, even if the originator subsequently became insolvent, the receivables would still flow into the SPV under the contracts assigned to it, provided that the originator's contractual obligations have been or are still performed (and such receivables are no longer part of the originator's assets to be liquidated to satisfy *its* creditors) and its repayment obligations under the notes would continue to be met from such receivables. (While traditional lending structures can provide for payment priorities through covenants and the provision of security, the lender would nevertheless ultimately have to rely on being able to enforce its rights against the originator along with other creditors in the event of the insolvency of the originator. This is avoided by moving the receivables which will service the debt into the insolvency remote SPV and beyond the reach of the originator's creditors).

C3.124 Such 'credit enhancement' (ie reducing the possibility of default by the borrower) is a fundamental characteristic of securitisation and means that the valuation of any security granted to the lender becomes secondary. This is because its attention is refocused away from whether, in the event of default, the lender will be able to recover its loan by realising the value of any such security. Instead, the value of security on default will be of secondary concern if the SPV's acquired income stream is regarded as being strong and stable enough to service its repayment obligations so that default becomes a remote possibility (and securitisations could be implemented without any security being granted if the quality of the securitised income stream makes the possibility of default sufficiently unlikely). This concentration on income stream values rather than fixed asset values allows companies which generate strong revenues using fixed assets with relatively low alternative use values to borrow more than they would otherwise be able to borrow against the value of such assets. In this way such borrowers can utilise their high value 'future' assets (ie its income streams) to raise finance[1].

1 In the sports sector the sums received recently by Southampton and Leicester City Football Clubs on the sale of their old stadia, for example, were £5m and £2.5m respectively, whereas they raised £25m and £28m in their respective securitisations.

C3.125 The SPV's 'insolvency remoteness' can be further enhanced by ensuring that:

(i) it undertakes no activities (which could lead to it incurring liabilities which might have to be satisfied in priority to the SPV's obligations to the noteholders) other than those necessary for the securitisation (eg few if any employees should be engaged by the SPV);
(ii) it covenants with the noteholders (or a security trustee acting on their behalf if there are a large number of them) that counterparties to any of its other contractual relationships (such as the originator) will be required to acknowledge that their debts and any security they have will be subordinated to any granted to the noteholders by the SPV, and that they will in no circumstances petition for the winding up of the SPV; and
(iii) there are appropriate restrictions on who may serve as its directors or be its shareholders.

C3.126 Further limitation of the risk of default on the notes can be provided by the grant of guarantees and security to the lender by other companies within the group structure, such as the originator or its parent, although this additional protection may not be necessary if the SPV is sufficiently insolvency remote and the securitised receivables are sufficiently strong to cover the SPV's repayment obligations. The likelihood of default can be further reduced by the lenders ensuring that their loans are 'over-collateralised'. This means that a significant margin is built in between the amount that will be required to service the loans and the anticipated value of the SPV's revenue stream, so that even if the income stream falls significantly it will still be sufficient to cover the payment obligations under the notes.

C3.127 By reducing the possibility of default on the loans made by the noteholders, the rate of interest payable on them should be lower than that which the originator could obtain if it borrowed similar amounts from other sources[1]. The lender's assessment of risk, and consequently the interest rate payable, may be further reduced (or the attractiveness of the notes to lenders enhanced) by obtaining a credit rating for the notes from a recognised rating agency, such as Fitch, Standard and Poors or Moody's[2]. (Reducing the cost of borrowing obviously increases the amount of funds that the SPV can borrow and channel to the originator).

1 For example, the interest reported to be payable by Ipswich Town on the £25m it raised from its securitisation was reported to be 8.29%.

2 In the sporting context, the £55m securitisation implemented by Newcastle United in 1999 was not rated, but various other means of credit enhancement, such as guarantees and security, were included. By contrast, the £30m securitisation by Everton Football Club implemented in 2002 was 'triple B' rated by Fitch.

C3.128 Another reason why institutional investors are far more likely to subscribe for the notes issued by the SPV than lend directly to the originator is that by reducing the risk of default credit enhancements make issuing long-term notes feasible, but with liquidity also provided to investors if the notes are listed. Such institutions, whilst ordinarily seeking long-term investments[1], need to maintain the flexibility to alter their investment portfolio by having the ability to easily dispose of the notes in the market.

1 Investors in UK football securitisations have tended to be UK and US pension providers as they seek to match their long-term obligations to provide pensions to long term fixed rate investments such as bonds.

C3.129 As well as enabling the originator to tap into debt funding from sources that, and possibly at lower rates than, would otherwise be unavailable, securitisation can also increase its overall capacity to raise finance. The debt raised by the issue of the notes will not appear as debt on the originator's balance sheet[1] because the notes are issued, and the debt to the noteholders is owed, by the SPV. Instead, the originator's balance sheet will show the receipt of the lump sum payment from the SPV in exchange for the receivables assigned to it. Consequently, the securitisation should not have a negative impact on the originator's gearing[2] which remains free to borrow further funds against its assets which have not been securitised, up to the limits on its gearing.

1 Provided that the SPV is an 'orphan' as described at para C3.122.
2 See para C3.83 et seq.

C3.130 Suitability of Securitisation to Sport At first glance, many sports entities would appear to be prime candidates for securitising their revenue streams, as the economic profile of many such entities is that they have revenues such as gate receipts (and particularly season ticket sales) which often display the 'classic' securitisable characteristics of being stable and high-value whilst being generated by the sports entity's tangible assets (the most valuable of which is likely to be its stadium)[1] which in isolation would give a lender little alternative use value if charged as security for traditional borrowing[2]. Inflation is likely to mean that gate receipts increase during the term of the fixed-rate notes issued, working to the borrower's advantage by increasing the revenue stream used to finance its debt service obligations, which are fixed at the outset of the borrowing.

1 For example, in football, even if a club chooses to show the 'value' of its players on its balance sheet, these 'assets' are not suitable as security for a lender as they would have difficulty in enforcing the security over (effectively the player's contract) by taking over the player's contract and selling his registration to another club. The *Bosman* ruling (meaning they can leave the club at the end of their contract without the club receiving a transfer fee) also means that the value of such 'assets' depreciates rapidly over the term of the contracts.
2 See para C3.92.

C3.131 However, a problem faced by sport in this context is that in most cases a sports entity's significant income streams will not be debts owed to it under contract and which can therefore be assigned to an SPV and then securitised. Taking football as an example again, the most significant contractually-obligated receivables that a club is likely to have are sponsorship revenues and (under quasi-contractual obligations of membership of the FA Premier League or Football League) its share of distribution of centrally sold media rights, and such contractually-obligated revenue streams have been securitised[1]. Equally, in motor racing, SLEC, the owner of a licence of the commercial rights to Formula One motor racing, securitised the revenues generated under contract by its exploitation of such commercial rights in 1999[2]. However, most other sports entities do not have significant (and therefore securitisable) broadcast, sponsorship or other contractually-obligated income. Also, even in sports where such income is significant, it may be sold centrally by the relevant governing body and each club's share in distributions of such income may fluctuate greatly according to its league position and other factors such as the number of times it appears on television. Similarly, sponsorship payments may also be dependent to some degree on sporting success which gives additional exposure (such as appearance in European competitions). Therefore, by far the most significant and predictable source of revenue for the vast majority of sports entities is ticket revenue received from people paying to enter their stadia. Even football clubs, the UK sports entities in receipt of the most significant broadcast and sponsorship revenues, still generate a significant proportion of their income at the gate[3]. Also, most supporters of sports entities tend to show admirable loyalty to their clubs even in difficult times (often more so in difficult times) so that such gate receipts display the stability and predictability that lenders will look for in a securitisation.

1 In July 2001, Leicester City raised £28m by securitising its league media payment distributions and other commercial revenues.

2 Such revenues were estimated at approximately US $240m per year at the time and were securitised in a $US 1.4 billion Eurobond issue.

3 Deloitte and Touche Sport's *2002 Annual Review of Football Finance* indicated that Premier League clubs' income from television (£348m) in the 2000/01 season exceeded their matchday income (£248m) for the first time. Nevertheless, three Premier League clubs securitised their ticket revenues during or immediately after that season. Deloittes' report for the 1999/2000 season shows that Football League clubs' matchday income (£123m) far exceeded their TV income (£35m). Even in the 2000/01 season, when they were in receipt of a £47m advance on the ITV Digital television deal, the total they received from television (£80m) was exceeded by matchday income (£155m).

C3.132 Consequently, a sports entity's gate receipts would appear to be its most suitable revenue source to securitise, were it not for the fact that such revenue is not a future 'stream' owed under contracts that can be assigned to an SPV, but is paid at the gate on matchday, or at best a the start of a season in the form of season ticket payments. However, notwithstanding the absence of assignable ticket debts, securitisation structures have been developed which allow such predictable and stable revenues to be securitised even though they are not owed under contracts that can be legally assigned to the SPV to back the notes which it issues. Anticipated (rather than contractually owed) revenues from a variety of sources can be securitised as long as the lenders are comfortable that they will nonetheless provide relatively secure and stable income to the SPV. This is particularly so if the revenues are of a similar nature to each other, but receivable from a variety of individual sources, so that cash flow is not overly dependant on one payer (again, many sporting entities' gate receipts satisfy these requirements). The basic structure of such 'future flow' securitisation is the same as the classic 'true sale' securitisation described above but is modified to deal with the non-assignability of anticipated revenues which are not owed under contracts. This is usually done by the isolation of the asset which gives the owner the right to receive the relevant revenue stream which is being securitised (ie the stadium which gives the owner to receive ticket income in exchange for allowing spectator's to enter its private land) rather than by the isolation of the revenue stream itself[1].

1 This structuring is described in more detail at para C3.158 et seq.

C3.133 In addition to the issue of assignability, as an anticipated revenue stream is, by its nature, less predictable than receivables owed under contract, the risk that it will not be sufficient to cover the SPV's obligations to the noteholders will consequently be greater. This may be particularly true of a sports entity which does not participate in a closed league, so that the club may be relegated and suffer a resultant decline in its gate receipts. Whilst lenders will recognise that the loyalty of some club's fans means that its gate receipts can be remarkably resilient in the event of relegation, certainly in the short term[1], many clubs do not have such a loyal fan-base and gate receipts can decrease very rapidly in a short period of time if it is relegated[2]. Even support for clubs with the most loyal of fans can wane during a sustained period without success which cannot be ruled out over the course of long-term lending[3]. Also, there are very few sports entities that are so successful that the effects of relegation can be ignored or given minor consideration[4]. Relegation can also effect other revenue streams such as sponsorship, league distributions[5] and other income generated by the sale of commercial rights (eg sponsorship contracts may include a provision reducing the amount paid to the club by the sponsor in the event of relegation).

1 For example, Manchester City Football Club's average attendance in the 1998/99 season, when they were playing in the Second Division of the Football League (ie the old Third Division) after two successive seasons ended in relegation, was over 28,000, 83% of its stadium capacity (Deloitte & Touche Sport's *Annual Review of Football Finance* (August 2000)).
2 For example, Wimbledon's average gate fell by over 50% after its relegation from the Premier League at the end of the 1999/2000 season (Deloitte & Touche Sport, see n 1).
3 The notes issued under most UK football club securitisations mature after 25 years.
4 For example, Blackburn Rovers were Premiership Champions in the 1994/95 season but relegated four seasons later.
5 Although in UK football, these reductions can be smoothed somewhat by 'parachute' payments made by the Premier League to clubs relegated from it.

C3.134 Consequently, the possibility of relegation can significantly hinder a sports entity seeking to securitise its gate receipts or any other of its revenue streams[1] and any securitisation that is implemented will undoubtedly include a level of over-collateralisation designed to cover this possibility. The additional credit enhancements described in the previous Section (such as security, parent or other guarantees) are also likely to be required. Further assurance that the noteholders will receive repayment can be given by the establishment of reserve accounts to ensure that the revenues that are received by the stadium-owning company are used to satisfy such obligations and not for other purposes. However, such credit enhancement may not be sufficient to reduce the risk to a level which is acceptable to institutional lenders being targeted, or to reduce the rate of return that they require to a level that justifies the expense of establishing the securitisation structure.

1 In most sports, in addition to a fall in the gate, income from other sources is also likely to decline after relegation. As mentioned in earlier, Leicester City raised £28m by securitising its media, sponsorship and league revenues in 2001, but were relegated at the end of the 2001/02 season. Although it is understood that the effects of a possible relegation on such revenues were factored into the transaction, and in particular in the level of over-collateralisation that was included, nevertheless (as a result at least in part of the effect that the reduction in distributions that will be received by the Football League's clubs as a result of the breakdown of its deal with ITV Digital in 2002) the SPV's ability to meet its obligations to the noteholders has been hindered to the extent that, notwithstanding a restructuring of the club's debt repayment obligations and efforts to cut the club's other outgoings (for example, by cutting players' salaries) the club applied to be placed into administration in October 2002.

(c) Securitisation: the Football Model

C3.135 As mentioned above, because football is the most commercially developed sport in the UK, with the most significant and, historically at least, the most stable revenue streams, securitisation in the UK sports sector has been used predominantly by football clubs. Consequently, the securitisations that have been implemented by football clubs represent current market practice as far as UK sports sector securitisations are concerned. The seven securitisations that were completed by FA Premier League clubs between December 1999 and September 2002 (being Newcastle United, Southampton, Leicester City, Ipswich Town, Leeds United, Everton and Manchester City) raised between £25m and £60m for each club and a total of £253m. Under the first, implemented by Newcastle United in 1999, the notes issued had a maturity of 17 years, but the notes issued under each subsequent scheme have had a 25-year term. The model used in these securitisations, and the adaptations to the traditional model described above which where included to take account of the peculiarities of football, are examined in more detail below.

C3.136 Football Revenue to be Securitised As described above, whilst the proportion of a Premier League football club's income that is provided by the sale of broadcast and other commercial rights under contractual arrangements is increasingly signficant, five of the six football club securitisations referred to in the preceding paragraph were 'future flow' securitisations of the club's ticket and corporate hospitality revenues as described above (Leicester was the exception as it instead securitised its media distributions from the league and other commercial income). The institutions purchasing the notes issued by each of these clubs therefore had to be convinced that it had a history of a loyal and sufficiently sizeable following and be relatively confident that sufficient numbers of the season tickets, executive boxes and matchday tickets would also be sold over the term of the notes, even in the event of relegation[1]. However, as will be seen from the description of the structure which is set out below, the stability of these clubs' gate receipts alone was not sufficient to secure lending from the institutions without further credit enhancement being provided.

1 In the 2000/01 season, four of these clubs had average attendances of between 97% and 99% of their stadium's capacity. Leicester's was 92% and doubts over the reliability of its gate receipts may have led it to securitise media and commercial revenues instead. By contrast, Newcastle United's securitisation in 1999 was completed despite the fact that it was in the relegation zone of the Premier League at the time (albeit early in the season). The investors' view of the robust nature of its ticket revenues was undoubtedly enhanced by the fact that the club enjoyed the only 100% attendance record in the Premier League in the previous season. Equally, a spokesman for Manchester City stated that, when presenting the proposal for its £30m securitisation of its ticket receipts to lenders (which could rise to £44m) 'the fact that [the club] had 28,000 fans in the Second Division was crucial'. However, the gate/hospitality securitisation was implemented by Everton whose average attendance was only 85% of the capacity of Goodison Park during that season, the second lowest average among the Premier League clubs, although both Ipswich and Southampton, with lower capacity stadia, had lower aggregate attendances. Nonetheless, a senior managing director of Bear Stearns (the arranging bank in the Everton securitisation) stated that: 'Even if [Everton] were relegated, supporters would be loyal and we expect the deal to go very well' (Attendance figures from the Deloitte and Touche Sport *Annual Review of Football Finance* for the relevant season).

C3.137 Structure of Football Securitisations Although, as stated above, some football clubs have securitised other assets or used the funds raised for other purposes, ticket securitisations undertaken to finance stadium relocation or redevelopment have been the most common form to date and we will therefore focus on that form. A relatively 'standard' structure has been used for these securitisations and the principal elements can be summarised as follows and are illustrated in figure [1] below:

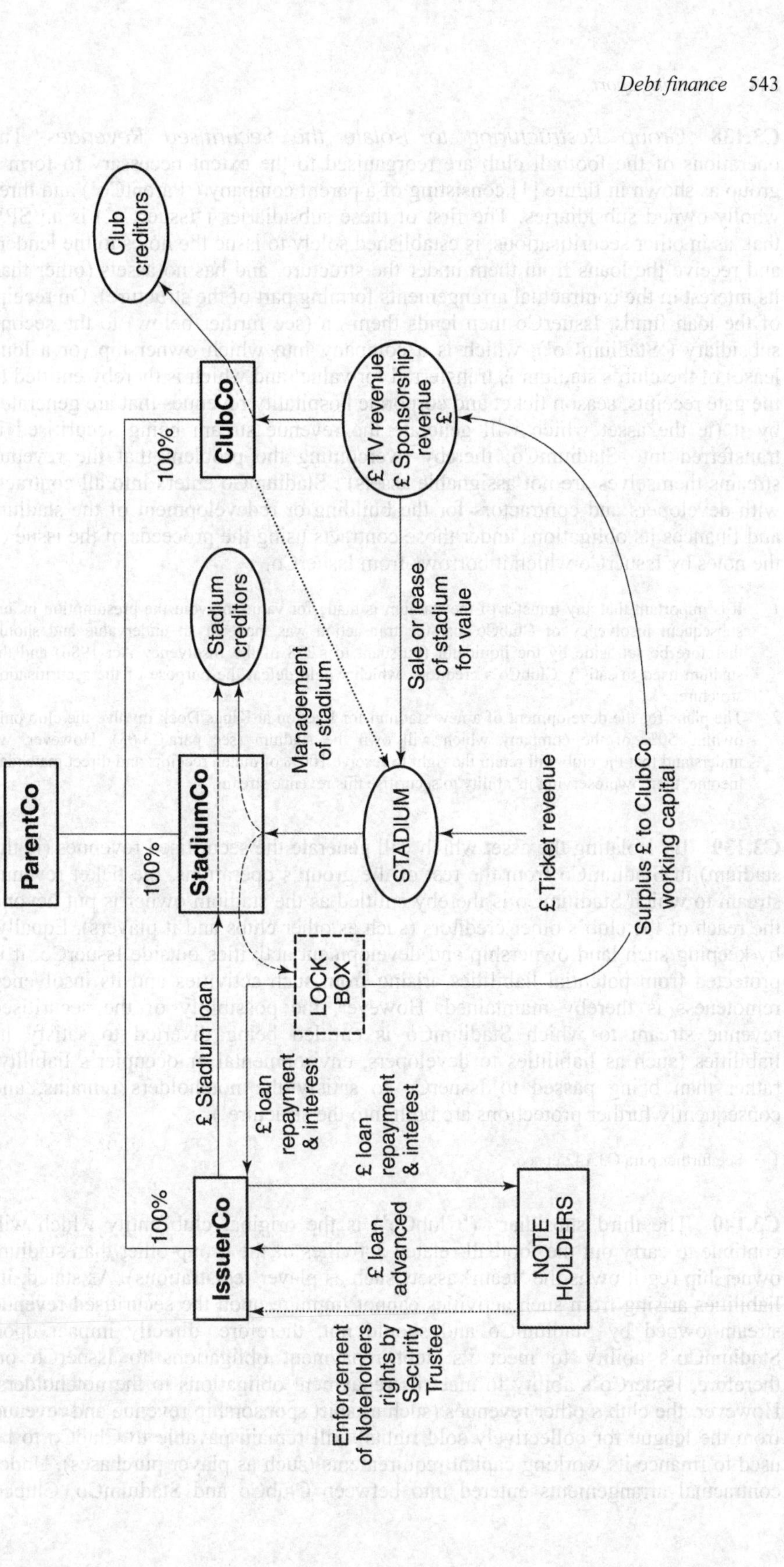
ParentCo
100%
IssuerCo
100%
StadiumCo
100%
ClubCo
Club creditors
Stadium creditors
£ Stadium loan
£ loan repayment & interest
LOCK BOX
Management of stadium
STADIUM
Sale or lease of stadium for value
£ TV revenue £ Sponsorship revenue £
£ Ticket revenue
Surplus £ to ClubCo working capital
£ loan repayment & interest
£ loan advanced
NOTE HOLDERS
Enforcement of Noteholders rights by Security Trustee

C3.138 *Group Restructuring to Isolate the Securitised Revenues* The operations of the football club are reorganised to the extent necessary to form a group as shown in figure [1] consisting of a parent company ('ParentCo') and three wholly-owned subsidiaries. The first of these subsidiaries ('IssuerCo') is an SPV that, as in other securitisations, is established solely to issue the notes to the lenders and receive the loans from them under the structure, and has no assets (other than its interest in the contractual arrangements forming part of the structure). On receipt of the loan funds, IssuerCo then lends them on (see further below) to the second subsidiary ('StadiumCo'), which is a company into which ownership (or a long lease) of the club's stadium is transferred for value[1] and which is thereby entitled to the gate receipts, season ticket and corporate hospitality revenues that are generated by it (ie the asset which will generate the revenue stream being securitised is transferred into StadiumCo, thereby overcoming the problem that the revenue streams themselves are not assignable assets)[2]. StadiumCo enters into all contracts with developers and contractors for the building or redevelopment of the stadium and finances its obligations under those contracts using the proceeds of the issue of the notes by IssuerCo which it borrows from IssuerCo.

1 It is important that any transfer of the stadium is made for value to avoid the presumption in any subsequent insolvency of ClubCo that the transaction was made at an undervalue and should therefore be set aside by the liquidator (pursuant to s 238 of the Insolvency Act 1986) and the stadium used to satisfy ClubCo's creditors, which would defeat the purpose of the securitisation structure.

2 The plans for the development of a new stadium for Everton at Kings Dock involve the club only owning 50% of the company which will own the stadium (see para C3.63). However, we understand that the club will retain the right to receive 100% of match receipts and direct matchday income, thereby preserving its ability to securitise this revenue stream.

C3.139 By isolating the asset which will generate the securitised revenues (ie the stadium) in StadiumCo from the rest of the group's operations, the ticket revenue stream to which StadiumCo is thereby entitled as the stadium owner is put beyond the reach of the club's other creditors (such as other clubs and it players). Equally, by keeping such land ownership and development activities outside IssuerCo, it is protected from potential liabilities arising from such activities and its insolvency remoteness is thereby maintained. However, the possibility of the securitised revenue stream to which StadiumCo is entitled being diverted to satisfy its liabilities (such as liabilities to developers, environmental or occupier's liability) rather than being passed to IssuerCo to satisfy the noteholders remains, and consequently further protections are built into the structure[1]).

1 See further para C3.142 et seq.

C3.140 The third subsidiary ('ClubCo') is the original club entity which will continue to carry out the football-related activities of the group other than stadium ownership (eg it owns the 'team' assets such as player registrations). As stated, its liabilities arising from such activities cannot impinge upon the securitised revenue stream owned by StadiumCo and should not, therefore, directly impact upon StadiumCo's ability to meet its debt repayment obligations to IssuerCo or, therefore, IssuerCo's ability to meet its repayment obligations to the noteholders. However, the club's other revenues (such as shirt sponsorship revenue and revenue from the league for collectively sold rights) will remain payable to ClubCo to be used to finance its working capital requirements (such as player purchases). Under contractual arrangements entered into between ClubCo and StadiumCo, Clubco will also manage the stadium for StadiumCo and carry out StadiumCo's obligations under the securitisation structure as manager or agent. This delegation of management activities by StadiumCo further reduces its susceptibility to incurring unexpected liabilities which could consume the securitised revenues before they can be paid to the SPV to satisfy the noteholders (as StadiumCo effectively does nothing other than own the stadium, receive the finance raised by IssuerCo from the issue of the notes by way of loan from IssuerCo and repay such loan from the proceeds of the securitised revenue streams to which it is entitled by virtue of its ownership of the stadium).

C3.141 *Funds Flow* The notes are issued by IssuerCo (ordinarily by way of private placement with institutions rather than an offer to the public)[1] to the noteholders and entitle them to a fixed rate of interest payable annually and repayment of principal over the life of the notes[2], which is usually 25 years. IssuerCo lends the aggregate amount raised from the noteholders to StadiumCo, often for use in developing the existing stadium or building a new one (the 'Stadium Loan'). The interest and principal payment obligations owed by StadiumCo to IssuerCo under the Stadium Loan mirror the aggregate obligations of IssuerCo to the noteholders, enabling IssuerCo to use the repayments of the Stadium Loan that it receives from StadiumCo to satisfy those obligations. StadiumCo uses the ticket revenues to which it is entitled as owner of the stadium (and which are collected on its behalf by ClubCo) to make repayments of the Stadium Loan to IssuerCo, and such ticket revenues are thereby 'securitised' as they provide the 'backing' for the securities (ie the notes).

1 All of the UK football securitisations have involved a private placement of the notes.

2 Some structures allow multiple drawdowns of the funds during the term of the notes, so that interest payments can be reduced by drawing down only when funds are required. However, investors do not favour this structure and may seek the ability to reset the interest rate during the term of the notes if this structure is used.

C3.142 *Credit Enhancement* In order to minimise the possibility that sufficient securitised funds do not flow from StadiumCo to IssuerCo to enable it to meet its obligations under the notes, ClubCo (which receives such revenues on behalf of StadiumCo) is required to pay them into a designated account (a 'lockbox' account) until sufficient sums are accrued in such account to cover the next payment of principal and interest under the Stadium Loan which is due to be made by StadiumCo to IssuerCo, plus a specified amount to be reserved in respect of future payments periods. The level of such 'debt service reserve' required to be maintained is commonly 50% of the following 12 months' payments of principal and interest under the Stadium Loan (although requirements can be higher if certain conditions are not fulfilled). Any further ticket revenue received by ClubCo on behalf of StadiumCo after the lockbox account has been filled[1] in any period can be used by StadiumCo as it wishes (eg to pay for further stadium development or to pass to ClubCo to supplement its non-securitised income, such as television and player transfer income, to meet its working capital requirements for transfer fees, wages etc, allowing the club to utilise any surplus of such funds which is not required to service the debt to be used to meet its operating costs). This is particularly important to the borrowing group if the securitisation builds in a large element of 'over-collateralisation' whereby the revenues which are securitised are anticipated to be far in excess of what will actually be required to service the debt under the notes[2], as it will not want such excess amounts of revenue tied up in the securitisation structure unnecessarily. However, it should be noted that, although ClubCo covenants to pay the requisite amounts into the lockbox account and StadiumCo covenants not to use those funds other than to make payments on the Stadium Loan, the sums in such lockbox account will nevertheless constitute funds of StadiumCo rather than IssuerCo until they are paid by StadiumCo from the lockbox account to IssuerCo on the relevant payment date under the Stadium Loan, and are therefore not put beyond the reach of StadiumCo's creditors (such as developers) until such payment is made. Consequently, the risk of default by StadiumCo (and consequently IssuerCo) remains, and further credit enhancements are included in the structure as described below.

1 If the club's ticket revenues are weighted towards season tickets (such that the revenues generated by season ticket sales alone is likely to be sufficient to cover the season's payments under the notes) such lockbox account is likely to be filled a short time after season ticket prices are announced and season ticket renewal payments are received by ClubCo.

2 UK football securitisations have generally worked on a debt coverage:service ratio of 3:1, meaning that the annual income that the securitised revenue streams are expected to generate should be at least three times the annual debt service obligations under the notes annually. Using a simple example, if the securitised revenue streams are projected to generate £15m per year and the interest plus capital repayment on the notes will be 10% annually, the maximum debt that can be serviced per year is £15m/3 = £5m. Consequently £50m can be borrowed by issuing notes backed by those revenue streams at the total service rate of 10%.

C3.143 In addition to the lockbox mechanism, a series of charges are granted to give the noteholders further assurance that IssuerCo's repayment obligations under the notes will be met. Charges are granted by IssuerCo over its assets (essentially its right to receive the payments of principal and interest from StadiumCo under the Stadium Loan). StadiumCo's payment obligations to IssuerCo under the Stadium Loan are secured by charges over the stadium[1], as is its interest in the agreements to which it is party under the securitisation structure in favour of IssuerCo. ClubCo also often provides IssuerCo with an unsecured guarantee of StadiumCo's obligations under the Stadium Loan (although as its guarantee is unsecured, ClubCo remains able to grant higher ranking security to other parties in order, for example, to raise working capital such as player acquisition finance). The unsecured guarantee by ClubCo of StadiumCo's obligations to IssuerCo is itself the subject of a guarantee from ParentCo which can be called on if both StadiumCo and ClubCo default in their obligations to IssuerCo,which is secured by both a fixed charge over ParentCo's shares in StadiumCo and a floating charge over the assets of ParentCo. All such security granted to IssuerCo is assigned to the noteholders (or held on trust for them by the security trustee if they are numerous[2]) ultimately giving them the ability to enforce the security against the group companies (including ParentCo whose assets comprise 100% of the shares in IssuerCo, StadiumCo and ClubCo and so ultimately include the assets of those companies, such as the stadium and the playing assets) in the event of default under the notes. However, although the fixed charge over its shares in StadiumCo can be enforced to give IssuerCo control of the stadium and the income it generates in the event of default under the notes, the floating charge over ParentCo's other assets, including its shares in ClubCo is 'lightweight' and so can only be enforced if steps are taken to liquidate ParentCo.

1 If the funds are financing the building of a new stadium, it should be owned by StadiumCo and should replace the old stadium as security once the team starts playing there.

2 This will be the case if the notes are issued publicly.

C3.144 Further enhancement of credit is provided by the group companies giving the noteholders (or the security trustee on their behalf) various assurances relating to the group and the securitised assets. These include:

(i) representations and warranties, such as the absence of default under material contracts by members of the borrowing group and the absence of environmental issues relating to the stadium;
(ii) positive covenants, such as to maintain approvals, insurance etc relating to the stadium;
(iii) negative covenants, such as restrictions on the creation of encumbrances over assets of the group (other than permitted encumbrances such as encumbrances required by providers of working capital to the group which are subordinated to the noteholders' security), restrictions on the sale of the stadium or the moving of the team to another stadium (other than if a new stadium is built during the life of the notes, in which case it will replace the old stadium in the structure), restrictions on disposals, issues or redemptions of shares in any of the group companies, restrictions on selling other assets and restrictions on reducing ticket prices; and
(iv) limits on other indebtedness that can be incurred by StadiumCo and ClubCo.

Whilst restrictions relating directly to ticketing and StadiumCo are clearly required to ensure that the securitised ticket revenue stream remains sufficient to fund the payment obligations over the life of the notes, restrictions aimed at ensuring ClubCo does not incur excessive debt[1] which could lead to *its* insolvency are also necessary to ensure that the team continues playing at the stadium, as the securitised revenue streams will disappear if there is no ClubCo team to play at the stadium. However, what the structure cannot ensure is that poor management of the club will not lead to a lack of sporting success and a consequent decline in gate receipts, particularly in the event of relegation. The only real protection for the lenders against this eventuality is the over-collateralisation of the loans to build in a sufficient margin to allow for such decline in the securitised revenues[2].

1 The 'other' debt of the group (excluding loans under the notes) is understood to be generally limited to under 50% of the group's other income (ie its non-securitised income).
2 See further paras C3.148 to C3.150.

C3.145 Whilst the enhancements that have been incorporated in UK football securitisations to date have not completely negated the advantages of securitisation for the relevant clubs, other clubs or sports with less robust revenue streams may find this to be the case. Also, notwithstanding the credit enhancements included in the 'standard' UK football securitisation model, some have nevertheless failed to gain a rating from the rating agencies[1].

1 However, as US institutions will not subscribe for unrated notes, two of the UK football securitisations were privately rated 'BBB' by Fitch.

C3.146 *Alternative Use of Funds* The majority of UK football ticket securitisations have been used to finance stadium building or redevelopment. This is 'neat' presentationally as nowadays stadium development should result in an increase in the club's gate capacity[1], thereby enhancing the revenue stream that is being securitised, completing a somewhat virtuous circle. However, it is not necessary for the finance raised by ticket securitisations to be used for stadium finance, provided that the lenders are comfortable that the securitised ticket revenue will nevertheless be sufficient to meet the SPV's payment obligations under the notes. For example, the £60m raised by the 2001 securitisation of Leeds United's ticket and corporate hospitality revenue were to be used to repay existing debt and for working capital such as player purchases rather than being spent on its stadium[2]. The lenders must therefore have been convinced that the club's existing ticket revenues were sufficient to cover the SPV's payment obligations and that the funds raised did not need to be spent on the stadium to enhance its ability to generate such revenues. It should be remembered that player acquisitions are intended to improve the performance of the team on the field, which should in turn increase gate revenues, even if average attendances are at or close to capacity, by increasing the number of European and domestic cup games played at the stadium.

1 Stadium improvements made after football stadium tragedies in the 1980s focused on safety and invariably reduced rather than increased capacities, but such improvements have now been completed.

2 Funds raised by the most recent securitisation, implemented by Everton, will be used to develop the club's training facilities, develop its youth academy and purchase players.

C3.147 However, if securitisation proceeds are used to finance a club's working capital requirements rather than stadium development, the restrictions on further borrowing which the club will be required to accept as a condition of the securitisation may make it difficult for it to subsequently raise further finance for significant stadium development during the life of the notes, unless its other unencumbered sources of revenue are sufficient to raise such finance. This may be possible for clubs such as Leeds whose other revenue streams are almost as significant as its gate receipts, but this will not be the case for an entity that does not have another comparable source of revenue. Consequently, football securitisations have tended to utilise gate revenue to finance ground development (thereby enabling clubs to access long-term loans to finance a long-term asset, namely the stadium), leaving the club's less significant revenue streams and any surplus of the securitised revenues which are not needed to finance the loan repayments to finance its working capital requirements, such as player acquisition and salary costs.

C3.148 Testing the Football Model As the model described above has now been used and refined in a number of such transactions, the costs involved in setting up and documenting further football club securitisations should be significantly less than they were in relation to the first UK football securitisation implemented in 1999. The investors who purchase the notes are also becoming more familiar and comfortable with such securitisations of gate receipts and other revenue streams. Such reduced costs and market familiarity may mean that smaller clubs are now able to raise finance through securitisation, provided that the model does not have to be significantly altered to take account of the vagaries of their revenue streams and finance requirements. However, at the time of writing it is interesting to note that two of the clubs that have implemented securitisations, Leicester City and Ipswich Town, were relegated at the end of the 2001/02 season. This will test the securitisation structure and in particular whether adequate credit enhancement and other protections have been built into the securitisation structures to cope with any reduction in the securitised revenues (gate receipts in Ipswich Town's case and league and other commercial revenue in Leicester City's) that these teams suffer as a result.[1] If this proves not to be the case, revisions to the model are likely to be made in any subsequent UK football securitisations.

1 In the case of Leicester City, events have shown that the level of lender protection built into the securitisation structure has not been sufficient to protect its noteholders as, after its relegation from the Premier League at the end of the 2001/02 season, the club first sought to restructure its loan repayments to noteholders and then, in October 2002, applied to the High Court to be placed into administration (a process by which the court appoints a qualified insolvency practitioner to run a company during a moratorium period during which its creditors cannot enforce their rights against it, in order to protect the company against precipitative enforcement action by creditors, with a view to ensuring its survival (perhaps by agreeing an arrangement with such creditors), or at least maximising the assets that will be distributed to its creditors in the event of its liquidation). However, the situation faced by Leicester is probably an extreme one which would not necessarily be faced by other clubs which are relegated after implementing a securitisation (as has been demonstrated, to date, by the fact that Ipswich Town have not experienced such extreme difficulties). This is because, unlike most other securitisations that have been implemented in UK football, Leicester securitised its television and other media income, rather than its gate receipts. As has been well-publicised, the breakdown of the Football League's TV deal with ITV Digital, just as Leicester City were relegated, and its replacement by a much less lucrative deal with BSkyB, has meant that the 'baseline' figures that would have been built into the securitisation structure to allow for the contingency of relegation were too high, being based on the anticipated ITV Digital revenues, meaning that the club was unable to meet its debt repayment obligations from its much reduced securitised revenues (even allowing for the 'parachute' payments that clubs receive from the Premier League in the first three seasons after relegation).

C3.149 In addition to testing the securitisation model from the lenders' point of view, the relegation of Ipswich and Leicester may also demonstrate the effect of securitisation on each club's ability to regain its position in the top flight. As discussed above, lack of sporting success in any 'open' league which operates a promotion and relegation system can be a downward spiral and this has been proven to be the case in football[1]. A club's revenue can fall dramatically in the season after it is relegated, particularly from the Premier League (even though this effect may be cushioned by 'parachute' payments that the club receives in the seasons following relegation)[2]. Whilst attendances may be maintained at least in the short term (particularly if the club, playing against weaker opposition, enjoys more success on the field than it did in the previous relegation season), sponsorship, broadcast and other commercial revenues are likely to decrease immediately. A relegated club is therefore usually faced with the dilemma of whether to gamble financially by maintaining its level of costs (such as player wages) and/or spending on new players in search of a swift return to the division from which it has been relegated, or to begin cutting its cloth according to its reduced means immediately by reducing its costs, probably by eschewing big signings and allowing highly-paid players to leave thereby increasing the likelihood of a continued lack of success and reduction in revenues[3]. If a club has entered into a ticket securitisation structure, its gate receipts must still be used after relegation to fill its 'lockbox' account before any additional gate revenues can be diverted to fund other spending. The fact that this filling of the lockbox account usually takes place after the announcement of season ticket prices for the following season, which is likely to take place in the summer after a relegation season, and will swallow the first portion of such funds received, may make it very difficult for a relegated club to sign players or offer existing players new contracts at a time when much transfer activity and player contract renegotiation is conducted (particularly if the club is uncertain as to how far relegation will reduce the value of the gate revenue which will become available to it after the lockbox is filled). Therefore, unless its revenues remain sufficiently strong, and particularly if the notes are insufficiently overcollateralised so that too much has been borrowed and there is little securitised revenue left after it is serviced, the consequent reduction in the club's ability to spend money to improve its chances of sporting success may consign it to further seasons in the lower divisions. Such continued lack of success is likely to further reduce the club's revenues (and is more likely to have an impact on attendances) and therefore its ability to spend its way back to the top, unless it can secure significant further finance from other sources. However, the covenants given by the club group in the securitisation will usually make this difficult, as the football model usually requires the club to accept restrictions on further borrowings and on raising equity finance without the consent of the noteholders or security trustee. In this way, the aspects of securitisations that are intended to reduce the likelihood of default under the notes could eventually have the opposite effect if the restrictions on the club's ability to spend in the short-term cause sustained failure on the field and a consequent decline in its revenues. In circumstances where such a downward spiral seems possible, it remains to be seen whether the noteholders or trustee would consider whether a short-term relaxation of these restrictions would be beneficial to them in the long-term[4].

1 Both Bristol City and Wolverhampton Wanderers suffered three successive relegation seasons in the eighties, taking them from the top division to the bottom division of the Football League. Neither has since regained its top-flight status.

2 Such parachute payments amounted to just over £3m per club in 2000/01 season. Even so, the 'cost' of revenue in terms of loss of income to clubs relegated from the Premier League at the end of that season was estimated to be £5m to £7m (see para C3.4, n 6).

3 If the club has implemented the securitisation in order to finance the stadium development which has commenced prior to relegation, it is unlikely to be able to reduce the ongoing costs of completing the project to any significant degree. Therefore, pressure on it to reduce costs by reducing the quality of its playing staff will be even greater. This is the situation that Leicester City faced after its relegation in the 2001/02 season shortly before the completion of its new stadium in the summer of 2002. However, somewhat paradoxically, at the time of writing, despite its players agreeing to a reduction in their wages (albeit with the possibility of them being supplemented by bonuses payable upon promotion) and the sale of some players, Leicester sat close to the top of the Division 1 table whereas Ipswich, which is not facing such financial pressures, sit much closer to the bottom.

4 It is understood that the institutional holder of the notes issued by Leicester City was amenable to some form of restructuring of its repayments, but that this was not sufficient to enable the club to avoid administration (see para C3.148).

C3.150 One final point worth reiterating in relation to securitisations, and particularly the protections that are built into the structure to try to ensure that sufficient revenues generated by the group's operations are isolated and passed to IssueCo to enable it to meet its obligations to the lenders, rather than being used to meet the club's other financial commitments, is that if such protections lead to the demise of the club itself they are likely to prove relatively worthless to the noteholders. This could be the case if such protections result in ClubCo being so starved of funds that even cost-cutting measures as described above[1] do not enable it to pay its own creditors (ie creditors other than the noteholders). In such circumstances, the club risks insolvency and winding-up, in which event the noteholders' rights over the revenue received by StadiumCo will be worthless if there is no longer a team playing at the stadium. The noteholders will at that point probably only have meaningful recourse to the stadium itself as an asset over which it has a charge[2], but the sale of the stadium is unlikely to cover the value of the loans made under the securitisation structure (for the reasons set out at para C3.92).

1 See para C3.149.

2 See para C3.143.

(d) Securitisation in Other Sports

C3.151 Entities in other sports may also be able to securitise revenue streams using an adaptation of the model described above. However, the challenges that they face are likely to be even greater than those faced by football clubs[1]. If their gate receipts or other income streams cannot match those of football clubs in terms of size such revenue streams will naturally generate a lower level of finance whereas structuring costs are unlikely to be proportionally reduced. Equally, if the reliability of a sports entity's revenue streams are not of the quality of a football club's (eg it may not have such a loyal or established fan base or significant other commercial income) noteholders are likely to require greater credit enhancements to protect themselves against default caused by a significant reduction in the securitised revenue streams (eg as a result of relegation or a rise in the popularity of a competing club or sport) than the enhancements that have been included in football club securitisations to date. For some entities this will mean that the advantages of securitisation over other methods of finance are eliminated.

1 This will be even more so if any of the football club securitisations that have been implemented end in default by the borrowing club.

C3.152 However, one way in which such smaller sports entities may be able to take advantage of securitisation would be by making use of conduit vehicles. These have been used in other industry sectors as a means of achieving securitisation for businesses whose individual revenue streams are not sufficiently strong or sizeable to justify securitisation by themselves, but which can be pooled with similar revenue streams of other businesses to back notes issued by a 'multi-seller' SPV, normally established by a bank. In this way, transaction costs are reduced and the finance raised can be utilised as a facility which the multiple originators can draw down from the SPV. Particularly given the likelihood that an entity operating in a particular sport will have income streams which are of a similar nature to other entities competing in the same sport or similar sports, conduit securitisations could be a valuable source of finance for smaller sports entities. Similarly, certain sports may involve the collective selling of club rights by the sport's governing body which then distributes the proceeds to the clubs, but which individual distributions are too small to be securitised. Such governing bodies could instead securitise the revenues it receives as a result of such collective selling and then distribute the proceeds of the securitisation back down to its member clubs.

C Other forms of debt financing structures

C3.153 Two other ways in which sports entities can finance their activities other than by attracting shareholder investment are worth mentioning briefly.

C3.154 Firstly, there has been a move in some countries for sports facilities to be financed along the same lines as public sector projects using structures similar to the PFI or DBFO schemes described above[1]. However, rather than funding projects through a combination of public and private investment, these stadium development schemes essentially involve the sports entity and the construction company (and perhaps its sub-contractors and some outside investors) investing in a special purpose vehicle company ('SPV') specially established for the purpose. The SPV is responsible for the design, build, finance and operation of the new stadium (which it will then sub-contract to third parties). Whilst the SPV receives some of the required funding[2] from these parties by way of equity investment, most of the project costs are borrowed by the SPV which will service the debt using income from the stadium, which the SPV will either lease long-term from the sports entity or own and transfer to the sports entity at the end of the DBFO period (which will be long enough to repay the debt and give the investors a return. However, unlike securitisation, because ownership and control of the stadium will rest with the SPV which is not wholly-owned by the sporting entity (unlike StadiumCo in the securitisation model described above) building stadia under DBFO schemes requires UK sporting entities to move away from the premise that they must own their stadium (an emphasis which is not as strong in other European countries) towards simply leasing them. However, this perceived abdication of control can meet with resistance from those in charge of, and supporters of, sports entities.

1 See para C3.29 et seq.
2 Often as little as 10%.

C3.155 Another alternative method of raising non-equity finance for sports entities which is becoming more prevalent, particularly in football, is sale and leaseback arrangements. This structure has been used to spread the cost of acquiring players over the term of their contracts, which might not otherwise be possible under league rules[1] or acceptable to the selling club. It essentially involves the sale by a club of a new player (ie the player registration it has just acquired) to a finance company for a sum equal to the transfer fee paid for the player by the club. The finance company then leases the player back to the club in return for regular payments spread over the term of the player's contract which will, in aggregate, repay to the finance company the sum paid to the club together with a commercial return. Alternatively, the club can enter into sale and lease back arrangements in relation to the registrations of its existing players in order to raise funds for other purposes. The cost of raising funds is this way is usually marginally higher than other methods because, as the player is 'owned' by the finance company, it bears more of the risk of this 'asset' losing its value than it would by simply making loans to the club which are secured on the asset but can be funded from other sources (consequently the finance company usually to protect its asset using insurance). However, as the club is not borrowing money but making leasing payments, and the player's registration is not an asset of the club over which the finance company takes security, the arrangements have the advantage that they should not fall foul of any negative covenants that the club has given not to make further borrowings or give further security.

1 Rule M.28 of the Rules of the FA Premier League provide that at least 50% of any transfer fee payable by one Premier League club to another must be paid immediately, and any balance within one year. By contrast, the Football League's Regulation 44.2.1 simply requires 'a percentage' of the fee to be paid immediately and any remainder within the period of the player's contract with his new club.

Query, however, whether sale and leaseback arrangements that involve an actual transfer of the player registration comply with the applicable league rules on clubs holding player registrations. See para C3.156, n 1.

C3.156 If the club wishes to transfer the player, it will have to reacquire the player registration from the financier by paying off the remainder of the sums owed under the leaseback arrangements. However, it is yet to be seen how easily a finance company can realise its asset (ie the player registration) by organising a transfer of the player from it (rather than the borrowing club) to a new club in the event of default[1].

1 These schemes are in their infancy, and it is not clear to the authors how they are operated within the FA Premier League Rules and the Regulations of the Football League which envisage only the holding and transfer of player registrations by and between football clubs. However, at the time of writing, this issue may soon be tested if the creditors of clubs which are subject to insolvency procedures owe sums to finance companies under such player sale and leaseback arrangements.

C3.157 Sale and leasebacks of clubs' stadia have also been explored as a means of raising substantial finance for them (sometimes in preparation for the club to move to a new stadium and the redevelopment of the old one by the new owner after it has been vacated by the club). However, as with DBFO schemes, this requires the clubs to recognise that ownership of their ground is not essential (particularly if the arrangement is only intended as a short-term measure).

7 EQUITY FINANCE

A Types of equity, characteristics and securing investment

C3.158 As discussed above[1], for the reasons identified earlier[2], many sports entities may prefer to raise equity rather than debt finance or may need to do so because the debt finance that it is able to raise is insufficient to meet its financing requirements. Whilst having essentially different characteristics to debt, an incorporated sports entity can adapt the structure of its share capital, as it can structure its debt, in order to attract equity investment and suit its own needs[3]. Different classes of shares can be created carrying different rights, allowing the sports entity to attract investment by creating particular classes of shares which match the requirements of particular potential shareholders in terms of the return they are seeking and the level of risk they are prepared to accept. At the same time, by tailoring the rights that it gives to its shareholders appropriately, a sports entity can ensure that its obligations to its shareholders are not overly burdensome when aggregated with its other obligations. The degree of control over the sports entity given over to new investors generally or on specific matters can also be limited.

1 See para C3.79 et seq.
2 See para C3.29 et seq.
3 The term 'equity' or 'risk' capital it is often used to refer only to ordinary shares carrying basic rights relating to voting, dividends and distributions of capital rather than shares with enhanced rights. However, in this Chapter the term 'equity' is used to describe shares of any class.

C3.159 The combinations of rights that a company can attach to its shares are virtually unlimited. However, each variation will essentially involve either improving (or, less commonly, reducing) the rights of the holders of a particular class of shares relative to the rights of holders of the company's basic ordinary shares in one or more of the following respects:

(i) sharing in the profits of the company that the company distributes by way of dividend;
(ii) exercising influence over the company by voting in meetings of the company; and
(iii) having its investment returned to it, perhaps together with a share of any surplus assets of the company that remain after its creditors are paid off, in the event that the company is wound-up.

C3.160 An entitlement to receive a share of the profits that the company is able to distribute, and/or to capital returned in a winding up, in preference to the holders of other classes of shares obviously reduces the risk that an investor in such shares will not recoup his investment together with the anticipated return. Consequently, such shares (known as 'preference shares') may attract investment from less speculative investors who may regard an investment in ordinary shares as being too risky. However, the *quid pro quo* for such limitation of risk is usually a limitation of the investor's potential 'upside' as such shareholders' priority entitlement to distributions of profit and capital is often capped at a fixed amount so that they do not participate in any distributions of profit or capital that the company makes which exceed their 'fixed' entitlement. Preference shares also normally carry limited or no voting rights, which may appeal to a sports entity whose existing shareholders are looking to raise equity funding without ceding control over the sports entity to new investors (although this will come at the price of being entitled to share in the profits of the entity only after the new investors' entitlement has been satisfied in full)[1].

1 However, 'participating preference shares' can be issued which entitle the holders to participate in distributions in excess of their 'fixed' entitlement and/or exercise voting rights. Such 'uncapping' of entitlements may, however, have implications under company law (such as on the ability of the company to issue such shares without first offering them to its existing shareholders). Such implications are beyond the scope of this chapter. Please refer to *Tolley's Company Law* (Tolley).

C3.161 Other enhancements of the rights attaching to preference shares can be used to make them more attractive to certain investors. For example, they can be convertible into ordinary shares at the option of the holder (often at a specified time or upon a specified event), giving the investor the opportunity to benefit from an increase in the capital value of the company's ordinary shares which may not accrue on the preference shares (for example, because they do not carry voting rights which often command a premium, particularly in the event of a takeover bid). Alternatively, the company may issue preference shares which are redeemable by it at the shareholder's option, giving them an ability to recoup their investment in circumstances other than when they are able to sell the shares or in a winding-up (in which circumstance they may not recoup their investment in full)[1].

1 Although the provisions of company law mean that it may not be possible for the company to redeem shares at a particular time, particularly if they are to be redeemed for more than their nominal value. See Summer 'Redeemable Shares' in *Tolley's Company Law* (Tolley) for a further explanation of the restrictions on redemption of shares.

C3.162 The rights attaching to shares can also be designed to suit the needs of the issuing company (in addition to its need for finance). For example, if preference shares are redeemable at the option of the company or convert automatically on a particular date, this can give its existing shareholders assurance that their rights to a share of its distributed profits will only be subordinated to those of the new preferred shareholders for a limited time. A redemption option exercisable by the company also gives it flexibility to repay the capital provided by the investor, in the same way that it could pay off the principal amount outstanding on a loan, if it found itself no longer in need of the funds (thereby increasing its gearing without increasing borrowings) or if it is able to obtain funding on terms, or from a source, more suitable to it at that time.

C3.163 The adaptation of the rights attaching to preference shares can make them somewhat of a hybrid between 'pure' equity and debt, thereby attracting investors seeking certain advantages of each. The fixed rate of return potentially payable on preference shares is similar to interest (although it will not be payable if the company is not sufficiently profitable) and the absence (or limitation to particular issues) of preference shareholders' right to vote gives them a similarly limited degree of control over the running of company to that of a lender. However, additional rights attaching to preference shares when compared with debt (such as convertibility[1]) means that they will often carry a lower dividend than the rate of interest that the company would have to pay on a similar amount of borrowing. Also, as they do not actually constitute debt, they can be attractive to companies who might otherwise prefer to raise debt financing but are restricted from doing so by limitations on their power to borrow or their gearing ratios[2].

1 Although debt may also be convertible: see para C3.102.
2 See para C3.81 et seq.

C3.164 Sports entities have adopted such creativity in structuring their share capital in order to attract equity investment, sometimes in multiple rounds. For example, in January 1995 Celtic plc (the parent company of the football club) made a public issue of ordinary shares and convertible preference shares of 60p each (carrying a 6% dividend and convertible into ordinary and deferred shares from June 2001), raising approximately £10m, with the vast majority of these being subscribed for by its fans[1]. However, despite the tendency of 'emotional' investors (ie fans) to be satisfied with acquiring a small stake and voice in their club and therefore not being valuable as a source of further investment for the club after they have acquired an initial shareholding, when Celtic sought further equity funding from existing shareholders, season ticket holders and new investors in 2001, a significant proportion of the 90% takeup of the offer was from supporters[2]. 18.5m 'convertible preferred ordinary shares' of £1 each were issued at a subscription price of £1.25, raising approximately £22.5m for the club. Such shares carried an initial dividend of 4%, but with the prospect that this could rise to 10% depending on the team's progress in the UEFA Champions' League (and it was anticipated that the proceeds of the offer would be used primarily for team strengthening, although they did help to reduce net debt from just under £30m in June 2001 to under £12m at the end of 2001[3]). Therefore, whilst inherently appealing to 'emotional' investors like any other football club share offering, such appeal was enhanced by linking the financial return to investors directly to the successful application of their investments to achieve success on the pitch[4]. Also, the share offering served further purposes as this linking between financial returns and sporting success meant that the interests of supporters and investors were aligned more closely, helping to dispel the notion that the club could not serve these two 'masters' simultaneously. (Also, the issue was viewed as further incentivising the man seen as largely responsible for on-field success, the manager Martin O'Neill, to stay at the club as he acquired £2m worth of the shares in the issue[5]).

1 See Morrow 'If You Know The History – A Study of Celtic' (Department of Sports Studies, University of Stirling), published in Singer & Friedlander's *Football Review, 1999/00 Season*.
2 Approximately £5.5m, with the bulk of the remainder being invested by existing shareholders with significant holdings.
3 See Celtic plc Interim Report 2001.
4 Also, subscribers' initial capital investment of £1.25 per share was protected in the conversion into ordinary shares to take place automatically in 2007, as the conversion price was fixed at £1.25 in the event that the market price of those shares at that time is at or above that level (giving the investors the opportunity to realise a capital gain at that point), but will otherwise be equal to the market price of the ordinary shares if it is below £1.25 at that time to give holders of the shares an equivalent value of ordinary shares upon conversion.
5 At the time of writing, despite interest from other clubs, Mr O'Neill has remained at Celtic.

C3.165 Other sports entities can similarly structure equity offerings creatively to appeal to the particular groups from whom they are seeking investment whilst also suiting their own particular requirements. However, the ability of a sports entity to bring in equity investment simply by being creative with its share capital should not be overestimated. Ordinary shares carrying basic dividend and voting rights will still be the basic building block of any incorporated sports entity's share capital, and the majority of the shares issued by most sports entities when raising equity funding have been ordinary shares. Whilst enhanced rights are attractive to investors, the overriding consideration for potential 'financial' (rather than 'emotional') investors when making a decision as to whether to invest in a sports entity will be whether its business is likely to be sufficiently successful to generate the financial returns that they are hoping to receive as a result of such investment. Being at the front of the queue for distributions made by a sports entity is of little value if it does not generate any profit to distribute[1].

1 Similarly, capital gains in the value of the shares in a company will generally only accrue (certainly in the long-term) if it generates profit to distribute to its shareholders.

C3.166 It should not be assumed that any new funding that a sports entity requires cannot be provided entirely by its existing shareholders subscribing for the requisite amount of further shares. However, if they are unable or unwilling to provide such funding, the raising of funding from new equity investors will necessarily entail the dilution of the influence of current shareholders over the company and their share of any distributions which it makes. Clearly, they will only accept such dilution of their rights if they think that the benefits to the company (and thereby to their, albeit diluted, shareholding) of receiving such further funding will outweigh such dilutive effects. Company law requirements ensure that such a dilutive issuance to third parties cannot occur unless the existing shareholders have approved it or been given the opportunity to prevent it by acquiring the new shares themselves. (In general terms, a simple majority of its existing shareholders' votes is required if a company is to create new shares of an existing class and authorise its directors to allot them[1]. If a new class of shares is to be created, the necessary amendment to the company's articles of association will require the approval of 75% of the shareholders' votes[2]. Such 75% majority will also be required for a company to issue any shares directly to a party other than its existing shareholders without first offering such shares to them in proportion to their existing shareholdings on the same or better terms as those offered to the incoming investor[3].) However, as discussed below, as the financial demands of participating in sport have increased, it is increasingly common for existing shareholders to seek to fund such demands by attracting equity investment from 'outsiders' rather than increasing their own financial commitment. Consequently, existing shareholders in sport have increasingly welcomed 'incoming' equity investment.

1 Companies Act 1985, ss 121 and 80.
2 Companies Act 1985, s9.
3 Companies Act 1985, ss 89 and 95.

B Shareholding models in commercial sport

C3.167 For a long time, the majority of sports entities which incorporated as companies limited by shares did so to take advantage of the benefits of limited liability[1], rather than as a means of raising finance. Consequently, this historical 'model' of shareholding in sport involves a limited number of individual founders of a sports entity, usually having a very strong emotional attachment to the sport or the club itself, becoming its shareholders (perhaps with one predominant controlling figure amongst them) and funding the entity by subscribing for more shares or providing 'soft' loans (ie loans on non-commercial terms, perhaps giving little prospect of repayment). Such shareholders tended to regard owning shares in a sporting entity as a benevolent activity, rather than as a means of generating a profit. This model is still predominant in many sports. However, as mentioned above, as the financial demands of being involved with some sports has increased dramatically, they have often outstripped the ability of such founders to meet them, resulting in the development of new shareholding models as equity investment from different sources is sought by those involved in, and attracted into, sport. These shareholding models can be broadly grouped within the main categories described below and the owners of, and advisers to, a sports entity considering raising equity finance should consider whether any one or more of these models is particularly available, or suited to its or their needs.

1 See para C1.40.

(a) Significant Individual Shareholder

C3.168 Essentially, this is an update to the traditional 'founder' model which involves one wealthy individual benefactor (invariably an investor who is making an 'emotional' as well as a financial investment because he is a follower of the sport or club) investing heavily in a sports entity, often at a time when it is in financial difficulty[1], and then effectively bankrolling it. As with founders, the emotional aspect of the investment is often greater than any financial considerations and the benefactor may not expect to be rewarded by a financial return on his investment, but may be more interested in simply being involved in the running of the sporting entity and his money bringing increased success to it (although with some benefactors the value of the publicity that can be generated by such benevolence should not be disregarded).

1 If the entity is in financial crisis, the incoming investor can obtain a significant or even controlling interest in the sports entity for a relatively small initial investment, thereby ensuring that he can exercise sufficient control over it before committing further funds.

C3.169 Most benefactors' motivation in funding a sporting entity is not totally philanthropic however (if they were, they could simply make a gift to it rather than subscribing for shares). Even if their primary motivation is to lead the sports entity or club to former or new levels of sporting success, the investor is nevertheless likely to require control of it and of how the money is spent. As well as providing the sports entity with new funds in return for newly issued shares, the investor may also seek to build his influence over the sports entity by purchasing shares already held by existing shareholders (which purchase monies will go to the selling shareholder rather than the sports entity)[1]. The degree of control that is given by a shareholding of a particular size will depend in part on the spread or otherwise of the voting rights attaching to the other shares in the sports entity. A shareholder can exercise a significant degree of control over a sports entity without holding the majority of the votes attaching to shares, particularly if the rights and controls carried by the shareholding under the constitutional documents of the entity or the law are enhanced. For example, the investor can enter into formal or informal alliances with other shareholders[2] or makes his investment conditional upon some or all of the other shareholders and the company entering into an agreement, or the constitutional documents of the entity being amended, to give his shareholding additional powers of control, such as veto rights or guaranteed board representation[3]. However, acquiring the majority of the voting rights, in the sports entity will in any event give the investor the greatest influence over in the running of it (although certain matters may be reserved to the holders of certain shares[4]). If an individual investor has a very significant majority of the voting rights (ie 75% or more of the voting rights) he can effectively control almost all of the decisions taken by the sports entity. In addition to exercising his votes on issues to be decided by the shareholders directly, a holder of the majority of the voting rights can also control the appointment of the sporting entity's directors, enabling the investor to appoint himself and/or his associates to such positions, thereby also giving him control over the day-to-day running of the sports entity which is delegated to the board.

1 Although if the sports entity is a public company, the investor should be aware of the rules restricting the way in which it can build up its stake under the City Code on Takeovers and Mergers.

2 Although again, the rules of the City Code on Takeovers and Mergers should be observed if the sports entity is a public company.

3 For example, the shareholders may want to specify that any shareholder wishing to sell his shares must first offer them to the other shareholders before selling them to a third party, providing the new shareholder with further opportunities to build his stake and influence.

4 See para C3.181.

C3.170 Although still prevalent in sports which are less demanding financially, as with the 'founder' model, this single majority shareholder model has also fallen out of favour in sports which involve very high financial demands as the finance now required for an entity to compete in such a sport is beyond the means of all but the most wealthy individuals[1]. In such sports, the model has developed into one in which existing shareholders raise further equity funding required from a small number of high net worth individuals or companies, each of whom (often together with the founders who retain a significant interest) owns a significant minority shareholding giving them a measure of, but not overriding, control. This model can work well when there is general consensus amongst these significant shareholders as to the direction in which the entity should be taken, but can lead to difficulties if there are serious or continuing differences of opinion between them.

1 Football at the elite level in England is such a sport. Bob Murray, the Chairman of Sunderland AFC, which is listed on the Official List of the London Stock Exchange, has been quoted as saying in 2001 (the club having offered its shares publicly and listed on the London Stock Exchange) that the club 'wouldn't be seventh in the Premiership and wouldn't have a 48,000-seater stadium unmortgaged if it wasn't for being in the City because I can't bankroll that'. Nevertheless, a very wealthy individual can still finance a football club competing amongst the elite, as Mohammad Al Fayed's reported £80m investment in Fulham Football Club has demonstrated.

C3.171 Ironically, the emotional element inherent in sport which leads some individuals to invest heavily in it has also driven some of them from it (and probably discouraged some other individuals from making similar investments). Significant or controlling shareholders in sports entities can be subjected to personal vilification by its fans if the blame for its sporting failures are laid at their door as a result of a perceived insufficiency of ongoing financial investment (often disregarding the size of the initial investment made), mismanagement, or because they are regarded as seeking a financial return (or at least protection of their financial investment) at the expense of the return sought by the fans, namely sporting success[1]. Investments in other sectors may be regarded as being a far less troublesome option as customers in other sectors do not usually react so strongly to the failure of a businesses that they patronise. These factors have contributed to the decline in the popularity of this model in some sports. Fans often seem not to recognise that, whilst they might not always like how the money put into their club by an investor is spent, it is often better for their club than not having it at all.

1 For example, Alan Sugar during his chairmanship of Tottenham Hotspur FC.

(b) *Significant Corporate Shareholder*

C3.172 This model is similar to the 'significant individual shareholder' model described above, but with the major difference that a sports entity will not be able to attract investment from a corporate shareholder on a purely 'emotional' basis, as it would from some individuals, without offering a reasonable prospect of a commercial return being generated on its investment. Unlike an individual who is free to make an investment without the prospect of any reasonable return if he so wishes, the board of a corporate investor has a duty to act in the best interests of that investing company, which ordinarily means maximising its profitability. Therefore, they cannot simply decide to put the company's money into a sports entity unless it can be objectively justified as being beneficial to the company making the investment. Corporate investors such as venture capital funds or financial institutions are likely to assess these potential benefits purely in terms of the financial return that they foresee making from the investment in the form of dividends and growth in the value of its shares in the sports entity[1].

1 Some investment companies such as ENIC have focused exclusively on the sports sector as an industry sector in which to invest. However, these investments have not yet generated any significant financial returns.

C3.173 However, equity investment may also be attracted from companies considering not only the potential direct financial return that they can make on that investment, but also the strategic benefits that the investment can bring to the investor's existing business if it is complemented by the sports entity's activities. For example, this strategy has been used by media companies looking to take a significant minority equity stake in one or more football clubs, not only to exploit and profit from synergies between their operations (eg co-operating on the exploitation of the clubs' media rights) but also to possibly benefit from having an influence on both sides of the table when collectively sold football media rights come up for resale. Media companies such as Granada Media and Ntl have pursued such a strategy recently (with Granada acquiring equity stakes of 9.9% in both Arsenal and Liverpool and Ntl acquiring similar stakes in Aston Villa, Leicester City, Newcastle United[1] and a smaller stake in Middlesbrough). However, a company wishing to make such a strategic investment may find that, perhaps to counter the anti-competitive effect that such influence may have, it is restricted from acquiring undue influence on matters such as the collective selling of media rights by acquiring an overly significant shareholding in a sports entity. For example, the broadcaster BSkyB, which at the time held live broadcast rights to Premier League football, was prevented by the Monopolies and Mergers Commission from acquiring a shareholding of 10% or more in Manchester United, on the grounds that such an interest in Manchester United would give BSkyB an anti-competitive advantage over other broadcasters bidding for broadcast rights, even if other clubs were taken over by other broadcaster or media companies (due to the pre-eminent positions of BSkyB and Manchester United in their respective markets)[2].

1 However, Ntl appears to be revising this strategy, probably as a result of its mounting debts, and has recently sold its shares in Newcastle United plc to one of the director shareholders of the club at a significant loss. It is also reported to be exchanging its equity stakes in clubs for other interests in them (such as media rights). A spokesman for Granada is also reported to have said that it paid too much for its interests in football (*Football Insider* (December 2001))

2 See further paras B2.336 to B2.338. Aside from the anti-competitive aspects of the proposed merger, the Monopolies and Mergers Commission also concluded that the merger would 'reinforce the trend towards greater inequality of wealth between clubs, weakening the smaller ones', 'would give BSkyB additional influence over Premier League decisions relating to the organisation of football, leading to some decisions which would not reflect the long-term interest of football' and that '[t]his adverse effect would be more pronounced if the merger precipitated other mergers between broadcasters and Premier League clubs.' (DTI press release, 9 April 1999 and Monopolies and Mergers Commission report *British Sky Broadcasting Group Plc and Manchester United Plc – a Report on the Proposed Merger*, April 1999 (Cm 4305). Therefore, it seems that authorities such as the Monopolies and Mergers Commission may take sporting considerations into account when determining such issues.

C3.174 Similarly, to maintain competition on the playing field as well as in commercial markets, investors have been restricted from acquiring significant shareholdings in different sporting entities which may compete against each other. Otherwise, such common ownership could inhibit sporting competition between those entities[1]. Such restrictions on multiple holdings can apply equally to restrict investments by individuals as well as by corporate shareholders[2], and may also prevent one sporting entity from making a strategic investment in another in order to establish a 'feeder' arrangement between the two[3].

1 Such rules are described in detail at paras C3.95 and C3.96.

2 The Football League introduced such rules in the late 1980s after media mogul Robert Maxwell acquired significant interests in Derby County and Oxford United and transfers were made between the clubs which were seen by some as being at less than their market values.

3 Although if there is no possibility of the two entities competing in the same competition, such arrangements should be possible. For example, at the time of writing Newcastle United is reported to be considering investing in a Chinese club side.

(c) Public Share Ownership

C3.175 If a sports entity reaches a stage of its commercial development where it needs to raise substantial finance and favours doing so by an issue of shares, but it cannot raise the amount required from a single or limited number of private investors, it may seek to raise such finance by an issue of its shares to the public[1]. Such an issue can be combined with securing a listing of the shares to be issued on a recognised investment exchange such as the London Stock Exchange, thereby providing liquidity to the new shareholders which will make the shares more attractive, and also providing existing shareholders with a means of 'exiting' the sports entity by disposing of part or all of their shareholding (thereby realising their investment, hopefully at a gain) if they so wish[2]. Most of the same considerations and legal obligations that would have to be taken into account by a sports entity offering debt securities to the public will apply similarly to the issue of shares to the public[3].

1 For a discussion of what will constitute an offer to the public, see para C3.115 et seq.

2 When the shares of Manchester United were floated on the London Stock Exchange in 1991, one of its directors, Maurice Watkins, stated that: 'One of the primary purposes was that it released cash to shareholders' (quote from Conn *The Football Business* (Mainstream Publishing).

3 See para C3.98 et seq and Gleeson 'Prospectuses and Public Issues' in *Tolley's Company Law* (Tolley)

C3.176 As with a public issue of debt securities, any sports entity which is considering raising finance by the issue of listed shares to the public will have to consider whether the finance that it can raise as a result of such a public share issue will justify the expense of re-registration as a public company, the expense of engaging advisors and undertaking the necessary procedures involved in obtaining a listing of its shares and submitting to the stricter regulatory regime to which it will be subject as a public listed company[1]. However, once the sports entity has gone through the re-registration and listing process, the process of raising further finance by the issue of more shares to the public will become easier, particularly if such offers are made only to its existing shareholders (for example, by way of a 'rights issue' or 'open offer')[2].

1 For a detailed analysis of these issues, see Gleeson 'Prospectuses and Public Issues' in *Tolley's Company Law* (Tolley)
2 Ie an offer made only to existing shareholders to purchase shares in proportion to their existing shareholdings, usually at a discount to their market value. For a detailed analysis, see Creamer and Mullen 'Rights Issues' in *Tolley's Company Law* (Tolley)

C3.177 As well as giving it access to a greater number of potential investors (and therefore potentially to more finance), obtaining a listing for the shares of any sports entity on a public market should enhance their value by increasing their liquidity and visibility, thereby making the shares more attractive to potential investors and enabling the sports entity to receive a higher price per share than they might if such shares were unlisted (thereby reducing the dilutive effect of the issue on existing shareholders). The credibility of the sports entity, both with investors and third parties with which it has commercial dealings, may also be enhanced as a result of the increase in its profile and (more tangibly) the greater degree of regulation imposed upon it by the relevant exchange, and its share value can thereby be increased[1].

1 Bob Murray, the Chairman of Sunderland which is listed on the Official List of the London Stock exchange has been quoted as saying: 'Because we are listed and we have corporate governance, people will lend us more money than they would have done'.

C3.178 A sports entity offering its shares publicly may also benefit from the offering's appeal to 'emotional' investors (ie its supporters) as well as those only taking financial considerations into account. Interest from supporters can increase demand for the shares and consequently the price at which they can be offered. Targeting shareholders can also help to sell the concept of flotation, as clubs can present it as an opportunity for fans to invest in, and have a say in the running of, 'their' club. However, as noted above, it is not always the case that sufficient new shares will be issued to shift control of the club away from the existing controlling shareholders. Also, a greater proportion of new shares issued by a sports entity upon and after flotation are likely to be taken by institutional financial investors rather than fans. Part of the reason for this will of course be that such institutions have more money to invest than fans, even in aggregate, are likely to have. Also, whilst possibly paying lip service to the idea of 'fan enfranchisement', the club may prefer not to have a large proportion of its issued share capital in the hands of 'emotional investors'. This is because fans are likely to measure the return on their investment in terms of the sporting success that the club attains by spending the funds raised (giving them an 'emotional' return on the investment), rather than the financial return that they receive on the shares. In fact, receipt of a financial return could even be regarded unfavourably by a supporter because, as he is likely to have only a very small minority shareholding in the club, the financial return received by way of a dividend paid out by the club to an individual supporter will be relatively minor when compared with the aggregate outflow of funds from the club to its shareholders (including the financial investors seeking such a financial return on their investment) that will result from such a dividend declaration. As such, the supporter is likely to prefer that such funds are instead retained by the club to increase the chances of a valuable 'emotional' return being received on the investment (such as a league championship), rather than being used to give him a meagre financial return on his investment (although he may recognise that unless it delivers a financial return to its shareholders, the club is unlikely to be able to raise further equity funding from financial investors).

C3.179 Similarly, whilst sporting success usually improves club's financial position and vice versa, some actions taken by a sports entity may be viewed as being aimed more at satisfying shareholders financially than achieving success, preferably immediately, on the field of play[1]. Consequently, the sports entity may find it very difficult to satisfy both its emotional and financial investor groups simultaneously. (However, some clubs have attempted to more closely align the interests of their financial and emotional investors through the linking of financial return to emotional return[2].)

1 For example, fans of some football clubs that have issued shares publicly to financial investors have viewed the sale by the club of highly valued players, or a refusal to sign 'big-name' players, as being motivated by a wish to appease 'financial' shareholders more interested in the health of the club's balance sheet than achieving immediate success on the field of play. The sale of Rio Ferdinand by Leeds United to Manchester United (for a £15m profit over a period of less than two years) has been regarded by fans as being good for the business but bad for the team, certainly in the short term (and most fans tend not to think long term). However, as discussed throughout this Chapter, the long-term success of the team is likely to be reflected in its balance sheet. Interestingly, Manchester United's share price fell when the likelihood of the transfer increased, presumably because, notwithstanding the likely improvement on the teams chances of success that the acquisition of the player would have, financial investors were concerned that the net effect on the club's financial health would be negative if it agreed to pay too high a transfer fee and/or wages for him. Also, a dispute between the Chairman of West Bromwich Albion and its manager over the amount of funding that would be made available for new players after its promotion to the Premier League in 2002 (the Chairman insisting that the club be financially prudent in the short and long-term) led to the resignation of the Chairman.

2 See the description of the preference shares offered by Celtic plc at para C3.164.

C3.180 Another reason why a sports entity may prefer not to issue a large proportion of its share capital to fans is that this may have a negative impact on its ability to raise equity finance in the future. Once they have given their club some financial support and have acquired a say, however small, in its affairs as a result (usually simply the right to attend and vote at general meetings of the sports entity) such emotional investors often have the have no desire (or the means) to increase the level of their influence to any meaningful level. Consequently, emotional investors may not be a significant source of further investment for a sports entity (for example, by taking up their entitlement in a rights issue) after they have participated in its initial public offering, whereas institutional financial investors are more capable of making further equity investments[1].

1 However, Celtic Football club successfully raised approximately £9.4m from an issue of shares in 1995, the majority coming from supporters (assisted by low cost loans made available by the club's bank), and a further £22.5m from a further issues of shares in 2001, with approximately £5.5m of that being subscribed by supporters.

C3.181 Although the foregoing analysis may suggest that a sports entity will be inclined to disregard sporting considerations and look to satisfy only its 'financial' investors after making an initial public offering of its shares, this is not always the case. The balance between sporting considerations and financial considerations can be shifted somewhat in favour of the former (if the sports entity sees this as desirable) by the creation of 'golden' shares carrying enhanced or veto rights in relation to particular sporting issues. These can be issued by the sports entity to parties whose primary considerations will be sporting rather than financial[1]. However, any shifting of the balance of power towards the 'emotional' investors in this way will almost inevitably decrease the attractiveness of shares in the sports entity to investors looking purely for a financial return (as their purpose is to prevent the maximisation of financial returns if this is to be achieved at the expense of sporting considerations). (For obvious reasons, such 'golden' shares issued to those entrusted with safeguarding sporting interests should be non-transferable or transferable only in limited circumstances).

1 For example, when Loftus Road plc acquired Wasps Rugby Club (along with Queen's Park Rangers Football Club) in preparation for its flotation on AIM in 1996, to address concerns that the rugby club's links to traditional enthusiasts would be eroded, the club remained in existence as an unincorporated association whilst transferring most of its assets to the plc (some assets relating to junior, amateur and social activities were retained). In return for the asset transfer the trustees of the unincorporated club received a 'golden' share and preference shares in the plc. The golden share gave the holder the right of approval or veto over certain matters (such as the disposal of Wasps' ground or any playing assets) and the preference shares gave the club a revenue stream to meet its expenses. Ordinary shares were then issued to the new investors. Similarly, when Hampshire County Cricket Club's parent company, Rose Bowl plc, made a public offering of shares in 2002, its share capital included a non-participating special share issued to the trustees of the cricket club which gave the holder no rights other than a right of veto over any disposal or proposal that would result in the cessation of first class cricket at the Rose Bowl ground.

C3.182 For the reasons outlined above (and notwithstanding any veto rights that it may offer to persons concerned with purely sporting matters) a sports entity considering making a public offering of shares may consider 'placing' all or a significant proportion of them with investors such as financial institutions. However, such a strategy may itself cause unrest amongst its supporters who may thereby feel that the club is deliberately disenfranchising them. Also, it may be impossible for a sports entity to ignore investments from its supporters if it cannot attract financial investors because they have been discouraged from investing in sport by the relatively poor track record of sporting shares (particularly in UK football), by the financial performance and prospects of that particular sports entity[1], or simply by the particular unpredictability that is inherent in any business that is reliant, at least to some extent, on 'sporting chance'[2].

1 For example, Norwich City Football Club plc's 2002 share offering was basically predicated on the club's pressing need for further funds as a result of a reduction in the finance it receives from the central selling by the Football League of broadcast rights. The Chairman's letter in the offer document was actually addressed to 'Dear Canary Supporter' and its stated dividend policy was that 'the Board does not expect to recommend any dividend on Ordinary Shares for the forseeable future'. Whilst the 'B' preference shares also offered carried a right to receive a cumulative 4.5% dividend, in order to subscribe for one B share investors had to purchase four ordinary shares. The club was clearly not in a position to attract equity investments from financial investors and the offering was therefore very clearly aimed at its supporters.

2 Relegation in particular can have a significant negative effect on the share price of listed football clubs and therefore the prospects of investors receiving a capital gain on their shares (for example, Leicester City's share price fell 38% to a new low of 8p (having opened at £1.10 on listing in 1997) after its relegation at the end of the 2001/02 season). Even clubs enjoying a period of relative success may find that their share capital is unattractive to investors. For example, a placing and open offer of shares in Preston North End Football Club in May 2000 raised under £3m of the £7.5m being sought.

C3.183 If a sports entity decides to offer listed shares to the public, it can choose from a variety of different exchanges on which to list these shares[1]. The choice of which exchange to choose will be governed by the different characteristics of the exchange (such as prestige, the stringency of the regulatory requirements and the associated costs of obtaining and maintaining a listing, etc) and their suitability to the needs of the sporting entity. (There is no requirement for a company to list on an exchange of the country in which it is incorporated, although in most cases an exchange established in the same country as the sports entity will be most appropriate). Of the listed UK football clubs (being the UK sports entities that have most often obtained a listing) roughly equal numbers have obtained a listing on the Main Market and the Alternative Investment Market ('AIM') of the London Stock Exchange[2]. Additionally, some football clubs' shares are traded on a system known as OFEX which is a quasi-listing (the shares are not traded or quoted on the London Stock Exchange but are traded 'off-exchange' via a dealing facility incorporating a network of brokers who match potential buyers and sellers) and applies less onerous requirements than the Main Market or AIM. Therefore, it tends to suit smaller companies than those that apply for a listing on the Stock Exchange and also companies which are not actively seeking to raise new capital from the public but who want to give their shareholders some liquidity by providing a dealing facility for their shares without having the burden and expense of meeting the Exchange's regulations[3].

1 For example, the Alternative Investment Market or the Official List of the London Stock Exchange.
2 AIM has less stringent entry and ongoing requirements but, for that reason, is seen as less prestigious.
3 For example, the shares in Arsenal, Bradford City and Manchester City are traded on OFEX.

C3.184 A detailed description of the mechanics of obtaining a listing is beyond the scope of this Chapter[1] and some aspects of the process will be peculiar to the particular exchange on which a particular sports entity is seeking a listing. In general, a prospectus will need to be produced[2] and the process of pricing, marketing and underwriting the share offering completed before applications are received and the shares finally listed and issued. However, in all cases a sports entity seeking to obtain a listing and make a public offering of its shares will need to assemble a team of advisers, comprising of a merchant bank, accountants, lawyers and brokers, to navigate it through the complex procedures involved.

1 For a detailed analysis of these issues, again, see 'Prospectuses and Public Issues' (Simon Gleeson) in *Tolley's Company Law* (Tolley).
2 See para C3.116 et seq.

C3.185 Notwithstanding the benefits of raising finance from the public described above, some companies find that, having raised finance from the public in this way, the ongoing requirements of the relevant exchange's regime are too onerous and that its listing is of little ongoing benefit if its requirements for, or prospects of raising, further finance from the public are limited. In such circumstance, the sports entity may consider 'dropping down' to an exchange with less onerous requirements[1]. Alternatively, some of its shareholders may even seek to return it to private ownership by purchasing a sufficient number of shares from other shareholders to give them sufficient voting power to pass the resolutions necessary to de-list its shares and reregister as a private company[2].

1 For example, Millwall Holdings plc was floated on the Main Market of the London Stock Exchange in 1989 but have since dropped down to AIM.

2 The process of re-registration requires the approval of 75% of the votes attaching to its shares, although minority shareholders can apply for cancellation of the resolution. (See further the Chapter on 'Formation and Types of Company' (Ken Dierden) in *Tolley's Company Law* (Tolleys)). At the time of writing, certain significant shareholders of Newcastle United plc have been increasing their stake by acquiring shares from other shareholders and it has been speculated that these acquisitions are being made as a precursor to taking the club back into private ownership.

8 SUMMARY

C3.186 As should be clear from the foregoing, there are a very wide variety of methods (and combinations thereof) by which a sports entity can raise finance to supplement any revenue it can generate from sporting and associated commercial activity. In deciding which avenues to pursue, it is important for a sports entity not only to carefully consider the uses to which it intends to put such finance, but also its ability to meet the obligations which will arise from its receipt. Often, obtaining expert advice on which sources of finance are likely to best suit its requirements can save a sports entity significant time and money which it might otherwise spend in pursuing a source of finance that will ultimately be unavailable or unsuitable. Whilst, at one end of the scale, a small community sports club is likely to face a choice only between seeking finance directly from its members or applying to grant-making bodies, at the other extreme some major sporting projects may be too large or complex to be funded by a single source or method of finance and must therefore be structured to access multiple sources of finance and satisfy the requirements of the providers of such finance[1].

1 See para C3.62 et seq on the funding of the Wembley Stadium and Kings Dock developments.

C3.187 Whichever method or methods of raising finance that a sports entity chooses to utilise, it should proceed with caution. When negotiating the terms of any finance provided by investors seeking a commercial return, a sports entity should satisfy itself that it will be able to meets its financial obligations under the terms of the financing and that the expectations on which the financing is based are realistic (and will continue to be so in a worst-case scenario such as relegation). A great deal of care should also be taken to ensure that the sports entity is able to, and does, observe any restrictions and conditions applicable to such finance in order to avoid having to repay funds received and/or the officers of the entity incurring personal liability for any breaches of such restrictions or conditions. Whilst sports entities seeking additional finance obviously hope that its receipt will enable them to move onwards and upwards, sports entities which find that they are unable to fulfil their obligations in relation to finance that they have received can find that such financing actually has catastrophic consequences, which may include the insolvency and ultimate demise of the sports entity, no matter how long it has been in existence up to that point[1]. This can be particularly true in sports where a club which finds itself in an insolvency situation is prevented by the rules governing the sport in which it competes from generating further commercial income (for example, if such rules provide for the suspension of the club from participation in the league). Whilst such rules are often intended to protect other participants in the sport, their effect can be that once a sports entity finds itself in serious financial difficulty it may find it impossible to climb its way back out[2].

1 For example, in 2002 Notts County Football Club, a founder member of the Football League, came close to being placed into administration. For a detailed description of the consequences of insolvency and the processes involved, see the various Chapters on 'Insolvency' by Shashi Rajani in *Tolley's Company Law* (Tolley).

2 For example, FIA rules provide that if any Formula One motor racing team registered at the start of a season fails to take part in any race (as was, for example, a possibility for the Arrows team at the 2002 British Grand Prix because its engine supplier refused to supply engines until it had been paid) the team faces substantial fines and forfeits its rights to take part in subsequent events. Similarly, the FA Premier League's Rule C.39 allows it to suspend a club from its competitions if the club is the subject of any insolvency proceedings.

C3.188 Even if 'rescue' finance from new investors can be secured in such perilous situation, the existing owners of the sports entity are likely to find that such new investors are able to demand a very favourable deal in terms of the rights that they acquire in return for providing such rescue finance, and so such existing owners are thereby likely to lose control of the sports entity in any event, even if it does survive[1]. However, if finance from suitable sources and on appropriate terms is secured by a sports entity, it can undoubtedly enable such sports entity to achieve its aims, whether they be modest ones, such as simply ensuring continued participation in a sport, or more ambitious ones, such as competing at the elite level of an international professional sport.

1 For example, after Bryan Richardson was ousted as chairman and chief executive of Coventry City Football Club in February 2002 after a vote of no confidence in him (despite remaining its largest single shareholder) he told the Coventry Evening Telegraph that the biggest mistake he made was allowing the club to accept £10m in loans from another shareholder who then led the move to oust him, 'not so much because of who they came from, but more so the fact that [the club] took on extra debt at that time': *Soccer Investor Weekly* (5 February 2002).

CHAPTER C4

RISK MANAGEMENT

Trevor Watkins (Clarke Willmott & Clarke), **Elizabeth Leggatt** (Clarke Willmott & Clarke) and **David Walker** (Clarke Willmott & Clarke)

Contents

1 INTRODUCTION

A What is risk management?

C4.1 Risk management is a process of assessing and then controlling risk. If successfully implemented, it is a concept that should underpin any organisation and provide it with a firm foundation on which to base its business operation. Its growing significance rests on many factors – the substantial increase in volunteer participation in sporting events, the inherent risks such programmes bring, the growth in the economic value of sport and the heightened awareness of what rights individuals hold. These have all highlighted the need for those in the sports sector to have a robust risk management strategy.

C4.2 Proper risk management involves an undertaking, be it a sports club, participant event organiser or spectator sport manager in:

(i) considering the operation as a whole and its activities, then identifying unfavourable incidents that might occur as a consequence of any part of those;
(ii) assessing the probability of and potential for those unfavourable incidents to occur;
(iii) evaluating the likely severity of consequences if a potential unfavourable incident became a reality;
(iv) devising and implementing a strategy to reduce, prevent or avoid the risk of the unfavourable incident occurring which is proportionate to the probability, potential and likely consequence of each unfavourable incident identified and the related costs of dealing with it balanced against the resources available to that organisation.

C4.3 Whilst general principles do apply to any risk management analysis, a successful approach must be tailored to the individual organisation and its particular activities. Risk management does not aim to remove all risk from any given activity – arguably it would be impossible to do so – but it seeks to remove those more probable or at least minimise the risk of their occurring. In devising a successful strategy to deal with risk it is imperative that an organisation involves all levels of its operation – its members, participants and those it does business with – if it is to produce a meaningful result. Rather than a 'one off' task, risk management analysis is a living programme that needs reviewing and amending regularly to reflect organisational changes and legal developments. If implemented properly it should enhance the overall programme offered by any organisation, produce commensurate benefits for the participants and ensure long term cost benefits.

B Why is risk management important?

C4.4 Risk management, if considered and implemented properly, will ensure that an organisation is run well and makes the best use of its resources. Its secondary effect is that it helps an organisation to comply with its legal obligations; it also protects the people involved with that organisation from exposure to unnecessary risk and its effects.

C4.5 Effective risk management will identify the potential exposure to risk, so enabling an organisation to take positive steps to eliminate, minimise or make financial provision for that risk. Identification of risks reduces the chance of a claim being made against the organisation and damage being incurred by people or property. In addition, if a claim is made or damage is suffered, an organisation that can show it took all reasonable steps to manage risk will be in a stronger position to defend any claim. It will also arguably have avoided many other claims if it makes changes identified as necessary in any risk management process.

C4.6 Other benefits may include potential reductions in premiums payable for insurance. Insurers are, subject to their satisfaction with the manner of the risk assessment, likely to take these steps into account when making decisions on the terms of any insurance offered. This benefit may well extend to participants who themselves can refer to the organisation's risk management programme and safety record when obtaining their own insurances.

C4.7 Good risk management is also important from a public relations perspective. By reducing the exposure to risk it may assist in avoiding incidents which would create negative publicity that can have a serious impact on an organisation. An effective risk management strategy may even enhance an organisation's reputation. It illustrates that the organisation cares about the health and well being of all of the people that play a part in it. This is particularly relevant in the volunteer sector where charities seek to raise monies by encouraging volunteers to participate in fundraising events.

C4.8 Secondary considerations also apply. Any organisation seeking to obtain legal expenses cover may do so on better terms if it can demonstrate a risk management programme that reduces the prospects of litigation (which in itself is time consuming, otherwise costly and also damages goodwill). Equally, property insurers will be more amenable to insuring a risk if an organisation can show it has minimised the risk to the insured interest. Risk management should also enable an organisation to better plan for its future by identifying and insuring against the potential loss of key people within it – whether a star soccer player, managing director or other vital member of staff. More importantly, however, risk management enables an organisation to identify those risks that might be less than obvious and otherwise ignored in insurance considerations where no risk management programme had been adopted. If used properly it is a tool to ensure an organisation protects itself as much as possible against potential negative events of the future.

C4.9 Risk management in essence provides an organisation with a better chance to deal with the unknown through a parallel strategy of eliminating risks that can be dealt with and minimising those that cannot. Virtually any risk is insurable on terms; its identification, management and insurance can in itself protect the future of an organisation. For those organisations who do not take those steps, that failure can in itself be the reason why its future growth is either greatly diminished or even its existence brought to an abrupt end.

C How is risk management relevant to sports organisations?

C4.10 Risk management is relevant to sporting organisations in the same way as it applies to all other associations and businesses.

C4.11 Sporting organisations, however, need to give careful consideration not only to their employees and contractors but also the participants, spectators and volunteers that may play a part in their operation.

C4.12 Sports organisations are exposed to a wide variety of risks. As with most businesses, they will own or occupy land, buy and sell goods and employ people but they each have their own peculiar function and activity that requires special consideration. For example, the owner of a Formula One racetrack will have to consider specific regulations of the FIA ('Federation Internationale d'Automobile'); a professional soccer club owner must abide by the rules of the Football League or FA Premier League; the organiser of a volunteer event must follow the particular rules and regulations that may apply nationally and locally.

C4.13 Risk management involves a meaningful assessment of specific risks associated with a particular sport, the likelihood of their becoming a reality and the preparation of a strategy for recovery should they do so. More often than not this will involve determining what practical actions an organisation might take pre- and post- an incident occurring. It combines risk avoidance and management of situations as they arise (as they will even when the likelihood of a risk occurring has been minimised).

C4.14 The significant financial considerations and consequences of modern professional sports have increased the importance of a prudent approach to risk management. An injury to a top player, driver, rider or other sportsman can have serious consequences for a sports organisation as well as the participant.

C4.15 An incident at a racetrack might primarily cause injury to a driver or spectator. The injured party may have a substantial claim against the venue owner and/or event organiser. Apart from the injuries suffered, the consequential losses may soar, particularly in high profile sports such as Formula One, given the amounts earned by participants outside of their racing contracts. An inability to perform other contracts due to injuries suffered in an event could lead to significant claims being made. The consequences, however, go beyond the initial affected parties. Any suggestion that an event or venue is unsafe may in itself deter others from competing there or coming to watch. In extreme circumstances, without action before or after an incident a racetrack might have its licence to hold such events revoked. Similarly, a governing body is likely to impose its own sanction for instances where a breach of safety is found to have occurred.

C4.16 Although rights fees for major sporting events appear to have tailed off, they still involve substantial sums. Organisations may well find themselves in breach of agreements with sponsors should they fail to ensure that they run a safe event. In addition, proper risk management extends to ensuring the rights of those with whom an organisation deals are not infringed. For example, a core sponsor is likely to have demanded exclusivity in its contract. An organisation must take all steps to ensure that the risk of that contract being breached by unlicensed activities is minimised. Contingency insurance, in particular, where specific incidents are insured against, is of benefit and is addressed below.

C4.17 Each undertaking will have exposure to a unique blend of risks and will have its own priorities, aims and resources which will influence the risk strategy which is adopted. A general risk management strategy will in itself address no more than surface issues.

2 RISK MANAGEMENT STRATEGY

A Assessment of potential exposure and evaluation of consequences

C4.18 An organisation must first assess its undertaking as a whole, identify those affected by it and set out in detail what causes or could cause harm and the potential unfavourable effects. It is important that the risk assessment is carried out by those who understand the organisation and its activities but who also may provide a different outlook. For example, by combining persons from within an organisation with outside parties involved in insurance, health and safety, the local authority or the emergency services, an altogether more wide ranging risk assessment will take place.

C4.19 There are arguably too many considerations for any organisation to cover every potential risk that could affect it. The process will include consideration of legal duties, their nature and to whom they are owed. These duties will necessarily relate to all whom the organisation deals with – employees, contractors, volunteers, participants, spectators, local authorities, government bodies – or who are involved in the organisation's business.

C4.20 A risk management report will identify and grade the severity of risk stemming from each activity/relationship/class of people involved. This will involve an assessment of the likelihood of a risk becoming a reality and the severity of the consequence if it does so; a grading of likelihood (highly unlikely, unlikely, possible, probable or almost certain) is attached to a severity of consequence (none, minor, medium, major or catastrophic affect for the organisation). It is important to remember that a risk management assessment is a living tool. The result of the assessment should enable the organisation to prioritise its management of the risks identified. How that organisation deals with the risks it has identified will necessitate an examination of the resources available (both financial and in manpower terms) as a whole to change its operation. In some instances, monies might be used in purchasing insurance; in other cases, modifications or improvements to a system of operation costing nothing in itself might reduce the risk. It is likely, however, that an organisation will need to make critical decisions as to how to implement a policy as not every risk will be capable of being addressed immediately.

C4.21 An athletic club might rate the risk of a slip on the running track as having medium or major effect (loss of athlete, claim for damages, effect on sponsors) but likely; whilst the crash of an aeroplane on their stadium is catastrophic but has little chance of happening. A motor racing circuit will need to consider the impact of thousands of spectators viewing a race together with the inherent dangers of the sport itself; event managers must assess the likely consequences of changes in weather; a charity race organiser will need to review the complete arrangements (roads, permits, campsite, food) for the volunteers seeking to raise money by participating in a cycle ride.

(a) Contractual Duties

C4.22 Entering into a contract will create certain duties and obligations between the parties that will be set out within it. A risk management assessment must include a review of existing contracts and commercial agreements and the procedures applied when new contracts are entered into.

C4.23 Commercial agreements should clearly set out the duties and responsibilities of each contracting party. It is usual for them to apportion liability between the contracting parties. Proper negotiation prior to entering into an agreement offers a key opportunity to limit exposure to risk. A contract entered into on unfavourable terms by an organisation can create a significant exposure to risk that was easily avoidable.

C4.24 Although a contract will contain core terms, additional obligations can be implied; for example, there is an implied obligation on an employer to provide a safe place and system of work. Equally it is impossible to exclude liability for death or personal injury within a contract and only insofar as it is reasonable in respect of other damage[1].

1 Sections 1(3) and s 2(2) of the Unfair Contract Terms Act 1977.

C4.25 The potential risks arising from existing contracts and proposed agreements should be identified. Professional advice should be taken to ensure that the implications of any contract are fully understood and that the contracts are enforceable.

C4.26 Often an event may occur that whilst identified as a possibility by the parties would be out of their control. 'Force Majeure' or 'Act of God' clauses are incorporated into contracts to limit liability for risks arising from such events. The contents of 'force majeure' clauses vary but the purpose is to exclude liability where a party is prevented from performing its obligations under the contract by circumstances which are beyond its control. This exclusion usually applies for as long as the relevant circumstances continue.

C4.27 Most sporting organisations will also be bound by applicable regulations drawn up by the governing body for that particular sport. The growing prevalence of self-regulation, with governing bodies attempting to confer their own jurisdictional powers, is an important factor in assessing risk. Often tensions will occur where differing standards are applied by separate governing bodies who may affect one event at which an organisation is involved, for example where a national and international association are both involved in administering an event. Again, a proper understanding of those regulations is imperative in dealing properly with risk.

C4.28 The consequences of failing to comply with such regulations may be significant particularly where rules are applied in an arbitrary manner. In many instances the judicial system has also refused to step in and review decisions made by bodies such as the Football Association or Jockey Club. Organisations must ensure they understand how the rules/regulations are to be interpreted if they are to reduce risk.

(b) Tortious duties

C4.29 Over time courts have been ready to establish a 'tortious' duty of care in specific situations owed by one party to another, even in the absence of a contract between them. Courts have also set standards that should be met if that duty is to be fulfilled. A failure to meet the required standard amounts to a breach of that duty; it can then give rise to a liability to redress any damage caused by that breach to the other party to whom the duty was owed.

C4.30 How does an aggrieved party establish that another is liable to redress damage? It must first show that a duty of care exists between the parties and then demonstrate that the offending party has breached that duty. To have redress for any damage it has suffered, a party must also demonstrate a causal connection between the breach and the damage and show that it was reasonably foreseeable that the type of damage which occurred to the offended party could result from that conduct.

C4.31 Typically, a duty of care results in liability for consequences such as personal injury and damage to property but it can also extend to (amongst other things) damage to reputation and any negative impact on business interests.

C4.32 Liability resting in negligence is established by considering the conduct of the party and contrasting it to accepted standards within that activity and in general. A failure to meet those standards (for example, by a failure to meet regulations imposed by a governing body) gives rise to a liability to compensate an aggrieved party for damage flowing from the breach. Organisations should, however, also be mindful of cases where strict liability arises (that is, the liability is automatic and without defence nor any assessment of the conduct concerned).

C4.33 A consumer has the right to claim damages if a product is dangerous and has caused damage to them or their property. Sporting organisations often sell goods to consumers. Even if the products have been manufactured elsewhere, the organisation will be under an obligation to take all reasonable steps to ensure that they are safe. A consumer will also benefit from contractual rights (either express or implied) and statutory protection. When sports organisations are also heavily involved in merchandising, product endorsement and licensing, it will be important to ensure that all proper safeguards are followed.

C4.34 A sporting organisation should be particularly conscious of its duty to take reasonable care to avoid injury to persons. If it fails to take such care it will be liable for injury which occurs as a result. This extends not only to participants in an event, for example a fun run, but also to the volunteers and employees involved – and further to any injury caused by those volunteers and employees during their association with the organisation. It is beyond the scope of this chapter to set out all potential breaches of duty which could cause serious consequences but for illustrative purposes consider:

(i) When allowing people to use its equipment an organisation must ensure the equipment is safe and arguably that its proper use has been explained by an organiser to participants in the event (the duty extends to ensure those who give such instruction are also properly trained).
(ii) Fundraising events necessarily involve volunteers and outside contractors, to whom the organiser will have a duty of care. Both could act in a manner that creates potential liability to third parties on behalf of the organiser (in this particular regard the contract between the organiser and volunteer or contractor must be properly drafted to reflect the relationship and this possibility).
(iii) Sporting events often attract large numbers of spectators and participants. The organiser must ensure the event is safe for both those watching and those participating in the event.
(iv) Recent events have shown the particular hazards that can occur when sporting organisations are affected by weather; for example the onset of heavy rain leading to a swollen river or a sudden storm affecting a canoe trip can lead to dangers that may have been avoided by prudent risk management (even as simple as not proceeding with such activity having checked local information and weather reports).
(v) As an employer the organisation may be held liable for the acts of its employees if these are in the course of the employment. Although contracts may include a right of indemnity from the employee, invariably it is the employer who foots the bill and makes no recovery, because courts are loathe to enforce indemnity provisions. This highlights the need for proper training, education and development of employees by the employer to minimise the risk of such liabilities arising.

C4.35 Whilst the human side of a sports organisation – the employees, participants and volunteers — is important, clearly the need to assess risk does not end with their participation. The risk assessment extends to venues, equipment and all other potential sources of risk.

(c) *Statutory duties*

C4.36 Statutory duties that affect risk management are briefly outlined below:

C4.37 Health and Safety Legislation As an employer, an organisation will be subject to various statutory duties imposed by the Health and Safety at Work Act etc 1974 ('HSWA 1974') and subsequent regulations.

C4.38 Section 2 of the HSWA 1974 imposes a duty on employers to ensure, as far as is reasonably practicable, the health, safety and welfare of its employees. This duty requires that the employers provide a safe place of work, adequate supervision, guidance and training.

C4.39 There is an obligation on employers under s 3 of the HSWA 1974 to ensure that the business is conducted in such a way as to ensure as far as is reasonably practicable, a person not in his employment who may be affected by the undertaking is not exposed to health or safety risks or so affected.

C4.40 An employer is under a legal duty to assess certain risks, for example the health risk arising from hazardous substances involved in the business in any way. There is also an obligation in relation to all public buildings to meet minimum fire safety standards.

C4.41 The organisation must implement a health and safety policy if it has five or more employees. Compliance with health and safety provisions is a key part of risk management. The health and safety requirements do not apply in full where the organisation has no employees and is run by volunteers. It remains good practice, however, to comply with the health and safety obligations as far as it is possible to do so.

C4.42 An organisation may often have a difficult decision to make in deciding whether to rely on volunteers. Volunteers need the same standard of training as employees and can also create liabilities that the organisation may have to meet. For example, trackside marshals are often volunteers who find themselves in particularly precarious situations dealing with extreme hazards. Merely turning up on an event day and taking on a range of tasks may no longer be a realistic option if risks are to be minimised; the day of the enthusiastic amateur could be over given the proliferation of duties and liabilities that now arise.

C4.43 It is important to note that any organisation employing staff should register with the Health and Safety Executive. An assessment of the risk of injury and a proper response to emergency situations is vital. The emergency services and local authorities are usually keen to assist in helping a business make such provisions.

C4.44 Discrimination Legislation Employment and other policies need to be reviewed to ensure compliance with the Sex Discrimination Act 1975, Disability Discrimination Act 1995 and the Race Relations Act 1976. A failure to do so is likely to increase the risk of claims being made. Under s 21 of the Disability Discrimination Act service providers will be under a duty to ensure that there is suitable access to premises for disabled people. This section is not yet in force but will be a significant obligation on many sports organisations[1].

1 See further para E3.47.

C4.45 Occupier's Liability Under the Occupiers' Liability Act 1957, an occupier must take such care as is reasonable to ensure that a visitor will be reasonably safe in using the premises for the purposes for which he is invited or permitted to be there. Leaving open holes in the ground without being fenced off, not providing proper safety fencing or not highlighting potential risks can all give rise to liability.

C4.46 **Licences** Sports organisations may be obliged to obtain licences in order to carry out certain activities. Failure to obtain such a licence where required is likely to have serious consequences. If a licence is obtained it is likely to be granted subject to terms and conditions which have to be adhered to. In each circumstance, a local authority or legal adviser will be able to give guidance[1].

1 See eg discussion of safety certificates for designated sports grounds at paras A1.61 et seq and D2.11 et seq.

C4.47 Breaches of statutory provisions usually carry penalties involving financial payments and in some circumstances a criminal record. They can also form a useful basis for civil actions.

3 RISK CONTROL

C4.48 Significant responsibilities fall upon any sporting organisation. Proper risk assessment and management will diminish the exposure an organisation faces. Having identified the issues which it needs to consider, the next step is to formulate a risk management strategy to avoid, reduce or limit those risks. This will need to take into account the financial constraints and limits on resources available to deal with risk management.

C4.49 As noted above, a proper risk management strategy will take the severity of consequence and balance it with the likelihood of the risk becoming an actuality. By making this comparison an organisation can prioritise its risk management. Those risks more likely to occur can be dealt with in priority by considering the severity of consequences. An organisation must compare the benefit in addressing the risk with the cost of doing so. The organisation must also consider the potential cost of failing to take such a step. It is difficult to determine an exact science in implementing risk management strategy. The decision will be particular to each organisation but by implementing risk management, at the very least the more serious risks/consequences that are likely to occur can be addressed.

C4.50 There are various practical steps that can be taken to avoid risk. Clearly the appropriate steps will depend on the particular risk being considered but they may include:

(i) the implementation of policies dealing with risk and taking appropriate steps to ensure that these policies are complied with;
(ii) taking professional advice from experts such as lawyers and doctors where appropriate particularly with regard to ongoing developments;
(iii) the provision of suitable training and supervision for employees, directors and volunteers;
(iv) keeping up to date with relevant sporting regulations and recommendations, understanding them and ensuring they are implemented;
(v) undertaking proper planning, including contingency plans, for events and adhering to these plans unless there is good reason to amend them;

(vi) highlighting risks to all relevant individuals and making them aware of contingency plans;
(vii) in relation to participants in sport, ensuring they have a good level of fitness and are involved at an appropriate level of the sport (for example, ensuring undue risks are not created by mismatching participants by age or skill);
(viii) ensuring that equipment is regularly checked and tested;
(ix) implementing a planned programme of maintenance and site inspections;
(x) implementing an ongoing procedure for recording risks and hazards on a reasonable timescale with proper updating mechanisms.

4 DEALING WITH RESIDUAL RISK – INSURANCE

C4.51 Minimising the risks identified will help to reduce an organisation's potential exposure but it is impossible to eliminate all risk. Sporting organisations should therefore consider taking out insurance to deal with all or some of the residual risks.

C4.52 The specific insurance requirements will vary but the cover needs to be tailored to deal with the particular risks identified. Insurance cover should be checked at least annually and arranged through brokers with an understanding of the organisation's business. It can take a number of forms, including but not limited to the following:

A Employer's Liability Insurance

C4.53 Section 1 of the Employers' Liability (Compulsory Insurance) Act 1969 requires that every employer take out an approved policy against liability for personal injury or disease arising in the course of their employment. As a matter of best practice this should be extended to cover volunteers.

B Key Person Insurance

C4.54 Clearly there will be key people within the organisation, both in terms of management and participants, without whom the business would suffer. Insurance is available to help deal with the loss of a key person. When deciding whether this type of insurance is appropriate the organisation will need to assess the impact of a loss of that person on the organisation.

C4.55 Key person insurance can be taken out to cover, inter alia, death, injury, illness or loss or revenue. In professional sport it is usual for this to be taken out; in the case of soccer players it is normal to ascribe to an insured player a 'transfer' value should a player lose the ability to play through injury.

C4.56 From a practical point of view the key person must be made aware of the policy terms and comply with them. A top sportsman who breaks a leg whilst on an unauthorised winter sports holiday may be entitled to their salary under their contract of employment but the employer might not be able to recover the insured sum given the nature of the occurrence that lead to the claim. It is important that the organisation is noted as loss payee on the insurance policy in the event that the insurance is paid out.

C4.57 Although an evaluation of a risk is subjective, its potential ramifications can be ascertained by reference to the financial performance of the business, any substantiated benefits the individual would have brought to the business and the effect of the loss on the future performance of the business. As many sports provide for continued payment of a contract at full rate, it is also normal for cover to include those ongoing salary costs.

C Contingency Insurance

C4.58 It is possible to insure against almost any contingency, from adverse weather conditions to civil unrest. As set out above, the occurrence of one event may lead to various significant consequences for the organisation and often these are events which are beyond the control of the organisation. Cancellation or postponement is likely to be the consequence of most unfavourable incidents occurring. Clearly in this situation the financial implications could be huge.

C4.59 Where organisations borrow against future income, the benefit of such policies is considerably heightened. This is more common in North America where the securitisation of future revenues has become commonplace[1]. A policy can cover as much or as little finance as is required but the loss must be ascertainable. For example, it may be taken out to insure against the non-appearance of a star performer due to injury including lost ticket sales or alternatively to cover only expenses incurred in organising an event.

1 See further para C3.119 et seq.

C4.60 It is also imperative to ensure cover for business interruption is considered. This can usefully cover temporary cessation or a reduced performance of a business; for example, the cost of relocating to temporary offices after a flood or fire and the likely downturn in business resulting on a temporary basis.

D Public Liability Insurance

C4.61 Almost every sporting organisation involves members of the public. Liability insurance is commonly used as a risk control method. Public liability insurance covers the organisation in the event that a member of the public suffers injury, death or damage to his or her property for which the organisation is liable.

C4.62 The elements covered by the insurance will again depend on the particular risks identified and may extend to include individual liability cover for coaches and referees, the risk of participation in sport, product liability cover and cover for property and equipment. An experienced broker will be able to properly advise an organisation against the background of existing duties[1].

1 See generally Chapter E5.

C4.63 Volunteers play a very significant part in many sporting organisations and it is best practice to protect them to ensure their continued support. Arrangements should be made to insure them against litigation arising from their involvement in the organisation.

C4.64 Consideration should also be given to obtaining cover for the following.

C4.65 Professional indemnity Where the organisation has professionals involved in its activities such as medical or professional coaches, it should consider taking out insurance cover to protect the organisation and the individual for any claims that a person has breached their professional duty or been negligent. Although professionals commonly have such insurance, existing policies may not cover that individual if their involvement in the organisation/event is outside of their normal activities.

C4.66 Director and officers liability Where the organisation is a company, it should review its Memorandum and Articles of Association to see whether it is required to indemnify its officers whilst they are acting in their capacity as officers of the organisation. If the organisation is unincorporated it should check its constitution to identify whether such an indemnity is given. If the organisation's constitution does indemnify its officers this poses a potential risk and this risk can be insured against.

5 CONCLUSION

C4.67 Sports organisations find themselves in an ever more complex and potentially dangerous working environment. To grow and be successful it is important that an organisation fully understands its business and the risks inherent within. A proper programme of risk assessment should lead to a detailed risk management strategy. By implementing this programme an organisation will be better organised, more respected and also much less open to the potential pitfalls of its business costing money and management time and hindering or even reversing progress.

C4.68 Above all risk management is about making the whole business to which it relates safer not only for the organisation but its employees, participants and volunteers who together make it what it is[1].

1 For further reading, see Greenberg and Gray 'Designing and Implementing a Sports Based Risk Management Programme' [1997] 5(3) SATLJ 49; O'Brien 'Sports Liability Insurance' [1997] 5(2) SATLJ 58; Green 'Insurance and Sports' [1997] 5(2) SATLJ 61; Stoner 'An Assessment of Risk' [1997] Sports Law Administration & Practice LAP Jan/Feb, p 8; Felix 'Risk Management and the Role of Sport – Part 1' (1998) 1(4) Sports Law Bulletin; O'Brien 'Risk Management and the Role of Sport – Part 2' (1998) 1(5) Sports Law Bulletin; 'Special Report: The Risk Business' *Sports Business* 31 (March 1998), pp 17–20; 'Risk Management' *Sports Business* 39 (November 1999), pp 23 and 24; Glendinning 'Always Look on the Upside' *Sports Business* 46 (June 2000), pp 22 and 23; *Managing the Risks: Insurance Guidelines for Sports Organisers, Sportsmen and Women* (Sports Council, Running Sport Series).

PART D

THE COMMERCIALISATION OF SPORTS EVENTS

CHAPTER D1

PROPRIETARY RIGHTS IN SPORTS EVENTS

Jonathan Taylor (Hammonds) and **Clive Lawrence** (McCormicks)

Contents

1 INTRODUCTION

D1.1 Part D of this book deals with the commercialisation of sports events. This chapter lays the foundation for that discussion by describing how and to what extent, under English law, an event organiser is able to create and exploit commercial rights in sports events, and to protect those rights from infringement by third parties.

D1.2 The first and most fundamental point is that English law does not recognise the existence of proprietary rights in a sports event per se. There is no such thing, for example, under English law, as 'broadcasting rights' or 'sponsorship rights' in a sports event[1].

1 See para D1.5 et seq.

D1.3 This is not to say, of course, that such rights do not exist as a matter of fact; the millions of pounds in rights fees that change hands in the sector each year attest that they do. Instead, it means that from a legal angle they are created, exploited and protected not as *sui generis* rights (such as exist, for example, in the field of employment law or human rights law), but by virtue of the application in combination of principles of real property law, contract law and intellectual property law. Specifically, the traditional model of sports commercial programmes is based on a foundational matrix of:

(a) exclusive rights of access to the sports venue and its environs, enabling control of the public, the media and others by admission only on specified terms and conditions[1];
(b) contractual control in addition over the conduct of event participants and commercial partners[2]; and
(c) the creation of various intellectual property rights in elements of the event that are protectable from unauthorised exploitation by third parties[3].

1 See para D1.14 et seq.
2 See para D1.28 et seq.
3 See para D1.36 et seq.

D1.4 It is this matrix that provides the foundation for the exclusive creation and exploitation of sports rights under English law. It is also this matrix that forms the basis for protection of the event from ambush marketing[1].

1 See para D1.116 et seq.

2 THE FOUNDATIONS OF A COMMERCIAL PROGRAMME FOR A SPORTS EVENT

D1.5 Those active in the sports marketing arena commonly refer to the following rights as arising in relation to a sports event: image rights[1]; broadcast and new media rights[2]; sponsorship, endorsement and official supplier rights[3]; merchandising and licensing rights[4]; hospitality rights[5]; and many others[6].

1 See Chapter D3.
2 See Chapter D4.
3 See Chapter D5.
4 See Chapter D6.
5 See Chapter D7.
6 See eg paras D8.10 and D8.11.

D1.6 In contrast to many overseas jurisdictions[1], however, English law simply does not recognise the existence of proprietary rights in a sports event per se.

1 See generally Wise 'A "Property Right" in a Sports Event: Views of Different Jurisdictions' [1996] 4(3) SATLJ 63.

D1.7 The leading authority for this proposition is an Australian case from 1937, *Victoria Park Racing v Taylor*[1]. The plaintiff operated a racecourse in Sydney, Australia. One of the defendants owned residential property adjacent to the racecourse. He allowed the other defendants to erect a scaffolding tower on his front lawn that overlooked the high boundary fences around the racecourse and enabled them to produce a commentary of the races that they then broadcast live on the radio.

1 *Victoria Park Racing and Recreation Grounds Co Ltd v Taylor* (1937) 58 CLR 479, HC of A.

D1.8 The plaintiff asserted that, having invested money and other resources into the organisation and staging of the races, it had a quasi-property right in them with which the defendants had unjustly interfered, and that the court had a general equitable discretion to grant an injunction to stop such free-riding.

D1.9 The Australian High Court rejected the claim as a matter of law on the basis that the defendants had not infringed any right belonging to the plaintiff. Latham CJ said:

> It has been argued that by the expenditure of money the plaintiff has created a spectacle and that it therefore has what is described as a quasi-property in the spectacle which the law will protect. The vagueness of this proposition is apparent on its face. What it really means is that there is some principle (apart from contract or confidential relationship) which prevents people in some circumstances from opening their eyes and seeing something and describing what they see. The court has not been referred to any authority in English law which supports the general contention that if a person chooses to organise an entertainment or to do anything else which other persons are able to see he has a right to obtain from a court an order that they shall not describe to anybody what they see … [T]he mere fact that damage results to the plaintiff from such a description cannot be relied upon as a cause of action … A 'spectacle' cannot be 'owned' in any ordinary sense of the word[1].

1 *Victoria Park Racing and Recreation Grounds Co Ltd v Taylor* (1937) 58 CLR 479 at 496 and 497, HC of A.

D1.10 Dixon J agreed that the right claimed 'was not an interest falling within any category protected by law or equity'. He said:

> If English law had followed the development that has recently taken place in the United States[1], the 'broadcast' rights in respect of the races might have been protected as part of the quasi-property created by the enterprise, organisation and labour of the plaintiff in equipping a racecourse and doing all that is necessary to conduct meetings. But courts of equity have not in British jurisdictions thrown the protection of an injunction around all the intangible elements of value … which may flow from the exercise by an individual of his powers or resources whether in the organisation of a business or undertaking or the use of ingenuity, knowledge, skill or labour. This is sufficiently evidenced by the history of the law of copyright and by the fact that the exclusive right to invention, trade marks, designs, trade names and reputation are dealt with in English law as special heads of protected interests and not under a wide generalisation[2].

1 This was a reference to the decision of the US Supreme Court in *International News Service v Associated Press* 248 US 215, 63 L Ed 211, 39 S Ct 68 (1918), enjoining INS from copying AP's news bulletins and then selling the data in competition with the AP, on the grounds that this constituted an unfair misappropriation of the fruits of AP's labours. This decision is the basis for the doctrine of US law that the organiser of a sports event owns a property right in that event that he is entitled to have protected from misappropriation by a third party. See eg *Pittsburgh Athletic Co v KQV Broadcasting Co* 24 F Supp 490 (WD Pa 1937): discussed at para D4.11. See generally Wise 'A "Property Right" in a Sports Event: Views of Different Jurisdictions' [1996] 4(3) SATLJ 63.

2 *Victoria Park Racing and Recreation Grounds co Ltd v Taylor* (1937) 58 CLR 479 at 508–509, HC of A.

D1.11 Therefore, the organiser of a sports event has to find some right in the event or any element of it that is protected by the law, rather than rely on a general proprietary right in the event itself. In other words, the event organiser must identify breaches of recognised rights to provide indirect protection for its commercial interests in the event per se[1].

1 For example, if a promoter cannot control access to the venue of the event, and therefore cannot stop an unauthorised person attending and recording audio-visual footage of the event, the promoter cannot stop that person by invoking some proprietary right in the event per se: see para D4.17. However, 'to the extent that the promoter can assert ownership to component works, and can make it physically impossible to broadcast the event without a reproduction of a substantial part of those

works, the promoter benefits from an indirect mechanism to manage the television rights in the event': Blais *The Protection of Exclusive Television Rights to Sporting Events Held In Public Venues: An Overview of the Law in Australia and Canada*, (1992) 18 Melbourne University Law Review 503, 529.

The same holds true of so-called 'image rights'. See Laddie J in *Elvis Presley Trade Marks* [1997] RPC 543, at 548: '[personalities] can only complain if the reproduction or use of the likeness results in the infringement of some recognised legal right which [he/she] does own'. See generally Chapter D3.

D1.12 This is of course a matter of great concern to sports event organisers, because:

> Legal uncertainty as to what subject matter is being purchased and sold, and to what extent, if at all, third parties may be prevented from engaging in piratical activities, is both detrimental and a disincentive to commercial and sporting activity[1].

However, it is possible to create a coherent and valuable package of rights that is capable of protection from third parties (and therefore is capable of being granted exclusively to, and exploited exclusively by, official commercial partners) based on the careful design, creation and implementation of a commercial programme based on the following three elements:

- Access rights to the venue at which the sports event is held. The event organiser must have the right to exclusive possession of the venue as a matter of real property law, and must be able in practice to control access to the venue, to stop unauthorised persons entering and exploiting the commercial value of the event, and to ensure through the use of terms and conditions that the public and the media admitted to watch the event confine themselves to watching and reporting respectively and do not stray into commercial exploitation of their own.
- Further contractual restrictions on:
  (a) the participants in the event (both clubs and individual players), to ensure that the central commercial programme for the event is not undermined or diluted by their own personal sponsorship or endorsement deals; and
  (b) the official commercial partners, to ensure that they neither overstep their own contractual rights nor inadvertently assist others in hijacking the goodwill in the event.
- The creation, protection and enforcement of the range of copyright, database rights, registered and unregistered trade marks and other intellectual property rights that may subsist in many of the elements that go to make up a sports event.

1 Blais 'The Protection of Exclusive Television Rights to Sporting Events Held In Public Venues: An Overview of the Law in Australia and Canada' (1992) 18 Melbourne University Law Review 503, 538.

D1.13 We now consider each of these foundational elements of a commercial sports rights programme in turn.

3 ACCESS RIGHTS

D1.14 Under English law many sports rights, including two of the biggest revenue earners, ticketing rights and broadcasting rights, are predicated on the event organiser having exclusive control over access to the stadium or other venue at which the sports event is held.

D1.15 This crucial 'control of the park' is grounded in the law of real property, contract and tort. Real property law provides the ownership, leasehold or licence interest in the land that allows the event organiser to claim and enforce the right of exclusive possession and control of the sports venue[1]. Contract law gives the event organiser the ability, and the legitimate right, to place restrictive terms and conditions on entry to the venue to protect the commercial value of the event, and to exclude those who do not accept or will not abide by those terms and conditions[2]. Tort law makes a trespasser of anyone who enters the land without permission, or enters with permission but then infringes the terms and conditions of that permission[3].

1 See generally Chapter D2.
2 See Latham CJ in *Victoria Park Racing and Recreation Grounds Co Ltd v Taylor* (1937) 58 CLR 479, 494, HC of A: 'At sports grounds and other places of entertainment it is the lawful, natural and common practice to put up fences and other structures to prevent people who are not prepared to pay for admission from getting the benefit of the entertainment'. See also *Said v Butt* [1920] 3 KB 497, 502 ('Every contract for admission is subject to the implied condition that the person admitted shall behave properly'); *Sports and General Press Agency Ltd v Our Dogs Publishing Co Ltd* [1917] 2 KB 125, 128, CA ('No doubt the Ladies' Kennel Association had the grounds for the day, and also the right of allowing those persons to enter of whom they approved and excluding those of whom they did not, and that right carried with it the right of laying down conditions binding on the parties admitted').
3 See *Clerk & Lindsell on Torts* (18th edn, Sweet & Maxwell), paras 18-01 and 18-52.

D1.16 A clear difficulty arises in the case of sports played in public places, to which it is not possible to control access to the event. Examples would include the Tour de France, the Boat Race and the London Marathon. Save where the government is prepared to enact special protective legislation (usually only for major events, such as the Olympics), or bid cities are prepared to implement local ordinances[1], it is only practicalities that prevent an unauthorised party seeking to exploit the event (for example, by creating and broadcasting audio or audio-visual coverage of the event)[2].

1 See paras D1.124, D4.17 and D4.18.
2 See generally Blais 'The Protection of Exclusive Television Rights to Sporting Events Held In Public Venues: An Overview of the Law in Australia and Canada' (1992) 18 Melbourne University Law Review 503. See further paras D4.17 and D4.18.

A Broadcasting rights

D1.17 Sports broadcasting rights, under English law, consist of a licence to enter the venue, film the proceedings and transmit the footage to the public[1]. Modern technology allows a 'fan' to bring into the stadium in his pocket any number of means – eg mobile phone, digital or analogue camera, palm-top computer – to send moving pictures, commentary and/or text-based reports and statistics outside the ground to others accessing them through television receivers, web-sites, radios, mobile phones and pagers. Therefore, in order to ensure that it can deliver the *exclusive* broadcasting rights that it has promised to its broadcasting partners, the event organiser has to be sure that it can prevent people entering the venue with filming/recording equipment, and that the actual act of filming/recording is in breach of the conditions of entry, and so can be prevented without argument. This it can do through conditioning the contractual rights of access (usually the admission ticket) on acceptance of such restrictions.

1 See para D4.14 et seq. In relation to the copyright that subsists in relation to the footage created by the broadcaster, see paras D1.54 to D1.56 and D4.22 to D4.24.

D1.18 In *Sports and General Press Agency Ltd v Our Dogs Publishing Co Ltd*[1], the Ladies' Kennel Association had granted the plaintiff photographic agency the 'exclusive' right to take photographs at a dog show run by the association. An independent photographer gained access to the show, took his own photographs and sold them to a publisher who produced and sold a successful photo-journal of the show. When sued, the publisher pointed out that no one had imposed a term of admission forbidding the taking of photographs. This turned out to be dispositive. Lord Justice Swinfen Eady explained[2]:

> It is said that the association had been put to trouble and expense in organising the show, which was their property and which included the right to take photographs themselves and to grant the same right to others, and that they in fact granted it to [the plaintiff]. In my opinion it is not right to speak of the right of taking photographs as property. No doubt the Ladies' Kennel Association had the grounds for the day, and also the right of allowing those persons to enter of whom they approved and excluding those of whom they did not, and that right carried with it the right of laying down conditions binding on the parties admitted; it might be a condition that they should not use cameras or should not take photographs or make sketches. But they did not lay down any such conditions … The answer to the plaintiffs' argument is that they could have acquired by contract such a right as they claim, and that they failed to do.

1 [1917] 2 KB 125, 128, CA.
2 [1917] 2 KB at 127–128. Mr Justice Lush put it more succinctly (at 128): 'if those who promote shows and exhibitions wish to prevent the taking of photographs, they must make it a matter of contract'.

D1.19 Similarly, in *Victoria Park Racing*[1] Mr Justice McTiernan noted that an event organiser was entitled 'to impose on the right it granted to any patron to enter the [venue] that he would not communicate to anyone outside the [venue] the knowledge about the racing which he got inside', and failure to observe that condition would be a breach of contract by the patron and a tortious inducement to breach by the recipient and subsequent broadcaster of the information.

1 *Victoria Park Racing and Recreation Grounds Co Ltd v Taylor* (1937) 58 CLR 479 at 526–527, HC of A.

D1.20 Furthermore, any person who has entered a venue by means of a ticket that incorporates the appropriate restrictions on conduct and use who then acts in breach of those terms and conditions thereby acts outside the licence he or she has been given to enter onto the land, and becomes a trespasser, liable to immediate ejection[1].

1 See paras D1.15 and D1.128.

D1.21 Therefore there should be a provision in the ticket conditions that prevents a spectator filming or making any other recording of the match. For example:

The purchaser of this ticket does not have the right to make a recording or transmission, in any medium, of events taking place within the stadium. Entry to the stadium will be denied to persons with audio, visual and/or audio-visual recording equipment of any sort, including without limitation cameras, video cameras, cassette recorders and microphones. In any event, no photographs, video recordings, sound recordings or similar may be taken or made in the stadium.

OR

You may not use recording equipment or camera devices for any purpose other than for private and domestic use … Images and sound recordings of the event taken by you with camera, video or audio equipment cannot be used for any purpose other than for private and domestic use, ie you may not sell, license, broadcast, publish or otherwise commercially exploit them.

D1.22 If there is also a concern about 'real-time' reporting of match data for commercial purposes[1], then the ticket conditions might also state:

Mobile telephones are permitted within the ground, provide they are used for personal and private use only.

1 See para D1.47.

D1.23 Under English law, however, ticket conditions are only enforceable if they were brought to the attention of the purchaser, and thereby incorporated into the contract of sale, prior to the sale taking place[1].

1 *McCutcheon v David MacBrayne Ltd* [1964] 1 All ER 430, [1964] 1 WLR 125, HL; *Thornton v Shoe Lane Parking* [1971] 2 QB 163, [1971] 1 All ER 686, CA.

D1.24 There may be notices posted on the matter at the venue, for example in the form of ground regulations[1], but the spectator could argue that this restriction was not brought to his attention at the time he purchased the ticket and therefore it is not enforceable against him.

1 See para D2.84.

D1.25 Instead, therefore, however many ticket distribution channels there may be for a particular event[1], in each case care must be taken to bring the ticket conditions to the attention of purchasers prior to or at the time the sale takes place.

1 For example, tickets may be sold by the sales office at the venue, in person and by mail; over the Internet, via the issuer's web-site; by a commercial agency such as Ticketmaster (phone and on-line sales); to member clubs (or, via those clubs, to their members); or to stadium debenture-holders.

D1.26 Ideally, written confirmation from each purchaser should be obtained that he/she has had the ticket conditions brought to his/her attention prior to sale and acknowledges and accepts them as a condition of sale[1]. Obviously, however, that may not always be practicable. If any telephone sales take place, one option would be to have an automated reply system that tells callers that ticket conditions apply, gives them an option to listen to someone reading out the ticket conditions, and makes them choose a specific option to say that they acknowledge and accept the ticket conditions, all *before* any purchase is allowed to take place. E-commerce operators should be instructed to make sure that a would-be purchaser, prior to making the purchase on-line, is given clear notice that ticket conditions apply to the purchase, and an opportunity to read those conditions. Ideally, the purchaser should have to take some positive act prior to purchase (for example, ticking a box) to acknowledge that he has read and acknowledges and accepts the ticket conditions. Similarly, a commercial agency such as Ticketmaster should be asked to agree to bring the conditions of sale of the tickets to the attention of the purchaser and to obtain firm evidence of the purchaser's acknowledgement and acceptance of those conditions prior to allowing any sale to take place[2].

1 For example, the application form for tickets for the Wimbledon tennis championships reproduces the ticket conditions in full on the back of the form, and the purchaser has to complete and sign a slip confirming that he/she accepts them.

2 The Society of Ticket Agents and Retailers ('Star') is a self-regulatory body that operates within guidelines supported by, among others, the Office of Fair Trading, the British Tourist Authority, the London Tourist Board and the Society of London Theatre. Star's Code of Practice is aimed at encouraging high standards of service in the ticketing industry, providing confidence to the ticket-buying public, and promoting better and clearer information for the ticket-buying public. Under the code, Star's members 'shall ensure that the terms and conditions attached to tickets are fully explained [to the purchasing customer]. Restrictions on transferability should be made clear, as well as any cancellation rights which the customer may have'. See Star Code of Practice, para B1.3.

D1.27 In similar fashion, the terms of accreditation of news media to the event should prohibit commercial use (as opposed to use for the purpose of reporting on the event) of the images, data and other information gathered during the reporting process. In addition to the general prohibition, they might include more specific restrictions designed to protect against particular commercial uses. For example, the terms of accreditation of media at FA Premier League and Football League clubs provide:

> Reporters are only permitted to produce or file articles. Unless they have an appropriate licence they shall not record or transmit or compile any audio commentary, moving pictures, photographs, audio, visual, text or data streaming any statistics, score updates or performance data, other than for inclusion within the article. Copy may be filed at any time during the match but resulting reports can only be published as follows:
> (i) one report between the 20th and 25th minute;
> (ii) one report at half-time;
> (iii) one report between the 65th and 70th minutes;
> (iv) further reports at the end of the match and thereafter;
> (v) in the event of injury time a further report can be published at the end.

4 CONTRACTUAL RESTRICTIONS ON PARTICIPANTS AND COMMERCIAL PARTNERS

D1.28 After ticketing and broadcasting rights, the next most important source of commercial value is a sponsorship programme that grants one main ('title') sponsor[1] and/or a 'family' of event sponsors[2]. The value here comes from an association of the commercial brand with the strong values of the sporting brand[3], and therefore depends upon clear and uncluttered affiliation and an absence of conflicting messages. The event organiser's ability to deliver this value to event sponsors depends upon its ability to control all aspects of the environment in which the event is held, and in particular to keep in check the commercial aspirations of the various participants in the event[4].

1 Such as Barclaycard's sponsorship of the FA Premier League, Nationwide's sponsorship of the Football League and Football Conference, Zurich's sponsorship of rugby union's Premiership, or Embassy's sponsorship of the World Professional Darts Championship.

2 Such as the sponsorship packages in relation to the England national football team granted by the Football Association to Nationwide, Carlsberg and others, or the packages in relation to the UEFA Champions League granted by UEFA to Amstel and others.

3 See generally Chapter D5.

4 A classic example was the dispute that arose in relation to the ICC Champions Trophy in September 2002. The ICC had sold the central commercial rights (principally, broadcasting and sponsorship) to that and other ICC events, including the 2003 and 2007 Cricket World Cups, to Global Cricket Corporation, for US $550m. As part of the deal, ICC promised that teams and individual players participating in ICC events would not be allowed to do sponsorship endorsement

deals that conflicted with rights and exclusivity granted by GCC to event sponsors. Disputes relating to the Indian team's proposed sponsorship by Sahara (in conflict with an event sponsor, South African Airways), and to the requirement that players not conduct any endorsement activity either during or for sixty days on either side of the event, prompted threats of boycotts and lawsuits that were only resolved at the last minute. See eg 'ICC rejects India's sponsor in Champions Trophy clash' (2002) Sportcal.com, 2 September; 'No contract deal despite ICC meeting with Indian cricketers' (2002) Sportcal.com, 5 September; 'Will the BCCI play ball?' www.sportbusiness.com (9 September 2002); 'Cricket sponsors: we won't back down again over clash' (2002) Sportcal.com, 13 September.

D1.29 Therefore, where the event organiser is hiring the venue(s) in which the event is held, or the event involves a number of clubs, each hosting matches in the event at its own home ground, the event organiser must ensure that its contracts with the host(s) or other venue owner(s) guarantee delivery of a completely 'clean' venue. For example, in a multi-club competition played at the various clubs' home grounds, the participation agreement or rules of the event might provide:

> Each Club shall procure, at no cost to the Event Organiser, that the venue at which it plays its home matches in the Event is a clean venue, ie a venue that is completely free, for the period commencing 48 hours prior to each match and ending 24 hours after such match, from any and all third party or Club messages, branding or advertising of whatever nature (including but not limited to commercial or promotional messages on tickets, car park passes and accreditations, tunnels and dressing rooms, advertising displays, pitch branding of whatever nature, concessions and branded vending facilities of any kind and the clothing of any ball boys, photographers and other accredited personnel), save only for those items installed, erected or otherwise authorised by the Event Organiser.

D1.30 As another example, cl 61(1) of the Olympic Charter provides:

> No kind of demonstration or political, religious or racial propaganda is permitted in the Olympic areas. No form of publicity shall be allowed in and above the stadia and other competition areas which are considered as part of the Olympic sites. Commercial installations and advertising signs shall not be allowed in the stadia, nor in the other sports grounds.

D1.31 Similarly, the teams and the athletes that play on the teams must also be 'clean', ie not carrying the baggage of sponsorships or endorsements that conflict with the central marketing programme of the event[1]. The resolution of this conflict will very much depend upon the relative bargaining positions of the parties[2]. However, the event organiser should always be seeking to include provisions in the participation agreements for the event that restrict participating teams and clubs from wearing branded clothing, using branded equipment, and/or co-operating with commercial advertising that seeks to imply an association between their personal sponsors and the event.

1 Or perhaps even any advertising message, conflicting or otherwise, since any message will increase the clutter and detract from the prominence enjoyed by the central sponsor.

2 For a discussion of one high profile conflict on this issue, relating to the ICC's international cricket events, see para D1.28, n 4.

D1.32 For example, in relation to clubs competing in an event, the participation agreement or event rules might provide:

> - The Event Organiser is the absolute and outright legal and beneficial owner of all of the Commercial Rights in and to the Event and all of the matches in the Event.

- The Event Organiser has absolute discretion with respect to the Commercial Rights. It may exploit some of the Commercial Rights itself; it may authorise others (including, for the avoidance of doubt, any Club) to exploit all or some of the Commercial Rights; and/or it may decide not to exploit (or to allow others to exploit) some of the Commercial Rights. The Event Organiser may also appoint a third party to act as broker or agent on behalf of the Event Organiser with respect to some or all of the Commercial Rights[1].
- The Event Organiser hereby authorises each Club, acting individually and not collectively with any other Club, to exploit the following rights – the 'Club Rights' – and to retain the income generated thereby (provided that the Club shall be responsible for all taxes and other levies thereon): *[list of rights devolved to the Clubs, such as ticketing, programmes, perimeter advertising, shirt sponsorship, catering concessions, pourage rights etc]*, provided always that the Club shall not grant any Club Rights to any third party whose products or services are in the Reserved Categories [ie those brand categories in which the Event Organiser wishes to preserve exclusivity for its commercial partners].
- All Commercial Rights other than the Club Rights are reserved to the Event Organiser (the 'Reserved Rights'), to be exploited (or not) as the Event Organiser in its absolute discretion shall see fit. For the avoidance of doubt, no Club is authorised or entitled to sell, license or otherwise exploit any of the Reserved Rights.
- Each Club shall support the programme established by the Event Organiser for the exploitation of the Reserved Rights. In particular (although without limitation):
  – No Club shall, without the prior written approval of the Event Organiser, exploit any Club Rights in conflict with the terms of these rules or in a manner that, in the opinion of the Event Organiser, detracts from the primacy of the programme established by the Event Organiser for the exploitation of the Reserved Rights;
  – Each Club shall use its best endeavours to assist the Event Organiser in combating activities that undermine the Event Organiser's commercial programme for the Reserved Rights, including so-called 'ambush marketing' activities such as (without limitation): unauthorised competitions and promotions based around the Event and/or individual matches; unauthorised creation and/or use (including but not limited to broadcasting, narrowcasting and/or webcasting) of video footage and/or audio commentary of matches; and unauthorised distribution, by any medium (including but not limited to internet, intranet, online service, interactive TV service, WAP or other telephony service or other interactive media content distribution service), of (a) any live, delayed or recorded textual or narrative match commentary or 'match tracker'-type commentary; and/or (b) any live or point by point scoring.

1 See Chapter D8.

D1.33 Where the event organiser will only be contracting with the participating teams, and not directly with the individuals playing on those teams, it will also want each contracting team to agree:

> to procure that each of its players, as well as each of its directors, officers, members, employees and members of staff involved in any way in the Club's participation in the Event, is made aware of and agrees to be bound by, to observe and to comply with the terms and conditions of participation.

D1.34 Ideally, however, there would be a contract between the event organiser and the individual players, in an entry form or other type of participation agreement signed by the players, or in the event rules and incorporated by reference into such participation agreement[1], with specific provisions requiring the player to support, and preventing the player from undermining, the central commercial programme. A particularly detailed example would be the following:

A 'Rights' shall mean such rights as the Player has:

(1) to use, reproduce and/or publish, in connection with any promotion, sponsorship, endorsement or other commercial arrangement or otherwise, the Player's name, likeness, autograph, biographical details, reputation, image and/or voice in his capacity as a participant in the Event, and/or

(2) to authorise any third party or third parties to do any of the foregoing.

B 'Promotional Services' means attendance at and participation as required, *all solely in the Player's capacity as a participant in the Event*, in advertising, marketing, promotional and other commercial activities specified by the Event Organiser, to assist in the exercise of the Rights as well as to support the rest of the commercial programme organised by the Event Organiser around the Event, including but not limited to personal appearances, public relations events, pre- and post-Match functions, official presentations, official dinners, hospitality events, photographic, filming or recording sessions, signing merchandise and other items, live and/or recorded Internet web chats, broadcasts and/or recording sessions, and benevolent activities including visits to schools, hospitals and charitable organisations.

C The Player represents, warrants and undertakes, with respect to the grant of the Rights and the provision of the Promotional Services, that:

(i) he has not to date done any of the following, and he will not do any of them during the Event or at any time thereafter:

(a) exploit any of the Rights himself;

(b) authorise or otherwise assist or enable any third party to exploit any of the Rights;

(c) directly or indirectly restrict or otherwise adversely affect the Event Organiser's exploitation of the Rights; and/or

(d) authorise or otherwise assist or enable any third party to restrict or otherwise adversely affect the Event Organiser's exploitation of the Rights;

(ii) he has not made to date, and from this date he shall not make, any commercial use of:

(a) the word marks relating to the Event,

(b) the registered trade mark of the logo of the Event and/or any other mark, words or logo capable of being confused with that mark, and/or

(c) his association with the Event Organiser and/or the Event;

(iii) he has not authorised and he will not authorise the use during the Event of his name, likeness, signature, reputation and/or image, whether directly or indirectly, in an individual or a group capacity, as a participant in the Event or otherwise, to endorse or promote in any way any product or service of a competitor of any Event Sponsor;

(iv) he will, throughout the Event, make himself available for, report promptly to, attend and participate in, all in his capacity as a participant in the Event, all Promotional Services required of him by the Event Organiser;

(iv) he will, throughout the Event, during all Event-related activities:

(a) wear such clothing (including any clothing displaying the name and/or branding of Event Sponsors) as the Event Organiser may provide,

(b) not wear any clothing or use any sports bag or other equipment featuring or in any way giving exposure to any product or service other than those of the Event Sponsors. If the Player wishes to wear any item of clothing or equipment not provided by the Event Organiser, any branding that is marked on the item shall be covered so that it is neither visible nor identifiable, and

(c) not provide any personal appearances to anyone other than as directed by the Event Organiser.

D At all relevant times, including press conferences, interviews and photo calls, the Player shall wear official branded clothing and shall not wear any clothing bearing any other brands or logos or marks.

Disputes between individual participants (usually, and most effectively, negotiating collectively) and event organisers as to the scope of such provisions, how much freedom individual participants have to continue their own individual endorsement programmes in and around the event, have become a commonplace feature of major sports events[2].

1 For example, para 4 of the Byelaw to Rule 45 of the Olympic Charter provides: 'Except as permitted by the IOC Executive Board, no competitor who participates in the Olympic Games may allow his person, name, picture or sports performances to be used for advertising purposes during the Olympic Games'.

2 See for example para D1.28, n 4.

D1.35 It will also be appropriate for the event organiser to require commercial partners to acknowledge the organiser's ownership of commercial rights in the sports event, and to agree not to exploit those rights save as specifically authorised in the agreement between them[1]. Indeed, ideally the agreement would go further and require the licensee not to do anything or to assist any third party to do anything that would undermine the value of the central commercial programme.

1 See further paras D1.131 to D1.134.

5 INTELLECTUAL PROPERTY RIGHTS IN SPORT

D1.36 The law encourages and rewards creativity and invention by giving to those who expend time, energy and talent (and research and development funds) in creating original brands, works or properties legally enforceable rights in the fruits of their creative labours. These rights, described generically as 'intellectual property rights', give the creator a degree of exclusivity in respect to the use and exploitation of his or her creation. On the other hand, the law also wants to encourage free competition and trade. Monopoly rights in intellectual property can translate into monopolies in related market sectors. Therefore, there are clear (and sometimes not so clear) limits placed on the degree of protection that intellectual property law will confer on rights owners. It is at the margins of this protection that the battle between event organisers and 'ambush marketers' takes place[1].

1 See paras D1.116 to D1.134.

D1.37 Contractual provisions will give an event organiser strong protection against unauthorised activities by its contractual partners, but only limited and indirect protection against unauthorised exploitation of the event by third parties with whom the event organiser does not have a contractual relationship. The event organiser's major weapon against such third parties is intellectual property law, through the skilful use of which the event organiser can deter or successfully take action against most unauthorised third party exploitation of the event.

D1.38 As noted above[1], whereas under English law there are no proprietary rights in a sports event per se, intellectual property rights may subsist in elements of the event that enable the rights owner to control and protect exploitation of at least some aspects of the event. The most relevant intellectual property rights in the sports sector are copyright, database rights, trade marks, 'unregistered trade marks' (passing off), and patents[2]. Each of these obviously represents an enormously important area of the law in its own rights, and a work of this type cannot do more than cover the basic features of the rights and highlight their main relevance and application in the sports sector[3]. Those requiring fuller treatment should refer to one of the many excellent intellectual property treatises available[4].

1 See para D1.11.
2 So-called 'image rights' have a chapter of their own: Chapter D3.
3 For an illuminating case study, see Chapple 'Introduction to Intellectual Property Rights' in Griffith Jones (ed) *Law and the Business of Sport* (1997, Butterworths). See also Phelops 'Can Sport Move in Mysterious Ways?' Copyright World (September 1996), p 17; Harrington 'Sport and Intellectual Property' (1999) 6(1) Sports Law Administration & Practice 1.
4 Such as Cornish *Intellectual Property* (4th edn, 2001, Sweet & Maxwell) or Copinger & Skone *James on Copyright* (14th edn, 2002, Supplement 1).

A Copyright

D1.39 Copyright is an intellectual property right of central importance to the sports industry. On its own or in combination with other intellectual property rights and contractual rights, it underpins ownership and exploitation of some of the key products and services that drive commercial revenues in sport.

D1.40 Section 1 of the Copyright Designs and Patents Act 1988 ('CDPA 1988') provides that copyright subsists in original[1]: literary, dramatic, musical and artistic works; sound recordings, films, broadcasts and cable programmes; and the typographical arrangements of published editions. Section 2(1) of the CDPA 1988 confers upon the owner of copyright in a work the exclusive right to: copy the work; issue copies of the work to the public; rent or lend the work to the public; perform, show or play the work in public; broadcast the work or include it in a cable programme service; or make an adaptation of the work or do any of the above in relation to an adaptation. Section 3(2) of the CDPA 1988 provides that copyright arises at the time a qualifying work (literary, dramatic and musical works) is created (ie recorded in material form). It arises automatically; copyright does not have to be registered to be enforceable.

1 Originality is not an enormous hurdle in this context. It effectively requires only that the works should not be copied but should originate from the author: *Ladbroke (Football) Ltd v William Hill (Football) Ltd* [1964] 1 All ER 465, [1964] 1 WLR 273, 291, HL.

D1.41 The copyright is owned by the author of the work, ie its creator[1]. For sound recordings, this is the producer; for films, it is the producer and principal director; and for broadcasts it is the maker of the broadcast[2]. Where the author created the work in the course of his employment by another, the employer is the first owner of the copyright, subject to any agreement to the contrary[3]. Where the author created the work on commission by another, the author will remain the owner unless he has assigned it in writing to the other[4]. However, in the absence of a written assignment of the copyright, the courts may infer a beneficial assignment, or a licence to use the copyright, from the nature of the transaction and the conduct of the parties[5].

1 To qualify a work for protection under the CDPA 1988, the author must at the material time have been a British national, or domiciled or resident in the United Kingdom (or another country to which the relevant part of the Act extends), or a body incorporated under the law of Britain (or such other country). See ss 154 and 157 of the CDPA 1988. There are also special rules as to which broadcasts qualify for protection. See s 153 of the CDPA 1988.
2 Section 9 of the CDPA 1988. See paras D1.54 to D1.56 and D4.22 to D4.24.
3 Section 11(2) of the CDPA 1988.
4 Section 90(3) of the CDPA 1988.
5 *Warner v Gestetner Ltd* [1988] EIPRD 89, Ch D.

D1.42 The general rule is that a work remains subject to copyright protection for a period of 70 years from the end of the year in which the author dies[1]. In relation to broadcasts and sound recordings, the copyright subsists for 50 years from the end of the calendar year in which it is made[2].

1 Section 12 of the CDPA 1988.
2 Sections 13A and 14 of the CDPA 1988.

D1.43 Copyright can be bought and sold and exploited like any other form of property. Many commercial deals in the sports sector are based on an assignment or licence of copyright, usually in return for a royalty[1]. Assignments and licences can be complete, ie authorising all of the acts that would otherwise be restricted by copyright, and can cover the entire copyright period, which would put the assignee or licensee in the same position as the original author[2]. Alternatively, they can be limited so as to apply to one or more but not all of the acts restricted by copyright and/or to part but not the whole of the period for which the copyright is to subsist[3]. Therefore a copyright work can be the subject of various assignments and licences for various periods of time, and many people apart from the copyright owner can be involved in the exploitation of a copyright work[4].

1 As to sports broadcasting contracts, see paras D1.52 to D1.54 and D4.22 to D4.24. There is nothing in theory to stop the securitisation of future royalty streams from the licensing of the use of copyright archives, eg to Olympic Games or World Cup Finals. On securitisation, see para C3.119 et seq.
2 Under s 92 of the CDPA 1988 exclusive assignees and licensees of the entire copyright in a work are authorised to exercise a right otherwise exercisable exclusively by the copyright owner to the exclusion of all other persons, including the person granting the licence.
3 Section 90(2) of the CDPA 1988.
4 This is particularly true of the copyright in broadcast footage of a global sports event, such as a FIA Formula One grand prix. There will be dozens of broadcasters licensed by the copyright owner to broadcast that footage, in particular territories, during particular time windows, on particular platforms. See generally paras D4.30 to D4.45.

(a) Works capable of copyright protection

D1.44 Literary works 'Literary works' within the meaning of s 3 of the CDPA 1988 means any work, other than a dramatic or musical work, which is written, spoken or sung. This obviously covers news articles, magazines and books. So, for example, copyright subsists in the vast amount of original written material generated about sport, including rules and regulations, match reports, newspaper and magazine articles, event programmes and books and encyclopaedias, as well as in calendars of events, fixture lists and databases of statistical information.

D1.45 Information itself, such as football results, is not subject to copyright, but the way the information is expressed may be. In *Football League Ltd v Littlewoods Pools Ltd*[1], the House of Lords held that copyright subsisted in the League's fixture list because (1) it was not possible to separate the arrangement of the fixtures from the mere making of the chronological list of fixtures, and (2) even if it had been possible, the preparation of the chronological list itself involved sufficient labour, skill and expertise to justify copyright protection. As a result, pools companies, betting offices and the media have had to enter into royalty-based licence agreements for the right to reproduce such fixture lists[2].

1 [1959] 2 All ER 546, HL. See also *Bookmakers' Afternoon Greyhound Services Ltd v Wilf Gilbert (Staffordshire) Ltd* [1994] FSR 723 (creation of race-card involved sufficient skill and judgment to afford it copyright as an original literary work). But see para D1.46, n 2.
2 See further para D1.47.

D1.46 'Literary works' can also encompass databases. The literary work comprised by a database is original if, and only if, by reason of a selection or arrangement of its contents, the database constitutes the author's own intellectual creation[1]. However, databases are now also protected by sui generis database rights[2]. Databases of sports information have traditionally been used as form guides, by scouts but also in the gambling industry. They are becoming more significant, and more commercially valuable, as the demand for sports data increases not only in the gambling industry (for products such as spread betting) but also in connection with interactive television, on the Internet (to provide content that drives traffic) and also for fantasy games in newspapers, 'realistic' computer games and the like.

1 Section 3A of the CDPA 1988.
2 See paras D1.63 to D1.75. Indeed, the fact that fixture lists probably amount to databases within the meaning of the new UK database law may affect the claim to copyright in such lists. Under the new law, databases only qualify for protection which 'by reason of the selection or arrangement of their contents constitute the author's own intellectual creation', which is a higher test for originality than exists under traditional copyright law. See para D1.40, n 1.

D1.47 The FA Premier League and the Football League, who between them organise the top four divisions of professional football in England, have formed a separate company, Football DataCo Ltd, to secure, protect and exploit the commercial value of data generated by the matches they organise. In addition, the Scottish Premier League and Scottish Football League have each appointed Football DataCo Ltd to perform the same role in respect of their competitions. This involves the traditional licensing of pools companies, betting offices and the media to reproduce the fixture lists, but it also involves the gathering of statistical data from a game (goals, scorers, substitutions, yellow cards, red cards etc), for exploitation on a real-time basis using the Internet and mobile telephony, but also on a long-term basis in (for example) form guides for betting, interactive television and fantasy football games[1]. The value is created and protected by means of copyright and database law in relation to the data that is generated for exploitation by Football DataCo Ltd. It is also created and protected by requiring members of the media and public seeking access to football matches to agree, via press pass terms and conditions for the media, and ticket conditions and ground regulations for the public, not to seek to create and/or transmit data about the match for commercial exploitation, on a 'real-time' basis or otherwise[2].

1 Lecture on Football DataCo Ltd by Brian Phillpotts, Commercial Director, FA Premier League Ltd, KCL Postgraduate Course in Sports Law (21 March 2002).
2 See paras D1.21 and D1.22.

D1.48 'Literary works' also encompasses items such as tables or compilations (other than databases), computer programmes and preparatory design materials for computer programmes (often called the 'source code'). So, for example, copyright will subsist in the source code and programming for the various computer products that track player performance during a match (and thereby generate statistics for commercial and non-commercial use), as well as for the vast array of sports-related computer games.

D1.49 Musical works Copyright in musical works can also be of relevance in sport. Copyright would subsist, for example, in an official theme tune to an event, or in a team anthem. It would subsist in both the composition of the music itself and separately in any sound recording or broadcast of the work.

D1.50 Artistic works Artistic works include photographic works and graphic works of any nature, irrespective of artistic quality[1]. Photographic images of sport are used not only to illustrate match reports and other printed material relating to sport, but also to convey messages and illuminate themes of other news articles, especially in the marketing of a broad range of products and services[2]. Copyright subsists in such photographs, which must be cleared prior to use. It also subsists in venue designs, such as for golf courses and motor-racing circuits. It also subsists in the artwork relating to sport – such as team and event logos[3], mascots, livery of team kits, badges, posters and flags – that forms the basis for sports sponsorship and sports merchandising and licensing programmes[4].

1 Section 4(1)(a) of the CDPA 1988.
2 A casual scan through any edition of the Law Society Gazette, for example, will usually reveal half a dozen sporting images, used by editors to illustrate non-sports-related stories and especially by law firms in the recruitment ads, seeking to portray positive images of themselves to potential recruits.
3 For an analysis of the issues arising in relation to composite logos (ie logos that combine the mark of the event with the mark of the sponsor), see Fitzpatrick and Thompson 'Being distinctive – the problem of creating composite logos' (2002) 5(1) Sports Law Bulletin 5.
4 See further Chapters D5 and D6. Such artwork may also amount to a design capable of protection under English law, as a registered or unregistered 'design right'. For an example of when this intellectual property right might add usefully to the armoury in a sports context, see Chapple 'Introduction to Intellectual Property Rights' in Griffith-Jones (ed) *Law and the Business of Sport* (1997, Butterworths), p 198.

D1.51 Dramatic works A dramatic work is one that is capable of being performed, such as by acting or dancing[1]. Sports events generally do not qualify as dramatic works within the meaning of the CPDA 1988[2]. This is because the sporting spectacle is by its nature not scripted but improvised; indeed, uncertainty of outcome is its very essence. Therefore, while copyright may subsist in the footage recorded of a sports event[3], it does not subsist in the sports event itself[4].

1 Section 3(1) of the CDPA 1988.
2 Section 180(2) of the CDPA 1988 defines 'performance' as 'a dramatic performance (which includes dance and mime), a musical performance, a reading or recitation of a literary work or a performance of a variety act or any similar presentation given by one or more individuals'. A sporting event does not fall into any of those categories.
3 See paras D1.54 to D1.56 and D4.22 to D4.24.
4 See Phelops 'Can Sport Move in Mysterious Ways' (1996) 63 Copyright World 16.

D1.52 To the extent that aspects of a sporting performance are scripted, then arguments can be made that copyright subsists in them. For example, ice-skating or gymnastic routines performed as a set series of manoeuvres to music might be argued to qualify for copyright protection under this head[1]. Where the routine is effectively a form of dance, there seems to be no reason in principle why the fact that the dance is performed as part of a sporting event should disqualify it from protection as a dramatic work. There is still uncertainty of outcome, in the sense that the participants are competing against each other, but the competition takes the form of a series of scripted individual performances, all judged against a common (artistic or quasi-artistic) standard. The performances of the competitors are conducted in isolation from each other, so that one competitor cannot have a direct impact on his or her competitors' performances but can only perform him or herself to the highest possible standard in the hope that it will be better than the performances of his or her competitors.

1 See Blais 'The Protection of Exclusive Television Rights to Sporting Events Held in Public Venues: An Overview of the Law in Australia and Canada' (1992) 18 Melbourne University Law Review 503, 528 ('Figure skating, gymnastics, synchronised swimming, aerobatic skiing or rhythmic gymnastics routines are arguably choreographic works provided they are given a material form and are thus protected dramatic works').

D1.53 Contrast that with a sport where the contest involves interaction between its participants. If a coach draws out or otherwise plots in writing a specific move such as a free kick routine in football or a backs' move in rugby, could it be argued that the original plan by the coach will qualify for copyright protection as a literary work or graphical work or both? What then takes place on the field of play could then be said to be effectively an exercise of the copyright owner's right to perform that work in public. The point has not been tested and there is no specific statutory prohibition on such an interpretation, but the authors regard it as untenable. The scripted free kick routine or backs' move would be a mere incidental feature or component part of a total match or encounter, the vast majority of which was entirely improvised, and the routine itself would necessarily be affected by the interaction of its 'performers' with opponents who are not party to any 'performance'. There is nothing in the CDPA 1988 to suggest that that Act was intended to protect sporting (as opposed to artistic) endeavour, and it would be straining the statutory intent to find that copyright protection should nevertheless be given to such a narrow element of an otherwise wholly improvised sporting contest[1].

1 See Phelops 'Can Sport Move in Mysterious Ways' (1996) 63 Copyright World 16.
Two types of right closely related to copyright are moral rights and performance rights. Moral rights are: (a) the right to be identified as the author of a work or director of a film (CDPA 1988, ss 77 and 78); (b) the right to object to derogatory treatment of one's work (CDPA 1988, s 80); (c) the right not to be falsely attributed as the author of a work (CDPA 1988, s 84); and (d) the right to privacy in relation to photographs or films that were commissioned for private or domestic purposes (CDPA 1988, s 85). Performance rights are the right not to have one's performance of a work exploited (in particular, recorded for commercial exploitation) without one's consent (CDPA 1988, s 183). Neither type of right is of central importance in the sports sector. Moral rights cannot be assigned or licensed; they can only be asserted or waived (CDPA 1988, ss 87 and 94). And as noted above, most sports events will not qualify as 'performances' for the purposes of the CPDA 1988.

D1.54 Sound recordings, films, broadcasts and cable programmes
Copyright (again in combination with other rights) underpins the enormous industry that surrounds the creation and broadcast of audio-visual images of sports events, driving subscriptions to pay-TV channels, attracting traffic to websites and generating spin-off products such as videos and computer games.

D1.55 'Sound recordings' will include player interviews, audio files and tapes of radio broadcasts. 'Films' are defined as recordings on any medium from which moving images may by any means be produced[1], which obviously encompasses audio-visual footage of sports events as well as the news conferences, training sessions and player interviews that surround them, interspersed with coverage of pundits in a studio or otherwise. Therefore, while there may not be any copyright inherent in a sporting performance per se[2], if that performance is recorded on audio and/or video-tape, that recording and its subsequent broadcast[3] will be protected by copyright.

1 Section 5B(1) of the CDPA 1988.
2 See paras D1.51 to D1.53.

3 Section 6 of the CPDA 1988 defines a 'broadcast' as the transmission by wireless telegraphy of visual images, sounds or other information capable of being received by members of the public lawfully or transmitted for presentation to members of the public. This would include for instance a satellite broadcast. A 'cable programme' is an item included in a 'cable programme service', ie a service consisting in sending visual images, sounds or other information by means of a telecommunication system other than wireless telegraphy for reception in two or more places or for presentation to members of the public.

D1.56 The owner of the copyright in the recording of a sports event is prima facie the party that produces it[1]. However, the CPDA 1988 specifically allows a present assignment of a future copyright, ie a copyright in a work that has not yet been created[2]. For example, if Sky Sports records and broadcasts coverage of an FA Premier League football match, then the owner of the copyright in the broadcast footage is BSkyB Ltd. However, in its broadcasting agreement with BSkyB, the FA Premier League will have taken an assignment of copyright in the broadcast from BSkyB, and licensed back to BSkyB the right to show the broadcast on Sky Sports channels for a specific (or unlimited) number of times during the term of the agreement[3].

1 Section 9 of the CDPA 1988. See para D1.41.
2 Section 91 of the CDPA 1988.
3 See further paras D1.21 to D1.24, and D4.69 and D4.79. If the event organiser fails to do this, then going forward it will be the broadcaster, and not the event organiser, who owns (and therefore controls the commercial exploitation of) archive footage of the event.

(b) Infringement of copyright

D1.57 Anyone who exercises any of the rights of the copyright owner (ie copying, selling or renting, performing, broadcasting or adapting[1]) with respect to the whole or a substantial part[2] of the work without the authorisation of the copyright owner thereby infringes copyright in the work[3].

1 Section 2(1) of the CDPA 1988. See para D1.40.
2 Section 16(3)(a) of the CDPA 1988. The test for the copying of a substantial part is more qualitative than quantitative. See *Ladbroke (Football) Ltd v William Hill (Football) Ltd* [1964] 1 WLR 273, HL per Lord Reid at 276: 'The question whether the defendant has copied a substantial part depends much more on the quality than the quantity of what he has taken'.
3 There are also secondary infringements such as importing infringing copies of a work, possessing or selling or distributing infringing copies in the course of business, providing means for making infringement copies, or permitting the use of premises or providing apparatus for the manufacture of infringing copies. See ss 22 to 26 of the CDPA 1988. These forms of infringement are particularly aimed at those who seek to make copyright infringement into a business proposition, such as those who (for instance) run illegal copying plants.

D1.58 Unlike some types of intellectual property, copyright does not confer a monopoly on the copyright owner in relation to the work once created. It simply prevents another person from committing the acts restricted by copyright as noted above. There is nothing for instance to stop another person independently creating the same work and if that new creation is not based upon an act restricted by copyright there is no infringement of copyright.

D1.59 In addition, copyright protects the work itself, and not any underlying concepts. Put another way, it protects the way an idea is expressed, but not the idea itself[1]. So, for example, it would be breach of copyright to copy the script of 'Space Jam' but not to create a film about cartoon characters playing basketball with 'real' characters.

1 *Football League v Littlewoods Pools Ltd* [1959] 2 All ER 546, HL.

D1.60 Furthermore, not all use of a copyright work constitutes copyright infringement. For example, 'incidental inclusion in an artistic work … film, broadcast or cable programme' does not infringe copyright[1]. In addition, 'fair dealing' is permitted in copyright works. 'Fair dealing' is not a defined statutory term; it is intended to cover acts that do not damage the commercial rights of the copyright owner. Therefore, use of copyright materials for research and private study purposes, or for purposes of criticism or review, does not infringe copyright. Nor does use of such materials for the purpose of reporting current events, provided that the use is accompanied by sufficient acknowledgement (no acknowledgement being required in relation to broadcast news programmes)[2]. This is most relevant in the sports context in the context of television news, whereby one channel shows short clips from another channel's coverage of a sports event, usually the goals or other key action. Such use has been held to be 'fair dealing' and therefore not copyright infringement, notwithstanding that it was by definition the key parts of the copyright work that were being reproduced[3]. The different news organisations periodically enter into voluntary codes for the reproduction of each other's footage for purposes of news reporting[4].

1 Section 31 of the CDPA 1988.
2 Sections 29 and 30 of the CDPA 1988.
3 *BBC v British Satellite Broadcasting Ltd* [1992] Ch 141, Ch D.
4 See para D4.82.

(c) *Remedies for infringement of copyright*

D1.61 If infringement can be established, the copyright owner has the right to damages and to an injunction to prevent further infringement. He can also obtain an order for delivery up of infringing copies. The CDPA 1988 even gives him the right, subject to certain procedures, to seize and detain infringing copies[1].

1 Sections 96 to 100 of the CDPA 1988.

D1.62 It is also a criminal offence to make for sale or hire, to import into the United Kingdom otherwise than for private and domestic use, or in the course of a business to possess, sell or hire, offer for sale or hire, exhibit in public or distribute an article that one knows or has reason to believe is an infringing copy of a copyright work[1]. It is also a criminal offence to make an article specifically designed for making copies of a copyright work, or to possess such an article, knowing or having reason to believe it is to be used for making infringing copies for sale or hire or for use in the course of a business[2]. Finally, where copyright is infringed by way of reception of a broadcast or cable programme, by public performance of a literary, dramatic or musical work, or by the public playing or showing of a sound recording or film, then anyone who has caused the work to be so performed, played or shown is guilty of an offence if he knew or had reason to believe that to do so would amount to an infringement of copyright in the work[3].

1 Section 107(1) of the CDPA 1988.
2 Section 107(2) of the CDPA 1988.
3 Section 198 of the CDPA 1988.

B Database rights

D1.63 As sports data becomes an increasingly valuable form of commercially exploitable 'content'[1], so the ability to protect such content from use by third parties assumes greater and greater importance.

1 As is becoming the case in football (see para D1.47) and horseracing (see paras D1.68 and D1.69).

D1.64 Although the CDPA 1988 encompasses databases as 'literary works'[1], the creator of the database may not own the copyright in the underlying data, and while he may have copyright in the way he has selected and arranged the data, that copyright may not be infringed by someone who takes the information from the database and arranges it in a different way. The Copyright and Rights in Databases Regulations 1997 (the 'Regulations')[2], which incorporated into English law the EC Directive on the legal protection of databases (the 'EC Directive')[3], created a new sui generis 'database right' that avoids these difficulties.

1 See para D1.46.
2 SI 1997/3032 (18 December 1997).
3 Directive 96/9/EC of 11 March 1996 of the Council and the European Parliament on the legal protection of databases.

D1.65 Regulation 6 of the Regulations defines a database as 'a collection of independent works, data or other materials arranged in a systematic or methodical way and individually accessible by electronic or other means'. Whilst copyright may subsist in the database as a literary work[1], in addition, if there has been 'substantial investment in the obtaining, verifying or presentation of the contents' of the database, the person who makes that investment thereby obtains a 'database right'[2].

1 See para D1.46. But see para D1.46, n 2 for the different test for originality for a database work.
2 Article 1.2 of the EC Directive; reg 13(1) of the Regulations.

D1.66 A database right is similar in many respects to a copyright in the database: anyone who extracts or re-utilises all or a substantial part of the contents of the database without the owner's consent thereby infringes the owner's database rights[1]. Repeated and systematic extraction or re-utilisation of insubstantial parts may amount to extraction or re-utilisation of a substantial part[2].

1 SI 1997/3032, reg 16(1).
2 SI 1997/3032, reg 16(2).

D1.67 The term of protection afforded by the database right is 15 years from the end of the calendar year in which the making of the database was completed[1]. However, substantial change to contents, including the investment entailed by an accumulation of successive additions, deletions or alterations, qualifies the resulting modified database for its own fresh term of protection. Therefore, basic maintenance and updating of a database may give rise to a rolling period of protection.

1 SI 1997/3032, reg 17(1).

D1.68 In *British Horseracing Board Ltd v William Hill Ltd*[1], the English courts considered the EC Directive and the Regulations for the first time. The British Horseracing Board ('BHB') is the governing body of horseracing in Britain. It compiles a huge amount of data relating to horseracing, including details of horses, their owners and trainers, their handicap ratings, jockeys, fixture lists, venues, dates, times, race conditions, entries and runners. The collection, verification and inputting of that data costs the BHB approximately £4m per year. It was not disputed that the requisite substantial investment in obtaining, verifying or presenting the content of the database had been made out for purposes of establishing a 'database right' under the Regulations.

1 *British Horseracing Board Ltd v William Hill Organisation Ltd* [2001] RPC 612 (Laddie J, 9 February 2001). See Duthie 'Database Rights – The Form Guide' (2001) 8(2) Sports Law Administration & Practice 1; Reid and Roy 'British Horseracing Board v William Hill' [2001] 9(2) SATLJ 105; Reid and Iqbal 'Horse Racing Case Establishes New Right for Sports Bodies' (2001) Sportcal.com, 27 February; Savvides 'Database Rights – A Powerful New Monopoly' (2001) 15 Sports and Character Licensing 30; Charlton 'Database Right: Stronger than it looks' (2001) 23(6) EIPR 296.

D1.69 William Hill is a major UK bookmaker. It was licensed to use information derived from the database in the course of its betting office and telephone betting business. BHB accepted that it had expressly or impliedly consented to much of that use. However, it had not authorised William Hill's reproduction of part of that information on its internet site. BHB contended that the information on William Hill's website derived from the unauthorised extraction and reutilisation of a substantial part of the contents of its database, thereby infringing BHB's database rights[1]. In the alternative, it contended that the repeated and systematic extraction or reutilisation of insubstantial parts of the contents of the database amounted to an infringement of its database rights[2].

1 Article 7(1) of the EC Directive; and reg 16(1) of the Copyright and Rights in Databases Regulations 1997.
2 Article 7(5) of the EC Directive; and reg 16(2) of the Copyright and Rights in Databases Regulations 1997.

D1.70 In its defence, William Hill first argued that the information that it had used was not part of the BHB's database in the relevant sense: it is the extent to which information is arranged and systematised and made accessible that is protected, and acts that do not make use of that arrangement or accessibility (eg taking the data and presenting it in a different form) do not infringe the database right. In other words, the database right subsists in the nature of the database as such, rather than transmitting through the database and attaching to the underlying component works that have been arranged to form the database.

D1.71 Laddie J rejected this argument, ruling that it confused the form that has to exist in order for the database right to be recognised, ie the arrangement and accessibility, with what is protected once the database is recognised, ie the investment made in obtaining, verifying and/or presenting the data. Interpreting the EC Directive, Laddie J ruled that the prohibition is on certain kinds of use or manipulation of parts of the contents of the database and that a collection of data from the database must be part of its contents.

D1.72 William Hill also argued that, even if its use did constitute use of the database, it was not use of a substantial part of the database. The basis for such argument was that the database was continually updated, thereby creating new databases separate from the previous databases. As such, William Hill argued that it used only a tiny amount of the information available on each new database as opposed to a substantial part of the collection of updated databases. Laddie J held that the test was quantitative but also qualitative, so that William Hill's assessment of the importance of the data extracted was relevant. William Hill wanted to use the data because it was complete and accurate, which was a direct result of the BHB's investment in collating and verifying the information. Therefore, the part of the database used by William Hill was sufficiently substantial to constitute an infringement.

D1.73 Thirdly, William Hill argued that its use did not amount to an extraction of the contents of the database: it had simply used the data that had already been extracted by a BHB licensee. Laddie J ruled that all that was required was the transfer of a substantial part of the contents of the database to a new medium, and therefore there had been an extraction by William Hill within the meaning of the Regulations.

D1.74 Finally, William Hill argued that its actions did not amount to re-utilisation within the meaning of the Regulations, because all of the information on its website was already available to the public. Laddie J ruled there was no requirement that the information not be available to the public by any other means.

D1.75 William Hill duly appealed, and on appeal the court primarily considered Laddie J's ruling on the first point, ie that the form of database was what gave rise to a database right, but once it existed, it was the element of content or investment that was protected. William Hill had argued that there must be a special quality of 'database-ness' which is protected, as opposed to the data itself, and pointed to the potential impact of Laddie J's ruling on this point: information that may be considered to have entered the public domain and to be freely usable might prove to have been derived from a database the right in which was protected even though the user was unaware of that ultimate source and right. The Court of Appeal decided[1] to refer a number of questions to the European Court of Justice, including Laddie J's interpretation of the Directive on this first issue[2]. A decision from the Swedish courts, which puts a far narrower interpretation on the Directive, is also being referred[3]. At the time of writing, the European Court of Justice had not provided any response to the questions referred. If Laddie J's interpretation stands, however, it will create a powerful protection for the owners of the numerous databases of sports data that are the source of content for a wide variety of commercial deals[4].

1 *British Horseracing Board Ltd v William Hill Organisation Ltd* [2001] EWCA Civ 1268, [2001] All ER (D) 431 (Jul) (Gibson, Clarke and Kay LJJ). See Porter 'Database Right – Reference to ECJ' EIPR 2001, 23(12).

2 Other questions referred to the European Court of Justice include whether a database that is constantly updated, creates new databases separate from the previous database; and whether a subscriber to a service provided by a licensee of the database right owner may make public that part of the database which he receives from such licensee.

3 *Fixtures Marketing Ltd v Svenska Spel AB*, Gotlands Tingsrätt, Case No. T 99-99 (Gotland District Court, 11 April 2000). The Swedish case, along with parallel proceedings in Finland (*Fixtures Marketing Ltd v Oy Veikkaus AB*, Vantaa District Court and Helsinki Court of Appeals, 1999 MMR 93), relates to the unauthorised use of British soccer fixture lists for pools betting competitions. The plaintiff sued for infringement of its copyright and database rights in the fixture lists. The copyright claims were dismissed on the basis that the fixture lists did not meet the required standards of originality under Nordic law. In addition, the claim for infringement of database rights was rejected on the basis that the Swedish law that purported to incorporate the EC Directive into Swedish law required more in the way of taking and reproduction of the contents of the database than had been committed by the defendants. See also *MV Holding Maatschappij de Telegraaf v Nederlandse Omroep Stichting* (Court of Appeal of the Hague, 30 January 2001).

4 Porter 'Database Right – A New Revenue Stream for Sports Bodies?' (2001) 3 Sport and the Law Journal 138; Greenwood and Davis 'Database right – developing IP protection for the Internet age' IHL Issue 100, 36; Porter and Roy 'All Bets are Off' (2001) 12(8) Ent LR.

C Registered trade marks

D1.76 A trade mark is a mark that denotes the nature or origin of goods or services. Its purpose is to exploit the goodwill enjoyed by the producer of the goods or the supplier of the services, either in itself or in relation to its goods or services. Since the most popular sports entities are brands in and of themselves, generating enormous (and uncritical) goodwill amongst their supporters[1], many of them have developed trade marks that represent the goodwill in that brand, and have based substantial commercial programmes around the use of, or the grant to third parties of the right to use, those marks in connection with their products and services[2].

1 One thinks of the petrol stations reportedly opened in Spain under the brand of Barcelona FC, that have been commercially successful notwithstanding that they sell exactly the same petrol as their competitors, but at a higher price.
2 See generally Chapters D5 and D6.

D1.77 Section 1 of the Trade Marks Act 1994 (the 'TMA 1994')[1] defines a trade mark as 'any sign capable of being represented graphically which is capable of distinguishing goods or services of one undertaking from those of other undertakings. A trade mark may, in particular, consist of words (including personal names), designs, letters, numerals or the shape of goods or their packaging'. This definition is not exhaustive: a distinctive colour or combination of colours or a distinctive sound or smell may constitute a trade mark, so long as it is capable of being represented graphically.

1 The TMA 1994, which replaced the Trade Marks Act 1938, was enacted to implement EC Directive 89/104/EC, which sought to approximate the laws of EC member states relating to trade marks.

D1.78 Although the law does provide some protection for unregistered trade marks[1], a trade mark is far easier to protect if it has been registered. Marks are registered in one or more of 45 different classes of goods and/or services. If validly registered in accordance with the applicable statutory regime[2], the trade mark confers certain exclusive rights on its owner with respect to its use in relation to the particular classes of goods and services in which it has been registered.

1 See paras D1.103 to D1.111.
2 Trade marks are granted on a territorial basis. In other words, a trade mark registered with the United Kingdom Trade Mark Registry is enforceable in the UK and may be infringed by conduct that takes place in the UK, but it will not be infringed by conduct that takes place in a foreign jurisdiction, unless it has also been registered in that jurisdiction's trade mark registry (or, within the European Community, if it has been registered as a Community Trade Mark). Therefore, an event organiser with an international brand (eg FIA Formula One World Championship) will have to consider a registration programme encompassing all commercially valuable territories around the world.

D1.79 There are certain grounds of absolute refusal of registration under the TMA 1994. For example, a mark will not be registered if it is devoid of distinctive character[1]. Thus, 'Aspirin' is a generic mark, in sufficiently distinctive of its manufacturer to be registrable as a trade mark. Nor will a mark be registered if it consists exclusively of signs or indications that serve to designate the kind, quality, quantity, intended purpose, value, geographical origin or other characteristics of goods or services[2]. In addition, there are certain specially protected emblems[3], such as royal arms and insignia, national flags and emblems or coats of arms granted by the Crown.

1 Section 3(1)(b) of the TMA 1994.
2 Section 3(1)(c) of the TMA 1994.
3 Section 4 of the TMA 1994.

D1.80 In *RFU and Nike v Cotton Traders Ltd*[1], Cotton Traders was selling classic England rugby jerseys bearing the 'England rugby rose'. The RFU had registered an updated version of the rose as a Community trade mark. It sued Cotton Traders for trade mark infringement and for passing off. Cotton Traders argued that the rose was not validly registered: the public perceived it not as a mark of trade origin, distinctive of the RFU, but as a national emblem or symbol associated with the England rugby team. Lloyd J agreed, finding that as of the 1996 registration date the rose was a generic national emblem or symbol, not associated with the RFU, and was not distinctive of goods produced by or associated with the RFU, nor did it acquire such distinctiveness after registration. Therefore, the trade mark infringement claim failed. For the same reasons, the RFU did not have goodwill in the English rose, and therefore its passing off claim also failed[2].

1 [2002] EWHC 467 (Ch), [2002] All ER (D) 417 (Mar). See Miles 'The Use of Sporting Trademarks in Merchandising' [2002] 11 EIPR 543.
2 As to passing off, see paras D1.103 to D1.111.

D1.81 Similarly, word marks such as 'World Cup' would be difficult to register as trade marks on the basis that they are insufficiently distinctive in a trade mark sense to overcome the absolute grounds of refusal: they would be taken as a reference to the tournament itself, not as identifying the trade origin of any goods or services[1].

1 See eg Tebay and Vale 'Law Makes Its World Cup Mark' (1998) 23 Sports Business 8; Bragiel 'Intellectual Property Rights and the World Cup' New Law Journal (12 June 1998), p 884.

D1.82 There are also relative grounds of refusal of registration. For example, a mark will not be registered if it is identical to a mark previously registered by a third party (and intended to be used on identical goods), or if it is similar to a registered mark (and intended to be used on identical or similar goods), and as such its registration would create confusion with the earlier mark[1]. Nor will a mark be registered if use of the mark would amount to passing off or would infringe copyright, design rights or registered designs[2]. An exception to this is if the applicant for registration of the later mark can show honest concurrent use of that mark[3].

1 Section 5(3) of the TMA 1994. See further para D6.47 et seq.
2 Section 5(4) of the TMA 1994.
3 Section 7(3) of the TMA 1994.

D1.83 Subject to the foregoing, it may be possible to register as trade marks the names, logos, badges and crests of teams, clubs and events[1], graphic representations of mascots, and patterns and livery applied to sports equipment. For example, 'Manchester United' is a registered trade mark, as is the British Lions badge and the Six Nations logo. Names and nicknames, portraits and images of individual athletes might also be registrable[2].

1 See Davidson 'Event names – strategies for protection' (2000) 3 Sport and Character Licensing 26.
2 See para D3.41.

D1.84 Once registered, a trade mark subsists for a period of 10 years from the date of registration. It is then subject to renewal for further periods of 10 years each. Theoretically, registrations can be renewed indefinitely, but non-use for five years can lead to a successful challenge to the registration[1] while unauthorised but unchallenged use of the mark by third parties may cause the mark to lose its distinctiveness and become generic[2].

1 Sections 46(1)(a) and (b) of the TMA 1994. There is a discretion not to revoke registration on these grounds where sufficient reason exists: *Glen Catrine's Trade Mark* [1996] ETMR 56, Ch D.
2 Section 46(1)(c) of the TMA 1994.

D1.85 Like other forms of intellectual property, registered trade marks can be bought and sold, assigned, licensed, securitised and otherwise commercially exploited.

(a) Trade mark infringement

D1.86 Types of infringement Section 10 of the TMA 1994, which identifies infringement of registered trade marks, is lengthy and involved, and what follows is an outline only of some of the main issues that arise, particularly in a sports context:

(1) Section 10(1) of the TMA 1994 provides that use in the course of trade of a sign identical with the registered mark in relation to goods and services identical with those for which the mark has been registered constitutes infringement of the registered mark.
(2) Section 10(2) of the TMA 1994 provides that use of a sign identical with or similar to the registered mark with respect to identical or similar goods or services is an infringement, but only where the trade mark owner can show a likelihood of confusion in the minds of the public, which includes the likelihood of association with the registered mark.
(3) Finally, s 10(3) of the TMA 1994 provides that use in the course of trade of a sign identical with or similar to a registered mark in relation to dissimilar goods or services will constitute an infringement if that use takes unfair advantage of or is detrimental to the distinctive character or repute of the registered trade mark.

D1.87 Therefore, ownership of a registered trade mark puts the owner into a strong but not an impregnable position. Whether or not various unauthorised acts infringe the owner's rights in that mark will depend upon various value judgments and/or evidence of similarity or confusion.

D1.88 Use as a trade mark To establish infringement, the owner of a registered mark will have to show that the defendant has made unauthorised 'use' of the mark. Section 10(4) provides that a person uses a mark in a trade mark sense if he affixes it to goods or packaging, offers or exposes goods for sale using the sign, puts them on the market or stocks them for those purposes under the sign, offers services under the sign, imports or exports goods under the sign, or uses the sign on business papers or in advertising. However, that definition is neither exhaustive nor definitive. It does not automatically follow that any use of that nature amounts to infringement.

D1.89 In *Trebor Bassett Ltd v Football Association*[1], the Football Association sought to stop Trebor Bassett including in sweet packages cards bearing photographs and descriptions of England footballers wearing the national team strip, including the Three Lions logo, on the grounds that the logo was identical to a registered trade mark of the Football Association and was being used on a class of goods in relation to which the mark had been registered. The court ruled that such incidental reproduction of the logo was not 'use' as a trade mark in the sense proscribed by s 10(1) of the TMA 1994:

> It is of the essence of a trademark that its purpose is to distinguish goods and services of one undertaking from those of other undertakings … It cannot seriously be argued that by publishing and marketing, on the cards concerned, photographs of players wearing the England team football strip (including the Three Lions logo) Trebor Bessett is in any sense using the logo in respect of the cards on which the photographs appear.

1 [1997] FSR 211, Ch D.

D1.90 In *Arsenal Football Club plc v Reed*[1], Arsenal FC sought to restrain street trader Matthew Reed from selling football shirts and other merchandise bearing the Arsenal crest device and the 'cannon' device on the basis that such sale infringed its rights as the owner of the registered trade marks in those devices. A disclaimer on Reed's stall that the merchandise was unofficial was held to prevent any consumer confusion, which precluded claims based on passing off or trade mark infringement under s 10(2) of the TMA 1994. However, Arsenal also sued for infringement under s 10(1) of the TMA 1994, ie use of the identical mark on identical goods, for which no proof of confusion is required. Reed argued however that his use of the devices was not use of the device 'as a trademark' within the meaning of s 10(1): each device as affixed to the football shirt or other merchandise functioned not as a 'badge of origin' (ie denoting that the product was manufactured or licensed by Arsenal Football Club Plc) but as a 'badge of allegiance' (ie denoting that the purchaser of the merchandise was a fan of Arsenal FC). Laddie J accepted this argument and rejected Arsenal's claim for trade mark infringement, staging:

> In my view … the Arsenal signs on Mr Reed's products would be perceived as a badge of support, loyalty or affiliation to those to whom they are directed. They would not be perceived as indicating trade origin.

However, since the point turned on construction of the TMA 1994, whether infringement of the registration of a trade mark would occur by the use of that trade mark in a non-trade mark sense, and since the TMA 1994 implemented the EC Trade Mark Directive (89/104/EEC), Laddie J referred the question to the European Court of Justice for a ruling.

1 *Arsenal Football Club plc v Matthew Reed* [2001] RPC 922. See Farnsworth 'An Own Goal for Arsenal?' (2001) 18 Sports and Character Licensing 7; Whittaker and Rudgard 'An Own Goal, or Merely Extra Time?' (2001) 1 Sport and the Law Journal 107; Miles 'The Use of Sporting Trade Marks in Merchandising' [2002] 11 EIPR 543.

D1.91 On 14 May 2002, the European Court of Justice held an oral hearing on the reference, and on 13 June 2002 the Advocate General issued his opinion[1]. The Advocate General took a more pragmatic and even traditional view of the question than had the English court. He refused to accept any limitation of the function of a trade mark to a mere indication of trade origin. He accepted that a trade mark acquires a life of its own, making a statement about quality, reputation and even in certain cases a way of seeing life. A consumer may buy trade-marked goods for a number of reasons, not exclusively because he considers that trade mark to denote the origin of the goods. The Advocate General saw no cause why those other functions of the trade mark should not be safeguarded as well as the function of denotation of origin.

1 *Arsenal Football Club plc v Matthew Reed* Case C-206/01 (13 June 2002, unreported). See Couchman 'Sports Merchandising: Paradise Lost, and Regained?' (2002) 9(4) Sports Law Administration and Practice 1; Hornsby 'Opinion on Arsenal case is music to brand-owners' ears' (2002) Sportcal.com, 19 June; Miles 'The Use of Sporting Trade Marks in Merchandising' [2002] 11 EIPR 543.

D1.92 The Advocate General therefore considered that a registered proprietor is entitled to prevent third parties using a mark identical to a registered trade mark in relation to the same goods or services where such use is capable of giving a misleading indication as to the origin, provenance, quality or reputation of the goods or services to which the mark is affixed. The decisive factor is not the feeling that the consumer buying or using the goods harbours towards the registered proprietor of the trade mark but the fact that they are acquired because the goods are associated with the trade mark. The vivid example is given of the purchase of a football shirt of a rival team simply for the purpose of burning it. Even in that case, the decision to purchase was made on the basis of the identification of the article with the mark.

D1.93 The Advocate General focused the analysis on why the person who is not the proprietor of the trade mark placed goods on the market with the same distinctive sign affixed to them. If he did so with the intent of exploiting the mark commercially, then in the Advocate General's view he should be deemed to be using it 'in a trade mark sense'.

D1.94 The Advocate General's opinion is not binding on the European Court of Justice, and the court may not go quite as far as the Advocate General did when it eventually issues its judgment in the matter, but certainly rights-holders will be hoping that the European Court of Justice agrees that the English court's construction of the TMA 1994 was too restrictive.

D1.95 Similar marks Whether two marks are similar or not is obviously a matter of fact. However, there are certain guiding principles. The court should take into account all relevant factors including the extent of fame of the mark, the degree of straightforward similarity, and the likelihood of any association between the marks. In some ways the tests for similarity and likelihood of confusion are allied: if the mark is similar it is more likely that there will be confusion and vice versa, often as a result of the possibility of imperfect recollection by members of the public or the belief that one mark is an extension of another[1].

1 *Wagamama Ltd v City Centre Restaurants plc* [1995] FSR 713, Ch D.

D1.96 Similar goods or services As to whether the goods or services in relation to which the marks are used are similar, a number of other factors are important, including the nature and the respective uses and users of the goods or services, the trade channels through which they reach the market, and the manner in which they are likely to be marketed. For instance, the producers of the famous 'Baywatch' television series had registered trade marks in class 9 (for video tapes and video disks featuring music, action-adventure, comedy, animation, sports or exercise). The defendant broadcast on the Adult Channel a series of programmes called 'Babewatch', which effectively amounted to a parody of 'Baywatch' but included pornographic material. The court rejected a claim for trade mark infringement brought under s 10(2) of the TMA 1994, on the ground that the pornographic programmes were not similar goods to the 'Baywatch' programmes, and that there was no likelihood of confusion between the two. It also rejected a claim for trade mark infringement brought under s 10(3) (dissimilar goods but use of the trademark that was unfair and detrimental to its distinctive character or reputation) on the same grounds of lack of confusion[1].

1 *Baywatch Productions Co Inc v Home Video Channel* [1997] FSR 22, Ch D. The need for confusion in relation to s 10(3) creates certain conceptual problems. The better known and more notorious a mark is, the less likely the public are to be confused by imitations. This would mean in certain circumstances that if all that was on the statute was s 10(2), then given the requirement to prove confusion, well-known marks might never be infringed on the basis that people would never actually mistake the 'counterfeit' goods for the goods of the legitimate mark holder. Section 10(3) gives an alternative cause of action for such well-known marks.

D1.97 Invalidity Even if a trade mark has been accepted for registration by the Trade Mark Registry, and even if the unauthorised user of that mark did not oppose such registration at the time, the registration does not preclude that user from asserting (either in an application to the Trade Mark Registry or in defence of infringement proceedings) that the mark should not have been registered – whether on absolute grounds or on relative grounds[1] – and should be declared invalid[2]. In response, the registered owner might seek to argue (for example) that subsequent to registration the mark has acquired distinctive character in relation to goods and services in the classes for which it was registered[3].

1 See paras D1.79 to D1.82.
2 Section 47 of the TMA 1994.
3 See proviso to s 3(1) of the TMA 1994. See also *British Sugar v James Robertson & Sons Ltd* [1996] RPC 281.

D1.98 In addition, registered trade marks may be revoked if they have not been used for five years without good reason[1], or if they have simply lost distinctiveness by becoming a common name for the product or service[2], or where as a result of the use made of the registered trade mark it is now liable to mislead the public, particularly as to the nature, quality or origin of the goods or services to which it is affixed[3].

1 Section 46 of the TMA 1994.
2 Section 46(1)(c) of the TMA 1994. A trade mark owner should therefore take positive and regular steps to distinguish his/her own trade mark name from the generic name used for substitutes, so as to retain the distinct product association with the trade mark name.
3 Section 46(1)(d) of the TMA 1994.

(b) Remedies for infringement of trade marks

D1.99 The civil remedies for trade mark infringement are damages, accounting for profits, injunctive relief and orders for delivery up of infringing articles[1].

1 Sections 14 to 16 of the TMA 1994.

D1.100 The TMA 1994 also criminalises various unauthorised uses of registered trade marks[1]. Where a rights owner is able to persuade the relevant authorities to get involved, the enforcement powers (particularly the provisions of the Trade Descriptions Act in relation to the power to make test purchases, to enter premises, inspect and seize goods and documents) can greatly strengthen the rights-owner's own anti-counterfeiting strategies.

1 Sections 92 and 93 of the TMA 1994.

(c) Brand Protection Programmes

D1.101 Notwithstanding the various pitfalls mentioned above, if the size of the commercial programme warrants it, a domestic or international trade mark registration programme can provide a relatively straightforward mechanism to prevent misuse of an event logo or other sports-related mark. In certain territories (for example in South America or South Africa) where first registration rather than first use is regarded as proof of ownership of a mark, defensive registrations should be promptly made in order to avoid pirates from claiming rights. Other considerations shaping the nature and extent of any international trade mark registration programme will include the life expectancy of a mark, the time required to effect registration and the identification of the important markets, product categories and potential licensees. The registrations will also have to be updated periodically to take account of new categories of licensing opportunity.

D1.102 To maintain proprietorship[1], once registered the marks should be used systematically and consistently in accordance with set procedures identified in a 'good practice' manual. These procedures should include the use of the appropriate trade mark notice (and copyright notice) wherever the mark is used together with indications of the relevant official status, for example 'Official Product' or 'Officially Licensed Product'.

1 See paras D1.97 and D1.98.

D Unregistered marks/passing off

D1.103 The TMA 1994 specifically states that its concern is registered trade marks and not unregistered marks, but also states that nothing in the TMA 1994 affects the law relating to passing off[1]. That law, which is the closest thing that English law has to a law against unfair competition, prevents a trader from wrongfully exploiting the goodwill built up by another by passing off his goods or services as the goods or services of that other.

1 Section 2(2) of the TMA 1994.

D1.104 The tort of passing off is made out where the claimant can show that:

(a) it owns goodwill in relation to a particular trade or particular goods or services;
(b) the defendant has in the course of its trade made a misrepresentation to the public to the effect that the goods or services that it supplies emanate from or are connected to the claimant;
(c) there is a real likelihood of confusion in the mind of the public between the goods and services of the claimant and those of the defendant; and
(d) damage has resulted to the claimant's business or goodwill[1].

To the extent that such passing off is achieved by the use of marks indicative of the claimant but that have not been registered and therefore do not qualify for protection under the TMA 1994, the law of passing off can be said to provide common law protection for unregistered 'trade marks'.

1 See for instance *Warnink v Townend* [1979] AC 731, HL.

(a) Misrepresentation

D1.105 The claimant must prove a misrepresentation to the public going to the provenance of goods or origin of services rather than mere quality, and aiming to associate the goods or services with the reputation of the claimant. The representation can be express or implied, but it must take place in the course of the defendant's business. Even a statement that is factually true might amount to a misrepresentation for purposes of passing off, depending on the impression made in the minds of the public[1].

1 See *John Brimsmeade & Sons Ltd v Brimsmeade and Waddington & Sons Ltd* (1913) 29 TLR 706, CA.

D1.106 For passing off to be established, the public needs to be led to understand that the legitimate rights-owner had in some way assumed responsibility for an important aspect (such as the quality) of the goods or services of the defendant[1]. For example, in *BBC World Wide Ltd v Pally Screen Printing Ltd*[2], the claimant sued producers of t-shirts depicting the Teletubbies characters, but was denied summary judgment because there was an unresolved factual dispute as to whether the public would or would not assume the t-shirts had been manufactured by or under the supervision of the claimant.

1 *Harrods v Harrodian School Ltd* [1996] RPC 697, 713, CA per Millett LJ. See also *Taverner Rutledge Ltd v Trexapalm Ltd* [1977] RPC 275, CA.
2 [1998] FSR 665, Ch D.

(b) Confusion

D1.107 Whether or not the requisite consumer confusion exists is a question of fact in each case. Much of what is said in relation to trade marks[1] is equally valid in relation to confusion in the context of passing off. Confusion on the part of a substantial part of the public, even if that substantial part is only confused because of a lack of technical knowledge in relation to the goods, will be enough for an injunction to be granted[2]. If it can be shown that ordinary sensible members of the public simply would not be confused, then there is no liability[3].

1 See para D1.95.
2 *J Bollinger v Costa Brava Wine Co Ltd (No 2)* [1961] 1 All ER 561, Ch D.
3 *Newsweek Inc v BBC* [1979] RPC 441, CA.

D1.108 Claims for passing off failed in *RFU & Nike v Cotton Traders*[1] and *Arsenal v Reed*[2] in relation to reproduction of team crests on sports merchandise because of the lack of evidence adduced of consumer confusion as to the origin of the merchandise.

1 [2002] EWHC 467 (Ch), [2002] All ER (D) 417 (Mar). See para D1.80.
2 [2001] RPC 922. See para D1.90.

(c) Goodwill/common field of activity

D1.109 Where traders seek to use the marks of popular sports teams and individuals to sell merchandise and other products, the usefulness of passing off as a remedy has historically been limited by court decisions insisting that the claimant must be operating in the same field of activity as the defendant[1].

1 See eg *McCulloch v May* [1947] 2 All ER 845.

D1.110 For example, in *Lyngstad v Anabas Products Ltd*[1], t-shirts were produced featuring pictures of the pop group Abba. Abba's organisation sued for passing off. The court held that as Abba were not in the business of producing clothing there was no common field of activity between the group and the producers of the t-shirts. Abba therefore did not have any relevant goodwill in respect of the manufacture of t-shirts, so that the acts complained of could not amount to the tort of passing off.

1 [1977] FSR 62, Ch D.

D1.111 However, more recent authority has shown unease with this restrictive analysis[1] and now the case of *Irvine v Talksport Ltd*[2] may breathe new life into the tort of passing off as a useful protection for sports rights-holders. Talksport Limited publicised its coverage of the forthcoming British Grand Prix to media advertisers by means of a flyer showing a photograph of Eddie Irvine, the racing driver. The photograph was used with permission of the photographer and therefore there was no copyright infringement[3]. However, in the original photograph Eddie Irvine was holding a mobile telephone. In Talksport's flyer, the mobile telephone had been replaced by a portable radio showing the words 'Talk Radio'. Irvine successfully claimed that this amounted to actionable passing off. Talk Sport sought to rely on the lack of a common field of activity, but the court took judicial notice of the common practice of famous individuals exploiting their names and their images by way of endorsement, not only in the field of expertise with which they are primarily associated, but also in more disparate contexts[4].

1 *Mirage Studies Co Ltd v Counter-Feat Clothing Ltd* [1991] FSR 145, Ch D.
2 [2002] EWHC 367 (Ch), [2002] 2 All ER 414.
3 See para D1.50.
4 For further discussion of the *Irvine* case, see paras D3.52 to D3.57 and D6.19 to D6.24.

E Patents

D1.112 Patent law protects new inventions or industrial processes that constitute an advance on the state of the art in relation to processes or things that are capable of industrial application. Like the trade mark regime, the Patents Act 1977 allows the owner of a patent to register it in a particular territory and thereby secure the exclusive right to make, use and exploit the patented product or process in that territory.

D1.113 Section 1 of the Patents Act 1977 specifically provides that the following are not capable of being inventions for the purposes of the Act and therefore cannot be protected as patents: discoveries, scientific theories or mathematical methods; literary, dramatic, musical or artistic works or any other aesthetic creation; schemes, rules or methods for performing mental acts, playing a game or doing business; programmes for a computer, and the presentation of information.

D1.114 Clearly this makes patent law inapplicable to many parts of the sports sector that are served by copyright and/or trade mark law. Suggestions that particular sports moves might be patented (eg the 'Cruyff turn') seem far-fetched[1]. However, the protection of patent law can be sought by manufacturers of sports goods for technological improvements to equipment, processes and materials used in the manufacture of sports goods, and processes for the manipulation of images in sports broadcasts (such as insertion of virtual advertising in broadcast footage[2]).

1 See 'Whose Move is This?' (1996) Times, 30 July.
2 See para D4.103.

F Statutory Intellectual Property Rights

D1.115 The Olympic Symbol etc (Protection) Act 1995[1] creates certain rights in respect of the Olympic five rings symbol, the Olympic motto and certain words such as 'Olympic', 'Olympiad' and 'Olympian'. A mark that incorporates these elements is not to be registered unless the application is made by or with the consent of the British Olympic Association[2]. In addition, the British Olympic Association is protected from infringement of those elements in the same way as if they were registered trade marks under the TMA 1994[3].

1 See Mellstrom 'Statutory Protection for Olympic Merchandise' [1996] 4(3) SATLJ; Bogdanowicz 'Protecting the Olympic Movement in the UK' (2000) 4 Sport and Character Licensing 10.
2 Section 4(5) of the TMA 1994.
3 See para D1.86 et seq.

6 AMBUSH MARKETING[1]

D1.116 A successful, well-organised and well-managed sports event generates commercial value not simply through selling access to the event itself (by admission tickets, television broadcasting, betting etc) but also by creating sponsorship and licensing programmes that exploit the enormous goodwill generated in the event among its fans and the broader public. Merchandisers exploit that goodwill directly, by selling event-branded products; sponsors and endorsees exploit it indirectly by associating their goods and services with the event's brand values[1].

1 This last section of this chapter is based on articles written on ambush marketing between 1995 and 2000 for Townleys Solicitors by Steve Townley, Nic Couchman and Dan Harrington.

D1.117 Ambush marketing (also known as 'parasitic' marketing[1]) is any sort of unauthorised association by a business of its name, brand, products or services, through any one of a range of marketing activities, with a sports event[2]. The term 'ambush' is used because the main actors are competitors of 'official' sponsors or suppliers of sports events, who pounce in the build-up to or during the event, to maximise commercial impact. The activity is often carefully planned to take advantage of inadequacies in an event's commercial programme and real or apparent loopholes in the legal protection available to event owners and sponsors.

1 See generally Bitel 'Ambush Marketing' [1997] 5(1) SATLJ 12; Mandel 'Case Study: Coca Cola' (2000) 4 Sport and Character Licensing 22; Garrigues 'Ambush Marketing: Robbery or Smart Advertising?' [2002] 11 EIPR 505.
2 The IOC's Olympic Marks and Imagery Usage Handbook defines ambush marketing as 'a planned attempt by a third party to associate itself directly or indirectly with Olympic Games to gain the recognition and benefits associated with being an Olympic Partner'.

D1.118 Ambush marketing constitutes a real threat to the ability of the event organiser to realise the full commercial value of the goodwill in its event. Commercial partners pay significant rights fees for exclusive rights of association and exploitation with respect to an event. They therefore expect the event organiser to deliver on commitments to a 'clean' event and to react speedily and decisively to attempts by their competitors to ambush the event. If the event organiser does not react in this way, or if the law simply does not allow it to do so, then the official sponsor may eventually decide that it should simply join the ambush marketer in exploiting the event without paying for the organiser's authorisation to do so.

A Types of ambush marketing

D1.119 Ambush activity can vary enormously in scale and seriousness and can be domestic or international in scope. However the underlying objective will invariably be to exploit the goodwill inherent in the event in some way, either by creating products around the event or by persuading consumers that the ambusher's product or service has been authorised, sanctioned or endorsed by, or is otherwise associated with, the sports event.

D1.120 Examples of ambush marketing involving products created around the event include corporate hospitality packages including tickets to major events, unofficial publications or merchandise sold on temporary stalls around the venues, or even 'big screen' broadcasts of the event in pubs seeking to attract supporter custom.

D1.121 Examples of ambush marketing that seeks to associate a brand with the event include Benetton's famous two-page newspaper advertisement featuring five giant rolled-up condoms in various colours parodying the Olympic rings around the time of the Barcelona Games, and the draping of an enormous Nike banner over the front of the car park opposite the Millennium Stadium in Cardiff on the opening day of the 1999 Rugby World Cup. A less obvious but no less applicable example would be using tickets for an event as a prize in a promotional competition run in a national newspaper[1].

1 Another would be using the event name as part of the domain name address for a website, as to which see para A5.140; and Reid 'Combating 'New Age' Ambush Marketing' (2001) 4(4) Sports Law Bulletin 10. See also 'Threat to official Games site from Aussie rival' (2000) Sportbusiness.com, 20 July.

D1.122 These types of activities may be carried out as 'one-off' stunts or may be part of an orchestrated marketing campaign around an event[1]. Save where they cross the line from ambushing to out-and-out counterfeiting, they may or may not involve any clear and direct breach of the proprietary rights in an event.

1 For further examples, see eg Bitel 'Ambush Marketing' [1997] 5(1) SATLJ 15; Elliot 'Tackling Ambush Marketing' (2002) Sportbusiness.com, 16 July.

B Fighting ambush marketing

D1.123 Given the failure of English law to recognise proprietary rights capable of legal enforcement in a sporting event per se[1], the ability of the event organiser to protect its event and its commercial programme from ambush marketing will largely depend on the following:

- the extent to which the ambushers are making use of elements of the event – such as emblems, logos, mascots, photographs and audio-visual footage – in which the event organiser owns or controls legally enforceable intellectual property rights;
- the extent to which other laws (ie outside the realm of intellectual property rights) gives the organiser remedies to deal with ambush marketing, such as laws relating to unfair competition, misleading advertising, false trade descriptions, street vending and appropriation of goodwill; and
- the extent of protection and control that the event organiser has obtained over the venue, surrounding areas and airspace, the public watching the event, the media reporting on the event, the clubs and individuals participating in the event and the official commercial partners looking to exploit the event[2].

1 See paras D1.6 to D1.12.

2 For discussion of the anti-ambush marketing techniques used at specific sporting events, see Bitel 'Ambush Marketing' [1997] 5(1) SATLJ 12 and (2000) 3 Sport and Character Licensing 18 (London Marathon); 'Caveat emptor: danger of ambush' (1999) Sportbusiness.com, 1 January (1999 Cricket World Cup); Roper-Drimie 'Sydney 2000 Olympic Games – A Case Study on How To Combat Ambush Marketing' (2001) 7(7) Sports Law Administration & Practice 1 (2000 Olympic Games); MacLaverly 'How Euro 2000 organisers tackled ambush marketing' (2000) 8 Sports and Character Licensing 6 (UEFA European Championships 2000); Naidoo 'Ambush Marketing Innovative Ideas for Salt Lake City 2002' (2002) 5(1) Sport and the Law Bulletin 9 (2002 Olympic Games); 'Mastercard backs FIFA "anti-ambush" strategy' www.sportbusiness.com (30 November 2001) (2002 FIFA World Cup Finals). See also generally Wall 'The Game Behind the Games' (2002) 12 Marquette Law Review 557; Whitehead 'Righting Commercial Wrongs' (1999) 50 Sports Marketing 15; Reid 'Sponsorship: Avoiding an Ambush' (1998) 34 Sports Marketing 4.

(a) *Using intellectual property rights to combat ambush marketing*

D1.124 To the extent that the ambush marketer has reproduced photographs, badges, logos, emblems or other works in which the event organiser owns the copyright, civil and/or criminal proceedings for infringement of copyright may lie[1]. Where an event badge or mark is used in a manner that confuses the public into believing that the associated brand or goods or services are associated with the event organiser, if the mark is a registered trade mark then infringement proceedings may be available under the TMA 1994[2], and if not then an action may be available for passing off[3]. In each case, careful analysis of the facts will be required to determine whether each of the requisite elements of the claim can be made out and whether any cognisable defences will be available to the defendant[4].

1 See paras D1.57 to D1.62.

2 See paras D1.86 to D1.100. See also 'FIFA legal threat to Visa over ambush marketing' www.sportcal.com (13 September 2002): Visa forced to withdraw on-line promotion that reproduced World Cup trade mark; 'FIFA's Pepsi Challenge' www.sportbusiness.com (7 June 2002).

3 See paras D1.103 to D1.111. See also *PGA Ltd v Evans* (25 January 1989, unreported), Ch D (Vinelott J) (injunction granted to stop unofficial corporate hospitality provider using the 'Ryder Cup' event mark to pass off its hospitality packages as official).

4 See for example, Bragiel 'Intellectual Property Rights and the World Cup' [1998] NLJ 884.

D1.125 Where the defendant is a counterfeiter or other truly pirate organisation, it may be a 'fly-by-night' operation looking for a one-off 'score' from a major event.

In such cases, civil proceedings might be impractical, and criminal proceedings under the CDPA 1998 or the TMA 1994 (including private prosecutions where necessary) might be more appropriate[1].

1 See paras D1.62 and D1.100.

(b) Using other laws

D1.126 Those representing event organisers plagued by ambush marketing need to be inventive as to both legal and extra-legal remedies. There are a variety of other legal and practical measures than can be used in appropriate cases, including actions for defamation, injurious falsehood, unjust enrichment and conspiracy to defraud, and complaints to the relevant advertising authority under the Control of Misleading Advertising Regulations 1988. It is also worth examining applicable national and local laws prohibiting activities such as peddling and street vending[1], ticket-touting[2], unauthorised display of advertising hoardings or aerial advertising.

1 For example, the Peddlars' Acts 1871 and 1881 can be of assistance. Where persons travel from one venue to another in order to sell goods, they must have a licence under the 1871 Act; to sell goods without such a licence is a criminal offence. Usually sale of articles from stalls positioned in the streets requires the grant of a street trading permit from the relevant local authority; otherwise such stalls can constitute illegal trading (and thus a criminal offence under local bye-laws) and an obstruction of the highway. Liaison with local police, both from the point of view of safety considerations as well as commercial considerations, and the relevant departments in local government, can be very helpful.

2 See Bitel 'Not quite the ticket' [1995] 3(1) SATLJ 31.

D1.127 It is important to maintain strong relations with all applicable agencies. This includes not only local Trading Standards Departments, who operate powers in respect of criminal offences arising under trade marks and copyright legislation, but also Customs and Excise in relation to counterfeit imported goods, and also for their taxation jurisdiction: street traders will not be registered for VAT in all likelihood and will not welcome the attentions of Customs Excise. In appropriate circumstances, local customs officers should be briefed to prevent unauthorised goods from overseas entering the country.

(c) Control over the environs of the event

D1.128 As noted above[1], the event organiser can also limit ambush marketing by ensuring that its contracts with the host(s) or other venue owner(s) guarantee delivery of a completely 'clean' venue[2]. The venue should be defined to include not only the field of play, the perimeters, stands, public areas, bars and eating areas, but also the airspace above[3]. Indeed, in appropriate circumstances it should extend beyond the venue itself to the surrounding environs[4]. For example, cities bidding for Olympic events need to guarantee delivery of a clean 'city', which may involve the use of local bye-laws to prevent ambushing efforts using advertising sites along the routes to a particular venue[5]. Announcements over public address systems, and on local radio and television stations regarding pirate products, may assist in informing and directing people to the licensed merchandise concessionaires. Local radio and television stations as well as news agencies should be informed of the details of any sponsor protection programmes in place and the need for their acquiescence in these programmes. Self-help can also be important, for example, in the form of careful selection of camera angles to avoid giving exposure to unauthorised advertisements and obscuring those that cannot be avoided[6].

1 See para D1.28.
2 The IOC's publication *Ambush Prevention and Clean Venue Guidelines* runs to 132 pages.
3 In the run up to the Atlanta Olympic Games in 1996 for example, the Federal Aviation Authority, under pressure from the local organising committee, banned all unauthorised flights within the city limits for the duration of the Games to prevent aerial ambush advertising. See also Bitel 'Ambush Marketing' [1997] 5(1) SATLJ 12 (similar arrangements in relation to the London Marathon). An interesting case, in this context, is *Gulf Oil (Great Britain) Ltd v Page* [1987] Ch 327, [1987] 3 All ER 14, CA (injunction granted to restrain defendants' conspiracy to injure plaintiff by using aircraft to display derogatory banner in airspace over sports event).
4 Britcher 'Zoning the big events' (2000) Sportbusiness.com, 11 December.
5 See 'IOC orders outdoor media buy-up in war on parasites' (1997) Sportbusiness.com, 1 October. See also Naidoo 'Ambush Marketing – Innovative Ideas for Salt Lake City 2002' (2002) 5(1) Sports Law Bulletin A 9 (describing forbearance agreements with building owners, use of local ordinances, governing street vending, signage, handbills etc).
6 See Bitel 'Ambush Marketing' [1997] 5(1) SATLJ 12, 16.

D1.129 Some forms of ambush marketing can be stopped through enforcement of the terms and conditions incorporated into the contract for the sale of admission tickets to the event[1]. These should include a non-transferability condition:

Tickets remain the property of the Issuer at all times. Unless with the express written agreement of the Issuer, tickets are issued for the purchaser's personal use only. It is not permitted for the purchaser to sell or otherwise transfer tickets to others, to exploit them commercially or non-commercially, to use them for promotional purposes or campaigns or to transfer and/or dispose of the tickets in any way.

OR

This ticket may not, without the Issuer's prior consent, be re-sold at a premium or used for advertising, promotional or other commercial purposes (including competitions or trade promotions) or to enhance the demand for other goods or services …

Any ticket obtained in breach of these conditions shall be void and all rights conferred or evidenced by such ticket(s), including without limitation the right of entrance, shall be immediately nullified and withdrawn. The Issuer shall have the right to confiscate such ticket(s), to deny access to the ticket-holder(s), or to eject anyone who has used such ticket(s) to gain access, all without any obligation to refund the purchase price to the purchaser.

This condition has several purposes. For example, to the extent that the issuer sets its ticket prices below market rate in order to ensure that genuine fans can get access to the games, the resale of those tickets on the black market could be said to subvert an important governing body imperative[2]. Specifically, in the context of ambush marketing, however, the condition provides a weapon against unofficial corporate hospitality and/or travel packages, as well as against the use of tickets as prizes in competitions, since such unauthorised commercial use of the tickets is a breach of contract by the purchaser of the ticket while third parties can be liable for inducing that breach, and also for purporting to offer for sale or as a prize a ticket that is void and therefore will not entitle the recipient to admission to the event[3].

1 See para D1.15.
2 See paras B2.12 to B2.15.
3 See paras D1.19 and D1.20. See also *PGA Ltd v Evans* (25 January 1989, unreported), Ch D (Vinelott J) (unsuccessful application for injunction restraining defendant from inducing breach of non-transferability ticket condition).

D1.130 The ticket conditions can also seek to ensure 'clean' spectators. For example, para 5.2 of the ticket conditions for the Sydney Olympics stated that those attending the Games could not:

> engage in ambush marketing ... display commercial or offensive signage ... sell any goods or services...wear or give away political, advertising or promotional materials ... [or] engage in any other activities which SOCOG considers dangerous or otherwise inappropriate.

Security staff at the Wimbledon tennis championships confiscate branded hats and signs that have been distributed by would-be ambushers to those waiting in queues[1].

1 'Hats off at Wimbledon' (2001) Sportbusiness.com, 29 June.

D1.131 Similarly, as noted above[1], the terms of accreditation of the media should prohibit commercial use (as opposed to use for the purpose of reporting on the events) of the photographs, data and other information gathered by the media.

1 See para D1.27.

(d) Control over the participants in the event and the event's official partners

D1.132 The entire network of participants in an event must be made aware of the anti-ambush programme and contractually bound to adhere to it. It is vital to get clear acknowledgment of the teams and the players of the central commercial programme, and an undertaking not to undermine that programme through their own commercial activities[1]. It is also important to get support for the anti-infringement programme from the event's official commercial partners.

1 See paras D1.29 to D1.35.

D1.133 For example, broadcast partners might be required to give official sponsors rights of first refusal over programme sponsorship or advertising airtime around broadcasts of the event, and/or (more unusually) to lock out the official sponsors' competitors from those opportunities[1]. Furthermore, there should be strict prohibitions on broadcasters adding 'virtual advertisements' to the 'clean' stadium broadcast by using computer-generated image manipulation techniques[2].

1 Glendinning 'Broadcast sponsorship is driven into line' (1999) Sportbusiness.com, 1 October.
2 Enser 'Regulating a virtual world' (2001) Sportbusiness.com, 17 May. See para D4.103.

D1.134 Official licensees within a sports commercial programme must be prevented from acquiescing or assisting in non-licensees' marketing activities by, for example, providing official merchandise to ambushers for distribution as prizes in competitions, participating in joint promotions that give credence to an ambusher's attempts to imply official association with an event, and/or allowing misleading advertising by ambushers in official publications.

D1.135 Depending on the circumstances, it might be appropriate to include provisions: giving the organiser right of approval over all of the licensee's promotional material; prohibiting the distribution of licensed merchandise as premiums; prohibitions on joint promotion of any kind connected with the event (save with other licensees); prohibitions against sub-licensing, sharing or assignment of licensed rights; rights of first refusal for sponsors/suppliers to advertise in official publications; prohibitions on licensees advertising in pirate event publications as designated by the licensor; requirements for licensees to use official corporate hospitality facilities only; and prohibitions on licensees selling or distributing ticket allocations other than to employees and bona fide guests of licensees.

CHAPTER D2

VENUES

Richard Moran (M[c]Cormicks)

Contents

1 INTRODUCTION

D2.1 The venue for sporting events will always be at the heart of any sporting operation. Firstly and most obviously, it is the place where any sporting event will take place. Secondly, whilst revenue for any sporting organisation (which for the purposes of this chapter will be described as a club) may derive from a number of core business areas including broadcasting, sponsorship, merchandising and ticket sales, each of these core revenue streams is inextricably linked to the operation, management and exploitation of the venue.

D2.2 It is crucial that any club considers its venue arrangements and how those arrangements will impact both operationally and upon revenue streams. Traditionally, clubs have tended to own their sporting venues outright. However, it is increasingly the case that venues are shared by a number of clubs and may be owned by one of those clubs, by a connected third party or by a separate commercial organisation. Recent years have seen an increasing number of clubs sell off prime sites to generate cash and to use that cash to part fund the construction of new stadia for use by themselves or alternatively make the switch to ground sharing arrangements.

D2.3 A number of preliminary issues arise in any consideration of the operation, management and exploitation of a venue. This chapter will consider both ownership and commercial exploitation of venues and set them in the context of the relevant regulatory framework. The chapter is divided into the following principal areas:

(1) the regulatory framework governing venues;
(2) ownership and terms of occupation;
(3) the venue as a revenue generator;
(4) match day control and exploitation.

D2.4 This chapter is written primarily from the club's viewpoint. Clearly many of the issues will be common to the owner, operator, user or spectator but may need to be approached from a different perspective. This chapter seeks to address general points of principle which will act as a starting point in any negotiations relating to the terms of ownership, use or exploitation of a venue. By their very nature the key factors will vary from venue to venue according to the respective requirements of the parties and the relevant regulatory backdrop.

D2.5 Much of the legislation and many of the examples will be drawn from association football, as the headline drivers for many of the exploitation issues have been in relation to football. The principles however will extend to other sporting environments. In each case, careful consideration will need to be given to the control and impact of any governing body or centrally pooled arrangements for exploitation in the context of the relevant sport.

2 THE REGULATORY FRAMEWORK

A General Issues

D2.6 There are many issues which arise in relation to sports venues which are not specific to sport and will arise in the context of the operation and management of venues and some of these are set out in general terms at para D2.7. The purpose of this text is however to focus on the impact of the regulatory framework specifically in the context of sport and accordingly no detailed consideration has been given in this chapter to those general issues.

D2.7 General issues which would need to be addressed in relation to any venue are likely to include the need to comply with all planning requirements and (during any construction and redevelopment) all safety and other requirements particularly where a venue is to be operational during a period of redevelopment. The operators of any venue will need to give due consideration to general liquor licensing and entertainment licensing issues as they arise. In addition to specific issues relating to safety certification, general compliance with fire certificate requirements would be essential (save to the extent it is covered by a general safety certificate[1]. Likewise, employer's liability and public liability insurance will need to be considered[2].

1 See para D2.17.
2 See further paras C4.53 et seq and C4.61 et seq.

B Occupiers' Liability

D2.8 Any occupier having control associated with and arising from its presence in and use of or activity in premises owes a duty of care to all visitors under the

Occupiers' Liability Act 1957. The operator should take such care as in all the circumstances of the case is reasonable to see that the visitor will be reasonably safe in using the premises for the purposes for which he is invited or permitted by the occupier to be there. The standard of care which can be expected of the occupier is broadly the same as that in an ordinary action in negligence. Any steps required to be taken in order to discharge the duty will inevitably vary both in the context of the circumstances of the venue and in the context of the individual to which the duty is owed. For example, in relation to young or disabled spectators the requirements are likely to be substantially varied and require that the facilities which have been provided to that particular class of spectators are indeed safe.

D2.9 Where an occupier is using the premises for his business, any breach of that occupier's duty under the Occupiers' Liability Act 1957 will give rise to a liability. Occupiers will typically seek to limit their liability by way of giving appropriate warnings of any potential dangers which may arise. The Unfair Contract Terms Act 1977 precludes occupiers from limiting or excluding liability for death or personal injury where the premises are occupied for the business purposes of that occupier.

D2.10 Under the Occupiers' Liability Act 1984, there is a general exception in relation to recreational or educational purposes not being considered to be business use. That exception however is unlikely to assist sporting clubs, because sport is their very business.

C Safety of Sports Grounds Act 1975

D2.11 In addition to the general legislation in relation to occupiers liability, specific legislation has been introduced in relation to sports grounds under the Safety of Sports Grounds Act 1975 ('SSGA 1975'). The SSGA 1975, taken in conjunction with subsequent amending legislation, provides a scheme for the licensing and control of sports stadia[1].

1 See para A1.61 et seq.

D2.12 The regime of control applies to large sports stadia. Large sports stadia are defined as those having a capacity for the watching of any sport of more than 10,000 visitors[1]. At these stadia the Secretary of State can require the venue owner to obtain a current safety certificate issued by the local authority.

1 In the case of association football at certain stadia, 5,000: as amended by Safety of Sports Ground (Accommodation of Spectators) Order 1996.

D2.13 Most major sport stadia in the country have been brought within the SSGA 1975 pursuant to designating orders.

D2.14 Under s 17 of the SSGA 1975, a sports ground is defined as a place where sports or other competitive activities take place in the open air and where accommodation is provided for spectators which consists either of artificial structures or adapted natural structures. Further provisions govern indoor sporting events[1].

1 See ss 42–43 of the Fire Safety and Safety of Places of Sport Act 1987.

D2.15 The regime gives a substantial amount of power to the local authority to determine the requirements necessary to secure reasonable safety. A safety certificate may specify the following:

(a) maximum number of spectators permitted into the stadium;
(b) number, size and situation of entrances, exits and crush barriers;
(c) any other steps (including alterations and additions) required to be taken as pre-conditions to the grant of any safety certificate.

The local authority may issue a prohibition notice when it considers a serious risk attaches to the admission of spectators. The authority is able to restrict access or if appropriate prevent admission until remedial steps have been taken.

D2.16 Under the Fire Safety and Safety of Places of Sport Act 1987. Notwithstanding that a stadium may not be designated under the terms of the SSGA 1975, any stand which provides covered accommodation for 500 or more spectators must also have a safety certificate in force. The powers of the local authority in respect of such stands are broadly similar to those set out above in relation to the SSGA 1975.

D2.17 Careful consideration needs to be given to the terms of a safety certificate in the context of any stadium. A safety certificate may either be general or special. Special certificates apply to a designated class of events and accordingly this can have an impact on the ability to operate a non-designated event in a multi-use stadium. Given the potential for the stadium to be closed in the event of non-compliance, ongoing liaison with the local authority is essential.

D Football Spectators Act 1989

D2.18 Association football clubs must additionally comply with the statutory framework set out in the Football Spectators Act 1989 ('FSA 1989'). The FSA 1989 provides for a scheme for licensing of football grounds and a national football membership scheme at designated football matches in England and Wales[1]. Under s 11 of the FSA 1989, the Secretary of State may require conditions relating to seating to be included in any admission arrangements for designated football matches. This sets out a scheme requiring all FA Premier League and Football League clubs to have all seater stadia.

1 See further paras A1.62 and A1.64 et seq.

D2.19 The Football Licensing Authority, created under the FSA 1989, sets a structure for the issuing of licences to venue operators and regulates the conditions of ticketing for designated grounds. Its role also overlaps with that of the local authority: it supervises the local authority's duties under the SSGA 1975, in relation to grounds at which designated association football matches are played. It may require a local authority to impose certain conditions under the safety certificates it issues with respect to such grounds.

D2.20 Pursuant to s 11(1) of the FSA 1989, the Football Spectators (Seating) Order 1994 was made giving a general direction to local authorities, requiring that they impose seating only requirements for spectators at designated matches. There have been a number of subsequent orders governing further stadia.

E Governing Body Requirements

D2.21 In addition to the legal requirements set out above, the governing bodies of individual sports may impose minimum ground grading standards with which member clubs must comply. Careful attention must be paid to the rules of the particular governing body to ensure that clubs meet or exceed the requisite minimum standard[1].

1 Stevenage Borough was denied promotion from the Conference to the Football League for failure to meet the League's ground grading requirements. Its subsequent challenge to that denial of access was rejected on grounds of delay. See para A3.151 et seq.

F Disability Discrimination Act 1995

D2.22 Provisions for disabled spectators have improved substantially at sports grounds in recent years. The provisions of the Disability Discrimination Act 1995 obliges service providers to take reasonable steps to change any practice, policy or procedure which makes it impossible or unreasonably difficult for disabled people to use a service and to provide an auxiliary aid or service which would enable disabled people to use the service and to overcome physical barriers which make it impossible or unreasonably difficult for disabled people to use a service by providing the service by reasonably alternative methods. Similar goals are achieved by reviewing the impact of building regulations on any new development or redevelopment of stadia[1].

1 See further paras E3.46 and E3.47.

G Alcohol Control and Licensing

D2.23 The general principles of licensing, as set out primarily in the Licensing Act 1964, are also applicable to sporting events. In addition, however, specific regulations have been introduced under the Sporting Events (Control of Alcohol etc) Act 1985 and the Sporting Events (Control of Alcohol etc) Amendment Act 1992. Under s 3 of the 1985 Act, where licensed premises are situated within the area of a designated sports ground, as defined under s 9 of the 1985 Act, intoxicating liquor may not be sold or supplied in the premises or consumed in or taken off the premises from two hours before the start of such an event until one hour after the event.

D2.24 An exception to the rule may be made by an order of the local licensing justices where such an order may specify the exact hours when intoxicating liquor can be supplied subject to any conditions they deem fit to impose. An order under this exception is not permitted in respect of any part of the premises from which the sporting event may be directly viewed, unless where such viewing takes place from private facilities, in which case the relevant period where the exception cannot apply is the period from fifteen minutes before the start of the event and after the end of the event[1].

1 See s 5A of the Sporting Events (Control of Alcohol etc) Act 1985.

3 OWNERSHIP AND TERMS OF OCCUPATION

D2.25 The club is likely to be either the exclusive occupier of the venue (as the freehold owner or the leaseholder) or alternatively it may share use of the ground on a non-exclusive licence basis.

A Exclusive Occupation

D2.26 Freehold ownership by one sporting organisation is, assuming there is no sub-leasing or licensing of the venue to other organisations, the least complex arrangement. The general principles as set out above will apply and the club will take into account the general obligations applicable to anyone operating a venue and also the regulatory framework relating to sport and in particular the sport played at that venue.

D2.27 If the ground is to be sublet or licensed for other purposes, due consideration will need to be given to the ability to sub-licence including the requirement for any amendment to the safety certificate and any other regulatory requirements.

D2.28 It is increasingly common for the club to cease to be the freeholder of a stadium having disposal of the property by way of some form of sale and leaseback arrangement and having a lease or licence of the existing stadium often on a temporary basis and subsequently (once constructed) a new stadium. In any such arrangement the principles of landlord and tenant law, as applied to any commercial arrangement, will need to be taken into account. In addition, there will need to be a specific allocation of responsibilities between the landlord and tenant in relation to venue-specific requirements such as safety certificates and liquor and entertainment licensing. In an exclusive leasing arrangement these matters would typically fall to the tenant to address.

B Ground Sharing

D2.29 The cost of development of stadia and the overheads associated with the running of the stadia means that increasingly stadium ownership, development and management are separated from the individual sporting clubs that use the stadium. The commercial advantage of being in a position to maximise use of a stadium by way of multiple occupation is obvious. Facilities which may otherwise be dormant on all but say twenty match days a year can be used on another twenty or more match days, allowing the venue and/or the club to maximise revenue from ticket sales, hospitality and banqueting, pourage arrangements and commercial concessions.

D2.30 The difficult issue for any club will be the extent to which any revenue stream that can be generated must then be shared with either the stadium owner or management company or any third party brought in to operate any aspect of revenue generation in relation to the venue to the potential exclusion of any separate arrangements the club may wish to enter into.

D2.31 Nevertheless, ground sharing is likely to increase, particularly given the improvement in playing surfaces which makes disruption of one user by another's damaging the pitch less of a risk.

D2.32 In addition to commercial issues which have been referred to above, consideration will need to be given by the club to any rules of the relevant governing body. These issues frequently come to light in association football, rugby league and rugby union and have been critical in relation to both a proposed move to new or different stadia and/or in circumstances where a club may achieve promotion but be denied the ability to take up what it considers to be its rightful place because either its stadium facilities[1] or its ownership arrangements[2] are not considered to be satisfactory. This may relate to long term ownerships or rights in respect of the venue or such matters as ground capacity. It is imperative that any sporting club obtains the requisite consent from its professional body for the use of any stadium.

1 See para D2.21, n 3.
2 Rotherham RFC was denied promotion to the Zurich Premiership for the 2002/2003 season because it did not have 'primacy of tenure' in its ground-share arrangements at Rotherham Football Club's ground.

D2.33 The complexities are inevitably compounded when it is considered that any league will need to consider the other commitments being made in respect of the stadium when it looks to schedule its programme for the season. This will arise where for example two football clubs share the same stadium or indeed where different sports are played at the same stadium.

D2.34 Multiple occupation is of equal concern to local authorities in terms of planning and safety, particularly where stadia may involve adjacent arenas and there is the potential for overlap of events, which can have significant impact not only on operations and safety but also public transport, traffic and the effect on the local community.

D2.35 There are three structures likely to be found in ground-sharing arrangements:

(i) ownership by one sporting club with another club or clubs given a licence to use the venue;
(ii) a stadium company which owns and operates the stadium, granting licences to use the venue to one or more sporting clubs;
(iii) a stadium company granting licences to one or more sporting clubs where the sporting clubs also have an equity stake and certain rights of control over the stadium company.

D2.36 Any ground-sharing occupant will need to consider the terms of licence in respect of the venue, ie the terms and conditions of its use of the venue.

D2.37 The licence requirements will inevitably vary according to the circumstances of the case but many of the core elements will be the same, and these are considered below

D2.38 Any licence arrangement needs to encompass a number of essential elements relating to match or event days:

- that the playing surface meets the club's (and indeed the governing body's) requirements. This may encompass any range of matters including the dimensions, markings and quality of the pitch;
- requirements in respect of operational facilities are met. This is likely to encompass playing facilities, changing facilities, access to and use of any other backroom facilities on match days;
- access to seating and use of corporate hospitality facilities on match days including any special members clubs that may be operated at the facility;
- facilities for the sale of merchandise on match days at the stadium;
- control of all ticketing for events and for these purposes access to any centralised ticketing computers and the ability to use where applicable any smart card technology installed to regulate access to events;
- the extent to which any concessions (which may include merchandising facilities, beverages or restaurants) are to be controlled by the club for specific events; and
- the extent to which the club will have rights to control its own sponsorship arrangements in respect of the venue for its own event. Sponsorship rights will include perimeter boards, electronic screens, scoreboards and public address systems.

D2.39 Any licence must include exclusive control and ownership of all broadcasting rights relating to any relevant events to include television (whether terrestrial, satellite or by way of any cable or club channel) and radio. In addition to all such rights being exclusively vested in the club, the club will require all relevant rights of access for itself and any third parties to the stadium. This may include access to press boxes and any relevant camera points. Access is likely to be required to all cabling, power and transmission arrangements. In addition, access may be required to be able to operate an electronic screen where instant replay may be relevant or in some cases required. Due consideration in respect of broadcasting will need to be given to any requirements of the relevant governing body or in relation to any centralised deal that may have been negotiated on behalf of the club and the club will need to bear in mind that such requirements may change from time to time.

D2.40 Consideration will need to be given to the extent to which the venue is required on non-match days, for example:

- for the use of the venue for sporting lunches or community programmes;
- for the operation of any club shop either on an individual basis or jointly with other parties;
- for the operation of common ticketing offices and facilities.

D2.41 Consideration needs to be given to any training facilities that may be attached to the stadium and access that may be required to both the stadium itself and to any other relevant facility such as gymnasia, treatment rooms, training pitches and the like.

D2.42 The club will need to consider the extent to which it wishes to limit other uses to which the stadium might be put. Whilst on one level this may include, for example, use of the venue by rival clubs, what may potentially be of significantly more importance is the ability to ensure the playing field would not be damaged by other users and that events will not be run in such close proximity so as to damage the ability of the club to have free access to a 'clean stadium' in terms of sponsorship and signage and the operation of concessions. The impact on a clean stadium of the grant of any stadium naming rights should be considered[1].

1 See generally para D1.128.

D2.43 The significance of a club being able to raise commercial revenue from use of the venue other than on match days should not be overlooked. This could include conference and training facilities and other events where people may be attracted to use the venue because of the association with that club rather than merely because of the existence of the facilities. Sharing in the equity of the stadium ownership or management company may assist in generating revenue from such sources, but it is also appropriate to consider arranging these as part of arm's length licensing arrangements.

D2.44 Where a club is entering into a long-term arrangement for use of facilities, it should consider what other specific long-term rights may be required. This could include, for example, the need to develop further training facilities or merchandising opportunities such as a club shop, at which point consideration would need to be given to who should bear the cost of developments and who should share in any rights and revenue streams that might be generated.

D2.45 The club may wish to have some form of option to acquire the venue and/or specifically a right of first refusal in the event of the venue being sold to a third party. For example, if a number of clubs were using the facility the balance of control could significantly shift if it were to be acquired by one of the other licensees.

D2.46 As always in such long-term licensing scenarios, flexibility would be required on the part of the club in the event of any change to obligations which it may have to its professional body. This may extend to ownership rights in respect of any owner/operator of the venue where a governing body may take the view that certainty of ownership and therefore control of the venue requires a minimum stake or control in an owner/operator. Expansion, upgrading and redevelopment requirements all need to be carefully considered in any long-term arrangement.

D2.47 The availability of stewards, security arrangements, gate staff, ticketing staff and banqueting staff will all need to be considered. Will these be separate staff brought in by the licensee or will these be the same staff that are used by the venue for all events and controlled by an operating company?

D2.48 If the owner/operator is to be responsible for a safety certificate and/or liquor and entertainment licensing, then the club will need to ensure that these are adequately and satisfactorily addressed, managed and renewed at the appropriate time. Consideration will need to be given to any remedies that might be available in the event of default by the owner/operator.

D2.49 A club should look for its licence to provide for meetings, reviews and co-ordination with the venue owner with regard to the operation of the facility and in particular to enable the club to meet its obligations to its governing body in relation to the scheduling of events. In a multi-occupation stadium, the competing interests and requirements of the parties can even in the best planned circumstances be difficult, especially when the requirements of the TV schedules disrupt existing arrangements. Care needs to be taken to ensure that as far as possible the various parties' requirements can be accommodated.

D2.50 In finalising any terms of a licence of occupation, a club will need to consider any obligations it has in relation to the premises in terms of reinstatement and this will need to be backed by relevant insurance. Indemnities will probably be required by the owner in respect of damage. Damage might result from trouble from fans or general use of the premises. Any club should consider its insurance in the context of these indemnities and any owner is likely to require evidence of satisfactory insurance arrangements.

D2.51 The owner is likely to restrict the club's freedom to use the premises, to avoid what the owner regards as inappropriate use. Consideration must be given to the effect any such imposed limits may have both operationally and financially upon the club.

D2.52 In situations of multi-occupancy, consideration will also need to be given to any need for parity as between current and potential licensees and this may have a significant impact on operational issues and revenue generating opportunities for the club.

D2.53 The relevant licence fee will need to be agreed. All of the above terms may affect negotiations on any appropriate licence fee particularly in respect of the terms and the extent to which the club will get a clean stadium and be able to generate revenue itself from the venue. Licence fees will typically either be a fixed fee calculated by reference to a sporting season, a year or an event or series of events or may be linked to a percentage of revenue raised by the club in relation to the venue. An element based on percentage of revenue can, if well structured, protect the club against the worst excesses of a downturn in its fortunes. If any licence fee is to be based in part on a share of turnover (or indeed profits) then an appropriate mechanism for payment and audit arrangements will need to be addressed.

D2.54 In any new stadium development or redevelopment of an existing stadium, the availability of funding in relation to a particular sport may have an impact on the structuring of the relationship between the owner/operator and the club. This can be an important part of any negotiations for rights at any new or redeveloped stadium and such considerations and discussions will need to take place at a very early stage of any proposal. The terms of any licence may have an impact on the ability for a club to obtain commercial funding in addition to development and redevelopment funding that might be obtained in respect of the particular sport. The structure of any occupation arrangements may also have implications for any future and ongoing fundraising issues including securitisations over ticketing and also security considerations for any lender in the absence of freehold or long leasehold rights[1].

1 See generally Chapter C3.

4 THE VENUE AS A REVENUE GENERATOR

D2.55 Any sporting club will need to consider the opportunities it has for raising commercial revenue both in relation to matches played at the venue and also in the context of non-match related events.

D2.56 Match day revenue is likely to be generated from sponsorship and signage, audio-visual screens and public address systems, ticket sales, corporate hospitality, food and drink, merchandise sales, programme sales, lotteries and competitions and other sponsorship opportunities connected with the venue. The hierarchical nature of sponsorship opportunities and the increasingly fragmented nature of these opportunities provides for the possibility of exploitation at all levels.

D2.57 Bearing in mind that a sporting arena is often only used for a very limited number of days or times of the year for sport, then opportunities arise for non-event related revenue. The existing facilities required for match days can often readily be adapted to enable their use for conferences, exhibitions, large banqueting events, Christmas parties, PR launches and civil weddings and receptions to name but a few. In addition to having readily available resources which often exceed the scale of resources that can be provided by local hotels, the venue also has the attraction of being connected with the relevant sporting club.

D2.58 Where any club is either the freehold owner or has an exclusive lease of the premises it will want to consider opportunities for licensing the premises for other uses. Equally the owner/operator of any stadium used on a licensed basis will want to retain the right to licence the facilities for other events.

D2.59 In addition to sharing the facilities with other clubs, opportunities can arise for grounds to be used for the playing of reserve games for other bigger clubs or for rock and pop concerts, boxing matches and (in appropriate arenas) show jumping, basketball and ice hockey. A stadium can even be turned over for the use of religious festivals and other large gatherings.

A Stadium Naming Rights

D2.60 Typically the attraction of stadium naming rights for a sponsor will be the opportunity to be associated with all positive aspects of the club in a high profile way. The rights may become more associated with a particular stadium or with a particular club depending upon whether that club is the sole occupier of the venue. Such rights can be valuable, but they can obviously only be exploited by a club if it has exclusive rights in relation to a stadium.

D2.61 Stadium naming rights can and often are associated with the funding of brand new stadia which provide an ideal opportunity for a fresh name to be attached to a stadium rather than its traditional name. If clubs wish to maintain some form of continuity they will wish to ensure that some form of name remains in addition to that of the new stadium sponsor. For example, Bolton Wanderers now play at the Reebok Stadium and if this were to be renamed there would be no form of continuity with the previous name. This can be contrasted with the scenario at Middlesbrough where the stadium will always be known as the Riverside as well as any associated stadium naming. The implications and potential consequences in terms of choice of stadium naming can have a different impact from that of a club sponsor or a shirt sponsor. Club and shirt sponsor deals are typically shorter in duration and changes to the sponsors occur on a periodic basis. Stadium naming is far more likely to be a long term deal particularly where it is tied in to the funding of a new stadium development.

D2.62 The effect of the longer term is that it is more difficult for both the club and the proposed sponsor to determine the value which should be attached to the rights.

D2.63 In addition, the club and the sponsor are seen to be closely associating themselves and both risk damage to their brand by the conduct or failure of the other. By way of example, long term poor performance or indeed a poor reputation or (in worst case scenarios) allegations of corruption at the club could have a negative impact on the sponsor and equally it is possible that the reverse can also be true whereby the sponsor's reputation is tarnished possibly by corporate scandal or a lack of corporate social responsibility.

D2.64 An additional concern to any club may be the ability of the sponsor over an extended period to meet the payment terms where sponsorship monies are not going to be paid upfront. The recent difficulties in respect of ITV Digital[1] have only sought to highlight potential damage that can result from revenue streams which have been relied upon but which are unexpectedly reduced or cut off.

1 See para D4.5.

D2.65 In any stadium naming deal, consideration needs to be given by the club to the impact that the stadium naming may have on its other rights which may be available for exploitation. A very strong association of stadium naming may dilute the value of sponsorship to a club sponsor, shirt sponsor or stand sponsor. Equally, the naming of a stadium in the context of say the brewing sector may impact on the value or marketability of pourage rights at the stadium if the two are not negotiated together. A stadium sponsor in the telecoms industry might equally restrict the ability of the club to sell other rights to other interested parties within that same sector.

D2.66 In addition to naming rights, any stadium sponsor will expect and a whole host of further rights connected with the stadium, which may include internal and external displays, perimeter advertising, name checks on PR announcements, as well as its name appearing on tickets and other literature connected with the venue.

D2.67 The grant of stadium naming rights is to make a clean stadium in sponsorship terms impossible to deliver to any licensee. For example, stadium naming may potentially have an impact on the choice of any governing body wishing to use that stadium for a particular event such as an international game or a cup semi-final or final to be played at a neutral venue and may impact upon the negotiation of centralised rights deals.

D2.68 Negotiations for stadium naming rights can be long and hard fought. For example, in the context of funding new developments, consideration will need to be given to the length of term for which the sponsorship rights will be granted. A limited and agreed period would be necessary for certainty on the part of all parties. Extended periods of sponsorship can lead to the name being associated with the stadium to such an extent it becomes always known as that stadium, which can have a detrimental effect on the value of any future sponsorship rights. The parties would also typically need to consider whether any payment rights should be associated with any success on the field of play. Negotiations may become more complicated if a number of clubs use the venue under the licence. In such circumstances the sponsor's name may be associated with the venue rather than simply the club.

D2.69 Clearly both parties will want to consider circumstances in which termination automatically occurs and circumstances in which the club may be entitled to buy out the sponsorship arrangement so that it can resell the rights.

B Signage and Sponsorship

D2.70 Stadium signage may be a substantial revenue generator for clubs. The ability to maximise revenue in this area will be very much dependent upon the terms of arrangements that have been arrived at by the club's governing body, which may have already granted the rights on a centralised group basis. In addition, other licensees, or even the stadium sponsor, may have demands on the available signage category exclusivity (ie veto rights over competitors being able to advertise within the venue). The effect of ambush marketing is dealt with in Chapter D1. Its importance in this field cannot be underestimated.

D2.71 A club will want to consider the extent to which any restrictions can and should be agreed because of the potential effect on the value of sponsorship and advertising rights.

C Broadcasting

D2.72 Broadcasting is of course an entire subject in its own right and is dealt with in Chapter D4. Venue arrangements are critical to any broadcasting deal. Subject at all time to governing body rules in relation to broadcasting rights, the club will need to ensure it has in place appropriate and complete contractual arrangements with all parties to enable it to create and exploit broadcasting rights to events held at its venue.

D2.73 Consideration will need to be given to the division between central broadcasting deals through governing bodies and other rights which the club may have retained itself such as local radio broadcasting arrangements.

D2.74 The club may also want to consider its own arrangements for recording of events and may enter into a separate arrangement with a production company. This is a developing area particularly in the context of giant screens and the possibility for instant replays.

D2.75 Contractual arrangements for audio visual recording will need to be considered in the context of any central broadcasting agreements to ensure that there is no conflict. Particular consideration may need to be given to the availability of closed circuit TV and early edited highlights for use in post-match reviews and at hospitality events following matches.

D2.76 For both broadcasting and audio visual recording arrangements, careful consideration will need to be given to access rights to a venue particularly where this is the subject of a leasing or licensing arrangement. Flexibility will be required to ensure that the changing needs of broadcasters and the club can be met.

5 MATCH DAY CONTROL AND EXPLOITATION

D2.77 Ticketing will always remain an important component of any sports business, whether it be in terms of the revenue stream generated, the security and control aspects of the running of an event, or the ability to maximise the number of spectators attending. Clubs need to consider exactly how they will manage the ticketing process and the extent to which this may be sub-contracted in whole or in part to a third party.

D2.78 In terms of public order, control of ticketing is an essential part of the management of the venue. Control over the terms of ticket issue allow (where appropriate) segregation of supporters and the incorporation of the club's ground rules. When dealing with ticketing and the incorporation of terms, the club will need to consider the following key issues.

D2.79 The terms and conditions of use and general ground rules must be incorporated at the point of sale to ensure that all tickets are sold subject to the conditions whether they are sold by the club itself or by a third party on its behalf[1].

1 See further paras D1.25 and D1.26.

D2.80 If possible the terms and conditions and the ground regulations should be incorporated on the ticket itself or a document accompanying the ticket. This is more practical in the context of corporate hospitality and sponsorship packages and with season tickets as opposed to individual tickets sold on a one-off basis.

D2.81 Notices should also be displayed at the entrance to grounds making it clear that the right of entry is subject specifically to ground regulations.

D2.82 It is likely that those regulations will need to be agreed in conjunction with the stadia owners and operators, as well as the sports governing body, the local authority and the local police.

D2.83 As a bare minimum, the conditions should include the right to refuse entry to the stadium and to confiscate the ticket upon breach of the ticket conditions and/or ground regulations. Season tickets and hospitality package tickets should at all times remain the property of the club to enable it to recover possession in the context of any breach. In addition to such forfeiture the club should reserve the right to eject the relevant person where it considers any breach has taken place.

D2.84 Below is a typical sample set of ground regulations:

NOTICE

Entry to the Ground is expressly subject to each and all of these Ground Regulations

1. Permission for any person to enter the Ground notwithstanding possession of any ticket by that person is at the absolute discretion of the stewards and officers of the Club and/or any police officer.
2. No guarantees can be given by the Club that the Event will take place at any particular time or on any particular date and the Club reserves the right to reschedule the Event without notice and without any liability for so doing.
3. In the event of the postponement or abandonment of the Event refunds of ticket prices if any will be made at the absolute discretion of the Club. The Club will have no legal liability to make a refund or to pay any form of consequential or indirect damage such as loss of enjoyment or travel costs.

4. The Club reserves the right to search any person entering the Ground and to refuse entry to any person refusing to submit to such a search.
5. The following are articles which must not be brought within the Ground (eg knives, glasses, fireworks, smoke canisters, air-horns, flares, bottles, weapons of any sort or banners and signs exceeding certain dimensions). Any person in possession of such items will be refused entry at the discretion of any steward or officer of the Club and/or any police officer.
6. All persons entering the Ground may only occupy the seat allocated to them by their ticket and must not move from any one part of the Ground to another without the express permission or instructions of any steward or officer of the Club and/or any police officer.
7. No object may be thrown within the Ground.
8. No foul or abusive language, singing, chanting or other offensive words such as racial or sexual abuse may be used within the Ground.
9. Nobody entering the Ground shall be permitted to climb any structures within the Ground.
10. Nobody may stand in any seating area whilst play is in progress.
11. No alcohol may be consumed within the Ground except in those areas specifically designated for such purposes.
12. No person may take photographs or use any video recording equipment inside the Ground without the express written permission of the Club.
13. No articles, periodicals, publications, flyers or goods of any nature may be offered either free or for sale by any person save only the Club within the Ground without the express written permission of the Club.
14. Any person entering the Ground must at all times comply with any and all instructions of any steward of officer of the Club and/or any police officer. Failure to comply within a reasonable time with any such instruction will lead to immediate ejection from the Ground.
15. Any individual who has entered any area of the Ground designated for the use of any group of supporters to which he does not belong may be ejected from the Ground either for the purposes of his own safety or for any other reason.
16. No tickets may be offered for resale within the Ground. Any such tickets offered for sale may be confiscated by any steward or officer of the Club or any police officer.
17. The Club reserves absolutely the right to eject from the Ground any person failing to comply with each and all of the Ground Regulations.

D2.85 The club must be vigilant to ensure that the ground regulations will apply to any spectator, including corporate hospitality customers, and therefore when selling packages must ensure that rights and obligations are adequately incorporated to cover all members of a party.

D2.86 Concern has arisen on occasions in relation to sponsors' tickets and the allocations of those tickets particularly where they are released to third parties. This has had an impact on segregation arrangements at events which may affect the safety of spectators. The terms of any arrangements with sponsors should incorporate restrictions on the way in which those tickets are disposed of or used, to restrict the availability of those tickets on the black market.

D2.87 Equally, if tickets are to be used by sponsors for competitions and marketing, consideration will need to be given to segregation and to ensuring that any winners or users of tickets meet any requirements.

D2.88 Any club will wish to consider how best to protect its image and satisfactorily control spectators. Careful consideration needs to be given to stewarding and security arrangements and the extent to which those are contracted out to third parties. Equally a club will need to consider carefully its arrangements and relationship with the local police to ensure that order is maintained. Appropriate policies will need to be developed to deal with fans who have been banned from the ground either by the club itself or by the courts.

D2.89 Ambush marketing has been dealt with elsewhere in this work[1]. However, when considering the venue consideration should also be given to its environs. A club will wish to review the extent to which it is able to control the approaches to and area immediately outside a stadium as well as the internal aspects. Ownership of land and policing and control of external sites can add not just to the good orderly conduct of the event but also to avoiding or limiting ambush marketing.

1 See paras D1.116 to D1.135.

CHAPTER D3

IMAGE RIGHTS

Jonathan Taylor (Hammonds), **Stephen Boyd** (Selborne Chambers) and **David Becker** (Hammonds)*

Contents

1 INTRODUCTION

D3.1 This chapter addresses the legal and practical issues that arise from the commercial exploitation of a sportsman's name, image and/or other identifying characteristics (such as his nickname, reputation, voice, persona, signature and initials).

* The authors acknowledge with gratitude the assistance provided on tax matters addressed in this chapter by Bernard McIlroy of Hammonds.

D3.2 After surveying the use that is made in modern marketing practice of the popularity of individual sportsmen and women[1], the chapter examines the extent to which English law recognises and protects the right of an individual to control the commercial use of his name and image[2]. It will be demonstrated that the law in this country does not properly reflect modern marketing practice, in that (in contrast to many overseas jurisdictions) it does not recognise an individual's proprietary interest in his image per se, but rather forces him to cobble together limited and piecemeal protection through the inventive use of various disparate legal doctrines.

1 See para D3.6 et seq.
2 See para D3.11 et seq.

D3.3 However, the fact that it is possible, by identifying and exploiting the loopholes and limitations of common law protection in this area, to use a sportsman's name and image without paying a rights fee to the sportsman for the privilege, only takes one so far. It is not only easier but also far more attractive from a practical point of view to enter into a commercial arrangement with the sportsman that secures his consent to the use of his persona, as well as his co-operation to facilitate that use. Of course, if the party seeking to use the image is the sportsman's club, then the need is even greater to come to an arrangement as to the commercial exploitation of the sportsman's name and image with which the sportsman is entirely comfortable and happy. Furthermore, if the product or service is being promoted beyond just the UK, that will bring into play foreign laws that do recognise an individual's right to control the commercial use of his persona. As a result, at the elite levels, notwithstanding the lack of recognition of 'image rights' as proprietary rights enforceable under English law, substantial contractual activity takes place in relation to the grant to clubs and other third parties of the right to use the sportsman's name and image, and for the provision of 'promotional' services by the player to assist in the exploitation of those rights. Some of those arrangements are surveyed below, including consideration of specific contractual clauses[1].

1 See para D3.67 et seq.

D3.4 The cynic would say that the emergence of 'image rights' has less to do with developments in marketing techniques and more to do with salary caps and tax dodges. However, in 2000 the Special Commissioners of the Inland Revenue rejected a challenge by the Inland Revenue to image rights arrangements involving Arsenal and two of its leading players (Dennis Bergkamp and David Platt), finding that the payments for the players' 'promotional services' were not disguised salary payments contrived to avoid income tax and National Insurance contributions, but rather were genuine commercial transactions for the acquisition of rights that were of independent value over and above the playing services that the players provided for their employer clubs. Section 5 of this chapter addresses the nature and scope of that ruling, and examines how the commercial exploitation of sportsmen's image rights can be structured so as to be most tax-efficient.

1 See para D3.78 et seq.

D3.5 Before going any further, however, it is necessary to address briefly correct terminology. At its most basic, this area of sports rights is simply about (as the Special Commissioners in the tax case referenced above recognised) 'the ability to make money out of the fact that one was very well known'[1], but that is too cumbersome for use as a label. The rights at issue have been described variously, in the UK and/or in other jurisdictions, as 'personality rights', 'character rights', 'rights of privacy', 'rights of publicity', 'endorsement rights' and 'image rights'[2]. Each has its advantages and disadvantages. The problem with 'personality rights' and 'character rights' is that some of those sportsmen who make most money in this area have little of either. 'Rights of privacy' does not work because the topic has nothing to do with privacy and everything to do with (sometimes rather extreme forms of) public exposure. However, 'publicity rights' sounds peculiar and evokes images of exhibitionists rather than sophisticated commercial operators. There is a lot to be said for the label 'endorsement rights', but while that covers most of the activity in this field it omits (for example) the substantial commercial enterprise of character merchandising[3], as well as the modern phenomenon of newspapers and magazines buying access to the personal lives of sports stars (weddings, baptisms, World Cup send-off parties) not to endorse any product or service[4] but simply to sell copies. Therefore, the authors prefer to use the term 'image rights', with 'image' used not in the narrow sense of 'likeness' but in the broad sense of 'persona' or (better) 'brand'.

1 *Sports Club, Evelyn and Jocelyn v Inspector of Taxes* SpC00253 (SC Brice and Everett, 8 June 2000), Simons Tax Cases [2000] STC (SCD) 443.

2 Cf *Sports Club, Evelyn and Jocelyn v Inspector of Taxes* SpC00253 (SC Brice and Everett, 8 June 2000), Simons Tax Cases [2000] STC (SCD) 443, para 8: 'During the hearing, and in the documents, the promotional agreements were sometimes referred to as "image rights agreements". As it was agreed that in England there is no property in a person's image we do not find the expression "image rights agreement" as being sufficiently descriptive of the contents of the agreements in issue in this appeal. As the agreements concerned promotion, publicity, marketing and advertising we refer to them as promotional agreements except where the context requires a reference to image rights'.

3 For a discussion of the distinction between endorsements and merchandising, see paras D3.56, n 1 and D6.20.

4 Anthea Turner and her chocolate bar excepted.

2 THE USE OF IMAGE RIGHTS IN MODERN MARKETING PRACTICE

D3.6 Much of the commercial value of sport in the 21st century resides in the massive popular appeal of the individual superstars who play the sport. Some sports are more oriented towards the individual than others[1], but even in team sports, where club brands (eg Manchester United, Leicester Tigers) or event brands (eg FA Premier League, FIA Formula One World Championship) may be strong, there has developed a strong cult of the individual based around star players whose fame transcends their sport and their ability in that sport and makes them 'celebrities' in their own right[2].

1 For example, golf and tennis may have team events (Ryder Cup, Davis Cup/Fed Cup), but more often an individual competes on behalf of him or herself. In contrast, in sports such as football, rugby and cricket the competition is essentially between teams. Somewhere in between is Formula One motor-racing, where the racing drivers are stars but the team and event brands are also very strong.

2 'However, the popular status of sports stars now transcends the authorisation of sports merchandise. Sporting fame is no longer confined to appropriate sports fora. Sporting heroes and heroines are household names, pin ups and increasingly fashion models': Gannon 'Sporting Glory?' [1996] NLJ 1160. See also Couchman 'Protection for personalities' (1997) 12 Sports Business 26: 'Personalities are increasingly becoming "marketing properties" in their own right: they are becoming like "brands" which, when associated with goods and services, can add tremendous value to the proposition'.

D3.7 Newspapers, magazines and on-line media all seek to exploit that celebrity to pull in readers, by printing vast numbers of stories and features about sports stars and their activities. Huge amounts of merchandise (such as sticker collections and playing card products) are based on the reproduction of the images of sports stars, as are often the hugely popular computer games that simulate top sports events[1]. In addition, marketing agencies have seized on the enormous appeal of the leading sports stars (in particular, their appeal to attractive demographic groups) as an ideal platform for the promotion of the brands, products and services of those agencies' clients[2]. Whether the image is 'role model' or 'anti-hero', the popular appeal can be vast.

1 See eg Hooker A and Ogden M 'The Name of the Game' (2000) 10 Sports and Character Licensing 14 (discussing factors that might lead computer games manufacturers to base games on individual sportsmen).

2 See eg Rowan 'Pepsi and Coke go into battle for Becks' (2002) London Evening Standard, 9 April.

D3.8 Clubs and national teams also seek to use their players' celebrity status to market the goods and services produced by the club, and to promote its sponsors and commercial partners. In doing so, they must battle[1] for space with the players' agents, who might originally have confined themselves to arranging their clients' playing contracts with their clubs, but now take a far broader role, securing endorsement and merchandising deals for their clients with commercial companies. It has come to the stage where the superstar footballers, such as Michael Owen, have at least three separate personas for commercial purposes – that of an individual, a club player and an international – with separate commercial programmes built around each of them.

1 Witness the brief strike by the England national rugby union team in September 2000 over the RFU's attempts to grant its sponsors the right to use the players' names and images in their own advertising and marketing materials. See 'England players in dispute over image rights' (2000) Sportcal.com, 25 September. Witness also the dispute in 2002 about the rights of Indian cricket players to endorse products conflicting with those of ICC sponsors in and around the ICC Champions Trophy. See para D1.28, n 1.

D3.9 The value of such activity can be substantial. In 1999, Anna Kournikova reportedly earned nine times more from endorsements than her earnings from playing tennis; whereas Michael Schumacher earned US $52.5m (70% of his total earnings) from licensing his name and image (the Schumacher product line consists of 350 articles, with the latest additions a vacuum cleaner and a scooter board)[1]. It has been reported that Real Madrid paid Luis Figo US $56m for his image rights, and that it subsequently paid Zinedine Zidane £21.6m for 90% of his image rights, on the basis that it could raise £21m from the sale of replica shirts alone[2]. In addition, the image rights of nine Premiership players have been were estimated to be worth between £3.5m and £7.25m per year, including Michael Owen at £7.25m and David Beckham at £6.5m[3].

1 (2000) 12 Sports Business 3.
2 (2001) London Evening Standard, 29 October.
3 See 'Owen's battle to make his mark' (1998) Times, 15 August.

D3.10 It is easy to overstate the position. Below the ranks of Kournikova, Schumacher, Owen and Beckham, there are thousands of sports 'stars' who would scarcely prompt a second glance off the field of play[1]. Even David Beckham, who has attained an unquestionable celebrity status that transcends his position as star for Manchester United and captain of England, is worth far more to his club on the field than off it[2]. However, the commercial exploitation of a sportsman's issue is not only an emotive issue in these days of increasing player power, particularly as players, their clubs and their national teams each seek to deliver value to their own sponsors and commercial partners. It can also make a significant difference to a sportsman's pay packet, particularly with careful tax planning, and therefore can be an important factor in the market for the services especially of overseas players (whose tax savings can be greatest)[3]. As a result, the topic of image rights is likely to remain at the front and centre of the sports marketing arena[4].

1 See Blood M 'Footballers' Image Rights in the UK' (2001) 15 Sports and Character Licensing 23: 'It is debatable whether or not such image rights outside of the sphere of football are as valuable as the egos of the players and their agents would like to think. David Beckham excepted, how many of the top 25 European footballers playing in the Champions League would be recognised, never mind valued by their image alone without their club or national uniforms? The beauty of football is the teams and therefore the potential customers' loyalty to their clubs. It is the clubs and not the players who are the core brands within the sport. This is the dilemma for individual players who are

attempting to exploit their own images in a European and UK Football culture which has yet to be overtaken with a fascination and infatuation with stars ...'

See also Jon Smith of First Artist Corporation (2002) Evening Standard, 9 April, p 16: 'Image rights are fashionable but worthless in many cases: you need a popularity beyond football and the UK. Beckham has a fan base way beyond Manchester United'.

2 Reports that David Beckham would receive more for his image rights than for his playing services in his latest contract with Manchester United ('United looking to brand Beckham' (2001) Guardian, 6 February) were obviously overstated. In fact, the club reportedly agreed to pay him £20,000 a week for the right to exploit his image, as opposed to £80,000 per week for his playing services. See (2002) Sportbusiness.com, 15 July. Nevertheless, this is certainly far more than has previously been paid for image rights in domestic football, reflecting Beckham's fairly unique iconic status.

3 See para D3.78 et seq.

4 The biggest source of commercial income for sports events remains broadcasting income. See para D4.2. Broadcasting involves the reproduction of the images of the players on the television screens of the nation. However, those images are not being used (at least directly) to promote brands or services or products of commercial partners, but rather are simply part of the sporting spectacle. That is not to say that players accept they are not entitled to a share of broadcasting revenues. Apart from the fact that broadcasting income finances player wages, the PFA takes the position that the cut of television revenues that the PFA receives from each of the FA Premier League and the Football League is paid in lieu of player appearance fees, which the players (in a show of solidarity with each other) have agreed to forego. The threatened PFA strike in 2001 arose out of a dispute between the PFA, the FA Premier League and the Football League as to the size of that cut in relation to the massive broadcasting fees committed by BSkyB and ITV to the FA Premier League and by ITV Digital to the Football League in 2001.

3 THE LEGAL STATUS OF A SPORTSMAN'S IMAGE RIGHTS

D3.11 The commercial value of any right, including image rights, can be undermined by the inability to protect that right at law from unauthorised use:

> The existence of goods and services bearing the individual's name or image (and therefore the possible implied suggestion that the individual has approved or endorsed the products) without authorisation can in some cases seriously damage the value of a sporting personality's licensing rights in his image. Not only does the individual suffer the loss of royalties he might have earned but also his image may depreciate in value by the affixing of his name and image to inferior goods or materials. It may also deprive him of another lucrative endorsement contract due to loss of exclusivity[1].

1 Steele 'Personality Merchandising, Licensing Rights and the March of the Turtles' [1997] 5(2) SATLJ 14.

D3.12 As Jones states:

> The damage caused by unauthorised manipulation or appropriation of a person's image for commercial purposes comes in two forms, the first being the invasion of the subject's privacy and the related loss of control or autonomy over the use of his or her image and the second being the loss of control inherent in the defendant's reaping an economic benefit from another person's image and the reputation and goodwill associated with it ... with the resultant reduction in the scope of future potential licensing opportunities in the market sector[1].

1 Jones 'Manipulating the Law against Misleading Imagery: Photo Montage and Appropriation of Well-Known Personality' (1999) 1 EIPR 28.

D3.13 Whether the sports star can prevent the unauthorised exploitation of his or her image and seek compensation from the opportunist marketeer or merchandiser depends upon whether, and to what extent, the law in the relevant country recognises and protects image rights. The law in many jurisdictions outside the UK has developed in tandem with the growth of the commercial value of the image of celebrities and a specific image right is recognised in many countries, including most of those in the European Community. It is worth briefly surveying the approach in such jurisdictions to set a context (and a contrast) for the approach under English law.

A Overseas jurisdictions

(a) United States of America

D3.14 The arguments for a discrete law dealing with image rights, or 'rights of publicity', as they are known in the USA, have been extracted from the American cases and summarised as follows:

(a) significant expenditure of time, effort, talent and finance is necessary to succeed as a sports person and as a result he or she justifiably deserves any money flowing from his or her fame;
(b) the population is incentivised to undertake socially enriching activities by ensuring that the sports person who undertakes such activities reaps the financial reward;
(c) the unauthorised use of a sports person's identity may saturate the market, thus injuring him or her by reducing the demand for his or her image; and
(d) every man and woman should have autonomy over what he or she endorses, be it an idea, a political candidate or a product[1].

1 Frackman and Bloomfield 'The Right of Publicity: Going to the Dogs' (The UCLA Online Institute for Cyberspace Law and Policy), p 2.

D3.15 As a result, the laws of many American states recognise:

> the inherent right of every human being to control the commercial use of his or her identity. The right of publicity is a state-law created intellectual property right whose infringement is a commercial tort of unfair competition. It is a distinct legal category not just a 'kind of' trade mark, copyright, false advertising or right of privacy. Whilst it bears some family resemblances to all these neighbouring areas of the law, the right of publicity has its own unique legal dimensions and reasons for being. The right of publicity is not merely a legal right of the 'celebrity' but is a right inherent to every one to control the commercial use of identity and persona and recover in court damages and the commercial value of an unpermitted taking[1].

For example, the California Civil Code provides a cause of action where:

> any person knowingly uses another's name, voice, signature, photograph, or likeness in any manner, on or in products, merchandise or goods, or for purposes of advertising or selling, or soliciting purchases of products, merchandise, goods or services, without such person's prior consent[2].

1 McCarthy *The Rights of Publicity and Privacy* (2nd edn, 2000, Clark Boardman Callaghan), paras 1-2 and 1-3.
2 California Civil Code s 3344 (2002). There is a limited exception that allows such use without consent in connection with 'news, public affairs or sports broadcast or account, or any political campaign'.

D3.16 In addition, at the federal level, s 43(a) of the Lanham Trade Mark Act prohibits use of any 'word, term, name, symbol or device, or any combination thereof, or any false designation of origin, false or misleading description of fact or false or misleading representation' that is likely to cause confusion, mistake or deception as to the affiliation, connection, association, origin, sponsorship or approval between a party and the goods, services or commercial activities of another.

D3.17 'The courts enforce this body of law vigorously, consistently and extensively. A person's right to control the commercial use of his or her personality is quite complete'[1].

1 Anderson 'The failure of American Privacy Law' in *Protecting Privacy* edited by Basil S Markesinis ('Markesinis') at p 146. For examples of use of US laws to protect celebrities' image rights, see Harrington 'Unauthorised use of a sports stars' image in the UK and internationally – a level playing field?' (1999) 1(1) Sport and Character Licensing 16.

(b) Canada

D3.18 The Canadian courts have also recognised that a person 'has a proprietary right in the exclusive marketing for gain of his personality, image and name, and that the law entitles him to protect that right if it is invaded'[1]. This right is protected by the tort of appropriation of personality, first recognised by the Ontario Court of Appeal in *Krouse v Chrysler Canada Ltd* in 1973[2], which is said to be 'the unique contribution of Canadian common law' to the development of legal principles in this area[3]. According to the *Krouse* case, a professional athlete has a commercial proprietary right with regard to his photograph or likeness when it is used in advertisements. However, where a photograph is not used to suggest an endorsement of a product by the athlete, but is only used to illustrate the sport in which he participates, no cause of action lies.

1 *Athans v Canadian Adventure Camps Ltd* (1977) 17 OR (2d) 425, 435. The Jamaican Supreme Court adopted a similar approach in *Bob Marley Foundation v Dino Michelle Ltd* 1994 Supreme Court No CLR115 of 1992.
2 (1973) 40 DLR (3d) 15.
3 Potvin, Howell and McMahon in *International Privacy, Publicity and Personality Laws* edited by Michael Henry ('Henry') at para 7.53.

(c) Australia

D3.19 There is no right in Australia equivalent to the American 'right of publicity' or the Canadian tort of appropriation of personality. However, s 52 of the Trade Practices Act 1974 provides that:

> [a] corporation shall not, in trade or commerce, engage in conduct that is misleading or deceptive, or is likely to mislead or deceive;

and s 53 of the Act provides that:

> [a] corporation shall not, in trade or commerce, in connection with the supply or possible supply of goods or services or in connection with the promotion by any means of the supply or use of goods of services–
> (a) represent that goods or services have sponsorship, approval, performance, characteristics, accessories, uses or benefits they do not have;
> (b) represent that the corporation has a sponsorship, approval or affiliation it does not have.

Although designed to protect consumers from buying goods or services that have been falsely associated with another product or a personality, 'the Act, albeit tacitly, serves to protect against the unauthorised exploitation of reputation or personality'[1].

1 Henry, para 3.79.

D3.20 Further, Australian common law also offers protection against the unauthorised use of personal identity in advertising and commercial promotion, through the tort of passing off. In *Henderson v Radio Corpn*[1], the plaintiffs were well-known ballroom dancers who successfully sued the defendant record manufacturer for passing off after it produced a dance music record with a photograph on the cover showing the two of them dancing. The court found that the target market would probably believe that the photograph indicated the plaintiffs' endorsement or approval of the record, and that the only possible reason for the defendant's use was to attract attention to the product and increase sales[2].

1 [1969] RPC 218.
2 The defendant sought to rely on the English precedent of *McCulloch v May* (see para D3.50), which required the plaintiff in a passing off case to show that it shares a 'common field of activity' with the defendant. Chief Justice Evatt did not agree with the narrow view of Wynn Parry J in that case: 'The remedy of passing off is necessarily only available where parties are engaged in business, using that expression in its widest sense to include professions and callings. If they are, there does not seem to be any reason why it should also be necessary that there be an area, actual or potential, in which their activities conflict': 1969 RPC at 234. In the recent *Irvine* case, Laddie J preferred the approach in *Henderson* to the *McCulloch* approach. See paras D3.52 and D3.53.

D3.21 Following *Henderson*[1] and another leading case in which the actor Paul Hogan established passing off against a shoe company whose advertisement was a spoof of the '*This* is a knife' scene from Crocodile Dundee[2], the current position in Australian law appears to be as follows:

> [A] personality who can be said to be in business – and the term is very broadly understood – is always free to grant or withhold his endorsement, and therefore any unauthorised claim to such endorsement damages him by depriving him of the fee he could otherwise have insisted on. It is irrelevant that the plaintiff may have no existing licensing business or may prefer not to grant licences. Nor does it matter that the defendant may have derived no benefit from the supposed endorsement, and would not voluntarily have paid a fee. Misrepresentation must still be shown, and the misrepresentation can be found in the public supposing there to be some sort of commercial arrangement of an unspecified kind between the plaintiff and the defendant. Given the existence of such a misrepresentation, it does not appear to have been one on which the public actually rely or to which they attach any importance, and by the same reasoning it does not have to be calculated to cause damage over and above the loss of a licensing fee[3].

1 As approved by the full High Court of Australia in *Campomer Sociedad Ltda v Nike International Ltd* (2000) 46 IPR 481.
2 *Hogan v Pacific Dunlop Ltd* (1989) 14 IPR 398. See also *Hogan v Koala Dundee Pty Ltd* (1988) 83 ALR 187 (Federal Court of Australia, Queensland District).
3 Christopher Wadlow *The Law of Passing Off* (2nd edn), pp 298 and 299. The question arises as to the extent to which, following the *Irvine* case discussed below, this description also accurately states the law in England. See paras D3.52 to D3.57.

(d) Sweden

D3.22 The 1979 Act on Names and Pictures in Advertising provides that a business man in Sweden may not use the name or picture of any individual without permission when promoting goods or services:

An athlete whose name or portrait is used for commercial purposes without consent is entitled to damages which as a rule amount to what the athlete normally would have charged for such services. Damages may be awarded also for non-economic harm. Moreover, under the Act intentional or grossly negligent use of an individual's name or portrait is a criminal offence punishable by fines[1].

1 Hober and Nilsson 'Sports Personality Rights in Sweden' (2001) 15 Sports and Character Licensing 25.

(e) France

D3.23 Under French law[1], 'personality rights' are 'fundamental rights attached to the persona of the human being, intended to protect non-patrimonial attributes or manifestations of the person'[2].

> [A]s of the 1960s more and more celebrities submitted claims to the French courts that their right to their image had been infringed by unauthorised commercial use. The issue was mainly one of protecting the celebrity against the free ride or risks of tarnishment of his or her name because of apparent endorsement of advertised products or services. The courts, struggling to find a legal ground to sanction this unauthorised use not hurting plaintiffs' privacy, affirmed an 'absolute right in one's image'[3].

A general right to privacy was recognised in 1970 when it was incorporated in the new Art 9 of the Civil Code. In 1995 the Constitutional Council 'consented to consecrate the "right to privacy" as a constitutional right, or more accurately, as a "constitutional principle"'[4].

1 See Frilet 'Image Rights in France' (2000) 5 Sports and Character Licensing 25.
2 Elizabeth Logeais 'The French Right to One's Image – A Legal Lure' (1994) 5 Ent LR 163 at 164.
3 See n 2 at p 165.
4 Professor Etienne Picard 'The Right to Privacy in French Law' in Markesinis, ch 3, p 51.

D3.24 'Generally speaking, the content of this [personality] right is considered in a negative manner: it is the right to prohibit the production and distribution of an individual's likeness without the subject's consent. The jurisprudence has nevertheless exposed several exceptions to the exercise of the right:

(i) when the image is incidental and was taken in a public place;
(ii) when it concerns a subject of a current event and is published soon after;
(iii) when it concerns the reporting of a trial (whose proceedings are public); and
(iv) when it concerns the likeness of a public figure in his public life'[1].

However, such publication must be made for the purpose of providing information and not for publicity purposes or for commercial exploitation[2].

> When concerned with the publication or distribution of the likeness of public figures, the judge may refer to the going rate (established by expert witness if necessary) in order to award on the basis of lost earnings, at most the sum equivalent to what could have been paid contractually, in accordance with the principles of the allocation of damages by virtue by Articles 1382 and 1383 of the Civil Code[3].

1 Henry, para 11.119.
2 Henry, para 11.123.
3 Henry, para 11.132.

D3.25 Using these laws, supermodel Linda Evangelista was able to take successful legal action under Art 9 of the Civil Code against a right wing French political party that used a photograph of her dressed as Joan of Arc in its advertising. Another famous case involved Eric Cantona, who was awarded damages for the unauthorised use of his image on the cover of a video[1].

1 See Harrington 'Image Rights – Overview of Protection in Key Markets' (2002) 9(2) Sports Law Administration & Practice 11, 12.

(f) Italy

D3.26 Similarly, Italian law protects the personality of any person, including their name and image. The relevant provisions are Arts 2 and 3 of the Italian Constitution, Arts 6 to 10 of the Italian Civil Code and Art 21 of the Italian Trade Mark Law. Accordingly, a company wishing to make commercial use of a sports person's name or image can only lawfully do so with that person's permission. However, courts tend not to enforce these rights where the use is merely informative[1].

1 See Harrington 'Image Rights – Overview of Protection in Key Markets' (2002) 9(2) Sports Law Administration & Practice 11, 12.

B The position under English law

D3.27 Professor Cornish notes that English law, in contrast:

> has steadfastly refused to adopt any embracing principle that a person has a right to his or her name, or, for that matter, to identifying characteristics, such as voice or image. An entitlement simply to demand that such characteristics without more amount to property in personality is highly regarded as a commodification too far[1].

1 See Cornish *Intellectual Property* (4th edn), para 16-34.

D3.28 The case most often cited for the rejection of a property right to prevent unauthorised use of identity in advertising is *Tolley v Fry*[1], where Greer LJ stated that:

> some men and women voluntarily enter professions which by their nature invite publicity, and public approval or disapproval. It is not unreasonable in their case that they should submit without complaint to their names and occupations and reputations being treated … almost as public property[2].

1 [1930] 1 KB 467, CA.
2 [1930] 1 KB 467 at 477.

D3.29 In the *Elvis* case, the Court of Appeal again rejected the idea of a proprietary right in a personality. Simon Brown LJ said:

> … all the English cases upon which [the plaintiff] seeks to rely (Mirage Studios not least) can be seen to have turned essentially upon the need to protect copyright or to prevent passing off (or libel). None creates the broad right for which [counsel for the plaintiff] contends here, a freestanding general right to character exploitation enjoyable exclusively by the celebrity. As Robert Walker LJ has explained, just such a right, a new 'character right' to fill a perceived gap between the law of copyright (there being no copyright in a name) and the law of passing off was considered and rejected by the Whitford Committee in 1977. Thirty years earlier, indeed, when it was contended for as a corollary of passing

off law, it had been rejected in *McCulloch v May*. I would continue to reject it. In addressing the critical issue of distinctiveness there should be no a priori assumption that only a celebrity or his successors may ever market (or licence the marketing of) his own character. Monopolies should not be so readily created[1].

1 *Elvis Presley Enterprises Inc v Sid Shaw Elvisly Yours* [1999] RPC 567, 597–598, CA. See Whybrow 'Elvis Presley: Celebrity Names and Images Have No Monopoly under English Law' (1999) 117 Trademark World 36; Cordery and Watts 'Character Merchandising: All Shook Up?' [1999] 5 Ent LR 155. It is germane to point out that the Whitford Committee referred to by Simon Brown LJ in the passage quoted from his judgment was considering 'character rights' under copyright law in connection with fictitious characters and the report contained the following passage: 'An unfair competition law would probably provide the most satisfactory solution but we make no recommendation for a further extension of the law of copyright'. See Cmnd 6732, para 909.

D3.30 In the absence of a discrete proprietary right in the commercial exploitation of one's own personality, a celebrity can only complain 'if the reproduction or use of [his/her] likeness results in the infringement of some recognised legal right which he/she does own'[1]. Or, as Goodenough puts it, 'plaintiffs lacking the real thing must rely on a confusing number of analogues and neighbouring doctrines'[2]. It is to these 'analogues' and 'doctrines' – a variety of statutory rights and common law principles, none of which is specifically designed to protect against the unauthorised use of a sportsman's name or image – that we now turn.

1 Per Laddie J in *Elvis Presley Trade Marks* 1997 RPC 543 at 548, Ch D.
2 Goodenough 'Re Theorising Privacy and Publicity' (1997) 1 IPR 37 at 65.

(a) Defamation

D3.31 The law of defamation does not prohibit the unauthorised use of the name or image of the claimant; rather, it protects the reputation of the claimant.

> [T]he gist of the action is that the defendant either lowers the plaintiff in the estimation of reasonable, right thinking members of society, or causes such citizens to shun or avoid him[1].

1 *Street on Torts* (10th edn), p 435.

D3.32 In *Tolley v Fry*[1], Mr Tolley, an amateur golfer in the days when there was a clear divide between 'gentlemen' and 'players', succeeded in a claim for defamation when he was depicted in an advertisement with a packet of Fry's chocolate sticking out of his pocket. The defamatory meaning of the advertisement was said to be that Mr Tolley had 'prostituted his reputation as an amateur golfer for advertising purposes'.

1 [1930] 1 KB 467, CA.

D3.33 Given that these days all sports stars with image rights worth exploiting are professional, it seems unlikely that defamation will ever assist in the protection of image rights again. It has been suggested that 'the use of a well known teetotaller or ex alcoholic to promote beer, for example, or a well known vegetarian to promote bacon, might provide a cause of action in defamation'[1], but the requisite harm to reputation does not seem clear-cut in such examples. If a footballer signed an exclusive boot deal with Nike in a blaze of publicity, and proclaimed loudly how he always wore Nike boots because they were the best, and then Reebok used the footballer's name and image to endorse its rival boots, an action might lie for defamation based on the alleged innuendo that the footballer did not honour his contracts, but again it would not be straightforward. The most likely claim might be from the unauthorised use of an image not for commercial but for political purposes, as happened in France, where a right-wing party used Linda Evangelista's image to promote its views[2].

1 Harrington 'Image Rights – Part Two' (2002) 9(3) Sports Law Administration & Practice 11 at 13.
2 See para D3.25.

(b) Malicious Falsehood

D3.34 The tort of malicious (or injurious) falsehood is related to defamation, but protects interests in goodwill and economic reputation. '[A]n action will lie for written or oral falsehoods … where they are maliciously published, where they are calculated in the ordinary course of things to produce, and where they do produce actual damage'[1]. 'The essence of the tort is that the defendant's lies should have caused economic damage to the plaintiff'[2]. The tort would in theory appear to be broad enough to cover a false endorsement scenario: in *Kaye v Robertson*[3], a claim for injurious falsehood was upheld in relation to a false representation of a commercial association between the parties. However, the authors are not aware of any case where the tort has been used in response to the unauthorised use of a celebrity's name or image for endorsement or merchandising purposes.

1 *Ratcliffe v Evans* [1892] 2 QB 524 at 527, CA.
2 *Street on Torts* (10th edn) at p 137.
3 [1991] FSR 62, CA.

(c) Trade Descriptions Act 1968

D3.35 Section 1(1) of the Trade Descriptions Act 1968 provides that:

> [a]ny person who, in the course of a trade or business–
> (a) applies a false trade description to any goods; or
> (b) supplies or offers to supply any goods to which a false trade description is applied,
> shall, subject to the provisions of this Act, be guilty of an offence.

Section 2 defines 'trade description' as 'an indication, direct or indirect, and by whatever means' given of any of a number of matters with respect to the goods, including:

> (g) approval by any person or conformity with a type approved by any person.

Section 14 provides similar protection in respect of services. Section 3(4) of the Act defines 'false trade description' to include 'a false indication, or anything likely to be taken as an indication which would be false, that any goods comply with the standard specified or recognised by any person or implied by the approval of any person'.

D3.36 On its face, it appears that this might again cover a case of use of a celebrity's name or image to imply falsely that he or she has endorsed the products or services in question. However again the authors are not aware of any case in which such an approach has been followed.

(d) *Regulatory Codes*

D3.37 There are a number of regulatory bodies overseeing both print and broadcast media, some of whose regulations would appear to encompass and prohibit the unauthorised commercial exploitation of a celebrity's image. However, these bodies are largely toothless and are unlikely to provide much comfort to an aggrieved celebrity; in particular, there is no scope for any award of damages to compensate for the celebrity's loss[1].

1 For a fuller treatment, see Smith *Image Persona and the Law – Special Report* (2001, Sweet & Maxwell) at para 5-166 et seq.

D3.38 Regulation 2(2) of The Control of Misleading Advertisements Regulations 1988[1] provides:

> For the purposes of these regulations an advertisement is misleading if in any way, including its presentation, it deceives or is likely to deceive the persons to whom it is addressed or whom it reaches and if, by reason of its deceptive nature, it is likely to affect their economic behaviour or, for those reasons, injures or is likely to injure a competitor of the person whose interest the advertisement seeks to promote.

Regulation 4(1) imposes a duty on the Director General of Fair Trading to consider any complaint made to him that an advertisement is misleading. Where the Director considers that an advertisement is misleading, and is satisfied that the complainant has exhausted all alternative avenues of redress, he may bring proceedings for an injunction to restrain further publication of the advertisement. By reg 6(5):

> the court shall not refuse to grant an injunction for lack of evidence that–
> (a) the publication of the advertisement in question has given rise to loss or damage to any person;
> (b) the person responsible for the advertisement intended it to be misleading or failed to exercise proper care to prevent it being misleading.

1 SI 1988/915.

D3.39 The British Codes of Advertising and Sales Promotion[1] provide that all advertisements should be legal, decent, honest and truthful (para 2.1); all advertisements should be prepared with a sense of responsibility to consumers and to society (para 2.2); all advertisements should respect the principles of fair competition generally accepted in business (para 2.3); and no advertisement should bring advertising into disrepute (para 2.4). Paragraph 13.1 of the Advertising Code, dealing with 'protection of privacy', provides that:

> [a]dvertisers should not unfairly portray or refer to people in an adverse or offensive way. Advertisers are urged to obtain written permission before: …
> b. referring to people with a public profile …
> c. implying any personal approval of the advertised product …

An individual who believes his said rights have been infringed by an advertisement may complain in writing to the Advertising Standards Authority. If a complaint is upheld, however, the sanctions are limited:

> The media, contractors and service providers may withhold their services or deny access to space; adverse publicity, which acts as a deterrent, may result from rulings published in

the ASA's monthly report; pre-vetting or trading sanctions may be imposed or recognition revoked by the medias, advertisers, promoters or agency's professional association or service provider and financial incentives provided by trade, professional or media organisations may be withdrawn or temporarily withheld[2].

1 (10th edn, 1 October 1999) with Addendum 1 added on 23 April 2000.
2 See n 1 at para 68.39.

D3.40 The Broadcasting Act 1990 makes it the statutory duty of the Independent Television Commission ('ITC') to draw up and enforce a code governing standards and practice in television advertising and the sponsoring of programmes. Paragraph 15 of the ITC Code, dealing with the 'Protection of Privacy and Exploitation of the Individual', provides that '[i]ndividual living persons must not be portrayed or referred to in advertisements without their permission except in circumstances approved by the Commission'. Anyone who is so portrayed or referred to may complain to the television company concerned or directly to the ITC. In the event that a complaint is upheld, the ITC may enforce the code by, for example, issuing formal warnings to, and fining, the licensee.

(e) Copyright

D3.41 The law of copyright in the UK confers a property right in original literary, dramatic and artistic works, as well as in sound recordings, films, broadcasts and cable programmes, and in the typographical arrangements of published editions[1]. 'Artistic works' include photographs, sculptures and graphic works[2]. Copyright is not of great use, however, for an individual seeking to control the exploitation of his image rights[3]. There is no copyright in a face[4] or in a name[5]. There is copyright in graphical representation, for example, of a cartoon character, but this will not help real people. There may be copyright in a signature. There is also copyright in a photograph, but (absent a contractual assignment) it belongs to the photographer, not to the subject of the photograph[6].

1 Section 1(1)(a) of the Copyright Designs and Patents Act 1988 ('CDPA 1988'). See para D1.40 et seq.
2 Section 4(1)(a) of the CDPA 1988.
3 See generally Abell 'Protecting Personalities: Time for a New Form of Copyright' (1998) 82 Copyright World 33.
4 *Merchandising Corpn of America Inc v Harpbond Inc* [1983] FSR 32 (case concerning 'Adam Ant').
5 *Exxon Corpn v Exxon Insurance Consultants International Ltd* [1982] Ch 119, [1981] 2 All ER 495.
6 Section 11(1) of the CDPA 1988.

(f) Trade Marks

D3.42 Section 1(1) of the Trade Marks Act 1994 defines a trade mark as 'any sign capable of being reproduced graphically which is capable of distinguishing goods or services of one undertaking from those of other undertakings. A trade mark may, in particular, consist of words (including personal names), designs, letters, numerals or the shape of goods or their packaging'[1]. Thus, a name, image or likeness of a sports star may be instantly recognisable, but it will not qualify for registration as a trade mark unless it is 'capable of distinguishing goods or services of one undertaking from those of other undertakings'.

1 See further para D1.76 et seq.

D3.43 Alan Shearer and Ryan Giggs are two famous footballers who have been allowed to register their names as trademarks; in contrast, Mark Hughes' application to register his name was rejected on grounds of lack of distinctiveness. To circumvent such lack of distinctiveness, some players have registered nicknames: Paul Gascoigne Promotions Ltd registered 'Gazza' as a trademark; and David Seaman registered 'Safe Hands'. Jacques Villeneuve and Damon Hill each registered images of themselves, in Hill's case an image of his distinctive eyes viewed through the visor of his helmet[1].

1 See generally Harrington 'Unauthorised commercial uses of a sports stars' image in the UK and internationally – a level playing field?' (1999) 2 Sports and Character Licensing 24.

D3.44 The main problem with trying to use trade mark law to protect against the unauthorised use of a celebrity's name or image is that that use is likely to be merely descriptive of the character of the goods to which the name is attached, rather than an indication of trade origin, and therefore not an infringement of the trade mark owner's rights[1]. For example, the owner of the copyright of footage of Alan Shearer playing football could include his name in the packaging of a video of that footage, notwithstanding the fact that Shearer's name is registered as a trademark, because it would be being used merely to describe what was inside the packaging, not to indicate that Alan Shearer himself had produced or authorised the production of the video.

1 See also para D4.79.

D3.45 Indeed, in the case of sports and character merchandising, where the name and image of the celebrity are reproduced on products as diverse as key rings and bars of soap[1], people buy the products not because they see the name and image as indicating that the product is produced or endorsed by the celebrity, but simply because the name and image are on the product. As stated in the following passage from the Court of Appeal's judgment in the leading case of *Re Elvis Presley Trademark Application*:

> the judge was right to conclude that the Elvis mark has very little inherent distinctiveness. That conclusion was reached by a number of intermediary steps, one of which was the judge's finding that members of the public purchase Elvis Presley merchandise not because it comes from a particular source, but because it carries the name or image of Elvis Presley. Indeed the judge came close to finding that for goods of the sort advertised by Elvisly Yours, the commemoration of the late Elvis Presley is the product and the article upon which his name appears (whether a poster, a pennant … a mark or a piece of soap) is little more than a vehicle[2].

1 See generally Chapter D6.
2 *Elvis Presley Enterprises Inc v Sid Shaw Elvisly Yours* [1999] RPC 567, 597–598, CA.

D3.46 To make out a claim for infringement of a registered trade mark, it is necessary to show that the defendant is using the mark 'as a trade mark', ie as a badge of origin, and in certain cases it is also necessary to show a likelihood that use of the mark will confuse the public[1]. Neither will be possible if the case involves production of merchandise bearing the celebrity's name and image and the public are buying the merchandise solely because it bears the likeness of the celebrity, and not because they believe the reproduction of that likeness indicates that the celebrity him or herself is associated with the production of the merchandise:

[W]hether a registered trade mark comprising the name of a celebrity is infringed by use on china, posters, t-shirts and the like will depend on the circumstances, both of the use by the proprietor and the type of use by the alleged infringer. If the public has been educated that the mark is a badge of origin (in the widest sense including approval, selection and endorsement) perhaps by the use of words such as 'licensed by' or 'official', there will be infringement. However, if the purchaser of a mug with the name (and/or photograph) of their hero or heroine decorating it is indifferent as to who makes it or is responsible for the name being on it, this should not constitute infringement of the trade mark[2].

1 See paras D1.88 to D1.95.
2 *Kerly's Law of Trade Marks and Trade Names* (13th edn), para 22.56. See also *Halliwell v Panini* (6 June 1997, unreported), Ch D (Lightman J) at para D3.56, n 2.

D3.47 The recent authority of *Arsenal Football Club plc v Reed*[1], although addressing the sale of merchandise bearing a club crest rather than a player's image, nevertheless supports the proposition that the mark must be used in a trade mark sense, ie to indicate trade origin, for an infringement action to lie. Where the purchaser wants to display the mark as a sign of affiliation or support for the club (or, by extension, the individual) represented by the mark, that is not, in Laddie J's view, use of the mark as a trade mark[2]. However, the case has been referred to the European Court of Justice, and while the court itself is yet to rule on the matter, the opinion of Advocate General Senor Ruiz-Jarabo Colomer[3] takes a far more expansive (and some would say contemporary) view:

Given the functions of those distinctive signs and the objective pursued by the Directive, the decisive factor is not the feelings with the consumer who buys the goods which the trade mark represents, or even the third party using it, harbour towards the registered proprietor, but the fact that they are acquired because, by bearing the sign, the goods identify the product with the trade mark – irrespective of what the consumer thinks of the mark – or even, as the case may be, with the proprietor.

It does not matter whether the reason for the decision to purchase is that the purchaser sees the trade mark as a sign of distinction or as a guarantee of quality or whether, on the contrary, he engages in an act of rebellion as an adherent to the cult of bad taste … The key to the problem is that he has decided to purchase it on account of the fact that the article is identified with the trade mark and, through it, with its proprietor, that is to say with the team.

The debate must be moved on to a different ground. Given that, where there is identity, the consumer purchases the goods because they bear the sign, the base from which the answer to the High Court must be provided is that of the person exploiting it without being the proprietor. It is not the reason for which a person buys goods or services that I must examine but the reason which has led the person who is not the proprietor of the trade mark to place the goods on the market or to provide the service using the same distinctive sign. If, regardless of the reason which motivates him, he attempts to exploit it commercially then he can be said to be using it as a trade mark and the proprietor will be entitled to object within the limits and to the extent allowed under Article 5 of the Directive.

1 [2001] RPC 922. See para D1.90, n 1.
2 See paras D1.90, D6.38 and D6.39.
3 *Arsenal Football Club plc v Reed* Case C-206/01 (13 June 2002, unreported), ECJ. See paras D1.91, n 1, D6.41 and D6.42.

D3.48 If the Advocate General's expansive approach is followed by the European Court of Justice, then the English law of trade marks could become somewhat more useful for a celebrity seeking to stop the unauthorised use of his persona, at least where the use is of aspects of that persona (name, nickname or image) that have been considered sufficiently distinctive for an application for registration as a trade mark to be accepted.

(g) Passing off

D3.49 The tort of passing off prevents parties passing their goods or services off as the claimant's goods or services, ie exploiting without authority the goodwill[1] that the claimant enjoys in the marketplace[2]. On its face, it would appear to provide a useful remedy against the unauthorised use of the name or image of a sportsman or woman to endorse goods or services. Until recently, that has not been the case, as the courts have shown a reluctance to use the tort to protect celebrities from the unauthorised use of their names and images. However, the recent case of *Irvine v Talksport*[3] has come closer than any other to according recognition and protection to the right of a sportsperson to control his or her image.

1 Goodwill 'is the benefit and advantage of the good name, reputation and connection of a business. It is the attractive force which brings in custom': Per Lord MacNaghten in *IRC v Muller and Co's Margarine Ltd* [1901] AC 217.

2 See generally *Clerk and Lindsell on Torts* (18th edn), para 26-01. See also paras D1.103 to D1.111 and D6.15 et seq.

3 See para D3.52 et seq.

D3.50 The source of the problem historically was the idea (derived from the concept of the tort as 'passing off your goods for the goods of the claimant') that the claimant had to be engaged in the same field of activity as the defendant. The leading case was *McCulloch v Lewis A May Ltd*[1]. The plaintiff was a well known children's radio broadcaster under the name 'Uncle Mac'. The defendant began distributing puffed wheat under the name 'Uncle Mac's Puffed Wheat', and the plaintiff sued for passing off. The court held that, as the plaintiff was not engaged in any degree in producing or marketing puffed wheat, there was no field of activity common to the plaintiff and the defendant and the defendant therefore could not be said to have invaded any proprietary right of the plaintiff or to have passed off the goods or the business of the plaintiff. Wynn-Parry J was:

> satisfied that there is discoverable in all those [cases] in which the court has intervened the factor that there was a common field of activity in which, however remotely, both the plaintiff and the defendant were engaged and that it was the presence of that factor that grounded the jurisdiction of the court[2].

1 [1947] 2 All ER 845, Ch D.

2 [1947] 2 All ER 845 at 851, Ch D.

D3.51 In other words, the sports star would have to show he or she was in engaged in the actual marketing and selling to the public of products or services endorsed with his or her name or image. Otherwise, in the view of the English courts, the commercial practice of character merchandising and licensing was not sufficiently widespread that the public would assume that any product using the sportsman's name or image was endorsed or authorised by the sportsperson[1].

1 See further cases discussed at para D1.56, n 2.

D3.52 This requirement had severely restricted the usefulness of the tort of passing off, in the sports sector as elsewhere. In the recent case of *Irvine v Talksport*[1], however, the *Uncle Mac* approach was disapproved and not followed. Eddie Irvine was a prominent driver in the FIA Formula One World Championship.

Talksport runs an eponymous radio station. In 1999 it embarked on a special promotional campaign to mark the rebranding of the station from Talk Radio to Talksport, and its acquisition of the right to broadcast coverage of the FIA Formula One World Championship. It sent just over 1,000 media buyers a flyer bearing a photograph of Mr Irvine. The original photograph, the right to copy which had been acquired from a sporting photograph agency (so that copyright in the photograph was not an issue), showed Mr Irvine holding a mobile telephone. The agency manipulated the photograph to cut out the mobile telephone and replace it with an image of a portable radio to which the words 'Talk Radio' had been added. Mr Irvine contended that the distribution of the brochure bearing that manipulated picture of him falsely implied that he endorsed Talksport, and was an actionable passing off.

1 *Edmund Irvine Tidewell Ltd v Talksport Ltd* [2002] EWHC 367 (Ch), [2002] 2 All ER 414 (Laddie J). See Sloper and Cordery 'Personality Endorsement – New Brands Hatch?' [2002] Ent L R 106.

D3.53 Laddie J noted that 'the law of passing off responds to changes in the nature of trade', and that the old cases may not reflect recent developments. He referred to the Australian passing off case of *Henderson*[1], which rejected the 'common field of activity' requirement, as well as the English case of *Harrods v Harrodian School Ltd*[2] where Millett LJ (with whom Beldam LJ agreed) said:

> There is no requirement that the defendant should be carrying on a business which competes with that of the plaintiff or which would compete with any natural extension of the plaintiff's business. The expression 'common field of activity' was coined by Wynn-Parry J in *McCulloch v May* … when he dismissed the plaintiff's claim for want of this factor. This was contrary to numerous previous authorities (see, for example, *Eastman Photographic Materials Co Ltd v John Griffiths Cycle Corpn Ltd* (1898) 15 RPC 105 (cameras and bicycles); *Walter v Ashton* [1902] 2 Ch 282 (*The Times* Newspaper and Bicycles) and is now discredited.

Having surveyed the authorities, Laddie J concluded that:

> [T]he law of passing off now is of greater width than as applied by Wynn-Parry J in *McCulloch v May*. If someone acquires a valuable reputation or goodwill, the law of passing off will protect it from unlicensed use by other parties. Such use will frequently be damaging in the direct sense that it will involve selling inferior goods or services under the guise that they are from the claimant. But the action is not restricted to protecting against that sort of damage. The law will vindicate the claimant's exclusive right to the reputation or goodwill. It will not allow others to so use goodwill as to reduce, blur or diminish its exclusivity. It follows that it is not necessary to show that the claimant and the defendant share a common field of activity or that sales of products or services will be diminished either substantially or directly at least in the short term … Even without the evidence given at the trial of this action, the court can take judicial notice of the fact that it is common for famous people to exploit their names and images by way of endorsement. They do it not only in their own field of expertise but, depending on the extent of their fame or notoriety, wider afield also … Manufacturers and retailers recognise the realities of the market place when they pay for well known personalities to endorse their goods. The law of passing off should do likewise. There appears to be no good reason why the law of passing off in this modern form and in modern trade circumstances should not apply to cases of false endorsement[3].

1 See para D3.20.
2 [1996] RPC 697, CA.
3 *Irvine v Talksport Ltd* [2002] EWHC 367 (Ch), [2002] 2 All ER 414 at 426b–427e. Laddie J showed perhaps less appreciation for the 'realities of the market place' when he awarded Irvine damages of only £2,000 on the basis that this was a 'reasonable endorsement fee': LTL 29 April 2002 (unreported elsewhere).

D3.54 Laddie J's ruling that 'Mr Irvine has a property right in his goodwill which he can protect from unlicensed appropriation consisting of a false claim or suggestion of endorsement of a third party's goods or services'[1] is a very significant step forward in the recognition of image rights under English law. It provides a proper cause of action that reflects modern marketing practice, and makes the inventive use of other causes of action less imperative[2]. Provided that a celebrity who is the victim of a false endorsement can show that at the time he had a significant reputation or goodwill (which does not have to be trading goodwill but rather can come simply from his being famous, eg as a sportsman), and that the defendant has sent a false message that a not insignificant section of the market would take to mean that his goods have been endorsed by the celebrity, then the celebrity will have a prima facie claim for passing off.

1 *Irvine v Talksport Ltd* [2002] EWHC 367 (Ch), [2002] 2 All ER 414 at 436h.
2 See Harrington 'Irvine's image rights victory sets UK sports law precedent' (2002) Sportcal.com, 15 March.

D3.55 Indeed, it was not long before the *Irvine* precedent was used by ex-England cricketer Ian Botham to extract a settlement payment of several thousand pounds from Diageo for using his image, without his authority, to promote Guinness[1]. The case involved an image of Mr Botham playing in the 1981 Ashes series against Australia. The image was unmanipulated, ie Guinness was promoted simply against a backdrop of Mr Botham playing cricket, which could fairly be argued to distinguish the case from the *Irvine* case[2]. Clearly, however, Diageo did not want to take the chance.

1 'Botham wins settlement in image rights dispute' (2002) Sportcal.com, 13 September.
2 'Will Botham case test limits on image rights breach awards?' www.lawdirect.co.uk (27 August 2002).

D3.56 It is important to note the limits of the *Irvine* ruling, however. Laddie J carefully distinguished cases involving the unauthorised use of a celebrity's name and image for endorsement purposes from cases involving the unauthorised reproduction of the name or image of the celebrity on merchandise (ie character merchandising)[1]. He said:

> In my view nothing said above touches on the quite separate issues which may arise in character merchandising cases … In those cases the defendant's activities do not imply any endorsement. For example, although it was a trade mark registration case, in Elvis Presley Trade Marks much of the argument turned on whether the appellant had merchandising rights in the name of Elvis Presley or in his image. It wanted to prevent third parties from selling products such as bars of soap and drinking mugs bearing the name of the performer and photographs of him. There could be no question of the performer endorsing anything since he had been dead for many years. So the argument being advanced was one which amounted to an attempt to create a quasi-copyright in the name and images. The Court of Appeal's rejection of that is, with respect, consistent with a long line of authority[2].

1 Laddie J highlighted the difference between the two forms of commercial activity at [2002] 2 All ER 414 at 418b–e: 'When someone endorses a product or a service he tells the relevant public that he approves of the product or service or is happy to be associated with it. In effect he adds his name as an encouragement to members of the relevant public to buy or use the service or product. Merchandising is rather different. It involves exploiting images, scenes or articles which have become famous … an example of merchandising is the sale of the memorabilia relating to the late Diana, Princess of Wales. A porcelain plate bearing her image could hardly be thought of as being endorsed by her, but the enhanced sales which may be achieved by virtue of the presence of the image is a form of merchandising'.

2 [2002] EWHC 367 (Ch), [2002] 2 All ER 414 at 427f–j.

In *Lyngstad v Anabas Products* [1977] FSR 62, Ch D, the members of Swedish pop group 'Abba' sued the defendants for making and distributing, without their permission, badges, t-shirts and pillowcases featuring the band's name and picture. Oliver J doubted that any confusion could arise, because the plaintiffs carried on no business other than that of musicians and singers: 'I am entirely unsatisfied that there is any real possibility of confusion. I do not think that anyone … receiving the goods … could reasonably imagine that all the pop stars … were giving their approval to the goods offered or that the defendants were doing anything more than catering for a popular demand among teenagers for effigies of their idols. There is no business of the plaintiffs here with which in my judgment the defendant's goods could possibly be confused. To suggest that there is some proprietary right in the plaintiffs' name which entitled them to sue simply for its use is contrary to all the English authorities'.

Similarly, twenty years later in the *Halliwell v Panini* case (6 June 1997, unreported) (Lightman J), Panini made unauthorised use of images of the five members of the Spice Girls group in a sticker book collection. The court declined to grant an injunction to restrain launch of the collection in the UK, because it did not think that the public would be misled into believing the Spice Girls had formally endorsed the product, not so much because they did not endorse products (they did), but because those products that they had endorsed were labelled 'official' goods, and so the public would not think that Panini's sticker collection that had no such label was officially endorsed. However, in a reflection of the reasoning in the *Elvis* case (see para D3.43), the court also noted that it thought that the public cared only that the product contained pictures of the Spice Girls and did not care who made the product, ie they cared about the likeness, not the source.

D3.57 However, Laddie J did leave the door slightly ajar to the development of further protection for the celebrity in this context, stating:

> Whether such a new right may be created either by development of the common law or as a result of the passing of the Human Rights Act, is not relevant to this action[1].

1 [2002] 2 All ER 414 at 428a. See paras D3.58 to D3.64.

(h) Human Rights Act 1998

D3.58 The Human Rights Act 1998 ('HRA 1998')[1] incorporates into English law the provisions of the European Convention for the Protection of Human Rights and Fundamental Freedoms[2]. As a result of the passage of the HRA 1998, the courts of this country are now obliged to take into account the rights provided by the Convention and not to act in a way which is incompatible with a Convention right[3]. Two rights are relevant for present purposes, namely the right to privacy and the right to peaceful enjoyment of property.

1 See Mulcahy *Human Rights and Civil Practice* (2001, Sweet & Maxwell), particularly ch 16. The authors gratefully acknowledge the assistance derived from the submissions provided to us on the effect of the HRA 1998 prepared by counsel, Lindsay Lane, at the invitation of Laddie J for the purposes of the *Irvine* case.

2 See generally Chapter A4.

3 *Douglas v Hello! Ltd* [2001] 2 WLR 992, CA per Sedley LJ at paras 111, 128–130 and per Keene LJ at para 166. See paras A4.30 and A4.31.

D3.59 The right to privacy Section 8(1) of the HRA 1998 provides that '[e]veryone has the right to respect for his private and family life, his home and his correspondence'. In this context, 'private life' includes a person's physical and psychological integrity and the guarantee afforded by the right to privacy is intended to ensure the development, without outside interference, of the personality of each individual in his relations with other human beings[1]. Section 8 imposes a positive obligation on the state to provide effective respect for private life including in the sphere of the relations of individuals between themselves[2]. Thus, it must be taken into account by the courts of this country when applying private law rights between private parties[3].

1 *Botta v Italy* (1998) 26 EHRR 241 at para 32.
2 *Douglas v Hello! Ltd* [2001] 2 WLR 992 per Brooke LJ at paras 81–91, Sedley LJ at para 130 and the ECHR cases cited therein. See eg *X and Y v Netherlands* (1985) 8 EHRR 235, ECtHR: 'The Court recalls that although the object of Article 8 is essentially that of protecting the individual against arbitrary interference by the public authorities, it does not merely compel the State to abstain from such interference: in addition to this primarily negative obligation, there may be positive obligations inherent in an effective respect for private life. These obligations may involve the adoption of measures designed to secure respect for private life even in the sphere of individuals between themselves'.
3 *Douglas v Hello! Ltd* [2001] 2 WLR 992, CA.

D3.60 The right to privacy covers the right to establish and develop relationships with other human beings and the outside world and includes activities of a professional and business nature[1]. It can be interference with a person's private life, contrary to the s 8 right to privacy to publish the photograph of an individual, even if that individual:

- was photographed in a public place. See for example, *Peck v United Kingdom*[2] in which the European Court of Human Rights found that the complaints of the applicant relating to the disclosure to and publication by the press of closed-circuit television footage of him trying to commit suicide filmed by Brentwood Borough Council raised serious issues under Art 8 of the European Convention and therefore would not be declared inadmissible[3].
- has sold some part of the privacy he seeks to protect. In *Douglas v Hello! Ltd*[4] for example, there was found to be an arguable case of interference with the claimants' right to privacy by publishing unauthorised photographs of their wedding even though the claimants had sold the rights to take photographs of their wedding to OK! magazine. This was because the claimants had retained one element of privacy, namely, the right to control publication of their photographs.

1 *Niemetz v Germany* (1992) 16 EHRR 97 at para 29.
2 Application No 44647/98.
3 It is of interest in this regard to note the view of the Matrix Media and Information Group in *Privacy and the Media – the Developing Law*, para 7.14: 'The scope of private life in Article 8 is potentially much wider than the concept of privacy in any tort of invasion of privacy … We suggest that, as a matter of principle, it is possible to have a reasonable expectation of privacy even in a public place and so the taking of photographs and their subsequent publication without consent should fall within the scope of Article 8(1). This does not mean that it will be impossible, or even necessarily very difficult, to take or publish such photographs. It simply means that the public authority concerned must be able to justify its behaviour under Article 8(2). This view is supported by the approach taken by the Supreme Court of Canada in *Aubry v Les Additions Vice-Versa* (1998) 1 SER 591 and by the English Court of Appeal in the pre-Human Rights Act case of *R v Broadcasting Standards Commission, ex p BBC* [2001] QB 885. It is also consistent with the approach taken in the PCC Code which recognises that a person may have a reasonable expectation of privacy in a private or public place'.
4 [2001] 2 WLR 992 per Sedley LJ at para 140.

D3.61 It remains to be seen how broadly the courts will construe the right to privacy conferred by s 8 of the HRA 1998 but it may be that that right may not be limited to the publication of photographs taken surreptitiously of people in private, or sometimes even in public places, but may extend to a more general right to control one's image:

> [A]s the right of publicity evolved directly from the right to privacy in the US, any new privacy law is an important development towards the protection of image and likeness in the UK[1].

1 Smith *Image Persona and the Law – Special Report* (2001, Sweet & Maxwell), para 5-70.

D3.62 The right to peaceful enjoyment of property Article 1 of Protocol 1 of the HRA 1998 provides that '[e]very natural or legal person is entitled to the peaceful enjoyment of his possessions'. This right is primarily concerned with protecting an individual's property against arbitrary interference by the state and not with relationships of a contractual nature between private individuals[1]. Further, the fact that a judicial authority provided a forum for the determination of a private law dispute does not necessarily amount to an interference by the state with the right of property[2]. However, it is clear that in some cases the state must take positive steps to protect the enjoyment of possessions[3] and the courts of this country have taken into account Art 1 of Protocol 1 in a number of cases between private individuals concerning legislative interpretation[4].

1 *Gustafsson v Sweden* (1996) 22 EHRR 409 at para 60.
2 *Ruiz-Mateos v United Kingdom* Application No 13021/87 at p 5 of the transcript.
3 See, for example *James v United Kingdom* (1986) 8 EHRR 123 at paras 35–36; and *Whiteside v United Kingdom* (1994) 18 EHRR CD 126.
4 See, for example *Wilson v First County Trust Ltd (No 2)* [2001] EWCA Civ 633, [2002] QB 74, [2001] 3 All ER 229.

D3.63 The European Court has explained that 'the right to dispose of one's property constitutes a traditional and fundamental aspect of the right of property'[1]. In the *Irvine* case, involving unauthorised use of the claimant's image, manipulated to suggest he used and/or endorsed the defendant's product[2], Laddie J invited submissions in relation to Art 1 of Protocol 1 (as well as Art 8 of the HRA 1998 itself), particularly in the light of the European Court's decision in *Van Marle v Netherlands*[3]. In that case, the applicants had practised as accountants for some years before 1974, when a new statute required them to seek registration if they wished to continue to practise. Their application for registration was refused in 1977, and their appeal was rejected. They complained that (among other things) the decision infringed their right to peaceful enjoyment of possessions under Art 1 of Protocol 1. The court held that Art 1 of Protocol 1 was applicable, although on the facts there had been no violation of that article:

> 39. The applicants further claimed to be victims of breaches of Article 1 of Protocol 1 … they alleged that, as a result of the Board of Appeal's decisions, their income and value of the goodwill of their accountancy practice had diminished. They maintained that they had thereby been subjected to an interference with the exercise of their right to the peaceful enjoyment of their possessions and to a partial deprivation thereof without compensation.
>
> 40 … the Government … pointed out that as a matter of Dutch law there was no such thing as a "right to goodwill" which could be regarded as property for the purposes of the Article …
>
> 41. The Court agrees with the Commission that the right relied upon by the applicants may be likened to the right of property embodied in Article 1; by dint of their own work, the applicants had built up a clientele; this had in many respects the nature of a private right and constituted an asset and, hence, a possession within the meaning of the first sentence of Article 1. This provision was accordingly applicable in the present case.

1 *Marckx v Belgium* (1979) 2 EHRR 330 at para 63.
2 See paras D3.52 to D3.57.
3 (1986) 8 EHRR 483.

D3.64 Thus, under Art 1 of Protocol 1, every person is entitled to the peaceful enjoyment of his or her goodwill, and any deprivation or interference can only be justified if it is in the public interest. To the extent that image rights are not protected by the law, celebrities lose the ability to agree to, and charge for, the use of their image and thereby suffer loss of income. This clearly constitutes an interference with peaceful enjoyment of their goodwill, and such unauthorised commercial exploitation would appear to offer little in the way of justification in the public interest. The courts are under an obligation, as a public body, to develop and apply the law in a way that respects Convention rights[1]. There would appear therefore, at least in theory, to be room for a claim under Art 1 of Protocol 1 to prevent the unauthorised use of celebrity's name or image.

1 See paras A4.30 and A4.31.

C Summary overview

D3.65 Even as late as 1990, the Calcutt Committee on Privacy concluded there was 'no pressing social need to provide any additional remedy for those such as politicians and actors, whose images or voices are appropriated without their consent for advertisement or promotional purposes'[1]. However, this really seems too unrealistic and outdated a view in the modern marketplace. As McCarthy says:

> … English law often seems tied to the legal categories of the past and, up to the present, unable to accommodate itself to the modern commercial realities of licensing and merchandising[2].

In *University of London Press Ltd v University Tutorial Press Ltd*, finding a copyright in examination papers, Peterson J said:

> There remains the rough practical test that what is worth copying is worth protecting[3].

As Abell points out:

> In the modern age, this principle should arguably apply to names and likenesses as much as it did to literary works in 1916: if the image of a personality is worth exploiting without authorisation, it should be protected by the law[4].

1 Cm 1102, para 12.8.
2 McCarthy *The Rights of Publicity and Privacy* (2nd edn), para 6-286.
3 [1916] 2 Ch 601 at 610.
4 Abell 'Protecting Personalities: Time for a New Form of Copyright' (1998) 82 Copyright World 33. See also Abell 'The Need for a UK Personality Right' *Managing Intellectual Property* (December 1997), p 19.

D3.66 However, there have recently been some positive signs in this regard. In particular, the *Irvine* case has made clear that a celebrity has a property right in his goodwill that he can protect from unlicensed appropriation consisting of a false claim or suggestion of endorsement of a third party's goods or services. In the same case, Laddie J also alluded to the possibility that the time may be coming for the reassessment of merchandising cases, either by reference to the HRA 1998 or by the development of the common law. Such reassessment may be encouraged by the opinion of the Advocate General in *Arsenal v Reed*[1].

1 Case C-206/01 (13 June 2002, unreported), ECJ. See paras D3.47 and D3.48.

4 IMAGE RIGHTS CONTRACTS

D3.67 In any event, whatever the legal position, the fact is that there has developed a substantial industry dealing with the grant and exploitation of the right to make commercial use of the images/personae of elite sportsmen. The legal position is important to note, in particular when addressing grants of exclusivity and the kinds of warranties and indemnities that are often sought in endorsement and licensing contracts[1]. However, so long as image rights can be granted as a matter of contract, the fact that English intellectual property law does not recognise any proprietary rights in a sportsman's image per se is no bar to their exploitation[2]. In this section of the chapter, therefore, there is a review of the main types of contracts and contractual provisions currently used to exploit the commercial value in a sportsman's image.

1 See further paras D6.66 et seq and D6.94 et seq.

2 See Couchman N 'Image Rights – The State of Play' (2001) 15 Sports and Character Licensing 11: 'the real issue here is perhaps not so much what the law says or does not say on the subject but what the marketplace says … The more contractual image rights deals that take place, the greater the acknowledgement by the market (and potentially by the courts) that they exist and have a value. Legitimate operators will increasingly want to ensure that where such rights exist, they are cleared'. Of course, contracts can not only grant image rights but also protect them from unauthorised use. See Rose 'Will sports stars stand up for their image rights?' (2000) 51 Sports Business 26: 'the reality is that the best known players (and the ones with the most valuable images) are using their contractual bargaining power to ring fence (in contract) the ability of others to use their image'.

A Contracts with clubs

D3.68 The current standard FA Premier League/Football League player contract[1] was drafted several years ago, when image rights were hardly recognised, let alone constituting the hard currency they are now. This is reflected in the (lack of) provisions in the contract addressing the commercial exploitation of the player's name and image. Most of the provisions relate solely to the terms of provision of playing services[2]. The only provisions relating even indirectly to marketing and commercial exploitation of image rights are the following:

> 7b. The Player agrees to be available for community and public relations involvement as requested by the Club management, at reasonable times during the period of the contract (eg 2/3 hours per week) …
>
> 11b. The Player shall not without the previous consent of the Club be engaged either directly or indirectly in any trade, business or occupation other than employment hereunder …
>
> 13. The Player shall permit the Club to photograph the Player as a member of the squad of players and staff of the Club provided that such photographs are for use only as the official photographs of the Club. The Player may, save as otherwise mutually agreed and subject to the overriding obligation contained in the Rules of the Football Association not to bring the game of Association Football into disrepute, contribute to the public media in a responsible manner. The Player shall, whenever circumstances permit, give to the Club reasonable notice of intention to make such contributions to the public media in order to allow representations to be made on behalf of the Club if it so desires …

1 Reproduced in *The Football Association Handbook 2001/02*, pp 361–365.

2 See Chapter E1.

D3.69 Obviously this is entirely inadequate to address modern commercial practice, from the point of view of both the player and the club. The player needs the club to acknowledge that, standard cl 11b notwithstanding, he does have a personal commercial programme of endorsement deals and personal appearances; while the club needs far more specific acknowledgment of its right to use the image of the player (in his capacity as a member of the club) for its own commercial programme. Therefore, a practice has developed (fuelled by the influx of foreign stars from jurisdictions that do recognise image rights[1]) of supplementing the standard contract with an addendum that (among other things) gives the club the non-exclusive right to use the player's image in its promotional and merchandising materials[2] or even entering into a separate contract addressing commercial matters with far more specificity than does the standard form. Whatever form those arrangements take (whether a straight assignment or licence of the rights direct from the player to the club, or via an intermediary service company), the key issues to be addressed are:

(1) the right of the club to use the player's name and image, in his capacity as a member of the club, to promote the brand, products and services of the club and its commercial partners;

(2) the obligation of the player to make personal appearances, attend photo shoots and provide other services to support that use; and

(3) the player's right to use his name and image for his own benefit, but not while on club service, nor using club colours, nor (if the club's bargaining power is strong) in relation to brands, products or services that compete with the brands, products or services of the club's sponsors[3].

1 See for example, paras D3.22 to D3.26.

2 See Blood M 'Footballers' Image Rights in the UK' (2001) Sports and Character Licensing 23. Blood also refers to clubs' use of 'player pools', ie pooling for distribution to the entire squad the appearance fees paid for media and other promotional work undertaken on behalf of the club. See also Smith 'Putting Players in the Picture' (2002) Football Business International 14. Another option is to insert relevant provisions in the club's rules, which are incorporated by reference into the standard playing contract. See para E1.18.

3 But see Owen 'Football cashes in on star players' (2002) Financial Times, 14 March, for a description of the recent trend among overseas clubs to take an assignment of all of the player's image rights, in his individual as well as in a club capacity, usually splitting resulting commercial revenues equally with the player.

D3.70 The practice will become more standardised if the draft revised standard playing contract that an FAPL/Football League working party has been considering for some years now is adopted in its current form. That draft takes the following approach in relation to image rights:

(1) the player must make himself available for up to three hours per week for appearances, interviews and photographic opportunities with sponsors and commercial partners of the club and/or the League[1], and the club and sponsors and commercial partners can use the photographs and other material to promote themselves and their brands, products and services, provided that the photographs and other materials are not used in such a way as to imply that the player is endorsing any particular brand or product[2];

(2) otherwise, the player is free to exploit his own image as he sees fit, provided that he gives the club reasonable notice of his commercial activities, and they do not interfere with his playing duties, except that:

(a) the player cannot, save for pre-existing agreements, endorse products or services competing with products or services of the club or the club's two main sponsors/commercial partners or the League's principal sponsor[3];

(b) the player cannot exploit images of himself in a 'club context', ie wearing club kit or other identifying characteristics; and
(c) while on club business, the player must wear approved clothing and not wear conflicting brands (except as to boots and goalkeeper gloves)[4].

1 It is noteworthy that the event organiser is using the redrafting exercise to ensure some support and protection for its central commercial programme as well.
2 The industry practice in this regard is that the inclusion in a photograph of at least three players in club kit is usually enough to avoid any inference of individual endorsement by any one player, as opposed to endorsement by the club itself.
3 See n 1.
4 Boots (and by extension goalkeepers' gloves) have always been treated as a special case, on the basis that they are 'tools of the trade' and choice as to the brand or type to use is highly personal to the individual player.

D3.71 However, the current draft also expressly provides that the club and player are able to enter into further arrangements in relation to his promotional services. Therefore, while this may become the standard approach, there remains free scope for variations, to reflect the particular needs (and/or bargaining power) of the parties in each case.

B Contracts with governing bodies

D3.72 Of course, a player may play not only for his club but also for his country, and will therefore also enter into contractual relations with his national governing body[1]. The national team will in turn have its own commercial programme, including its own sponsors who will want to use the players' images to endorse their products and services. Therefore, arrangements have to be established similar to those set out above between the player and his club.

1 See further para E1.3.

D3.73 The arrangements made by the Rugby Football Union with respect to players picked for the England squad are of interest in this respect. Each player enters into a standard contract to provide his playing services to the RFU for national representative duty. In addition, however, all of the players assign their image rights to a company that:

(1) grants to the RFU the right to use each player's name or image (including photographs or audio-visual footage) for sponsorship, advertising or merchandising purposes, but only in his capacity as a member of the England squad;
(2) promises to procure the services of the player at promotional events to enable the exploitation of those rights; and
(3) promises to procure that the player–
  (a) wears only official clothing when on England squad duty;
  (b) does not make any commitments in his personal commercial programme that prevents him from carrying out promotional services in relation to the England squad; and
  (c) does not promote products or services in his capacity as a member of the England Squad without the RFU's consent.

D3.74 Whether the contract is between the club and the player directly, or between the club and an intermediary service company, many of the provisions will be absolutely standard, and can be taken from any relevant precedent, eg as to confidentiality, termination etc. However, some of the more particular clauses are identified below.

C Sample provisions

(a) Club-player contract

D3.75 The following are examples of some of the more specific clauses to be found in a standard player-club image rights contract:

1 **Definitions**

1.1 'Image Rights' means the right to use the Player's name, nickname, slogan and signatures developed from time to time, image, likeness, voice, logos, get-ups, initials, reputation, shirt number, biographical information, graphical representation, electronic, animated or computer-generated representation and/or any other representation and/or right of association and/or any other right or quasi-right anywhere in the Territory of the Player and/or his performances;

1.2 'Personal Appearances' means occasions and events at which the Club requires the Player's personal attendance including without limitation all photographic sessions, audio-visual recording sessions, live and/or recorded internet, radio and/or television interviews, discussions or other appearance, attendances at charitable, educational, promotional or marketing events, at which the Player shall wear, carry and/or endorse such items of clothing, accessories, apparel and equipment as the Club may direct from time to time;

1.3 'Rights' means the Image Rights and the Underlying Rights;

1.4 'Underlying Rights' means trademarks and service marks (whether or not registered), copyrights, design rights (whether or not registered), moral rights, design rights, patents, performance rights, database rights, internet, WAP or other new media registrable rights, names, logos and codes, rights of publicity, personality and/or privacy and/or any other intellectual property rights that may subsist or be capable of registration in respect of the player and the Image Rights which may exist in any jurisdiction in the Territory …

2 In consideration of the payment of the Retainer and Royalty, the Player shall make available to the Club and to any and/or all of the group companies of the Club, the Image Rights and the Underlying Rights and grants to the Club and to any and/or all of the group companies of the Club the sole and exclusive right and licence within the Territory and during the Contract Period to use, exploit, protect, enforce, licence and sub-licence any and/or all of the Image Rights and Underlying Rights, now or in the future existing or to be developed, free from encumbrances [save those items set out at Schedule 2 ('Existing Contracts')].

3 During the Contract Period neither the Player nor any of the Rights shall be associated with or be permitted to be associated (whether intentionally or inadvertently) with any third party for the purposes of any promotional, advertising, endorsement or sponsorship activities or campaigns without the prior written consent of the Club and the Player shall take such steps as the Club shall reasonably require to prevent or put an end to any such association.

4 During the Contract Period the Player shall not set up or run any business which requires the use of the Rights or any personal association with the Player without the prior written consent of the Club.

5 The Player shall attend and participate in Personal Appearances as directed by the Club from time to time free of charge, save for reimbursement of reasonable travelling expenses. The Club shall when practicable give written notice to the Player of each proposed Personal Appearance as far in advance as is reasonably practicable.

6 Upon termination of this agreement, the Club shall retain full title, right and ownership of including, without limitation, any product, image reproductions, materials, audio-visual recording or any other items featuring the Image Rights and the Underlying Rights and created during the Contract Period.

7 The Player shall be entitled to receive:
£[ ] per appearance of 0–8 hours duration; or
£[ ] per appearance of 8+ hours duration; and
[X]% of all net profits derived from Club shop sales of merchandise bearing solely any of the Rights. In calculating such net profits, the Club shall be entitled to deduct from revenue all costs of manufacture, sale, distribution and supply and any taxes payable in respect of such revenue derived solely from such merchandise sales. Revenue derived from such merchandise sales bearing any Image Rights or Underlying Rights in conjunction or in connection with the Club and/or any other players of the Club shall not be included in calculating the Royalty.

(b) *Club-company contracts*

D3.76 Where the player has assigned all of his image rights to an image rights company, the club will need to contract with that company for the right to use the rights and for the promotional services of the player to enable the club to exploit those rights[1]. In appropriate circumstances, the club may wish to insist that the player is made a party to the contract to guarantee performance of the obligations undertaken by the company[2].

1 See eg para D3.73.
2 See cl 9 of para D3.77.

D3.77 The following are standard provisions often seen in a contract of this type:

1. The player is a professional [____] player who has entered into a playing contract with the Club;
2. The Company is authorised to grant licences relating to the provision of promotional services by the Player relating to the use of the name, image, signature and other characteristics of the Player, and is willing to grant the Club such a licence on the terms set out below;
3. 'Merchandising' means:
   (a) the manufacture, sale, advertisement, distribution, licensing, marketing and promotion of products or services, by or on behalf of the Club or any sponsor or licensee of the Club, that carry the Club's marks or regalia or relate in any way to the Club,
   (b) the promotion of the Club, and/or
   (c) the promotion and assistance of the Club's sponsors and licensees in relation to their marketing activities that relate to the Club;
4. 'Player's Image' means the Player's name, nickname, initials, signature, endorsement, reputation, voice, shirt number, video or film portrayal, computer-generated or animated portrayal, photographs, licences, biographical information, graphical representations, images or facsimile image and all other characteristics of the Player;
5. 'Rights' means the intellectual property rights and other rights now existing or in the future arising in the Player's Image, including but not limited to so-called 'personality rights', so-called 'image rights', so-called 'rights of publicity', so-called 'rights of privacy', patents, trade marks, service marks, logos, get-up, trade names, internet domain names, rights in designs, copyright (including rights in computer software) and moral rights, performance rights, database rights, in each case whether registered or unregistered and including applications for registration, and all rights or forms of protection having equivalent or similar effect anywhere in the world;

6. In consideration for the Club's performance of its obligations under this Agreement:
6.1 during the term of this Agreement, upon reasonable notice, the Company shall procure that the Player shall co-operate with the Club and its licensees and sponsors in promoting the Merchandising Activities and the products and services promoted thereunder, including (without limitation) giving them all reasonable facilities and opportunities to take photographs and/or moving pictures of the Player;
6.2 the Company hereby grants to the Club for the term of this Agreement a worldwide right and licence to use and exploit, and/or to assign to sponsors and licensees the right to use and exploit, in any medium, the Player's Image and the Rights in relation to the Merchandising Activities. At all times (a) the Player's Image and the Rights shall remain the property of the Company and/or the Player absolutely; and (b) all rights in any products or services marketed by or on behalf of the Club that make use of the Player's Image and/or the Rights, and any goodwill arising as a result, shall remain the property of the Club absolutely; and
6.3 the Company shall procure that the Player performs the Services in a diligent manner and complies with and observe all lawful proper directions which may from time to time be given to the Company and/or the Player by a Club Official pursuant to the terms of this Agreement.
6.4 the licence granted at cl 6.2, above, shall:
6.4.1 be exclusive only to the extent that neither the Company nor the Player shall exploit, or authorise anyone else other than the Club to exploit, the Player's Image and the Rights in relation to the Merchandising Activities; and
6.4.2 save as referred to in cl 6.4.1 be non-exclusive, which for the avoidance of doubt shall mean that nothing in this Agreement shall prevent or prejudice the Company and/or the Player from licensing third parties to use the Player's Image and the Rights in connection with the marketing and promotion of products and services that do not carry the Club's marks or regalia or otherwise relate to the Club; and
6.4.3 survive the termination of this Agreement but only until the expiry of the last of any agreements to exploit the Rights (and for the purposes of those agreements) entered into by the Club during the term of this Agreement;
6.5 The Company shall ensure that any sponsorship advertising or similar promotional commitments which the Company or the Player may undertake do not conflict with or prevent the Player from participating or being otherwise involved in the Merchandising Activities and/or the Services and/or any sponsorships, advertising or similar promotional activity or agreement undertaken or concluded by the Club, provided that this obligation shall not apply to any endorsement or other promotional or advertising commitment undertaken by the Player in relation to his capacity as a member of a national squad;
6.6 Subject to cl 6.2(a), All intellectual property rights in or arising out of any use or exploitation of the Rights by the Club or its sub-licensees or assignees and/or provision by the Company and/or the Player of the Merchandising Activities and/or the Services will be and remain the exclusive property of the Club or its assignees, as the case may be;
6.7 The Company shall procure that the Player will during the term of this Agreement in performing the Services:
6.7.1 follow all reasonable instructions given to the Company and/or the Player by the organiser of any event or activity to which the Services relate;
6.7.2 conduct himself in an orderly and respectable manner suitable to the relevant event or activity and any relevant audience; and
6.7.3 undertake any interviews and co-operate with any reporters or other representatives of any media organisations as a Club or the relevant organiser may reasonably direct;

6.8 This Agreement constitutes a contract for the provision of services and is not a contract of employment and accordingly the Company shall be fully responsible for the Player and the Company's own tax and national insurance, social security contributions and Value Added Tax liabilities in connection with the performance by the Company of its obligations under this Agreement[1];

6.9 The Company and the Player jointly and severally represent, warrant and undertake to the Club that each of them:

6.9.1 has full power and authority to enter into and perform its obligations under this Agreement and to grant to the Club all of the rights and licences granted hereunder;

6.9.2 has not done and shall not do anything that would impair the Club's free and unrestricted exercise of the rights and licences granted under this Agreement, such as itself/himself exploiting, or authorising anyone else other than the Club to exploit, the Player's Image and the Rights in relation to the Merchandising Activities; and

6.9.3 The Player and the Company shall provide their reasonable co-operation to the Club in (a) combating any unauthorised use by any third party of the Player's Image or the Rights in connection with the Club; and/or (b) defending any claim that the rights of any third party is infringed by this Agreement;

7. The Company shall procure that the Player shall provide the Club with promotional and marketing services on an 'as required' and non-exclusive basis which shall include without limitation (subject to the Club providing the Company with reasonable notice):
   (1) interviews on television, radio or to newspaper or magazine journalist by the Player;
   (2) ensuring the availability of the Player for Club social or Club sponsor events;
   (3) attendance by the Player at filming, photographic or recording sessions and permitting the Club to use and publish such films, videotapes, recordings for the profit of the Club and similar images or voice of the Player for its own requirements;
   (4) making the Player available at any promotional and marketing events organised by or on the behalf of the Club;
   (5) use of the Image Rights for any of the Club's products or services or events;
   (6) making the Player available at any benevolent or charitable activities arranged by the Club;
   (7) attendance by the Player at visits by and to third parties at Club matches or training or any matches or events at the Club's premises;
   (8) the Player on behalf of the Company undertaking public speaking duties; and
   (9) the Player assisting with specialist motivation activities;

8. In full and final consideration for the grant of the various rights and licences under this Agreement the Club shall pay the Company in respect of the Services a retainer of [ ] Pounds (£[ ]) per annum plus value added tax or any similar tax. This is calculated on an hourly basis on the expected level of usage by the Club of [ ] hours per month of the Player's time. Should the average monthly usage exceed 150% of the expected usage then the Company has the right to charge the Club an excess fee equal to an agreed hourly rate;

9. In consideration of the Club entering into this Agreement with the Company, the Player guarantees to the Club as principal obligor and not merely as surety the full due and punctual performance and observance by the Company of all its obligations under or pursuant to this Agreement, including (without limitation) the obligations of the Company to procure the services of the Player hereunder. This is a continuing guarantee that shall remain in force until all obligations of the Company under this Agreement have been fully satisfied.

1 In relation to tax issues, see para D3.78 et seq.

5 TAX ISSUES

D3.78 One of the reasons to separate out a sportsman's provision of promotional services from his provision of playing services is to reduce the tax burden on the sportsman by trying to structure his affairs so that payments for promotional services do not incur income tax liability. The tax issues relating to image rights are a relatively new area of expertise, and the reader is encouraged to take specialist tax advice. In particular, there are a number of anti-avoidance provisions that could possibly apply[1], detailed discussion of which is beyond the scope of this chapter. What follows can only be a general introduction to the issues.

1 In particular Pt XVII Ch III of the Income and Corporation Taxes Act 1988 (transfer of assets abroad) and s 775 of the same Act (sale by individual of income derived from his personal activities).

D3.79 The first question is whether or not the sportsman has an 'image' that is capable of exploitation in its own right, ie that has a commercial value separate and apart from the skills of the sportsman in his particular area. This is a question of fact, and one on which the tax authorities can be expected to take a tough approach.

D3.80 The next question is whether the sportsman is domiciled in the UK or outside the UK. The tax position changes markedly depending on the answer to this question. An analysis of domicile is determined for tax purposes is beyond the scope of this book, and the reader should refer to a specialist work[1]. For current purposes, it is sufficient simply to note that 'domicile' is a concept of private international law that refers to a person's 'spiritual home' (as opposed to the place where he or she resides from time to time).

1 For example Booth *Residence, Domicile and UK Taxation* (6th edn, Tolley).

A UK domiciliary

D3.81 The following analysis relates to the UK tax position of a sportsman, resident and/or ordinarily resident and domiciled in the United Kingdom, who is employed by the club for which he plays[1].

1 It is possible for a sportsman to provide his playing services as an independent contractor (pursuant to a contract for services) rather than as an employee (contract of service). See paras E1.6 to E1.10.

D3.82 In such a case, the payment made by the club to the sportsman for his playing services is clearly Schedule E employment income on which the sportsman must pay income tax and with respect to which the sportsman and the club must make National Insurance contributions ('NICs'). The club is required by law to account for income tax and the sportsman's NICs under the PAYE system[1].

1 See para C2.64 et seq.

D3.83 This liability is substantial: most sportsmen will be taxed at the highest marginal rate of 40%, in addition to their NICs; while employer NICs add significantly to the cost to the club of the sportsman's salary package. However, avoidance of such tax is difficult if not impossible. Interposing a service company between the sportsman and the club would be artificial and would not change the basic position that the sportsman is providing services as an employee of the club.

The Inland Revenue would most likely challenge the arrangement on the basis that the sportsman remains, essentially, an employee[1].

1 This challenge would be under the provisions contained in Sch 12 to the Finance Act 2000, commonly known as 'IR 35', as to which see paras D3.106 to D3.113.

D3.84 On the other hand, a sportsman may also provide 'promotional' services, both to his club and to third parties, in the form of personal appearances, publicity shots, endorsements of their goods and/or services, and so on. That income is related to but is not directly connected with his employment by the club. In relation to that income, an intermediary service company may be a useful tax mitigation/deferral tool. However, care needs to be taken to insulate the arrangement, insofar as is possible, from attack by the Inland Revenue. There are two related but separate issues:

(1) is the arrangement a sham? and
(2) does IR 35[1] apply to the arrangement?

1 See para D3.83, n 1.

(a) Using an intermediary personal service company

D3.85 The sportsman establishes a personal service company (an 'image rights company') and transfers his image rights to such company, usually via a licensing agreement[1]. The sportsman also contracts with the image rights company to perform promotional activities and services as directed by the image rights company. The image rights company in turn contracts on behalf of the sportsman with third parties (such as his club and his national team) for the exploitation of those image rights and also for the performance of certain promotional services by the sportsman. All earnings and royalties derived from the performance of the promotional services and the exploitation of the image rights accrue to the image rights company. See fig 1 below.

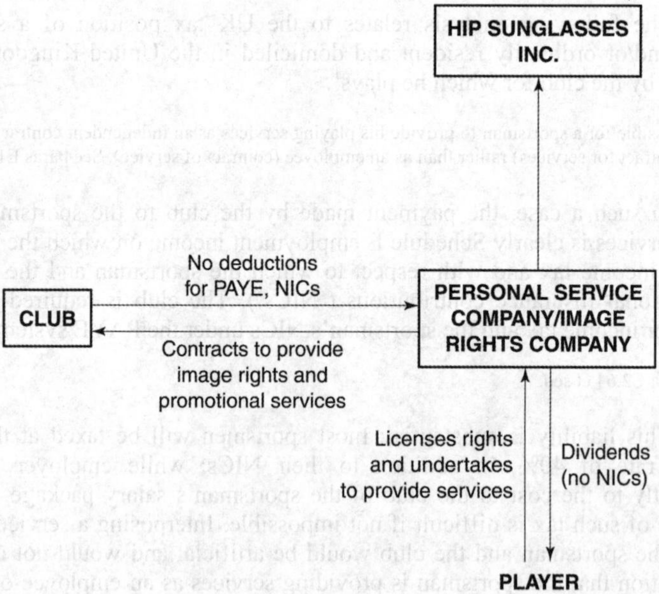

1 It should be noted that the transfer of the image rights from the sportsman to the image rights company is prima facie a disposal of an asset for capital gains tax purposes, and therefore subject to a capital gains tax charge. There will usually have been no payment made by the company for the rights, and therefore the Inland Revenue will calculate capital gains tax liability based on fair market value, determined by reference to (among other things) the length of the grant and the status of the player (which makes it better, on balance, to set up the transfer early in the player's career), with a discount applied to reflect contingencies such as the risk of injury. Although certain reliefs may be available, it is important to consider whether the benefits of setting up this structure for the exploitation of the player's image rights outweigh this and the other costs of setting up the structure.

D3.86 The sportsman's playing contract with his club should reflect the provision only of playing services, not of promotional services[1]. The promotional services should be provided by the image rights company to the club pursuant to their separate contract[2]. In that way, as there is no direct contract between the club and the sportsman for these services, the income derived by the sportsman in respect of such activities should not be regarded as income from his employment. The effect is that the Schedule E and NIC legislation does not apply to the amounts that the club pays to the image rights company in respect of the services provided. In other words, the club pays the gross amount of the agreed fee to the image rights company; it does not have to deduct PAYE or employee NICs on the fee, nor does the club itself have to pay employer NICs on the fee.

1 Cf the current (para D3.68) and proposed (para D3.70) standard contractual provisions in professional English football.
2 See para D3.77.

D3.87 All parties benefit from this arrangement. The club avoids an NIC liability of its own; while the image rights company, having received its fee gross, then has a degree of flexibility over how it is paid out.

D3.88 The image rights company could pay a salary to the sportsman, but that would involve payment of Sch E income tax and NICs[1].

1 See paras D3.82 and D3.83.

D3.89 Alternatively, the image rights company could pay the corporation tax due on profits each year (at a rate of between 10% and 30%, depending on the level of profits[1]) and either pay dividends to the sportsman or 'roll up' undistributed post-tax profits. It should be noted that although the sportsman (as a shareholder) will pay income tax at an effective rate of 25% on his dividend income, the overall tax burden will depend on the rate of corporation tax paid by his image company, because dividends can only ever be paid out of post-tax profits. If, however, the profits are not distributed but rather are 'rolled up', then it may be possible to liquidate the service company in a tax-efficient manner at some point in the future.

1 See paras C2.20 to C2.23.

(b) The Sports Club *case*

D3.90 In the *Sports Club* case[1], the Inland Revenue attacked image rights arrangements as described above as a sham designed solely to disguise salary payments as image rights payments and so avoid the payment of income tax and NICs under the PAYE system.

1 *Sports Club, Evelyn and Jocelyn v Inspector of Taxes* SpC253 (Special Commissioners Brice and Everett, 8 June 2000), Simons Tax Cases [2000] STC (SCD) 443, para 39.

D3.91 Footballer Dennis Bergkamp had had his own image rights company (incorporated in the Dutch Antilles) since 1991. He had assigned his image rights to the company and agreed to provide promotional services to the company for the exploitation of such rights. That company then sub-licensed the rights to an intermediary company incorporated in the Netherlands, owned by Bergkamp's agent, which in turn sub-licensed the rights to his club for certain defined uses and to Reebok in relation to a boot deal.

D3.92 Fellow footballer David Platt also had an offshore image rights company, which contracted with certain commercial third parties (but not with his club). In 1995, Platt wound up the company and set up a new UK image rights company, with himself and his wife as directors and shareholders. He assigned to that company the right to exploit his name, image, signature and voice, and was separately employed by the company to be 'the physical representative of the company's intellectual property rights'[1]

1 *Sports Club, Evelyn and Jocelyn v Inspector of Taxes* SpC253 (Special Commissioners Brice and Everett, 8 June 2000), Simons Tax Cases [2000] STC (SCD) 443, para 59.

D3.93 In the summer of 1995, Bergkamp and Platt were both transferred to Arsenal Football Club. They each signed playing contracts with Arsenal. No one disputed that these amounted to employment contracts or that income paid under those contracts was assessable to tax under Schedule E. However, Arsenal subsequently signed separate agreements with the players' respective image rights companies[1], pursuant to which Arsenal agreed to pay fees to the respective companies in return for the companies granting Arsenal the right to exploit the players' image rights and supplying certain promotional services of the players to assist in that exploitation.

1 In Bergkamp's case, the contract was with the Dutch BV that held a sub-licence from his Dutch Antilles company.

D3.94 The parties also agreed that, if the Inland Revenue did not accept that the payments in relation to image rights and promotional services were not emoluments of the employment, then the payments made under the agreements would be reduced by an amount 'equivalent to that which would be deductible under the PAYE Regulations' were they to apply, this amount to be retained by Arsenal against the possible tax liability[1].

1 *Sports Club, Evelyn and Jocelyn v Inspector of Taxes* SpC253 (Special Commissioners Brice and Everett, 8 June 2000), Simons Tax Cases [2000] STC (SCD) 443, para 39.

D3.95 In April 1997, the Inland Revenue issued a Notice of Determination that the payments made to the image rights companies constituted income from the players' employment and therefore were subject to the normal deductions for income tax. Arsenal, Bergkamp and Platt appealed to the Special Commissioners, who handed down their ruling on 8 June 2000[1].

1 In anonymised form: *Sports Club, Evelyn and Jocelyn v Inspector of Taxes* SpC253 (Special Commissioners Brice and Everett, 8 June 2000), Simons Tax Cases [2000] STC (SCD) 443.

D3.96 The primary issue, then, was whether the payments for 'image rights' and related services were 'emoluments of employment' within the meaning of s 19 of the Income and Corporation Taxes Act 1988. The Inland Revenue argued that in each case the payments made by Arsenal to the image rights company were inextricably linked to the player's employment as a footballer by Arsenal, that they had been structured and presented as payments pursuant to agreements to provide promotional services in the exploitation of the image rights solely in order to circumvent Arsenal's wage structure; and they were not genuine commercial transactions.

D3.97 Arsenal and the players argued in response that the exploitation of the players' image rights had a value independent of the playing services they provided to Arsenal. They accepted that English law does not recognise individuals' 'image rights' per se[1], but pointed out that an individual's consent to the use of his image in an advertisement was required by the applicable advertising codes[2], and was also required from a practical viewpoint, ie to obtain the individual's co-operation in the creation of the advertisement.

1 See para D3.27 et seq.
2 See paras D3.39 and D3.40.

D3.98 The Special Commissioners heard evidence that commercial organisations were prepared to pay substantial sums for the right to use sportsmen's names and images to promote their products and services, and that image rights companies and separate image rights contracts were not uncommon mechanisms for exploiting such rights. The evidence also showed that Bergkamp and Platt were 'world class player[s] of international standing'[1], whose image rights companies had been able to generate significant income from licensing their image rights to third parties for commercial exploitation.

1 *Sports Club, Evelyn and Jocelyn v Inspector of Taxes* SpC253 (Special Commissioners Brice and Everett, 8 June 2000), Simons Tax Cases [2000] STC (SCD) 443, paras 12 and 42.

D3.99 The Special Commissioners also heard evidence that the promotional contracts included both positive and negative obligations on the players. The promotional contracts required them positively to endorse products and make personal appearances, over and above the obligations imposed on other squad members by the standard playing contract[1]. The promotional contracts also prevented them from providing similar services to others.

1 See para D3.68.

D3.100 The Special Commissioners held that the agreements were capable of having and did have independent value over and above the playing services that the players provided to Arsenal, being genuine commercial agreements for full consideration to provide promotional services that the parties could seek to enforce[1].

1 *Sports Club, Evelyn and Jocelyn v Inspector of Taxes* SpC253 (Special Commissioners Brice and Everett, 8 June 2000), Simons Tax Cases [2000] STC (SCD) 443, para 83.

D3.101 The Inland Revenue had argued that the transactions in issue were simply 'a smokescreen or window dressing', a device to circumvent Arsenal's own internal salary structure. Arsenal was not in the business of exploiting image rights; the payments were 'in reality rewards for the players acting [as] or becoming employees'[1].

1 *Sports Club, Evelyn and Jocelyn v Inspector of Taxes* SpC253 (Special Commissioners Brice and Everett, 8 June 2000), Simons Tax Cases [2000] STC (SCD) 443, para 87.

D3.102 The Special Commissioners rejected this argument in relation to both players. In relation to Bergkamp, they relied on the fact that Bergkamp's company had been set up many years before his transfer to Arsenal, and had entered into similar relationships with his previous club. They noted that the transaction with Arsenal proceeded from the beginning that image rights would have to be acquired separately from playing services. They also found that Arsenal had fully intended to exploit the image rights at the time that it acquired them, and indeed that it got a third party valuation of those rights and its lawyers went to significant lengths to ensure that Arsenal secured those rights. The fact that in the event Arsenal did not exploit the rights did not overcome this showing[1].

1 *Sports Club, Evelyn and Jocelyn v Inspector of Taxes* SpC253 (Special Commissioners Brice and Everett, 8 June 2000), Simons Tax Cases [2000] STC (SCD) 443, para 90.

D3.103 In relation to Platt, the decision was considerably more marginal, mainly because the image rights company was set up for Platt specifically in relation to the Arsenal transfer, and was not used previously at his other clubs. Moreover, his agent had referred to the structure as a 'method of remunerating' the player. Nevertheless, Platt had previously granted the right to exploit his image rights to third parties, thereby demonstrating the commercial value of those rights; an image rights contract was discussed at an early stage with Arsenal, before any global figures were discussed; and when a global figure was discussed a particular value was ascribed to the image rights element of it. Again, the rights had not subsequently been properly exploited, but this was partly due to Platt's subsequent injuries. Again, then, the Special Commissioners found that the transaction was not a sham[1].

1 *Sports Club, Evelyn and Jocelyn v Inspector of Taxes* SpC253 (Special Commissioners Brice and Everett, 8 June 2000), Simons Tax Cases [2000] STC (SCD) 443, paras 92–94.

D3.104 Finally, the Special Commissioners concluded that the payments made for image rights and promotional services were not emoluments of the players' employment by Arsenal within the meaning of s 19 of the Income and Corporation Taxes Act 1988:

> We note that the promotional agreements and the consultancy agreement were contracts for full consideration and so would be excluded from tax under section 19 for that reason alone. Also, we find that the payments under those agreements were made in return for promotional rights and consultancy services respectively and were not made 'in reference to' the playing of games which was the service rendered by each player by virtue of his player's agreement with [Arsenal]. Neither were the payments under the promotional and consultancy agreements a reward by [Arsenal] for their services of the players; they were paid by [Arsenal] for the promotional rights and the consultancy services respectively[1].

1 [2000] STC (SCD) 443, para 100. The Special Commissioners also rejected the Inland Revenue's contentions that the payments were taxable under Schedule E as (1) 'benefits in kind' within the meaning of s 154 of the 1988 Act; and/or (2) pension benefits within the meaning of s 595 of the 1988 Act. With respect to the former, again the Special Commissioners relied on the fact that Arsenal paid the companies '"by reason of" the separate commercial contracts to provide promotional services and not by reason of the employments to play for the club': para 114. With respect to the latter, the Commissioners similarly held: 'we do not agree that the sums were paid "with a view to the provision of any relevant benefits". They were paid with the view to the provision of rights under the promotional agreement': para 126.

D3.105 The *Sports Club* decision depended very much on the facts of the case, which obviously affects its precedential effect. However, the following principles can be taken from the case:

(1) It is entirely possible and legitimate for sportsmen to separate their playing services from their image rights and promotional services in such a way that the latter do not form part of their contract of employment, provided that this is a genuine arrangement.
(2) It will be necessary to show that the name and image of the sportsman in question has a commercial value to third parties, for the endorsement of their products and services, that exists separately from the sportsman's employment by his club. Therefore, it is likely to work only for elite sportsmen.
(3) It would be helpful from an evidential point of view (but not essential) for the image rights company to be established long before the transaction in question.
(4) The payments for playing services must be distinguished from payments for the grant of image rights throughout the negotiations.
(5) It would also be helpful for the club actually to exploit the rights acquired from the image rights company!
(6) Finally, the split between the salary element and the payment for the provision of promotional services and image rights needs to be commercially sensible and justifiable. The image rights elements of the package should be reasonable in relation to the commercial value of the rights and not obviously incorporating an element of what the market would pay for the player's playing services. The actual split will be dependent upon the particular circumstances of the sportsman involved and how marketable and valuable his image rights are. Essentially, however, salary and 'image rights' payments must be negotiated as two separate commercial contracts.

(c) The application of IR 35

D3.106 On 6 April 2000, legislation was introduced to prevent employees avoiding liability for income tax and NIC by providing their services to their employers through personal service companies. The legislation applies where a worker provides services to a client via an intermediary in circumstances such that if the contract had been made directly then the worker would have been treated as an employee of the client for tax purposes. These anti-avoidance provisions are contained in Sch 12 to the Finance Act 2000, more commonly known as 'IR 35' (after the Inland Revenue press release that announced the introduction of the rules).

D3.107 Where IR 35 applies, the effect is to regard the fees paid to the intermediary service company not as company revenue upon which corporation tax is payable after deduction of allowable expenses, but instead as deemed salary to the worker. The worker is therefore subjected to Schedule E income tax and employee NICs on that deemed salary. The intermediary service company is liable for the collection of that tax and NICs, together with payment of its own employer NICs on the deemed salary. The third party client remains unaffected and can continue to make gross payments as before.

D3.108 The *Sports Club* case did not address whether the structure put in place for Bergkamp and Platt was potentially subject to IR 35.

D3.109 There is an argument that IR 35 is potentially applicable to image rights company schemes entered into by sportsmen, as the sportsman could be said to be providing his promotional services to the club via an intermediary, within the meaning of the new legislation.

D3.110 Following such an argument, the key issue would be to determine whether the circumstances are such that if the promotional services were provided under a contract directly between the sportsman and the club, the sportsman would be regarded as an employee of the club for income tax purposes (by reference only to such promotional activities).

D3.111 It has been argued that, in order to avoid being classified as an employee under the legislation, the sportsman should be seen to be using the image rights company as a separate trading vehicle that conducts business in its own right with a variety of third parties[1]. According to this view, the important point is for the sportsman's image rights to be licensed to the club on a non-exclusive basis, so that other licences can be and are entered into with third parties for the use of the same rights, because the sportsman will then meet the test of a self-employed person rather than an employee[2].

1 See Odendaal 'Taxation of Sportpersons' Image Rights Company Schemes and Potential Application of IR 35' [2001] 9(2) SATLJ 118.
2 See n 1.

D3.112 The authors do not agree with this argument. The basic ruling in the *Sports Club* case was that sportsmen can separate their playing services from their image rights and promotional services in such a way that the latter do not form part of their contract of employment, provided that this is a genuine arrangement. On the one side, there is the payment being made by the club direct to the player for his playing services: this is an employment relationship. On the other side is the payment being made by the club to the image rights company for a separate asset that is independent of the sportsman's playing services and capable of being exploited in its own right, namely his image rights. Payment for the right to use such rights, and for the provision of promotional services by the sportsman to assist in the exploitation of those rights, is not being paid in respect of the sportsman's duties as an employed player, but in respect of that separate asset. So long as that income is not simply disguised salary, but arises from a genuine commercial contract that is separate from the sportsman's playing contract with the club[1], then it should not be regarded as employment income and the sportsman would not be caught by IR 35 in respect of that income[2].

1 Where the image rights company is in fact a sham, and is being used solely as a mechanism to divert income from the club that would otherwise have been paid to the sportsman under his employment contract, the Inland Revenue would be entitled to look through the image rights company and regard the sportsman as an employee under IR 35.
2 See Maas 'Bend the tax rules like Beckham' (2002) Tax Journal, 27 May.

D3.113 The key conclusions, then, remain the same as after the *Sports Club* case. The arrangements in terms of which the image rights are exploited must be genuine; and the amounts paid for the exploitation of the image rights and the provision of the promotional services should not be disguised salary but must be genuine payments made over and above salary, commensurate with the value of the image rights and promotional services being acquired. Accordingly, these schemes will only tend to work for top-level high profile sportsmen who can truly be said to enjoy celebrity status, separate and apart from their sports skills, that is of value to the marketplace.

B Non-UK domiciliaries

D3.114 Non-UK domiciliaries generally do not have to pay UK tax on income and capital gains arising abroad (provided that the foreign source income or gains are not actually remitted to the UK). Through careful planning, income paid by a foreign player's English club for use of his image rights can arise abroad, thereby potentially avoiding UK tax.

D3.115 Jurisdictions outside the UK tend to recognise and give legal protection far more readily to the 'personality' rights of individuals[1]. As a result, the commercial exploitation of image rights is well-established[2], and many foreign sportsmen coming to play in the UK already have an established image rights company in an offshore location prior to becoming a UK resident, as was the case with Dennis Bergkamp[3]. Again, then, the club can contract with the player directly for the provision of his playing services, and with the image rights company for a licence to use his image rights and for the provision of his promotional services.

1 See paras D3.14 to D3.26.
2 Dennis Bergkamp's agent told the Special Commissioners in the *Sports Club* case that 'all the players in [Bergkamp's] first club team had image rights contracts': *Sports Club, Evelyn & Jocelyn v Inspector of Taxes* SpC253 (Special Commissioners Brice and Everett, 8 June 2000), [2000] STC (SCD) 443, para 14.
3 See para D3.91.

D3.116 In such circumstances, the Inland Revenue may find it hard to distinguish the *Sports Club* case and treat the payments to the image rights company as employment income for the player. Rather, the payments are likely to stand up as royalty payments or licensing fees in exchange for the grant of use of the image rights and promotional services[1].

1 See paras D3.100 to D3.105.

D3.117 The Inland Revenue is likely to insist that the club levies withholding tax on those (pure income) payments[1]. However, it may be possible to use existing double tax treaties to avoid such withholding tax. For example, the double taxation treaty between the Netherlands and the UK provides that no withholding tax will be levied on a payment of licence fees by a UK resident person to a Dutch resident person, where the Dutch recipient is the beneficial owner of the licence fees it receives[2].

1 Section 349 of the Income and Corporation Taxes Act 1988.
2 The Dutch recipient would need to apply to the Inland Revenue Financial Intermediaries and Claims Office to obtain confirmation that the UK sports club can pay the licence fee at the reduced 'treaty rate' of withholding, which in the case of the Netherlands is nil.

D3.118 So, for example, the player could grant an exclusive 'image rights' licence to a Jersey Trust (fig 2, n 1). The Jersey Trust assigns the licence to Jersey Image Co in exchange for shares in Jersey Image Co (fig 2, n 2). Jersey Image Co then grants a sub-licence to a Dutch BV, an independent Dutch licensing conduit company (fig 2, n 3). Finally, the Dutch BV grants an 'image licence' to the club (and other third parties) (fig 2, n 4).

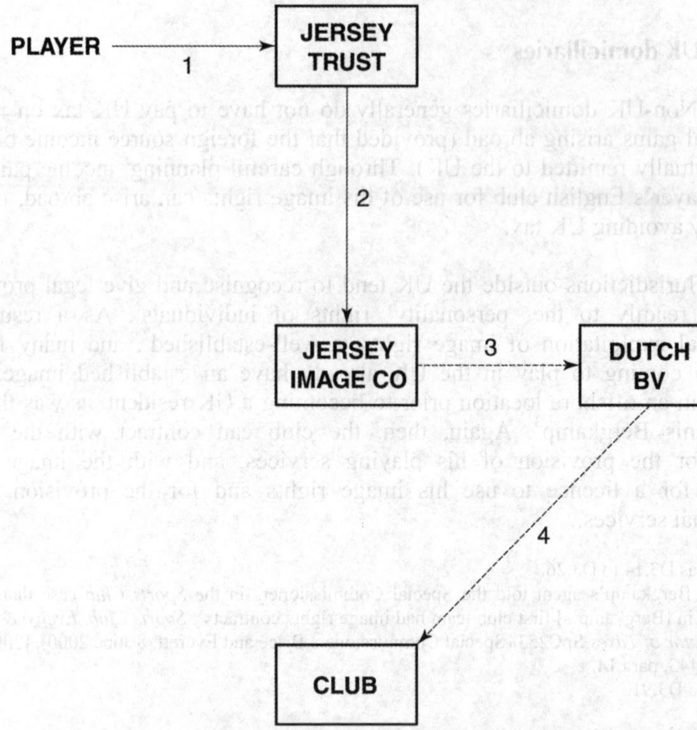

D3.119 To take account of the requirement that the Dutch resident must be beneficial owner of the licence fees received from the club, the Dutch BV should be independent and should take a commercial fee prior to payment of the licence fees to Jersey Image Co. This will also help avoid the Inland Revenue treating the Dutch BV as being managed and controlled in the UK, and therefore to be treated as a UK resident for tax purposes. For the same reason, the Dutch BV should avoid completing and signing licence agreements in the UK itself.

D3.120 The Dutch tax authorities will not levy withholding tax on the onward payment of licence fees from the Dutch BV to Jersey Image Co. In this way, no tax would be levied in Holland or the UK; the only payment would be a commercial fee paid to the Dutch BV. (In the absence of a commercial fee, the Dutch authorities tax a 'spread' of the licence fees received by the BV. The amount taxable is between 2% and 7% of the gross licence fees received, depending on the level of income).

D3.121 To avoid a capital gains tax charge, the initial grant of the exclusive licence should be made before the player becomes UK resident. However, 'gift' tax in the player's home jurisdiction may be an issue[1].

1 See para D3.85, n 1.

CHAPTER D4

BROADCASTING AND NEW MEDIA

Matthew Eccles (Octagon CSI Limited)*

Contents

1 THE IMPORTANCE OF SPORTS BROADCASTING RIGHTS

D4.1 This chapter addresses various legal and practical issues relating to the sale of broadcasting rights to sports events. If this book had been written as little as five years ago, it may well have been sufficient for this chapter simply to deal with television, video and radio rights. However, those last five years have seen the exploitation of sport on a range of new media platforms, in particular the Internet, and new ways of carving up and exploiting the overall package of sports broadcasting rights that make this a far more involved topic than it once was.

* The author gratefully acknowledges the input of Jonathan Higton of Hammonds and Dan Harrington of Couchman Harrington Associates.

D4.2 The sale of sports broadcasting rights[1] is of fundamental importance to the commercial programmes of most sports rights-holders. For many sports, broadcast rights have replaced ticket income as the single most important source of revenue. Throughout the 1990s and the start of this millennium, sports with major television appeal, the 'must-have' programming such as elite football, enjoyed something of a bonanza in rights fees:

- Broadcasting money accounted for almost forty percent (40%) of the revenues of most FA Premier League clubs in the 2000/2001 football season[2].

- The FA Premier League media rights deals signed around the summer 2000 have reportedly netted over £1.2 billion. This represents an increase of almost £1 billion over the amount received by the FA Premier League from its first broadcast deals, struck in 1992.
- Also, in summer 2000, the Football League secured a £315m rights fee deal with ITV Digital (then On Digital) for the television rights to Nationwide League and Worthington Cup games, followed by a £105m joint venture rights deal with Premium TV (a subsidiary of ntl) to run the official Football League Internet portal[3].
- A US $1.2 billion 10-year marketing and media rights deal between the ATP Tour and ISL in respect of the 'Super 9' tennis tournaments (which do not include any of the four majors).

1 The term 'broadcasting rights' is used as short-hand in this chapter to encompass any and all rights to transmit audio, audio-visual, text and other data on television or any other medium, excluding the print media.

2 Deloitte & Touche's *Report on England's Premier Clubs* (June 2002). Broadcasting revenues includes revenues from television and radio deals both domestically and internationally. This figure compares with a total of 12% for the 1995/95 season and is likely to increase substantially for the 2001/2002 season, which is the first season of the FA Premier League's latest broadcasting and media arrangements (although the clubs received an advance on the new deal).

3 Time will tell whether this deal comes to be seen as the high watermark of rights fees. Of course ITV Digital's failure to pay this rights fee has been well documented.

D4.3 Following deregulation in the 1980s, technological and economic conditions in the media and technology sector (particularly television) have changed enormously. These changes provided the competitive environment and technological developments that drove up the market value of elite sports broadcasting rights and produced the degree of inflation noted above. New distribution platforms carrying new channels have been developed and launched, often at huge expense. First came satellite and cable television, then pay-television (in particular dedicated subscription sports channels) and later the Internet. More recently, we have seen the development of interactive and enhanced television, broadband cable and now distribution to handheld devices using mobile telephony networks. Since the summer of 2000, we have seen rights holders seeking to exploit most if not all of these platforms or modes of delivery, particularly for the most valuable sports. The ability to carve up the overall package of broadcasting rights to a sporting event across platforms, territories and time zones has made it possible to put together smaller packages of sports content that complement (or at least do not compete with) each other, thereby maximising exposure and commercial value for the rights-holder[1].

1 This process of fragmentation of rights packages is addressed in further detail at paras D4.30 to D4.45.

D4.4 Perhaps the most fundamental factor in the expansion of the sports broadcasting market has been the recognition of broadcasters, particularly subscription-based broadcasters such as Rupert Murdoch's News Corporation (in the UK, BSkyB), that sports programming, along with first-run Hollywood films, are 'must-see' programming, ie required viewing that people will pay to see notwithstanding the availability of 'free' programming on the other channels. To fall into this category, the rights have to be to the elite sports, particularly football, but also (in the UK) the very best rugby, cricket, tennis and motor-racing[1]. Additionally, the rights have to be live and exclusive, to ensure the uncertainty of outcome that creates the true attraction of the sporting spectacle and so that people wishing to watch the event have no choice but to pay to access them[2]. Rupert Murdoch identified such rights as 'the battering-ram' to achieve market penetration for his subscription-based television channels, and his strategy has been an outstanding success[3].

1 Although the need for a large inventory of sports programming to fill the schedules of dedicated sports channels around the elite events can create demand for sports rights that are really at best only 'must see' programming for their own dedicated followers.

2 Very few events are sufficiently attractive to have simultaneous coverage on more than one channel. However attractive the event, multi-channel coverage would simply not work for subscription-based broadcasters such as BSkyB, because no subscriptions would be driven by the showing of an event that was accessible for free on another channel.

3 Channel 5 used the same strategy in February 1999, just months after its launch, paying a substantial fee for the exclusive right to broadcast in the UK the England national team's European Championship qualifying match away to Poland, thereby forcing millions of viewers who had not previously bothered to tune their televisions to Channel 5 to find the new channel on their dials so as not to miss the match.

A further strategy followed by BSkyB, which aims to protect BSkyB's previous and future investments in sports rights, has been taking equity stakes in football clubs and the provision of consultancy services to look after the clubs' media interests. Carlton, Granada and NTL quickly followed BSkyB's lead. See para C3.173.

D4.5 The spring 2000 dot.com boom may have represented the high-water mark for sports broadcasting rights fees. The subsequent crash in the dot.com market and in the advertising market, as well as recessionary economic conditions generally, have hit the sports broadcasting market very hard[1], and new media platforms have struggled to start generating the returns required to justify their enormous investment costs. In the UK the market has seen the collapse of ITV Digital, the new digital platform launched by Carlton and Granada, largely due to the costs of acquisition of sports rights (particularly the Football League rights bought in June 2000) for its ITV Sport channel, and the serious scaling back of NTL's Premium TV operation and the new British Eurosport Channel. Further afield, there has been the collapse of ISL (previously the most powerful sports rights agency in the world) largely due to huge exposure on tennis and motorsport contracts, and Kirch Media, the rights and free-television of the giant German media group, which declared itself insolvent in April 2002. As a result, two of the huge sports broadcasting rights deals referred to at para D4.2 defaulted and were subsequently terminated[2].

1 It is not just macro-economic conditions that can have a dramatic effect on the sports broadcasting market. To take just one example, the decline in rights fees for tennis in Germany from the mid-1990s onward was due in no small measure to the fact that the careers of Germany's most successful tennis players, Boris Becker, Steffi Graf and Michael Stich, were all coming to an end.

2 In the lawsuit that followed ITV Digital's collapse, the Football League's efforts to recover the deficit from ITV Digital's shareholders, Carlton and Granada, failed when the court ruled that in the absence of a written guarantee signed by those companies, promises of parent company support in ITV Digital's tender document were not sufficient to render them liable for its default: *Carlton and Granada v Football League* [2002] All ER (D) 1, QBD.

D4.6 Despite these recent problems, there is no doubt that televised sport has always had and will continue to have the ability to deliver substantial and loyal audiences. Indeed sporting events are capable of delivering some of the highest ever viewing figures. For example, a British television audience of around 27m people watched the Argentina v England penalty shoot-out in the second round of the 1998 World Cup Finals and audiences for the 2002 World Cup in Japan/Korea were as high as 16.8m for the England v Denmark second round clash, despite the difficulties with time zones in Japan/South Korea. Only Royal Weddings in the early 1980s and major story-lines in top soap operas can get anywhere near the viewing figures delivered by the highest level of sport. The ability to deliver audiences of this level and the consistent success of sports to deliver loyal viewers who have attractive demographic profiles to sponsors and/or advertisers remains the key factor driving demand for sports programming.

D4.7 One thing that is for certain is sports broadcasting has come a long way since the first single camera sports television broadcasts of the 1930s which were greeted with sceptical comments in the press of 'It'll never catch on' and 'television is too tame to capture the excitement of sport'.

2 WHAT ARE SPORTS BROADCASTING RIGHTS?

D4.8 When a broadcaster spends millions of pounds buying the rights to broadcast a sporting event on its television channel or other media platform, what exactly is it buying?

D4.9 In the case brought in 2000 by the BBC against Talksport, the commercial radio station[1], Laddie J described a sports broadcasting right as 'the right to broadcast on radio and television, live coverage of the matches from within the stadia where they are taking place'. But does the law recognise rights in a sporting event or spectacle per se, or is it a combination of other, recognised legal rights that creates the valuable broadcasting rights in the event? Different jurisdictions take vastly different approaches to this fundamental question.

1 *BBC v Talksport Ltd* [2001] FSR 53 (Laddie J).

D4.10 In France, the approach is straightforward. The government sees sport as part of its public responsibility and sport is heavily regulated, with only those authorised by the government being allowed to organise particular sport and sanction competitions in that sport. In relation to commercial exploitation of such events, the Loi du Sport provides:

> broadcasting rights to sporting events belong exclusively to the concerned sporting federation or to the legal person in charge of the management of the professional sector by delegation of authority[2].

In other words, the federation licensed by the state, or its designee, has a statutory monopoly right to exploit the broadcasting rights to the events that take place in that sport. Competing claims (such as from professional clubs participating in the event) are precluded.

1 See paras A1.10 and A1.11.
2 Translation of Loi no 84-610 du Juillet 1984.

D4.11 In the United States a quasi-property right in sporting events is recognised as part of the doctrine of commercial misappropriation developed by the US courts. The leading case involved the Pittsburgh Pirates baseball team[1]. The owners of the team sued a radio station that was broadcasting commentary of the Pirates' ballgames. The radio station had leased buildings overlooking the ballpark and had paid observers to watch and commentate on the Pirates' games from those buildings. The court held that the Pittsburgh owners had a proprietary right in news disseminated from the ball-park and the right to control use of that news for a period after the game. Schoonmaker J said:

> For it is our opinion that the Pittsburgh Athletic Company, by reason of its creation of the game, its control of the park, and its restriction of the dissemination of news therefrom, has a property right in such news, and the right to control the use thereof for a reasonable time following the games.

1 *Pittsburgh Athletic Co. v KQV Broadcasting Co* 24 F Supp 490 (WD Pa 1937).

D4.12 In contrast, English law recognises no stand-alone broadcasting or other proprietary rights in a sporting event. This was established in 1937 in the Australian case of *Victoria Park Racing v Taylor*[1]. The facts are similar to those in the *Pittsburgh Pirates* case, but the result was very different. The plaintiff operated a racecourse. The first defendant owned adjacent land and let the other defendants erect a tower on that land to see into the racecourse for the purpose of commentating on races for broadcasting over the radio. The plaintiff argued that it had a quasi-property right in the races that the defendants should be prevented from infringing, but this claim was rejected by the Australian High Court. Latham CJ stated:

> It has been argued that by the expenditure of money the plaintiff has created a spectacle and that it therefore has what is described as a quasi-property right in the spectacle which the law will protect. The vagueness of this proposition is apparent on its face. What it really means is that there is some principle (apart from contract or confidential relationship) which prevents people in some circumstances from opening their eyes and seeing something and describing what they see. The court has not been referred to any authority in English law which supports the general contention that if a person chooses to organise an entertainment or to do anything else which other persons are able to see he has a right to obtain from a court an order that they shall not describe to anybody what they see … the mere fact that damage results to the plaintiff from such a description cannot be relied upon as a cause of action. I find difficulty in attaching any precise meaning to the phrase 'property in a spectacle'. A 'spectacle' cannot be 'owned' in any ordinary sense of the word[2]

1 *Victoria Park Racing and Recreation Grounds Co Ltd v Taylor* (1937) 58 CLR 479, HC of A.
2 (1937) 58 CLR 479 at 496 and 497.

D4.13 However, Latham CJ did accept in *Victoria Park Racing*, that relevant rights could be created as a matter of contract[1]. The leading case in this area involved a dog show run by the Ladies Kennel Association, who licensed the 'exclusive' rights to take photographs of the dog show to the plaintiff photographic agency[2]. Unfortunately for the plaintiff, an independent photographer gained access to the show and took his own photographs which he sold to a publisher for use in an illustrated photo-journal of the show. The agency sued the producer of the photo-journal for infringing what it claimed was its exclusive right to appoint a photographer. The court denied the relief claimed on the basis that no one had made it a term of admission that photographs may not be taken. Lord Justice Swinfen Eady explained:

> It is said that the association had been put to the trouble and expense in organising the show, which was their property and which included the right to take photographs themselves and to grant the same right to others, and that they in fact granted it to

[the plaintiff]. In my opinion it is not right to speak of the right of taking photographs as property. No doubt the Ladies' Kennel Association had the grounds for the day, and also the right of allowing those persons to enter of whom they approved and excluding those of whom they did not, and that right carried with it the right of laying down conditions binding on the parties admitted; it might be a condition that they should not use cameras or should not take photographs or make sketches. But they did not lay down any such conditions … The answer to the plaintiffs' argument is that they could have acquired by contract such a right as they claim, and that they failed to do[3].

1 His colleague in that case, Mr Justice McTiernan, explained that an event organiser was entitled 'to impose on the right it granted to any patron to enter the [venue] that he would not communicate to anyone outside the [venue] the knowledge about the racing which he got inside', with any failure to comply amounting to a breach of contract by the patron and a tortious inducement to breach by the recipient and subsequent broadcaster of the information: *Victoria Park Racing* (1937) 58 CLR 479 at 526–527.

2 *Sports and General Press Agency Ltd v Our Dogs Publishing Ltd* [1917] 2 KB 125, CA.

3 [1917] 2 KB at 127–128.

D4.14 Given that there is no stand-alone proprietary right in the sporting event and that there is no law to prevent third parties from exploiting the event organiser's sporting property, what is it that broadcasters are buying when they spend millions of pounds for the right to broadcast (for example) football matches? The answer is that although there is no single UK law that gives rise to ownership of a sporting event, the law of real property, contract and intellectual property can be used to establish exclusive ownership and control over a sporting property akin to a monopoly right through:

(a) control of access to the venue;
(b) control of the activities of persons attending the venue; and
(c) ownership of the copyright in content created at the venue[1].

1 See further paras D1.5 to D1.13 (proprietary rights in sports events generally), and paras D1.17 to D1.22 (broadcasting rights to sports events).

A Control over access to the venue

D4.15 If the event organiser controls the venue at which a sporting event takes place, it will be possible to control those individuals permitted access to the venue to watch the event. This means that the event organiser is in a position to permit access to a camera crew from its television broadcast licensee and/or a commentary team from its radio broadcast licensee, and to ensure their exclusivity by forbidding access to any other camera crew or broadcast team.

D4.16 Such control can be secured either by ownership of the freehold or leasehold interest in the land on which the venue is sited, or by a contract with the owner or controller of the venue that gives the event organiser the exclusive right to occupy the site and to determine who has access and on what conditions[1]. That contract should also address:

(a) access to utilities and facilities such as electricity, water and parking facilities for outside broadcast units, availability of camera gantries, commentary positions and studio facilities for host and licensed broadcasters, access to any broadcast production facilities that may be available on-site; and
(b) authority to use (as part of the broadcast and film) any related intellectual property rights such as the name of the stadium.

1 See paras D1.14 to D1.16 and D2.25 to D2.54.

D4.17 Where the event takes place in a public area, so that access cannot be controlled, as with ocean races, the Tour de France, marathons, boat races and surfing events, the ability to prevent unauthorised filming and broadcasting of the event is curtailed. For example, in a case involving the Boston marathon[1], a broadcaster not authorised by the race organiser sent cameras onto the streets of Boston to film and broadcast the race. The race organiser sought to prevent the broadcast of that unauthorised coverage of the race, but it was held that any television station could broadcast coverage of the race because the race organiser did not own the race as it unfolded on the streets. Although this is a US case, it can probably be inferred that, because of the UK's greater reluctance to recognise a sports broadcasting right in an event per se, the UK courts would follow a similar ruling[2].

1 *WCVB-TV v Boston Athletic Association* 926 F 2d 42 (1st Cir 1991).
2 See generally Blais 'The protection of exclusive television rights to sporting events held in public venues: an overview of the law in Australia and Canada' (1992) 18 Melbourne University Law Review 503.

D4.18 There are solutions to this problem, such as the introduction of special legislative protection. For example during the Sydney 2000 Olympic Games, the Sydney Games Legislation effectively gave the Sydney Organising Committee of the Olympic Games control of the streets of Sydney during certain Olympic events. This may involve the local authority regulating broadcasting in public spaces by a system of granting licences and permits[1]. Without such special provisions, it is simply practicalities (such as the expense of creating broadcast quality coverage) that prevent an unauthorised party exploiting an event held in public areas[2].

1 One of the IOC bidding conditions for the hosting of future Olympic Games is an undertaking on the part of the City governing authorities to ensure broadcast exclusivity for public venue sports.
2 See generally Blais 'The protection of exclusive television rights to sporting events held in public venues: an overview of the law in Australia and Canada' (1992) 18 Melbourne University Law Review 503.

B Control over the activities of persons attending the event

D4.19 The law will recognise and enforce conditions placed on the rights of access granted to those who wish to attend a sports event[1]. Terms and conditions printed on tickets form part of the contract under which individuals are permitted access to the venue and as such can be used to control the activities of spectators at the venue[2]. Similarly, terms of accreditation (the conditions under which media are permitted entry) can be used to control the activities of the media.

1 See paras D1.18 and D1.22 and D4.13.
2 Care needs to be taken to bring the conditions to the attention of the purchaser of the ticket prior to sale, to ensure incorporation into the contract and therefore enforceability. See further paras D1.23 to D1.26.

D4.20 For example ticket conditions could be used to prevent spectators taking photographs or video of the action for commercial purposes[1]. Or media accreditation could prevent accredited media from reproducing data on certain media, such as the internet or mobile telephony[2].

1 See for example the sample ticket conditions set out at para D1.21.
2 See further para D1.27.

D4.21 Anyone in breach of the ticket conditions to an event is likely to be found to be in breach of contract. Furthermore, a ticket is a licence from the person with exclusive possession of the property to enter that property. Anyone found to be acting outside the terms of that licence will be trespassing at the venue (in addition to any breach of contract) and could be ejected from the premises[1].

1 See para D1.20.

C Ownership of the copyright in the content created

D4.22 Provided that the appropriate qualifying criteria are met[1], UK copyright law provides that copyright will subsist automatically in the sound recordings, films, broadcasts or cable programmes created by the broadcast partner[2]. The table at figure one below, sets out the qualifying criteria necessary for copyright to subsist in each of those separate elements. The table also identifies who will be the first owner of the copyright and the duration of the relevant protection. Section references are references to the Copyright, Designs and Patents Act 1988 (unless otherwise stated).

Figure One

Copyright or Protectable Element	Qualifying Criteria required to obtain copyright protection	First Owner of Copyright	Term of Protection
Film (moving images)	Must be recorded on any medium from which a moving image can be produced *s 5(b)(i)*	Producer and the principal director *s 9(2)(a), (b)*	50 years from end of year in which it is made *s 13(b)(9)*
Sound recording	Must be a recording of sounds which allows the sounds to be reproduced *s 5(a)(i)*	Producer *s 9(2)* International sound (ambient crowd noise) *host broadcaster*	50 years from end of year in which it is made *s 13(a)(2)(a)*
Broadcast	Must be a transmission by wireless telegraphy of visual images, sounds capable of being received by the public or other information *s 6*	Broadcaster *s 9(2)(b)*	50 years from end of year in which broadcast first made *s 14(2)*
Cable programme	An item contained in a 'cable programme service', ie a service consisting of sending visual images, sounds or other information by means of a telecommunication system other than wireless telegraphy for reception in two or more places or for presentation to members of the public *s 7(1)*	The cable service provider *s 9(2)(c)*	50 years from the end of the year in which the cable programme was first broadcast *s 14(2)*

Copyright or Protectable Element	Qualifying Criteria required to obtain copyright protection	First Owner of Copyright	Term of Protection
Commentary	Must be recorded in some form *s 3(2)*	Commentator *s 11(i)*	Life of commentator plus 70 years *s 12(2)*
Broadcast graphics (literary and/or artistic works)	Must be fixed as recordings *s 4(1)(a)*	Person who creates the work *s 11(i)*	Life of author plus 70 years *s 12(2)*

1 See s 153 of the Copyright Design and Patents Act 1988.
2 See further paras D1.39 to D1.53 and in particular paras D1.54 to D1.56.

D4.23 The broadcaster (as the originator) would be the first owner of the copyright in the film, sound recordings and broadcasts of the event[1]. Unless the event owner acquires the right to use such copyright material, either by way of copyright assignment or an exclusive licence, it would be the broadcaster and not the event organiser that could authorise broadcasting of the live event footage and highlights or clips across the range of territories and media options.

1 The broadcaster would own the copyright provided that its terms of engagement with any non-employee production crew/commentators, etc contain appropriate copyright assignments: CDPA 1988, s 90(3). Where a copyright work is created by an employee during the course of his employment, his employer will be the first owner of the copyright: CDPA 1988, s 11(2).

D4.24 It is standard for event organisers to seek a full assignment (usually by way of assignment of future copyright[1]) of the copyright arising from the broadcaster's production of match footage. This copyright assignment is usually included in the broadcast rights contract between the rights holder and the host broadcaster[2]. In return for the assignment of copyright (and payment of any rights fee), the rights holder will then grant the host broadcaster a limited licence to broadcast the match in its licensed territory[3].

1 Assignments of future copyright are expressly envisaged and permitted by s 91 of the CDPA 1988.
2 See para D4.69.
3 See n 2.

D Provisos

(a) Off-tube coverage

D4.25 The protection offered by copyright law from unauthorised use of the broadcast is not complete. One specific problem is off-tube coverage, where a commentator watches someone else's transmission of a sports event and simultaneously without the consent of the rights-holder, produces his own commentary, which could either be audio or text based, and could be broadcast over any of the usual media platforms, the most likely candidates being radio and internet.

D4.26 A recent example demonstrating unlicensed use of off-tube coverage comes from the case of *BBC v Talksport*[1]. The BBC, as a UK member of the

European Broadcasting Union (EBU), had acquired from UEFA the exclusive right to broadcast radio commentary of matches in the Euro 2000 football tournament staged in Belgium and Holland. Talksport, a commercial competitor of the BBC that does not qualify as a public broadcaster within the meaning of the EBU membership rules and therefore is not eligible for membership of the EBU, decided to broadcast commentary produced by its employees sitting in hotel rooms in Belgium and watching Belgian live television coverage of the event. Talksport's unofficial broadcasts included ambient sound effects to simulate crowd noise and atmosphere, and it advertised its commentary of the matches as 'live'.

1 *BBC v Talksport Ltd* [2001] FSR 53 (Laddie J).

D4.27 As the 'official' rights-holder, the BBC sought to protect the rights it had acquired, applying for interim relief restraining Talksport from presenting its off-tube coverage. However, the BBC's legal options were severely limited by the fact that English law does not recognise proprietary rights in sports events. Talksport had not obtained unauthorised access to the venue, nor had it infringed any ticket conditions: the Belgian television coverage gave it a 'virtual' stepladder over the fences of the venues, from which 'vantage point' it could see and therefore commentate on the event. The commentary produced did not infringe any copyright since Talksport was not broadcasting what the television commentator was saying, but instead had its own employees producing their own commentary. Instead, the BBC attempted to rely on the tort of passing off[1], alleging that Talksport's use of the words 'live broadcast' and simulated ambient crowd noise amounted to a misrepresentation to the public that Talksport's commentaries were live broadcasts made by commentators at the venues, and alleging further that this misrepresentation damaged the BBC's reputation and goodwill as a live sports broadcaster. Unsurprisingly, notwithstanding Laddie J's disapproval of Talksport's actions, he declined to grant the BBC an injunction, on the basis that it could not prove the requisite goodwill in any particular sign or symbol that was being used by Talksport. The case was settled prior to trial, with Talksport agreeing to make it clear in future off-tube broadcasts that the commentary was not coming live from the event[2].

1 For a basic outline of which, see paras D1.103 to D1.111.
2 The settlement reached between Talksport and the BBC is becoming something of an industry standard. Virgin Radio, the national commercial radio station, offered its listeners live 'completely unofficial' commentary of England's matches in the FIFA World Cup 2002.

D4.28 The problem posed by off-tube broadcasts depends on the extent to which such broadcasts undermine the commercial value of the official rights packages granted by the rights-holder. Clearly it will be far more of a problem for the official radio or text broadcaster than for the licensee of audio-visual rights. However, it does illustrate the limitations of the legal protection that can be constructed for official broadcast licensees and it should therefore be borne in mind when negotiating warranties relating to action to be taken against unauthorised pirating of the package of rights being granted.

(b) Competition rules

D4.29 The other important proviso at this stage is that the party that controls access to the venue does not necessarily control the broadcasting rights to events held at the venue. For example, an FA Premier League club will usually own its own ground and therefore control access to the ground. However, the rules of the FA Premier League ('FAPL') competition, like the rules of many other competitions, prevent member clubs from granting any broadcasting rights to FAPL matches without the consent of The FA Premier League Limited[1]. That rule is used to create a package of the broadcasting rights to all matches played at the home grounds of member clubs, ie to all of the matches in the FAPL championship, that can be sold centrally and revenues received centrally and distributed to the member clubs in accordance with predetermined criteria[2].

1 Thus, FAPL Rule 7 provides: '(1) The Company shall enter into commercial contracts in respect of broadcasting in accordance with the Memorandum and Articles of Association. (2) The Clubs undertake to provide such rights, facilities and other services as may be necessary to enable the Company to fulfil such contracts, including but not limited to providing access to enable television companies to film League Matches at the grounds of the relevant Clubs. (3) No League Matches shall be televised or recorded or transmitted by satellite or cable or any similar method without the written consent of the Board, save in the case of closed circuit television within the ground of the Club where the League Match is being played'.

2 For the competition law issues raised by such arrangements, see para B2.249 et seq.

3 EXPLOITATION OF BROADCASTING RIGHTS: RIGHTS PACKAGES

D4.30 Having established ownership and control of the content created at the event, the rights-holder is then in a position to exploit that content commercially. The traditional model was to sell all of the broadcasting rights to an event exclusively in one package to a single broadcaster. That model has bee superseded by an approach that carves the rights into separate packages, so as to maximise revenues and exposure for the sport. The packages can be divided up by content type (eg audio-visual, audio, text, data, photographs or combinations of these); by territory (regional, national, global); by time window (live, deferred as live, delayed highlights, clips); by level of exclusivity; by authorised language; and by mode of use. The packages can also be designated for exploitation by different media/on different platforms, such as television (which could be sub-divided into terrestrial, free-to-air, premium, pay-per-view, video-on-demand, interactive television, etc); radio; internet (audio-visual streaming, audio streaming, data); and mobile telephony (3G, WAP, SMS, MMS, internet[1]).

1 3G (third generation mobile telephony) is the next generation of wireless communication. When launched in the UK, 3G technology will make it possible to transmit video clips, stills, text, digitised voice and video conferencing material to mobile devices. Effectively, 3G will be able to provide the same (or similar) services to people on the move as they can now receive at home or in the office. At the time of writing, autumn 2002 is the earliest any of the UK mobile operators expect to launch 3G services. WAP is Wireless Application Protocol, which is the technical language designed to provide internet content on mobile phones. SMS is Short Messaging Service, which supports text messaging on mobile phones. MMS is Multimedia Messaging Services, which supports not only text messaging but also images, graphics, voice, video and audio clips.

D4.31 Using the above defining characteristics (and any others that may be relevant to a particular case), the rights-holder is able to 'carve' the overall broadcasting rights package into separate distinct packages of rights. Provided that the rights packages have been designed correctly, so that they complement rather than undermine each other, the rights-holder will be able to offer each rights package on an exclusive basis. It obviously becomes crucial, in the contractual documents, to define correctly and precisely every element of the rights granted to a particular licensee, particularly as technological developments continue[1].

1 For example, with mobile telephones becoming more capable of receiving the real internet (rather than just WAP), it becomes difficult to make clear distinctions between so-called mobile rights and internet rights.

D4.32 The crucial package is usually the package that includes the right to show the event live, 'as it happens', since this is usually the most valuable to broadcasters. Until broadband technology develops, the likeliest medium for this type of coverage remains television, although within that category choices will have to be made[1] between the increased rights fees and production innovations of pay-TV and the greater exposure delivered by free-TV[2] (as well as the potential for enhanced television services on digital platforms). Any other packages will have to be designed so as not to undermine the value of that exclusivity. The aim is to extract the greatest possible revenue out of the whole sporting property. To achieve that aim, the rights-holder may have to accept less revenue from its mobile telephony or internet partner in order to protect the value of the live television deal.

1 If they are not made for the rights-holder by the government. See the detail on the 'listed events' rules in the Broadcasting Act 1996 at para A1.81 et seq.
2 Which may in turn increase the demand for sponsorship rights to the event. See further para D4.84, on the use of 'minimum coverage' obligations to ensure the delivery of value to sponsor partners.

D4.33 The current strategy adopted by rights-holders seeking to protect the value of live broadcast rights is to restrict exploitation on other media/platforms by time window and by length of footage permitted to be exhibited (commonly referred to as a 'holdback'). In particular, the licensee of the live rights will usually insist that no other licensee can broadcast any part of the event on any other media platform until after (ideally long after) the licensee's live broadcast is complete.

D4.34 No doubt, the use of holdbacks that restrict the availability of premium content on new media will restrict the extent of exposure of the sport and could even be argued to stifle the advancement of the technology itself. However, this appears to be the inevitable price to be paid for protecting valuable live television rights.

D4.35 In terms of territorial packages, the carve-up is usually driven by the overseas demand for the event, as well as the global coverage of the broadcasters. Where the demand for the event is close to global, as in (for example) the FA Premier League, not even a multi-national media conglomerate such as News Corporation is going to have sufficient coverage to exploit all of the markets itself. An alternative would be to sell or license the overseas package to a specialist distributor.

D4.36 One key issue to be addressed when creating exclusive territorial packages is that of 'overspill'. 'Overspill' is the term given to the reception of a television signal in a territory in which the signal is not intended to be received. Overspill is inherent in broadcasting, particularly (but by no means only) in satellite broadcasting, because television signals do not recognise international frontiers. As such, viewers from outside a licensed broadcaster's contract territory can often (possibly with the use of the necessary decoding equipment) receive television signals that are not intended for them. The possibility of the exclusivity offered to one licensed broadcaster being undermined through overspill of a television signal from another licensed broadcaster should be dealt with in the contract with the licensed broadcaster[1].

1 See para D4.87.

D4.37 Many sports rights-holders seek to carve out so-called 'clip' or 'library' rights from the exclusive grant of rights to broadcast partners. Retaining clip or library rights within a licensed territory permits a rights-holder to authorise clips of the sporting event to be transmitted in 'magazine' style shows and elsewhere[1]. This may be particularly useful to organisers of less popular sports as it increases the sport's exposure, perhaps to a global audience and therefore hopefully its popularity.

1 Examples include Transworld Sport and Gillette World of Sport.

D4.38 In terms of the different media available for broadcast of aspects of the sports event, the rights packages should be designed so as to make the most of the particular strengths of the various media on offer. For example, viewing video footage of a sport on a mobile telephone screen will never replace video viewing on a television. However, the mobile telephone has the advantage of being always to hand. As such, the mobile device lends itself neatly to being a 'news medium'. For example, if a key incident occurs in a sporting event, anyone with a mobile phone could be alerted by a text message. Taking this further, once the requisite technology is launched, the mobile device will be an ideal medium on which to view short clips of sporting action soon after the incident has happened. The clip could be accompanied by a short piece of text updating the viewer on the current score or state of play in the event.

D4.39 Whereas mobile telephony may be seen as a 'hot news' medium, the Internet can perhaps be considered to be an 'information' medium. The Internet is where the sports enthusiast can search out information about a particular sport. The Internet rights package should be designed to fit with these strengths. For example, the Internet package could offer the sports enthusiast the chance to access delayed video clips of the event from a video archive, together with data and statistics about the event.

D4.40 If the mobile device can be considered a news medium and the Internet an information medium, then television is the 'entertainment' medium. Although doubtless the continued effect of 'convergence' will be to shrink the boundaries further between these technologies, it will take a massive shift in viewers' habits for television not to remain the main entertainment medium. As such, despite convergence, making these distinctions between the various media is likely to continue to be helpful in determining what rights should be available on which media.

D4.41 A good example of how sports rights have been carved up into different rights packages in practice is to look at the most recent media rights arrangements of the FA Premier League, which controls all media rights centrally[1]. The latest FA Premier League media deals commenced at the beginning of the 2001/02 football season and run for three seasons, ending after completion of the 2003/04 football season. The deals were negotiated during summer 2000 at the height of the dot-com boom, at which time there was unprecedented competition between broadcasters for sports rights. The Premier League took advantage of the market conditions by offering more separate packages of rights than had previously been seen in the sports broadcasting rights market (see Figure Two).

Figure Two

FAPL Rights Package	Licensee	Content
Live television (plus interactive)	BSkyB	66 live matches a season including interactive services
Pay-per-view television	BSkyB, ntl, ITV Digital	40 live matches a season
Highlights television (terrestrial broadcasts)	ITV Network	Match highlights on a delayed basis
Video-on-Demand	Video Networks	Deferred rights to the 106 live matches a season broadcast by BSkyB and the PPV operators
Mobile Telephony	Hutchison 3G	Clips of key match footage shortly after the event, broadcast by MMS
Club Rights	FAPL Clubs	Deferred rights to all the particular Club's Premier League matches for exhibition on Club Channel[2] or Club Website

1 See para D4.29.
2 At the time of writing, Manchester United, Chelsea and Middlesborough are the only Premier League clubs with dedicated Club television channels.

D4.42 The pay-per-view television, video-on-demand, mobile telephony and club rights arrangements were all new rights packages. The pay-per-view deal was the first (and at the time of writing still the only) pay-per-view offering in the UK for an on-going sporting competition, rather than just a one-off event, such as a boxing match.

D4.43 An objective of the latest FA Premier League agreements was to test the possibilities brought by the availability of new media platforms. An example of this is the agreement with Hutchison 3G for 3G mobile telephony rights, which to the best of the author's knowledge was the first UK based arrangement for the exploitation of sporting content on 3G telephones.

D4.44 The mobile network operators seem to have identified the acquisition of sports rights as a key strategy to attract customers to their particular network, perhaps in the belief that acquisition of premium sports content can act as the 'battering ram' for 3G phones as it did for subscription television. Following Rupert Murdoch, the mobile operators' strategy appears to be to use exclusive premium sports content as a way of differentiating their mobile network from that of their competitors, in what is a highly competitive market.

D4.45 The latest Premier League media deals also included more separate packages for television rights than had previously been offered in relation to one sporting property[1]. Both live packages (the 66 live matches acquired by BSkyB and the 40 live matches acquired by the pay-per-view consortium) allow the broadcasters to offer interactive services in conjunction with the live broadcasts. Interactive television lends itself to sports events. At the touch of a button, the user can access a menu through which he can place a bet on the match he is about to watch and/or access various statistics and information on the event and the teams and players. The availability of interactive services brings into focus the importance for a rights holder of securing ownership of data connected to the sporting event. If the rights holder can establish ownership of data relating to the sport that is not available elsewhere and that data attracts some form of copyright or other intellectual property rights protection[2], the rights holder can license use of that data as part of the interactive television package. The real value in owning or controlling exclusive data relating to sporting events comes from being able to license use of such data for betting purposes. Interactive television including the availability of interactive betting is regulated by the Independent Television Commission[3].

1 No doubt a crucial reason for this is to avoid a repeat of the Office of Fair Trading's action against The FA Premier League and its broadcasters in respect of the previous television arrangements. See para B2.264 et seq.
2 See para D1.63 et seq for a fuller discussion.
3 See paras D4.108 and D4.109.

4 CREATION OF BROADCAST FOOTAGE IN PRACTICE

A Host broadcasters

D4.46 Having considered how a rights holder can establish ownership of sports rights and can carve those rights up for exploitation as separate, complementary rights packages, this next section looks at the practicalities of creating footage of sporting events for access by licensees of the various rights packages for broadcast in accordance with the rights they have acquired. The focus will be on the creation of live coverage of the event, since almost all rights packages are based on access to this coverage. There may of course be events (ocean racing, extreme sports) where practicalities or production mixing requirements mean that there is no live broadcast, but rather editing in the studio, but this is the exception rather than the rule.

D4.47 **Host broadcaster arrangements** The 'host broadcaster' is the term commonly applied to the entity that produces the main live coverage, or 'live feed' for an event. Historically, the role of host broadcaster is performed by the broadcaster (or broadcasters) licensed to exhibit coverage of the event in the territory where the event takes place. The contractual arrangements with that broadcaster will oblige it to attend the event to produce the live feed and perform other duties, such as co-ordinating access to the feed by broadcasters from other territories. Usually the live feed created by the host broadcaster will be used by other licensed broadcasters for their own productions.

D4.48 The host broadcaster therefore has two distinct elements to its contract with the rights owner. Firstly it is responsible for providing services for production of the live feed on behalf of the sport rights holder and for servicing the needs of the international broadcast (and other media) licensees. Secondly, as a 'licensed broadcaster' itself, it will enjoy limited rights to broadcast the coverage it has produced in its territory.

D4.49 Delivery of feed and provision of services to licensed broadcasters The host broadcaster will generally accept an obligation to provide other licensed broadcasters with access to the feed at a suitable point. The coverage accessed by the licensed broadcaster, will either be a live signal or in tape delay format. Access to a live signal might be through a PTT (an international telecommunications gateway such as the BT Tower) or (more commonly today) at an Outside Broadcast Unit at the venue. Occasionally the point of access will be after up-link to a distribution satellite. Generally there will be no charge for accessing the live feed, but the host broadcaster will be entitled to charge for any extras provided. Where the feed is delivered by tape this will include tape, duplication and delivery costs. Additionally the host broadcaster may be obliged to deliver to the rights holder a complete copy of the feed on tape within a reasonable period following conclusion of the live event for archive purposes.

D4.50 Independent production companies Another option (often used when there is no demand for a live broadcast and therefore no host broadcaster willing to produce the feed as part of the cost of acquiring the live rights) would be for the sports right-holder to commission a specialist independent production company to produce coverage of the event. Any such arrangement should include an assignment of the copyright in the film produced by the producer to the rights-holder[1]. The rights-holder would then be able to control the exploitation of the resulting programming in some edited form (such as highlights or perhaps as part of a broader 'magazine' style programme).

1 See para D4.23.

D4.51 Rights-holder's own productions As an extension of the independent production model, some sports have grown to such a level of commercial maturity and sophistication that it makes commercial sense for them to produce their own coverage 'in-house'. This is usually done through a company controlled by the rights holder[1] or by an organisation specially established to produce the live coverage[2].

1 For example the feed for the FIFA World Cup Finals is produced by Host Broadcast Services, a company that is 100% owned by Kirch Media, holders of the broadcast rights for the 2002 and 2006 FIFA World Cups.

2 For example, the Sydney Olympic Broadcasting Organisation and Salt Lake Olympic Broadcasting Organisation were responsible for producing the feeds from the 2002 Summer and Winter Games respectively

B Licensed broadcasters

D4.52 The remainder of this section looks at how the licensed broadcasters (such as broadcasters in other territories) or other licensees (such as the mobile telephony partners) access the match footage and create their own bespoke programming or content.

D4.53 Licensed broadcasters' productions It is usually a requirement that the live feed produced by the host broadcaster will be free of graphics, save for those directed by the rights-holder (eg official timing and technology partners) with sound (crowd noise known as 'international sound') on a separate track. The licensees of other rights packages sold by the rights holder will then customise this 'clean' feed to create their own bespoke broadcasts, with commentary, studio presentation and commercial breaks as seen by viewers in their respective territories.

D4.54 It is also common at major events for licensed broadcasters to be given access to studio space or other facilities at the venue of the event, for the purpose of producing their own supporting commentary, presenter links and interviews. Adaptation of the live feed would have to be contractually permitted in the licensed broadcaster agreement and the scope of what is available will be worked out with the host broadcaster, who will provide additional services, facilities and equipment, charging on a rate-card basis.

D4.55 For exploitation of the match footage on other media, in particular internet or by mobile telephony, the licensee will need to access the live feed (or other coverage), which will then be edited, stored, re-formatted and re-purposed (if necessary) for exploitation, within the limits agreed, via these platforms.

D4.56 Broadcast services suppliers In addition to the above arrangements, a wide range of service providers operate within the sports broadcasting market (such as graphics suppliers, virtual imaging suppliers, timing partners, data and results services) to provide enhancement services. Contractual relationships will arise between these suppliers and sports rights holders, production companies, host broadcasters and licensed broadcasters.

D4.57 Audio-only production/coverage The production of audio-only coverage is a significantly simpler matter to organise than full international television quality coverage. The host broadcaster's role is to equip and co-ordinate facilities and services for other licensed broadcasters, who will generally wish to produce their own commentary with stadium ambience. The internet provides another potential platform for audio coverage with many radio stations being simultaneously transmitted via their websites, on-line and/or operators producing commentary for on-line exploitation.

D4.58 Fixed Media Fixed media, ie platforms such as video or DVD, will rarely require their own production arrangements at the venue. Instead it would be usual to use the host broadcaster's feed, edited and packaged for exploitation via these media.

5 SPORTS BROADCAST CONTRACTS

D4.59

(i) This section examines the key provisions of the host broadcaster, independent production, and licensed broadcaster contracts.

A Host broadcaster contract

D4.60 Parties An appropriate level of due diligence should be undertaken by both the rights-holder and the host broadcaster. The host broadcaster will wish to satisfy itself that the rights-owner can in fact deliver the rights to the event and secure all necessary consents and obligations from participants and stadium owners[1]. The rights-holder will look to the host broadcaster's ability to produce a live feed of the requisite quality and to meet its financial obligations[2].

1 See para D4.29.
2 See para D4.5, n 2.

D4.61 The Events The contract should set out the exact scope and nature of the sports event, which can be hard to pin down, particularly in the context of modern major sports events in which pre-match entertainment, opening ceremonies, presentation ceremonies and press conferences are the norm. For some major events, there are numerous qualifying rounds that will need to be included or excluded from the ambit of the host broadcast contract. If a match could result in a replay, this will need to be factored into the contract. Equally, the question arises as to whether the host broadcaster must arrange for all matches forming part of a tournament to be covered (and if so, to what standard) or whether just the most appealing ties will be covered (and if so, who makes the selection). A detailed schedule of timings and locations of events if available will often be attached to the contract.

D4.62 Scope of production The host broadcast contract will also need to address exactly what it is that the host broadcaster is to produce. This will usually include provision of the live feed to a required technical specification. It is usual for coverage of the live feed to start around 10 minutes before a match and end 10 minutes after (or longer if there is to be a presentation or closing ceremony or other activity, such as a coin toss, to be covered). However, in addition to the live feed, the rights-holder may wish the host broadcaster to produce regular highlights or 'round-up' or 'news' packages from other fixtures (such as all the goals from fixtures played in a particular league). Clear obligations and responsibilities need to be set out to confirm exactly what the rights-holder requires the host broadcaster to produce.

D4.63 Production Quality The host broadcast contract will seek to set minimum standards for the quality of the production. Whilst both parties wish for the event to be show-cased in a high quality production, there may be different views as to what constitutes 'high quality' (often depending on who is responsible for production costs). The host broadcast contract should set out a technical specification for the production together with minimum production standards and editorial parameters. These terms can be hard to define and in long-term contracts may become dated. Therefore, a more general standard warranty would be to produce programming of 'a high standard to be expected of a world class sporting event suitable in all respects for international broadcast purposes'.

D4.64 The contract should also contain more objective measurable provisions relating to specific technical production facilities and attributes (such as the minimum number and location of cameras, personnel and slow motion replays). Where a rights-holder is seeking a 'common look' from a number of producers, the specification will need to be detailed and should reserve a position for the rights-holder to provide further instruction if it is considered necessary.

D4.65 Editorial control It may be appropriate for the host broadcast contract to include provisions relating to editorial control. Broadcasters naturally do not wish to cede editorial control to sports administrators. On the other hand, rights-holders are likely to be sensitive to how the event is portrayed by the broadcast media. The issue is somewhat irrelevant for live coverage or for programming where speed of production (eg within two hours of the event) dictates that it is not possible to go through a protracted editorial approval process. However, the contract can be used to set out guidelines for the broadcaster to follow, including:

(1) a prohibition on any interruption of coverage during periods of play for commercial breaks[1];
(2) warranties that the production will not be obscene, blasphemous, libellous, infringe third party proprietary rights or be detrimental to the image of the relevant sport, event or its participants or bring them into disrepute;
(3) obligations to include the logos of official timings and graphics partners and the URL of the official event web site and to use the official event logos (where broadcast regulations permit);
(4) obligations not to obscure, replace or add advertising banners and other sponsorship media, by means of virtual advertising[2] or otherwise;
(5) obligations to discuss prior to the event the style and other editorial parameters for presentation of the event and related graphics, scheduling, set designs, running orders and presentational formats;
(6) detailed obligations as to the duration and scheduling of highlights;
(7) detailed commitments to on-air promotion for the event and the broadcasts; and
(8) general support for event sponsors, titles, advertising boards and backdrops.

1 This is obviously more relevant to some sports than others. For example, interruptions in coverage may not concern organisers of a golf tournament to the same extent as an organiser of a football match.
2 See para D4.103.

D4.66 Access to the venue and essential facilities and utilities There should be a provision setting out the conditions under which the host broadcaster's personnel and equipment are permitted access to the venue and to those facilities at the venue (power supply, parking for outside broadcast units, camera gantries, commentary positions, production suites etc) that are needed to produce the feed. The rights-holder should be able to grant access to these facilities either free of charge or at cost, depending largely on the terms that the rights-holder has been able to negotiate in the host venue contract. Sample wording for a venue access clause would be:

'[Rights Holder] shall procure access for the [Host Broadcaster] to the [Venues] without charge before, during and after the [Event] (at reasonable times to be agreed between the parties) for the purpose of [Host Broadcaster] performing its role as host broadcaster (including but not limited to site survey, installation, and removal of equipment, coverage of the Event).

Whilst every effort will be made by [Rights Holder] to assist [Host Broadcaster] with the installation and operation of equipment (in order to provide the very best level of television coverage and the best camera positions) it is acknowledged by [Host Broadcaster] that the installation and operation of equipment must not interfere unduly with the organisation of the [Event] and consultation should take place with [Rights Holder] as soon as practicable before the [Event] to ensure any disruption is minimised. Any displacement of seats or other facilities at the [Venue] which may reduce income available to [Rights Holder] whether for the purpose of installing equipment or otherwise, may only be effected with the prior consent of [Rights Holder].

Access to the [Venues] shall be given to accredited staff of [Host Broadcaster] who are necessary for it to perform its role as host broadcaster, together with reasonable access for vehicles.

Access to services, facilities or equipment already existing at the [Venue] which [Rights Holder] is able to make available, including but not limited to electricity, water, floodlights, commentator positions and interview rooms shall be provided to [Host Broadcaster]. Where such services, facilities or equipment are not available without charge to [Rights Holder], then [Host Broadcaster] shall meet the costs thereof.

[Host Broadcaster] shall be solely responsible for any damage, death or injury causes by its staff representatives or contractors whilst at the [Venue] and shall indemnify [Rights Holder] fully in that respect and further shall under the guidance of [Rights Holder] repair promptly any damage caused at the [Venues] by its staff, representatives or contractors[1].

1 The contract may also contain a warranty that the host broadcaster has adequate public liability insurance to cover all risks associated with producing the feed and being present at the venue.

D4.67 Delivery of feed and provision of services to licensed broadcasters The host broadcaster contract should set out the conditions under which other licensed broadcasters or media partners of the rights-holder can access the live feed produced by the host broadcaster. This should include free access to the live feed; specification that the live feed will be a 'clean' feed; identification of the point of access to the live feed (eg at the venue or telecommunications gateway such as the BT Tower), and arrangements for tape delivery.

D4.68 The host broadcaster may also be required to deliver a service (either the international feed or a version of its broadcast signal) to various corporate hospitality boxes within the venue and/or for exhibition on big screens. The rights-holder may also require the feed and any and all additional camera angles/material to be provided, at no cost, for purposes of adjudication of sporting decision by video referees and third umpires, and for after the match for disciplinary purposes.

D4.69 Intellectual property rights in the feed As set out in the table at Figure One (para D4.22), copyright will subsist in the film of the event produced by the host broadcaster and the sound recording made of the event and any broadcast. The host broadcaster contract should therefore include an assignment of copyright from the host broadcaster (as first owner of the copyright) to the rights-holder. From the rights-holder's perspective, this assignment will not only include the final version of the film created and/or any resulting programming but also all other material. Example wording of such a clause is as follows:

[Host Broadcaster] hereby assigns to [Rights Holder] by way of assignment of future copyright all copyright whether vested, future or contingent and all other intellectual property rights in its film and/or broadcast and/or recording of the Events including the picture sound and commentary tracks. To the extent that the benefit of such rights cannot be assigned under English law, then [Host Broadcaster] acknowledge that such rights are held and exercisable for the sole benefit of [Rights Holder] and hereby waives any and all so-called moral rights to the same[1].

1 Where the host broadcaster is also a licensed broadcaster within (for example) a defined territory, the contract will also need to contain an appropriate licence of copyright back from the rights-holder to the host broadcaster. See para D4.79.

D4.70 In respect of any works included within the broadcast feed and/or productions of the host broadcaster (such as music, broadcast graphics and/or scripted links), all intellectual property and related rights must be fully cleared for domestic and international distribution in all media. The host broadcaster should procure full releases and authorisations from presenters, commentators and interviewees.

B Contract with independent production company

D4.71 The contractual arrangement with an independent production company should deal with all of the key terms set out above in relation to the host broadcaster, and the following additional clauses.

D4.72 Clearance of third party rights The production company should be required to ensure that all third party copyright works (including any background music) used in the production are fully cleared for domestic and international television (and other media if necessary) distribution. This will be particularly relevant in respect of extreme sports and magazine style programming, which often feature numerous clips of sporting action set to music. Appropriate synchronisation licences will be required to cover the use of such music. The terms of such licences must be broad enough to cover the anticipated use of the programming.

D4.73 Factors to be considered when negotiating clip and music clearance provision include the number of exhibitions required, the credits required (if any), the territorial extent of the licence, which media must be covered (eg television only, or all forms of media 'whether now known or hereafter invented'), and payment (usually flat fee but sometimes a specified royalty in respect of each exhibition).

D4.74 Editorial control There is greater scope for sports rights-holders to secure editorial control over programming that they commission from independent producers, as opposed to host broadcaster productions. Where the programming does not consist of a live feed but rather of a finished weekly magazine or highlights package, then it is not uncommon for the sports rights-holder to have full rights of approval over the storyboard, running order and even the finished product. Thus, sports programming production contracts usually contain a schedule containing a full 'treatment' or editorial description of the show to be produced and rights of examination/rejection.

C Licensed broadcaster agreements

D4.75 Some of the provisions of the host broadcaster contract will also be of relevance in relation to the licensed broadcaster agreement (and of course the host broadcaster may also be granted certain rights as a licensed broadcaster).

D4.76 Payment[1] With licence fees for some sports broadcast rights running into hundreds of millions of pounds, great care and attention must be paid to the payment clause, including any instalment schedules, and in particular any comfort being offered. The ITV Digital debacle[2] has focused attention on the need to seek appropriate financial comfort, particularly in relation to start-up joint ventures, in the form of parent company or other (eg financial) guarantees.

1 In some instances the rights owner will accept the host broadcaster obligations in lieu of a rights fee.
2 See para D4.5, n 2.

D4.77 Another factor to consider taking account of in the payment clause is the inherent risk involved in televising live sports events. Matches and events can be cancelled or delayed for a number of reasons: public transport problems; floodlights failing; crowd disorder; political unrest; or even war. Whilst some or all of these events will be covered under force majeure clauses, it may be prudent from the broadcaster's perspective to agree a formula in advance to adjust the payments due if one or more events are cancelled or unduly delayed. Similarly, sports rights-holders may wish to introduce a formula to adjust the licence fee upwards if for any reason, the licensed broadcaster wishes to show more sporting action than was originally anticipated. Alternatively, if agreement is impracticable in advance, provision may be made for any non-delivery of rights to be referred to an expert to determine the value of the rights not delivered and therefore the compensation due to the licensed broadcaster[1].

1 See further para A5.13.

D4.78 It will also be important to include provisions dealing with minimisation of the risks of withholding tax and co-operation regarding recovery of the sums withheld. This may require including within the contract particular provisions detailing where and how payment is to be made to achieve the most tax efficient result.

D4.79 Licence The licensee and the rights-holder must both be fully aware of exactly what rights are being granted under the agreement. Given the recent proliferation in available media distribution platforms and modes of content exploitation, the scope for disputes regarding the extent of rights granted is significant unless the extent of the licence is very tightly defined. The exact grant of rights can be distinguished by the various defining characteristics discussed at paras D4.30 to D4.33. The basic grant could be, for example:

Subject to the provisions of this Agreement and in consideration of the payment of the licence fee by the [Broadcaster] the [Rights Holder] hereby grants to the Broadcaster on an exclusive basis the right to exhibit [Live Footage] of the Event by means of [Subscription Television] with commentary in the English language within the Territory only.

D4.80 The above is only a very basic example of the wording required to grant the appropriate licence. In practice, the contract would have to provide watertight definitions for 'Subscription Television', 'Event', and 'Live Footage' and would also deal with any ancillary rights such as news access and clip/library rights.

D4.81 Exclusivity The agreement will also set out the level of exclusivity on which the relevant rights are granted. Usually licenses of major events will be granted on an exclusive basis, ie the rights holder will not grant the same or similar rights to anyone else. However, these exclusive licences will usually be subject to certain exceptions such as news access, clip (or library) rights and overspill[1].

1 See paras D4.36, D4.37, D4.82 and D4.87.

D4.82 One carve-out from exclusivity that broadcasters have little choice but to accept is that of news access. Section 30 of the Copyright Designs and Patents Act 1988 ('CDPA 1988') introduced a 'fair dealing' exception that had not previously been available under UK law applying to the use of copyright film, sound recordings and broadcast material owned by third parties for the purpose of reporting news of the event[1]. The copyright position was tested by the BBC in an attempt to challenge British Satellite Broadcasting's (BSB)[3] use of clips from the BBC's live broadcast of the 1990 Football World Cup Finals in Sky news bulletins. The court held[2] that the use by BSB in scheduled news bulletins of recorded material taken from live transmissions fell squarely within the definition of 'fair dealing' under s 30 of the CDPA 1988. The court's decision means that recordings of key moments from sports events, such as the goals from the FA Cup Final, may be accessed and broadcast by other broadcasters in their news bulletins. In light of the court's decision, UK broadcasters drafted and agreed to adhere to the 'News Access Code of Practice'[4], which set limits and guidelines on the use of clips in news bulletins as follows:

(1) extracts can only be used within 24 hours of the original transmission and credit such as 'pictures courtesy of ITV' must be granted to the original broadcaster;
(2) extracts can only be included in news/regional news and not any sports news, sports magazine, sports review or any other programme;
(3) the news broadcaster must try to eliminate commentary contained in the original broadcast; and
(4) extracts may not be shown more than six times in news bulletins on any one channel within 24 hours of the original transmission.

1 The fair dealing exception set out in the predecessor to the CDPA 1988 did not apply to film, sound recordings or broadcasts.
2 *BBC v British Satellite Broadcasting Ltd* [1992] Ch 141, Ch D.
3 BSB is the satellite broadcaster that brought us the 'squariel' satellite dish. It merged with Rupert Murdoch's Sky television in 1992 to form BSkyB.
4 The BBC, ITV Network Ltd, ITV Regions, Channel 4, ITN, BSkyB, GMT, Channel 5 and MUTV all signed the News Code of Access.

D4.83 Holdbacks As explained above[1], it is becoming common practice for licensed broadcast contracts to set out detailed holdback periods that restrict the rights-holder's exploitation of the match footage on other media platforms. For example, there might be a 'live' window for subscription television before highlights can be broadcast on free television; no live transmission on the Internet; and specific use of very limited excerpts on a 'hot news' basis by mobile telephony operators. Sample wording would be:

Except as may be agreed in writing by the [Broadcaster], the [Rights Holder] warrants and undertakes that it shall not make available (and shall not authorise any other person to make available) live or delayed feeds, film or other material comprising moving audio-visual representations of [Matches] in the [Event] by any means or media whether now know or hereafter devised except as set out in the exceptions below:

Internet Rights and Mobile Rights

The Rights Holder or its licensees may exploit the [Internet Right] and/or [Mobile Rights]:

(i) up to a total of [5] (minutes) of excerpts from the first half of the [Match] during half-time; and

(ii) a total of [10] minutes of the [Match] following the end of the [Match].

1 See para D4.33.

D4.84 Minimum commitment To promote the sport generally, and specifically to maximise the value that it can deliver to its sponsors and other commercial partners, the rights-holder will wish to secure a minimum commitment from the broadcaster in relation to the channel on which the event is broadcast, the time of broadcast, and for how long and how often. Broadcasters are naturally reluctant to accept too restrictive a position regarding scheduling of programmes, wishing instead to maintain as much flexibility as possible.

D4.85 The rights-holder's ability to negotiate the minimum commitment it requires can depend not only on the viewing interest in the programming in question but also on the broadcaster in question. In general, it should be easier to negotiate the required minimum commitment with a pay television operator to include the event on its dedicated sports channel than it would be with a major terrestrial broadcaster to broadcast the event on its leading general entertainment channel, where the competition for airtime and values required to be delivered are much higher.

D4.86 Sub-licensing/assignment It is important for rights-holders to maintain control of exploitation of the rights in their events. Usually the licensee will not be permitted to sub-license any of its rights without the prior written approval of the rights-holder.

D4.87 Overspill Overspill is the reception of a television signal outside the territory in which it is intended to be received. Overspill provides a threat to the exclusivity offered to a licensed broadcaster within a specific territory. From the rights-holder's perspective, there should be contractual protection to minimise the potential impact of overspill both into and out of the licensed territory. Firstly, the contract should contain wording that the exclusivity granted to the broadcaster in its particular territory is subject to the possibility of overspill from licensed broadcasters in other territories, and that such overspill shall not be considered a breach of any exclusivity or other rights granted to the licensed broadcaster. Secondly, if the licensed broadcaster is a pay-television operator, it should be obliged to take steps to prevent sale and/or distribution of decoders and/or smart cards used to receive encrypted satellite transmissions outside of its contract territory[1]. Sample clauses would be:

the [Broadcaster] acknowledges that transmissions made primarily for reception outside the Territory may be capable for reception within the Territory due to the inherent inability of satellites to beam down signals which are confined to territorial boundaries ('Overspill') and the occurrence of such Overspill shall not constitute a breach of this Agreement by [Rights Holder].

the [Broadcaster] shall procure that all transmissions of the [Event] (including all point to point transmissions made for the purposes of fulfilling any signal delivery obligations) which due to Overspill are capable of outside reception outside the Territory during the Term shall be encrypted and shall not be receivable by any person outside the Territory in unencrypted form and that no device (including, but not limited to, any 'smart card' and/or any decoding equipment which is necessary to decode or decrypt such transmission) shall be knowingly authorised or enabled by or with the authority of the [Broadcaster] so as to permit any person to view any such transmission outsider the Territory during the Term in an intelligible form.

1 This was the case with the negotiations in Germany between Kirch Media and the broadcasters ARD and ZDF in relation to television rights to the 2002 FIFA World Cup Finals. The broadcasters wished to boost the profile of their recently-launched digital satellite service by broadcasting World Cup matches unencrypted via satellite. Kirch Media noted that the unencrypted service would be capable of being received across Europe and that this would undermine the exclusivity of its other television rights deals. ARD and ZDF were requested either to pay a rights fee that reflected the fact that the broadcast would be available throughout Europe, or encrypt the broadcasts such that they were only accessible to German viewers. Both ARD and ZDF opted to encrypt their broadcasts. Kirch's stance protected the investments made by licensed broadcasters, particularly those operating pay-TV channels, in territories in which ARD or ZDF's coverage would have been receivable.

D4.88 Reporting requirements Usually an obligation will be placed upon the licensed broadcaster to deliver detailed audience viewing figures for its broadcasts, together with other appropriate information such as demographic profiling. This information will be used by the rights-holder in relation to the sale of sponsorship and broadcasting rights to future events.

D4.89 Access to Live Feed The broadcast licence agreement should set out the arrangements under which the licensed broadcasters will access the live feed produced by the host broadcaster. Access to the feed is likely to be free at the venue or telecommunications gateway. In practice, the licensed broadcaster will often liaise directly with the host broadcaster for such access. Sample wording would be:

In relation to any [Match] or part of the [Event] attended by the Host Broadcaster in fulfilment or exercise of its coverage obligations [Rights Holder] hereby grants to [Licensed Broadcaster] free of charge access to the [Feed] at the Venue from the Host Broadcaster's production truck or at [the British Telecom Tower] for the purposes of exercising the [Rights] granted to it under this Agreement.

D4.90 Broadcast sponsorship Broadcast sponsorship is the broadcast of the event, rather than the sponsorship of the event[1]. In effect it is a form of television advertising whereby brands are able to associate themselves with sports programming more closely than by simply purchasing airtime in scheduled advertising slots. Broadcast sponsorship in the UK is characterised by opening and closing credits and 'break bumpers' (the short sponsored clips or graphics immediately before and after the broadcast of the programme and either side of commercial breaks).

1 See para D4.102 for a brief discussion of regulatory aspects of broadcast sponsorship.

D4.91 Broadcasters tend to claim ownership of the right to sell broadcast sponsorship rights because it is the broadcast of the programming that is the subject of broadcast sponsorship rather than the event itself. However, the rights-holder has an interest in maximising the benefit and exposure for its own event sponsors and should also look to prevent a competitor of an event sponsor 'ambushing'[1] the event sponsorship by securing broadcast sponsorship rights[2]. The potential for conflict is obvious[3]. A widely-used compromise is for the contract with the licensed broadcaster to require that:

(a) the broadcaster first offers the right to sponsor the broadcast to existing event sponsors; and

(b) if the event partners do not take up the offer to sponsor the broadcast, the broadcast sponsor appointed by the broadcaster may not be a competitor in the brand sector of any of the event sponsors.

For example:

[Rights Holder] hereby confirms that [Broadcaster] may enter into programme sponsorship agreements in relation to the [Television Rights] subject to the following conditions:

(a) no such programme sponsor shall other than with the prior written approval of [Rights Holder] be a competitor in business or product category of any existing [Event Sponsor] or [Official Supplier] of the [Rights Holder];

(b) [Broadcaster] shall first offer the opportunity to become programme sponsor to the existing [Event Sponsor] and if the [Event Sponsor] declines to accept such offer Broadcaster shall then offer the opportunity to become programme sponsor to all other [Official Suppliers] of the [Rights Holder] on a first come first served basis. Said offers to be on reasonable terms. In the event that the [Event Sponsor] and all other [Official Suppliers] decline said offer within 14 days then [Broadcaster] may negotiate with other commercial entities to become programme sponsors PROVIDED THAT [Broadcaster] shall not enter into any such programme sponsorship agreement on terms more favourable to the programme sponsor than those declined by any Event Sponsors without first giving such Event Sponsor the right to accept such terms; and PROVIDED FURTHER THAT [Broadcaster] shall not in any event appoint as programme sponsors any company whose products or services compete with the products or services of the Event Sponsor or the [Official Suppliers].

1 See para D1.132.

2 For example, UEFA retains all broadcast sponsorship rights for the Champions League, and so Ford and Amstel beer (both of whom are official Champions League sponsors) have sponsored ITV's coverage of the Champions League.

3 See further paras D5.199 and D5.120.

D4.92 Event sponsorship The rights-holder will also look for the licensed broadcasters to support any official sponsor's rights directly, including (subject to prevailing broadcast regulations) obligations on the broadcaster to refer to a title sponsor when referring to the name of the event in commentary and/or on broadcast graphics. To further protect the event sponsor's rights, the rights holder should consider including provisions prohibiting the modification or obscuring of sponsors' banners and signage by virtual imaging or other means[1].

1 See para D1.132.

D4.93 Access to venue and production rights The agreement may contain provisions entitling the licensed broadcaster is able to access the venue for the purposes of adding its own commentary, presenter links and interviews to the live feed. Such additions mean that the broadcast of the event in a particular territory may be customised in accordance with the presentation style of the particular channel. The contract will also need to address whether or not broadcast graphics may be added to the live feed to customise it further to the requirement of the licensed broadcaster. Where access to the venue is to be granted, this will be a matter for liaison with the host broadcaster.

D4.94 Additional rights The licensed broadcaster contract should also address the rights and obligations of broadcasters to use content and/or otherwise associate themselves with the event and promote their coverage on websites and other media. It is necessary to protect the value of these rights for the rights-holder and to protect their other commercial partners but also to enable full promotion to take place on complementary media. Host broadcasters are sometimes granted rights to place signage on pitch-side advertising hoardings. In addition broadcasters expect that tickets will be available and for very popular events will specify a number of tickets to be provided. Other advertising opportunities or hospitality opportunities may also be required.

D Other content licence agreements

D4.95 The foregoing discussion will also apply with respect to other content licence agreements, such as arrangements for exploitation of sports content on mobile phones or via the internet. The main difference between a licensed broadcast agreement and (for example) an agreement for exploitation of content on mobile telephony will be the extent of the licence granted. The two rights packages will offer differing content, delivered to end users by different means and on different technology, all of which will need to be addressed in the grant of rights in the licence and in the holdback and other restrictive provisions.

6 REGULATION OF SPORTS BROADCASTING

D4.96 One of the most important bodies of external regulation for purposes of the exploitation of sports broadcasting rights is EC (and UK) competition law. Because of the market power that exclusive rights to elite sports programming are perceived to confer on their licensees, and because of the perceived need for a free and open market in those rights to encourage investment and innovation in the media and technology markets, the EC and UK competition regulators have looked at the sports broadcasting market with more intensity than they have considered any other aspect of the sports sector. The competition regulators have considered issues such as collective selling of broadcasting rights, collective purchasing of broadcasting rights (by the European Broadcasting Union), the length and scope of exclusive grants of broadcasting rights to particular events, black-out rules, and other matters. The competition regulators' views on these issues have had a substantial impact on the ability of the holders of elite sports rights to exploit those rights as they see fit, and their rulings must therefore be studied carefully. However, these matters are dealt with at length elsewhere in this book[1] and therefore will not be repeated here.

1 See Chapter B2.

D4.97 Also covered elsewhere in this book[1] is the highly significant 'listed events' legislation, which protects public access to certain designated sports events by prohibiting the grant of exclusive broadcasting rights to those events to anyone other than the BBC, ITV or Channel 4 save in very narrow circumstances.

1 See para A1.81 et seq.

D4.98 Instead, this section of this chapter addresses the other main bodies of regulation of the sports broadcasting rights market.

D4.99 Broadcast Regulation In most countries television and radio broadcasting is a highly regulated area, certainly more so than the Internet. Reasons why broadcasting is so heavily regulated include the fact that until the introduction of multi-channel digital television, there was only a limited range of broadcast frequencies available and it was considered that this limited range of frequencies should be allocated to broadcasters producing programming in accordance with the public interest. A further reason for regulation is that television is a passive medium: if a viewer switches on to a particular channel, they will see whatever is being broadcast at that time. By this reasoning, the more that television becomes an interactive media, the less it will require regulation.

D4.100 The main European regulation is the EU Directive 'Television without Frontiers' ('the Directive')[1]. The Directive seeks to regulate broadcasting across the EU and EEA, because (according to the preamble to the Directive) broadcasting is one way of pursuing the Community objective of establishing a closer union amongst the European population. The main relevance of the Directive for present purposes is the mechanism it provides for reciprocal recognition and enforcement by member states of other member states' 'listed events'[2].

1 Directive 89/552 EEC.
2 See Chapter A1.

D4.101 In the UK, commercial broadcasting[1] is regulated by the Independent Television Commission (ITC), which was established under the provisions of the Broadcasting Act 1990. All UK broadcasters other than the BBC[2] must have the appropriate ITC licence in order to operate a broadcasting service. All ITC licensees are required to comply with the various Codes drawn up by the ITC, which among other things governs standards and practice in programme content, advertising and programme sponsorship. The ITC Codes also bring into effect certain provisions from the Directive. The ITC Codes with the most relevance to sports broadcasting are the ITC Code of Programme Sponsorship and the ITC Code on Sports and Other Listed Events. Full-length versions of these Codes (and all other ITC Codes) can be found on the ITC's website[3].

1 Ie all television channels other those operated by the BBC.
2 Although not an ITC licensee, the BBC is subject to the legislation on listed events and therefore the regulations on listed events as set out in the relevant ITC Code. See para A1.88 et seq.
3 See www.itc.org.uk.

D4.102 The Sponsorship Code The ITC Code of Programme Sponsorship sets out the rules for the sponsorship of television programmes and gives effect in the UK to a number of requirements relating to television sponsorship set out in the Directive. The sponsorship code provides regulations relating to (amongst other things) maximum length of sponsor's clip, the wording of the sponsor's credit and prohibited sponsors[1].

1 See further paras D4.112 to D4.118.

D4.103 Use of Virtual Advertising[1] Virtual advertising is the name given to electronic imaging systems used to insert advertising or other commercial messages on the broadcast footage of an event[2]. This technology could be used to expand the market for event sponsors by altering (or adding to) the received broadcast of advertising at events to suit different markets. The technology would enable a sponsor of an international event to target different markets by advertising different brands in each receiving country. The rights-holder could sell the same advertising space many times over to different advertisers in each receiving nation. However, virtual advertising is heavily regulated by various different jurisdictions.

1 See Enser 'Regulating a Virtual World' (2001) Sportbusiness.com, 17 May.
2 For example, it is possible to use this technology to insert an advert for Coca-Cola within the centre-circle during a football match, such that for television viewers it appears as if the branding is actually present on the pitch.

D4.104 For example, the ITC has developed guidelines[1] for use of electronic imaging systems that are intended to regulate use of the technology for a trial period. The ITC's position is that because virtual advertising works by altering the broadcast signal, precautions must be taken to ensure that the broadcaster (ie the ITC licensee) does not lose editorial control of the television signal. The key ITC guidelines are:

(a) where a programme uses electronic imaging systems, this must be made transparent to viewers, ie there should be some form of notice explaining that the technology is being used[2];
(b) electronic imaging systems may only be used to replace existing advertising signage at an event;
(c) the broadcaster must have the contractual right to refuse to carry an electronically altered signal, such right to be exercised at the broadcaster's reasonable discretion; and
(d) the broadcaster must not in any way be involved in selling 'virtual' advertising to advertisers.

1 The full text of the guidelines is available on the ITC website, www.itc.org.uk.
2 Suggested wording from the ITC is: 'This broadcast uses electronic imaging to replace some of the actual advertising billboards at the sports arena with advertising aimed at the UK market'.

D4.105 FIFA has its own guidelines that apply to the use of virtual advertising during the broadcast of football matches. These guidelines allow use of virtual advertising only on the pitch when the teams are not on the field and on areas in the stadium that are already used for advertising or other flat areas that could potentially be used for advertising.

D4.106 Although the Directive does not expressly mention virtual advertising, Chap IV, Art 10(1) of the Directive provides that advertising should be recognisable as such and should be kept separate from the programme service. Therefore, if use of virtual advertising is such that the advertising is no longer separate and distinct from the programming, this could amount to a breach of the Directive. Although they are not expressly stated as such, the guidelines of the ITC on virtual advertising provide an interpretation of the relevant provisions of the Directive.

D4.107 A UK commercial television broadcaster wishing to broadcast a football match would have to comply with both the FIFA and ITC Guidelines and also the Directive. Rights-holders wishing to exploit the potential of virtual advertising may well find these guidelines restrictive. Rather perversely (given that it does not carry advertisements) the BBC may well present the best opportunities for rights-holders wishing to exploit virtual advertising technology. The BBC is not subject to the ITC Guidelines and it might accept the use of virtual advertising on its programmes if this means paying lower rights fees[1].

1 The BBC would have to clear use of virtual advertising in line with the BBC's charter.

D4.108 Interactive Television[1] The ITC has produced a guidance note on Interactive Television[2], to be read in conjunction with the other ITC Codes. The note sets out the ITC's approach to regulation of the content of interactive television services, including interactive television betting. In summary, the ITC has taken the view that interactive television requires a light regulatory touch and that it would not be appropriate to develop 'new regulation' for interactive services. The rationale behind this approach is that unlike in standard linear one way television, viewers of interactive television are 'pulling' content; having chosen an interactive option, they are by definition exercising control over it. Their expectations, as a result, can be different.

1 See para D4.45.
2 ITC *Guidance to Broadcasters on the regulation of interactive television services* (February 2001), available from the ITC website at www.itc.org.uk.

D4.109 The ITC's main regulatory concerns for interactive television are to ensure that viewers are clear about what kind of environment they are in, and that programme integrity is effectively maintained. In practice, this has meant that broadcasters wishing to offer interactive betting have ensured that the viewer must go through certain processes to be able to place a bet and cannot do so simply by pressing one button whilst watching a programme.

CHAPTER D5

SPORTS SPONSORSHIP

Warren Phelops (Nicholson Graham & Jones)*

Contents

1 CURRENT TRENDS IN THE UK MARKET

D5.1 The global sports sponsorship market was valued at US $15 billion last year[1]. It is estimated that the global sports sponsorship market will grow to $16.8 billion by the end of 2005, $4.9 billion of which will be in Europe[2]. There was an estimated £422m spent on sports sponsorship in the UK in 2001[3]. As the growth in the value of sports rights fluctuates in a period of uncertainty, sponsorship appears to be re-emerging as a key revenue stream to sports rights holders. One recent report[4] estimates that whilst the growth in the value of European sports television rights will slow from 30% per year (1995 to 2000) to 8% per year (2001 to 2005), European sports sponsorship's growth will decline at a much slower rate from 15% per year (1995–2000) to 10% per year (2001–2005). If accurate, the sports sponsorship market will become relatively increasingly important to sports rights owners.

* With the assistance of other members of the Nicholson Graham & Jones Sports Group.

1 Dresdner Kleinwort Wasserstein's *The business of sport* (May 2001) quoting its source as Sponsorship Research International, Zenith Media, DKWR.
2 Arksports, June 2002.
3 Sport Business Group Information Resources, Ipsos UK Sportscan.
4 Oliver & Ohlbaum Associates Ltd *Prospects for European Sport Business to 2006* (November 2001).

D5.2 Whilst companies came under increasing pressure to slash the amount they were spending on advertising during the second half of 2001, sponsorship seems not to have been so affected. One factor is that sponsorship deals are generally for reasonably long periods and more difficult to withdraw from as the sponsor is contractually committed to paying the rights holder. Others include the continuing television channel proliferation creating fragmented viewership and new technologies (such as TiVo) both of which are reducing the potency of media advertising.

D5.3 There were also new sponsorships last year including Toyota committing itself to paying £80m over four years to sponsor ITV's Formula One coverage and Norwich Union investing £20m, over a five year period, in UK athletics[1]. 2002 may also prove a good year. Unilever was reported to be substantially moving its marketing investment towards sponsorship, adding an extra US $200m to its sponsorship budget for 2002[2].

1 Hollis Sponsorship & Donations Year Book 2002.
2 'Sponsorclick Revamps Its Forecast Up For Global Sponsorship Market Growth' *Pressbox.co.uk* (26 May 2002).

2 WHAT IS SPONSORSHIP?

D5.4 The term sponsorship describes an investment in cash or kind in an activity, in return or access to the exploitable commercial and marketing potential associated with that activity. Sports sponsorship is generally either of an event, a league, a governing body, a particular team or individual or the broadcast of an event. Those capable of being sponsored are, in marketing speak, commonly referred to as 'properties', and the ability to associate oneself with a property is known as a 'right'.

D5.5 Sponsorship is a 'below the line' form of advertising, that is, advertising which is not carried by the traditional media. Rather than actually paying for brand advertising in the media, a sponsor is able to raise awareness indirectly, such as by its name being mentioned in an event title, or having its logo on athletes' clothing or on stadium advertising boards.

3 WHY SPONSOR SPORT?

D5.6 Sponsorship has historically enabled accurate targeting of, and often provided a more cost effective outlet to, the public than television and radio advertising. Sports fans appear intensely loyal to particular sports and particular events. Sponsorship also generally provides a constant clutter free platform where marketing messages can be delivered free from those of competitors. Contrast this with television advertising where the platform is intermittent (ie during programme breaks) and can include competitor advertising. Accordingly, sponsors are likely to continue to compete furiously to be associated with prime sports properties.

D5.7 Particular sporting events have the advantage of delivering a large number of viewers and spectators within a very narrow demographic band. When the brewers Bass needed to attract a target market of 18 to 24 year old men in the 'C1/C2' social group for its Carling Black Label brand, it successfully identified football sponsorship as a vehicle for its marketing given the enormous slice of this target group which is exposed to Premier League football. More recently, telecoms company Redstone has used its association with the Welsh Rugby Union not only to raise awareness, but to launch its brand to a specific corporate market.

D5.8 Sports sponsorship is also a tool used by little known brands to create quickly mass brand awareness. Green Flag's public awareness was greatly heightened by its England Team sponsorship. Axa, the French based insurance and financial services company, has used sports sponsorship successfully to build its brand. Initially it sponsored the English Cricket County Championship, and then turned its attention to a four year sponsorship of the FA Cup in 1999. A quoted report from Axa stated that prompted awareness of the Axa name grew from 36% to 77% over the term of the sponsorship, while spontaneous awareness grew from 3% to 10% over the same period[1]. Once a company such as Axa has developed brand awareness it can use this as a basis to develop consumer knowledge in its products.

1 (2002) Financial Times, 20 May.

D5.9 Well established brands have long used sports sponsorship to maintain public awareness. Coca-Cola has a long term relationship with the Wimbledon Tennis Championships, the Olympics and the FIFA World Cup. Heineken was the first, and remains the, title sponsor of club rugby union's European Rugby Cup. NatWest has a well established association with English cricket, first by sponsoring a domestic knock-out cup and then by its current sponsorship of international one day cricket taking place in England. Sports events have also become synonymous with their sponsors because they have been sponsored by one brand for so long. The Embassy World Snooker Championship taking place annually at the Crucible Theatre in Sheffield is an excellent example.

D5.10 Increasingly, some sponsorship relationships are becoming more innovative so that those involved have developed what is far more than a simple rights owner/sponsor relationship. One of the most talked about sponsorship deals is that between Nike and the Brazilian football federation. It is reported that this ten year, £250m, shirt sponsorship deal commits the Brazilian national team to playing five (now reduced to two) Nike sponsored games each year[1]. Nike can then sell or place the worldwide TV rights in these games, further enhancing its global exposure and image by associating itself with one of football's all time great brands.

1 'Game, Set and Match' *Marketing Week* (28 August 1997).

4 HOW DO SPONSORSHIP AND ADVERTISING INTERACT?

D5.11 Sponsorship and advertising are not mutually exclusive. They are communication tools that are commonly used in tandem. The questions asked when deciding on a marketing campaign are how much money is there to spend and what are the objectives? If the objective is to communicate a detailed product message, advertising may be more appropriate. If the objective is to raise general brand awareness, sponsorship may be more appropriate. However, if there is little public awareness about a company's goods or services, that company will not get as much value out of a sponsorship opportunity if it is not backed up with an advertising campaign.

D5.12 When deciding to sponsor an event, a key point is how much extra leverage can be gained from related activities. The sponsor should ensure it has the rights, for example, to run promotions, competitions or advertisements that focus on the sponsorship. As a good, but non-sports example, Nescafe launched its sponsorship of the Friends television series with a party in Central Park, New York. It also placed short advertisements directly before and after each segment of the television programme showing people sitting around drinking Nescafe coffee.

5 VALUING SPONSORSHIP

D5.13 The valuation of sponsorship rights is not an exact science – there is no universally agreed measure. From the sponsor's perspective, valuation techniques are constantly evolving due to the increasingly complex ways that exposure may be given through various media. A company may sponsor an event for many different reasons, from brand awareness even to the corporate hospitality on offer. The valuation will, therefore, depend upon the sponsor's objectives. The sponsor must set out the realistic objectives it hopes to achieve from the sponsorship and then decide how it intends to measure these objectives. If the intention is to reach the widest possible audience then figures based upon television audience or website hits can assist in putting a value on the sponsorship. Some sponsors view the 'ancillary' rights as equally or more valuable – for example, a shirt sponsorship by telecoms companies who may acquire content rights for their platforms as part of the arrangements.

D5.14 One difficulty with valuing sponsorship where it is used as a tool to enhance general brand awareness rather than a particular product, is that it then becomes difficult to measure whether there is any direct influence on sales. The most obvious way to value sponsorship is to use general tracking and marketing studies to determine the effect the sponsorship has on public awareness about a sponsor's brand and image. However, this can be contrasted with some sponsorships by fast-moving consumer goods companies, who will launch specific new brands/varieties of their products linked directly to the sponsorship and use the anticipated profits on sales of the new products as the yardstick for valuing the sponsorship.

D5.15 A sponsor may be able to compare the worth of its sponsorship to the cost of purchasing a similar amount of advertising time. It can add up the total amount of time its brand and logo was visible during a broadcast or its name was mentioned on television or radio and calculate whether the sponsorship is cost-effective. It is for the sponsor to decide whether the coverage is worth the same as a unique advertising space. A sponsor should consider the worth of quality media exposure with favourable coverage rather than just the volume of exposure.

D5.16 From the event owner's perspective, it will want to value the rights as high as possible. The event owner will need to determine the lowest price acceptable and to do this it will need to determine the actual cost of obtaining and running the sponsorship. Items of cost will include tickets, hospitality, signage production and erection, marketing, legal and accountancy costs. The owner can then factor in the profit margin it wishes to achieve and have some indication on the sort of price it should be asking.

6 TYPES OF SPONSORSHIP

D5.17 The various ways in which a sponsor can be associated with a sports 'property' are set out below.

D5.18 **Stadium or venue sponsorship** The Reebok Stadium in Bolton is an obvious example. Often a 'naming rights' deal is a crucial part of financing a new sports venue – as with Leicester City's new ground, the 'Walker's Bowl'[1].

1 Leicester City PLC interim results for the six months ended 31 January 2002.

D5.19 **Title or event sponsorship** This is where a company is the sole or main sponsor of an event and is discussed in great detail later in this chapter. Often it is accompanied by the right for the sponsor to have its name in the event's title, for example, in football the FA Barclaycard Premiership and in rugby the Zurich Premiership. In such arrangements, the title sponsor generally has the pick of the advertising and promotional opportunities which are available. Secondary sponsors are only able to take subordinated or ancillary rights to the title sponsor. Occasionally, a title sponsorship arrangement will prohibit any other sponsors being associated with the event or having core rights (such as perimeter signage) associated with any sponsorship.

D5.20 **Secondary sponsorship** For example, of one of the matches or races forming part of the event. In horse racing, individual sponsors often select a particular race on the card rather than sponsor the whole race meeting.

D5.21 **Official supplier status** The sponsor becomes the official supplier of a product or service or range of products or services it wishes to associate with the event for marketing purposes.

D5.22 **Broadcast sponsorship** Namely sponsorship of the television, radio, online or other media platform broadcast of the event. The sponsor of the broadcast enters into a separate arrangement with the broadcaster and, therefore, the broadcast sponsor may be different to the event sponsor.

D5.23 **Player sponsorship** These are generally characterised as individual endorsements and commonly involve sponsoring an individual to wear kit made by the sponsor, to display the sponsor's mark and/or otherwise for the sports star to associate him or herself with the sponsor's products or services. Associating a brand with an individual tends to be a more risky strategy than sponsoring an event, team or federation. In allying itself so closely with one individual, a sponsor becomes dependent on the whims of an elite athlete's personality or performance. If that individual behaves erratically or badly, or if his or her standard of performance dips significantly, this can adversely impact on the sponsorship message (as would an individual being seen using a competitor's products). Although a sponsor can negotiate what is often referred to as a 'morality clause' into a contract[1], often it is too late to rely on such a contractual remedy before any public relations damage is done.

1 See para D5.131.

D5.24 Brands such as Pepsi and Walker's Crisps have long used personalities to promote their products. Police sunglasses have used David Beckham's association as a launch for their product. Indeed sportswear manufacturers such as Nike and Adidas see it as an absolute necessity to have their equipment worn by top athletes. Contrast this with other leading brands who shy away from using personal endorsements for product promotion, as, in their view, consumers tend to pay more attention to the personality than the product being promoted. Whilst image rights and endorsement are dealt with more fully in Chapter D3, the following are some of the key provisions for any brand owner to consider when entering into any endorsement arrangement:

- A grant in favour of the brand owner of an exclusive right to use the athlete's endorsement (name, likeness, photograph, signature etc) within a particular territory. The exclusivity may be limited to the brand owner's area of products or services.
- A restriction on other sponsorships being undertaken by the athlete. Any brand owner must be particularly careful to ensure that the athlete is not sponsored by a brand in the same market sector.
- An obligation on the athlete to display the brand owner's logo on his clothing and when he or she should do this. The contract should specify the size and shape of the logo, and its precise location on the athlete's apparel (ie centre of helmet, left shirt sleeve etc). It is advisable to specify the location as precisely as possible, using measurements where necessary.
- An obligation for the athlete to make a certain number of personal appearances at the brand owner's promotional days, such as to appear in the brand owner's hospitality tent at a sporting event or attend photo shoots. The contract should specify the amount of time for which the athlete should attend and the circumstances in which an attendance can be cancelled – limited to illness or injury, if possible. The athlete should also be placed under an obligation at least to reimburse the brand owner's costs in the event that he or she fails to appear.
- If the athlete fails to comply with his or her obligations to perform, unless the contract has been structured carefully, there is a limited amount that any brand owner can do other than take court action seeking damages. Sensible drafting of the payment clause should ensure that payment is staged, enabling a brand owner to withhold further payments if services are not performed. Payment may also be linked to athlete playing performance, for example establishing a payment link between a golfer's accrual of Tour Championship points and payment. In reality, however, many brand owners will have to accept the possibility of poor playing performance as a risk in any sponsorship arrangement.

D5.25 The remainder of this chapter focuses on title sponsorship of a major sports event which takes place inside a stadium. Other types of sports events present their own problems for sponsors, for example 'grass roots' sponsorship, where, for instance, peculiar financing considerations may apply. These include the possibility of funding from lottery monies or from the government's Sportsmatch Scheme (administered by the Institute of Sports Sponsorship (ISS)) which matches £1 for £1 monies invested by a sponsor in a qualifying, grass roots scheme[1].

1 See further paras C3.65 to C3.70.

D5.26 The ISS itself aims to promote best practise in sponsorship and works closely with sports bodies, the government and the media to improve understanding. It keeps its members informed of important legislation concerning sports sponsorship and members can get advice on specific matters such as contract negotiation and sponsorship valuation[1].

1 Further information can be obtained from the ISS website at www.sports-sponsorship.co.uk.

D5.27 This chapter will now review the issues peculiar to these types of sports 'properties'.

7 RIGHTS AND PROPERTIES – LEGAL OWNERSHIP

D5.28 So far use has been made of the commercial vernacular of sponsorship 'rights' owned by, or attaching to, sports 'properties'. In the UK sponsorship rights are owned or, perhaps, better described as 'controlled' through a series of contracts entered into by the entity running and organising the event (described in this chapter as the event owner).

D5.29 There is no such thing as a proprietary right in a sports event in English law[1]. Cases normally relied on as authority for this are from Australia and Canada and have held that no such property right exists[2]. This seems to have been accepted by implication in *BBC v Talksport*[3] where Blackburne J identified the broadcasting rights to Euro 2000 as the 'right to broadcast on radio and television, live coverage of the matches from within the stadia where they are taking place'. By implication such rights of the owner of the event cannot extend to coverage outside the stadia. The event owner's rights must, therefore, rest on owning or controlling access to the stadia and not on any proprietary right in the event itself.

1 See generally paras D1.5 to D1.13.
2 See for example, *Victoria Park Racing and Recreation Grounds Co Ltd v Taylor* (1937) 58 CLR 479; and *NHL v Pepsi Cola Canada* (1995) 122 DLR (4th) 412. See para D1.7 et seq.
3 *BBC v Talksport Ltd* [2001] FSR 53.

D5.30 Neither is there any intellectual property right in most types of sport or sports activity[1], as sports events (except for anomalies such as ice dancing) are not dramatic works protected by the Copyright Designs and Patents Act 1988 and, therefore, are not capable of copyright protection in their own right[2].

1 See Phelops 'Can Sport Move In Mysterious Ways?' *Copyright World* (September 1996), p 17.
2 See *FWS Joint Sports Claimants v Copyright Board* (1991) Canadian Federal Court of Appeal 81, PLR 4th 412 3 June 1991. See further paras D1.51 to D1.53.

D5.31 In the US the position is less clear. In one case, it was decided at first instance that the defendants had engaged in unfair competition in violation of

New York common law through their commercial misappropriation of the plaintiff's proprietary interests in the plaintiff's games[1].

1 *National Basketball Association and NBA Properties Inc v Sports Team Analysis and Tracking Systems Inc* 939 F Supp. 107 (SDNY 3 September 1996).

D5.32 However, on appeal in January 1997[1], the Second Circuit Court of Appeals in New York reversed the original decision and held that the appellants had not engaged in unlawful misappropriation. The court held that, whilst there is copyright in a recorded broadcast of a sports event, there is no property right in the event itself (also, seemingly, the UK position). There has been criticism of the decision and, therefore, the US position may be re-visited.

1 105 F 3d 841 (2d Cir 1997).

D5.33 One of the keys to maintaining control of (and thereby maintain the ability to grant exclusive rights in relation to) a sports event is to control access to that event. This can be problematical for events which take part on, or near, publicly accessible land. Preventing non-authorised access to, or television coverage of, events such as marathons or sailing or speed boating events is incredibly difficult. In such circumstances an event owner has to be absolutely sure that, in practice, it can deliver the exclusive rights which it has contractually committed to do.

D5.34 A sponsor should, therefore, ensure that the event owner has secured all the necessary constituent rights from third parties such as contracting with participants in the event, the venue owner, any relevant governing body or federation and arranging television coverage.

8 THE SPONSORSHIP CONTRACT

D5.35 The key provisions of the contract between the sponsor and event owner are set out below.

A The Parties

D5.36 The sponsor should ensure it is contracting with the right party, that is, the owner of the rights. This will involve requiring the event owner to produce copies of the relevant contracts with third parties to confirm the event owner's capacity to grant to the sponsor the necessary rights it will require.

D5.37 Both parties must have capacity and authority to enter into the contract. Commonly, a UK event owner will be a sports governing body often legally constituted either as an unincorporated association or as a company limited by guarantee[1]. The constitutional documents (the rules in the case of the former, and the memorandum and articles of association in the case of the latter) will need to be checked to ensure the event owner can enter into the agreement.

1 See generally Chapter C1.

D5.38 For unincorporated associations, those persons claiming authority to enter into the sponsorship contract on behalf of the association must be verified by checking the rules (or, in the case of trustees entering into the contract, the trust deed) to confirm their power to contract and bind association members.

D5.39 Where the event owner is a representative body, the sponsor should ensure that its members (normally the participating clubs) have ceded to the representative body, either under its constitution or its rules or through a separate arrangement, sponsorship and other marketing and media rights necessary for the sponsor to carry out its full marketing programme contemplated by the contract.

D5.40 Where a sponsorship package is being bought from an agent, it must be absolutely clear that the agent has all the rights it is purporting to sell. Furthermore, it is crucial that a sponsor should be comfortable that if the agent should get into financial difficulties or even falls bankrupt or insolvent, that the sponsor will either get all of its money back or have the rights delivered in full. Sponsors would be wise to have the relevant rights owner as a party to the contract with its agent. If not possible then, as a bare minimum, the sponsor should insist on a separate rights owner guarantee or, if not possible, comfort letter confirming that the rights owner will step into the agent's shoes in the event of difficulties with delivery by, or the insolvency of, the agent[1].

1 See further Chapter D8.

B The Term

D5.41 The duration of the grant of the rights can be agreed in a number of ways. For example, if the event is a cup competition or a season, the duration will be linked to a period defined by the duration of the competition in any one or more years.

D5.42 If the sponsorship is to be of a number of events within a specified term, the contract should provide not only for the duration of the sponsorship but also the number of events that it is to cover within that period.

D5.43 Often there is an option to renew at the end of the fixed period. The renewal option could be absolute or conditional, often on matching the best offer made by a third party on any sale of the rights once the original term expires in circumstances where the event owner and incumbent sponsor's original renewal discussions did not lead to agreement.

C The Territory

D5.44 Generally a sponsor will require world-wide rights. Any exploitation of these rights on a world-wide basis will, however, depend on a number of factors, including the coverage of the event.

D5.45 Ideally the sponsor will not want the event owner to split the sponsorship rights territorially. However, new technology regarding manipulation of audio-visual footage of the event, such as the ability to superimpose different advertisements electronically on advertising boards at the venue[1], could permit the rights owner to sell the sponsorship or advertising rights to sponsors in different territories, which may not be an issue to the sponsor if it does not wish to target those territories. On the other hand, a sponsor with world-wide rights may wish to take advantage of the new technology and use it to promote different brands in different territories.

1 See para D4.103 et seq.

D The Sponsor's Rights

D5.46 Most event sponsorship arrangements will include many of the following rights.

(a) Naming rights

D5.47 The right to incorporate the sponsor's name in the title (and trophy) of the event in all pre- and post-event publicity (such as match programmes, posters, websites, television, radio and other media promotions).

D5.48 The parties must consider whether such rights are exclusive, how the sponsor may be described (which may be by a particular or range of products or services the sponsor wishes to profile or the corporate entity in its entirety) and what the event name should be. Depending upon bargaining strength, the event may be named after the sponsor, for example, the Worthington Cup, or retain its current name, but expressed to be 'supported by' or 'in association with' the sponsor, for example, the FA Cup sponsored by Axa. The latter, of course, proffers less profile to a sponsor and the event is less likely to become synonymous with the sponsor's name.

D5.49 Included in naming rights are rights of 'designation', ie rights for a sponsor to describe itself in a way that explains its relationship with the event, such as the 'official' or 'sole' sponsor of the 'property'.

(b) Official supplier rights

D5.50 The right to supply exclusively key services or products required for the staging of the event. This might include IT solutions and technology equipment, clothing for players, balls, etc. Particular care is required for official suppliers using that designation especially where the products supplied to the event by the sponsor are sports equipment for use at the event. Following a complaint by a Danish tennis ball importer about the Danish Tennis Federation's (DTF) designation of just three types of first grade ball as 'official', the European Commission in 1998 took the view that, unless the 'official supplier' label can be justified on technical grounds (in this instance it could not since others also manufactured top grade balls), granting its use would mislead consumers by unjustifiably attributing a label of quality to the products. Therefore, it must be clear from the label that the relationship is of a sponsoring nature. The solution in the DTF case was to refer to the 'official' suppliers as simply a 'sponsor of the DTF'[1].

1 *Danish Tennis Federation Commission* OJ [1996] C 138/6, [1996] 4 CMLR 885, Commission's XXVIIIth Report on Competition Policy (1998), p 160. See further paras B2.207 to B2.211, B2.316 and B2.317.

(c) Advertising and branding rights

D5.51 As part of the package, a sponsor will want to advertise at the venue. Where advertising is on static, fixed advertising hoardings placed around the perimeter of the playing area, the contract should provide for the number of hoardings and their location. Location value will be determined by the positioning of television cameras. A site plan should be scheduled to the contract marking chosen sites. Often the sponsor is obliged, at its own cost, to produce, install, and maintain signage boards and will generally employ specialist agents to do so. Therefore, the sponsor and the agents will need rights of access to the venue for these purposes.

D5.52 Signage might also cover rotating signage boards (where the sponsor may need to agree time of availability during play as they generally exhibit only one advertiser on all boards at any one time), signage on seats, around scoreboards or computer display screens, on the playing surface, in goal nets and corner flags.

D5.53 Regardless of the position or nature of the signage, a sponsor will want assurances that such branding is not obscured during the event. This may well require the event organiser to employ a service team around the venue to ensure that any obstructions or interferences with branding are removed immediately should they occur.

D5.54 The parties will also need to clarify the period prior to, during, and after each match or race of the event when the advertising will be displayed.

D5.55 Sponsors will also want protection against their competitors or unauthorised third parties being able to take advantage of advertising opportunities. A sponsor will often want to ensure the event venue(s) will not be used by unauthorised third parties for publicity purposes. The sponsor may also seek an entitlement to review and veto the appointment of fellow sponsors, or at least an undertaking that the event organiser will not appoint as sponsors any of its competitors or organisations whose image may be incompatible with that of the sponsor. This has led to the development of the concept of 'clean' venues to ensure an event owner can control advertising at the event stadia. For example, a club hosting a UEFA Champions League match must provide a 'clean' stadium, which means that no advertising except that officially authorised by UEFA may be located within normal camera range. The club must also ensure that advertising boards are within the unimpaired range of view of the main camera[1].

1 See para 4.2, Annexe VII of the UEFA Champions League Regulations 2001/2002.

D5.56 Although the concept of 'clean' venues protects the inherent value of the sponsorship package, it does not protect the sponsor against ambush marketing outside the venue. Whilst it is relatively easy to control 'unofficial' advertising within a venue, it can be difficult to do so outside the venue unless the event owner or sponsor has secured rights to hoardings and other advertising sights close to the venue and in its environs.

D5.57 Sponsors will also be keen to ensure that internet rights are included in the sponsorship package. Having an online presence is, in today's marketplace, an important means of reaching your target market. A sponsor will therefore want to ensure that it has the right to include its logo on the event owner's website and that links are maintained between the event owner's website and the sponsor's website. Another possibility is for the event owner and sponsor to create an event-specific co-branded website with links to the event owner's website and the sponsor's website. Access to broadcast feeds for the webcasting of an event, or highlights of an event, may also be an important component of the bundle of sponsorship rights.

D5.58 Branding rights will include the right to incorporate the sponsor's branding on as many elements of the event as possible, for example competitors' clothing, messages on scoreboards and computer display screens, branding at press conferences and interviews with participants. Broadcasting regulations, including, in the UK, the Independent Television Commission's (ITC) Codes, must be complied with[1].

1 See para D5.115 et seq.

D5.59 Branding rights for an event or team can be limited by regulations at both European and national level. For example, France's Loi Evin law bans all advertising of alcohol at French based events and restricts the appearance of alcohol brand related signage for events held elsewhere but screened in France. This prevented Anheuser-Busch, one of the 12 official sponsors of the World Cup 1998 in France, from displaying perimeter advertising for its Budweiser brand at any of the ten grounds where matches were played. It was also the reason why, in March 1995, French television channels refused to broadcast coverage of Arsenal v Auxerre in the UEFA Cup and of England v Scotland in the Five Nations Championship – there was alcohol advertising present at the venues of those events and they were concerned that broadcasting coverage of the event including such advertising would be deemed to be television advertising of alcohol brands and so an infringement of the Loi Evin[1].

1 For details of a challenge to the Loi Evin on EC free movement grounds, see paras A3.36, n 4 and B3.20.

D5.60 Alcohol advertising is also regulated at a European level by the Television Without Frontiers Directive ('TVWF Directive')[1]. The aim of this Directive was to lay down common standards in television broadcasting applying across all member states so as to create a true single market in television broadcasting. Amongst its provisions, the TVWF Directive prevents advertising directed at the abuse of alcohol, rather than banning its use entirely, and reflects the general acceptance that alcohol is not a harmful substance if consumed responsibly. The restrictions on alcohol advertising in the TVWF Directive are directed at the content of TV advertising. In particular, advertisements must not:

- be aimed at children or depict children consuming alcoholic drinks;
- suggest that alcohol consumption enhances social or sexual success;
- link alcohol consumption to enhanced physical performance or driving; or
- encourage 'immoderate consumption'.

1 Council Directive 89/552/EEC, amended by Directive 97/36/EC.

D5.61 So far, steps have not been taken by the EU to prohibit alcohol advertising in the same way it has attempted to do so for tobacco advertising.

D5.62 In the UK, tobacco advertising is currently regulated by the Voluntary Agreement on Sponsorship of Sport by Tobacco Companies in the UK ('the 'Voluntary Tobacco Agreement'), signed on 31 January 1995 by the Government, the Tobacco Manufacturers' Association and the Imported Tobacco Products Advisory Council. The European Union has attempted to impose a Europe wide ban on tobacco advertising by way of a Directive[1] which came into force in July 1998. However, the tobacco industry and the German government successfully challenged the validity of this Directive so that it was annulled by the European Court of Justice. In May 2001, the European Commission issued a new proposal for a Directive on advertising and sponsorship of tobacco products which would take this ruling into account. The draft Directive proposes, inter alia, to:

- ban tobacco advertising on any website that sells advertising space for tobacco advertisements;
- ban all forms of radio tobacco advertising and sponsorship of radio programmes by tobacco companies; and
- prohibit tobacco sponsorship of events involving or taking place in several EU member states, or otherwise having cross-border effects, as well as the free distribution of tobacco products in the context of such sponsorship.

1 Tobacco Advertising Directive (Council Directive 98/43/EC).

D5.63 This Directive is likely to be adopted by the end of 2002 and the proposal requires member states to comply with its terms by 31 July 2005. This does, however, depend on when, and if, the Directive is finally adopted.

D5.64 As a result of the annulment of the EU Directive, the UK Government issued a draft bill, the Tobacco Advertising and Promotion Bill, in March 2001 to implement the policy agreed under the EU Directive which would supersede the Voluntary Tobacco Agreement. This bill has yet to pass in to law. The bill aims to:

- ban all tobacco advertising and promotion of tobacco including sponsorship by tobacco companies;
- place restrictions on the display and promotion of tobacco products in shops – that is, at the point of sale;
- restrict or prohibit the advertising of non-tobacco products sharing tobacco branding (such as, Camel boots); and
- prohibit the distribution of free cigarettes or other tobacco products.

D5.65 As currently drafted, the bill permits the Secretary of State to make regulations to specify when the ban on tobacco sponsorship is to take effect, but this effective date may not be later than 1 October 2006.

(d) *Hospitality rights*

D5.66 These will include tickets to the event, food, beverage and other hospitality. It might also include the use of office and other facilities at the event's site. The contract will need to clarify how many tickets the sponsor will want, for which matches or races forming part or the whole of the event, of what standard and at what cost, if any. Rights of resale (for example to the sponsor's own customers) or for use in the sponsor's other, unconnected promotional activities (such as prize competitions) should be covered[1].

1 See generally Chapter D1.

D5.67 Hospitality facilities (including catering and its quality) should also be covered. Sometimes the venue will have its own caterer with whom the event owner has no relationship. In these circumstances the sponsor should arrange hospitality direct.

(e) Merchandising rights

D5.68 This may include the right for the sponsor to manufacture or license the manufacture of t-shirts or other types of 'premium items' branded with the event owner's logo and the sponsor's logo, (or any composite logo) for distribution at, or outside, the event or inclusion in hospitality packages. It is common for there to be a prohibition on sales of premium items as this would undermine the event owner's merchandising programme.

(f) Presentation rights

D5.69 These will typically include the right to present the championship trophy to the competition winners at a ceremony and, possibly, to use the trophy for specified periods, either before or after the event, as well as a right to make man of the match or tournament awards.

(g) Association marketing rights

D5.70 A licence to use the event mark (sometimes a composite logo of the sponsor's mark and the event owner's mark) on the sponsor's products, in its marketing literature, on its website and in promotional and advertising campaigns. This assumes the event owner owns the event mark or otherwise has power to licence its use. The event owner will likewise need a non-exclusive licence to use the sponsor's mark for specified purposes. These rights and marks may be protected by an anti-infringement programme being implemented by the parties whereby each party agrees to assist the other in the protection of the rights and marks.

D5.71 The sponsor may wish to use other intellectual property owned by the event owner, such as its fixture lists. A licence should be obtained from the event owner for any use of that nature. To avoid any subsequent dispute, the parties should also agree branding and use of web sites including which domain names the sponsor can register in relation to the event for its own promotional purposes.

(h) Filming rights

D5.72 The sponsor may want its own film footage (which, as copyright owner, it could exploit as it wished) for its own advertising or promotion purposes, such as for use on its own web site. The sponsor will need access to the event's venue to produce this footage. The terms of access should be clarified in the contract. For example, will recording equipment be allowed in dressing rooms and on the perimeter of the playing area? Will parking facilities and electric feeds be available? Alternatively, the sponsor could be granted the right to use footage created by the broadcaster of the event for specified purposes. The event owner must obtain the right to license this use from the broadcaster. The parties will need to agree what type of footage and of what amount.

(i) Approval rights

D5.73 The sponsor will also want rights of approval over certain matters including contracts with key third parties necessary for the success of the event. For some sports or events, sponsors are seeking a greater say over the 'property' they are sponsoring[1].

1 See para D5.82 et seq.

D5.74 In some contracts the approval may be watered down to a duty imposed upon the event owner to consult with the sponsor and use reasonable endeavours to incorporate the sponsor's requirements into such contracts. In others, where the sponsor's requirements are fundamental to the sponsorship, the sponsorship contract will be conditional upon the event owner entering into the specified contracts with the relevant third parties incorporating terms specified in the sponsorship agreement (such as the venue contract obliging the venue owner to remove existing branding of rivals at the event venue) or on terms satisfactory to the sponsor.

D5.75 As an alternative, the sponsor will insert a right of fee claw-back if its demands are not adhered to. From the sponsor's viewpoint this may be less desirable than being able to ensure its rights can be fully exploited, for at this stage it will have embarked on a marketing plan, of which the sponsorship cost is only part. However, claw-back provisions may be more attractive than, and an equally valuable encumbrance on the event owner as, a right to terminate for breach of contract.

E Exclusivity

D5.76 To maximise the sponsor's commercial opportunities, it will ideally wish to be the only sponsor of an event. From the event owner's standpoint, particularly for prime events, exclusivity of this nature will generally radically reduce the return from sponsorship exploitation. The compromise has been the creation of product categories and granting exclusivity in each category, although the concept developed for other reasons.

D5.77 It was first used with enormous success for the Los Angeles Olympics in 1984. Prior to that time, sports events had traditionally had no formal structure to their sponsorship arrangements so that one event might be supported by a range of soft drinks or restaurants, for example. Now the generally accepted theory is that by offering sponsors exclusivity, a rights owner can sell fewer, but higher value exclusive packages and, thereby, raise more sponsorship income from fewer sponsors.

D5.78 Defining the sponsorship category is key. Inevitably, the event owner will want a category to be drafted as narrowly as possible, whereas a sponsor will want its exclusive category to be as wide as possible. Contrast the 'drinks' category with the 'non-alcoholic, non-carbonated, fruit juices' category. This definition is often the cause of much debate, but must be well thought through to avoid arguments at a later stage.

D5.79 Such exclusive arrangements may raise competition concerns under Art 81 of the EC Treaty which prohibits agreements that may affect trade between member states and which have as their object or effect the prevention, restriction or distortion of competition in the common market. Where an event owner grants exclusive rights to a particular sponsor this inevitably has the effect of excluding other sponsors from taking up that opportunity and, accordingly, such arrangements may distort competition by giving an unfair advantage to that sponsor. This advantage may also have an effect on trade between member states where the sponsor sells its products or services in the EU.

D5.80 EC competition law requires an agreement to have an appreciable effect on competition for it to infringe Art 81. Guidance from the European Commission states that an agreement will not have an appreciable effect where it is made between non-competitors each having less than a 15 per cent market share. Defining market share for a sport event is difficult given the difficulty of defining the relevant market. There are also relatively few cases so far in relation to sponsorship agreements[1]. From the cases to date, the recommended approach to seek to avoid competition law infringements is to:

- Ensure that there is a transparent tender process for sponsorship opportunities such that competing sponsors are given equal opportunity to put their best terms forward to the event owner.
- Ensure that the duration of any exclusivity is objectively justifiable. The DTF case referred to a period of two years; any term exceeding five years would be unlikely to be regarded as acceptable.
- Where the sponsorship includes the provision of equipment carefully choose the designation wording. In the DTF case the European Commission viewed the use of such language as potentially misleading to customers of the products concerned, since it appeared that the DTF was saying only those balls met the required standards. The use of the word official in reference to products or services should be objectively justifiable by reference to technical standards, rather than simply a reflection of the fact that it is a product made by the sponsor.
- A sponsorship agreement should avoid any attempt at price fixing (either on the event owner in terms of ticket pricing, etc. or on the sponsor, in terms of the pricing of its goods or services perhaps for other events). Such a provision is likely to give rise to fines being imposed on the parties by the European Commission.
- Any other restrictions contained in the agreement, other than the exclusivity itself, should be scrutinised closely to see whether they are objectively justifiable. For example, a sponsor's attempt to restrict other events that may be put on by the event owner are likely to be regarded as unacceptable.

1 Although see the *Danish Tennis Federation* case referred to at para D5.50.

D5.81 In any event where an agreement appears to raise competition concerns, it may be advisable to seek the comfort from the competition authorities (either the European Commission or a national regulatory authority). Comfort may be obtained either in form of informal guidance, or a formal exemption – available under Art 81(3) where the benefits of the agreement to the economy and consumers outweighs its anti-competitive effects. Given the sums involved in the sponsorship of a major event, obtaining such comfort may well be viewed as an attractive form of insurance. This is especially so where the sponsor or the event owner is aware that competitors or customers are likely to wish to challenge the proposed arrangements[1].

1 For further discussion of competition issues in relation to sponsorship agreements, see paras B2.306 to B2.317.

F Sponsor's control over event organisation

D5.82 The sponsor may wish to be involved in organising, or controlling the organisation of, certain aspects of the event, particularly publicity for, and marketing of, the event. It may wish the event owner to hold a high profile pre-event draw or to stage a victory procession with the sponsor's branding imprinted upon it.

D5.83 Some sponsors are rethinking the sponsorship relationship and structure and increasingly seek to acquire greater control over the events or properties that they sponsor. This could be achieved by entering into a joint venture relationship with the property owner into which the rights associated with the event are transferred. This allows the sponsor representation on the board or committee of the joint venture entity. The sponsor will, therefore, be able to exert direct control over the organisation (or certain aspects) of the event.

D5.84 A further advantage of this structure for the sponsor may be the offsetting of a profit and loss expense (that is, the sponsorship fee) with balance sheet assets (those being the shares in the joint venture, where of a corporate nature).

D5.85 The degree to which the sponsor involves itself in the organisation of the event will affect its legal responsibility for what happens at the event. By exerting greater control over events, sponsors may become unwittingly liable to third parties where previously only the event owner would have been liable. These liabilities can include to those (such as spectators) injured at sports events who may look to a sponsor for redress, possibly on the grounds that the sponsor:

- is negligent;
- is an 'occupier' of the event venue under the Occupiers Liability Act 1957;
- is the event owner's agent;
- is a joint tortfeasor;
- controls the event; or
- is responsible under the Consumer Protection Act 1987 for defective products manufactured for the event on behalf of the event owner, but incorporating the sponsor's trade mark.

G The Sponsor's obligations

D5.86 The sponsor's main obligation will be to pay the sponsorship fee. Other obligations may arise depending on the nature of the sponsorship. These may include for the sponsor:

- to comply with any regulations of that sports governing body;
- to agree not to exploit any association with the event or, in the case of an individual, the athlete, once the contract has expired or been terminated;
- not to bring into disrepute the event owner, sports body, or the event; and
- to confirm it has requisite authority to enter into the arrangement.

H The Event Owner's Obligations

D5.87 In essence, these mirror the rights granted to the sponsor. They include the factors set out below.

(a) *To organise and run the event*

D5.88 The key elements of this undertaking will be to procure that the event is held in accordance with an agreed format set out in a schedule to the contract, that the venue has all the necessary facilities to enable the performance of the event owner's obligations to the sponsor and that participants of an appropriately high quality attend, and take part in, the event.

(b) *No conflicting arrangements*

D5.89 It is common for the event owner to warrant that the event owner has not entered into, and will not enter into, any conflicting agreement nor grant to any third party rights, licences or permissions which may conflict with the sponsor's rights. This warranty may throw up disclosures which can affect the sponsor's investment. This was illustrated by Bass' sponsorship of the FA Premier League and the conflicting deals already entered into by certain clubs (for example Liverpool and Carlsberg). The rules of the FA Premier League allow the League to enter into sponsorship agreements subject to individual clubs' existing arrangements[1].

1 Rules C.17 and C.20 of The FA Premier League Rules for season 2001/2002.

(c) *Format and Scheduling*

D5.90 Another key event owner obligation centres on format and scheduling and being obliged not to alter either as the sponsorship's value depends on them. For example, the existing format may anticipate sudden death, knock-out matches of a guaranteed minimum number weighted so that the most attractive teams play the most matches. If the competition structure changes so the weighting favours less attractive teams, the sponsorship value will decrease. However, minor alterations may not be fatal for a sponsor and it is common to give an event owner some leeway by allowing non-material alterations.

D5.91 Scheduling is important. Sponsorship is often one of the elements of a particular marketing strategy (involving for example, promotions, advertising and direct mailing) which needs to be carefully planned throughout a specific period. Should the dates of matches comprising the sponsored competition change, this may significantly disrupt the sponsor's pre-planned marketing activities during that period.

D5.92 Whilst a sponsor should demand that its consent is obtained before the format and schedule as represented to it (normally scheduled to the sponsorship contract) is materially altered, scheduling times and dates often change at the behest of the broadcaster, beyond the event owner's control. Broadcasting fees are generally much more valuable to event owners and broadcasters will not accept scheduling alteration rights subordinated to sponsor's wishes. Whilst claw-back of sponsorship fees, in such circumstances, may be one solution, the sponsor would be well advised to have its own separate arrangement with the broadcaster to deal with such eventualities.

D5.93 An alternative for a sponsor may be to cherry pick sponsorship of, and pay for, selected games forming part of an event, rather than sponsoring the event as a whole, leaving the event owner free to re-schedule or re-format the remaining games as it wishes.

I The Sponsorship Fee

D5.94 The sponsorship fee is normally a cash sum, although increasingly sponsors may offer non-cash alternatives as part consideration, sometimes described as a 'barter' arrangement. For example, an airline title sponsor may offer free flight tickets to overseas participants in the event.

D5.95 The payment dates are often contentious. The event owner will want up-front payments at the commencement of the event to assist cash flow. The event owner will commonly have financial obligations to participants or a third party governing body who has granted the event owner the right to stage the event, which fall due at the beginning of the event. The event owner may, therefore, want back to back payment obligations from the sponsor, that is, the sponsor is required to pay the fee at the same time that the event owner's expenses/financial obligations become due. Where front-ended payments are agreed, the sponsor should include repayment provisions if key undertakings are broken, for example, as mentioned elsewhere in this chapter, a lack of television coverage, changes to the format and structure of the event substantially reducing the sponsorship's value or cancellation of whole or part of the event.

D5.96 The sponsor, by contrast, should try to ensure that payments are performance related. The threat of non-payment of fees is the main weapon in the sponsor's armoury for breach by an event owner, particularly for major breaches, such as re-scheduling or materially altering the event's format, reduced or no television coverage, loss of a key venue or competitors.

D5.97 The threat of terminating the agreement may not be as effective as performance-related payment because although in the former a right of action for damages may arise, on termination the sponsor will lose the marketing benefits of the sponsorship and frustrate what may be a three to five year programme, whilst the event owner has already received the fee. Seeking to restrain the event owner from organising, promoting or exploiting its competition is unlikely to be successful as a court is likely to hold that money is an adequate remedy and in any event such an application would be unrealistic and unlikely to be granted as it affects many other innocent parties such as the competitors.

D5.98 A sponsor may also have concerns that if all of the fee is paid up front, there may be a risk that a badly managed event will dissipate the funds.

D5.99 In practice, a compromise of payment in tranches is often reached, linked either to commencement, the final and key performance stages such as completion of a certain number of rounds or matches, or to periodic payment dates covering the contract's term.

D5.100 If either party is relatively new, of limited financial stature, or a subsidiary of a larger parent, or if the size of the deal so merits, the other party would be well advised to obtain a suitable guarantee of the principal's payment (in the case of a sponsor) or repayment (in the case of the event owner) obligations. In 2002, the Football League lost its claim against Carlton Communications plc and Granada plc alleging that they had guaranteed the financial obligations of ITV Digital, which had contracted with the Football League for certain media rights and subsequently went into administration having allegedly defaulted on its obligations to the Football League[1].

1 See para D4.5, n 2.

J Tax

D5.101 The event owner as recipient of the fees generally makes a taxable supply for VAT purposes. Therefore, fees must clearly state whether they are inclusive or exclusive of VAT. Where the contract is silent, the fees will be deemed to be VAT inclusive for UK purposes. Provision for the supply of VAT invoices for the sponsor to recover input tax should be included. Particular care is required where part of the consideration is not cash, since there could then be VAT supplies by the sponsor to the event owner and vice versa, which may give rise to valuation difficulties.

D5.102 However, if either the sponsor or the event owner is based outside the UK, the VAT position will be different. For example, if the event owner is based in the UK, but the sponsor is based and registered for VAT in another EC member state, then generally no UK VAT will be chargeable by the event owner. The sponsor may, of course, be subject to VAT in his member state under the 'reverse charge' procedure described elsewhere in this work[1].

1 See para D7.77.

D5.103 For income or corporation tax purposes, the fee will be tax deductible for the sponsor provided it is wholly and exclusively expended for the purposes of the sponsor's trade, profession or vocation[1]. Where the event owner or sponsor is tax resident outside the UK, provisions dealing with grossing up and withholding tax may also be relevant.

1 Section 74(1)(a) of the Income and Corporation Tax Act 1988.

K Media Coverage

D5.104 Television and, increasingly, other media coverage of the event is invariably fundamental to sponsorship value. It is the principal medium for distributing the sponsor's branding or product message to a wide domestic and, perhaps, international audience.

D5.105 Generally, the event owner commissions a television producer and distributor or the ultimate end-users, the broadcasters, before selling sponsorship. A title sponsor will want the event owner to warrant and confirm this. Where the warranty cannot be given, the event owner should undertake as a fundamental obligation that it will procure that these contracts will be secured at least a certain period prior to the staging of the event. Alternatively, this should be a condition precedent to the sponsorship contract.

D5.106 The key areas where the sponsor will want comfort from the event owner, commonly in the form of warranties are set out below.

(a) The quality of television coverage

D5.107 The television producer's name or the names of bidders for producing the pictures if one has not been appointed should be disclosed, so that the sponsor can determine whether current or proposed arrangements are satisfactory. Obligations regarding transmission of the sponsor's branding (for example, in promotional messages, in videos and backdrops used for television interviews and draws) and on-screen credits when referring to the event or to thank the sponsor for supporting the event are important.

(b) The extent, quantity and scheduling of television coverage

D5.108 This covers timing, frequency and length of coverage. It should also include coverage of 'event-related matters' such as result services, draws, winning parades, interviews with players. All such coverage should include sponsor's branding at a level and in a manner that will vary for each sponsorship arrangement.

D5.109 In *Northern & Shell v Champion Children*[1], a dispute arose over the timing of a broadcast. HRH Diana, Princess of Wales, was due to present awards to children at a celebrity event and the ceremony was to be broadcast on television and sponsored by the publishers of *OK! Magazine* for a fee of £160,000. She was unable to take part and was replaced by HRH the Duchess of Kent. It was acknowledged that there might be less public interest as a result and fresh terms were negotiated. The sponsorship fee was reduced by £90,000 and any reference to estimated television viewing figures was removed. Clause 6 of the sponsorship agreement, however, stated that:

> In the event that the Event … is not broadcast by the BBC at a time and date acceptable to the Sponsor in its reasonable discretion, all monies paid under this Agreement by the Sponsor shall be repaid upon demand by the Sponsor, and no further sums shall be due.

Originally, the show was to be transmitted on a Sunday afternoon with an anticipated audience of six million viewers but as that was no longer seen as capable of attainment, all that was specifically provided for was the transmission of a one hour network programme to be transmitted as a pre-Christmas 1997 special. The first sponsorship instalment of £45,000 was paid, but subsequently *OK!* sued Champion for the return of the first instalment. *OK!*'s grounds included that the scheduling of the broadcast did not live up to Champion's 'pre-contractual proposal and other representations' that the show would be broadcast at peak time and attract an audience of at least six million. On appeal, it was held that cl 6 did not say anything about viewing figures and that *OK!* had got what it had bargained for: free publicity from a public service channel on the back of an event watched by hundreds of thousands of potential readers of the magazine. The sponsorship money was not conditional on a specific range of slots or viewing figures and it was, therefore, unreasonable for *OK!* to demand its money back.

1 *Northern and Shell plc v Champion Children of the Year Awards Ltd* [2001] EWCA Civ 1638, [2001] All ER (D) 407 (Oct).

(c) *The identity of broadcasters domestically and internationally and the type of coverage*

D5.110 Will the coverage be live (simultaneous) or deferred (unedited but not simultaneous) or highlights? Terrestrial coverage has wider audience reach than, for example, satellite, cable, or digital broadcasts and, even more so where pay per view is contemplated, and therefore, greater sponsorship value.

D5.111 For UK events, regard should be had to the Listed Events under the ITC Code on Sports and Other Listed Events, drawn up pursuant to the Broadcasting Act 1996, with the aim of ensuring particularly significant sporting events can be enjoyed by the public generally and are not restricted to say exclusive pay-per-view coverage. Certain of the listed events (Group A Events – including the Olympics, the World Cup, the FA Cup Final and Wimbledon) are those events which may not be covered live on an exclusive basis unless certain criteria are met. The other listed events (Group B Events – including the Ryder Cup, Test Matches in England, the Commonwealth Games) are those events that may not be broadcast live on an exclusive basis unless adequate provision has been made for secondary coverage. Secondary coverage must include rights for the provision of edited highlights or delayed coverage amounting to at least 10% of the scheduled duration of the event, or the play in the event taking place on any day[1].

1 See further para A1.81 et seq.

D5.112 Certain requirements are also placed on broadcasters that are under the jurisdiction of the UK and broadcasting to other European Economic Area (EEA) States to ensure that such broadcasters do not circumvent the rules on Listed Events which apply in those states. Reciprocal arrangements exist for preventing broadcasters established in other EEA States from circumventing the UK Listed Events rules[1].

1 See further paras A1.88 et seq and B1.49 to B1.53.

D5.113 If international television exposure is critical to the sponsorship's value, provision must be made either for overseas distribution to be procured or the consequences of a failure to secure this. The consequences may include claw-back of the sponsorship fee or an obligation on the event owner to grant international distribution rights to the sponsor to exploit as it chooses.

D5.114 In some cases sponsors may want to acquire certain television rights themselves to ensure desired distribution either by bartering them (that is, generally, supplying television material in exchange for advertising slots), selling them or supplying them for free to overseas broadcasters.

L Regulatory Compliance

D5.115 The parties must consider regulatory issues, and for the sponsor particularly where the sponsor is the broadcaster as well as the event sponsor. In the UK sponsorship of broadcasts or events which are broadcast is governed by the BBC's Sponsorship Guidelines[1] and the ITC's Code of Programme Sponsorship (including the ITC Rules concerning Advertiser Involvement in Programmes) (the 'Code') and, for tobacco sponsors, the Voluntary Tobacco Agreement[2].

1 Contained in the BBC Commercial Policy Guidelines and the BBC Producer's Guidelines.
2 See para D5.62.

D5.116 The BBC's Sponsorship Guidelines cover event sponsorship. Sponsors and event organisers are specifically prohibited from paying for any part of the programme costs. In relation to BBC events, the governing principle is that the public should not have reason to suspect that the BBC's integrity has been compromised by the influence of a sponsor. In relation to non-BBC events, the Guidelines state that coverage should not be used as a means of 'back door' advertising. Accordingly:

- there are rules governing the use and positioning of placards and banners, including reflections of sponsor messages painted on the pitch;
- rules on the content of credits; and
- for BBC events, strict rules to ensure that the BBC is not seen to be endorsing the sponsor or the sponsor's products or services. For example, there is an absolute ban on product placement.

D5.117 The Broadcasting Act 1990 imposed a statutory duty on the ITC to draw up and to review from time to time a code setting out the standard and practice in the sponsoring of programmes. The Code applies to all television programme services licensed by the ITC under the Act (including ITV, GMTV, Channels 4 and 5, BSkyB, but not the BBC).

D5.118 The ITC can impose sanctions, such as financial penalties, on licensees not complying with the Code.

D5.119 The Code distinguishes between programme sponsorship and event sponsorship. Programme sponsorship is defined so that a programme is deemed to be sponsored if any part of its costs of production or transmission is met by an organisation or person other than a broadcaster or television producer, with a view to promoting its name, goods or services.

D5.120 There are two key principles governing the regulation of programme sponsorship:

- the content and scheduling of programmes must not be distorted for commercial purposes. Accordingly, there must be no visual or oral reference to the sponsor (or the sponsor's product or service) in the programme it is sponsoring. This extends to generic references to the sponsor's (unbranded) product, service or business. The only exception to this absolute prohibition is where the broadcast and event sponsor are one and the same[1]; and
- programmes must maintain a distinction between advertising and sponsor credits. Sponsor credits are not counted as part of advertising minutage. Strict rules govern the placing and content of credits to ensure that sponsor credits are used primarily to create an association between the sponsor and the programme rather than to advertise the sponsor or the sponsor's goods or services.

1 See para D5.122 et seq.

D5.121 The Code sets out specific rules governing coverage of events (broadly defined as recognised sporting occasions and one off or annual events). The rules are intended to ensure that coverage is focused on the event rather than on any incidental advertising. Accordingly:

- visual or oral reference to any advertising, signage or branding must not exceed that which may be justified by the editorial needs of the programme. Event sponsors should be aware that the Code specifically cautions against branding 'which seems to be deliberately positioned for the cameras, or positioned in such a place that makes prominent television exposure likely'[1]; and
- there is an absolute prohibition on oral references to the sponsor's business, product or service during the coverage of the event.

1 Code Rule 19.2.1.

(a) Broadcast sponsorship

D5.122 The event sponsor will want comfort that the event producer/broadcaster is obliged to maximise the value and profile of the event sponsorship. This should ideally include an offer of further marketing opportunities (television advertising and sponsorship) in preference to others and an obligation to prevent ambush marketing. The event sponsor will want assurances that the media contracts between the event owner and the media producer/broadcaster(s) include provisions permitting the event owner to:

- provide an options package to a sponsor (that is a first and/or last option for the event sponsor to become additionally the sponsor of the broadcast and to acquire slots in advertising breaks around the event transmissions);
- incorporate a title sequence and promotional clip prior to the event with sponsor identification as desired by the sponsor;
- protect the sponsor from 'ambush' (such as by a competitor acquiring slots during advertising breaks around coverage of the event or in tele-marketing associated with coverage of the event);
- ensure the broadcast sponsor is not an industry competitor of the sponsor;
- ensure the broadcast is not doctored to obscure the event sponsor's marketing, including, signage at the event. Technological advances have led to the creation of 'virtual billboards', whereby the broadcast pictures can be doctored to display to viewers watching the broadcast a different perimeter signage advertiser to the advertiser actually being displayed on signage at the event venue. This can be done without corrupting on the broadcasted pictures other elements of the event, such as the movement of players on the pitch. The 'virtual advertising' technology and its use during event coverage must, in any event, where applicable to the broadcaster(s) comply with the ITC Sponsorship Guidance Note on 'Virtual Advertising'. For example, the Guidance Note requires that the use of electronic imaging systems to supply virtual advertising be disclosed to viewers, either at the beginning or end of a broadcast. These systems may also be used only to replace existing advertising signage at a venue – true 'virtual' advertising is not permitted[1].

1 See further paras D4.103 to D4.107.

D5.123 The rights to be granted as listed above should be expressed to apply to exploitation of the event on any other media, whether developed at the date of the agreement or at any time after. This would cover, for example, webcasts, streaming through mobile phones and interactive television features. A reference to 'technology developed after the date of the agreement' is particularly important given the rapid rate of development of new media platforms and the current classification of sport as 'premium content'.

M The Venue

D5.124 The quality, status and infrastructure of the event venue(s) must include facilities to enable full exploitation of the sponsorship rights granted. In certain circumstances the sponsor may prefer its own direct arrangement with the venue owner. For example, where the venue already has potentially conflicting commercial arrangements such as signage advertising competitor's products, or arrangements enabling a competitor's, rather than the sponsor's, products to be used on the field of play. This latter issue arose during the 1996 Coca Cola Cup final where Coca Cola, the event sponsor and exclusive soft drink provider to Wembley and Lucozade, the official drinks supplier to both finalists, each claimed exclusive rights to have bottles with their branding on the field of play at that match.

D5.125 As mentioned above, the sponsor should check with the venue owner whether it can control advertising sites immediately outside and around the ground and if not, who does, for unless these sites are controlled event marketing may be hijacked by advertising on them by businesses not officially associated with the event[1]. The contract should also provide for alternative suitable venues, should the desired ones be unavailable.

1 See para D1.128.

D5.126 The sponsor will also want protection from fans being supplied with and/or wearing clothing with competitors' branding that will be visible during the event[1].

1 See para D1.130.

N Copyright/Trade Mark Protection

D5.127 Use of the event logo and other intellectual property rights of the event owner has been discussed elsewhere in this book and is equally relevant here[1]. As a short summary of some of the key points, the contract should include warranties from the parties that:

- each owns the marks that the other is contractually entitled to use or has the exclusive right to grant a licence for their use;
- all marks to be used, including the event logo, have been registered in the relevant class(es) at the Trade Marks Registry and in other appropriate jurisdictions.

1 See Chapters D1 and D6.

D5.128 The contract should make provision for sub-licensing, for ownership of goodwill attaching to the event marks, and that both parties will co-operate in policing the use of the event mark and take action where there has been infringement. The allocation between the parties of the costs of such action should also be specified. The uses to which the event mark may be put should be set out, including (for example) the type and quality of event-elated merchandise.

D5.129 Other relevant issues, whilst not strictly intellectual property issues, include protecting the reputation and integrity of the event and sponsor. What this means varies for each circumstance, but is often regarded as a sweeper clause to protect against a party riding roughshod over the other's interests.

D5.130 One particularly tricky area is the composite logo, a logo made specifically for the sports event which combines elements of both the sponsor's and event owner's logos. The usual considerations apply here, such as ownership of goodwill and the logo itself, but so do certain special considerations. The sponsor and event owner would want to restrict the other's use of the composite logo as it would not want its mark or brand name being used indiscriminately and without its permission by the other party.

O Termination

D5.131 The following are common events conferring rights of termination seen in sponsorship contracts:

- either party going into liquidation;
- material breaches not remedied after notice;
- specific matters – such as, breaches enabling a reduction or withholding of the sponsorship fee. For example, if the event is cancelled or rescheduled, the sponsor may want the right to terminate the agreement and recover all, or at least a portion, of the sponsorship fee. To the extent that the claw-back provisions in the agreement are insufficient the sponsor may wish to have a right to terminate the agreement if, for example, the club it is sponsoring does not play in important matches;
- if there is a change of control in either party; or
- if either party's image or reputation is brought into serious disrepute. For sponsors, such clauses are particularly useful where a scandal in the sport involving the governing bodies or participants might create public relations problems for sponsors who are associated by their commercial arrangement with that sport. Examples include:
  (a) Glenn Hoddle's removal as England manager for his controversial views on reincarnation and the disabled. Nationwide Building Society was then sponsoring the England team, but did not terminate its arrangement as a result;
  (b) Lawrence Dallaglio's removal as England captain in the summer of 1999 following his unwitting revelations to News of the World reporters posing as potential sponsors. Two of his sponsors at the time were Nike and Lloyds TSB;
  (c) the drugs scandal that affected cycling in 1998, which, according to one press report, caused a key team sponsor to reduce its sponsorship after that year's Tour de France[1].

1 (1998) Financial Times, 9 October.

P Insurance

D5.132 The sponsor should ensure that the event owner is adequately insured for the following risks:

- public liability covering injury and loss to spectators and third parties;
- cancellation or abandonment of the event;
- television transmission interruption or failure;
- product liability for defective event products incorporating the sponsor's branding. A sponsor may be liable for a defective product where it puts its name on the product or uses a trademark or other distinguishing mark in relation to the product[1]. Whilst the sponsor's liability for defective event-branded goods (including its logo) is not entirely clear, the sponsor should negotiate an indemnity from the event owner and insurance protection;
- trophy insurance to cover loss, theft and damage to the trophy normally supplied by the sponsor;
- participants' insurance; and
- defamation insurance for literature produced in association with the event.

1 Section 2(2) of the Consumer Protection Act 1987.

9 OTHER MATTERS

D5.133 There are a variety of less key matters for the contract to cover or matters of a non-specific sponsorship nature such as boilerplate issues. One that may be particularly pertinent is supervening illegality, bearing in mind, for example, what is being proposed for tobacco sponsorship, outlined above in this chapter[1].

1 See para D5.64.

CHAPTER D6

MERCHANDISING AND LICENSING

Clive Lawrence (M[c]Cormicks)

Contents

1 INTRODUCTION

D6.1 Licensing and merchandising are generic names given to agreements which provide for the use of the name, logo, trade marks, livery colours and other properties of and relating to a sports person, club or organisation to brand or publicise goods and services which are not directly connected with the core business of that person, club or organisation (defining the core business to be the provision of sporting services of one kind or another).

D6.2 The potential licensors of rights in this context include governing bodies, tournaments, clubs and sports organisations, individual players, teams and others. Effectively any party which has a genuine property in his, her or its identity within sport, and has a means of capitalising upon that property beyond the most immediate facets of participation in the sport, can participate in licensing and merchandising activity. One of the growth areas of debate is whose rights are involved in any merchandising deal, and who has the right to do the deal. That will be dealt with below but for the general clarity of this chapter, the name 'Licensor' should be considered to apply to the rights-owning party entering into the deal.

D6.3 Another point which should be made at the outset relates to the nature of the transaction with which this chapter deals. The types of licensed articles, materials or merchandise which could be covered by the subject-matter of this chapter are bounded only by the human imagination (or, in the case of certain merchandising lines, an imagination altogether more demonic). At its core however is the familiar content of replica kit, endorsed sporting equipment, publications, souvenirs and so forth. One distinction which should be made however is that this chapter is concerned with those deals where the design, manufacture, production and distribution or any major element of those disciplines in relation to the items is conducted not by the Licensor but by a third party company. It is that element of licensing out the properties held by that Licensor for such use by another party which gives rise to the specific issues dealt with here. There are of course some companies, clubs and organisations which effectively produce their own lines of merchandise and branded goods, or simply engage manufacturers to construct those items to their specifications. Whilst there are clearly issues which arise in those contexts which are also covered incidentally in this chapter, those are effectively simple commercial manufacturing and supply arrangements for the relevant organisation.

D6.4 The breadth of materials covered by the issues in this chapter is as stated above immense. The extent of economic activity in this sector is likewise enormous. Although revenues from merchandising and licensing may be considered to have peaked for certain key organisations, in that the very biggest players in the market may have seen their record profits from these income streams from a few years ago taper down over recent times, there are now more and more Licensors in the market. Clubs, organisations and individuals for whose licensed products the market at its peak may have had no place are now entering the market as 'commercialisation' spreads through the entire range of sporting endeavour. In other words, what the core products in the market may have lost in novelty they have gained in familiarity and the ubiquity of licensed and merchandised goods is one of the facts of contemporary existence. In addition, the novelty mug may not be at the cutting edge of a sports club's commercial strategy but video games, websites, television channels, mobile telephony services and so forth undoubtedly are, and many of the issues discussed in this chapter are of direct relevance to what are after all (independently of their specialised elements) licensed products and services in most cases. If a sports club, player or property is doing deals with third parties where it effectively 'hires out' its identity to that third party, then irrespective of the idiosyncratic elements unique to that specific deal alone, the core issues of that deal are principles set out in this chapter.

D6.5 For further ease of reference, where this chapter refers to the owner of the relevant rights to be licensed as the Licensor, the person, firm or company to whom those rights are licensed will be referred to as the Producer.

A Objectives

D6.6 To understand fully the nature of the transaction, it is useful first to deal in outline with the objectives of the respective parties. Dealing first with the Licensor, the obvious and primary object of entering into an agreement of this nature is to generate revenue. However, profit is not the sole object of the exercise. It is also frequently the case that the availability of licensed goods and services, particularly in certain overseas markets such as South East Asia, can lead to greater visibility, and therefore greater potential support available for the Licensor. Where the Licensor is, for instance, a football club, to have a broad range of merchandise in a given market place can almost act as a self-fulfilling prophecy: the visibility that then gives to the club can generate an interest in the Club and a support for it in markets where the usual historical ties to the Club do not exist. Goods which are perceived to have a certain quality can in some intangible manner validate the Club they represent. If the Licensor is an individual player, the creation of a range of goods on a viable commercial footing not only increases that individual's income, it also can increase the individual's kudos and visibility in relation to other potential income sources such as personal appearances and so forth; and where an individual might be selling his or her services to organisations or clubs, it can increase their value in that context. For instance, where a footballer has an established track record of being the subject of licensed goods, that player may be in a position to make additional charges over and above the charge made by way of his wages for his playing services by way of image rights[1].

1 See generally Chapter D3.

D6.7 Finally, and in some ways related to the above, there is the elusive question of brand development. Every Licensor has a brand and every Licensor wants to develop it! There is a very real sense in which sheer visibility for a brand leads to development. In other words, a clear brand strategy is crucial for every company which is based (as the majority of potential Licensors to a greater or lesser extent are) on the successful exploitation and development of its corporate identity, corporate image and brand. The proper structuring of the licensing and merchandising functions behind those top-line commercial strategies is an issue of crucial importance which must not be neglected in the consideration of the more directly legalistic issues outlined below. This issue will be dealt with in further detail below but it is a crucial issue when dealing with brand development to identify that for brands to a large extent familiarity breeds favourability, and that the key question for the brand owner is to ask what the associations with the brand are. Having identified the core messages and associations, it must ensure these are maintained and used to focus all its activities in this sector. Sports brands have occupied a high level of visibility over recent years in a general trend towards the greater identification of branding with aspirational aspects of life style. In addition, there are the issues of health, fitness, excellence, stability, tradition and other such values which must be communicated through the brand and conserved through any deals discussed in this chapter.

D6.8 From the point of view of the Producer, the objectives to a certain extent are very similar. Once again, the primary driver will be income generation; or at least, it should be. One of the other issues of importance to a Producer is its market positioning and the creation and maintenance of its brand portfolio in competition with other Producers. There are of course economies of scale involved in producing a broad range of fairly similar articles to be branded with various different identities, and there are also major issues of prestige involved (quite separately from the financial models in some cases) in carrying a particularly highly-rated Licensor amongst one's range of clients for licensed articles. From the point of view of a Producer, the brands for which it produces licensed articles are in themselves the strongest recommendation of that Producer to other Licensors. There is therefore on occasions (particularly if not uniquely in the sports industry) a premium in terms of value over and above that yielded by a solely financial model, to a Producer in completing its portfolio, disrupting a competitor's portfolio, breaking into another arena which might previously have been controlled by a competitor, or in having a household name as a client in order to impress its perhaps less glamorous but more remunerative core markets. A Licensor looking for a Producer should be aware of those issues and seek to extract value from them. The same basic issues arise under another guise in a slightly different context for a Producer, namely that of exclusivity, and the extent to which the rights granted are controlled by the Licensor and granted solely to the Producer. This one of the core areas for any Producer in any deal of this nature and can of course be a battleground.

B Risks

D6.9 Having dealt with the purposes and objects of such a deal, it is only perhaps prudent to refer to the risks which are attendant upon doing deals of this nature. From the point of view of a Licensor, a badly structured deal or one which fails to maximise the potential of a given market will lead to a loss of presence in that market and a potential loss of momentum for the brand. If goods are substandard or are sold in the wrong markets or in the wrong manner, or are inappropriate for the brand, there will be a serious effect on brand value. That damage to the brand can extend and form a general malaise affecting all that the brand represents.

D6.10 Some mention has been made above about the completion of a Producer's portfolio. Beware being the trophy client! More dangerous yet is the prospect of purchase by the Producer of the right to produce a given licensed article for the Licensor in order to kill the product in the market: in other words where the Producer fails properly to capitalise on the right it acquired, specifically in order to clear the competitive room in the market for its other brands. The Licensor which is a victim of that manoeuvre will be rightly aggrieved but may only have itself to blame in terms of the manner in which it has structured the deal or permitted it to be structured. Certainly complaints made after the event and based upon nebulous ideas to the effect that the Producer lacked the intention or desire to attain its potential market share are unlikely ever to prove attractive, either as grounds for termination of an agreement or for proceedings under generalised warranties. It is important therefore for the Licensor to ensure the deal is structured in such a way that the Producer has to attempt to maximise the market in good faith for the deal to work for it commercially. Some knowledge of the market is crucial in identifying the relevant factors. A minimum guaranteed royalty is the obvious first choice[1].

1 See para D6.85.

D6.11 The risks for the Producer are, perhaps paradoxically, less drastic. The first obvious risk is overbidding. Many deals in this area will be conducted on the basis of competitive tenders either in a formal sense or informally, and in the first flush of enthusiasm or in order to establish a bridge-head into a new market Producers have commonly turned deals in the sports industry into loss leaders, sometimes at risk to the entire company. It is likewise a real risk for the Producer that (as alluded to above) it may fail to obtain sufficient exclusivity from the Licensor, or (perhaps even more dangerously) proceed on a false premise as to the extent of exclusivity available to it. It is the Producer's nightmare to bid on the basis of obtaining under any deal effective control of a given area of the market, and then to find that competitive products proliferate. This will be addressed further under the heading of due diligence below[1]. Suffice it to say now that in the absence of such due diligence and the requisite warranties and indemnities to back it up from the Licensor, the value of merchandising and licensing deals can prove entirely illusory.

1 See para D6.54 et seq.

D6.12 Finally, the Producer has to be aware of safeguarding its own interests. Often the proposal from a Producer is to develop a new area or product line for the Licensor. It is crucial that if the Producer is occupying that development role it secures for itself a share of the future of that product line. In other words, it is does not want to expend its research and development funds, commit its expertise and promotional efforts to the project, and find that as soon as the proposition becomes profitable it is being exploited by the Licensor on its own or by way of another Producer.

D6.13 Many of the above issues turn on matters of competition in the market place, and the parties must be alert to the risk that their transaction could be argued to have an appreciable detrimental effect on competition on that market. It may be the case that in certain markets certain sports brands can occupy a dominant position, be they proprietary brands for clothing and equipment, or even organisations within that given sport. Alternatively, there may be issues relating to distribution channels, including the fixing of minimum and maximum prices.

C Core Rights

D6.14 It is important to bear in mind the nature of the rights which form the subject-matter of the agreements discussed in this chapter. Firstly, much of what appears here is concerned with issues relating to brands. Brands are primarily transformed in a legal environment into trade marks. Limitations of space in this chapter permit only the following outline introduction and/or reminder of the issues in this area[1].

1 See further paras D1.36 to D1.115.

(a) Passing off

D6.15 'Trade mark' is a phrase used in two main contexts. The first is in a colloquial context where it can be used as a signifier for the general goodwill of a business or brand. Sometimes there is discussion of 'common law' or 'unregistered' trade marks. These are difficult to identify positively as they only exist in effect where the law considers that they are entitled to protection under a tort known as passing off. Goodwill in the general sense of the general customer connection and business reputation of a company or a brand does have a definite value, and forms a major element of the value of a business (for instance on sale of that business) whether or not that is represented by registered marks; and important rights of this nature do need to be acquired by Producers from Licensors even where those rights are not registered. However, in the absence of registration those rights can be nebulous. Where no registration exists, as outlined below[1] it is better for a Producer to be inclusive in its definition of the rights licensed under the agreement and further to allow for their nebulous nature by obtaining the appropriate warranties and indemnities from the Licensor. Examples would include warranties to the effect of there not being any use by any third party of like or similar marks in any manner interfering with the rights granted to the Producer under the agreement and indemnities against any claims that the Producer's use of the rights will infringe third party rights.

1 See para D6.66 et seq.

D6.16 The tort of passing off is complex in its details but its essential elements are simple. The name of the tort arises from the phrase 'to pass off your goods as those of another'. A passing off claim is made out where the legitimate owner of the rights purportedly infringed can show:

(a) that it owns goodwill in relation to those rights in that there is a genuine trade reputation for those rights, and
(b) that the offending person or company has in the course of their trade made a misrepresentation to the public to the effect that the goods or services they supply in the manner purportedly infringing the rights emanate from or have in some way an important connection to the legitimate owner of the rights, and
(c) that there is a real likelihood of confusion in the mind of the public who might use those goods or services between the goods and services of the offending person and the goods and services of the legitimate rights holder, and
(d) that damage has resulted.

D6.17 A word here should be spared for particular dangers which might arise in the sport market with which this book deals, and a new authority which may open up new avenues for rights holders to defend their rights. Firstly, the nature of the goodwill owned by the legitimate owner of the rights needs to be considered. For instance, referring back to the components of passing off set out above[1], in a case exemplifying the traditional approach of the courts, *Lyngstad v Annabas Products Ltd*[2], t-shirts were produced picturing the pop group Abba. Abba's organisation sued for passing off. The court held that as Abba were not in the business of producing clothing there was no common field of activity between the group and the producers of the t-shirts and the use of the picture of the group in that context did not amount to passing-off. As Abba therefore had no relevant goodwill in respect of the manufacture of t-shirts, the acts complained of did not infringe any goodwill owned by Abba.

1 See para D6.16.
2 [1977] FSR 62.

D6.18 In addition, the connection which is deemed to have been established between the goods complained of and the legitimate rights owner is again an important issue. From that point of view there has to be a likelihood that the public will believe there to be more than just any connection: the connection must be relevant. It has been specifically stated in the sporting context in relation to sponsorship that the public generally is used to companies sponsoring sporting events and does not therefore consider that a sponsoring company is the promoter or organiser of the event[1]. For passing-off to be established in such a connection the public needs to be led to understand that the legitimate rights-owner had some way assumed responsibility for an important aspect such as the quality of the goods or services which are considered to infringe its rights. An instance of this is given in *BBC Worldwide Ltd v Pally Screen Printing Ltd*[2]. Here the BBC took proceedings in passing off against unauthorised printers of t-shirts depicting the 'Teletubbies'

TV characters. The BBC was denied summary judgment because it was considered at least to be a possibility that the public would not consider the t-shirts to have any relevant connection to the BBC in that they were not assumed to be manufactured by or under any form of supervision by the BBC, but would consider them merely to illustrate the characters.

1 *Harrods Ltd v Harrodian School* [1996] RPC 697.
2 [1998] FSR 665.

D6.19 A recent authority which cast an interesting cross-light on some of the authorities referred to above is *Irvine v Talksport Ltd*[1]. In this case, Talksport Limited, then operating under the name 'Talk Radio', wished to publicise to its potential customer base of media advertisers its coverage of the forthcoming British Grand Prix. It produced a flyer that included a photograph of Eddie Irvine, the racing driver. The photograph was used with permission of the photographer and therefore there was no copyright infringement[2]. However, in the original photograph Eddie Irvine was holding a mobile telephone. As used in Talksport's flyer, the image had been manipulated to cut out the mobile telephone and to replace it with the image of a portable radio showing the words 'Talk Radio'. This was done without consent from Irvine and it was held that this amounted to actionable passing off for which Talksport was liable in damages to Irvine.

1 [2002] EWHC 367 (Ch), [2002] 2 All ER 414. See paras D3.49 to D3.57.
2 Query as to whether there could have been objection raised as a result of the unauthorised doctoring.

D6.20 The judgment in some ways reflects the current unsettled state of the law in relation to passing off and trade mark infringement in the context of sporting endorsement and merchandising deals. It seeks to clarify the law and to take into account commercial realities. Indeed, specific judicial notice was taken of the common practice of famous individuals exploiting their names and their images by way of endorsement, not only in the field of expertise with which they are primarily associated, but also in more disparate contexts. For this purpose a distinction was drawn between endorsement cases (characterised as being those cases where the famous individual involved had specifically 'told' the relevant public that he approves of the product or service or is happy to be associated with it) and merchandising cases (characterised in the judgment as typified by film merchandising, where products or services using images from the film are sold to members of the public who want a reminder of it). The distinction is not entirely novel but nor is it entirely clear. There is a broad range of deals which are done in the endorsement and merchandising market which are based on various implicit statements on behalf of personalities and organisations and lead to various assumptions on the part of the public to whom they are directed. To categorise all of these deals conveniently into the 'endorsement' pigeon-hole or the 'merchandising' pigeon-hole will be difficult and controversial, and the courts (it is suggested) are not the best qualified to do it, at least on the evidence of the crude distinction that the *Irvine* court sought to draw.

D6.21 Having decided that this was an endorsement case, the *Irvine* court then distinguished the leading case of *McCulloch v May*[1], which had for a long period been treated as a bar to celebrities obtaining judgment in passing off cases where their endorsement was used without consent, based on the lack of a 'common field of activity' between the celebrity and the producer of the product[2]. In *Irvine*, that authority was treated as being discredited and not (in the author's view) before time: the criticisms which had been levelled against McCulloch over the years were well founded; in effect, it was a case which confronted a new problem with an almost touching devotion to old tools and methods.

1 (1947) 65 RPC 58.
2 As in the Abba case referred to above, see para D6.17.

D6.22 *Irvine* therefore breathes life into the remedy of passing off, at least where the defendant is seeking to imply that the claimant has endorsed a product when in fact he has not. An action for passing off will be available if the claimant can show (1) that at the time of the alleged passing off, he enjoyed a valuable reputation or goodwill, and (2) that the defendant's actions amounted to a representation to a not insignificant section of the market that its goods had been endorsed by the claimant. He will also have to show (3) damage, but this will be made out by proof that the defendant's unauthorised use of his goodwill has reduced, blurred or diminished its exclusivity. It will not be necessary to show a common field of activity or more direct damage.

D6.23 The *Irvine* case clearly states that the same does not apply in relation to merchandising deals, but the distinction is not clear and will need to be developed in further case law.

D6.24 One interesting footnote is that Irvine was awarded damages of only £2,000. But even if the victory was a largely pyrrhic one for him, the precedent he has established does create new lines of argument which it can be expected with some confidence will be refined over coming years by those seeking to strengthen the inventory of rights that can be exploited in the sports and wider context. Some of the concepts which have been used to decide the case will require considerable gloss before they have a real meaning, but the door has been opened.

D6.25 Pending such development, it must remain the case that it is by no means established that, in the absence of a registration of a trade mark, passing-off will provide sufficient protection for the Licensor or Producer.

(b) Trade marks

D6.26 In the less colloquial and more technical sense, of course, a trade mark is a graphic device registered on a national or international basis according to rules of registration which are largely harmonised internationally. The United Kingdom has of course its own trade mark registry, as does the European Community, and as indeed does just about every developed economy in the world. There are various international treaties which look to link trade marks registered in one territory to other territories by way of conferring priority in terms of time in relation to subsequent applications for registration in the second territory. The territorial nature of trade marks however, must be understood: a registered trade mark in Britain does not provide a remedy in any other territory when it is treated there in a manner which would constitute an infringement in Britain.

D6.27 Trade marks properly so called are items of property which arise from registration. Those matters which are capable of registration are set out in s 1(1) of the Trade Marks Act 1994:

> In this Act a 'trade mark' means any sign capable of being represented graphically which is capable of distinguishing goods or services of one undertaking from those of other undertakings. A trade mark may, in particular, consist of words (including personal names), designs, letters, numerals, or the shape of goods or their packaging.

D6.28 It is important to note therefore that not only the more straightforward badges of identity and business names are registrable, but also some more arcane things, such as scents which are capable of being represented graphically, music and so forth. To be registrable, a trade mark must comply with this definition. It must have a distinctive character: anything which is completely devoid of such distinctive character is not registrable. In addition, if a mark simply indicates the kind, quality, purpose, value, or origin of the goods – in other words if it is simply descriptive of what the goods are – it will not be registered. Finally, if the mark is simply a customary sign of a trade, such as the familiar sign for pawnbrokers, it cannot be registered. These are known as the absolute grounds of refusal. If any of these grounds is maintained against a mark it will not be granted registration as a trade mark in any circumstances.

D6.29 There are also relative grounds of refusal. These are grounds which will only arise where certain circumstances external to the proposed mark exist. If therefore the trade mark for which registration is sought is identical with an earlier mark, or similar to an earlier mark and to allow that similar subsequent mark to be registered would create confusion with the earlier mark to which it is similar, then again registration will be refused.

D6.30 A trade mark does not confer a monopoly upon its owner. It does however confer upon the trade mark owner certain rights which are unique to it. Trade marks are registered in specific classes in an overall system of more or less universal classifications throughout the world, and within each of those classes any trade mark registered is the subject of a specific description of the goods or services for which it is registered. These matters become particularly relevant in relation to trade mark infringement below.

D6.31 Trade mark infringement is governed by s 10 of the Trade Marks Act 1994. That section is lengthy and raises a number of issues for detailed consideration elsewhere, but an outline summary is as follows. Infringement is effectively constituted in four different permutations of offending act and external circumstances as follows.

D6.32 The first way infringement of a registered trade mark is made out is if an *identical* mark is used for *identical* goods or services to those for which the registered mark holds its registration. Whilst that is the most simple and straightforward type of trade mark infringement, one very serious limitation in the context of the current chapter of an action pursued on this basis is outlined below in relation to the *Arsenal Football Club Plc v Matthew Reed* case[1].

1 [2001] RPC 922.

D6.33 An *identical* mark used for *similar* goods or services to those for which the registered mark holds its registration can also constitute an infringement, but only where there is an addition a likelihood of there being confusion in the minds of the public of a nature somewhat analogous to that required for passing-off to be made out as outlined above[1] (which would include the likelihood of confusion as to there being a relevant association between the goods complained of and the registered mark).

1 See para D6.16.

D6.34 Thirdly, use of a *similar* mark on *identical* or *similar* goods and services to those for which the registered mark holds its registration will again constitute an infringement, again provided that there is that likelihood of confusion referred to above.

D6.35 Finally, if an *identical* or *similar* mark to the registered mark is used for goods or services which are in fact dissimilar to those for which the registered mark has its registration, but that use takes unfair advantage of or is detrimental to the distinctive character or repute of the registered trade mark, and that trade mark has a reputation in the United Kingdom, then that will also constitute an infringement.

D6.36 As will be seen immediately, the formulation of infringement necessarily can involve many layers of value judgement to be made by the parties to any dispute and ultimately by the court. Evidence of matters such as similarity or confusion is always difficult in that they are subjective judgments or states of mind not necessarily amenable to empirical testing. The experience of taking such matters to court can be bitter in that in the absence of evidence of such things as confusion in the minds of the public the relevant trade mark owner may be criticised, and when such evidence is produced the court will devote considerable time to criticism of its methodology! Suffice it to say that a caveat should be entered as to the extent to which ownership of the registered trade mark will necessarily transform any act which the trade mark owner thinks is illegitimately capitalising upon the mark or its goodwill in that mark into a trade mark infringement in the technical sense.

D6.37 Where the Trade Marks Act 1994 requires a showing of likelihood of confusion, the arguments outlined above in relation to passing off, such as in *BBC Worldwide Ltd*[1], may be relevant, ie that there may be confusion but not relevant confusion, or that for all that the public see a similar trade mark being used, they would not associate that similarity with the trade mark in a sense which ties the infringing item to the provenance or origin denoted classically by the trade mark.

1 [1998] FSR 665. See para D6.18.

D6.38 That brings the discussion, however, to the seminal case of *Arsenal v Reed*[1]. This case raises fundamental issues in the context of professional football merchandising, as to the nature of trade mark use and the extent of protection offered by a registered trade mark. Mr Reed was a street trader of some long standing who sold merchandise displaying Arsenal Football Club's trade marks on stand near Highbury. He would sell woolly hats, scarves and other items of clothing with the registered trade marks 'Arsenal', 'the Gunners' and the club badge displayed upon them. Mr Reed's stall prominently displayed however a disclaimer of any formal connection between himself and Arsenal Football Club or any official endorsement of the goods he sold by the Club. It stated that this was unofficial merchandise. This effectively denied Arsenal the opportunity to suggest that there existed any likelihood of confusion, either in the context of passing off or in the context of s 10 of the Trade Marks Act 1994.

1 [2001] RPC 46. See para D1.90, n 1.

D6.39 However, leaving those causes of action to one side, Arsenal could still have had some cause for optimism in that it held registrations in relation to its trade marks for goods of an identical nature to those sold by Mr Reed. The first limb of trade mark infringement, therefore, namely an identical mark used in connection with identical goods or services to those for which the registered mark holds its registration, seemed to be made out. Mr Reed argued however that his use of the trade mark was not use 'in a trade mark sense'. In other words, relying on previous authorities which had indicated that the incidental reference to a trade mark in a comparatively descriptive sense, or in a sense which did not identify the goods or services as being those of the trade mark owner, was not infringement, Mr Reed argued that the trade marks when displayed upon the goods sold by him were not 'badges of origin', ie badges which identified the goods as being those of Arsenal Football Club, but rather 'badges of allegiance' whereby – on the analogy of reasoning similar perhaps to that used in cases such as that of *BBC Worldwide Ltd v Pally Screen Printing Ltd*[1] – the badge simply constituted a depiction of the identity of the football club to which the wearer owed allegiance as a football supporter, devoid of any connotation of that club having any role or responsibility in the origin, quality or nature of the goods. This argument was accepted by the court.

1 See para D6.16.

D6.40 As indicated above, that point has now been referred to the European Court of Justice. It has excited much interested comment both academically and commercially. Certain other cases from other jurisdictions have been referred on a like point and to a certain extent the sports merchandising industry is holding its breath. Affirmation of the view that use of club regalia on shirts and similar items was use as a 'badge of allegiance' not a 'badge of origin' and therefore was not use in a trade mark sense would not constitute a fatal blow to the merchandising or licensing industry, but it would severely affect the market. There would be a much broader range of rights or properties which currently are considered to be controlled by Licensors which would become free for Producers to exploit without licence by capitalising upon that interpretation of the law. The extent to which that would have a liberalising effect on the market or would allow the market then to give effect to the understanding deemed to exist amongst its potential consumers is perhaps a topic for a different work. Suffice it to say however that this is an important issue for all concerned in the industry.

D6.41 On 14 May 2002, the reference was heard before the ECJ and on 13 June 2002, the Advocate General's opinion was issued. Such an opinion is not binding on the ECJ, but is often an indication of what the ECJ may decide. The opinion perhaps took certain constituencies by surprise in that, rather than follow the reasoning outlined above in relation to use 'in a trade mark sense', the Advocate General took a more pragmatic and even traditional view of the question. The Advocate General refused to accept any limitation of the function of a trade mark to a mere indication of trade origin. He accepted that a trade mark acquires a life of its own, making a statement about quality, reputation and even in certain cases a way of seeing life. A consumer may buy trade marked goods for a number of reasons, not exclusively because he considers that trade mark to denote the origin of the goods. Those other reasons are numerous and the Advocate General saw no cause why those other functions of the trade mark should not be safeguarded as well as the function of denotation of origin. He therefore considered that a registered proprietor is entitled to prevent third parties from using a mark identical to a registered trade mark in relation to the same goods or services where such use is capable of giving a misleading indication as to the origin, provenance, quality or reputation of the goods or services to which the mark is affixed. The decisive factor is not the feeling the consumer buying the goods or using them harbours towards the registered proprietor of the trade mark but the fact that they are acquired because the goods are associated with the trade mark. The vivid example is given of the purchase of a football shirt of a rival team simply for the purpose of burning it. Even in that case, the decision to purchase was made on the basis of the identification of the article with the mark[1].

1 See para D1.91, n 1.

D6.42 The Advocate General focused the analysis on why the person who is not the proprietor of the trade mark placed goods on the market with the same distinctive sign affixed to them. If he did so with the intent of exploiting the mark commercially, then in the Advocate General's view he should be deemed to be using it 'in a trade mark sense'.

D6.43 If the ECJ does adopt the Advocate General's approach, then the initial shockwave sent by this authority through the industry will subside to some extent.

(c) Copyright

D6.44 In addition to trade marks there are also other aspects of intellectual property law and types of property or rights which are relevant in these contexts. Copyright is created and subsists in literary, artistic, musical, graphic and photographic works (amongst other things) independently of registration and effectively as a legal by-product of the creative process. That copyright is then enforced to a greater or lesser extent throughout the world by reciprocal enforcement provisions enshrined in international treaties. The copyright owner, ie the author of the work (save where the work is created in the course of employment, in which case it will usually belong to the employer) effectively enjoys the exclusive right to make copies of, adapt, publish, broadcast, affix to goods and otherwise use (ie reproduce) that work. That right can then be made the subject of the licences and provisions referred to in this chapter.

D6.45 Where for instance a club's badge, the representation of a player's signature, a photograph or depiction of a player, team, or venue, or other text or graphics, sights, pictures or sounds recorded in any material form are to form part of any deal, they are all the subject of copyright and must all therefore be controlled by the Licensor as core elements of its brand and dealt with by the Producer only as set out in any agreement.

D6.46 For example, whether or not reproduction of a club badge on a replica shirt constitutes infringement of registered trade mark rights in that badge[1], the badge is also a copyright work and the copyright owner has the right to restrain the reproduction of that work on items offered for sale to the public.

1 See para D6.38 et seq.

(d) *Registered designs*

D6.47 There has for a long period of time been a regime of design registration in the United Kingdom. That regime had fallen largely into disuse and disrepute, but since the Registered Designs Regulations 2001[1] came into force there is the likelihood of a revival of interest.

1 SI 2001/3949.

D6.48 Under the new regime designs may be registered for a period of up to 25 years (by five yearly renewals). A 'design' is defined in the new Regulations as:

> the appearance of the whole of part of a product resulting from the features of, in particular, the lines, contours, colours, shape, texture or materials of the product or its ornamentation.

Of particular interest is that under the new Regulations the owner of the registered design has the exclusive right to 'use' the design and any design which does not produce on the informed user a different overall impression. Such 'use' includes making, offering, putting on the market, importing, exporting or using of a product in which the design is incorporated or to which it is applied[1].

1 Section 7 of the Registered Designs Act 1949, as amended by SI 2001/3949.

D6.49 Such a design registration therefore might confer upon such items as official badges, official design and livery features and so forth a form of exclusivity in connection with any manifestation of that design in any product, its packaging and components, as opposed to the simple manifestation in one product only. This is a substantial advance on previous design registration law. There is a genuine question mark over the robustness of such a registration in due course (which will only be seen in practice) but a number of familiar sports properties might ideally be protected by design registration under the new law as an ancillary protection to that provided by trade marks.

D6.50 However, old design items for which design registrations have not yet been made may not be so protected. To qualify for registration the design must be novel and must possess individual character. Novelty in this context means that if a design has been used more than 12 months prior to the application to register it is not registrable. As a result, a retrospective registration programme to take advantage of the new law is not possible. Instead, regard should be had in respect of new design elements to the availability of such registration.

D6.51 Finally on this topic, an EC registered design will shortly come into force, providing protection analogous to that under UK law as above throughout the EC area.

(e) *Image rights*

D6.52 The phrase 'image rights' is generally used to identify the right to represent an individual's name, fame, image, likeness, photograph, signature and other signifiers of his identity in a manner implying direct endorsement by that player of goods or services. Those rights arise not only in endorsement contracts with the individual sportsman himself, but also in sponsorship contracts with his team or governing body. They are dealt with in detail in Chapter D3.

2 THE PRINCIPAL ELEMENTS OF A MERCHANDISING/LICENSING AGREEMENT

D6.53 There follows an outline discussion of the principal elements of a licensing or merchandising deal, including provision of skeleton draft clauses to illustrate a point where appropriate.

A Due Diligence

D6.54 It is of course trite advice to suggest that the first task of any contracting party is to find out that it is dealing with the right organisation. Apart from the usual searches and investigations which should take place before entering into any deal, however, there is in the context of sports licensing the crucial question for any Producer as to whether it has identified the correct organisation as Licensor to provide the rights required.

D6.55 Each sport can have its own idiosyncrasies in this regard. The place to start investigating the matter is almost always going to be the principal constitutional document governing the sport. This will often be the constitution and/or rules of the sport's governing body. A fairly standard structure for most sports is for there to be a general world governing body, of which all local governing bodies and their sub-divisions are members. In football, the pyramid from FIFA down to UEFA down to the Football Association in England and Wales is a familiar example. In the same pyramid structure, beneath the local governing body there will in many sports be the club or team which then acts as the employer for the players. Given the nature of the rights which will be required in any deal of this nature, locating where those rights are held in the relevant structure, and under what limitations arising out of constitutional arrangements as to their use such rights have to operate, are crucial initial investigations.

D6.56 For instance, to take a particularly rights-intensive form of agreement, where a Producer wishes to produce a video game involving all the teams in a given league or competition and incorporating league tables, management and statistical elements and a game simulating mechanic, there will be a host of rights which ideally would need to be acquired. If the game were a motor-racing game incorporating a drivers championship, a constructors championship and a race simulator, there would be the potential to incorporate the name, identity and logos of the championship or racing formula concerned; the names, logos and liveries of the various teams of car constructors; the liveries and marks of the well-known technical suppliers and main competition sponsors; and those of the main team sponsors and suppliers; the names, images and virtual representations of drivers and even team managers; the branding used and positioned in line with television cameras by major race track sponsors; the layout of racetracks and depictions of other venue specific items; and so forth. In constructing that deal, the Producer will have to work out which organisation to adopt as its Licensor and ensure that the chosen organisation either holds or acquires all the rights it requires to produce the product so that it can grant the same to it.

D6.57 In the example given, if the Producer chooses to sign up with the main promoter or organiser of the competition, then it is at least likely that promoter will have the rights necessary to grant the necessary licence of its trade marks and the necessary copyright licences in respect of statistics, formats and so forth for the competition specific elements. However, it is questionable to what extent it can grant rights in connection with the constructors' or teams' logos, liveries etc. It may be, however, that as part of the constitution of the sport the governing body has the right to grant the rights in respect of those logos on a collective basis for all the teams. That is frequently the case where leagues exist and collective commercial transactions are entered into by the league as a whole. It is a useful way of pooling the resources of the individual teams, not all of whom might not be able to sustain a viable deal on their own, and for all of whom any possible deal would almost definitely incorporate trespassing into rights owned by other teams and require elements of co-operation and reciprocation altogether too difficult to organise on a piecemeal basis.

D6.58 Having checked therefore that there is the relevant degree of centralisation at that level, and assuming that the governing body can grant on a collective basis rights sufficient to satisfy the Producer as to the competition and team elements thus far, the next level to be considered would be the sponsors of the teams. It is very questionable that the relevant rights in this regard are held by any governing body and in certain circumstances it is questionable as to whether they are held or controlled by the teams themselves. These rights may therefore simply not be obtainable in that context without doing a separate deal or forcing the Licensor to do a separate deal with the relevant parties. The extent to which then any failure to obtain such rights detracts from the realism of the product may then have an effect on the price payable by the Producer. It will be too late if the price has been fixed in a binding manner before all investigations are complete.

D6.59 As for the right to reproduce images of the drivers, there are three possible holders of those rights. Firstly, it may be that a chain of agreements or constitutional provisions vests the relevant rights (or at least the right to grant sufficient rights) in the teams, who then vest those rights in the governing body by the chain of authorisation embedded in the constitution of the sport. For instance, certain sports provide for standard terms and conditions of employment of players, managers and other key personnel which are negotiated on a collective basis. Those standard employment terms may vest in the employing team certain rights in relation to the depiction of the players, coaches, managers and other relevant personnel in the team's context (for instance where such personnel are depicted wearing the team's livery, strip or branded clothing or in some other way which necessarily links them to the team, as opposed to a depiction in a purely 'civilian' sense without any such branding or context, or in the guise or context of a national or representative team or any other team of which they are members before or after the team in question). The rules of the sport may then provide that the team must provide to the governing body any rights they require derived from the players via the employment contract in the governing body. In the absence of such a standard employment arrangement and governing body rules it may be that instead there is separate provision in the individual players' agreements each on its own individual basis with the teams which vest the necessary rights in the teams. The final possibility is that the players hold those rights themselves independently of the teams and that negotiations may be necessary either with players' organisations, if the players choose to exploit their collective strength, or with the players' individual representatives, in order to acquire the relevant rights. An equal likelihood to any of the situations outlined above in many sports is that the position is fluid and even a matter of ongoing dispute between the various interested parties.

D6.60 This element of due diligence is therefore crucial and it is necessarily twofold. Firstly, the Producer must identify the rights it requires, and secondly it must satisfy itself as to who holds them and stipulate, where it is contracting with a Licensor which it is not confident holds all the relevant rights, that where the rights provided for in the agreement are not held by it the Licensor at its own expense will obtain them to the extent necessary to make good its grant. It is clear that the Licensor should be pressed to give warranties and indemnities as to the nature and integrity of the rights it holds or controls, such that it confirms it can control the same as a minimum to the extent necessary to grant all rights stipulated in the agreement to the Producer.

D6.61 One other element of due diligence is equally important and (however obvious) deserves mention: the Producer must satisfy itself as to whether the rights it is acquiring exist as rights at all. The question is similar to the question as to whether in law the purported rights in question are of a nature where the grant to the Producer can be made exclusive or not. In other words, a Producer should not get into a situation where it is effectively paying an extra component of value for a purported right or a component of a purported right which is not in fact controlled or controllable by any person. If that right is in fact simply an element of identity which is not properly speaking the property of any one person, and which anybody therefore has the right to use or reproduce, it should firstly not be paying for it, and secondly should not put itself in the position of demanding exclusivity from the Producer in that regard. Most importantly, perhaps, it should not build any of its projections or commercial proposals on the basis that nobody else can use or reproduce it.

D6.62 This issue would arise, for instance, in a team sport where a very generic representation of a strip such as an all white strip may be sufficient to identify a given team (such as the England Rugby Union team) within the game in the sense that a fan will recognise it as a shorthand indicator for the team, but does not display sufficient identifying features, or the representation of it does not necessarily copy designs or copyright works to a sufficient extent to provide any remedy to any purported rights owner where that representation is depicted without authorisation.

D6.63 In this regard, any Producer assessing a grant of rights, especially one purporting to give the Producer the exclusive right to use the rights, must bear in mind the ability of the Licensor, under existing intellectual property law, to make good that grant, ie to prevent unauthorised use of the rights by third parties. For example, if the ECJ in the *Arsenal v Reed* decides to follow the English court rather than its own Advocate General's opinion, and hold that use of club regalia on a shirt or similar is not use of the mark 'in a trademark sense'[1] then the Licensor will not be able to stop third parties using that mark on such items without its authorisation, at least not on trade mark grounds.

1 See para D6.38 et seq.

D6.64 Another case in point arose in connection with the England Rugby rose device. In *Rugby Football Union and Nike European Operations Netherlands BV v Cotton Traders Ltd*[1], the Rugby Football Union, as the governing body of English rugby union and the organiser of England's national representative team, had registered as a trade mark the rose device that had been worn on England team shirts since 1920. However, its action for infringement of that registered trade mark failed, the court ruling that the rose was treated as a national emblem or an emblem of the England rugby team and did not generate in the minds of the public any direct association with the RFU such that it denoted the trade origin of the goods to which it was applied. Whether that is the test to be applied in future may depend on the outcome of the *Arsenal v Reed* case detailed above[2]. Even more starkly, however, Cotton Traders succeeded in arguing that the RFU should never have been allowed to register the device as a trade mark because at the time of registration it was used by many parties on rugby shirts and similar goods and therefore was not distinctive of goods produced by the RFU but rather was a generic mark; nor had it acquired distinctiveness after registration. On the same basis, it was found that the RFU did not own any goodwill in the rose device, use of which by a third party therefore could not be said to amount to a representation that the goods to which the device was fixed were produced by or associated with the RFU. In that case therefore again any exclusivity given to the main licensee (which in this case was one of the claimants in the action) was at least seriously compromised. These considerations also become relevant in considering any obligations imported in any agreement to take any proceedings or defend any article against counterfeiting.

1 [2002] EWHC 467 (Ch), [2002] All ER (D) 417 (Mar).
2 See para D6.38 et seq.

D6.65 Producers should also be vigilant as to claims as to the ownership of necessary rights which are made by interested parties which contradict the settled assumptions of potential Licensors. For instance, producers of video games who have entered into legitimate deals with governing bodies and teams in various sports have been contacted and sometimes even threatened with proceedings by representatives of individuals who feel that rights belonging to them have been infringed, notwithstanding that both Licensor and Producer proceeded in good faith on a different assumption. Examples of this are the disputes involving depictions of individual footballers on video games where the Producer has contracted with the sports' governing bodies: players' representatives have demanded payment to the individual players irrespective of the position of the governing body.

B Grant

D6.66 A golden rule in respect of any grant of rights or even description of rights is that it has three dimensions: nature, territory and term. Discussed above is the requirement for the clear identification of the rights required by the Producer, effectively as intellectual raw materials, and where those are held[1]. The Licensor too has an interest in ensuring absolute clarity in the description of those rights which are to form the subject matter of the agreement. It should not permit any vague or all-inclusive formulations, and it should be clear where applicable that the rights referred to in the agreement are only those that operate within the relevant territory and for the relevant term.

1 See para D6.54 et seq.

D6.67 It is of course a familiar form of dispute for the broad formulation of rights proposed by a Producer to be countered by a restrictive definition proposed on behalf of the Licensor. In particular, if a Producer believes that competition for the award of the contract has caused it to overbid, it may seek to compensate by filling the agreement with more rights than the Licensor initially thought that it was selling.

D6.68 It is crucial that any specific exclusions from the grant either in terms of the intellectual raw materials to be used in the formulation of the licensed articles or in the nature of the licensed articles or the markets into which those can be sold are also specifically identified. For instance, if all of Europe is the territory save that a preceding deal exists in Spain, or the Licensor owns trade marks throughout Europe save Spain, this must be dealt with clearly.

D6.69 Having clearly identified the rights being granted, it is then crucial that there is equal clarity given to the next level of rights, namely the grant by the Licensor in respect of the nature of the use that can be made of them. The distinction is straightforward: the first right is (for instance) a United Kingdom trade mark, and the second is the right to affix it to a t-shirt. The nature of the licensed articles or services to which the agreement relates should be very clearly circumscribed as this will also become a crucial issue in the context of exclusivity. See Example 1 below for some possible provisions:

Example 1

Definitions

'Licensed Articles'	means training shoes in all relevant sizes as approved in all respects in writing by the Licensor pursuant to the terms of this Agreement to which the Trade Mark is affixed
'Trade Mark'	means that UK registered trade mark a copy of the registration certificate issued in respect of which is set out at Annexure A
'Term'	means the period commencing on the date of this Agreement and terminating on the third anniversary thereof subject to earlier termination in accordance with the terms of this Agreement
'Territory'	means the United Kingdom of Great Britain and Northern Ireland the Isle of Man and the Channel Islands

Grant

The Licensor hereby grants to the Producer the right (which shall be exclusive upon the basis set out at clause [ ] and subject to the terms of this Agreement) for the Term to manufacture distribute market and sell the Licensed Articles within the Territory upon the terms set out in this Agreement.

D6.70 A good rule of thumb for Licensors to use as a starting position is that no element or extent of exclusivity should be granted to any Producer which is broader or more extensive than the area occupied in the relevant market by the product which is actually going to be produced. To take the example therefore of a video game, if the video game is only to be sold in a box in a CD-Rom format in the United Kingdom on a specified games platform, then not only should the definition of the rights granted make that absolutely clear, but also the exclusivity granted to the Producer should arguably not include any other territory, any other games platform, or any allied or similar product of services such as online gaming. The rule of thumb counterpart position from the point of view of a Producer is that it must have a sufficient exclusivity from or in respect of all relevant parties to ensure that no other person can produce the same product, or even a product capable of being confused with the licensed product.

D6.71 A Producer will always want to be the only Producer producing licensed articles of the nature dealt with in the agreement. It will also have very strong ideas, based doubtless on the best market research, as to the nature of the competition it faces in respect of the licensed articles or services to be provided for in the agreement. For example, a manufacturer of a soft drink may consider that its competition is not only other soft drinks but also alco-pops, crisps, chocolate bars and so forth – in other words, anything that competes for the pound coin in the pocket of the person aged eight to 18. From the point of view of the Licensor, the competitive market is simply other sugar and water drinks. In the distance between those positions will lie the substance of the argument and hopefully the reasonable resolution.

D6.72 Another key issue which can derail the process is the requirement by a Producer for a level of exclusivity which the Licensor simply cannot deliver. To take our example about video games in motor-racing, it may be that the governing body of the specific racing formula can give exclusivity in relation to that racing formula: as the governing body of that formula, it will not grant rights to a third party to produce a like game covering the entirety of the sport, and nobody else has the right to make any such grant. That is a straightforward exclusivity provision. The governing body may not however be able to stop the teams it represents producing game formats which deal only with their team. For instance, the teams may produce a game which is largely similar to the governing body's game and based upon test driving and so forth, or in which the player can only drive their teams' car through a largely generic environment, or even crossing over with the team between formulas, of which the relevant governing body's formula is just one component. Likewise, to add two examples together, the governing body may have been specifically authorised to enter into an agreement whereby an exclusive licence is given to a Producer to create a boxed game but on the basis that each of the teams is free to exploit online games to their hearts' content. The Licensor needs to be assiduous in obtaining as many rights as possible for delivery to the Producer; the Producer needs to be equally assiduous in ensuring all angles have been covered. See Example 2 below for some possible provisions which may be sought to balance the position in the light of the above. These examples tend to favour the position sought by the Licensor in circumstances where an element of uncertainty may exist:

Example 2

Definitions

'Competitive Articles'	means training shoes [and/or sports shoes/exercise footwear/football boots/rugby boots/running shoes/ footwear/etc/etc] in any relevant sizes to which the Trade Mark or any mark similar to or likely to be confused with the Trade Mark is affixed

1. The Licensor hereby agrees that it shall not grant to any person save to the Producer the right during the Term to manufacture distribute market or sell Competitive Articles in the Territory
2. The Licensor shall use its best endeavours [subject to the terms of this clause [ ].3] to procure that in the event that any person manufactures distributes markets or sells in the Territory and during the Term Competitive Articles any and all steps reasonably practicable are taken to prevent the same at the earliest possible opportunity including but not limited to the taking of all relevant and applicable court proceedings
3. Without prejudice to its obligations arising under clause [ ].2 no warranty is given by the Licensor

3.1 that no Competitive Articles will be manufactured distributed marketed or sold without its permission or consent in the Territory and during the Term and/or
3.2 that in the event such Competitive Articles are so manufactured distributed marketed or sold that the same may be prevented and/or
3.3 that no Competitive Articles will be manufactured distributed marketed or sold by or on behalf of [ ] in respect of any of which the Licensor shall have no obligations to take any steps whether pursuant to clause [ ].2 or otherwise]

D6.73 There is no substitute for clarity on both sides as to the nature of the deal they are entering into before the formulation of heads of terms and certainly prior to the formulation of any legally binding deal or the closure of the bidding process. Frequently, and for understandable commercial reasons, outline heads of agreement are entered into, sometimes on a legally binding basis, which fail to address with sufficient clarity these fundamental issues. Licensors should be absolutely clear as to what rights they have to sell and what level of exclusivity they have to confer. Often, however, one party will be able to capitalise on some naivety of the other in order to create a position from which that other can find it difficult to extricate itself. Even if binding engagements have not been entered into, where a public announcement has been made or an industry has become aware of the award of the contract to a specified Licensor, if these details then need to be sorted out in retrospect the Licensor is in a weak position given that the alternative potential Producers will have gone away and spent their budgets on other properties. It is now in effectively exclusive negotiations without much comfort in any direction.

C Approval Mechanisms

D6.74 It is crucial for the maintenance of brand value by the Licensor that only such goods as it has specifically approved in all relevant respects (eg design, safety, materials and construction) are sold. It is crucial for the Producer that it does not waste its time making products which are then rejected by the Licensor. Therefore, if the product is to be developed as a new product under the agreement then the Licensor will need – and will be required by the Producer – to involve itself in all elements of the design process.

D6.75 Likewise, a major element of the agreement is likely to be the right the Producer has to use the relevant brand and identity rights in order to support, publicise and advertise the availability of the licensed articles or services provided for under the agreement. For that reason therefore, the Producer, in addition to using the more straightforward rights such as the right to reproduce the logo and certain specific elements of livery and so forth in that context, may also require for promotional purposes more arcane properties such as clips of highlights from the competition in which the Licensor is concerned, player appearances, promotional events on site at the Licensor's premises, and so forth. Again, however, the Licensor will usually want strict veto rights over all proposed promotional uses. This is not just because as a matter of good practice a Licensor should always insist on veto rights whenever prominent use is made of its brand, mark or identity. It can also be necessary to protect other aspects of its commercial programme. For instance, if a clip of a certain type of action is required for a TV advertising campaign, it is crucial that the use of that clip does not infringe the broadcasting arrangements entered into by the Licensor.

D6.76 It is also crucial, however, for the Producer to have certainty. Licensors cannot hold the process up forever or be capricious, or even dilute rights down to inconsequence by failure to give reasonable approvals. Timings must be harmonised with production and promotion requirements, dates for key market launches and so forth. Ultimately, the Licensor must be in a position where it has either acted reasonably and taken its necessary role in the development process, or be stuck with what the Producer has been forced to create in a vacuum.

D6.77 Clear procedures therefore should be laid down in the agreement. Clear timings should also be laid down. There should be provision for the Licensor to have sufficient time to make up its mind as to whether it approves the relevant materials or not, perform any tests required, or sound out any third parties it needs to consult, before the materials are used or produced. However, as outlined above, from a Producer's point of view, there will be a legitimate concern that the Licensor cannot take forever in doing so. It is frequently provided therefore that approval of goods is deemed to have been given if an approval deadline is passed without the express approval or disapproval of the relevant materials by the Licensor. This can be a tricky matter for negotiation on certain occasions: Licensors do not want to be held to ransom for mistakes or oversights. It is, however, often the only way that the legitimate interests of the two parties can be reconciled.

D6.78 It is also a legitimate demand by a Producer that all approvals and consents required in respect of all relevant materials are only withheld on a reasonable basis, giving reasons and giving details of how adaptations to the relevant materials or proposed uses will lead to their approval. If a Licensor is uncomfortable having its discretion fettered in this way, it should give further thought to the clarity of the definitions applied to the rights granted. In other words, if it is not to have broad discretion at the approval stage it can derive comfort from having been as specific as possible as to what nature of items can be produced and what nature of promotional materials might be used and how. The less latitude in that regard permitted to the Producer, the less discretion required by the Licensor. From the Producer's point of view however, clarity is never a problem so long as it represents an acceptable position, and if the grant is strictly circumscribed the remaining potential for the Licensor to intervene in the process should be minimal.

D6.79 A skeleton of a clause dealing with the main points arising above appears as Example 3 below:

Example 3

Definitions

'Promotional Materials'	means any advertising marketing or promotional materials in any medium intended to be used or used in any way in connection with the manufacture distribution marketing or sale of the Licensed Articles and/or depicting the Trade Mark or otherwise referring to the Licensor

Approvals

[ ].1 Prior to any manufacture distribution marketing or sale of any item of or project constituting or intended to constitute Licensed Articles and/or Promotional Material the Producer shall obtain the written approval of the Licensor in the manner set out in this clause [ ] (such approval not to be unreasonably withheld or delayed) as to the design materials used performance manufacture and quality and all relevant characteristics of any Licensed Articles and as to the nature and content and any

form format or medium in which any Promotional Material is to be used and any and all countries or regions in which the same is to be used in the said form format or medium.

[ ].2 At Producer's own expense Producer shall ensure that as early as reasonably practicable but in any event no later than ten (10) business days prior to any intended commencement of manufacture (in the case of Licensed Articles) or distribution (in the case of Promotional Materials) Producer shall supply or procure the supply to the Licensor of a sample and (in the case of any Promotional Material wherever relevant) the Licensor's proposals as to all matters to be approved by the Licensor to enable the Licensor to exercise its said approval. If the Licensor fails to notify Producer of its approval or disapproval in writing within ten (10) business days of a request for approval the Licensor's approval shall be deemed to have been given.

[ ].3 Where the Licensor for any reason notifies its disapproval of any Licensed Articles and/or Promotional Materials pursuant to clause [ ].2 it shall notify in writing to Producer the reason for such disapproval and any steps which are to be taken by the Producer in order to procure approval by the Licensor.

[ ].4 Partner shall ensure or procure that any Licensed Articles and/or Promotional Material manufactured distributed marketed or sold in connection with this Agreement shall conform to the samples approved by the Licensor in all material respects unless otherwise agreed in writing by the Licensor.

D Intellectual Property

D6.80 Apart from the fundamental issues of what intellectual property rights exist and what exclusivity they confer[1], further intellectual property issues will arise out of the operation of the agreement itself. For instance, each party will in all likelihood acquire the right under the agreement to use the other party's trade marks in certain contexts. Approval on the part of the Licensor for use by the Producer has been dealt with above and there may well be the need for reciprocal provisions along similar lines for use by the Licensor of the Producer's mark.

1 See para D6.14 et seq.

D6.81 In addition, many if not all licensed articles, services and advertising materials created by the Producer under the agreement are the subject themselves of important intellectual property rights. To stay with the example given above of a video game, that video game in itself will be a copyright work. It will have in all likelihood a separate brand and possibly therefore a separate trade mark for its brand name. It will have a distinctive livery which may be an amalgam of the livery of the Producer and the Licensor. It will generate its own goodwill in the market place, and may give rise to spin-off games, or like games in the same format, following the success of the original. The agreement needs to recognise this in advance and to stipulate expressly who owns the relevant intellectual property rights in and in relation to the licensed articles, services and even advertising and marketing materials.

D6.82 This is often a complicated and difficult conversation. It needs to be understood that Producers will often be investing their own research and development and their own core competences and unique abilities in the development of the licensed articles – that is often why they have been selected to be the Producer. In some cases, they will only make the investment on the basis that the expenditure will accrue for their own benefit in terms of long term 'ownership' of the resulting articles or materials. In the video game example, therefore, if the Producer then develops a format which is transferable to other Licensors, it would expect to be able to take at least the generic component on to that alternative Licensor. From the Licensor's point of view however, it would not wish to be the test environment upon which its competitors or even colleagues can then capitalise by taking over with no strings attached a format it has helped to develop or at least in which it has risked its goodwill and intellectual property. The extent to which creation of licensed articles can be a collaborative process should be acknowledged and provided for where relevant in any agreement. In some ways, this is a parallel conversation to a pricing conversation based on the extent of research and development funds committed: the Producer cannot expect to pay a low royalty rate on sales of the licensed product on the basis that it is expending research and development funds if it then wishes the result of that research and development to accrue for its own unique benefit. The converse is also true: the Licensor cannot expect the price not to reflect the research and development to be undertaken by the Producer if the Licensor is also seeking to take the product of that research and development with it.

D6.83 Some middle ground is usually sought but co-ownership is not often a useful compromise. It may be the only available compromise but the two things are not exactly the same! Regard has to be had to the prospect that at the conclusion of the period of the agreement, the product may still be a viable concern but the Licensor and the Producer may no longer wish to be in business together. Any form of co-ownership in the classical sense requires two co-owners to act as one or not at all. There may therefore need to be genuine creativity in this context, such as ongoing royalties to be paid following even expiry of the agreement, 'buy out' provisions in the event of there being no subsequent agreement, and so forth.

D6.84 In addition to these issues of principle, there are also the standard 'boilerplate' provisions in this context, such as that use of trade marks may take place only as stipulated by the trade mark owner, acknowledgement of ownership be given to the relevant intellectual property owner in each relevant regard (in terms for instance of statements as to the manufacture of the licensed articles under licence by the Producer), and specific disclaimers in relation to elements not represented in the deal (such as, for instance, that where necessary a statement that no endorsement by or on behalf of any of the teams or individual drivers involved in the motor sport championship and depicted in the video game in the example above should be incorporated in the packaging). There should be a specific stipulation that any goodwill accruing to the Producer in relation to any rights licensed to it by the Licensor should be assigned back to the Licensor (and vice versa if a pre-existing product is to be badged with the Licensor's identity). Reciprocal provisions should exist if either party wishes to apply for further registrations of its respective trade marks or requires any assistance in registration of the other as a registered user of those trade marks or even assistance from the other in relation to the defence of those marks in the case of infringement. The relevant costs will usually be required to be paid by the party requiring the assistance; it may wish to provide that it will only pay costs necessarily incurred to third parties, rather than the 'internal' or administrative costs of the other party.

E Payment

D6.85 The legal effect of the payment clause will be minimal but there are practical points which should be outlined at this point. Firstly, in the context of pricing the deal as a whole, there has to be a proper balance struck between the element of minimum royalty guaranteed by the Producer to the Licensor and the ongoing royalty rate. In almost all merchandising or licensing deals, the payment mechanism is a royalty on sales actually made. The minimum guarantee is a periodic sum which is paid on a non-refundable basis on account of those ongoing royalties irrespective of whether they are earned. The sum is however recoupable in that as the mainstream ongoing royalty is calculated on actual sales there is then set against any payment due the sums already paid by way of minimum guarantee on account of those royalties.

D6.86 Where there is no minimum guarantee, because sports related products can have a promotional value which is not automatically the case with other properties, there needs to be a specific provision to the effect that even if there is a transfer of ownership in the licensed articles by the Producer for no consideration or for something other than monetary value or cash, royalties continue notwithstanding to be paid on such transactions.

D6.87 The other standard provisions in this context – that full books and records of accounts should be kept by the Producer throughout the term of the agreement and for a minimum of two years thereafter, and that the Licensor should be entitled (on a reasonable number of occasions only!) on notice during office hours to inspect and take copies of those books and records itself or by its accountants (and in the event that discrepancies of accounting are ascertained to a given level the cost of any such inspection be paid by the Producer) – are important in all contracts where royalties provide the primary method of payment.

D6.88 Likewise, standard provisions in relation to payments common in all commercial contracts as to the method of payment, the currency, the applicability of VAT and other taxes, and the ability between the parties to set off other sums owing between them should be dealt with meticulously.

F Indemnities and Limitations on Liability

D6.89 This is perhaps an area where the considerations in relation to sport are no different to those in relation to any other market sector. From the point of view of the Licensor, the starting position obviously will be to limit the possible liability accruing to it, particularly based upon notional or anticipated profitability of the licensed articles, loss of bargain and opportunity and so forth. Consequential loss and economic loss should therefore be excluded wherever possible by Licensors. An overall cap on its aggregate potential liability of whatever nature under the contract will also be a crucial area of concern.

D6.90 The Producer of course will have misgivings about this, both generally in that it must have some security for its investment of time, money and opportunity, and particularly in relation to any indemnities that are given in connection with intellectual property rights. A Producer is entitled to demand a full guarantee of the integrity of the rights it is acquiring, which means backing up the warranty that the Licensor owns or controls the rights granted with a form of indemnity. Too low a cap on that indemnity will seriously undermine the Producer's protection against claims of infringement by third parties.

D6.91 The manner in which the negotiations proceed obviously will be individual to each agreement but it is perhaps prudent to point out that the 'crude' solution that the position should be entirely reciprocal and equal is not necessarily the best position for the parties. There may need to be appreciation of the legitimate extent to which either party is prepared to be at risk under the agreement. It may therefore be that the final position is a permutation of options from general caps on liability, exclusions of certain heads of damage or liability, and the identification of specific clauses in the agreement to which either or both of those options do not apply.

D6.92 Also under this heading it is right to consider which party owns the right to take or defend proceedings where there has been infringement of intellectual property licensed either way or owned by either party under the agreement. The Producer will ideally want the Licensor to back up its warranties as to the integrity of the intellectual property rights granted under the agreement with acceptance of an obligation to take proceedings against third parties who infringe that intellectual property, and to take conduct of and indemnify the Producer against proceedings issued against the Producer by third parties who allege it has infringed their rights. Likewise, the Licensor will want to have control of any such proceedings in either direction. However, the interests of the parties may diverge when it comes to the question of whether the Licensor is obliged to take proceedings in the first case and the extent to which it is obliged to defend proceedings in the latter. The Licensor may be in a position where it would like to abandon proceedings at a given point (subject always to the indemnities given to the Producer as to the resulting settlement) but the Producer may in those circumstances wish it to continue with those proceedings to eliminate illegitimate competition in a given market.

D6.93 Some outline clauses from which these complex deals may be assembled are given in Example 4 below:

Example 4

Indemnity and Limitation of Liability

[ ].1 The [Producer] [Licensor] hereby agrees fully and effectively to indemnify and to keep indemnified the [Licensor] [Producer] against and hold it harmless from all claims actions loss or liability direct indirect and consequential losses of whatever nature ([excluding] [including but not limited to] [reasonable] legal fees [and] [but excluding] pure economic loss) arising out of:

[ ].1.1 any alleged unauthorised use of [any patent process copyright and/or trade marks (including but not limited to the Trade Mark) idea method or device] [the Trade Marks] used by the [Licensor]/[Producer] in connection with the Licensed Articles and/or the Promotional Materials [save] [where such use is pursuant to the Licensor's authorisation];

[[ ].1.2 any use of and/or alleged defects in the Licensed Articles and/or the Promotional Materials or out of instructions for use of the Licensed Articles or lack of the same (including without limitation all public and product liability)]

[ ].2 If any claim or threat of action ('Proceedings') in respect of which the [Producer] [Licensor] seeks indemnity pursuant to clause 9.1 is received by or comes to the notice of the [Producer] [Licensor] the [Producer] [Licensor] shall as soon as practicable give or procure to be given to the [Licensor] [Producer] written notice of the same and shall make no comment or admission to any third party in respect thereof. Such notice shall be accompanied by a copy of the relevant document(s).

[[ ].3 Save to the extent that the Proceedings relate to the Trade Mark in any way (in which event the Licensor shall have sole discretion as to what action if any is to be taken subject only to the provisions of clause [ ])]:

[ ].3.1 the [Producer] [Licensor] shall allow the [Licensor] [Producer] to have conduct on its behalf of any litigation or settlement negotiations in relation to any Proceedings in respect of which the [Producer] [Licensor] seeks indemnity pursuant to clause [ ].1; and

[ ].3.2 if so requested in writing by the [Producer] [Licensor] the [Licensor] [Producer] shall take such action as the [Licensor] [Producer] may reasonably request (with the [Licensor] [Producer] to reimburse the [Licensor's] [Producer's] reasonable expenses in so doing) to avoid dispute resist appeal compromise or defend such Proceedings.

[ ].4 This clause and clauses [ ].5 to [ ].7 inclusive set out the [Producer's] [Licensor's] entire liability (including any liability for the acts and omissions of its employees agents and sub-contractors) to the [Licensor] [Producer] in respect of:

[ ].4.1 any breach of its contractual obligations arising under this agreement, and

[ ].4.2 any representation or tortious act or omission including without limitation for negligence arising under or in connection with this Agreement,

save only in respect of those matters expressly stated in this clause [ ] of this Agreement to give rise to an obligation set out therein of the [Licensor] [Producer] to indemnify the [Licensor] [Producer].

[ ].5 Any act or omission on the part of the [Licensor] [Producer] or its employees agents or sub-contractors falling within clause 9.4 above shall for the purpose of this clause 9 be known as an 'Event of [Licensor's] [Producer's] Default'.

[ ].6 The [Licensor's] [Producer's] liability to the [Producer] [Licensor] for death or injury resulting from its own negligence or that of its employees agents or sub-contractors shall not be limited.

[ ].7 Save as set out at clause [ ].1 and subject to the provisions of clause [ ].6 and [ ].8 the [Licensor's] [Producer's] entire aggregate liability howsoever arising and of whatever nature in respect of any and all Events of [Licensor's] [Producer's] Default of whatever nature and howsoever arising shall be limited to [ ].

G Warranties and Undertakings

D6.94 The nature of the warranties and undertakings to be given on either side are to a large extent self-evident. Many have been outlined above. The Producer would be entitled to expect from the Licensor a warranty as to its ownership or control of the rights granted under the agreement, its authorisation and competence to enter into the agreement, that (for instance in relation to any element of rights not directly under the Licensor's control) it has any separate authorisations specifically required from third parties where relevant, and as to its intention not to grant similar rights to any third party or to operate them itself where the deal in question is an exclusive deal.

D6.95 There will also be warranties required by the Licensor from the Producer, as to the nature and quality of the design, manufacture and materials used in connection with the licensed articles, and any advertising or promotional materials used in connection with them, and where for instance those licensed articles perform any particular function such as children's toys, that the same are safe and comply with all relevant standards (both in terms of legal obligations and otherwise) in all relevant markets. To take the earlier example of a computer game, there should not be any obscene blasphemous or defamatory material held within that game, nor should the game offend certain canons of taste, and/or the same must achieve certain certifications. All appropriate explanations, warnings and instructions for use should be supplied and all relevant insurance obtained against any product liability or similar claims. Where intellectual property in the licensed articles themselves is to vest in the Producer, it should be clear that the Producer is under an obligation at all relevant times to defend the licensed articles against infringement and to provide from time to time to the Licensor details of the steps being taken to secure the licensed articles against unauthorised copying or reproduction. Where any further consents from parties other than the Licensor are required by the Producer in order to produce the licensed articles, the Licensor should ensure that the Producer is obliged to obtain them.

H Confidentiality and Press Release

D6.96 In the course of formulating and performing the agreement, various confidential details as to the other's plans and business may be obtained by each party and it is important that where applicable the relevant confidentiality clause covers those issues. It should also be provided that if there is to be a press release as to the successful conclusion of the deal, this is agreed by both parties and released only in the agreed form.

I Distribution and Promotion

D6.97 Reference is made above[1] to the potential danger posed by those Producers who might buy the rights to produce certain licensed articles or services in order to ensure that their competitors do not get hold of them, or do not use them in order to avoid competition with that Producer's main product lines. In the absence of a minimum guaranteed royalty that places clear incentives on the Producer to maximise sales[2], there should be a provision providing that distribution and promotion should take place to the best of the Producer's ability in accordance with the Producer's legitimate business policies. A general obligation upon the Producer to do all things necessary to maximise sales may be legitimately resisted by the Producer on the grounds that it best knows its markets and must have the discretion to use that knowledge, but the discussion should at least be had to give the Licensor some comfort in this regard.

1 See para D6.10.
2 See para D6.85.

D6.98 It may be also that there are certain channels of distribution which are prohibited. Regard has to be had of course to competition law as and when this arises, but it is surely legitimate to provide that the licensed articles should be distributed only through reputable and recognised business channels and not by way of (for instance) door to door hawking, sale in street markets, as free gifts, and so forth.

D6.99 If promotional budgets can be agreed and marketing plans set in stone then that may be of benefit but the individual facts and considerations in each case will determine the relevance of these issues.

J Duration and Termination

D6.100 There should be a standard clause as to the term of the agreement, providing that either party can terminate early in the event of unremedied breach of contract or insolvency on the part of the other. However, regard should also be had to those instances where termination on either side may be desirable in respect of occurrences or circumstances which may not in themselves constitute breach of the contract.

D6.101 In this regard, therefore, from the point of view of either party a force majeure clause should be considered. If the instances beyond the party's control are to be reduced to specific examples it may be legitimate to include as an example sport-specific items such as a ruling or determination by a governing body of sport the effect of which, if the Licensor is forced to comply, would be to deprive either party of the substantial entirety of its rights under the agreement.

D6.102 Further issues also need to be considered in this context, particularly to allay certain legitimate concerns on the part of Producers. Any Producer which has contracted to obtain rights from any Licensor needs to hedge against the possibility that the Licensor may cease to control those rights for reasons beyond its control during the course of the agreement. In particular, a governing body may find itself the subject of a breakaway whereby some or all of its major component teams join or form another governing body. This can obviously seriously affect the value of the deal for the Producer. Likewise, if the Licensor is a team, and it is relegated from a given division, or ceases to participate at a given level of the sport altogether, that again will need to be factored into a termination clause.

D6.103 Reference was made above to the value of the brand licensed to the Producer by the Licensor, and the connotations of that brand[1]. If the brand is fundamentally degraded, such as by the conviction of a team or organisation of doping offences, or a major financial scandal or so forth, the relevant Producer will want to have the opportunity to terminate the agreement.

1 See para D6.7.

D6.104 A Licensor should be very wary, however, of the alternative proposition, namely that the payments to be made under the agreement should be subject to re-negotiation in such circumstances. This simply creates a huge area of uncertainty. It is better perhaps for all concerned for there to be either a specific reduction in fees or alteration of terms pre-agreed against the possibility of foreseeable events, such as relegation of a team from a given league, or even a right to terminate in the event of certain such events if that is considered an appropriate response. It would still be open to the parties to renegotiate at that stage to avoid the termination, but omitting an express right to renegotiate would avoid uncertainty and endless bargaining.

D6.105 If a Licensor is a player, the Producer will want the right to terminate if the Licensor ceases to play the game professionally, drops out of a top level, suffers injury or disgrace or even dies. Perhaps the starkest environment for such clauses will be that of such direct player endorsement agreements, where, on top of the matters outlined above (so called 'death and disgrace' clauses), even something as apparently innocuous as an exceptional change in the appearance of the player may have a drastic effect, and this may need to give rise to or right for the Producer to terminate the agreement. An example would be for instance where a player has an agreement with a hair care product and then shaves his head.

K Effect of Expiry

D6.106 There should be specific provisions relating to the extent to which the Producer can continue, following the expiry or termination of the agreement, to sell the licensed articles. It may be legitimate for a Producer to have three months to sell off the licensed articles in order to clear its stocks. Provided this does not tread on the toes of the next incumbent Producer, that is often acceptable. However, the Licensor may not have the same charitable feelings where the agreement is ended as a result of the Producer's breach of contract. The Producer may also want a better hedge against unplanned events in the event that it is forced to terminate as a result of the Licensor's breach. The ramifications of these positions are fairly obvious. Somewhere between the extremes of the stock being destroyed at the behest of the Licensor at the one end of the spectrum to a free and unlimited period of sell-off of stock on the other, will lie what is hopefully a rational situation at the conclusion of the process.

D6.107 A final note would simply be to identify certain clauses in the agreement such as those relating to intellectual property, warranties, indemnities, the taking or co-operation in proceedings, confidentiality and so forth which should be specifically identified as surviving the termination of the agreement.

L Boilerplate

D6.108 Finally, of course, any agreement of this nature should contain the standard 'boilerplate' provisions one would expect in this context. For example, it should be considered essential by any Licensor to have strict control over the right of the Producer to assign or sub-license any rights licensed to it under the agreement or to share with any third party in any exploitation of any such rights in any manner. Even a sub-licence within the Producer's own group of companies should be subject to control by the Licensor, since the Licensor must not let the rights it has granted get beyond its direct and effective control.

D6.109 Finally, a word in relation to notification of the agreement for negative clearance or exemption to competition authorities. It will sometimes be the case that the parties cannot agree entirely as to whether a given agreement is suitable for such notification or otherwise and this can be dealt with by an agreement to meet with the other party to agree and formulate a notification if the parties consider that appropriate. It may also be necessary to provide that, in the event that any competition authority chooses to intervene and declare any provision of the agreement unenforceable or illegal with the effect that either party is deprived of any substantial benefit calculated to accrue to it under the agreement, the parties should renegotiate, and ultimately in the event of such re-negotiation not bearing fruit or not being able to restore the parties to the respective positions they bargained for at the outset, there should be the opportunity for either party affected to terminate the agreement. It goes without saying that it is important for both parties to circumscribe the circumstances in which such rights arise very strictly.

3 SUMMARY

D6.110 The above is intended to be a basic outline as to the main commercial and legal considerations in formulating a merchandising or licensing agreement in the sports industry. It is never going to be exhaustive and the point should be made simply for the record that there will always be legitimate commercial or tactical reasons for departure from practically every single piece of advice set out above on the facts of a given agreement.

CHAPTER D7

HOSPITALITY AGREEMENTS

Warren Phelops (Nicholson Graham & Jones)*

Contents

1 INTRODUCTION

D7.1 The UK hospitality market is estimated to be worth approximately £700m per annum[1]. It has developed from a recognition that a sports event offers a relaxed and informal environment for discussing business and to forge strong business relationships. It is also thought that the glamour and excitement of a sports event will be reflected on the entertainer, the theory being that if the client has a positive experience of the event, so he or she will have a positive view of the company providing the entertainment. Hospitality is also a good medium for a business to show its interest and enthusiasm in working for a particular individual or entity. However, there is a school of thought that hospitality could, in certain circumstances, place undue business pressure on those entertained. This concern has led the Law Commission to consider whether it should, in some cases, fall within the anti-corruption legislation[2]. Hospitality provision is constantly innovating as traditional formats sometimes become tired, repetitive and dull. In current times the tried and tested formula of tickets to, and food, beverage and entertainment at, a sports event does not always achieve the business objectives described above. Hospitality providers recognise that entertainment must fit the target and now also offer more interactive packages, such as the 'Twickenham Experience' and its themed marquee at English Rugby's HQ. This innovation is not confined to sport. Novel events outside sport, such as cookery lessons with celebrity chefs, dinners with celebrities and yoga classes are increasingly vying with non-major events in the hospitality market.

* With the assistance of other members of the Nicholson Graham & Jones Sports Law Group.
1 Corporate Hospitality Event Association Ltd Website, www.cha-online.co.uk.
2 See paras D7.81 and D7.82.

D7.2 Hospitality at sports events is usually provided either by official, specialist hospitality operators who secure the tickets and sites by contracting directly with the event owner (and generally the owner or controller of the event venue), or unofficial operators who acquire tickets and sites for entertainment from unofficial or unauthorised sources, and in each case package them with hospitality. These providers charge a premium for combining a ticket, entertainment, food and beverage. Event organisers and stadia owners often justify this pricing structure by claiming that, as an additional source of revenue, it enables them to keep down ticket prices for the average fan by means of a cross-subsidy from the 'corporate' market. Consequently, the provision of hospitality has become a core part of event/venue owners commercial programme in recent years. Often stadia are rebuilt or redesigned to maximise the opportunities for selling hospitality packages. An example is the £100m development of Chelsea Football Club's Stamford Bridge Stadium, completed in 2001. The £30m West Stand now includes six new hospitality areas, including an upper tier of corporate suites to accommodate up to 600 people[1]. The state-of-the-art national stadium due to be built at Wembley by 2005 is reported to set aside 15,000 'premier' seats out of its 90,00 capacity for corporate hospitality and wealthy guests[2].

1 Sports Venue Technology website, www.sportsvenue-technology.com.
2 '15,000 VIP Seats At New Wembley' (2001) Guardian, 15 December.

D7.3 This chapter focuses on the legal issues surrounding the provision of hospitality at sporting events. It will be divided into four main sections:

(1) the commercial rationale for an official hospitality arrangement;
(2) the key provisions that appear in a hospitality agreement between an event owner and an official hospitality provider (official provider) at a major sporting event;
(3) criminal rules relevant for hospitality providers; and
(4) the rights of purchasers of hospitality packages.

2 COMMERCIAL RATIONALE FOR OFFICIAL HOSPITALITY ARRANGEMENTS

A What is hospitality?

D7.4 It is important to identify at the outset what is meant by hospitality in the context of sporting events so that the parties understand the terms of the agreement and what is expected of each party and, from a competition perspective, in order to define the relevant market. The hospitality provided by the official provider will generally include tickets to the event, entertainment, food and beverage. All of these elements are of a certain standard and provided at a pre-determined location (not necessarily where the event is taking place). Management and administration services, transportation, arranging accommodation, booking facilities, company care, marketing and other materials and services are also incorporated into some packages.

B Advantages of official providers

D7.5 If a purchaser buys a hospitality package from a specialist operator, and the package is not delivered, the only redress is a claim for breach of contract, which often does not give compensation for the loss of business opportunity and embarrassment from letting down those invited to be entertained. Whilst bonding arrangements entered into by some agents can help to ameliorate the position by affording some comfort in case of a failure to provide the package[1], the best security for purchasers is provided by contracting with official providers as they are most likely to be able to provide the package contracted, as perhaps its most crucial elements (the tickets and sites) are obtained by those operators direct from the event owner[2].

1 See paras D7.80 and D7.90.
2 See for example, *Professional Golfers Association Ltd v Evans* (25 January 1989, unreported), Ch D.

D7.6 The official stamp used by official providers in their brochures is the event mark reproduced under licence from the event owner to demonstrate that their supply of tickets and hospitality sites and facilities can be guaranteed. Therefore, an official sanction from an event owner is attractive to a provider as it induces public confidence in its ability to deliver the packages offered. Past scandals, including sales of illicit 'hospitality packages' for high profile events, have dented the public's confidence in unofficial suppliers and, accordingly, any 'official' status will both underline the credibility of the package in the eyes of the public and enable the official provider to sell its packages at a greater premium.

D7.7 From the event owner's viewpoint, making an official provider appointment reduces the prevalence of unofficial activity, provides another revenue stream and secures the provision and quality of hospitality packages as far as possible.

3 HOSPITALITY AGREEMENTS – KEY PROVISIONS

D7.8 The main elements of a hospitality rights agreement (the 'agreement') focus on:

- rights granted;
- territory provisions;
- consideration;
- exclusivity;
- guarantees;
- warranties;
- restrictions on official providers; and
- tax issues.

A Rights granted

D7.9 The official provider will want to ensure that the agreement guarantees the provision of tickets and all facilities necessary for it to sell the hospitality packages. It also wants to ensure that it can use the event logo as an official stamp of approval from the event owner in its sales campaign to attract customers.

D7.10 The event owner, by contrast, will need to address to what extent it can guarantee the provisions of these elements of the proposed packages and to consider the rights that have been or will be granted to its other commercial partners (such as sponsors and travel and tour providers) to ensure there is no conflict.

(a) Due Diligence

D7.11 It is, therefore, vital for both parties that the rights available for grant are confirmed. The due diligence should include disclosure and review of the agreements the event owner has with the venue owners, owners of the environs, the governing body authorising the event, the participants and other relevant third parties.

D7.12 Rights to licence use of the event name and logo will also need to be checked and warranties should be sought not only for contractual protection, but to assist in the due diligence process. Both of these matters are expanded upon below.

D7.13 The key rights are:

(a) to purchase tickets for resale to customers;
(b) to sell hospitality packages;
(c) to use official status;
(d) to use event logo(s);
(e) to use photographs; and
(f) of access.

(b) Ticketing

D7.14 The right to purchase tickets from the event owner of the desired quality and quantity is fundamental for the success of a hospitality programme. Tickets for seats in inferior positions within the event venue will reflect badly on the reputation of the official provider and, arguably, the event owner. Also, those being entertained will not be impressed by a poor view of the action.

D7.15 It is essential to identify either on a map of the stadium scheduled to, or in the provisions of, the agreement the location of the seats provided. Where specific allocation is not possible at the time of contracting, an alternative is to include wording referring to normal highest or second highest face values or some other formula for events that have taken place or will take place at that stadium or those stadia. Further, the practitioner should consider whether it might be possible to identify general positions of tickets, such as in nominated stands at the relevant venue(s).

D7.16 The price (or face value) of tickets is also important in pricing hospitality packages and profit margins. Therefore, prices or formulae (which can be particularly complex where the event takes place in more than one jurisdiction) and dates for supply of tickets must also be agreed to enable the official provider to make plans for its administration.

(c) Authority to sell hospitality

D7.17 The right to sell hospitality packages (as defined in the agreement) must be provided for expressly in the agreement.

(d) Official status

D7.18 The official provider will want to make reference in its marketing brochures to its official appointment. Great care should be taken over how this right will be exploited.

D7.19 The 1998 European Commission investigation into official tennis ball suppliers should be considered when drafting the provisions granting the provider official status[1]. As a result of the Commission's examination of the appointment by the Danish Tennis Federation (DTF) as an official tennis ball supplier, the DTF dropped the words 'official ball' and 'official supplier' from its arrangements with that particular supplier. The Commission was concerned that the use of these words indicated that the supplier's tennis balls were of superior quality to any other brand as a result of their endorsement by the DTF, thereby misleading consumers.

1 *Danish Tennis Federation Commission* OJ [1996] C 138/6, [1996] 4 CMLR 885, *Commission's XXVIIIth Report on Competition Policy* (1998), p 160. See further paras B2.207 to B2.211, B2.316, B2.317 and D5.50.

D7.20 An official provider might be examined on similar grounds by the Commission. However, unlike an equipment manufacturer, the official provider by using its 'official' status in marketing literature is seeking to illustrate a link to the event in order to give comfort to the public as to its performance, rather than to suggest that its services are of a higher quality than its trade competitors. However, there has been no published European decision on this in a hospitality context.

(e) Use of event logo(s)

D7.21 The official provider will want to use the official logo(s) for the event in its sales and promotional material because (as mentioned above) it will be perceived by the public as a type of kite mark guaranteeing quality and performance. It will require a grant of rights (licence) from the event owner in the agreement permitting the use of the relevant mark(s).

D7.22 The official provider's rights to use the event owner's logo should be set out clearly in the agreement. The following questions must be considered in the early stages of negotiation:

- what is (are) the trade mark(s) or the logo(s) that the official provider may use? The exact form of the logo to be used should be appended to the agreement and any colour, size and other use restrictions specified;

- how can the official provider use the logo? In combination with other stipulated words (for instance, 'official'), freely or only in isolation? and
- where can the official provider use the logo (for example, printed publicity materials, advertising hoardings)? Are the rights exclusive within the hospitality product category?

D7.23 The official provider should carry out the due diligence on the quality of the event owner's relevant intellectual property rights. Ownership of registered trade marks can be checked by searching either the UK or European trade mark registers. Even if the marks are unregistered, it is advisable to search the trade marks register for any similar marks as owners of such marks may object to the official provider's use of the logo. This will be of most concern for a new or one-off event for which a logo may have been recently created.

D7.24 The event owner may be using the trade mark under licence. If so, the terms of this licence also need to be checked to ensure, in particular, that it has the right to sub-license to the event sponsor and that the appropriate warranties and reassurances are given regarding ownership of the marks.

D7.25 It is important to establish who owns the copyright in the logo. Of key importance is who designed the logo. If the designer was an employee of the event owner then, subject to any agreement to the contrary, the copyright will automatically be owned by the event owner. If the designer was a third party contractor, the copyright assignment from the designer to the event owner should be reviewed to ensure that all the rights were transferred to the event owner.

(f) Use of photographs

D7.26 An official provider may also want to use and reproduce photographs of players participating in an event in its sales and marketing material. These may or may not be photographs that the event owner owns or has authority to use. The official provider must obtain permission from the copyright owner (the photographer, his or her employer or assignee) or check permission given to the event owner. Otherwise, any such reproduction would be infringement of copyright in the photograph.

D7.27 What about consent from the players themselves? Until recently, it was generally acknowledged that personality rights (that is, the right of a person to restrict photographs of themselves) do not exist in English law. However, in *Edmund Irvine v Talksport*[1] the High Court held that in using a picture of the British Formula 1 racing driver Eddie Irvine which had been manipulated to show him listening to a radio marked 'Talk Radio', Talk Radio was liable to Mr Irvine in damages for passing off. The court decided that Mr Irvine's image had been misused to create a false message in the minds of those viewing the promotional material. Although decided under the law of passing off, this decision goes some way to acknowledging rights in personalities' images. This reinforces the requirements of the British Codes of Advertising and Sales Promotions which 'urge' advertisers to obtain written permission before referring to people with a public profile[2].

1 *Edmund Irvine and Tidswell Ltd v Talksport Ltd* [2002] EWHC 367 (Ch), [2002] 2 All ER 414, Ch D. See paras D3.52 to D3.57.

2 (1999 edn, revised 23 April 2000), Advertising Code, principle 13.1(b). See generally Chapter D3.

D7.28 The strip that players are wearing in the photographs must also be checked and provided for. Under trade mark law, if the appearance of any trade marks, such as logos on the players' strips in the photographs, is merely incidental, this will not constitute trade mark infringement[1].

1 *Trebor Bassett Limited v Football Association* [1997] FSR 211. See para D1.89.

D7.29 However, rather than relying on 'incidental inclusion' or taking risk on the rapidly-developing area of 'personality rights', if the event owner has authority, it is preferable to impose obligations on the event owner to secure all necessary consents, licences and assignments to give the official provider access to, and the right to use, player photographs.

D7.30 The official provider should require the event owner to undertake to take action against infringers (particularly hospitality infringers) making unauthorised use of the logo. If this is the case it should be clearly stated in the agreement.

(g) Access to sites

D7.31 The parties will need to establish what land (including at the venue(s)) the event owner controls or has rights to use for the event. The parties must then agree whether the official provider should be allocated the best of those facilities and/or sites on that land or whether they will be reserved for the event owner's other commercial partners. It is also important to prevent 'piracy' by ensuring that unofficial providers cannot get access to the best facilities and/or sites.

D7.32 The access rights the official provider will require include:

- a right of occupation;
- rights to use power and water supplies and other necessary facilities; and
- rights of access to and from other areas of the stadium which the official provider's clients and staff may need to use.

D7.33 All terms of access must comply with all relevant laws and regulations, particularly health and safety. The agreement should also set out which party is responsible for third party liability, particularly for injury to persons.

B Territory provisions

D7.34 The agreement should clarify the geographical area for which the official hospitality rights are granted.

D7.35 Many major sporting events with international interest have at least one officially appointed travel and tour provider providing packages of tickets purchased from the event owner with travel and/or accommodation (principally for overseas clients).

D7.36 Many hospitality companies market and sell packages either themselves or through agents in territories outside where the events will be held, which are also the tour operator's prime selling markets. There is, therefore, considerable scope for conflict and the event owner may seek to limit the official provider's right to sell packages outside the countries where the event is being held unless an accord is made with the official tour provider.

D7.37 The event owner will need to balance the risk that denying the official provider the opportunity to market overseas may provide the unofficial hospitality agents with a free run in these territories against the risk that allowing an official provider a worldwide sales territory will devalue the official travel and tour provider's rights.

D7.38 Where territorial restrictions are imposed on the official provider it will want comfort that the official travel and tour provider will not compete with it by offering free food, refreshment and/or otherwise similar entertainment in its packages or by sub-contracting hospitality provisions to a third party commercial partner[1].

1 See paras D7.47–D7.60.

D7.39 Key nowadays in the discussion on territoriality is the advertising of packages for sale on the internet. As websites are accessible globally, the official provider may risk breaching any territorial restrictions imposed upon it.

D7.40 One solution would be to allow the official provider to use the internet for marketing and sales provided that the website states that it only has rights to sell packages to persons within the event's jurisdiction or specified jurisdictions and that the website is designed only for customers in those jurisdictions. The parties could also specify in the agreement that the prompt boxes for any purchaser placing an order for hospitality in response to an internet advertisement specify that the return address for the ordered packages should be in the same jurisdiction (or other relevant territory) where the event is being held.

D7.41 There is, however, still a risk for the event owner if rights are only granted to the official provider for a limited part of Europe. Although it is acceptable under EU law to restrict active sales (that is, to prevent the official provider from actively seeking customers from other jurisdictions within Europe), passive sales cannot be legitimately restricted[1]. Therefore, if someone from, for example, Spain accessed the website, ignored the statement that the website was offering packages to customers only in the UK and requested packages from the official provider, the event owner could not restrict the official provider from supplying the ordered packages despite the fact that this may be selling outside the permitted territory.

1 Commission Regulation EC/1983/83.

D7.42 One possible solution on a practical level is to prescribe that the functionality of the website should require address details for sale of packages and not allow entry of addresses outside the permitted jurisdictions (for example, by only including certain countries in the 'country' part of the address).

C Consideration

D7.43 The event owner may have acquired the rights to host the event and commercially exploit the event (including the right to sell tickets to the event) from a third party (for instance, a sport governing body) in return for payment. Therefore, the event owner will want to secure this payment obligation from rights buyers, including the official provider, by demanding a fixed fee from the official provider independent or irrespective of hospitality sales or revenue. The fee may be characterised as a licence fee paid up front for use of the event name and logo or a minimum guaranteed amount of the event owner's agreed entitlement to a share of hospitality sales revenues.

D7.44 If a minimum guarantee, this is generally paid in instalments, after contracting but prior to the commencement of the event, rather than a single up-front payment. The event owner will want comfort that instalments payments due after, rather than upon, signing the agreement will be paid on time and will commonly seek a guarantee for this obligation[1].

1 See paras D7.61 and D7.62.

D7.45 The minimum guarantee commonly reflects a fair valuation of the rights being granted. This valuation will be made on an assumed basis so the official provider will want contractual provisions to vary the guaranteed amount if any of the assumptions in the agreement are incorrect. Sometimes this is dealt with by warranties alone or by both warranties and terms for calculating the reduction. The assumptions will generally include such matters as the price of tickets, the participants and the number of events.

D7.46 In addition to the fixed fee or minimum guarantee described above, the event owner may demand further sums equal to either, or both, of:

- the cost of the tickets to be included in the packages. (If the ticket prices have not been determined at the contract date a contractual mechanism for calculating the price will be required at the time of contracting. Otherwise there will be an unacceptable level of uncertainty for the official provider. Where the event will take place in more than one jurisdiction or the tickets are priced in more than one currency, provisions dealing with currency conversion to calculate the event owner's entitlement are necessary); and/or
- a percentage of either hospitality sales revenues, profits derived from hospitality sales, and/or the face value of the hospitality tickets (off-set against any minimum guarantee or, perhaps, fixed fee).

D Exclusivity

D7.47 There are obvious advantages to both parties in limiting the number of appointed hospitality providers. From the official provider's standpoint an exclusive, official appointment:

- enables it to stand out from unofficial agencies and to provide the best hospitality in the best locations;
- enables it to use the event logo exclusively as a mark guaranteeing performance and quality in the consumer's eyes; and
- should minimise the risk of any potential criminal law concerns[1].

1 See paras D7.80–D7.82.

D7.48 From the event owner's point of view an exclusive, official appointment:

- protects the value of a key asset, the event marks, as it can control which agencies will be licensed to use them;

- makes policing and control over the official hospitality market easier;
- generally maximises the value of the rights; and
- is administratively easier and cheaper because the cost and time in negotiating one, rather than numerous, licencees is less.

When drafting exclusivity clauses the issues outlined below should be addressed.

(a) *Look out for others*

D7.49 To protect the official provider's interests, it should be clearly stated in the agreement that neither the event owner nor anyone else on its behalf or authorised by it can sell hospitality for the event.

(b) *No conflicting arrangements*

D7.50 It is important to ensure that there are no conflicting arrangements with other parties with whom the event owner contracts to stage the event, such as existing arrangements between the venue owner (as distinct from the event owner) and stadia sponsors or debenture or box holders which allow those persons, for example, to dine in restaurants or to receive hospitality at the stadium at all events held there. It is important to consider all of the existing arrangements and agree the terms upon which the official provider operates in conjunction with these other arrangements.

(c) *Policing unofficial sources*

D7.51 Providers who have obtained tickets from unofficial sources who are not permitted under the ticketing conditions to sell tickets for hospitality should be restrained as far as possible[1]. This is particularly difficult for major events and whilst an event owner will usually be unable to procure that this does not happen, the parties should agree the steps to be taken to prevent this as far as possible. Examples include:

- inserting provisions in contracts (including on the tickets themselves) with those whom the event owner supplies or sells tickets, prohibiting them either from using the tickets for hospitality or from transferring them without the event owner's consent. The official provider must be exempted from these provisions in respect of the tickets it receives;
- ensuring all tickets carry security codes and means of identifying the original recipient of a ticket;
- including a provision in the agreement that the event owner will refer any persons interested in hospitality to the official provider only; and
- publicising the official provider and the prohibition on others using tickets (or hospitality) and sanctions for breach (including court action and publicising the action). Both parties will need to agree where, how often and who bears the cost of the publicity. It is becoming more common to set up a telephone hotline service so members of the public can confirm the validity of tickets and obtain hospitality information.

1 See for example, *Professional Golfers Association Ltd v Evans* (25 January 1989, unreported); see also para D1.129.

(d) Other commercial partners

D7.52 The parties will need to clarify what hospitality arrangements are intended to be made for the event owner's official guests and other commercial partners (sponsors, official licensees, and so on) and who is entitled to the better locations.

(e) Competition law issues

D7.53 Exclusive hospitality arrangements may fall within the scope of UK and EC competition rules[1].

1 See Chapter B2.

D7.54 Article 81(1) of the EC Treaty prohibits agreements which may affect trade between Member States and which have as their object or effect the prevention, restriction or distortion of competition. Article 82 prohibits any abuse by one or more undertakings of a dominant position within the common market or in a substantial part of it in so far as it may affect trade between Member States. Similar provisions now exist under UK law courtesy of Chapters I and II of the Competition Act 1998 (which came into force on 1 March 2000).

D7.55 If an agreement infringes Art 81(1) then it will be void and unenforceable (unless the offending provisions can be severed from the agreement). Such an infringement also gives rise to the risk of fines: under EC Regulation 17/62 the European Commission may fine infringing parties up to 10% of their total worldwide turnover.

D7.56 Agreements falling within the scope of Art 81(1) may benefit from an exemption under Art 81(3) where they give rise to economic benefits, confer a benefit on consumers, and are no more restrictive than is required to achieve those aims. The parties seeking an exemption must notify their agreement to the Commission.

D7.57 In assessing whether Art 81 (or the Chapter I prohibition under UK law) has been infringed, the key question is whether the arrangements in question have an appreciable adverse effect on competition on the relevant market. This will depend to a large extent on whether the hospitality agreement has been entered into on an exclusive basis and, therefore, whether there remains an opportunity for a competing provider of hospitality to provide their services at the same event[1].

1 But see paras B2.85 and B2.219 for a consideration of the preliminary question of how to define the relevant market, which may assist greatly in demonstrating that even exclusive appointments have no appreciable effect on competition on the market properly defined.

D7.58 Whilst not dealing specifically with hospitality agreements, the 1992 Commission decision concerning distribution of package tours for the 1990 World Cup[1] is relevant. The organising committee of the 1990 World Cup granted a package tour operator exclusive rights worldwide to acquire ground entrance tickets for the purpose of selling package tours that included those tickets. The Commission held that the exclusive rights granted infringed Art 81(1) as the effect was to restrict competition between tour providers in the common market. No fines were imposed.

1 *Distribution of Package Tours During the 1990 World Cup* OJ [1992] L326/91, [1994] 5 CMLR 253. See para B2.227.

D7.59 More recently, on 20 July, 1999, the Commission decided[1] that the ticketing arrangements for the 1998 World Cup in France were anti-competitive. The organiser of the tournament was held to have acted in breach of Art 82 by abusing its dominant position in distributing over 570,000 tickets only to those with an address in France and 181,000 tickets for the final stage games at a draw in Paris six months prior to the event. However, it was only fined €1,000. The token fine reflected the Commission's view that the parties were unlikely to have appreciated in advance the abusive nature of the conduct.

1 *1998 Football World Cup* OJ [2000] L5/55, [2000] 4 CMLR 963. See para B2.227.

D7.60 In practice, hospitality arrangements for most events are unlikely to give rise to competition concerns. Concerns may arise in relation to exclusive deals for larger events, or the entry into long-term arrangements whereby a particular hospitality provider is given access to a venue or event for a period of years thereby excluding others. Concern may also arise where hospitality arrangements are linked to general ticket distribution and, therefore, limit the ticket distribution channels. Appropriate discussions should be held prior to the event with the competition authorities in order to gain some comfort that the proposals will not be viewed as anti-competitive.

E Guarantees

D7.61 The event owner will usually require some form of security for the payment of instalments of the minimum guarantee amounts, fixed fee and other agreed payments, such as, the percentage of hospitality sales revenue. Such security is often provided by way of a bank guarantee or letter of credit arranged by the official provider. A bank will almost always insist upon its own standard letters of credit/guarantee terms and would typically require a separate counter-indemnity, sometimes cash-backed, from the applicant for the letter of credit guarantee, whether the official provider or a related company.

D7.62 Guarantees are not commonly provided to secure performance obligations given the difficulty any party would have in stepping into the shoes of another to carry out its business. However, in certain circumstances (for example, where the guarantor operates in the hospitality industry) the parent company or other associated company may be prepared to procure the performance of the official provider's obligations, for example, by way of a novation of the obligations of the official provider triggered by the latter's failure to perform. This arrangement can be set out in the agreement by joining in the parent or associated company, or alternatively in a separate agreement between them and the event owner.

(a) Trust account

D7.63 Sometimes, a pre-agreed amount of the official provider's revenue is held on trust for the event owner in a trust account to meet the cost of providing the packages to the purchasers in the event the official provider fails to deliver. The terms of the trust account deposit can be such that funds could be released at certain performance milestones, such as the provision of packages for the early rounds of a tournament.

D7.64 The official provider will also be interested in the funds and may require security for the return of an amount equal to the funds at some point in the future, to be agreed between them, for example, if the event does not take place, the event owner commits a breach entitling the official provider to recover any losses or, on the achievement of certain milestones, such as provision of packages for the early rounds of the tournament.

F Warranties

(a) Event Owner's Warranties

D7.65 Time often prevents a proper prior due diligence exercise from being undertaken leaving the official provider reliant on building appropriate warranties into the agreement, which in any event encourages disclosure by the event owner. Examples of warranties the official provider should try and obtain include that:

- the event owner has all the necessary authority and consents (including, if appropriate, from the relevant sports governing body) to grant the rights, such rights are unencumbered and that it will not enter into conflicting arrangements;
- the quality of participants in the event is of an agreed standard;
- the level of organisation of the event is of an agreed standard;
- the event owner has the right to grant the licences under the agreement so that the use of the logo will not infringe third party intellectual property rights. This warranty is commonly backed by an indemnity;
- the arrangements with venue owners include a right to use land for the hospitality sites granted to the official provider by the event owner;
- all enquiries about hospitality will be referred to the official provider;
- the event owner has complied with the relevant laws such as those relating to health and safety;
- the event will take place at a certain time, at specified venues and be of a certain format; and
- insurance for cancellation or abandonment of the event is in place and that the official provider is covered by such insurance.

D7.66 The event owner will also want to ensure that the purchasers of hospitality packages actually receive the tickets and hospitality and will be particularly concerned to safeguard that event, such as on the insolvency of an official provider. While a number of different structures can be used to achieve the same commercial result, the legal structure ultimately used will depend on the nature of the applicable legal system, such as whether common law or codified, and therefore whether it recognises concepts such as trusts and agency arrangements. One of the devices used frequently in common jurisdiction is the trust account 'flawed asset structure'.

(b) Official Provider's Warranties and Undertakings

D7.67 A key concern for the official provider will be to develop and protect the reputation and image of the event. In allowing the official provider to use the logo, in particular if this is in combination with the word 'official', the reputation of the event is on the line; clients attending or enquiring about the official provider service will associate the official provider with the event.

D7.68 The degree of control required will depend on the size of the event, but the event owner should consider including the following controls over the official provider in the agreement principally in relation to the manner in which the official provider sells packages:

- an undertaking as to the quality of the service that the official provider must provide (for example, a broad description such as high quality standard of service);
- a specification of the quality of the sales and marketing materials on which the logo is reproduced;
- a right to inspect stocks of sales and marketing materials;
- a right to prior approval of all printed sales and marketing materials;
- a right to veto uses of any sales and marketing materials that the event owner considers of substandard quality;
- an acknowledgement of the event owner's rights to the logo and trade mark and that all goodwill from official provider's use of them accrues to the event owner;
- an obligation on the official provider to report any complaints about itself or about the event to the event owner;
- a provision for early termination of contract including destruction or return of all materials bearing the logo to the event owner and undertakings not to use the trade mark or logo; and
- an obligation on the official provider to inform the event owner if it is aware of any infringement of an event owner's intellectual property rights.

G Restrictions on official providers

D7.69 There are certain areas where the event owner may wish to limit the scope of the official provider's activities. The matters covered commonly include:

- a prohibition on the provider from sourcing tickets from third party persons;
- restrictions on the use of the event owner's intellectual property rights and the freedom of the provider to instigate its own marketing campaign;
- restrictions on the use of income and in some cases tickets received by the official provider from hospitality sales prior to delivery of the packages[1];
- restrictions on sub-contracting to caterers or hospitality infrastructure providers without consent and specifying terms that must be included in those contracts;
- restrictions on sub-contracting to other hospitality providers and sub-licensing the right to use the event logo;
- obligations to use event sponsors' products, where relevant; and
- steps to prevent the official provider's clients from branding hospitality areas.

1 See paras D7.63 and D7.64.

H Tax issues

D7.70 The tax treatment of the transaction will vary depending on the rights supplied by the event owner and the payment method.

(a) Income/corporation tax

D7.71 Each party will be liable to tax on its profit element in the country where it is resident for tax purposes, although it may also be liable to tax in the country in which the event is staged, if it can be said to be carrying on a trade there.

(b) Value added tax

D7.72 VAT is a tax on supplies of goods and services. The proper VAT treatment can be complicated particularly where the event takes place in a number of different countries.

(c) Inside the United Kingdom

D7.73 Assuming that the parties and the event are based in the UK, the sale of the ticket by the event owner to the official provider is a taxable supply for UK VAT purposes by the event owner. (The sale of a match ticket would seem to constitute the grant of a right to occupy a seat or other accommodation at a sports ground which is mandatorily standard rated)[1]. Equally, the grant of hospitality rights and any licence to use logos or other intellectual property rights will be a taxable supply, on general principles.

1 Value Added Tax Act 1994, Sch 9, Pt II, Group 1, Item 1(l) (VATA 1994).

D7.74 The event owner should be registered for UK VAT and invoice the official provider. On general VAT principles the official provider will be able to recover the VAT charged to it by the event owner provided that it makes fully taxable supplies in the course of its business. The current view in the UK is that, assuming the official provider charges one price to its customers for the hospitality package, the official provider is making a single supply (called a composite supply) to its customers for VAT purposes with the predominate element being the supply of the match ticket and the other services, such as the supply of food, being incidental. This is because the customers are obliged to buy the match ticket and the other services as a package.

D7.75 The result is that the VAT supply by the official provider will be treated as taking place in the UK, where the event is being staged in the UK, and UK VAT must be charged to customers on the total amount charged by the official provider. Consequently, the official provider should register for UK VAT if its supplies exceed the VAT registration threshold and it should be able to reclaim the VAT charged to it by the event owner.

(d) Outside the United Kingdom

D7.76 Where any of the events are to be held outside the UK, the VAT implications are more complicated. Irish law, for example, treats the sale of the hospitality package by the official provider as sporting services which will be treated as being supplied for VAT purposes where the official provider has its business establishment. This may not be where the event is being staged. However, the event owner may be based in the same jurisdiction as the event and may, under that local law, be obliged to charge local VAT on some of the rights being provided to the official provider, such as the tickets. The official provider may have to recover that local VAT separately (for example, under the Eighth EC Directive 79/1072 dealing with arrangements for the refund of VAT to taxable persons), which will be an administrative burden with possible adverse cash-flow consequences.

D7.77 Other rights, such as the grant of licences by the event owner to use trade marks, may require the official provider to account for UK VAT under the reverse charge procedure. For example, if the official provider is established in the UK and is paying a French event owner for the use of its trade marks, there is no French equivalent of VAT payable but the official provider must treat itself as supplying the services in the UK[1]. So, it has to account for output tax on the supply made to it by the French event owner, but it also has a corresponding input tax reclaim. Assuming the official provider is fully taxable, it will be able to recover the input tax in full and there will be no actual VAT cost.

1 Section 8 of the VATA 1994.

(e) Withholding

D7.78 VAT problems are not the only difficulties caused by an overseas connection. If the event owner is based outside the UK and grants the official provider the right to use, say, copyright, withholding tax (an amount of tax deducted at source from interest, dividend, royalty or licence fee payments) may have to be deducted from payments by the official provider to the event owner for use of those rights, although an applicable double tax treaty may reduce or eliminate that withholding tax. This may give rise to a cash-flow cost for the event owner, if there is no grossing up clause in the agreement (that is, a clause obliging the official provider to pay an amount which after any tax deducted leaves the event owner with the amount it would have received had tax not been deductible) or to an additional cost to the official provider, if there is a grossing up clause.

D7.79 Whilst this is only an indication of some of the areas to consider, it highlights the need for both parties to agree between themselves and, possibly, with the relevant tax authorities, at an early stage what services they are providing and for what payment, so that the appropriate structure can be reflected in the agreement for the benefit of each party.

4 CRIMINAL LIABILITY

A Currently

D7.80 In supplying tickets as part of a hospitality package, the official provider should consider the following English criminal law designed to control the secondary ticket sale market in case the official provider's activities might fall foul of any of those offences:

- It is an offence for an unauthorised person to sell, or offer or expose for sale, a ticket for a designated football match in any public place or place to which the public has access or, in the course of a business, in any other place[1].
  A person is unauthorised if he is not authorised in writing to sell tickets for the match by the home club or by the organisers of the match. Currently the

offence only extends to designated football matches (which includes most cup or league matches in England or Wales). As a hospitality package provider can commit an offence under s 166 of the Criminal Justice and Public Order Act 1994 if it supplies a ticket to a designated football match as part of a hospitality package without being authorised, this makes official sanction attractive. The Act also gives the Home Secretary power to extend the application of s 166 to other sporting events.

- It is an offence for any unauthorised person offering to resell tickets not to give information, prior to their supply, about the original price of the ticket, the rights conferred to the holder of the ticket, the location of the seat and any features (obstruction, and so on) which would adversely affect the purchaser's use or enjoyment of the seat[2]. This applies to the supply and resale of tickets for any gathering, amusement, exhibition, performance, game, sport or trial of skill or similar event. In addition, unless the purchase of the ticket is by telephone, the information must be given in writing.

  These obligations do not apply to the holder/promoter of the event or any person acting on the behalf of the holder or promoter of the event. An official provider appointed or authorised by the event owner should, therefore, be exempt. They also do not apply where the supply of tickets comes within a package to which the Package Travel, Package Holidays and Package Tours Regulations 1992 apply.

  The Package Travel, Package Holidays and Package Tours Regulations 1992 could apply to hospitality. These Regulations apply to packages (and this would include hospitality packages) that contain any two or more of the following elements: transportation, accommodation or other tourist services not ancillary to accommodation or transportation and accounting for a significant proportion of the package. An example of other tourist services could include grandstand tickets to watch the Monaco Grand Prix when included in a hospitality trip to Monaco.

  The Regulations provide that certain information must be contained in the sales brochure for the package; the circumstances where particulars in brochures are binding on the package provider; the form of the supply contract and that the package provider must provide a bond or other form of financial security to refund consumers' prepayments and repatriate them in the event of insolvency. The final requirement means in practice that all package providers covered by the regulations must be bonded to a professional association (such as ABTA) or a suitable trust account or insurance policy must be in place. Where the package includes a flight, the provider must have an Air Travel organisers' licence (ATOL) issued by the Civil Aviation Authority.

  Unless a hospitality package provider is organising packages to events including either transportation and/or accommodation in the package, the Regulations do not presently affect the hospitality industry. However, future EU legislation, especially in light of the problems encountered with the 1998 World Cup could extend the regulation to the hospitality package industry and lead to bonding becoming compulsory for all hospitality package providers. At present the bonding scheme open to hospitality package providers operated by the Corporate Hospitality & Event Association Ltd (CHA) for its members is voluntary[3].

- It is an offence for any person in the course of any trade or business to make a statement which he knows to be false or recklessly to make a statement which is false concerning the provision, nature and location of any services, accommodation or facilities, the time at which or the manner in which such services are provided and by whom, or the examination, approval or evaluation of such services by any persons[4]. Hospitality package providers, therefore, need to have verified the facts behind any claims they make about the content and quality of the package in any literature given to consumers concerning the package to be offered.

1 Section 166 of the Criminal Justice and Public Order Act 1994. See further para A1.66, n 1.
2 Regulation 4 of the Price Indications (Resale of Tickets) Regulations 1994.
3 See further paras D7.90 and D7.91.
4 Section 14 of the Trade Descriptions Act 1968.

B The Future

D7.81 The criminal law's impact on hospitality has been under review. The Law Commission published a report in March 1998 on the updating of the Prevention of Corruption Acts 1889 to 1916[1]. It proposed the creation of two new offences: corrupt performance by an agent of his functions as an agent; and receipt by an agent of a benefit which consists of, or is derived from an advantage that the agent knows or believes to have been corruptly obtained. The Home Office has accepted the Law Commission's recommendations in this area[2]. However, relevant legislation has yet to be introduced.

1 *Legislating the Criminal Code: Corruption* Law Com no 248.
2 Home Office White Paper *Raising Standards and Upholding Integrity: The Prevision of Corruption* (26 June 2000).

D7.82 These proposed offences could have a large impact on the corporate hospitality industry. For example, if hospitality was provided by a company to an individual employee of a potential client company in the expectation of receiving a contract or order in return, the company offering the hospitality and, in certain circumstances, the company receiving the free entertainment would be likely to be committing an offence under the proposed legislation. In order to avoid any liability, companies would have to have clear policies on both the offering and acceptance of corporate hospitality packages by employees to avoid any inference of corruption.

5 THE RIGHTS OF PURCHASERS OF HOSPITALITY PACKAGES

D7.83 When a person buys a hospitality package, the rights of redress depend upon the terms of the contract entered into between the purchaser and the official provider.

A Outright cancellation

D7.84 The official provider will usually reserve the right to cancel without penalty up to a certain number of days before the event. If proper notice is given, the purchasing company would usually not be able to claim. If no notice or inadequate notice is given, the company could claim damages for breach of contract[1].

1 See para D7.86.

B Partial delivery

D7.85 If the official provider gives notice in advance that a fundamental part of the package will not be provided (for example, the tickets are provided but catering arrangements may be cancelled on the day) the purchaser has a choice. It can:

- affirm the contract (that is agree to take partial delivery) and claim damages for that part of the contract that is not provided. If the consumer decides to affirm the contract it cannot later decide to cancel the contract on the basis of that breach; or
- cancel the contract and claim damages for the entire loss. The right to cancel outright will only arise if the official provider has committed a fundamental breach of contract.

C Damages

D7.86 The aim of contractual damages is to put the parties into the position they would have been in had the breach not occurred (ie had the contract been properly performed). For outright cancellation the company should be entitled to claim a full refund of any money paid, plus any consequential damages, including, for example, any wasted costs of travel to the event and possibly loss of enjoyment (although there are limits on the extent to which a company purchaser, as opposed to an individual purchaser, can claim for loss of enjoyment).

D7.87 For partial delivery, heads of loss may include: the cost of alternative catering arrangements; compensation for lower quality tickets than were promised and/or compensation for lower quality accommodation than was promised.

D7.88 The loss must be in the reasonable contemplation of the parties at the time the contract is made, and must arise naturally from the breach, under general *Hadley v Baxendale* principles. It would, therefore, be difficult to succeed in a claim, for example, for loss of business opportunity because, in addition to the difficulty in establishing that the failure of the official provider to perform properly its obligations actually caused any loss of business, the loss is likely to be regarded as too remote, save perhaps in circumstances where the official provider has been specifically made aware by the purchaser of the business opportunity expected to arise from the event.

D Other remedies

D7.89 A company may, if applicable, report the provider to Trading Standards or to the Department of Trade and Industry to investigate possible criminal action under the Trade Descriptions Act 1968 or the Price Indications (Resale of Tickets) Regulations 1994[1].

1 See paras D7.80–D7.82.

D7.90 It may be possible to make a claim under a bond, if the operator is bonded pursuant to the CHA bonding scheme. The CHA[1] is the main representative body in the hospitality industry, although it has no statutory authority. It maintains a code of practice regulating the activities of its members, requiring them to act in a responsible and professional manner and to be ethical and fair at all times. However, the code does not contain any explicit protection for customers of members of the CHA in the event of a failure to supply tickets. Its role is to educate companies that buy hospitality packages so that they are aware of the pitfalls in booking packages from non-officially appointed agents and the precautions they should take, such as vetting the supplier in question and checking with the organiser and/or official agent that the supplier will receive tickets to the event in question.

1 For further information, see the CHA website, www.cha-online.co.uk.

D7.91 Due to the possibility of EU regulation being extended to cover the hospitality industry and in order to increase consumer confidence following the bad publicity during the World Cup 1998, the CHA has recently introduced a voluntary bonding scheme for full fee paying members. This provides a degree of protection for customers if the hospitality provider becomes insolvent up to a limit of £300,000.

E Limitations of liability

D7.92 The official provider will often seek to limit its liability in its standard terms of business by:

- limiting liability to the price paid;
- excluding liability for consequential damages;
- requiring complaints to be made within a specific time period;
- reserving the right to alter packages; and
- reserving the right to offer reasonable alternative packages.

D7.93 These limitations will be enforceable if they satisfy the requirement of reasonableness[1]. In deciding whether or not the requirement of reasonableness is satisfied, the courts will consider: the relative strength of the parties' bargaining position; any inducements offered to the company to agree to the term; whether the company has known of the extent of the exclusion; whether it was reasonable to expect that compliance with the term was practicable[2].

1 Section 3 of the Unfair Contract Terms Act 1977 (UCTA 1977).
2 UCTA 1977, Sch 2.

F Offers of alternative packages

D7.94 Official providers may attempt to limit their liability in the event that the contracted package is unavailable by offering alternative packages. Whilst it is open for the purchaser to accept such an offer, if the offer is unacceptable the purchaser will generally not be bound to accept and the official provider will be unable to rely on its purported exclusion of liability. The purchaser should, however, bear in mind that it is under a duty to mitigate its loss. If the offer is reasonable the purchaser should consider it carefully.

G Claims against the event owner

D7.95 In some circumstances a purchaser may be able to buy hospitality direct from an event owner, though for big events and stadia this is increasingly rare. In those circumstances, the same principles as set out above will apply.

D7.96 If the purchase is through a hospitality provider, there will be no direct contract between the purchaser and the event owner. Subject to rights that may exist under the Contracts (Rights of Third Parties) Act 1999[1], claims against the event owner will, therefore, be limited to claims in tort. Possible actions include:

- misrepresentation. If, for example, the event owner had endorsed the hospitality provider by granting official status and that status had led the purchaser to believe that purchasing from such operators was the only way to guarantee tickets; and
- procuring breach of contract. If it can be shown that the event owner was aware of the contract between the purchaser and the official provider and intended to cause a breach of that contract. This is likely to be difficult to prove.

1 See para D7.97.

D7.97 With the implementation of the Contracts (Rights of Third Parties) Act 1999, the position regarding the possibility of a purchaser of hospitality making a contractual claim against an event owner may change. The Act amends the rule of privity of contract and, in certain circumstances, allows a third party to enforce a contractual term between two other parties. Broadly speaking the contract must purport to confer a benefit on the third party (for instance, the provision of tickets), and the enforcement of the term must not be inconsistent with the other terms of the contract. Therefore whether any such claim could be made will depend upon the terms of the agreement between the event owner and official provider.

CHAPTER D8

REPRESENTATION AGREEMENTS

Richard Verow (Octagon Worldwide)

Contents

1 BASIC PRINCIPLES

D8.1 In a sports context, a representation agreement is usually an agreement between a sports Rights-Owner and a specialist sports marketing agency. In this contract a 'Rights-Owner' is usually a governing body, event owner, league, sports club, individual athlete or other sports rights-owning body (the 'Rights-Owner'). The Rights-Owner may seek to exploit the 'commercial rights' that it owns or controls in a sports event or property by engaging the services of a commercial agent of some description (the 'Agent'). On one level, a representation agreement between a Rights-Owner and an Agent is similar to an agreement between a home owner and an estate agent: the Rights-Owner appoints the Agent to find a potential buyer (a 'Commercial Partner'), and to negotiate and ultimately sell a property (in this case a bundle of commercial sports rights) to the Commercial Partner on its behalf for a fee or an agreed commission. In the majority of cases, this is a commission-based structure. However, split fee and commission arrangements are common in situations where additional services – such as event organisation or sponsorship consulting services – are also being supplied as part of the same arrangement.

D8.2 Describing the arrangement as similar to that of home owner and estate agent is by no means the end of the matter. Whilst the sales element of the agreement is all important – without that the Agent will not receive any commission – there will be additional services supplied as part of the agreement which will include evaluating the marketplace and value of the rights as well as advising on the structure, packaging and marketing of the rights and identifying potential Commercial Partners for the rights in question.

D8.3 This type of arrangement is common for any number of sports 'properties'. This includes top level international events such as Rugby World Cup, European Rugby Cup, the UEFA Champions League and European Championship events as well as the commercial rights owned by national federations and associations such as the RFU, the British and Irish Lions, the Football Association, US Track and Field, UK Athletics, the IAAF and any number of other event organisers.

D8.4 The Rights-Owner's Motivation There may be a number of assumptions and factors that drive the Rights-Owner to appoint an Agent, such as:

- limited available staffing and resourcing for the Rights-Owner to find a number of Commercial Partners;
- the availability of financial guarantees from Agents effectively to underwrite a certain amount of commercial revenue and thereby offset some financial risks and provide guaranteed income levels for the Rights-Owner;
- the Agent's knowledge and expertise in the marketplace for both the valuation and the sale of the available commercial rights;
- a desire to revitalise an existing event or set of rights with new ideas and new streams of commercial revenue.

D8.5 The actual appointment process is also becoming increasingly sophisticated. For example, it is common during the negotiation phase of any Rights-Owner–Agent relationship for the parties to agree on a 'lock-out' period of exclusivity during which neither party will negotiate with anyone else[1]. Any such arrangement is only enforceable under English law to the extent that it can prevent either party (usually the Rights-Owner) from negotiation with any other agency[2]. The parties are not locked into a binding commercial representation agreement at this stage; they are simply precluded from negotiations with another party for a specified period of time. Such agreements commonly also contain binding confidentiality provisions.

1 See further para D8.47.
2 *Walford v Miles* [1992] 2 AC 128 at 138, HL.

D8.6 A Rights-Owner will also commonly become involved in a full formal presentation and tender procedure. It will produce an 'Invitation to Tender' document that may contain draft legal documentation (such as a draft form of commercial representation agreement and a standard sponsorship and licensing agreement) for comment. An agency may be concerned to know that such a procedure is a genuine tender situation rather than a 'stalking horse' arrangement simply designed to motivate an incumbent agency. A tender will then involve a presentation and a process of whittling down a group of agencies to the two or three stronger contenders, and then the final appointee.

2 DEFINITIONS AND COMMON TERMS

D8.7 There is no industry-wide glossary of standard terms for the 'common and garden' representation agreement. The main relationship may be described as an 'agency agreement', a 'rep agreement', a 'commercial rights agreement', a 'marketing rights agreement', or just a plain old 'agreement' or contract.

D8.8 The assumption behind all of these labels is that there will be a contractual relationship between a 'Rights-Owner' and an 'Agent' or 'Consultant'. The contract will relate to a set of 'rights'. Again the 'rights' in question are referred to by any number of different names such as 'commercial rights', 'sponsorship rights', 'marketing rights' or even 'licensing rights' (this latter description might also be taken as referring to 'merchandising rights')[1].

1 As to commercial rights in a sports property generally, see Chapter D1. As to sponsorship rights, see Chapter D5. As to licensing and merchandising rights, see Chapter D6.

D8.9 This highlights a particular issue for both the Rights-Owner and the Agent, namely the relationship between the rights which are the subject matter of the representation agreement in point and other rights owned or controlled by the Rights-Owner. There are any number of additional rights which are themselves capable of separate definition and exploitation such as 'perimeter advertising rights', 'television rights', 'audio visual rights', 'radio rights', 'interactive games rights', 'publishing rights', 'music rights', 'on line rights', 'new media rights' and '3G rights'[1].

1 See further Chapter D4.

D8.10 Despite the abundant (and apparently ever-increasing) number of potential revenue streams in sport, the main commercial rights available for realistic exploitation and the main attendant streams of revenue currently break down as follows:

- Television rights revenue – usually defined by reference to delivery system and payment mechanism eg subscription satellite/free to air terrestrial[1];
- Sponsorship rights revenue – usually by reference to 'title rights' and/or 'partner packages' and/or 'secondary partners' and/or 'official suppliers'[2];
- Perimeter advertising boards sales; and
- Merchandising rights and sales revenue[3].

1 See further Chapter D4.
2 See further Chapter D5.
3 See further Chapter D6.

D8.11 There are a number of ancillary revenue streams, some of which have greater or lesser potential and interest to Agents, covering some or all of the following:

- hospitality rights[1];
- pourage rights;
- premium rate telephone services;
- data rights (often results, scores and specific news and text services)[2];
- official travel agents and tour operators;
- ticketing; and
- general on-site franchises and catering.

1 See further Chapter D7.
2 See paras D1.22 and D1.47.

D8.12 The representation agreement may cover some or all of the rights elements listed above. For the remainder of this chapter, it is assumed that rights in the nature of television and audio-visual rights are not dealt with in the agreement. These rights are covered in detail in Chapter D4. In addition, the phrase 'Commercial Partner' will be used to cover any third party who enters into a binding agreement with the Rights-Owner and/or the Agent for the exploitation of some or all of the 'commercial rights' listed and discussed above.

3 WHAT ARE 'SPORTS RIGHTS'?

D8.13 Just as there is no one agreed specified industry standard definition of 'commercial rights', there is not (in the UK at least) any set legal definition or category of 'sports rights'. There may be sports lawyers and accountants specialising in sports work, there may also be arguments for (and against) specific legislation protecting sports rights (one example of which is legislation protecting the Olympic rings and words)[1]. However the legal protection of sports rights is a 'hotch potch' of differing legal disciplines[2]. For the purposes of a representation agreement, the Rights-Owner and the Agent will need to consider the specific legal protections available or potentially available for the rights in question. These protections are likely to consist of a combination of intellectual property rights, goodwill, as well as a network of contractual and regulatory restrictions (such as governing bodies rules, participation agreements, employment contracts, ticketing requirements, venue hire agreements)[3]. The Rights-Owner and the Agent will often conduct their own (or a combined) due diligence or audit of the available rights and any attendant protections and restrictions on use.

1 The Olympic Symbol etc (Protection) Act 1995: see para D1.115.
2 See generally Chapter D1.
3 See n 2.

D8.14 An Agent will wish to ensure that the Rights-Owner is aware of and owns or controls its intellectual property rights (such as its own event and association marks and logos) as well as copyright in all relevant audio-visual and broadcast materials and that they are available to be exploited. The Agent will also seek to ensure that other proprietary rights such as those of ingress and egress from any venue or stadium are controlled by the Rights-Owner.

D8.15 The Agent's interest is in ensuring that it has rights to offer which are deliverable and wherever possible legally protected. It can then offer some or all of these rights to potential Commercial Partners. A Rights-Owner that is reluctant or unable to offer comfort to the Agent on such matters may find it difficult to deliver rights to Commercial Partners.

4 LEGAL RELATIONSHIP BETWEEN RIGHTS-OWNER AND AGENT

D8.16 In some cases, an 'Agent' will actually buy the rights from the Rights-Owner outright, taking an assignment of the rights and thereafter being entitled to deal with the rights as principal as far as possible and as it sees fit[1] (subject to any restrictions included in the assignment to protect the value of any rights held back by the Rights-Owner). Legally, the concept of an 'assignment' in this context is tenuous, since the rights in question are not proprietary; the assignment is of the benefit of the contractual and proprietary rights the Rights-Owner holds. More usually, however, the Agent is appointed simply to take the rights to market, locate potential Commercial Partners, negotiate a proposed deal, even prepare a detailed letter of intent and/or long-form agreement, and bring the contract and final deal to the Rights-Owner for approval. Notwithstanding its title, the 'Agent' may not have actual authority to bind the Rights-Owner to any particular deal that the Agent sources. Usually the Rights-Owner reserves the right to decide whether or not to enter into a binding legal agreement (the Agent might seek agreement that approval will not be unreasonably delayed or withheld but this will be strenuously resisted by the Rights-Owner). Given that an Agent acting without actual authority but with ostensible authority can bind the Rights-Owner with respect to third parties, care needs to be taken from all sides that the Agent does not exceed the bounds of its authority.

1 See further para D8.53.

D8.17 Although the Agent may be the exclusive agent in respect of all the available commercial rights, it is unlikely that the Rights-Owner will authorise the Agent to offer those rights outside of an agreed commercial plan and for agreed minimum amounts of money. This provides some protection for the Rights-Owner as to the method in which rights are offered to the market, ensures that this is done in an agreed and organised manner and also affords the Agent the opportunity at an early stage to agree with the Rights-Owner the way that it (the Agent) is to approach the market and the 'packages' it is to offer.

5 APPOINTMENT AND GRANT OF RIGHTS

D8.18 The Agent will seek to be appointed exclusively[1] to exploit a certain set of defined commercial rights throughout a defined territory (usually the entire world or at least the territory in which the event or events in question are being held) for a specified period of time[2] and in return for which it will receive a payment of some form[3].

1 See para D8.23 et seq.
2 See para D8.42 et seq.
3 See para D8.51 et seq.

D8.19 A relatively standard form of representation agreement will grant the Agent the right to market the 'marketing rights' or 'commercial rights', defined to cover some or all of the following matters, depending on the particular situation of the contracting Rights-Owner:

'Marketing Rights' mean –

All sponsorship and licensing rights in relation to the Events [as defined] which includes [without limitation] the following:

- All perimeter board advertising boards located at venues along with all other advertising at the venues;
- Use of approved designations such as 'official partner';
- Available concessions, franchising, display, sampling, demonstration and sales rights;
- Promotional and related commercial opportunities;
- Promotional and advertising opportunities and publications owned or controlled by the Rights-Owner;

- Exclusive right to use specified trade marks and logos;
- Advertising and related rights on tickets and invitations used in connection with the Events such use being in connection with the Rights-Owner and its events;
- The right to produce premiums and give away items;
- The right to promotional opportunities such as man of the match and other Event related prizes;
- The right to an agreed number of tickets and hospitality;
- Advertising in-match programmes;
- Access to content and hypertext links on the Rights-Owners and Event related websites;
- Branding on Event related print activity;
- The use of photos and audio-visual content relating to the Events;
- Press conferences and press releases announcing the appointment of the Agent and/or Commercial Partners;
- Interview backdrops;
- Access and invitations to Event related functions and events;
- Appearances from players and management teams.

D8.20 The parties may also wish to specify the minimum and maximum number of rights packages that it may be offered to potential sponsors and the minimum rights that each such package will contain. For example, a Rights-Owner may seek a maximum of eight sponsor partners for an event, who will each be entitled to a basic 'partner package' of rights which could include the following:

- eight perimeter advertising hoardings;
- product category exclusivity;
- up to 50 tickets each;
- agreed hospitality and parking;
- the use of the Event marks and logos;
- internet site links;
- sampling and promotional opportunities;
- programme advertising; and
- other agreed rights.

D8.21 There may also be links to and from the official event website as well as other specific rights such as 'man of the match' prizes. In general the package of rights available for offer to Commercial Partners will reflect the definition of marketing or commercial rights listed above.

D8.22 The Agent will seek to ensure that the grant of rights is backed up with appropriate provisions relating to exclusivity and additional warranties and undertakings securing the delivery and protection of the Agent's appointment and the rights on offer. The common concern of the Rights-Owner and Agent will be to maximise income from the agreed commercial programme whilst taking account of any number of constraining factors which can limit the Rights-Owner's ability to offer and exploit its rights free from conflicts.

6 EXCLUSIVITY AND 'CONSTRAINING FACTORS'

A Exclusive appointment

D8.23 It is usual for an Agent to require that the grant of rights is exclusive to the Agent. Effectively this means that no other person (including the Rights-Owner) can offer the rights for sale or exploit the rights. The Agreement will usually state that the appointment of the Agent and/or the grant of rights is an 'exclusive' appointment/grant, and will elaborate on this as follows:

- A provision making it clear the Rights-Owner must not exploit the rights itself, or authorise any one else to exploit the rights.
- An obligation on the Rights-Owner to refer all enquiries regarding the rights to the Agent.
- The Rights-Owner may draft the financial provisions of the agreement to make it clear that if the Agent does not actually source a deal, then that income is not commissionable income. However, the Agent will resist such a provision on the basis that its appointment is exclusive and it should lead and preferably control the commercial sales programme. Accordingly if the Rights-Owner is obliged to refer enquiries to the Agent, the Agent can take the lead (in accordance with the agreement) in negotiating and concluding a contract. Practically speaking the Agent will insist on all agreements being subject to commission payments since there will always be a considerable input of the Agent's time in all deals and (in cases where there is a financial guarantee) the Agent's financial risk.
- There will usually be a provision excluding the Rights-Owner from appointing another Agent or exploiting any of the rights itself for a certain period of time prior to expiry of the term of the existing representation agreement, ie a grace period for the existing Agent to attempt to agree terms for the extension of its appointment. The Rights-Owner will usually insist that any renewal negotiations take place during the term of the representation agreement rather than following its expiry. This lessens the risk of disruption and smooths the transition from one representative's term to the next, if there is a change.
- There may also be restrictions on how commercial rights held back by the Rights-Owner (eg broadcasting rights) can be exploited, including whether or not the Agent has a 'first look' at additional rights. The Rights-Owner will resist this since it can restrict its ability to exploit the rights itself or to appoint other agencies to do so. The Rights-Owner should seek to retain some control and flexibility over its ability to appoint other agencies to exploit unrelated rights. On the other hand, there should be a common interest in agreeing restrictions, to ensure that there is no conflict in the way the range of commercial rights controlled by the Rights-Owner are exploited, and also to ensure that each Commercial Partner receives what it has been promised, in terms of exclusivity and otherwise. A good example relates to broadcast sponsorship: a sponsor will at the very least want some assurances that the broadcast partner will not grant broadcast sponsorship rights to the sponsor's competitors. Increasingly, therefore, broadcast sponsorship rights are included in the package of rights covered by the representation agreement, even if the broadcast rights are held back.

B Existing agreements / 'clean venues'

D8.24 The Agent's exclusivity relates not only to its appointment by the Rights-Owner but also to its ability to exploit the rights free from interference. There may be various factors that affect its ability to do so and these factors tend to mirror the concerns of potential sponsors in a sport. Can the Rights-Owner deliver 'clean venues'? If it cannot do so, what agreements are already in place and how do they affect the grant of rights and the commercial value of the rights? What are the relations with and restrictions on participants in the event regarding their own sponsorship arrangements whilst competing?[1]

1 See further para D1.31.

D8.25 A Rights-Owner may also have a number of existing agreements in place, and will usually want it to be clear that they fall outside the representation agreement and no commission is payable to the Agent for income received under them or a renewal of the agreement with the incumbent sponsor. The Rights-Owner will usually agree that the rights covered by such existing agreements revert to the if they are not renewed by the incumbent.

D8.26 The Agent and the Rights-Owner should consider the commercial structure of the rights, existing agreements that participants in an event have in place and their ability to ambush the rights and materially affect the commercial value of the rights and relations with commercial partners. The ideal situation for an Agent is often that it has the rights completely 'clean' of any other commercial interests, whether for participants, venues, television companies, previous agents and sponsors or otherwise. Accordingly participants should be required to participate free of sponsorship (especially whilst actually competing in the events)[1]. In practice, however, the larger the event the greater the likelihood of there being numerous competing interests of this nature. In such a situation the Agent will seek to safeguard its position and its financial interests as far as possible.

1 See para D1.31.

C Ambush marketing[1]

D8.27 The most basic form of ambush marketing protection that the Agent would require would relate to the protection and enforcement of intellectual property rights owned and controlled by the Rights-Owner. It would also require the Rights-Owner to put in place and as far as possible enforce participation agreements, venue agreements as well as agreements with all other Commercial Partners, ensuring that for all factors which are directly within the Rights-Owner's control there will be no conflict and no possibility of ambushing[2]. For example, if the Agent does not control the merchandising and licensing rights to a property, then the Agent would require the Rights-Owner to ensure that any merchandising or licensing partner which it appoints or which is appointed on its behalf is not able to do joint promotions with anyone other than the sponsors or other Commercial Partners sourced by the Agent[3]. This would help to ensure that a retailer who has not paid to acquire commercial rights of its own is not able to piggyback on the goodwill of the property in an uncontrolled manner.

1 See further paras D1.116 to D1.135.
2 See para D1.132 et seq.
3 See para D1.135.

D8.28 In practice ambush marketing and related issues are as important for the Rights-Owner as they are for the Agent and all Commercial Partners. The extent to which the Rights-Owner will contractually commit to protect rights and the extent to which it is legally able to do so are a matter for the Rights-Owner who, in general, will seek to ensure the lowest practical level of contractual commitment with the prospect of a significant discretionary albeit non-contractual commitment if any ambush marketing issues arise.

D8.29 Alternatively, the Rights-Owner may seek to place much more of the onus on the Agent to police the rights and control ambush marketing. The Agent is likely to resist any such obligation for very similar reasons to the Rights-Owner. If there is no available budget to police the rights or indeed some of the rights cannot be protected using available intellectual property or contractual remedies, then an outright obligation to prevent ambush marketing is likely to be impractical and something which the Agent cannot deliver. In practice a well thought out policy of trademark protection and licensing[1], along with appropriate 'on the ground' policing[2], is likely to discourage some of the more obvious ambush marketing tactics employed by third parties.

1 See para D1.124.
2 See paras D1.126 and D1.127.

D8.30 The Agent needs to be aware that exclusivity by its very nature relates only to the rights actually granted by the Rights-Owner, and accordingly it should always seek appropriate protections from the Rights-Owner relating to the matters listed above.

D Scope of rights package – number of events

D8.31 The grant of rights will normally relate to specific events organised by the Rights-Owner. There should be reasonably detailed terms dealing with the Rights-Owner's obligation to organise and stage the events and put in place all necessary contractual and other arrangements to ensure that the events are actually held. The Agent should consider whether any new or additional events will be added to the existing package of events and if so what those events might be, when they may be added and whether the Agent would wish to acquire such rights itself. Any major governing body is likely to run a number of different events at different age levels as well as different types of competition such as league and cup competitions incorporating national as well as international teams and competitors. The Rights-Owner will often have very good commercial and practical reasons not to use one agency for the exploitation of all its rights and in general for all but the smallest sports and commercial programmes the Agent will be willing to accept such a limitation. The prospect of the event(s) covered by the representation agreement reducing in scope should be considered along with any effect this may have on the value of the rights and packages on offer and therefore on the viability of a minimum guarantee[1].

1 See para D8.54.

E Event management

D8.32 The representation agreement must be clear as to the relationship between the Agent's sales role and any event management role. For example, does the Agent's role include mainly the implementation of sponsors' rights, as well as perimeter advertising, production and the staging and day to day management of an event. If the event management role and the general production role are to be assigned to the Agent, then the representation agreement should deal specifically with this and incorporate appropriate terms. The Agent is unlikely to accept a specific event management role without a fixed fee remuneration which will be entirely unrelated to any commission arrangements relating to sales. If the event management role is not in any way contingent on rights sales and no additional budget is made available then the Agent may obviously find itself in financial difficulties if it is not able to recover sufficient commission to cover staffing and related costs of event management. Although both matters may be dealt with in one agreement, in financial terms they should generally be kept quite separate.

D8.33 Even if the Agent is not undertaking an event management role as well as a sales role, it will have a definite interest in maintaining some hands-on role as far as relationships with Commercial Partners are concerned and so will doubtless have some presence at all events. For example, the Agent may undertake some basic brand protection work, or it may produce a style bible and guidelines for use by Commercial Partners. The Agent may be required to co-ordinate delivery of the rights to Commercial Partners and to hold regular meetings with them to ensure that their requirements (whether contractual or otherwise) are being met so far as is practical.

D8.34 Occasionally the Rights-Owner will grant the Agent very limited exclusivity. It may only authorise the Agent to approach certain named companies (sometimes only in certain territories) in relation to the rights on offer. Although many of the terms of the representation agreement would remain the same, in the case of such a limited exclusivity the Agent is likely to be less prescriptive over the other terms of the Agreement discussed above and elsewhere in this chapter.

F Conflicts of interest

D8.35 Although the Agent will expect to be exclusively appointed, it would usually make it clear to the Rights-Owner that it only provides its services non-exclusively and that it is free to take on other projects. The Rights-Owner may seek to limit this in a number of ways, for example to ensure that there is no conflict between its project and the other projects that the Agent may take on. It may require the right to veto other projects in the same sport. In any event, the Agent should ensure that there is no conflict of interest between its role for the Rights-Owner and its role on any other projects that it may be undertaking. For example, if the Agent also undertakes consulting work for clients who are Commercial Partners of the Rights-Owner, then the Agent should ensure that there is no direct conflict of interest between those two roles. The Agent may also wish to ensure that it can undertake consulting work for Commercial Partners that are successfully contracted and sign with the Rights-Owner. In general this should not cause any conflict of interest between the Rights-Owner, the Agent and the Commercial Partners so long as the relationship is properly managed and only takes effect following signature.

7 RIGHTS-OWNERSHIP AND CONTROL

D8.36 The starting point in the Rights-Owner's agreement with an Agent and indeed its arrangements with any other Commercial Partners is that it owns or controls the rights which it is offering or purporting to offer to the Agent and its

Commercial Partners. There should normally be a general warranty and/or representation to this effect in the Agreement along with a warranty and representation that it has the exclusive right and full authority to enter into and perform the terms of the Agreement.

D8.37 The Rights-Owner may have some basic due diligence and housekeeping of its own to do before entering the Agreement to ensure that it can offer a detailed and unified package of rights. For example, does it have clear title and direct and enforceable relationships with the constitutional members/participants of the Rights-Owner.

D8.38 The basic warranty protection required to supplement the terms outlined above will be that the calendar for the event in question is fixed and set, that there will be participants for the events, that the events will be organised and managed properly, and that there will be no changes to the events or the structure of the events or any material problems with rights delivery. These factors are all relevant to the Agent's ability to sell the rights in a competitive market place as well as the Agent's own financial protection.

D8.39 In a more detailed representation agreement, the Agent will seek to ensure that the rules and regulations of the event are set in an agreed form and that they do not vary, at least as far as the commercial rights are concerned, so as to detract from the value of the packages that the Agent may offer under the representation agreement. Ideally the Rights-Owner will ensure that all participants agree to be bound to the rules and regulations prior to their participation in the competition. The Rights-Owner should then also undertake that it will ensure compliance with the rules.

D8.40 The Agent may also require the Rights-Owner to ensure that the quality of participants is of a certain minimum standard and may even require the Rights-Owner to ensure that specific participants take part. There may also be requirements not only to the quality of the competitors but also to the benefits of winning the competition. For example, in some team events the benefits of winning the competition may involve promotion or eligibility for another cup or league competition. In addition to a warranty or a representation in dealing with this type of matter the Agent may want to negotiate a right of termination if its commercial criteria, such as those outlined above, are not met.

D8.41 The Agent may also require some or all of the following warranties and/or undertakings to back up the basic protections relating to the Rights-Ownership and control:

- co-operation of the participants with the commercial programme;
- enforcement of the terms of relevant participation and commercial rights agreements;
- co-ordination of the calendar to ensure there is no conflict with other major sporting events;
- delivery of rights from and to broadcasters;
- compliance by the Rights-Owner with its financial obligations with third parties when necessary for the proper functioning of the events;
- entering into agreements with venue owners for the event in particular regarding the availability of advertising sites at the venues and ensuring that there are no conflicts with the rights that the Agent has been appointed to market to potential Commercial Partners;

- obtaining all necessary consent and clearances (including where necessary from participants) to perform all obligations and exercise rights; and
- the development of standard form agreements and offer letters/letters of intent for potential Commercial Partners.

8 DURATION AND TERMINATION

D8.42 The basic duration of the representation agreement should be defined as well as the circumstances in which termination may occur prior to normal expiration. Assuming there is no breach of the agreement or other event giving rise to termination, the representation agreement should normally expire simply by passage of time. There may also be terms relating to the renewal or extension of the Agreement. The duration of the representation agreement will also be governed by the type of rights/events which are the subject matter of the agreement. If it is simply a one-off event which will not be repeated, then it is likely to be a short term agreement (with no renewal provisions). If the agreement relates to a cycle or series of events, it is likely to be longer term. In any event there should be clarity over the duration of the agreement. For example, the agreement may state:

> This Agreement shall have effect from [insert date] and shall continue in force until [*insert number of days*] after the final match forming part of the Event in the [*insert season*] subject always to earlier termination or extension in accordance with the terms of this Agreement.

D8.43 As far as termination of the Agreement is concerned, there are a number of terms which are considered 'standard' in any commercial agreement, as follows:

- A termination right if there is a non-remediable or material breach of any term of the Agreement. There would normally be a requirement of notice and an opportunity to cure, with a time limit of (say) 28 days from notice in which to cure the breach.
- Termination rights where there is any suggestion that either party cannot meet its debts as they fall due, any creditors meeting with the appointment of any supervisor, receiver, administrator or administrative receiver, any partition for the winding up of bankruptcy or dissolution or anything other than insolvent reorganisation of either party.

D8.44 In addition to the more usual terms outlined above there will be other specific concerns which the Rights-Owner and Agent may have. For example:

- The Rights-Owner may require a termination right if the Agent does not hit a minimum sales or revenue target; alternatively the representation agreement could become non-exclusive if such a target is not met.
- The Rights-Owner may require key person provisions although again the Agent should always resist such terms on the basis that it restricts the way in which it can do business and also gives a named individual an undue amount of control over certain key accounts or rights.
- There may also be provisions relating to the timing of the rights sales – in particular the event may require early funding some of which will be driven by commercial rights sales. Accordingly if a sale is not made by a certain date the Rights-Owner (and indeed the Agent) may need to review the terms of the representation agreement and possibly terminate it.

- In certain circumstances the Agent is likely to raise issues over the constitution of the governing body and the threat (if any) of any breakaway or rival competition. This may also be a concern of the Rights-Owner and some suitable acceptable mutual provisions may be agreed relating to termination in such circumstances.
- The Agent and other Commercial Partners may wish to ensure they have the right to terminate if there is a major drugs or doping scandal which hits the sport. The difficulty for the Rights-Owner is the potential conflict of interest: it may also have an obligation to police the event and conduct drug testing, in which case it could effectively be penalised for performing its role.
- The Agent will want to ensure that there is a minimum number of events forming part of the package and if those are not delivered there may be a termination right.
- Where the broadcasting rights are retained by the Rights-Owner, the Agent may want the right to terminate if minimum broadcast coverage is not secured (because this is so vital to the creation of sponsorship value).

D8.45 If the termination right is exercised, there should be provisions in place regarding the effect of termination on the party's rights. There is likely to be a general survival clause which will cover accrued rights and obligations of the parties and maintain their right to take action for any existing breach of terms of the representation agreement. Further terms may deal with the following:

- handing back of ownership of property and intellectual property rights in materials used and developed in relation to the rights;
- physical delivery of such materials;
- any ongoing commission and payment obligations as well as the obligation to collect money due;
- any terms of the Agreement which remain in force (such as confidentiality and intellectual property provisions).

Provisions should also be considered as to the position in relation to existing agreements (particularly entitlement to commission on future payments) and (if the Agent enters into contracts with Commercial Partners in its own name) whether such agreements are consigned/transferred.

9 RENEWAL RIGHTS

D8.46 Assuming that the representation agreement is not terminated by reason of breach or for any of the other specific causes set out in the agreement, then the Agent is likely to require some commitment from the Rights-Owner regarding renewal of the Agreement. This may be an enforceable option to renew the Agreement for a further period of time. If there is an option, then this would usually be on agreed financial and commercial terms making it an enforceable provision (otherwise, it is at risk of being deemed an unenforceable 'agreement to agree'). Effectively a notice would be served and the representation agreement would continue in force as varied by the terms of the option for a further set period of time.

D8.47 If it is not possible to negotiate an option, then the Agent may try to negotiate a 'first look' or 'right of first negotiation' over the extension or renewal of the representation agreement. As a matter of English law, this does not mean that the Rights-Owner is required to agree terms for an extension or renewal, only that it is required to negotiate exclusively with the Agent for the 'lock-out' period[1].

1 See para D8.5, n 2.

D8.48 The Agent may further attempt to negotiate a last look or matching right if it is unable to agree terms for renewal following a lock-in or exclusive right of negotiation period. The Rights-Owner is unlikely to agree such provision as it tends to hamper its ability to negotiate with a third party agency for exploitation and offering for sale of the rights since very few agencies or commercial partners will negotiate in a situation where they know that the rights will then be offered back to another party who will have an enforceable right and ability to match the offer.

10 FORCE MAJEURE

D8.49 The representation agreement should also deal with cancellation, postponement and force majeure events. In each of these situations the agreement should define the circumstances in which the event may be cancelled or postponed or in which the parties' obligations are suspended due to force majeure. There should be some terms which deal with unexpected events requiring action. If an event is simply cancelled then, assuming this is done in circumstances which do not amount to a breach of contract, there will need to be terms dealing with the effect on the representation agreement. Unless the Agent is offering a financial guarantee based upon a certain minimum number of events, the cancellation may only affect the value of the rights and/or existing third party agreements. If an event is simply postponed but takes place at a later stage, then the representation agreement can simply state that it continues in force in respect of the postponed event and is extended accordingly.

D8.50 When an event of force majeure interferes with and suspends the parties' obligations, then the representation agreement would usually state a maximum period of time in which the obligations will be suspended before the agreement can be terminated by the party not affected. The clause should also deal with the effect of termination in such circumstances, including any refunds.

11 FINANCIAL TERMS

D8.51 There are a number of alternative financial arrangements for most representation agreements. The most common form of arrangement is that an Agent is paid a commission (usual between 5% and 25% depending on the events in question) of gross fees and on benefits or value in kind arising from rights sales. Alternatively there may be a set fee structure in place which may take the form of a basic retainer for the provision of certain services such as rights sales and consulting, or there may be a mixed commission and fee arrangement. In general, care needs to be taken to set out whether commission is due on (for example) income received under extensions of agreements where the Agent secured the original agreement but the extension was agreed after the representation agreement expired.

D8.52 In certain circumstances, the financial terms of the agreement are similar to banking arrangements in that the Agent may agree to buy out all the commercial rights for a set amount of money or may offer a guarantee against minimum rights sales fees.

A Buy-outs

D8.53 A buy-out works quite simply in that the Agent will pay a set-fee against an agreed payment schedule in return for which the commercial rights are assigned to and (in so far as it is possible) vest in the Agent. If the Agent has the right to enter into agreements directly with Commercial Partners then the Rights-Owner will deliver all rights against those agreements. In such circumstances, the Agent will have the same interests as any Commercial Partner in the scope, nature and ability to protect and enforce the exclusivity of the rights being granted. On the other hand, if the agreement does operate as a buy out or if it operates in any way so that the Agent enters into agreements directly with commercial partners, the Rights-Owner should ensure that if there are any problems with the financial stability or viability of the Agent the agreements are automatically assigned or novated over to the Rights-Owner, thereby protecting the income stream and its Commercial Partners. There may be quite detailed contractual procedures in place depending on who enters into agreements.

B Minimum guarantees

D8.54 In relation to certain major sporting properties, Agents will be prepared to offer guarantees against the amount of income which can be raised from rights sales. A guarantee can generally operate in a number of ways. The actual guarantee itself only operates to the extent that the Agent fails to raise sufficient income from the sale of commercial rights. One common mechanism is for the agreement simply to provide that the first specified amount of money (for example £100,000) raised from rights sales is passed directly to the Rights-Owner, without deduction of any commission by the Agent. The next slice of income (say £20,000) will pass directly to the Agent. All monies above that figure will be split in agreed proportions. Alternatively, all monies raised from right sales will be split between the parties in an agreed proportion and at the end of each year or sometimes more regularly the income will be totalled and any deficiency or any excess dealt with according to the terms of the representation agreement.

D8.55 A minimum guarantee anticipates that the Agent will pay the Rights-Owner the minimum guaranteed amounts against a payment schedule set out in the Agreement, irrespective of the amount of income being generated from the exploitation of the rights that are the subject of the representation agreement. Assuming that the minimum amounts are raised and received then the payment schedule should not apply and monies should be distributed as they are received. If however the Rights-Owner requires an immediate payment in return for simply granting the rights to the Agent then that payment may be made on signature of the Agreement and instalments at agreed dates following that date, allowing the Agent to collect all income until it has covered the guarantee and its first slice of commission.

D8.56 Although guarantees are superficially attractive to Rights-Owners, shifting the financial risk over to the Agent, the availability or offer of a guarantee from an Agent is only one of a number of factors that a well-advised Rights-Owner will take into account when considering the appointment of an Agent. The actual ability to meet the guarantee commitment as well as the ability to sell and exploit the rights and make the most of the available commercial opportunities is to also be considered. A guarantee may mean (provided sufficient protections are in place) that the Rights-Owner will receive a minimum amount of money; it does not guarantee that the Agent will do an excellent job of exploiting the commercial rights to the events covered by the representation agreement.

C Net profit sharing

D8.57 In addition to the financial arrangements outlined above, it is also possible for a net profit sharing arrangement to be agreed. In return for the grant of commercial rights in an event, the Agent will share with the Rights-Owner the net profits of staging and organising the event. This is more likely to apply to a one off or new event rather than a major set of commercial rights to an existing sports event.

PART E

ISSUES FOR INDIVIDUAL SPORTSMEN AND WOMEN

CHAPTER E1

PLAYERS' CONTRACTS WITH CLUBS, TEAMS AND EVENT ORGANISERS

Paul Goulding QC (Blackstone Chambers), **Jane Mulcahy** (Blackstone Chambers) and **Paul Harris** (Monckton Chambers)

Contents

1 INTRODUCTION

E1.1 This chapter considers the contractual relationships between individual players and their clubs, teams and event organisers.

A Defining terms

E1.2 For the purpose of this chapter the term 'players' encompasses:

(1) all employees of clubs – managers, coaches and players – as well as trainees and apprentices;
(2) those who, albeit self-employed, find themselves in quasi-employment relationships with teams (for example, racing drivers contracted to one particular constructor for a period of time[1]); and
(3) those contracting directly with event organisers (for example, a tennis player contracting with the All England Tennis Club to take part in the Wimbledon tennis championship, or a darts player contracting with the British Darts Organisation to take part in the Embassy World Professional Darts Championship[2]). In so far as some of the principles discussed below relate only to those who in law can be defined as 'employees', then this more specific term will be used.

1 Eg *Nichols Advanced Vehicle Systems v De Angelis* (21 December 1979, unreported), Oliver J; *Walkinshaw and Arrows Grand Prix v Pedro Diniz* [2001] 1 Lloyd's Rep 632, Tomlinson J.
2 See para E1.96 et seq.

B The web of relationships

E1.3 The possible contractual relationships surrounding players can be many and varied. For example, a footballer is employed by his club yet, under his employment agreement, he is subject to contractual terms imposed by football's governing bodies, as well as personal terms negotiated with his club. He may also play for the national team, which is overseen by the national football association, and enter into a further agreement in respect of that role. So, during the 2002 World Cup Finals, the England players were under contract to the English Football Association ('the FA'). Their agreements with the FA provided for a disciplinary procedure to deal with allegations of misbehaviour in much the same way as that in a 'normal' contract of employment, save that any breach had to be dealt with more quickly[1]. Nor did the complex matrix end there. The Fédération Internationale de Football Associations ('FIFA'), the World Cup organiser, has its own rules too and entered into participation agreements with the various football associations that gave FIFA the ultimate say on discipline and any team's (or player's) continued involvement[2].

1 'If any of the England players do a Keane …' (2002) Times, 28 May, Law Supplement, p 7. Similarly, in rugby, British Lions Limited contracts directly with players from the four home unions for their playing and promotional services in connection with the quadrennial Lions tour. Disciplinary proceedings arose in relation to the 2001 Lions tour to Australia, involving Austin Healey, and were resolved by reference to the disciplinary code incorporated into British Lions Limited's contract with Healey. In athletics, there is a contract between the British Athletic Federation (now UK Athletics) and an athlete who agrees to compete under its rules: *Diane Modahl v British Athletic Federation Ltd (in administration)* [2001] EWCA Civ 1447, [2002] 1 WLR 1192. See further paras A3.122 to A3.125.
2 Five players from four squads were suspended by FIFA for at least the opening matches of the 2002 World Cup Finals. One, Jose Luis Chilavert, Paraguay's goalkeeper, was serving the last of a three-match ban imposed for spitting at Brazil's Roberto Carlos in a South American qualifying game. And Rivaldo was fined £4,500 by FIFA for play-acting in Brazil's opening match against Turkey (and getting a Turkish player sent off in the process).

E1.4 As well as such employment and quasi-employment relationships, footballers enter into agreements with agents, normally to assist in negotiations with their clubs[1]. In these agreements the footballer is the principal in the relationship: legally he calls the tune. A boxer is also, in strict legal terms, the principal in his relationship with his manager, but this relationship is of a different order: the boxer is normally the subordinate party[2]. In reality a manager will control the boxers who 'employ' him and they will depend on him for work (ie by arranging fights via contracts with others) and hence remuneration. The relationship is more akin to the manager as employer and the boxer as employee (unless, presumably, the boxer is Lennox Lewis). As such, a boxer is more reliant on his agent than, for example, professional golfers, snooker players and tennis players (who may also employ agents). The latter generally have more economic independence and are more obviously self-employed professional sportsmen.

1 See paras E2.31 and E2.106 et seq. Although football agents in practice sometimes do negotiate on behalf of players, they have no authority actually to enter into a contract on a player's behalf. See, for example, cl 14(b) of the Standard Football League Player Contract which states: 'The Club and the Player shall arrange all contracts of service and transfers of registration to any other Football Clubs between themselves.'

2 Gardiner *Sports Law* (2nd edn, 2001, Cavendish), p 529.

E1.5 Another category of contract often entered into by a player is the sponsorship/promotional agreement. These agreements do not form the subject-matter of this chapter, save to mention that they have in the past given rise to litigation[1], and will no doubt do so again in the future.

1 *Conchita Martinez v Ellesse International* (20 March 1999, unreported), CA (Martinez' claim for a $550,000 bonus to be paid on her ranking as number two in the world failed since she was in truth ranked number three. The House of Lords refused Martinez leave to appeal); *Gerhard Berger v Vijay Mallya* (19 March 1998, unreported), Tuckey J (Berger claimed he was entitled to receive $750,000 in return for displaying the Kingfisher beer logo on his racing helmet during the Formula 1 racing season: application to strike out the claim for irregular service failed); *Bain Budgen Sports Ltd v Hollioake* (8 December 1997, unreported), Pumfrey J (application for injunction against Hollioake by sports goods supplier refused, although speedy trial ordered); *Mobil Oil New Zealand Ltd v Bagnall and Maher* [2001] UKPC 57, (11 December 2001, unreported) (claim by Mobil to recover NZ$220,000 plus tax and interest under guarantees after planned races did not take place); *Don King Productions Ltd v Warren* [1998] 2 Lloyd's Rep 176 (dispute arising out of partnership agreement between boxing promoters).

2 WHO IS AN EMPLOYEE?

E1.6 English law differentiates between employees, who work under a contract of service, and those who are self-employed, who work under contracts for services. The distinction is important because the rights and obligations of the parties depend on the categorisation of the relationship. In particular, only the former can take advantage of statutory dismissal rights[1].

1 The distinction explored in this section between employed and self-employed has generated a considerable amount of case law. This chapter does not propose to deal with anything apart from the key cases. A full and detailed appraisal of the area can be found in *Harvey on Industrial Relations and Employment Law* (Butterworths), Div A at paras [1] to [250].

E1.7 An employee, in entering into a contract of service, sells his labour. An independent contractor, entering into a contract for services, sells the end product of his labour. However, it is not always so easy to tell the two apart. For this reason the law has developed various tests to help the courts in their task. These tests have historically focused on whether there is personal service ('the personal service test'), whether the employer 'controls' the employee ('the control test'), and/or whether or not a worker is integrated into the organisation, or is truly independent of it ('the organisation/economic reality test'). More recently, the approach has been to amalgamate these tests and to deny that any one approach to the problem is conclusive ('the multiple test').

E1.8 In the case of *Montgomery v Johnson Underwood Ltd*[1] the Court of Appeal emphasised three conditions which are required to be fulfilled under a contract of service:

(i) 'mutuality of obligation', ie that in consideration for a wage or other remuneration, a servant will provide his *own* work and skill in the performance of some service for his master. (This encompasses the notion of *personal* service[2].);
(ii) an express or implied agreement that performance of the service would be subject to the control of the party employing (an emphasis on the control test); and
(iii) that the provisions of the contract are consistent with it being a contract of service (ie that no aspect of the agreement is sufficient to detract from a finding that the worker is an employee).

In trying to determine whether a contract of service exists, whilst the nature and extent of the mutual obligations and control may vary, these concepts certainly cannot be dispensed with altogether[3]. This appeals to common sense. If a contract allowed a famous rugby player to nominate a stand-in on the day of an important game, then his contract with his club could not be considered to be a contract of employment since there would be no concept of personal service at all. As for control, the simple fact that a player is skilled does not mean that he is put beyond the control of a club that pays him[4].

1 [2001] EWCA Civ 318, [2001] IRLR 269 at para 18. This restates and approves the guidance of McKenna J in *Ready Mixed Concrete (South East) Ltd v Minister of Pensions and National Insurance* [1968] 2 QB 497 at 515.

2 A sports instructor working for Glasgow City Council who was entitled to arrange for a replacement to take her sessions was not necessarily barred from employee status: [2001] 9(2) SATLJ 36. She was allowed not to work in person, but only if she was unable to attend. Further, the replacement needed to be taken from a council-approved list, and the council itself sometimes organised the replacement, paying him or her direct.

3 *Montgomery v Johnson Underwood Ltd* [2001] EWCA Civ 318, [2001] IRLR 269 at para 23. The Court of Appeal accepted that 'in many cases the employer or controlling management may have not more than a very general idea of how the work is done and no inclination directly to interfere with it'. However, 'some sufficient framework of control must surely exist. A contractual relationship … in which a party has no control over the other could not sensibly be called a contract of employment': para 19.

4 In *Walker v Crystal Palace Football Club* [1910] 1 KB 87, CA, Cozens-Hardy MR stated at p 92: 'It has been argued before us … that there is a certain difference between an ordinary workman and a man who contracts to exhibit and employ his skill where the employer would have no right to dictate to him how he should play football. I am unable to follow that. He is bound according to the express terms of his contract to obey all general directions of the club, and I think in any particular game in which he was engaged he would also be bound to obey the particular instructions of the captain or whoever it might be who was the delegate of the authority of the club for the purpose of giving those instructions. In my judgment it cannot be that a man is taken out of the operation of the [statute] simply because in doing a particular kind of work which he is employed to do, and in doing which he obeys general instructions, he also exercises his own judgment uncontrolled by anybody'. Gardiner notes that the emphasis on the authority of the team captain seems out of place in the context of the modern footballer (Gardiner *Sports Law* (2nd edn), p 528) although Sir Alf Ramsey considered that Bobby Moore, while playing for England in the 1960s and early 1970s, was his authority on the field. In cricket, by contrast, cl 5(a) of the Contract For Professional Cricketers requires a cricketer to 'obey all the lawful and reasonable directions of the captain or deputy captain': Gardiner *Sports Law* (2nd edn), p 528.

E1.9 The other tests[1] continue to have a role to play once the key requirements of mutuality of obligation and control are satisfied. So, if a person is 'employed as part of the business' rather than his work being merely accessory (and not integrated), he is more likely to be an employee (the organisation test)[2]. But if he appears to be working on his own account he will not be an employee (the economic reality test). Hence a footballer is much more likely to be an employee than a golfer, even though the latter will have to contract to compete[3].

1 See para E1.7.

2 In *Withers v Flackwell Heath Football Supporters Club* [1981] IRLR 307 a bar manager described as self-employed was nevertheless held to be an employee as the terms of his contract showed that he could not be considered 'his own boss'.

3 Footballers, rugby players and cricketers are almost always employees. Snooker players, on the other hand, work on their own account (albeit under management): *Hendry, Williams and Sportsmasters Network Ltd v World Professional Billiard & Snooker Association Ltd* [2002] UKCLR 5, [2002] ECC 8, [2001] Eu LR 770 (Lloyd J); as do rally/racing drivers (albeit contracted to constructors under contracts for services): *Subaru v Burns* (11 December 2001, unreported, Deputy Judge Strauss; *Nichols Advanced Vehicle Systems v De Angelis* (21 December 1979, unreported), Oliver J. Boxers 'employ' managers (albeit under unequal relationships in practice) and hence remain self-employed: *Watson v Prager* [1991] 1 WLR 726; *Warren v Mendy* [1989] 1 WLR 853.

E1.10 Other matters to consider are whether an amount of salary is paid; who provides the 'tools of the trade'; whether the worker is regarded by the employer as free to work elsewhere; how the parties themselves see the relationship, and whether there is a power of dismissal (which points to a contract of service)[1]. However, the tax position is not conclusive either way. A worker may be regarded as an employee for the purposes of unfair dismissal despite the fact that he is held to be self-employed for tax purposes[2].

1 See *Harvey on Industrial Relations and Employment Law*, A[52]. It is an essential ingredient of a contract of employment that the employer has a power to dismiss: *Hopper v Lincolnshire County Council* (24 May 2002, unreported), EAT.

2 *Airfix Footwear Ltd v Cope* [1978] IRLR 396. Similarly, in *Young and Woods Ltd v West* [1980] IRLR 201, CA, the worker was an employee despite an agreement with his employer that he be paid gross.

3 FORMATION OF THE CONTRACT

E1.11 Assuming a player has the capacity to enter into a contract[1], normally the first and most important task is for him or her to agree terms. However, for those from outside the UK who do not have an automatic right to earn remuneration here, the first step is for their prospective employer to obtain a work permit to enable the player to work.

1 See paras E1.80 to E1.83.

A Work permits

E1.12 Work permits are dealt with by the Government department Work Permits (UK), previously known as the Overseas Labour Service[1]. Nationals of a European Union ('EU') or a European Economic Area ('EEA') country do not have to apply for a work permit. However, those from outside the EEA without settled status do. There is a specific category for sportspeople and entertainers applying for permits. This category enables employers to recruit 'people who are internationally established at the highest level in their sport, and whose employment will make a significant contribution to the development of that particular sport in this country at the highest level'[2].

1 The name changed on 2 April 2001, and the department can be contacted via www.workpermits.gov.uk. In the financial year 2000/2001 some 110,000 work permit applications were considered. Around 150,000 were expected in the year 2001/2002.

2 Government Guidance 2002, para 10(a). Coaches must also be suitably qualified at the highest level.

E1.13 Guidance is periodically issued in relation to work permits for sportspeople, although the Secretary of State and those bodies consulted by him must take care not to apply any relevant criteria too rigidly[1].

1 In *R v Secretary of State for Education and Employment, ex p Portsmouth Football Club* [1998] COD 142 the court quashed the decision to refuse the 24 year old Australian international, Zeljko Kalac, a work permit. The Overseas Labour Service, as it then was, had taken into account the views of football's governing bodies which appeared to believe that the criteria were determinative rather than illustrative. Interestingly, the 2001/2002 criteria stated that Work Permits (UK) would not consult with the governing bodies on individual applications, indicating that the process had changed.

E1.14 The most recent guidelines came into force on 1 April 2002 and were expressed to last until 1 September 2002 ('the 2002 guidance'). These stated that the criteria for work permit applications are agreed following consultation with the appropriate sports governing bodies, but that it is necessary to contact the Sportspeople and Entertainment Team of Work Permits (UK) to find out what the criteria are for any particular sport[1]. This was a change in approach: previously criteria were published by the Home Office on its internet site and there was therefore easy access to the guidelines for football, cricket, horse racing, rugby league, rugby union, speedway and ice hockey. In relation to football, for example, international players of the highest calibre were considered to be those:

(i) who had played for their country in at least 75% of competitive 'A' team matches for which they were available for selection during the two years preceding the date of the application; and
(ii) whose country was at or above 70th place in the official world FIFA rankings when averaged over the two years preceding the date of the application[2].

As stated above[3], these criteria are only illustrative. For example, the Home Office previously publicly stated that exclusion from international matches due to injury would be taken into consideration[4]. The need to consider carefully a multitude of factors that might affect eligibility means that many football cases succeed on appeal even though initially refused[5]. However, obtaining a work permit *prior* to signing a football player from a non-EEA country is now crucial in the light of new FIFA rules which prevent the validity of a contract being made conditional on the acquisition of a work permit[6]. There is some tension between this approach and Work Permits (UK)'s preference for a signed copy of the employment contract to be provided when a work permit application is made[7].

1 Sportspeople and Entertainments Team, Work Permits (UK), Immigration and Nationality Directorate, Home Office, Level 5, Moorfoot, Sheffield, S1 4OQ. Tel: 0114 259 3710; fax: 0114 259 4987; email: ents.workpermits@wpuk.gov.uk.

2 Prior to July 1999, a foreign footballer would not generally have been eligible unless he was one of the six highest earners for the UK club concerned. Further, a work permit applied only for a single season. The wage requirement has since gone and work permits are issued in line with the length of the contract up to a maximum of five years.

3 See para E1.13.

4 This was echoed in *R v Secretary of State for Education and Employment, ex p Portsmouth Football Club* [1998] COD 142 per McCullough J: 'The 75% test is simply illustrative of the way in which the necessary ability may be, and no doubt will be, able to be demonstrated, but it is not an exclusive test … Everyone should recognise that although 75% was chosen, having regard to the fact that in many cases it would no doubt be difficult to be satisfied that the player lost matches through injury, if it can be shown on reliable evidence that a player of stature had lost the opportunity of selection and would have been selected but for the fact of injury, that is a material factor which ought to be taken into account by those who recommend and by those who have the responsibility to decide'.

5 For example, Liverpool FC successfully appealed against the OLS's decision to refuse a work permit to the American goalkeeper Brad Friedel because he did not satisfy the 75% test: he had been sharing international duties with Leicester City's Kasey Keller: Beloff et al *Sports Law* (1999, Hart Publishing), para 4.71. Two Turkish footballers joined Blackburn Rovers in the 2001/2002 period, but not without a fight. Tugay Kerimoglu was granted a work permit in July 2001, but only after an appeal. Delays similarly held up the work permit of Hakan Unsal in February 2002. In a separate case, many clubs tried to sign Canadian Jason Bent, but all failed to obtain a work permit. Plymouth Argyle's first application was denied because of Canada's poor rating in the FIFA rankings. However, they succeeded on appeal and Bent was signed on 22 September 2001.

6 Article 30(1) of the FIFA Regulations for the Status and Transfer of Players, dated 5 July 2001. The status of this rule in any dispute between a player and club is considered below at para E1.21. According to Art 30(2) of the same Regulations: 'The player's prospective new club shall be required to make any necessary investigations … or to take any appropriate action *before* concluding the contract, otherwise it will be liable to pay the full amount of compensation … agreed upon (and/or the amount of the salary due)' (FIFA's emphasis).

7 See para 5 of the 2002 guidance.

E1.15 In deciding on an application, Work Permits (UK) will consider the availability of qualified 'resident workers' in some sports, although it recognises that there are likely to be shortages in various areas. Where this is so, work permit applications do not need to be supported by evidence of the non-availability of such workers. Otherwise, however, employers have to show why they cannot fill any vacant position with home-grown talent.

E1.16 The requirement to obtain a work permit clearly treats non-EU/EEA nationals differently. However, this does not breach European law since there is no discrimination against nationals of EU/EEA member states[1].

1 See further para B3.24 et seq.

B Express terms

E1.17 Players contracting with teams or event organisers almost invariably enter into written agreements setting out the rights and obligations of the parties[1]. These agreed express terms are paramount, unless overridden by law[2].

1 The great thing about written agreements is that they are (relatively) clear. Oral contracts become very problematic when the two parties disagree as to what was said. Rugby player Julian White had the worst of both worlds in his dispute with Bristol Rugby Ltd: *Julian White v Bristol Rugby Ltd* [2002] IRLR 204, Havelock-Allan J. White entered a three-year written agreement to play for Bristol commencing in July 2001, and was paid £15,000 on signing up. To that extent his obligations were clear. However, he then had second thoughts. White claimed that, when the contract was made, he had been given an option orally to cancel at any time prior to July 2001, in which case he would have to repay the money. Bristol denied any such thing. At trial White failed to establish that the option had existed. There was no record in the contract or any contemporaneous documentation and White's own recollection of the relevant conversations was poor. In the face of this and Bristol's denials, the court was influenced by the fact that there appeared to be no good reason for Bristol to have given any such option.

2 *Rank Xerox Ltd v Churchill* [1988] IRLR 280, EAT; *Harvey on Industrial Relations and Employment Law*, A[253].

(a) Examples

E1.18 In employment agreements between players and clubs, the same express terms normally arise in one form or another. On the club's part there will be an obligation to pay wages (normally while the player is fit and while the player is incapacitated[1]). On the player's part there is normally an obligation to avoid unnecessary injury and to behave appropriately.

1 The current standard Premier and Football League playing contract (see para E1.19) provides that, should a player become incapacitated by sickness, the club will, at a minimum, pay his basic salary plus sickness benefit for 28 weeks, followed by a further 28 weeks at the basic salary, during the playing season (cl 9). In the event of permanent incapacity the club is entitled to terminate the contract, but must give the player a minimum of six months' notice (cl 10).

E1.19 Commonly a contract will incorporate terms agreed at governing body level, as well as terms personal to the particular player. Football is a good example. A player must sign the standard FA Premier League and Football League playing contract ('the League contract')[1] as well as personal terms dealing with matters such as salary and bonuses (and, in relation to the more successful players, image rights and the like)[2]. The former deals with a host of matters. For example, under the League contract the player agrees:

(i) to play to the best of his ability[3] and to attend all matches as directed (cls 2 and 3);
(ii) to observe the rules of the club (subject to the rules of the authorities[4]) (cl 5);
(iii) not to indulge in any sport, activity or practice that might endanger a high standard of physical fitness or invalidate any insurance policy (cl 7(a));
(iv) to make himself available for community and public relations involvement for a few hours a week (cl 7(b));
(v) to undergo such medical treatment as the club may reasonably require (cl 8); and
(vi) not to live anywhere the club deems unsuitable for the performance of his duties[5] (cl 11(a)).

The player is also subject to the overriding obligation contained in the FA rules not to bring the game or the club into disrepute (see, for example, cl 13). Any serious or persistent misconduct by the player may result in termination of the agreement (cl 16), although any such decision by a club is subject to a right of appeal (and further appeal from that decision if requested)[6]. Similarly a player can terminate for serious or persistent breach by the club, subject to the same appeals process (cl 17)[7]. Breach by a player short of serious or persistent misconduct can be punished by a fine or suspension (cl 18)[8].

1 The League contract was, at the time of writing, being redrafted both generally, and also specifically to take account of the new FIFA rules.
2 See para D3.69 et seq.
3 It is unheard of for a player to be sacked because he does not play to the best of his ability, clubs instead preferring to sell a player who is under-performing.
4 This contract expressly makes the player subject to the rules of the Football Association and either the Premier League or the Football League, depending on his club's status. In the case of conflict, the governing body rules take precedence over the employment agreement and the rules of the club. This arrangement is of course different from that found to exist in the context of athletics, where the athlete contracts direct with the governing body: *Modahl v British Athletic Federation Ltd (in administration)* [2001] EWCA Civ 1447, (12 December 2001, unreported), CA. See paras A3.122 to A3.125.

5 It is this provision that allows football clubs occasionally to dictate where their players live. For example, Leeds wanted Jonathan Woodgate to move away from Teesside and nearer to the club. Football manager Lou Macari also agreed to a residence clause: *Macari v Celtic Football and Athletic Co Ltd* [1999] IRLR 787. His failure to comply with the obligation to reside within a 45-mile radius of George Square, Glasgow, was one of the reasons for his dismissal, which was found by the Scottish Court of Session to be lawful. Curiously, Macari's contract also included a clause that he could be dismissed 'if … [he] shall have become addicted to intemperance'. This clause did not figure in his case, but would no doubt cause others in football to think twice before signing.

6 An English player has the right to appeal to the Board of the Premier League or the League. Either the club or the player may appeal against that decision to the Football League Appeals Committee. In 2002, Dennis Wise's contract with Leicester City was terminated by the club when he broke team-mate Callum Davidson's jaw in a hotel room incident while on a pre-season tour. Wise challenged that termination before a League tribunal, on procedural and substantive grounds. The tribunal solved the procedural problems by hearing the case de novo, and found Wise guilty of serious misconduct. However, it said Leicester was simply using the incident to extricate itself from an expensive contract (Wise was being paid a reputed £30,000 per week) that it now regretted. Leicester appealed that decision, and the appeal tribunal upheld the appeal, finding that, given that Wise had committed serious misconduct, it was up to the club whether simply to fine him or to terminate his contract. Wise did not give up. In October 2002, his solicitors announced that he was suing Leicester in the High Court for wrongful termination of his playing contract, seeking more than £2.3m in damages (an indication of how much less his new club, Millwall, was paying him) and was also bringing employment tribunal proceedings for wrongful dismissal.

In Scotland, the same process exists save to the Scottish equivalents. Kevin Thomas took up both options before bring unfair dismissal proceedings against St Johnstone FC in the Dundee employment tribunal (Case Number S/300307/2001, heard in September 2001).

7 In September 2002, it was reported that Derby County player Danny Higginbottom had served notice of termination of his contract after Derby failed to pay amounts owing to him thereunder. Derby subsequently paid up.

8 See para E1.44 et seq.

E1.20 Similar provisions can be found in the standard Contract for Professional Cricketers and the England and Wales Cricket Board's Rules and Regulations[1]. In particular, both football and cricket have the catch-all offence of 'bringing the sport into disrepute'[2].

1 Gardiner *Sports Law* (2nd edn, 2001, Cavendish Publishing), p 535. The Rugby Football Union has standard recommended terms for players contracts but member clubs are not obliged to use them: *Julian White v Bristol Rugby Ltd* [2002] IRLR 204 (Havelock-Allan J).

2 See paras E1.19 and A2.45.

(b) Incorporation

E1.21 As noted above[1], the professional footballer's contract expressly incorporates the rules of the Football Association and either the Premier League or the Football League, depending on the status of his club. They also incorporate the club's standard player rules. In the case of conflict, the governing body rules take precedence over the employment agreement and the rules of the club. In other instances, incorporation is not so clear. The question whether, and if so what, extraneous rules and regulations are incorporated is a straightforward question of construction of the language of the agreement. For example, a clause specifying that a boxing bout shall be conducted in conformity with the rules and regulations of the World Boxing Organisation ('WBO') was not sufficient to incorporate the WBO rules into a contract between promoters and a boxer[2]. The rules applied only to the bout itself.

1 See para E1.19, n 4.

2 *Clansman Sporting Club Ltd v Robinson* (5 May 1995, unreported) (Johnson J).

(c) Restrictions

E1.22 Express terms may be included into players' contracts in an attempt to prevent them from playing in particular circumstances during the term of the agreement, or to curtail their freedom after the contract has come to an end. The contract will be partially or wholly void if such terms are found to be in unreasonable restraint of trade[1].

1 Gardiner *Sports Law* (2nd edn, 2001, Cavendish Publishing), pp 227–235 and 540–546; Beloff et al *Sports Law* (1999, Hart Publishing), paras 4.49–4.54 and 4.73–4.79. For further discussion of the doctrine of restraint of trade in relation to playing contracts, see para E2.32 et seq.

E1.23 Since an employee has a duty to be loyal to his employer while the contract subsists, there is little room for a complaint of restraint of trade during the term of the agreement. A professional footballer, for example, agrees not to participate professionally in any other sporting or athletic activity without the written consent of his club[1]. He or she would have a hard job persuading a court that such a restriction was unreasonable.

1 See cl 7(a) of the Football League contract.

E1.24 Nevertheless, it has been suggested that the *duration* of a contract can of itself give rise to an unreasonable restraint of trade. In *Watson v Prager*[1] the contract between a professional boxer and his manager was for an initial period of three years, as prescribed by the Boxing Board of Control, but also contained an option for the manager to extend for a further three years – which he purported to exercise. The boxer sought to establish that the contract was unenforceable. He succeeded. The contract fell within the doctrine because it was prescribed by the governing body rather than negotiated freely. Further, and in relation to the option, the manager's interest could have been protected by an extension of only eighteen months[2]. Strictly *Watson v Prager* addresses only those cases where terms have been imposed by a governing body. But in principle very long contracts may be susceptible even if freely negotiated[3].

1 [1991] 1 WLR 726, Scott J.

2 An option on a boxer's services in the event that he became champion, to last for three fights over the next 18 months, was not in unreasonable restraint of trade: *Clansman Sporting Club Ltd v Robinson* (5 May 1995, unreported), Johnson J. Similarly, an exclusive contract to drive for Subaru was not in restraint of trade. There was equality of bargaining power at the time the contract was entered into, the remuneration was substantial, and the duration of the contract was only two seasons: *Subaru v Richard Burns* (11 December 2001, unreported) (Deputy Judge Strauss).

3 Cases relating to the music industry certainly suggest this is the case: Beloff et al *Sports Law* (1999, Hart Publishing), paras 4.77–4.79. In *Instone v Shroeder Music Publishing Ltd* [1974] 1 WLR 1308, HL, a 10 year exclusive contract between a young songwriter and a music publisher was held to be in unreasonable restraint of trade. A similar argument was raised in relation to football player Nicolas Anelka when he wanted to leave Arsenal: Gardiner and Welch 'The contractual tie – Anelka' in Gardiner *Sports Law* (2nd edn, 2001, Cavendish Publishing), pp 563 and 564.

E1.25 The most notable instance of a *post*-termination restriction was professional football's former transfer system, which through its registration requirements effectively barred one club signing a player unless it paid a fee to his former club. This applied to all professional players, even when their contracts with their clubs had come to an end. The position under English law was that the transfer rules were valid and enforceable[1]. However, since the celebrated case of *Union Royale Belge de Sociétés de Football Assocation ASBL v Jean-Marc Bosman*[2], players who are aged 24 and over and who are out of contract are completely free to negotiate a new contract with any club.

1 *Eastham v Newcastle United Football Club* [1964] Ch 413, Wilberforce J. The transfer rules were coupled with powers of retention whereby a club could debar a player joining another club at the end of his contract simply by continuing to pay him a reasonable wage. The combined systems were in restraint of trade, but the rules enabling a club to require a transfer fee were upheld. See para E2.32 et seq.

2 Case 415/3 [1995] ECR I-4921, ECJ. See paras A3.172, n 1, B2.153 to B2.156, B3.40 et seq and E2.40 et seq.

E1.26 An alternative option for employers attempting to prevent employees downing tools and moving straight to a competitor is the so-called 'garden leave' clause. Typically such a clause provides that, in the event of the employer or the employee giving notice to terminate the contract, the employer may require the employee to spend all or part of the period of notice at home (whether gardening or not is a matter for him)[1]. The aim is normally that any confidential information that the employee has obtained in the course of his employment should go stale before he is released to work for a competitor[2]. Since the typical footballer or rugby player is a commodity ideally to be used or sold (rather than a receptacle of confidential information to be put in cold storage), such clauses are rare[3]. They nevertheless serve a purpose if attempting to delay a manager's departure, as Steve Bruce, then manager of Crystal Palace, discovered[4].

1 Such a clause should be express. If not the court will construe the contract to determine whether or not the employee has the right to work, in which case placing him on garden leave is a breach of contract: *William Hill Organisation Ltd v Tucker* [1998] IRLR 313, CA. Similarly, a court will be careful not to grant interlocutory relief to enforce a garden leave clause to any greater extent than would be covered by a justifiable covenant in restraint of trade: *William Hill* per Morrit LJ.

2 See *Harvey on Industrial Relations and Employment Law* (Butterworths), A[612]–[615.02].

3 For consideration of such a remedy in relation to footballers, see Paul McGrath 'Football Contracts – Fact or Fiction' [2001] 9(2) SATLJ 109–117.

4 *Crystal Palace v Steve Bruce* (22 November 2001, unreported), Burton J. In June 2001 Steve Bruce signed a two-year management contract with Crystal Palace, with provision for nine months' notice and a garden leave clause. He discovered the manager's position at Birmingham City had become available and wanted to leave. Crystal Palace would not let him talk to Birmingham and he resigned, claiming that the club had repudiated his contract (for various reasons). The club applied for an interim injunction requiring Bruce to comply with the garden leave provision. Despite undertakings given by Bruce not to approach fellow management staff or players, the court granted the injunction pending a speedy trial on the basis that staff and players might simply follow Bruce to Birmingham. Further, the court held it was arguable that he had confidential information on players and other matters, and was going to a direct promotion rival. See casenote by De La Mare in [2000] 2 ISLR 16. (For more on injunctions as a remedy, see para E1.68 et seq.)

C Implied terms

E1.27 If a term of an agreement is not express, it may be implied. However, no term will be implied unless it is something which the parties must be taken to have agreed. It is not enough to show that it would have been reasonable to include the term, nor that it would have been unreasonable not to have agreed to it. Rather it must be reasonable to assume that the parties did so agree – that their real intention was to include the term – even if they did not say so at the time[1]. Such terms may be classified as implied in various ways:

(i) by conduct;
(ii) by an 'officious bystander' (because it is so obvious)[2];
(iii) by custom;

(iv) to make the contract work ('business efficacy'); and
(v) by virtue of the nature of the agreement (ie it is a characteristic of the sort of agreement that all parties entering into such an agreement must necessarily have accepted such a term)[3].

Public policy also circumscribes the freedom to contract in some respects. For example, agreements between members and clubs will be found to include an implied term that any disciplinary hearing will be conducted fairly and in accordance with the rules of natural justice[4] (although the English courts have stopped short of implying such a term in employment contracts; instead statute creates such a right[5]).

1 See *Harvey on Industrial Relations and Employment Law* (Butterworths), A[255].
2 A term must be necessary such that the bystander would say it must be so: *Bournemouth and Boscombe Football Club Ltd v Manchester United Football Club Ltd* (1980) Times, 22 May, CA. Bournemouth sold a player to Manchester United, for a fee that increased if the player scored a certain number of goals. Manchester United sold the player before he was able to score the requisite number of goals. The Court of Appeal, by a majority, implied a term that Manchester United was bound to afford the player a reasonable opportunity of scoring the tally of goals in competitive first team football and found that the term had been breached since the player had been transferred without reasonable cause. The player might presumably have made the same argument himself if his contract of employment made a bonus contingent in the same way.
3 See *Harvey on Industrial Relations and Employment Law* (Butterworths), A[255]–[275.01].
4 *Lee v Showman's Guild of Great Britain* [1952] 2 QB 329, CA. In *Nolan v Aldwinians Rugby Union Football Club* (10 July 2001, unreported), Recorder Allen, the implied term was breached in various respects in the process of disciplining Nolan who was said to have deliberately stamped on the face of an opposing player. A contract was found to exist between Diane Modahl and the British Athletic Federation which included a term that disciplinary procedures should be fair: *Modahl v British Athletic Federation* [2001] 1 WLR 1192, CA. See further para A3.127, n 3.
5 Beloff et al *Sports Law* (1999, Hart Publishing), paras 7.53 and 7.76.

(a) Employment

E1.28 Employment agreements are a classic example of a contract into which terms will be implied by a court simply by virtue of the nature of the agreement. The most fundamental duty on an employer is to pay wages: this will be implied even if not dealt with expressly (and these days the rate will not be less than the minimum wage). Perhaps more crucially for well-remunerated players, however, the employer arguably has a duty to provide work, as well as to take reasonable care of his employee and to maintain mutual trust and confidence[1].

1 See *Harvey on Industrial Relations and Employment Law* (Butterworths), A[379]–[398]; Gardiner *Sports Law* (2nd edn, 2001, Cavendish Publishing), pp 536–538. A further duty is to provide, and monitor, a reasonably suitable working environment: *Waltons and Morse v Dorrington* [1997] IRLR 488, EAT, where the relocation of a secretary to a smoky area (and the refusal to move her) founded a claim for unfair constructive dismissal.

E1.29 Duty to provide work In relation to a duty to provide work, the traditional view was that the employer (as master of his servant) did not have to do so[1]. There might have been an express undertaking to provide work[2], or exceptionally such an undertaking might have been implied – for example in the case of actors, where publicity is vital[3]. But otherwise the employee could be left, in practice, unemployed.

1 'Provided that I pay my cook her wages regularly, she cannot complain if I take all or any of my meals out': *Collier v Sunday Referee Publishing Co Ltd* [1940] 2 KB 647.
2 *Marbé v George Edwardes (Daly's Theatre) Ltd* [1928] 1 KB 269.
3 *Herbert Clayton and Jack Waller Ltd v Oliver* [1930] AC 209, HL. This category could equally extend to skilled workers (see para E1.30) and 'even to chartered accountants': *Provident Financial Group plc v Hayward* [1989] ICR 160 at 168, CA per Dillon LJ.

E1.30 This view was challenged by the Court of Appeal in *Langston v Amalgamated Union of Engineering Workers*[1], at least in the case of skilled workers. The Court of Appeal said that it was arguable that there was an implied obligation on the part of the employer to provide a reasonable amount of work if there was work to be done. Broadly, an employer could not unreasonably withhold work having regard to a worker's interest in exercising and improving his skills.

1 [1974] IRLR 15.

E1.31 It is too much to say professional footballers, cricketers and the like must be allowed to play in the first team on the basis that, as for actors, publicity is vital[1]. It might, however, be argued that they have the right to play in reserve matches if fit because otherwise their skills will suffer and they will lose match fitness, although it would be a special case where this argument succeeded. (Arguably a club which fails to comply with this limited duty may give a player 'sporting just cause', if not simple just cause, for leaving[2].

1 See para E1.29.
2 See para E1.64.

E1.32 Duty to take care As to the duty of an employer to take care for the health and welfare of an employee, there is no argument: the duty exists and is threefold. An employer must:

(i) select proper staff;
(ii) provide adequate materials; and
(iii) provide a safe system of working[1].

Further, the duty extends to circumstances where a third party, whom the employer has entrusted with the performance of its duty to take reasonable care, is negligent[2]. Although the duty is normally regarded as tortious, the fact that it is also implied as a contractual term[3] allows an employee to claim constructive dismissal if a system of work is so unsafe as to be a repudiatory breach of contract[4].

1 *Wilsons and Clyde Coal Co Ltd v English* [1938] AC 57, HL.
2 *McDermid v Nash Dredging and Reclamation Co Ltd* [1986] IRLR 308.
3 In *Kieron Brady v Sunderland Football Club* (17 November 1998, unreported), CA, a concurrent duty in contract and in tort was accepted by the football club, but on the facts the duty was not found to have been breached. Brady was a talented young footballer who suffered from a vascular problem in his right leg which prematurely terminated his career. He sued Sunderland, alleging he should have been diagnosed at a much earlier stage, at which point he could have benefited from successful corrective surgery. However, he failed to establish that he had complained to the club's physiotherapist in such a manner as to prompt the physiotherapist to refer him to a specialist. Nor was there a duty on the physiotherapist to conduct a full medical examination of every patient no matter what the problem. Only unusual symptoms and/or symptoms that did not respond to treatment needed to be referred. In *Michael Watson v British Boxing Board of Control* [2001] QB 1134, CA, there was no such contractual duty. However there was a sufficient nexus between the parties for a duty to arise in negligence. The Board was in breach of that duty in respect of brain damage suffered by Watson, for failing to provide proper ringside medical services and equipment.
4 *British Aircraft Corpn v Austin* [1978] IRLR 332, EAT; *Graham Oxley Tool Steels Ltd v Firth* [1980] IRLR 135, EAT.

E1.33 Trust and confidence The implied duty of trust and confidence, which is mutual, is a modern concept that came of age with its recognition at the highest level in *Malik v Bank of Credit and Commerce International SA*[1]. It means that an employer should not, without reasonable and proper cause, conduct itself in a manner calculated or likely to destroy or seriously damage the relationship of trust and confidence with its employee[2]. The duty does not, however, apply to dismissal[3].

1 [1997] IRLR 462, HL. The claimants were formerly employed by BCCI before its notorious collapse. They sued the bank on the grounds that they had been stigmatised in the employment market by the circumstances of the failure. For the purpose of deciding whether there was a cause of action it was assumed that the collapse had been brought about by the corrupt, dishonest behaviour of others and that the claimants had indeed been handicapped in the labour market by virtue of their association with the bank, and had thereby suffered loss. The House of Lords held that such an action was sustainable. By behaving in a corrupt and dishonest manner an employer can breach the duty. In assessing whether or not a breach has taken place, conduct is to be viewed objectively, and not by reference to the motives of the employer.

2 *Woods v WM Car Services (Peterborough) Ltd* [1981] IRLR 347, EAT (affirmed in the Court of Appeal). In *Macari v Celtic Football and Athletic Co Ltd* [1999] IRLR 787, Celtic was in breach of the duty in its dealings with manager Lou Macari. Macari would have been entitled to accept the breach and treat the contract as terminated. However, he did not do so, instead remaining at the club and drawing salary under his contract. Macari was therefore obliged to comply with instructions given to him by the managing director (see para E1.35 et seq on the duty to obey a lawful instruction) and was lawfully dismissed when he failed to do so.

3 *Johnson v Unisys Ltd* [2001] UKHL 13, [2001] IRLR 279. *Malik* was not a wrongful dismissal complaint, but related to a breach owed *during* employment.

E1.34 The employee's duties The essential duty on the employee (and the corollary of the duty on the employer to pay) is to 'serve' the employer, ie to be ready and willing to work[1]. The employee also impliedly promises he is reasonably competent[2], will take reasonable care in the performance of his duties[3], will carry out reasonable instructions (duty of obedience), and will be loyal.

1 *Cresswell v Inland Revenue Board* [1984] IRLR 190.

2 Serious incompetence may justify dismissal at common law, but will probably be unfair for the purposes of the Employment Rights Act 1996 (see para E1.54 et seq) unless the employee has first been warned his performance is inadequate: *Cook v Thomas Linnell & Sons Ltd* [1977] IRLR 132.

3 *Lister v Romford Ice and Cold Storage Co Ltd* [1957] AC 555.

E1.35 Obedience Not every act of disobedience will justify summary dismissal at common law[1]. There has to be a deliberate flouting of the terms of the contract[2]. Nor is the employee obliged to carry out instructions that are outside his contract: if the employer insists, the employee can claim to have been constructively dismissed[3]. However, an employee cannot simply ignore lawful instructions in the face of a breach of trust and confidence by his employer if he chooses to remain employed. The obligation to comply with the instructions is not the counterpart of the implied term of trust and confidence (unless the instruction was issued in bad faith to embarrass or harm the employee)[4].

1 See para E1.47.

2 *Laws v London Chronicle* [1959] 1 WLR 698.

3 *O'Brien v Associated Fire Alarms Ltd* [1968] 1 WLR 1916, CA.

4 *Macari v Celtic Football Athletic Co Ltd* [1999] IRLR 787, Court of Session (per Lord Caplan in relation to bad faith). Macari failed to comply with instructions to abide by a contractual residence clause, to attend more regularly at Celtic's ground and to report to the managing director on a weekly basis. He was therefore lawfully dismissed notwithstanding Celtic's own breach of the duty of trust and confidence (which he had not treated as repudiating his contract of employment).

E1.36 Loyalty The duty of loyalty gives rise to various obligations on the part of the employee[1]. He must behave honestly, not make any secret profits[2], pass on to his employer any information that comes to him on his employer's behalf, not use or disclose confidential information obtained in his employment[3] (save as allowed by the Public Interest Disclosure Act 1998, ie whistleblowing), and not set up in competition with his employer[4].

1 See *Harvey on Industrial Relations and Employment Law* (Butterworths), A[405]–[441].
2 *Boston Deep Sea Fishing and Ice Co v Ansell* (1888) 39 Ch D 339.
3 *Faccenda Chicken Ltd v Fowler* [1984] IRLR 61.
4 *Hivac v Park Royal* [1946] 1 All ER 350. As stated above (para E1.23), cl 7 of the League contract expressly prevents footballers playing elsewhere without their club's consent. A similar provision exists in the contract for professional cricketers: Gardiner *Sports Law* (2nd edn, 2001, Cavendish Publishing), p 539.

(b) Incorporation

E1.37 The express incorporation of the rules of governing bodies is considered above[1]. Such rules may also be incorporated by implication but only if one of the legal tests for implication[2] is satisfied and no express term conflicts with the term sought to be implied. The possibility of implied incorporation was considered in relation to the World Boxing Organisation rules, but the rules were not implied in the circumstances of that case[3]. However, the need for fair disciplinary procedures was implied in the *Nolan* and *Modahl* cases[4].

1 See para E1.21.
2 See para E1.27.
3 *Clansman Sporting Club Ltd v Robinson* (22 May 1995, unreported), Johnson J. There was no necessity for the rules to be implied.
4 See para E1.27, n 4.

E1.38 An interesting issue arises in relation to FIFA's Regulations for the Status and Transfer of Players. For example, Art 30 prevents transfer or employment contracts being made conditional on the acquisition of a work permit[1]. It is not however clear how this term is to be incorporated into the contract between the club and the player. The League contract expressly provides for incorporation of the FA and League rules[2]. But there is no mention of FIFA, which might therefore be considered as intentionally excluded. The problem will be solved if the FA itself implements the FIFA rules, as the provision will then be expressly incorporated. Otherwise the question remains (as yet) unanswered[3].

1 'The validity of a transfer contract or of an employment contract between a player and a club cannot be made conditional upon the positive results of a medical examination or upon the acquisition of a work permit.'
2 See para E1.21.
3 The issue of whether the FA rules apply between clubs, as well as between the FA and each club, was raised in *Aylesbury Football Club (1997) Ltd v Watford Association Football Club Ltd* (12 June 2000, unreported), Poole J. However, the matter was not determined, the case being decided on normal principles relating to minors' contracts (see para E1.82).

4 PERFORMANCE OF THE CONTRACT

E1.39 With the contract signed, all the parties have to do is perform it. However, this is not always as straightforward as it sounds, particularly when it comes to one party paying up.

A Examples

E1.40 It is common for footballers' employment contracts to specify bonuses to be paid if they score a certain number of goals. These provisions are often reflected in the transfer contract between the footballer's old club and his new employer. Just such a term caused difficulties for Bournemouth and Boscombe Athletic Football Club after selling the player Ted MacDougall to Manchester United[1]. Under the terms of the deal Manchester United was to pay £25,000 to Bournemouth when MacDougall had scored 20 goals. However, three months into the contract Tommy Docherty took over as manager and quickly put MacDougall up for sale. Two months later MacDougall was out (to West Ham) and the goal bonus remained unpaid. Bournemouth sued for the amount. The majority of the Court of Appeal (including Lord Denning MR) were willing to imply a term into the transfer contract that Manchester United were bound to afford MacDougall a reasonable opportunity of scoring 20 goals in first team competitive football[2]. Further, that term had been breached by the transfer of MacDougall without reasonable cause[3]. The question arises as to whether the court would have taken the same approach had Manchester United been sued by MacDougall himself for any goal bonus he had failed to obtain by being transferred.

1 *Bournemouth and Boscombe Athletic Football Club and Co Ltd v Manchester United Football Club Ltd* (1980) Times, 22 May, CA.

2 This term was as devised by the judge below. Various alternative formulations of the implied term were put forward by the Court of Appeal. One was that Manchester United would not transfer MacDougall without just cause so as to deprive Bournemouth of its money.

3 It is difficult not to have sympathy with the dissenting judgment in this case. Brightman LJ reasoned that MacDougall had been sold because Doherty *bona fide* considered that he was not a satisfactory member of the team. It was this withdrawal from the team which led to the contract being terminated and the bonus not becoming payable. Since there was no express term requiring Manchester United to include MacDougall in the team Brightman LJ asked himself whether any term could be implied that, as a matter of course, MacDougall would be retained in the team contrary to the manager's discretion. The answer to that had to be no. However, such an inference must be implicit in the term the majority of their Lordships had implied. Limiting the manager's judgment in this way could not have been contemplated by the parties. (However, the position would be entirely different if there was a finding of bad faith against the manager.)

E1.41 Uruguayan footballer Milton Nunez found himself on the wrong side of an action by his club, Sunderland, to prevent his previous employer, Uruguay Montevideo FC, from obtaining the final transfer payment for his services[1]. Sunderland obtained an *ex parte* injunction restraining Montevideo from calling on a bank guarantee for the money on the basis that Nunez's agent had fraudulently misled Sunderland into believing that Nunez was registered with a first division club, Nationale, and not with Montevideo, a third division and unconnected club. However, Montevideo succeeded in having the injunction discharged. Nunez's agent had sent documents expressly referring to Montevideo rather than Nationale and Sunderland had been mistaken in confusing the two. There was therefore no seriously arguable case that fraud was the only realistic inference to be drawn[2].

1 *Sunderland Association Football Club Ltd v (1) Uruguay Montevideo Football Club, (2) Milton Nunez, (3) Mr Betencur* [2001] 2 All ER (Comm) 828.

2 Nunez was transferred to Nacional on 10 June 2001.

E1.42 Rugby player Julian White signed a three year exclusive playing contract commencing July 2001 with Bristol Rugby Club but then decided he did not want to join after all[1]. He had been paid a £15,000 advance when signing the contract in 2000 and claimed that, when the agreement was made, he had been given an option to cancel it at any time prior to July 2001 if he paid the money back. Unfortunately, the option did not appear in the contract nor any other contemporaneous documentation – and Bristol denied that any such option had ever been offered.

White sued the club for a declaration that the option had been exercised, alternatively for misrepresentation (that an option existed), alternatively for a declaration that the contract had been repudiated. He was granted an interim injunction to restrain Bristol from interfering with his attempts to play elsewhere in 2001/2002[2]. But at trial he was unsuccessful. His recollection was poor and the court was influenced by the fact that there appeared to be no good reason for Bristol ever to give such an option. His claims based on the option therefore failed. Further, there was no repudiation by Bristol[3].

1 *Julian White v Bristol Rugby Ltd* [2002] IRLR 204, Havelock-Allan J.
2 In the event, no other club would sign him until the situation was clarified because of the risk of having to pay a transfer fee to Bristol if White failed.
3 There was no attempt made by the club to restrain White's breach and thereby to compel performance of a contract for personal services, which is perhaps not surprising in the light of the authorities on such injunctions (para E1.68 et seq). However, in a happy ending, White joined Bristol after all.

E1.43 Southend United Football Club failed to pay its former manager, Colin Murphy, five per cent of the profit realised upon the transfer of Stan Collymore[1]. Murphy sued for the amount and succeeded, the court construing three separate agreements in his favour.

1 *Colin Murphy v Southend United Football Club Ltd* (18 March 1999, unreported), Eady J. However, Murphy had to give credit for six months' worth of his salary (£16,000) for leaving his employment early.

B Disciplinary breaches (short of termination)

E1.44 The Football League contract makes express provision for termination by a player or a club if the other is guilty of a serious or persistent breach of a player's employment agreement[1]. However, it also provides for action short of termination if there is simple misconduct or a non-repudiatory breach by a player[2]. It is this latter provision that has resulted in numerous footballers losing up to two weeks' wages for a variety of misdemeanours – and some more serious incidents. In fact, with Premiership footballers earning more in a week than most people earn in a year, it might seem that a ceiling of two weeks' wages is a little low for bad behaviour[3]. That certainly seems to have been the opinion of Leeds United when it fined Lee Bowyer four weeks' wages for being drunk on the night that Asian student Sarfraz Najeib was attacked[4].

1 Clauses 16 and 17. The contract specifies the procedure to be followed, ie 14 days' notice of termination followed by an appeal procedure if so requested.
2 Clause 18 states: 'If the Player is guilty of misconduct or a breach of any of the training or disciplinary rules or lawful instructions of the Club or any of the provisions of this Agreement, the Club may either impose a fine not exceeding two weeks' basic wages or order the Player not to attend at the Club for a period not exceeding fourteen days. The Club shall inform the Player in writing of the action taken and the full reasons for it and this information shall be recorded in a register held at the Club. The Player shall have a right of appeal as set out in Clause 16(a) [to the League Board] (exercisable within seven days of the receipt by the Player of such written notification from the Club) and the Club or the Player as the case may be shall have a further right of appeal as set out in Clause 16(b) [to the Football League Appeals Committee] of this Agreement. Any penalty imposed by the Club upon the Player shall not become operative until the appeals procedures have been exhausted'.
3 A fine is, however, unheard of in 'normal' life, where an employee is likely only to receive an oral or written warning. Without an express provision enabling an employer to stop an employee's wages, the employer would be in repudiatory breach of the contract in doing so, unless the

employee was not performing the contract at all: *Julian White v Bristol Rugby Ltd* [2002] IRLR 204, Havelock-Allan J. (Bristol refused to pay White because he refused to attend the club for training or for matches.) Simple under-performance by players does not justify stopping their wages, contrary to Portsmouth chairman Milan Mandaric's apparent belief in March 2002 when he announced he would do just that following a bad run of results. (In fact the players were paid.)

4 The total fine (which, if imposed unilaterally, would have been a breach of contract since it was for more than two weeks) was believed to have been in the region of £88,000, a sum which Bowyer initially refused to pay on the grounds that he was being victimised. Jonathan Woodgate, who was found guilty of affray, was fined eight weeks' wages (believed to be £104,000) and ordered to work with Leeds' community programme until the end of his contract.

5 TERMINATION OF THE CONTRACT

E1.45 At common law a contract can be lawfully terminated in whatever way the contract provides. So, if notice is required and notice is given the contract is brought to an end with no breach sounding in damages. Alternatively, one party can choose to accept the other's repudiatory breach, terminating the agreement as of the date of their acceptance. However, the matter is more complicated in relation to employment agreements, since legislation demands that a contract is ended not only lawfully but also fairly (and treats the end of fixed term contracts as dismissal[1]).

1 Section 95(1)(b) of the Employment Rights Act 1996 expressly provides that an employee is dismissed if a fixed term contract expires without being renewed.

A Termination by clubs/teams

(a) Reasons for termination

E1.46 In practice players' contracts are terminated for a variety of reasons. Managers are dismissed most commonly because results are not going well rather than because they have committed gross misconduct (although some are dismissed for that reason). With the parlous state of football's finances, increasing numbers of players are being made redundant. Others are dismissed because they are incompetent or for 'some other substantial reason'[1], such as refusing to accept changes in terms and conditions (where an employer is acting reasonably)[2] or being impossible to work with[3]. Dennis Wise was famously dismissed in September 2002 for breaking team-mate Callum Davidson's jaw in a hotel room incident arising out of a players card school on a pre-season tour[4].

1 See s 98(2) of the Employment Rights Act 1996.
2 *R S Components Ltd v Irwin* [1974] 1 All ER 41.
3 *Treganowan v Robert Knee & Co Ltd* [1975] IRLR 247.
4 See para E1.19, n 6.

(b) Dismissal at common law

E1.47 To dismiss a player summarily, without giving the notice specified in his contract of employment, is a wrongful dismissal – unless the employee is guilty of gross misconduct[1]. This will be the case if an employee breaches an express or implied term which goes to the root of the contract, or repudiates the contract in its entirety. A dismissal in these circumstances is simply the employer communicating to the employee that the latter's breach has discharged the employer from his obligations under the contract, and that the employer has consequently elected to regard the contract as terminated[2].

1 Under the standard Football League contract, dismissal for gross misconduct requires 14 days notice (cl 16).

2 Gardiner *Sports Law* (2nd edn, 2001, Cavendish Publishing), pp 573 and 574. An employer can elect to keep the contract alive, as happened when Julian White refused to train or play matches for Bristol Rugby Club because he claimed he had exercised an option to leave: *Julian White v Bristol Rugby Ltd* [2002] IRLR 204, Havelock-Allan J. Bristol could certainly have accepted his repudiation and terminated the contract, but did not do so as it wanted to retain White's services.

E1.48 An employee who disobeys a lawful and reasonable instruction given by his employer may commit gross misconduct, although one act of disobedience can justify dismissal only if it goes to show, in effect, that the employee is repudiating the contract[1]. Refusing to obey three separate lawful instructions was sufficient to allow Celtic to dismiss manager Lou Macari lawfully, even though the club itself had breached the implied term of trust and confidence between employer and employee[2].

1 *Laws v London Chronicle Ltd* [1959] 2 All ER 285, CA per Lord Evershed MR.

2 *Macari v Celtic Football and Athletic Co Ltd* [1999] IRLR 787, Court of Session. The period of notice in Macari's contract was not less that two years, and a further clause expressly provided for termination on material breach of the agreement or if Macari committed gross misconduct, as well as other eventualities. (No express clause is actually needed to provide for termination for material breach, including gross misconduct, since the principles of the common law apply regardless. The clause in this case was not found to supplant the common law principles.) However, following a fall-out with a new board of directors at the club, Macari failed to comply with a residence clause to move nearer to Glasgow, and did not attend Celtic Park at any time between 20 May 1994 to 11 July 1994. He was found to be in material breach in failing to comply with lawful and legitimate instructions to abide by a contractual residence clause, to attend more regularly at Celtic Park and to report to the managing director on a weekly basis. This was a repudiatory breach that Celtic was entitled to accept.

E1.49 In a rare case involving players claiming for breach of contract as a result of their dismissals, seven rugby league players from Wakefield Trinity won claims for compensation ranging from £3,000 to £25,000. The club, in financial crisis, had terminated the employment of all the players over 24[1]. It remains to be seen whether football's current financial difficulties will throw up more such cases. In October 2002, Dennis Wise sued Leicester City for wrongful termination, alleging it had used his altercation with team-mate Callum Davidson on a pre-season tour as an excuse to get out of what now seemed (after relegation) an unaffordable contract[2].

1 [2001] 9(2) SATLJ 34.

2 See para E1.19, n 6.

E1.50 Much more common are cases involving managers[1]. Tony Pulis was dismissed from First Division football club Gillingham for alleged misconduct, only to be subsequently expelled from same division Portsmouth for similar reasons. He brought actions against both clubs for wrongful dismissal. In the Gillingham case, the club claimed Pulis had broken the terms of his contract in various respects, including by holding clandestine meetings about possible employment with other clubs. Pulis denied any misconduct. The matter ended in an out of court settlement of £75,000[2]. At the time of writing Pulis's case against Portsmouth is continuing[3]. John Rudge, one of football's longest-serving managers, was dismissed by Port Vale, and took the club to a Football League arbitration tribunal to obtain compensation. When Southampton suspended Dave Jones for 12 months in 2000, replacing him with Glenn Hoddle as manager, Jones challenged the suspension before the FA Premier League's Managers' Arbitration Tribunal.

1 The 2001/2002 season was dubbed the 'year of the sacking' for football managers. As early as October 2001 John Barnwell, chief executive of the coaches' trade union, the League Managers' Association, warned that if the rate of dismissals continued at the then rate, two-thirds of managers in post would find themselves out of work. At that time 11 managers had been dismissed, compared to only four by that point in previous seasons: [2001] 9(3) SATLJ 44.
2 [2001] 9(2) SATLJ 34.
3 Pulis was dismissed from Portsmouth for alleged misconduct having been placed on leave in October 2000 to allow him to concentrate on fighting his High Court claim against Gillingham: [2001] 9(1) SATLJ 23.

E1.51 George Graham was summarily dismissed by Tottenham Hotspur Football Club after stating publicly that the club needed to spend money on new players. In July 2001 the matter was settled, with the payment to Graham of a sum 'reported to be not unadjacent to £1 million'[1]. Kenny Dalglish, on the other hand, had to commence proceedings against Celtic Football Club before obtaining £612,522 plus interest and expenses[2]. And a claim by Joe Royle for a larger pay off from Manchester City[3] is still to be determined.

1 [2001] 9(2) SATLJ 35 and [2001] 9(1) SATLJ 25.
2 Dalglish was dismissed from his position as Celtic's Director of Football at the end of the terrible 1999/2000 season which saw Celtic finish 21 points behind Glasgow Rangers and the ignominy of a home defeat in the Scottish Cup against Inverness Caledonian Thistle: [2001] 9(1) SATLJ 24.
3 Joe Royle was a victim of Manchester City's relegation from the Premiership to the Nationwide League. Following his dismissal he was given a £200,000 pay off. However, he argued the figure should have been £700,000. On his case he was still a Premiership manager when he was dismissed and the amount paid should have reflected his earnings in that capacity rather than the salary of a first division manager (a pay cut of 65 per cent): [2001] 9(3) SATLJ 44.

E1.52 In *Niall Hogan v London Irish Rugby Football Club Trading Ltd*[1] professional rugby union players claimed for damages for breach of contract arising out of the termination of their playing contracts at the end of the 1997/98 season. The club's chief coach had negotiated with the players to play for two seasons but, at the end of only one, the club informed each player that their services were no longer required and that the coach had had no authority to make a binding agreement. The court found that the terminations were unlawful, since the claimants had been allowed to play and train for a year, and had been paid at the rate agreed with the coach. The club had therefore ratified the contracts with each of the players.

1 (20 December 1999, unreported), Purchas QC.

E1.53 There is an interesting distinction between claims for wrongful and unfair dismissal when it comes to justifying termination. In cases of unfair dismissal it is not possible for an employer to justify dismissal after the fact, ie an employer cannot rely on a repudiatory breach by an employee discovered only *after* that employee is dismissed in order to make the dismissal fair[1]. But in wrongful dismissal claims, an employer can take such conduct into account[2]. So, if an employer subsequently discovers an employee committed some dire misconduct while in his employment, the employer can rely on that repudiatory breach even if he did not know about it at the time of the dismissal (and even if the real reason for the dismissal would not, of itself, have been sufficient to have discharged the employer from his obligations under the contract)[3].

1 *W Devis & Sons Ltd v Atkins* [1977] AC 931, HL. The repudiatory conduct may, however, go to the amount of compensation awarded, since such amount has to be just and equitable in all the circumstances.
2 *Boston Deep Sea Fishing and Ice Co v Ansell* (1888) 39 Ch D 339.
3 See generally, *Harvey on Industrial Relations and Employment Law* (Butterworths), D1[862]–[869].

(c) Statutory dismissal rights

E1.54 The right not to be unfairly dismissed is embodied in the Employment Rights Act 1996 ('ERA 1996'). It applies to all employees and is more employee-friendly than the common law since procedural failings may render a dismissal unfair even though, at common law, the dismissal was not wrongful.

E1.55 Unfair dismissal is a large and case-heavy area that is best dealt with by consulting a dedicated text[1]. However the key principles are summarised here:

(i) an employee must have been employed for at least a year to bring a claim;
(ii) the claim has to be made within three months of the effective date of termination (unless not reasonably practicable to do so);
(iii) the claim is made to, and heard by, an employment tribunal, which is a specialist forum for unfair dismissal (and other statutory employment) claims;
(iv) an employee is dismissed for the purposes of the Employment Rights Act 1996 if his contract is terminated by his employer (with or without notice), or he is employed under a fixed term and that fixed term expires, or he terminates the contract in circumstances in which he is entitled to do so by virtue of the employer's conduct (constructive dismissal)[2];
(v) a dismissal will be fair only if it is for a fair reason and the employer acted reasonably[3];
(vi) a reason is fair if it relates to capability or qualifications, or to conduct, or the employee is redundant, or could not continue to work without contravention of a statutory duty or restriction, or the reason is otherwise substantial ('some other substantial reason')[4];
(vii) an employer acts reasonably if he takes fair steps in line with the reason for the dismissal[5]; the sanction of dismissal must have been within the band of reasonable responses that an employer could reasonably make in the circumstances[6].

1 For example, *Harvey on Industrial Relations and Employment Law* (Butterworths), D1. For a consideration of the remedies for unfair dismissal, see para E1.72 et seq.
2 See s 95(1) of Employment Rights Act 1996.
3 See s 98 of the Employment Rights Act 1996.
4 See s 98(2) and 98(1)(b) of the Employment Rights Act 1996.
5 For example, in a misconduct case, the employer must be found by the tribunal (on a balance of probabilities) to have reasonably believed that the conduct had been committed, which belief must be based on reasonable grounds, following a reasonable investigation: *British Home Stores Ltd v Burchell* [1978] IRLR 379. It is not necessary for the employer to prove that the misconduct in fact took place, only that in the circumstances set out above it honestly believed that it had. It is not for the tribunal to substitute its own opinion, but to assess whether the employer acted as a reasonable employer would: *Whitbread plc v Hall* [2001] EWCA Civ 268, [2001] ICR 699.
6 *HSBC Bank plc v Madden* [2000] ICR 1283; *Whitbread plc v Hall* [2001] EWCA Civ 268, [2001] ICR 699.

E1.56 It seems fewer sports dismissal cases pass through the employment tribunal system than through the courts[1]. This is perhaps no surprise since many players' earnings are a good deal higher than average and there is a ceiling on unfair dismissal awards[2]. Players therefore tend to bring their claims in the High Court where damages are at large, or to institute proceedings in both the High Court and the employment tribunal[3], staying the latter pending determination of the former[4].

1 This comment takes into account the fact that employment tribunal level cases are much less likely to become public than High Court cases, which have a greater tendency to be reported.
2 From 1 February 2002, £52,600.
3 As in the case of Dennis Wise: see para E1.19, n 6.
4 This is to prevent relevant issues being determined in the employment tribunal before High Court proceedings for fear of it being argued that an estoppel prevents the same issues being raised twice.

E1.57 There are some examples of employment tribunal proceedings however. In *Thomas v St Johnstone Football Club Ltd*[1], footballer Kevin Thomas failed in his claim for unfair dismissal against the club. His contract was terminated after he was seen with another player in the toilet of a bar 'with a white substance on top of the toilet roll holder and [Thomas] with a rolled up £20 note in his hand'[2]. The Scottish club asserted that Thomas had been dismissed on the grounds of conduct, alternatively some other substantial reason[3]. However, Thomas complained of various procedural breaches, not least that he had not been told prior to a first meeting that the matter was to be discussed. His appeal under his League contract[4] to the Scottish Premier League Board was successful, the Board concluding that he was guilty of serious misconduct but quashing the decision to terminate. But the club's appeal to the Scottish Football Association's Appeals Committee was upheld and the contract terminated. The tribunal accepted that the initial disciplinary procedure was flawed. However, the procedural errors had been cured by the subsequent appeal by way of rehearing to the Scottish Premier League Board[5]. Further, the decision to dismiss fell within the band of reasonable responses which a reasonable employer may have adopted[6].

1 Case No S/300307/2001, Dundee employment tribunal (September 2001, unreported).
2 Employment tribunal decision, p 4 at 15.
3 The reasons for dismissal communicated to Thomas were that: (i) the taking of an illegal substance could not be condoned in any walk of life; (ii) he must have been aware of the potential consequences, and known the matter would be treated 'in the most serious manner'; (iii) players were role models and the club had to send out the appropriate signals to supporters and young players: Employment tribunal decision (n 1 above), p 12 at 1–10.
4 The Scottish League contract provides for the same appeal process as the English but to the equivalent Scottish bodies.
5 Employment tribunal decision (n 1 above), p 23 at 45.
6 Employment tribunal decision (n 1 above), p 25 at 10–15.

E1.58 In *Beck v Lincoln City Football Club*[1] Beck was dismissed for taking an unauthorised leave of absence to go on holiday. Worse still, he gave misleading statements for his absence, first claiming bereavement and then a breakdown in the relationship with his girlfriend. He had two previous written warnings for misconduct. In the circumstances, the tribunal considered Beck's dismissal was fair. In *Post Office v Liddiard*, however, an employment tribunal found the dismissal of an employee following his involvement with hooliganism was unfair, and the Employment Appeals Tribunal dismissed the Post Office's appeal. Nevertheless, the Court of Appeal set aside the decision and remitted the case to a different employment tribunal[2]. It found the employment tribunal had not really addressed the central issue of whether or not it was reasonable for the employer to dismiss the employee because it believed that his conduct had brought it into disrepute[3]. In another case, postman Tom Doherty was found to have been unfairly dismissed despite television pictures showing him assaulting a Galatasaray fan during disturbances at the Turkish club's match with Arsenal in Copenhagen in May 2000[4]. Further, the tribunal ordered his reinstatement[5].

1 Gardiner *Sports Law* (2nd edn, 2001, Cavendish Publishing), p 591.
2 (7 June 2001, unreported), CA.
3 In relation to Mr Liddiard's contention that s 98 of the Employment Rights Act 1996 should be construed in a way compatible with human rights, the Court of Appeal said no more than that nothing required the section to be construed any differently than before the Human Rights Act 1998 came into force.
4 The Post Office had argued that Doherty's actions caused harm to the image of the 'friendly postman'; however, it had based its decision on film footage that did not mention Doherty's association with the employer: [2001] 9(2) SATLJ 34.
5 The Post Office refused to reinstate Doherty: [2001] 9(3) SATLJ 44. For a discussion of reinstatement as a remedy, see para E1.72. The Post Office's refusal rendered it liable for increased compensation.

B Termination by players

E1.59 Players terminate their contracts for a variety of reasons. They may feel they are being treated badly or unfairly, personally or professionally[1]. Or they may want to take advantage of the fact that, for one reason or another, their stock is particularly high, making it the right time to move on. (A good performance at an event like the World Cup can turn a football player into a superstar with interest from the world's best teams. And a racing driver doing well in the rankings is bound to attract good offers from elsewhere.) In some cases an accommodation can be found that lets the player leave but compensates the team[2]. Alternatively, the team may take steps to try and stop the player leaving[3].

1 See, in relation to the latter, para E1.63 et seq.
2 See generally Chapter E2.
3 See para E1.68 et seq.

(a) Examples

E1.60 Drivers who have moved on have found themselves at the sharp end of litigation in various cases. Elio de Angelis jumped ship from the 'Shadows' team to drive for Lotus[1]. The 'Shadows' team applied for an interim injunction but failed to obtain one. Similarly, the Subaru team applied unsuccessfully for an injunction to stop Richard Burns driving for Peugeot[2]. And Pedro Diniz contracted with the Sauber team notwithstanding the existence of an exclusive contractual tie with Arrows. Fortunately for him the Judge concluded that the parties had tacitly agreed to bring the Arrows contact to an end, saving him from having to pay a $7m termination payment[3].

1 *Nichols Advanced Vehicle Systems Inc v De Angelis and Team Lotus* (21 December 1979, unreported), Oliver J.
2 *Subaru v Richard Burns* (11 December 2001, unreported), Deputy Judge Strauss.

3 *Walkinshaw & Arrows Grand Prix v Pedro Diniz* [2001] 1 Lloyd's Rep 632, Tomlinson J. There was a termination provision permitting either party to terminate at the end of the 1998 season on payment to the other of $7m. There was also a clause that allowed Diniz to terminate if the racing performance of the Arrows cars was beneath a certain threshold ('the performance clause'). The Arrows team sued Diniz after he left following a poor 1998 season, claiming that he terminated pursuant to the $7m clause, alternatively damages. (No attempt was made to obtain an injunction.) Diniz denied repudiation and argued that he had terminated pursuant to the performance clause, alternatively that Arrows had repudiated the contract. The facts surrounding the breakdown of the relationship were very complicated, with various communications and inconsistencies. In the end the judge took a common sense view that the parties had agreed to end the contract: this was not the same as exercising a right under the $7m clause. He also concluded that the performance clause was a warranty by Arrows of the results to be achieved. Since the Arrows team had not met the performance standards, Diniz was entitled to terminate under that provision too.

E1.61 In football, players who want to move on and are still under contract ask to be listed for transfer, or have their agents make various discreet enquiries behind the scenes. But because of the need for their registration to be transferred to a new club (which requires the co-operation of the old)[1] there are no instances of a player simply turning up in a different strip on a Saturday afternoon having decamped for pastures new. Managers are a different matter. Football's rules preclude a club from approaching an employee of a fellow club without the latter's approval[2]. But if a manager hears that a position has come free and wants to apply for a role it might be thought that there is nothing anyone can do to stop him. An injunction will not be granted to force him to work[3]. Crystal Palace, however, relied on a garden leave clause in manager Steve Bruce's contract when he left in a bid to take up a post with rival Birmingham[4]. An interim injunction was granted to prevent him going anywhere pending a speedy trial[5], although ultimately he joined Birmingham a few weeks later by agreement.

1 See paras E2.2 to E2.4.

2 Rule 20 of the Football League regulations states: '20.1: No Club shall take any steps (either directly or indirectly through any third party, including the making of statements to the media) to induce or attempt to induce another Club's employee to terminate his contract of employment with that other Club, whether or not such termination constitutes a breach of that contract. 20.2: No Club shall (either directly or indirectly through any third party) make contact with or enter into negotiations relating to the employment of another Club's employee. 20.3: The only exception to this Regulation is where the Club has obtained the prior written permission of the Chairman (or in his absence, a director or the secretary) of that other Club. Any such permission must set out any conditions attaching to it'.

3 See para E1.68 et seq

4 See para E1.71.

5 The matter was settled out of court and without the trial taking place. In a strange quirk of fate, Bruce went on to take Birmingham into the Premier League via the play-offs while Crystal Palace remained in the First Division under Birmingham's pre-Bruce manager, Trevor Francis.

E1.62 Some players have tried to walk away from contracts but failed. Julian White signed for Bristol Rugby Club, but then purported to terminate the agreement by exercising an option to do so, alternatively accepting Bristol's repudiation[1]. Both arguments failed at trial[2] and White stayed with Bristol[3]. For a while it looked like John Crawley would have to stay at Lancashire County Cricket Club for the remaining three years of his contract. Crawley failed in his bid in February 2001 to persuade the English Cricket Board that Lancashire had been guilty of 'serious or persistent breach' of the agreement. However, after almost six months in limbo, Lancashire accepted a compensation payment from Hampshire in return for releasing Crawley from his contract[4].

1 *Julian White v Bristol Rugby Ltd* [2002] IRLR 204, Havelock-Allan J.

2 See para E1.42.

3 This was not a case in which an attempt was made by the club to restrain breach of the contract. White could simply have left the agreement behind and been subject to an action for breach of contract. Interestingly, though, the court decided (although without full argument) that there was a legitimate interest in Bristol keeping White to his contract, even if he refused physically to play for them, because – whilst under contract – Bristol could have demanded a transfer fee. Query how much weight this would have had if Bristol had applied for an interim injunction to restrain White from leaving.

4 Aftab Habib bought out the last year of his contract with Leicestershire County Cricket Club when he wanted to leave.

(b) 'Sporting just cause'

E1.63 The FIFA Regulations for the Status and Transfer of Players that came into force in September 2001[1] allow footballers to terminate their contracts for a 'valid sporting reason ('sporting just cause')'[2] (as well as for 'just cause')[3]. Sporting just cause will be established on a case-by-case basis pursuant to the dispute resolution procedure set out in the regulations[4]. If sporting just cause is established, FIFA will determine whether compensation is payable and in what amount[5]. But if there is a unilateral breach without sporting just cause (or just cause), sports sanctions shall be applied and compensation payable[6]. The sanction for a player is a restriction of four months from the beginning of the season on his eligibility to play[7].

1 See generally Chapter E2. Contracts between players and clubs concluded before 1 September 2001 will continue to be governed by the previous regulations, which came into force on 1 October 1997, unless the agreements were signed after 5 July 2001 and the parties expressly agree to make them subject to the regulations: Art 46 of the regulations.

2 As discussed above (para E1.21), these regulations are not incorporated into players' contracts expressly, although they will be so if adopted by the Football Association (the rules of which are incorporated).

3 See Art 24 of the regulations. 'Just cause' is FIFA terminology for repudiatory breach that has always allowed a player to consider himself constructively dismissed: Gardiner *Sports Law* (2nd edn, 2001, Cavendish Publishing), p 579.

4 Article 24 provides: 'Each case will be evaluated on its individual merits, taking account of all relevant circumstances (injury, suspension, player's field position, player's age etc). Furthermore, sporting just cause shall be examined at the end of the football season and before expiry of the relevant registration period in the former club's national association'. The dispute procedure is set out in Art 42. The procedure is expressed to be 'without prejudice to the right of any player or club to seek redress before a civil court in disputes between clubs and players'. However, unless players and clubs expressly agree that termination is possible for 'sporting just cause', and hence a contractual provision subject to the jurisdiction of the courts (see n 2 above), the only forum for such disputes will be FIFA. (And only FIFA will determine whether sporting sanctions apply.)

5 See Art 24 of the regulations.

6 See Art 21. With contracts signed up to a player's 28th birthday, this is the case during the first three years. Where a contract is signed after that time, the same principles apply for only the first two years. After that time no sanctions will apply, although sports sanctions may be pronounced on a club and/or player's agent for inducing a breach of contract.

7 Article 22.1. This sanction will be applied if the breach occurs at the end of the first or second year of the contract. No sanctions will be applied if the breach occurs at the end of the third year (or second year if the contract is signed after the age of 28) unless there was a failure to give appropriate notice after the last match of the season. In that case 'the sanction shall be proportionate'. However, in the case of aggravating circumstances (such as failing to give notice or recurrent breach of contract) sports sanctions may be imposed for up to a maximum of six months. A club seeking to register a player who has unilaterally breached a contract during a prohibited period will be presumed to have induced a breach of contract and itself be subject to sporting sanctions including fines, deduction of points and exclusion from competitions: Art 22.2.

E1.64 Quite what constitutes 'sporting just cause' is not defined. The only example given[1] is if a player can show, at the end of a season, that he has not played regularly for the first team and participated in less that 10% of first team fixtures[2]. Another possible instance was Aston Villa's manager allegedly isolating David Ginola and accusing him of being too fat to play in the Premiership[3].

1 FIFA Circular on the Status and Transfer of Players (24 August 2001): [2001] 9(3) SATLJ 185–198.

2 This illustrates the difference between sporting just cause and breach of contract, since it is difficult to see how the latter could be established on these facts, providing the selection decisions were made in good faith. (Although, for a breach of a transfer agreement between clubs on a similar basis see *Aylesbury Football Club (1997) Ltd v Watford Association Football Club Ltd* (12 June 2000, unreported), Poole J (para E1.76). The inter-relationship with contract is explored further in Gardiner *Sports Law* (2nd edn, 2001, Cavendish Publishing), p 580. For example, will a club forego contractual rights when a player is entitled to terminate for FIFA's purposes?

3 In this case Gordon Taylor, chief executive of the players' union, the PFA, claimed that the remarks of the manager could amount to constructive dismissal: [2001] 9(2) SATLJ 35 and 36.

6 REMEDIES

E1.65 Where a contract has been breached, the usual remedy is in damages. Nevertheless, often the main concern for a club when a player is about to walk away from a contract is to stop him going. For this reason, there are various cases in the sporting arena about applications for injunctions, albeit that most such applications fail. An alternative type of remedy is for unfair (as opposed to wrongful) dismissal. These remedies are specified by statute and include orders to reinstate or re-engage employees as well as compensation for the loss of a job[1].

1 For a consideration of remedies in relation to football contracts, see Paul McGrath, 'Football contracts – fact or fiction' [2001] 9(2) SATLJ 109–117.

A Damages

E1.66 The normal rule in relation to contractual damages is that, where a party sustains a loss by reason of a breach of contract, he should be placed so far as possible in the position he would have been in had the contract been performed[1]. Therefore, in relation to a breach of a contract of employment, the prima facie measure of damages for wrongful dismissal is a sum equivalent to the wages that would have been earned between the time of actual termination and the time when the contract might lawfully have been terminated[2]. This sum should include any fringe benefits that the employee would have received during the same period[3]. If the contract incorporates a disciplinary procedure or some other administrative process that must be followed before notice of termination may be given validly, the time such a process may have taken, had it been followed, may also be added to the notice period when determining the period over which damages are to be assessed[4]. However, the employee is under a duty to look for other work to mitigate his loss, unless the contract provides for a termination payment to be by way of a debt (in which case the duty to mitigate does not apply)[5].

1 *Radford v De Froberville* [1977] 1 WLR 1262 at 1268 per Oliver J.

2 See *Harvey on Industrial Relations and Employment Law* (Butterworths), A[653].

3 *Silvey v Pendragon plc* [2001] EWCA Civ 784, [2001] IRLR 685.

4 *Focsa Services (UK) Ltd v Birkett* [1996] IRLR 325, EAT. However, this does not extend to include a claim that, had the procedure been followed, the employee may not have been dismissed: *Janciuk v Winerite Ltd* [1998] IRLR 63, EAT.

5 See *Harvey on Industrial Relations and Employment Law* (Butterworths), A[654]–[654.01].

E1.67 Since fixed term contracts (without notice provisions) are the norm in professional sport, the measure of loss for wrongful dismissal will be the earnings for the period of time that the contract has left to run, subject to the duty to mitigate. There is therefore an obvious potential for high awards of damages[1]. Sometimes, however, the contract cuts both ways. For example, although football managers are a prime example of sportspeople obtaining large awards when dismissed[2], their contracts often also include provision for termination payments to be paid to the employer should they walk away from the deal[3]. Care has to be taken with these clauses since, if they are intended to penalise the departing employee as opposed to representing a genuine pre-estimate of loss, they will be struck down as penalties[4].

1 Gardiner *Sports Law* (2nd edn, 2001, Cavendish Publishing), p 577. In fact, because of the football transfer system and the general nature of professional sport, clubs normally ensure the matter is dealt with by agreement.
2 See, for example, Kenny Dalglish and Joe Royle (para E1.51).
3 Glenn Hoddle was widely believed to have an £800,000 get-out clause in his contract with Southampton (prior to his moving to Tottenham Hotspur).
4 Paul McGrath, 'Football contracts – fact or fiction' [2001] 9(2) SATLJ 114. In *Murphy v Southend United Football Club Ltd* (18 March 1999, unreported), Eady J, former manager Colin Murphy conceded that Southend was entitled to a payment of six months' worth of salary (£16,000) by virtue of his premature termination of the contract. This was a counterclaim to Murphy's successful claim for 5 per cent of the profits on selling player Stan Collymore. See further para E1.43.

B Injunctions

E1.68 The principal difficulty for clubs and teams attempting to obtain injunctions to stop players leaving is the English law view that no injunctive relief will be given to enforce a contract for personal services[1]. The reason sometimes given for this rule is that to do so would smack of slavery, but the better reason is that it is impossible for the court to supervise such a contract[2]. The authorities nevertheless draw a distinction between a promise to work for one employer, where an injunction will not be granted, and a promise not to work for another, where an injunction is a possibility. So, where a singer was exclusively committed to one venue but was lured away to another, an injunction was granted to prevent her from going[3]. And similar reasoning led to a film studio obtaining an injunction to prevent the actress Bette Davis from appearing in any film made by another studio for the remaining three years of her contract[4]. However, the view in this line of authority, whilst never strictly overruled, has not been followed in subsequent cases[5]. In *Warren v Mendy*[6] the Court of Appeal endorsed the view in *Page One Records Ltd v Britton*[7] that it was necessary to look at the realities of the situation to determine whether, in fact, the defendant was likely to be indirectly compelled to return to his employer (the grant of an injunction thereby effectively enforcing the contract for personal services).

1 *Clark v Price* (1819) 2 Wills Ch 157; *De Francesco v Barnum* (1890) 45 Ch D 430; *Ehrman v Bartholomew* [1898] 1 Ch 671.
2 *C H Giles & Co Ltd v Morris* [1972] 1 WLR 307 at 318 per Megarry J.
3 *Lumley v Wagner* (1852) 1 De GM & G 604.
4 *Warner Bros Pictures Inc v Nelson* [1937] 1 KB 209.
5 For example, in *Mortimer v Beckett* [1920] 1 Ch 571 a boxing manager unsuccessfully sought to restrain a boxer from boxing for another manager in breach of his agreement.
6 [1989] 3 All ER 103.
7 [1968] 1 WLR 157.

E1.69 The arguments were played out in detail, pre-*Warren v Mendy*, in the case of *Nichols Advanced Vehicle Systems Inc v Elio de Angelis*[1]. De Angelis had jumped ship from the 'Shadows' team to join Lotus for the 1980 season, and Nichols applied for an interim injunction to restrain him from breaching his exclusive contract obligation. However, no such injunction was granted, despite Oliver J's disapproval of the way De Angelis had behaved[2], as to do so would have had the practical effect of compelling De Angelis to perform a contract for personal services[3]. Neither was an injunction granted in *Subaru v Richard Burns*[4], nor in *Pantano and Pantano Management v Supernova Ltd*[5] where the roles were reversed, and a driver sought an injunction to prevent the team fielding any driver in his place.

1 (21 December 1979, unreported) (Oliver J).
2 Oliver J was of the view that to grant the injunction would serve no other useful purpose than to mark the court's disapproval of De Angelis's behaviour. Curiously, it does not appear to have been argued that the 'Shadows' team would have had its competitive position in Formula 1 racing damaged by De Angelis racing for a rival team. Contrast the case of *Crystal Palace Football Club v Steve Bruce* (22 November 2001, unreported) (Burton J) (para E1.26, n 4), where this argument apparently carried some weight. Even so, the competitive point was argued in *Subaru v Richard Burns* (11 December 2001, unreported), Deputy Judge Strauss (see n 4), but did not ultimately persuade the judge to grant an interim injunction.
3 The nature of Formula 1 racing had an influence on Oliver J. He stated: '… there is something morally repugnant in the notion of shackling together in a relationship of mutual trust, dependence and daily personal contact, individuals who are at loggerheads or who have lost confidence in one another'. This was particularly the case where, given the inherent danger of the sport and the crucial nature of the teamwork required, the need for mutual trust and confidence was vital.
4 (11 December 2001, unreported), Deputy Judge Strauss. Burns, a rally driver, left Subaru to drive for Peugeot. Again the Judge was influenced by the need for the closest possible co-operation between the driver and the management (see n 3 above) in order to ensure safety and the proper operation of the car, and by the fact that an injunction would effectively compel Burns to drive for Subaru. In relation to the competition point, he considered there were two distinct parts of Burns' contract: driving and promotion. While it might benefit Subaru to prevent Burns driving, it would be of no benefit to Subaru to have Burns standing idle in relation to promotion.
5 (March 2002, unreported) (Enriques J). Giorgiou Pantano, a Formula 3 driver, was dismissed by his team not long before the 2002 Imola race. He sought an injunction on the basis that the team was bound to use his services and not anyone else's. However, the application was rejected on familiar *De Angelis* and *Subaru* grounds that the two parties should not be shackled together when the relationship crucially required trust and confidence. This was so notwithstanding that the injunction was sought by the employee and not the other way round.

E1.70 In *Warren v Mendy* itself[1], Frank Warren tried to obtain an injunction to stop fellow boxing agent Ambrose Mendy from dealing with boxer Nigel Benn, who was under an exclusive contract to Warren. An injunction was obtained without notice to Mendy but later discharged, which action was subsequently approved by the Court of Appeal. Their Lordships substantially followed the approach in *De Angelis*[2]. It was recognised that restraining a breach might effectively compel Benn to perform the contract with Warren for personal services, particularly when he needed to exercise his skill for his psychological and physical well being[3]. The fact that the injunction was not sought against Benn himself proved no impediment. The substance of the action was the same as if the injunction was being sought against the boxer. The court was not prepared to grant Warren '… by the back door relief which he could not obtain through the front …'[4].

1 [1989] 1 WLR 853.
2 See para E1.69.

3 [1989] 1 WLR 853 at 857. In other words, faced with the choice of giving up professional boxing altogether for the period of the injunction, or continuing to box under the management and promotion of Warren, Benn may effectively have been forced to do the latter, since he needed to box. That was something the court would not order.

4 [1989] 1 WLR 853 at 867. The Court of Appeal made three general statements of principle. First, compulsion is a question of fact in each case, to be viewed pragmatically. Secondly, '... the longer the term for which an injunction is sought, the more readily will compulsion be inferred': [1989] 1 WLR 853 at 867. Thirdly, there is less likely to be an injunction where mutual trust and confidence is key to the endeavour, but it no longer exists.

E1.71 An interim injunction was however granted in *Crystal Palace v Steve Bruce*[1]. The circumstances were different from the cases already discussed in so far as the club relied on an express garden leave clause in Bruce's contract that allowed it to specify that Bruce should not attend work for the period of his notice (nine months). The reasons for the court granting the injunction are rehearsed above[2] but Burton J was certainly influenced by the fact that a trial of the issues was possible within a matter of weeks, making the grant of an interim injunction a less prejudicial matter for Bruce[3].

1 (22 November 2001, unreported), Burton J. See also para para E1.46, n 4.

2 See para E1.46, n 4.

3 In 2001, Adrian Newey, the engine designer and key employee of McLaren, seemed about to join rival Formula 1 team Jaguar until McLaren persuaded him to remain with them. Proceedings were threatened but the parties reached agreement before the matter got to court.

C Statutory remedies

E1.72 There are three possible statutory remedies for unfair dismissal: compensation, reinstatement and re-engagement. Compensation is assessed under two heads. First there is the basic award, calculated in most cases in the same way as a statutory redundancy payment[1]. Secondly there is the 'compensatory' award which is designed to compensate for the actual loss suffered by the employee arising out of the unfair dismissal[2]. This is broadly calculated by assessing the loss flowing from the loss of employment, where appropriate reducing the amount by any sums paid by the employer, or sums earned by way of mitigation, or by an amount for contributory fault[3], and then, if the sum exceeds the maximum permitted (see n 2 below), reducing it to the maximum[4]. However, it is not in every case that an employee will be fully compensated, since the only obligation on the tribunal is to award what is just and equitable in the circumstances[5]. Further, if the employee would have been dismissed in any event, even had the dismissal not been unfair, in general he will have suffered no loss attributable to the unfair dismissal[6].

1 This award is based on a week's pay for every year in employment between 22 and 40, capped at a statutory figure. (For those under 22, the calculation is based on half a week's pay. For those 41 and over, the calculation is based on one-and-a-half week's pay). From 1 February 2002 the capped figure for a week's pay is £250.

2 This, too, is capped, from 1 February 2002 at £52,600.

3 Unlike wrongful dismissal, unfair dismissal allows a tribunal to reduce compensation to reflect any conduct by the employee which contributed to the dismissal.

4 For an in-depth consideration of compensation, see *Harvey on Industrial Relations and Employment Law* (Butterworths), D1[2501]–[2850].

5 See s 74(1) of the Employment Rights Act 1996.

6 See *Harvey on Industrial Relations and Employment Law* (Butterworths), D1[2544]. Similarly, if there is only a chance that the employee would have been retained, the award should be reduced to reflect that chance: *Polkey v AE Dayton Services Ltd* [1987] IRLR 503.

E1.73 One of the attractions of a claim in the employment tribunal for unfair dismissal is that the tribunal can order either that an employee be returned to his old job (reinstatement) or that he be re-engaged in another comparable capacity[1]. Once a tribunal has determined that a dismissal is unfair it must consider reinstatement or re-engagement. However, it will only make such an order if an employee wishes it. Further, the tribunal will consider whether it is practicable for the employer to comply with the order, and whether the employee has caused or contributed to his own dismissal.

1 See ss 114 and 115 of the Employment Rights Act 1996. See detailed exposition in *Harvey on Industrial Relations and Employment Law* (Butterworths), D1[2371]–[2500]. Should an employer refuse to comply with such an order, an extra amount of compensation will be awarded.

E1.74 Kevin Thomas made it clear in his employment tribunal claim that he wished to be reinstated as a player with St Johnstone Football Club if his employment tribunal claim was successful[1]. In the event, it was not[2]. However, a tribunal did order the reinstatement of postman Tom Doherty after he was found to have been unfairly dismissed (despite television pictures showing him assaulting a Galatasaray fan during disturbances at the Turkish club's match with Arsenal in Copenhagen in May 2000)[3].

1 *Kevin Thomas v St Johnstone Football Club Limited*, S/300307/2001, Dundee employment tribunal, (September 2001, unreported) at p 16, line 15.
2 See para E1.57.
3 See para E1.58.

7 PROCURING A BREACH OF CONTRACT

E1.75 If person A procures the breach by B of a contract between B and C, then C can sue A for damages for the tort of procuring a breach of contract[1]. There are various essential elements of the tort: (i) A must know of the existence of the contract between B and C. However it is not necessary that A knows of the precise terms, or that a contract definitely exists. Knowledge that there is almost certainly a contract in existence and a mere general knowledge of terms will suffice; (ii) A must intend to interfere with B's contract. The test of intention is objective, and recklessness by A as to the effect of his actions will suffice. There is no need to show malice or spite on the part of A; (iii) there must be an actual breach of B's contract. It is not a tort to procure the breach of a contract that is void for some reason, such as incapacity to contract[2], or unenforceable for another reason, such as restraint of trade. Procurement can consist of direct acts of persuasion, exhortation or enticement by A, but can also arise by A dealing inconsistently with the contract, or by A acting (or getting others to act) unlawfully in an indirect manner that brings about a breach of the contract between B and C[3].

1 The standard Football League contract between clubs and players provides that a player shall not induce or attempt to induct another player to leave: cl 14(a). And football governing body FIFA has made a club's commission of the tort the subject of its sports sanctions under certain circumstances: FIFA Regulations for the Status and Transfer of Players, Art 22.1, and para E1.63, n 7.
2 See para E1.76.
3 For a more detailed exposition of the tort, see *Clerk & Lindsell* (18th edn), ch 24.

E1.76 In *Aylesbury Football Club (1997) Ltd v Watford Association Football Club Ltd*[1] Lee Cook, only 16 and a talented young footballer, signed an exclusive contract with Aylesbury. Aylesbury did not attempt to register the contract until he was 17, at which time the FA refused to accept the registration. Shortly afterwards Cook signed a contract and FA registration form with Watford FC. Aylesbury sued Watford for damages for procuring Cook's breach of contract, but the action failed. The contract with Aylesbury was not enforceable as Cook was a minor at the time of signing and the contract was not for his benefit at the time it was made[2].

1 (12 June 2000, unreported) (Poole J).
2 See para E1.80. It was also argued by Watford that it did not have any intent to induce a breach of contract, because it knew that the contract been Aylesbury and Cook was unenforceable and had not been registered with the Football Association (meaning that it was not a contract pursuant to which Cook could be playing football). In theory this would have been a good defence but, in the event, the judge made no findings on this issue.

E1.77 In another case, boxing promoter Frank Warren alleged that agent Ambrose Mendy had induced the boxer Nigel Benn to breach his contract with Warren (and/or unlawfully interfered with their contractual relations)[1]. The matter came before the Court of Appeal on the issue of whether there should be an interim injunction restraining Mendy from behaving in the manner alleged[2]. The Court of Appeal approved the discharge of the injunctions that had earlier been granted, without notice to Mendy, on the usual ground that Benn should not be forced to box for Warren.

1 *Warren v Mendy* [1989] 1 WLR 853.
2 See para E1.70.

8 TORT OF UNLAWFUL INTERFERENCE

E1.78 If person A unlawfully interferes with the business of B with the object and effect of causing damage to B, then B can sue A for damages for the tort of unlawful interference. This tort is still developing and the law is not entirely clear but, in general terms, there are certain essential elements:

(i) there must be actual damage caused (or about to be caused);
(ii) there must be an intention to injure on the part of the tortfeasor;
(iii) the means used must be unlawful in themselves.

Breaching existing contracts is an example of such unlawful means[1]. Other examples include breach of copyright, breach of confidence, deceit and misfeasance in public office. Acting in breach of competition laws may also suffice[2].

1 *Warren v Mendy* [1989] 1 WLR 853. See also para E1.70.
2 For a more detailed exposition of the tort, see *Clerk & Lindsell* (18th edn), ch 24.

E1.79 An attempt was made to sue for this tort in *Watson and Bradford Football Club v Gray and Huddersfield Town Football Club*[1]. Gordon Watson was the victim of a late, high dangerous tackle by Kevin Gray in the opening stages of a First Division Yorkshire derby match. Gray was successfully sued for negligence in causing Watson's broken leg and Huddersfield was vicariously liable for his negligence. However, Bradford thought there was more to the challenge and that Gray may have been deliberately exacting retribution for an alleged incident moments earlier, or was reckless (knowing that there was a significant risk of injury but going ahead anyway). Bradford therefore sued Gray (and, vicariously, Huddersfield) for unlawfully interfering with Watson's contract with Bradford.

At trial deliberate intention was impossible to prove. Further, reckless intention was not made out on the facts: the challenge was appalling but not deliberately so. Had the facts been different, however, it seems the tort may well have been made out and Bradford would have been able to claim damages for its losses against Huddersfield.

1 (1998) Times, 26 November (Hooper J). See also para E5.33.

9 MINORS' CONTRACTS

E1.80 Minors – that is those under the age of 18, historically 21 – do not normally have the legal capacity to enter into a contract. However, a contract of employment (or contract for services) is considered to be a special case and is capable of being upheld as for a minor's benefit, if the facts bear this out.

E1.81 So, when a minor broke a contract to accompany a professional snooker player, damages were awarded since the contract was intended to benefit the minor by training him and helping him develop experience[1]. Similarly, a young boxer was bound by the rules of the British Boxing Board of Control since they were for his benefit: the rule that disqualified him, outlawing punching below the belt, was as much for his benefit as it was for his opponent's[2].

1 *Roberts v Grey* [1913] 1 KB 520.
2 *Doyle v White City Stadium Ltd* [1935] 1 KB 110.

E1.82 A football club did not, however, induce a breach of contract when it signed a 17-year-old player under contract with another club because the youngster could not be bound by that contract[1]. Aylesbury Football Club purported to contract with the player when he was 16, but could not subsequently recover damages from Watford FC for interfering with that contract because the contract was not for the minor's benefit. The court found the young player did not need to enter into a contract with Aylesbury to receive training and experience. Further:

(i) since the FA prohibited such arrangements[2], the minor's contract could not be registered;
(ii) for an initial period, at least, his wages were to depend upon the will of his employer; and
(iii) there were restrictive covenants in the agreement to prevent him playing for another club, or indeed any sport.

In the circumstances the contract was not to benefit him at all, but to ensure Aylesbury could negotiate for appropriate compensation.

1 *Aylesbury Football Club (1997) Ltd v Watford Association Football Club Ltd* (12 June 2002, unreported), Poole J. See also para E1.76.
2 See para E1.83.

E1.83 As indicated above, the FA has strict rules in relation to clubs contracting with minors. Players under 18 years of age and in full-time education may not enter into a contract of employment with a club, nor may players under 17 (whether at school or not) except as trainees or scholars as defined by the FA[1]. (The combination of these two rules means that the FA will register a contract with a 17 year old not in education, but not if he signed before he was 17[2].) Players between their 15th and 17th birthdays may be registered as trainees[3], and those of 14 and over may be offered scholarships[4]. FIFA's rules similarly protect minors, allowing international transfers of minors to be permitted only if strict conditions are met[5].

1 FA rules, C1(a).
2 *Aylesbury Football Club (1997) Ltd v Watford Association Football Club Ltd* (12 June 2002, unreported), Poole J. See also paras E1.76 and E1.82.
3 FA rules, C3(a).
4 FA rules, C3(b).
5 FIFA Regulations for the Status and Transfer of Players, Art 12. International transfers shall be permitted only if: (i) as a general rule, the family of the player moves to the country in which the new club is located for reasons that are not linked to football; and (ii) within the territory of the EU/EEA and in the case of players between the minimum working age in the new training club's country and 18, suitable arrangements are guaranteed for their sports training and academic education by the new training club.

10 SPECIAL FEATURES

A Salary caps[1]

E1.84 In the sporting world, a salary cap is a global limitation on the amount permitted to be paid to the playing staff of a team, over a given time period. Salary caps are already well established (in both sporting and legal cultures) in certain US and Australian team sports, such as basketball and rugby league[2]. A type of salary cap is also established in English professional rugby[3]. Renewed impetus has recently been given to the debate over salary caps, in the light both of the high player wages/salaries of some professional footballers and the financial turmoil besetting the Football League following the collapse of its broadcasting deal with ITV Digital. Salary caps are said to be one means of increasing 'competitive balance' in sport, a term used to describe the relative measure of sporting abilities amongst teams in the same competition. A degree of such balance is important, because nobody wants to see one team dominate all competitions in a sport, at least not on a continuous basis.

1 This section includes material from articles written by Paul Harris, first appearing in [1999] 7(2) SATLJ and [1999] 7(3) SATLJ.
2 Other examples include American football (the NFL) and Australian Rules football.
3 See para E1.85.

E1.85 English Rugby League (now known as the Super League) introduced a cap in 1998 when most professional rugby league clubs were in a state of financial crisis[1]. Historically its cap varied from team to team, broadly allowing clubs to spend up to 50% of their net income on all player payments. This meant richer clubs could spend more than poorer. So, in an effort to improve the competitive balance among clubs, the Super League has been forced to 'harden' its cap. Accordingly, a rule stipulating that a club may pay only 20 players more than £20,000 was introduced at the start of the 2000 season, so as to prevent bigger clubs from stockpiling the best players. This was further tightened by the introduction of an absolute ceiling of £1.8m on player wages from the start of 2002. Penalties for breach of the Super League's cap can be severe. Any clubs who have overspent may suffer points deductions and lose prize money at the end of the year.

1 Nicholas Tsatsas, 'Is it time for English football to adopt a salary cap?' [2001] 9(2) SATLJ 128.

E1.86 The potential introduction of a salary cap to a sport raises various important practical questions. For example, at what level should the cap be set? If set at the level of the highest earners then the cap will have no effect since the playing field will remain unlevelled. If at the lowest, the larger teams will be badly affected and have to sell players. In response to this difficult problem, salary caps for teams playing in Australia's major rugby league competition have, at times, been set at different levels to take into account the effect of expenditure on clubs' viability[1]. A separate issue arises concerning existing players. What if some take up a large proportion of the cap? One common solution has been to ignore the salary cap for these players altogether[2]. In the National Basketball Association ('NBA') league in the US, the salary cap rules have allowed teams to re-sign existing players outside the scope of the salary cap[3]. Unfortunately, the effect of this arrangement is simply to entrench the sporting disparity between teams rather than improve competitive balance[4].

1 *Adamson v NSWRL* (1999) 100 ALR 479.
2 This neatly avoids the problem that reducing payments in existing agreements would be a breach of contract. An alternative might be to announce a cap at a date some point in the future. This approach was adopted in rugby league in Australia, but simply allowed players to mount a successful legal challenge before the cap even began operation: *Adamson* (n 1 above).
3 Care needs to be taken in drawing direct lessons from the NBA since it operates a system of collective bargaining for players' wages. The point is, though, that for a long time certain players have been paid outside the cap under this so-called 'Larry Bird exception', though the most celebrated beneficiary has been Michael Jordan.
4 Wigan chairman Maurice Lindsay defended the Super League's decision to give the club a £500,000 leeway on its salary cap by pointing to existing contractual obligations which he said necessitate the exemption: [2001] (92) SATLJ 33.

E1.87 Any international sport presents the added difficulty that the introduction of a salary cap in one country alone would be to introduce a huge distortion in the market. (Imagine a salary cap being introduced into the English Premier League but not into La Liga and Serie A. It is easy to see where the best players would want to play.) Yet to try and impose a cap on an international basis involves solving the practical difficulties already outlined on an even grander scale, as well as opening the door much more obviously to challenges based on European free movement and competition law[1].

1 As to which, see generally Chapters B2 and B3, and (specifically as to salary caps) paras B2.187 to B2.190.

E1.88 The principal domestic legal problem is restraint of trade[1]. In general, sporting rules designed to promote competitive balance are interferences with, or restraints of, trade[2]. The legal battleground is, therefore, justification of those interferences or restraints by reference to the interests of the parties concerned, which justification is not easy to show. It is easy to envisage a case framed to highlight the direct, immediate harm to a range of players' interests while at the same time emphasising other, less restrictive measures that would probably be less discriminatory and more effective to improve competitive balance (such as better distribution of income). In such circumstances a cap may be unenforceable. However, the situation may be very different where the cap is vital to the continued existence of the sport on financial grounds[3].

1 See para A3.135 et seq.

2 See *Adamson v NSWRL* (1999) 100 ALR 479 in relation to the draft procedure in Australian professional rugby league; *Buckley v Tutty* (1971) 125 CLR 353, in relation to the retention and transfer system in Australian professional rugby league; *Rugby Union Players' Association Inc v Commerce Commission (No 2)* [1997] 3 NZLR 301, in relation to the transfer system in New Zealand professional rugby union. See also *Johnson v Cliftonville Football and Athletic Club* [1984] 1 NI 9, Ch D.

3 See further Paul Harris 'Salary Caps' [2002] 10(1) SATLJ 120.

B Player release

E1.89 When it comes to international duty, clubs have arrangements with governing bodies to release their players for the national team. For example, the FIFA Regulations on the Status and Transfer of Players make detailed provision for the release of players for national association representative matches[1]. The rules include the following:

(i) a club is obliged to release a player to whichever national association of which he is a national[2] for a total of five international matches per calendar year (and more if the player is required for the FIFA World Cup, or in other specified circumstances[3]);
(ii) a player shall also be released for the period of preparation, as specified[4];
(iii) the player shall resume duty with his club not later than 24 hours after the match to which he was summoned, although this may be prolonged to 48 hours if the match took place on a different continent from that on which he is registered[5];
(iv) a club is not entitled to financial compensation save for any agreed extended period of release[6];
(v) a club must continue to insure the player during the period of release[7];
(vi) as a general rule, 'any player registered with a club is obliged to respond affirmatively' when called upon to play for a national team[8].

If a club refused to release a player, it can be fined, cautioned, censured or suspended[9]. Disputes that have arisen in relation to such rules are discussed elsewhere in this book[10].

1 See Arts 36–41.

2 See Art 36.1.

3 See Art 36.2. It is not compulsory, however, for clubs to release players for friendly matches scheduled on dates outside the co-ordinated international match calendar.

4 See Art 36.5.

5 See Art 36.7. A breach of this obligation can lead to a shorter period of release to the national association or other sanctions: Art 36.8.

6 See Art 37.1. This obligation, and that in relation to insurance, prompted the G-14 group, which includes the likes of Manchester United, Real Madrid and Bayern Munich, to request that FIFA consider the possibility of organising compensation on the basis that national games carry the risk of player injury, and cause financial loss (since the clubs are effectively paying the players' wages while they are working for a different employer). The national associations greeted this proposal with alarm since they would face bills of thousands of pounds a year in insurance premiums and potentially be bankrupted if they had to pay the wages of top class players who happen to have been injured on international duty: [2001] 9(3) SATLJ 45. By contrast, the Welsh Rugby Union has a system whereby clubs receive money for each international player provided for the national side.

7 See Art 37.3. Although a similar rule exists in relation to international rugby union, many unions do insure players while they are on international duty.

8 See Art 38.1.

9 See Art 41.1.

10 See paras B2.113 to B2.115.

C Players' unions and strike action

E1.90 The concept of players being members of unions used to seem unusual. But in recent years players' unions have come to the fore, not least through threats of strike action. There are various unions that are now relatively well-known. Footballers are represented by the Professional Footballers' Association ('PFA'), which is affiliated to the Trade Union Congress, whereas football managers have their own body, the League Managers' Association ('LMA'). Cricketers have their own union, the Professional Cricketers' Association. (This was responsible for a collective agreement[1] negotiated with the Test and County Cricket Board[2] which has evolved into the standard contract for professional cricketers[3].)

1 Collective agreements for sport remain something of an alien concept in the UK (although not in the US, where professional sport is heavily unionised). Nevertheless, the EU began a dialogue with FIFPro, the umbrella organisation for football players' unions, with a view to regarding it as a social partner and to establishing procedures for the formation of collective agreements regulating footballers' employment contracts: FIFPro press release of 4 July 2001; Gardiner *Sports Law* (2nd edn, 2001, Cavendish Publishing), p 534.

2 The Test and County Cricket Board was replaced by the England and Wales Cricket Board in 1997.

3 Gardiner *Sports Law* (2nd edn, 2001, Cavendish Publishing), p 533.

E1.91 An important role for unions is to represent individuals who have a grievance, or who are being disciplined by their clubs. Both professional footballers[1] and professional cricketers have the contractual right to union representation at individual hearings[2]. Footballers may also be represented by the PFA before a transfer tribunal[3].

1 Clause 20 states that a player may be represented by a member of the PFA at any personal hearing of an appeal (whether the hearing of a grievance by the player or a disciplinary matter). Further the PFA will step in if the occasion demands it. In October 2001, the PFA intervened when the new Chairman of Swansea City, Tony Petty, attempted to dismiss seven players as well as to compel a further eight to accept greatly reduced terms. Petty told the players that their contracts were being terminated because the club could no longer afford to pay their wages. The PFA pointed out that his actions were in violation of Football League regulations: [2001] 9(3) SATLJ 42.

2 Gardiner *Sports Law* (2nd edn, 2001, Cavendish Publishing), p 533.

3 See n 2 above.

E1.92 Unions are, of course, also instrumental in organising industrial action. Football fans faced the appalling prospect of a weekend without the beautiful game at the end of 2001 when the PFA balloted its members over strike action and obtained a positive response. The action concerned the share that the PFA should receive of television revenue received by the FA Premier League and Football League. The PFA claimed there was a long-standing agreement that it would receive 5% of such income (although this had never been formally recorded in writing). That percentage would have netted the PFA £25m of the then current TV deals, but it was initially offered only £10m. The matter was heading for the courts when an accommodation was found[1].

1 The PFA held strike ballots twice before, in 1992 and 1996, on both occasions receiving more than 90% backing. However, agreement was reached each time, and strikes averted.

E1.93 Leading Welsh rugby union players were put on strike alert in 2001 following a disagreement between the Welsh Rugby Union ('WRU') and its top clubs over funding. Leighton Samuel, owner of Bridgend, warned that players could be withdrawn from internationals in November 2001 unless the WRU agreed to moderate the way in which it allocated cash to clubs. The clubs had previously been paid between £10,000 and £35,000 by the WRU for each international player they provided for the national side. They sought to replace this by pooling the money and distributing it among themselves. In the event, the clubs failed to carry out their threat[1].

1 [2001] 9(3) SATLJ 43.

E1.94 English rugby union has had problems of its own. Players went on strike from international representation after rejecting a pay deal from the Rugby Football Union ('RFU') in November 2000. They objected to the RFU retaining intellectual property rights covering the use of players' images and likenesses, and wanted increased match fees. The RFU had offered a deal that increased players' match fees and win bonuses by 35%, and promised a share of deals involving intellectual property, in a package that was said to total more than £6m over a four-year period[1]. The action was called off after a peace deal was struck. Then, in 2001, action was again mooted after the RFU threatened to impose life bans on players. Again the RFU backed down[2].

1 *CNN Sports Illustrated*, 21 November 2000.
2 [2001] 9(1) SATLJ 69 and 70.

E1.95 Nor is it just team players that consider industrial action. In late December 2000, Darren Campbell, Britain's Olympic 200 metres silver medal winner, suggested that top athletes might strike if UK Athletics did not improve its levels of assistance to younger and developing athletes. He was backed in this view by Jamie Baulch, world indoor 400 metres champion[1].

1 [2001] 9(1) SATLJ 26.

11 RELATIONSHIPS WITH EVENT ORGANISERS

E1.96 Not every player has to contract with a team in order to play. In individual sports, such as athletics, players instead contract with event organisers in order to take part[1]. This is the case even in the absence of a written agreement (in the appropriate circumstances)[2].

1 This is also the case with sports such as tennis, golf, and darts (see para E1.2).
2 *Diane Modahl v British Athletic Federation Ltd (in administration)* [2001] EWCA Civ 1447, [2002] 1 WLR 1192. Modahl appealed from a decision at first instance that she had no contract with BAF. (She argued that implied into that contract were conditions that BAF's Drug Advisory Committee would take all reasonable steps to ensure that those who sat on the disciplinary committee would be free from bias.) The Court of Appeal found that the basic structure for a contract could be seen. If a legally-enforceable contract could be created where an athlete expressly agreed in an entry form to be bound by the relevant rules, then there could be no escape from the conclusion that a contract could properly be implied when circumstances made it clear that that was what the athlete had in fact promised, as Modahl had done. However, the procedures of which Modahl complained had been carried out fairly. See further para A3.10, n 2.

E1.97 Virtually all snooker players are members of the World Professional Billiards and Snooker Association ('WPBSA'), which regulates professional snooker worldwide and organises and promotes professional snooker tournaments. The WPBSA's rules and practices were challenged, however, when two of its members wanted to participate in a separate tour but were prevented from doing so by the WPBSA rules[1]. Three rules and two practices were at the centre of the challenge in a trial heard in summer 2001. Ultimately, however, only one of the complaints was upheld, with the court finding that the WPBSA was not permitted to prevent participation in other tournaments without its sanction. This rule breached ss 2 and 18 of the Competition Act 1998 and was therefore void. It also breached EC law, and was unlawfully in restraint of trade[2].

1 See *Hendry & Williams v WPBSA* [2002] UKCLR 5, [2002] Eu LR 770 (Lloyd J). See also paras B2.131 to B2.141.
2 See n 1 above. See also Paul Harris 'Abusive Sports Governing Bodies' *Competition Law Journal* (2002), Issue 2.

E1.98 The most important aspects of any contract with an events organiser are the rules of participation and provision for a disciplinary process. For example, the participation agreement for the 2002 Embassy World Professional Darts Championship subjected a player to a strict framework. In entering into the contract a player agreed to be bound by the British Darts Organisation's ('BDO's') Eligibility Rule, Disciplinary Code, Policy on Drugs, Playing Rules (including the Player Dress Code), and the 2002 Championship Playing Rules and Format[1]. Each player also promised, amongst other things:

(i) not to enter the Professional Darts Council's World Championship in the same season[2], and to play in the BDO event in the following year (if he finished in the top four in the 2002 championship and had not retired)[3];
(ii) to participate in promotional activities for the event[4] and to display an assigned advertising patch on his shirt[5]; and
(iii) not to do anything, or omit to do anything, which would disrupt the Championship, or bring darts, the BDO or its commercial partners into disrepute[6].

These sorts of commitments are common to many such agreements.

1 Clause 1.
2 Clause 4.
3 Clause 4.2.
4 Clause 6.1.
5 Clause 6.2.
6 Clause 8.

CHAPTER E2

PLAYER TRANSFERS

Adam Lewis (Blackstone Chambers), **Paul Harris** (Monckton Chambers), **David Becker** (Hammonds) and **Parul Patel**

Contents

1 THE MEANING OF THE TERM 'PLAYER TRANSFER'

A Change of employment

E2.1 In those sports where the term 'player transfer' is used[1], it describes the arrangements that lead to a change of employment. The employers are the clubs, or teams, and the employees being transferred are the players.

1 Player transfer rules are dealt with at paras E2.76 to E2.80 and B2.152 et seq and in Beloff *Sports Law* (1999, Hart Publishing) and Gardiner *Sports Law* (2nd edn, 2001, Cavendish Publishing), chs 9 and 12.

B Registration

E2.2 In those sports, in addition to the player being employed for the purposes of contract and employment law, the national and international governing bodies' rules will broadly provide that a player must also be 'registered'[1] with a specific national governing body as being at a specific club. The rules will also provide that a player cannot be registered as being at more than one club. In this context, a player must be registered if he is to be permitted to play for that the club in any meaningful competition organised by the national governing body or by the international governing body of which it is a member. In the words of the latest FIFA Regulations governing the Application of the Regulations for the Status and Transfer of Players[2] 'the registration constitutes the licence for a player to play football'. Quite simply, in those sports that operate such a registration system, the player is not permitted to play without such a 'licence'.

1 Or 'licensed' by the governing body.
2 Available on www.fifa.com.

E2.3 The consequence of a player only being able to be registered as being with one club at any given time is that when there is a change in employment status there must also be a change in the registration status of the player, if the change in employment is to be effective.

C Meaning of the term 'player transfer'

E2.4 A 'player transfer' therefore involves not only the termination of a player's employment relationship with one club, followed by the creation of another such relationship with a different club, but also the de-registration of that player as being with the former club and his re-registration as being with the new club. If the transfer is international, the registration 'moves' from one national governing body to another. It is this combination of change in, first, employment status, and secondly, registration status that makes up the player transfer.

D Loans and temporary transfers

E2.5 In some sports, such as football, a player can go 'on loan' or 'temporary transfer' to another club. This might happen if, for example, a club was considering buying a player and wanted an opportunity to assess him in context before doing so. It might also happen if the employing club wanted to reduce its wage bill whilst not actually finally selling the player. When a player goes on loan there must still be a transfer of registration, although it may be classified as a temporary transfer of registration. In employment terms, the position may vary from case to case. In that the player is 'on loan' and is not being finally transferred, it will generally be the position that he remains employed by the lending club and does not enter into an employment contract with the borrowing club: the financial arrangements of the loan are between the two clubs. He would still be entitled to sue the lending club for his full contractual entitlement. As a matter of practice, however, the wages to which he was entitled from the lending club are likely to be paid to him by the borrowing club, ostensibly on behalf of the lending club. Furthermore, it may well be that a collateral contract does arise between the player and the borrowing club, so that the player cannot escape the general obligations owed by a player to his club. Usually also the borrowing club pays a loan fee upfront to the lending club, which is non-refundable. There is likely to be an option to buy as well, for a figure specified in the loan agreement. If the borrowing club wants to get round this and pay less, it can usually do so by simply indicating a willingness to exercise the option, but for a lower price.

E Transfer rules

E2.6 The peculiarity of player transfers is that they are not based *solely* on ordinary employment law principles of termination and formation of contracts between employer and employee: the transfer of registration is not an automatic procedure which follows a change in employment. Clubs agree contractually through the transfer provisions contained in the governing bodies rules to additional obligations between themselves. The principal such additional obligation is the rule that requires the acquiring club to pay the selling club a fee to secure the transfer of the registration, so that the player can play for the new club (a 'transfer fee' system)[1]. In the past such fees have been payable irrespective of whether the player was still under contract to the selling club, on the basis that the selling club retains the registration until it is prepared to release it (a 'retention' system'). More recently, fees have been payable if the player was under contract, but have ceased to be payable as soon as the contract expired. The latest development, in football and rugby at least, is that a compensation fee is payable in defined circumstances in respect of relatively younger players only. The justifications put forward for such rules have been, in general terms, that they enable clubs to secure compensation for their development of the player (not having had sufficient length of service from him to represent an adequate return for their investment), and they provide funding for the clubs lower down the pyramid that find and develop talent, with corresponding effects upon competitive balance and the development of a future player base. Plainly however, the rule also prevented players from moving when they want to do so. When a player was out of contract, they stopped him moving, even though he was under no contractual or other obligation not to play for a different club. Even when a player was in contract, the rule went further than a player's obligations under English contract and employment law at least, because a contract of employment will not be specifically enforced, and an employer is left to an action in damages if an employee decides to break contract and leave his or her employer before he is contractually entitled to do so[2]. Other obligations which governing bodies have imposed on clubs through transfer rules include a rule that players cannot be transferred on a date outside specified 'transfer windows'[3], rules designed to defeat sham transfers[4], rules in relation to temporary transfers[5], rules preventing players being transferred to a club outside a specific geographic area[6], and rules in relation to the negotiation of transfers[7].

1 See para E2.18.
2 See para E2.10.
3 See para E2.22.
4 See para E2.27.
5 See para E2.28.
6 See para E2.29.
7 See para E2.30.

F The price attached to release of registration

E2.7 The control of a player's registration by a club, coupled with the governing bodies' rules, allowed clubs to create a market in the release of the player's registration. Transfer fees in some sports, notably professional football, escalated far above the value of the loss of the player's services for the remainder of his or her contract and far above the cost of the development put into the player. In particular, transfer fees were payable to elite clubs, even when they had played no real role in the development of a player, perhaps because the player was already top class when he or she arrived at the club.

E2.8 Such arrangements have not surprisingly been the subject of a number of legal challenges on a variety of bases, and the extent of the additional obligations which governing bodies can lawfully impose in transfer rules is now considerably reduced[1]. In the remainder of this first section of this chapter the authors examine further the contrast with changes of employment outside the sports sector, which has provided the impetus for the legal challenges, and address the different additional obligations which governing bodies have sought to impose in transfer rules, some of which have been challenged by players and regulatory authorities, as well as the justifications offered by the governing bodies for those transfer rules. In the second section of this chapter the authors examine the legality of transfer rules in the light of the challenges that have been made. In the third section the negotiation of a transfer (including the role of players' agents in such negotiation) is addressed, and in the fourth section the authors address the disputes which can arise between clubs, and between clubs and players, in relation to transfers.

1 See also the statement of EU Commissioner Viviane Reding in relation to reform of the transfer rules: [2001] 9(1) SATLJ 80; McGrath [2001] 9(2) SATLJ 109.

2 CONTRAST WITH CHANGE OF EMPLOYMENT OUTSIDE THE SPORTS SECTOR

E2.9 In an ordinary non-sporting employment context, an ordinary employee might wish to change (transfer) employer. In the usual situation, if he hands in his notice of resignation, according to the terms of his current employment contract, and then works out his notice period before changing employer, then that is the end of the matter (subject to there being any enforceable restrictive covenants over his post-termination activities for a certain period[1]). Certainly in the ordinary case, there is no question of the employee, or the new employer, making a payment to the former employer in such circumstances, or of the new employer requiring the employee to discontinue a formal registration with the former employer and become formally re-registered with the new employer.

1 As to which see Chapter E1. Such covenants are themselves subject to the restraint of trade doctrine. In some contexts it is possible that the movement to a competing team of a player, or more particularly some other participant in a sport such as a manager or a vehicle designer, may raise breach of confidence concerns.

E2.10 Alternatively, if the employee (and/or new employer) wishes the employee to commence his new employment more quickly than the existing notice period allows, then, generally, it is open to the employee to breach the notice period of his existing contract by departing early and paying compensation for that breach of contract. The compensation is calculated on ordinary legal principles of putting the innocent party (the former employer) into the position that it would have been in had the contract not been breached. In other words, generally, the employee can 'buy his way out of' the notice period without any sanctions additional to compensation. In particular, the English courts will not enforce an employment contract by an order for specific performance[1].

1 See para E1.68 et seq; *Warren v Mendy* [1989] 1 WLR 853; *Nichols Advanced Vehicle Systems Inc v Elio de Angelis* (21 December 1979, unreported), Oliver J; *Subaru v Richard Burns* (12 December 2001, unreported), Deputy Judge Strauss; *Pantano and Pantano Management v Supernova Ltd* (6 March 2002, unreported), Enriques J. But cf *Crystal Palace v Steve Bruce* (22 November 2001, unreported), Burton J. In *Jaguar v McLaren* 16 June 2001, settled, [2001] 9(2) SATLJ 88, a key employee of McLaren, Newey, contracted to go to Jaguar. MacLaren lured him back again. Jaguar was unable to hold Newey to his contract.

E2.11 Of course, whether this option is sensible, or worthwhile, depends on all manner of considerations, including the cost, and the existence of enforceable restrictive covenants on the employee.

E2.12 For present purposes, though, the important points are, first, that there is no requirement to change any 'registration', second, that the payment comprises *exclusively* the amount required to compensate the former employer for the breach of contract, and, third, that the money paid to the former employer should come from (or be paid on behalf of) the party in breach of contract, namely, the employee, rather than from the new employer.

E2.13 Notably in the non-sporting context, the general intention is that there should be, broadly, a 'free market' for employees at all times. In that free market, employers should compete between each other for employees. If the new employer obtains a competitive advantage over the former employer as a result of recruiting one of its employees, at whatever time of the financial year, then that is regarded as simply a function of the free market. It is not the business of one employer to safeguard the interests of a competing employer by abstaining, or waiting, from recruiting its (best) employees; quite the reverse, it is in the interests of employers to seek to undermine competing businesses, including by recruitment policies.

E2.14 Further in this non-sports employment market, if an employee is himself developed, or trained, by the former employer, then that development or training is simply lost (to the former employer) when he departs, save to the extent that the former employer has been able to benefit from it prior to termination. It goes without saying that other former employers (that is, earlier in the employment life of the employee in question) also have no continued claim over the employee in respect of any training that they provided to him.

3 THE TRANSFER RULES THAT HAVE BEEN IMPOSED, AND WHY

E2.15 Certain needs in the context of professional team sports contrast sharply with the situation outside the sports context, leading governing bodies to seek to impose the additional obligations in transfer rules.

A Competitive balance

E2.16 First, as a matter of practical reality, there must be broad 'competitive balance' between sports clubs (employers) in order to preserve the integrity of the sporting competition. At one extreme, it is no use there being a sports competition in which one club (employer) is successful in driving out of business the other clubs (employers), because then the 'successful' club has nobody to compete against and would, itself, not be able to survive. Less extreme, but along similar lines, if one club (employer) can obtain all the best players (employees), then it is likely always to win the sporting competition in question. When a competition becomes predictable, experience shows that the spectators, and the public generally, find it less interesting; uncertainty of outcome and possibility of an upset is the spice of sporting competition. When the competition loses interest, it begins to wither because spectators, sponsors, broadcasters and advertisers begin to go elsewhere. Thus, again, there is a mutual self-interest amongst clubs (employers) and, indeed, players, in keeping a certain 'competitive balance' – certainly over the long term[1].

1 See further para B2.66 et seq.

E2.17 *If* unrestricted transfer of, and/or unrestricted competition for, players upsets the 'competitive balance', or presents a serious risk of increasing competitive *im*balance, it makes sense for restrictions on 'normal' free movement of, and/or unrestricted competition for, players to be agreed and/or imposed in the interests of the sport as a whole. The issue that arises, as discussed below[1], is the extent to which such restrictions are permissible in order to pursue the preservation of competitive balance.

1 See paras E2.32 to E2.65.

B 'Trickle down' and training compensation through transfer fees

E2.18 The second factor is linked to the first. Traditionally in professional team sports, training and development of players has occurred right throughout the various levels of the sport. Generally, younger players are initially sought or attracted by small, local clubs, and are then coached and trained as they develop and mature. These small clubs lower down the pyramid plant the seeds of what will become the professional player base, and occasionally they produce a top level player. Bigger, higher placed clubs will also develop players, but there are fewer such clubs (and limited training places at them) and a great many more small, local clubs. Therefore, the more small, local clubs that bring on players, the wider the player base. Some considerable revenue for a club providing training, including in particular for clubs at the lower level of the sport, has been generated by the requirement in governing body transfer rules of a payment to that club of transfer fees for players whom it has trained and developed, as a precondition for the release of the player's registration to the new club. To the extent that such transfer payments contribute to the survival, or even the development, of the clubs at the lower levels of the particular sport then they can be seen to contribute to the general 'competitive balance'[1]. Often this effect is referred to as the 'trickle down' effect; transfer fees, it is said, trickle from the upper levels of a sport down towards the lower levels when clubs at higher levels take transfers of players that have been trained at lower levels.

1 See paras E2.32 to E2.65.

E2.19 Care should be taken, though, not to press the competitive balance justification for transfer fees too far, because transfers tend to operate such that the best players leave the lower placed clubs and move to the clubs that are *already* higher placed. Accordingly, the competitive *im*balance between the higher and lower clubs can be further exaggerated. Whilst the lower placed clubs receive a transfer fee, it is generally too low to purchase sufficiently high quality players to reduce the competitive imbalance, not least of all because the established, better players are often already employed by clubs at a higher level (and their transfer fees – not to mention their wages – would likely be high). That said, 'trickle down' *does* contribute to the general competitive balance of a divisional structure; that is, where there are different institutionalised levels of competitive balance in different divisions. A divisional structure, provided that there is promotion and relegation between divisions, can directly affect competitive balance at the highest levels of the sport over the longer term.

E2.20 'Trickle down' also encourages the search for, and development of talent in players many of which, necessarily, have to commence at the lower levels of the sport. It thereby assists in widening the player base. It does so by rewarding, or compensating, the clubs that provide the scouting and training for having provided that service. The wider the player base, the greater the likelihood of talented players going to a wider range of top clubs, enhancing competitive balance at least amongst them, although as mentioned above, not necessarily between clubs at the top and clubs at the bottom. Furthermore, the developing club will have the benefit of the emerging talent until the player is sold, which it might not otherwise have at all. In any event, nurturing widespread talent is good for a sport as a whole, not only so that a sport can sustain itself and develop, but also so that it can foster and promote public interest, which is the key to its future success. Further, the wider the talented player base, the greater the pool of players from which representative and national sides can be drawn. These considerations rarely, if ever, apply to the market for non-sporting employees.

E2.21 *If* transfer fee rules promote and maintain this aspiration, and do so proportionately, then it can sensibly be said that the restrictions on free movement of, and/or free competition for, players that they entail may be a necessary evil. Again, whether or not that is the case is addressed further below[1].

1 See paras E2.32 to E2.65. The leading cases are *Eastham v Newcastle United Football Club 2* [1964] Ch 413 and *Union Royal Belge des Sociétés de Football Association ASBL v Jean-Marc Bosman* (C-415/93) [1995] ECR I-4921.

C Team and seasonal stability and transfer windows

E2.22 Third, team sports competitions tend to be seasonal. A team commences a season with a certain squad of players and faces other teams with their own squads for that season. Thus, at the outset, both the teams and the supporters know the nature of the competitive task that faces them. Further, team managers are able to plan around the players in their squad and make seasonal plans for their team. This last aspect is crucial. Team sports are, by definition, dependent on the performance of the team. If any, or all, members of the team were free to depart from the team on a whim, subject only to normal contractual principles of compensation (which compensation, in the event of a dispute, is ordinarily determined *after* the departure has already occurred), then planning for, and actual, team performance could be severely hampered, with a corresponding impact not only on the fortunes of that one particular team but, if the practice were widespread, on the integrity of the sport as a whole. In other words, the team sport could be badly undermined by the totally free movement of, and/or free competition for, any or all members of the team.

E2.23 At times the impact could be particularly acute. For example, towards the end of a season, it may be that certain teams are no longer in contention for any prizes, but are safe from relegation or other penalty. Simultaneously, other teams are still battling it out for, say, the national championship. Unrestricted transfers could lead to the best players from 'safe' teams being transferred, even temporarily, to championship contenders in order to boost their prospects, right at the crucial moment. Similar distortive practices could occur at the bottom of a division. Such behaviour would, again, undermine team planning as well as the seasonal nature of many competitions.

E2.24 Such behaviour would also be likely to lead to discontent among supporters, many of whom not only strongly support a particular team but also identify players with that team, at least during the course of one season. This 'tribalism' serves further to distinguish the sports employment market. If, say, a bank loses employees and provides inferior service as a result, then its customers would ordinarily feel no inhibition about changing banks – at whatever time of the year. Not so, however, in the case of supporters of a team; even if the whole squad of players were transferred to a rival club, there is little chance of most supporters switching allegiance, even if they were unhappy about what had happened.

E2.25 The requirement for team and seasonal stability has led governing bodies to impose 'transfer windows' within which it is possible for clubs to acquire other players, and outside which it is prohibited. The transfer windows may be different for different competitions, with the result that, for example, a newly acquired player could be played in the national league, but would be precluded from taking part in a cup campaign. Transfer windows may be imposed by reference to particular times of the season, or to particular periods before a match in the relevant competition.

E2.26 *If* transfer window rules address this concern properly and proportionately, then they may be said to justify the restriction on the free movement of, and/or competition for, players. This is also discussed below[1].

1 See paras E2.32 to E2.65. The leading case is *Jyri Lehtonen v Fédération Royal Belge des Sociétés de Basketball* (C-176/96) ECJ Judgment of 13.4.2000, OJ 2000/C192/06, [2000] ECR I-2681, [2000] 3 CMLR 409.

D Good faith and notification of transfer terms

E2.27 The governing body's rules[1] may impose an obligation that a transfer must be in good faith and that clubs may not act so as to allow a club to obtain a registration for the purposes of a special match. There may also be a requirement that a copy of any transfer arrangement be provided to the governing body. Such provisions are designed to prevent sham transfers (for example within the transfer window, if there is one), which would be followed by a transfer back to the selling club. The justification for such obligations is largely the same as that for transfer windows. It is permissible to sell players, but not to avoid the requirement that a player be registered to only one club at a time or to obtain a player for the purposes of particular problematic matches.

1 Such as the Football Association Rules.

E Obligations in the context of loans or temporary transfers

E2.28 The governing body's rules[1] may impose an obligation that a player on temporary transfer cannot play for the new club, and cannot be recalled and then play for the lending club, until the approval of the governing body has been obtained. Again, the justification is to prevent clubs avoiding the substantive rules and obtaining a player for a particular match.

1 Such as the Football Association Rules.

F Restrictions on the clubs to which a player may be transferred

E2.29 The pursuit of competitive balance may also be advanced as the justification for rules that allow governing bodies to prevent players being transferred to new clubs outside defined geographic limits, or theoretically to clubs identified on different bases. In Australia, New Zealand and Canada there have in the past been rules which require players to play for the team in the area in which they reside, and not for any other team, or which preclude transfer abroad[1]. In some competitions, notably in the United States, governing bodies organising competitions reserve the right to approve or refuse a transfer[2], so as to maintain competitive balance by stopping a concentration of players in the richest club or in the club in the most popular city. A particular aspect of this system has been to limit the number of foreign players that can be transferred to an individual club, which has also been justified on the basis of maintaining the standard of the national team[3].

1 See the cases at para E2.35, nn 1 to 3; *Hall v Victoria Football League* [1982] VR 64 (A rule of the governing body requiring Australian Rules Football players to play for the team in the area where they lived (in the interests of ensuring competitive balance) was declared in unreasonable restraint of trade); *Kemp v New Zealand Rugby Football League* [1989] 3 NZLR 463 (New Zealand League rule which prohibited a rugby league player moving from New Zealand to Australia to play rugby league there held in unreasonable restraint of trade).

2 Cf *R v British Basketball Association, ex p Mickan* (17 March 1981, unreported), CA (the Court of Appeal rejected the players' contention that the governing body had unreasonably refused to licence them to play for a different club than the club for which they had originally applied for a licence to play.)

3 Addressed in *Bosman* along with the validity of registration rules restraining players from moving after their contracts had expired. See para E2.37 et seq.

G Obligations in relation to the negotiation of transfers

E2.30 In addition, the governing body may impose a variety of rules in relation to the negotiation of transfers. The rules may prohibit clubs from approaching players, or managers still in contract to another club. They may limit the conditions that can be imposed in transfer agreements, for example by providing that a concluded agreement cannot be made subject to a player passing a medical or obtaining a work permit[1].

1 See para E1.14, n 6.

H The use of agents

E2.31 A principal function of players' and clubs' agents is to negotiate transfers of players. The governing body's rules are likely to set parameters for the activities of such agents. They may also impose obligations on clubs and players, for example not to use an agent who is unlicensed by the relevant governing body[1].

1 See E2.106 et seq.

4 THE LEGALITY OF TRANSFER RULES

A Restraint of trade: *Eastham*

(a) *Eastham v Newcastle United Football Club*

E2.32 The first mechanism used to challenge restrictive transfer rules, and in particular rules which allowed a club to retain a player's registration after the end of the player's contract and to secure a transfer fee for the release of the registration, was the common law restraint of trade doctrine[1]. In *Eastham v. Newcastle United Football Club*[2], George Eastham, the Arsenal and England forward, used the restraint of trade doctrine to challenge the then version of the transfer system in English professional football, and succeeded in having it declared illegal and unenforceable. The system as it then operated in England was significantly different to the system operated over the last few years in the UK (and elsewhere in the EU). In particular, in Eastham's time, the transfer system operated in tandem with a 'retention' system such that a player could be retained indefinitely by a club (and not be transferred anywhere at all), even though his contract had expired, simply by that club paying that player a reasonable wage and putting him on the 'retention list'. The retention system had particularly pernicious, restrictive effects upon a player's ability to move to exercise his trade, as the facts in *Eastham* themselves demonstrated.

1 See Farrell 'Transfer Fees and Restraint of Trade' [1996] 4(3) SATLJ 54; Stewart 'Restraint of Trade in Sport' [1996] 6(3) SATLJ 41. See para A3.135 et seq for further discussion in relation to the use of the restraint of trade doctrine to challenge the rules and decisions of sports governing bodies.

2 [1964] Ch 413.

E2.33 In *Eastham* Wilberforce J applied the test defined in *Nordenfelt v Maxim Nordenfelt Guns and Ammunition Co Ltd*[1] and examined whether the restraint was reasonable in the interests of the parties[2]. He held[3] that:

> the two systems when combined were in restraint of trade and, since [the League] had not discharged the onus on them of showing that the restraints were no more than was reasonable to protect their interests, were in unjustifiable restraint of trade, and that as such they were *ultra vires* …

Notably, the burden was regarded as being on the governing body to show that the restraint was reasonably necessary in the interests of the parties. Wilberforce J considered that the transfer system, if operated alone, would have been substantially easier to justify[4] than the actual tandem 'transfer and retention' system operated in practice. However, neither the transfer system nor the retention system, nor both together, were in fact demonstrated by the football bodies involved in the litigation[5] to be reasonable in the interests of the parties. That conclusion presaged the debate in *Bosman*, and thereafter, in that there is a degree of similarity between many of the 'interests' and 'justifications' put forward by the football bodies in *Eastham* and those advanced thereafter.

1 [1894] AC 535 at 565. Lord MacNaughten described the doctrine in the following terms: 'All interference with individual liberty of action in trading, and all restraints of trade of themselves, if there is nothing more, are contrary to public policy, and therefore void. That is the general rule … But there are exceptions: restraints of trade and interference with individual liberty of action may be justified by the special circumstances of a particular case. It is a sufficient justification, indeed it is the only justification, if the restriction is reasonable – reasonable, that is, in reference to the interests of the parties concerned and reasonable in reference to the interests of the public, so framed and so guarded as to afford adequate protection to the party in whose favour it is imposed, while at the same time it is in no way injurious to the public …' The key concepts for present purposes are those of 'reasonable in … the interests of the parties' and 'reasonable in … the interests of the public', since it is generally unlikely that the rules of a transfer system will fall outside the definition of a restraint on the ability of a player to pursue his trade. (See para A3.137).

2 See para A3.135 et seq for further discussion of the more recent debate as to how the test is to be applied in the context of challenges to the decisions of sports governing bodies (as manifested in the differences of approach of Blackburne J in *Newport v Football Association of Wales* (interlocutory hearing Jacob J [1995] 2 All ER 87, trial unreported Blackburne J 12 April 1995), who followed the *Maxim Nordenfelt* test in the same way as Wilberforce J in *Eastham*, and of Carnwath J who suggested in *Stevenage Borough Football Club v Football League* (1996) Times, 1 August (Carnwath J), (1996) 9 Admin LR 109, CA that the onus falls on the challenger to establish that the governing body's rule is unreasonable in a public law sense: neither case involved the transfer rules.

3 [1964] Ch 413, headnote.

4 [1964] Ch 413 at 437.

5 Newcastle United FC, the Football League and the Football Association.

E2.34 *Eastham* is an object lesson in the need for evidence and the unsatisfactory nature of mere assertion. For example, in relation to the 'trickle down' justification, it was held 40 years ago in *Eastham* that 'it was not shown either that clubs in general do spend any large sums in training professional players … or that if the retention system were to go they would cease to spend …'[1]. As to the competitive balance justification, Wilberforce J held that: 'I do not think that the evidence supports this rather far-fetched argument; indeed, I think that it is refuted by the evidence …'[2]. The following passage from the judgment is also worthy of note:

> … it was said that this system … is operated in all professional leagues and has been so operated for a long time. This is claimed as evidence that those who know best consider it to be in the general interest of the game. I do not accept this line of argument. The system is an employers' system … No doubt employers all over the world consider the system a good system, but this does not prevent the court from considering whether it goes further than is reasonably necessary to protect their legitimate interests …[3]

1 [1964] Ch 413 at 436.

2 [1964] Ch 413 at 436.

3 [1964] Ch 413 at 438.

(b) The Commonwealth decisions

E2.35 *Eastham* has been followed in the Commonwealth. In Australia, in *Buckley v Tutty*[1], it was held that transfer rules imposing a retention system, a transfer fee system, and a ban on transferring outside New South Wales, were illegal as in unreasonable restraint of trade. The court held that the doctrine applied to full time or part time professionals and irrespective of any contractual relationship. An argument that any restriction was integral to the organisation of the sport was rejected, as was an argument that the rule allowed the governing body a discretion and so should not be treated as restrictive. The test applied was the *Maxim Nordenfelt* test, with the onus on the governing body. In New Zealand, in *Blackler v New Zealand Rugby Football League*[2], it was held that a rule under which a player could be prevented from transferring from a New Zealand club to an Australian club was in unreasonable restraint of trade. In South Africa, in *Coetzee v Comitis*[3], football transfer rules were set aside.

1 (1971) 125 CLR 353, [1972] ALR 370 at para 15. *Buckley v Tutty* has been followed in a number of decisions in the Australian Courts: *Hall v Victoria Football League* [1982] VR 64 (residential tie); *Foschini v Victoria Football League* (15 April 1983, unreported), Crockett J (Victoria) (Lexis); *Hughes v Western Australia Cricket Association* (1986) 69 ALR 660 (disqualification as a result of playing unauthorised game abroad); *Barnard v Australian Soccer Federation* (1988) 81 ALR 51; *Adamson v NSW Rugby League* (1991) 100 ALR 479, 27 FCR 535, on appeal 103 ALR 319 (residential tie and draft arrangements held void), (1991) 31 FCR 242; *Nobes v Australian Cricket Board* (16 December 1991, unreported), Marks J (Victoria) (Lexis); *Robertson v Australian Professional Cycling Council* (10 December 1992, unreported), Waddell CJ (NSW); *Australian Rugby League v Cross* (1997) 39 IPR 111.

2 [1968] NZLR 547. *Blackler* has been followed in other New Zealand decisions: *Stinnato v Auckland Boxing Association* [1978] 1 NZLR 1 at 26 per Cooke J) and in relation to transfer rules in *Kemp v New Zealand Rugby Football League* [1989] 3 NZLR 463. See also *Rugby Union Players' Association Inc v Commerce Commission (No 2)* [1997] 3 NZLR 301 (challenge to revised transfer rules failed).

3 *Coetzee v Comitis* [2001] 4 BCLR 323. In relation to Canada, see *Johnson v Athletics Canada* (1997) 41 OTC 95 at paras 23 and 24; *Yashin v NHL* [2000] OTC 681.

(c) The similarity between the restraint of trade test and the test under the free movement rules and the competition rules

E2.36 The concept of reasonableness in the context of restraint of trade involves the proposition that the restraint must pursue a reasonable, legitimate objective, and must do so proportionately[1]. Similar considerations arise in the context of the free movement rules in Arts 39 (ex 48) and 49 (ex 59) EC and the competition rules in Arts 81 and 82 EC and the Competition Act 1998[2]. The restraints imposed must be no more than is reasonable. If they are no more than is reasonable, then they are probably justified under the free movement and competition rules and not rendered unenforceable by the restraint of trade doctrine. Importantly, a restraint will not satisfy the test, if a less onerous alternative can achieve the same object, such as in this context a more direct system of income redistribution between clubs.

1 See para A3.138, and note the debate as to whether the test ought to be different in the context of challenges to the rules and decisions of sports governing bodies.

2 Lord Woolf suggested in *Wilander v Tobin* [1997] 2 Lloyd's Rep 296 at 301, col 1 that the proportionality test under the free movement rules was equivalent to the reasonableness test under the domestic doctrine of restraint of trade and the implied quasi public obligations owed by sports governing bodies. In *Bosman* (para E2.21, n 1), Advocate General Lenz approached the problem on the basis that a solution could be found equally well under the free movement or competition rules. It however remains the case that in some instances a different result might be achieved under the various doctrines. For example in the context of the competition rules it is less clear that the reasons for a restraint can automatically be relied upon before a national court.

B Free movement: *Bosman* and *Lehtonen*

(a) Free movement of workers: Art 39EC

E2.37 Restriction on freedom to move Almost by definition, the need to transfer a registration before a player can move effectively to take up new employment inhibits that player's movement more than if no such obligation existed. At the bare minimum, there is an administrative hurdle to overcome, namely, arranging for the actual transfer of a name from (at least) one register to another, which hurdle may involve some time, expense and/or inconvenience. At the other extreme, the refusal or failure to transfer a registration altogether, whether because a fee demanded is not paid or otherwise, will effectively prevent the movement taking place at all. To the extent that the rule requiring a transfer of registration and/or a fee for such transfer operates so as to deter or prevent the free movement of nationals of EU/EEA member states amongst those member states, then it is prohibited under Art 39 EC (ex 48)[1], except to the extent that it is objectively justified and strictly proportionate to the legitimate aim being sought. It is unlikely that players would be subject to transfer rules and at the same time be providers of services rather than workers, but in any event Art 49 EC (ex 59) applies a parallel prohibition[2].

1 See further Chapter B3. Article 39 of the Treaty establishing the European Community (formerly Art 48) is the first Article in Title III, Free Movement of Persons, Services and Capital. It reads:

'1. Freedom of movement for workers shall be secured within the Community.

2. Such freedom of movement shall entail the abolition of any discrimination based on nationality between workers of the Member States as regards employment, remuneration and other conditions of work and employment.

3. It shall entail the right, subject to limitations justified on grounds of public policy, public security or public health:

(a) to accept offers of employment actually made;

(b) to move freely within the territory of Member States for this purpose;

(c) to stay in a Member State for the purpose of employment in accordance with the provisions governing the employment of nationals of that State laid down by law, regulation or administrative action;

(d) to remain in the territory of a Member State after having been employed in that State, subject to conditions which shall be embodied in implementing regulations to be drawn up by the Commission.

4. The provisions of this Article shall not apply to employment in the public service.'

2 When read together with Art 55 EC (ex 66) and Art 46 EC (ex 56).

E2.38 No need to establish discrimination There is no need for any discrimination against nationals of one member state as compared with nationals of other member states for Art 39 EC to apply. In other words, if the relevant (for example) French rule hinders the movement of Frenchmen as much as it hinders (in the sense of 'applies to' or 'potentially applies to') Germans or Italians, it may still be unlawful[1]. The crucial point is that there is a hindrance to free movement of an EU/EEA national seeking to work. There must be a cross-border dimension to the intended movement. In circumstances where there is no actual impact across member states borders, and no realistic potential effect, the Article cannot apply directly. In other words, in a *totally and purely* domestic context, the Article has no application[2].

1 See *Union Royal Belge des Societes de Football Association ASBL v Jean-Marc Bosman* (C-415/93) [1995] ECR I-4921, in particular the Advocate General's Opinion at 4991 and the Judgment at 5069, para 96.

2 Notably in the UK, the provisions of Chapter I of the Competition Act 1998 reproduce the substance of Art 81 EC (not Art 39 EC), but without the requirement for an actual or potential effect on inter-State trade.

E2.39 Objective justification If they are to survive in the EU/EEA, the restrictions on free movement encapsulated in the transfer rules of a sport, to the extent that they have an impact on cross-border movements between member states, must be objectively justified.

E2.40 *Bosman* A case study of the application of Art 39 EC to such rules has been provided by professional football in the EU/EEA. *Bosman* concerned a Belgian national playing professional football in the Belgian football league who had come to the end of his contract of employment with his club, RC Liege. Though his contract had expired, Bosman remained registered with RC Liege. He wished to transfer internationally into the French professional league. RC Liege, however, would not permit the transfer of his registration until they had received a transfer fee from the French club. There were doubts about the French club's ability to make the payment demanded by RC Liege. In the end, the payment was not made, the transfer of registration did not take place and Bosman's proposed move to France was stopped in its tracks, even though Bosman still wanted the move to take place. Bosman claimed that the refusal to permit him effectively to move to France to carry out his profession was an unjustified fetter upon his fundamental right freely to move across member states borders for such purposes. He also argued that the restriction on his ability to carry on his profession was anti-competitive within the meaning of Arts 81 EC and 82 EC. The case was brought in the Belgian courts against his club, and the Belgian football association, and UEFA, and was referred by the Belgian courts to the European Court of Justice ('ECJ'). All three defendants supported the rule permitting RC Liege to demand a transfer fee before allowing registration to be transferred. Given the actual facts, the battle focused on fees demanded for *international* transfers of *out-of-contract* players, rather than on all transfers, or on transfers of contracted players, or on other aspects of the transfer rules[1].

1 There was also a challenge to the rule limiting the number of players from other member states permitted to play for a particular club team. This challenge succeeded, because of the obvious discriminatory impact of such a rule upon free movement of players. See further paras B2.109 and B3.18.

E2.41 The justification offered The arguments advanced by the defendants in support of the transfer of registration and the corresponding fee fall into two of the three main categories referred to above, namely, the promotion of competitive balance and trickle down/training compensation. The third category referred to above, team/seasonal stability, played no role in the litigation, but has featured more heavily afterwards and in particular in the later case of *Lehtonen*[1], referred to below.

1 *Jyri Lehtonen v Federation Royal Belge des Sociétés de Basketball* (C-176/96) ECJ Judgment of 13.4.2000, OJ 2000/C192/06, [2000] 3 CMLR 409 [2000] ECR I-2681.

(b) *Competitive balance*

E2.42 Competitive balance is a legitimate aim The Advocate General in *Bosman* considered that competitive balance was a justifiable aim in the context of professional football. However, he considered that the evidence adduced before the ECJ did not show either that the transfer rules in question promoted or fostered competitive balance, or that there was no other arrangement, less restrictive of free movement, that would do so[1]. Nothing in the transfer rules in question prevented the richest clubs from securing the services of the best players. If anything, he concluded, the rules contributed to competitive *im*balance, because the lower level, financially weaker clubs could not afford to pay the transfer fees for the better players that would enable those clubs to improve their competitive position. This conclusion was important. One of the defendants' key justifications was fatally undermined because they had not addressed the question of smaller clubs being disadvantaged. Further, and by way of contrast with the then-existing transfer system, the Advocate General considered that a (largely hypothetical) system of redistribution of income received by clubs across the league, from whatever source, could contribute to competitive balance, whilst not restricting free movement of players at all. Again, this conclusion was important, and again, it had not been sufficiently addressed by the defendants. The ECJ agreed with the Advocate General.

1 [1995] ECR I-4921 at 5016 et seq.
2 [1995] ECR I-4921 at 5072, para 107.

E2.43 'Natural' limitations Of course, there are 'natural' limitations to competitive balance, or imbalance. The size of the squad, that is, the number of the best players, that even a rich club can employ is inevitably constrained by club finances. Player ambition is another 'natural' constraint; the best players do not invariably wish to languish for lengthy periods in the reserve teams of a large squad. Another is the inertia of players with family ties and commitments. Thus, it is unlikely that one club could ever employ all the best players over any length of time. These 'natural' limitations on competitive imbalance, however, have nothing to do with transfer, or other, rules. Indeed, they would continue to exist under a redistribution of income arrangement. These 'natural' limitations on competitive imbalance are also of limited effect. Under current transfer rules, experience in professional football demonstrates that the financially most powerful clubs can indeed assemble extensive squads comprising almost exclusively top-class international players, doing their best to satisfy player ambitions with a rotation policy. In the Premier League, at least, it has proven difficult to compete against these squads. In other words, the 'natural' limitations alone are not capable of maintaining competitive balance.

E2.44 Other 'artificial' measures to promote competitive balance So, in addition to these natural limitations, there may be a need for measures to promote competitive balance other than through transfer fees (if they have any such effect) and income redistribution. In *Bosman* one alternative advanced was collective wage bargaining for players. Keeping players' wages at a manageable, uniform level would, in theory, enable smaller clubs to register star players, thereby improving the club's competitive sporting position. Similarly, a salary cap arguably has an impact on competitive balance[1]. Another alternative is a formal limitation on squad size. Another option is a 'draft' system, such as practised in some American sports. Under a typical draft system, the lowest ranked teams at the end of one season are entitled to pick from the best new players emerging into the sport, with the highest ranked teams only getting to pick from lower down the 'draft'. The central difficulty, though, is that whilst some of these alternatives pursue the aim of competitive balance head-on, and with greater effect than transfer systems, many of them have an equally profound, or even greater, impact upon free movement of persons than transfer rules. If transfer rules have already been found to have a disproportionately and unjustifiably large impact on free movement (at least in respect of out of contract, international transfers), it is difficult to see how some of these other measures could ever be justified and proportionate.

1 See paras B2.187 to B2.190. See also Paul Harris 'What position do team salary caps play in the game of competitive balance?' [1999] 7(3) SATLJ 31; and Paul Harris 'The benefits of the team salary cap in English rugby league' [1999] 7(3) SATLJ 88.

E2.45 The need for evidence The real problem for the defendants in *Bosman* on the issue of competitive balance was that the evidence did not show that the restrictions upon free movement caused by the transfer rules involved had a targeted, or indeed any, positive impact on competitive balance, yet there were other options, some of which appeared to have a better focus, some of which appeared to have less impact on free movement, and some of which appeared to have both. In such circumstances, it is little surprise that the ECJ was unimpressed by this supposed justification.

(c) Trickle down/training compensation

E2.46 Trickle down/training compensation is a legitimate aim The Advocate General in *Bosman* again considered that this aim was justifiable in the context of football, but also considered that the means employed in the transfer rules to achieve that aim were defective. The principal difficulty was that the transfer fee did not reflect actual training costs properly, indeed at all. Rather, it related principally to the amount that the player had been earning prior to his transfer. Further, a transfer fee was required even in circumstances in which it could not be said that a player had been 'trained' by the transferring club, most obviously, for example, when the transferring player was already an experienced, fully trained professional at the time he had joined the transferring club.

E2.47 The need for evidence Again, there were evidential problems for the defendants. Leaving aside the (lack of) alleged link to training costs, the flow-of-money figures provided by the defendants did not even show an impressive trickle down in practice. Rather, the trickle down, on the figures provided, appeared to be minimal. In any event, of course, there is no 'trickle down' within a national football association when the transfer was international; all the money goes abroad. The ECJ again agreed with the Advocate General's analysis[1].

1 [1995] ECR I-4921 at para 109.

E2.48 Redistribution of income through other methods The better approach, it was held by the ECJ, would be to provide a system of redistribution of income in which significant monies actually did trickle down from the higher levels of the game to the bottom. Broadcasting rights were identified as a prime source of income available for partial redistribution. Further, if training fees were to be one aspect of that trickle down, then they had to be, in fact, directly related to the costs of actual training.

(d) Bosman*: outcome and ambit*

E2.49 A key lesson to be learned, therefore, from the *Bosman* case in relation to the two arguments made is that, if a justification for a fetter upon free movement is to be advanced sensibly, it has to be supported by convincing evidence –

particularly given that redistribution of income, with its lack of impact upon free movement, can always be held up as an alternative. It is no good for a governing body merely to assert supposed justifications. It is no good, either, merely to rely upon historic practices in an attempt to support unjustified rules[1]. These points alone ought perhaps to make some governing bodies sit up and take note. Indeed, the mere exercise of searching for evidence to justify a transfer rule will sometimes reveal that it cannot be supported and that, therefore, its existence or nature should be revisited.

1 Other subsidiary arguments in supposed justification of the transfer rules in issue in *Bosman* were also rejected by the Advocate General and the ECJ, principally on the bases that the rules were not shown, in fact, to promote the aims advanced and/or because there were less restrictive alternatives available, notably income redistribution.

E2.50 Accordingly, the outcome of *Bosman* was that where an EU/EEA national wished to transfer to a club in another EU/EEA member state at the end of his contract of employment with a club, the club that he was leaving could not demand a transfer fee as a condition of permitting the transfer[1]. It could not do so because the restrictions that such a demand placed upon the right to free movement of that national across EU/EEA member states' borders for the purpose of work were not objectively justified and/or proportionate to the aims advanced and/or sought to be achieved by the football governing bodies. The *principles* obviously apply to other sports[2], although the results of the analysis may not be the same and further different rules may be in issue. Notably, since competitive balance and trickle down/training compensation were, in part, the conceptual justifications for other aspects of the transfer rules not strictly in issue in *Bosman*, it could be that those other aspects might be vulnerable to later legal challenge, whether in the context of football or another sport.

1 Not only do the principles apply to players from the EU and from the EEA (which includes Norway, Liechtenstein and Iceland) when they move within that area but they have been extended by the courts to players from outside the EU but who come from countries with an equal treatment agreement with the EU. Once playing within the EU, such players are entitled to the same free movement rights as EU players: see *Lilia Malaja v Fédération Française de Basketball* Case no VC 99 NC 00282 Administrative Appeal Court, Nancy. Malaja was Polish. She was contracted to a French club. The governing body's rules confined clubs to a maximum of two non EEA nationals. Malaja argued successfully that she had to be treated the same way as an EEA national because of the Association Agreement between the EU and Poland, Art 37 of which provided that workers of Polish nationality who were lawfully employed in the EU could not be discriminated against on grounds of nationality. See also *Auneau* [2000] 2 Revue Trimestrielle de Droit Europeen, p 389. The Court of Arbitration for Sport (or 'CAS') addressed the issue of an out of contract player going from Scotland to Monaco in *Celtic v UEFA* CAS 98/201, *Digest of CAS Awards II 1998–2000* (2002, Kluwer), p 106, discussed in more detail at para E2.123. It held that although the player was going to a club strictly outside the EU, the *Bosman* ruling applied and Celtic was not entitled to demand a transfer fee from the new club because the club was affiliated to the French federation and the transfer was therefore rightly treated as a transfer within the EU. Ostensibly, the principles do not apply in the context of transfers from, or to, outside the EU/EEA. That said, it is plain that many governing bodies, such as FIFA, may adopt rules which make no distinction.

2 *Malaja* and *Lehtonen* involved basketball. Many governing bodies, such as the International Rugby Board, changed their rules as a result of the *Bosman* ruling and later developments. Equally there may be some that have failed to do so, at least in some respects.

(e) *Team/seasonal stability:* Lehtonen

E2.51 As to the third category of justification, seasonal/team stability, the ECJ has more recently held in *Lehtonen*[1] that some restrictions on free movement in a system of transfer rules may be objectively justified on this basis. The rules in *Lehtonen* involved the timing of transfers rather than transfer fees.

1 *Jyri Lehtonen v Federation Royal Belge des Societes de Basketball* (C-176/96) ECJ Judgment of 13.4.2000, OJ 2000/C192/06, [2000] 3 CMLR 409 [2000] ECR I-2681.

E2.52 ***Lehtonen*** This case concerned a Finnish basketball player who played in the Finnish professional basketball league. In both Belgium and Finland a registration system for players operated, under the auspices of the international basketball federation, such that, without registration in a national league, a player was not eligible to play. In other words, as in professional football, registration constitutes the player's 'licence' to play. Lehtonen sought to transfer in order to play for a club in Belgium during the play-off stages of the Belgian league, late in the season. A transfer rule of the Belgian league prohibited transfers into the Belgian league of overseas players who were coming from another European country after 28 February. Another rule prevented such transfers for overseas players coming from non-European countries after 31 March. Lehtonen transferred into the Belgian league after 28 February, notwithstanding the rule referred to, and was fielded by a Belgian professional club in a play-off game. The club was fined by the national association pursuant to the transfer rules and, effectively, was forced to resile from its relationship with Lehtonen.

E2.53 On a reference to the ECJ it was held that there could be valid sporting reasons connected with team stability and 'regularity of sporting competition' for allowing transfers only during certain 'windows', notwithstanding the obvious hindrance that such rules would have on free movement of persons. For example, the ECJ held that

> late transfers might be liable to change substantially the sporting strength of one or other team in the course of the championship, thus calling into question the comparability of results between the teams taking part in that championship, and consequently the proper functioning of the championship as a whole[1].

That was particularly so in a league that operated a play-off system. Strictly, the ECJ left to the national court the questions whether or not the particular rules of the Belgian federation were justified for purely sporting reasons and did not go beyond what was necessary for achieving the aim pursued. However, the ECJ gave a clear indication that the difference in dates of transfer 'windows' for players depending on the country from which they were moving appeared unjustifiable (meaning that the actual case was likely to succeed back before the national court).

1 [2000] ECR I-2681 at para 54.

E2.54 Thus, in contrast to the attempts to justify transfer fees (at least for out of contract players) as measures contributing to competitive balance and trickle down/training compensation, transfer 'windows' do appear justifiable and, depending on how they are structured, may be proportionate to the sporting aims of team/seasonal stability. The judgment demonstrates that some elements of a transfer system are capable of being justified, notwithstanding an obvious direct impact on free movement[1].

1 See also Paul Harris 'Recent sports-specific case law of the ECJ' (2000) 3(3) Sports Law Bulletin.

C Competition law

(a) *Restrictive agreements contrary to Art 81 EC and the Chapter I prohibition*

E2.55 A market for the employment of players of a sport is not free if it is bound by various transfer restrictions. For example, a transfer window prevents a club freely competing for the services of a player altogether, except at a certain time. The obligation to pay a fee for the transfer merely of a registration is another impediment to free competition for that player's services. Both are restrictions or distortions of the way in which the market would otherwise work[1].

1 See the contrast with an ordinary employment market referred to above at paras E2.9 to E2.14.

E2.56 Article 81(1) EC[1] prohibits as incompatible with the common market all agreements between undertakings, decisions of associations of undertakings and concerted practices which may affect trade between member states and which have as their object or effect the prevention, restriction or distortion of competition within the common market. Such prohibited agreements are automatically void pursuant to Art 81(2) EC, but are capable of being exempted from Art 81(1) EC by the European Commission under the terms of Art 81(3) EC[2]. The prohibition in s 2, Chapter I of the Competition Act 1998 mirrors Art 81. The Chapter I prohibition applies even where there is no effect on cross border trade, which is required under Art 81.

1 See generally Chapter B2. Article 81 EC (formerly Art 85) is the first Article of Title VI ('Common Rules on Competition, Taxation and Approximation of Laws') of the Treaty establishing the European Community.

2 Article 81(3) EC reads:

'The provisions of paragraph 1 may, however, be declared inapplicable in the case of:
– any agreement or category of agreements between undertakings;
– any decision or category of decisions by associations of undertakings;
– any concerted practice or category of concerted practices;

which contributes to improving the production or distribution of goods or to promoting technical or economic progress, while allowing consumers a fair share of the resulting benefit, and which does not:

(a) impose on the undertakings concerned restrictions which are not indispensable to the attainment of these objectives;
(b) afford such undertakings the possibility of eliminating competition in respect of a substantial part of the products in question.'

E2.57 Transfer rules are agreements subject to competition law In *Bosman*, the Advocate General considered the application of Art 81(1) to the transfer rules there in issue[1], although the ECJ itself did not[2]. There can be no doubt that Art 81(1) does apply to sport and sporting rules, except to the limited extent that the rules are of purely sporting interest and significance: for example the offside rule[3]. The rules on transfers are not such rules; they directly regulate and impact upon the market for the services of players. Professional sports clubs are 'undertakings' and professional sports associations are 'associations of undertakings' (that is, associations of the clubs, notwithstanding that there may be other members/associates), or arguably 'undertakings' in themselves. Transfer rules are 'decisions of associations of undertakings' or, arguably, 'agreements between undertakings' (clubs) through the mechanism of rules agreed jointly under the auspices of a sports association.

1 [1995] ECR I-4921 at 5026–5036.

2 The ECJ decided that there was no need to consider the application of the EC competition laws, because it had already decided that the transfer rules at issue more than justifiably restricted free movement pursuant to Art 39 EC (see paras E2.41 to E2.48).

3 See paras B2.56 to B2.61. This principle has been consistently maintained through the ECJ case law from *Walrave and Koch* [1974] ECR 1405 and *Donà v Mantero* [1976] ECR 1333 through to *Lehtonen*, [2000] ECR I-2681, [2000] 3 CMLR 409 and *Christine Deliège v Ligue Belge de Judo ASBL*, ECJ Judgment of 11.4.2000, OJ 2000/C176/02; [2000] ECR I-2549.

E2.58 Transfer rules affect trade between member states By definition, *international* transfers within the EU/EEA 'may affect trade between member states', because trade is not limited to trade in goods or products, but extends to all economic services and activities. Of considerable practical importance, it does not follow that, simply because a transfer is not itself international, it cannot have an actual or potential effect upon cross-border trade, or patterns of trade. Taking a simple hypothetical example, if there is a restrictive system of domestic transfers in England, but not in Italy or Spain, then a Spanish national playing in Spain wishing to transfer might be deterred from transferring to England for fear of the difficulty of further transfers thereafter. Instead, he might prefer to transfer within Spain, or transfer to Italy. In theory, this, or similar types of argument, could succeed in making an apparently domestic transfer subject to Art 81EC depending on the exact facts.

E2.59 In any event, the impact of this requirement is considerably reduced by the application in the UK of s 2 of the Competition Act 1998 which mirrors the substance of Art 81 EC, save that the requirement is for an effect on 'trade within the United Kingdom'.

E2.60 Transfer rules restrict competition The Advocate General in the *Bosman* case concluded that the rules were anti-competitive within the meaning of that provision. It is apparent that the object and effect of transfer rules is, at least in part, precisely the prevention, restriction or distortion of competition. That is because, of course, inherent in the concept of 'competitive balance' that underlies the transfer rules is the object, indeed hopefully the effect, of restraining an otherwise free market for the services of players.

E2.61 But the restriction may be justified On the face of matters, therefore, transfer rules are in breach of Art 81 EC. The focus accordingly shifts to whether they are justified and proportionate. For the same reasons as given in *Bosman* and *Lehtonen*, there are at least three potentially available justifications for all, or parts of, the rules: competitive balance, trickle down/training compensation and seasonal/team stability. It appears likely, however, that the ECJ would consider that most restrictions go further than is necessary or proportionate, that is, they are not 'indispensable' to the aims pursued[1]. In the same way that it did in the context of free movement of persons, the sword of income redistribution (or some other less restrictive measure) hangs over the heads of the justifications advanced in support of the restrictions. It has been the threat of proceedings under Art 81 that has enabled the European Commission to bring the 'football family' to the table and to negotiate the current agreement in relation to football transfer rules.

1 See para E2.62.

E2.62 *Tibor Balog* In *Tibor Balog v Charleroi Sporting Club*[1], the application of the competition rules to the post *Bosman* transfer system was considered by the

Advocate General, but the case did not progress to the court because it was settled and the reference withdrawn before that could happen. The case carries little authority therefore, but is nevertheless of interest when examining the legality of other rules decided in relation to the football transfer rules. The case had been referred to the Court of Justice by the Charleroi Court of First Instance on 2 July 1998. The Advocate General decided that it was contrary to the competition rules for a club in an EU/EEA member state to require payment of a transfer fee for a player from outside the EU who was out of contract, whether the buying club was in or outside the EU/EEA.

1 C-264/98 A-G's Opinion released on 29 March 2001and withdrawn after case settled.

(b) Abuse of a dominant position contrary to Art 82 (EC) and the Chapter II prohibition

E2.63 Article 82 EC[1] prohibits abuses of a dominant position in a relevant market. Abusive conduct is conduct that is not objectively justified.

1 See generally Chapter B2. Article 82 EC reads (in first part): 'Any abuse by one or more undertakings of a dominant position within the common market or in a substantial part of it shall be prohibited as incompatible with the common market insofar as it may affect trade between Member State.'

E2.64 The most obvious market involved here is that for the transfer/employment (ie the services) of players in the EU/EEA. That is a market between players and clubs, since it is clubs that transfer/employ the players. It is a market in which clubs compete with each other for the players. There are too many clubs in the EU/EEA for any single club sensibly to be said to be dominant. Further, insofar as the transfer rules are agreed between all the clubs, it is difficult to see how any one club could be said to be abusing any position it had. Accordingly, there appears to be no scope for the application of Art 82 EC to this market[1]. Although there can be 'collective dominant positions' ie groups of undertakings that, collectively, are dominant (for example, groups of clubs together in one league or in one national association), it makes no sense to speak of such a collective dominant position in this context, because – as a collective unit – the clubs are not operative on the relevant market. Only clubs acting unilaterally operate on the relevant market.

1 See Advocate General Lenz on this issue in *Bosman* [1995] ECR I-4921 at 5036–5039.

E2.65 It could, however, sensibly be argued that the national or international governing body of a sport, for example the FA or UEFA, is itself in a dominant position (in some respects) with regard to both clubs and to players, on the market for the organisation and promotion of leagues and tournaments, and indeed arguably on the market for the regulation of the sport more generally[1]. Although neither the FA nor UEFA is active in the most obviously relevant market, namely, the market for the services of players, it is possible to construct an argument that they cannot abuse their dominant position by promulgating rules that are not objectively justified.

1 See for example, *Hendry v World Professional Billiards and Snooker Association Ltd* (5 October 2001, unreported), QBD (Lloyd J), in which it was found that the WPBSA was dominant on the market for the organisation and promotion of professional snooker tournaments. See further paras A3.170 and B2.131 et seq.

D Developments since *Bosman*: the FIFA arrangements agreed with the European Commission

(a) *Unfinished business*

E2.66 Though the *Bosman* case was officially concluded in December 1995 its ramifications continue to the present day. First, as mentioned above, the legal reasoning behind the free movement argument that succeeded on the facts of the *Bosman* case itself was capable of being used to attack other aspects of the transfer system not then directly in dispute. For example, why should principles other than normal employment law principles apply to cross-border transfers of players still under contract, particularly if the conceptual 'justifications' put forward by the football bodies for the transfer system *as a whole* had been exposed as factually weak? Secondly, there was no formal conclusion by the ECJ itself on the competition law arguments advanced in *Bosman*, but the Advocate General had concluded that Art 81(1)EC did apply and his analysis appeared persuasive. Again, conceptually, there was reason to suppose that these arguments would apply to other aspects of the transfer system, including to contracted players. As described above[1], the *Tibor Balog* case (albeit abandoned before there was any judgment from the Court of Justice) involved a step beyond the position under *Bosman* being made on the basis of the competition rules. Thirdly, the ruling endangered what 'trickle down' there was of monies from the upper levels of the sport to the lower levels. Indeed, in the case of out-of-contract players, it was cut off altogether. Fourthly, the ruling created an inconsistency between purely domestic transfers and international transfers that was illogical from a sporting perspective yet increasingly noticeable in an ever more pan-European football transfer market. Fifthly, the continued increase in revenue to football clubs and associations from the sale of broadcasting rights contributed to the upward spiral of transfers fees, ensuring both that they would continue to be in the headlines and that there would be the finances available to mount a further legal challenge to the transfer system. Sixthly, the pan-European competitions, notably the UEFA Champions' League, appeared to coincide with the emergence of a handful of clear sporting leaders in many of the domestic football leagues. One consequence of perennial candidates from domestic leagues for European honours has been renewed calls for measures to increase competitive balance in domestic leagues. Not surprisingly, including for the above reasons, the football transfer system was forced to undergo a thorough overhaul in light of *Bosman*.

1 See para E2.62.

E2.67 To the distress of the football bodies, the European Commission intervened and acted as a catalyst in the revision of the European football transfer system, arguing consistently that free movement and free competition laws dictated fundamental changes to the remainder of the system that had not been directly affected by *Bosman*. A Statement of Objections was served on FIFA[1]. Eventually, in March 2001, a hard-negotiated agreement was reached between FIFA/UEFA and the Commission as to a new framework for international transfer rules[2].

1 See Draft Preliminary Guidelines on the Application of the Competition Rules to Sport (unpublished Commission memorandum, 15 February 1999).
2 See FIFA Circular at www.fifa.com.

E2.68 At one point it looked as if FIFPro, the international players federation, was not prepared to accept the compromise. With its support, proceedings were commenced which would have put in issue the validity of the compromise, effectively 'Bosman II'. FIFPro considered, in essence, that the changes to the rules did not go far enough and did not protect adequately the fundamental principles of free movement of players and/or freedom of competition for players' services. They were also concerned to protect the position of very young players in the transfer market. The difficulty faced by FIFPro however was that the tools in the hands of their lawyers were rather blunt. If the legal challenge succeeded on the issues of principle, the existing system fell to be declared invalid as a whole: even though there would be nothing there to replace it. Moreover, a totally 'free' market would not meet the concerns that FIFPro shared with the football bodies, that is, to promote competitive balance, provide for trickle down/training compensation, maintain team/seasonal stability and protect young players. Consequently, after certain marginal further concessions to FIFPro were made in the proposed new system, the proceedings were settled.

(b) The new FIFA Regulations

E2.69 The outcome is two sets of Regulations and a lengthy explanatory text setting out the principles and rules applicable from September 1st 2001[1]. The intention is that the national associations will draw up their own domestic rules in conformity with the principles set out in these documents and that all new contracts with players entered into after that time will also conform[2]. The new FIFA regulations clearly reflect a compromise between, on the one hand, the promotion of the features referred to above, namely competitive balance, trickle down and team/seasonal stability and in addition the protection of very young players and, on the other hand, the fundamental principles of free movement and free competition.

1 See www.fifa.com.
2 The new FIFA Regulations are not clear and leave many issues unresolved. It remains for the national associations to implement them and at present they apply only to international transfers, with the local association's rules continuing to govern domestic transfers. In Section 5 below the authors describe a step-by-step approach to a transfer.

(c) The continuing threat of challenge

E2.70 It is hoped by the parties involved in the negotiations that, to the extent that the negotiated outcome restricts free movement and competition, it is objectively justified and proportionate. If not, notwithstanding the lengthy and, at times, tortuous negotiations, it may remain vulnerable to legal attack. The agreement between the European Commission and FIFA has no formal status. It remains open for a new 'Bosman II' action to be commenced in a national Court. However in the negotiations all concerned have been a great deal more alive than in *Bosman* to the need for evidence to support their assertions as to why the rules are justified. Any challenge to come in the future would have to overcome the evidence that has now been amassed.

(d) Evidence on the redistributive effect of transfer fees

E2.71 In particular, on the one hand, the football bodies have employed specialist consultants[1] to analyse flows and amounts of transfer fees, specifically in the English Premier League and Football League, in order to support the 'trickle down' justification[2] for the present, restrictive system of transfers. Undoubtedly, the actual figures do provide a measure of support for the trickle down justification. For example, the Premier League has provided a net total of £96m in transfer fees to the Football League as a whole in the five years to 1999/2000[3]. This amount has enabled the clubs of the Football League to cover a substantial proportion, namely around a quarter to a third, of their operating losses during that period. In other words, without the transfer fees trickling down, the operating losses of the Football League clubs would be considerably worse. Another way of putting it is that the trickle down to Division 3 in 1999/2000 was sufficiently large to keep three clubs in business[4] in that season.

1 Deloitte and Touche Sport worked with the FA, Premier League, Football League and UEFA to produce a study on 'the economic impact of the transfer system'. See also their 'Annual Review of Football Finance, August 2001' and their report on 'England's Premier Clubs, April 2001'.
2 The same degree of effort does not appear to have been spent on addressing, separately at least, the 'competitive balance' justification.
3 Deloitte and Touche Sport 'Annual Review of Football Finance, August 2001', p 28, Table 3.2
4 See n 3 at p 29.

E2.72 On the other hand, it is plain both that the trickle down redistribution could be substantially greater, given the amount of income generated by the modern game of professional football, and that the redistributive effect of transfer fees has failed to prevent the gap in size and resources between rich and poor clubs, and upper and lower, divisions from growing ever larger[1]. In other words, on one view, the competitive imbalance is getting worse.

1 See, generally, Chapter 1 'Profitability of Clubs' in the 'Annual Review of Football Finance, August 2001', including Table 1.2 'Financial results by division and "The Gap"' and see the first two chapters of 'England's Premier Clubs, April 2001'.

E2.73 Probably the only safe conclusion to draw is that the jury is still out on how far the current statistics of redistribution go in justifying the restrictions of the (old) transfer system. It is even less clear how much justification the statistics of redistribution will provide under the new transfer rules, because nobody yet knows what those new statistics are or will be. The present authors remain sceptical as to the legal weight of justification that could be demonstrated both under the old system and under the new system, principally because of the theoretical ability to construct a more redistributive system, with greater impact on competitive imbalance and with greater trickle down, yet less impact on free movement and free competition. That is so notwithstanding the extensive efforts made in the recent negotiations better to focus and target the restrictions inherent in the system on justifiable objectives.

E2.74 There is an uneasy relationship, however, between theory and practice. The realities are that any alternative system – including any other more 'pure' system of income redistribution – has to be acceptable to the football bodies, or it will not get off the ground at all. There is no real point in proposing that the most successful clubs 'donate' 50 per cent of all their income every year to the least successful clubs: that destroys the incentive to succeed and would be totally unacceptable to any successful club. So, therein lies the rub: the blunt instruments of Arts 39 and 81 EC remain available, but they have the potential if applicable to smash the system wide open, with nothing left to replace it. But a totally 'free' player employment market is an outcome that virtually nobody desires. It remains to be seen whether, probably as a result of actual or threatened legal action by disaffected players or their unions, even the revised system will have to be amended.

5 NEGOTIATION OF AN INDIVIDUAL PLAYER TRANSFER

E2.75 Different transfer systems exist for different sports, and there may be different systems within a sport dependent upon whether a transfer is across borders or within the jurisdiction of a particular national governing body. The common strand however is that in the absence of a specific transfer system in regulations imposed by the relevant governing body, the arrangements are governed solely by the general law (in particular the law of contract and employment). When any transfer is negotiated therefore, the constraints are contained both in the general law and in the specific governing body regulations themselves. In this section, by way of example, the authors briefly address the main constraints imposed by the governing body regulations on transfers of professional footballers. In any given case, close attention will have to be given to the applicable regulations in the context of the specific facts arising.

A International and domestic regulations in the context of football transfers

(a) The new FIFA regulations governing the transfer and status of players

E2.76 The FIFA Regulations[1] have attempted to create a balance between the principles of freedom of contract, freedom of movement for players and free competition, whilst still ensuring redistribution of income to those clubs involved in training and developing players. This has been achieved through the mechanisms set out below, which apply to international transfers.

(i) Protection of clubs from players leaving mid-contract during the 'protected period'[2] by the introduction of 'sporting sanctions'[3]. Sporting sanctions can be avoided if, in the circumstances, the player has unilaterally terminated his contract for 'just cause' or 'sporting just cause'. Exactly what these terms mean will be determined on a case by case basis by FIFA's Players' Status Committee. An example of 'sporting just cause' is if the player has not been played in at least 10 per cent of games (for which he was fit and available for selection) in any season (determined at the end of any such season). An example of 'just cause' would be failure to pay the player his due remuneration.

(ii) Permitting players unilaterally to terminate fixed term contracts early outside of the 'protected period', subject only to the payment of a compensation fee for breach of contract. Calculation of the compensation fee is discussed later in this section[4].

(iii) Permanent transfers to take place during one of two transfer windows and the imposition of a limit of only one transfer per player per year[5]. In Europe these windows were to be in January and June/July (during the closed season). It was recommended that the January window should be restricted to transfers required for sporting reason (such as technical adjustment to the squad, injuries in a squad or other exceptional circumstances).

(iv) Contracts to be for a period of between one to five years[6].

(v) Clubs to be entitled to receive a 'training and development fee' for any players that it has trained if the player leaves such club up to the age of 23. All clubs involved in the player's training and development from the player's 12th birthday up to when training and development have been completed (maximum age of 21) will be entitled to a proportion of the total 'training and development fee' calculated in accordance with the Regulations and the categorisation figures provided by each National Association.

1 The FIFA Regulations were adopted on 5 July 2001, but only came into force on 1 September 2001, and are applicable only to those contracts entered into after 1 September or to those entered into prior to that date by express agreement

2 The 'protected period' is the first three years of a contract for players who were under 28 when entering into the contract and the first two years of a contract for players who were 28 or over when entering into the contract.

3 In the case of a breach of contract by a player after the first or second year (for players signed when the player was under 28), a player could face suspension of four months from the beginning of the national championship. No sanction will be imposed at the end of the third year (second year if the contract was signed when the player was aged 28 or over), unless no notice is given by the player. A player could face a suspension of up to six months for aggravating circumstances eg a recurrent breach of contract. Sporting sanctions will be imposed from the start of the 2002/2003 season.

4 See para E2.87 et seq.

5 See Art 5 of the FIFA Regulations.

6 See Art 5 of the FIFA Regulations.

(b) Domestic Transfers

E2.77 The FIFA regulations referred to above govern only international transfers, in other words transfers of players between different countries. National associations govern transfers relating to players within their own jurisdiction ('domestic transfers'). While the system may change, the current English system is not the same as the FIFA system[1]. First, domestic transfers are not wholly subject to transfer window restrictions. Furthermore, there is no provision for the imposition of any 'sporting sanctions' but equally there is no right for a player to terminate his contract prior to its expiry date save as provided under the standard player agreement[2] for 'serious or persistent breach of the terms and conditions' of the contract or as a provided by common law (e.g. on grounds of constructive dismissal for fundamental breach of contract).

1 The English football authorities have been in debate over the harmonising the domestic system with the international system. The Football League and the Professional Footballers' Association are of the view that the domestic system should remain unchanged, whilst some club managers, such as Sir Alex Ferguson, have come out in favour of the proposed restricted transfer windows period. At the time of writing, transfer windows have been imposed on the FA Premier League, but the Football League have been granted the opportunity to transfer players outside the January transfer window.

2 Clause 17 under the 2001/2002 version of the standard player agreement. The standard player agreement is currently under review. The 2002/2003 FA Premier League Handbook has not yet been issued and the clause number may change from time-to-time.

E2.78 The only sanctions against a player who seeks to terminate his contract prior to its expiry or requests a transfer are purely financial in that he loses his right to payment of the remaining part of any signing-on fee[1] (if such a fee was agreed as part of his playing contract) and may also be sued for breach of contract. This may become increasingly complicated if the player in addition to or as part of his playing contract had entered into a contract for the licence or assignment of his 'image rights' or 'personality rights'[2]. On the other hand, if a transfer prior to the expiry of a contract is instigated by the employing club, the player is entitled to receive the entire signing-on fee upon completion of the transfer and could sue the club for breach of contract.

1 As provided by the FA Premier League Regulations and the Football League Regulations for Premier League players and Football League players respectively.

2 See paras D3.68 to D3.71.

E2.79 The practical reality is that clubs may indicate their intention to terminate a player's contract by placing the player on the notional 'transfer list'. However, the player's contract is not in fact terminated until a new club is found to which the player may be transferred subject to the player agreeing acceptable terms with the transferee club. In this way the player's contract is never terminated and any claim for breach of contract the player might have had is eliminated.

E2.80 This system has developed for historical reasons. Previously the value of a transfer fee was associated with the value of the player's registration. Consequently, if a club no longer wanted to retain a player's services, it was not commercially prudent to terminate the player's contract as this would mean that the club would lose its right to hold the player's registration and thereby lose the right to receive a 'transfer fee'. Additionally the club would put itself at risk of having to pay damages for breach of contract to the player.

B How negotiations begin and are conducted

E2.81 Against this background of the currently different international and domestic regulatory systems in football, the authors examine below some aspects of the practical procedure involved in commencing and conducting a transfer. The authors do this by reference to three different situations. First, transfers of player aged 23 or over and without an existing contract ('out-of-contract transfers'); secondly transfers of players aged 23 or over and subject to a contract ('in-contract transfers); and thirdly transfers of players under the age of 23 ('trainee transfers'). In each case the authors highlight the difference between international and domestic transfers.

(a) Out-of-contract transfers

E2.82 The least regulated and procedurally simplest form of transfer is the 'out-of-contract transfer'. An out-of-contract transfer is one where the player whose registration is to be transferred is not engaged under a contract of employment by any football club. However the last club with whom the player had a contract would remain the registered holder of the player's registration, hence the necessity for a transfer of that registration. In such circumstances no transfer fee is payable to the club holding the player's registration by the club to whom the player is to transfer. This has not always been the case. Previously there existed a system whereby the club holding a player's registration was entitled to compensation for its transfer to another club whether or not the player was serving such club under a contract and regardless of the player's age.

E2.83 Consequently, for transfers in relation to players who are out-of-contract, the only negotiation that is required relates to the player's personal terms with the new club.

E2.84 To this end, the player's agent or representative will need to identify a club that is interested in engaging the player's services and commence negotiations. There are no restrictions on the agent in approaching such clubs as the player is no longer under contract and is free to negotiate and enter into a playing contract with any club with whom he can agree terms.

E2.85 Once it appears that it will be possible to agree terms, the steps and documentation set out below should be completed:

(i) Ensure that the player has passed the appropriate medical examinations. It is crucial to note that under Art 30 of the FIFA Regulations, playing contracts (and indeed transfer contracts) cannot be made subject to a condition either that the player pass a medical examination satisfactorily or that a work permit be obtained[1]. Consequently these matters must always be resolved to the club's satisfaction prior to completion of any transfer and the conclusion of any binding agreement. If they are not the club runs the risk that it will have entered into a binding contract which, so far at least as FIFA is concerned, is not subject to these conditions. This means that the club may be held to the agreement, or be financially liable on it even if the player then fails a medical or a work permit is not obtained[2].

(ii) Obtain the appropriate work permits[3] and visas (if required) to allow the player to enter and work in the country of the club to which the registration is to be transferred.

(iii) Obtain an international transfer clearance certificate (ITC) issued by the national association to which the club holding the player's registration is affiliated. The club holding the registration will need to consent to the issue of the ITC, before it will be issued by the national association concerned[4]. Consent to the issue of the ITC may only be refused by a club if there is an outstanding contractual dispute (not relating to any compensation fee) in relation to the playing contract.

(iv) Sign the playing contract containing agreed terms, and simultaneously complete the relevant documentation as specified under the national association regulations to record that the player is registered with the new club. In England this consists of the Football Association Forms H1 (Transfer of Registration signed by transferor and transferee clubs and the player) and G2 (Player Registration form). These need to be filed with the Football Association together with a copy of the playing contract (including any associated 'image rights' agreement).

1 See para E1.14, n 6. Notwithstanding this regulation, several clubs continue to insert clauses to this effect in player's contracts. See further para E2.125 et seq.

2 This has proved a costly mistake for a number of clubs. The precise ambit of the obligation is however unclear. In order to prevent the application by a domestic court of the condition, which is likely to be valid as a matter of domestic contract law, it would have to be shown that the FIFA regulations were in some way implicitly incorporated into the contract (an argument rejected, albeit in a different context, by Morland J in *Barry Silkman v Colchester United Football Club* (15 June 2001, unreported). In practice however this factor may offer little comfort, since the FIFA Players' Status Committee is unlikely to be impressed by such an argument.

3 Again this must be done before any binding contract is entered into. Note that in the UK work permits will not be granted for players who arrive on a loan. The basic criteria for obtaining a work permit in the UK for footballers are that the player must have appeared in at least 75 per cent of the national team matches over the course of the preceding two years and the national team for which the player plays is ranked 70 or above in the FIFA world rankings table. If either of these criteria are not satisfied a work permit will not be granted at first instance. However, there is a right of appeal which follows and a work permit may be granted at that stage if the club applying for the work permit can show that the player has an international reputation and will add to the value of the English game and the club and that it has not been able to identify any other players of equal value and quality available within the EU. These factors were set out by McCullough J in *R v Secretary of State for Education and Employment, ex p Portsmouth Football Club* [1998] COD 142. Injuries will be taken into account, as well as evidence that the player would have achieved the required percentage were it not for exceptional circumstances, such as that the player missed an international match in order to play in an Under 23 match in the Olympics. The appeal is heard by a specially appointed panel of football-related adjudicators.

4 See Art 6 of the Regulations.

E2.86 A domestic out-of-contract transfer follows the same procedure except that there is no need to obtain an ITC. Football Association Form H1 does however require the confirmation of the appropriate consent to the registration transfer. The player's registration will effectively be cancelled and he will re-register with the new club[1]. An important practical point to note is that a fresh work permit application will still need to be made if the player is a non-EU/EEA citizen as work permits are non-transferable and granted exclusively for the benefit of the employing club.

1 See r 41.3 of the Football League Regulations.

(b) *In-contract transfers*

E2.87 This is where the player concerned is under contract with a club which has not expired. In this situation, a player's registration may be sought to be transferred at either the club's request (usually done via the notional 'transfer list' as explained above[1]), or at the player's request. This has always been the case. The difference following the introduction of the FIFA Regulations is that the consequences of the requests are different. Previously, for players under contract, players had the right to request a transfer but the club could refuse to transfer the registration thereby preventing the player from leaving the club, or at least from playing elsewhere. Under the FIFA Regulations, a club can no longer refuse to transfer the registration: a player would be in breach of contract but he cannot ultimately be stopped from going and from playing for a new club. Instead, the club has available to it other remedies, the extent of which depend on the point at which when the player leaves the club. The principal remedy available to the club is the right to compensation as a result of the player leaving early: how this is calculated is discussed below under the heading 'arriving at a transfer fee' below[2]. This compensation can be regarded as compensation for breach of contract, which it is if the player unilaterally leaves, but it is also the basis for a club to reach agreement on the fee for which a player will be released from his contract. In addition to the compensation however, the player may be subjected to some form of sporting sanction, as discussed above[3].

1 See para E2.79.
2 See para E2.91.
3 See, with regard to the effect of the 'protected period' in this context, para E.100.

E2.88 During the final six months of the player's contract, approaches may be made to and by other clubs in relation to a contract for the period commencing after the expiry of the existing contract without any restriction or sanction (unless of course the player has contractually agreed otherwise). However, if terms are agreed with a new club to take effect after the expiry of the player's existing contract, it is an emerging practice for the club and the prospective transferee club to enter into a form of agreement to enter into a formal playing contract at a future date on pre-agreed terms. Most famously this technique was used in relation to the transfer of Emanuel Petit from Barcelona to Chelsea. Again it is essential for a club to satisfy itself on fitness and on the work permit situation before entering into a binding agreement.

E2.89 If a transfer[1] is to take place mid-way through a contract, the steps set out below should be taken.

- **Step 1** – the proposed transferee club must first (at least in theory) contact the transferor club to get permission to speak with the player (or his representatives on the player's behalf).
- **Step 2** – negotiations must be initiated between the transferee club and the transferor club to agree a level of compensation for early release of the player from his contract and subsequent transfer of his registration. Simultaneously, negotiations must be initiated between the player (or his representative) and the transferee club as regards the player's personal terms with the transferee club. In the event that the two clubs cannot agree a mutually acceptable fee or in the event that the transferor club does not give consent to the transferee club to speak with the player, the player may nevertheless leave the club (albeit in breach of contract) and the transferor club will have a choice of forum[2] in which to have the level of compensation for the breach of contract assessed and any other sanction imposed[3].
- **Step 3** – follow the same procedural steps as set out above for out-of-contract transfers. Even if a mutually acceptable compensation fee has not been agreed between the transferor club and transferee club, the transfer may nevertheless be completed and the compensation fee assessed at a later date by the Dispute Resolution Chamber of FIFA's Player Status Committee ('DRC'). However, if this is to be done, the transferee club should act in the knowledge that the assessment of the DRC (or the Arbitration Tribunal of Football ('TAF') on appeal) will be binding. The player should also note that the transferor club may choose instead to sue the player for breach of contract in the national court of law.

1 In the case of a transfer of a player on loan during the term of his contract, the transferor club will need to enter into a loan agreement (as opposed to a transfer agreement) with the transferee club, which sets out the terms of the loan, including the loan fee payable for the loan of the player. Usually, the transferee club will take over the obligations of the transferor club towards the player for the duration of the loan period. The player's registration will be transferred temporarily, for the duration of the loan period, after which it will revert to the transferor club. See para E2.5.

2 This may be through the local law courts, or the Dispute Resolution Chamber (or 'DRC') of the Players' Status Committee. The decision of the DRC will cover whether the termination was in breach of contract, whether there was 'just cause' or 'sporting just cause' for the breach and the level of compensation (if any) and any sporting sanction to be imposed. The decision of the DRC may be appealed to the Arbitration Tribunal of Football ('TAF'). The DRC should give its decision within 60 days of the referral. See further paras A5.135 to A5.138.

3 The amount of compensation and the imposition of sanctions will depend on whether the breach took place within the 'protected period'. In the case of a breach within the first three years by a player who signed a contract before aged 28 (two years in the case of a player who signed the contract at age 28 or over), compensation will be due and sporting sanctions may be imposed.

E2.90 Domestic in-contract transfers are not governed by the new FIFA Regulations, but are instead governed by the Football League Regulations, the Premier League Rules and the Football Association Rules. In practice the procedure is virtually identical to international in-contract transfers. A few differences are worth noting, however. First, no transfer windows exist domestically[1]. Second, as domestic transfers are not governed by the new FIFA Regulations, a club is still able to refuse to allow a player to transfer his registration. In reality, however, this may well have the long-term effect of having a de-motivated player on the club's wage books, which is not in the club's best interests. The player may also argue that such a failure to allow for a transfer of registration amounts to an unreasonable restraint of trade, although this has yet to be tested in the courts. No sporting sanctions are provided, as in the case of international transfers. The payment of compensation fees is governed by the Football League Regulations[2] and the

Football Association Rules[3] and the transferee club is required to pay to the Football League a levy of five per cent of the total compensation fee paid by that club. Disputes as to payment of compensation fees are referred to the Football League Board and an appeal procedure is provided via the Football League Appeals Committee.

1 See para E2.77. There is also, however, a transfer deadline as stipulated in Section M.1 of the Football Association Rules, being 5pm on the fourth Thursday in March of each season.
2 See r 44 of the Football League Regulations.
3 Section M.26 of the Football Association Rules. See M.23–25 for the provisions relating to the calculation of the compensation.

(c) Trainee Transfers

E2.91 There are special rules for the transfer of players up to the age of 23. A player under the age of 18 cannot be transferred internationally unless his parents are moving to a different country for non-football related reasons. The same procedures need to be followed for players under 23 as apply to transfers of players over 23 (as detailed above). However, for players under 23, in addition to any compensation fee payable in respect of the breach of contract, there will also be a 'training and development fee' payable. There is a fixed formula to calculate this training and development fee based on the age of the player and the category of clubs involved in his training and development between the age of 12 and 21 (or earlier if the player's training is deemed to have been completed). The calculation and distribution of the training and development fee is the responsibility of the transferee club who must make the payments within 30 days of the transfer. The formulae set out in the next section may be used to assist in the calculations.

C Arriving at a transfer fee

E2.92 We deal first with the assessment of the training and development fee and then turn to the assessment of compensation for a player leaving before his contract has expired.

(a) Training and Development Fee Calculation

E2.93 The training and development fees due to the clubs[1] involved in the player's training excluding the transferor club are calculated by applying the formula **A x B = C**, where:

- **A** is the annual cost fixed for the category of the club training the player between the age of 12 and 21[2];
- **B** is the number of years the player was trained by the relevant club; and
- **C** is the total training and development fee payable to the training club.

1 If there was more one such club then the calculation needs to be done for each club and totalled together to arrive at the total amount of compensation payable.
2 For the purposes of calculating **A**, one must refer to the category of club as determined by the national associations. In England, the categories and **A** costs have been provisionally defined by the FA for each player as follows:
(i) Category 1 (38 teams from the FA Premier League, and Football League Divisions 1 and 2): £286,724;
(ii) Category 2 (54 teams from Football League Divisions 1, 2 and 3): £179,284;
(iii) Category 3 (approximately 220 teams from below the Football League): £34,545;
(iv) Category 4 (amateur clubs): £1,000.

E2.94 The total amount of training and development fee payable in relation to the transferor club is calculated by using the formula **E x F = D,** where:

- **E** is –
  - (a) zero if the transfer is to a category 4 club; or
  - (b) the annual training and development cost of the lower category club if the transfer is from a higher to a lower category club (that is not a category 4 club); or
  - (c) the average of the training and development costs of the two clubs for a transfer from a lower to a higher club;
- **F** is the number of years training provided by the transferor club; and
- **D** is the total training and development cost payable by the transferee club in relation to the transferor club's training and development.

E2.95 The total training and development fee payable by the transferee club is the sum total of C for each club involved in the player's training (except that relating to the transferor club) plus D. Once the total training and development fees have been calculated, adjustments may need to be made for redistributions in accordance with paras E2.95 to E2.97.

E2.96 Where there is a transfer from a category 3 or 4 club to a higher club all clubs involved in the training of the player are entitled to a proportion of the difference between **D** and **C**: 75 per cent of the difference between **D** and **C** is to be distributed on a pro-rata basis to all clubs (excluding the transferor club) involved in the training and development of the player. The transferor club will retain the remaining 25 per cent of the difference between **D** and **C**.

E2.97 Where there is a transfer from a category 2 club to a category 1 club the proportion of the difference between **D** and **C** to be distributed to lower level clubs is 50 per cent pro-rata to all clubs (excluding the transferor club) involved in the player's training and development and 50 per cent of the difference retained by the transferor club.

E2.98 Where there is a transfer between clubs of equal category levels, 10 per cent of **D** should be distributed on a pro-rata basis to all clubs (other than the transferor club) involved in the player's training and development.

E2.99 In addition to redistribution of the training and development fees, clubs involved in a player's training and development will be entitled to continuing payments via the 'solidarity mechanism'. This is a system which redistributes five per cent of any compensation fee payable in relation to the player throughout the currency of his football career[1]. The five per cent contribution is distributed based on the age of the player whilst at each club involved in his training and development[2].

1 This is five per cent of the compensation fee, and not five per cent on top of the compensation fee, as has been argued by some clubs.

2 The proportions of this five per cent that are distributed to each club under the solidarity mechanism are as follows. The club that trained the player at age 12–13 gets five per cent of the five per cent. The club that trained the player at age 13–14 also gets five per cent. The club that trained the player at each of age 14–15 through to 22–23 gets 10 per cent.

E2.100 In its attempt to increase transparency and protect smaller clubs critical to the ecosystem of football, FIFA has incorporated the above system for rewarding clubs involved in the training of players. The system is entirely new and appears complicated to operate. The system will take some time to settle into a user-friendly mechanism, but once this is done, the system should prove to be a more efficient method to redistribute income to all clubs contributing to the football family.

(b) Compensation for a player leaving before his contract has expired

E2.101 The compensation fee (which is now the replacement of what was formerly referred to as a transfer fee), is assessed using the criteria used by common law principles for assessing damages, but taking into account the specificity of sport and other objective criteria. These criteria may include the level of remuneration and other benefits under the existing contract and/or the new contract (the latter being relevant as a good indicator of what the player is worth, and also because of the principle that the player should not be allowed to profit from his breach); the length of time remaining on the existing contract (which is up to a maximum of five years under the FIFA Regulations); the amount of any fee or expense paid or incurred by the former club, amortised over the length of the contract; and whether the breach occurs during a 'protected period'[1].

1 It is unclear whether the level of compensation is intended to be greater if the breach has occurred within the 'protected period'. This would have the effect of providing the protection for contracts sought by FIFA. Ultimately the amount of compensation will be dictated by the common law principles of the country in which the 'losing' club is situated. FIFA have merely indicated that this factor is one of the objective criteria to take into account in calculating damages in addition to the amount of damages calculated under general common law principles.

E2.102 Whilst these are the criteria that would be used by the Dispute Resolution Chamber of FIFA's Player's Status Committee to assess the compensation fee payable, there is still a reluctance to use this system because of the uncertainty of the findings of the DRC. Such reluctance is likely to remain until there have been a number of precedent cases by which players and clubs alike may seek guidance from the level of award being made by the DRC. As a result, compensation fees still remain subject to 'out of tribunal' negotiations and agreements between transferor and transferee club. Early indications do not suggest that there has been any change in value of 'compensation fees' (the level of fee still depends almost entirely on market value) and in fact they have retained the popular term 'transfer fees'.

E2.103 Prior to the advent of the FIFA Regulations, the domestic system in England made similar provision in that a compensation fee was payable to a club transferring a player mid-way through the player's contract. In the absence of the transferor and transferee club coming to an agreement as to the amount of transfer fee, the matter could be submitted to arbitration. However, the same uncertainty existed which had resulted in clubs being reluctant to submit to the jurisdiction: largely because there was no way for the transferee club to assess the level of compensation that might be awarded by the arbitration panel (despite the availability of a list of criteria that might be taken into account). The uncertainty and time delay between agreeing the transfer and calculation of the transfer fee have proved to be effective deterrents for clubs from submitting to such arbitration proceedings.

E2.104 Consequently, most (if not all) transfers that go through to completion have done so by the transferor and transferee club agreeing a transfer fee or compensation fee. Time has seen the development of a variety of creative mechanisms for the payment schedule and conditions of the transfer fee, including: staggered payments over the course of one or more seasons; payments conditional upon the transferee club attaining promotion/avoiding relegation/qualifying for European competition; payments conditional upon the performance of the player (for example by reference to the number of goals scored, number of appearances per season, number of clean sheets maintained and so on); and payments which are linked to a percentage of any future transfer fee attained in relation to a player over and above a set figure.

E2.105 Transferor clubs generally seek to maximise the amount of guaranteed payment because there is no risk that the payment may not become payable and also because the more conditional payments there are, the greater the need for administrative policing of the conditions to check when payments are due and ensure that the payments are made. However, conditional payments can be a useful and lucrative tool in relation to developing players (whose value is almost impossible to assess due to the absence of any substantial track record) and also in relation to key players (engaged to help avoid relegation, achieve promotion and so on).

E2.106 Perhaps if decisions of the DRC become more frequent and there is an increase in numbers of clubs submitting cases to the DRC to assess compensation fees, the use of these more creative compensation fee payment agreements will diminish. However, at this stage, there is no indication that this will happen and because of the limited practical difference between the old system and new system and also because of the strength of existing business practice, it is envisaged the current method of negotiating compensation fees will remain largely unaltered. The Regulations and increased transparency of the criteria used for calculating the compensation fee, may have the effect of slowing down the acceleration of compensation fees if clubs threaten submission to the DRC to assessment of the compensation fee. This is unlikely, however, as this has not materialised to date under the domestic system which already made similar provision. The effect has been that either the clubs agree a fee or the transfer remains incomplete: such is the fear of the unknown.

D The role of a player's agent

(a) FIFA Regulations governing Licensed Player Agents

E2.107 These Agent Regulations[1] are based on six key requirements:

(i) A player may only be represented by immediate family (a parent or sibling), a lawyer or a licensed agent[2].

(ii) There must be a written agreement between the licensed agent and the player or club he/she represents[3] setting out the financial terms of representation and confirming that the parties agree to be bound by the Agent Regulations. As a matter of practice, the percentage of commission demanded by player agents ranges from as little as three per cent of the player's gross guaranteed income, to as much as 15 per cent. If the agreement is silent as to the level of remuneration, an agent will be entitled to five per cent of the value of the player's contract negotiated by him/her (if the agent is a player representative). If the agent represents a club, a fixed fee must be agreed at the outset of negotiations.

(iii) Player representation agreements must last for no longer than two years including any automatic right of renewal/extension in favour of the agent.
(iv) An agent must not represent more than one party in any particular contract negotiation and must receive remuneration only from the party whom he/she represents in such negotiation.
(v) All licensed agents must agree to be bound by the Licensed Agent's Code of Conduct and the Agent Regulations upon receiving their licence.
(vi) Licensed agents must provide adequate professional indemnity insurance or deposit a bond of CHF 100,000 with FIFA and pass an entrance examination before they may be awarded a licence[4].

1 The Regulations to govern the conduct of players' agents licensed by FIFA (via national associations affiliated to FIFA) came into force in March 2001. For a discussion of the changes to these regulations forced on FIFA on competition law grounds, see paras B2.182 to B2.186. The licensing system, previously operated by FIFA itself is now operated by the national associations on its behalf.
2 This has always been the requirement, even before the March 2001. It is for players and clubs to ensure that unlicensed agents are not used and FIFA has a penalty system for players and clubs that do use or deal with unlicensed agent. Unlicensed agent here refers to anyone who is not licensed, nor is an immediate family member or lawyer of a player.
3 Despite the threat of sanctions for failure to comply with this regulation, and the emergence of a greater need to show evidence of a mandate in the competitive world of player representation, many agents still choose to have no written agreements with their clients. A standard representation agreement is attached to the Agent Regulations at Annexe C, although it should be noted this agreement is generally regarded as being inadequate on its own, and is usually supplemented by a further agreement with more detailed terms and conditions.
4 Previously agents were obliged to make the bond deposit to be awarded a licence. There was no testing procedure about FIFA regulations or basic contract law as is now the case. There was also no option to provide professional indemnity insurance as an alternative to the bond deposit.

E2.108 Prior to March 2001 agents could obtain one of two licences in relation to player dealings[1]. They could either obtain an international FIFA licence issued and awarded by FIFA direct at a bond cost of CHF 100,000, or a domestic licence issued by the national association in whose jurisdiction the agent intended to practice. This licence came at a bond cost of CHF 50,000. A domestic licence only authorised dealing in domestic negotiations and transfers specific to the national association that had issued the licence.

1 There are also licences available to govern agents who organise matches or tournaments called 'Match Agents'. This section of the chapter relates only to matter concerning players.

(b) Roach

E2.109 Under the Agent Regulations there is now only one type of licence: the international licence. However, this new breed of licences is issued by national associations by virtue of authority delegated by FIFA. If there is any breach of the Agent Regulations it is for the national association to resolve, investigate and impose an appropriate sanction. This has not always been the case as the Football Association ('FA') realised when they attempted to investigate and subsequently discipline players' agent, Dennis Roach. Mr Roach held a FIFA international licence entitling him to acting in domestic and international transfer negotiations. During one such negotiation, Mr Roach negotiated on behalf of the player that the buying club should discharge the player's commission obligation to Mr. Roach. The FA attempted to discipline Mr Roach accordingly for accepting payment from a club in relation to the negotiation of a player's contract on behalf of the player which the FA alleged was contrary to the FA Rules. Mr Roach brought proceedings challenging the FA's jurisdiction to discipline him, on grounds that he was a FIFA licensed agent and not an FA licensed agent and that FIFA regulations did not permit the FA to discipline him for breach of FIFA regulations. The FIFA regulations prohibited a players' agent from acting for two sides in a negotiation, but did not prohibit the player's commission obligation being discharged by the buying club. The FA acceded to judgment after Mr Roach brought a CPR 1998, Pt 8 action against the FA challenging its jurisdiction.

E2.110 The situation in which Mr Roach found himself shows the complexity of the practical issues surrounding the payment of an agent's commission, which is further illustrated by the following hypothetical example. There is an Italian footballer playing under contract with an Italian club. It has been widely speculated in the press, supported by statements of the Italian club, that they might be willing to sell the player for the right price. The player has an agent. The agent is approached by an English football club, to ascertain the status of the player at the Italian club. The agent tells the Italian club that there is potential interest for the transfer of the player. Negotiations begin between the English club and the Italian club. The agent brokers a deal between the two clubs for the transfer of the player. Once the deal has been brokered, the agent negotiates the playing terms and conditions for the player with the buying English club and the termination package to be paid by the Italian club (as the early release was at its instigation). A medical examination is completed successfully by the player, an ITC is obtained from the FIGC (Italian Football Federation) with the consent of the Italian club and forms H1 and G2 together with the playing contract are filed with the English Football Association. The question arises in these circumstances of who pays the agent?

E2.111 The agent in these circumstances could theoretically have been paid by the player or either club. First the agent might take a commission from the clubs for brokerage services in respect of the agreement between the clubs. However, a formal agreement to this effect would be required and such an agreement would be essential to avoid any future suggestion that the buying club had paid the player's agent in respect of the playing contract negotiations.

E2.112 The second, and most straightforward proposition is that the agent is entitled to a commission from the player for representation and negotiation of the player's contract on behalf of the player[1]. As mentioned at para E2.106, in the absence of an agreed fee, the agent will be entitled to five per cent of the player's annual basic gross income under the employment contract in accordance with the provisions of the Agent Regulations.

1 Under Art 12 of FIFA's Players' Agent Regulations, the amount of commission is based on the player's annual basic gross income (excluding other benefits such as a car, flat, point premiums and/or any kind of bonus or privilege) that the player's agent has negotiated for him in the employment contract.

E2.113 The reason why agents should not receive payment from both club and player is that if an agent knows that his commission is to be paid by the transferor club or not at all then there would arise a substantial conflict of interest. It would not be transparently clear that the agent had acted in the player's best interests in accordance with the agent's duty to the player. Furthermore, the club and the agent may find themselves in difficulties with the Inland Revenue and Customs & Excise if the payment by the club to the agent is not invoiced or accounted for properly.

E2.114 If a club is to discharge a player's obligation to pay commission this must be set out in the remuneration schedule of the playing contract as a benefit in kind and reported on Form P11d as a taxable benefit in kind received by the player. Furthermore, the invoice for the commission must be addressed to the player as it was the player who was the beneficiary of the services, not the club. The invoice may be marked as payable by the club, so long as it is made clear that it is addressed to the player. These are additional issues that need to be considered in addition to any sanctioning implications (the player could be fined or his licence revoked) that may be imposed by a national association for breach of the Agent Regulations[1].

1 The practical implication of having the licence revoked would be that the agent would not be able to apply for a further licence for a period of two years (timed by reference to the examination date for the agent's licence).

E2.115 As an alternative and legitimate solution to the issue of agents recovering commissions from players, agents often factor into the signing-on fee or playing contract their commission costs, so that the player does not lose out (in that he gets paid extra to reimburse him for his agent's commission), the club is not seen to be paying the player's agent and the player's agent is not seen to be receiving payment from the club.

(c) The agent's role

E2.116 Whilst it is not obligatory for player or clubs to engage the services of agents, players these days almost without exception engage the services of agents. Players are often approached by agents as soon as they show signs of excellence (this can be from ages of 12 upwards). More commonly, however, agents will nurture a relationship of trust and confidence with potential professional players with a view to entering into a formal representation agreement when the player reaches professional status or approaches professional status.

E2.117 The FIFA licence regulates only the aspects of an agent's activities related to the representation of a player in his playing contract negotiations and in relation to the transfer of a player. In addition to these basic services, agents are increasingly offering other enhanced services ranging from representation in all commercial agreements (eg endorsement and sponsorship, advertising) to assistance and day to day management of all financial (tax and investment), accounting and legal services.

E Checklist – Transfers, Player Contracts and Agent Contracts

(a) Transfers

E2.118 A list of factors which need to be considered when conducting a player transfer is set out below:

- Will an agent be used to broker the deal? If so, the agent should be engaged on formal terms agreeing the nature of the services to be provided and the financial terms for the services.
- Notify the club with whom the player is currently contracted that the transferee club wishes to speak with the player about a transfer.

- Contact the player or his agent regarding the player's desires about transferring.
- Commence negotiations between the transferor and transferee club about a compensation fee.
- Calculate the training and development fee (if any).
- Commence negotiation of the player's personal terms.
- Is an international transfer clearance certificate required? If so, make the application with good time to ensure that the ITC is available as soon as the transferor club grants its consent (this would usually be done at the time the transfer is completed).
- Is a work permit required? If so, prepare the application and check that the player satisfies the basic criteria for a work permit to be granted. If these criteria are not satisfied, prepare for an appeal in order to obtain the work permit.
- Once it appears likely that agreement can be reached on all financial terms as between transferee and transferor club and transferee club and the player, arrange a medical examination of the player. Take care not to enter into a binding agreement before the results of the examination and the application for a work permit have been resolved.
- If the work permit is granted and the medical examination is positive, then prepare all the appropriate contractual and regulatory documentation: transfer of registration form (signed by all parties); transfer agreement (between the transferee and transferor clubs); registration form and playing contract (signed by player and the transferee club).
- Register documentation with the national association of the transferee club.

(b) Player contracts

E2.119 A list of factors which need to be considered when acting on behalf of a player in the negotiation of his contract with the club for which he will be playing, is set out below:

- **What is the signing-on fee to be?**
  This is usually payable by equal annual instalments over the course of the full term of the playing contract and becomes immediately payable in its entirety in the event that the club seeks to transfer the player to another club.
- **What is the weekly salary to be?**
  Usually this is paid in arrears, however, it is possible to negotiate payment in advance, particularly if the player is coming from abroad and needs 'settling in' money. In addition, it may be possible to negotiate payment of salary for that period where the player is training with the club but is waiting for documentation to be executed or the ITC to be issued.
- **Accommodation**
  The agent may wish to consider seeking to negotiate accommodation 'to the reasonable satisfaction of the player' and 'within reasonable distance of the training facilities'.
- **Reimbursement of expenses and relocation costs**
  The reimbursement of expenses and relocation costs can be a significant factor, particularly if the player is coming from abroad[1].
- **Car**
  This benefit could take the form of the provision of a car, or a car allowance. In either case, factors such as running costs, insurance and maintenance need to be negotiated and agreed.

- **Flights**
  Should the player be coming from a location abroad, a club may provide one or two return air tickets per annum as part of his contract. In addition, agents may wish to consider requesting that this include provision for the player's partner and children.
- **Performance bonuses**
  Usually clubs will have standard bonus provisions which cover all those contracted by the club. However, if the player is a striker, for instance, the agent should consider negotiating goal scoring bonuses, or if he is a goalkeeper, bonuses for keeping a 'clean sheet'. Bonuses can also be negotiated based on the performance of the team in competitions, if these are not included in the club's standard bonus scheme. Many clubs are now beginning to structure remuneration so that there is less guaranteed income for the player but greater performance-related income.
- **Bonuses based on future transfer fee attained**
  Often an agent may be able to secure for the player a percentage of a future transfer fee. The application of the new Regulations post-1 September 2001 should not, in principle, prevent an agent from negotiating a similar percentage in respect of compensation fees.
- **Early release provision if a third party club offers a minimum transfer fee**
  This may prevent a club from refusing to transfer a player once an offer of a certain minimum amount has been received by a third party club.
- **Post-termination non-competition restrictions**
  Any such restrictions need to be negotiated and drafted in specific detail to ensure that such provisions would be enforceable if contested.
- **Licence[2] to use the player's 'image rights' and an appropriate fee[3] for such use**
  As a matter of practice, usually only those clubs in the FA Premier League would consider paying a licence fee to the agent in order to secure use of the player's image rights. It has become common amongst the leading players in the Premier League to establish personal service companies, to which they license their image rights, for tax reasons. The use of such image rights are then granted by the service company to the club in a separate commercial agreement. The Inland Revenue has recognised that such a structure is legitimate provided that the player can show that he has a valuable and distinguishable image, that the agreement is a genuine commercial arrangement, and that the level of remuneration paid for the use of such image rights is commensurate to their value[4]. Agents who represent players transferring from abroad may negotiate an agreement between the club and a personal service company registered in an off-shore jurisdiction, preferably one which has a double tax treaty with the UK which reduces the level of withholding tax payable by the club[5].
- **Personal idiosyncrasies**
  Players may have certain other quirky requirements, such as the need to play in a particular shirt number, be served a particular chocolate prior to a match and so on.

1 In the UK, the Inland Revenue currently allows a maximum of £8,000 for this.
2 Some players may agree to a full assignment of all image rights in relation to the player as a member of the club and the player in his personal capacity. See generally para D3.67 et seq.
3 This could include a variation of fixed fees, royalties on a per usage or revenue related basis and/or using a minimum guarantee or other such creative payment mechanism. See para D3.67 et seq.
4 *Sports Club plc v Inspector of Taxes* [2000] STC (SCD) 443, involving the players Dennis Bergkamp and David Platt. See paras D3.90 to D3.107.
5 See further para D3.114 et seq.

(c) Agent Representation Contract

E2.120 The contract between the player and his agent should contain, at the very least, provisions dealing with the matters set out below:

- **The parties to the contract**
  Is it a company agency through whom a FIFA licensed agent is to provide agency services to the player or club, or the individual agent in his personal capacity?
- **Term**
  How long is the representation agreement to last?
- **Territory**
  Is the agent to be the player or club's agent in all territories or only specified territories (for example worldwide, Europe, England, worldwide excluding a particular country or territory)?
- **Exclusivity**
  Can the player or club use another other agent at the same time to provide similar services?[1] An exclusivity provision is made more effective if supported by a positive obligation on the principal to refer all enquiries direct to the agent and to not progress any negotiations covered by the representation agreement on his/its own behalf without the involvement of the agent[2].
- **Services to be provided**
  For example, player contract negotiation only, full commercial and financial management, brokering or negotiating a particular transfer.
- **Commission payable**
  Including all details about payment dates, accounting and invoicing provisions, late payment provisions and variations for different services.
- **Right to use the principal's name in promoting/endorsing the agent**
- **Right of the agent to represent other players**
- **Acknowledgment of the player having taken independent legal advice**
- **Termination provisions**
  Including how and when the contract may be terminated, whether there will be any continuing entitlement to commission for negotiations and contracts concluded prior to termination or contracts concluded post-termination for which negotiations were substantially carried out prior to termination.

1 The industry norm is for such agreements to exclusive to a particular territory and a specified term or specific task – this is to avoid duplication of work, avoiding the situation where two agents seek to be paid giving rise to a dispute as to who should get paid.

2 The FIFA Players' Status Committee have held that even an exclusive representation agreement cannot prevent a player from managing his affairs on his own. However, the Players' Status Committee have also held that an agent may still claim commission even if they have not actively been involved in a transfer, if a clause to this effect is explicitly and unequivocally stipulated in the representation agreement.

6 DISPUTES IN RELATION TO INDIVIDUAL PLAYER TRANSFERS

A Dispute as to remuneration payable by one club to another

E2.121 The transfer of a player from one club to another, whether domestically or internationally, is a matter of contract and the general principles of contract law therefore apply. As mentioned above[1], clubs often come up with creative mechanisms for the payment of a transfer fee. For instance, a club may link part of the remuneration to be paid for the player to the performance of that player over a period of time. This can lead to disputes over whether the player has achieved that performance target or indeed been given a reasonable opportunity to achieve such a target.

1 See para E2.103.

E2.122 In one such case, *Bournemouth and Boscombe Athletic v Manchester United Football Club*[1], Edward MacDougall, a striker, was transferred from Bournemouth and Boscombe Athletic to Manchester United for the sum of £200,000. An amount of £175,000 was paid up-front by the club, and the remaining £25,000 was to be paid when the player had scored 20 goals for Manchester United. Mr O'Farrell was the manager of Manchester United at the time. During the period from October to December 1972, MacDougall did relatively well, scoring four goals in eleven matches. O'Farrell was then dismissed and the new manager, Mr Docherty, dropped the player shortly thereafter. It was clear that the player did not feature in Mr Docherty's plans for the first team going forward, and in fact he let it be known that the player was up for sale. Bournemouth claimed that they were entitled to payment of the £25,000 on the basis that there was an implied term in the contract to the extent that the player would be given a reasonable opportunity to score the 20 goals necessary to trigger the additional payment. The Court of Appeal upheld the judgement of the High Court by a split majority, ruling that there was indeed a breach of an implied term that the player would be given a reasonable opportunity to score the 20 goals, and he had not been provided with that reasonable opportunity.

1 (1980) Times, 22 May, CA.

E2.123 This case raised interesting questions about the degree of discretion a manager would have when his club has entered into a contract containing such a clause. Does this mean that a manager would then be bound to select a player even when the player has lost form? This was dealt with in the dissenting judgment of Lord Justice Brightman in the Court of Appeal[1]:

> It seems to me unlikely to have been the intention, and certainly ought not to be assumed as a matter of necessity to have been the intention, of Manchester United and Bournemouth that the contract between them should interfere in any way with a bona fide exercise of the discretion of the manager of Manchester United … Such an [implied] term, in my view, hampers the manager of Manchester United in the exercise of his judgement in a manner that cannot have been contemplated by the parties.

However, as Lord Justice Donaldson pointed out in his judgment as part of the majority judgment[2], the obligation under the implied term is to provide the player with a *reasonable* opportunity:

> If it is clear that he has lost his form and is not going to recover it, there is no obligation to play him at all. What is required is a reasonable opportunity, and it is not reasonable for him to expect to be played or for Bournemouth to expect him to be played if he has wholly lost his form through no fault of Manchester United.

The Court of Appeal ruled that, in the circumstances, the player had not lost form, but did not fit into the plans of the new manager, and thus the reasonable opportunity had not been provided. This decision would appear to have important implications for a new manager who discards a player who is the subject of such a contractual clause, simply because that player does not fit into the new manager's plans.

1 (1980) Times, 22 May at p 11H, CA.
2 (1980) Times, 22 May at p 9D, CA.

E2.124 *Celtic v UEFA*[1], which was adjudicated before the Court of Arbitration for Sport ('CAS') in Switzerland, provides a useful indication of the adjudication process before the governing bodies in football, as well as dealing with the question of compensation for a player out of contract. Celtic, a club in the Scottish Premier League, had contracted with a player until 1 July 1996. On 27 June 1996, the player entered into a playing contract with Monaco, with effect from 1 July 1996. Monaco is affiliated to the French Football Federation ('FFF'), as the Principality of Monaco has no national association of its own. Celtic claimed that they were entitled to compensation for training and/or development of the player on the basis of Art 14 of the FIFA Regulations governing the Status and Transfer of Football Players. The matter was referred to UEFA, the governing body of European football. UEFA considered that it was not competent to take a decision on the question of Celtic's entitlement to compensation for training and/or development of the player, only on the question of the amount of such compensation. As there were no regulations of the confederation dealing with the question of entitlement to compensation, the matter was referred to FIFA's Player Status Committee. FIFA's Player Status Committee ruled that, in light of the *Bosman* ruling[2], Monaco was not bound to pay any compensation to Celtic, as both clubs were bound by the EC Court ruling in this regard (Monaco being affiliated to the FFF, which was in EU territory. Celtic submitted the matter to arbitration before CAS in accordance with the UEFA Statutes, arguing that UEFA had erred in referring the matter to FIFA and that the matter should have been adjudicated upon by UEFA's Board of Experts in accordance with the UEFA Statutes. CAS ruled that UEFA had acted correctly, as the confederation had not exercised its option to draw up its own rules to settle differences as to the question of entitlement of compensation, only in respect of the question of the amount of compensation. CAS also upheld the decision by FIFA, to the extent that Celtic was not entitled to compensation for training and/or compensation for the player, as the matter was governed by the *Bosman* ruling in that the player's contract had expired, the player was a citizen of the EU, and the player was transferring from one EU country to another (the player had still had the status of a worker employed in the territory of the EU, even though he was employed by Monaco).

1 CAS 98/201, *Digest of CAS Awards II 1998–2000* (2002, Kluwer), pp 1 and 6.
2 Described in paras E2.40 to E2.50.

B Enforcement of a contract with a minor

E2.125 In *Aylesbury Football Club v Watford*[1], the High Court was asked to rule on the enforceability of a contract concluded between a 17 year old footballer, Lee Cook, and Aylesbury. Aylesbury instituted a claim for damages against Watford on the basis that Watford had induced Lee to break his contract with Aylesbury and sign for Watford. The claim against Watford failed because Aylesbury's contract with Lee, who was a minor, was unenforceable in any event and therefore Watford could not have procured its breach. The court held that, apart from breaching the rules of the Football Association[2], the contract was not to the player's benefit in that it contained unduly onerous terms and the payment of wages depended on the will of the Aylesbury. Whilst the facts of this case were fairly unusual, it is an indication to clubs that the courts will be quick to come to the aid of a minor when entering into an ostensibly prejudicial contract with a club.

1 (12 June 2000, unreported), Poole J (ref 00/TLQ/873).
2 Under r 18 of the Football Association Rules, Aylesbury had failed to specify the emoluments in the contract, and had also failed to register the contract with the Football Association, in effect preventing him from playing under the contract.

C Identity, quality and fitness of a player

E2.126 In general, football clubs are fairly cautious when entering into contracts to purchase a player, not least because of the costs that may be involved in such a purchase. Clubs will employ scouts to identify and watch certain players, will invite players to undertake trials at the club, and, ultimately, arrange for players to undergo medical and fitness tests prior to the conclusion of contract for the transfer of a player. Nothwithstanding this, cases have arisen where the buying club purchases a player only to find that the quality and characteristics of the asset that they have bought is different to that expected by the club. Clubs appear on occasion to be prepared to base their decisions on anecdotal information of dubious value: a Premiership club reputedly bought a player whom it believed to be the cousin of the Liberian international George Weah, only to find out that he was not and that he was not as good a player as they expected. Where however there has been a genuine and material breach of an express term, or representation, as to the identity or quality of a player there might be an argument on which the buying club could seek to get out of the contract. The difficulty is in proving such a term or representation. The fact that clubs will normally want to satisfy themselves as to the quality of a player means that it is very difficult to show that they have relied on any representation as to quality, or that it is included as an implied term. In a case which came before the Scottish Courts[1], Dundee United terminated a playing contract of a player on the basis that the player had induced the club to enter into the contract by making a material pre-contractual misrepresentation as to the condition of his knee, and also on the basis that the player was in serious breach of the terms of the contract by continuing to misrepresent the condition of his knee. Prior to entering into the contract on 8 August 1996, the Club had the player medically examined by the club doctor and club physiotherapist, as is the normal course. The Club's case was that, when asked during the examination about his right knee, the player said he had had no problem with or medical treatment to his right knee. The player maintained he disclosed that he had received one injection to his right knee during the medical examination. In October 1996 the player sustained an injury to his right knee and in December of that year the player was forced to stop training and playing as a result. Following an internal investigation by the Club, the Club terminated the contract on the basis of the reasons stated above. The player appealed to the Scottish Football League Appeals Committee in this case, and was successful in his appeal[2]. However, players should be aware of the consequences of failing to disclose what may later be regarded as conditions material to their ability to play football. A material misrepresentation by omission which induced the Club to enter into the contract would enable the Club to lawfully terminate that contract.

1 *Dundee United Football Co Ltd v Scottish Football Association* 1998 SLT 1244, OH.
2 Dundee United later appealed against this decision to the Scottish Football Association Appeals Committee, on the basis that no reasons had been given for the finding by the Scottish Football League Appeals Committee. This appeal was dismissed by Lord Bonomy in the Outer House for the reason that the League Appeals Committee had been represented at the Association Appeals Committee hearing in order to provide an additional explanation of its decision as might be required by the Association.

E2.127 Further, it will probably not be possible for a club to argue that it relied on a representation, or that an implied term arises, that a player is, or will remain, fit. Article 30 of the FIFA Rules governing the Status and Transfer of Players makes it clear that the validity of a transfer contract or indeed a player's contract between a player and a club cannot be made conditional upon the results of a medical test or upon the acquisition of a work permit. This reflects the belief that it should be up to a club to satisfy itself of a player's fitness, before entering into a binding contract, and that players should not be left exposed.

E2.128 Nothwithstanding, it is clear that the nature of negotiations in practice often puts clubs in a position where an agreement in principle has been reached between them and there is a desire to regularise that in some sort of document immediately, subject to the player agreeing terms. This has often led to the situation where clubs have entered into forms of agreements which they have purported to make subject to medical examination or the obtaining of a work visa, as well as the player agreeing terms. On some occasions, the player may even have agreed terms. This practice may pose a substantial problem for the transferee club if the player fails the medical. Under Art 30 of the FIFA Regulations, the condition is invalid. If an agreement which was otherwise binding was entered into, the transferee may find itself having acquired a broken down player, with no recourse.

E2.129 Faced with this situation, a club must argue, first, that no binding agreement for the purposes of Art 30 was entered into. This will depend upon an analysis of what actually happened and how the document is expressed, and what effect that has under the applicable law. Obviously if the final transfer agreement and player contracts have been entered into and contain the condition, there is not much room for this argument. In practice however the form of document entered into in advance of the medical tends to be in shorter form and the intention is generally to sign a formal transfer agreement afterwards. The problem here is that although the intention might have been to enter into a further agreement subsequently, the earlier document may be a binding agreement in itself. Care must be taken to ensure that it is not. The other side of the coin however, is obviously that often clubs want the earlier agreement to be binding, because they want more security than the parties having simply recorded the terms on which they will be prepared to enter into an agreement in the future. At this level, the issue becomes one of which adverse risk the club wants to take: the player turning out to be unfit, or the deal disappearing.

E2.130 The second approach is to ensure that there is some other mechanism of cancelling the earlier agreement other than one of those impugned under Art 30. This could be contained in a simple clause giving the buying club an absolute discretion to cancel. Consideration should also be given to arguments based on frustration, total failure of consideration and impossibility of performance. If a player cannot enter a country it is difficult to see how at least the intention behind the contract is achieved. The difficulty is that the essence of the transfer contract is the consent to the release of the registration and agreement as to the compensation for the selling club for no longer having the player. Furthermore, such arguments are likely to find more favour before a domestic court than before the Players' Status Committee.

E2.131 Thirdly, as a matter of domestic contract law, it is not entirely clear that Art 30 operates to defeat an otherwise validly agreed condition. As a matter of English law, it is arguable that while clubs might be in breach of FIFA Regulations by introducing a particular condition, that does not alter the fact or content of the contract itself. In *Barry Silkman v Colchester United Football Club*[1], an agent sued for his fees. The club sought to rely on the FIFA Regulations which supposedly precluded payment by the club to the agent in the particular circumstances. Morland J held that whilst the agreement between club and agent might be in breach of the FIFA regulations, such an agreement was not thereby unlawful or unenforceable as a matter of English law. This situation is different to the situation where two clubs depart from the rules, but it nevertheless raises the possibility of an argument that the condition making a transfer or playing contract subject to a medical test might indeed be enforceable before an English court. The difficulty is that the Players' Status Committee, in contrast to the courts, will not hesitate to apply Art 30 in any dispute that comes before it.

1 (15 June 2001, unreported), Morland J.

E2.132 It should also be borne in mind that if a transfer does not go through because of a failed fitness test, but for the reasons given above there was nevertheless a binding agreement which has been breached, the loss suffered by the selling club may actually be significant. If a price was negotiated which was a price for a fit player, the loss will be the difference between that price and the price that can subsequently be obtained for an unfit player.

E2.133 The lesson for purchasing clubs is undoubtedly to ensure that a binding transfer contract and playing contract are only signed and concluded once the player has passed the medical test and obtained the work permit, where necessary. Where fitness is in doubt, there may be other approaches that can be taken to the structure of the deal to protect the purchasing club. For instance, the purchasing club may seek to pay the amount of compensation based on the number of appearances by the player on the field for the purchasing club. This occurred in the case of Paul Gascoigne when transferring to Everton from Middlesbrough, where Middlesbrough received an amount per game played by Gascoigne, up to an agreed maximum amount.

D Identity of the Selling Club

E2.134 Despite the due diligence conducted by buying clubs when seeking to buy a player, in the rush to complete a transfer deal mistakes can be made with regard to issues as fundamental as the identity of the selling club. This is particularly the case where the selling club is in a foreign jurisdiction and negotiations are conducted through agents and interpreters. This is evident from the case of *Sunderland Association Football Club v Uruguay Montevideo FC*[1], which came before the High Court in April 2001. The dispute involved the transfer of the Honduran international Milton Nunez from a club in Uruguay to Sunderland. Under the agreement, the transfer fee was to be split into three payments: a sum of money was due to be paid within seven days of the registration, a further sum after six months, and a final fee after twelve months. The second and the final payments were the subject of a bank guarantee in favour of the first defendant, Uruguay Montevideo

FC. The claimant, Sunderland, had obtained an interim injunction without notice preventing the first defendant from calling on the bank to perform their guarantee in its favour in the sum of US $500,000, on the basis that Sunderland had a seriously arguable case that it had been deliberately misled by the club and the agent of the player into believing that it was acquiring a player whose registration was owned by top Uruguayan club Nacional which played in Montevideo, when in fact it was owned by the third division amateur Uruguayan club known as Uruguay Montevideo FC. Sunderland's position was that it would not have bought the player had it known the true position. The player had originally played for Nacional, and had been on loan to Greek club FC Paok, but through an arrangement unknown to Sunderland the player's registration came back to Uruguay Montevideo FC. The defendants sought to discharge the injunction in the High Court, the claimant to maintain it. Because the payment was through a guaranteed banking arrangement, Sunderland had to establish a seriously arguable case of fraud.

1 [2001] 2 All ER (Comm) 828.

E2.135 Sunderland was unable to show that there was a seriously arguable case of fraud and the injunction was dismissed. Mr Justice Blofeld held that a genuine misunderstanding had arisen between Sunderland's agent and the agent of the player, who also appeared to act for the selling club, because of linguistic difficulties. Sunderland mistakenly considered 'Uruguay Montevideo FC' to be the formal name of the club known as Nacional, but it had not been deliberately led into that belief. Consequently the guaranteed payment was made. Sunderland amended, and continued the action on the basis of innocent misrepresentation and mistake, to recover the payments made. The matter was settled before trial.

E2.136 The case is another salutary warning that buying clubs must take great care to satisfy themselves of all the facts in advance of concluding a binding agreement.

E Disputes between clubs over approaches

E2.137 Under Section J of the Premier League Rules, a club may not, except in limited circumstances, approach a player registered with another club without the prior written consent of that club. A major issue for clubs is the unauthorised approaches made by other clubs to players still under contract. Many of these matters are resolved by arbitration before an FA panel; however on occasion an action is brought against a club for seeking to induce a breach of contract.

E2.138 In a recent case, Liverpool FC and the German international Christian Ziege were fined £20,000 and £10,000 respectively in a Premier League disciplinary hearing after Middlesbrough FC had issued a complaint to the Premier League over an alleged illegal approach by Liverpool in respect of the player. Liverpool's illegal approach allowed them to discover and activate a clause in Ziege's contract allowing him to leave Middlesbrough for a sum of £5.5m. Rangers and Chelsea had each offered Middlesbrough £7.5m for the player, and, in the absence of knowledge of the relevant clause in the player's contract, Liverpool may well have offered more than £5.5m. Middlesbrough subsequently filed proceedings against Liverpool claiming an amount of £2m, based on the argument that if Liverpool had not known of the activation clause, they would have been forced to pay the market value of the player, which was alleged to be £7.5m. Middlesbrough also claimed an amount of approximately £4.5m based on loss of income

Middlesbrough would have received had the player been playing for the club during the 2000/2001 season. The loss of income was alleged to include loss of merit award (for league placing in the Premiership), loss of gate receipts, loss of profits from ancillary sales (presumably, at the ground), and loss of television facility. Liverpool applied to strike out the claim on the ground that there was no real prospect of succeeding in the allegations of loss and damage, and successfully appealed the Master's dismissal of that application to Astill J[1]. Mr Justice Astill found that in respect of both the claim for £2m, and the claim for approximately £4.5m, Middlesbrough had no real prospect of success in proving the loss claimed. Mr Justice Astill's reasons were, in respect of the claim for £2m, that the Chief Executive Officer of Liverpool had stated that the club would not have paid more than £5.5m for the player in any event. In addition to that, the player, having been sold to Liverpool for £5.5m, was later sold to Tottenham Hotspur Football Club for £4.5m. Mr Justice Astill held there was no market value for the player at that time, considering the player's own statement that he would have joined no other club besides Liverpool. In addition, in what is perhaps a warning to clubs including 'on-sale' clauses in player contracts, Mr Justice Astill held that:

> By its own hand, [Middlesbrough] had removed itself from the negotiating process by agreeing to the inclusion of clause f7 in Mr Ziege's contract.

Mr Justice Astill dismissed as speculative the claim for approximately £4.5m. His comments in this regard raised the difficulties in establishing the exact loss to a club in monetary terms when a key player is not playing. It is doubtful whether a court would ever award damages for loss of league positioning, gate receipts, television coverage, and profits from the sale of food because a key player is not playing. Whilst no doubt a blow to the club, establishing causation (that the loss would not have occurred but for the unavailability of the player) and quantum will always be difficult in these circumstances. Unfortunately, the small amount of the fine imposed by the FA Disciplinary Hearing on Liverpool in this matter, hardly acts as a deterrent to the larger clubs in the Premiership, who can afford to run the risk of the imposition of a small fine in return for what could be great financial gain. The illegal approach by Liverpool in this matter could cynically be viewed as a good business decision on behalf of Liverpool. Unless the Football Association intervenes more regularly in this area, and imposes higher sanctions for breach of the Premier League Rules, the financially weaker clubs will remain vulnerable to predatory tactics from the larger, wealthier clubs.

1 *Liverpool Football Club and Athletic Grounds plc v Middlesbrough Football and Athletic Grounds plc* Queens Bench, 2002/PTA/0186. Judgment delivered on 21 May 2002.

E2.139 In *Crystal Palace v Bruce*[1] the High Court were also asked to rule recently on what was alleged to be an approach in respect of a club manager, namely former footballer Steve Bruce. Bruce had been appointed as manager of Crystal Palace. Shortly after his appointment, he discovered the manager's position at Birmingham City had become available (on Crystal Palace's case because he had been approached) and he wanted to leave. Crystal Palace would not let him talk to Birmingham and he resigned, claiming that the club had repudiated his contract (for various reasons). Crystal Palace alleged that his resignation was in breach of his employment contract but refused to accept his resignation, and sought an injunction enforcing his contract of employment, more particularly a nine-month 'garden leave' provision, in terms of which Bruce would still be paid by the club but would not be required to attend at his place of work nor be entitled to contract with another employer. This was a somewhat unusual case, in that traditionally courts have been reluctant to grant specific performance of an employment contract, in effect forcing employer and employee to continue working together. However, in this case it was contended that Crystal Palace might well have been prejudiced had Bruce been allowed to join Birmingham City, on the basis that staff and players might simply follow Bruce to Birmingham, he had confidential information on players and other matters, and was going to a direct promotion rival. Despite undertakings given by Bruce not to approach fellow management staff or players, Mr Justice Burton granted the injunction which effectively enforced the 'garden leave' provision. The matter did not proceed to trial, however, as it was settled between the parties at a stage after the two clubs had played each other and once Birmingham City's former manager Trevor Francis had been appointed manager of Crystal Palace and adequate compensation had been agreed between the two clubs[2].

1 *Crystal Palace v Steve Bruce* (22 November 2001, unreported), Burton J, [2002] 2 ISLR SLR–81 to 87.

2 See de la Mare 'Legal eagles: the Crystal Palace case' [2002] 2 ISLR 16. See also para E1.71.

E2.140 Apart from the two cases cited above, there has been no other court litigation over the so-called 'tapping up' of players or managers. This is because, notwithstanding the Premier League rule prohibiting this conduct, it is very much part of an ongoing practice amongst clubs and their agents and scouts, and also very difficult for the governing bodies to police.

F Resolution of Transfer Disputes

E2.141 In general, disputes between clubs will be settled by arbitration. The rules of the Premier League, Football Association, Football League, UEFA and FIFA all provide for the settlement of disputes by arbitration[1]. However, in circumstances where urgent relief is required claimants still turn to the court. This can be seen in the Sunderland case, for instance, where Sunderland sought an injunction to prevent Montevideo from calling up a guarantee given by a bank[2].

1 See paras A5.40 to A5.68.

2 See para E2.133.

E2.142 In matters involving a dispute between a player and a club, the Football League rules provide for the convening of a Football League Panel prior to arbitration. Whilst this ensures that many disputes are settled before going to arbitration, the Panel hearings, along with the arbitration procedure, can take several weeks. The effect is that players who seek urgent relief in respect of a dispute with their club are often forced to go via the courts to obtain such urgent relief. Provided that the applicant can show all the legal requirements for obtaining such urgent relief, courts have generally been prepared to hear these disputes, notwithstanding the provisions in the Football League Rules dealing with dispute resolution.

E2.143 The question of jurisdiction can be a complicated one in the event of disputes between clubs located in different countries. It would therefore be prudent for clubs to ensure that a governing law clause is included in transfer contracts, as well as a clause conferring exclusive jurisdiction on the English courts, if they are located in England.

CHAPTER E3

DISCRIMINATION

Dinah Rose (Blackstone Chambers) and **Claire Weir** (Blackstone Chambers)

Contents

1 INTRODUCTION TO THE LEGAL FRAMEWORK

E3.1 'Discrimination', in its positive sense, is at the heart of competitive sport, since the whole purpose of competition is to single out and reward the fastest, strongest and most skilful players. In order to achieve that object, it is essential that unfair discrimination, in its negative sense, should be eliminated. In one of the great clichés of discrimination law, there must be a level playing field.

E3.2 The right to equal treatment without unjustified discrimination is recognised in national and EU law, and under a range of international human rights instruments[1]. In general, professional sportsmen and women have the same rights to equal treatment as other workers, with some limited, specific exceptions, while those involved in amateur sport may be protected against discrimination as consumers of publicly-available facilities and services. This chapter is not intended as a comprehensive survey of discrimination law, but, rather, is concerned with the impact of discrimination law on both amateur and professional sport.

1 See, for example, European Convention on Human Rights, Art 14; International Covenant on Civil and Political Rights 1966, Arts 2, 3 and 26; International Convention on the Elimination of All Forms of Racial Discrimination 1966; Convention on the Elimination of all Forms of Discrimination Against Women 1979; Declaration on the Elimination of All Forms of Intolerance and of Discrimination Based on Religion or Belief, 1981.

A Common law

E3.3 Since the 1960s, the United Kingdom has developed an elaborate statutory framework for the prohibition of discrimination on the grounds of sex, race and disability, and (in Northern Ireland) religion. Discrimination claims are now almost invariably based on statute. Before the enactment of these statutes, however, courts had already recognised that arbitrary discrimination might be an unlawful restraint of trade, and contrary to public policy as a matter of common law. Thus, in *Nagle v Fielden*[1] the Court of Appeal refused, on this ground, to strike out an action brought by a woman who was refused a racehorse trainer's licence because of her sex. This principle might still be of relevance in a situation not covered by the existing discrimination legislation in the UK, such as an arbitrary refusal to grant a licence on the ground of age, or sexual orientation[2].

1 [1966] 2 QB 633.
2 Although, depending on the status of the licensing body, this situation might now be covered by Art 14 and Protocol 1, Art 1 of the European Convention on Human Rights, enacted in the UK by the Human Rights Act 1998, with effect from 2 October 2000: see further paras A4.70, A4.71, E3.6 and E3.7. The principle of equality has been described as a general axiom of rational behaviour: *Matadeen v Pointu* [1999] 1 AC 98 at 109B.

E3.4 Discrimination in the operation of a contract or a rule potentially in restraint of trade would also be a factor in assessing the reasonableness of the restraint[1].

1 For the general principles of restraint of trade and their application in the sports sector, see para A3.135 et seq.

B The statutory framework

(a) *The anti-discrimination legislation*

E3.5 The main anti-discrimination legislation in Great Britain comprises the Equal Pay Act 1970 ('EqPA 1970'), the Sex Discrimination Act 1975 ('SDA 1975'), the Race Relations Act 1976 ('RRA 1976') and the Disability Discrimination Act 1995 ('DDA 1995')[1]. The structure of this legislation is considered in more detail below[2].

1 In Northern Ireland the Fair Employment and Treatment (Northern Ireland) Order 1998 additionally prohibits discrimination on the ground of religious belief or political opinion. Treatment of this legislation is outside the scope of this work.
2 See para E3.16 et seq.

(b) *The Human Rights Act 1998*

E3.6 The Human Rights Act 1998 ('HRA 1998') incorporated the European Convention for the Protection of Human Rights and Fundamental Freedoms ('the Convention') into UK law with effect from 2 October 2000. The operation of the HRA 1998 and the Convention in the sports sector is considered in more detail in Chapter A5.

E3.7 Article 14 of the Convention prohibits discrimination in the enjoyment of the other rights secured by the Convention on any ground, including sex, race, colour, language, religion, political or other opinion, national or social origin, association with a national minority, property, birth 'or other status'[1]. It is important to note that Art 14 is not a free-standing prohibition on discrimination; discrimination is prohibited only in relation to the exercise of rights conferred by other articles of the Convention. An individual seeking to rely on Art 14 must therefore show that the treatment of which he complains falls within the ambit of a substantive Convention right[2]. The HRA 1998 is also restricted in scope, in that it only prohibits acts of 'public authorities' that are incompatible with the Convention[3]. Conduct such as a refusal of a licence on the ground of sexual orientation, or on some other prohibited ground, would be likely to engage Art 14 , in conjunction with the property rights protected by Art 1 of the First Protocol to the Convention, or with Art 8, which guarantees the right to respect for private and family life. In such a case, the body that had committed the act of discrimination would be required to demonstrate that the discrimination was objectively justified[4].

1 See further paras A4.70 and A4.71.
2 See for example, *Inze v Austria* (1987) 10 EHRR 394; *Botta v Italy* (1998) 26 EHRR 241, para 39 and 40.
3 As defined in s 6(3) of the HRA 1998. See further paras A4.14 to A4.27.
4 See further para A4.71.

C EC Law

(a) Treaty articles

E3.8 Article 12 of the EC Treaty prohibits discrimination on the ground of nationality in areas covered by the Treaty[1]. Article 13 of the EC Treaty is a free-standing article which enables the Community, within the areas covered by the Treaty, to adopt measures to combat discrimination on the grounds of sex, racial or ethnic origin, religion or belief, disability, age or sexual orientation.

1 See, in a sporting context, Case 36/74 *Walrave and Koch* [1974] ECR 1405 (discriminatory rules relating to the nationality of pacemakers in cycling contests held to be incompatible with the precursor provision to Art 12, and with the free movement provisions).

E3.9 The rights to individual freedom of movement under EC law[1] also comprise an entitlement not to be discriminated against on the ground of nationality in the exercise of those rights[2]. The *Bosman*[3] case was partly concerned with a discriminatory rule restricting the number of professional players from other member states who could be fielded by football clubs. The prohibition against discrimination only applies, however, to economic activities within the ambit of the EC Treaty, and not to matters, rules or events of an exclusively sporting nature[4]. In *Edwards v British Athletic Federation and International Amateur Athletic Federation*[5], for example, it was held that disparate sanctions as between member states in relation to drug-taking could not be challenged under EC law since the rules were of purely sporting significance[6].

1 See generally Chapter B3.
2 See, for example, Arts 39(2) and 54 of the EC Treaty.
3 *Union Royale Belge des Sociétés de Football Association ASBL v Jean-Marc Bosman* [1995] ECR I-4921.

4 See for example, *Walrave and Koch v Association Union Cycliste Internationale* [1974] ECR 1405 (above, para E3.8); *Donà v Mantero* [1976] ECR 1333 (Italian Football Federation affiliation limited to Italian nationals); *Lehtonen and Castors Canada Dry Namur-Braine ASBL v Fédération Royale Belge des Sociétés de Basketball* [2000] ECR I-2681 (rules preventing fielding of basketball players transferred from other member states after a particular date in breach of Treaty unless capable of objective justification on sporting grounds).

5 [1997] Eu LR 721. See also *Wilander and Novacek v Tobin and Jude (ITF)* [1997] 2 CMLR 346, CA.

6 For further discussion of the 'sporting exception' to EC law, see paras B2.56 to B2.61.

E3.10 Article 141 of the EC Treaty guarantees the right to equal pay for equal work or work of equal value, and includes both cash payments and payments in kind. Article 141 is directly effective in English law and has informed the development of much of the SDA and EqPA case law.

(b) Directives

E3.11 Several directives prohibiting discrimination have been adopted pursuant to the EC Treaty. The main directives are the following.

E3.12 The Equal Pay and Equal Treatment Directives Council Directive 75/117/EEC ('the Equal Pay Directive') and Council Directive 76/207/EEC ('the Equal Treatment Directive') are directly effective in English law. The Equal Pay Directive requires member states to eliminate discrimination on the ground of sex with regard to all aspects and conditions of remuneration where men and woman are performing the same work or work of equal value. The Equal Treatment Directive requires member states to ensure equal treatment for men and women in relation to access to employment, promotion, vocational training and working conditions.

E3.13 An amended Equal Treatment Directive was adopted by the European Council and Parliament on 18 April 2002. The amended Directive, which will come into force in 2005, prohibits harassment on the ground of sex. Sexual harassment is defined for the first time as a matter of European law, reflecting the same approach as much of the existing English case law. Indirect and direct discrimination are also defined, again in line with existing English law. The amended Directive also requires employers to take 'preventive measures' against discrimination.

E3.14 The Race Directive Directive 2000/43/EC ('the Race Directive') was introduced under the auspices of Art 13 of the EC Treaty[1]. It requires member states to ensure equal treatment on the ground of race or ethnic origin (but not nationality) in the fields of employment, vocational training and access to publicly available goods and services, amongst other things. Member states are required to implement the Directive by 8 August 2004.

1 See para E3.8.

E3.15 The Framework Directive Directive 2000/78/EC ('the Framework Directive') was also passed pursuant to Art 13 of the EC Treaty. It requires member states to take measures to outlaw discrimination in employment, promotion, access to vocational training and working conditions on the grounds of religious belief, disability, age and sexual orientation. The United Kingdom is required to implement the Directive in so far as it relates to religion and sexual orientation by 2 December 2003, and insofar as it relates to disability and age, by 2 December 2006.

2 WHAT IS DISCRIMINATION – THE STRUCTURE OF THE LEGISLATION

E3.16 As mentioned above[1], the prohibition of discrimination in England and Wales is largely achieved by four main statutes: the Sex Discrimination Act 1975, the Race Relations Act 1976, the Disability Discrimination Act 1995 and the Equal Pay Act 1970.

1 At para E3.5.

E3.17 In the employment field, sex discrimination in relation to pay and other contractual benefits falls within the remit of the EqPA 1970. Sex discrimination in relation to non-contractual matters falls within the scope of the SDA 1975.

E3.18 The structure and wording of the SDA 1975 and the RRA 1976 are similar in many respects. Pt I of both Acts defines 'discrimination'. Parts II and III of the Acts define the circumstances in which discrimination is unlawful. Part II is concerned with discrimination in the employment field, and Pt III with discrimination in other fields, such as the supply of goods, facilities and services to the public. In order for an act to be challenged as unlawful under the SDA 1975 or RRA 1976, it must be shown to constitute discrimination, as defined by Pt I of the relevant Act, and to fall within the scope of the provisions of Pt II or Pt III of the Acts. Part IV sets out ways, other than personal liability for a direct act of discrimination, in which individuals and bodies can be liable under the Acts. Part V contains exceptions from the Acts. Part VIII contains the enforcement provisions.

E3.19 The structure and provisions of the DDA 1995 are significantly different from the SDA 1975 and RRA 1976. Parts II and III set out the circumstances in which discrimination is unlawful, but 'discrimination' is defined at various places throughout the Act. Part VII contains further provisions about liability. Enforcement is contained in Pts II and III and Sch 3.

A The SDA 1975 and RRA 1976

(a) 'Discrimination'

E3.20 There are three main forms of discrimination under the SDA 1975 and the RRA 1976:

(i) direct discrimination;
(ii) indirect discrimination; and
(iii) discrimination by way of victimisation[1].

1 Consideration of the detail of the domestic discrimination legislation is outside the scope of this work. For fuller consideration, see *Halsbury's Laws of England*, Vol 13, Discrimination (4th edn reissue), paras 301–558; *Harvey on Industrial Relations and Employment Law* (Butterworths), Division L – 'Equal Opportunities'.

E3.21 Direct discrimination Direct discrimination occurs where a person is treated less favourably, on a prohibited ground, than a comparable person[1] is, or would be, treated[2]. For example, it would be directly discriminatory to refuse to consider granting a professional boxing licence to a woman on the grounds of her sex. The question is whether sex is the reason or a principal reason for the treatment in question. The benign motives of a discriminator do not preclude a finding of discrimination[3]. Direct discrimination within the circumstances identified at Pts II and III of the SDA 1975 and RRA 1976 is unlawful save where expressly permitted by a statutory defence. By contrast with the position under the HRA 1998, and the position in relation to indirect sex and race discrimination, there is no general defence of justification for direct race or sex discrimination.

1 See s 5(3) of the SDA 1975; and s 3(4) of the RRA 1976. See *Ice Hockey Super League v Henry* (11 July 1999, unreported), EAT, decision of 2 March 2001 (Canadian hockey player with UK ancestry could not compare himself with non-EU/EEA players, since they required a work permit and he did not, a materially different circumstance).
2 See s 1(1)(a) of the SDA 1975; and s 1(1)(a) of the RRA 1976.
3 See for example, *Birmingham City Council v Equal Opportunities Commission* [1989] AC 1155 at para 30, HL, applied in *James v Eastleigh Borough Council* [1990] ICR 554, HL.

E3.22 *Harassment* Direct discrimination includes racial and sexual harassment and abuse. In *Hussaney v Chester City Football Club and Ratcliffe*[1] a member of the club's youth squad, informed by his friends that the club's manager had called him a 'black cunt', successfully claimed that the club and the manager were guilty of unlawful race discrimination[2].

1 EAT 203/98, unreported, decision of 15 January 2001 (EAT).
2 Mr Hussaney was awarded £2,500 compensation. See also a pending action brought against the San Francisco Giants by baseball players from the Dominican Republic alleging they had been sexually harassed by the Giants' Latin American scout.

E3.23 An employer who fails to take adequate steps to protect his employees from harassment emanating from third parties with whom the employee comes into contact at work may also be liable under the SDA 1975 and RRA 1976[1]. This principle operates where, by the application of good employment practices, the employer could have prevented the harassment or reduced its extent. This principle might apply in the context of the racial abuse of players by spectators or members of opposing teams, at least where the players' club was aware of the problem and had failed to take steps to mitigate it[2]. It would be prudent for a club that is aware of a problem of racist abuse to do all it reasonably can to discourage it, for example, by reiterating in match programmes its commitment to the CRE's 'Let Kick Racism out of Football' Campaign, or by evicting from the ground any spectator caught using racist language, having signalled its prior intention to do so in match programmes[3].

1 *Burton and Rhule v De Vere Hotels* [1996] IRLR 596, EAT: see para E3.40.
2 See for example, *Tamanivalu v Western Australian Rugby Union* [1994] HREOCA 25, decision of Australian Human Rights and Equality Commission of 29 August 1994 (racist abuse by spectators and opposition players not something for which a rugby union player's club was liable in the absence of evidence demonstrating that the club was aware that there was a particular problem with racist abuse that the club had done nothing about). Cf the case of Tony Bowry, a black batsman for Lightcliffe Club, who was subjected to racist abuse by an opposing player during a league match. When his captain complained to the umpire, the umpire refused to take any disciplinary action, and the captain was disciplined by Bradford Cricket League. The League subsequently pledged to apologise to Mr Bowry for its failure to take effective action and also pledged to ensure he received an apology from the umpire.
3 It is an offence pursuant to s 3 of the Football Offences Act 1991 to take part in indecent or racist chanting at certain football matches. See para A1.65.

E3.24 Indirect discrimination Direct discrimination is concerned with the less favourable treatment of comparable people, on prohibited grounds. Indirect discrimination addresses treatment that is formally equal, but that has an unequal effect on members of particular groups. It occurs where a requirement or condition is applied equally to individuals of different sexes or racial groups, but operates in such a way that a substantially smaller proportion of women (or men) or members of a particular racial group are able to comply with it, and the complainant suffers a detriment because he or she is unable to comply[1]. Indirect discrimination is lawful if the application of the requirement or condition in question is shown by the discriminator to be objectively justified. The discriminator must show that there is a reasonable relationship of proportionality between the requirement and the aim sought to be achieved by it, which must itself be untainted by discrimination[2]. For example, a requirement that those who wish to join a particular sporting team must reach minimum height or strength thresholds could be indirectly discriminatory on the grounds of sex (or, potentially, race). Such a requirement is, however, very likely to be justified.

1 See s 1(1)(b) of the SDA 1975; and s 1(1)(b) of the RRA 1976. Following amendments to s 1 of the SDA 1975 with effect from 12 October 2001 by the Sex Discrimination (Indirect Discrimination and Burden of Proof) Regulations 2001, SI 2000/2660, the test for indirect sex discrimination in the employment field is now slightly different from that set out above. By s 1(2)(b) of the SDA 1975, indirect discrimination now requires the application to a woman (or man) of a provision, criterion or practice that is applied equally to a man (or woman), but that is such that it would be to the detriment of a considerably larger proportion of women than of men. The significance of the amended wording remains to be seen.
2 See for example, *Enderby v Frenchay Health Authority*, C-127/92 [1993] IRLR 591, ECJ.

E3.25 Victimisation Discrimination by way of victimisation occurs when a person is treated less favourably, not on the ground of his or her race or sex, but on the ground that he or she has done a 'protected act', as set out in the RRA 1976 and the SDA 1975[1]. These acts include bringing proceedings against the alleged discriminator under the relevant Act, and alleging (unless the allegation is false, and was not made in good faith)[2] that the discriminator, or any other person, has committed an act that would contravene the relevant Act. In *Hussaney*[3] for example, Mr Hussaney was released from the club following his complaint about the manager's racist comment. He subsequently brought a claim for discrimination by way of victimisation[4].

1 See s 4(1) and (2) of the SDA 1975; and s 2(1) and (2) of the RRA 1976.
2 See s 4(4) of the SDA 1975; and s 2(2) of the RRA 1976.
3 See para E3.22.
4 The Tribunal found that there was no victimisation. In its decision of 15 January 2001 the EAT held that the Tribunal had erred and remitted the case to the Tribunal for rehearing.

(b) Prohibited grounds

E3.26 The SDA 1975 prohibits discrimination against both women and men[1] on the grounds of their sex and/or their marital status[2].

1 See ss 2(1), 2A(5), 3(2) and 4(3) of the SDA 1975.
2 See s 3 of the SDA 1975.

E3.27 The SDA 1975 also prohibits discrimination against transsexuals in relation to employment and vocational training only. The provisions relating to transsexuals apply only to professional sports, and not to amateur clubs.

Discrimination is prohibited 'on the ground that a person intends to undergo, is undergoing, or has undergone, gender reassignment'[1]. The ambit of this protection is still unclear, and is potentially of significance in the context of sport. As the law currently stands, the sex of transsexuals is treated as remaining unchanged, even where they have undergone gender reassignment surgery[2]. Difficult questions may arise particularly where the sexes are segregated. For example: could a man who has undergone gender reassignment be lawfully prevented from joining a women's cricket team? If so, could he also be lawfully prevented from joining a men's cricket team? The genuine occupational qualifications contained at ss 7 and 7A of the SDA 1975 would apply to exclude transsexuals from many single sex sports. For example, professional clubs involved in contact sports may be able to rely on ss 7(2)(b) and 7A of the SDA 1975, exempting from the SDA 1975 employment that needs to be held by a man because it is likely to involve physical contact with men, in circumstances where men might reasonably object to its being carried out by a woman, and vice versa. The exception at s 44 may also apply[3].

1 See s 2A(1) of the SDA 1975; read with s 82(1).
2 See *Bellinger v Bellinger* [2001] EWCA Civ 1140, [2002] Fam 150, currently on appeal to the House of Lords, applying *Corbett v Corbett* [1970] 2 All ER 33. See also the decision of the European Court of Human Rights in *Goodwin v United Kingdom* [2002] 2 FCR 577.
3 See paras E3.54 and E3.55.

E3.28 The RRA 1976 prohibits discrimination on the grounds of colour, race, nationality or ethnic or national origins[1]. 'National origin' is a wider concept than 'nationality' or 'citizenship'[2] and ethnic origin is wide than 'racial origin'[3]. In *Ice Hockey Super League v Henry*[4], a Canadian ice-hockey player with a UK ancestry stamp challenged the inclusion of a four week probationary period in his contract on the ground of nationality, in circumstances where a player originating outside the EU/EEA would not have had a similar clause in his contract[5]. In *Henderson v NBL Management Ltd and Australian Basketball Federation Inc*[6], a professional basketball player who was a naturalised Australian citizen challenged the NBL and ABF's requirement of a three-year period of continuous residence in Australia before he could be registered as a non-restricted player with an NBL club. The HREOC held that there was no discrimination on the ground of nationality, since the three-year delay applied to any change of nationality for the purpose of the rules, irrespective of the national origin of the player.

1 See s 1(1) of the RRA 1976; read with s 3(1)–(3).
2 *BBC Scotland v Souster* [2001] IRLR 150 (Court of Session) (English rugby journalist entitled to bring claim of race discrimination based on his national origin when contract terminated by BBC Scotland).
3 *Mandla v Dowell Lee* [1983] 2 AC 548, HL, giving guidance on the circumstances in which a group may be considered to constitute an 'ethnic group'.
4 EAT 1167/99, unreported, decision of 2 March 2001 (EAT).
5 The League's appeal against the Tribunal's finding of discrimination succeeded before the EAT on the basis that, in seeking to compare himself against non-EU/EEA players, Mr Henry was not comparing like with like, as required by the legislation, since non-EU/EEA players required a work permit, and Mr Henry did not.
6 Unreported, decision of the Australian Human Rights and Equal Opportunity Commission of 25 May 1992.

E3.29 Discrimination on the grounds of sexual orientation[1], age[2] and for religion[3] is not currently covered by the legislation[4].

1 See for example, *Secretary of State for Defence v MacDonald* [2001] IRLR 431 (Court of Session); *Smith v Gardner Merchant Ltd* [1998] IRLR 510, CA (verbal abuse).

2 Although it may be possible to characterise an age requirement or threshold as indirectly discriminatory on the ground of sex, and therefore as falling within the scope of the SDA 1975, see for example, *Harvest Town Circle Ltd v Rutherford* [2001] IRLR 599.
3 Save in Northern Ireland: see para E3.5.
4 Although this will change once the Framework Directive (see para E3.15) is implemented. It has also been suggested (see, for example, *Pearce v Governing Body of Mayfield Secondary School* [2001] EWCA Civ 1347, [2001] IRLR 669, paras 15–18, per Hale LJ, in relation to sexual orientation) that discrimination or harassment on these grounds may be covered by the ECHR as incorporated into domestic law by the HRA 1998.

B The DDA 1995

(a) 'Discrimination'

E3.30 The DDA 1995 has a different structure from the other discrimination legislation. There are three types of discrimination under the DDA 1995: discrimination by way of less favourable treatment, discrimination by way of failure to make reasonable adjustments, and victimisation. Important guidance on the application of the DDA 1995 is contained in secondary legislation and Codes of Practice[1].

1 See for example, the Disability Discrimination (Providers of Services) (Adjustment of Premises) Regulations 2001, SI 2001/3253, the Disability Discrimination (Services and Premises) Regulations 1996, SI 1996/1836, the Disability Discrimination (Meaning of Disability) Regulations 1996, SI 1996/1455, the Code of Practice on Rights of Access to Goods, Facilities, Services and Premises, the Code of Practice for the Elimination of Discrimination in the Field of Employment Against Disabled Persons or Persons who have had a Disability and Guidance on Matters to be Taken into Account in Determining Questions Relating to the Definition of Disability. Codes of Practice are admissible in any proceedings brought under the DDA 1995: s 53(5). By s 3(3) of the DDA 1995 a court or tribunal is required to take Guidance into account in determining whether a person has a relevant disability within the DDA 1995.

E3.31 Less favourable treatment A person discriminates against a disabled person if, for a reason that relates to that person's disability, he treats him or her less favourably than he would treat a person to whom that reason did not apply, and he cannot show that the treatment in question is justified[1]. For example, a refusal to permit a rally driver with insulin-controlled diabetes to enter a competition on the ground of safety would be discriminatory in the absence of proper justification for the refusal[2]. In *Hall v Victorian Amateur Football Association*[3], an Australian Rules Football player was successful in his claim that the defendant had unlawfully discriminated against him by refusing him registration on the basis of his HIV-positive status.

1 See ss 5 and 20(1) of the DDA 1995.
2 See para E3.38. As mentioned at para E3.21, direct discrimination (discrimination by way of less favourable treatment) on the grounds of race or sex cannot be justified.
3 Unreported, decision of Victorian Civil and Administrative Tribunal of 23 April 1999, [1999] 7(2) SATLJ 66.

E3.32 Failure to make reasonable adjustments Where arrangements, policies, procedures, or the physical features of buildings or premises place a disabled person at a substantial disadvantage by comparison with people who are not so disabled, there is a specific statutory duty in certain cases on those who are responsible for those arrangements or premises to take reasonable steps to prevent the arrangements or policies having that effect[1].

1 See ss 6 and 21(1) of the DDA 1995.

E3.33 Unjustified failure to comply with a duty to make reasonable adjustments constitutes discrimination[1]. For example, it might be necessary to permit blind swimmers to touch lane dividers with their hands.

1 See s 20(2) of the DDA 1995.

E3.34 In *PGA Tour Inc v Martin*[1], a case in the US involving an analogous discrimination statute, the US Supreme Court held that the PGA was required to allow a competitor with a circulatory disorder to use a golf-cart on its tours and in qualifying. The PGA accepted that allowing Martin to use a golf cart was a necessary modification, but contended that it would alter an essential aspect of the game, and was therefore not an adjustment that was required. The Supreme Court held that the adjustment was reasonable, on the basis that there was nothing in the Rules of Golf that required players to walk the course. Golf was a game in which it was impossible to guarantee that all players would play under exactly the same conditions in any event, and Martin endured greater fatigue than his fellow-competitors even using a golf-cart.

1 Unreported, decision of the US Supreme Court of 29 May 2001 (Scalia and Thomas JJ dissenting).

E3.35 Victimisation Discrimination by way of victimisation is prohibited under the DDA 1995[1]. The prohibition is materially similar to that applicable to race and sex discrimination[2].

1 See s 55 of the DDA 1995.
2 As to which, see para E3.25.

(b) Definition of 'disability'

E3.36 The protection against discrimination afforded by the DDA 1995 is only granted to 'disabled persons', as defined by the Act. A 'disabled person' is someone with a 'disability'[1], namely a physical or mental impairment, which has a substantial and long-term adverse effect on his ability to carry out normal day-to-day activities[2]. Arthritis, epilepsy and diabetes are therefore all potentially covered by the DDA 1995. Progressive conditions such as HIV and cancer may also be covered[3]. Some conditions are expressly excluded from the definition of disability, including hayfever[4]. The DDA 1995 also covers people who have been disabled in the past[5].

1 See s 1(2) of the DDA 1995.
2 See s 1(1) of the DDA 1995; read with Sch 1. Guidance on the scope and application of this definition is given in the Disability Discrimination (Meaning of Disability) Regulations 1996, SI 1996/1455 and the Guidance on Matters to be Taken into Account in Determining Questions Relating to the Definition of Disability. By s 3(3) of the DDA 1995, a court or tribunal is required to take the Guidance into account in determining whether a person has a relevant disability within the DDA 1995.
3 Progressive conditions are covered from the stage at which any impairment first has some (not necessary substantial) effect on ability to carry out day to day activities: DDA 1995, Sch 1, para 8 The government has recently indicated its intention, subject to consultation, to extend the coverage of the DDA 1995 to include HIV from the point at which it is diagnosed, and cancer from the point at which it is diagnosed as being a condition that is likely to require substantial treatment: 'Towards Inclusion – Civil Rights for Disabled People', Department for Education and Skills (June 2001).
4 See reg 4(2) of the Disability Discrimination (Meaning of Disability) Regulations 1996, SI 1996/1455.
5 See s 2 of the DDA 1995; read with Sch 2.

(c) Justification

E3.37 Treatment of disabled people that would otherwise amount to a discriminatory failure to make reasonable adjustments or less favourable treatment will be lawful if justified under the DDA 1995. Discrimination in employment and training may only be justified where the reason for the treatment is both material to the circumstances of the case and substantial[1]. If the employer is under a duty to make reasonable adjustments, but fails without justification to do so, any less favourable treatment by him can only be justified where it would have been justified even if he had made the reasonable adjustments that he was under a duty to make[2].

1 See s 5(3) and (4) of the DDA 1995.
2 See s 5(5) of the DDA 1995.

E3.38 In relation to discrimination in the provision of goods, facilities and services, discriminatory treatment is only justified where, in the opinion of the alleged discriminator, one of a number of specified statutory conditions[1] is satisfied, and it is reasonable in all the circumstances for the alleged discrimination to hold that opinion[2]. The conditions include that the less favourable treatment is necessary in order not to endanger the health and safety of any person, including the disabled person. In the example of the rally driver with diabetes given above[3], therefore, the refusal to allow him to compete might be justified on the ground of safety. To satisfy the requirement of reasonableness it is likely, however, that the organisers would have had to made a reasonable attempt to assess the likely safety risk of the disability in the circumstances of the individual driver, and be prepared to justify their decision, if necessary by reference to objective material. Generalised assumptions about diabetes and safety would not be sufficient.

1 See s 20(4) of the DDA 1995.
2 See s 20(3)(b) of the DDA 1995.
3 See para E3.31.

E3.39 The test of reasonableness is also unlikely to be satisfied where there is evidence that the same result could be achieved by means less restrictive of an individual sportsman's or sportswoman's rights. In *Hall*[1], for example, the Tribunal held that although banning an HIV-positive player from Australian Rules football would inevitably achieve the desired aim, namely to prevent any risk that other participants in games would be infected, the same result could be achieved by implementing proper risk-reduction procedures.

1 See para E3.31.

C Forms of liability

E3.40 A person may be directly personally liable for an act of discrimination under the DDA 1995, the RRA 1976 or the SDA 1975. They may also be vicariously liable for the acts of another[1], or liable for knowingly aiding and abetting those acts[2]. In *Hussaney*[3], for example, the claim against the club's manager was based on his having aided and abetted the club to discriminate against Mr Hussaney by deciding not to offer him a professional contract. It is unlawful under the RRA 1976 and the SDA 1975 to instruct someone in a subordinate position to discriminate, or to attempt to procure them to do so[4]. It is further unlawful to pressurise someone to discriminate[5]. Finally, an employer may be liable for the discriminatory actions of a third party towards his or her staff where that action was sufficiently under his or her control that he or she could have prevented it or reduced the extent of it[6].

1 See s 41 of the SDA 1975; s 32 of the RRA 1976; and s 58 of the DDA 1995. See *Lister v Hesley Hall Ltd* [2001] UKHL 22, [2001] IRLR 472.
2 See s 42 of the SDA 1975; s 33 of the RRA 1976; and s 57 of the DDA 1995. See *Anyanwu v South Bank Students' Union* [2001] UKHL 14, [2001] IRLR 305.
3 See para E3.22.
4 See s 39 of the SDA 1975; and s 30 of the RRA 1976.
5 See s 40 of the SDA 1975; and s 31 of the RRA 1976.
6 See further para E3.23 and the examples given there.

D The EqPA 1970

E3.41 The EqPA 1970 inserts a statutory 'equality clause' in a woman's employment contract. By this statutory term, where a woman is employed on like work, work rated as equivalent, or work of equal value to that of a man in the same employment, and a term of her contract of employment is or becomes less favourable than a similar term in the man's contract, her contract is treated as modified so as to be no less favourable than that of her comparator[1]. 'Employment' means not only employment under a contract of service, but also a contract 'personally to execute any work or labour'[2]. These provisions could, therefore, be wide enough to apply to participants in a tournament or competition. For example, the provision of prizes of lower value to female competitors at Wimbledon might be vulnerable to challenge under the EqPA 1970[3]. However, an equality clause does not operate in relation to a variation between a woman's contract and that of her male comparator if the employer proves that the variation is genuinely due to a material factor that is not the difference of sex. Thus, the All England Club might argue that the lower pay of women competitors is due not to their sex, but to the fact that they play a maximum of only three sets rather than five in a match.

1 See s 1 of the EqPA 1970.
2 See s 1(6)(a) of the EqPA 1970.
3 See s 1(3) of the EqPA 1970. For the extensive case law on the interpretation of s 1(3), see *Harvey on Industrial Relations and Employment Law* (Butterworths), K[200]–[313].

3 WHEN IS DISCRIMINATION UNLAWFUL: THE SCOPE OF THE LEGISLATION

A Employers and Agencies

E3.42 In relation to the discrimination laws, sporting bodies are no different from other employers. They are subject to the ordinary requirements of the SDA 1975, the RRA 1976 and the DDA 1995 prohibiting discrimination against contract workers[1], employees[2], and applicants for employment[3]. In *Sterling v Leeds Rugby League Club*[4] a professional rugby league player was successful in his claim for race discrimination against the club and its coach following the club's decision that he would not be selected for the first team, apparently irrespective of his performance during the season. Mr Sterling also succeeded in claims of victimisation against the club, its managing director and its chief executive on the basis that they had failed properly to investigate his complaint of race discrimination.

1 See ss 4(1), (2) and 12 DDA 1995; read with ss 5 and 6; ss 4(1), (2) and 7 of the RRA 1976; and s 6(1), (2) and 9 of the SDA 1975. See for example, *Grant v Lancashire County Cricket Club*, case no. 2407757/99, unreported, decision of Employment Tribunal of 2 November 2000 (woman awarded £15,000 after a Tribunal found that Club had discriminated against her in refusing to appoint her to two positions at the club, inter alia, on the basis that members would not want a woman to chair meetings); see also *Kingstonian Football Club v Cummins*, EAT/1130/98, unreported, decision of the Employment Appeal Tribunal of 21 October 1998 (Kingstonians liable for sexual harassment of office administrator).

2 Defined as including people employed under contracts 'personally to execute any work or labour': SDA 1975, s 82(1); and RRA 1976, s 78(1).

3 For example, *Saunders v Richmond-Upon-Thames London Borough Council* [1978] ICR 75 concerned sex discrimination in the questions put to a female golfer applying for the post of club professional. Detailed consideration of the extent and nature of these obligations is outside the scope of this work. For further information, see *Harvey on Industrial Relations and Employment Law* (Butterworths), Div L (Equal Opportunities).

4 [2001] ISLR 201, decision of the Employment Tribunal of 13 October 2000. Mr Sterling was subsequently awarded £10,000 for injury to feelings.

B Organisations conferring qualifications or authorisations

E3.43 It is unlawful for a body that can confer an authorisation or qualification that is needed for, or that facilitates, engagement in a particular profession or trade to discriminate in the terms on which the authorisation or qualification is offered, by refusing to offer it, or by withdrawing it or varying the terms on which it is held[1]. This type of discrimination is unlawful under the SDA 1975 and the RRA 1976 but not the DDA 1995. 'Profession' includes any vocation or occupation[2].

1 See s 13 of the SDA 1975; and s 12 of the RRA 1976.

2 See s 82(1) of the SDA 1975; and s 78(1) of the RRA 1976.

E3.44 In *British Judo Association v Petty*[1] the award of a national refereeing certificate to a woman, subject, in effect, to the proviso that she did not referee men's matches, was held to be discriminatory contrary to s 13 of the SDA 1975. The EAT emphasised that it was not necessary for the applicant to demonstrate that her job prospects had in fact been affected by the discriminatory arrangement. In *Couch v British Boxing Board of Control*[2] a female boxer successfully relied on s 13 of the SDA 1975 to challenge the refusal of the British Boxing Board of Control to grant her a licence to box professionally, on the grounds, inter alia, that women were emotionally unstable and accident-prone because they suffered from pre-menstrual syndrome[3].

1 [1981] ICR 660, EAT.

2 Case No 2304321/97, decision of Employment Tribunal of March 31, 1998.

3 See also *Hardwick v Football Association*, EAT/1036/97; EAT/54/98, unreported, decision of Employment Appeal Tribunal of 30 April 1999, [1999] 7(3) SATLJ 23 (woman successfully challenged Football Association's discriminatory refusal of an Advanced Coaching Licence in circumstances in which she had performed better on the required training course than certain men: awarded £16,000 compensation); *Thompson v Professional Pool Players' Association*, Case Nos 15898/91 and 47323/91, decision of Employment Tribunal from 1991 (unlawful refusal of membership of the PPPA where membership amounted to the grant of professional status).

C Organisations providing vocational training

E3.45 It is similarly unlawful for a body which provides, or make arrangements for the provision of, facilities for vocational training to discriminate against someone seeking or undergoing such training[1]. Again, such discrimination is unlawful under the SDA 1975 and the RRA 1976 but not the DDA 1995. 'Training' includes any form of education or instruction[2]. In the *Hardwick* case[3], Mrs Hardwick's claim, based on the refusal of an advanced football coaching certificate, was brought both on the basis that the FA was a qualifying body, and on the basis that it was concerned with the provision of vocational training.

1 See s 14 of the SDA 1975; and s 13 of the RRA 1976.
2 See s 82(1) of the SDA 1975; and s 78(1) of the RRA 1976.
3 See para E3.44, n 3.

D Providers of goods, facilities and services

(a) Scope

E3.46 It is unlawful for any person concerned with the provision of goods, facilities or services to the public or a section of the public to discriminate against a person who seeks to obtain or use those goods, facilities or services[1]. This section applies whether the goods, services or facilities are provided free or for payment[2]. It is unlawful for such a person to refuse or omit to provide such services, or to provide them in a less favourable way or on less favourable terms[3].

1 See s 29(1) of the SDA 1975; s 20(1) of the RRA 1976; and s 19(1), (2) of the DDA 1995.
2 See n 1.
3 See s 29(1) of the SDA 1975; s 20(1) of the RRA 1976; and s 19(1)(a), (c) and (d) of the DDA 1995.

E3.47 It is additionally unlawful, on the ground of disability, for such a person to fail to comply with his or her duty to make reasonable adjustments to practices, procedures or procedures that make it impossible or unreasonably difficult for disabled persons to make use of a particular service[1]. Where an auxiliary aid or service, such as the provision of information on tape or sign language, would enable a disabled person to make use of a public service, or facilitate his or her use of the service, the service provider is under a further duty to take reasonable steps to provide that aid or service[2]. With effect from 1 October 2004, providers of services will also be required to make reasonable modifications to physical features of buildings making it impossible or unreasonably difficult for disabled people to make use the services provided[3]. Services and facilities covered by the legislation include any place that members of the public are permitted to enter[4] and facilities provided for entertainment, recreation or refreshment[5]. Sports stadia are therefore covered[6].

1 See s 19(1)(b) of the DDA 1995; read with s 21(1). This provision is subject to various exceptions: see for example, s 21(6) and (7).
2 See s 19(1)(b) of the DDA 1995; read with 21(4). This provision is subject to various exceptions: see for example, s 21(6) and (7).
3 See s 19(1)(b) of the DDA 1995; read with s 21(2); brought into force by the Disability Discrimination Act (Commencement No 9) Order 2001, SI 2001/2030. See also the Disability Discrimination (Providers of Services) (Adjustment of Premises) Regulations 2001, SI 2001/3253; the Disability Discrimination (Services and Premises) Regulations 1999, SI 1999/1191; and the DDA Code of Practice: Rights of Access, Goods, Facilities, Services and Premises, in force from May 27, 2002. This provision is subject to various exceptions: see for example, s 21(6) and (7).

4 See s 29(2)(a) of the SDA 1975; s 20(2)(a) of the RRA 1976; and s 19(3)(a) of the DDA 1995.
5 See s 29(2)(e) of the SDA 1975; s 20(2)(e) of the RRA 1976; and s 19(3)(f) of the DDA 1995.
6 DDA Code of Practice: Rights of Access, Goods, Facilities, Services and Premises, in force from May 27, 2002, para 2.14.

E3.48 It is also unlawful for a person who manages premises to discriminate against a person occupying those premises[1].

1 See s 30(2) of the SDA 1975; s 21(2) of the RRA 1976; and s 22(3) of the DDA 1995.

E3.49 Private Clubs[1] In *Charter v Race Relations Board*[2] it was held that the provision of goods, services or facilities to 'the public or a section of the public' did not cover private members' clubs, on the basis that there is no 'public' element where a personally selected group of people met in private premises. This exemption is still applicable to discrimination by all private members' clubs on the grounds of sex and disability[3]. Private members clubs that have 25 or more members and that are not trade unions are, however, required not to discriminate on the ground of race[4].

1 There is a further exception in the SDA for voluntary bodies: see para E3.57.
2 [1973] AC 868, HL. See also *Dockers' Labour Club v Race Relations Board* [1976] AC 285.
3 The Sex Discrimination (Amendment) Bill, currently before the House of Lords, would make it unlawful, however, for private clubs that admit both men and women, to admit women only to an inferior class of membership, such as associate membership.
4 See s 25 of the RRA 1976.

E3.50 It is therefore lawful for private clubs to refuse to admit woman and disabled people to membership, or to admit them to inferior membership (for example, only admitting women to associate membership of a golf course, which in turn restricts the times at which they are entitled to use the course)[1]. Where, however, a private members club allowed both members and non-members to use its facilities, or where there was an insufficient degree of 'personal selection' in determining access, a refusal to allow access to women or the disabled would constitute unlawful discrimination. In *Anderson v Professional Footballer's Association*[2] the refusal of the PFA to allow a female agent to attend the PFA's annual awards dinner was held not to fall within the 'private clubs' exemption, the judge noting that he could see no difference between the degree of personal selection and screening that the PFA claimed to have exercised in relation to those attending the dinner and that exercised by a restaurateur.

1 See, however, para E3.49, n 3.
2 [2000] ISLR 74 (C Ct.)

(b) Access as a competitor

E3.51 In *Martin v PGA Tour Inc*[1] golf tours were held to fall within the Americans with Disabilities Act 1990 on the basis that the events occurred on golf courses, which were places open to the public, and that the PGA, as a lessor and operator of golf courses, must not discriminate against any individual in the enjoyment of the goods, services and facilities of those courses[2]. The circumstances in which women are entitled to take part in mixed competitions or to play against men are considered fully below[3].

1 See para E3.34.

2 The PGA did not contend that it was a private club exempt from the coverage of this part of the Act. It suggested, however, that as a competitor Martin was a provider of entertainment and services rather than a consumer, and, as such, was outside the scope of this part of the Act. This argument was comprehensively rejected by the US Supreme Court, which noted that competitors paid the PGA for the privilege of competing in the tours, and were therefore its customers.

3 See para E3.54.

(c) *Access as a spectator*

E3.52 The topic of access for spectators is most likely to be relevant in the context of disabled spectators. As mentioned above[1], the operators of sports stadia and other premises open to the public will be under an obligation, with effect from 1 October 2004, to make reasonable modifications to features of those premises that make it impossible or unreasonably difficult for disabled people to use those facilities. Where, for example, disabled seating was arranged in such a way that those using it regularly had their view blocked by able-bodied persons standing up in front of them to see the action, or where disabled seating did not make sufficient provision for companions, those might be considered to be features arising from the design of the building that made it unreasonably difficult for those people to make use of the stadium, and therefore unlawful[2].

1 See para E3.47.

2 Compare the Americans with Disabilities Act 1990, which requires a specific proportion of the seating capacity in facilities built after 1990 to be allocated to wheelchairs, that disabled accessible seats have comparable lines of sight to those for able-bodied spectators, and that disabled accessible seats be provided throughout the facility. In August 1999 the City of New York (which owns Yankee Stadium) and the New York Yankees settled a claim brought by a group of disabled fans alleging that seating provided at the Stadium was too scarce, did not make sufficient provision for companions, had poor lines of sight and was not of a comparable admission price.

4 STATUTORY EXEMPTIONS

E3.53 Both the RRA 1976 and the SDA 1975 contain exceptions permitting limited discrimination in sporting activities in certain circumstances. There is no need for any specific sporting exception in the DDA 1995, since the tests of discrimination, including failure to make reasonable adjustments, and justification, are sufficiently flexible to cover the situation where, even with reasonable adjustments, a disabled person is not reasonably able to take part in a sporting event or competition with less disabled competitors or the able-bodied.

A Single-sex sporting activities

E3.54 Section 44 of the SDA 1975[1] renders single-sex competitions lawful 'in relation to any sport, game or other activity of a competitive nature' where the 'strength, stamina or physique of the average woman puts her at a disadvantage to the average man'. The reference to 'sport, game or other activity of a competitive nature' would appear to exclude activities of a non-competitive nature, such as training or coaching sessions. Section 44 was applied to prevent a schoolgirl playing football under the auspices of the FA in *Bennett v Football Association and Nottinghamshire Football Association*[2]. It has been held not to apply to all-female boxing[3], all-female professional wrestling[4], to a woman referee in an all-male judo contest[5], or to mixed snooker[6]. In Australia, in *South v Royal Victoria Bowling Association*[7], a similar provision was held not to exempt a rule restricting access to affiliation for a female bowler who wished to play in men-only competitions. This section of the SDA 1975 has been heavily criticised and there have been numerous calls for its repeal[8].

1 The RRA 1976 naturally contains no similar exception in relation to single-race or nationality sports, although it does sanction limited discrimination on the ground of nationality, place of birth or length of residence in selecting teams for sports or in setting competition rules (see para E3.56).
2 Unreported, decision of July 28, 1998 (CA), partially extracted in *GLC v Farrar* [1980] ICR 266 at 271H–272C (EAT). It appears that the decision in *Bennett* proceeded on the basis that football was an activity generally excepted from the statute in circumstances where women (of whatever age) wanted to play in mixed teams or against men. No consideration was apparently given to the comparative strength and stamina of men and women at the age of the complainant. It is notable that a similar Australian legislative provision, namely s. 66 of the Equal Opportunity Act, expressly provides that the exception does not apply to sporting activity for children under the age of 12.
3 *Couch v British Boxing Board of Control* (para E3.44).
4 *GLC v Farrar* (n 2).
5 *British Judo Association v Petty* (para E3.44).
6 *French v Crosby Links Hotel*, unreported decision of May 7, 1982 (Gt. Yarmouth CCt).
7 Unreported, decision of Victorian Civil and Administrative Tribunal of February 28, 2001.
8 See for example, Dr D McArdle 'Discrimination in Sport' [1998] 6(1) SATLJ 80; David Pannick 'Sex Discrimination in Sport' (EOC pamphlet, March 1983).

E3.55 It is unclear whether 'sex' in s 44 would be interpreted as meaning biological sex. If so, a rule that prevented a male to female transsexual playing in an all-female cricket team would be justified under this section, even in circumstances where the claimant had undergone gender reassignment.

B Nationality discrimination in competition rules and team selection

E3.56 The RRA 1976 permits limited discrimination on the grounds of nationality, place of birth and length of residence in the selection of representative teams and in setting competition eligibility rules[1].

1 See s 39.

C Voluntary bodies

E3.57 The SDA 1975[1] allows non-profitmaking voluntary bodies to restrict their membership to one sex, or to choose to provide benefits, facilities and services to one sex only, even though membership may be open to the public or to a section of it. So, for example, an all-female golf-club would be entitled to refuse membership or access to men, provided that the club was not set up pursuant to any enactment and did not carry out its activities for profit.

1 See s 34.

D Mixed facilities

E3.58 It would be lawful for a sports club or organisation to restrict access to certain facilities or services to prevent serious embarrassment to male users at the presence of women, or where users are likely to be in a state of undress and a male user might reasonably object to the presence of a woman[1]. This provision is most likely to apply in the context of changing facilities.

1 See s 35(1)(c) of the SDA 1975.

E3.59 It would also be lawful for a club or organisation to restrict access to facilities or services to men in circumstances where the facilities or services are such that physical contact between users is likely, and a male user might legitimately object if other users were women[1].

1 See s 35(2) of the SDA 1975.

5 REMEDIES

E3.60 The remedy for breaches of Pt II of the RRA 1976, the SDA 1975 and the DDA 1995 and for breaches of the EqPA 1970 is by way of application to an Employment Tribunal[1]. The remedy for breaches of Pt III of the RRA 1976, the SDA 1975 and the DDA 1995 is by way of action in the county court[2]. Where the complaint is that a person has been instructed to carry out an act of race or sex discrimination, or placed under pressure to discriminate on grounds of race or sex, enforcement must be through the Equal Opportunities Commission or the Commission for Racial Equality[3]. Claims must be brought within certain specified time limits[4].

1 See s 63 of the SDA 1975; s 54 of the RRA 1976; s 8 of the DDA 1995; and s 2(1) of the EqPA 1970.
2 See s 66 of the SDA 1975; s 57 of the RRA 1976; and s 25 of the DDA 1995.
3 See s 72 of the SDA 1975; and s 63 of the RRA 1976.
4 See 76 of the SDA 1975; s 68 of the RRA 1976; Sch 3 to the DDA 1995; and s 2(4) of the EqPA 1970.

CHAPTER E4

THE REGULATION OF DRUG USE IN SPORT

Charles Flint QC (Blackstone Chambers), **Jonathan Taylor** (Hammonds) and **Adam Lewis** (Blackstone Chambers)*

Contents

1 INTRODUCTION

E4.1 The fight against the illicit use of drugs in sport is one of the greatest challenges facing today's sports regulators. The essence of the sporting spectacle is a contest on a level playing-field, the outcome of which is determined solely by the individual merit of the participating athletes[1]. Illicit drug use strikes at the very heart of that spectacle by adding a further surreptitious factor that makes the outcome dependent not on individual merit but rather on unnatural performance enhancement. Illicit drug use can also pose grave health risks to the athletes, whose ability to make rational choices may be affected by the high stakes of modern competition. These fundamental dangers obviously mandate a rigorous regulatory response. However, too unyielding an approach – for example, adopting a strict liability approach to doping charges, with a tariff of substantial fixed or minimum sanctions, including suspensions from the sport for lengthy periods, without any ability to take account of the relative culpability of the individual athlete – risks compromising basic fairness and respect for participants' individual rights. The regulators are challenged with resolving these conflicting imperatives in a manner that both respects the interests of the athletes and vindicates the broader public interest in the sport itself. If the regulators fail to get the balance right, their anti-doping programmes will be subject to forceful challenge.

* The authors are grateful for the helpful comments of Richard McLaren and Deborah Jevans.

1 The term 'athlete' will be used in this chapter to refer to participants in any sport. In addition, for sake of convenience, the male gender will be used.

E4.2 It has been suggested that drug-use has always been part of sport, going right back to Ancient Greece[1]. However, the regulatory response started in earnest only in the late 1960s, after the deaths from amphetamine abuse of Danish cyclist Kurt Jensen during the 1960 Rome Olympics and English cyclist Tony Simpson during the 1967 Tour de France. The Council of Europe first tabled a resolution against the use of drugs in sport in 1960. The International Olympic Committee ('IOC') established its Medical Commission in 1967, and quickly introduced a programme for testing for stimulants and narcotics at the 1968 Olympic Games in Mexico City. At the 1972 Games in Munich, over 2000 samples were tested. In 1974, the IOC expanded the scope of its programme from merely protecting the health of athletes to preventing cheating; it banned anabolic steroids, and started testing for them at the 1976 Montreal Games. In 1983, the ability to detect prohibited substances in athletes' urine samples took a great leap forward with the introduction of gas chromatography and mass spectometry techniques. In 1984, the Anti-Doping Charter proposed by the Council of Europe's Committee of Sports Ministers was adopted.

1 See eg ASDA *The history of drug use in sport* www.ausport.gov.au/asda/drugs1.html.

E4.3 If these developments engendered any complacency among regulators, that vanished when Ben Johnson tested positive for a banned steroid after his victory in the 100 metres sprint at the 1988 Seoul Olympics, and had to be stripped of his gold medal[1]. The Dubin Inquiry in Canada, established in response to that debacle to look into the use of prohibited drugs in sport, found that 'the use of drugs as a method of cheating has reached epidemic proportions', and concluded: 'the evidence shows that banned performance-enhancing substances and in particular anabolic steroids are being used by athletes in almost every sport, most extensively in weightlifting and track and field'[2]. Further, after the fall of the Berlin Wall in 1989, evidence emerged of systematic state-sponsored misuse of drugs in the former East Germany, prompting criminal prosecutions of doctors and coaches for causing grievous bodily harm by giving steroids to minors[3]. In 1996, a report by Italian physiologist Sandra Donoti was made public, documenting widespread abuse of illicit hormones in professional cycling. In July 1998, the Festina team was expelled from the Tour de France after criminal investigators uncovered evidence of systematic drug use. Further evidence implicated other teams, some of which withdrew, leaving only 15 of the original 21 to compete. This scandal (and in particular the opprobrium heaped on sport for its perceived failure to police itself) prompted the IOC to organise the World Anti-Doping Conference at Lausanne in February 1999, whose delegates sought to identify ways to take the regulatory response to a new level of co-ordination and effectiveness. The upshot was the establishment of the new World Anti-Doping Agency that is now in the process of assuming sole responsibility for the anti-doping functions historically performed by the IOC[4].

1 See Houlihan 'The World Anti-Doping Agency: Prospects for Success' in *Drugs and Doping in Sport* (2001, Cavendish), pp 125–127.
2 Mr Justice Charles Dubin, Report of the Commission of Inquiry into the Use of Drugs and Banned Practices Intended to Increase Athletic Performance (Ottawa 1990) at p 517.
3 See eg (1998) Times, 19 March; www.wired.com/news/politics/18 July 2000.
4 See para E4.42 et seq.

E4.4 There are not many commentators who would suggest that the regulators in the field of anti-doping have yet got the balance right. There is a popular perception (among athletes as much as the public) that drug 'cheats' are getting off doping charges on technicalities, and yet there is also a growing concern that some of the weapons being used in the fight against doping require too great a sacrifice of the rights of the accused athlete in favour of the public image of the sport overall, resulting in essentially innocent athletes being wrongly branded as cheats. The governing body is caught in the cross-fire. One governing body (the British Athletics Federation) has already gone bankrupt, in October 1997, reportedly as a result of the costs of the *Modahl* case, and its successor (UK Athletics) has warned that its level of spending on doping issues is also unsustainable[1].

1 'Moorcroft set to throw in towel on drug cases' (1999) Times, 27 November.

E4.5 This chapter starts with a brief critique of the rationales offered for regulating drug use in sport[1]. It then briefly surveys the somewhat bewildering array of sports bodies and public bodies, national and international, who claim authority to regulate drug use in sport[2]. There follows a detailed analysis of the methods used to regulate drug use in sport, including in particular the type of provisions typically included in anti-doping programmes, and how the ban on illicit drug use is policed and enforced[3]. The chapter concludes by going step-by-step through the disciplinary process where an athlete is charged with a doping offence[4].

1 See para E4.6 et seq.
2 See para E4.15 et seq.
3 See para E4.53 et seq.
4 See para E4.242 et seq. This chapter addresses only incidentally the challenges that have been made in the English courts to the actions of sports bodies and tribunals in the anti-doping sphere, because that subject is dealt with in some detail in at paras A3.10, A3.122, A3.146, A3.168 and A3.175.

2 WHY REGULATE DRUG USE IN SPORT?

E4.6 The primary justifications offered for regulating the use of drugs in sport are:

(i) the prevention of cheating; and
(ii) the protection of the health of the athletes[1].

1 See eg Preamble to the Olympic Movement Anti-Doping Code (Lausanne 2001): 'the Olympic Movement Anti-Doping Code is essentially intended to ensure respect for the ethical concepts implicit in Fair Play, the Olympic Spirit and medical practice and to safeguard the health of athletes'. See also Council of Europe Explanatory Report on the Anti-Doping Convention (Strasbourg 1990): 'Doping is contrary to the values of sport and the principles for which it stands: fair play, equal chances, level competition, healthy activity. Doping endangers the health of athletes, as they are using substances in ways that they were not designed for; sport is meant to be a life-enhancing activity, not one that imperils life'.
For a broader view of the rationale behind anti-doping, discussing how doping subverts the 'fundamental values' of sport, see Art 1 of the draft World Anti-Doping Code, E-Version 1.0, issued 10 June 2002. See also Houlihan *Dying to Win* (2nd edn, 2002).

E4.7 According to the first rationale, consumption of performance-enhancing drugs[1] gives the athlete an unfair advantage and is against the spirit of free and fair competition[2].

1 In the case of sports involving animals, there will also be a concern about substances that *hinder* performance. See eg *G v FEI*, CAS 91/53, award dated 15 January 1992, Digest of CAS Awards 1986–1998 (Berne 1998) at p 79 (administration of tranquilliser to a horse was a doping offence under the FEI Veterinary Regulations).

2 See Samaranch, Foreword to *Doping: An IOC White Paper* (Lausanne 1999): 'such behaviour makes a mockery of the very essence of sport, and of the soul of what our predecessors, like ourselves consider to be sacrosanct ideals: the inner desire to surpass one's own limits, the social need to compete with others, to find one's identity within society and to develop at all levels'.

E4.8 This is not just a moralistic objection. The integrity of the sporting spectacle depends upon the contest being conducted on a level playing-field, so that the outcome is uncertain and the determining factor will be the skill, endurance and other abilities of the individual contestants[1]. A primary responsibility of any sports regulator must be to protect and preserve that integrity; indeed, it is the objective that underlies many sporting rules and regulations, expanding well beyond the anti-doping arena[2]. Doping scandals can discredit an entire sport, particularly as other athletes may believe they are forced to join in to make the playing-field level once more[3].

1 See eg Beloff 'Drugs, Laws and Versapaks' in *Drugs and Doping in Sport* (2001, Cavendish), pp 39 and 40.

2 Other examples would include anti-corruption rules, rules restricting common ownership of competing teams, and rules restricting the kinds of equipment that can be used by participants in a sport or in a specific class of a sport. Indeed, rules relating to central selling of commercial rights have the same objective, being used to ensure revenues are distributed in a manner that ensures competitive balance (and therefore uncertainty of outcome): see para B2.262 et seq.

3 See eg IOC President Jacques Rogge (2002) Sportcal.com, 4 February: 'I call on the whole sports community to wake up to this terrible danger and do everything possible to protect the athletes. Doping is not just an attack on ethics and fair play. It is a mortal danger to the credibility of the sports world'.

Put simply, 'sport that is rigged is no sport at all'. Dyer and Owen, 'Drug tests may condemn the innocent and miss the cheats' (2002) Financial Times, 30 May.

See also Mike Rowbottom (2002) Independent, 9 March: 'As we meander into the 21st century it is doping, more than anything else, which threatens to rob sport of its meaning … As every new doping case emerges, the question "What am I watching? What have I seen?" has to be applied with even greater rigour'.

In addition, where the sport depends on revenues from betting (eg horseracing), loss of public confidence in the integrity of results can have a direct financial impact.

E4.9 It is therefore common to present anti-doping regulations in general and drug testing in particular as a method of protecting the reputation of the clean athlete, validating his achievements by removing any suspicion of cheating, and also ensuring he does not feel he too has to take drugs in order to have any chance of success[1]. It is no surprise, therefore, that many athletes lead the calls for more testing of competitors and for strict and uncompromising application of the rules, including substantial bans for those who fail drug tests[2].

1 See Verroken, 'A time for re-evaluation: the challenge to an athlete's reputation' in *Drugs and Doping in Sport* (2001, Cavendish) at p 31: 'Athletes need supporting evidence; how many times do we hear suggestions of drug-induced performance when an athlete breaks a record, or when a competitor plays out of his or her socks? Part of the function of testing is to reduce the doubt about sports performance'.

Similarly, the Jockey Club stated that the intent behind the 'dawn raid' out-of-competition tests that it staged at five stables on 26 February 2002 was to dispel allegations circulating in the media since December 2001 (see (2001) Daily Telegraph, 20 December) that illicit drug use was rife in horse racing. When the samples tested negative, the Jockey Club proclaimed 'the crucial all-clear which signalled that British racing is officially overwhelmingly "drug free"'. See 'Dope tests leave yards in the clear' and 'Hill confident his team can catch EPO dopers' (2002) Daily Telegraph, 28 February.

2 See eg 'Radcliffe calls for random blood tests' (1999) Daily Telegraph, 13 July; 'Radcliffe turns up heat on Moorcroft; British captain says stricter approach is needed in doping cases' (2000) Guardian, 9 March; 'British women's team captain makes her point against doping' (2001) Daily Telegraph, 11 August.

E4.10 On the other hand, it can be hard to draw a principled distinction between doping and other forms of performance-enhancement that are deemed to be legitimate[1]. More fundamentally, some commentators argue that the aim of a drug-free sport is unrealistic. Even now, it is accepted that most blood doping techniques[2] are undetectable, and the potential to abuse future scientific developments (for example, gene therapy[3]) suggest that the determined cheater will always stay at least one step ahead of the testers. Many therefore argue that the utopia of an absolutely level playing-field is an impossible and unhelpful dream. As a result, calls periodically surface to legalise the use of performance-enhancing drugs in sport[4].

1 See eg Mick Hume (1999) Times, 9 August: 'Why should we make such a distinction between drugs and the many other artificial aids which are considered perfectly alright – such as painkillers and diet supplements, or computer-designed running shoes and high-tech equipment?' See also Chris Jones 'Drugs Sports & Ethics' (1994) 1 *Relay* 16. Another often-cited example is the use of 'hypoxy' tents, which allow athletes to train at sea-level while sleeping in conditions that simulate sleeping at altitude.

2 See para E4.144.

3 See (2001) 4(5) Sports Law Bulletin 1.

4 Most notably in *The Daily Telegraph* of 26 July 1998, which reported the view of then-IOC President Juan Antonio Samoranch that 'substances that do not damage a sportsman's health should not be banned'. See also (1998) 1(2) Sports Law Bulletin 1, reporting similar comments by Great Britain coach Wilf Paish.

E4.11 In addition, many sports ban the use of 'social' drugs, eg marijuana, alcohol and various narcotics, ie drugs that are considered to be recreational rather than performance-enhancing[1]. The usual explanations (in addition to health concerns) include wanting to encourage parents to allow their children to take up the sport, and the need to uphold the image and reputation of the sport for the benefit of commercial sponsors[2]. However, there appears to be far less support among athletes for such rules, which some see as 'just moralistic judgements dressed up as sporting concerns'[3]. For example, the IOC Athlete's Commission has stated:

> While the IOC has a strong interest in preserving the fairness of Olympic competition, and while it has strong grounds in sport ethics for seeking to eliminate doping, it is on far riskier ground if it seeks to mandate moral rules unrelated to sport. It is not clear why the rules of eligibility for sport should include all recreational drugs used in all countries. If sports federations or the IOC wish to take a stand against recreational drug-use (or tobacco, or alcohol abuse, or other social problems) then this should be done through codes of conduct and education, rather than rules that govern eligibility for sport competition[4].

1 For example, the Football Association tests for 'a comprehensive list of social drugs'. Hodson *Ethical Dilemmas: Defining Cheating*, UK Sport Seminar, Tackling Ethical Issues in Drugs and Sport (October 1996).

2 See Verroken, 'A time for re-evaluation: the challenge to an athlete's reputation' in *Drugs and Doping in Sport* (2001, Cavendish) at p 36: 'the argument that there is "no perceived performance enhancement benefit" fails to take into account the role model responsibilities that come with being an elite athlete representing your country, as well as the responsibility you have towards your fellow athletes, sponsors and sport'.

For a contrary view, see Welch 'A snort and a puff: recreational drugs and discipline in professional sport' in *Drugs and Doping in Sport* (2001, Cavendish) at pp 75 et seq.

3 Mick Hume (1999) Times, 9 August.

4 IOC Athlete's Commission *The Athlete's Anti-Doping Passport*, 22 March 2000. The current IOC list of prohibited substances gives sports federations the choice whether or not to ban cannabinoids. See para E4.143. The draft World Anti-Doping Code, which is set to become the fundamental anti-doping instrument in world sport (see para E4.45), would exclude use of such drugs from doping codes, allowing sports instead, if they so choose, to make the use of such drugs a violation of a separate code of conduct. See draft World Anti-Doping Code, E-Version 1.0, issued 10 June 2002, cl 8.3.5.

E4.12 As for the second commonly proposed rationale for anti-doping regulation (protecting the health of athletes), it is certainly true that drug use can have various detrimental side-effects, which can be significant or even life-threatening[1]. There is also evidence that athletes focused on competing at elite levels can make irrational decisions regarding such serious health risks[2]. Nevertheless, there are those who remain uncomfortable with this paternalistic approach[3].

1 See para E4.138 et seq. See generally 'The medical consequences of taking performance-enhancing and other drugs in sports' – ch 3 of *Drugs in Sport: The Pressure to Perform* (2002, BMA).

2 See Goldman and Klatz *Death in the Locker Room 2* (1992) Chicago: Elite Sports Medicine, p 23, extracted in Gardiner *Sports Law* (2nd edn, 2001, Cavendish Publishing), pp 300 and 301 (reporting that more than 50% of athletes say they would take a drug that was guaranteed to kill them, if it was first guaranteed to help them become Olympic champions). See also Bamberger and Yaeger 'Over the Edge: Special Report' *Sports Illustrated*, May 1997; Radford, 'The fight against doping in sport: the last five years' (1992) 33(1) *Sport & Leisure* 1; (1998) The Economist, 6 June. See generally *Drugs in Sport: The Pressure to Perform* (2002, BMA).

3 See eg Chris Jones 'Drugs Sports & Ethics' (1994) 1 *Relay* 16: 'providing that the risks are known and the choice is voluntary and that no-one else is harmed, then is this a matter for the sporting authorities?'

E4.13 However, the weaknesses in the various anti-doping rationales are of little practical importance. The fact is that condoning drug use in sport would not only be perceived to threaten the core characteristics of sport that give it such massive popular appeal (and consequent commercial value); it would also compromise the 'war on drugs' being waged in society in general. It is therefore very unlikely to happen[1].

1 See eg IOC press release, 8 July 1999: 'The IOC wishes to reiterate its total commitment to the fight against doping, with the aim or protecting athletics' health and preserving fair play in sport. Any declarations which go against these principles are both wrong and misplaced'; Conclusions of the Anti-Doping Working Party at the First EU Conference on Sport, Olympia May 1999: 'The slightest permissiveness is not tolerated in the fight against doping'; European Commission, *Salt Lake City Winter Olympics: success for Europe and a step closer to zero tolerance on doping*, press release dated 25 February 2002, IP/02/309 (same).

E4.14 On the other hand, a less narrow approach would help all sides. The advocates for a crushing regulatory response plainly believe it helps the cause of anti-doping to establish a black and white system based on strict liability principles[1]. In the authors' view, however, an approach that does not differentiate on any level between those who set out to cheat and those who do not, does far more harm than good to the fight against drugs in sport. Branding an athlete a cheat, disqualifying him from the event in question, and banning him from future participation in the sport based (for example) on the inadvertent presence of a prohibited substance of a nature and/or in a quantity that cannot on any basis have enhanced his performance, risks bringing the system into disrepute[2].

1 Typical of this approach is the following extract from *Doping: An IOC White Paper* (Lausanne 1999), written by Prince Alexandre de Merode, the Chairman of the IOC's Medical Commission: 'The sports world, concerned by the rapid expansion of doping, tried to circumscribe its effects and set limits. In vain. Each definition whose philosophical content was satisfactory failed to withstand the legalistic precision of the man of law, a phenomenon that allowed the guilty to proclaim their innocence, to escape well-deserved sanctions, and even to make their fortune at the expense of trusting and naïve organisations by means of morally unjustifiable damages'.

2 See further para E4.101 et seq.

3 WHICH BODIES REGULATE DRUG USE IN SPORT?

E4.15 Over time, a wide array of national and international organisations, from sport and from government, has asserted the right to regulate drug use in sport, alongside or even in priority to other regulators. While some of the claims to regulatory authority might be relatively easy to dismiss on grounds of marginal relevance[1] and/or credibility[2], the field remains relatively crowded. The inconsistencies of approach from sport to sport and from country to country (particularly with regard to definitions of doping and sanctioning tariffs) do nothing to aid the war on drugs[3]. Greater harmonisation of effort between all competent parties remains a pressing objective, and the number one priority of the World Anti-Doping Agency[4].

1 For example, neither the United Nations' Drug Control Program nor the World Health Organisation's substance-abuse programme appears to have had much direct practical impact in this area.

2 Whereas the European Commission has perhaps deemed it politically unacceptable not to be seen to be responding strongly to expressions of concern from the Council of Ministers and the European Parliament about the scourge of doping in sport (hence the frequent press releases announcing action plans), nevertheless it is difficult to discern a sound legal basis for the Commission's claims to jurisdiction in this area. See further paras B1.39 to B1.47 and especially B1.48.

3 See eg paras E4.89 to E4.104 (lack of harmonisation of definitions of doping offence) and E4.338 et seq (lack of harmonisation on sanctions).

4 See para E4.42 et seq.

A Regulation by the state

E4.16 Illegal drug use is a threat to public health, which traditionally it is the government's responsibility to protect. The governments of some states have used this as the justification for adopting legislation regarding drug use in sport that often includes provisions for state-sponsored doping controls and for *criminal* investigation (including search and seizure), liability and sanction[1].

1 Certain states (eg Greece, Belgium, France, Italy) impose criminal penalties, including imprisonment, on those who supply athletes with drugs and sometimes even (eg Greece, Belgium) on the athletes who use them, provided knowledge and intent are shown. See generally *Rules Governing Doping and Drug Trafficking in the Various Countries*, Report of the Working Group on The Legal and Political Aspects of Doping, World Conference on Doping in Sport, Lausanne (February 1999), Appendix One.

The French criminal authorities carried out searches and seizures during the 1998 Tour de France that uncovered evidence of EPO use that would not have been uncovered by sample collection and analysis. Such high profile police investigations have culminated in criminal trials. See eg *Cycling's 'Drugs Doctor' Ferrari Begins Trial Today* (2001) Sportcal.com, 24 September; 'Doping probe threatens to disfigure football' (2002) Financial Times, 20 May.

E4.17 Consistent with its non-interventionist approach to the regulation of sport generally, however[1], the UK government has traditionally taken a relatively hands-off approach to the regulation of drug use in sport. The UK has endorsed the Olympic Movement Anti-Doping Code[2]; and it is also a signatory to the Council of Europe's 1989 Anti-Doping Convention[3], and to the International Anti-Doping Arrangement[4]. However, it has not passed any specific legislation to incorporate the provisions of these international instruments into domestic law, or to require sports bodies to adopt anti-doping programmes reflecting their provisions[5]. Instead, the regulation, policing and enforcement of anti-doping rules in sport in the United Kingdom are left largely to the respective sports governing bodies.

1 See generally Chapter A1. In contrast, interventionist states such as France and Italy have issued codified anti-doping regulations that sports federations must adopt and enforce, or else face being stripped of their right to govern their respective sports. See eg French Law no 99 222 of 23 March 1999 and the Italian Law no 376 of 14 December 2000, both on 'Discipline of health protection in sports activities and of fight against doping'.
See generally Chaker *Study on national sports legislation in Europe* (1999, Council of Europe Publishing), p 78 et seq.

2 See para E4.23.

3 The Anti-Doping Convention (Council of Europe – European Treaties – ETS No 135) was adopted in 1989. Thirty-eight member states of the Council of Europe have signed it, including the UK. It is currently the main legal instrument for the harmonisation of doping rules at government level but consists only of statements of general principle, with each signatory left to decide how to implement it at national level. See further para B1.42.

4 The International Anti-Doping Arrangement (MOU 1990) outlines the commitment of its signatories (the UK, Australia, Canada, New Zealand, Sweden, the Netherlands and Norway) to co-operate and promote anti-doping in sport.

5 Similarly, while EU member states are entitled to require pharmacists to print warnings on medicines that are banned from use in sport – see Council Directive 92/27/EEC of 31 March 1992, OJ L 13, 30/04/1992, pp 8–12 – again the UK government has not implemented any national legislation to that effect.

E4.18 That statement is subject, however, to two important provisos. First, it does not take account of the government's indirect regulation of drug use in sport through the work of UK Sport's Ethics and Anti-Doping Directorate[1]. Secondly, a sports governing body can only impose sport-specific sanctions, ie disqualification from the event in question and a ban from further participation in the sport[2]. It cannot punish those not involved in the sport, which makes it powerless against suppliers and other non-athlete transgressors[3]. Only the state has that ability, through the criminal law. In the UK, the Misuse of Drugs Act 1971[4] makes it a criminal offence (subject to certain restrictions and qualifications) to:

(i) import or export a controlled drug (s 3(1));
(ii) produce or 'be concerned in' the production of a controlled drug (s 4(2));
(iii) supply or offer to supply a controlled drug or to be concerned in the supply or offer of supply of a controlled drug by another (s 4(3));
(iv) be in possession of a controlled drug (s 5(2)); or
(v) be in possession of a controlled drug with intent to supply it to another (s 5(3)).

1 See para E4.33 et seq.

2 See para E4.325 et seq.

3 The draft WADA code imposes a responsibility on governments 'to regulate the conduct of athlete support personnel who violate anti-doping rules including the possibility of professional discipline, penal sanctions and other punishment beyond that which sports bodies can impose': draft World Anti-Doping Code, E-Version 1.0, issued 10 June 2002, para 5.3.5.

4 See also the Misuse of Drugs Regulations 1985 and the Medicines Act 1968. See generally Lowther 'Criminal Law Regulation of Performance Enhancing Drugs' in *Drugs and Doping in Sport* (2001, Cavendish), p 225.

E4.19 There are three classes of 'controlled' drugs (A, B and C, listed in Sch 2 to the Act). The range of potential penalties depends on the harmfulness of the drug in question: possession of a Class A drug with intent to supply another is punishable by an unlimited fine, seizure of assets and/or up to life imprisonment; possession of a Class B drug with intent to supply is punishable by a fine of up to £2,500 and/or up to 14 years in prison; and possession of a Class C drug with intent to supply is punishable by a fine of up to £1,000 and/or up to five years in prison[1].

1 However, the police reportedly have a policy of not prosecuting Class C drugs offences. See Moore *Sports Law and Litigation* (2nd edn, CLT Professional Publishing) at p 161.

E4.20 Importantly, the Misuse of Drugs Act 1971 is aimed at society as a whole, not sport in particular, and there is no necessary correlation between the Act and the anti-doping rules adopted by sports governing bodies. In particular, while many substances that are 'controlled' drugs under the Act are also banned from use in sport – eg cocaine, diamorphine (Class A), amphetamine (Class B), stanozolol, clenbuterol and testosterone (Class C)[1] – many substances are banned from use in sport that do not appear on Sch 2 to the Act. Indeed, many substances that are prohibited in the sporting context (eg caffeine, ephedrine) are available over the counter or by prescription in the UK.

B Regulation by the International Olympic Committee

E4.21 The IOC, working through its Medical Commission, has traditionally presented itself as the figurehead of the fight against drug use in sport. A Court of Arbitration for Sport panel has opined that the ultimate 'source of competence with regard to rules against doping' is the Olympic Charter, which gives the IOC 'fundamental competence with regard to the fight against doping'[1].

1 *Re International Cycling Union and Italian National Olympic Committee*, CAS 94/128, *Digest of CAS Awards 1986–1998* (Berne 1988) at p 495.
The Olympic Charter states (in relevant part) that the role of the IOC is (among other things) to 'lead the fight against doping in sport' and to 'take measures the goal of which is to prevent endangering the health of athletes': Olympic Charter, Chapter One, cl 2(8) and 2(9).

E4.22 In September 1988, the IOC adopted the 'International Olympic Charter Against Doping in Sport'. In 1994, it signed an agreement with the Summer and Winter Olympic Federations and National Olympic Committees to unify anti-doping rules and procedures based on a list of the prohibited substances and methods established by the IOC Medical Commission[1], and in September 1994 it presented a Medical Code relating to the use of drugs in sport, which included the first IOC List of Prohibited Substances and Prohibited Methods[2].

1 IOC *Preventing and Fighting against Doping in Sport* (Lausanne 1994).
2 For a discussion of which, see para E4.136 et seq.

E4.23 This first attempt at harmonisation had limited results[1]. In November 1998, therefore, the IOC adopted a single unified Medical Code, which it professed should be applied throughout the Olympic Movement. The delegates at the World Anti-Doping Conference held in Lausanne the following year declared their commitment to make the Medical Code – renamed the Anti-Doping Code – 'the basis for the fight against doping in sport'[2]. Thus, the Olympic Movement Anti-Doping Code came into effect on 1 January 2000. Although it is contemplated that the World Anti-Doping Agency will replace the Olympic Movement Anti-Doping Code with its own Code once the current review and consultation process is over[3], until that time the Olympic Movement Anti-Doping Code remains in full force and effect and is the cornerstone anti-doping text for sport.

1 See generally Vrijman 'A Commentary on Current Issues and Problems' in *Drugs and Doping in Sport* (2001, Cavendish), p 147.
2 *Declaration on Doping in Sport*, World Anti-Doping Conference (Lausanne 1999).
3 See para E4.45.

E4.24 The Olympic Movement Anti-Doping Code applies, as a matter of contract, to all events held as part of the Olympic Games, whatever the sport[1]. In addition, any international federation that wants to be recognised by the Olympic Movement as *the* governing body for its sport theoretically is required to adopt the Code not only for its Olympic events but also for all events held under its auspices, throughout the sport. This requirement has been interpreted as non-mandatory[2], and not effective to make the Olympic Movement Anti-Doping Code applicable to non-Olympic events absent a specific provision in the international federation's rules to that effect[3]. However, most international federations do currently follow the Olympic Movement Anti-Doping Code, at least for the most part[4].

1 See para E4.61. Both the IOC and the international federation of the sport in question will deal with a doping offence committed at the Olympic Games. The IOC disciplinary procedure will apply, but the IOC will only decide whether to disqualify an athlete and expel him from the rest of the particular Olympiad. The file will then be passed to the international federation for a decision in relation to any broader ban. Thus, for example, in *Baxter v IOC* (see para E4.134), the IOC's decision was solely a decision to disqualify the athlete and strip him of his medal, not a decision to ban him prospectively. It was the FIS that was charged with considering a prospective ban. It decided that the circumstances of the case called for a lenient sanction of only three months suspension. See (2002) Daily Telegraph, 4 June.
2 See *Re International Cycling Union and Italian National Olympic Committee*, CAS 94/128, *Digest of CAS Awards 1986–1998* (Berne 1998), pp 495, 507 at para 28: 'where doping is concerned, as its rules currently stand, the IOC itself imposes unification neither on the [National Olympic Committees], nor, moreover, on the [International Federations], any more than it obliges the [National Olympic Committees] to impose their own rules on the [National Federations]. Playing to the full its role as supreme authority of the Olympic Movement, it encourages such unification without imposing it, outside those cases provided for by the Medical Code … But the Code does not draw from these provisions the conclusion that any organisation which does not adopt the provisions of the Code thereby excludes itself from the Olympic Movement … The sole obligation of the [International Federations] and [National Olympic Committees] recognised by the IOC at the time of the adoption of the Code is to inform the IOC of the dates by when the necessary modifications will be adopted, without penalties being foreseen in the event of a violation of such obligation'.
3 See eg *Re International Cycling Union and Italian National Olympic Committee*, CAS 94/128, *Digest of CAS Awards 1986–1998* (Berne 1998), pp 495, 508. An IAAF arbitration panel ruled that the fact that the Olympic Movement Anti-Doping Code does not apply in non-Olympic events unless and until specifically adopted in the federation's rules for those events, even if the federation has committed itself to such application, meant that the athlete was subject to the IAAF's strict liability rules and could not rely on an Olympic Movement Anti-Doping Code provision departing from a strict liability approach. *Bavilacqua*, IAAF Arbitration Panel decision dated 25 November 1996, in Tarasti *Legal Solutions in International Doping Cases* (2000, SEP Editrice) at pp 143–146, para 5. See also *Haga v FIM*, CAS 2000/A/281/1, award dated 22 December 2000, *Digest of CAS Awards II 1998–2000* (2002, Kluwer), p 410.
4 See para E4.26.

C Regulation by international governing bodies

E4.25 The Olympic Charter specifically recognises the competence of international federations to conduct the fight against doping in their respective sports according to the specific characteristics and requirements of those sports[1]. According to the Court of Arbitration for Sport, therefore:

> [a]t all events, the [international federations] possess the principal competence with regard to establishing rules in the fight against doping which appears to be the best solution, given the necessity of ensuring the application of identical standards wherever the competitions relating to a specific sport are taking place[2].

1 It contemplates in particular that they may prohibit certain procedures and substances (Charter Rule 31, cl 2.6), administer medical controls and examinations (cl 2.2), and impose penalties for infractions (cl 2.7). Furthermore, even if the infraction takes place at the Olympic Games, the IOC will concern itself only with the athlete's result at the Games. It will leave it to the relevant international federation to determine whether the athlete should be banned from further events for a period. See para E4.24, n 1.

2 *Re International Cycling Union and Italian National Olympic Committee*, CAS 94/128, *Digest of CAS Awards 1986–1998* (Berne 1998), p 495, 504 at para 19.

E4.26 Some federations do provide for the application of the Olympic Movement Anti-Doping Code to all of their events, even outside the Olympic Games. Others have adopted anti-doping programmes that use the Olympic Movement Anti-Doping Code as a reference point but depart from it in various more or less material respects where deemed necessary to reflect the specific circumstances of their particular sports[1]. For example, they might limit testing to fewer classes of prohibited substances than appear on the IOC List, and/or they might modify the sanctions that would apply under the Olympic Movement Anti-Doping Code in the event that a doping charge is upheld. The result is an alarming divergence of approach from sport to sport[2].

1 See generally Vrijman 'Harmonisation: A Commentary on Current Issues and Problems' in *Drugs and Doping in Sport* (2001, Cavendish), p 147.

2 See eg para E4.340 et seq.

E4.27 Periodically since 1994, the IOC has written to international federations within the Olympic Movement, asking them to confirm that they have implemented the Olympic Movement Anti-Doping Code throughout their sport. To the knowledge of the authors, at least one major international sports federation has responded by confirming substantial compliance with the Olympic Movement Anti-Doping Code, but noting specific deviations that it deemed necessary for that sport, without suffering any adverse consequence[1].

1 On the other hand, the authors have also heard anecdotal evidence that the provisional recognition of at least one international federation under the Olympic Charter was not confirmed after the standard two-year probationary period, allegedly because of its poor doping record. In the same vein, *The Daily Telegraph* of 5 February 2002 reported the comments of Dick Pound, World Anti-Doping Agency Chairman, that the US domestic athletics federation should be thrown out of the Olympic Movement for failing to report all positive results of its athletes to the International Association of Athletics Federations ('IAAF'), as required by the IAAF's rules. See generally Report dated 11 July 2001 of the Independent International Review Commission on Doping Control – USA Track & Field, available on www.wada.org.

E4.28 Furthermore, it seems that the regulatory autonomy of international federations in doping matters will increase once the World Anti-Doping Agency regime comes fully into force[1].

1 See *World Anti-Doping Code, Explanatory Document C-103/01-0.6* (Lausanne 2002): 'Unlike the [Olympic Movement Anti-Doping Code] and its predecessor, the IOC Medical Code, the World Anti-Doping Code is not intended to be a comprehensive set of anti-doping rules which provides all

of the detailed specifications for sample collection, sample analysis and results management. Rather, the World Anti-Doping Code should be a shorter more general document which provides the framework upon which the specific anti-doping rules and regulations of all stakeholders are based. To encourage the adoption of effective anti-doping rules and regulations by the stakeholders, the World Anti-Doping Agency will publish model anti-doping rules and regulations and other models of best practice for each category of stakeholder … Some stakeholders may choose to adopt the model rules and regulations and other models of best practice verbatim. Others may decide to adopt the models with modifications. Still other stakeholders may choose to develop their own rules and regulations consistent with the general principles and specific requirements set forth in the Code'.

E4.29 In the anti-doping sphere, where there is a pressing need for the application of uniform standards throughout the sport, at every level and in every country, the international federation is likely to include in its rules fairly specific anti-doping provisions that it will apply directly to cross-border competitions held under its auspices, and that it will require member national federations to apply to domestic events held under their own auspices with the sanction of the international federation[1]. Different international federations will then be more or less active in policing and enforcing those standards, depending on their relative commitment, resources and practical authority.

1 See eg IAAF Rule 58 (Responsibility for Doping Control).

D Regulation by national governing bodies

E4.30 The degree of discretion allowed by an international federation to a national governing body in crafting anti-doping regulations at a national level will vary[1]. The international federation will tend to want to delegate responsibility to the national governing body for testing and management of results, including initial disciplinary proceedings. However, the international federation will generally want to retain control over the system and the ability to challenge decisions taken by national governing bodies with which it disagrees.

1 See eg IAAF Rule 2.2: 'The rules and regulations of an elected national governing body must be in conformity with and not wider than IAAF eligibility rules'.

E4.31 However, the fact that a national governing body has an interest in a clean image and in the availability of its top athletes to represent the governing body in international competition creates a potential conflict of interest for the national governing body, not only at the drafting stage but also (indeed, in particular) at the policing and enforcement stage[1]. This has led on occasion to conflict between the national governing body and the international federation, for whom uniform application and enforcement of anti-doping norms throughout the sport is essential[2].

1 Of course, the same could also be said of international federations, and indeed of the IOC. See eg Bamberger and Yaegas, 'Over the Edge: Special Report' *Sports Illustrated* (May 1997): 'Exposing star athletes could create enough publicity to send sponsors packing, and it might also disillusion a sports-watching public that assumes that the overwhelming majority of Olympic athletes are clean'.

2 See further paras E4.32 and A3.124.

E4.32 For example, the rules of the International Association of Athletics Federations (IAAF) give that body the power, where a member national association fails to take action against an athlete following a positive drugs test, to suspend the athlete pending an adjudication of his case[1]. Ultimately, the IAAF can suspend a national association from membership if it fails to take sufficient action against an athlete suspected of having committed a doping offence[2], and it can also challenge any decision of a member's doping tribunal that it believes to be in error[3]. FINA's rules provide, in contrast, that positive tests by four of a national association's swimmers in one 12-month period will result in a two-year ban of that association from international competition[4]; while WADA's draft Code authorises the punishment of national federations that fail to cooperate in anti-doping efforts or who are deemed, because of the number of positive tests, to be 'not committed to eliminating doping by competitors within its jurisdiction'[5].

1 IAAF Rule 59.2. In 1997, when USA Track & Field took no action after US athletes Mary Decker Slaney and Sandra Farmer-Patrick tested positive, leaving them free to continue to compete, the IAAF intervened under Rule 59.2 and suspended both of them from competition pending the brining of disciplinary proceedings by USA Track & Field.

The UCI has a similar rule. See *UCI v A*, CAS 97/175, award dated 15 April 1998, *Digest of CAS Awards II 1998–2000* (2002, Kluwer), p 158.

In *Walker v UKA and IAAF* (7 July 2000, unreported), QBD (Toulson J.), 25 July 2000 (Hallett J), one of the issues was whether the IAAF could retrospectively apply an additional rule allowing it to suspend athletes cleared by the national body pending the hearing of its challenge to that decision before an IAAF arbitration panel. The events in question had taken place before the rule was introduced. After Hallett J gave a strong indication that retrospective application would not be legitimate, the IAAF backed down. See paras A3.124 and E4.368.

2 IAAF Rule 20.2(c). Cf (2002) Daily Telegraph, 5 February, reporting the comments of Dick Pound, World Anti-Doping Agency Chairman, that USA Track & Field should be thrown out of the Olympic Movement for failing to report all positive results of its athletes to the IAAF, as required by the IAAF's rules. Mr Pound dismissed as baseless USA Track & Field's reported defence that US privacy laws prevented such disclosure until all avenues for legal challenges have been exhausted. See generally Report dated 11 July 2001 of the Independent International Review Commission on Doping Control – USA Track & Field, available on www.wada.org.

3 See para E4.366. A number of well-known cases took this form, reported at [2001] 4 ISLR: *Sotomayor* at p 254; *Ottey* at p 260; *Walker* at p 264; *Christie* at p 270; *Cadogan* at p 273. Only in *Ottey* did the IAAF fail. *Sotomayor* offers the most extreme example of national body recalcitrance.

4 FINA Doping Rules (2002).

5 Draft World Anti-Doping Code, E-Version 1.0, issued 10 June 2002, cl 8.8.10.

E Regulation by national anti-doping agencies

(a) UK Sport

E4.33 In a clear indication of a lack of faith in the ability of sports governing bodies to police their sports transparently and effectively, the policy statement drawn up by the signatories to the International Anti-Doping Arrangement[1] specifies that:

> [a] national organisation independent of the national sport organisations, and with full integrity in the anti-doping field, shall have responsibility for ensuring the enforcement of the anti-doping sport policies, laws and/or regulations[2].

1 See para E4.17, n 4.

2 ISDC Policy Statement 3.1 (National Anti-Doping Organisations).

E4.34 Thus, notwithstanding the UK government's unwillingness to take direct responsibility for the regulation of drug use in sport[1], it does in fact regulate the area indirectly, via UK Sport and the regional sports councils[2], by conditioning recognition of an entity as the governing body of its sport (and therefore access to public funds for that sport) on compliance with UK Sport's Anti-Doping Policy[3].

1 See para E4.17.

2 As to which, see para A1.47 et seq.
3 Article 4.2 of the Council of Europe's Anti-Doping Convention (see para E4.17, n 3) requires signatories to 'make it a criterion for the grant of public subsidies to sport organisations that they effectively apply anti-doping regulations'. UK Sport *Statement of Anti-Doping Policy* states (at para II): 'UK Sport as the national anti-doping organisation for the UK will put in place an anti-doping programme designed to prevent the misuse of drugs in sport and to penalise those who are guilty of it contravening this policy. The Sports Councils will work in partnership with the governing bodies of sport and sports organisations within the UK to achieve effective anti-doping policies and procedures. As a condition of recognition and eligibility for funding of governing bodies and sports organisations the Sports Councils will place certain requirements on them to ensure the effectiveness of this programme'.

E4.35 Claiming legitimacy from the ISDC Policy Statement[1], and exercising de facto power through its control of the public purse-strings, UK Sport's Ethics and Anti-Doping Directorate pursues its declared role of setting out the policy framework for anti-doping, delivering a testing programme against agreed standards, monitoring the outcome of test results, and keeping the sporting community educated and informed about anti-doping matters[2].

1 See para E4.33, n 2.
2 See eg UK Sport *Anti-Doping Report 2000/01* at p 2.

E4.36 Governing bodies seeking public funding are required to submit their own anti-doping policies to UK Sport for approval. To be approved, those policies have to conform to the provisions of UK Sport's Anti-Doping Policy[1]. A central tenet of that policy is accountability:

> UK Sport must be able to independently review all governing body anti-doping policies and procedures, and any information on the testing of athletes from international competitions must be shared with UK Sport by the governing body in the UK[2].

Once the policy has been approved, failure to comply with it 'may result in immediate suspension of UK Sport and Home Country Sports Council funding'[3]. In addition, continued eligibility for funding will depend on meeting the targets for testing[4].

1 See UK Sport *Anti-Doping Policy*, Annex A: 'As a condition of recognition and eligibility for lottery and exchequer funding from the Sports Councils, all governing bodies will be required to put in place and observe an Anti-Doping Policy consistent with what is set out below'. See also UK Sport *Model Rules and Guidelines for Anti-Doping 2002*.
In contrast to national anti-doping agencies in certain other states, UK Sport recognises that an international governing body may impose conflicting requirements. '[P]roviding the national policy standards are not weakened by the adoption of the [International Federation's] rules, no approval for changes would be withheld by the UK Sport'. See UK Sport *Anti-Doping Report 2000–01*, p 3. See also UK Sport's *Anti-Doping Policy*, commentary para III, and at the preamble to Annex A. Tellingly, however, there is no mention of what would happen if the international federation required a variation that UK Sport considered to be unacceptable.
2 UK Sport *Anti-Doping Report 2000–01*, p 3.
3 UK Sport *Anti-Doping Policy* at para IV. See also UK Sport *Anti-Doping Policy* at para VIII: 'If a governing body fails to agree an Anti-Doping Policy with UK Sport, or is found by UK Sport to be in breach of that policy, the Sports Councils will be entitled to cease any payments by way of lottery and exchequer funding to the governing body and seek claw-back of any payments made during the period of default'.
4 UK Sport *Anti-Doping Policy* at para VI.

E4.37 UK Sport claims to reserve the right to test athletes for prohibited drugs 'wherever and whenever it deems appropriate'[1]. In fact, however, its jurisdiction currently depends entirely upon a sport's reliance on public funds. At events held under the auspices of national governing bodies who rely on public funding and therefore must comply with UK Sport's Anti-Doping Policy, UK Sport is certainly able to insist that it be allowed to conduct testing of participants. However, where a sports governing body has no need to apply for public funds, as an ostensibly private body with no express public authority or function[2] it is under no legal obligation to participate in the anti-doping activities of UK Sport. In such circumstances, UK Sport has no right to require the governing body to comply with UK Sport's Anti-Doping Policy, nor does it have the right to test athletes participating in the governing body's events[3]. However, the governing body or event organiser, if it implements its own independent anti-doping programme, is of course free to contract with UK Sport (or any other service provider) for the provision of sample collection and testing services at its events[4].

1 UK Sport *Anti-Doping Programme Annual Report 1999–2000* at p 6.
2 See paras A1.19 and A3.62.
3 On the other hand, if the sport is an Olympic sport and the national governing body wants to send a team to the next Olympic Games, it must comply with the regulations of the British Olympic Association, which means allowing testing by UK Sport.
4 According to the commentary to UK Sport *Anti-Doping Policy*, para III, UK Sport will only provide anti-doping services to such sports bodies if their anti-doping rules comply with that policy.

E4.38 Notwithstanding the activities of UK Sport in this area, however, the government's commitment has clear limits. In September 2001, for example, representatives of UK Athletics and the British Olympic Association reportedly met with the Minister of Sport, Richard Caborn, seeking a commitment by the government to underwrite the legal costs of prosecuting doping cases[1]. The authors are unaware of any positive response.

1 *UK Athletics: We Need Financial Help to Fight Doping* (2001) Sportcal.com, 11 September.

(b) Other countries[1]

E4.39 A UK athlete may well find himself competing in international events staged overseas. In a small but increasing number of countries, domestic anti-doping legislation has been passed, specific to sport, that gives national authorities (often the National Olympic Committee, but in some cases government agencies or even the police) the right to conduct investigations into suspected drug abuse in sport (including carrying out drug testing), to bring disciplinary proceedings (directly or through the national sports federation) against transgressors, with lengthy bans from the sport among the possible sanctions, but also in some cases to bring criminal charges against those that supply banned drugs to athletes, and even against athletes that knowingly use such drugs[2].

1 Space constraints make it impossible to deal, in this section, with all of the various anti-doping agencies operating outside of the UK. Instead, the section simply flags some of the major issues of which a UK athlete competing abroad needs to be aware.
2 See para E4.16, n 1.

E4.40 UK athletes competing overseas can therefore be required to submit to drug-testing not only by the event organiser, under the rules of the competition, but also by a foreign governmental agency, under the mandate of local law. The athlete may find himself asked to provide a sample to a local authority whose jurisdiction he has not agreed to and whose procedures he has not vetted. The team manager might be allowed to accompany him during sample collection, to identify any discrepancies in collection procedures, but thereafter the sample disappears for analysis, and there can be few if any discernible protections for the athletes in the procedures that follow. In addition, the tests may be for different substances from those on his governing body's list, and the potential sanctions may vary from his governing body's rules. Indeed, they may include possible *criminal* sanctions.

E4.41 With sports governing bodies, on the one hand, seeking to preserve the global uniform application of the anti-doping rules they have fashioned for their sports, and national authorities, on the other, jealously protective of the nation's sovereign right to regulate drug use within its territorial boundaries and suspicious of the sports movement's good faith, fundamental jurisdictional clashes are inevitable. In some cases, the national authorities' anti-doping programmes are claimed to 'trump' the international governing bodies' own programmes. Indeed, the claim is sometimes made that testing carried out by or on behalf of international federations on a state's territory infringes that state's sovereign jurisdiction. In other cases, the two regulatory systems are said to run in parallel with each other. In both cases, serious problems arise[1]. Various protocols have been negotiated between governing bodies of various sports and foreign governmental agencies that seek to reconcile the desire of the governing body for global enforcement throughout its sport of a uniform set of rules with the foreign agency's insistence that 'its' law must be applied in its territory. The jury remains out on the long-term efficacy of such a compromise solution.

1 For example, UEFA reported that in 1997 a national anti-doping organisation carried out out-of-competition tests on participants in UEFA matches played within that organisation's territorial jurisdiction, without even notifying UEFA beforehand. UEFA said it would not recognise any positive findings identified or sanctions imposed as a result of such tests. Discussion paper of the Anti-Doping Convention Monitoring Group, *The Problem of Conflicting Jurisdiction between Sports Federations and the National Anti-Doping Agencies*, 20 February 1997, T-DO (96) 26 Rev at para 7. The paper's authors concluded that better communication and co-ordination were required.

F Towards uniformity: the World Anti-Doping Agency

E4.42 Quite clearly, this confusing and contradictory regulatory thicket threatens to compromise the one thing that unites the various would-be regulators, namely the desire to fight drug use in sport. In February 1999, at the IOC-hosted World Conference on Anti-Doping in Sport in Lausanne, delegates from the Olympic Movement, international federations, the United Nations, governments, national anti-doping agencies, athletes and the medical profession took a first step towards cutting through that thicket and getting sports bodies and governments to work towards a consistent and coordinated approach. Specifically, they agreed to establish an independent international anti-doping agency in time for the 2000 Sydney Olympics, with a mandate 'to co-ordinate the various programmes necessary to realise the objectives that shall be defined jointly by all the parties concerned'[1].

1 Declaration on Doping in Sport, World Anti-Doping Conference (Lausanne 1999). See generally Houlihan 'The World Anti-Doping Agency: Prospects for Success' in *Drugs and Doping in Sport* (2001, Cavendish), p 125.

E4.43 The World Anti-Doping Agency was formally established on 10 November 1999. With headquarters in Montreal, Canada, it has a board of 40, of whom 17 are from the Olympic Movement, 17 from public authorities (four each from the Asias, Asia and Europe, three from Africa and two from Oceania) and six appointed by the board.

E4.44 The World Anti-Doping Agency's mission is 'to promote and co-ordinate at international level the fight against doping in sport in all its forms'. Its principal task is 'to co-ordinate a comprehensive anti-doping programme at international level' in concert with the international federations. It has taken over from the IOC's Medical Commission custodianship of the List of Prohibited Substances and Prohibited Methods, as well as laboratory accreditation. It will spearhead the development of out-of-competition testing programmes; will develop uniform standards and procedures for sample collection and analysis; will work towards the harmonisation and unification of anti-doping rules, disciplinary procedures and sanctions; and will promote education and research into anti-doping in sport. It also proposes to encourage coordinated action by national governments on issues such as adopting harmonised anti-doping legislation, taking strict measures to limit the availability of prohibited substances (including strict penalties against traffickers and also sanctions against doctors and pharmacists who mis-prescribe or mis-dispense prohibited substances), proper labelling of medicaments, coordination of public action through one responsible body in each state, support for education and research programmes, and financial support for doping control programmes[1].

1 See WADA Mission Statement. See also *Anti-doping body hands out $5m to fund doping research* (2001) Sportcal.com, 4 June. The IOC Medical Commission will confine itself in the future to issues relating to sports medicine. For example, it will continue to examine concerns relating to developments in gene therapy. See (2001) 4(5) Sports Law Bulletin 1.

E4.45 The World Anti-Doping Agency has committed to developing the Olympic Movement Anti-Doping Code into a World Anti-Doping Code for approval and adoption by all stakeholders by April 2003, in time for implementation at the Athens Olympics in 2004[1]. The first draft was issued for public comment on 12 June 2002[2]. The World Anti-Doping Agency is also considering mechanisms that would allow individual governments to adopt the Code directly into national law[3]. The Intergovernmental Consultative Group[4] has stated that the Convention 'should act as the reference point for the development of a world wide legal instrument' that would give the World Anti-Doping Agency's rules and pronouncements legally binding effect[5]. Initially, the World Anti-Doping Agency itself talked of governments 'ratifying' the Code as part of an international convention, but it has since replaced that plan with a vague reference to 'identifying tools by which governments may adopt the Code'[6]. Whether or not this aim is realistic, in the meantime the World Anti-Doping Agency will rely on the more traditional, indirect methods of compulsion, such as conditioning inclusion in the Olympic Movement on compliance.

1 See *World Anti-Doping Code: Project Plan*, Version 1.4 (Lausanne, December 2001): 'If WADA is going to be successful in the achievement of a uniform and consistent world-wide approach to deter the use of drugs in sport, an overall framework of relevant policies, principles, standards, procedures, guidelines, recommendations etc within anti-doping must be in place – labelled as the World Anti-Doping Code'.

2 Draft World Anti-Doping Code, E-Version 1.0.

3 See World Anti-Doping Code: Project Plan, Version 1.4 (Lausanne, December 2001): 'But WADA has limited formal authority to implement an anti-doping code. IFs, IOC and Governments and NADOS should accept to implement the Code if it is to be effective as a tool to achieve real harmonisation'.

4 See para E4.48.

5 IICGADS Declaration (Montreal, February 2000).

6 Compare Art IV of the *Draft framework of the Code, RY-01.10.22* (Lausanne 2002) to Art IV of version RY 01.11.17 of the same document.

E4.46 The prospect of co-ordinated and harmonised action not only within the private sports movement but also among governments, bringing together sport-specific measures and state-backed sanctions, all working from the same set of objectives, has excited many of those fighting on the front line of the war on drugs. To date, however, the effectiveness of the new organisation, particularly in driving inter-state co-operation but also in winning the confidence of key sports federations, is yet to be proven[1].

1 See generally Houlihan, 'The World Anti-Doping Agency: Prospects for Success' in *Drugs and Doping in Sport* (2001, Cavendish), pp 125 and 145.

E4.47 Initially, various governmental bodies expressed concern about the independence, transparency and 'precise remit' of the World Anti-Doping Agency, given the IOC's heavy involvement[1]. The World Anti-Doping Agency has taken various steps to resolve these concerns, including agreeing on equal representation of sports bodies and governments on the WADA board[2], and a rotation of the chair between the two constituencies.

1 See eg European Commission press release IP/99/767. The Commission said that '[g]overnments would not accept an agency which was merely an appendage of sports organisations': *The Fight Against Doping in Sport*, Working paper for the First European Sports Conference (Olympia, May 1999). Tellingly, the work undertaken at the first meeting of the Intergovernmental Consultative Group on Anti-Doping in Sport, in February 2000, included formulating 'recommended principles of governance for WADA'. UK Sport *Anti-Doping Programme Annual Report 1999–2000* at p 14.

2 See para E4.43.

E4.48 Different authorities also seem to be finding it difficult to give up what they see as their regulatory priority in this area. Based on work done at the International Summit on Drugs in Sport held in Sydney in November 1999, various countries formed the International Intergovernmental Consultative Group on Anti-Doping in Sport, whose premise is that 'governments have a major role to play in developing a worldwide doping control programme' and whose objectives include:

> resolv[ing] the processes for co-ordinated world-wide governmental participation in WADA … and harmonis[ing] policies in areas that are exclusively the jurisdiction of government …[1]

1 Declaration adopted at the First Meeting of the International Intergovernmental Consultative Group on Anti-Doping in Sport (Montreal, February 2000).

E4.49 The UK is a member of the International Intergovernmental Consultative Group on Anti-Doping in Sport. UK Sport has stated:

> It is expected that WADA will interface with existing National Anti-Doping Organisations rather than duplicate current work of an established international standard … WADA would concentrate on assisting development in areas without an infrastructure for anti-doping under sport or government support[1].

1 UK Sport *Anti-Doping Report 2000–01* at p 5.

E4.50 The Council of Europe has made it plain that it does not intend to curtail the activities of the Anti-Doping Convention Monitoring Group[1]. And after a long-simmering dispute, European Union funding has been withheld from the World Anti-Doping Agency, and the European Commission is developing its own autonomous 'zero tolerance' anti-doping policy[2].

1 As to which, see para B1.42.
2 *EU Sports Official Targets Drugs*, Associated Press (6 December 2001); COM (2002) 220 from the Commission to the Council concerning the Commission's participation in WADA and its funding, 6 May 2002 (announcing decision to withdraw Community representative as observer on WADA board and not to provide EC funding to WADA). See further paras B1.44 and B1.45.

E4.51 On the other hand, the Lausanne Declaration made it clear that the private sports movement was not capitulating to the competence of the various governmental organisations on anti-doping issues, stating:

> The IOC, the [International Federations] and the [National Olympic Committees] will maintain their respective competence and responsibility to apply doping rules in accordance with their own procedures, and in co-operation with the [World Anti-Doping Agency][1].

To date, some sports have proved a lot more amenable than others to establishing links with the World Anti-Doping Agency.

1 Declaration on Doping in Sport, World Anti-Doping Conference (Lausanne 1999).

E4.52 One apparent success has been the World Anti-Doping Agency's out-of-competition testing programme. Further to agreements signed with various international federations, the World Anti-Doping Agency organised 2,500 tests in 2000, and planned 3,500 and 4,500 respectively for 2001 and 2002. It has also developed an Independent Observer programme as a means of quality assurance for governing body-sponsored testing. It has contributed to the work done on developing a reliable test for EPO[1]. It has stated that it wants to establish itself as 'a clearing-house for worldwide testing'[2], and many sports have called on it to take over the collection and testing process completely.

1 See para E4.192.
2 WADA Out-of-Competition Testing Program Report (8 February 2002).

4 HOW IS DRUG USE IN SPORT TO BE REGULATED?

E4.53 An effective sports anti-doping programme requires a clear acceptance by athletes participating in the sport[1] of an anti-doping programme that clearly and proportionately defines exactly what is prohibited[2] and gives the governing body the ability to police the prohibition, including a drug-testing system of unquestionable integrity and reliability[3], as well as the disciplinary authority to prosecute fairly and effectively those who transgress[4].

1 See paras E4.54 to E4.74.
2 See paras E4.75 to E4.173.
3 See paras E4.174 to E4.185 and E4.186 to E4.214.
4 See paras E4.215 to E4.241.

A The contractual commitment to anti-doping regulations

(a) The anti-doping programme

E4.54 In the United Kingdom, the regulatory and disciplinary authority of a sports governing body over the participants in the sport is not public but private in nature, deriving not from the sovereign authority of the state but from the consent of the participants[1].

1 See paras A1.19 and A3.62. See eg *Wilander and Novacek v Tobin and Jude (No 2)* [1997] 2 Lloyd's Rep 296, CA per Lord Woolf LJ: 'Assuming, but not deciding, that the [Anti-Doping] Appeals Committee is not a public body, this does not mean that it escapes the supervision of the High Court. The proceedings out of which this appeal arose are part of that supervision. The Appeals Committee's jurisdiction over the plaintiffs arises out of a contract'.

E4.55 It is therefore incumbent upon the governing body to ensure that its anti-doping programme is clear and unambiguous and is properly and validly incorporated into its constitution so that it can legitimately be said to form part of the contractual agreement between the governing body and participants in the sport[1]. If ambiguity does exist in the anti-doping programme, it is likely to be construed in favour of the athlete and against the governing body[2]. This is particularly true when a strict liability approach[3] is taken in the programme[4]. This subject-area is littered with authorities showing how, in the absence of clear 'constitutional' authority, and properly drafted and thought-out regulations, disciplinary efforts can quickly become undermined[5].

1 See eg *Wilander and Novacek v Tobin and Jude (No 2)* (26 March 1996, unreported), CA, per Neill LJ: 'it is important that, in the case of international bodies of the standing of the ITF who are responsible for major international sports, the rules which govern their affairs should be most carefully drafted so that the possibility of confusion and doubt is removed. These sports now assume multi-million pound, or multi-million dollars, dimensions and it is therefore incumbent on those responsible to make sure the rules are absolutely clear, and drafted so that the possibility of confusion is avoided'.

See also *USA Shooting and Quigley v Union Internationale de Tir*, CAS 94/129, award dated 23 March 1995, *Digest of CAS Awards 1986–1998* (Berne 1998) p 187, 197–98 at para 55: 'The fight against doping is arduous, and it may require strict rules. But the rule-makers and the rule-appliers must begin by being strict with themselves. Regulations that may affect the careers of dedicated athletes must be predictable. They must emanate from duly authorised bodies. They must be adopted in constitutionally proper ways. They should not be the product of an obscure process of accretion. Athletes and officials should not be confronted with a thicket of mutually qualifying or even contradictory rules that can be understood only on the basis of the de facto practice over the course of many years of a small group of insiders'.

2 As a matter of contract law. This is the contra proferentem principle. See eg *Aanes v FILA*, CAS 2001/A/317A, award dated 9 July 2001, p 15; *Ime Akpan*, IAAF Arbitration Panel, award dated 10 April 1995, in Tarasti *Legal Solutions In International Doping Cases* (SEP Editrice 2000) at p 135, para 4; *Tuck & Sons v Priester* (1887) 19 QBD 629 at 638 per Lord Esher MR.

Cf *Modahl v BAF Ltd* (28 July 1997, unreported), CA, per Lord Woolf: 'The BAF Rules are the rules for implementation in this country of requirements parallel to those contained in the IAAF Rules. If there is any ambiguity as to the interpretation of the BAF Rules then the IAAF [Rules] can be used to resolve that ambiguity'. See also Art 26(6) of the FILA Doping Regulations (200): 'Bearing in mind that the anti-doping code of the Olympic Movement has been drawn up in close co-operation with the International Federations, … any problems of interpretation of any article in these Regulations or for any question not dealt with here, must be referred to the IOC's Anti-Doping Code Lausanne 2000'.

Cf also *UKA v Walker* (2000) unreported UKA Disciplinary Committee decision dated 25 January 2000, para 30 (rejecting suggestion that phrase in anti-doping rules should be disregarded entirely because of lack of clarity, because that would 'amount to a charter for systematic steroid drug abuse').

3 As described at para E4.89 et seq.

4 See *USA Shooting and Quigley v Union Internationale de Tir,* CAS 94/129, award dated 23 May 1995, *Digest of CAS Awards 1986–1998* (Berne 1998), p 187, para 71: 'if the UIT adopts a strict liability test, it becomes even more important that the rules for the testing procedure are crystal-clear, that they are designed for reliability, and that it may be shown that they have been followed. Otherwise, the door will be open to a surfeit of litigation'.

5 See eg UK Sport *Anti-Doping Report 2000–01*, p 19 (reporting that a boxing governing body 'decided not to proceed with the case [against a boxer who tested positive for a metabolite of nandrolone] until regulations are changed in line with recommendation of appeal stewards'). For

further examples, see paras A3.10 and E4.90 et seq. See generally Young *Problems with the Definition of Doping: Does Lack of Fault or the Absence of Performance Enhancing Effect Matter?* – paper delivered at CAS arbitration seminar (Lausanne, 8 December 1998): 'The most publicised controversies in the war against doping in sport have involved attacks on the collection and testing process. However, the more fundamental problems in doping control are not the responsibility of the technicians and laboratory scientists. They are the responsibility of the lawyers and sports officials who write and enforce the doping rules. Ultimately, courts and arbitral tribunals are not going to enforce rules that are not clearly written and consistently applied. This is particularly true when the athlete testing positive is a sympathetic figure whose career is on the line. Unfortunately, most sports organisations do not have clear doping rules which unequivocally say what the organisation means. One of the biggest problem areas in this regard involves confusion over what the rules say in answer to the following two questions: Does it matter that the athlete testing positive was not at fault? Does it matter that the athlete's performance was not enhanced by the banned substance in question? A sports organisation may choose to answer these questions differently when defining a doping offence than it does when establishing rules for sanctions. It may also choose different rules for different banned substances. What is critical is that the organisation think through the implications of these questions and make sure that its rules answer them clearly. Otherwise, sports organisations are going to continue to get surprised by adverse judicial and arbitral decisions, and the perception that doping control really does work will be further undermined'.

E4.56 In drawing up its anti-doping rules, the governing body or event organiser will have to consider (among other things) what substances and methods to ban; whether to make doping a strict liability offence; whether to include ancillary offences and to bring non-athlete participants within the scope of the programme; whether to impose interim suspensions and (if so) whether to have a Review Board assessment of the evidence first; and what discretion (if any) to build in for the disciplinary tribunal with respect to sanctions and reinstatements[1]. The rules must set out how the governing body intends to enforce the programme, including the scope of any drug testing programme; must clearly explain the responsibilities of the participants to submit to testing and otherwise cooperate with the anti-doping efforts of the governing body; must respect the substantive and procedural rights of individual athletes; and must state clearly the potential sanctions for offenders[2].

1 See Young, para E4.55, n 5.
2 All of these issues are dealt with in the following sections of this chapter.

E4.57 On each issue, the governing body's room to manoeuvre may be limited. If the sport is in or has aspirations to join the Olympic movement, then the Olympic Movement Anti-Doping Code will have to be applied in Olympic events and theoretically in non-Olympic events as well, even if there may be latitude for variations that take into account the specific characteristics of the sport in question[1]. If the sport is not an Olympic one, the domestic governing body will have to determine how much freedom of action it is given under the international governing body's rules[2]. In addition, if the sport is dependent on public funding, then the domestic governing bodies in the UK will have to comply with UK Sport's model anti-doping code[3].

1 See para E4.25.
2 See para E4.30.
3 See para E4.36.

(b) The athlete's consent

E4.58 Assuming that the rulebook of the governing body contains a clear and unambiguous anti-doping programme, setting out the prohibitions, how they will be policed, and the disciplinary procedures and sanctions available upon proof of transgression[1], the next issue is to ensure that the provisions of the programme will be enforceable against a particular athlete. Evidence will be required that the athlete agreed to abide by and to be bound by the provisions of the anti-doping programme and any decisions made pursuant to that programme. Because of the significant intrusions that an anti-doping programme involves into the personal privacy of an athlete, and the onerous sanctions to which a positive finding may lead, when it comes to enforcement of that programme against an athlete there are good arguments that the governing body should have to demonstrate that the programme and its implications are set out clearly in its rulebook, were specifically brought to the attention of the athlete, and were understood and accepted by him[2].

1 See para E4.56.

2 See generally *Interfoto Picture Library Ltd v Stiletto Visual Programmes Ltd* [1989] QB 433. Petr Korda cited *Interfoto* in support of his argument that cl V(3) of the International Tennis Federation's ('ITF') anti-doping programme (which gave the ITF the right to appeal against doping decisions of the first instance tribunal) was particularly onerous and therefore, in order to bind Korda, should have been brought specifically to his attention. Mr Justice Lightman accepted the *Interfoto* principle but distinguished Korda's case on its facts: *Korda v ITF Ltd* [1999] All ER (D) 84, QBD.

E4.59 So, for example, the IAAF requires every member federation to include a specific provision in its own rules allowing the IAAF to carry out not only in-competition but also out-of-competition tests on that member federation's athletes[1]. The IAAF further provides that no athlete may compete in his federation's national championships, or in international competitions, unless he has agreed to submit to such out-of-competition testing[2].

1 IAAF Rule 57.1(ii) and (iii). See also FIS Doping Rules, Rule 6, para 18 (FIS Medical Guide 2001/02) (same).

2 IAAF Rule 57.3. Cf The Olympic Charter, Bye-Law to Rule 59: 'As a condition precedent to participation in the Olympic Games, every competitor shall comply with all provisions contained in the Olympic Charter … The NOC [National Olympic Committee] which enters the competitor ensures under its own responsibility that such competitor is fully aware and complies with the Olympic Charter and Medical Code'.

E4.60 The question is how such consent on the part of the athlete may be demonstrated.

E4.61 Consent established by writing The best evidence of the athlete's consent is of course a written agreement signed by that athlete. A sport following best practice in risk management will seek to obtain the written consent to its rules of all athletes falling under its jurisdiction. This might be accomplished by incorporating the anti-doping programme into the terms and conditions of participation in the sport, or the rules for a particular event in the sport, and requiring the athlete to sign a membership form (for the sport) or an entry form (for a particular event) that sets out his acknowledgement of and agreement to comply with and abide by the provisions of the anti-doping programme[1].

1 See eg The Olympic Charter, Bye-Law to Rule 49, cl 5.1: 'The entry form must include the text of the eligibility conditions and the following declaration to be signed by the competitors: … "I also agree to comply with the Olympic Charter currently in force and, in particular, with the provisions of the Olympic Charter regarding the eligibility for the Olympic Games … [and] the IOC Medical Code (Rule 48) … and arbitration before the Court of Arbitration for Sport (Rule 74)"'.

E4.62 If the form is presented to the athlete just before the event in which he wishes to participate, and signature is made a condition to participation, it may be possible for the athlete subsequently to argue that the 'consent' obtained was not voluntary[1].

1 See further para A5.161 et seq.

E4.63 The IOC has proposed the introduction of an 'Athlete's Anti-Doping Passport', which amounts to an agreement by the athlete bearer to submit to testing not only during the Olympic Games but also between Games, in competition and out-of-competition. The passport would also contain a record of tests on the athlete. The World Anti-Doping Agency has now taken over this initiative, and is sponsoring pilot projects (including one that was conducted at the 2002 Salt Lake City Games), to be phased in for full operation at the 2004 Olympics[1].

1 See www.WADApassport.org.

E4.64 The athlete's consent also has to be informed. This means giving the athlete copies of the rules to which he is being asked to submit, or at least access to such copies, and an opportunity to read them and to discuss them with his advisors prior to commitment. Vague references to acceptance of 'obligations under the rules' are not enough[1].

1 *Modahl v BAF Ltd* (14 December 2000, unreported), QBD (Douglas Brown J). See para E4.69.

E4.65 If the athlete is a minor, then his parent or guardian should be asked to agree on his behalf to the application of the anti-doping rules and to the obligation to submit to testing[1].

2 But see the *Chela* case, ATP Tour Anti-Doping Tribunal, decision dated 30 March 2001, para 33: 'The final argument raised by Mr Chela's counsel against the finding of a doping offence was that Mr Chela was only 20 years old when he signed the Tour's Player Consent Form. It was never clear to the Tribunal whether the age of majority in Argentina for purposes of the validity of contracts is 18 or 21, however the answer makes no difference here. The Tour's Rules provide that all players may be drug tested. Drug testing is a part of the rules of the game which all players accept along with the opportunity to participate on the Tour. Mr Chela can not enjoy the benefits of the Tour and then ignore the responsibilities set forth in the Rules. It was not necessary for the Tour to have a signed contract with Mr Chela in order for the Tour to drug test him or to impose discipline on him for a positive drug test. In the Tribunal's experience, many sporting bodies conduct drug testing on their athletes without having the athletes sign any contract or other form of consent'.

E4.66 Consent established other than by writing However, it would be unrealistic to expect that evidence in the form of written consent will always be available. In such cases, there are two other possible routes to establish the necessary consent on the part of the athlete to the anti-doping rules, namely by inference from:

(1) his participation in the sport; and
(2) his submission, upon a positive test, to the disciplinary authority of the sport's anti-doping tribunals[1].

1 See paras E4.65, n 1 and A3.123, n 1.

E4.67 Given that the authority of sports bodies to govern their sports is founded, under English law, on the contractual relationship between those bodies and their respective members[1], it would seem natural to infer consent to the rules simply from participation in the sport[2]. In the *Wilander* case, for example[3], there was no dispute that there was a contractual relationship between the athletes and the International Tennis Federation ('ITF') that incorporated the ITF's Anti-Doping Programme, although the only basis even referred to for such a contract was the fact of participation by the athletes in ITF-sanctioned events[4]. This is now express in the draft WADA Code[5].

1 See para E4.54.
2 See eg ITF Anti-Doping Programme 2002, cl B(1): 'Any player who enters or participates in an event or activity organised, sanctioned or recognised by the ITF or who has an ATP Tour or WTA Tour ranking, shall comply with and be bound by all of the provisions of this Programme'. See also UK Sport *Model Rules and Guidelines for Anti-Doping*, cl 1.4: 'To be eligible to participate or assist any participant in any event or activity organised or authorised or held under the rules of the Association wherever held, a person must comply with these Rules'.
3 Professional tennis players Mats Wilander and Karel Novacek provided urine samples at the French Open in June 1995. Each sample tested positive for a metabolite of cocaine. When the B samples also tested positive, the ITF notified the players, who protested their innocence and appealed to the Appeals Committee. However, in January 1996, just before the hearing before the Appeals Committee was to take place, the players applied to the High Court for an injunction restraining the ITF from taking any further proceedings against them, on three separate grounds: (a) the ITF's Anti-Doping Programme was in unreasonable restraint of trade and therefore void and unenforceable; (b) the ITF's procedure was so defective that the finding of doping violations was unreliable; and (c) the ITF had committed three separate breaches of contract that amounted to a repudiation of its contract with the players on which its disciplinary authority was founded. Those arguments were rejected, first by the High Court and subsequently by the Court of Appeal. See *Wilander and Novacek v Tobin and Jude* (19 March 1996, unreported), QBD (Lightman J), CA 26 March 1999.
4 This is also the approach taken in the draft WADA Code (E-Version 1.0, issued 10 June 2002), at para 4.1.1: 'Athletes, including minors, and athlete support personnel are deemed to accept the Code by virtue of their participation in competitive sport'.
5 Draft World Anti-Doping Code, E-Version 1.0, Art 4.1.1: 'Athletes, including minors, and athlete support personnel are deemed to accept the Code by virtue of their participation in competitive sport'.

E4.68 In the *Korda* case, Petr Korda resisted the notion that he had contracted to comply with the ITF's anti-doping programme. In his May 1998 application to the All England Tennis Club to compete at that year's Wimbledon Championship, however, he had acknowledged the application of anti-doping regulations 'imposed on the Championships … by the governing bodies of the game'. Mr Justice Lightman therefore had 'no doubt that such a contractual relationship has been established'[1].

1 *Korda v ITF Ltd* [1999] All ER (D) 84. Mr Justice Lightman rejected Korda's suggestion that this was simply a submission to the jurisdiction of the Appeals Committee 'rather than such as to establish in the circumstances the creation of a contractual relationship. This appears to me to be totally unreal. Any submission to the jurisdiction of the Appeals Committee must in the circumstances be part of an acceptance of a contractual relationship on the terms of the Programme which defines the status, jurisdiction and procedures of the Appeals Committee'.

E4.69 In the *Modahl* case[1], it was the athlete, Mrs Modahl, who was seeking to establish a contractual relationship, and her governing body, the British Athletic Federation ('BAF'), which disputed the existence of the contract. Mrs Modahl argued first that a contract arose by virtue of her acknowledgement, in her application form for membership of Sale Harriers, of her 'obligations under the BAF rules'. Secondly, she argued that a contract could be inferred from her participation in an event sanctioned by the BAF. Thirdly, she argued that a contract could be inferred from her submission, upon notification of a positive finding, to the jurisdiction of the BAF Disciplinary Tribunal. At trial, Mr Justice Douglas

Brown rejected all three submissions on the basis that the essentials of a legally enforceable contract (offer and acceptance, consideration and intent to create legal relations) were not present[2]. Although the Court of Appeal upheld Mr Justice Douglas Brown's dismissal of the claim on other grounds[3], two members of the court held that a contract had in fact arisen. According to Lord Justice Mance:

> The [BAF] rules, in my view, contain a framework of rights and duties of sufficient certainty to be given contractual effect with regard to the athlete's entitlement and ability to compete. Consideration exists in the athlete's submission to the rules and to the [BAF's] jurisdiction, in [BAF's] agreement to operate the rules and to permit the athlete to compete in accordance with them and in both parties' agreement on the procedures for resolution of any disputes contained in the rules … [T]he necessary implication of [Mrs Modahl's] conduct in joining a club, in competing at national and international level on the basis stated in the rules and then submitting herself to both in and out-of-competition doping tests is that she became party to a contract with the [BAF] to the relevant terms of the rules … [W]hile the courts should avoid inventing contracts, they should not be unduly hesitant about giving contractual effect to a continuous long-term relationship based on a programme and rules couched in language of contractual character and purporting to impose mutual rights and obligations[4].

1 *Modahl v BAF Ltd* (14 December 2000, unreported), QBD (Douglas Brown J), [2002] 1 WLR 1192, CA. Mrs Modahl was originally banned by a BAF internal tribunal after testing positive for testosterone. However, an appeal tribunal overturned the ban because of uncertainties regarding deterioration of the sample prior to testing, and exonerated Mrs Modahl. See para A3.10, n 2. In February 1996, Mrs Modahl instituted proceedings against the British Athletics Federation in the High Court. She alleged that the rules of the BAF, read against the background of the rules of the IAAF, formed the basis of a contract between her and the BAF, and that the BAF's conduct in suspending her and initiating disciplinary proceedings against her in the circumstances of her case constituted a breach of a duty that the BAF owed her as part of that contract to exercise its powers under the programme fairly. She sought damages to compensate her for the losses flowing from that breach, namely the expenses she incurred in fighting the charges (£250,000) and the financial loss she suffered from the wrongful ban from competition of almost a year (£230,000). Her claim went up to the House of Lords once and the Court of Appeal twice before ultimately failing. See further paras A3.89, A3.90 and A3.122 to A3.125.

2 *Modahl v British Athletics Federation* (14 December 2000, unreported), QBD.

3 [2002] 1 WLR 1192, CA.

4 [2002] 1 WLR at 1222–1225. Lord Justice Latham also held that a contract had arisen. [2002] 1 WLR at 1209. The dissenting view was that of Lord Justice Jonathan Parker. He saw nothing in the record that allowed him to infer a contract between Mrs Modahl and the BAF from her contract with her club. He also thought participation in the event in question an insufficient basis to infer such a contract, since the event at which Mrs Modahl provided the sample in question was not even organised by the BAF. Nor, in his view, was submission to the BAF's disciplinary jurisdiction sufficient, because neither side intended thereby to create legal relations. [2002] 1 WLR at 1214. See further para A3.125.

E4.70 Even if a contractual relationship is established by one of these routes, however, the absence of a written agreement setting out clearly the athlete's consent to the stringent provisions of the anti-doping programme may well make the task of enforcement of specific provisions of that programme more difficult[1].

1 See eg Gray 'Doping Control: The National Governing Body Perspective' in *Drugs and Doping in Sport* (2001, Cavendish) at p 29: 'Whilst Art 6 [European Human Rights Convention] rights may be waived by contract, it is suggested that a sporting governing body may have difficulty in establishing a genuine and voluntary agreement to waive individual human rights if this consists of no more than a "deeming provision" where, by virtue of membership of an affiliated club, a participant is deemed to accept the jurisdiction for doping control purposes of a national governing body. It is felt to be unlikely that a court will accept a voluntary waiver in the absence of full equality of bargaining powers'.

(c) Binding non-athletes

E4.71 Many anti-doping programmes, including the Olympic Movement Anti-Doping Code[1] and UK Sport's Anti-Doping Policy[2], proscribe not only the use of prohibited substances and methods but also 'aiding and abetting' such use, 'inducing' such use, and 'trafficking' in prohibited substances[3]. This is of course aimed against athletes themselves drawing other athletes into doping abuse, but it is also aimed at non-athletes who are close to athletes and in a position of influence over them, such as doctors, coaches and other officials.

1 See para E4.23.
2 See para E4.34.
3 See para E4.160 et seq.

E4.72 The signatories to the Council of Europe's Anti-Doping Convention called for the harmonisation of:

> procedures for the imposition of effective penalties for officials, doctors, veterinary doctors, coaches, physiotherapists and other officials or accessories associated with infringements of the anti-doping regulations by sportsmen and sportswomen[1].

The Olympic Movement Anti-Doping Code is expressly made applicable to 'all Participants'[2], which term is defined to include:

> any athlete, coach, trainer, official, medical or para-medical personnel working with or treating athletes participating in or preparing for sports competitions of the Olympic Games, those competitions to which the IOC grants its patronage or support and all competitions organised under the authority, whether direct or delegated, of an [International Federation] or [National Olympic Committee][3].

The draft World Anti-Doping Code takes a similar approach[4], but uses the term 'athlete support personnel', defined as:

> any coach, trainer, official, medical or para-medical personnel working with or treating athletes participating in or preparing for sports competition[5].

1 Anti-Doping Convention of 16 November 1989 (Council of Europe – European Treaties – ETS No 135), Art 7(e).
2 Olympic Movement Anti-Doping Code (Lausanne 2001), Chapter One, Art 2.
3 Olympic Movement Anti-Doping Code (Lausanne 2001), Chapter One, Art 1. However, athletes are warned not to try to use this provision to avoid personal responsibility. See Olympic Movement Anti-Doping Code (Lausanne 2001), Chapter One, Art 3: 'Notwithstanding the obligations of other Participants to comply with the provisions of this Code, it is the personal responsibility of any athlete subject to the provisions of this Code to ensure that he/she does not use or allow the use of any Prohibited Substance or Prohibited Method'.
4 See para E4.67, n 5.
5 Draft World Anti-Doping Code, E-Version 1.0, issued 10 June 2002, App One.

E4.73 Getting written agreements from such non-athletes to abide by anti-doping programmes presents obvious practical difficulties. In the absence of a membership or licensing requirement that encompasses these categories of participant in the sport[1], the only obvious mechanism for obtaining a written commitment would be its insertion into the terms of accreditation for which such persons must apply to gain access to non-spectator areas at particular events. However, this cannot be relied upon to provide proper coverage. For example, it does not cover those who coach or assist the athlete off-site. Therefore, those seeking to enforce an anti-doping programme against non-athlete participants may be forced to fall back on inferring consent from participation in the sport generally, as is done in the Olympic Movement Anti-Doping Code:

> Participants shall accept the individual or joint obligation to submit disputes concerning the application of this Code to the Court of Arbitration for Sport. Such acceptance is presumed by the very fact of participation by the Participants in the Olympic Movement. Any de facto refusal of such acceptance shall result in the Participants being considered as having excluded themselves from the Olympic Movement[2].

1 The World Anti-Doping Conference contemplated that not only athletes but also coaches and officials would have to take the Olympic oath, promising to observe (among other things) the Olympic Movement Anti-Doping Code: Declaration on Doping in Sport (World Anti-Doping Conference, Lausanne 1999).

2 Olympic Movement Anti-Doping Code (Lausanne 2001), Chapter Three, Art 6. A similar approach is taken in the draft World Anti-Doping Code. See draft World Anti-Doping Code, E-Version 1.0, issued 10 June 2002, para 4.1.1 ('Athletes, including minors, and athlete support personnel are deemed to accept the code by virtue of their participation in competitive sport').

E4.74 If the aider and abettor is a coach or trainer, not only will the inference of consent to the rules be easier; it will also make the standard sanction for a doping offence – suspension from participation in the sport[1] – a relevant one[2]. If not, however, not only the application of the rules but also identification of an appropriate sanction would be more problematic[3].

1 See para E4.332.

2 For example, in *V v FINA*, CAS 95/150, award dated 28 June 1996, *Digest of CAS Awards 1986–1998* (Berne 1998) p 265, a coach who had inadvertently given his swimmer a headache tablet that contained a prohibited substance was banned from all swimming activities for one year by the international governing body, FINA. He was said to have acted recklessly in that he did not consult with the team doctor before giving her the tablet. On appeal, the Court of Arbitration for Sport upheld the finding of a doping offence, finding that the failure to consult the doctor meant that his conduct 'fell far below the standard of care and vigilance required of him in his professional duty as a swimming coach', but decided that mitigating circumstances warranted reduction of the suspension to time served, ie seven months.

See also paras E4.3, n 3 (criminal prosecutions of East German coaches) and E4.16, n 1 (French prosecution of doctors working in professional cycling).

3 The IAAF therefore tries to leave itself the most freedom of action possible, providing that if a non-athlete is found guilty of assisting or inciting others to commit a doping offence, 'the Council may, at its discretion, impose an appropriate sanction': IAAF Rule 56.3. See also FIS Doping Rule 2, para 9 (FIS Medical Guide 2001/02). The breadth of this discretion betrays the weakness of the sports federation's position.

B Definition of what is prohibited and construction of the rules

E4.75 Bearing in mind the onus that is on the governing body to provide clear and understandable regulations[1], the starting-point in any anti-doping programme must be to identify with precision what actions (or omissions) are prohibited and therefore would constitute a doping offence. This will certainly be the starting-point for any tribunal called upon to resolve charges brought under such a programme[2].

1 See para E4.55.

2 See Art R58 of the CAS Code of Sports-Related Arbitration: 'The Panel shall decide the dispute according to the applicable regulations and the rules of law chosen by the parties … '.

E4.76 Commentators are agreed that 'faulty, contradictory or weak definitions' of doping can greatly undermine efforts to take effective action against doping in sport[1]. The reasons are clear. Any lack of precision will be construed in favour of the athlete[2]. For example, a definition of an offence that refers to intent to improve performance as an element cannot be construed as a strict liability offence, whatever the draftsman may have intended[3]. However, according to the same commentators[4], surprisingly few sports bodies have heeded the call for clarity and precision[5].

1 Vrijman 'Harmonisation: A Commentary on Current Issues and Problems' in *Drugs and Doping in Sport* (2001, Cavendish), p 147. See also Gay *Constitutional aspects of testing for prohibited substances* (1992, London).
2 See para E4.55.
3 See eg *USA Shooting and Quigley v Union Internationale de Tir*, CAS 94/129, award dated 23 May 1995, *Digest of CAS Awards 1986–1998* (Berne 1998), p 187, 194; *Lehtinen v FINA*, CAS 95/142, award dated 14 February 1996, para 32.
4 Vrijman 'Harmonisation: A Commentary on Current issues and Problems' in *Drugs and Doping in Sport* (2001, Cavendish), p 147; Gay *Constitutional aspects of testing for prohibited substances* (1992, London).
5 For example, cl 3.1 of the English Cricket Board's Anti-Doping Regulations provides that: '[t]he provision by a Cricketer of a sample of urine … which contains any prohibited substance (as defined in Schedule A) shall constitute an offence contrary to these Regulations …'. That looks like a strict liability approach. However, cl 4 provides that: '[i]t shall be an offence under these Regulations for an Cricketer *knowingly* to use any prohibited substance as set out in Schedule A' (emphasis added).

(a) *Applicable law: general principles of law in the sports context*

E4.77 It is impossible to address the difficult issues arising under this topic without being clear as to the system of law that governs the construction of the rules and the basis upon which an athlete may be found guilty of a doping offence and banned from international competition.

E4.78 In essence, the legal principles that apply in this area are international, not national, in nature, consisting of general principles of international sports law (or 'lex ludorum'[1]) derived from decisions of the Court of Arbitration for Sport and other arbitral panels and courts that have been called upon to apply or construe anti-doping rules in sport.

1 Variously described elsewhere as a 'lex sportiva' – see Beloff et al *Sports Law* (1999, Hart Publishing), p 256; Reeb, *Digest of CAS Awards II 1998–2000* (Kluwer 2001) – and a 'lex ludica'. *AEK Athens and Slavia Prague v UEFA*, CAS 98/200, award dated 20 August 1999, *Digest of CAS Awards II 1998–2000* (2002, Kluwer), pp 38, 102–103.

E4.79 The anti-doping rules at issue will be derived from global anti-doping programmes promulgated by international sports federations. The determinations of doping offences under those programmes will conventionally be made initially by tribunals appointed by national member federations[1]. Appeals will then generally lie to an international appellate body, most often (as a result of the mandate given in the Lausanne Declaration on Sport[2]) the Court of Arbitration for Sport (or 'CAS')[3].

1 See generally Chapter A2.
2 See para E4.358. Appeals from decisions of the IOC Disciplinary Commission relating to doping offences at the Olympic Games may also be appealed to the Court of Arbitration for Sport.
3 As to the CAS as an institution, see para A5.84 et seq.

E4.80 The role of national law should, in the doping context, be limited. The athlete is likely to be deemed to have entered into a contract with the national sports body, and perhaps also with the organisers of the event in question, or even the international federation under whose auspices the event in question is held[1]. In the absence of an express choice of law, the proper substantive law of that contract will be the system of law with which the contract has the closest connection[2], which in the case of rules derived from an international doping regime is unlikely to be English law. Rather, the tribunal should be looking to apply the general principles of international sports law that have been developed, by the CAS and other bodies, in interpreting the international doping regime in question. This must be right in principle, as it would clearly be contrary to the interests of sport for the same international rules to be given a different meaning and legal effect in different jurisdictions. This is especially so given that, in the event of an appeal to the CAS, those same rules will be interpreted not by reference to national law, but by reference to general principles of law.

1 *Modahl v British Athletics Federation Ltd* [2002] 1 WLR 1192, CA. See paras A3.125 and E4.66 et seq.

2 See Art 4 of the Rome Convention on the Law Applicable to Contractual Obligations, incorporated into English law by the Contracts (Applicable Law) Act 1990.

E4.81 While the procedural rules of the Court of Arbitration for Sport might suggest that that court will determine doping appeals by reference to one system of national law[1], in practice the CAS makes its decisions by reference to internationally accepted general legal principles, applying a much less rigorous approach to the literal wording of the rules in issue than would be employed by the English courts. The CAS has stated that it:

> is of the opinion that all sporting institutions, and in particular all international federations, must abide by general principles of law. Due to the transnational nature of sporting competitions, the effects of the conduct and deeds of international federations are felt in a sporting community throughout various countries. Therefore the substantive and procedural rules to be respected by international federations cannot be reduced only to its own statutes and regulations and to the laws of the country where the federation is incorporated or of the country where its headquarters are. Sports law has developed and consolidated along the years, particularly through the arbitral settlement of disputes, a set of unwritten legal principles – a sort of *lex mercatoria* for sports or, so to speak, a *lex ludica* – to which national and international sports federations must conform, regardless of the presence of such principles within their own statutes and regulations or within any applicable national law, provided that they do not conflict with any national 'public policy' ('*ordre public*') provision applicable to a given case. Certainly, general principles of law drawn from a comparative or common denominator reading of various domestic legal systems and, in particular, the prohibition of arbitrary or unreasonable rules and measures can be deemed to be part of such *lex ludica*. For example, in the CAS award *FIN/FINA* the Panel held that it could intervene in the sanction imposed by the international swimming federation (FINA) 'if the rules adopted by the FINA Bureau are contrary to the general principles of law, if their application is arbitrary, or if the sanctions provided by the rules can be deemed excessive or unfair on their face'[2].

1 See Art R58 of the CAS Code of Sports-Related Arbitration: 'The Panel shall decide the dispute according to the applicable regulations and the rules of law chosen by the parties or, in the absence of such choice, according to the law of the country in which the federation, association or sports body which has issued the challenged decision is domiciled'.

In exercising its jurisdiction over cases arising from the Olympic Games, the CAS will apply Swiss principles of private international law. See eg Art 7 of the Arbitration Rules of the XXIV Olympic Winter Games at Salt Lake City.

See also Beloff 'Drugs, Laws and Versapaks' in *Drugs and Doping in Sport* (2001, Cavendish) at pp 39 and 56: 'As trading nations developed a lex mercatoria, so, little by little, a lex sportiva is in gestation. On the CAS Ad Hoc Panels in Atlanta in 1996 and Kuala Lumpur in 1998 on which I served, the Panel were [sic] obliged to apply, inter alia, "general principles of law and the rules of law, the application of which it deems appropriate". Those general principles and rules are the common heritage of major systems of laws applied in a sporting context'.

2 *AEK Athens and Slavia Prague v UEFA*, CAS 98/200, award dated 20 August 1999, at para 156, *Digest of CAS Awards II 1998–2000* (2001, Kluwer), 38, 102–103 (citations omitted).

E4.82 The 'general principles of law' referred to in the passage quoted in the preceding paragraph are the common building blocks with which the various national and international legal systems are built. They include the following well-known principles, which not surprisingly bear a marked resemblance to English public law principles[1]:

- **Legality** – rules must be construed and applied consistently with their own terms and on the basis that there can be no sanction without a law or rule providing for it[2].
- **Legal certainty and retrospective application** – the rules and how they can be applied must be clear and capable of being predicted at the time of the events in question[3]. In general, rules cannot be construed as allowing retrospective application, or be applied retrospectively[4].
- **Legitimate expectation and acquisition of rights** – rules must be construed and applied in a way that respects the legitimate expectations and acquired rights of those affected[5].
- **Good faith** – rules must be construed and applied openly and honestly, and not in bad faith, arbitrarily or capriciously[6].
- **Fairness** – the sports governing body must act in a procedurally fair manner[7].
- **Non-discrimination** – like cases must be treated alike and different situations differently[8].
- **Proportionality** – rules must be construed and applied in a way that goes no further than is reasonably necessary to pursue a legitimate aim. The benefit supposedly achieved by an approach must not be out of proportion to the detriment suffered by the applicant[9].
- **Fundamental rules** – rules must be construed and applied in accordance with the fundamental rights protected under the European Convention on Human Rights[10].
- Lastly, there are a number of additional general principles of construction that must be followed:
  (a) rules must be purposively construed[11];
  (b) rules must be construed in favour of the athlete or club and against the body imposing the rules (the contra proferentem rule)[12];
  (c) where they give rise to penal sanctions, rules must be construed narrowly, in the sense that a sanction can only be imposed that is clearly provided for by the provision[13]; and
  (d) rules must be construed consistently so that force is given (if possible) to each provision in the material part of the code, and no such provision is rendered useless.

1 The general principles of law applied as part of European Community law are derived from the common principles of the legal systems of the various member states, and form a good starting point for the assessment of the general principles of law applied when measuring the actions of sports governing bodies. See Vaughan *Law of the European Communities Service* (Butterworths looseleaf), Pt 2, chaps 7 and 8, paras 1105–1324. See also Schwarze *European Administrative Law* (1992, Sweet & Maxwell).

2 Cf Vaughan *Law of the European Communities Service* (Butterworths looseleaf), Pt 2, chaps 7 and 8, para 1221. See also Beloff et al *Sports Law* (1999, Hart Publishing), p 11.

3 Cf Vaughan *Law of the European Communities Service* (Butterworths looseleaf), Pt 2, chaps 7 and 8, paras 1243–1261.

4 *Waddington v Miah* [1974] 1 WLR 683, HL; *Walker v UKA & IAAF* (7 July 2000, unreported), QBD (Toulson J.), 25 July 2000 (Hallett J); see para A3.124. In *Re International Cycling Union and Italian National Olympic Committee*, CAS 94/128, opinion dated 5 January 1995, *Digest of CAS Awards 1986–1998* (Berne 1998), p 495, the CAS panel took the view that modifications to the IOC rules do not apply automatically in sports governed by such rules unless the sport's rules specifically provide for immediate application. It also stated its view that athletes sanctioned for a doping offence must be afforded the benefit of a rule change reducing the applicable sanction for such offence if the rule change occurs prior to the execution of the sanction imposed under the old rule.

5 *AEK Athens v UEFA*, CAS 98/200, interim relief decision, paras 50–60 and as described in the final decision, *AEK Athens and Slavia Prague v UEFA*, CAS 98/200, award dated 20 August 1999, *Digest of CAS Awards II 1998–2000* (2002, Kluwer), p 42; *Watt v Australian Cycling Federation*, CAS 96/153. See also Beloff et al *Sports Law* (1999, Hart Publishing), p 10. Cf Vaughan, *Law of the European Communities Service* (Butterworths looseleaf), Pt 2, chaps 7 and 8, paras 1262–1282.

6 *AEK Athens and Slavia Prague v UEFA*, CAS 98/200, award dated 20 August 1999, at paras 155–166, *Digest of CAS Awards II 1998–2000* (2002, Kluwer), pp 38 and 102–03; *Cullwick v FINA*, CAS 96/149, award dated 13 March 1997, *Digest of CAS Awards 1986–1998* (Berne 1998), p 251. See also Beloff et al *Sports Law* (1999, Hart Publishing), p 10–12.

7 *AEK Athens and Slavia Prague v UEFA*, CAS 98/200, award dated 20 August 1999 at paras 58–60 and 156–158, *Digest of CAS Awards II 1998–2000* (2002, Kluwer), pp 38, 64–65, 102–03. Cf Vaughan *Law of the European Communities Service* (Butterworths looseleaf), Pt 2, chaps 7 and 8, paras 1224–25. See also Beloff et al *Sports Law* (1999, Hart Publishing), pp 217 and 218.

8 *AEK Athens and Slavia Prague v UEFA*, CAS 98/200, award dated 20 August 1999, at paras 63 and 156, *Digest of CAS Awards II 1998–2000* (2002, Kluwer), pp 38, 66–67, 102–03. See also Beloff et al *Sports Law* (1999, Hart Publishing), p 12. Cf Vaughan *Law of the European Communities Service* (Butterworths looseleaf), Pt 2, chaps 7 and 8, paras 1226–1230.

9 *AEK Athens and Slavia Prague v UEFA*, CAS 98/200, award dated 20 August 1999, at para 156, *Digest of CAS Awards II 1998–2000* (2002, Kluwer), pp 38, 102–03. See also Beloff et al *Sports Law* (1999, Hart Publishing), p 12. Cf Vaughan *Law of the European Communities Service* (Butterworths looseleaf), Pt 2, chaps 7 and 8, paras 1241–42.

10 Cf Vaughan *Law of the European Communities Service* (Butterworths looseleaf), Pt 2, chaps 7 and 8, paras 1222–23.

11 *Perez v IOC*, CAS OG 00/0005, award dated 19 September 2000, paras 26–28, *Digest of CAS Awards II 1998–2000* (2002, Kluwer); *AEK Athens and Slavia Prague v UEFA*, CAS 98/200, award dated 20 August 1999, at para 156, *Digest of CAS Awards II 1998–2000* (2002, Kluwer), pp 38, 102–03. Identifying the purpose behind rules precludes interpreting them by reference to current political concerns. *Reel v Holder* [1979] 1 WLR 1252; affd [1981] 1 WLR 1226, CA. See also *Celtic v UEFA*, CAS 98/201, award dated 7 January 2000, paras 25 to 31, *Digest of CAS Awards II 1998–2000* (2002, Kluwer), pp 106, 118–19. See also Beloff et al *Sports Law* (1999, Hart Publishing), p 11.

12 *B v ITU*, CAS 98/222, award dated 9 August 1999, para 31, *Digest of CAS Awards II 1998–2000* (2002, Kluwer), pp 106, 118–19; *Korda v ITF*, CAS 99/A/223, award dated 31 August 1999, paras 25 and 48, *Digest of CAS Awards II 1998–2000* (2002, Kluwer), pp 345, 354 and 359. See also Beloff et al *Sports Law* (1999, Hart Publishing), p 11. Cf Vaughan *Law of the European Communities Service* (Butterworths looseleaf), Pt 2, chaps 7 and 8, paras 1188–89.

13 *USA Shooting & Quigley v Union Internationale de Tir*, CAS 94/129, award dated 23 May 1995, para 34, *Digest of CAS Awards 1986–1998* (Berne 1998), pp 187, 197–98; *B v IJF*, CAS 99/A/230, award dated 20 December 1999, para 10, *Digest of CAS Awards II 1998–2000* (2002, Kluwer), pp 369 and 374. See also Beloff et al *Sports Law* (1999, Hart Publishing), p 11.

E4.83 A further point arises from the fact that the anti-doping regimes customarily provide that appeals, if not the primary determination by the national domestic tribunals, are by way of arbitration. Once it is appreciated that these bodies derive their jurisdiction from consensual submission to arbitration, by the athlete and the sporting organisation respectively, then the role of substantive and procedural national law must be diminished. Even considerations applying from the European Convention on Human Rights may have very limited application, as the effect of submission to arbitration is to waive many of the protections derived from Art 6[1].

1 See para A4.36.

E4.84 If on proper analysis the rules providing for a determination of the doping charge constitute an arbitration agreement, then under English law, by virtue of the Arbitration Act 1996, the substantive determination of facts and law is to be left by the courts to the arbitral tribunal, subject only to very narrow grounds of potential challenge to the arbitral award in the courts. Thus the classic legal principle that matters of law, including the interpretation of the rules, are for the determination of the courts, not for the domestic tribunal[1], no longer applies in most doping disputes.

1 As enunciated (for example) by Lord Denning in *Lee v Showman's Guild* [1952] 2 QB 329, CA.

E4.85 As a result, an athlete facing doping proceedings before an English-based tribunal acting under a national federation's rules should in principle find it very difficult to persuade an English court to set aside or intervene in those proceedings. If the proceedings are properly treated as an arbitration, then any challenge could only be brought under the Arbitration Act. In any event, in many cases the rules will provide that an appeal lies to an international arbitral body, thus as a matter of contract impliedly excluding any right to seek court intervention[1].

1 Even the procedural protections of the Arbitration Act 1996 will generally only apply to that part of the process under which determinations are being made by a national tribunal whose seat is in England and Wales, and not to that part of the process that is determined by an international arbitral body whose seat is outside the jurisdiction of the English courts. See s 2 of the Arbitration Act 1996. There are limited exceptions to this rule.

E4.86 Furthermore, while the Court of Arbitration for Sport is subject to the jurisdiction of the Swiss courts, the Swiss Federal Tribunal recognised in 1993[1] that the CAS offers sufficient guarantees of independence and objectivity for its awards to be final and enforceable by the Swiss courts. In practice, its awards will be enforceable internationally[2] and will only be susceptible to challenge in national courts on a very limited number of grounds[3].

1 See paras A5.95 and A5.96.
2 By virtue of the New York Convention on the Recognition and Enforcement of Foreign Arbitral Awards 1958.
3 See para A5.176.

E4.87 It is clear that in principle anti-doping regulation should be harmonised so as to avoid court challenges in one jurisdiction to disqualifications ordered by a national or international tribunal situated in another state. The anti-doping programmes are international, applying wherever the sport is played[1]. Therefore, even if a programme is expressly governed by English law, the English court should in its interpretation apply the principles adopted by the CAS. Just as under English law the meaning of international conventions is to be determined by reference to international jurisprudence[2], so the English courts should seek to interpret the anti-doping rules of sports bodies in accordance with the jurisprudence of the CAS in interpreting the same or similar anti-doping regimes. As noted above, this means interpreting the rules by reference to internationally accepted legal principles, applying a much less rigorous approach to the literal wording than would conventionally be employed by the English courts[3].

1 For example, in *Modahl v British Athletics Federation Ltd* [2002] 1 WLR 1192, CA, although the breach of contract claim was argued through the English courts exclusively by reference to English law, on the basis that the contract (the disciplinary rules propounded by the British Athletics Federation) was governed by English law, to the extent that the substance of the doping dispute remained in issue the rules in question were actually the international rules of the IAAF, and the alleged doping offence occurred in Portugal. The role of the BAF's anti-doping tribunal was solely to hear and determine the case, in accordance with those international rules, and an appeal lay to the IAAF Arbitration Panel sitting in Monaco. The IAAF rules did not provide for their meaning or effect to be governed by any national system of law, and (as noted above) it would clearly be contrary to the interests of sport for the same international rules to be given a different meaning and legal effect in different jurisdictions.

2 *Fothergill v Monarch Airlines* [1981] AC 251.

3 See para E4.81. Although Scott J took a different approach in the leading English case of *Gasser v Stinson* (15 June 1988, unreported), QBD (see para E4.110), that case was anomalous both in its jurisdiction and its result. Sandra Gasser was Swiss, the doping offence occurred in Italy, and the defendant was an English representative of the IAAF. The fortuitous location of the headquarters of the IAAF in England led the English court to assume jurisdiction and to apply English principles of restraint of trade to an international regime. The decision of the English court on the merits (see para E4.110) was inconsistent with that of the Swiss courts, which overturned the application of the mandatory penalty on Sandra Gasser.

The IAAF has since moved to Monaco in an attempt to avoid the jurisdictional reach of the English courts: this approach has not proved particularly successful, mainly because the national governing body is generally sued as well, making the joinder of the IAAF legitimate. See *Walker v UKA and IAAF* (7 July 2000, unreported), QBD (Toulson J), where a challenge to the jurisdiction over the IAAF was rejected. See also *Edwards v BAF and IAAF* [1998] 2 CMLR 363 (Lightman J).

E4.88 It would therefore be wrong in principle to approach questions relating to construction of the rules in anti-doping cases from the insular viewpoint of English common law. Instead, the provisions of international anti-doping regimes fall to be assessed by reference to the general principles of sports law referred to above[1]. The English cases have proceeded to date on a legal basis that has failed adequately to recognise the international dimension of sports anti-doping regimes.

1 See paras E4.81 and E4.82. Contra McLaren 'Doping Sanctions: What Penalty?' [2002] 2 ISLJ 23 and 33 ('CAS should not look to general principles of law unless the parties have expressed such a choice of law').

(b) *Sample definitions*

E4.89 The 2002 Anti-Doping Programme of the International Tennis Federation (ITF) states:

> Doping is forbidden and constitutes a Doping Offence under this Programme. Doping occurs when:
> (a) a Prohibited Substance is found to be present within a player's body; or
> (b) a Doping Method is used by a player[1].

The first alternative is clearly a strict liability offence, predicated solely upon proof of the presence of the substance in the athlete's body; the second alternative requires proof of 'use' and therefore, at least arguably, of intent[2].

1 See ITF Anti-Doping Programme 2002, cl C(1).
2 See para E4.94.

E4.90 The IAAF's definition is very similar[1] but adds a third doping offence: when 'an athlete admits having used a prohibited substance or taken advantage of a prohibited technique'[2].

1 See IAAF Rule 55.2.
2 See IAAF Rule 55.2(iii).

E4.91 In contrast, Art 2.1 of the Council of Europe's Anti-Doping Convention[1] defines doping as 'the administration to sportsmen and sportswomen, or the use by them, of pharmacological classes of doping agents or doping methods'. This could be read to require proof of intent in all cases[2]. Similarly, the European Group on Ethics has offered the following definition:

> the use of substances, dosages or methods with the intention of enhancing sporting performance, which are banned mainly because they may have a harmful effect on sportsmen/women's health and which may compromise the generally accepted conditions of fair play[3].

This would clearly seem to require proof of intent to enhance performance (and in addition, arguably, of risk to health).

1 See para E4.23.
2 Through the word 'use': see para E4.94.
3 Opinion on the Ethical Aspects of the Struggle Against Doping in Sport, Annex 2 to the Commission's Communication to the Council, etc, Brussels 1/12/1999, COM (1999) 643 at para 2.2. See also International Amateur Wrestling Federation, International Rules, para A(1): 'Doping is defined as the administration or use of any substance for the purpose of artificially increasing the physical or mental performance of the athlete during the competition'.

E4.92 The draft WADA Code[1] defines doping as:

> the presence of a substance in an athlete's bodily specimen, or the use or evidence of any substance or method, that has the potential to enhance sports performance and which either poses an unnecessary risk of harm to athletes or is otherwise contrary to the spirit of sport[2].

Pending finalisation and adoption of that Code, however[3], the Olympic Movement Anti-Doping Code remains the cornerstone anti-doping text. However, each of the two alternative definitions of doping that appears in the Olympic Movement Anti-Doping Code[4] raises a series of questions.

1 See para E4.45.
2 Draft World Anti-Doping Code, E-Version 1.0, issued 10 June 2002, Art 2.
3 See para E4.45.
4 Olympic Movement Anti-Doping Code Chapter One, Article Two. Various international federations have adopted the Olympic Movement Anti-Doping Code definition in full, including the International Ski Federation (see FIS Doping Rules, FIS Medical Guide 2001/02, Rule 1).

E4.93 The Olympic Movement Anti-Doping Code definition: first limb The first limb of the Olympic Movement Anti-Doping Code definition defines doping as 'the use of an expedient (substance or method) which is potentially harmful to athletes' health and/or capable of enhancing their performance'[1].

1 Olympic Movement Anti-Doping Code Chapter One, Art 2(1).

E4.94 Some have suggested that the active term 'use' connotes some form of deliberate act, and therefore means that proof of knowledge/intent is required to establish doping under this limb[1].

1 See *N v FINA*, CAS 98/202, award dated 22 December 1998, para 15, *Digest of CAS Awards II 1998–2000* (Kluwer 2002), pp 234 and 248. The Olympic Movement Anti-Doping Code defines 'use' as 'the application, ingestion, injection, consumption by any means whatsoever of any Prohibited Substance or Prohibited Method. Use includes counselling the use of, permitting the use of or condoning the use of any Prohibited Substance or Prohibited Method'. Olympic Movement Anti-Doping Code Chapter One, Art One.

In *C v FINA*, CAS 95/141, award dated 22 April 1996, *Digest of CAS Awards 1986–1998* (Berne 1998) pp 215, 219–20, the CAS panel held that a definition of doping based on 'use' is 'unequivocal. It admits only the strict liability of the athlete and does not allow the concepts of fault or intent to intervene'. In contrast, however, the ex-Chairman of the IAAF arbitration panel apparently took the view that the phrase 'the use of a prohibited substance' (as opposed to 'the presence of a prohibited substance') made it unclear whether or not a strict liability approach was being taken. See Tarasti *Legal Solutions in International Doping Cases* (SEP Editrice 2000), p 88, n 90.

E4.95 Further concerns arise from the definitions of the categories of banned expedients. Those categories are open-ended and therefore create great uncertainty as to the scope of the proscription.

E4.96 For example, the first category – expedients that are 'potentially harmful to athletes' health' – is patently overbroad. Indeed, read literally it would render any athlete who smoked nicotine (ie cigarettes) subject to sanction.

E4.97 The second category – substances or methods that are 'capable of enhancing performance' – is also patently overbroad, since (again, read literally) it would encompass (for example) substances such as fruit and vegetables and methods such as weight-training. There are very many substances that are claimed to enhance performance that are not on the IOC List of Prohibited Substances[1].

1 For example, creatine is alleged to have performance-enhancing characteristics. However, it is also said to be present in meat and fish. Because it has not been possible to agree a cut-off point beyond which ingestion by meat or fish consumption can be ruled out (see further para E4.258 et seq), creatine has not been designated a prohibited substance.

E4.98 The Olympic Movement Anti-Doping Code definition: second limb The second limb of the Olympic Movement Anti-Doping Code definition defines doping as 'the presence in the athlete's body of a Prohibited Substance *or* evidence of the use thereof *or* evidence of the use of a Prohibited Method'[1].

1 Olympic Movement Anti-Doping Code Chapter One, Art 2(2) (emphasis added).

E4.99 The second and third alternatives require evidence of 'use', and therefore arguably of intent[1].

1 See para E4.94.

E4.100 However, the first alternative requires proof only of 'the presence in the athlete's body of a Prohibited Substance'. In other words, liability is strict, ie not dependent on any showing of intent, recklessness, negligence or other fault. It is established 'as soon as the presence of a banned substance has been detected in an athlete's body, independent of any element of intention'[1]. This approach has been carried over into the draft WADA Code, which lists as its primary anti-doping violation 'the presence of a prohibited substance or its metabolites or markers in an athlete's bodily specimen'[2]. It is also the approach that UK Sport mandates for all governing bodies that wish to receive public funds[3]. And yet fundamental concerns arise from this definition of a doping offence, which are discussed in the next section of this chapter.

1 IOC Explanatory Memorandum to the Olympic Movement Anti-Doping Code, 9 December 1999, p 9. See Scott J in *Gasser v Stinson* (15 June 1988, unreported), QBD: 'The disqualification does not depend upon any guilty intent on the part of the athlete. He or she may not have known that the substance was being ingested. The disqualification depends upon no more than the finding of the prohibited substance in the athlete's urine'.

Some sports underline their absolute approach with further provisions that seek to remove any room for doubt. See eg ASFGB Doping Control Rules, cl 10: 'The finding in a person's body tissue or fluids of a prohibited substance shall constitute an offence and such person shall be sanctioned in accordance with this Rule 10.1, regardless of whether such person can establish that he did not knowingly ingest the prohibited substance'; ITF Anti-Doping Programme 2002, cl C(3): 'A player is absolutely responsible for any Prohibited Substance found to be present within his body. Accordingly, it is not necessary that intent or fault on the player's part be shown in order for a Doping Offence to be established … ; nor is the player's lack of intent or lack of fault a defence to a Doping Offence'; IAAF Rule 55.4: 'It is an athlete's duty to ensure that no substance enters his body tissue or fluids which is prohibited under these Rules. Athletes are warned that they are responsible for all or any substance found in their body'.

And yet, the IAAF's accompanying 'help notes' to athletes state, in the third sentence of the introduction: 'Doping is the use of methods or taking of substances (usually various forms of medication) which artificially increase physical performance'. This could be cited to suggest that a doping offence under the IAAF rules requires proof of both intent (through use of the word 'use' – see para E4.24 – and/or 'taking') and actual performance enhancement. But see *Walker* case, IAAF Arbitration Panel, 20 August 2000, para 13, [2001] 4 ISLR 264: 'athletes may not ignore the Rules and simply rely on the Help Notes. The Help Notes are there purely for guidance of athletes and not for the purpose of interpreting either the Rules or the Guidelines themselves.'

2 Draft World Anti-Doping Code, E-Version 1.0, issued 10 June 2002, para 8.1.1.1.

3 UK Sport *Statement of Anti-Doping Policy 2002*, Annex A, para 1.

(c) *Strict liability*

E4.101 Introduction At the outset it is necessary to distinguish between different questions which may arise under the general rubric of 'strict liability' in doping. The basic distinction is between:

(1) strict, or absolute, liability imposed by the rules in respect of the proved presence of a prohibited substance found in the body of an athlete; and
(2) the imposition of a mandatory scale of penalties in the event of infringement, irrespective of the circumstances of infringement.

The considerations applicable to those questions must also be differentiated from the question of whether, in the event of a prohibited substance being found, the athlete should be permitted to retain the assumed competitive advantage obtained in the event in which he competed under the influence of the prohibited substance. Thus in principle different approaches could be taken to the questions:

(a) has the athlete committed a doping offence?
(b) should he be disqualified from the event in question?
(c) should he be disqualified from future events in accordance with the prescribed scale of penalties?

E4.102 At the core of this area is the basic question of the extent to which moral fault, in the sense of deliberate conduct or negligence, is implicit in the doping regimes. Again one must distinguish between the principle of implying moral fault in the anti-doping regime, and the means by which fault is established or inferred. In this area presumptions, such as the presumption that presence of a prohibited substance should imply fault on the part of the athlete, may play a significant part.

E4.103 There are two particular considerations that underlie the need for a process of disqualification. The first is the overriding need for fairness in competition, which is in principle independent of any question of moral fault. If, retrospectively, it can be objectively determined that an athlete has competed under the influence of a substance that did enhance, or may fairly be assumed to have enhanced, his performance in any way then the need for fairness to other competitors should dictate that the offending athlete be disqualified and lose his ranking and benefits derived from the particular event, even if the athlete was himself not at fault. But the second consideration is that of deterrence of drug abuse in sport and it is only that factor that could justify the imposition of prospective periods of disqualification. That aspect should be viewed from a penal viewpoint and fundamental questions of fairness should dictate that there is found, or inferred, at least some element of moral fault before the athlete is so penalised.

E4.104 It has been suggested[1] that a strict approach to the issue of liability for a doping offence is legitimate provided that the rules allow the athlete's lack of moral fault to trigger a lesser sanction[2] and/or early reinstatement, ie before the ban has been fully served[3]. Indeed, it has been suggested that provisions for lesser sanctions or early reinstatement have been adopted for that very purpose[4]. However, this approach is fundamentally flawed: even if sanctions are reduced, the athlete is still branded a cheat in the eyes of his competitors, his sponsors and the public[5]. For this reason, whatever the approach on sanctions, the justification for a strict approach to liability for a doping offence can be challenged. However, if the tribunal has no discretion to reflect the relative lack of culpability of the athlete in the sanction imposed, and/or there is no mechanism for early reinstatement, the position becomes all the harder to justify.

1 See Gay *When is a positive finding a doping offence?* UK Sport Seminar, Tackling Ethical Issues in Drugs and Sport (October 1996): 'the power of reinstatement is an important safety valve to the absolute offence doctrine and one which I think mitigates its severity in an individual case'.
2 See para E4.315 et seq.
3 See para E4.372 et seq.
4 Beloff 'Drugs, Laws, and Versapaks' in *Drugs and Doping in Sports* (2001, Cavendish), pp 39 and 45.
5 See *NWBA v IPC*, CAS 95/122, award dated 5 March 1996, *Digest of CAS Awards 1986–1998* (Berne 1998), pp 173 and 178: 'This is perhaps unfortunate phraseology, because the word "guilty" suggests reprehensible conduct and does not allow the outsider to distinguish between cheaters and inadvertent violators'.

See also Kerr 'Doped or Duped? The Nandrolone Jurisprudence' [2001] 3 ISLR 97 and 98: 'To be banned for a doping offence is about the worst thing that can happen to an athlete in his or her career. Many at the top are now effectively professional and their livelihood as well as their reputation may be ruined at a stroke. The accusation is so serious because doping is seen as cheating, and cheating dishonours sport. The point that doping offences, as defined in the relevant rules, need not involve cheating at all, is one often lost on the press and public'.

See also Griffith-Jones QC 'The Need for a World-wide Anti-Doping Code' (2002) 5(1) Sports Law Bulletin 3: 'Whilst the right to make such an application [for reinstatement] softens the harshness of the rules, a process which allows the circumstances of an offence to be taken into account only by such means is cumbersome, potentially unfair and unnecessary. Whilst an opportunity to seek early reinstatement in appropriate circumstances should perhaps remain, all primary issues of punishments should best be addressed when sentence is passed. The sentencer should have the primary obligation to ensure that "the punishment fits the crime". Far better this than to require an individual who, although "guilty" of a strict liability "offence", establishes circumstances apt to mitigate the seriousness of his offence, to a standard punishment, thereby tarring him with the same brush as those with no saving mitigation, leaving him subsequently for the (perhaps arbitrary) exercise of discretion to allow him back into the fold of sporting competition. Generally, sport and the general public want to see harsh penalties imposed on those who deliberately cheat by taking performance-enhancing drugs. Similar penalties imposed on those who are shown not to be morally culpable, are likely to undermine confidence in the system and bring the whole process into disrepute, thereby letting the cheats win'.

E4.105 The fight against doping is said to require strict rules, but those rules must be consistent with the fundamental rights of athletes to a fair determination of the doping offence and a proportionate restraint on the ability to earn a livelihood by participating in competition. Too often pragmatic considerations, sometimes rather too glibly stated, are advanced in justification of draconian rule structures that, if they are to stand, should be founded on respectable principle.

E4.106 Applicable law Questions of strict liability, as in the case of any other question of construction of an anti-doping rule, are likely to be considered by reference to the general principles referred to at paras E4.77 to E4.82.

E4.107 The objective basis of liability It is clear that it is for the sporting body bringing an anti-doping charge to establish the objective elements of the offence to the necessary standard of proof[1]. The objective elements of a normal case will be the presence in the athlete's body of a substance that is indeed prohibited. Those elements will be proved by establishing that the sample was taken properly from the athlete, that the chain of custody is verified and that the laboratory analysis, by an IOC approved laboratory, complied with current standards[2].

1 See paras E4.248 to E4.252.
2 See para E4.253 et seq.

E4.108 Under the conventional anti-doping regime, the sports body is required only to prove that a prohibited substance was present in the athlete's body. It is not required to prove affirmatively that the prohibited substance was ingested or administered with any particular intent or in any particular circumstances[1]. The justification offered is that the sports body is only in a position to establish the presence of the prohibited substance. How that substance came to be in the athlete's body could not be proved by the sports body in all but the most exceptional cases. If proof of an offence required, directly or indirectly, proof of the circumstances of administration or ingestion, then there is a strong argument that the anti-doping regime would become unenforceable[2].

1 See para E4.100.
2 See eg *Aanes v FILA*, CAS 2001/A/317A, award dated 9 July 2001, *p* 19: 'it would put a definite end to any meaningful fight against doping if the federations were required to *prove* the necessary subjective elements of the offence, ie intent or negligence on the part of the athlete. In fact, since neither the federation nor the CAS has the means of conducting its own investigation or of compelling witnesses to give evidence, means which are available to the public prosecutor in criminal proceedings, it would be all too simple for an athlete to deny any intent or negligence and to simply state that he/she has no idea how the prohibited substance arrived in his/her system' (citations omitted).

E4.109 This concern has been expressed in two slightly different ways. First, it has been expressed as a difficulty of expense:

> a requirement of intent would invite costly litigation that may well cripple federations - particularly those run on modest budgets in their fight against doping[1].

Secondly, and perhaps more forcefully[2], it is expressed as a matter of efficacy: it would be not just costly but impossible to prove intent on the part of the athlete, and therefore the floodgates would be opened to drug cheats in sport.

1 *USA Shooting & Quigley v Union Internationale de Tir*, CAS 94/129, award dated 23 May 1995, para 36, *Digest of CAS Awards 1986–1998* (Berne 1998), pp 187 and 193. See also Gray 'Doping Control: The National Governing Body Perspective' in *Drugs and Doping in Sport* (2001, Cavendish) at pp 14 and 15.
2 A lack of means can never be a sufficient justification for adopting unfair rules, particularly when (as noted at para E4.113) that unfairness makes the decisions made pursuant to those rules susceptible to successful challenge before the courts.

E4.110 For example, Scott J, in the leading English case of *Gasser v Stinson*[1], rejected the contention that the IAAF's strict liability doping rules were in unreasonable restraint of trade, on the basis that a less absolute rule would not be effective to fight the evil of doping in sport:

> But the consequences if the absolute nature of the offence were removed or if the length of the sentence became discretionary and not mandatory must be considered. Suppose an athlete gives evidence that he or she did not take the drug knowingly and that it must therefore be inferred that the drug was ingested unknowingly. How is the IAAF to deal with such an explanation? How can credibility be tested? Suppose a third party, perhaps a member of the athlete's team of coaches, perhaps a medical adviser, perhaps a malicious prankster, gives evidence that he or she administered the drug to the athlete and that the athlete had no knowledge that this was being done. How is the credibility of that third party's evidence to be tested? The pressure for success in international athletics, as well as in domestic athletics, and the national pride and prestige that have become part of international athletics have to be borne in mind. Will the credibility of the athlete or the third party vary depending upon the nation to which he or she belongs? If a competitor or third party from nation A is to be believed, what will be the position when similar evidence is given by a competitor or third party from nation B? The lengths to which some people will go in order to achieve the appearance of success for their nation's athletes in athletics competitions is in point … Cynicism, sadly, abounds. Mr Holt, in his evidence, said that in his view, if a defence of moral innocence were open, the floodgates would be opened and the IAAF's attempts to prevent drug-taking by athletes would be rendered futile. He had, in my opinion, reason for that fear[2].

1 (15 June 1988, unreported), QBD. At the 1987 World Championships in Rome, Sandra Gasser, a Swiss international middle-distance runner, gave a urine sample that subsequently tested positive for a metabolite of methyl-testosterone, a banned anabolic steroid. Ms Gasser contended (among other things) that she had not knowingly taken any banned substance. In September 1987, the IAAF suspended Ms Gasser from competition for two years, which meant she would miss the 1988 Seoul Olympics. She and the Swiss athletic federation challenged the ruling on various grounds, none of which was accepted by the IAAF Arbitration Panel. (See para E4.281). In March 1988, Ms Gasser commenced an action in the English High Court, seeking (among other things) a declaration that the IAAF's ban was unlawful and she was therefore entitled to continue to compete in official competitions, including the 1988 Olympics. Ms Gasser argued that anti-doping rules suspending athletes from competition for a doping offence were an unreasonable and therefore unenforceable restraint of trade. She contended that a strict liability rule could not be shown to be reasonable, because 'a rule which did not permit an athlete even to try and establish his or her moral innocence, either in resisting conviction or in mitigation of sentence, was unreasonable and unjustifiable'.

2 Scott J's ruling in *Gasser v Stinson* was followed in *Wilander and Novacek v Tobin and Jude* by both Mr Justice Lightman (19 March 1996, unreported), QBD and the Court of Appeal ((1996) Independent, 26 April).

E4.111 The first response to this argument is that the force of pragmatic considerations cannot be allowed to eradicate the search for a principled basis of liability. There is in principle something objectionable in an athlete being found guilty of a doping offence, thus suffering a severe moral stigma and the loss of a career, if in truth there was no moral fault on his part[1]. Although in the vast majority of cases, the reason for the presence of the prohibited substance will be unexplained or unclear, there will be some cases in which the cause of the presence of the prohibited substance can be convincingly established. If those circumstances negate any moral fault on the part of the athlete[2], it may well be that disqualification of the tainted result itself remains necessary in order to protect other athletes disadvantaged by the inadvertent presence of the drug[3], but the suggestion that the athlete should be found guilty of a doping offence (thereby branding him a cheat) and punished by means of a prospective ban from participating in future events seems unsustainable as a matter of principle[4].

1 See para E4.104, n 5.

2 For example, the athlete may be able to prove that the prohibited substance was present in his body without his knowledge and without any fault on his part, perhaps because of prescribing error by a doctor or dispensing error by a chemist, or even because someone maliciously 'spiked' his food. See eg *John Skeete* case, UK Athletics, unreported decision dated 29 March 2001 (GB sprinter's father admitted he had spiked his son's health supplements with anabolic steroids after his son left his training group). The father was eventually banned from coaching for two years (see (2001) Guardian, 27 September at p 30; and (2001) Daily Telegraph, 27 September 2001 at p 83), but under the IAAF rules the UK Athletics tribunal had no choice but to find the 'morally innocent' son guilty of a doping offence and ban him for two years, leaving as his only recourse an application for early reinstatement under the 'exceptional circumstances' rule (as to which, see para E4.372 et seq).

Similarly, Young in *Problems with the Definition of Doping: Does Lack of Fault or the Absence of Performance-Enhancing Effect Matter?*, paper delivered at the CAS arbitration seminar (Lausanne, 8 December 1998), cites the case of a Russian weightlifter, 1996 Olympic Gold medalist Aleksi Petrov, whose lifetime ban was rescinded by the IWF when his former girlfriend confessed that she had spiked his food with the banned substance found in his sample.

See also (2001) Guardian, 27 September, citing the case of Ludmila Engquist who had a doping ban lifted by a Russian court in 1996 after her husband admitted he had spiked her drink with anabolic steroids after she asked him for a divorce); *Chela* ATP Tour Doping Tribunal decision dated 30 March 2001 (two-year ban was reduced to three month ban because of proof doctor had prescribed steroid without athlete's knowledge, as part of vitamin and supplement cocktail).

3 The fact that the athlete had the benefit of a banned substance justifies cancelling his result, whether or not he ingested the substance intentionally, 'for obvious questions of sports equity'. See *Aanes v FILA*, CAS 2001/A/317, decision dated 9 July 2001, pp 16–18 ('[I]t is perfectly proper for the rules of a sporting federation to establish that the results achieved by a "doped athlete" at a competition during which he was under the influence of a prohibited substance must be cancelled irrespective of any guilt on the part of the athlete. This conclusion is the natural consequence of sporting fairness against the other competitors. The interests of the athlete concerned in not being punished without being guilty must give way to the fundamental principle of sport that all competitors must have equal chances'); *SJ v FEI*, CAS 92/71, award dated 10 October 1992, *Digest of CAS Awards 1986–1998* (Berne 1998), pp 135 and 140; *N v FEI*, CAS 94/126, award dated 9 December 1998, para 6, *Digest of CAS Awards II 1998–2000* (2002, Kluwer), pp 137 and 141.

In other words, if, retrospectively, it can be objectively determined that an athlete has competed under the influence of a substance that enhanced (or may fairly be assumed to have enhanced) his performance in any way then the need for fairness to other competitors should dictate that the offending athlete be disqualified and lose his rankings and other benefits derived from the particular event, even if the athlete himself was not at fault. The analogy would be to an athlete who inadvertently took a short-cut in a cross-country race. He or she would be disqualified regardless of culpability. See Tarasti *Legal Solutions In International Doping Cases* (SEP Editrice 2000) at p 85. See also Beloff 'Drugs, Laws and Versapaks' in *Drugs and Doping in Sport* (2001, Cavendish), pp 39 and 45: 'there can be no objection in principle from disqualifying anyone who has won a race with the aid of drugs, even though he, she or it was entirely innocent in the matter. The fact remains that the advantage has been obtained – and, in objective terms, unfairly'.

Query the position, however, where the substance found in the athlete's sample plainly and incontrovertibly has *no* performance-enhancing effect. (See further paras E4.134 and E4.292).

4 See eg Oschutz 'Harmonization of Anti-Doping Code Through Arbitration: The Case Law of the Court of Arbitration for Sport' [2002] 12 Marquette Law Review 675, 689 ('the principle of strict liability cannot be justified if additional suspensions [ie beyond cancellation of the tainted result] are at stake').

E4.112 The argument that the fight against doping would become virtually impossible if liability were not strict does not provide a principled answer to this concern[1]. Nor is it clear why in practice a requirement for lack of fault to be taken into account, if proved, should undermine doping regimes.

1 See *Aanes v FILA*, CAS 2001/A/317, award dated 9 July 2001, p 18: 'It is obvious that it would be an important weapon in the fight against doping if the federations were able to impose sanctions on athletes who have tested positive, without having to establish any element of guilt on the part of the athlete. However, this argument, which is one of prevention and deterrence, loses sight of the general objective of doping sanctions, namely the punishment of the athlete for having violated the rules'.

E4.113 The pragmatic concern that this may generate costly litigation is unpersuasive when it is recognised that the imposition of strict liability, without any regard to moral fault, risks bringing the system into disrepute and would lead to findings that would be set aside by courts in many jurisdictions, thus doing more serious damage to the war against doping.

E4.114 The concern that without strict liability the floodgates would open[1] is based on the misconception that the only alternative to strict liability is to require the sports body to prove intent. In fact, it is clear that:

> there are other means, in particular when allocating the burden of proof, to ensure an effective fight against doping without accepting the risk of sanctioning an athlete who is not guilty of an offence or whose level of guilt does not justify the full extent of the sanction[2].

1 See para E4.109. See also Prof Ron Maugham of Aberdeen University, quoted in (2002) Financial Times, 30 May: 'Do we frame the rules so that no innocent athlete is prosecuted but 90 per cent of cheats get away with it, or do we run the risk of convicting some innocent people in order to catch the cheats?'

2 *Aanes v FILA*, CAS 2001/A/317A, award dated 9 July 2001, *p* 18.

E4.115 Specifically, the rules may make fault an element of the offence, but allow that fault to be presumed from the presence of the prohibited substance in the athlete's body[1]. Such a presumption is in principle justified by the nature of the offence and the need to control drug abuse in sport[2].

1 See eg FISA Rules of Racing and Related Bye-Laws, Pt 7, r 80, para 6.3: 'Every sample A declared positive must be treated as scientific proof of a breach of the Anti-Doping Bye-laws, and shall carry a presumption (revocable) of being a voluntary act'.

2 See *Aanes v FILA*, CAS 2001/A/317A, award dated 9 July 2001, pp 20, and 21–22: 'Doping only happens in the sphere of the athlete: he/she is in control of his/her body, of what he/she eats or drinks, or who has access to his/her nutrition, of what medication he/she takes etc. In these circumstances, it is appropriate to presume that the athlete has knowingly or at least negligently consumed the substance which has led to the positive doping test'.

E4.116 However, the athlete ought to be given the opportunity to rebut that presumption by adducing evidence that the presence of the substance in his body was not due to any intent or negligence on his part[1]. Importantly, that will be a very heavy burden: it has been stated that the athlete has to provide evidence that demonstrates with near certainty that he was not at fault[2]. It would *not* be sufficient for the athlete simply to assert, however credibly, that he just does not know how the substance came to be in his sample, and to rely on assertions of good faith and lack of motivation to cheat[3]. Instead, it would be necessary to adduce cogent evidence showing:

(1) how the substance came to be in his sample; and
(2) that he in no way controlled, was aware of or could be held responsible for such ingestion or administration[4].

1 In most cases, the athlete would not be able to discharge this burden. See eg *Chagnaud v FINA*, CAS 95/141, award dated 22 April 1996, *Digest of CAS Awards 1986–1988* (Berne 1998), pp 215, 224–21; *Aanes v FILA*, CAS 2001/A/317A, award dated 9 July 2001, *p* 20.

2 *Chagnaud v FINA*, CAS 95/141, award dated 22 April 1996, *Digest of CAS Awards 1986–1998* (Berne 1998), pp 215, 220–21 ('to be able to rebut satisfactorily the presumption of guilt on the part of an athlete who has tested positive, it is vital that such athlete provide counter-evidence which allows it to be established with near-certainty that he has not committed a fault'); cited with approval in *B v IJF*, CAS 98/214, award dated 17 March 1999, para 16, *Digest of CAS Awards II 1998–2000* (2002, Kluwer), pp 308 and 319.

3 *W v FEI*, CAS 92/86, award dated 19 April 1993, *Digest of CAS Awards 1986–1998* (Berne 1998), pp 161 and 164: 'to admit such (moreover unproven) allegations would amount to emptying [the FEI anti-doping rules] of their substance, which would result in making any fight against doping futile'. See also McCutcheon 'Sports Discipline, Natural Justice and Strict Liability' (1999) 28(1) Anglo-American Law Review 37, 67: 'A mere assertion of lack of fault by an athlete who has tested positive is unlikely to be successful and it would be open to the tribunal to draw the natural and proper inferences that arise from the evidence. At the very least the athlete would bear an evidential burden in relation to a contention of lack of fault and, in the absence of credible evidence, would run the risk of a determination of guilt'.

4 Tarasti *Legal Solutions in International Doping Cases* (SEP Editrice 2000) at p 112: 'Explanations of what might have happened are as a rule not credible. Only facts count. The [positive] finding is normally the only fact the sports organisations have at their disposal. The counter-evidence must also be facts, not beliefs or claims'.

In *P v FINA*, CAS 97/180, award dated 14 January 1999, para 9, *Digest of CAS Awards II 1998–2000* (Kluwer 2002), pp 184, 195, the CAS panel ruled that 'as far as exculpatory evidence is concerned, strict standards must be imposed', and applied this rigorous approach in rejecting evidence adduced by the athletes that their food had been spiked (including the 'confession' of the supposed saboteur).

E4.117 In this context moral fault includes not only deliberate contravention but also negligence, most widely defined[1]. The regime is based on the assumption that an athlete, and his coach, will be alert to any possibility of prohibited substances being present in any medication or athletic food supplements. Any failure to heed general warnings from the sporting authorities[2] or to make rigorous enquiries as to the constituents of novel supplements will be sufficient to constitute fault[3].

1 For example, a rider who left her horse in a box without cleaning out litter or fodder left by the previous occupant was found to be culpably negligent and therefore guilty of a doping offence under the FEI Rules when the horse's sample tested positive for a banned substance. *G v FEI*, CAS 91/53, award dated 15 January 1992, *Digest of CAS Awards 1986–1998* (Berne 1998), pp 79, 89: 'G has not shown herself to have taken all the precautions which would have enabled her to clear herself of the presumption of negligence which results from the presence, in the urine of her horse, of a Prohibited Substance'. See also *N v FEI*, CAS 92/63, award dated 10 September 1992, *Digest of CAS Awards 1986–1998* (Berne 1998), pp 115, 122.

2 See para E4.184. A wrestler at the 2000 Sydney Olympics tested positive for metabolites of nandrolone and was disqualified from the Olympic Games and banned from all competitions for two years. He subsequently blamed a nutritional supplement that his sponsor had given him, the label to which revealed no prohibited substances, but which was subsequently found to contain nandrolone precursors. While the panel declined, in light of Swiss law, to apply a strict liability standard (see para E4.130), the wrestler's failure to stop taking the supplement when warnings were issued about labelling failures in such products was deemed sufficiently negligent to warrant the finding of a doping offence and the imposition of a 15-month suspension: *Aanes v FILA*, CAS 2001/A/317A, award dated 9 July 2001.

3 Tarasti *Legal Solutions in International Doping Cases* (SEP Editrice 2000) at p 93: 'Different kinds of explanations may previously have been credible when the general knowledge of doping and prohibited substances was low. But today at least in athletics, where some 15,000 doping tests are performed yearly, and when a wide educational programme is carried out, all athletes who are competing internationally are well aware of their duties. An athlete who says that a trainer or girlfriend has given him some pills whose content is unknown, means today that the athlete has in most cases made himself guilty of negligence, if a doping substance has been detected. In this respect, the liability of a top athlete for negligence is much higher than the liability of ordinary people'.

E4.118 Some regimes may allow for proof of 'exceptional circumstances' to negate the offence or mitigate the penalty[1], but in general the wording of the rules does not easily allow a tribunal to acquit an athlete, even if the circumstances of wholly innocent ingestion can be established. The basis for adoption of this approach has to be to apply a broad and purposive interpretation of the rules[2], against the background of a number of decisions in other jurisdictions that strict liability would be contrary to general principles of law[3].

1 See para E4.315 et seq.
2 See paras E4.77 to E4.82.
3 See *In the Matter of Arbitration between Jessica Foschi and US Swimming Inc*, AAA Case No 77190003696 (1 April 1996) (FINA's strict liability drug rule 'so offends our deeply rooted and historical concepts of fundamental fairness as to be arbitrary and capricious' and is therefore unenforceable); *Baumann v DLV*, OLG Frankfurt/Main, judgment of May 18 2000, 13W29/00, p 15 (rules imposing punishment without fault incompatible with German law). See generally Wise '"Strict liability" drug rules of sports governing bodies' [1996] NLJ 1161, 1163: 'It is submitted that under Swiss law and the laws of most civilised countries, neither CAS panels nor any other court, arbitral tribunal or domestic tribunal can or should uphold the legality of a "strict liability" drug regulation'.

E4.119 The principle of implying into the anti-doping rules a requirement of moral fault has been clearly stated not to apply to the disqualification of an athlete from the event at which he is found to have competed with a prohibited substance in his body. In that respect the principle of fairness in competition outweighs the need to establish moral fault, so that the athlete must be found guilty of a doping offence and be deprived of the benefits of his unfair competitive advantage. It is only in respect of prospective disqualification that the absence of moral fault on the part of the athlete could be material[1].

1 See para E4.111.

E4.120 Thus the approach adopted in *Gasser v Stinson*[1] is questionable on a number of grounds. Firstly, it fails to distinguish between the legitimacy of upholding a disqualification from the event in question on a strict liability basis, and imposing a prospective disqualification on a basis of mandatory penalties unrelated to the moral fault of the athlete. Secondly, it fails to address the approach of interpreting the rules on the basis that they raise only a rebuttable presumption of fault, rather than an absolute offence. Thirdly, there would seem no reason in principle why sporting tribunals, which are dealing with matters of great importance, should not be able to examine the credibility of witnesses and decide whether the athlete has indeed provided convincing evidence to explain away the presence of a prohibited substance. Once the onerous nature of the defence is appreciated, there is no reason why the admission of a possibility of the proof of innocence should derail the disciplinary process when conducted by experienced and expert tribunals armed with a considerable degree of scepticism[2]. Fourthly, the concern about the intrusion of litigation into anti-doping disputes does not support an argument for strict liability. Those concerns should in any event be met by a proper appeal arbitration process, and as a CAS panel has observed it is equally subversive to the fight against doping for a disqualification later to be annulled by a court on the grounds that the strict liability approach is in breach of fundamental rights[3].

1 See para E4.110.
2 See McCutcheon 'Sports Discipline, Natural Justice and Strict Liability' (1999) 28(1) Anglo-Am LR 37 at 67: 'Courts and tribunals on a daily basis face questions of this type and it is hardly unreasonable to expect the same of a sports tribunal'.
3 *Aanes v FILA*, CAS 2001/A/317A, award dated 9 July 2001.

E4.121 Summary of general discussion On this approach liability in doping cases should be described as being 'strict' but not 'absolute'. The presence of a prohibited substance is sufficient to establish the offence but if it is affirmatively proved by the athlete that the substance was ingested or administered without any fault on his part then in principle he should have a defence, at least to a prospective penalty[1]. This approach provides no solace to cheats, and certainly opens no floodgates.

1 See Tarasti *Legal Solutions in International Doping Cases* (SEP Editrice 2000) at pp 112 and 13: '[The accused athlete] has to abolish the presumption of negligence when prohibited substances have been detected. Strict liability means here mostly interpretation of negligence … According to my opinion, strict liability in sport has its own content. The case will be settled usually when after a positive finding the burden of proof has been shifted to the athlete and the presumption of negligence of the athlete including an active duty to avoid doping prevails. This determines the content of strict liability'.

E4.122 The objectives of the anti-doping rules are stated to be the prevention of cheating and protection of the health of athletes[1]. A rule that gives the athlete a defence to a prospective disqualification penalty if he can affirmatively and convincingly prove that the substance entered his body without his knowledge and in circumstances for which he cannot be blamed does not undermine these objectives. Therefore, the justification for adhering to the absolutist approach to strict liability is questionable, both under the general principles of international sports law and even under the English law of restraint of trade.

1 See para E4.6.

E4.123 The English cases of *Gasser* and *Wilander*, reached without reference to the substantial body of CAS and European jurisprudence, cannot safely be relied upon[1]. Certainly the English cases will not be accepted as persuasive by those international tribunals, principally the CAS, who have the task of interpreting the international anti-doping regimes. It would be illogical, and ultimately futile, for the English courts and domestic English tribunals entrusted with interpreting the anti–doping rules to apply those rules in a manner inconsistent with the accepted international jurisprudence as it is developing in the CAS decisions[2].

1 See also Beloff 'Drugs, Laws & Versapaks' in *Drugs and Doping in Sport* (2001, Cavendish), pp 39 and 46.
2 See para E4.124 et seq.

E4.124 CAS decisions on strict liability The decisions of the Court of Arbitration for Sport have not been entirely consistent as to the permissibility of a strict liability approach, at least in part due to the fact that they have had to examine the issue in the context of varying rules of different organisations, and in the context of different consequences (liability, disqualification, discretionary ban, mandatory ban).

E4.125 Certain of the CAS decisions that discuss and analyse the arguments for and against conclude that a strict liability approach *is* permissible, but they set various parameters on it. The decisions supporting an absolutist approach include the following:

- The CAS panel in *USA Shooting & Quigley v Union Internationale de Tir*[1] said that it 'would as a matter of principle be prepared to apply a strict liability test', because requiring the governing body to prove fault (and thereby allowing an athlete to avoid liability based on lack of fault):
  (a) would be unfair to his competitors in the tainted event;
  (b) would probably be too difficult to prove and therefore would open the floodgates to drugs cheats; and

(c) would certainly be too expensive to prove.

The first objection is addressed, however, by disqualifying the athlete from the event in question; the second two have been answered above[2].

- In *Lehtinen v FINA*[3], the CAS panel noted, with apparent approval, that previous CAS panels 'have always supported the application of such 'strict liability' standard in other doping cases', provided the applicable rules are clearly articulated as such. It noted the contention that punishment (a prospective ban) without proof of fault was illegal under Swiss law, but did not need to address that issue on the facts of the case before it. This case, then, does not take us much further either way.
- In *N v FINA*[4], the CAS panel held that the FINA rules imposed a strict liability offence. The CAS panel pointed out that earlier FINA cases before the CAS that contemplated that lack of intent was a defence[5] involved differently drafted rules and that the CAS cases that endorsed a strict liability construction[6] involved analogous rules to those under consideration. The CAS panel concluded that under the FINA rules the question of intent only came into play when sanction, and not liability, was under consideration. The panel did however expressly state that it did not have to examine whether the FINA rules 'would be compatible with general principles of law in so far as they purport to prevent a competitor from establishing his innocence by showing conclusively that the presence of a prohibited substance in his bodily fluid was the product of an ingestion which was neither intentional nor negligent, eg where his drink is "spiked"'. The case therefore left open the possibility that the general principles of law might be relied upon to undercut strict liability in some contexts.
- In *Bernhard v ITU*[7], the CAS panel held that strict liability was essential and indispensable for an effective fight against doping in sport and for the protection of fairness towards all competitors and of their health and well-being. The panel stated that the concept of strict liability went further than establishing a presumption of guilt: it made the athlete liable regardless of guilt. The panel hypothesised that the only exceptions to strict liability might be 'force majeure' or the wrongful act of a third party. Accordingly, it was irrelevant if the athlete could establish that he had not acted intentionally or negligently. According to the panel, this was 'the only interpretation capable to ensure [an] efficient fight against doping'. The panel also held however that the principle of strict liability only made fault irrelevant: it did not extend to absolving the relevant federation from showing to the comfortable satisfaction of the panel that a metabolite in the athlete's sample came from an exogenous prohibited substance. Again, therefore, the CAS left open the possibility of exceptions, and confined strict liability to the question of fault.
- In *Raducan v IOC*[8], the CAS panel stated that it had been repeatedly confirmed in CAS jurisprudence that the Olympic Movement Anti-Doping Code made doping a strict liability offence, so that in order to prove liability no intentional element or competitive advantage had to be established. It was enough instead simply to prove the presence of a prohibited substance. This rule was applied in *Raducan* notwithstanding that the athlete had taken Nurofen for a headache and the amount of the drug in her sample would not have produced a positive result if she had not had a very low body weight of 37kg. The CAS panel held that in balancing the interests of the athlete with the need to achieve drug free sport, the Anti-Doping Code had to be enforced without compromise.

1 CAS 94/129, award dated 23 May 1995, para 36, *Digest of CAS Awards 1986–1998* (Berne 1998), pp 187, 193. See generally *UCI v Moller*, CAS 99/A/239, para 10 (surveying CAS cases upholding strict liability approach); Young *Problems with the Definition of Doping: Does Lack of Fault or the Absence of Performance Enhancing Effect Matter?*, a paper delivered at CAS arbitration seminar (Lausanne, 8 December 1998) (surveying US and CAS decisions upholding strict liability approach on same grounds as in *Quigley*).

2 See paras E4.113 and E4.114.

3 CAS 95/142, award dated 14 February 1996, *Digest of CAS Awards 1986–1998* (Berne 1998), pp 225, 230.

4 CAS 98/208, award dated 22 December 1998, paras 12–17, *Digest of CAS Awards II 1998–2000* (2002, Kluwer), p 234.

5 *S v FINA,* CAS 91/56, award dated 25 June 1992, *Digest of CAS Awards 1986–1998* (Berne 1998), p 93; *F v FINA,* CAS 96/156.

6 In particular *Korneev & Gouliev*, CAS Atlanta 1996/003–4, award dated 4 August 1996. See paras E4.151 and E4.251.

7 CAS 98/222, award dated 9 August 1999, paras 15–44, *Digest of CAS Awards II 1998–2000* (2002, Kluwer), p 330, 336–337.

8 CAS Sydney 2000/011, award dated 28 September 2000, *Digest of CAS Awards II 1998–2000* (2002, Kluwer), p 665.

E4.126 It is clear from even these cases that a degree of disquiet was often felt by CAS panels as to the fairness of a strict liability approach. This was reflected in statements to the effect that 'rules attempting to impose strict liability and to allow no defences at all should be "absolutely crystal clear and unambiguous"' and that any ambiguity in such rules should be construed in favour of the accused athlete[1].

1 *Bernhard v ITU*, CAS 98/222, award dated 9 August 1999, para 31, *Digest of CAS Awards II 1998–2000* (2002, Kluwer), pp 330, 339, quoting *F v FINA*, CAS 96/156, para 13.3.

E4.127 In addition, cases started to emerge from other jurisdictions that ruled unlawful under local law a strict liability approach that punishes an athlete irrespective of whether or not he is at fault[1].

1 See para E4.118, n 3.

E4.128 This concern was clearly acknowledged in *Chagnaud v FINA*[1]. Faced with a challenge to FINA's strict liability anti-doping rule, the CAS panel accepted that requiring a sports body to prove intent would undermine the war on doping, but also noted that not allowing any scope for proof of lack of fault would be unprincipled and disproportionate. It reconciled the position by focusing on the distinction between disqualifying the athlete from the tainted event and banning him from participation in further events:

> The Panel is of the opinion that the system of strict liability of the athlete must prevail when sporting fairness is at stake. This means that, once a banned substance is discovered in the urine or blood of an athlete, he must automatically be disqualified from the competition in question, without any possibility for him to rebut this presumption of guilt (irrebutable presumption) …
>
> In conjunction with such a sporting sanction, a disciplinary sanction may also be involved in doping cases. In the majority of cases this is suspension of the athlete who tested positive. On this precise aspect of the issue, the Panel believes that the different sports rules on sanctions in doping cases should make allowance for an appreciation of the subjective elements in each case. For it is indeed the task of the sports authorities to establish the guilt of an athlete in order to fix a just and extricable sanction …
>
> It has been noted above that the fact of leaving the burden of proof to the competent sports authority would lead to serious uncertainty of the law. Thus the Panel considers that generally speaking the principle of presumption of the athlete's guilt may remain but that,

by way of compensation, the athlete must have the possibility of shifting the burden of proof by providing exculpatory evidence. The athlete will thus be allowed to demonstrate that he did not commit any fault intentionally or negligently …

1 CAS 95/141, award dated 22 April 1996, *Digest of CAS Awards 1986–1998* (Berne 1998), pp 215, 220–21, followed in *P v FINA*, CAS 97/180, award dated 14 January 1999, para 9, *Digest of CAS Awards II 1998–2000* (Kluwer 2002), pp 184, 193; and also in *B v IJF*, CAS 98/214, award dated 17 March 1999, para 16, *Digest of CAS Awards II 1998–2000* (2002, Kluwer), pp 308, 318–319; but not followed (although not expressly mentioned) in *N v FINA*, CAS 98/208, award dated 22 December 1998, para 16, *Digest of CAS Awards II 1998–2000* (2002, Kluwer), pp 234, 248 (lack of intent relevant only to mitigation); and also not followed in *Bernhard v ITU*, CAS 98/222, award dated 9 August 1999, paras 17 and 18, *Digest of CAS Awards II 1998–2000* (2002, Kluwer), pp 330, 337.

E4.129 The *Chagnaud* panel was not prepared to go as far as to say that such an approach should be followed even in the face of clear wording in the sport's anti-doping rules that proof of fault was not required[1]. However, the CAS panel in *Haga v FIM*[2] was not so reticent, ruling that the admission of exculpatory evidence 'is required in accordance with common principles of law and the human rights of the accused athlete even if the federation rules do not expressly provide for it'.

1 CAS 95/141, award dated 22 April 1996, para 19, *Digest of CAS Awards 1986–1998* (Berne 1998), p 215, 221. Instead, finding no room for manoeuvre in the wording of the rules themselves, the CAS panel created some by pointing to a prior inconsistent application of the rules by FINA itself. See para E4.312.

2 CAS 2000/A/281, award dated 22 December 2000, *Digest of CAS Awards II 1998–2000* (2002, Kluwer), p 410 (outlining 'the jurisprudence of CAS with respect to doping cases').

Other CAS panels have also simply interpreted 'strict liability' doping definitions as shifting the burden onto the athlete to prove his lack of fault. See eg *FCLP v IWF*, CAS 99/A/252, para 7.4.3; *Luyckx v FEI*, CAS 2000/A/275, para 26.

E4.130 ***Aanes v FILA*** This approach was then confirmed in the now leading CAS judgment of *Aanes v FILA*[1]. Fritz Aanes, a Norwegian wrestler, tested positive at the Sydney Olympics for nandrolone metabolites. The IOC disqualified him from the rest of the Games, and subsequently FILA banned him from all competitions for two years. The ban was automatic upon the finding of a prohibited substance; proof of intent or fault was not required. Aanes challenged FILA's ban before the Court of Arbitration for Sport. He disclaimed any intent to dope or negligence and blamed food supplements provided by his sponsor (which were not labelled as containing any prohibited substance but were subsequently found to do so). He contended that a strict liability rule could not be enforced against him because he could not be punished by the imposition of a ban without fault.

1 CAS 2001/A/317, award dated 9 July 2001.

E4.131 The CAS panel decided that, in the absence of an express choice of another law, and given that FILA was based in Switzerland, the FILA rules had to be interpreted in light of Swiss law[1], which includes the general principles of law set out above[2]. It rejected FILA's contention that the FILA anti-doping rules were clear, making fault irrelevant to liability to a ban and relevant only to reduction of sanction based on 'specific and exceptional circumstances'. However, it also ruled, in a crucial passage[3], that the clarity or otherwise of the anti-doping rules was irrelevant; even if the rules unambiguously eschewed fault as an element of an offence leading to a ban, the CAS panel would have to admit evidence of lack of fault as an exculpatory factor:

However, the panel is of the opinion that as a matter of principle and irrespective of 'specific and exceptional circumstances' an athlete cannot be banned from competition for having committed a doping offence unless he is guilty, ie he has acted with intent or negligence. Even if the rules and regulations of the Sports Federation do not expressly provide that the guilt of the athlete has to be taken into account the foregoing principle would have to be read into these rules to make them legally acceptable.

CAS panels have to interpret the rules in question in a way which seeks to discern the intention of the rule maker, and not to frustrate it. In interpreting the FILA rules the Panel does not find any indication that they intended to ignore the subjective elements as such. Since the Panel is of the opinion that under Swiss law an athlete cannot validly be banned in the absence of any fault, an interpretation to the contrary would lead to the rules being void which would frustrate the objective of a fight against doping pursued by the entire sporting world.

Before explaining the reasons for the principle of guilt, the Panel wishes to clarify that this principle does not apply to the disqualification of a 'doped athlete' from the event at which the doping test was conducted. It is therefore perfectly proper for the rules of a sporting federation to establish that the results achieved by a 'doped athlete' at a competition during which he was under the influence of a prohibited substance must be cancelled irrespective of any guilt on the part of the athlete. This conclusion is the natural consequence of sporting fairness against the other competitors. The interests of the athlete concerned in not being punished without being guilty must give way to the fundamental principle that all competitors must have equal chances.

1 See para E4.81, n 1.
2 At paras E4.77 to E4.82.
3 *Aanes v FILA*, CAS 2001/A/317A, award dated 9 July 2001, pp 16 and 17.

E4.132 On the facts before it (ingestion by means of nutritional supplements in the face of numerous IOC warnings about contamination of such supplements), the CAS panel in *Aanes* found that the wrestler could not rebut the presumption of negligence, and therefore it upheld FILA's finding that a doping offence had been committed[1]. However, it took the wrestler's relative lack of fault into account by reducing the sanction from a suspension of two years to a suspension of 15 months.

1 See para E4.117, n 2. Similarly, in *M v Swiss Cycling*, CAS 2001/A/345, award dated 28 January 2002, p 20, the CAS panel noted that, based on *Aanes* and its progeny, an athlete had to be given an opportunity to rebut the presumption of guilt arising from the presence of the prohibited substance in his sample. To do so, however, the athlete 'would have had to demonstrate and prove that the EPO established did not enter his body through intent or negligence', which the claimant was not able to do.

E4.133 This is consistent with longstanding authority: CAS panels have often been persuaded to depart from 'fixed' sanctions set out in the relevant rules, usually on the ground that the fixed sanction was not proportionate to the seriousness of the offence, and specifically did not reflect the relative lack of moral guilt of the athlete concerned[1]. Relying on some of that authority, the CAS panel in *Aanes* expressly noted that it would have considered itself entitled to depart from the 'fixed' sanctions in the rules even if the rules had not expressly provided for a reduction of the otherwise mandatory sanction in the case of 'exceptional attenuating circumstances'[2].

1 For example, FINA's four-year ban for a first offence involving steroids has been reduced to two years, while a two year judo ban has been reduced to fifteen months. See, respectively, *Meca-Medina and Kajcan v FINA*, CAS T 2000/A/270; *Bouras v IJF*, CAS 98/214, award dated 17 March 1999, para 21, *Digest of CAS Awards II 1998–2000* (2002, Kluwer), pp 308, 322–323. See also *Chagnaud v FINA*, CAS 95/141, award dated 22 April 1996, *Digest of CAS Awards 1986–1998* (Berne 1998), pp 215, 222; *N v FEI*, CAS 92/73, award dated 10 September 1992, *Digest of*

CAS Awards 1986–1998 (Berne 1998), pp 153, 159; *FIN v FINA*, CAS 96/156, award dated 23 April 1997, *Digest of CAS Awards 1986–1998* (Berne 1998), pp 351 358–59. See generally McLaren 'Doping Sanctions: What Penalty?' [2002] 2 ISLR 23 at 29.

But cf *Susin v FINA*, CAS 2000/A/274, award dated 19 October 2000, paras 230–235, *Digest of CAS Awards II 1998–2000* (2002, Kluwer), pp 389, 408–409 (holding itself bound to apply four-year fixed ban, irrespective of mitigating factors).

2 CAS 2001/A/317, p 24.

E4.134 In *Baxter v IOC*[1], the Scottish skier Alain Baxter sought to test the conclusion in *Aanes* that strict liability could justify a disqualification as opposed to a ban. Baxter had innocently used a nasal decongestant that in the United States contained an additional substance to the same branded product in the UK. The first issue was whether that additional substance was itself a prohibited substance, and Baxter argued that it was not. He went on to argue, however, that even if it had been, there was no lawful basis (in the light of the general principles of law outlined at paras E4.77 to E4.82) to disqualify him where not only had he acted innocently but also there was no basis on which the substance could have enhanced performance. The justification offered for the proposition in *Aanes* was that whether or not the athlete had acted entirely innocently, the other athletes against whom he competed must be protected against his having enjoyed an advantage. Baxter argued that in the absence of that consideration, the justification for a disqualification, which was in itself very damaging, was undercut[2]. His appeal before the CAS was dismissed in October 2002.

1 CAS 2002.

2 Note however the *Raducan* case (para E4.125), where it was held that the governing body did not have to prove the existence of a performance-enhancing effect.

E4.135 Conclusion on strict liability The decisions of the CAS are not yet uniform in their approach to the issue of strict liability in doping cases. However, the forceful and principled judgment in *Aanes* indicates the likely development of the law in this area. On that basis the general position may be stated as follows:

- the mere presence of a prohibited substance establishes a doping offence, and a presumption of moral fault;
- that finding will require the athlete to be disqualified from the event in question;
- unless the athlete convincingly rebuts the presumption of moral fault, then he will be subject to disqualification from future competition; and
- even if the rules prescribe mandatory periods of disqualification, those mandatory penalties should not be applied without any regard to the circumstances of the case.

The commentary provided by the drafters of the WADA Code indicates that this is how they understand the strict liability rules should operate in practice[1].

1 The World Anti-Doping Code, Annotated with Explanatory Comments, E-Version 1.0, pp 17–19.

(d) The IOC List of Prohibited Substances and Prohibited Methods

E4.136 Given that the mere presence of a prohibited substance in the body gives rise to (at least) a presumption of fault[1], if not establishing the offence in its entirety[2], it would seem important to have absolute clarity on what is or is not a prohibited substance. One would expect there to exist a very definitive list of prohibited substances. However, because of the concern of providing a loophole for 'designer drugs'[3], in fact the IOC List of Prohibited Substances and Methods[4] is not a definitive list of prohibited substances but rather a list of categories of prohibited substances, including non-exhaustive lists of 'examples' in each category.

1 See para E4.135.
2 See para E4.100.
3 See para E4.147.
4 Appendix A of the Olympic Movement Anti-Doping Code. This list is regarded as at least the first reference point for anti-doping regulations in sport.

E4.137 Prohibited substances Part I of the IOC List sets out five different classes of prohibited substances, and provides several examples of each (and there is a further list of more examples at the end of the appendix).

E4.138 Class A is ***stimulants***. Stimulants have a direct stimulating effect on the central nervous system, increasing (among other things) cardiac output. These effects tend to be short-term, and stimulants are therefore considered 'performance-day enhancers'[1]. Listed examples include amphetamines, caffeine, cocaine, strychnine and ephedrine, as well as Beta-2 agonists[2]. They can have various harmful side effects, including hallucinations, hypertension and hypothermia.

1 Which is why they are not tested for in samples collected out of competition. See para E4.197.
2 As to Beta-2 agonists, see also para E4.140.

E4.139 Class B is ***narcotics***. Narcotics are analgesics, reducing or disguising pain. Regular ingestion can lead to addiction, as well as breathing and digestion difficulties. Listed examples include codeine, heroin, diamorphine, methadone, morphine and pethidine.

E4.140 Class C is the male sex hormone ***testosterone*** and other agents that are synthetic variations of testosterone, ie *anabolic (growth-promoting) and androgenic (masculinising) steroids* such as nandrolone, stanozolol and nostenedione. Testosterone stimulates protein production and so promotes muscle growth and development. These are long-term effects and therefore steroids are regarded as 'training enhancers'. Elevated testosterone has physiological side-effects (eg facial hair in women, breast growth in men) and carries a risk of infertility, heart failure and liver tumours. Class C also encompasses ***Beta-2 agonists***. Examples include clenbuterol, fenoterol, salbutamol, salmeterol and terbutaline. These are stimulants[1] and also (depending, in some cases, on the amount ingested) anabolic, increasing muscle size and strength. Possible adverse side effects include blood pressure and arrhythmia.

1 See para E4.138.

E4.141 Class D is ***diuretics***, such as bumetanide and triameterine. Diuretics increase the excretion of potassium, sodium and water, and so aid weight loss. As a result, they could assist athletes in sports where competition is organised by weight class, such as boxing, judo and weight-lifting. Side effects include alkalosis, disturbed metabolism and low blood sugar. Diuretics also dilute, and so reduce, the concentration of drugs in the urine, and therefore their use also constitutes a prohibited method[1].

1 See para E4.144.

E4.142 Class E is ***peptide and glycoprotein hormones*** (substances produced by glands in the body to control specific bodily functions) *and their analogues* (man-made drugs with similar effects), *as well as all respective releasing factors (and their analogues)* of those substances. Examples of peptide hormones are human growth hormone (HGH), erythropoietin (EPO) and darbepoetin. HGH (a treatment for dwarfism) quickens muscle recovery from workouts and therefore allows more intensive training, which helps athletes who rely on strength. Those relying on endurance would use EPO (a treatment for kidney disease), which enables the blood to produce more oxygen-carrying red cells. Adverse side effects for HGH include disfigurement through bone growth, and for EPO include hypertension, blood clots and encephalopathy.

E4.143 Part III of the IOC List identifies further substances that may be banned or restricted in certain specified circumstances. Specifically, alcohol, cannabinoids and beta-blockers[1] are banned only if the rules of 'a responsible authority' (ie the relevant sports governing body) so provide[2]. For example, alcohol is banned in motor racing, shooting and fencing; cannabis is prohibited in football, swimming, motorcycling and rugby league. Use of certain local anaesthetics and corticosteroids (anti-inflammatories) is permitted in cases of genuine medical need, but only if administered by one of the methods specified in the IOC List[3].

1 The Council of Europe's Anti-Doping Convention (see para E4.17, n 3) includes beta-blockers as a sixth class of prohibited substance, ie absolutely banned, without scope for variation from sport to sport. The IOC used to take the same approach. However, while beta-blockers have a calming effect that may enhance performance in sports such as archery, diving and shooting, by the same token beta-blockers would inhibit performance in aerobic and endurance sports requiring prolonged periods of high cardiac output. Therefore, the IOC's current approach, giving governing bodies flexibility to address the specificities of their sports, seems more sensible. For example, the Amateur Swimming Federation of Great Britain bans beta-blockers for diving and synchronised swimming, but not for other disciplines. See ASFGB Doping Control Rules, cl 2.3.

2 A governing body that wishes to prohibit the use of any of the Pt III substances must not only adopt the IOC List but must also specifically provide in its rules that the Pt III substances are banned. A CAS panel at the Nagano Olympics found Ross Rebagliati, the snowboard gold medallist, not guilty of any doping offence, notwithstanding that his urine sample tested possible for a metabolite of marijuana, because the FIS had not specifically prohibited marijuana. See *Rebagliati v IOC*, NAG OG/92/002, award dated 12 February 1998, *Digest of CAS Awards 1986–1998* (Berne 1998), pp 419, 424: 'We do not suggest for a moment that the use of marijuana should be condoned, nor do we suggest that sports authorities are not entitled to exclude athletes found to use cannabis. But if sports authorities wish to add their own sanctions to those that are edicted by public authorities, they must do so in an explicit fashion. That has not been done here … We must decide within the context of the law of sports, and cannot invent prohibitions or sanctions where none appear'.

3 See para E4.167 et seq.

E4.144 Prohibited methods Part II of the IOC List identifies two categories of prohibited methods:

- **Blood doping** – ie injecting oneself with one's own previously extracted blood or someone else's blood to increase the amount of circulating red blood cells and/or improve oxygen transport.
- **Pharmacological, chemical and physical manipulation** – ie the use of substances or procedures that alter or affect the integrity of urine or other samples used in anti-doping programmes and/or mask the use of prohibited substances ('masking agents')[1]. Examples range from the crude (urine substitution or tampering[2]) to the more subtle, such as administration of masking agents such as diuretics (to dilute and therefore manipulate the concentration of substances in the urine), probenecid or bromantan (which

temporarily block the excretion of anabolic steroids from the kidney to the urine) and epitestosterone (to hide elevated testosterone levels, since those are measured as a ratio to the level of epitestosterone in the urine)[3].

1 See eg IAAF Procedural Guidelines for Doping Control (2000 edn), p 21.
2 For example, Michele de Bruin, the Irish swimmer, was found guilty of a doping offence because the test disclosed the presence in her urine not of any prohibited substance, but rather of a level of whisky that would have been fatal, if digested, and therefore must have been added to the sample ex post facto as a masking agent. In August 1998, FINA banned de Bruin for four years for using a prohibited method, a decision subsequently upheld by the Court of Arbitration for Sport. See *Bruin v FINA*, award dated 7 June 1999, *Digest of CAS Awards II 1998–2000* (2002, Kluwer), p 255.
3 See para E4.261.

E4.145 Supplementing the IOC List Because new pharmaceutical substances are constantly being developed, specific provision is made for supplementing the IOC List, and it is regularly updated:

> The list of Prohibited Substances and Prohibited Methods contained in this Code may be changed by the IOC Executive Board upon recommendation by the Council of the International Anti-Doping Agency (IADA) and will come into effect three months, or such shorter delay as shall be specified in cases of medical necessity, after the International Federations and National Olympic Committees have been notified, in such manner as shall be determined by the IADA[1].

1 Olympic Movement Anti-Doping Code Chapter One, Art 4. IAAF Rule 55.3 provides that its list of prohibited substances 'shall be constantly reviewed by the Anti-Doping Commission and may be added to or amended by them. Such addition or amendment must be approved by the Council, and shall come into force three months from the date of such approval'.

E4.146 The World Anti-Doping Agency has a similar provision in its draft Code, save that it specifically contemplates a period of consultation prior to adding a substance to the list[1]. The draft Code also lists criteria for including a substance or method on the list, including requiring 'a reasonable opinion, based on scientific evidence, pharmacological effect or experience that the substance or method has the potential to enhance sport performance'[2]. However, '[t]he inclusion of a Prohibited Substance or Prohibited Method in [the Olympic Movement Anti-Doping Code] is not subject to appeal'[3], on this or any other basis; and nor would it be under WADA's proposed replacement code[4].

1 Draft World Anti-doping Code, E-Version 1.0, issued 10 June 2002, at para 8.3.1.
2 Draft World Anti-Doping Code, E-Version 1.0, issued 10 June 2002, cl 8.3.3.
3 Olympic Movement Anti-Doping Code (Lausanne 2001), Chap Three, Art 3.
4 Draft World Anti-Doping Code, E-Version 1.0, issued 10 June 2002, cl 2.

E4.147 Related substances The IOC List contains 'examples' of substances prohibited under each class of prohibited substances, but the list of examples in each class concludes with the term 'and related substances', and many substances that are not mentioned on the list are said to be prohibited under that term. This approach is considered 'essential because otherwise compounds not intended as drugs but with the desired pharmacological effect would be used to circumvent the control based upon a comprehensive list of drugs'[1]. Once they are identified, they can be added to the IOC List[2], but in the meantime they can only form the basis of a successful doping charge if they are demonstrated to be a 'related substance' to a substance on that list.

1 Professor Arnold Beckett 'The Problem of Drugs in Sport', *Dictionary of Medical Ethics* (2nd edn, 1981), p 41. See also IOC *Doping: An IOC White Paper* (Lausanne 1999), p 24: 'The rationale for prohibiting related substances is to prevent unscrupulous chemists or persons from promoting new drugs or chemicals that act like prohibited substances but are not specifically named. The term "designer drug" refers to a drug that is nearly identical to a prohibited drug yet possesses a slight difference which enables cheaters to argue that the drug is not on the prohibited list. Thus, the use of the phrase "and related substances" is a very helpful way of preventing the introduction of new drugs'.

See eg *Korneev and Gouliev v IOC*, CAS Arbitration (Atlanta) NO 003–41, *Digest of CAS Awards 1864–1998* (Berne 1988): 'The ongoing fight against the use of drugs in sport would be severely hampered by there being an exclusive list of substances being the only substances whose use was prohibited'.

2 See para E4.145.

E4.148 The Olympic Movement Anti-Doping Code defines 'related substance' as 'any substance having pharmacological action and/or chemical structure similar to a Prohibited Substance or any other substance referred to in this Code'[1]. The ITF Programme defines 'related substances' as 'those substances that are structurally, chemically, pharmacologically or physiologically similar to the substances listed within each Class of Substances'[2]. The IAAF rules speak not of 'related substances' but of 'chemically or pharmacologically related compounds'[3].

1 Olympic Movement Anti-Doping Code (Lausanne 2001), Chap One, Art One.

2 ITF Anti-Doping Programme 2002, Sch 1.

3 IAAF Procedural Guidelines for Doping Control (2000 edn), Sch One. In his submissions to the UKA Disciplinary Committee, Doug Walker argued that the phrase 'chemically or pharmacologically related' in the IAAF rules was unclear and therefore the phrase should be disregarded. The Disciplinary Committee rejected the contention that it was unclear, but also said that any lack of clarity would not mean the phrase should be disregarded, because this would 'amount to a charter for systematic steroid drug abuse. If a drug had to be specifically listed in order to be prohibited, that would be an open invitation to devise compounds which differed chemically in some minor respect only from those listed but which had substantially the same pharmacological effects, and for athletes to use such products at will until a test at some point led to their disclosure to the athletics authorities'. *UKA v Walker*, unreported, UKA Disciplinary Committee, 25 January 2000, para 30. Subsequently, each side in the *Walker* Case effectively proceeded on the basis that 'chemically related' meant 'having substantially the same chemical structure' and 'pharmacologically related' meant 'having substantially the same pharmacological effect by the same means'. See para E4.156.

E4.149 Clearly, this makes the parameters of the IOC List, and therefore the scope of (potentially strict) liability, far less clear-cut. The former President of the IAAF Arbitration Panel has therefore stated that in such cases (ie where it is alleged a substance is prohibited even though it is not expressly mentioned on the list, because it is a 'related substance' to a substance that is mentioned on the list), 'it is the claimant's duty to show that this substance has the same impact on the athlete and his/her performance as the substance mentioned in the list, ie that a near relation exists between these substances'[1]. That seems unobjectionable. More controversially, however, he has also said that 'it is necessary to present sufficient evidence that the athlete in question has been or ought to have been aware of this before the athlete can be considered to have liability for using such substance'[2].

1 Tarasti *Legal Solutions In International Doping Cases* (SEP Editrice 2000) at p 83.

2 See n 1.

E4.150 In point of fact, most sports put the risk of using a 'related substance' firmly on the athlete[1]. Moreover, the former President of the IAAF Arbitration Panel slightly contradicted himself when he said:

All efforts should be made to ensure that there is no space for such 'related compounds', because without the help of a specialist an athlete cannot know these substances[2].

1 See eg UK Athletics *Doping Rules and Procedures* (2001), cl 9: 'It is the duty of all athletes to ensure that no substances enter their body tissues or fluids which are prohibited under these Rules. Athletes are warned that they are responsible for all and any substance detected in samples given by them'.

2 Tarasti *Legal Solutions in International Doping Cases* (SEP Editrice 2000), p 45.

E4.151 Athletes have been able to challenge successfully the assertion that the substance found in their urine is 'related' to a banned substance and therefore is itself banned, not on the basis of a lack of knowledge on their part but on the basis of a lack of sufficient proof of the necessary chemical or pharmacological relationship between the two substances. For example:

- In September 1992, East German athletes Katrin Krabbe, Grit Breuer and Manuela Derr each tested positive for Clenbuteral. It was found that they had each systematically taken a medication containing Clenbuteral from April 1992 to August 1992. Clenbuteral was not mentioned on the IOC List but it was alleged to be pharmacologically related to anabolic steroids on the list. On this basis, all three athletes were banned from competition for four years. The Legal Committee of the German Athletic Association revoked that ban on the ground (among others) that it had not been properly shown that Clenbuteral was 'related' to banned anabolic steroids[1].
- A Russian swimmer and a Russian wrestler at the 1996 Atlanta Olympics tested positive for Bromantan. Bromantan was not mentioned at that time on the IOC List but the IOC concluded that it had stimulant properties and the athletes were therefore charged on the basis that Bromantan was 'related' to banned stimulants. A CAS panel rejected the charges on the basis that the scientific evidence submitted to it was not sufficient to establish 'to the relevant and high degree of satisfaction necessary' that Bromantan was a stimulant within the meaning of the IOC List. Objective evidence of 'the actual chemical composition and qualities' of the substance was required[2]. To avoid this difficulty recurring in the future, the IOC Medical Commission subsequently added Bromantan to the IOC List.
- In the *Walker* case, UKA's Disciplinary Committee found that UKA had not met its burden of showing beyond reasonable doubt that either 19-norandrostenedione or 19-norandrostenediol was chemically or pharmacologically related to nandrolone[3], but the IAAF Arbitration Panel disagreed[4]. Again, each substance was subsequently added to the IOC List.

1 The Legal Committee did impose a one-year ban for misconduct (taking a prescription drug purchased on the black market without medical need). In August 1993, the Council of the IAAF unilaterally and without a hearing extended that ban for a further two years, and the IAAF Arbitration Panel rejected the German Athletic Association's appeal. *Breuer, Derr, Krabbe* case, IAAF Arbitration Panel decision dated 20 November 1993, in Tarasti *Legal Solutions in International Doping Cases* (SEP Editrice 2000), pp 129–131. Krabbe took her challenge to the German civil courts, who in March 1996 upheld the Legal Committee's one-year ban but ruled the IAAF's additional two-year ban illegal on the grounds (among others) that the disproportionate sanction and the lack of a hearing infringed Ms Krabbe's constitutional rights. Decision of the High Regional Court of Munich of 28 March 1996, Sport und Recht, 4/96, pp 133 et seq. In 2001, a Munich court fixed the damages at DM1.2m plus interest from 1994; the IAAF appealed but subsequently, in a 2002 settlement, agreed to pay Ms Krabbe damages to compensate her for lost earnings while wrongfully banned. See *The Observer* of 5 May 2002.

2 *Korneev and Gouliev v IOC*, CAS Arbitration (Atlanta) 96/003-4L, award dated 4 August 1996, at p 20, quoted in length by Beloff in 'Drugs, Laws and Versapaks' in *Drugs and Doping in Sport* (2001, Cavendish) at p 51. See also Justice Vince Bruce *The ANZSLA Commentator*, Vol 9, No 1, p 15.
3 See para E4.156.
4 See para E4.159.

E4.152 Metabolites of listed substances and related substances Metabolism is the chemical process by which complex substances are decomposed in the body after ingestion or administration and converted into metabolites of the substance originally ingested or administered. For example, if cocaine is ingested, little or no cocaine is found in the urine. Rather, benzoylecoginine, a metabolite of cocaine, is found. To take account of this, anti-doping regulations usually provide that '[t]he expression "prohibited substance" shall include a metabolite of a prohibited substance'[1].

1 See eg IAAF Rule 55.6. See also ASFGB *Doping Control Rules*, cl 2.2: 'In these Rules and Protocols the expression prohibited substance shall include all metabolites of any substance on the FINA List, and any related substances'.
Cf Olympic Movement Anti Doping Code (Lausanne 2001), Chap One, Art 2.2: 'Doping is … the presence in the athlete's body of a Prohibited Substance or *evidence of the use thereof* …' (emphasis added).
The draft World Anti-Doping Code (E-Version 1.0, issued 10 June 2002) refers to 'markers or metabolites' (at para 8.1.1.1). At Appendix A, it defines a 'marker' as 'a compound, group of compounds or biological parameters that indicate the use of a prohibited substance or prohibited method', and a 'metabolite' as 'any substance produced by a biotransformation process'.

E4.153 What if a substance found in the urine may be a metabolite of a banned substance but also may be a metabolite of a substance that is not banned? For example, a substance may be a metabolite of nandrolone, which is banned, but also of norinyl, a contraceptive pill, which is not. Is the athlete entitled to the benefit of the doubt? Authority exists that in such circumstances, the burden is on the charging body to show the substance metabolised from the prohibited substance, not on the athlete to show it metabolised from the non-prohibited substance, and that therefore in the absence of sufficient evidence on the issue, the charging body has not sustained its burden of proving the presence of a banned substance in the athlete's urine[1]. The case of Great Britain athlete Doug Walker[2] is on point.

1 *Ime Akpan*, IAAF Arbitration Panel decision dated 10 April 1995, in Tarasti *Legal Solutions in International Doping Cases* (SEP Editrice 2000), pp 135–136 (when metabolite could have come from nandrolone but could also have come from norinyl, a non-prohibited contraceptive declared by the athlete on her doping control form, the IAAF had the continued burden of proving, beyond a reasonable doubt, that nandrolone and not norinyl caused the presence of 19-nandrolone); *Re Bernhard v ITU*, CAS 98/222, award dated 9 August 1999, *Digest of CAS Awards II 1998–2000* (2002, Kluwer), p 330 (if mere presence of prohibited substances establishes liability, then governing body must be able to demonstrate that the metabolites were exogenous, not endogenous). Cf *Jason Livingston* case, decision of BAF Appeal Panel (1993, unreported) (dismissing defence based on speculation that metabolite might possibly have derived from an unidentified non-prohibited substance, where no scientific evidence to support the speculation). But see the dissent in that case: 'In view of the fact that, albeit in only one known example, the main metabolite of a prohibited substance, nandrolone, has been found to be identical with a metabolite of a non-prohibited substance, namely progesterone, I believe that corroboration is required in the case where only a single principal metabolite of a prohibited substance is found. This corroboration may be from the presence of at least one other metabolite recognised as being characteristic of the prohibited substance, or from conventional non-scientific evidence, such as a confession or observance by a third party'.
2 See para E4.154 et seq.

E4.154 On 1 December 1998, Walker gave an out-of-competition urine sample. The sample tested positive for 19-norandrosterone. On 7 January 1999, UK Athletics suspended Walker from all competition with immediate effect. When the analysis of his B sample confirmed the initial positive result, UK Athletics charged Walker with a doping offence.

E4.155 Before the Disciplinary Committee, it was accepted that the 19-norandrosterone had metabolised from one of the 19-norsteroids (ie nandrolone, 19-norandrostenedione or 19-norandrostenediol). It could not be shown, however, from which of those it had metabolised. Therefore, the Disciplinary Committee ruled, UK Athletics had to show that each of them (nandrolone, 19-norandrostenedione *and* 19-norandrostenediol) was a prohibited substance.

E4.156 At the time, only nandrolone was expressly mentioned on the IOC List, and therefore UK Athletics had to show that each of 19-norandrostenedione and 19-norandrostenediol was 'chemically or pharmacologically related to' nandrolone. This it failed to do to the satisfaction of the Disciplinary Committee.

E4.157 This meant that the 19-norandrosterone in Walker's urine could have metabolised from a substance that was not prohibited. As a result, the Disciplinary Committee found that UK Athletics had not shown beyond a reasonable doubt that a metabolite of a prohibited substance was present in Walker's sample[1].

1 *UKA v Walker* (25 January 2000, unreported), UKA Disciplinary Committee.

E4.158 The IAAF Council referred the decision to the IAAF Arbitration Panel, contending that UK Athletics' Disciplinary Committee had misdirected itself or otherwise reached an erroneous conclusion when it exonerated Walker[1]. The IAAF contended that a substance qualifies as a 'metabolite of a prohibited substance' if it could be derived from a prohibited substance, even if it could equally be derived from other, non-prohibited substances. UK Athletics contended that such a showing would not be proof to the requisite standard of the presence of a prohibited substance in the sample. Instead, to meet that standard, the prosecutor would have to show that the metabolite could only have derived from a prohibited substance.

1 See para E4.364.

E4.159 The IAAF Arbitration Panel avoided ruling on that issue by finding, on the scientific evidence before it, that 19-norandrostenediol and 19-norandrosterone were both chemically and pharmacologically related compounds of nandrolone[1]. Nevertheless, in the authors' view it is to be doubted that a doping offence could be established on the basis of the presence of a metabolite that could have come from a non-prohibited substance, simply because it could also have come from a prohibited one.

1 *Walker* case, IAAF Arbitration Panel, 20 August 2000, para 19, [2001] 4 ISLR 264. In other words, the subsequent additions of those substances to the IOC List (as of 31 January 1999) had been redundant, simply confirming the position that had existed all along, rather than supplementing it.

(e) Ancillary offences

E4.160 Effective doping control requires the cooperation and participation of the athletes. Therefore, most anti-doping programmes make it an offence to fail or refuse to comply with drug testing procedures[1], and/or with any other provision of the anti-doping programme[2]. To give the rules some teeth, they may also provide that proof of such refusal or failure carries the same lengthy ban as an offence involving the use of anabolic steroids[3].

1 See eg IAAF Rule 56.1.
2 See eg ITF Anti-Doping Programme 2002, cl C(2)(b); UK Sport *Model Rules and Guidelines for Anti-Doping*, cl 2.2(vi). Under the Olympic Movement Anti-Doping Code, in contrast, such refusal is not a doping offence in itself but rather an exacerbating factor triggering the application of a more onerous range of sanctions. See para E4.336.
3 See eg ITF Anti-Doping Programme 2002, cl G(4): 'A failure or refusal to submit to testing or to comply with the provisions of the Programme shall be treated as a Doping Offence involving a Class 1 Prohibited Substance …'.

E4.161 One issue is whether an athlete may argue that his failure or refusal to comply with the provisions of the anti-doping programme was justified and/or should be excused. Some sports allow such a defence but put the onus on the athlete[1]; others do not allow it at all[2]. The position may be slightly different where the sample to be taken is not urine but blood[3].

1 See eg ECB Guidelines for Anti-Doping Regulations (2001), cl 3.1: 'A Cricketer who asserts that his failure to take a Doping Control Test was "reasonable" will have the onus of proving that to the Disciplinary Panel which hears his case'.
2 In the *Ngugi* case, an athlete was sanctioned for refusing to provide a sample out-of-competition even after the consequences of refusal were explained to him. Although the athlete cited various language and other difficulties, the IAAF Arbitration Panel upheld the sanction on the basis that the offence was one of strict liability and the points raised by the athlete therefore went only to the issue of whether exceptional circumstances existed sufficient to warrant early reinstatement by the IAAF Council. *Ngugi v Kenyan AAA and IAAF,* IAAF Arbitration Panel decision dated 5 November 1994, in Tarasti *Legal Solutions in International Doping Cases* (SEP Editrice 2000) at pp 133 and 34.
3 See IAAF Rule 56.1: 'An athlete shall only be entitled to refuse to provide a blood sample in circumstances where the mandatory procedures and safeguards set out in the "Procedural Guidelines for Doping Control" are not observed'.

E4.162 Difficult issues can arise particularly in the context of no-notice out-of-competition testing: there might be a host of innocent reasons why the athlete is not where his training timetable says he should be. Therefore, sports with out-of-competition testing programmes have developed complex rules for determining when 'non-availability' amounts to a failure to submit to drug testing[1].

1 See para E4.204.

E4.163 Many anti-doping programmes also make it an ancillary offence 'if a person assists, induces, encourages or causes another to use a prohibited substance, a prohibited technique or to commit any offence under these Rules'[1]. More specifically, 'trading, trafficking, distributing or selling any prohibited substance otherwise then in the course of a recognised profession or trade' is a very serious offence[2].

1 See eg ASFGB Doping Control Rules, cl 3.1.5. See also UK Sport Model Rules and Guidelines for Anti-Doping, cl 2.2(iii); Olympic Movement Anti-Doping Code Chapter Two, Article 1(3); IAAF Rule 56.4.

The ECB Anti-Doping Regulations, at cl 6, provide: 'Any person or body subject to the jurisdiction of the ECB who knowingly assists and/or encourages and/or incites a Cricketer to commit any breach of the Anti-Doping Regulations, himself commits an offence for which he is liable to be referred to the Disciplinary Committee by way of complaint and subsequently dealt with by way of the procedures set out under the Disciplinary Standing Committee Regulations'.
2 See eg IAAF Rule 56.4.

E4.164 Clearly, making such conduct a doping offence under the rules expands the scope of the programme significantly, not only in terms of the type of behaviour covered[1], but also in terms of the potential defendants to disciplinary charges, since the offence implicates not only athletes but also coaches, trainers, doctors, relatives and beyond[2].

1 Clearly, intent (or at least fault of some kind) is going to be a necessary element of such offences.
2 See para E4.71 et seq.

E4.165 It may also be made a doping offence under the sport's anti-doping programme for an athlete to be convicted of a criminal offence involving a prohibited substance, whether or not (apparently) the predicate facts of that offence would also constitute a doping offence[1].

1 See UK Sport *Model Rules and Guidelines for Anti-Doping*, cl 2.2(iv). Cf ECB Anti-Doping Regulations, cl 4.2: 'Any criminal conviction relating to the use of such prohibited substance should be regarded as incontrovertible proof that the Cricketer has knowingly used such substances'. Alternatively, such conduct might be dealt with under the standard disciplinary offence of bringing the sport into disrepute. See para A2.45.

E4.166 Canadian anti-doping regulations include as an 'accessory' offence the charge of 'turning a blind eye to the use of prohibited substances or practices'[1]. Clearly, this is a significant further expansion of the scope of the prohibition, imposing an affirmative obligation on an athlete to report suspicions of drug use by his team-mates and competitors. Many might regard this approach as a step too far, and the authors are unaware of its adoption outside Canada.

1 See www.cces.ca.

(f) Exemptions for therapeutic use

E4.167 An athlete may need to use a prohibited substance to treat a medical condition. The most common example is exercise-induced asthma, which affects approximately 10 per cent of young people. Asthma narrows the airways and thereby affects the performance of the lungs. The commonly prescribed treatments are beta agonists, such as salbutamol, terbutaline and salmeterol, which have a stimulant and (over certain concentrations) an anabolic effect[1], as well as corticosteroids, which are also said to have a stimulant effect. Similarly, insulin is required to treat athletes with insulin-dependent diabetes. In addition, local anaesthetics can be necessary in certain circumstances.

1 See para E4.140.

E4.168 The IOC List therefore sets out general circumstances in which these otherwise banned substances may be used. Asthma medications (formoterol, salbutomol, salmeterol and terbutaline) are 'permitted by inhaler only and must be declared in writing, prior to the competition, to the relevant medical authority'. Insulin is 'permitted only to treat insulin-dependent diabetes. Written notification prior to the particular competition of insulin-dependent diabetes by an endocrinologist or team physician to the Relevant Medical Authority is necessary'. Certain specified local anaesthetics are permitted but may only be administered by local or intra-articular injections, and 'only when medically justified, upon written notice prior to the particular competition to the Relevant Medical Authority, when applicable, or during the competition in matters of medical urgency'.

Corticosteroids are allowed for topical use only, by inhalation or by intra-articular or local injections[1].

1 IOC List *Olympic Movement Anti-Doping Code* (September 2001), App A, p 39.

E4.169 The specific mechanics for securing an exemption for therapeutic use are left to the rules of each sport[1]. Most rules provide for prospective exemption only, expressly ruling out retrospective exemption[2]. Some allow retrospective exemption[3]; while others may simply allow the fact that the athlete was entitled to a medical exemption but failed through oversight to get one in advance to be considered as a mitigating factor in relation to sanction, a doping offence being deemed to have been committed[4].

1 For example, under cl E(3)(b) of the ITF Anti-Doping Programme 2002, it is the Review Board (see para E4.228, n 2) that is responsible for considering exemption requests. Under clause 5.5 of the IAAF Procedural Guidelines for Doping Control (2000 edn), the relevant body is the IAAF Doping Commission (or, for asthma medications, the relevant body of the athlete's national federation). See also IAAF Procedural Guidelines for Doping Control (2000 edn), cl 5. In common with many other sports, the IAAF grants an exemption for only one-year, which means (in the case of chronic conditions) the athlete having to repeat the process each year. See also ASFGB Doping Control Rules, cl 2.10. The IAAF also requires (cl 5.4) an explanation from the qualified physician 'as to why a non-listed drug cannot be used'.

2 See eg ECB Anti-Doping Regulations, cl 5.4.

3 See ITF Anti-Doping Programme 2002, cl J(5) (limiting discretion to cases where: (1) an application prior to the event for an exemption would have been granted; and (2) the Review Board considers that the prohibited substance was not used to enhance performance).

4 See eg Six Nations Championship Anti-Doping Programme 2002, cl 5.4: 'Where the Doping Offence involves one or more of the Prohibited Substances listed at clause 2.5 above [ie the therapeutic use exemption provision], and the Player is able to prove on the balance of probabilities that he was entitled to use the Prohibited Substance in accordance with clause 2.5.2 but had failed to submit a medical declaration in accordance with the provision, then the Judicial Tribunal shall have discretion with regard to the sentence it may impose'.

E4.170 In any event, the exempting authority should be satisfied that the use merely cancels out a medical disadvantage and does not create a competitive advantage. There should also be provision for continuous review[1].

1 See eg ASFGB Doping Control Rules, cl 2.12 (contemplating exemption only when the medical officer 'is satisfied that an exemption is medically justified and will not create a competitive advantage for such a person').

E4.171 Even if the athlete has secured a prior exemption, if subsequently asked to provide a sample he should still declare the medication in question on the sample collection form[1].

1 See para E4.207.

E4.172 What of an athlete who requires use of a prohibited substance to treat a medical condition other than those specifically referenced on the IOC List? The IOC had a subcommittee to review such cases. Consistent with its policy that 'no athlete will be banned from competing because of an illness that requires a prohibited drug', its mandate was to 'find a way for the diseased athlete to compete'[1]. If no such pre-screening mechanism is available, the athlete should save a copy of any prescription he is given by his doctor and, if subsequently required to provide a sample, should declare it to the sampling officer. However, he should by no means assume that his use of that prohibited substance will be excused.

1 IOC *Doping: An IOC White Paper* (Lausanne, 1999), p 14.

E4.173 The present system of exemptions, which can require applications not only to be renewed each year but also to be filed with several different bodies, can seem unnecessarily burdensome. The World Anti-Doping Agency has suggested that the code it is developing to replace the Olympic Movement Anti-Doping Code[1] 'could either set forth the principles upon which exemption should be granted or perhaps the responsibility for granting medical exemptions should be centralized'[2].

1 See para E4.45.

2 The World Anti-Doping Agency, *Draft Framework of the Code 0.7* (Lausanne 2002), Art 9.3. In fact, the first draft of the Code (E-Version 1.0, issued 10 June 2002, at cl 8.3.4), simply sets very broad guidelines for exemptions, leaving it to the party with responsibility for results management to put a proper mechanism in place.

C Enforcing the prohibition: methods other than drug testing

(a) *Investigative powers*

E4.174 UK Sport's model rules confer discretion on the anti-doping authority to 'conduct investigations into the activities of any person who it has reasonable cause to believe may have committed an offence under these Rules and that person shall co-operate with those investigations'[1].

1 UK Sport *Model Rules and Guidelines of Anti-Doping*, cl 2.3.

E4.175 This can be a double-edged sword. On the one hand, it allows the governing body to be pro-active in the face of public allegations of drug use in its sport, and so to bolster public confidence that effective steps will be taken to keep the sport clean. Indeed, without the ability to investigate other than by means of drug-testing, it would be practically impossible to police a ban on ancillary activities such as aiding and abetting and trafficking.

E4.176 On the other hand, apart from concerns based on principle – some question whether such a 'bloodhound' role is appropriate for a sports governing body – there are also practical concerns. For one thing, a broader investigative ambit creates opportunities for the malicious athlete to persecute the innocent. The governing body will have to exercise discretion as to whether or not to bring charges, without the relative certainty of a case to answer that a positive sample analysis provides. Its decisions will have to be justified publicly to maintain public confidence in the sport.

E4.177 There are also doubts about the efficacy of a broader investigative ambit than drugs-testing, particular since the governing body does not have the power to confiscate evidence or to compel the giving of testimony, at least as far as non-participants in the sport are concerned[1].

1 The Australian Olympic Committee reportedly included in its athletes' participation agreement for Sydney 2000 a clause consenting to search of person and possessions at any Olympic venue, and seizure for analysis of any suspicious substances found as a result of such searches. See *Report of the Working Group on The Legal and Political Aspects of Doping*, World Conference on Doping in Sport (Lausanne, February 1999), pp 11 and 12.

E4.178 As a result, some sports specifically limit investigations to cases where an athlete's sample has tested positive for a prohibited substance[1].

1 See eg ITF Anti-Doping Programme 2002, cl C(4).

(b) Whistle-blowing

E4.179 The draft WADA Code requires athletes to 'blow the whistle' on illicit drug use[1].

1 Draft World Anti-Doping Code, E-Version 1.0, issued 10 June 2002, at cl 5.1.5 (one responsibility of athletes is 'to report anti-doping rule violations of which they have knowledge to an appropriate anti-doping agency').

E4.180 There is also 'whistle blowing' on one's self. An especially enlightened approach is taken in the ITF Anti-Doping Programme 2002, which provides that:

> [a]ny player who voluntarily discloses to the Medical Liaison that he has a problem involving chronic drug use or drug dependency, and who has not at that time been required to submit to in-competition or out-of competition testing under this Programme, will not be subject to any penalty. However, in such circumstances, the Medical Liaison may recommend that the player seek medical evaluation and, if appropriate, treatment[1].

1 ITF Anti-Doping Programme 2002, cl O. Cf IAAF Rule 55.2(iii) and 55.8 (making admission of illicit drug use a stand-alone doping offence).

(c) Education

E4.181 A more positive form of enforcement of the prohibition against drugs in sport is education regarding the ethical values of sport and the dangers of doping[1]. The parties to the Council of Europe's 1989 Anti-Doping Convention undertook:

> to devise and implement, where appropriate in co-operation with the sports organisations concerned and the mass media, educational programmes and information campaigns emphasising the dangers to health inherent in sport and … harm to the ethical values of sport. Such programmes and campaigns shall be directed at both young people in schools and sports clubs and the parents and adult sportsmen and sportswomen, sports officials, coaches and trainers[2].

1 See eg Browne, Lachance and Pipe 'The ethics of blood testing as an element of doping control in sport', *Official Journal of the American College of Sports Medicine* (April 1999), pp 497 and 500 (in preference to unreliable blood testing, 'a vigorous educational program to articulate and inculcate the advantage of drug-free sport should go forward'); Dubin *Report of the Commission of Inquiry into the Use of Drugs and Banned Practices Intended to Increase Athlete's Performance* (Ottawa 1990) at p 523: 'While testing will always be necessary, we must ground the integrity of the sport on the firmer base of fair play, ethics and a sense of what is right.'

2 Anti-Doping Convention of 16 November 1989 (Council of Europe – European Treaties – ETS No 135), Art 6.1.

E4.182 One example is the Clean Sport Guide, prepared by the Netherlands Centre for Doping Affairs, under the auspices of the Council of Europe's Anti-Doping Convention Monitoring Group and the European Union, which proposed model education materials, including a module highlighting legitimate ways of optimising performance. UK Sport also provides published resources for use in educating and informing participants in the sport of the dangers of drug misuse[1].

1 See also 'IAAF Finalises E-Learning Anti-Doping Project' (2002) Sportcal.com, 25 January.

E4.183 On a more practical level, various sports bodies (for example, the International Tennis Federation) provide help-lines that athletes can call to find out the status of particular substances. UK Sport in early 2002 launched an on-line database to allow athletes, doctors, pharmacists and others to determine the status of particular substances[1].

1 UK Sport Anti-Doping Report 2000–01 p 36. See www.uksport.gov.uk/did.

(d) Labelling

E4.184 Of course, knowing what is and is not a prohibited substance only helps if the ingredients of products are clearly listed on the packaging[1]. A panel of scientists commissioned by UK Sport issued a report in January 2000, expressing concern about inadequate labelling of sports supplement products[2]. In September 2001, an IOC-commissioned study reported that a quarter of 600 over-the-counter nutritional substances had tested positive for prohibited substances not mentioned on the packaging[3]. The World Anti-Doping Agency has identified this as an area where coordinated government action is required to enforce strict labelling obligations on manufacturers of such products[4]. The ideal would be a requirement that packages be marked with a warning about use of the product when involved in competitive sport.

1 This is especially so since a claim that the substance was not listed is not accepted as a defence to a doping charge: *Aanes v FILA*, CAS 2001/A/317, award dated 9 July 2001, p 23.
2 UK Sport Nandrolone Report and 19-Norsteroids Fact Sheet (January 2000).
3 *IOC: 20 per cent of supplements contain nandrolone* (2001) Sportcal.com, 21 September; *IOC Medical Commission Reissues Supplements Warning* (2001) Sportcal.com, 28 September. See also 'British products fail IOC dope tests' (2002) Independent, 5 April.
4 See para E4.44. Potential regulation of the supplements industry was debated in Parliament on 23 April 2002. See *Hansard*, 23 April 2002, col 46WH.

(e) Addressing the calendar

E4.185 A packed competitive calendar that requires athletes to strain their bodies to the limits and does not give them time to recover properly from injury and/or fatigue could be said to encourage doping in sport[1]. The Legal Working Group at the Lausanne Conference noted that:

> it would therefore be useful to thin out the competition timetable and promote the establishment of charters between athletes, their sponsors and their federation with the aim of achieving this[2].

However, the authors are aware of no follow-up on this issue.

1 See Cleary (2002) Daily Telegraph, 7 May; European Commission press release dated 18 March 2002, IP/02/424.
2 *Report of the Working Group on the Legal and Political Aspects of Doping*, World Conference in Doping in Sport (Lausanne, February 1999), p 12.

D Enforcing the prohibition: drug testing

E4.186 Drug testing – the extraction of body fluids from the athlete and analysis for evidence of prohibited substances and methods – remains the most popular method of enforcing the ban on drug use in sport, because of its perceived deterrent effect. Thus, for example, the Olympic Movement Anti-Doping Code provides that:

> [a]ll athletes are subject to doping controls (urine analyses, blood tests and other authorised techniques for detecting prohibited substances or methods)[1].

1 Olympic Movement Anti-Doping Code, Chap One (Lausanne 2001), Art 2(1). This amendment to the original was adopted in Rio de Janeiro on 24 May 2000.

E4.187 Drug-testing in sport started in the late 1960s, but has been and continues to be refined in an effort to increase its usefulness in detecting banned substances and methods. Advanced techniques of chromotographic and spectroscopic analysis now make it possible to detect small quantities of drugs in a sample, sometimes even several months after their administration. Developments in DNA analysis are also promising[1].

1 See eg Verroken 'A time for re-evaluation: the challenge to an athlete's reputation' in *Drugs and Doping in Sport* (2001, Cavendish) at p 35: 'In the future, it is possible that DNA testing will assist us in providing a comprehensive testing programme that has its own unique identification system built in. This could aid the sample identification process and perhaps even reduce the need for supervised collection. Questions of sample manipulation could be dealt with more easily'.

E4.188 Nevertheless, it remains the case that not all prohibited substances on the IOC List can be detected by sample analysis. In particular, certain glycoproteins and peptides cannot yet be unambiguously detected[1].

1 See paras E4.192 to E4.195.

E4.189 Sample collection is highly intrusive, and sample analysis is a mystery to most athletes (and their representatives). However, it is vital that athletes have faith in the efficacy and reliability of doping controls. The procedures for sample collection and analysis therefore have to be clear, straightforward and well thought out.

(a) Using drug-testing agencies

E4.190 Governing bodies and event organisers do not have sufficient in-house expertise to run their own sample collection and analysis programmes, and even if they did they would still suffer from the conflict of interest issues identified by various government-sponsored enquiries[1], which concluded that the collection and testing of samples should be undertaken by trained officials who are independent of the sports governing bodies[2]. Therefore, governing bodies and event organisers will look to engage an outside agency to conduct the doping control for them[3].

1 See eg Moynihan/Coe Report *Misuse of Drugs in Sport* (London 1987); see also Black Enquiry, interim report, Senate Standing Committee of the Environment, Recreation and the Arts (May 1989).

2 An alternative would be for an independent body such as the World Anti-Doping Agency to observe the tests, an initiative rejected by FIFA in relation to testing at the 2002 World Cup in Japan and Korea. See FIFA refuses help with its dope tests' (2002) Financial Times, 29 May.

3 There is usually specific provision for this in the rules, so that athletes cannot say they did not agree to it. See eg IAAF Rule 55.12: 'The IAAF or its Members may delegate the collection of samples to any Member, governmental agency or any other third party that they deem suitable'.

E4.191 UK Sport will conduct drug tests on athletes in sports that receive public funding[1]. UK Sport also makes this service available on a fee-paying basis to sports that do not obtain public funding but need sample collection services for the anti-doping programmes that their international federations require them to operate[2]. UK Sport's sample collection service has ISO 9002 (now 9001:2000) (International Standard for Doping Control) certification[3]. Independent Sampling Officers are trained and approved before being appointed by UK Sport to a national register; thereafter, they receive continuing mentoring and training.

1 The governing body of the sport may use a doping control agency other than UK Sport, without jeopardising its access to public funding, provided that the other agency is 'suitably qualified', ie it has the same ISO and ISDC certification as UK Sport. See UK Sport *Anti-Doping Policy*, App A, para 3.

2 For example, in 2002 the Six Nations Committee, the organiser of the annual Six Nations Championship, contracted with UK Sport to provide doping control services at matches held in England, Scotland and Wales. It also contracted with the Irish Sports Council to provide doping control services at matches held in Ireland, and with IDTM to provide doping control services at matches held in France and Italy.

For its testing programme (see para E4.52), the World Anti-Doping Agency contracts with the Drug-Free Consortium, a consortium of sample collectors made up of UK Sport, eleven other national anti-doping agencies, and IDTM.

3 ISO Doping Control Common Procedure (ISO/PAS 18873: 1999). This certification is reconfirmed each year throughout external auditing by the British Standards Institute. See UK Sport *Anti-Doping Report* 2000/01, p 2.

(b) Sample collection

E4.192 Currently, many programmes collect and test urine samples only. However, it is argued that urine analysis is of limited use in detecting the emerging range of peptide hormones and mimetics and their analogues[1], partly because it is slow and expensive but also because of questions over its reliability. The high profile case involving athlete Olga Yegorova illustrated the difficulties[2]. Tests that are quicker, cheaper and reportedly more reliable have been developed based on analysis of blood, and therefore more and more sports are now providing for the collection of blood samples[3].

1 Category E on the IOC List; see para E4.142.

2 Yegorova provided a urine sample after a Golden League meeting in Paris in July 2001. The French laboratory announced that analysis of the urine tests revealed excessive haemoglobin levels. However, there was no positive from a blood sample to confirm the result of the urine analysis, as the rules required. Yegorova subsequently passed an IAAF blood-screening test and was therefore free to compete in the World Championship in Edmonton in August 2001, prompting protests by fellow athletes. See para E4.9, n 2.

For a useful discussion and defence of the urine test for EPO, see *UCI v H*, CAS 2001/A/343, award dated 28 January 2002.

3 See eg IAAF Procedural Guidelines for Doping Control (2000 edn), cl 1.3: 'for purposes of IAAF Rules and these Procedural Guidelines the body fluids analysed are urine and blood. The IAAF Council reserves the right to order testing to be conducted on any other fluids if advances in the detection of the prohibited substances indicated that such analysis would be helpful'.

On the compatibility of blood testing with the common law and the Human Rights Act, see Beloff M and Beloff R 'Blood Sports – Blood testing, the common law and the Human Rights Act 1998' [2000] 2 ISLR 43.

E4.193 Blood sample analysis can have a role to play even if the urine-only test is accepted for EPO. For the EPO test, the urine has to have been continually frozen since collection, which is extremely costly. Therefore, in some sports blood is tested first, and if that test reveals irregular levels of haemoglobin, then the urine sample is frozen in order that it can be tested for EPO. This filtering system is said to minimise the time and costs that have to be committed to the urine tests without undermining the effectiveness of the drug controls[1].

1 See I-news, IDTM Newsletter, September 2001: *IDTM launches onsite EPO Screening in Edmonton*. See also 'Hall confident his team can catch EPO dopers' (2002) Daily Telegraph, 28 February (recounting 24 hour turn-around of blood-screening results from samples taken from stables on 26 February 2002).

E4.194 The IOC was questioning the reliability of blood analysis as late as May 1997[1]. Therefore, individual sports have led the way. Cycling was the first to adopt blood tests for EPO, followed by biathlon, skating, skiing, swimming and athletics[2]. For example, blood and urine were collected for analysis at the 2000 Olympics in

Sydney, the 2001 IAAF World Championships in Edmonton and (for the first time in Britain) at the 10th World Half Marathon Championships in Bristol in October 2001. All endurance sports at the Winter Olympics at Salt Lake City in 2002 were covered[3], as was the FIFA 2002 World Cup in Japan and Korea[4].

1 Report by the Chairman of the Sport and Law Commission, IOC Executive Board/Summer IFs, Monaco, 22 May 1997. See also Brown, Lachance and Pipe 'The ethics of blood testing as an element of doping control in sport' (1999) Official Journal of the American College of Sports Medicine 497 (arguing that blood tests should not yet be introduced because of unanswered scientific, ethical and legal questions).

2 It should be noted that some blood-screening, done just before an event is to start, is not specifically for anti-doping purposes but rather simply to identify haemoglobin volumes that would make it dangerous to compete. In such cases, the athlete is barred from taking part in the event, not as a sanction, but to protect the athlete's health, and no further disciplinary measures are taken. See eg FIS Procedural Guidelines for Doping and Medical Control, Section A, Blood Screening (FIS Medical Guide 2001/02); UCI Cycling Regulations, Pt XIII (Sporting Safety and Conditions). See also cl 8.3.7 of the Draft World Anti-Doping Code, E-Version 1.0, issued 10 June 2002.

3 See WADA Out-Of-Competition Testing Program Report (8 February 2002).

4 'FIFA acts to boot out World Cup drug fears' (2002) Times, 28 February.

E4.195 IOC-funded scientists are said to have developed a reliable blood test for HGH, but it has not yet been implemented[1].

1 'New drugs fear; Olympic chiefs bring in new tests but leave loophole for the hormone cheats' (2000) Daily Mail, 29 August.

E4.196 In-competition sample collection A lot of drugs testing still takes place 'in competition', ie at the event itself. Athletes are usually selected for testing either by pre-defined criteria (eg anyone who reaches the quarter-finals, anyone who finishes in the top three, anyone who breaks a world record[1]) or randomly (eg drawing cards[2]), although the governing body may reserve residual discretion to target particular players for testing in appropriate circumstances[3].

1 See eg ASFGB Doping Control Rules, cl 4.5.

2 For example, in rugby union's Six Nations Championship, a draw is held just prior to kick-off at which the coaches for each side draw three cards from a pack numbered 1 to 15. The first two players corresponding to those numbers will be tested after the match, with the third held in reserve in case of serious injury to one of the first two that precludes testing. The coaches are not told which numbers they have selected, so that the players do not learn of their selection for doping control until after the match is played, from which point they are constantly chaperoned until they have provided a sample. See eg 2002 Six Nations Championship Anti-Doping Programme, App 4 (Sample Collection Guidelines).

3 See eg ECB Anti-Doping Guidelines (2001), cl 3.3: 'The ECB has the power to require a Cricketer to take a Doping Control Test other than in the random circumstances provided for, that is, to "target" test a Cricketer. This is a power which the ECB will not exercise unless the circumstances demand it, but the ECB will not hesitate to use it in appropriate cases'. See also ITF Anti-Doping Programme 2002, cl G(2); IAAF Procedural Guidelines for Doping Control (2000 edn), cls 2.3–2.5.

E4.197 Out-of-competition sample collection Many drugs (particularly anabolic steroids) are ingested months before the event to increase muscle mass and strength. This can mean there are no traces of the drug in the body by the time of the competition, which renders in-competition testing ineffective[1]. Therefore, most sports now recognise that, for an anti-doping programme to be truly effective, there must be specific provision allowing for a comprehensive short-notice and/or unannounced out-of-competition testing programme[2]. In other words, the athlete is subject to testing any time and anywhere[3]. The testing may be done on (short) notice, usually making an appointment, or it may be completely unannounced[4].

1 By the same token, it is unnecessary to test out-of-competition for substances that provide only short-term effects, such as stimulants. The Olympic Movement Anti-Doping Code authorises the exclusion of such substances from out-of-competition testing. It recommends testing only for the training enhancers, ie substances in Class C (anabolic agents), Class D (diuretics), Class E (peptide hormones, glycoprotein hormones and analogues) and Class II (prohibited methods). See IOC Explanatory Memorandum concerning the application of the Olympic Movement Anti-Doping Code, 9 December 1999, at p 11. Under the IAAF rules, for example, samples collected out-of-competition are tested only for anabolic agents and peptide hormones. See IAAF Rule 57.7 and Procedural Guidelines for Doping Control (2000 edn), cl 5.3.

2 In 1988, the Committee of Ministers of the Council of Europe adopted a Recommendation to Member States on the Institution of Doping Controls Without Warning Outside Competitions, No R(88)12. The signatories to the Anti-Doping Convention thereafter confirmed their desire (Art 7.3a) for the introduction of out-of-competition testing. The IAAF introduced out-of-competition testing in 1990 and now conducts many more tests out-of-competition than in competition. The importance of out-of-competition testing was also stressed in the Lausanne Declaration and it has become a major tenet of the World Anti-Doping Agency's mission. See eg WADA Out-of-Competition Testing Program Report (8 February 2002); and see further para E4.198.

3 Many anti-doping programmes specify that testing can take place not only at the athlete's training camp but also (for example) at his 'accommodation or any other place where the athlete is likely to be found'. IAAF Procedural Guidelines for Doping Control (2000 edn), cl 3.6. UK Sport has suggested that there is no right to insist the athlete submit to testing at his home, UK Sport *The Human Rights Act and Anti-Doping* (2000). UK Athletics would not send sampling officers to the athlete's place of work. See *Athlete's Guide*, UK Athletics Anti-Doping Policy and Support Team (2002).

4 See eg IAAF Procedural Guidelines for Doping Control (2000 edn), cl 3.6.

E4.198 Many international federations have contracted the World Anti-Doping Agency to conduct all or part of their out-of-competition testing programmes. Before the 2000 Sydney Olympics, the World Anti-Doping Agency coordinated 2,500 out-of-competition tests, and the Olympic federations themselves conducted another 2,500. From January 2001 to 8 February 2002, just before the 2002 Salt Lake Olympics, the World Anti-Doping Agency conducted 162 tests across seven International Olympic Winter Sports Federations, including 193 EPO blood tests[1].

1 WADA Out-of-Competition Testing Program Report (8 January 2002).

E4.199 In the UK, under UK Sport's Out-of-Competition Testing Programme, in 1999-2000, 45% of the 6,141 tests conducted by UK Sport were out-of-competition tests, mainly in football, rugby union and athletics[1]. In 2000-01, 452 samples were taken out-of-competition from UKA's elite athletes, 139 of which were from powerlifters and 144 from weightlifters[2].

1 See UK Sport *Anti-Doping Programme Annual Report 1999–2000* at p 10.

2 UK Sport *Anti-Doping Report 2000–01*, pp 8 and 9.

E4.200 In 2002, the FIFA World Cup Finals tournament in Japan and Korea became the first World Cup Finals tournament to incorporate out-of-competition testing[1].

1 'Drugs tests for Croatia and Italy' (2002) Daily Telegraph, 28 May.

E4.201 A high-profile casualty of out-of-competition testing was Michelle de Bruin, the Irish swimmer, who was visited by a sampling team at her home in Ireland in January 1996, gave a sample that was found to have been contaminated with alcohol, a masking agent for prohibited substances, and was banned for four years[1].

1 See para E4.144, n 2.

E4.202 The main differences between in-competition testing and out-of-competition testing lie in how the athlete is selected and located for testing. While in both cases selection may be random or targeted[1], practicality requires that an out-of-competition testing regime covers only a limited set of athletes, for whom sufficient information is available to enable their location to be tracked all year round, both in season (at competitions and in training) and out of season. In practice, this means that a governing body will identify a number of elite athletes, for example all those selected for international competition in the past twelve months, and will require those athletes to provide proper contact details, updated as necessary, to enable the sampling team to locate them at all times[2]. These details are then kept in a register[3].

1 For in-competition testing, see para E4.196. The IAAF targets mainly athletes ranked in the world top 20 in their discipline. See Dolle *The IAAF and Its Fight Against Doping in Athletics* (Monaco 1999). Cf ITF Anti-Doping Programme 2002, cl H(1) (normal rule is random selection for out-of-competition-testing); cl. H(2) ('A player may be specifically selected by the APA and ITF Executive Director, Medical if (1) he has previously submitted a specimen resulting in a positive test for a Class 1 Prohibited Substance that has been disqualified …, or (2) a player has previously been found to have committed a Doping Offence or (3) a player is subject to follow-up testing based on the recommendation of the Review Board, or (4) a player is subject to testing under Section (R) of this Programme [ie after conviction of a criminal offence involving a prohibited substance]'.

2 See eg ASFGB Doping Control Rules, cl 4.6: 'As part of its general unannounced out-of-competition testing programme, ASFGB may from time to time maintain a register of elite athletes. Anyone appearing on such register will be notified. Upon receiving a notification a person must (1) keep the ASFGB informed of the addresses or location and contact telephone numbers where he may be contacted to undergo a doping test at any time; and (2) should at all times carry with him a valid and conclusive form of identification'.

See also IAAF Rule 57.4: 'On the request of the IAAF to the relevant Member Federation, an athlete shall be required to keep a current address on file with the IAAF or the athlete's National Federation. The athlete shall immediately inform the IAAF or the National Federation, as the Case may be, of any change in that address for more than three days for any reason other than participation in international competitions in athletics, in which event he shall inform the IAAF or his National Federation of the temporary address at which he may be contacted. The athlete may also be required to keep on file a training schedule, showing the times and places when he may routinely be found training'.

3 See eg UK Sport *Anti-Doping Report 2000–01*, p 12 (describing registers containing training details of eligible athletes mentioned in athletics, weightlifting, powerlifting and Scottish rugby union). UK Sport maintains a register of (1) all athletes receiving World Class Performance Funding; and (2) suspended athletes seeking reinstatement.

E4.203 In team sports, squad training sessions are an obvious focus for out-of-competition tests. Otherwise, however, and especially in non-team sports, the logistical difficulties are clear, especially when one takes into account the various departures that an athlete may take as a matter of course and entirely innocently from his normal training routine. Yet such a mundane matter assumes great importance where a failure to submit to testing constitutes a doping offence[1].

1 See para E4.204, n 2.

E4.204 The rules may provide that failing to notify the governing body of a change of address within a set period is a doping offence[1], or that failing to be available at the notified address for a specified number of times will be considered a failure to submit to a test[2]. For example, UK Sport reports 'non-availability' when the athlete has not been located for testing even though the sampling officer has visited his registered address three times in a five day period (including day one and day five)[3].

1 See eg ASFGB Doping Control Rules, cl 4.7 (48 hours). See also Art 8.1.1.4 of the draft WADA Code, E-Version 1.0.

2 See eg UK Athletics Anti-Doping Policy & Support Team, Athletics' Guide 2002: 'If the athlete is not at the address on the register, it is assumed that they are avoiding testing, and non-collection is treated in the same way as a positive test result, meaning that the athlete would be subject to disciplinary action'. See also IAAF Rule 57.4: 'The failure by an athlete to keep an address (including any temporary address) or, if required, a training schedule on file, or the filing of false information, will be considered a doping offence. If it is documented that, on three or more consecutive occasions on separate days, a testing official has been unable to find the athlete, that documentation may be introduced as evidence of the commission of this offence'. On the other hand, under IAAF Rule 60.4, the sanction for such an offence is relatively light, at least for the first offence (public warning) but also for the second (minimum three month supervision). Cf ASFGB Doping Control Rules, cl 4.8.

3 UK Sport *Anti-Doping Report 2000–01*, p 12. Cf ITF Anti-Doping Programme 2002, Sch 3, cl 12: 'Where an appointment has been made, it is the player's responsibility to ensure that there is no possible confusion over the date, time and precise location where the specimen location is to take place. The APA or his designee will wait for up to two hours beyond the time agreed but thereafter will report to the ITF that a player did not attend testing. In these circumstances the player may be deemed to have refused or failed to submit to a doping test or to have refused or failed to comply with the Tennis Anti-Doping Programme'. See also IAAF Procedural Guidelines for Doping Control (2000 edn), cl 3.8.

E4.205 The IAAF takes a pragmatic approach. An athlete must have at least two out-of-competition drug tests each calendar year in order to be eligible to collect winnings from Grand Prix events and world championships[1]. If he fails to provide the necessary information about his whereabouts for such tests to be conducted, he will not receive his prize money. According to reports, about 25 to 30 athletes fell foul of this provision in 2001[2].

1 Dollé, *The IAAF and its Fight Against Doping in Sport* (Monaco 1999).

2 See www.news.findlaw.com/aps/2080 (27 November 2001).

E4.206 The World Anti-Doping Agency has identified the issue of 'maintaining and receiving regular and accurate athlete whereabouts information from International Sports Federations' as one of its 'future challenges'. It has stated that it intends to commence a pilot project with certain federations to develop information systems that track athletes' whereabouts for purposes of out-of-competition testing[1].

1 WADA Out-Of-Competition Testing Program Report (8 February 2002). Similarly, UK Sport is developing 'athlete timetable' forms in which an athlete will list details of primary and secondary residences and training grounds and other regular residences.

E4.207 The sample collection process The basic sample collection process[1] is the same for both in-competition testing and out-of-competition testing, consisting of the following elements:

- **Selection of athletes for testing** – This could be random or targeted[2].
- **Athlete notification** – The sampling officer should produce proper identification and authorisation documents. He or she should provide the athlete with a doping control notification form, explain the athlete's rights and responsibilities, and get the athlete to sign the form to acknowledge receipt of notice that he has been selected for a drug test and is required to report for that test. In certain circumstances (particularly in out-of-competition testing), the athlete may also be required to provide identification.
- **Accompanying the athlete to the doping control room** – The athlete may be allowed to complete any training or treatment he was undergoing

at the time he was notified of his selection for a test, but he must report to the doping control station within a specified time-limit (usually one hour) after notification, and in the meantime he must be chaperoned at all times.

- **Procedures at the doping control room** – The doping control room should have testing facilities and equipment. Sealed drinks (non-alcoholic, decaffeinated) should be available for athlete consumption in case of dehydration. The athlete can be accompanied by a colleague until he is ready to give a sample.
- **Urine sample collection** – The athlete selects a collection kit from a selection of sealed packs and confirms that the identification numbers match and that the seals are all intact. He is observed while he provides the sample (to rule out use of a catheter or other tampering). A minimum amount of urine (usually 70 ml) is required to allow the laboratory to complete its procedures. Special provisions exist relating to the collection of a partial sample and how to store that sample and then combine it with a later sample to reach the minimum[3]. The sampling officer tests the acidity (pH) and specific gravity of the sample (to ensure it has not been diluted to manipulate concentrations)[4]. The usual provision is that the pH must be between 5 and 7 and the specific gravity 1.010 or higher. The sample is then split into two, an 'A' sample and a 'B' sample. The athlete seals the bottles, then the samples are put in a transport bag, which is also sealed. Elaborate coding systems are used to ensure a demonstrable chain of custody[5].
- **Blood sample collection** – The procedures for blood sample collection reflect the fact that this procedure is far more intrusive and carries far more health risks for the athlete. For example, the IAAF rules provide that the sampling officer must be medically qualified (and able to demonstrate such qualification to the athlete prior to sample collection). They forbid the taking of a blood sample unless the athlete there and then signs a further consent to blood testing. If he does not, no sample will be taken, but an unjustified refusal will be regarded as a doping offence[6]. Further, they limit the site on the body from which the blood may be drawn and how much blood may be drawn (25 millilitres)[7].
- **Athlete sign-off** – The athlete is asked to sign a sample collection form, to confirm the details of the sample collection and that he is 'satisfied with the sample collection procedure and that the samples collected have been sealed and numbered as above'. An athlete should be sure he is happy with the procedures before signing off, as his signature may be taken as a waiver of any objection based on facts known to the athlete at the time[8].
- The form also asks the athlete to declare any medications taken in the previous seven days. While declaring a medication on the form does not excuse its use if it turns out to contain a prohibited substance[9], it may assist the athlete in providing a therapeutic use explanation for a positive result[10] or in credibly arguing that a metabolite may have come from something other than a prohibited substance[11].
- The form is counter-signed by the sampling officer, to attest that 'the competitor provided a sample under my supervision and that the sample collection procedures were correctly carried out'. Each of the athlete and the sampling officer keeps a copy of the form, and a 'blind' copy (ie one not revealing the athlete's identity, but identified only by an anonymous code, to safeguard the objectivity of the scientific analysis) goes with the sample to the laboratory.

- **Storage and transport to laboratory** – The samples are packed and sealed into a secure transport bag, which is transported by a secure chain of custody to the laboratory.

1 See eg IAAF Procedural Guidelines for Doping Control (2000 edn).

2 See paras E4.196 and E4.202.

3 See eg International Rugby Board Regulations Relating to the Game (2002), reg 20 (Anti-Doping), Sch One, cl 8 (Partial Sample).

In the *Gasser* case, a failure to collect more than 45ml of urine was ruled irrelevant, because it did not affect the laboratory's ability to test both the A sample and the B sample properly. *Gasser and SLV v IAAF*, IAAF Arbitration Panel, award dated 18 January 1988, in Tarasti *Legal Solutions in International Doping Cases* (SEP Editrice 2000) at p 118.

4 See *Cadogan* case, IAAF Arbitration Panel decision dated 20 August 2000, para 15, [2001] 4 ISLR 273. Cf *B v FINA*, CAS 98/211, award dated 7 June 1999, *Digest of CAS Awards II 1998–2000* (2002, Kluwer), pp 255, 259 (purpose is 'to determine if urine is sufficiently concentrated to enable the sample to be satisfactorily analysed').

5 The need for careful and detailed provisions should be clear. As Lord Justice Neill observed in *Wilander and Novacek v Tobin and Jude (No 2)* (26 March 1996, unreported), CA: 'It will be obvious that any system which requires an athlete to be subject to tests of body fluids which are then sent away for analysis requires a very careful arrangement to make certain, first, that the fluids are properly preserved and, secondly, that there exists no possibility of confusion of one sample with another. It is for that reason that a chain of custody procedure should be laid down and observed'.

6 IAAF Procedural Guidelines for Doping Control (2000 edn), cl 2.29. The only circumstances in which a refusal will be deemed justified (under cl 2.33) are: (i) if the sampling officer does not provide evidence that he is medically qualified; (ii) if the packaging of the equipment to be used is not clean, sealed and intact; or (iii) if the officer tries to collect more than the specified maximum 25ml of blood.

7 The IAAF's rules specify that blood can only be drawn from the athlete's arm, 'from a superficial vein, preferably in the anti-cubital region … as painlessly as possible'. IAAF Procedural Guidelines for Doping Control (2000 edn), cl 2.32.

The FIS rules provide that '[t]he total number of phlebotomy attempts is limited to 3 on each arm'. FIS Procedural Guidelines for Doping and Medical Controls, Rule 7.5, Collection of Blood Samples (FIS Medical Guide 2001/02).

8 See eg ECB Anti-Doping Regulations (2001), Sch B, cl 7: 'A signed Doping Control Test form without notification of dissatisfaction shall be conclusive proof that the DCT test was carried out to the Cricketer's satisfaction'.

See also IAAF Procedural Guidelines for Doping Control, cl 2.19 ('If the athlete feels the procedures were not carried out satisfactorily, he should declare so on the Doping Control Form and state the reasons for dissatisfaction. In the absence of any such declaration the athlete shall be deemed to have waived any alleged procedural breach'.), cl 2.36 (same) and cl 3.18 (same). See also ITF Anti-Doping Programme 2002, Sch 3, cl 9.

In the *Reynolds* Case, the IAAF Arbitration Panel relied upon (among other things) Mr Reynolds' declaration on the sample form that he was satisfied with the sample collection procedures in rejecting his subsequent attack on the reliability of the procedures followed. Tarasti *Legal Solutions in International Doping Cases* (SEP Editrice 2000), p 121, para 8. See also *Bunn v FEI*, CAS 2000/A/313.

9 *Lehtinen v FINA*, CAS 95/142, award dated 14 February 1996, para 42: 'it should be noted that a declaration in the test form … is not in itself sufficient to turn a banned substance into a permitted one. If a certain banned substance has been identified, a prior declaration in the test form still does not justify the use of such substance'.

But see UK Sport *Anti-Doping Report 2000–01*, reporting positive test for a beta-blocker in shooting ('Rules of governing body permit the taking of prescribed medication provided they are declared prior to an event. Competitor has declared taking substance on entry form for the event therefore governing body is satisfied that the rules have been followed').

10 See *Lehtinen v FINA*, CAS 95/142, award dated 14 February 1996, para 42: 'The declaration essentially serves the purpose of supporting the laboratory in analysing the test sample. The absence of a declaration does not in itself constitute a doping offence. However, the Panel agrees with FINA that failure to comply with the duty to declare a certain medication in the test form may indeed raise serious doubts about the medical necessity to use that medication and even lead to the assumption that there was a doping offence'.

11 See eg *Ime Akpan* in Tarasti *Legal Solutions in International Doping Cases* (SEP Editrice 2000), p 135, para 4.

(c) Sample analysis

E4.208 Sample analysis, in order to enjoy the confidence of athletes, administrators and fans, must be independent, quality-assured, uniform and reliable.

E4.209 The IOC, through its Medical Commission, has developed requirements for accreditation of laboratories to conduct analysis of samples against the IOC List[1]. This form of external quality assurance is to be taken over by the World Anti-Doping Agency. It is a standard provision in an anti-doping programme, intended as a protection for the athlete, that samples may only be tested at properly accredited laboratories[2].

1 IOC, *Procedures for Accreditation of Laboratories*, Olympic Movement Anti-Doping Code (Lausanne 2001), App Two.

2 See eg FIS Anti-Doping Rules, r 5, para 15.3 (FIS Medical Guide 2001/02). UK Sport requires that the laboratory also be certified as ISO 17025 compliant by an independent internationally recognised accreditation body. UK Sport Anti-Doping Policy, Annex A, para 11.

E4.210 The Olympic Movement Anti-Doping Code sets out procedures for an accredited laboratory to follow in analysing the sample[1]. The sample is coded for anonymity, to safeguard the objectivity of the scientific analysis. The laboratory checks the integrity of the sample upon receipt, and proceeds to analysis only if satisfied with the external chain of custody and that there is no evidence of tampering.

1 Olympic Movement Anti-Doping Code (Lausanne 2001), App D (Laboratory Analysis Procedures).

E4.211 There then follows a number of screening tests in the form of instrumental analysis, usually gas chromatography. Any positive findings are confirmed by mass spectrometry analysis[1]. If the presence of a prohibited substance is confirmed in this way, then a fresh part of the sample is tested. If that test confirms the presence of the prohibited substance, then an adverse report is issued[2].

1 For a detailed account of the analytical process, see *Gasser v Stinson* (15 June 1998, unreported), QBD (Scott J). See generally Prof Dr J Segura *Doping Control in Sports Medicine* (1996) 18(4) Ther Drug Monit.

2 See Prof D Cowan 'When is a positive finding a doping offence?' UK Sport Seminar *Tackling Ethical Issues in Drugs and Sport* (October 1996).

The IOC-recommended reporting format is (1) administration (code number, date of receipt, confirmation seals intact, etc); and (2) analytical results (generic name of identified substance; pH, density and appearance of sample; summary of analytical procedures and copies of analytical data). See IOC List, *Olympic Movement Anti-Doping Code*, App D, cl 1.3 (Reporting Results).

E4.212 In the case of EPO blood screening, three parameters are measured: the haematocrit level, the haemoglobin level and the reticulocytes level. If the readings are above the cut-off levels, more blood from the sample is tested. If it confirms levels above the cut-off, the instrument itself is checked with an internal control. If it passes that check, the urine is analysed. Portable equipment can be used for on-site screening of blood samples[1].

1 *i-news* IDTM newsletter (September 2001).

E4.213 Apart from those cases where a minimum threshold is specified[1], the amount of the prohibited substance detected is irrelevant[2]. However, the laboratory will usually include the information in its report.

1 See para E4.258 et seq.
2 Olympic Movement Anti-Doping Code (Lausanne 2001), Chap Two, Art IV. See eg draft World Anti-Doping Code, E-Version 1.0, issued 10 June 2002 at para 8.3.2: 'Excepting those substances for which a quantitative threshold is specifically identified on the Prohibited List, the detected presence of any quantity of a prohibited substance in an athlete's sample shall constitute an anti-doping rule violation'.

E4.214 The laboratory will report the results to the doping control agency and/or directly to the governing body that has required the tests. It will store the B urine sample for a minimum of 90 days[1], in case a confirmatory analysis is required[2]. Some rules require storage until the end of any judicial process commenced following testing.

1 IOC List, Olympic Movement Anti-Doping Code App D, cl 1.4 (Long-term storage).
2 See para E4.231 et seq.

E Results management

E4.215 The next stage of the process is results management, which encompasses the receipt of test results (or 'failure to comply' reports), gathering and assessing relevant information and determining the validity of the result or report.

E4.216 Traditionally, at this point, the collecting agency hands over the baton to the governing body of the sport in question, and leaves the governing body to process the results and bring any charges as appropriate. For example:

> UK Sport will send by special delivery to the nominated results officer of the governing body or international federation normally within one working day of receipt by UK Sport a package of documentation including the laboratory report, the chain of custody documentation [and] sample collection forms, and identify any irregularity evident to UK Sport that may affect or influence the reliability of the analytical result as evidence of a prima facie case … UK Sport will provide the documentary evidence to the governing body on the understanding that it will be shared with all relevant parties[1].

1 UK Sport *Anti-Doping Policy*, Annex A, paras 13 and 14.

E4.217 However, the conflict of interest problem remains; indeed, it can be even more pressing at this stage. The government signatories to the International Anti-Doping Arrangement[1] have therefore declared that the national anti-doping organisation should be responsible for such results management[2]. UK Sport's rules provide:

> To ensure that the review process is fair and accurate UK Sport will appoint an Independent Scrutiny Committee to monitor the reporting of results to governing bodies of sport. The ISC will monitor the standards of the results management process of UK Sport and will be available to advise on individual cases should a governing body want a further independent opinion as to whether the evidence of a reportable doping offence is sufficient. This advice to governing bodies will be charged for at a fixed fee. The ISC will also monitor the decision of any governing body review and where this decision does not agree with the initial determination of UK Sport will investigate the alleged deficiencies in the evidence. The ISC may publish the conclusions of its investigation and ask the governing body to reconsider its decision. The right to challenge and provide an independent reporting structure is an essential element in the public accountability and transparency of the UK's anti-doping system[3].

1 See para E4.48.
2 IADA Policy Statement – Results Management (2.6).
3 See UK Sport *Anti-Doping Policy 2002*, p 18. This is a noticeably more assertive position than UK Sport has previously taken.

E4.218 Even if the governing body does not have to answer to UK Sport, it may be subject to scrutiny by its international federation[1].

1 See para E4.364 et seq.

E4.219 In the context of a particular event – eg the Olympic Games, the Six Nations Championship – the entire sample analysis and results management process may be accelerated to allow sanctions to 'bite' at the event itself.

F Confidentiality

E4.220 The potential harm to an athlete's reputation if an allegation of doping becomes public is immense, even if the athlete is subsequently cleared of the offence. Therefore, the anti-doping programme should include a commitment to keep the allegation confidential[1]. Where there is provision for interim suspension of the athlete pending the disciplinary hearing[2], the allegations must be confidential at least until that point[3]. Otherwise, however, the allegations should be confidential unless and until the disciplinary panel upholds the doping charges and imposes a permanent sanction[4].

1 See eg ITF Anti-Doping Programme 2002, cl S; FIS Procedural Guidelines for Doping and Medical Controls, r 9.6 (FIS Medical Guide 2001/02).
2 See para E4.235 et seq.
3 See eg IAAF Procedural Guidelines for Doping Control (2000 edn), cl 2.61. The draft WADA Code (E-Version 1.0, issued 10 June 2002, para 8.10.1) requires confidentiality at least until completion of the independent review of the case. See para E4.226 et seq.
4 See eg UK Athletics, Doping Rules and Procedures (2001), para 9.

E4.221 Whatever the position in theory, however, in practice confidentiality cannot be guaranteed, mainly because various review bodies, suspicious of the conflicted governing body, will be insisting upon transparency and accountability[1].

1 Some governing bodies try to address the concern by making their procedures more transparent. See eg *UK Swimming Body to Reveal All Doping Test Results Online* (2002) Sportcal.com, 14 January.

E4.222 For example, UK Athletics' rules provide that a positive test is to be kept confidential until a disciplinary hearing has been held and has confirmed a doping offence. However, information often seems to leak out of the system prior to that point. Indeed, the IAAF, suspicious of UK Athletics' motives, has several times refused and/or failed to observe the confidentiality agreement, both while the case is pending (as in the case of hurdler Gary Cadogan)[1], and even (in the case of pole-vaulter Michael Edwards) after UK Athletics has decided the athlete has no case to answer[2]. Any refusal to share information with the international body is generally met with a very hostile reception[3].

1 See eg 'Cadogan joins list of Britain's drug test failures' (1999) Guardian, 21 July.
2 'Britain's credibility on the line as drug crisis worsens' (2000) Daily Telegraph, 14 February.
3 See para E4.32, n 2.

E4.223 In addition, a governing body dependent upon public funding must include in its anti-doping programme provisions for the reporting to UK Sport of:

> such information and assistance as UK Sport may request concerning any alleged breach of its Anti-Doping Policy or any practice concerning the misuse of drugs in sport, including the names and test results of any athlete member of that body who returns a positive A test result outside the UK Sport programme; [and] the name and relevant circumstances of any person whom it knows, or reasonably suspects, has committed an infraction of this policy …[1]

1 UK Sport *Anti-Doping Policy*, Annex A at para 8.

E4.224 UK Sport reserves the right in its rules not only to publicise the outcome of any disciplinary proceedings, but also to:

> report in confidence to the [British Olympic Association], or relevant Commonwealth Games Association, or Sports Council, or other similar organisation regarding the progress of a doping case in so far as the case has direct relevance to the eligibility of an athlete to represent the UK or any country or countries within the UK at any level or to receive funding[1].

1 UK Sport *Anti-Doping Policy*, Annex A, para 44. The accompanying commentary states: 'In reporting to another organisation in confidence UK Sport will use its best endeavours to secure agreements on confidentiality but cannot be held liable for any negligence on behalf of that organisation. The right of the international federation or World Anti-Doping Agency or legal requirements of another country to take action are not affected by this agreement on confidentiality. In general public disclosure may be made after the athlete has been notified of the result, however in principle details of the case (substance, athlete's name) should only be disclosed at the completion of the process'.

E4.225 Similarly, under the Olympic Movement Anti-Doping Code, testing laboratories are required to report positive tests not only to the authority submitting the sample but also to the IOC Medical Commission and also the relevant international federation. The Olympic Movement Anti-Doping Code provides that '[a]ll organisations and Participants which use IOC accredited laboratories are deemed to agree to provide the information listed in this article'[1]. Here, however, the information required to be provided does not include the name of the athlete.

1 Olympic Movement Anti-Doping Code (Lausanne 2001), Chap Five, Art 4.

G Review process

E4.226 Charging an athlete with a doping offence is clearly extremely harmful to his reputation. This can be true even if he is subsequently cleared, given the prevailing perception that most athletes charged with a doping offence are guilty but get off on technicalities. Therefore, many programmes provide for the safeguard of a preliminary review of the evidence by medical, technical and legal experts to determine whether sufficient evidence exists that the athlete has a case to answer before such charges are brought[1].

1 See eg Draft World Anti-Doping Code, E-Version 1.0, issued 10 June 2002, para 8.6.2.3. Some programmes (eg the ITF Anti-Doping Programme 2002) proceed on the basis that a positive test result from a laboratory is an 'analytical positive' only, ie based solely on the data before the laboratory, which cannot form the basis of a doping charge unless and until it has been verified.

E4.227 UK Sport's model Anti-Doping Policy allows a governing body to proceed merely on the basis of the information provided by UK Sport[1], or to have an independent review, either by the Independent Scrutiny Committee (ISC) set up by UK Sport[2] or by the governing body's own review board appointees, the latter being subject to ISC scrutiny:

> [T]he governing body may accept the notice of determination from UK Sport as evidence of a potential doping offence (ie a determination) and proceed to the disciplinary stage. Alternatively the governing body may wish to seek a further independent opinion that the evidence in respect of ownership, security or integrity is complete. It may require UK Sport to refer the evidence to the Independent Scrutiny Committee (or instigate its own review answerable to the ISC; any review arranged by the governing body must meet the same high standards as the Independent Scrutiny Committee). The Independent Scrutiny Committee will review the evidence and respond to the Governing Body, copy to UK Sport. The Independent Scrutiny Committee will consist of independent experts (that is independent of the sport and UK Sport), with appropriate medical, legal and administrative expertise to consider the available evidence and decide whether the evidence is sufficiently complete and strong that the athlete should be called upon to answer for it. The Independent Scrutiny Committee will need to be satisfied that the evidence contained in the [testing agency's report, including the laboratory report, chain of custody and sample collection forms] is in order including evidence that the identification and integrity of the samples has been maintained throughout the process[3].

1 See para E4.216.
2 See para E4.217.
3 UK Sport *Anti-Doping Policy*, Annex A, paras 20 and 21.

E4.228 Although this review is said not to constitute a hearing[1], UK Sport does contemplate that the governing body will have given the athlete an opportunity by (or at least at) that stage to state any objections to the test results on the grounds of deficiencies in the collection process or chain of custody or other irregularity, and the review body is required to consider such objections and resolve any dispute about the integrity of the sample collection process, including 'call[ing] for further evidence of the issues of concern in the collection, transportation of analytical process where this is deemed to be relevant to the discussion'[2].

1 UK Sport *Anti-Doping Policy*, Annex A, para 21. See commentary to para 21: 'It is simply an assessment of the sample collection documentation and laboratory analysis to determine whether sufficient evidence exists to refer the matter to a disciplinary hearing'. Leading authority suggests that the review board may base its assessment that there is a case to answer on evidence that would not be admissible in a court of law: *Modahl v BAF Ltd* (28 July 1997, unreported), CA (Lord Justice Morritt).
2 UK Sport *Anti-Doping Policy*, Annex A, paras 19, 22 and 23.
Under clause J of the ITF's Anti-Doping Programme 2002, a slightly different approach is taken. A positive test result is reported to the Anti-Doping Programme Administrator (the 'APA'). The APA reviews the file to see that the collection process, the chain of custody and the proficiency data are all in order. He or she then make recommendations to a Review Board, which is made up of 'an outside group of experts with medical, technical and legal knowledge of anti-doping procedures'. The Review Board reviews the file to determine whether (a) there has been a positive result (b) that should not be 'disqualified', eg because there is an approved medical exemption request on file, or 'procedural irregularities exist that materially affect the validity of the test'. If the Review Board gives the green light for the Case to proceed, the athlete is notified and given ten days 'to offer medical information and/or medical documentation which may explain the presence of the Prohibited Substance or use of a Doping Method'. The Review Board then considers, based on that submission, 'whether there are sufficient medical reasons to support the players use of the Prohibited Substance or Doping Method'. If not, the matter proceeds to analysis of the 'B' sample. (See para E4.231 et seq). A positive result from the B sample also goes back to the Review Board, which can disqualify it (and therefore bring the matter to a close) 'if procedural or analytical irregularities exist that materially affect the validity of the test'.

E4.229 Similarly, under the IAAF's rules, an athlete is given the opportunity to provide an explanation within a set period. If an adequate explanation is received, that is the end of the matter. If not, the test is regarded as positive and the matter proceeds[1].

1 IAAF Procedural Guidelines for Doping Control (2000 edn), cls 2.51, 2.54.

E4.230 The review board may also consider whether the athlete qualifies for an exemption from the ban, allowing him to use the prohibited substance found in his sample on medical grounds[1]. If so, the matter proceeds no further[2].

1 See para E4.167 et seq.
2 See eg ITF Anti-Doping Programme 2002, cl J(3).

H Testing the B sample

E4.231 A further safeguard comes in the form of provisions giving the athlete the right to insist upon analysis of the B sample[1]. The laboratory will only test the B sample for the prohibited substance found in the A sample. If the analysis of the B sample does not confirm the presence in the athlete's sample of the prohibited substance identified as a result of the test of the A sample, then the positive findings with respect to the A sample are rejected and the matter is discontinued.

1 See eg IAAF Procedural Guidelines for Doping Control (2000 edn), cl 2.57. See generally *Gasser v Stinson* (15 June 1988, unreported), QBD (Scott J).

E4.232 The applicable rules may give the athlete the right to insist that the B sample analysis take place at a different laboratory[1]. He will almost invariably be give the right to attend the B sample analysis, and/or to send a representative, and if he does neither then the rules may provide for the appointment of a surrogate to attend and observe on his behalf[2]. The main purpose is to allow the athlete to confirm that the B sample bears the correct identification code number, remains sealed and has not been tampered with, but the representative may also be a scientist who checks the procedures followed.

1 See eg the anti-doping rules of the Jockey Club. In one case, a jockey's A sample tested positive for cocaine but at an extremely low level. The jockey exercised his right to have the B sample tested at a different accredited laboratory, following his own privately undertaken tests that did not reveal the presence of the drug. The Jockey Club could not find a second accredited laboratory with equipment sensitive enough to test down to the levels of the A test result, even if it had been valid. The B sample was eventually tested at a second laboratory and found to be negative.
Cf Draft World Anti-Doping Code, E-Version 1.0, issued 10 June 2002, para 8.5.3: 'The determination of whether analysis of the B sample, or other analysis, will be performed at another WADA-accredited laboratory will be made by the anti-doping agency initiating the test'.
2 See eg ITF Anti-Doping Programme 2002, cl J(9); Draft world Anti-Doping Code, E-Version 1.0, issued 10 June 2002, para 8.6.1.

E4.233 The athlete may be required to pay for the B sample analysis. If he waives the B sample analysis, for this or any other reason, he may be deemed to have waived any right to challenge the reliability of the A sample test results. Therefore, notwithstanding that the chances of exoneration through the B sample analysis are slight[1], the athlete probably is usually best advised to insist on the B sample analysis, and to be present himself or through a representative to observe the procedures followed. In such circumstances, if no objection is raised at the time to the procedure followed by the laboratory in conducting that analysis, the athlete may be barred from raising the objections in subsequent disciplinary proceedings[2].

1 The authors are aware of only two instances (one detailed at para E4.232, n 1) where the analysis of the B sample did not confirm the presence of a prohibited substance identified by the analysis of the A sample. On the other hand, in *UCI v H*, CAS 2001/A/343, award dated 28 January 2002, the acquittal of a cyclist whose A sample tested positive for EPO was upheld because the levels of EPO in the B sample did not cross the designated threshold. See also *Report of the Independent International Review Commission on Doping Control – USA Track & Field*, 11 July 2001, p 86 (reporting B samples that did not test positive for substances found in A sample, most likely because of delay in undertaking B sample test).

In *Gasser v Stinson* (15 June 1988, unreported), QBD (Scott J), the test of the B sample confirmed the presence of methyl-testosterone detected upon analysis of the A sample. However, steroids were also detected in the B sample that had not been detected in the A sample. Ms Gasser's representatives argued that this raised a doubt as to the reliability of the test results, and in particular suggested that the A and B samples were not from the same person. The testing doctor testified, however, that the different results were not caused by the fact that the urine came from two different people, but rather were the result of oxidisation of the ether reagent used in the testing of the B sample. Both the IAAF Arbitration Panel and the English High Court accepted that the different findings did not undermine the reliability of the positive finding of methyl-testosterone. See para E4.281.

2 See *N v FINA*, CAS 98/208, award dated 22 December 1998, para 30, *Digest of CAS Awards II 1998–2000* (2002, Kluwer), pp 234, 251. Cf UK Sport Model Rules and Guidelines on Anti-Doping, cl 4.3 (while any dispute of positive findings on grounds of deficiency in collection process or chain of custody or other irregularity should be presented within seven days of receipt of B sample results, failure to do so will not preclude raising of such objections at subsequent disciplinary hearing).

E4.234 Sometimes the rules allow the governing body to have the B sample tested even if the athlete waives that right, to shore up the positive A sample test against future challenge[1].

1 See eg IAAF Procedural Guidelines on Doping Control (2000 edn), cl 2.59. Under the UK Sport model, the review panel would make this decision. See UK Sport Model Rules and Guidelines on Anti-Doping, cl 6.4.

I Interim suspensions

E4.235 Anti-doping programmes often[1] allow for the interim suspension of an athlete charged with a doping offence, pending adjudication of the charges[2]. In addition, where the athlete is a recipient of public funding, the relevant Sports Council may suspend that funding pending adjudication of the charges[3].

1 But not always. For example, under the ITF rules, no suspension is imposed unless and until both the A and B sample have been confirmed to be positive, the Review Board has completed its review and the Anti-Doping Tribunal has found a doping offence has been committed. See ITF Anti-Doping Programme 2002, cl J(15); L(7); N(1).

2 See eg ECB Anti-Doping Regulations (cl 3.5.2) and Guidelines (cl 14); ASFGB Doping Control Rules, cl 6.1.

3 UK Sport *Anti-Doping Policy*, Annex A, para 39: 'where the Review of Evidence finds there is prima facie evidence that a doping offence has been committed … , the relevant Sports Council will normally suspend funding to the athlete, coach or other person concerned immediately, pending the final outcome of the full disciplinary process. Payments during the period of suspension will be paid into a suspension account. In the event that the disciplinary process decided that no doping offence has been committed, the payment will be forwarded in full to the athlete, coach or other person concerned'. Cf UK Sport *Anti-Doping Policy*, para IX(a), which could be read to suggest the suspension of funding in these circumstances is automatic.

E4.236 Some international federations require their member national governing bodies to suspend an athlete from competition automatically once it has been decided that there is a case to answer[1]. Others would leave it to the discretion of the individual national governing body whether or not to impose an interim suspension[2]. However, an international federation might reserve the right to impose an interim suspension if the national governing body fails to do so[3]. Furthermore, where a national governing body clears an athlete, some rules allow the international federation to impose a suspension if it is challenging the national governing body's acquittal of the athlete[4].

1 See eg IRB Regulations Relating to the Game (2001), reg 20.11, which provides that an interim suspension is automatic upon the Review Board deciding there is a case to answer, even before the B sample analysis takes place.

Similarly, IAAF Rule 59.2 provides that '[t]he athlete shall be suspended from the time the IAAF, or, as appropriate, an Area or a Member, reports that there is evidence that a doping offence has taken place'. In practice, this means that if the athlete is not able to provide a proper explanation for a positive test of his A sample within the time-limit set by the IAAF, he shall be provisionally suspended forthwith. See IAAF Procedural Guidelines for Doping Control (2000 edn), cl 2.54.

2 See eg UK Sport *Anti-Doping Policy*, Annex A, para 23.

3 See eg IAAF Rule 59.2: 'If, in the opinion of the IAAF, a National Federation has failed properly to impose a suspension, the IAAF may itself impose that suspension'. For example, UK Athletics decided not to impose an interim suspension on Linford Christie after he tested positive for nandrolone (see para E4.294). The IAAF intervened and suspended Christie under IAAF Rule 59.2.

4 See para E4.361.

E4.237 The power (or even the obligation) to impose an interim suspension, prior to any final finding that a doping offence has been committed, is a controversial one, especially given the harm that will be done to the athlete's reputation. An instructive analogy is to an application for a preliminary injunction in a civil matter.

E4.238 There is no doubt that the positive drugs test, especially when coupled with the safeguard of an independent review panel reviewing the evidence and deciding that there is a case to answer, would clearly meet the hurdle of establishing a serious issue to be tried, at least when the offence charged is one of strict liability.

E4.239 The balance of convenience is finely set:

(a) The justification usually offered for the suspension is that sport depends entirely upon the supporter's faith in the sporting spectacle as a contest on a level playing-field to be determined by sporting prowess alone, which faith will be utterly undermined if it later transpires that someone charged with (and later convicted of) a doping offence had been allowed to compete. In addition, there is no reliable way to review the results of sports events retrospectively so as to wipe out the effects of the tainted competitor, or to compensate the non-tainted athlete whose place was taken by the drugs cheat.

(b) On the other hand, if an athlete is suspended on an interim basis and the doping charge is not made out, not only will the athlete's reputation be damaged forever. In addition, the athlete will have missed out on competing in events during that suspension, the effect of which on his career could never be known. Therefore, even if the athlete could show that the charges were brought in breach of some contractual or other duty, so that the governing body is theoretically liable to him in damages[1], the fact is that his losses are unquantifiable and therefore cannot be compensated by money damages. On the other hand, once a doping offence has been established, the governing body could revoke all results achieved in the meantime[2].

(c) Nevertheless, the few judicial pronouncements on interim suspension provisions in anti-doping programmes have not been hostile (as long as those provisions were not retrospectively applied)[3]. Lord Justice Pill remarked in *Modahl* that:

'[t]he effect of suspension may be very serious for the athlete and [involve missing important athletics events] … I understand the need for that sequence of measures in order to guard against the damages of drug-taking immediately before a big event. It would be little comfort to other competitors if the defaulter could be punished only after the event had taken place'[4].

In the same case, Lord Hoffman noted, without criticism:

'I think that the IAAF adopted its system of instant suspension followed by disciplinary proceedings in the belief that although it might sometimes cause injustice in the individual case, it was necessary in the wider interests of the sport'[5].

1 The authors are aware of no anti-doping programme that provides for a governing body to give a suspended athlete a cross-undertaking in damages in case it is subsequently unable to make out its charges.
2 See eg ITF Anti-Doping Programme 2002, cl N.
3 See para E4.366.
4 *Modahl v BAF Ltd* (28 July 1997, unreported), CA.
5 *Modahl v BAF Ltd* (22 July 1999, unreported), HL.

E4.240 One point that it is certainly fair to make is that a defendant always has the right to be heard on an application for an interim injunction against him. It is certainly well arguable that anti-doping rules providing for interim suspensions should similarly have at least some limited right for the athlete to be heard prior to any such suspension coming into force[1]. It has been forcefully argued that the omission of such a right is unlawful[2]. However, the draft WADA code currently provides that an interim suspension may be imposed 'prior to any hearing' (and prior to B sample confirmation), so long as a Review Board has decided there is a case to answer[3].

1 See eg ECB Anti-Doping Regulations, cl 3.5.2(c). See also IAAF Procedural Guidelines for Doping Control (2000 edn), cls 2.51, 2.54 (athlete given opportunity to explain before test will be regarded as positive, only suspended where no adequate explanation is forthcoming), cl 2.55 (athlete may make representations to IAAF at any time); cl 2.56 (IAAF may lift suspension and drop proceedings 'if the athlete raises matters which the IAAF thinks indicate that a doping offence has not been committed').
2 Nick Bitel, November 2001 lecture on the KCL Postgraduate Certificate in Sports Law course, citing as authority the Human Rights Act 1998 as well as the remark of Mrs Justice Ebsworth in *Jones v Welsh Rugby Union* (1997) Times, 6 March, that 'it is properly arguable that a system which in effect prohibits a party from challenging by question or by evidence the factual basis of the allegations against him on its face lacks basic fairness, even if the end result may seem to have been justifiable … '. But see *Guest v Commonwealth Games Federation and Triathlon Canada* CAS CG02/001, award dated 2 August 2002: 'under English law … or indeed under general principles of law, a hearing before an interim suspension is not normally required by principles of fairness (see eg *Lewis v Heffer* [1978] 1 WLR 1061); moreover an interim or provisional suspension without a hearing is common in the rules of other governing bodies concerned with the problem of doping in sport: see eg those of the IAAF referred to in CAS arbitration SYD 15 *Melinte v IAAF*, para 8a). The rationale for summary reaction to a positive test is obvious: the public interest of the sport trumps the private interests of the athlete. It should be emphasised that such suspension, decided on an urgent basis, does not deprive the applicant of a proper hearing at a later stage with the potential for an appropriate remedy'.

In the United States, there is clear authority to support the proposition that an athlete must be given an opportunity to be heard before an interim suspension is imposed. See *Harding v US Figure Skating Association* 624 NYS 2d 723 (1994); *Lindemann v American Horse Shows Association* 851 F Supp 1476 (1994). See also Report of the Independent International Review Commission on Doping Control – USA Track & Field, 11 July 2001, p 12 ('While USATF declined to impose provisional suspensions before final adjudication of a case, its refusal to do so is premised on its understanding that a federal US statute and the USOC consultation prohibit USATF from depriving an athlete of the opportunity to compete without a full adjudicatory hearing'). The Commission's comment (at pp 65 and 66) is of interest: 'As a policy matter, the Commission believes that by not allowing pre-hearing suspensions under any circumstances, any incentive for an athlete to co-operate in the prompt adjudication of a doping case is reduced. The foot-dragging tactics employed by some athletes and their trainers contribute significantly to the chronic delays in the disposition of the USATF doping cases. Some athletes may have no reason to seek swift resolution, because as long as the final adjudication is put off, they can continue to compete. Moreover, the notion that athletes who have positive "A" and "B" samples may continue to compete and enjoy the benefits of successful competition is an imposition on the rights of all clean athletes, who are entitled to a level playing field. Accordingly, the Commission believes that consideration should be given to a policy that would permit the suspension of athletes, at least upon a receipt of a confirming "B" sample and a preliminary review of the case, during which the athlete has the opportunity to make a submission'.

3 Draft World Anti-Doping Code, E-Version 1.0, issued 10 June 2002, para 8.6.3.1.

E4.241 Clearly, if there is to be an interim suspension pending a determination of the charges, the rules should also provide for the full hearing to take place without delay[1].

1 See eg draft WADA Code, E-Version 1.0, issued 10 June 2002, para 8.7.1: 'The hearing shall be held without unnecessary delay and shall be expedited when circumstances warrant (eg when an athlete has been provisionally suspended or when necessary to resolve eligibility prior to an upcoming event)'; IAAF Procedural Guidelines for Doping Control (2000 edn), cl 2.62: hearing to take place 'as soon as possible and under normal circumstances not later than three months after the final laboratory analysis'. See UK Sport *Anti-Doping Policy*, Annex A, para 29 ('The Disciplinary Committee hearing shall normally be convened within 4 weeks of the decision of the Review of Guidance. The hearing may be opened and adjourned to seek further information at the discretion of the Chair of the Disciplinary Committee for example in order to allow time for the athlete to prepare his/her case').

5 DISCIPLINARY PROCEEDINGS

A An overview

E4.242 In many ways, disciplinary proceedings based on doping charges are no different from disciplinary proceedings relating to non-drugs-related charges, and law and practice relating to the latter is all relevant to the former[1]. For example, the general principles of natural justice (in particular, the right to notice of the charges and the right to a fair and proper opportunity to be heard in defence of those charges, by an independent and impartial tribunal) apply to doping proceedings as much as to any other disciplinary proceedings[2].

1 See generally Chapter A2.

2 Article 7 of the Council of Europe's Anti-Doping Convention provides that sports bodies should exercise their disciplinary powers in doping cases by 'applying agreed international principles of natural justice and ensuring respect for the fundamental rights of suspect sportsmen and sportswomen; these principles will include: (i) the reporting and disciplinary bodies to be distinct from one another; (ii) the right of such persons to a fair hearing and to be assisted or represented; [and] (iii) clear and enforceable provisions for appealing against any judgment made …'.

Similarly, para 5 of the Declaration on Doping in Sport (World Anti-Doping Conference, Lausanne 1999) states: 'In order to protect athletes and their rights in the area of disciplinary procedure, the general principles of law, such as the right to a hearing, the right to legal assistance, and the right to present evidence and call witnesses, will be confirmed and incorporated into all applicable procedures.'

See also para 8.7 (Right to a Fair Hearing) of the Draft World Anti-Doping Code, E-Version 1.0, issued 10 June 2002.

The Court of Arbitration for Sport has also ruled that the right to be heard is 'one of the fundamental principles of due process' which has to be respected during internal proceedings of federations. See eg *G v FEI*, CAS 91/53, award of 15 January 1992, *Digest of CAS Awards 1986–1998* (Berne 1998), pp 79, 86 and 87. See also cases cited at para A3.9, n 7.

E4.243 Thus, there should be provision for the athlete to receive proper details of the charge against him, of the procedure to be followed, and of the possible sanctions if an offence is established[1] and perhaps also for the disciplinary panel to be given an outline of his defence in advance of the hearing. A directions hearing may be appropriate to address issues that the parties are not able to agree, such as any areas of specific disclosure of documents or other information requested by one party (usually the athlete) and resisted by the other.

1 UK Sport *Anti-Doping Policy*, Annex A, para 14.

E4.244 Usually, the rules will provide that the substantive proceedings shall be heard in private. Traditionally, this has been seen as a benefit for the accused athlete, but that orthodoxy has recently been questioned[1]. The ideal is to give the athlete the choice. Whether the hearings are public or private, the rules should give the accused a full and fair opportunity to challenge the evidence adduced against him, including by cross-examination of witnesses and through the right, if a case to answer is established, to adduce documentary and fact and expert witness evidence of his own. More difficult is whether the athlete is entitled to legal representation. The preferable view is that this should be allowed[2].

1 It has been cogently argued that confidence in the system would be improved if, once an athlete is suspended, the disciplinary process continued in public. See Curtis 'Running scared: an athlete lawyer's view of the doping regime' in *Drugs and Doping in Sport* (2001, Cavendish) at p 122. UK Sport's rules purport to require the governing body to 'invite an observer from UK Sport to any disciplinary hearing or appeal to confirm that fair and open procedures have been followed'. UK Sport *Anti-Doping Policy*, Annex A, para 49.

2 See para A3.102, n 8.

E4.245 In the anti-doping context, the specialist nature of the charges means that the tribunal must be not only independent and impartial[1] but also competent in the area. Thus, for example, UK Sport's model Anti-Doping Programme provides:

> The membership of the panels and/or committees that manage the investigation and disciplinary process will be drawn from individuals who are independent from (ie having no conflict of interest in) the issue or its outcome and have appropriate legal, scientific, medical or administrative expertise and experience. Unless otherwise required by the rules of the International Federation it is recommended that the chair of the Disciplinary Committee and Appeal Panel should be legally qualified and drawn from a panel of lawyers who have not represented the governing body or advised the governing body in any capacity[2].

1 See paras A4.50 and A4.51.

2 UK Sport *Anti-Doping Policy*, App A, para 5. The commentary by UK Sport to this provision refers the reader to the Sports Dispute Resolution Panel, as to which see para A5.124 et seq.

E4.246 Apart from these and other safeguards[1], the accused athlete is also entitled to protection from undue delay, particularly when he is subject to an interim suspension[2]. For example, Mr Justice Lightman said in *Korda v ITF* that:

> a tight timetable designed to secure an expeditious procedure for the final determination of charges of doping offences … [is] plainly necessary for the proper conduct of the sport of tennis, to ensure public confidence in its administration and to safeguard the interests of players. Any sustained period of uncertainty as to the outcome of proceedings whilst they take their course is likely to be highly damaging to all concerned[3].

Furthermore, there should be a right of appeal from the decision of the original tribunal, to a further appellate tribunal organised under the auspices of the national or international federation, and/or to the Court of Arbitration for Sport[4].

1 See further para A3.101 et seq.
2 See para E4.235 et seq.
3 *Korda v ITF* [1999] All ER (D) 84, QBD (Lightman J), cited with approval by the Court of Appeal in that case: [1999] All ER (D) 337, CA. See also *Bray v New Zealand Sports Drug Agency* [2001] 2 NZLR 160, 166 (NZCA), which notes 'the public policy concern that, in the interest of those tested, those that may be competing against before the test results are known and the wider public interest in encouraging drug free sport, the processes under the sports drug testing regime be carried out without any undue delay'.
4 See para E4.357 et seq.

B Presenting a doping charge

E4.247 Usually, a sport's anti-doping programme will confer responsibility on a designated official of the governing body (the 'Anti-Doping Officer') to investigate and pursue doping charges. Unless he is legally trained, given the many legal complexities and traps of the disciplinary process the Anti-Doping Officer may be well advised to enlist the help of the in-house lawyer or external counsel.

(a) Burden and standard of proof

E4.248 UK Sport's model code provides that '[t]he burden of proof shall be with the governing body in any hearing before the Disciplinary Committee and with the Appellant in any hearing before the Appeal Panel'[1]. This is an important requirement of fairness and means that, unless the Anti-Doping Officer submits competent proof of each of the elements of the doping offence with which the athlete is charged, then the athlete has no case to answer and is entitled to have the charges dismissed without having to submit any proof of his innocence[2].

1 UK Sport *Anti-Doping Policy*, Annex A, para 36. See also Olympic Movement Anti-Doping Code (Lausanne 2001), Chap Two, Arts 1 and 2.2.
2 On the other hand, if that burden is discharged, then the onus will be on the athlete to establish exceptional circumstances or other mitigating factors: see para E4.315 et seq.

E4.249 The proof submitted must meet the required standard. In light of the quasi-criminal nature of a doping charge, UK Sport's model code prescribes a very high standard of proof: '[u]nless [International Federation] rules specify otherwise, a doping offence will have to be proven beyond a reasonable doubt'[1]. The IAAF requires the same under its anti-doping rules[2].

1 UK Sport *Anti-Doping Policy*, Annex A, para 36.
2 See IAAF Rule 59.6.

E4.250 Where anti-doping programmes require proof only on the balance of probabilities, English disciplinary tribunals will construe that requirement strictly:

> the criterion of balance of the probabilities must be applied by reference to the general seriousness of the allegations for any player accused of a doping offence. We accept that, for a player, an allegation of a doping offence is a very serious matter[1].

Indeed, one English doping panel stated:

> We take the view that the relevant standard of proof is the civil standard of proof (ie on the balance of probabilities), but that in the light of the nature and gravity of the matter in issue and the potential effect on Mr Livingston there is in this case no practical difference between [the civil] standard of proof required and the criminal standard of proof. In other words, Mr Livingston is entitled to succeed in his appeal unless the evidence has made us sure that Mr Livingston has committed a doping offence[2].

1 *ITF v Korda*, unreported decision of ITF Appeals Committee dated 22 December 1998, para 13. See also *Korda v ITF*, CAS 99/223/A, award dated 31 August 1999, para. 25, *Digest of CAS Awards II 1998-2000* (Kluwer 2002), p 345; *N v FINA*, CAS 98/208, award dated 22 December 1998, para 13, *Digest of CAS Awards II 1998–20002* (Kluwer 2002), pp 234, 247.

2 *Jason Livingston* decision of the BAF Appeal Panel (1993, unreported).

E4.251 In the *Korneev and Gouliev* case at the Atlanta Olympics, the Court of Arbitration for Sport panel ruled that the requisite standard of proof under the Olympic Movement Anti-Doping Code 'is greater than a mere balance of probabilities but less than a standard which may be expressed as beyond reasonable doubt. In our view, an appropriate expression of the standard of proof required is that the ingredients must be established to the comfortable satisfaction of the Court having in mind the seriousness of the allegation which is made. It follows that the more serious the allegation being considered the greater is the degree of evidence which is required to achieve the requisite degree of comfortable satisfaction necessary to establish the commission of an offence. In addition, the nature of the offence is one of strict liability if a prohibited substance is used. Accordingly, this is a further factor which may require a higher degree of satisfaction than may otherwise be appropriate'[1]. This is also the approach that is proposed to be adopted in the draft WADA Code[2].

1 *Korneev and Gouliev v IOC*, CAS (Atlanta) No 003-4L, award dated 4 August 1996; followed in *N v FINA*, CAS 98/208, award dated 22 December 1998, *Digest of CAS Awards II 1998–2000* (2002, Kluwer), pp 234, 247; *UCI v H*, CAS 2001/A/343, award dated 28 January 2002, para 14, and in *M v Swiss Cycling*, CAS/2001/A/345, award dated 28 January 2002, pp 13 and 14.

2 Draft World Anti-Doping Code, E-Version 1.0, issued 10 June 2002, at para 8.2.1.

E4.252 However, where the offence is one of strict liability, predicated merely upon proof of the presence of a prohibited substance in the athlete's body, the fact remains that a laboratory report that a sample taken from the athlete tested positive for a prohibited substance is usually going to be sufficient to make out a prima facie case, whatever the formulation of the standard of proof[1]. It will then be up to the athlete to submit evidence (to the extent permitted by the relevant rules[2]) that disturbs that showing[3]. It is however to be noted that where there is doubt as to the status of the substance found as a prohibited substance, or as to whether a metabolite was derived from a prohibited substance, or as to whether it might have been endogenously produced[4], the standard of proof will become much more important.

1 Mrs Modahl's counsel contended that '[a]lthough the burden of proof beyond reasonable doubt is upon the Federation, the certified result of the test goes so far to discharge that burden that in practice the athlete will have to adduce evidence which raises a reasonable doubt': *Modahl v BAF Ltd* (22 July 1999, unreported), HL (Hoffman LJ). The former President of the IAAF Arbitration Panel agrees that 'in practice the burden of proof moves rapidly to the athlete's side': Tarasti *Legal Solutions in International Doping Cases* (SEP Editrice 2000) at p 66.

2 See paras E4.278 and E4.287.

3 In the Court of Appeal in *Wilander and Novacek v Tobin and Jude (No 2)* (26 March 1996, unreported), CA, Lord Justice Neill held that the placing of the burden of proof on the athlete in this way was reasonable, since the burden only went onto him if his urine had tested positive for a prohibited substance: 'prima facie, scientific evidence establishes that certain facts exists and it seems not unreasonable, in the context of a code of this kind, that it should be for the player to rebut the prima facie case against him'. On the other hand, Lord Justice Neill also said that the athlete's burden should be rebuttable by proof 'on the balance of probabilities', ie the civil standard rather than the criminal standard or something in between.

4 As in (respectively, and for example) *Korneev and Gouliev v IOC*, CAS (Atlanta) No 003-4L, award dated 4 August 1996 (doubt as to status as prohibited substance) (see para E4.151); *Ime Akpan*, IAAF Arbitration Panel decision dated 10 April 1995, in Tarasti *Legal Solutions in International Doping Cases* (SEP Editrice 2000), pp 135-36 (doubt as to origin of metabolite) (see para E4.153); and *Ottey*, decision of IAAF Arbitration Panel dated 3 July 2000, [2001] 4 ISLR 260 (doubt as to exogenous ingestion) (see para E4.298).

(b) Elements of the offence

E4.253 The elements of the offence, ie the matters that the Anti-Doping Officer must prove to the requisite standard in order to establish a prima facie case, obviously depend on how doping is defined in the applicable rules, and what specific doping offence is being alleged.

E4.254 For example, if the athlete is alleged to have committed the strict liability offence of having a prohibited substance present in his body, then the Anti-Doping Officer will have to show that the substance found was indeed a prohibited substance, that the sample was taken properly, that there was a complete chain of custody of the sample on its way to the laboratory and that the analysis of the sample was 'state of the art'[1]. The Anti-Doping Officer does not have to establish how the substance got there or that the athlete ingested it or administered it to himself intentionally, recklessly or even negligently[2]. Nor does the Anti-Doping Officer have to show that the prohibited substance enhanced the athlete's performance[3]. Generally, and subject to the rules, the *amount* of the substance found is irrelevant[4].

1 *Aanes v FILA*, CAS 2001/A/317, award dated 9 July 2001, p 19.

2 See para E4.100.

3 The IOC has clarified 'that Article 2(1) and 2(2) [of the Olympic Movement Anti-Doping Code – see paras E4.93 to E4.100] are not linked and that a prohibited substance or method may be qualified as doping without necessarily meeting the criteria provided in Article 2(1)'. IOC Explanatory Memorandum to the Olympic Movement Anti-Doping Code (9 December 1999) at p 7. In other words, substances included on the list are illegal per se; they do not have to be shown to be capable of enhancing performance. See also Olympic Movement Anti-Doping Code, Chap Two, Art 4(4): 'The success or failure of the use of a Prohibited Substance or Prohibited Method is not material. It is sufficient that the Prohibited Substance or Prohibited Method was used or attempted for the offence of doping to be considered as consummated'.

This approach has been upheld on several occasions by the Court of Arbitration for Sport, on the basis that otherwise the fight against doping would become very difficult, if not impossible. See eg *N v FEI*, CAS 94/126, award dated 9 December 1998, para 7, *Digest of CAS Awards II 1998–2000* (2002, Kluwer), pp 137, 142.

4 See para E4. 213. See eg *N v FEI*, CAS 92/63, award dated 10 September 1992, *Digest of CAS Awards 1986–1998* (Berne 1998) pp 115, 119 and 120; *N v FEI*, CAS 92/73, award dated 10 September 1992, *Digest of CAS Awards 1986–1998* (Berne 1998) pp 153, 156.

E4.255 Even if the tribunal insists upon reading a requirement of fault into the rules, it will most likely presume that fault from the mere presence of the substance in the body[1], so that the Anti-Doping Officer will still have to do nothing more to establish his prima facie case. If, however, the doping offence in question is one that requires actual proof of intent or other fault[2], then obviously the Anti-Doping Officer will have more work to do.

1 See para E4.131.
2 See para E4.267 et seq.

E4.256 Prohibited substance The Anti-Doping Officer will obviously rely on the laboratory report to establish that the sample provided by the athlete contained a prohibited substance. The report should clearly state what prohibited substance has been detected, and (in cases where the substance is only a positive over a certain threshold[1]) in what quantity, and should provide thorough data in support of that finding. The report is not beyond challenge, and it can be surprising how much 'scientific' evidence can be in dispute, but the report is usually at the least sufficient prima facie evidence of a finding of a particular substance in the sample to meet the Anti-Doping Officer's burden on the issue.

1 See para E4.259 et seq.

E4.257 It may not be clear, however, whether the particular substance found in the sample qualifies as a prohibited substance. This is particularly the case when the substance is not specifically mentioned on the IOC List but is said either to be another example under the general head, or to be 'related' to a substance that is specifically listed[1], or alternatively is said to be a metabolite of:

(i) a listed substance; or
(ii) a substance related to a listed substance[2].

In such cases, the Anti-Doping Officer will have more work to do.

1 See para E4.151 (citing cases requiring substantial objective evidence of the actual chemical composition and qualities of the substance to establish its chemical and/or pharmacological relationship to a listed substance). Cf para E4.149 (analysing suggestion it must also be proved athlete was aware of relationship).
2 See para E4.147 et seq.

E4.258 The Anti-Doping Officer will also have more to do if the substance found in the athlete's sample is one of those that can be produced endogenously or alternatively ingested innocently by consuming normal food products or over-the-counter medicines.

E4.259 Many substances that are on the IOC List are produced naturally, in small quantities, by the body. For example, every sample will test positive for testosterone, because every athlete produces testosterone naturally in his (or indeed her) body. Such endogenous production cannot be allowed to render an athlete liable for a doping offence. Strangely, however, most anti-doping regimes do not state this explicitly[1]. Rather, it is to be inferred from their inclusion of a mechanism that allows a distinction to be drawn between endogenous (ie naturally produced) testosterone and exogenous (ie externally administered) testosterone[2].

1 Cf the decision of IAAF Arbitration Panel in the *Walker* case, 20 August 2000, [2001] 4 ISLR 264: 'Neither the [IAAF] Rules nor the [Procedural Guidelines for Doping Control] presently consider the presence of naturally produced nandrolone or its metabolites in the determination of a doping offence'.

2 See eg decision of IAAF Arbitration Panel in the *Marlene Ottey* case, 3 July 2000, [2001] 4 ISLR 260. See also *Bernhard v ITU*, CAS 98/222, award dated 9 August 1999, para 25, *Digest of CAS Awards II 1998–2000* (2002, Kluwer), pp 330, 338 (requiring sports body to prove clearly and indisputably that nandrosterone was not endogenously produced).

E4.260 Where the prohibited substance found in the sample could have been endogenously produced, the Anti-Doping Officer will have to adduce evidence that demonstrates the concentration of the substance found in the sample 'so exceeds the range of values normally found in humans as not to be consistent with normal endogenous production'[1]. He is assisted, in this respect, by the quantitative thresholds established by the applicable rules[2]. If the threshold is not met, the presence of the substance is attributed to endogenous production and/or consumption of the food products. If the threshold is met, then there is a presumption that the substance has been exogenously administered.

1 Decision of the IAAF Arbitration Panel in the *Walker* case, 20 August 2000, para 9, [2001] 4 ISLR 264.
2 See *S v FINA*, CAS 2000/A/274, award dated 19 October 2000, *Digest of CAS Awards II 1998–2000* (2002, Kluwer), pp 389, 397 (T/E rule is 'one method for proving the exogenous administration of testosterone … [A T/E ratio of greater than 6:1] constitutes presumptive evidence of an exogenous administration of testosterone'); *B v IJF*, CAS 98/214, award dated 17 March 1999, *Digest of CAS Awards II 1998–2000* (2002, Kluwer), pp 308, 319 (once amount above trigger is shown to be present, burden is on athlete to prove substance was endogenously, and therefore innocently, produced).

E4.261 For example, the IAAF Rules provide that 'a sample will be deemed to be positive for testosterone where either the ratio in urine of testosterone (T) to epitestosterone (E), or the concentration of testosterone in urine, so exceeds the values normally found in humans as not to be consistent with normal endogenous production'[1]. Scientific evidence that 'very few' out of 'thousands' of athletes tested have T/E ratios above 6:1 led the IAAF Arbitration Panel to accept a 6:1 T/E ratio as the upper limit for endogenous production[2], and this is now a generally accepted cut-off point[3], although it triggers a rebuttable presumption rather than an absolute finding[4].

1 See IAAF Procedural Guidelines for Doping Control (2000 edn), p 18.
2 See Tarasti *Legal Solutions in International Doping Cases* (SEP Editrice 2000), p 80. The 6:1 T/E ratio threshold was reportedly set to accommodate the less than 10 in 1,000 men with a ratio of more than 5:1. It has been criticised as encouraging testosterone use among men (most of whom have a natural T/E of a 1.3 to 1 or lower) and especially women. Bamberger and Yaeger, 'Over The Edge: Special Report' *Sports Illustrated* (May 1997). However, it remains the standard uniformly applied.
3 *Decker Slaney*, IAAF Arbitration Panel decision dated 25 April 1999, in Tarasti *Legal Solutions in International Doping Cases* (SEP Editrice 2000), p 155 (T/E ratio of 9.5:1 so exceeded range of values normally found in humans as not to be consistent with normal endogenous production); *Mitchell* case, in Tarasti *Legal Solutions In International Doping Cases* (SEP Editrice) at 167 ('Since the threshold ratio of 6:1 includes a large margin of safety in relation to the normal value it is irrelevant to which extent the T/E ratio found in a specific case exceeds the ratio 6:1; Mr Mitchell's case [7.3:1] is not a borderline case').
4 Thus, the IOC List now provides that '[t]he presence of a testosterone (T) to epitestosterone (E) ratio greater than six (6) to one (1) in the urine of a competitor constitutes an offence unless there is evidence that this ratio is due to a physiological or pathological condition, eg low epitestosterone excretion, adrogene production of tumor, enzyme deficiencies. In the case of T/E higher than 6, it is mandatory that relevant medical authority conduct an investigation before the sample is declared positive. A full report will be written and will include a review of previous, subsequent tests and any results of endocrine investigations. In the event that previous tests are not available, the athlete should be tested unannounced at least once per month for three months. The results of these investigations should be included in the report. Failure to cooperate in the investigations will result in declaring the sample positive': Olympic Movement Anti-Doping Code (Lausanne 2001).

For an analysis of the presumption in action, see para E4.300 et seq, as well as *UCI v S*, 98/192, award dated 21 October 1998, *Digest of CAS Awards II 1998–2000* (2002, Kluwer), pp 205, 219.

E4.262 Alternatively, scientists have now developed a new technology, Isotopic Ratio Mass Spectrometry, involving comparing the carbon isomers of endogenous and exogenous testosterone, which is said to provide direct and conclusive evidence that the testosterone is (or is not) endogenous, doing away with the need for evidential presumptions based on elevated T/E ratios; indeed, if this test shows exogenous administration of testosterone, then the Anti-Doping Officer's burden is met even if the T/E ratio is less than 6:1[1].

1 See para E4.304.

E4.263 Similarly, some substances can be ingested by consuming certain common foods and over-the-counter medicines. For example, caffeine can obviously be consumed from coffee and many other products. Many over-the-counter cough, cold and hay fever medications, as well as certain herbal products such as ginseng, contain mild stimulants. Therefore again a threshold is specified in the IOC List, below which any finding is deemed to be attributable to consumption through food or over-the-counter medicine, rather than to doping, and therefore not an infraction of the rules[1].

1 See eg IOC List, Olympic Movement Anti-Doping Code (Lausanne 2001), App A: 'For caffeine the definition of a positive is a concentration in urine greater than 12 micrograms per millilitre'.

E4.264 In many cases, therefore, the Anti-Doping Officer will require expert scientific evidence to support the charges he is bringing. For that reason, the event organiser's service contract with the laboratory[1] will usually contain a provision requiring the laboratory personnel to assist as necessary in disciplinary proceedings, including appearing to give evidence in support of the positive finding. However, it may also become necessary to obtain evidence from another independent expert.

1 See para E4.190.

E4.265 Present in the athlete's body fluids Assuming he can show that the sample contained a prohibited substance, the Anti-Doping Officer will also have to satisfy the tribunal to the requisite standard that the prohibited substance was present in the athlete's bodily fluids. This means showing that:

(a) the sample was taken from the athlete and stored securely;
(b) there is a complete record of the chain of custody of the sample to the laboratory;
(c) the sample arrived at the laboratory intact; and
(d) the sample was properly tracked at the laboratory and was not confused with other samples.

It also means showing that the sample was kept in proper conditions at all times, thereby ruling out the possibility of degradation or contamination of the sample after it was taken from the athlete.

E4.266 The Anti-Doping Officer will usually rely, in this respect, on the document pack produced by the sample collection team, including the doping control form signed by the athlete, the declaration of medications, the chain of custody documents and the sampling officer's report[1]. This should be enough to establish a prima facie case on the point. Indeed, if there were any holes, they would likely have been spotted by the review board prior to charges being brought[2]. However, if it appears that at the hearing the athlete will be questioning the chain of custody to try to throw doubts on the reliability of the evidence against him, further statements can be obtained from the sampling officer, the courier service, the laboratory, and so on, so that the whole process is tracked.

1 See para E4.216.
2 See para E4.226 et seq.

E4.267 Fault Even if the anti-doping programme that the Anti-Doping Officer is applying purports to adopt a strict liability approach, it is possible (if not likely) that the tribunal hearing the case will require proof of fault, by one means or another[1]. Alternatively, the anti-doping programme in question may not follow a strict liability approach, or it may include various offences that do require proof of intent. An obvious example would be the ancillary offence of trafficking[2].

1 For example, by finding the programme to be unclear and construing the ambiguity in favour of the athlete (see para E4.126); or by pointing to a previous case where the strict liability approach was not rigorously enforced (see para E4.312); or simply by holding that the programme would be illegal and therefore unenforceable if a fault requirement could not be implied (see para E4.130).
2 See para E4.163.

E4.268 Less obviously, however, the offence of using prohibited methods[1] may require proof of intent in certain circumstances:

- Where the prohibited method involves use of a masking agent that can be detected by analysis of a sample, then liability might be predicated (or at least established prima facie) simply upon the presence of that substance in the sample[2].
- In the case of other prohibited methods, however, a strict liability approach is not sustainable. For example, in the *Krabbe* case, samples supposedly taken from three different female athletes were found to be from the same person. The IAAF Arbitration Panel ruled that 'the offence of using or taking advantage of a prohibited technique … is not one of strict liability. It requires proof that an athlete actively and knowingly used or took advantage of the technique. Obviously a body such as the DLV [the German Athletic Association] in taking procedures to investigate and establish such an offence needs evidence from which the athlete's involvement can be clearly established or inferred'[3]. In that case, the panel thought the DLV was right to have pressed such charges and questioned whether the rejection of these charges was correct, but did not have to come to a view because the case was dismissed on other, unrelated grounds. Similarly, in *B v FINA*[4], the CAS panel noted that 'an allegation of manipulation includes an element of mens rea and attributes dishonesty to an athlete (whereas other doping offences may be ones of strict liability)'.

1 See para E4.144.
2 Tarasti *Legal Solutions In International Doping Cases* (SEP Editrice 2000) at p 70. See also *N v FINA*, CAS 98/208, award dated 22 December 1998, *Digest of CAS Awards II 1998–2000* (2002, Kluwer), p 234. Alternatively, the rules may provide that proof that the athlete's sample tested positive for that masking agent gives rise to a presumption that the athlete ingested that substance with intent to mask the presence of a prohibited substance. Such presumption will be rebuttable but the burden will have shifted to the athlete to show he did not ingest or administer the agent knowingly.
3 *Breuer, Krabbe, Moller* IAAF Arbitration Panel decision dated 28 February 1992, in Tarasti *Legal Solutions In International Doping Cases* (SEP Editrice 2000) at pp 125-128.
4 CAS 98/211, award dated 7 June 1999, para 27, *Digest of CAS Awards II 1998–2000* (2002, Kluwer), pp 255, 266.

E4.269 Even if intent is not an element of the doping offence charged, it can still be relevant. Under the Olympic Movement Anti-Doping Code, for example, proof of intent is an exacerbating factor in determining what sanctions should be imposed[1]. In this respect, the Olympic Movement Anti-Doping Code provides that intent 'can be proved by any means whatsoever, including presumption'[2]. On the other hand, intent (or lack thereof) may also be relevant when it comes to mitigation[3]. Therefore, the Anti-Doping Officer will need to be prepared to address the issue.

1 See para E4.336.
2 Olympic Movement Anti-Doping Code (Lausanne 2001), Chap Two, Art 4(1).
3 See para E4.315 et seq.

C Defending a doping charge

E4.270 For most athletes, the instinctive reaction, upon notification of a positive test, is to proclaim one's innocence on the basis that one did not knowingly take any prohibited substance and has no idea how it got into one's system. Of course, however, if the rules adopt a strict liability approach, then lack of knowledge or other evidence of 'moral' innocence is irrelevant.

E4.271 Under a strict liability system, the athlete has limited options: basically, he needs to raise a sufficient doubt that the sample is his, or as to the reliability of the laboratory test results (because of deterioration or contamination of the sample, or otherwise), or as to the status of the substance identified in the charge as a prohibited substance. On the other hand, if fault is an element of the offence, or lack of fault is a defence to the charge, or if proof of performance-enhancement is required, then he will have more options.

E4.272 The athlete has the right to challenge the Anti-Doping Officer's evidence by cross-examination, in an effort to raise sufficient doubt in the minds of the tribunal members as to whether a prima facie case has been established to the requisite standard. However, if the Anti-Doping Officer's evidence does establish a prima facie case, it remains open to the athlete to adduce evidence of his own in an effort to rebut that showing by raising sufficient doubt in the minds of the tribunal to warrant rejection of the charges and/or to support any defence afforded by the rules.

E4.273 Furthermore, if the athlete believes that the disciplinary tribunal hearing the charges against him lacks jurisdiction, or is following flawed procedures, or applying illegal rules, he must raise the issue before the tribunal itself, or else risk waiving the argument[1].

1 See *Modahl v BAF Ltd* [2002] 1 WLR 1192, CA; *UCI v A*, CAS 97/175, award dated 15 April 1998, *Digest of CAS Awards II 1998–2000* (2002, Kluwer), pp 158, 166 and 167.

E4.274 On the other hand, fighting doping charges can be prohibitively expensive. Legal aid is not available, while any lottery funding will probably have been suspended pending resolution of the charges[1]. Moreover, apart from paying his own lawyers and experts, if his defence is unsuccessful the athlete may be exposed to an order requiring him to pay the other side's costs[2].

1 See para E4.235.
2 See paras E4.355 and E4.356.

E4.275 Therefore, assuming that the rules give the tribunal discretion to consider exculpatory evidence when considering sanctions[1], and in particular where the rules contain realistic provisions for the (early) reinstatement of the athlete[2], the athlete may want to consider pleading guilty and concentrating his efforts on obtaining as limited a sanction and/or as quick a reinstatement as possible. Indeed, sometimes the anti-doping programme provides that an early admission may be considered in mitigation[3].

1 See para E4.315 et seq.
2 See para E4.372 et seq.
3 See eg English Cricket Board Anti-Doping Guidelines (2001), cl 15: 'Cricketers are also invited to note that the Discipline Standing Committee is likely to act more leniently in the case of a Cricketer who admits at an early stage that he has taken a Prohibited Substance'. See also *UCI v C and FFC*, CAS 2000/A/289, award dated 12 January 2001, *Digest of CAS Awards II 1998–2000* (2002, Kluwer), pp 424, 428 (discussing similar UCI rule).

(a) Disclosure and cross-examination of witnesses

E4.276 To what extent is the athlete entitled to disclosure of relevant materials by the collection agency, the laboratory and/or the governing body? Generally, the rules will provide for the governing body to disclose to the athlete copies of all materials relating to the collection, transportation and analysis of his sample[1]. These may be enough, as in *Modahl*[2], for the athlete's legal and scientific advisors to raise a material doubt regarding the Anti-Doping Officer's case.

1 See eg UK Sport *Anti-Doping Policy*, Annex A, para 14: 'UK Sport will provide the documentary evidence [regarding sample collection, chain of custody and sample analysis] to the governing body on the understanding that it will be shared with all relevant parties'. Cf IAAF Procedural Guidelines for Doping Control (2000 edn), cl 2.64 (authorising parties' withholding of legal advice and other privileged information).
2 See para E4.284.

E4.277 Quite apart from the relevant documentation, the athlete may also want to cross-examine members of the sample collection team, or the couriers responsible for transport of the samples to the laboratory, or members of the laboratory's staff. If the rules do not entitle him to do so, or if the Anti-Doping Officer is unable or unwilling to produce the witnesses required, and/or if the tribunal lacks the power to enforce their presence, then clearly in appropriate cases, where it is clear that the inability to question a witness has denied the athlete the ability to defend himself properly, the basis exists for a challenge to any adverse award on the ground that the process was unfair[1].

1 See further para A3.102 et seq.

(b) The anti-technicality rule

E4.278 Another threshold issue of strategy and proof relates to the anti-technicality rule, which is included in one form or another in most well-drafted anti-doping programmes.

E4.279 In any doping case, but particularly one where the offence charged is one of strict liability, with liability (and often mandatory sanction) depending solely on proof of presence of a prohibited substance in the athlete's body, the athlete and his representatives will have little choice but to dissect every step in the sample collection and analysis process, seeking to find some departure from the guidelines laid down or other discrepancy that could be used to challenge the reliability of the drug-testing results. And the fact is that a tribunal that is barred by the strict liability approach from taking the athlete's alleged lack of fault into account might be inclined to look sympathetically at evidence of discrepancies as a means of avoiding conviction.

E4.280 To ensure that this ground for challenge is not overused by tribunals to compensate for the perceived unfairness of a strict liability approach, and in particular to ensure that the focus is on irregularities that actually do call the test result into question, governing bodies often specify in their rules that the procedures laid down there are 'guidelines' only, and that a departure from the procedural guidelines laid down for drug testing 'shall not invalidate the finding that a prohibited substance was present in the sample or that a prohibited technique has been used, unless this departure was such as to cast real doubt on the reliability of such a finding'[1].

1 IAAF Rule 55.11. See also draft World Anti-Doping Code, E-Version 1.0, issued 10 June 2002, at para 8.2.2.2: 'Departures from established standards or other irregularities in sample collection, sample analysis or other aspects of doping control shall not invalidate a positive test results or other basis upon which an anti-doping rule violation may be established unless such irregularity or departure casts substantial doubt on the reliability of the positive test result or the factual basis for any other anti-doping rule violation'.

Cf Olympic Movement Anti-Doping Code, Chap Six, Art 5: 'Minor irregularities, which cannot reasonably be considered to have affected the results of otherwise valid tests, shall have no effect on such results. Minor irregularities do not include the chain of custody of the sample, improper sealing of the container(s) in which the sample is stored, failure to request the signature of the athlete or failure to provide the athlete with an opportunity to be present or be represented at the opening and analysis of the "B" sample if analysis of the "B" sample is requested'. See also UK Sport Model Rules and Guidelines on Anti-Doping 2002, cl 3.7.

Contra *Bray v New Zealand Sports Drug Agency* [2001] 2 NZLR 160 (NZCA), where the provisions of the New Zealand Sports Drug Agency Act were held to require the quashing of a positive test where the statutory requirement to get the sample to the laboratory as soon as practicable had not been met, notwithstanding the contention that the delay had had no impact on the reliability of the finding.

E4.281 In such circumstances, it is not enough for the athlete simply to show that there were departures by the collection agency or the laboratory from the sample collection and/or testing procedures that are set out in the programme and/or that constitute accepted practice. He will also have to show that the departure raises a material doubt as to the reliability of the evidence proffered against him[1]. Otherwise, the departure will be discounted as a harmless 'slip'. This issue – and the robustness of the tribunal's approach to it – is often dispositive:

- In *S v International Equestrian Federation*, the CAS panel ruled that the analysis of the B sample could not confirm the positive result of the A sample analysis 'unless all of the provisions of Annex III of the Veterinary Regulations have been scrupulously observed, in such a way as to eliminate any possibility of manipulation'. The panel accepted the rider's evidence that the B sample jars had not been sealed in the manner required by the FEI rules, so that it was 'not possible to exclude definitely the possibility of manipulation and thus contamination'. As a result, the CAS panel ruled, 'doubt exists which must be to the benefit of' the rider, and therefore the FEI's doping conviction was overturned[2].

- In contrast, in *G v International Equestrian Federation*, an identically-composed CAS panel dismissed more speculative attacks on the collection and testing procedures followed, and stated that 'the legal presumption of guilt of the person responsible will be destroyed only if the alleged and proved flaw is of a nature to call into question the result of the analysis'[3].
- Similarly, while Ms Gasser and the Swiss Athletic Federation were able to demonstrate to the satisfaction of the IAAF Arbitration Panel that proper procedures had not been followed in her case in two respects:
  (a) Ms Gasser was only able to provide 45 ml of urine, rather than the recommended minimum of 70 ml; and
  (b) defective ether was used during the B sample test;
  the panel ruled that mere proof of departures from the guidelines in itself was not enough to avoid conviction; the athlete also had to show that the failures 'affected or could have affected the finding on the analysis of his or her urine of a doping substance therein'. It ruled that the failures in that case did not cast any significant doubt on the correctness of the laboratory's findings, and therefore upheld the sanction[4].
- Ms Gasser took her argument to the English High Court, where she argued that a failure to follow the procedural guidelines for the collection and testing of samples 'in any material respect' renders the result of the test inadmissible as a basis for the suspension of the athlete concerned. Mr Justice Scott rejected this submission, accepting instead the submission of the IAAF that the defect in procedure must have 'rendered the result of the test unreliable or unfair to the athlete'. He did not specify who should bear the burden on this point, but he did say: 'If important safeguards for the athlete provided by the Guidelines have not been observed, prima facie at least it seems to me that the failure would require a conclusion that the testing procedure adopted could not be regarded as reliable or fair …'. On the facts, however, he found that the failures did not render the test results unreliable in Ms Gasser's case[5].
- The Court of Appeal in *Modahl*[6] confirmed that the intent of the anti-technicality rule 'is to avoid technical points being taken which lack any real merit'. It ruled that Mrs Modahl's challenge based on the alleged lack of accreditation of the laboratory fell into this category, since Mrs Modahl did not argue that the alleged lack of accreditation cast any doubt on the reliability of the finding. However, Lord Justice Morritt noted that 'the point will be available where it is apparent that the requisite analysis may not have been carried out either under proper conditions or, perhaps, at all due to the nature of the organisation from which the report of the analysis has been received'[7].
- In *Korda v ITF Ltd*, the ITF Appeals Committee agreed with Korda's criticisms of the procedures for the collection of partial samples, but held, invoking the anti-technicality rule in Section U of the ITF's Anti-Doping Programme, that the flaws did not affect the integrity of the test result, a finding upheld by the Court of Arbitration for Sport on appeal[8].

1 See eg *N v FINA*, CAS 98/208, award dated 22 December 1998, para 25, *Digest of CAS Awards II 1998–2000* (2002, Kluwer), pp 234, 250 ('where there is a substantial risk of contamination of a sample, the results of that sample ought, save exceptionally, to be disregarded'). The rule may explicitly put the burden on the athlete to prove that the departure from the guidelines raises a material doubt as to the reliability of the positive finding. See eg ITF Anti-Doping Programme 2001, cl U (standard: 'on the balance of probabilities'). Otherwise, such a burden will probably be implied.

2 *S v FEI*, CAS 91/56, award dated 28 June 1992, *Digest of CAS Awards 1986–1998* (Berne 1998), pp 93, 97.

3 *N v FEI*, CAS 92/63, award dated 10 September 1992, *Digest of CAS Awards 1986–1998* (Berne 1998), pp 115, 121.
4 See *SLV and Gasser v IAAF*, IAAF Arbitration Panel, decision dated 18 January 1988, reported in Tarasti *Legal Solutions in International Doping Cases* (SEP Editrice 2000), pp 117–119.
5 *Gasser v Stinson* (14 June 1998, unreported), QBD (Scott J).
6 *Modahl v BAF Ltd* (28 July 1997, unreported), CA (Lord Woolf MR).
7 See n 6.
8 *ITF v Korda*, CAS 99/A/223, award dated 31 August 1999, *Digest of CAS Awards II 1998–2000* (2002, Kluwer), pp 345, 354 ('The formal premises (i) that there was a deviation (ii) that such deviation casts material doubt as to the reliability of the procedure were not made out …'). In *Wilander and Novacek v Tobin & Jude*, (1996) Independent, 21 April, CA, a previous case arising under the ITF Anti-Doping Programme, the players contended that the Review Board did not have sufficient material to entitle it to conclude that the A samples had been properly tested (and therefore should not have proceeded to the test of the B sample), because (a) they could not be satisfied of a proper intra-lab chain of custody; and (b) there was no information to confirm that the pH and density of the urine tested were within the prescribed limits. Lord Justice Neill rather ducked this point, simply stating 'that it would be quite inappropriate for this court to reach a conclusion about the nature and effect of the scientific evidence that was before the Review Board at their hearing in August 1995', and therefore leaving the issues to the Appeals Committee. He concluded that there was not even an arguable case that the procedures adopted had been so defective that the court ought to intervene.

E4.282 It is however to be doubted that any reliance could be placed on the anti-technicality rule (subject to its express wording) *in advance* of the slip sought to be excused. In a Jockey Club case, the jockey's A sample tested positive, at an extremely low level, for cocaine. The jockey's own tests suggested that the drug was not present. Under the rules he was entitled to have his B sample tested at a second 'UK accredited' laboratory. A second laboratory was agreed, but the Jockey Club cancelled the test when it found out that the second laboratory's equipment was not sensitive enough to test down to the result found by the first laboratory, even assuming that the first result had been valid. The Jockey Club appears to have discovered that in fact, no other UK accredited laboratory could test that low, because it sought to have the B sample tested at a second laboratory outside the UK, which would arguably be a 'slip' within the meaning of the anti-technicality rule in the Jockey Club rules. The jockey rightly objected. The anti-technicality rule cannot protect knowing departures from the rules before they happen, only unknowing ones after the event. The B sample was duly tested at the agreed second UK accredited laboratory, and proved negative, exonerating the jockey[1].

1 See para E4.232, n 1.

(c) Challenging the integrity of the sample

E4.283 Although the exhaustive chain of custody documentation now in use[1] makes it unlikely that a positive sample could belong to someone else, sometimes the analytical evidence may raise some doubts[2].

1 See para E4.216.
2 See eg *Gasser v Stinson* (15 June 1988, unreported), QBD (Scott J).

E4.284 On the other hand, the athlete may try to show that the integrity of the sample he provided has been impaired by the conditions in which it was transported and/or stored, rendering the subsequent positive finding insufficiently reliable to support a doping conviction. This is what happened in the *Modahl* case[1]:

- On 18 June 1994, Diane Modahl, the English 800 metre runner, competed at the Santo Antonio athletics meeting in Lisbon, Portugal. The Portuguese

Athletic Federation (PAF) had a drug-testing team on site, which collected a sample from Mrs Modahl. That sample was then sent to a laboratory in Lisbon, which subsequently reported that the A sample had tested positive for testosterone at a ratio to epitestosterone of 42:1, well in excess of the 6:1 threshold specified in the rules[2]. On 24 August 1994, the PAF notified the IAAF, the IAAF notified the BAF, and the BAF notified Ms Modahl, withdrew her from its team at the Commonwealth Games, and organised a test of the B sample, which produced the same result.

- On 6 September 1994, the BAF suspended Modahl and commenced disciplinary proceedings against her. At a hearing on 13 December 1994, Mrs Modahl argued that degradation of the sample and failures in the testing procedures used by the laboratory made the test results unreliable. The five-member Disciplinary Committee accepted that there had been serious flaws in the testing procedures, but nevertheless ruled that Mrs Modahl had failed to carry the burden of providing a satisfactory explanation for the level of testosterone in her sample. The Disciplinary Committee therefore decided that the case had been proved beyond reasonable doubt, and unanimously found Mrs Modahl guilty of a doping offence and banned her from competition for the then-mandatory four years.
- Mrs Modahl appealed and on 26 July 1995 the Independent Appeal Panel, having re-heard the case, including new scientific evidence, unanimously upheld her appeal and set aside the finding of the Disciplinary Committee, on the basis that the BAF had not discharged its burden of establishing beyond reasonable doubt that the laboratory test was reliable. Specifically, the Appeal Panel accepted the expert scientific evidence submitted on behalf of Mrs Modahl that it was possible that the level of testosterone in her sample had been caused by degradation arising from bacterial action as a result of the failure to refrigerate the sample after collection. The suspension was therefore vacated and Mrs Modahl was reinstated with immediate effect. She subsequently launched a claim for damages that went to the House of Lords once and the Court of Appeal twice before being dismissed[3].

1 *Modahl v BAF Ltd* [2002] 1 WLR 1192, CA.
2 See para E4.261.
3 See para A3.10, n 2.

(d) *Challenging the reliability of the test results*

E4.285 Apart from challenging the evidence that the sample in question is his, or querying whether its integrity has been undermined by the manner in which it has been stored or handled, the athlete may also seek to challenge the reliability of the analysis undertaken by the laboratory[1].

1 The CAS panel in *USA Shooting and Quigley v Union Internationale de Tir*, CAS 94/129, award dated 23 March 1995, para 70, *Digest of CAS Awards 1986–1998* (Berne 1998), p 187, ruled that an athlete could defeat charges by showing that the test results were unreliable *even if* he had admitted taking the substance in question.

E4.286 Once again, the first point of reference will be the documents produced by the laboratory to support the positive finding. Retaining an expert can be crucial. It has been pointed out that the science underpinning drug-testing is hardly unimpeachable: scientists' evidence may consist as much of opinion as of fact, and therefore may be vulnerable to competent challenge[1].

1 Nick Bitel, Anti-Doping lecture on the KCL Postgraduate Certificate in Sports Law course (November 2001).

E4.287 Once again, however, as with the anti-technicality rule[1], the anti-doping programme may place obstacles in the way of such an attack. For example, the Olympic Movement Anti-Doping Code provides as follows:

> Accredited laboratories are presumed to have conducted testing and custodial procedures in accordance with prevailing and acceptable standards of scientific practice. This presumption can be rebutted by convincing evidence to the contrary, but the accredited laboratory shall have no onus in the first instance to show that it conducted the procedures other than in accordance with its customary practices[2].

1 See para E4.278 et seq.

2 Olympic Movement Anti-Doping Code (Lausanne 2001), Chap Three, Art 4. This provision has been carried over to the draft WADA Code (E-Version 1.0), issued 10 June 2002 at para 8.2.2.1.

E4.288 Therefore, unless the athlete can show that the laboratory used was not properly accredited[1], if he wishes to argue that his sample was not stored or was not tested properly, he will have to support his argument 'by convincing evidence' sufficient to overcome the presumption of propriety. This is a heavy burden for the athlete and one that will rarely be met[2].

1 The laboratory involved in the *Modahl* case, although formally IOC-accredited, had failed to notify the IOC that it had moved the site of its facilities, and had carried out the analysis of Diane Modahl's sample at the new site. Diane Modahl therefore argued that it did not qualify as an IOC-accredited laboratory. This argument received short shrift before from Lord Justice Hoffman in the House of Lords. See *Modahl v BAF Ltd* (22 July 1999, unreported), HL.

On the other hand, the accreditation procedures for laboratories include provisions for 'yellow cards' for laboratories that have failed to comply with all applicable requirements. See Olympic Movement Anti-Doping Code (Lausanne 2001), App B, Annex IV (Restrictions for Laboratories Failing Re-Accreditation Tests). It would not be a surprise to see an athlete seek to rely on such an event in an effort to persuade the tribunal to question the reliability of the laboratory's positive finding with respect to his sample.

2 See eg *Bruin v FINA*, CAS 98/211, award dated 7 June 1999, para 36, *Digest of CAS Awards II 1998–2000* (2002, Kluwer), pp 255, 268 (rejecting efforts to impugn laboratory procedures based on missing documentation). But cf *USA Triathlon v Smith*, CAS 99/A/241, paras 68–70 (giving athlete benefit of doubt regarding reliability of test procedure).

(e) *Challenging the status of the substance in issue as a 'prohibited substance'*

E4.289 Because the IOC List of Prohibited Substances and Prohibited Methods is far from a definitive, black and white document[1], the athlete may be able to raise a doubt as to whether the substance found in his sample is in fact a prohibited substance. There are numerous potential lines of attack.

1 See para E4.136 et seq.

E4.290 Is the substance actually prohibited? Where the sample that tested positive was taken at a non-Olympic event, it may be that the IOC List does not apply. For example, the sport may not have adopted the IOC List in its entirety[1], or it may have adopted a prior version of the IOC List and not yet updated it at the time the sample was taken, so that the substance found in the sample is not on the relevant list[2]. Alternatively, the sport may have adopted the current IOC List in its entirety, but the substance may not have been added to the IOC List until after the athlete gave his sample[3]; or it may be one of the 'optional' substances on the IOC List that is only prohibited if the athlete's governing body has deemed it to be so, and that body may not have done so[4]. If the substance is in fact prohibited, however, it is not open to the athlete to argue that it should not be prohibited[5].

1 See eg UK Sport *Anti-Doping Report 2000–01*, p 21 (reporting no action taken in equestrian racing after findings of ephedrine and phenylephnine because 'substance not banned under governing body rules').

2 A 1997 survey found that '36 [of 54] International Federations apply the most recent IOC list of banned classes and methods of doping. Seven International Federations apply a "non-current" version of the IOC doping list, while 17 International Federations appear to have adopted a list of banned doping classes and methods completely different from that of the IOC'. See Vrijman, *Towards Harmonisation: A Commentary on Current Issues and Problems*, update of a paper presented at the International Symposium, Doping in Sport and Its Legal and Social Control (Alabama 1996). By 2001, compliance was much better, 28 out of 29 federations surveyed having adopted the most recent IOC list. Vrijman 'Harmonisation: A Commentary on Current Issues and Problems' in *Drugs and Doping in Sport* (2001, Cavendish), p 147. Vrijman mentions the case of Spanish cyclist Pedro Delgado, who tested positive for Probenecid during the 1988 Tour de France. Since Probenecid was on the then-current IOC list but not on the out-of-date version of the IOC list that the UCI had adopted, Delgado could not be suspended and went on to win the Tour. But see *UCI v A*, CAS 97/175, award dated 15 April 1998, *Digest of CAS Awards II 1998–2000* (2002, Kluwer), pp 158, 168 and 169 (holding Bromontan to be prohibited because at the relevant time it was on the IOC list, although not on the UCI list).

3 It is impermissible under English law and the general principles of law set out at paras E4.77 to E4.82 to give rules retroactive effect. See para E4.82, n 4.

4 See para E4.143, n 2.

5 See para E4.146.

E4.291 Is the substance expressly listed on the IOC List? If the substance in question is not expressly mentioned on the IOC List, then the Anti-Doping Officer will have to show that it is either:

(1) a substance that can be classified under one of the five general classes (stimulants, narcotics, steroids, diuretics and hormones)[1]; or
(2) a substance that is 'related to' (ie similar in pharmacological action or chemical structure to) a prohibited substance[2]; or
(3) a metabolite of a prohibited substance or of a substance related to a prohibited substance[3].

The athlete may well be able to challenge this showing, as the authorities discussed elsewhere in this chapter demonstrate[4].

1 See paras E4.137 to E4.142.

2 See para E4.151 (requirement of substantial objective proof, by reference to chemical composition and qualities of substance, that it is chemically and/or pharmacologically related to listed substance); para E4.149 (suggestion of requirement of proof athlete was aware of relationship).

3 See para E4.152 et seq.

4 See para E4.137 et seq.

E4.292 A slightly different argument was deployed in the *Baxter* case[1]. The IOC List refers to methamphetamine as an example of a banned stimulant. Methamphetamine is a commonly-abused stimulant which is a dextro rotatory isomer. A separate substance, known as 'levmetamfetamine', is a lelo rotatory isomer. Although *chemically* similar, the latter is only a nasal decongestant, with no performance-enhancing effects. In US drug programmes, a test for methamphetamine is not deemed positive unless it has been shown, by isomer separation analysis, that the results have not been caused by levametamfetamine. Baxter argued before the IOC Disciplinary Commission that the IOC had to do the same in order to discharge its evidential burden of establishing the presence of a banned stimulant in his body: he had used a Vicks nasal inhaler bought in the US that, unknown to him, included an additional ingredient not contained in the same inhaler bought in the UK and that was a permitted product in the UK. The IOC Disciplinary Commission rejected that argument, saying that methamphetamine was banned and methamphetamine was what had been found in Baxter's sample; levmetamfetamine was banned just as much as methamphetamine; there was no need to go on to establish which was present and there was no need to go further and show that what had been found in the sample was performance-enhancing. The Court of Arbitration for Sport rejected Baxter's appeal in October 2002.

1 CAS 2000. See para E4.134.

E4.293 Was the substance produced endogenously? Where the substance found in the athlete's sample is one of those that can be produced endogenously, then unless scientific evidence exists to establish the substance in the sample is exogenous[1] the Anti-Doping Officer will have had to adduce evidence that demonstrates the concentration of the substance found in the sample 'so exceeds the range of values normally found in humans as not to be consistent with normal endogenous production'[2]. The rules may set thresholds beyond which exogenous ingestion will be presumed[3], but the athlete may seek to submit evidence to rebut the presumption and establish endogenous production or innocent exogenous ingestion[4].

1 See para E4.262.
2 See para E4.261.
3 See para E4.260.
4 This option is expressly set out in the IOC list with respect to testosterone (see para E4.261) but has also been held to apply with respect to nandrolone (see *Ottey* case, IAAF Arbitration Panel decision dated 3 July 2000, para 15, [2001] 4 ISLR 260; *Walker* case, IAAF Arbitration Panel, decision dated 20 August 2000, para 32, [2001] 4 ISLR 264), and there is no reason in principle why its application should stop there. Cf Kerr, 'Doped or Duped? The Nandrolone Jurisprudence' [2001] 3 ISLR 97, 101 (depicting the defence as applied in *Ottey* to nandrolone as 'an artificial creation outside the published rules').

E4.294 Nandrolone Nandrolone, also known as nortestosterone, is on the IOC List as a Class C anabolic steroid[1]. It came sharply into public focus in the late 1990s, when there were a number of positive findings, including against some very high-profile athletes. In the UK alone, in 1999 and 2000, four leading British track athletes – Linford Christie, Doug Walker, Gary Cadogan and Mark Richardson – each tested positive for nandrolone[2].

1 See para E4.140.
2 It was reported that there were 343 positive tests for nandrolone across all sports in 1999, including Merlene Ottey of Jamaica and Dieter Baumann of Germany: (2000) Associated Press, 8 February.

E4.295 In the face of this rash of positives, people looked for an innocent explanation. Claims were made that the nandrolone found in the tests had been produced naturally in the body, or had been ingested by eating the flesh of animals that had been injected with steroids[1]. Suspicions were voiced that many nutritional supplements on the market (particularly those sourced from the completely unregulated US supplements market) were contaminated with substances such as nandrolone that were not disclosed on the labels.

1 See eg *Meca-Medina*, CAS 99/A/234 and CAS 99/A/235. In the *Korda* case, the athlete's expert witness suggested that either endogenous production or consumption of meat of animals injected by steroids could explain the metabolites of nandrolone found in his sample. However, the CAS panel accepted the ITF's evidence that endogenous production and/or consumption of tainted meat would only explain trace amounts of nandrolone metabolites, and could not explain concentrations as large as those found in the athlete's sample: *ITF v Korda*, CAS 99/223/A, decision dated 31 August 1999 at para 50. See discussion of similar cases in Beloff, 'Drugs, Laws and Versapaks' in *Drugs and Doping in Sport* (2001, Cavendish) at p 52.

E4.296 The various claims were complicated by initial controversy regarding the appropriate cut-off to rule out endogenous production of nandrolone. IOC research established the laboratory reporting cut-off for nandrolone (and therefore by default the generally accepted threshold for a nandrolone positive, ie the quantity beyond which any innocent explanation is ruled out) at two nanograms per millilitre for men and five nanograms per millilitre for women[1]. However, certain 1999 CAS decisions suggested that there was a 'grey area' between two nanograms per millilitre and five milligrams per millilitre, where tests should not be declared positive without further investigation[2].

1 See IOC guidance document for accredited laboratories, *Analytical Criteria for Reporting Low Concentrations of Anabolic Steroids* (August 1998), appended to Nandrolone Review, Report to UK Sport (January 2000)).

2 *Bernhard v ITU*, CAS 98/222, award dated 8 August 1999, *Digest of CAS Awards II 1998–2000* (2002, Kluwer), p 330; *UCI v Mason*, CAS 98/212, award dated 24 February 1999, *Digest of CAS Awards II 1998–2000* (2002, Kluwer), p 274; and *Boujas v FIJ*, CAS 98/214, award dated 17 March 1999, para 40, *Digest of CAS Awards II 1998–2000* (2002, Kluwer), p 308. See generally Young *Survey of Major Issues in CAS Doping Cases*, paper presented to CAS seminar (Lausanne, December 1998).

E4.297 In March 2000, it was reported that research commissioned by FIFA had suggested that physical and mental stress could raise the level of nandrolone occurring naturally in the body above the IOC-specified two nanograms per millilitre cut-off for endogenous production[1]. An expert committee commissioned by UK Sport concluded otherwise in January 2000[2], but in July 2000 the UKA Nandrolone Working Party concluded, based on 'preliminary results', that a 'combination of exercise and dietary supplements, none of which appears to contain a prohibited substance, can result in a positive'[3].

1 Garroson and Harverson 'IOC warned over steroid' (2000) Financial Times, 2 March. As a result, according to the same report, FIFA had been advised that the IOC's rules regarding nandrolone were 'not legally sustainable'.

2 *Nandrolone Review*, Report to UK Sport (January 2000).

3 Report of the UK Athletics Nandrolone Working Party, 25 July 2000, relying on research undertaken at the University of Aberdeen.

E4.298 The British athletes were cleared by UKA disciplinary tribunals, on the basis that it could not be proved beyond a reasonable doubt that the substance in the sample was not endogenously produced. However, the IAAF Council referred the cases to the IAAF Arbitration Panel, which rejected the various arguments made to explain the positive findings. The IAAF Arbitration Panel accepted the IOC-established cut-offs of two nanograms per millilitre for men and five nanograms per millilitre for women; it rejected as scientifically unreliable the research upon which the Nandrolone Working Party[1] based its contrary view. It found that the levels of nandrolone found in the samples of Walker (12.59ng/ml), Christie (181.8ng/ml) and Cadogan (9.8ng/ml), being over that threshold, so exceeded the range of values normally found in humans as not to be consistent with normal endogenous production. In the case of Merlene Ottey, the panel accepted that the IAAF had not proved that levels of 4.53 ng/ml could not have been produced endogenously because it fell below the threshold[2]. Court of Arbitration for Sport panels seem to have come round to accept the same threshold[3].

1 See para E4.297, n 3.

2 See para E4.293, n 4. See generally Kerr, 'Doped or Duped? The Nandrolone Jurisprudence' [2001] 3 ISLJ 97.

3 See *Meca-Medina v FINA*, CAS 99/A/234 para 10.1 (accepting IOC cut-off, rejecting any 'grey area' between 2 and 5 nanograms per millilitre); *FLCP v IWF*, CAS 99/A/252, para 7.5.6 (same).

E4.299 It is now generally considered that many of the positive nandrolone tests are attributable to contaminated nutritional supplements[1].

1 See para E4.184. See also *Dutch Athletes Asked to Stop Using Dietary Supplements* (2002) Sportcal.com, 7 January. This of course provides no defence to a strict liability charge. Query whether it could be a fertile ground for mitigation. See *Aanes v FILA*, CAS 2001/A317, award dated 9 July 2001, p 22 ('the sporting world has, for quite some time, even before the 2000 Sydney Games, been well aware of the risks in connection with using so called nutritional supplements').

E4.300 **Testosterone** In the case of testosterone, while a ratio of testosterone to epitestosterone of more than 6:1 raises a presumption of exogenous application[1], the IOC List says such a finding cannot be ruled a positive until the possibility that the elevated testosterone is due to a physiological or pathological condition has been ruled out[2].

1 See para E4.261.
2 See para E4.261.

E4.301 The IAAF Rules put the burden in this respect firmly on the athlete, providing that, if the 6:1 ratio is met, nevertheless:

> [a] sample will not be regarded as positive for dihydrotestosterone or testosterone where an athlete proves by clear and convincing evidence that the abnormal ratio or concentration is attributable to a pathological or physiological condition[1].

The IAAF Arbitration Panel has said this means the proof 'must convey a high degree of probability and not mere assertions'; it has suggested medical records, coupled with expert evidence, would be required[2].

1 IAAF Procedural Guidelines for Doping Control (2000 edn), p 18. There are similar provisions for (for example) all of the peptide hormones, mimetics and analogues (p 19) and caffeine (p 20). There is no similar express provision for nandrolone, but one has been implied by analogy, for reasons of fairness. See para E4.293, n 4.
The draft World Anti-Doping Code would similarly put the burden on the athlete, once any reporting criteria had been met, to prove that the cause was a psychological or pathological condition. See Draft World Anti-Doping Code, E-Version 1.0, issued 10 June 2002, clause 8.1.1.1.12.
2 *Decker Slaney* case, decision dated 25 April 1999, reported in Tarasti *Legal Solutions in International Doping Cases* (SEP Editrice 2000) at pp 157, 159, para 26. In the *Decker Slaney* case and the *Mitchell* case, the explanations proffered were held not to meet that standard. See para E4.302.

E4.302 Two prominent American athletes, Mary Decker Slaney and Dennis Mitchell, relied on this provision to try to explain away the presence of abnormal amounts of testosterone in their respective samples. Decker Slaney blamed her contraceptive pills, alcohol consumption, her menstrual cycle and/or the ageing process for the testosterone found in her sample[1]. Mitchell blamed dietary supplements, alcohol and/or stress caused by sexual activity and lack of sleep the night before the test[2]. In each case, USA Track & Field accepted the explanation and acquitted the athlete of a doping offence. However, the IAAF Council referred those acquittals to the IAAF Arbitration Panel, which ruled in each case that the evidence submitted by the athlete had failed to establish to the requisite standard that the elevated ratios were caused by innocent pathological or physiological conditions[3].

1 (1999) Daily Telegraph, 27 April.

2 'Banned Mitchell may be back for Olympics' (1999) Times, 4 August.
3 Tarasti *Legal Solutions in International Doping Cases* (SEP Editrice 2000) at pp 155–164 (Decker Slaney) and pp 165–170 (Mitchell). Prior to the IAAF Arbitration Panel's ruling, Slaney filed suit in the Indiana courts against the US Olympic Committee and the IAAF for failing to investigate possible innocent explanations for the level of testosterone found in her urine. That case was dismissed in 2001: *Slaney v IAAF* 244 F 3d 80 (7th Cir 2001).

E4.303 In contrast, UK Sport reported in 2002 that a basketball player's elevated T/E ratio was 'felt to reflect unusual, but natural levels of testosterone. Not considered to be a doping offence – no further action'[1]. Similarly, after a sample taken from a rugby player revealed an elevated T/E ratio, endocrine tests and additional out-of-competition tests were carried out, following which it was concluded that there was 'no evidence of testosterone administration, and player's consistent and marginally irregular T/E ratio is due to a benign physiological abnormality'[2]. In February 2002, the World Anti-Doping Agency reported that a German cyclist found to have an elevated T/E ratio was not sanctioned because the ratio was 'naturally elevated'[3].

1 UK Sport *Anti-Doping Report 2000–01*, p 18.
2 UK Sport *Anti-Doping Report 2000–01*, p 24.
3 WADA Out-Of-Competition Testing Program Report (8 February 2002).

E4.304 In *S v FINA*[1], after the athlete submitted a sample with a T/E ratio of 6.9, her national federation conducted a medical investigation including a longitudinal hormonal study of the athlete, concluded that her elevated T/E ratio 'can be due to a pathological condition', and therefore decided not to sanction her. The FINA Executive referred that decision to a FINA Doping Panel, which overturned the decision and imposed a four year suspension on the athlete, on the basis that it was her burden, once a T/E ratio in her sample of more than 6:1 had been established, to show that the elevated testosterone 'is due to a physiological or pathological condition', which burden was not satisfied by an 'unverified hypothesis' that the finding 'may' have been caused by a pathological condition. The CAS panel rejected the athlete's appeal. The panel agreed with FINA that the presumption from the T/E ratio had not been rebutted, but relied principally on direct evidence, from isotopic ratio measurement[2], that the testosterone had been administered exogenously. The panel also found that such analysis could be relied upon as proof of exogenous administration of testosterone even if the T/E ratio was less than 6:1, and that if such proof existed, it was conclusive, and therefore it was not open to the athlete to seek to rebut it by claiming that the elevated testosterone was exogenously produced as a result of a physiological condition.

1 CAS 2000/A/274, award dated 19 October 2000, *Digest of CAS Awards II 1998–2000* (2002, Kluwer), p 389.
2 See para E4.262.

(f) Is the athlete entitled to use the substance for medical reasons?

E4.305 The IOC List provides, and the anti-doping programmes of the particular sports should also provide, a route to an individual exemption permitting use of specified prohibited substances where medical necessity is demonstrated[1].

1 See para E4.167 et seq.

E4.306 For example, the IOC List allows use of salbutamol, where ingested by inhalation, to treat exercise-induced asthma. To establish that he is entitled to such an exemption, the athlete must show that he declared his medical need for the salbutamol to the relevant authority, with the supporting evidence required by the rules (if any), within any time-limit required by the rules[1]. Secondly, he must be able to show that he took the salbutamol by inhalation; however, this will usually be presumed from evidence of asthma for which salbutomol is prescribed[2].

1 The Court of Arbitration for Sport has suggested that a doctor's certificate 'is in itself not conclusive: [the governing body] is fully entitled to double check, challenge and reject a formal notification in case of any abuse'. *Lehtinen v FINA*, CAS 95/142, award of 14 February 1996, para 40. The concern arises from the increase in number of 'asthmatics' in elite sport. At the 1984 Olympic Games, 1.7% of athletes declared a therapeutic requirement to use beta agonists; at Salt Lake City in 2002, the figure was 6.1%.

2 *Lehtinen v FINA*, CAS 95/142, award dated 14 February 1996, para 57.

E4.307 If there is a review panel function in the programme in question, that review panel will consider whether or not there is any question of an entitlement to an exemption[1]. However, even if the review panel resolves that there is not and the matter proceeds to formal charges, the issue may remain a live one before the disciplinary panel.

1 See para E4.230.

E4.308 For example, what if an athlete tests positive for salbutamol, did not file a request for an exemption prior to the event, as the rules clearly required, but produces a valid doctor's certificate pre-dating the test that confirms that he is an asthmatic who takes salbutamol by inhalation? What if he filed a request for an exemption, but only with the domestic governing body, and the event at which he tested positive is run by the international governing body, which only recognises requests that have been filed directly with it? What if he declared ventolin (the asthma medication that contains salbutamol) in the 'Declaration of medication taken recently' box on the doping control form he completed when he gave the sample? What if he said nothing on the doping control form?

E4.309 Some governing bodies have taken a hard line, insisting that taking salbutamol without having followed the pre-notification rules constitutes a doping offence, even if medical necessity can subsequently be shown[1]. The Court of Arbitration for Sport has endorsed this approach on policy grounds[2], saying an offence is committed if a notification has not been filed beforehand, even if a declaration is made on the doping control form at the time the sample is given[3]. It mitigates the effects of this by requiring strict proof of each element of the offence[4]. Others mitigate the effects by allowing the doping tribunal to depart from the otherwise mandatory sanctions in such cases if it is satisfied the athlete would have been entitled to the exemption[5].

1 See eg reg 16 of the IRB Regulations Relating to the Game (2001). Cf ITF Anti-Doping Programme 2002, cl J(5) (allowing retrospective exemptions in certain circumstances).

2 *Lehtinen v FINA*, CAS 95/142, award of 14 February 1996, para 40: 'the panel agrees with FINA that the admissibility of *a posteriori* notification of the medical necessity of salbutamol would encourage abuse and weaken the fight against doping … The duty of *prior* notification may serve as a strong deterrent against some forms of possible cheating. Therefore, the panel agrees with FINA that one should not admit any evidence to prove medical necessity otherwise than through prior notification'.

3 *Lehtinen v FINA*, CAS 95/142, award of 14 February 1996, para 42: 'if salbutamol has been found, the declaration [of salbutamol on the doping control form] itself neither gives evidence that its use was medically indicated nor does it show that it was applied by inhalation'.
4 *Lehtinen v FINA*, CAS 95/142, award of 14 February 1996.
5 See para E4.169, n 4.

(g) Lack of fault

E4.310 If the definition of doping in the relevant rules does make proof of intent a necessary element, or lack of intent a defence[1], then clearly the athlete has many more lines of argument potentially available to him. Depending on exactly how the rules are formulated, these may range from mere assertions of ignorance as to how the substance came to be in his sample[2], through specific evidence of inadvertent ingestion[3], to doctor misprescription, all the way to evidence of outright sabotage[4].

1 See paras E4.267 and E4.268.
2 But see para E4.116.
3 For example, Ross Rebagliata blamed the marijuana in his sample on passive smoking at a party. See para E4.143, n 2.
4 See para E4.111, n 2.

E4.311 The case law shows how a panel can be persuaded to read a fault requirement into unclear (and sometimes even into clear) strict liability programmes[1].

1 See para E4.130.

E4.312 The resourceful defendant athlete will also research prior decisions by the prosecuting sports body for inconsistencies in application that can be exploited. For example, a French swimmer tested positive for a banned substance given to her by her coach without her knowledge. FINA's rules mandated that she be banned for two years. However, in an earlier case involving Australian swimmer Samantha Riley, FINA had decided, based on the inadvertent nature of the use and the lack of performance-enhancing effect of the substance at issue, that it would only issue a 'strong warning'[1]. The French swimmer, suspended for two years without any such forbearance, relied on that inconsistency in her appeal to the Court of Arbitration for Sport, and won, with the CAS holding that FINA had to treat like cases alike[2].

1 See discussion by Beloff 'Drugs, Laws & Versapaks' in *Drugs and Doping in Sport* (2001, Cavendish), pp 39, 48.
2 *Chagnaud v FINA*, CAS 95/141, award dated 22 August 1996, *Digest of CAS Awards 1986–1998* (Berne 1998), p 215.

(h) Lack of performance-enhancing effect

E4.313 Similarly, an athlete may seek to persuade a tribunal (particularly one that is frustrated by its inability, under the strict liability approach, to take the athlete's perceived moral innocence into account) that references in the rules to a desire to stop performance enhancement should be read to require the Anti-Doping Officer to prove that the substance in question did in fact enhance the athlete's performance[1]. There are significant obstacles in the way of such a defence[2].

1 See cases cited at para E4.76, n 3.
2 See para E4.254, n 3. Cf *Haga v FIM*, CAS 2000/A/281, award dated 22 December 2000, *Digest of CAS Awards II 1998–2000* (2002, Kluwer), pp 410, 418 (where definition in rules of 'doping' referred to 'substances … which may lead to an artificial or unfair increase in performance in events', CAS panel held FIM 'needs to establish only that the substance found in the athlete's urine has the potential of enhancing performance').

(i) Data Protection Act 1998

E4.314 Failure to maintain sensitive personal data in confidence may amount to a breach of the statutory duty imposed by the Data Protection Act 1998. If the offence alleged is failure to submit to a test and the defence is lack of confidence in the integrity of the system, then evidence of such breach would support the defence, but it remains highly doubtful that it would succeed.

(j) Mitigation

E4.315 The rules may give the disciplinary tribunal discretion to take into account the relative (lack of) fault of the transgressing athlete in considering what sanction to impose[1]. The athlete should therefore be prepared to submit evidence as to his lack of fault, which would ideally consist not of mere protestations that he does not know how the prohibited substance got into his body but rather of evidence that the substance was ingested in circumstances for which the athlete cannot be blamed[2].

1 See para E4.334. And if they do not, the tribunal may imply it. See para E4.133.

2 For example, Dutch international footballer Ronald de Boer reportedly had his nandrolone ban reduced by UEFA from 12 months to 11 weeks because of evidence that contaminated food supplements had caused the positive result: *Soccer Star de Boer's Drug Ban Cut by UEFA* (2001) Sportcal.com, 30 July.

E4.316 For example, British swimming's Doping Control Rules provide:

> Where these Rules provide for a minimum period of suspension, the minimum may be lessened if the person found to have committed a doping offence can clearly establish how and when the prohibited substance got into such person's body tissue or fluids and that the prohibited substance did not get there as a direct or indirect result of any intent, fault or negligence of such person[1].

1 ASFGB Doping Control Rules, cl 10.9.

E4.317 Similarly, cl E(4)(c) of the ITF Anti-Doping Programme 1998 conferred discretion on the Appeals Committee to mitigate the suspension element of the sanction and also part of the forfeiture element, but 'only if the player establishes on the balance of probabilities that Exceptional Circumstances exist and that as a result of those Exceptional Circumstances the penalties as set out … in the Programme should be reduced. For the purposes of this paragraph, Exceptional Circumstances shall mean circumstances where the player did not know that he had taken, or been administered the relevant substance provided that he had acted reasonably in all the relevant circumstances'. The construction of this clause came into dispute in the *Korda* case.

E4.318 Petr Korda, a professional tennis player, provided a urine sample at the 1998 Wimbledon championships that subsequently tested positive for 19-norandrosterone and 19-noraetiocholanolone, both metabolites of nandrolone, a prohibited anabolic agent. The ITF's Independent Anti-Doping Review Board[1] decided there was no basis to disqualify the positive finding, and therefore the ITF notified Korda, in October 1998, that he was subject, under the Anti-Doping Programme, to a mandatory twelve-month suspension from all competition as well as forfeiture of ranking points and prize money won at the tournament where the sample was given.

1 See para E4.228, n 2.

E4.319 Korda asserted (among other things) that 'Exceptional Circumstances' existed within the meaning of cl E(4)(c) of the Programme, so that even if he had committed an offence the otherwise mandatory twelve-month suspension should not be imposed.

E4.320 The Appeals Committee agreed with Korda's criticisms of the procedures for the collection of partial samples but held that the flaws did not affect the integrity of the test results[1]. It also noted that the ITF Anti-Doping Programme adopted a strict liability approach, and therefore the ITF was not required to establish that Korda knew he had taken, or been administered, a prohibited substance in order to demonstrate that a doping offence had been committed. It ruled that mere proof of the presence of the nandrolone metabolites in Korda's urine established a doping offence.

1 See para E4.281.

E4.321 The Appeals Committee also ruled, however, that Korda had established that 'exceptional circumstances' existed 'in that [he] did not know that he had taken (or been administered) the relevant substance and he acted reasonably in all the relevant circumstances'. It said that Korda

> does not have to show the source of the positive test results. The Programme confers a discretion on this Appeals Committee where we are satisfied, on the balance of probabilities, that the Appellant acted innocently and reasonably … In our judgment, the Appellant has established that he acted reasonably (as well as innocently) in all the relevant circumstances. Whatever the cause of the positive results, we are satisfied that the Appellant could not be faulted in any relevant respect.

It therefore decided that the entire twelve-month suspension should be waived[1].

1 *Korda v ITF*, unreported decision of the Appeals Committee of the ITF, dated 22 December 1998.

E4.322 The ITF appealed the decision to the Court of Arbitration for Sport. It contended that the Appeals Committee had misconstrued the 'exceptional circumstances' provision, wrongly held that 'exceptional circumstances' were established and wrongly exercised its discretion by waiving any suspension. The ITF contended that 'I don't know how the substance came to be in my body' is not a sufficient basis to qualify for a departure from the otherwise mandatory suspension. Instead, the player had to be able to adduce specific evidence to demonstrate that, in the circumstances in which the relevant substance was ingested/administered, he did not know of such ingestion/administration and his conduct was reasonable, for example he did not fail to take appropriate precautions to prevent a prohibited substance from entering his body. The ITF contended that it follows that if he cannot provide evidence of how the prohibited substance entered his body, he cannot use this provision. It sought a declaration that the mandatory one-year suspension should be imposed.

E4.323 After a brief excursion to the courts to resolve Korda's claim that the ITF was not entitled under the rules to pursue such an appeal[1], the CAS panel held a de novo rehearing both as to fact and law. By decision dated 31 August 1999, the CAS panel reversed the ITF Appeals Committee's finding that 'exceptional circumstances' existed that warranted waiving any suspension. The CAS panel agreed with the ITF that a 'bald denial' of knowledge about how the substance was ingested or administered was not enough to qualify the player for relief. Rather, he would have to show that, in the circumstances in which the relevant substance was ingested/administered, he did not know of such ingestion/administration and his conduct was reasonable. A contrary interpretation was noted to be inconsistent with the strict liability approach adopted by the ITF's programme:

> it would be odd indeed if a player could be 'absolutely responsible' for the prohibited substance found to be present within his body, so that a doping offence was committed ipso facto without knowledge, intent or fault, but that he could mitigate penalty solely by absence of knowledge. The provisions as to penalty (if so interpreted) would, in our view, fatally contradict the rule and undermine the policy of the provisions as to liability.

The CAS panel held that Petr Korda could not meet the standard, properly interpreted:

> Even if … he unconsciously broke the anti-doping rules, he fell short of these standards of vigilance in relation to what he took, which is demanded of a player who wishes to establish 'exceptional circumstances' pursuant to ITF Rules[2].

1 See paras A5.150 to A5.155.

2 (1999) CAS 99/223/A, award dated 31 August 1999, para 59, *Digest of CAS Awards II 1998–2000* (2002, Kluwer), p 345.

E4.324 The athlete should also be ready to plead in mitigation that the substance found in his sample did not have any performance-enhancing effect[1].

1 See eg ECB Anti-Doping Guidelines, cl 16: 'the Committee will not *necessarily* draw any distinction in terms of the penalty to be imposed between the use of a non-performance enhancing drug and one which may be performance enhancing' (emphasis added).

D Sanctions

E4.325 The potential sanctions available to a tribunal that has found an athlete guilty of a doping offence include 'sporting' sanctions (ie revoking of results and forfeiture of any prize money, ranking points and other benefits earned from the tainted performance) as well as 'disciplinary' sanctions, such as a ban for a period from further participation in the sport and/or a financial penalty[1].

1 See generally McLaren 'Doping Sanctions: What Penalty?' [2002] 2 ISLR 23.

E4.326 Furthermore, in addition to the sanctions imposed by the tribunal, conviction of a doping offence may trigger further collateral sanctions, eg from funding agencies[1].

1 See para E4.349 et seq.

(a) Sporting sanctions

E4.327 Cancellation of results Article 3.3 of the Olympic Movement Anti-Doping Code provides that:

> any case of doping during competition automatically leads to invalidation of the result (with all its consequences, including forfeit of any medals and prizes), irrespective of any other sanction that may be applied …[1]

1 So, for example, Andrea Raducan was stripped of her Sydney gold medal and Alain Baxter was stripped of his Salt Lake bronze. See paras E4.125 and E4.134. The draft WADA Code (E-Version 1.0, issued 10 June 2002 at para 8.1.3) adopts the same approach.

E4.328 This is easiest to apply in sports played between individuals. Here, the anti-doping rules will usually provide for cancellation of results, certainly of results obtained at the event where the sample was given[1] and (if there has been no interim suspension after that time) at all subsequent events in which the athlete has participated prior to the hearing[2], but sometimes also at all events in which the athlete participated for a fixed period prior to the date of the positive sample[3]. Of course, if an individual's results count towards a broader competition, then the disqualification may have wider ramifications[4].

1 But see *Haga v FIM*, CAS 2000/A/281, award dated 22 December 2000, *Digest of CAS Awards 1998–2000* (2002, Kluwer), pp 410, 421 (where athlete took part in two separate races in same event in one day, and tested positive after the second race for ephedrine, CAS panel treated each race as a single competition, held that the positive test after the second race did not show that the first race was tainted, and so disqualified the athlete only from the second race).

2 See eg IAAF Rule 59.4; ITF Anti-Doping Programme 2002, cl N(4); draft World Anti-Doping Code, E-Version 1.0, issued 10 June 2002 at para 8.8.5. But see *B v IJF*, CAS 99/A/230, award dated 20 December 1999, *Digest of CAS Awards II 1998–2000* (2002, Kluwer), pp 369, 375 (in absence of provision in rules that sanctions should run from date sample is given, then athlete may not be disqualified from event based on positive test result with respect to sample taken in out-of-competition test prior to event).

3 See eg ASFGB Doping Control Rules (2001), r 10.1. It was reported that the international swimming governing body, FINA, backed down when Michele de Bruin threatened to sue if her 26 Irish records were wiped out: (1999) Daily Record, 14 October.

4 See eg *USA Shooting and Quigley v Union Internationale de Tir*, CAS 94/129, award dated 23 May 1995, *Digest of CAS Awards 1986–1998* (Berne 1988), p 187 (shooter's gold medal earned US a quota place for the 1996 Olympic Games; this was lost when he was disqualified).

E4.329 In team sports, the position is not so straightforward, at least where there is no suggestion that the team was responsible for the drug-taking by the individual member. Nevertheless, many programmes take a strict approach, penalising the entire team for an offence by one individual team member[1]. This approach has an obvious deterrent effect.

1 See eg International Paralympic Committee, r 1.1.4 ('if the competitor [found guilty of doping] is a member of a team, the match competition or event during which the infringement took place shall be forfeited by that team'), applied in *NWBA v IPC*, CAS 95/122, award of 5 March 1996, *Digest of CAS Awards 1986–1998* (Berne 1988), p 173. The alternative approach is for the team to be disqualified from the entire event only if more than one member is found guilty of a doping offence.

The draft WADA Code would leave this issue to the discretion of the international federation: E-Version 1.0, issued 10 June 2002, para 8.8.2.

E4.330 Forfeiture of benefits The rules will usually provide for the forfeiture by the athlete of any prize money, ranking points or other benefits earned as a result of his tainted performance[1].

1 See eg ITF Anti-Doping Programme 2002, cl N(3): 'If a player is found through the procedures set forth in this Programme to have committed a Doping Offence … then such player shall … forfeit all computer ranking points earned at the tournament or event where the player provided the positive specimen and forfeit and return to the ITF all prize money without deduction for tax earned at the tournament or event where the player provided the positive specimen'.

See also IAAF Rule 60.4: 'Where an athlete has been declared ineligible, he shall not be entitled to any award or addition to his trust fund to which he would have been entitled by virtue of his appearance and/or performance at the athletics meeting at which the doping offence took place, or at any subsequent meetings'.

Wise event organisers will also include in their rules a provision similar to cl N(8) of the ITF Anti-Doping Programme 2002: 'There will be no readjustment of prize money, ranking points or title for any player who lost to a player subsequently suspended pursuant to this programme …'.

E4.331 Again, this can be less straightforward in team competitions. At the 1992 Barcelona Paralympic Games, a member of the gold-medal-winning USA Wheelchair Basketball team tested positive for a prohibited substance. The organising committee ruled that the US team should forfeit the match and all team members should forfeit their medals. A Court of Arbitration for Sport panel, relying on IPC rule 1.1.4 ('if the competitor [found guilty of doping] is a member of a team, the match competition or event during which the infringement took place shall be forfeited by that team'), upheld the forfeiture ruling, and rejected the suggestion that the non-offending players should nevertheless be allowed to retain their gold medals. The panel recognised the unfairness of this, but noted that 'the implication of participating in a team sport means that the chain is no stronger than its weakest link'. The appellant did not ask for a ruling that they could have silver medals; therefore the CAS panel did not have to decide whether the forfeiture was of just the final match or of the whole event[1].

1 *NWBA v IPC*, CAS 95/122, award dated 5 March 1996, *Digest of CAS Awards 1986–1998* (Berne 1998), p 173.

(b) Disciplinary sanctions

E4.332 Few would argue that it is unfair to revoke tainted results and require forfeiture of benefits earned from the tainted performance, even when the athlete is able to establish that the prohibited substance in question was ingested innocently[1]. Far more controversial, however, are the suspensions that are also imposed, which keep the athlete out of the sport entirely[2] for long periods into the future. The arguments as to proportionality and fairness[3] are compounded by the complete lack of harmony of approach among different sports on this subject[4].

1 See para E4.111. Query where there is evidence that the substance in question had no performance-enhancing effect. See paras E4.134 and E4.392.
2 See para E4.345.
3 See para E4.111 et seq.
4 See generally McLaren 'Doping Sanctions: What Penalty?' [2002] 2 ISLR 23.

E4.333 The Olympic Movement Anti-Doping Code provisions on disciplinary sanctions The rules of some sports leave the tribunal no discretion in fixing sanctions once liability is determined; instead, they set out fixed sanctions that apply mandatorily upon proof of particular categories of doping offence[1]. This has the advantage of consistency, at least from the point of view of protecting the interests of the sport. By definition, however, it makes it impossible to take into account the facts and circumstances of the case at hand, and therefore could in theory be attacked for a lack of proportionality.

1 See eg ITF Anti-Doping Programme 2002, cl M (fixing periods of suspension from the sport, from three months to two years, depending on what class of prohibited substance is involved, or for up to life, if it is a repeat offence). But note that the ITF allows the exercise of discretion, in 'Exceptional Circumstances', to reduce these 'mandatory' sanctions. See para E4.317 et seq.

The approach taken (for example) by the IAAF is for the rules to fix the sanctions that the disciplinary panel must apply and leave it to the governing body itself to determine, on an application for early reinstatement by the athlete, whether exceptional circumstances exist that justify mitigation of the sanction in a particular case. Tarasti *Legal Solutions In International Doping Cases* (SEP Editrice 2000) at p 100.

E4.334 The rules of other sports include a flexible tariff of sanctions, sometimes with mandatory minimums. For example, the Lausanne Declaration declared that 'the minimum required sanction' for a first offence involving 'major' doping substances or prohibited methods should be a two year ban from all competition[1].

1 Declaration on Doping in Sport (World Anti-Doping Conference, Lausanne 1999).

E4.335 Following on from the Lausanne Declaration, the Olympic Movement Anti-Doping Code adopts a rising tariff of sanctions, depending upon:

(a) the class of prohibited substance used (the greater the performance-enhancement, the stricter the sanction); and
(b) whether it is a first, second or subsequent doping offence.

If the prohibited substance in question is ephedrine, phenylpropanolamine, pseudoephedrine, caffeine, strychnine or related substances, then the prescribed sanctions are:

(i) a warning;
(ii) a ban on participation in one or several sports competitions in any capacity whatsoever;
(iii) a fine of up to US $100,000;
(iv) suspension from any competition for period of one to six months[1].

If any other prohibited substance is involved, then the prescribed sanctions are:

(i) a ban on participation in one or several sports competitions in any capacity whatsoever;
(ii) a fine of up to US $100,000;
(iii) suspension from any competition for a minimum period of two years[2].

1 Olympic Movement Anti-Doping Code (Lausanne 2001), Chap Two, Art 3(1)(a)(4).
2 Olympic Movement Anti-Doping Code (Lausanne 2001), Chap Two, Art 3(1)(b). But see para E4.339.
It is worth noting that the IAAF, from 1991 to 1997, applied a four-year ban for steroid offences, and reduced this to two years only as a result of the German courts ruling that anything more than a two year ban was disproportionate and therefore illegal and unenforceable under German law. See *Edwards v BAI and IAAF* [1998] 2 CMLR 363 (Lightman J).

E4.336 However, if one or more exacerbating factors exists[1], then the range of sanctions goes up several notches. If the prohibited substance used is ephedrine, phenylpropanolamine, pseudoephedrine, caffeine, strychnine or related substances, then (unless it is a repeat offence) if exacerbating factors exist the sanctions prescribed by the Olympic Movement Anti-Doping Code are:

(i) a ban on participation in one or several sports events in any capacity whatsoever;
(ii) a fine of up to US $100,000;
(iii) suspension from any competition for a period of two to eight years[2].

If any other prohibited substance is involved, or if it is a repeat offence involving ephedrine, phenylpropanolamine, pseudoephedrine, caffeine, strychnine or related substances, then if exacerbating factors exist the prescribed sanctions are:

(i) a life ban on participation in any sports event in any capacity whatsoever;
(ii) a fine of up to US $1,000,000;
(iii) suspension (between four years and life) from all sports competition[3].

1 The exacerbating factors are: '(a) intentional doping; (b) the use of a Masking Agent; (c) manoeuvres or manipulation that may prevent or distort any test contemplated in this Code; (d)

refusal to undergo any test contemplated in this Code; (e) doping for which responsibility is imputed to an official or the athlete's entourage; (f) complicity or other forms of involvement in an act of doping by members of a medical, pharmaceutical or related profession': Olympic Movement Anti-Doping Code (Lausanne 2001), Chap Two, Art 3(2).

2 Olympic Movement Anti-Doping Code (Lausanne 2001), Chap Two, Art 3(2)(a).

3 Olympic Movement Anti-Doping Code (Lausanne 2001), Chap Two, Art 3(2)(b).

E4.337 The IOC has provided the following clarification of the flexible approach offered by the Olympic Movement Anti-Doping Code[1]:

> The sanctions enumerated in Chapter II, Article 3 may be applied alternatively or cumulatively, as stated in Article 3(7). They provide the decision-making bodies with a greater flexibility than was previously the case, to allow them to take into account all of the circumstances of a particular case and to impose the most appropriate sanction. Each component of the Olympic Movement will develop its own jurisprudence based on practices used to date and, notably, the sanctions established by the CAS. In this sense, a fine should not ever, in principle, replace a measure of suspension, but should rather complete such a sanction, particularly in those sports in which the financial element plays an important role.
>
> By way of example, a positive result for ephedrine could result in the following sanction(s):
>
> (a) Suspension from all competition for a period of six months [Art III(1)(a)(iv)].
>
> (b) Ban from participation in the next World Championships [Art III(1)(a)(ii)] (which might be taking place outside the six month period, but the measure could be justified if the athlete in question tested positive at the time of the World Championships and the IF did not wish to allow the athlete to participate in the following World Championships).
>
> (c) A fine, which could be fixed anywhere between US$0 and US$100,000 in Cases where a sport is involved in which the athletes stand to earn significant amounts of money and/or if the IF considers that such a measure would have a particular effect on the athlete in question.
>
> The order in which the different sanctions are enumerated in the Code is not of importance, since they are all available to the decision-making body. However, the sanction of suspension is the basic sanction and should, therefore, be the first in any enumeration.

1 IOC Explanatory Memorandum to the Olympic Movement Anti-Doping Code (9 December 1999) at p 7.

E4.338 Lack of harmonisation on sanctions The flexible approach allowed by the Olympic Movement Anti-Doping Code has led sports federations to develop their own respective sanctioning tariffs, within the broad framework of the Code provisions. This is unlikely to change once the World Anti-Doping Agency has developed its own code[1]. The resulting inconsistency between different sports is most acute when the substance involved is not a stimulant and therefore the Olympic Movement Anti-Doping Code's only parameter (for a first offence) is the recommended two-year minimum. In such a case, the IWF (weightlifting) imposes a fixed two year sanction; FINA (swimming) requires a minimum of four years; and FISA (rowing) mandates a life ban[2].

1 See *World Anti-Doping Code Explanatory Document C-103/01-0.5* (Lausanne 2002): 'The stakeholders may decide that total uniformity of sanctions is not required but that in addition to agreement on the common principles underlying the imposition of sanctions, certain minimum or maximum periods of suspension for particular offences will be mandated by the Code'.

2 See respectively IWF Anti-Doping Policy, cl 14.2(a); FINA Doping Control, cl DC 9.2(a); FISA Rules of Racing and Related Bye-Laws, cl 9.3.1(a).

E4.339 Indeed, even the two-year minimum is not sacrosanct. The delegates at the World Anti-Doping Conference representing football and cycling insisted that a carve-out be included in the Lausanne Declaration, and subsequently in the Olympic Movement Anti-Doping Code, allowing for downward departure from the two-year minimum 'based on specific, exceptional circumstances to be evaluated in the first instance by the competent IF bodies …'[1]. So, for example, the FIS Doping Rules provide that the sanction for an 'inadvertent use of doping' (first offence) shall be a three-month ban, whatever substance was found in the sample[2].

1 Olympic Movement Anti-Doping Code, Chap Two, Art 3(b)(iii).

2 FIS Disciplinary Procedures for Doping Offences (FIS Medical Guide 2001/02), p 36. In football, Dutch internationals Edgar Davids and Frank de Boer were banned for only three months and 12 months (subsequently reduced to 11 weeks) respectively for use of nandrolone.

E4.340 One respected commentator has suggested that the Olympic Movement Anti-Doping Code guidelines now provide a benchmark comparative guide when considering the proportionality of the sanctions imposed under a particular sport's anti-doping programme, ie that federation's sanctions will be considered prima facie disproportionate if markedly greater than the sanction that the Olympic Movement Anti-Doping Code would apply in the same circumstances[1].

1 McLaren, 'Doping Sanctions: What Penalty?' [2002] 2 ISLR 23, 32. However, he limits this to first offences, saying that 'once an athlete commits the same infraction twice, any penalty imposed by an IF will generally be deemed proportionate'.

E4.341 As noted above, CAS panels have been persuaded to depart from fixed sanctions set out in the relevant rules, usually on the ground that the fixed sanction was not proportionate to the seriousness of the offence, and specifically did not reflect the relative lack of moral guilt of the athlete concerned[1].

1 See para E4.133. See also Griffith-Jones QC, 'The Need for a World-wide Anti-Doping Role' (2002) 5(1) Sports Law Bulletin 2 (suggesting the Human Rights Act 1998 might provide the basis for a similar agreement under English law). Cf *R (Lichniak) v Home Secretary* [2002] QB 296, CA, in which the Court of Appeal rejected an analogous challenge to the statute mandating life imprisonment for murder, but only because such 'mandatory' sentences were in reality indeterminate (and therefore discretionary) and individualised.

Cf UK Sport Model Rules and Guidelines for Anti-Doping, r 12: 'The funding sanction applied by the Sports Councils is fixed and mandatory (subject to appeal) to ensure consistency in the UK as required by the Human Rights Act'.

E4.342 The draft WADA Code provisions on disciplinary sanctions The draft WADA code contains the following provisions on sanctions:

(a) for violations involving the presence or use of a prohibited substance or method, or refusal to submit to a doping test, a two-year ban for the first offence and a life ban for the second offence, unless the substance involved was a specified stimulant[1], and the athlete can 'clearly establish that the use of a specified stimulant was for therapeutic purposes and was not intended to enhance sport performance', in which case the ban will be between zero and six months for a first offence, six and 24 months for a second offence and two years to life for a third offence[2];

(b) for failing to provide proper whereabouts information for out-of-competition testing and/or missing such a test, a ban of between three and 24 months[3]; and

(c) in addition, 'parties accepting the Code may, at their discretion, choose to adopt rules imposing additional sanctions for anti-doping rule violations which are appropriate to the circumstances of the violation and the nature of the sport including: disqualification beyond the periods set forth in Article 8.8.3 from participation on national teams or from future competitions which they control or for which they establish eligibility criteria; recovery of costs incurred in the administration of anti-doping rule violation proceedings; fines; revocation of other rights or privileges during disqualification; and required testing prior to reinstatement'[4].

1 Ie one of the stimulants identified on the prohibited list as being 'particularly susceptible to inadvertent use because of their general availability and which are less likely to be successfully abused as doping agents': Draft World Anti-Doping Code, E-Version 1.0, issued May 2002, at para 8.8.3.1.
2 Draft World Anti-Doping Code, E-Version 1.0, issued May 2002, at paras 8.8.3.1 and 8.8.4.1.
3 Draft World Anti-Doping Code, E-Version 1.0, issued May 2002, at para 8.8.4.3.
4 Draft World Anti-Doping Code, E-Version 1.0, issued May 2002, at para 8.8.9.

E4.343 Practicalities The rules should include a provision specifying when any suspension imposed on an athlete is to begin. For example, it may start on the date that the verdict is published[1]. Where an athlete has been serving a provisional suspension pending the verdict, however, fairness suggests he should be credited for that time[2].

1 See eg reg 16 of the IRB Regulations Relating to the Game (2002).
2 See eg IAAF Rule 60.2(a)(i), 60.2(b)(ii); Tarasti *Legal Solutions in International Doping Cases* (SEP Editrice 2000) at p 103; draft World Anti-Doping Code, E-Version 1.0, issued 10 June 2002, at para 8.6.6.

E4.344 On the other hand, the rules may be concerned to ensure that a sanction is not rendered ineffective because all or most of it falls during the close season[1].

1 See eg *UCI v Mason*, CAS 98/212, award dated 24 February 1999, para 23, *Digest of CAS Awards II 1998–2000* (2002, Kluwer), pp 274, 281.

E4.345 Another practical question that the rules need to address is exactly what the suspension means. Clearly, it means that the athlete is ineligible to compete in sanctioned events. But does it extend further than that? For example, is the athlete allowed to coach others at sanctioned events? If this issue is not addressed in the rules, embarrassment can result when suspended athletes turn up at sanctioned events in some other capacity[1].

1 A good example of a nailed-down clause is DC 9.4 of FINA's Doping Control Rules, which provides that '"suspension" shall mean that the individual sanctioned shall not participate in any activities of FINA or any of its Member federations, in any discipline, in international competition, including acting as a competitor, delegate, coach, leader, physician or other representative of FINA or a Member federation'.

Cf UCI Anti-Doping Examination Regulations, Art 129 bis (suspension renders athlete ineligible for participation in competitions – which does not stop a banned cyclist from coaching in the sport).

E4.346 Sanctions for trafficking The Lausanne Declaration stated that '[m]ore severe sanctions shall apply to coaches and officials guilty of violations of the Olympic Movement Anti-Doping Code'[1]. In fact, the Olympic Movement Anti-Doping Code provides for life-bans for trafficking[2], whereas WADA's draft Code imposes a ban of four years to life[3].

1 Declaration on Doping in Sport (World Anti-Doping Conference, Lausanne 1999), para 3.
2 Olympic Movement Anti-Doping Code (Lausanne 2001), Chap Two, Art 3(6). See also IAAF Rule 60.2(c) (same).
3 Draft World Anti-Doping Code, E-Version 1.0, issued May 2002 at para 8.8.4.2.

E4.347 FINA's rules for swimming leave the sanction for trafficking to the discretion of its Doping Panel[1]. When Chinese swimmer Yuan Yuan and her coach Zhou Zhewen were discovered trying to smuggle large quantities of synthetic human growth hormone into Australia for the 1998 World Championships, each of them was found guilty of trafficking in a prohibited substance and banned from participation in the sport for 15 years[2].

1 FINA Doping Control Rules, cl DC 9.2 (f).
2 Gardiner *Sports Law* (2nd edn, 2001, Cavendish Publishing), p 313.

E4.348 Of course, trafficking in prohibited substances may also be a criminal offence in the jurisdiction where the trafficking takes place. The criminal authorities do not have power to disqualify a convicted trafficker from participation in a particular sport, so that criminal conviction and sanction does not render sports disciplinary proceedings redundant. However, the Anti-Doping Officer would have to exercise care in such circumstances, including even potentially suspending his investigation pending the outcome of the criminal case, in order to avoid prejudicing the athlete's rights.

(c) Collateral sanctions

E4.349 Public funding The UK is required, as a signatory to the Anti-Doping Convention, to:

> take appropriate steps to withhold the grant of subsidies from public funds, for training purposes, to individual sportsmen and sportswomen who have been suspended following a doping offence in sports during the period of their suspension[1].

1 Anti-Doping Convention (Council of Europe – European Treaties – ETS No 135), Art 4.3b.

E4.350 Under UK Sport's rules, therefore, an athlete who was receiving lottery funding will lose that funding, either temporarily or permanently. Specifically:

(i) where the offence is a first one and involves ephedrine, phenylpropanolamine, pseudoephedrine, caffeine, strychnine or related compounds, public funding is cut for one year[1];

(ii) where the offence is:
  (a) a second offence involving one of the foregoing substances; or
  (b) a first offence relating to any stimulant, narcotic or 'class of drug subject to certain restrictions' or 'any other substance specifically prohibited or restricted by the rules of the governing body';

  funding is cut for two years[2].

(iii) where the offence involves:
  (a) a third offence relating to ephedrine, phenylpropanolamine, pseudoephedrine, caffeine, strychnine or related compounds;
  (b) a second offence relating to any stimulant, narcotic or 'class of drug subject to certain restrictions' or 'any other substance specifically prohibited or restricted by the rules of the governing body';
  (c) an anabolic agent, peptide hormone, mimetic, analogue or any doping method; or
  (d) a refusal to submit to a test;

  then funding is cut for life[3].

1 UK Sport *Anti-Doping Policy* at para IX(d) and at Annex A, para 42.
2 UK Sport *Anti-Doping Policy* at para IX(c) and at Annex A, para 41.
3 UK Sport *Anti-Doping Policy* at para IX(b) and at Annex A, para 40.

E4.351 In each case, there is discretion to waive or vary the withholding of funding in the case of 'exceptional circumstances', but normally the 'express support' of the governing body will be required before any request by the athlete to exercise such discretion will be considered[1].

1 UK Sport *Anti-Doping Policy* at para XI.

E4.352 Access to public facilities UK Sport's rules provide that:

> [a] governing body shall not allow an athlete, coach or other individual banned for a doping offence to participate in a Sports Council funded programme, except where these are specifically part of the agreed rehabilitation programme in particular the independent counselling services provided through the ACE programme …[1]

1 UK Sport *Anti-Doping Policy*, Annex A, para 42.

E4.353 UK Sport's rules also provide that an athlete who is ineligible for funding by reason of a doping conviction is not entitled:

> to use lottery funded facilities, to participate in lottery funded training sessions or receive support services available through the World Class Performance Programme, except where these are specifically part of the agreed rehabilitation programme[1].

1 UK Sport *Anti-Doping Policy*, Annex A, para 45. Australia similarly denies anyone serving a doping suspension access to state-aided sports facilities. Linford Christie was therefore unable to train his athletes at such facilities in the run-up to the 2000 Olympics in Sydney.

E4.354 International representation Under the rules of the British Olympic Association, an athlete who is convicted of a doping offence is automatically banned for life from representing Great Britain in the Olympics[1]. There are provisions, however, for reinstatement[2].

1 BOA Byelaw of the National Olympic Committee: Eligibility for Membership of the GB Olympic Team of Persons Found Guilty of a Doping Offence.
2 See para E4.372 et seq.

E Costs

E4.355 Under UK Sport's model code, the original disciplinary committee and any appeal panel each has discretion to order one party to pay some or all of the other party's costs[1]. This would obviously assist an athlete who was successful in defending doping charges, but would further burden an unsuccessful one[2].

1 UK Sport *Anti-Doping Policy*, Annex A, para 37.
2 See UK Sport *Anti-Doping Policy*, Annex A, commentary following para 31: 'Regard should be given to any costs that might be incurred by the individual and care taken to balance the provision of a fair hearing with the necessary costs involved in a thorough investigation of the evidence'.

E4.356 On appeal to the Court of Arbitration for Sport, once again there is a cost-shifting rule, specifically based upon 'the outcome of the proceedings, as well as the conduct and financial resources of the parties'[1].

1 CAS Code of Sports-Related Arbitration, r 65.3.

F Appeals

E4.357 Mr Justice Lightman has suggested that in the absence of a provision for an appeal, a serious question would arise as to whether an anti-doping programme could be 'materially deficient and unfair and … [therefore] in unreasonable restraint of trade'[1].

1 *Wilander and Novacek v Tobin and Jude* [1997] 1 Lloyd's Rep 195, QBD (Lightman J).

E4.358 The Anti-Doping Convention requires its signatories to 'encourage' sports bodies to apply 'agreed international principles of … justice', including 'clear and enforceable provisions for appealing against any judgments made'[1]. And the sports governing body signatories to the Lausanne Declaration committed to provide that decisions of their internal tribunals could be appealed to the Court of Arbitration for Sport[2].

1 Anti-Doping Convention of 16 November 1989 (Council of Europe – European Treaties – ETS No 135), Art 7.

2 Declaration on Doping in Sport (World Anti-Doping Conference, Lausanne 1999).

E4.359 It is therefore virtually standard nowadays for anti-doping programmes to provide that the decisions of a first instance tribunal – as to liability, or sanction, or both – may be appealed to a further appellate body, whether an internal one or (more likely) an external one, in particular the Court of Arbitration for Sport in Lausanne[1].

1 See eg Olympic Movement Anti-Doping Code (Lausanne 2001), Chap Three, Art One: 'Any Participant affected by a decision rendered in application of this Code by the IOC, an [International Federation], an [National Olympic Committee] or other body may appeal from that decision to the Court of Arbitration for Sport, in accordance with the provisions applicable before such court'.

See also UK Sport's *Anti-Doping Policy*, Annex A, para 32: 'Where the decision of the Disciplinary Committee is disputed by either party then (subject to any appeal requirement by the relevant International Federation under its rules) the dispute may be referred to an independent Appeal Panel formed by the governing body, or by agreement between the parties to an independent body such as the Sports Dispute Resolution Panel or Court of Arbitration for Sport'.

Interestingly, the Draft World Anti-Doping Code (E-Version 1.0, issued May 2002, p 27, n 1) designates CAS as the exclusive appeal body but states that 'various issues still need to be resolved with CAS before it is designated as the exclusive appellate body under the Code'. It also provides that not only the athlete, the athlete's National Olympic Committee, national federation and national anti-doping organisation but also any anti-doping agency involved in the proceedings, the international federation, the IOC and WADA may appeal a decision (Draft Code, para 8.9.2), and that 'CAS decisions shall be subject to judicial review as provided by Swiss law': (Draft Code, para 8.9.3).

E4.360 An athlete found to have committed a doping offence should consider his appeal options carefully. The appeal mechanism may provide a ready means to clear one's name, even if the appellate body may be limited in the relief it may grant and therefore demands for compensation have to be taken to the courts. For example, Diane Modahl appealed successfully against her doping conviction to an Independent Appeal Tribunal set up by the British Athletics Federation. Her subsequent action was not a challenge to the decision but rather an attempt to obtain compensation[1].

1 See paras A3.10, n 2 and A3.122 to A3.125.

E4.361 There may also be tactical advantages to filing an appeal. The CAS appeal procedures give the Court of Arbitration for Sport power to suspend enforcement of the decision being appealed pending a ruling[1]. This may allow an athlete found guilty of doping and suspended just before a big event to compete in that event (subject to revocation of results achieved at the event of the doping finding is subsequently upheld)[2]. Contrast that with the IAAF's rules, which allow its Council, if it has decided to refer a member association's acquittal of an athlete to the Court of Arbitration for Sport (formerly to the IAAF Arbitration Panel[3]), to suspend the athlete pending the CAS decision[4].

1 CAS Code of Sports-Related Arbitration, R37.

2 For example, in *Lehtinen v FINA*, CAS 95/142, award dated 14 February 1996, the Court of Arbitration for Sport suspended enforcement of a two year ban, enabling Mr Lehtinen to participate in the 1995 European Championships in Vienna. The decision does not reveal the reasons for the interim ruling. However, the fact that the prohibited substance was salbutamol and the athlete was a confirmed asthmatic who had simply failed to make the proper declarations may have had something to do with it.

See also *Haga v FIM*, 2000/A/281, award dated 22 December 2000, *Digest of CAS Awards II 1998–2000* (2002, Kluwer), pp 410, 412 (relevant issues were likelihood on success or merits, irreparable harm if stay not granted, and balance of interests; stay granted because reasons for decision were not available and so it could not be determined whether decision violated FIM rules or rules of law and therefore whether appeal was likely to succeed on the merits).

In order to filter out unmeritorious appeals, UK Sport's model programme includes a requirement that the appellant obtain permission to appeal from the Chair of the Appeal Panel, which permission will not be granted when 'insufficient grounds' are shown for an appeal. UK Sport's *Anti-Doping Policy*, Annex A, para 33.

3 See Reeb 'The IAAF to recognise the jurisdiction of the Court of Arbitration for Sport' [2001] 4 ISLR 246.

4 See IAAF Rule 59.4.

E4.362 On an appeal to the Court of Arbitration for Sport, if the relevant rules do not specify the standard of review of the decision being appealed[1], then the CAS panel will require an athlete to show that:

> the rules adopted by … [the relevant sports governing body] … are contrary to general principles of law, [or that] … their application is arbitrary, or [that] the sanctions provided by the rules can be deemed excessive or unfair on their face[2].

The CAS Panel will have 'full power to review the facts and the law'[3]. There have been various instances where CAS panels have overturned doping convictions, on factual and/or legal grounds, or have reduced as disproportionate the sanction imposed by the tribunal below[4]. Of course, the governing body will often also be entitled to appeal a decision of the first instance tribunal[5], and may be able to persuade the appellate panel that the sanction should be increased[6].

1 For example, the IAAF's rules require the referring party (ie the IAAF Council or the athlete) to show that the first instance tribunal 'has misdirected itself, or otherwise reached an erroneous conclusion': IAAF Constitution Rule 21(3)(ii) and (iv).

2 *FIN/FINA*, CAS 96/157, award dated 23 April 1997, para 22, *Digest of CAS Awards 1986–1998* (Berne 1998), p 351.

3 CAS Code of Sports-Related Arbitration, Art R57.

4 See para E4.134.

5 See paras A5.150 to A5.155.

6 See eg *UCI v Abdoujaparov*, CAS 98/175, award of 5 April 1998 (ban increased from six to 12 months).

G Finality

E4.363 A decision by the 'final' appellate body should not, in every circumstance, be regarded as final. For one thing, the international governing body may reserve the right to review the decision of a disciplinary tribunal (including an appellate tribunal) convened by one of its member associations. For example, in the *Visagie* case, where a South African Rugby Football Union doping tribunal cleared an athlete who had tested positive for nandrolone, firstly on grounds of irregularities in the testing procedures, and secondly because of controversy over the cut-off for endogenous production of nandrolone[1], the International Rugby Board (IRB) relied on such a provision in its rules to review all of the documentation from the original proceedings and the appeal proceedings. It subsequently announced it would not refer the matter to an IRB Committee for further consideration, because of the irregularities in the testing procedures, but it specifically endorsed the IOC's two ng/ml threshold for 19-norandnosterone, and criticised the South African Rugby Football Union for causing 'unnecessary' difficulties by adopting anti-doping rules that differed from the IRB's own rules[2].

1 *SA Appeal Tribunal split on Visagie verdict* www.planet-rugby.com (15 May 2001). See para E4.296.

2 *IRB decision puts Visagie in the clear* www.planet-rugby.com (31 July 2001).

E4.364 Somewhat similarly, the IAAF Rules give the IAAF the right to appeal (formerly to an IAAF Arbitration Panel, now to the Court of Arbitration for Sport) decisions made by member national associations' doping tribunals exonerating an athlete 'where … the IAAF believes that in the conduct or conclusions of such hearing the member has misdirected itself, or otherwise reached an erroneous conclusion'[1]. Pending resolution of that appeal, the athlete is automatically suspended from competition[2].

1 IAAF Rule 21.3(iii). Historically, that rule provided for the appeal to be made to an IAAF Arbitration Panel. The decisions of that panel form an important part of sports anti-doping jurisprudence. See generally Tarasti *Legal Solutions in International Doping Cases* (SEP Editrice 2000). It was amended in 2001 to provide that the appeal will lie to the Court of Arbitration for Sport. See Reeb 'The IAAF to recognise the jurisdiction of the Court of Arbitration for Sport' [2001] 4 ISLR 246.

See also Rule C 17.7 of the FINA Constitution ('Where a Member Federation has held a hearing under DC8, and the FINA Executive believes that in the conduct or conclusions of such hearing the Member Federation has misinterpreted FINA Rules or otherwise reached an erroneous conclusion, the Executive may call for a hearing before a Doping Panel').

Cf FIS Doping Rules, Rule 7, para 23 (FIS Medical Guide 2001/02): 'sanctions [imposed by a National Ski Association] shall be reviewed at the next meeting of the FIS Council. At this meeting, the FIS Council will decide to accept or amend the sanction imposed by the National Ski Association in relation to the FIS sanction catalogue. Where sanctions have been amended, the decision of the FIS Council is final and binding upon all National Ski Associations. An appeal against the decision of the FIS statutory bodies may be made to CAS'.

2 IAAF Rule 59.4.

E4.365 The IAAF's use of these provisions to challenge decisions made by the US domestic governing body USA Track & Field is well-documented[1]. Prior to the 2000 Sydney Olympics, however, the IAAF also referred acquittals of several British athletes by UK Athletics' doping tribunal to the IAAF Arbitration Panel[2]. Each of those acquittals was overturned by the IAAF Arbitration Panel[3].

1 See generally *Report of the Independent International Review Commission on Doping Control – U.S.A. Track & Field* (11 July 2001), reproduced on www.wada.org.

2 Apparently, the IAAF wished to avoid a repeat of its embarrassment at the Atlanta Games in 1996, where each of Australian sprinter Dean Capobianco and Italian high jumper Antonella Bevilacqua competed despite having tested positive for banned substances, after their national governing bodies' respective disciplinary tribunals ruled in their favour. (Capobianco's tribunal ruled that the chain of custody procedures had been flawed; Bevilacqua's tribunal waived any ban because it was

persuaded she had taken the drug by mistake). The IAAF could not get the cases before the IAAF Arbitration Panel prior to the Games. After the Games, the IAAF Arbitration Panel found each of them guilty of doping offences, and gave Capobianco a four-year ban and Bevilacqua a three-month ban. Similarly, when USA Track & Field cleared Mary Decker Slaney of doping charges notwithstanding her positive test for excessive testosterone, the IAAF Council referred the case to the IAAF Arbitration Tribunal, which imposed a retrospective two-year ban. See Tarasti *Legal Solutions in International Doping Cases* (SEP Editrice 2000), at pp 143–46 (Bevilacqua), pp 147–150 (Capobianco) and pp 155–164 (Decker Slaney).

3 See para E4.298.

E4.366 In 1999, GB athlete Dougie Walker launched a High Court challenge to:

(a) the IAAF's right to refer the decision of UK Athlete's (UKA) Disciplinary Committee exonerating Walker to an IAAF Arbitration Panel; and
(b) UK Athletics' ability to comply with any IAAF Arbitration Panel ruling overturning its decision[1].

Walker advanced two grounds for the challenge:

(1) that there was no contract between him and the IAAF that gave the IAAF Arbitration Panel jurisdiction to declare him ineligible; and
(2) that on the basis of double jeopardy principles, the final decision of UK Athletics' internal appeal tribunal could not be overturned.

UK Athletics contended that its decision to exonerate Walker was correct, but also accepted that the IAAF did have the power to refer the matter to arbitration. UK Athletics therefore defended both the IAAF's challenge to its decision and Walker's challenge to its ability to abide by the result of the IAAF's challenge. The IAAF sought first to escape the jurisdiction of the English Court on the basis that it was based in Monaco. This was rejected by Toulson J The matter came on for a hearing before Hallet J as an application for an injunction restraining UK Athletics and the IAAF from holding an appeal arbitration or from acting on the result. The IAAF claimed that the athlete should be suspended pending the IAAF arbitration hearing on the basis of IAAF Rule 59.4, which stated that even where an athlete had been exonerated by his national federation, he could be suspended by the IAAF pending the IAAF's challenge to the exoneration. Both Walker and UKA contended that that rule could not apply to Walker, because it had been introduced after his offence and could not validly be applied retrospectively. Hallet J in argument showed support for this contention. The matter was settled on the basis that Walker withdrew his allegation that the IAAF could not challenge UK Athletics' decision, and the IAAF accepted that pending an arbitration award actually overturning UK Athletics' decision, Walker could not be suspended. This left the athlete free to seek to qualify for the 2000 Sydney Olympics. For fitness reasons, however, and because he had nearly served out the two year ban that an adverse IAAF arbitration award would re-impose, Walker decided not to run. This decision proved wise, as the IAAF arbitration decision went against Walker and UK Athletics[2].

1 *Walker v UKA and IAAF* (7 July 2000, unreported), QBD (Toulson J), 25 July 2000 (Hallet J). See para A3.124.

2 See para E4.298.

E4.367 Apart from any further internal disciplinary proceedings, there is always the possibility of challenging a decision of a disciplinary tribunal in the courts. This issue is addressed in some detail elsewhere in this work[1].

1 See para E4.5, n 1.

H Recognition of sanctions

E4.368 Usually, a suspension imposed by an international federation will be automatically binding upon and have to be recognised and enforced by every member federation, so that the suspension has a global effect throughout the sport[1].

1 See eg IAAF Rule 61.2: 'Where doping control has been carried out by the IAAF, every Member shall recognise the results of such doping control and shall take all necessary action to render such decision effective'. See also FIS Doping Rules, r 7, para 24 (FIS Medical Guide 2001/02).

E4.369 A suspension imposed by a competent internal tribunal of one member federation for a doping conviction will also usually be recognised and enforced by all member federations, either directly or via adoption by the international federation[1].

1 See eg ITF Anti-Doping Programme 2002, cl W: 'In the event of any positive result or any other Doping Offences obtained in the course of anti-doping tests carried out by or on behalf of a Member … [p]rovided that the Member's doping control programme substantially complies with the provisions of the ITF Anti-Doping Programme, the ITF Executive Director, Medical will refer the Case to the Review Board for consideration on behalf of the ITF … After consideration the Review Board will make its recommendations to the ITF. If the Review Board recommends that sanctions imposed by the Member be recognised by the ITF, the ITF shall be entitled to uphold the penalty on behalf of all its Members'.

Cf FIS Doping Rules, r 7, para 25 (FIS Medical Guide 2001/02): 'The FIS Council may recognise the results of doping control carried out by a sporting body other than the FIS, with rules and procedures different from those of the FIS, provided that the testing was properly carried out and the rules of the governing body conducting the test afford sufficient protection to the athlete'.

E4.370 Indeed, there is no reason in theory why one sport should not be able to recognise and give effect to a suspension imposed on a participant by a governing body in another sport, provided that the doping rules and standards of the two sports are not materially different. Indeed, the World Anti-Doping Agency is heavily promoting the adoption of rules to that express effect. Its draft Code provides:

> Subject to the right of appeal provided in Article 8.9, the sample collection and handling procedures, result management and hearing process and results (excluding any non-mandatory sanctions imposed pursuant to Article 8.8.9) of any party accepting the Code which are consistent with the Code and are within that party's competence, shall be recognised and respected by all other parties accepting the Code. Parties may recognize the actions of other bodies which have not accepted the Code if the rules of those bodies are otherwise consistent with the Code[1].

The Rugby Football Union already has a rule to that effect, which it applied in order to ban Perris Wilkins from participation in the sport of rugby union, following on from his ban from athletics by UK Athletics for using epimethandenione[2].

1 Draft World Anti-Doping Code, E-Version 1.0, issued 10 June 2002 at para 5.12.6. See Vrijman, 'Harmonisation: A Commentary on Current Issues and Problems' in *Drugs and Doping in Sports* (2001, Cavendish), pp 147, 159.

2 (2002) Daily Telegraph, 27 September, p 52.

E4.371 Difficulties can arise when a governmental agency claims authority to ban an athlete from participation in the sport within that agency's territorial jurisdiction, as is the case with, for example, France's Council for the Prevention of and Fight Against Doping. The profound clash in competing jurisdictions that can arise –

most governing bodies would claim the exclusive right to impose such 'sporting' sanctions within their sports, yet most governmental agencies will insist on applying 'the law of the land' – are usually resolved by the signing of a 'protocol' full of more or less workable compromises[1].

1 See para E4.41.

I Reinstatement

E4.372 Rehabilitation of transgressors is an important goal. Indeed, UK Sport requires governing bodies to include a provision in their anti-doping programmes allowing athletes who have been suspended from competition for a doping offence to apply for reinstatement either during or at the end of the ban:

> The governing body shall publish conditions of eligibility for reinstatement, including whether the athlete is required to participate in a programme of no notice testing and/or rehabilitation and involvement in education programmes throughout the period of suspension. This requirement shall be presented to the athlete at the time of notifying the penalty and the athlete's written agreement obtained to participate in the eligibility programme[1].

1 See eg ITF Anti-Doping Programme 2002, cl P(1)(c) (providing that an athlete will be required to pass a certain number of drugs tests prior to being reinstated). Cf IAAF Constitution, r 57.6 (three tests during suspension and one test for full range of substances just before end of suspension).

E4.373 Even governing bodies not dependent on public funding tend to follow this approach[1].

1 See eg IAAF Constitution, r 60.7.

E4.374 Some sports provide for automatic reinstatement upon completion of the suspension and satisfaction of any conditions, without the need for further application or showing[1]. UK Sport mandates the following procedure, to be followed whether the reinstatement is sought during or at the end of the ban:

> An athlete who has been suspended or banned from competition for a doping offence may apply for reinstatement either during or at the completion of the period of suspension or ban. The governing body shall appoint an independent tribunal to consider the application and normally require evidence of full compliance with the reinstatement conditions stated in the rules or procedures of that governing body and the International Federation to which it is affiliated. Members of the independent tribunal should be individuals who have no conflict of interest with the issue or the outcome and who have not been involved in the matter or dispute at any previous stage. UK Sport shall be notified about athletes who have applied for reinstatement and the conditions applying and the decision reached[2].

1 BOA Bye-Law of the National Olympic Committee: Eligibility for Membership of the GB Olympic Team of Persons Found Guilty of a Doping Offence, para 4. An alternative ground set out in that clause is that the doping offence was 'minor', ie carrying a suspension of no more than six months under the Olympic Members Anti-Doping Code.

2 UK Sport *Anti-Doping Policy*, Annex A, para 45. Where it is the international federation that considers the application, it could be deemed to be sitting as judge in its own cause.

E4.375 The IAAF's anti-doping rules also allow an athlete to apply (to its Council) for early reinstatement, but the burden is a heavy one:

> In exceptional circumstances, an athlete may apply to the Council for reinstatement before the IAAF's period of ineligibility has expired. Where an athlete has provided substantial assistance to a Member in the course of an inquiry into doping carried out by that

> Member, this will normally be regarded by the Council as constituting exceptional circumstances. A decision on exceptional circumstances shall be made only if the athlete is able to present three negative tests conducted by the Member or the IAAF, with a period of at least one month between each test. However it is emphasised that only truly exceptional circumstances will justify any reduction[1] …
>
> It is not possible to state comprehensively the circumstances in which the discretion to reinstate will be exercised by the Council. However, the Council will not regard as exceptional for the purposes of Rule 60 an allegation that the prohibited substance was given to an athlete by another person without his knowledge, an allegation that a prohibited substance was taken by mistake or a suggestion that medication was prescribed by a doctor in ignorance of the fact that it contained a prohibited substance. The Council may, however, consider that exceptional circumstances exist where an athlete has provided substantial evidence or assistance to a national federation or the IAAF in the course of disciplinary or legal proceedings brought against those dealing in prohibited substances or coaches or athletes representatives who are taking or inciting or assisting others to take such substances[2]

1 IAAF Constitution, r 60.9.

2 IAAF Procedural Guidelines for Doping Control (2000 edn), cl 4.1. For example, in June 2001, the IAAF granted early reinstatement to GB athlete Mark Richardson, before the end of his ban for nandrolone, based on his commitment to lecture to other athletes on the dangers of taking supplements that might be contaminated with prohibited substances.

E4.376 It has been suggested that the Court of Arbitration for Sport might effectively introduce a 'reinstatement' provision by the back-door when the sport itself has not included one in its rules, by applying a federation's fixed sanction:

> subject to the proviso that after a prescribed period of time an athlete would be able to apply to CAS for a reinstatement hearing … The athlete would then bear the onus of proving, on a balance of probabilities, that there existed exceptional circumstances surrounding the infraction. Examples of such circumstances might include the athlete's reliance upon inaccurate information that the athlete could not have reasonably verified and new evidence that otherwise impugns the test results or the athlete's culpability. A claim that the athlete had no knowledge of having taken a banned substance would not be, alone, enough to establish an exceptional circumstance[1].

So far, this idea has not gained great momentum, and it could certainly be argued to encroach upon the sport's right to have its own rules applied and enforced without rewriting by any review body.

1 McLaren 'Doping Sanctions: What Penalty?' [2002] 2 ISLR 23 at 33.

E4.377 If it is possible to apply for early waiver of the governing body's suspension, then arguably there needs also to be similar provision for the collateral sanctions that are triggered by such a ban[1]. Indeed, UK Sport's rules contains a mechanism for early reinstatement of public funding[2]; and the British Olympic Assocation also allows an athlete to apply for reinstatement of eligibility for membership of the GB Olympic team, on the basis of 'significant mitigating circumstances'[3].

1 See para E4.349 et seq.

2 UK Sport *Anti-Doping Policy*, para XI. The athlete will have to show on the balance of probabilities that there are exceptional circumstances justifying reinstatement. The following factors will be considered: age, remorse, circumstances surrounding the infraction, experience in sport, contribution to sport, prospects for rehabilitation, prior and post-infraction conduct, co-operation with investigating bodies and length of suspension served. See commentary to UK Sport *Anti Doping Policy*, para XI.

3 BOA Bye-Law of the National Olympic Committee: Eligibility for Membership of the GB Olympic Team of Persons Found Guilty of a Doping Offence, para 4. An alternative ground set out in that clause is that the doping offence was 'minor', ie carrying a suspension of no more than six months under the Olympic Members Anti-Doping Code.

CHAPTER E5

CIVIL LIABILITY FOR ON-FIELD CONDUCT

David Griffith-Jones QC (Devereux Chambers)

Contents

1 INTRODUCTION

E5.1 When competitors and other participants enter the field of play, they remain as much subject to the law of the land as any other citizen in any other circumstances. Any persisting idea that the law's writ does not run on the playing field and that sporting sanctions alone define the limits of accountability for on the field misdemeanours, has surely been dispelled in recent years by the increasing stream of cases coming before the courts in which claimants have sought recompense for injuries sustained in the course of their sporting endeavour.

E5.2 Where sport is carried out in structured relationships enshrined in or consequent upon one or more individual contracts, disputes resulting from particular incidents may sometimes be resolved, wholly or partly, by reference to the terms of such contracts. For example, in *Brady v Sunderland AFC*[1], where a professional footballer complained that his employer, his club, had failed to provide him with adequate medical facilities and had allowed a vascular problem in his leg to go undiscovered and unheeded, leading his continuing playing to cause a career terminating injury, his primary claim (which, in the event, failed on the facts) was formulated as a breach of the club's contractual duty to take reasonable care of his health and safety. Contractual claims are generally outside the scope of this chapter, which focuses on such general rights and obligations as may be engaged by events on the playing field regardless of the extent to which the participants and any relevant third parties may have bound themselves together by contract. Whether or not relevant relationships are enshrined in contracts, events on the field of play give rise to non-contractual rights and liabilities. Indeed, in Brady, in addition to making a contractual claim, Mr Brady was able to repeat his factual complaints in pursuit of an alternative (but equally unsuccessful) claim presented in negligence. Negligence represents by far and away the most common cause of action used for claims arising from on-field conduct. Another potential tort is that of 'trespass to the person' (assault/battery), appropriate where one individual sets out to injure another. Cases asserting such a tort are rare, if only because of the practical difficulty of proving a sufficient intent to injure[2], although, at the time of going to press, the world of football is awaiting developments after publication of Roy Keane's autobiography, in which the Manchester United player is said to have admitted intending to injure Alf-Inge Haaland in a tackle during a match against Manchester City in April 2001. Keane faces not just disciplinary action by the Football Association but litigation at the suit of his victim and Manchester City.

1 (17 November 1998, unreported), CA.
2 See eg *Watson and Bradford AFC v Gray and Huddersfield Town AFC* (1998) Times, 26 November (Hooper J); and para E5.49.

E5.3 For these reasons, the primary focus of this chapter will remain on the tort of negligence, for which no such intent is required and the concept of reasonable care provides the principal touchstone. In particular, the chapter will seek to identify in relation to particular categories of person operating within sport respectively the circumstances in which a duty of care is owed, to whom and by whom any such duty is owed and the scope and limitations of any such duty. Where appropriate, certain other potential causes of action will also be considered.

2 NEGLIGENCE

A Genesis

E5.4 In 1928, the House of Lords laid the foundations of the modern law of negligence in *Donoghue v Stevenson*[1], the case arising from the unwelcome discovery in a bottle of ginger beer of the remains of a snail and the gastroenteritis which resulted from its partial ingestion. Their Lordships addressed the question of when a relationship between individuals gives rise to a duty of care, breach of which sounds in damages. The result was their formulation of the classic 'neighbour principle'. In one of the most enduring statements of legal principle known to the common law, Lord Atkin said[2]:

> The liability for negligence … is no doubt based upon a general public sentiment of moral wrongdoing for which the offender must pay. But acts or omissions which any moral code would censure cannot in a practical world be treated so as to give a right to every person injured by them to demand relief. In this way rules of law arise which limit the range of complainants and the extent of their remedy. The rule that you are to love your neighbour becomes in law, you must not injure your neighbour; and the lawyer's question, *Who is my neighbour? receives a restricted reply. You must take reasonable care to avoid acts or omissions which you can reasonably foresee would be likely to injure your neighbour. Who then is my neighbour? The answer seems to be – persons who are so closely and directly affected by my act that I ought reasonably to have them in contemplation as being so affected when I am directing my mind to the acts or omissions which are called in question.*

In so formulating the principle, Lord Atkin gave qualified approval to the earlier statements of principle emanating from Lord Esher, firstly (as Brett MR) in *Heaven v Pender*[3] and later in *Le Lievre v Gould*[4]. In the former case, he had said[5]:

> Whenever one person is by circumstances placed in such a position with regard to another that every one of ordinary sense who did think would at once recognise that if he did not use ordinary care and skill in his own conduct with regard to those circumstances he would cause danger of injury to the person or property of the other, a duty arises to use ordinary care and skill to avoid such danger.

In the later case, Lord Esher had added this qualification[6]:

> If one man is near to another or is near to the property of another, a duty lies upon him not to do that which may cause a personal injury to that other, or may injure his property.

Lord Atkin took Lord Esher's qualifying remarks as being in line with the statement by AL Smith LJ in the same case[7]:

> The decision in *Heaven v Pender* was founded upon the principle that a duty to take care did arise when the person or property of one was in such proximity to the person or property of another that, if due care was not taken, damage might be done by the one to the other.

Accordingly, Lord Atkin went on to say[8]:

> I think this sufficiently states the truth, if proximity be not confined to mere physical proximity, but be used, as I think it was intended, to extend to such close and direct relations that the act complained of directly affects a person whom the person alleged to be bound to take care would know would be directly affected by his careless act.

1 [1932] AC 562.
2 [1932] AC 562 at 580.
3 (1883) 11 QBD 503.
4 [1893] 1 QB 491.
5 (1883) 11 QBD 503 at 509.
6 [1893] 1 QB 491 at 497.
7 [1893] 1 QB 491 at 504.
8 [1932] AC 562 at 581.

B The test

E5.5 There are a number of features arising from the above statements of principle. In particular:

(i) a duty of care is owed to those who ought reasonably to be in contemplation as being affected by a particular act;
(ii) the duty itself is simply to take reasonable care to avoid injury to the person or property;
(iii) because the existence and practical content of the duty and the identification of the individuals to whom the duty is owed are dependent in part on the concept of reasonableness, the particular circumstances of any given case will determine whether or not a duty is established and, if so, whether or not breach of such duty can be shown.

The third of the above three points is of particular importance when it comes to considering the issue of liability within different particular fields. It is important to keep in mind that, in all fields, the principles of law to be applied are the same. What may, however, make a difference to the result of a particular case, are the circumstances within which those principles of law fall to be determined. Hence it is often said that the categories of negligence are never closed. Fresh circumstances are always arising and will continue regularly to arise in which a decision is called for as to whether or not the duty of care exists or has been breached. Indeed, in laying down the principles, Lord Atkin well recognised that they were of a nature that cases would inevitably arise in which it would be difficult to decide upon their application[1]. The lack of scientific precision in the test, and the prominence given to the criterion of reasonableness, was reflected by Saville LJ's statement in *Marc Rich & Co v Bishop Rock Marine Co Ltd*[2]:

> It is necessary to consider the matter by enquiring about forseeability but also by considering the nature of the relationship between the parties and to be satisfied in all the circumstances it is fair just and reasonable to impose a duty of care … the so called requirements for a duty of care are not to be treated as a wholly separate but rather as convenient and helpful approaches to the pragmatic question whether a duty should be imposed in any given case[3].

1 See for example ([1932] AC 582) his comments on the potential difficulty in deciding whether or not a particular relationship is sufficiently close to give rise to the duty.
2 [1994] 1 WLR 1071 at 1077. The quoted passage was approved by Lord Steyn in the House of Lords [1996] AC 211 at 235.
3 See also *Caparo Industries v Dickman* [1990] 2 AC 605, in which the House of Lords articulated the test in three stages: (1) Is damage reasonably foreseeable? (2) Is there sufficient proximity between the parties? and (3) Is it fair just and reasonable to impose the duty?

3 NEGLIGENCE IN SPORT

E5.6 The cases tell us very clearly that, in considering issues of liability, sport is not a special case with its own discrete jurisprudence, divorced from established general principles. The position was put succinctly in 1927 by Swift J in *Cleghorn v Oldham*[1] in giving judgment for the plaintiff who had been injured when struck by the defendant's golf club during a demonstration swing:

> Games might be, and [are], the serious business of life to many people. It would be extraordinary to say that people could not recover from injuries sustained in the business of life, whether that was football, or motor racing, or any other of those pursuits which were instinctively classed as games but which everyone knew quite well to be serious business transactions for the persons engaged therein.

1 (1927) 43 TLR 465 at 466.

E5.7 The correct approach is to understand that ordinary principles apply, whilst also recognising that such principles require that, in a sporting context (as in any other context), the circumstances derived from that context go into the melting pot when judging the issues of reasonableness which are inherent within the principles themselves.

E5.8 In a sporting context, as in any other, whilst the issue of liability falls to be determined by reference to the ordinary general principles of law, it is that very context which will often fashion the decisions required in the application of those legal principles. Hence the decision on liability in relation to a blow inflicted by a punch or a kick may be different where the blow is landed in the context of some sporting conflict, in comparison with an identical blow inflicted on another occasion, such as in a public house. If, in an otherwise comparable situation, liability is to arise in the public house, but not on the playing field, the reason for the distinction in treatment lies not in the fact that different rules or principles of law are being applied in the two cases, but rather in the fact that the application of the principles of law involved depends upon the particular circumstances of the case being judged. This is because the principles of law are framed in terms of reasonableness and themselves require that all relevant circumstances are taken into consideration in their application.

A Changing values

E5.9 Another feature of the central role of the concept of reasonableness within the established legal principles is that, because reasonableness depends upon all the circumstances, individual judgments as to what is reasonable may change with time. What was regarded as reasonable in years gone by, may later be deemed unreasonable (or vice versa) because of the changing times and the different circumstances which they may bring. This results in the possibility that, whereas a given case may have given rise to no liability in the past, liability may nevertheless be established in a similar case today. This is not because different principles are applied today, but because the circumstances in which the principles are applied (and in particular the public's perceptions of what is and is not acceptable behaviour) have changed. This may explain why, for example, there has been an increase in recent times in the number of claims for damages arising from incidents occurring in the sporting arena. In the past, violence on the playing field may have been regarded as simply part and parcel of the game and something to be accepted to a far greater extent than is now the case. That such violent conduct within a sporting context is now more generally deprecated is one of the circumstances likely to influence the judges called upon to determine whether particular instances give rise to legal redress.

B The (sporting) circumstances are crucial

E5.10 It follows that it is fundamental to a proper understanding of the law of negligence to appreciate that the context of any incident being judged will help determine whether or not a duty of care can be established and, if so, whether or not it has been breached. The particular results of 'sports cases' which have come before the courts have depended in part upon the very sporting context within which the incidents concerned have occurred. In short, in 'sports cases', decisions on the issues of liability are likely to be fashioned by the particular sporting context within which they fall to be judged.

E5.11 It also follows that the application of established legal principles in a 'sports case' requires, first and foremost, an examination of those features of the sport in question which serve to identify the relevant sporting context within which such principles require to be applied. Such features will almost invariably have a significant bearing on the determination of the issues on which such a case depends. In a celebrated case in which the liability of a rugby referee was examined, *Smoldon v Whitworth*[1], the Court of Appeal reviewed the authorities and again confirmed the principle in terms which, although related to the facts of the particular case before the court, are of general application:

> The level of care required is that which is appropriate in all the circumstances, *and the circumstances are of crucial importance*. Full account must be taken of the factual context in which [a referee exercises his functions] …

1 [1997] ELR 115; on appeal [1997] ELR 249, CA.

E5.12 The point was particularly well illustrated by the recent decision of the Court of Appeal in the boxer, Michael Watson's, claim against his governing body arising out of the serious injuries which he sustained in and as a consequence of his fight with Chris Eubank. In *Watson v British Boxing Board of Control*[1], the Court of Appeal had to consider, for the first time, in what circumstances, if at all, a sports governing body owed a duty of care to a competitor to minimise the consequences of personal injury sustained in following the sport within its jurisdiction. Relying upon the particular circumstances in which the British Boxing Board of Control was able to enjoy almost total control over the conduct of the sport of professional boxing, the Court of Appeal had little difficulty in holding that the BBBC, in its exercise of that control, owed a duty to the boxers to ensure that proper medical facilities were in place to deal appropriately with any foreseeable injury sustained during the bout. That the Court of Appeal arrived at a decision which was fact specific and was not intending to lay down a principle of general application that, in all circumstances, all sports governing bodies owed a duty of care to the participants in their sports was made expressly clear by Lord Phillips MR, who gave the leading judgment[2].

1 [2001] QB 1134.
2 [2001] QB 1134 at at 1163.

E5.13 In the following parts of this chapter, therefore, although particular sections are devoted, as a matter of convenience, to the liability of particular categories of person within particular sporting relationships respectively, it should be remembered that, when it comes to issues of negligence, the *principles* to be applied are the same in each case. It follows that statements of principle in cases dealing with particular sporting relationships are likely to be worthy of application to other types of such relationship. Equally, it should be remembered that the features of a particular type of sporting relationship may well influence the particular decision in the application of such principles.

E5.14 In the context of professional sport it should also be remembered that, where an individual is accused of negligence whilst engaging in sport, he may not be the only potential defendant. In particular, if he was acting in the course of his employment by another, that other, additionally, is likely to have to accept any liability which may be established, under the ordinary principles of vicarious liability[1]. This may be of particular importance in circumstances where it is the employer alone who carries any relevant insurance. Indeed, the all enveloping embrace of the doctrine of vicarious liability as most recently expounded in cases such as *Lister v Hesley Hall*[2], suggests that an employer may now be held liable even for the deliberate assaults of his employee if committed during the latter's sporting endeavour on behalf of the employer. This was certainly the result in *Rodgers v Bugden & Canterbury-Bankstown*[3], an Australian case involving an assault by one rugby league player upon another during a match.

1 See for example, *Watson & Bradford City AFC v Gray & Huddersfield Town AFC* (1998) Times, 26 November; para E5.49.
2 [2002] UKHL 22, [2002] 1 AC 215.
3 (1993) ATR 81 – 246. The traditional view to the contrary (see eg *Racz v Home Office* [1994] 2 AC 45; *Makanjuola v Metropolitan Police Comr* (1989) 2 Admin LR 214) may need to be revised in the light of the modern test.

4 LIABILITY OF CONTESTANTS TO SPECTATORS AND OTHER ONLOOKERS[1]

A *Wooldridge v Sumner*

E5.15 In a seminal case, with important implications for issues of liability in many different types of sporting circumstances, the Court of Appeal considered the scope of a contestant's duty in *Wooldridge v Sumner*[2], a case where a horse competing in the Horse of the Year Show at the White City had bolted from the arena and into the spectators, injuring a photographer. The photographer sued the rider in negligence. In his judgment, Diplock LJ highlighted the remarkable fact that [at that time] there was:

> an almost complete dearth of judicial authority as to the duty of care owed by the actual participants to the spectators.

1 It is not unknown for a spectator to be held liable to a competitor! In *Karpow v Shave* [1975] 2 WWR 159, a spectator intervened after a fight between two competitors, one of whom was his brother. He was held liable for a punch which broke the competitor's nose. Another situation might be where a spectator negligently strays onto the course, for example in a cycling race, as has happened in the Tour de France.
2 [1963] 2 QB 43.

E5.16 The Court of Appeal looked at the circumstances of the relationship between contestant and spectator and accepted that there was a sufficient degree of proximity between them to give rise to a duty of care on the part of the contestant. On the facts, however, the court decided that there had been no breach.

E5.17 In rejecting the plaintiff's claim in negligence against the rider of the horse (and overturning the trial judge) Diplock LJ accepted that the rider had been guilty of an error of judgment, but went on[1]:

> That is not enough to constitute a breach of the duty of reasonable care which a participant owes to a spectator. In such circumstances something in the nature of a reckless disregard of the spectator's safety must be proved, and of this there is no suggestion in the evidence.

1 [1963] 2 QB 43 at 72.

B No formal requirement of recklessness

E5.18 This apparent introduction into the law of negligence in a sporting context of a requirement that, for him to be liable, the defendant should have acted with recklessness might be seen as novel. In other (non-sporting) contexts, an error of judgment or other similar lapse is often all that is required. It is, however, important to note that, properly understood, Diplock LJ was not purporting to modify the duty owed, which remained a duty simply to exercise reasonable care. Rather, he was indicating what was required, in the special circumstances of a particular type of sporting occasion, for a breach of that duty to be established. This is clear from an earlier passage, when he said[1]:

> Lord Atkin's statement of principle in *Donoghue v Stevenson* does not purport to define what is reasonable care and was directed to identifying the persons to whom the duty to take reasonable care is owed. What is reasonable care in a particular circumstance is a jury question and where, as in a case like this, there is no direct guidance or hindrance from authority it may be answered by inquiring *whether the ordinary reasonable man would say that in all the circumstances the defendant's conduct was blameworthy* … The law of negligence has always recognised that the standard of care which a reasonable man will exercise *depends upon the conditions under which the decision to avoid the act or omission relied upon as negligence has to be taken.*

1 [1963] 2 QB 43 at 66.

E5.19 In this passage, Diplock LJ was not departing from established principles so as to make recklessness a prerequisite of liability in sports cases[1]. Rather, he was simply identifying the practical content of the obligation to take reasonable care in the particular circumstances of the specific sporting context within which the issue of the defendant's liability required to be judged. This is clear from the passage where he went on to express his view as to what the reasonable man would say if asked to identify blameworthy conduct in such circumstances. He said[2]:

> A person attending a game or competition takes the risk of any damage caused to him by any act of a participant done in the course of and for the purposes of the game or competition notwithstanding that such act may involve an error of judgment or a lapse of skill, unless the participant's conduct is such as to evince a reckless disregard of the spectator's safety.

1 That recklessness is not a formal requirement of the tort of negligence in sports cases was reaffirmed by the Canadian cases *Unruh v Webber* (1994) 112 DLR (4th) 83; and *Zapf v Muckalt* (1996) 142 DLR (4th) 438. See also *Headcorn Parachute Club Ltd v Pond* QBD Transcript, 11 January 1995 (Alliott J).

2 [1963] 2 QB 43 at 68.

C The (sporting) circumstances are crucial

E5.20 In so expressing himself, Diplock LJ was doing no more than recognising that, as in all situations, the specific requirements imposed by a general obligation to exercise reasonable care depend upon all the circumstances. In the context of a competitive horse show, where the proper and accepted aim of the competitors was to attempt to win the competition, the Court of Appeal did not feel that mere errors of judgment were enough on which to found liability.

E5.21 Elsewhere in his judgment, Diplock LJ illuminated the criterion of reasonableness further, by making it clear that, in such a case, the reasonableness of the defendant's actions cannot be judged in isolation. The spectator's expectations require to be considered as well. As Diplock LJ said[1]:

> The matter has to be looked at from the point of view of the reasonable spectator as well as the reasonable participant; not because of the maxim *volenti non fit injuria*, but because what a reasonable spectator would expect a participant to do without regarding it as blameworthy is as relevant to what is reasonable care as what a reasonable participant would think was blameworthy conduct in himself …

1 [1963] 2 QB 43 at 67.

D The acceptance of risk

E5.22 In the two last quoted passages, Diplock LJ articulated a principle of fundamental importance to cases involving alleged negligence in the context, in particular, of a vigorous and competitive sporting occasion. The principle that spectators (and indeed others with a voluntary involvement, whether active or passive, in sport) must be taken to accept such risks as are 'inherent in' or 'incidents of' the game and that, accordingly, a competitor's duty of care does not extend to sheltering them from such risks is manifestly sound and uncontroversial. The broad principle was expressed in the United States of America by Chief Justice Cardozo in an entertaining and illuminating judgment in *Murphy v Steeplechase Amusement Co Inc*[1] when he said:

> One who takes part in such a sport accepts the dangers that inhere in it so far as they are obvious and necessary just as a fencer accepts the risk of a thrust by his antagonist or a spectator at a ball game the chance of contact with the ball … the antics of the clown are not the paces of the cloistered cleric …

1 166 NE 173 at 174 (1929).

E5.23 It might be said, however, that it is less immediately obvious that the inherent risks which have to be accepted may embrace the risk of injury through errors of judgment and lapses in skill by individual competitors. But it is suggested that any sensible analysis confirms the sense of such a proposition, the validity of which, as will be seen below, is not confined to issues of liability simply between competitors and spectators but extends to all such issues arising out of the frenzy of sporting activity itself. Diplock LJ's reasoning, in *Wooldridge v Sumner*[1], was that everyone knows and spectators (and other interested parties) are taken to accept that a reasonable participant in a competitive sporting contest (of the kind there before the court) will be likely to be pushing himself to the limit in an effort to win that contest and, where the competition is fast moving, he will be likely to have to act and exercise judgments decisively and swiftly. The decisions made and actions taken by such competitors in 'the agony of the moment' or 'the heat of battle' (viz in the 'flurry and excitement' of the competition itself) are, rightly, deserving of special allowance when it comes to such matters being judged by reference to the standard of reasonableness inherent in the criteria for legal liability. It is in the light of such considerations that a competitor in such a sporting event will only be likely to breach his duty, which however remains one of reasonable care, if he displays such a disregard for the safety of others (be they spectators, fellow competitors or others) that his actions may properly be categorised as reckless.

1 [1963] 2 QB 43.

E5.24 Sellers LJ expressed his judgment to similar effect[1]:

> … provided the competition or game is being performed within the rules and the requirement of the sport and by a person of adequate skill and competence the spectator does not expect his safety to be regarded by the participant. If the conduct is deliberately intended to injure someone whose presence is known, *or is reckless and in disregard of all safety of others so that a departure from the standards which might reasonably be expected in anyone pursuing the competition or game*, then the performer might well be held liable for any injury his act caused. There would, I think, be a difference, for instance, in assessing blame which is actionable between an injury caused by a tennis ball hit or a racket accidentally thrown in the course of play into the spectators at Wimbledon and a ball hit or a racket thrown into the stands in temper or annoyance when play was not in progress.

1 [1963] 2 QB 43 at 56.

E5.25 The distinction drawn by Sellers LJ between injury caused by actions during play and at other times, is simply a recognition that actions which are not part of 'the heat of battle' and are outside the 'flurry and excitement' of the competitive activity itself do not merit the same consideration.

E5.26 Thus in *Payne v Maple Leaf Gardens Ltd*[1], a spectator at an ice-hockey match recovered damages in respect of injuries sustained not due to an ordinary incident of the game of ice-hockey but as a result of a fight between two players. Further examples abound, particularly in the context of injuries to fellow competitors[2].

1 [1949] 1 DLR 369.

2 See, for example, *Cleghorn v Oldham* (1927) 43 TLR 465 in which the plaintiff was injured by the defendant demonstrating a golf swing otherwise than in the course of play. See also *Harrison v Vincent* [1982] RTR 8, discussed below primarily in relation to the liability of the promoters of a motor cycle race, in which however the rider of a motor-cycle was held liable to his combination passenger for negligence not during the race itself but during the preparation of his machine beforehand.

E A 'reasonable man of the sporting world'

E5.27 Another case where the court had to consider the potential liability of a competitor to a spectator was *Wilks (formerly infant) v Cheltenham Home Guard Motor Cycle and Light Car Club*[1]. There, a motorcycling scrambler lost control of his machine which left the course and injured two spectators. In finding that the rider was not liable in negligence, the members of the Court of Appeal gave their judgments in terms which cautioned against expressing the test generally in terms of recklessness. Edmund Davies LJ articulated the proper test to be applied in such circumstances in the following terms[2]:

> the proper test is whether injury to a spectator has been caused by an error of judgment that a reasonable competitor, being *a reasonable man of the sporting world*, would not have made.

1 [1971] 1 WLR 668.
2 [1971] 1 WLR 668 at 674.

E5.28 This touchstone of 'the reasonable man of the sporting world' is a useful gloss on the general expression of the test of negligence because it immediately brings the circumstances of the particular sporting context into the equation. The Court of Appeal plainly thought that a 'reasonable man of the sporting world' who attended a motor cycle scramble as a spectator expected the participants to be going all out to win and that, in such circumstances, provided they played within the rules and did not act in an obviously foolhardy way, such a person would not expect them to have any particular regard for his safety and would simply accept the foreseeable risk of injury inherent in the sport and its ordinary incidents. In the circumstances, the scrambler was held not to be in breach of his duty of care.

F Passers-by and other third parties

E5.29 Of course, there is the potential for a competitor to cause injury to others who are not strictly spectators but merely passers-by. In general terms, however, the test is the same. As always, what amounts to reasonable care will depend on all the circumstances. Particular circumstances which may well affect the equation include the extent, nature and likelihood of foreseeable harm. It is no more than common sense to say that less should be expected of a competitor to guard against small or insignificant risks than against substantial risks of significant injury/damage.

E5.30 Hence, in *Bolton v Stone*[1], it was held by the House of Lords not to be unreasonable and negligent for cricketers to ignore the (albeit foreseeable) risks of injury and damage from the ball being hit out of the ground, in circumstances where the chances of injury etc were assessed as negligible, the ball having been so struck only about six times in 30 years. On the other hand, in a case where such blows were struck regularly each season, the court held the cricketers liable[2].

1 [1951] AC 850.
2 *Miller v Jackson* [1977] QB 966. See also *Hilder v Associated Portland Cement Manufacturers Ltd* [1961] 1 WLR 1434.

E5.31 Further, in *Brewer v Delo*[1] where a golfer hooked his ball off the tee and struck another player on the next fairway, it was held that the risk of injury had been so small that a reasonable man would have been justified in ignoring it and judgment was given for the defendant.

1 [1967] 1 Lloyd's Rep 488. Compare *Lamond v Glasgow Corpn* 1968 SLT 291. See also *Ellison v Rogers* [1968] 1 OR 501; *Clark v Welsh* 1975 (4) SA 469; on appeal 1976 (3) SA 484; and *Finnie v Ropponen* (1987) 40 CCLT 155.

5 LIABILITY OF CONTESTANTS TO EACH OTHER

A Trespass to the person

E5.32 Where it is alleged that injury was inflicted by one competitor upon another with intent (that is, deliberately), it may be that a cause of action in assault and battery (trespass to the person) will be asserted. Such a claim asserts the inflicting of injury by the intentional application of force to which the 'victim' has not consented. This requirement of intent is quite specific. The kind of careless behaviour which (as explained above in relation to claims by spectators) is generally sufficient to establish a breach of the duty to take reasonable care in order to establish the tort of negligence will not suffice. As Lord Denning made clear in *Letang v Cooper*[1]:

> When injury is not inflicted intentionally, but negligently, I would say the only cause of action is negligence and not trespass.

1 [1964] 2 All ER 929.

E5.33 This additional requirement of intent (still coupled to the absence of consent) means, in the sporting context, that successful claims of assault are inevitably very much rarer and harder to establish than assertions of negligence[1]. For example, in *Watson & Bradford City AFC v Gray & Huddersfield Town AFC*[2], a tackle in a professional football match was held to have been made negligently but, even in circumstances where the tackle was described as 'very dangerous, appalling, diabolical and quite unacceptable' and it was part of the Claimants' case that Mr Gray had been intent upon exacting retribution upon Mr Watson for an earlier incident in which the latter's elbow had made contact with one of Mr Gray's teammates, the Claimants did not assert (or pursue) a claim of trespass to the person. This may have been in part because such a claim was strictly unnecessary in view of the negligence claim. It may also be explained by what appears to be a general 'gentlemen's' understanding, apparent in many of the cases, that professional footballers simply do not set out to injure each other. It may be that the position is different other, more physical sports, such as rugby league, in which allegations of assault have occasionally successfully been pursued, for example in the Australian case, *Rogers v Bugden & Canterbury-Bankstown*[3].

1 See, however, *Lewis v Brookshaw* (1970) unreported, noted at 120 NLJ 413. See also the Australian case of *McNamara v Duncan* (1971) 26 ALR 584. At the time of going to press, the footballer Alf-Inge Haaland and his club, Manchester City, has intimated an intention to claim damages against Manchester United and its captain, Roy Keane, as a result of injuries sustained by Haaland in a tackle by Keane in April 2001. This comes after Keane's apparent, if naïve, admission of intent in his recently published autobiography.
2 (1998) Times, 26 November.
3 (1993) ATR 81 – 246.

B Negligence

E5.34 Having identified, above, that the general duty owed by a competitor to a spectator is the same duty as is owed by any individual to his 'neighbour' in any circumstances (one of reasonable care) and that the implications of such duty in its application to a spectator depend upon the sporting context within which the duty is exercised, it will readily be understood that it is the same general duty which is owed by a competitor to his fellow competitors. It follows that the principles enunciated in cases such as *Wooldridge v Sumner*[1] and *Wilks v Cheltenham Cycle Club*[2] discussed above in the context of claims by spectators, are appropriate for application in cases between sporting contestants.

1 [1963] 2 QB 43.
2 [1971] 1 WLR 668.

(a) *Acceptance of inherent risks in the heat of battle*

E5.35 It follows further that, as with a spectator, a plaintiff competitor is taken to accept the risks of injury[1] from the ordinary incidents of his particular sport, which may involve errors of judgment and failures of skill, especially where the sport requires decisions to be taken and skill to be exercised at extremes of physical endeavour. Thus it was said in a Canadian case, *Agar v Canning*[2]:

> The conduct of a player in the heat of the game is instinctive and unpremeditated and should not be judged by standards suited to polite social intercourse.

1 For an example of an early case involving damage to *property*, see *Clarke v Earl of Dunraven, The Satanita* [1897] AC 59, where one yacht collided with another. See also *Headcorn Parachute Club Ltd v Pond*, QBD Transcript, 11 January 1995 (Alliott J).
2 (1965) 54 WWR 302 at 304. See also *St Laurent v Bartley* (1998) 127 Man R (2d) 121.

E5.36 It was on this basis that, in *McComiskey v McDermott*[1], the duty owed by a rally driver to his navigator was held to be to exercise such care as was reasonably to be expected of a driver going all out to win the rally. Manifestly, decisions taken in such circumstances would have to be judged in the context that they were taken in the 'flurry and excitement' of the event itself.

1 [1974] IR 75. See also *Stratton v Hughes, Cumberland Sporting Car Club Ltd & RAC Motor Sports Association Ltd* (17 March 1998, unreported), CA.

(b) Condon v Basi

E5.37 In recent years, such cases have arisen with increasing frequency and the reports and newspapers now abound with examples. In the landmark case of *Condon v Basi*[1] a footballer was held liable for breaking his opponent's leg in a tackle. Again, the Court of Appeal stressed the circumstances of the footballing context in identifying the particular implications of the general duty to take reasonable care. In doing so, Sir John Donaldson MR gave his approval to the words of Kitto J in the Australian case of *Rootes v Sheldon*[2]:

> The conclusion to be reached must necessarily depend, according to the concepts of the common law, upon the reasonableness, in relation to the special circumstances, of the conduct which caused the plaintiff's injury … the tribunal of fact may think that in the situation in which the plaintiff's injury was caused, a participant might do what the defendant did and still not be acting unreasonably, even though he infringed the 'rules of

the game'. Non-compliance with such rules, conventions or customs (where they exist) is necessarily one consideration to be attended to upon the question of reasonableness; but it is only one, and it may be of much or little or even no weight in the circumstances.

1 [1985] 1 WLR 866.

2 [1968] ALR 33. In that case a water skier sued the boat driver for damages arising out of an incident where the skier collided with an object, of which the driver had given no warning. The claim failed, the risk in question being held to be inherent in or part and parcel of the sport. A (Canadian) water skiing case where liability was established is *Pawlak v Doucette & Reinks* (1985) 2 WWR 588. There the driver of the tow boat, having first failed to establish that the plaintiff was a novice, had applied full power before the plaintiff was ready to start, causing the latter's fingers to become entangled in and severed by the rope. The driver's actions were held to fall outside the range of risks which the plaintiff was taken to have accepted in the circumstances.

E5.38 The Court of Appeal also made it clear that the proper approach in such circumstances is to see whether or not the defendant acted with reasonable care in all the circumstances, rather than to ask whether or not the plaintiff should be taken to have consented to the manner in which the defendant had acted so as, thereby, to *excuse* the defendant's lack of care.

E5.39 In other words, the issue of consent (in the sense of the acceptance of certain risks, namely those risks which are inherent in the game and its ordinary incidents) affects the practical implications of the duty to take reasonable care itself rather than provides a potential defence to an established breach of that duty. Logically this makes sense. The competitor is only liable to avoid inflicting injury upon his opponent by taking reasonable care, and what amounts to reasonable care depends upon all the circumstances, one of which is that he is competing against others who are, as 'reasonable men of the sporting world', expected to appreciate and accept the risk of injury occurring during the general run of play. Hence it is where the competitor steps outside the general run of play that the risk of injury will be less likely to be one which his opponents ought to be expected to accept. In such circumstances, the offending competitor is more likely to be held liable. Thus it was that Mr Basi was held liable for Mr Condon's broken leg, his sliding tackle having been adjudged to constitute 'serious foul play', to have been made in a reckless and dangerous manner (albeit without malicious intent), and to be worthy of a sending off.

(c) The rules of the game

E5.40 The clear implication from *Condon v Basi* is that, in the case of contact sports such as football, rugby etc, it will be almost impossible to establish liability unless the actions of the defendant are outside the rules of the game[1]. Indeed the Court of Appeal appeared to be saying that a breach of the rules is virtually a necessary, albeit not necessarily a sufficient, requirement for liability to attach. Again, there is nothing 'special' about sports cases in this regard. In various fields, it has regularly been held that the rules and standards laid down by professional bodies provide a good guide as to the standards of reasonabless expected of those who operate in the fields governed thereby[33].

1 In *Leatherland v Edwards*, QBD Transcript, 28 October 1998, the defendant was liable for negligence in a game of 'uni-hockey' because he was adjudged guilty of a serious breach of the rules in raising his stick above waist height.

2 See, for example, *Bolam v Friern Hospital Management Committee* [1957] 1 WLR 582; *Sidaway v Board of Governors of the Bethlem Royal Hospital* [1984] QB 493; *Gold v Haringey Health Authority* [1987] 2 All ER 888.

E5.41 Thus, in *Wright v Cheshire County Council*[1], for example, the fact that certain gymnastic activities were being conducted in a manner which was generally accepted, caused the Court of Appeal to overturn a finding of liability in respect of injuries caused.

1 [1952] 2 All ER 789.

E5.42 Equally, the 'customs of the slopes' were one ingredient which went into determining the issue of liability in a skiing accident case in *Gilsenan v Gunning*[1].

1 (1982)137 DLR (3d) 252. See also *Dyck v Laidlaw* (2000) 9 WWR 517, in which a skydiver was held to have been negligent, and liable for injuries to a fellow skydiver with whom he collided, for making a turn contrary to well established safety procedures.

E5.43 That a breach of the laws of the game should not necessarily be sufficient, however, to establish liability as a matter of law is surely self evident. As has been seen above, the duty owed by a competitor is directed towards avoiding the risk of injury which his fellow competitors are not taken to have accepted by their very participation. The law cannot confine its assumption that competitors accept particular risks to risks of injury inflicted by action falling strictly within the laws of the game. Were the position otherwise, injuries caused by fouls of one form or another would be expected to give rise to legal liability with a frequency which would be quite intolerable. Foul play is, therefore, regarded *up to a point* as being part and parcel of the game, or as part of 'the culture of sport' and as something which the participants have to accept. No one would sensibly suggest that the duty of care owed by one competitor to another should extend to a duty never to commit a foul. There must come a point, however, where a line has to be drawn beyond which the risk of injury should not have to be accepted. Precisely where such line should be drawn is incapable of definition. As Judge LJ said in *Caldwell v Maguire & Fitzgerald*, a recent case of a failed claim by one jockey against two others:

> the issue of negligence cannot be resolved in a vacuum. It is fact specific[1].

All the circumstances of each individual case will require to be considered. It is suggested, however, that in a game of high physical endeavour (such as rugby or football) it will be only in the case of a particularly bad foul, involving obviously blameworthy conduct[2], that it will be possible to prove a breach of the duty to take reasonable care by one of the participants in the game, thus rendering him liable for injury caused to a fellow competitor.

1 [2001] EWCA Civ 1054, [2001] All ER (D) 363 (Jun). See [2001] ISLR Issue 3 224. The case is discussed further below at para E5.45.

2 The temptation is to use terms such as 'recklessness', as was used by Diplock LJ in *Wooldridge v Sumner* [1963] 2 QB 43. Such terms are apt, provided only that their use is not permitted to introduce confusion as to the extent of the duty owed. Such duty is always to exercise reasonable care in the circumstances. It is the circumstances of a particular sporting occasion which may sometimes require an element of recklessness to be proven if breach of that duty is to be established. See *Smoldon v Whitworth* [1997] ELR 115; on appeal [1997] ELR 249, CA.

(d) *Disproportionate action*

E5.44 In certain sports, of course, part of the very object of the game is to land blows on one's opponent (with the inevitable consequence of causing injury of one form or another). Boxing is the obvious example. Plainly, in such circumstances, no action will lie in respect of such injury, at least where caused in accordance with the rules of the sport. A competitor in such a sport is taken to accept such risks, against which his opponent is not expected to guard. Once a competitor steps outside the rules (see the boxer Mike Tyson's bites of Evander Holyfield's ears) the potential arises for a possible claim. Thus, in *Lane v Holloway*[1], where the plaintiff challenged the defendant to a fight (after one of them had referred to the other's wife as a 'monkey faced tart'), in the course of which, however, the plaintiff was injured by a severe punch in the eye, the defendant was held liable, Lord Denning MR remarking that the defendant:

> went much too far in striking a blow *out of all proportion to the occasion.*

1 [1968] 1 QB 379 at 388.

E5.45 Although that case was one where the cause of action was of assault and the discussion centred on the issue of consent[1], it is suggested that the concept of acting 'out of all proportion to the occasion' is a useful one when considering the nature and extent of a sportsman's liability to his opponents and fellow competitors. The point is that the further outside the rules of the game that a competitor goes, the more likely it is that he will be found to have committed an act the risk of which his fellow competitor should not be taken to have accepted as part and parcel of the sport or the culture thereof (and that he will be held liable for any injury caused by his actions) and the less likely it is that the injury will be regarded as having been caused by an ordinary incident of the game and as involving no breach of the duty to exercise reasonable care. In the context of competitive sport (in which things necessarily may happen very quickly and judgments are exercised in the 'flurry and excitement' of the contest), practical realities suggest that a participant has to act in flagrant breach of the rules (in a manner that is deliberate, reckless or at least foolhardy) before the courts are likely to show an inclination to fix him with liability for injuries caused. Thus, a professional jockey who was badly injured in an accident resulting from an incident during a race, failed to establish liability against two other riders even though the Defendants were held by the Jockey Club to have been guilty of careless riding: in *Caldwell v Maguire*[2], Tuckey LJ reaffirmed that, whilst every contestant in a lawful sporting contest owes a duty of care to his fellow contestants, the scope of that duty is simply:

> to exercise in the course of the contest all care that is objectively reasonable in the prevailing circumstances for the avoidance of infliction of injury to such fellow contestants …

1 Whereas the question of consent is relevant in the tort of negligence (at least in the sporting context) to the practical content of the duty to take reasonable care, it may provide a defence to the tort of assault.
2 [2001] EWCA Civ 1045. See [2001] 3 ISLR 224.

E5.46 Moreover, he went on to reaffirm that, in the context of a horse race (or other similarly frenetic activity) the threshold for liability is in practice inevitably high and that there should be:

> no liability for errors of judgment, oversights or lapses of which any participant might be guilty in the context of a fast-moving contest. Something more serious is required.

(e) Recent footballing examples

E5.47 Many of the well publicised cases have concerned football. Further recent football cases in which the principles referred to above, first established in *Condon v Basi*[1], have been applied include the following cases.

1 [1985] 1 WLR 866.

E5.48 Elliott v Saunders[1] In this case the Chelsea player Paul Elliott failed to establish that Dean Saunders, then of Liverpool, had acted with such a lack of care as to be in breach of his duty to exercise reasonable care in all the circumstances, when the defendant's tackle had severed the plaintiff's cruciate ligaments. In so holding, Drake J appeared to accept that the circumstances were such that the plaintiff would have had to have been able to establish that the defendant had been guilty of dangerous and reckless play to get home. He went on to accept the evidence of the defendant that he had raised his feet in the tackle at the last moment in an instinctive attempt to avoid probable serious injury to himself. Such instinctive reactions were not such as, in the learned judge's view, to give rise to liability in law, occurring as they did in the heat of battle. In following *Condon v Basi*, however, Drake J did not agree with the obiter dictum in that case that there might be a higher standard of care required of a player in, say, the Premier League than of a player in a local football match. The standard of care required in each case was the same, although, as he was at pains to point out, the nature and level of the match in question (and, accordingly, the standards of skill to be expected from the players) would form part of the factual context within which such standard fell to be applied. This is surely right. In *McCord v Swansea City Football Club*[2] Brian McCord, a former Stockport County player, succeeded in his claim that John Cornforth, captain of Swansea City, had acted negligently in challenging for a loose ball by sliding down onto one leg, whilst raising his other leg above the height of the ball. In the circumstances, Ian Kennedy J found that Mr Cornforth had acted in a way which was inconsistent with his taking reasonable care. The defendants were, accordingly, liable to the plaintiff for his broken leg which ended his professional career.

1 QB Transcript, 10 June 1994.
2 QB Transcript, 19 December 1996.

E5.49 Watson & Bradford City AFC v Gray & Huddersfield Town AFC[1] Gordon Watson now joins the ranks of those few professional footballers who have successfully prosecuted a claim for damages for personal injury arising out of a foul tackle. He succeeded against Kevin Gray[2] and, vicariously, the latter's employer, Huddersfield Town in a claim arising out of a late tackle which resulted in a double fracture of the right leg. The test which the trial judge, Hooper J, chose to apply to determine liability was whether a reasonable professional player would have known that there was a significant risk of serious injury from a tackle such as that inflicted by Mr Watson on Mr Gray. Interestingly, Hooper J's articulation of the test in those terms is not illuminated by citation of earlier authority, and for this reason his judgment may be thought to carry little weight, particularly as he made it clear that he was not concerned with whether or not this test was appropriate for other cases. It is further clear that he considered that his test took account of the important concepts of consent and voluntary assumption of risk. In any event, it is likely that the ultimate conclusion of the case was foregone according to any formulation of the test for negligence, after the judge's acceptance that the tackle was appropriately described as *'very dangerous, appalling, diabolical and quite unacceptable.'* Although not expressly articulated, it is clearly to be inferred that he rejected any suggestion that, as a professional footballer, Mr Watson was to be taken as having consented to such a tackle or to have accepted the risk of injury therefrom. The case is noteworthy for the fact that Mr Watson's club, Bradford City, also claimed damages for the loss of use of the services of its business asset, Mr Watson. They framed their claim as one for unlawful interference with their contract with Mr Watson. They therefore had to establish in particular that the defendants knew of the contract (this would surely have been manifest) and that Mr Gray had, intentionally or (arguably) recklessly, interfered with it. In the event, the claim failed as the judge was not prepared to find that Mr Gray had acted recklessly, but the claim nevertheless serves as a warning as to the potential legal consequences of rash tackles and similar conduct in the field of professional sport.

1 (1998) Times, 26 November (Hooper J). Permission to appeal refused – CA, 22 April 1999.

2 Another example of a successful claim, this time in the context of rugby union, is *Ramsay Elshafey v Javed Clay*, QBD Transcript, 6 April 2001. The case is of anecdotal interest only, liability expressly having turned on which of two competing versions of the facts was preferred. The judgment contains no significant legal analysis.

E5.50 Pitcher v Huddersfield Town Football Club[1] Darren Pitcher failed in his claim for damages for injury resulting from a late tackle in a Nationwide Division One match between Crystal Palace and Huddersfield Town. The judge found that, although the tackle in question had been late and clumsy, it was no more than that and represented simply *'an error of judgment in the context of a fast moving game where [the Defendant] had to react to events in a matter of split seconds.'* In so holding, the judge went on to find that *'this was the kind of tackle which, although against the rules of the game, occurs up and down the country every Saturday of the football season in Division One matches'* and did not cross what the Judge described as the *'high threshold'* to attract any legal liability.

1 QBD Transcript, 17 July 2001 (Hallett J).

(f) Other sports

E5.51 Similar principles apply in relation to sports where the activity involved is less strenuous or frenetic than those such as football. In golf, for example, participants are required by the law to accept that wayward shots by others on the course constitute a risk which is part and parcel of the game and, within limits[1], has to be accepted.

1 Such limits cannot be defined. Each case will depend upon all its circumstances. It is, however, suggested that the rules and etiquette of golf may often provide a guide as to what should and should not have to be accepted – see eg *Ellison v Rogers* (1968) 1 OR 501. Thus, for example, a player who drives before the party in front of him has cleared the green or has otherwise proceeded beyond his range is likely to receive scant consideration if his ball should strike and injure a player in such party – see eg *McVety v Mahoney* (1980) 25 AR 173.

E5.52 Thus in *Clark v Welsh*[1], a player injured when a ball flew off the toe of another player's club had no redress, the offending player having been under no duty to prevent such an injury which derived from a risk inherent in the game itself[2].

1 1975 (4) SA 469; on appeal 1976 (3) SA 484.

2 See also *Feeney v Lyall* 1991 SLT 156n; and *Potter v Carlisle and Cliftonville Golf Club Ltd* [1939] NI 114.

E5.53 On the other hand, in *Lewis v Buckpool Golf Club*[1], a wayward shot which struck a player on an adjacent green gave rise to liability in circumstances where the pursuer, a high handicap golfer (and therefore, perhaps, prone to poor shots), could easily have waited to allow the injured player to clear the green before hitting off the tee.

1 1993 SLT (Sh Ct) 43. See also *Ratcliffe v Whitehead* [1933] 3 WWR 447; *Whitefield v Barton* 1987 SCLR 259; and *Finnie v Ropponen* (1987) 40 CCLT 1551.

E5.54 Similar principles apply elsewhere. In skiing, for example, certain dangers inherent in the sport, such as an occasional loss of control, have to be accepted. Thus in *Gilsenan v Gunning*[1] it was said:

> A skier's conduct has to be measured in relation to the circumstances of skiing … It is in the light of the very nature of the sport that one must consider what the standard of care is that ought to be applied to skiers' conduct[2].

1 (1982) 137 DLR (3d) 252 at 257. See also *Turanec v Ross* (1980) 21 BCLR 198.
2 To be pedantic, the court was guilty, in this passage, of confusing the *standard of care* (which was, as always, one of reasonableness) with the *practical content* of that duty in the circumstances of the case.

6 LIABILITY OF SPORTS PROMOTERS & EVENT ORGANISERS

E5.55 The promoter or organiser of a sports event is not exempt from the obligation to exercise reasonable care which forms the foundation of the tort of negligence. In addition, however, he may face additional causes of action[1]. In particular, if he is the occupier of the premises where the event is staged, an action against him may, in appropriate circumstances, be framed under the Occupiers' Liability Act 1957. Further, where the actions complained of are alleged to have interfered with another's use or enjoyment of land, or of some right in relation to land, the action may be framed in nuisance[2]. These additional causes of action will briefly be considered first.

1 For an example of a case involving liability of a participant to the organisers, see *Headcorn Parachute Club Ltd v Pond*, QBD Transcript, 11 January 1995, where the executors of a parachutist who died when she collided with the organisers' taxiing aeroplane were held 50% liable for the resulting damage. The organisers were themselves held 50% to blame, for failing to exercise proper control over the drop zone.
2 Where the rights infringed are to enjoyment of private land, the action is in private nuisance; where rights of access to or passage over the public highway are interfered with, the action lies in public nuisance.

A Nuisance

(a) Balancing of interests

E5.56 Whereas in a claim founded in negligence, the plaintiff's interest in avoiding injury is, in one sense, sacrosanct and the reasonableness of the defendant's actions is judged simply according to the steps which he could have taken to avoid causing injury to the plaintiff, in a claim founded in nuisance the reasonableness of the defendant's actions or activities are judged in balance with the rights of the plaintiff peaceably to enjoy (his) land. It is only if such actions or activities are adjudged unreasonable after balancing them against the defendant's competing interests that liability will be established. It is this balancing exercise which distinguishes nuisance from negligence[1]. As with negligence, however, all the circumstances have to be taken into account in judging the question of reasonableness. Particular considerations which are likely to be important include the extent, duration and seriousness of the alleged interference, the general nature of the locality and the ease with which the alleged interference might be curbed. Whether a nuisance has occurred will be a question of fact in each case. Moreover, the touchstone of reasonableness also plays a part in determining the appropriate remedy. In particular, an injunction may well be refused if the cost of compliance would be disproportionate to the injury thereby being avoided. Thus in *Goode v Owen*[2] the Court of Appeal overturned the judge's order requiring the owner of a golf driving range to erect a 40 foot high fence to prevent the egress of golf balls onto neighbouring farm land, on the grounds that the nature and extent of the nuisance could not justify such expense.

1 For an examination of the distinctions between the torts of nuisance and negligence, see *The Wagon Mound (No 2)* [1967] 1 AC 617 at 639; and *Goldman v Hargrave* [1967] 1 AC 645 at 657.

2 [2001] EWCA Civ 2101, [2002] 02 LS Gaz R 29.

(b) Examples

E5.57 In *Castle v St Augustine's Links Ltd*[1] damages were recovered by the plaintiff (who had the distinct advantage of represention by the 'dream team' of Sir Edward Marshall Hall KC and Norman Birkett) against a golf club as a result of being struck in the eye by a golf ball whilst using the highway adjacent to the course. The judge was influenced by his finding that balls had for some time and with regularity been sliced onto the highway in question.

1 (1922) 38 TLR 615.

E5.58 On the other hand, in *Stone v Bolton*[1], the plaintiff, Bessie Stone, failed in her attempt to recover damages as a result of being struck by a cricket ball, on the grounds that there was no evidence that a cricket ball had ever previously hit or inconvenienced anyone on the road where the plaintiff had been standing. The fact that balls had previously, but only occasionally, been hit onto the road over a period of 30 years was insufficient to make the playing of cricket on the ground a public nuisance.

1 [1949] 1 All ER 237 (affirmed on appeal as to nuisance, [1950] 1 KB 201, CA, and also on other grounds – [1951] AC 850, HL). See para E5.30.

E5.59 By contrast, in *Miller v Jackson*[1] the playing of cricket on a village green (which had been a feature of village life since the turn of the century) was held to amount to an actionable nuisance at the suit of the owners of an adjacent residence into whose garden balls had regularly been struck, even though the house in question was of relatively recent construction and had been acquired by the plaintiff only in 1972. Interestingly, however, in a dubious exercise of its discretion[2], the Court of Appeal discharged the injunction granted by Reeve J, the effect of which had been to prohibit further playing of cricket on the green, in deference to the interests of the other villagers. In this regard, the greater interest of the public was permitted to triumph over the hardship to individual householders, although damages were payable. Indeed, had the Court of Appeal felt able to do so, it would have determined that there was no actionable nuisance because the cricketers had been there well before the plaintiff. The court's hands were tied by binding authority, however, that such considerations did not provide a defence to a claim[3].

1 [1977] QB 966.
2 See *Kennaway v Thompson* [1981] QB 88.
3 See *Sturges v Bridgman* (1879) 11 Ch D 852; and *Bliss v Hall* (1838) 4 Bing NC 183.

E5.60 In either of the above cricket cases, the plaintiff's claims were additionally framed in negligence. Indeed, where physical injury is caused, it is likely that a claim in negligence will be determinative and that an additional claim founded in nuisance will add little to the plaintiff's prospects. The position may be different, however, where the interference alleged is through an assault upon the senses, for example by noise or smell. It is in such cases that the tort of nuisance is likely to be crucial.

E5.61 Thus in *Stretch v Romford Football Club*[1], for example, the defendants were held liable for an actionable nuisance when they started speedway racing at their football stadium and, in *Kennaway v Thompson*[2], a motor-boat racing club was held liable in respect of the noise from its events[3].

1 (1971) 115 Sol Jo 741.
2 [1981] QB 88.
3 Other examples include *Inchbald v Robinson* (1869) 4 Ch App 388 (circus); *Becker v Earl's Court Ltd* (1911) 56 Sol Jo 73 (a merry-go-round and other sideshows); *Thompson-Schwab v Costaki* [1956] 1 WLR 335 (brothel); *Prestatyn UDC v Prestatyn Raceway* [1970] 1 WLR 33 (trotting course); *Dunton v Dover District Council* (1977) 76 LGR 87 (playground); *Laws v Florinplace* [1981] 1 All ER 659 (sex shop in a residential area).

B The Occupiers' Liability Act 1957

E5.62 The Occupiers' Liability Act 1957 imposes a duty of care on 'occupiers' of premises towards 'visitors' thereto. For this purpose, an 'occupier' is not simply someone in physical occupation but extends to anyone with control over the premises, and a 'visitor' includes anyone who comes lawfully onto the premises[1]. Thus the organiser or promoter of a sporting event, to the extent that he controls the venue where it takes place, owes a duty under the Act to everyone who attends the event, from competitors and spectators to broadcasters and vendors etc. Equally, it is not beyond the realms of possibility that, in appropriate circumstances, a sponsor or a governing body may have such a close involvement in the organisation of an event as to have sufficient control of the venue to be categorised as an occupier thereof for these purposes.

1 See ss 1(2) and 2(6) and, for example, *Wheat v Lacon & Co Ltd* [1966] AC 552. Trespassers are not covered by the Act (but see the Occupiers' Liability Act 1984 which accords limited rights to trespassers.)

(a) The common duty of care

E5.63 The duty owed by an occupier to a visitor is simply the 'common duty of care' namely:

> a duty to take such care as in all the circumstances of the case is reasonable to see that the visitor will be reasonably safe in using the premises for the purposes for which he is invited or permitted to be there[1].

1 See s 2(2) of the Occupiers' Liability Act 1957.

E5.64 It can be seen, therefore, that the scope of an occupier's duty is essentially the same as at common law[1], although the Act expressly articulates certain circumstances to be taken into account by providing[2] that an occupier must expect children to be less careful than adults and is entitled to expect people exercising their calling (including, it is suggested, sportsmen and women) to appreciate and guard against risks incidental thereto, where free to do so. Such circumstances are little more than common sense and are equally likely to be regarded as relevant in appropriate cases at common law.

1 See, for example, *Simms v Leigh Rugby Football Club Ltd* [1969] 2 All ER 923, in which a rugby league player failed in a claim both in negligence and under the Act, in respect of injuries sustained after being shunted by a tackle into a wall some seven yards from the touch-line. See also *Gillmore v LCC* [1938] 4 All ER 331.

2 See s 2(3) of the Occupiers' Liability Act 1957

E5.65 Thus, for example, in *Morrell v Owen*[1], the organiser of a sporting event for the disabled was obliged to take account of the participants' disabilities in fulfilling its duty to take reasonable care for their safety, which duty (in its practical content) was accordingly more stringent than it otherwise would have been.

1 (1993) Times, 14 December.

E5.66 The correlation between the Act and the common law is further underlined by s 2(4)(a), which provides that a warning of danger will not absolve the occupier unless in all the circumstances the warning was enough to enable the visitor to be reasonably safe[1].

1 See, for example, *Jones v Northampton Borough Council* (1990) Times, 2 May, where the defendant council was held not liable in respect of injuries caused at its sports centre through slipping on a wet floor during a game of five a side football, it having given due warning of the fact that water had leaked onto the floor.

E5.67 The duty extends to taking reasonable steps to protect visitors from forseeable risks of injury. Further, such risks may stem from the state of the premises itself or from the activities conducted thereon. This may be so even where the activities are unauthorised. In *Cunningham v Reading Football Club Ltd*[1], for example, a football club was held liable in claims by police officers injured whilst policing a match when fans ran amok. The fans in question had a violent reputation and trouble was manifestly foreseeable, and yet the club had taken no adequate steps to prevent them from obtaining missiles, in the form of pieces of concrete ripped from the terraces (which were in a poor state of repair). The fact that the degree of foreseeability was such that it was 'very probable' that the fans would seek to use such missiles, meant that the intervention of such fans in inflicting the injuries on the plaintiffs did not break the chain of causation between the club's breach of duty and the damage complained of[2].

1 (1991) 157 LG Rev 481.

2 See also *Home Office v Dorset Yacht Co Ltd* [1970] AC 1004; *Lamb v Camden London Borough Council* [1981] QB 625; and *Perl Ltd v Camden London Borough Council* [1984] QB 342.

E5.68 Similarly, in *Hosie v Arbroath Football Club Ltd*[1], a football club was held liable in respect of injuries caused when a security door proved insufficiently robust to withstand the attentions of an unruly crowd which had surged at it.

1 1978 SLT 122.

C Negligence

(a) The obligation to minimise risk

E5.69 The passages and citations above have shown how, when it comes to the liability of competitors in sport, fellow competitors and spectators are expected to accept the risks which are inherent in the particular sport. Promoters and organisers, on the other hand, are expected to take appropriate steps to minimise such risks where reasonably practicable, by the provision of safety measures of one form or another. For them, decisions affecting the safety of spectators and others are not taken in the flurry and excitement of the competition. On the contrary, the fact that the competitors cannot be expected to guard against such dangers as are inherent in such competition, is itself a feature of the circumstances which are likely to affect the extent to which the promoters or organisers may be expected themselves to provide appropriate protective measures. For example, whilst racing drivers are not expected to hold back from the extremes of their competitive endeavour in order to shelter the spectators from danger, the obvious dangers from their activities will be expected, within the limits of reasonable anticipation, to be minimised by sensible safety measures put into place by the promoters/organisers. The nature and extent of the measures required to be taken will depend upon all the circumstances, because, once again as always, the duty is simply to take such care as is reasonable to avoid foreseeable accidents and injury. What amounts to reasonable care in each case will depend upon the context of the incident in question.

E5.70 The position was well put in a New Zealand case, *Evans v Waitemata District Pony Club*[1], by Speight J:

> If a plaintiff is a paying customer at a spectator sport, there are certain duties owed to him by both organisers and competitors but those are not absolute. He may well have volunteered to accept such risks (for example, a flying cricket ball from a big hit) as no reasonable precautions on the part of the organiser or observation of care on the part of the competitor could be expected to prevent and such risks can be said to be within the type of danger that the customer is prepared to run. *But it must be apparent that a spectator*[2] *only recognises and accepts the risks which prudent management and control and sensible competition cannot be expected to avoid* … Did the organisers fail to take sufficient precautions to make the area and the operations as safe as reasonable care and skill could achieve in the circumstances including the nature of the contest and the known vagaries of the … animals and competitors likely to be engaged?'[3]

1 [1972] NZLR 773 at 775. The case involved a claim by spectators at a pony club gymkhana who were injured when a tethered horse tethered to a fallen tree broke free and ran amok. The organisers were held liable for failing to provide a secure area where horses could be kept when not competing.

2 It is suggested, further, that this could equally be said of a competitor.

3 See also *Green v Perry* (1955) 94 CLR 606; and *Moloughney v Wellington Racing Club* [1935] NZLR 800.

(b) The beneficiaries of the duty

E5.71 Further, according to the general principles of negligence enunciated by the House of Lords in *Donoghue v Stevenson*[1], the duty is owed to all those who ought reasonably to be in contemplation as being affected by the acts in question.

1 [1932] AC 562.

E5.72 Thus, for example, in *Alcock v Chief Constable of South Yorkshire*[1], a case arising out of the Hillsborough disaster (at the home of Sheffield Wednesday Football Club), where 95 spectators at an FA Cup semi-final football match were crushed to death as a result of poor crowd control procedures, it was held by the House of Lords that a duty of care might be owed in appropriate (but limited) circumstances to prevent nervous shock (in the form of a recognisable psychiatric illness) even to those not present at the scene of such a disaster but who were linked to those who died by close 'ties of love and affection'[2]. As Lord Keith said[3]:

> It is common knowledge that such ties exist, and reasonably foreseeable that those bound by them may in certain circumstances be at real risk of psychiatric illness if the loved one is injured or put in peril …[4]

1 [1992] 1 AC 310.

2 Another case arising from the Hillsborough disaster was *Hicks v Chief Constable of South Yorkshire* [1992] 2 All ER 65, in which the House of Lords rejected claims for pre death pain and suffering on behalf of two sisters who had been killed, in the absence of evidence of any specific injury suffered before the girls lost consciousness. See also *White v Chief Constable of South Yorkshire Police* [1999] 2 AC 455, in which police officers at the scene failed to establish that their employer had owed them a duty to protect them from psychiatric, rather than physical harm (or the psychiatric effects of actual or threatened physical harm).

3 [1992] 2 All ER 65 at 110.

4 The limitations of a claim in such circumstances, however, were made clear by the House of Lords. In particular, the close ties of love and affection must be proved by positive evidence and the fact of a particular blood or other relationship will not necessarily suffice alone, save perhaps in the case of the closest relationships such as a parent/child or husband/wife. Further, the psychiatric illness must derive through sight or hearing of the acts complained of (or their immediate results) – in the circumstances of this case, even exposure to pictures of the scene generally on the television was not enough, the broadcasts having avoided pictures of suffering by recognisable individuals.

E5.73 In the event most of the claims failed, on the grounds either that the plaintiffs' relationship with those who died were insufficiently close or that their proximity to the disaster itself (through watching television, which generally did not dwell on depictions of the suffering of identifiable individuals) was too remote.

(c) The dangers of the place and of the entertainment

E5.74 In *Hall v Brooklands Auto-Racing Club*[1], spectators injured when two racing cars crashed and left the track claimed damages from the organisers. In dismissing their claims, the Court of Appeal drew a helpful distinction between 'the dangers of the place' and 'the dangers of the entertainment'. The organisers of a sporting event are taken to owe a duty (in negligence, as occupiers and even, in relation to a spectator, under the contract by which the spectator purchases his ticket to secure his right of entry) to take reasonable steps to guard against foreseeable risks from the condition of the premises where the event is staged, even where the danger in the condition of such premises derives from the fact that the event is being staged. In relation to the event or entertainment itself, however, in common with competitors themselves, the practical content of the duty to exercise reasonable care is fashioned by the tacit acceptance by all concerned of the risks which are incidental thereto. The duty in relation to risks from the conduct of a sporting event or occasion (as distinct from the condition of the premises in which the event is staged) was held not to extend to:

> an obligation to protect against a danger incident to the entertainment which any reasonable spectator foresees and of which he takes the risk[2].

1 [1933] 1 KB 205. See also *Horne v RAC Motor Sports Association* (24 May 1989, unreported), CA, where liability was established on the basis that marshals had failed to warn spectators at a rally that they were standing on a dangerous bend.
2 [1933] 1 KB 205 at 217 per Scrutton LJ.

E5.75 It was this principle which determined the result in *Murray v Harringay Arena Ltd*[1], where a spectator (a six year old boy) failed to recover damages for injuries sustained by a flying puck at an ice-hockey match. The arena in which the match had taken place was held to be as safe as was reasonably to be expected and the plaintiff's injury to have been the result of a danger inherent in the sport itself which the plaintiff was taken to have accepted and against which the organisers could not reasonably have been expected to guard.

1 [1951] 2 KB 529.

E5.76 Contrast, however, *Klyne v Bellegarde*[1], where a spectator at an ice-hockey match recovered damages for injuries sustained (from a hockey stick) whilst standing in an aisle alongside the rink which had no protective guards above the side boards. In these circumstances the organisers were held to have failed to take such steps as would reasonably have been expected to provide spectators with an arena where they would be protected from the obvious dangers to which they were liable to be exposed.

1 (1978) 6 WWR 743.

E5.77 In *Harrison v Vincent*[1] the Court of Appeal found that the organisers of a motor cycle combination race were negligent and liable for the injuries caused to the plaintiff (the passenger in the first defendant's combination) when the first defendant's machine suffered brake failure, the first defendant missed a gear and the machine left the course via a slip road only to collide with a recovery vehicle which was protruding into the plaintiff's escape route some 40 metres up it. The brake failure was held to be the result of the first defendant's negligent preparation of the machine (for which the first defendant and his employers were liable). Further, the organisers were also held liable on the basis that they ought to have contemplated that a competitor might leave the course and need the slip road and that, in allowing the recovery vehicle (itself, no doubt, part of the safety regime) to park in a position of relative danger, they were in breach of their duty to take reasonable care. The injuries sustained by the plaintiff were not the result of any risk which was inherent in the sport which the plaintiff should be taken to have accepted[2]. Rather, they derived from the condition of the premises on which the event was staged through the dangerous positioning of the recovery vehicle. Significantly, the rules of the international federation under whose auspices the race was organised provided for escape roads to remain unobstructed for 100 metres. As Sir John Arnold P said[3]:

> It is not of course conclusive that, because there is a general rule of this sort, every failure to comply with its terms in every circumstance would necessarily be negligent. Nevertheless, it is relevant to the matter that, if one is not to comply with such a rule, at least one must have a convincing reason for not doing so.

1 [1982] RTR 8.
2 See Watkins LJ at 19. See also *Craven v Riches* CA Transcript, 27 February 2001.
3 [1982] RTR 8 at 15.

(d) The significance of codes of practice and other recognised standards

E5.78 It should be noted that many sporting and other bodies, in addition, publish codes of practice for the safe conduct of particular types of sporting event. It is likely that the extent of any compliance or non-compliance with any such relevant code of practice will be a material consideration in appropriate cases. Such codes may well be regarded as an indication of acceptable conduct and a measure of the kind of safety measures which reasonably ought to be taken to provide protection from foreseeable risks. In particular, a contravened provision in a code may make it difficult for an organiser to plead that an injury was caused by a risk which was inherent in the sport which spectators and others were obliged to accept and against which there was no obligation, in exercise of a duty of reasonable care, to guard[1].

1 See, for example, *Wright v Cheshire County Council* [1952] 2 All ER 789; *Smoldon v Whitworth* [1997] ELR 115; on appeal [1997] ELR 249, CA; and *Bacon v White & Chartfield Associates Ltd* QBD Transcript 21 May 1998.

E5.79 Thus, in *Hinchcliffe v British Schoolboys Motorcycle Association*[1], a nine-year old moto-cross rider recovered damages after careering out of control into an inflexible perimeter rope, on the grounds that general practice at that time favoured the use of flexible tape for such perimeter fencing. Another example is *Slack v Glennie*[2] where the owners and operators of a leisure park used for motor cycle racing were held liable for the death and injury respectively of a rider and his sidecar passenger when they crashed into a fence on the inside of the track, in circumstances where published safety standards recommended that the inside of such tracks should be kept clear of obstruction. According to similar reasoning, in *Headcorn Parachute Club Ltd v Pond*[3], particular allegations of negligence against a parachuting club, in allowing parachutists to land in close proximity to areas used by landing and taxiing aircraft, were dismissed on the grounds that such a practice was regarded as *'the norm in parachuting circles'*.

1 (April 2000, unreported), QBD.
2 (19 April 2000, unreported), CA. Other examples include *Davis v Feasey* (14 May 1998, unreported), CA (motor-cross organisers liable for failure to adhere to the rules for the safe lay out of competitive tracks, by including a prohibited 'double jump', which resulted in injury to a competitor); *Stratton v Hughes, Cumberland Sporting Car Club Ltd & RAC Motor Sports Association Ltd* (17 March 1998, unreported), CA (motor rally organisers sited finish line contrary to RAC regulations – no liability, due to lack of causation).
3 QBD Transcript, 11 January 1995 (Alliott J). See also *Smith v Flintrace Ltd* (27 March 1998, unreported), CA (stock car race organisers not liable for crash injuries partly because they had complied with the relevant provisions of a code of practice subsequently endorsed by the appropriate governing body).

E5.80 On the other hand, adherence to a commonly accepted standard may not always be sufficient to avoid liability. In *Watson v British Boxing Board of Control*[1] the fact that the regulations adopted for the bout in which Michael Watson was badly injured may have been broadly the same as would have been adopted by other world boxing governing bodies provided the BBBC with no defence to Mr Watson's claim for damages arising from the inadequacies in the medical facilities made available at ringside pursuant to those regulations.

1 [2001] QB 1134. See also para E5.99.

(e) Real risks and minor risks

E5.81 Equally, the fact that no previous similar accident has previously occurred, of itself, provides no answer to a negligence claim. Thus, Sir John Arnold P, in *Harrison v Vincent*[1], went on to make it clear that the absence of any previous similar accident was no reason for not following the rule of the federation. In passing he made it clear that the test of reasonableness requires a person to take steps to reduce or eliminate real risks of which he knows or ought to know subject only to the qualification:

> that it is justifiable not to take steps to eliminate a real risk if it is small and if the circumstances are such that a reasonable man, careful of the safety of his neighbour, would think it right to neglect it[2].

1 See para E5.77.
2 Per Arnold P quoting from *The Wagon Mound (No 2)* [1967] 1 AC 617 at 642. See also *Bolton v Stone* [1951] AC 850 (above). See also *Simms v Leigh Rugby Club Ltd* [1969] 2 All ER 923, where a rugby club was held not liable for a player's broken leg, and where it was said (obiter) that even if there had been evidence to show that the injury had been caused by contact with the concrete retaining wall some seven yards from the touch-line, the club would not have been liable as the risk was sufficiently improbable that it was not necessary to guard against it (note, however the words of disapproval of Arnold P in *Harrison v Vincent* (see para E5.77)).

E5.82 It is suggested, however, that this qualification to the general principle (that risks which are reasonably foreseeable, and which are not to be regarded simply as the normal incidents of the sport in question, should be guarded against where practicable) should be treated with caution. It will be rare indeed that it will be held justifiable not to take steps to guard against a 'real risk'[1] and it may be that the better distinction is between 'real' or significant risks and minor risks. Thus the position was expressed, for example, by Lord Dunedin in *Fardon v Harcourt-Rivington*[2] in the following terms:

> If the possibility of the danger emerging is reasonably apparent, then to take no precautions is negligence; but if the possibility of danger emerging is only a mere possibility which would never occur to the mind of areasonable man, then there is no neglience in not having taken extraordinary precautions.

1 See for example *Whitefield v Barton* 1987 SCLR 259.
2 [1932] All ER Rep 81.

E5.83 Thus, for example, in *Gillon v Chief Constable of Strathclyde Police*[1], it was because the risk, although foreseeable, was minimal, that a police sergeant watching the spectators at a football match failed to recover damages in respect of injuries caused when a player, in losing control of the ball, cannoned off the pitch and collided with her.

1 (1996) Times, 22 November.

E5.84 Similarly, in *Bolton v Stone*[1], Bessie Stone's negligence claim in respect of her injuries after being struck by a cricket ball hit from the ground onto the highway failed because the risk of any such injury had been minimal, the evidence being that balls had only rarely reached such highway and that no one had previously been injured or otherwise inconvenienced[2].

1 [1951] AC 850.

2 Compare *Miller v Jackson* [1977] QB 966, where the decision went the other way, the evidence being that balls were regularly hit out of the ground. In the circumstances it was held that the risk of injury had been of such significance as to have required additional protective measures. Equally, in *Lamond v Glasgow Corpn* 1968 SLT 291, liability was established in respect of injuries caused by a wayward golf ball, the evidence being that balls were frequently hit from the course onto a disused railway line (even though the plaintiff's was the first recorded accident).

7 LIABILITY OF COACHES, REFEREES, SUPERVISORS AND SCHOOLS etc

A Positions of special responsibility

E5.85 Because a claim in negligence is founded upon the simple principle that the law requires the exercise of reasonable care to avoid injuring one's 'neighbour' and identifies one's neighbour as anyone who ought reasonably to be in contemplation as being affected by one's acts or omissions, it is immediately apparent that coaches, other supervisors and the like will be expected to exercise reasonable care in imparting their knowledge and skills to their charges.

E5.86 For example, in *Pawlak v Doucette & Reinks*[1], the owner of a motor boat was held to owe a novice water skier a duty of care where the owner had taken it upon himself to supervise the water-skiing activities.

1 (1985) 2 WWR 588.

E5.87 Similarly, an individual who, for example, takes it upon himself to coach a pupil on how to effect a proper (and, therefore, 'safe') rugby tackle may expose himself to legal liability if he gets things wrong with the result that his charge is injured in a match. An example of such a case (which, however, failed on the facts) is *Van Oppen v Clerk to the Bedford Charity Trustees*[1] where a schoolboy unsuccessfully claimed damages from his school for injuries sustained in a rugby tackle, on the basis that he had never been taught how to tackle properly. Indeed that case suggests, rightly in view of the nature of the relationships involved between coaches and players (particularly where the players are young pupils to whom the coaches are, to some extent, 'in loco parentis'), that a coach may be liable through failure to give appropriate instruction (negligence by omission) as well as in the more obvious case of giving advice which is wrong. Thus, for example, a weightlifting coach who fails to advise as to the way in which to lift heavy weights so as to minimise the risk of back injury may find himself exposed to liability when his charge sustains injury through the use of an unsafe technique. Hence, a schoolboy who broke his neck when diving from a starting block into the shallow end of a swimming pool succeeded in a claim for damages against his PE teacher who had failed to give him appropriate instruction on how safely to effect such a dive[2].

1 [1990] 1 WLR 235.
2 See *Gannon v Rotherham Metropolitan Borough Council* (6 February 1991, unreported). Interestingly, he also succeeded against the Amateur Swimming Association for failing to issue (to instructors) appropriate warnings as to relevant dangers.

E5.88 Similarly, in *Hedley v Cuthbertson*[1], a professional mountain guide was held liable for the death of his fellow climber because of his failure to take adequate safety precautions when proceeding with a manoeuvre. The decision was received with some dismay in the worlds of rock/mountain climbing and other inherently dangerous sports, partly because the manoeuvre was made urgent as a result of a perceived risk from a threatened rock fall. The basis of the judge's decision appears to have been his finding that the defendant had overestimated the potential danger posed by a rock fall, which (the judge also found) was unlikely. In the circumstances, the judge took the view that the guide's conduct had fallen below the standard to be expected of a competent mountain guide in the circumstances. In doing so, he was careful to point out that his decision was founded upon the special facts of the case, and ought not to be regarded as liable to open the floodgates to similar claims.

1 QBD Transcript 20 June 1997 (Dyson J) Compare the earlier case of *Pope v Cutherbertson* QBD Transcript 21 December 1995 (Deputy High Court Judge Diana Cotton QC), in which the guide was held not to blame for a rock climbing fall.

E5.89 Again, in *Bacon v White & Chartfield Associates*[1], a SCUBA diving instructor was held liable for the resultant death of his pupil when he had lost sight of her on her first open water dive, as a result of his failure to follow the safety code published by his governing body. The fact that the deceased had been a novice was especially significant in informing the practical content of the defendant's duty to take reasonable care.

1 QBD Transcript, 21 May 1998.

B In loco parentis

E5.90 In Canada, the courts have equated the duty of a teacher/instructor to the standard reasonably to be expected of a parent. In a case where a pupil suffered a catastrophic accident during a gymnastics class, which was poorly supervised[1], the duty was expressed as follows:

> [the] common law duty to take care of this pupil during this activity in the manner of a reasonable and careful parent, taking into account the judicial modification of the reasonable and careful parent test to allow for the larger than family size of the physical education class and the supraparental expertise commanded of a gymnastics instructor[2].

1 *Thornton v School District No 57, Board of School Trustees* (1976) 73 DLR (3d) 35 at 57. In England, see *Chittock v Woodbridge School* [2002] EWCA Civ 915, [2002] 32 LS Gaz R 33 in which Auld LJ articulated the duty in clear terms.
2 See also *Williams v Eady* (1893) 10 TLR 41, CA.

E5.91 An extreme example of the application of these principles is provided by the first instance decision of Leveson J, in *C (a child) v W School*[1], where a school was, at first instance, held liable for the catastrophic injuries sustained by a pupil aged seventeen and a half in an accident on a skiing trip. The school's liability was said by the trial judge to lie in its lack of adequate supervision of the claimant even in circumstances where his parents had signed a form authorising their son to ski unsupervised. The trial judge decided that an earlier incident of irresponsible behaviour had been such that the masters on the trip ought to have done more than, as they did, reprimand the claimant and should have taken steps to ensure that, in spite of the parents' authority, his future conduct was restrained and monitored. In the event, he was able to resume skiing unsupervised and a further incident of irresponsibility on his part led to his accident. Although, ultimately and not surprisingly, the decision was overturned on appeal[2], examples such as this undoubtedly fuel the anxiety of schools and other organisations, who appear increasingly to be deterred from organising skiing and similar trips for their pupils and from permitting them to engage in other high risk sports[3] partly because of the risks of possible litigation in the event of injury.

1 [2002] PIQR P13.
2 [2002] EWCA Civ 915 – the Court of Appeal held that the trial judge had imposed too high a duty of care
3 For example, the *London Evening Standard* of 19 June 2002 reported that a leading boys public school, Kings School in Ely, was planning to phase out the playing of rugby in favour of other less physically confrontational sports.

C *Smoldon v Whitworth* – the case of the negligent referee

E5.92 A striking example of the application of the principles of negligence in this area is provided by the well publicised case of the referee held liable for injuries sustained by a front row forward in a collapsed scrummage in a rugby union colts game, *Smoldon v Whitworth*[1]. The publicity which that case earned led to considerable anxiety, not to say hysteria, amongst referees up and down the country, which it is suggested, was largely misplaced. On the facts as found by the judge at first instance, the circumstances which led to his finding of liability against the referee, which finding was upheld by the Court of Appeal, were extreme indeed. Liability was established only by reason of a combination of circumstances, which included the facts that:

(a) the game in question was a colts (under 19) game;
(b) the laws of the game, as applied to colts, had been specifically revised by the International Rugby Football Board to reduce the risk of such injuries, in particular by requiring that scrummages should be required to form according to a defined sequence of crouch-touch-pause-engage;
(c) the International Board and the defendant referee's own Society of Referees had issued, respectively, directives and minutes emphasising the importance of correctly following the crouch-touch-pause-engage procedure and the dangers inherent in not doing so[2];
(d) prior to the scrummage in which the plaintiff sustained his injury, the referee in question had failed to apply and enforce those revised laws properly and the scrums had been allowed to 'come in hard' and this had lead to in excess of twenty collapsed scrummages[3];
(e) the referee had failed to take appropriate steps to enforce the laws, even in the face of a warning from one of his touch judges that someone would get hurt if he did not step in and in the face of shouts from spectators and complaints from certain of the players.

1 [1997] ELR 115 (Curtis J); on appeal [1997] ELR 249, CA.
2 Interestingly, the Staffordshire Rugby Union Society of Referees had previously expressly recognised the risk that a referee might be held legally liable in negligence for any injuries caused if the procedures were not properly enforced.
3 Significantly, the defendant referee himself accepted in evidence that 25 collapsed scrummages (he did not accept there had been so many, but his evidence was rejected by the judge) would suggest that the laws were not being enforced and that he had lost control of the game.

D No reason for hysteria

E5.93 The case was, therefore, an extreme one on the facts and should not lead to a flurry of referees prematurely hanging up their whistles. What is important about the case is that it underlines the fact that the principles of negligence are of universal application and that, accordingly, referees are not immune from their application[1]. As the Court of Appeal said:

> The case … is also of concern to many who fear that the judgment for the plaintiff will emasculate and enmesh in unwelcome legal toils a game which gives pleasure to millions. But we cannot resolve the issues argued before us on the basis of sympathy or personal predilection. We must instead endeavour to apply established legal principles, so far as applicable in this novel field, in order to draw on that public wisdom by which the deficiencies of private understanding are to be supplied.

1 It ought to come as no surprise that, in *Smoldon v Whitworth*, the judge expressly found that a referee does owe a duty of care to the players in the game under his charge. Indeed, the point had not been in issue between the parties.

E The (sporting) circumstances inform the practical content of the duty of care

E5.94 The Court of Appeal went on, however, to underline once again the crucial fact that the established legal principles require that the factual context within which particular events take place will inform the content of any duty to take reasonable care. For this reason, it did not accept as well founded the argument that a finding in favour of the plaintiff would open the floodgates to numerous claims by injured players. On the contrary, the Court of Appeal warned that it would be difficult ever to establish liability:

> The level of care required is that which is appropriate in all the circumstances, and the circumstances are of crucial importance. Full account must be taken of the factual context in which a referee exercises his functions, and he could not be properly held liable for errors of judgment, oversights or lapses of which any referee might be guilty in the context of a fast moving and vigorous contest. The threshold of liability is a high one. It will not easily be crossed … [the learned trial judge] did not intend to open the door to a plethora of claims by players against referees, and it would be deplorable if that were the result. In our view that result should not follow provided all concerned appreciate how difficult it is for any plaintiff to establish that a referee failed to exercise such care and skill as was reasonably to be expected in the circumstances of a hotly contested game of rugby football …

E5.95 In a further passage of unquestionable logic, the Court of Appeal also distinguished the practical content of the duty of reasonable care as owed by a referee to the players from that owed by, say, a competitor to a spectator (as in *Wooldridge v Sumner*[1] and *Wilks v Cheltenham Home Guard Motor Cycle and Light Car Club*[2]):

> In [the latter] cases it was recognised that a sporting competitor, properly intent on winning the contest, was (and was entitled to be) all but oblivious of spectators. It therefore followed that he would have to be shown to have very blatantly disregarded the safety of spectators before he could be held to have failed to exercise such care as was reasonable in all the circumstances. The position of a referee vis-à-vis the players is not the same as that of a participant in a contest vis-à-vis a spectator. One of his

responsibilities is to safeguard the safety of the players. So, although the legal duty is the same in the two cases, the practical content of the duty differs according to the quite different circumstances.

1 [1963] 2 QB 43.
2 [1971] 1 WLR 668.

E5.96 It follows that, as always, all the circumstances must be taken into consideration when it is sought to hold a referee liable for injury sustained during the course of a game. As the Court of Appeal made clear, the 'threshold of liability' is a high one. Referees may take comfort from the fact that, if they know the laws of their game and simply seek to apply them in a reasonable manner, they should have little to fear[1]. In particular, as has already been seen in relation to the liability of competitors between themselves, an individual competitor is taken to have accepted the risk of injury occurring in the ordinary run of the game, even as a result of all bar the more serious and flagrant of fouls. Similarly, it seems clear that in ordinary circumstances a player will be likely to be able legitimately to complain of errors by the referee in only the clearest cases of incompetence[2].

1 A clear lesson to be derived from the decision, however, is that referees should know the laws and be aware of the dangers inherent in a failure to apply them.
2 See for example *Carabba v Anacortes School District No 103* 435 P 2d 936 (1967); and *Kline v OID Association Inc* 609 NE 2d 564 (1992).

F Children

E5.97 But it has to be said that the age or other significant attributes of the players being refereed, is manifestly one of the circumstances to be taken into account in determining whether or not the referee has acted reasonably in all the circumstances – there is plainly less scope for the argument that a player must be taken to have accepted certain risks where the player is young and still learning generally about the game being played. In such a case the referee has a particular responsibility to see that the players in his charge are reasonably safe and are given appropriate protection. The same applies wherever the activities of children are conducted under supervision, in particular during school or other similar sporting activities[1]. Similarly, in a contact sport, where an adult coach participates in a demonstration or a practice game, his duty of care must take appropriate account of the difference in size and strength between himself and his students[2].

1 See, for example, *Gibbs v Barking Corpn* [1936] 1 All ER 115; *Ralph v LCC* (1947) 111 JP 548; *Wright v Cheshire County Council* [1952] 2 All ER 789; *Conrad v Inner London Education Authority* (1967) 65 LGR 543; *Fowles v Bedfordshire County Council* [1996] ELR 51; and *Thornton v Trustees of School District No 57* (1976) 57 DLR (3d) 438.
2 See for example, *Affutu-Nartoy v Clarke* (1984) Times, 9 February.

8 LIABILITY OF GOVERNING BODIES

E5.98 Thus far, most if not all the cases considered have concerned claims in which the allegation has been that the negligence of the Defendant has itself resulted in the infliction of injury on the Claimant.

A *Watson v BBBC*

E5.99 In *Watson v British Boxing Board of Control*[1], the boxer, Michael Watson, claimed not that the British Boxing Board of Control had inflicted injury upon him in his fight with Chris Eubank but that its failure to ensure that adequate medical facilities were in place at ringside had allowed the injury inflicted by Mr Eubank's punch to develop catastrophic consequences through a delay in treatment. The case posed novel questions not only in this regard but also because it was not the BBBC which had itself provided the ringside facilities – rather, through its rules it had imposed on the promoters certain mandatory minimum requirements, and additionally it had given advice, all of which was designed to secure the safety of boxers. The rules, for example, stipulated that two approved doctors should be present at ringside at all times and particular advice given included guidance as to the professional expertise appropriately to be expected of those doctors and the types of equipment which should be available to them. The promoters of the Watson/Eubank fight appear to have followed the BBBC's rules and advice. However, the Court of Appeal found that the professional expertise of the doctors at ringside and the equipment available to them had been inadequate to cope appropriately with Mr Watson's condition when he was knocked unconscious and that such deficiencies had meant that emergency treatment in the form of intubation, the insertion of an endotracheal tube, the administration of a diuretic to reduce swelling of the brain and the administration of oxygen had been delayed for about thirty minutes until Mr Watson had reached hospital. Had there been no such delay, the brain damage which, sadly, Mr Watson sustained would have been averted or reduced. In confirming the trial judge's finding that the BBBC was liable in negligence, the Court of Appeal accepted that the decision broke new ground. After all, the BBBC had not inflicted injury upon Mr Watson, nor had it itself provided the ringside medical facilities. Moreover, Mr Watson had been a willing participant in the fight, in which the infliction of injury on him had been one of the primary aims of his opposing fighter, Mr Eubank. Nevertheless, the Court of Appeal held that, in the circumstances, the BBBC had owed Mr Watson a duty of care. That duty had been to impose regulations requiring the promoters to take reasonable steps to ensure that any personal injury sustained was properly (and timeously) treated. It was the BBBC's assumption of responsibility, as found by the Court, to safeguard boxers from the consequences of such injury as might be inflicted by their opponents in the ring which had carried with it the duty to exercise reasonable care in addressing those needs. Moreover, this was the case even in circumstances where the BBBC's assumption of responsibility was at one stage removed from the action, being manifested, through its regulatory role, by the imposition of a mandatory code to be followed by others. In coming to this conclusion, the Court of Appeal endorsed what had been said by Hobhouse LJ in *Perrett v Collins*[2], a case in which a flying association had been held liable in negligence for the consequences of an aircraft crash after it had wrongly certified the aircraft as safe:

> It has never been a requirement of the law of the tort of negligence that there be a particular antecedent relationship between the defendant and the plaintiff other than one that the plaintiff belongs to a class which the defendant contemplates or should contemplate would be affected by his conduct. Nor has it been a requirement that the defendant should *inflict* the injury upon the plaintiff. Such a concept belongs to the law of trespass not to the law of negligence.

1 [2001] QB 1134.
2 [1998] 2 Lloyds Rep 255 at 261.

E5.100 The Court of Appeal also distinguished cases such as *Capital and Counties plc v Hampshire County Council*[1], in which it had been reaffirmed that the duty of care imposed on a 'rescuer' does not extend to reducing damage which would have occurred in any event in spite of the rescuer's intervention. As Lord Phillips MR said (at p 1160):

> There is a clear distinction between the role of the board and the role of a fire service or the police service. The latter have the role of protecting the public in general against risks, which they play no part in creating. There is a general reliance by the public on the fire service and the police to reduce those risks. In these circumstances there is no close proximity between the services and the general public. There are also reasons of public policy for not imposing a duty of care to individuals in relation to the performance of their functions … In contrast the injuries which are sustained by professional boxers are the foreseeable, indeed inevitable, consequence of an activity which the board sponsors, encourages and controls. The conduct of the activity of professional boxing carries with it … the need for the provision of medical assistance to treat the injuries that they sustain and minimise their adverse consequences … The board, however, arrogates to itself the task of determining what medical facilities will be provided at a contest by (i) requiring the boxer and promoter to contract on terms under which the board's rules will apply and (ii) making provision in those rules for the medical facilities and assistance to be provided to care for the boxer in the event of injury. In this way, the board reduces this aspect of the promoter's responsibility to the boxer to the contractual obligation to comply with the requirements of the board's rules in relation to the provision of medical facilities and assistance the board assumes the responsibility of determining the nature of the medical facilities and assistance to be provided. These facts bring the board into close proximity with each individual boxer.

1 [1997] QB 1004.

B A salutary warning to governing bodies

E5.101 This imposition of a duty of care in the fulfilment of an essentially regulatory function should serve as a warning to all sports governing bodies, although the wilder expressions of dismay with which the decision has been greeted in some quarters may derive from a misunderstanding of its true significance. The decision was expressly fact specific. The particular features which led the court to hold the BBBC liable included the important finding that:

> the board set out by its rules, directions and guidance to make *comprehensive provision* for the services to be provided to safeguard the health of the boxer. All involved in a boxing contest were obliged to accept and comply with the board's requirements. *So far as the promoter was concerned, these delimited his obligations* … at all material times, by reason of the *effective absolute control* over boxing that the board assumed, the board was in a position to determine, *and did in fact determine*, the measures that were taken in boxing to protect and promote the health and safety of boxers[1].

1 [1997] QB 1004 at 1149.

C Distinction between governing bodies' controlling and advisory roles

E5.102 As Lord Phillips MR made clear, if the BBBC had confined itself to giving advice rather than imposing mandatory requirements, it would have been *'strongly arguable'* that no duty of care would have been established, for want of proximity. As it was, because of the regulatory regime in place, Mr Watson had been entitled to rely, and had relied, upon the exercise of due care by the BBBC to safeguard his health and, in all the circumstances, it was fair just and reasonable to impose the duty.

E5.103 It follows that governing bodies may now find themselves torn between, on the one hand determining and requiring adherence to mandatory standards of safety and, on the other, leaving the responsibility for such matters in the hands of the organising and competing parties. In reality, whilst *Watson* has shown that sports governing bodies are indeed at risk, the hurdles facing a potential claimant remain high. *Watson* was, on its facts, an extreme case, the precise circumstances of which are unlikely to be replicated very widely across other sporting fields.

D *Agar v Hyde* – common sense, but questionable reasoning, from Australia

E5.104 Some of the difficulties facing a Claimant who seeks to pin liability for personal injury on his governing body are apparent from a recent case which came before the High Court of Australia, on appeal from the Court of Appeal of New South Wales. In *Agar v Hyde*[1] claims were brought against the International Rugby Football Board and certain of its constituent members asserting negligence in their failure to revise the scrummaging rules in the game of rugby union in time to prevent the two separate claimants' spinal injuries, caused in each case by the opposing scrum engaging before the claimants' respective front rows were ready. Because the IRFB and certain other named defendants resided overseas, the claims came before the court under applications under Australian rules of court for permission to proceed. Permission was refused in both cases on the grounds that the Claimants did not have even an arguable case that the Defendants were under a *'duty to take reasonable care in monitoring the operation of the rules of the game to avoid the risk of unnecessary harm to players'*. The judgments of the court are replete with the kind of statements of policy which may owe much to an Australian view that sport is good for you and rugby union is a sport played by men who delight in stretching themselves to meet the physical challenges which it poses and are prepared to run the risk of injury in order to do so. More significantly, the court relied upon the remoteness of the IRFB's effective control (if any) over the particular matches in which the Claimants were injured, and the fact that the risk of injury which was posed by the rules at that time was manifest and must be taken to have been voluntarily accepted by all participants in the matches, including the Claimants. Perhaps surprisingly, the four members of the six man court who handed down a joint judgment regarded it as absurd even to suggest, as was the necessary implication of the claimants' cases, that the IRFB owed a duty of care to each person, in any part of the world, who played rugby under its laws. As they stated[2]:

> If the laws of the game define the conduct to which an adult participant consents, the law-makers should not be liable because they could have made the activity that the participant chose to undertake less dangerous.

1 [2000] 201 CLR 552.
2 [2000] 201 CLR 552 at 583, para 89.

E5.105 Similar sentiments were expressed by Callinan J[1]:

> Rugby union is notoriously a dangerous game … Some positions, such as the front row, are almost equally notoriously more dangerous than others … The [claimants] could not possibly have been ignorant of any of these matters … Sport, particularly amateur sport, stands in an entirely different position from the workplace, the roads, the marketplace, and other areas into which people must venture. When adults voluntarily participate in sport they may be assumed to know the rules and to have an appreciation of the risks of the game. In practically every sport safer rules could be adopted. Should the international body controlling cricket have been held liable for not prescribing the wearing of helmets by batsmen before the West Indian cricket selectors unleashed upon the cricketing woirld their aggressive fast attack of the 1970s? Should cricket be played with a soft rather than a hard ball?

1 [2000] 201 CLR 552 at 600, para 126.

E5.106 Although some of the court's reasoning may be open to debate, the decision itself was manifestly sensible, if not inevitable on its facts. It should be noted however, that the claimants concerned were adults of whom the assumption that they had known and accepted the risks was plainly fair.

E Children

E5.107 The court was careful to make clear that different considerations might arise in the case of children (although many of the reasons for the court's decision, other than consent, would arguably still apply). In this regard, it is to be noted that, in 2001, the England and Wales Cricket Board issued an edict that, subject to a parent's written disclaimer, all youngsters playing cricket should be required to wear a helmet when batting and when standing up to the stumps when keeping wicket.

9 SOME ADDITIONAL CONSIDERATIONS

A Causation

E5.108 Liability in negligence requires proof of damage and damages are awarded only in respect of damage which is caused by the negligence complained of. In *Watson v British Boxing Board of Control*[1] the claimant succeeded only after he established to the court's satisfaction that the provision of immediate ringside medical care of the kind which was found to be lacking would have halted the development of the very serious consequences of his injuries which he in fact sustained. The Court of Appeal accepted the judge's finding that, but for the absence of appropriate and immediate treatment at ringside, Mr Watson *'would have made a good recovery …'*. By contrast, in *Stratton v Hughes, Cumberland Sporting Car Club Ltd & RAC Sports Association Ltd*[2], the organisers of a motor rally escaped liability arising from a crash because their failure to adhere to all accepted safety standards was found to have played no part in causing the Plaintiff's accident[3].

1 [2001] QB 1134.
2 (17 March 1998, unreported), CA.

3 See also *Chittock v Woodbridge School* [2002] EWCA Civ 915, [2002] 32 LS Gaz R 33 (see para E5.91), in which Auld LJ, after overturning the trial judge's finding of negligence, indicated that he would have allowed the school's appeal on the grounds of lack of causation in any event, on the basis that closer monitoring/supervision of the Claimant would not have prevented his skiing accident.

B Damage assessment

E5.109 The aim of damages in tort is to compensate the victim, to the extent that a monetary award can, by putting him in the position in which he would have been had the tort not been committed. General principles applicable to personal injury claims apply and it follows that damages may be awarded under various heads, including general damages for pain suffering and loss of amenity and special damage embracing both particular expenses incurred or likely to be incurred such as the costs of care, and particular losses suffered or likely to be suffered such as lost earnings, both to the date of assessment and for the future. To the extent that there may well be doubt as to how the victim's life would have progressed but for the accident, the court may be invited to evaluate particular chances. For example, a young professional footballer of promise, badly injured whilst playing for a lowly league club, may include a claim for the lost chance of future employment by a club in the Premier League. If the evidence suggests (almost certainly expert evidence would be required) that he would have had, say, a 40% chance of securing such employment within x years, the calculation of his damages will proceed on that basis, in accordance with ordinary principles, as expounded, for example, in *Chaplin v Hicks*[1]. Thus, in *Mulvaine v Joseph*[2] an injured golfer received damages to reflect his lost chance of tournament successes and of qualifying for the professional circuit. In quantifying the value of the lost chance, the court first assesses the value of the benefit on the assumption that the Claimant would indeed have received it, and then discounts its value according to the percentage chance which, according to the court's determination, he would in fact have had of receiving it.

1 [1911] 2 KB 786.
2 (1968) 112 Sol Jo 927.

E5.110 For a more detailed exposition of the principles involved in the assessment of damages for personal injury, the reader is referred to the specialist textbooks on the subject.

C Contributory negligence

E5.111 Where the damage suffered is a consequence not just of the defendant's negligence but also of the claimant's own lack of care, the award of damages is liable to be reduced in proportion to the claimant's own blameworthiness. Thus in *Bacon v White & Chartfield Associates*[1] the personal representatives of a deceased SCUBA diver recovered damages from the diver's instructor for his failure to follow approved diving rules, but those damages were halved on account of the diver's own failure to disclose relevant medical conditions which should have disqualified her from diving and which had contributed to her sad demise. Similarly, in *C (a child) v W School*[2], the damages awarded to a child on a school skiing trip arising from an accident when he was skiing unsupervised were reduced by 50% on account of the child's own lack of care[3].

1 QBD Transcript, 21 May 1998.
2 [2002] PIQR P13.
3 See also *Fowles v Bedfordshire County Council* [1996] ELR 51. In *Headcorn Parachute Club Ltd v Pond*, QBD Transcript 11 January 1995, the court attributed blame 50:50 between a parachutist who struck a taxiing aeroplane on landing and the owners of the aeroplane who were also the organisers of the parachute jump. The parachutist's negligence lay in her failure to keep a proper lookout, the organisers' in failing to keep proper control of the drop zone.

E5.112 Sometimes, the degree of blame attached to the Claimant himself may even exceed the causative effect of the Defendant's negligence, in which case the reduction of the award will exceed 50%, as happened, for example, in *Craven v Riches*[1], in which an award of damages against the organisers of an amateurs club day at a motor cycle racing circuit in respect of a member's broken neck and consequential quadriplegia as a result of a racing accident caused by the Defendants' negligence in allowing riders of different standards and experience (and, therefore, speeds) on the track at the same time was reduced by two thirds due to the Claimant's own careless riding.

1 CA Transcript, 27 February 2001.

D Volenti non fit injuria

E5.113 The maxim *volenti non fit injuria* describes a defence to a claim in circumstances where it is shown that the plaintiff had consented to the breach of the duty of care which is alleged and had agreed to waive his right of action in respect thereof. It can be seen, therefore, that the defence is founded upon the concept of consent. Further, such consent may be express, but is usually implied from particular circumstances.

E5.114 It is suggested that the maxim is not often likely to have any application to claims (at least those founded in negligence) in sporting contexts of the kind discussed in the preceding paragraphs. This is simply because, as has already been seen, the concept of consent or the acceptance of particular risks is already inherent in the identification of the practical content of the duty to exercise reasonable care in all the circumstances. Thus, as has been seen, in a sporting contest of one form or another, a competitor's duty to exercise reasonable care does not require him to avoid risks which are part and parcel of the game and its culture, such risks being taken as having been accepted (and consented to) by those willingly taking part in (or watching) the very same contest. It follows that, where such a risk materialises and results in injury, no breach of duty will be established to which the maxim '*volenti non fit injuria*' is needed to provide a defence. Further, if a breach of duty is established, the plaintiff will already have shown that the defendant's actions had gone beyond the indefinable line distinguishing between what was and was not part and parcel of the game to be accepted by all participants and that, accordingly, he had not consented thereto or accepted the risk of injury thereby.

E5.115 It followed, for example, in the 'referee's case', *Smoldon v Whitworth*[1], that the Court of Appeal gave short shrift to the defendant's alternative defence that, in the event that he was held to have been in breach of duty by allowing continual collapsed scrums, the plaintiff had consented to the risk of injury of the type sustained by him by voluntarily playing in the front row of the scrummage and thereby participating in the collapses:

> this argument is unsustainable. The plaintiff had of course consented to the ordinary incidents of a game of rugby football of the kind in which he was taking part. Given, however, that the rules were framed for the protection of him and other players in the same position, he cannot possibly be said to have consented to a breach of duty on the part of the official whose duty it was to apply the rules and ensure so far as possible that they were observed.

1 [1997] ELR 115; on appeal [1997] ELR 249, CA.

E5.116 The point is that, whereas a competitor or participant accepts the risks which are inherent within his sport and accordingly negligence will not be established by a failure to avoid such risks, such a competitor or participant does not, through his participation, accept untoward risks, that is risks which are not inherent within (or 'part and parcel of') the sport and its culture.

E5.117 There is no basis, therefore, for saying that a competitor or participant must be taken to have accepted the risk of injury caused by neligence. Thus in *White v Blackmore*[1], a case involving a claim by the dependents of a spectator killed whilst watching a jalopy race, Lord Denning MR said:

> No doubt the visitor takes on himself the risks inherent in motor-racing, but he does not take on himself the risk of injury due to the defaults of the organisers[2].

1 [1972] 2 QB 651 at 663.
2 See also *Cleghorn v Oldham* (1927) 43 TLR 465.

E5.118 The Court of Appeal in *Smoldon* went on, however, to give an indication of a particular set of circumstances in which a '*volenti*' defence might yet call for consideration. If the plaintiff had been identified as a prime culprit in causing the scrummage to collapse, then it might have required some consideration as to whether or not, by his actions, he should have been taken to have consented to the risk of injury and to have waived his right of action against the referee for breach of his duty of care[1].

1 Query whether in such circumstances, however, the referee would still have been held to be in breach. Arguably the concept of consent, as used to define the content of his duty in the circumstances, might simply have been extended so as to absolve him from any obligation to the plaintiff in the first place, to take account of the fact that, in the circumstances, 'the game' which the plaintiff was choosing to play was a game which ignored the relevant laws relating to set scrummages.

E Exemption clauses

E5.119 In certain sporting relationships and the potential liabilities arising therefrom, it may be necessary to consider the provisions of the Unfair Contract Terms Act 1977[1], which target 'business liabilities' namely liabilities arising from things done by a person in the course of a business (whether his own or someone else's) or resulting from the occupation of premises for business purposes[2].

1 Other legislation may affect issues of liability in particular circumstances. An extreme example is *Disley v Levine (t/a Airtrak Levine Paragliding)* [2002] 1 WLR 785, CA, in which it was argued, imaginatively but ultimately unsuccessfully, that a paragliding instructor's liability in negligence was excluded or limited by Schedule 1 of the Carriage by Air Acts (Application of Provisions) Order 1967 which implemented the Warsaw Convention.

2 See s 1(3) of the Unfair Contract Terms Act 1977.

E5.120 Section 2 is directed at liability for negligence[1] and provides:

> (1) A person cannot by reference to any contract term or to a notice given to persons generally or to particular persons exclude or restrict his liability for death or personal injury resulting from negligence.
> (2) In the case of other loss or damage, a person cannot so exclude or restrict his liability for negligence except in so far as the term or notice satisfies the requirement of reasonableness …

1 For this purpose, 'negligence' means breach of any obligation, by contract or at common law, to take reasonable care or exercise reasonable skill and includes the common duty of care under the Occupiers' Liability Act 1957. See s 1(1) of the Unfair Contract Terms Act 1977.

E5.121 Thus, in *Bacon v White & Chartfield Associates Limited*[1] a claim for damages against a SCUBA diving instructor arising from the death of one of his pupils was not defeated by the pupil's signature to a contractual exemption clause.

1 QBD Transcript, 21 May 1998.

E5.122 Section 2 of the Occupiers' Liability Act 1984, however, introduced an amendment to s 1 of the Unfair Contract Terms Act 1977, by providing that:

> Liability of an occupier … for breach of an obligation or duty towards a person obtaining access to the premises for recreational or educational purposes, being liability for loss or damage suffered by reason of the dangerous state of the premises, is not a business liability of the occupier unless granting that person such access for the purpose concerned falls within the business of the occupier.

E5.123 It should be noted, however, that this exemption will not apply to the conduct of sporting events and activities as a business but will only catch the gratuitous use of land for recreational activity, in which case the fact that the occupier carries on some unrelated business will not prevent him from excluding his liability. Further, even in that event, the only liability which may be excluded or limited is for loss or damage arising by reason of the dangerous state of the premises.

E5.124 Thus, in the case of professional sport at least, and wherever sport is being conducted as a business[1], liability in negligence for personal injury or death may not be excluded or restricted. This will apply, for example, to a sports promoter or event organiser[2], to the occupier of a particular sports stadium or other venue, to individual athletes or competitors, to coaches, referees governing bodies and, indeed, to anyone who potentially may have a liability to another in negligence.

1 Amateur sport is not necessarily exempt from the provisions of the Act. Although the sportspersons themselves may be truly amateur (as distinct from in name only), nevertheless their performance may be carried out in the course of another's business. Thus, for example, an amateur team may perform at a venue to which spectators pay to gain admission. Certain circumstances may give rise

to real issues as to whether or not actions take place 'in the course of a business'. The extent to which, for example, a charity may be regarded as conducting a business is open to question.

2 Thus the Unfair Contract Terms Act 1977 would, if enacted at the time, have changed the result of *White v Blackmore* [1972] 2 QB 651, where the organisers of a jalopy race avoided liability for the death of a spectator by reliance upon the exemption notices which they had posted at the scene.

E5.125 In relation to negligence liabilities other than death and personal injury, exclusions and limitations of liability are only permitted to the extent that they satisfy the 'requirement of reasonableness'. This is defined in s 11 as follows:

> (1) In relation to a contract term, the requirement of reasonableness … is that the term shall have been a fair and reasonable one to be included having regard to the circumstances which were, or ought reasonably to have been, known to or in the contemplation of the parties when the contract was made …
>
> (3) In relation to a notice (not being a notice having contractual effect), the requirement of reasonableness … is that it should be fair and reasonable to allow reliance on it, having regard to all the circumstances obtaining when the liability arose or (but for the notice) would have arisen …

E5.126 In determining whether a particular exclusion or limitation may be relied upon, a distinction is drawn between contractual provisions, which are judged for their reasonableness by reference to the circumstances when the contract was agreed, and other notices, which are judged according to the circumstances obtaining at the time of the alleged breach of duty. Further, no additional guidance is given as to the criteria to be considered when determining whether or not a provision satisfies the requirement of reasonableness as so defined[1] save that, by s 11(4), it is provided that where the provision purports to limit liability to a specified sum of money, particular consideration should be given to the defendant's available resources and to whether it was open to him to take out insurance. It is suggested that the relative extent to which insurance cover is readily available to the respective parties (otherwise than at prohibitive cost or on unreasonable terms) is something which will always be relevant to the requirement of reasonableness, as will such matters as the parties' respective resources, the extent to which the relevant provision was drawn to the attention of the affected party and the extent to which he had had any real option over exposing himself to the risk which the provision was designed to cover. As with the duty to exercise reasonable care itself, so the 'requirement of reasonableness' is sufficiently flexible to be capable of being moulded to suit the circumstances of any particular case. Indeed, the concept of reasonableness is such that no clear and binding principles beyond the wording of the Act itself can be derived from the cases[2].

1 This is in marked contrast to the requirement of reasonableness as applied, by ss 6 and 7, to contracts for the sale and supply of goods, where particular (non-exclusive) guideline criteria are spelt out in Sch 2. They include such things as the parties' relative strengths of bargaining power, whether the provision was known (or ought reasonably to have been known) to the affected party and whether or not the affected party had any option but to agree to the contract.

2 In this regard, see *George Mitchell (Chesterhall) Ltd v Finney Lock Seeds Ltd* [1983] QB 284, per Lord Denning MR at 299.

10 SOME PRACTICAL CONSIDERATIONS

E5.127 The new regime laid down by the Civil Procedure Rules 1998 demands, in effect, that any claim be thoroughly investigated, as to issues both of liability and damages, prior to the commencement of proceedings. This is reinforced by the

Pre-Action Protocol for Personal Injury Claims, one of the express aims of which is to put parties in a position where they may be able to settle cases fairly and early without litigation. A failure to adhere to the Protocol may attract costs sanctions. Similarly, the courts use of the doctrine of proportionality to limit the amount of recoverable costs awarded to a successful litigant makes it increasingly important that parties consider carefully whether and to what extent certain types of cost need to be incurred. For example, the traditional and almost invariable use of competing 'experts' to assist in determining liability in sports injury cases may need to be reconsidered. The extent to which such 'experts' can truly provide any great assistance to a judge by expressing opinions, for example on whether a particular tackle should be regarded as 'part and parcel of the game' is, in many instances, to be doubted. History discloses that, for most vigorous physical challenges, different views are debated by different 'experts' and many such views may be influenced, subconsciously or otherwise, by all kinds of extraneous motivations, stemming, perhaps, from an inclination on the part of some professionals (past or present) to protect their own, or perhaps from a pre-existing opinion about one of the party's reputation or even from a belief that, for example, centre forwards are generally worthy of greater/lesser protection than, generally, they are accorded!

E5.128 What is of far greater importance to the issue of liability in virtually every case is that the factual evidence be established with as much clarity as is possible. Video evidence generally proves decisive, as in *Watson & Bradford City AFC v Gray & Huddersfield Town AFC*[1], in which such evidence was fundamental to the decision in favour of the Claimant. It should be remembered, however, that video pictures are often of inferior quality in the first instance, and thought should be given in appropriate cases to seeking their enhancement through the engagement of some appropriate video post-production service. Similarly, still photographs, if available (perhaps from press photographers), can provide considerable assistance. In the absence of any video or other similar evidence, the litigation process may prove to be even more of a lottery than ever and a Claimant may face a struggle to establish liability. Oral evidence of what happened is often devalued by the fact that the majority of witnesses are likely to be either a team mate of or otherwise affiliated to one or other of the parties – all too often, litigation between contestants involves a reflection and repetition of the adversarial on-the-pitch contest. The extent to which either party is able to deploy evidence from eye witnesses who may properly be described as neutrals is likely to increase the prospects of that party correspondingly.

1 (1998) Times, 26 November: see above at para E5.49. It should be noted, however, that, in *Elliot v Saunders* (10 June 1994, unreported), Drake J was more impressed by the oral evidence than the video.

E5.129 Expert evidence may, of course, be crucial to the assessment of loss. Medical evidence is invariably likely to be required even if, as is usual in larger or more complicated cases, liability is addressed separately in the first instance. In addition, other experts may be needed, particularly in cases where questions arise as to what the future might have held for a particular victim had it not been for his injury. It seems increasingly likely that, in smaller to medium-sized cases at least, the court will consider ordering the appointment of a single joint expert to assist with such issues. Provided that agreement can be reached on a suitable appointment, that the expert's instructions are comprehensively prepared and that each side has sufficient opportunity (transparently) to inform the process of his consideration, such an order should not necessarily be seen as objectionable and should serve to limit the costs.

E5.130 Generally, in the spirit of the CPR 1998, litigation should be regarded as a last resort. Before committing to such a precarious process, it is suggested that parties should be encouraged to explore all other avenues of settlement, including mediation, expert adjudication and any other alternative dispute resolution mechanisms which may be appropriate to their particular circumstances, if necessary making use of one of the growing number of available ADR organisations, such as, for example, the Sports Dispute Resolution Panel[1].

1 See para A5.124 et seq.

CHAPTER E6

SPORTS PARTICIPATION AND THE CRIMINAL LAW

Dr Mark James (Manchester Metropolitan University)

Contents

1 SPORTS PARTICIPATION AND THE CRIMINAL LAW

E6.1 A line of authority dating back to a football match in the Victorian era holds that, in the context of sport, '[n]o rules or practice of any game whatever can make that lawful which is unlawful by the law of the land'[1]. This statement ensures that the rules of a sport cannot be used to oust the normal operation of the criminal law. Thus, the fact that an act is performed during participation in a sport does not automatically exempt its perpetrator from potential criminal liability.

1 *R v Bradshaw* (1878) 14 Cox CC 83 at 84 per Bramwell LJ.

E6.2 That the criminal law is applicable to on-field conduct is neither universally accepted by those connected with sport nor universally understood by them. For example, one defendant, a schoolboy rugby player, kicked a prone opponent in the face so hard that he broke his jaw. The defendant was convicted under s 18 of the Offences Against the Person Act 1861 for inflicting grievous bodily harm with intent and sentence to three months in a Young Offenders Institution. Following the trial, his father claimed that a term of imprisonment was unfair because his son was not a criminal[1].

1 *R v Calton* (2 September 1998, unreported), (1999) Yorkshire Post, 29 September.

E6.3 Although this is a somewhat extreme example, there is still a significant amount of debate surrounding the appropriateness of using the criminal law as a regulation mechanism where sport is concerned[1]. Some writers consider that all non-accidental injury-causing acts, particularly those that are contrary to the rules of the game, should be punished by the criminal law because '[w]ithout the Rule of

Law in Sport you have chaos'[2]. Others have argued that the use of the criminal law to control on-field conduct '[r]uns the risk of adversely and irreversibly changing the nature and dynamics of organised sports' and that instead governing bodies should use their own self-regulatory powers of punishment more effectively[3]. Throughout, however, the courts have taken a steady line that '[s]port is not a licence for thuggery'[4]. Thus, whatever the niceties of the debate about whether or not the criminal courts are an appropriate forum for these issues, those courts are prepared to hear any cases involving violence by participants in a sports event (referred to hereinafter as 'participator violence') that are brought before them.

1 See further Gardiner *Sports Law* (2nd edn, 2001, Cavendish), ch 15.
2 Grayson 'Sport and the Law: A Return to Corinthian Values?' [1998] 6(1) SATLJ 5.
3 Gardiner 'The Law and the Sports Field' [1994] Crim LR 513 at 515.
4 *R v Lloyd* (1989) 11 Cr App Rep (S) 36.

E6.4 This chapter will examine the ways that the criminal law can be used to respond to and punish misconduct by participants on the field of play including, but not limited to, participator violence. Section 2 of the chapter will examine the operation of the criminal law in respect of participator violence in contact sports. Section 3 will consider the status of combat sports and the difficulties that the law faces in dealing with new forms of limited rules fighting. Section 4 will review proposals for reform of the law in this area. Section 5 will deal briefly with the criminal law relating to match-fixing, a different form of misconduct by sports participants on the field of play[1].

1 Criminal liability for misconduct off the field of play, ie public order offences by spectators, is dealt with at paras A1.64 to A1.72.

2 PARTICIPATOR VIOLENCE

A General

E6.5 A player who has been the victim of participator violence and who wishes to see the perpetrator punished has two options[1]. Firstly, and most commonly, he can leave the matter to the internal mechanisms of the particular sport. These mechanisms – in-game penalties imposed at the time by the referee/match official, and/or further disciplinary sanctions imposed after the event by the governing body of the sport in question – are triggered by a breach of the rules of a sport and will cover most instances where a criminal act has occurred. In most sports, fines and/or playing bans are the usual sanction; playing bans can range from one match to life dependant upon the nature and severity of the attack[2]. Where little or no injury has been caused, an in-game penalty and/or subsequent ban or fine imposed by the governing body will serve the interests of all the concerned parties more than adequately. There is no general duty to report the incident to the police. Even where more serious injuries are concerned, sports participants are traditionally more likely to let the issue be resolved by the governing body of the sport by reference to the rules of the game than to have recourse to the law of the land. Where professional players are concerned, particularly professional footballers, the fines that can be imposed by a governing body will often be much higher than those that could be imposed by the criminal courts. In such circumstances, the punishment imposed by the governing body will be considered to be sufficient. Perhaps as a result, the incident of elite performers being convicted for acts of participator violence is low[3]. Most victims of acts of participator violence, then, will seek no further action beyond the sanction imposed on the perpetrator by the referee or governing body of the sport in which they are participating.

1 The recovery of compensation through the civil courts is discussed in Chapter E5.
2 See para A2.99.
3 For example, the incidents at issue in *Ferguson v Normand* 1995 SCCR 770; and *R v Devereux* (1996) Times 26 February, in football and rugby union respectively, are two of the few recent prosecutions involving professional sportsmen.

E6.6 The second option is for the injured victim to go ahead and report the incident to the police. Although the police can begin an investigation without a formal complaint from the victim, such action is extremely rare as it requires that they proceed without the evidence and/or co-operation of possibly the most important witness. In recent years there has been a marked increase in the number of cases of participator violence being brought before the criminal courts. However, it remains the case that there are relatively few criminal prosecutions for participator violence given the number of technically criminal acts that occur during participation in sport every week. The main explanation for this appears to be that the players themselves do not want to see the involvement of the criminal law in the sport that they play. They do not want, potentially, to be the next player prosecuted so they refrain from seeking the prosecution of someone who injures them by not reporting the incident to the police. Closely associated with this point is that, rightly or wrongly, most players see injury and foul play as an integral part of modern sport. The consent that they give to contacts that form a part of the game stretches, in their minds, to cover most of the injurious acts that could form the basis of a criminal action.

E6.7 Prosecutions arise more frequently at the amateur levels of sport than amongst the professionals, notwithstanding that the law would make little distinction as regards the playing status of the parties. The injured player will usually instigate criminal proceedings (by reporting the incident to the police) for one of two reasons:

(i) The first would be where the victim felt that the perpetrator was inadequately punished by the governing body, for example if the governing body imposed no penalty beyond any in-game sanctions imposed by the referee, or if it imposed a further ban or fine that was deemed insufficient by the victim. The victim might then seek to use the criminal system as a means of securing what he would perceive to be 'justice' in the form of a more substantial punishment of the perpetrator.

(ii) The second reason is where the victim wishes to receive compensation for his injuries, but civil action against the perpetrator would be futile because he is an uninsured 'man of straw'. The criminal law regime offers limited compensation to crime victims in the form of Compensation Orders against victims[1] as well as under the state-sponsored Criminal Injuries Compensation Scheme[2]. In order to make a claim under this scheme, the victim must co-operate with the police from the earliest possible time. This begins with reporting the incident to the police as soon as is practicable and providing them with sufficient information to investigate it adequately. Provided he does this, the victim is eligible for compensation under the scheme whether or not charges are subsequently filed against the perpetrator. However, where there is sufficient evidence and the perpetrator can be located, a prosecution may follow and the victim will be expected to co-operate with it.

1 See para E6.73.
2 See para E6.74.

E6.8 Whatever the motivation, once a complaint has been made to the police by the victim, the rest of the criminal process is largely out of his or her hands. The police will decide if there is sufficient evidence to hand over the case to the Crown Prosecution Service (CPS). The CPS will then decide whether or not the case should be prosecuted, applying the following two tests:

- **Is there sufficient evidence to provide a realistic prospect of conviction?** This test is dependant on the quality of the evidence unearthed by the police investigation. The normal criminal standard of proof applies. Proof of foul play alone is not sufficient for a prosecution to succeed[1]. The prosecution must prove beyond a reasonable doubt that the perpetrator had the requisite mens rea and that the act was performed without the consent of the victim. Where cases of participator violence are concerned, it can be evidentially very difficult to meet this burden.
- **Would prosecution be in the public interest?** This second test requires the exercise of prosecutorial discretion by the CPS. In general, the prosecution of violence will always be in the public interest[2]. Where participator violence is concerned, however, the issue is not so clear-cut, particularly as there are no written guidelines as to what conduct is acceptable in the name of sport and what is not[3].

1 See para E6.16 et seq.
2 *R v Brown* [1994] 1 AC 212 and Law Com no 134, *Consent and Offences Against the Person* (1994) London: HMSO, para 10.17.
3 For the position in Scotland, see para E6.61.

E6.9 In exercising its discretion, the CPS will consider similar factors to those that are taken into consideration when sentencing those convicted of acts of participator violence[1]. An incident will be deemed to be more serious and therefore more likely to be prosecuted where any of the following are present: the injury-causing act was unconnected with playing the game, such as a punch or head butt; it occurred off-the-ball or away from the play; it caused a significant degree of injury, particularly a fracture to the face; it was intended to cause injury to the victim; there was a chance of inciting a watching crowd to commit additional acts of violence and disorder; the perpetrator is a professional and therefore a potential role model. An incident will be deemed to be less serious and less likely to result in prosecution where: it was part of the normal playing of the game and there was no intention to cause harm, such as a mistimed tackle; only minor injuries were caused; and/or the matter has been dealt with adequately by the governing body, for example by fining the perpetrator and/or giving him a long ban from playing.

1 See para E6.68 et seq.

E6.10 If an injured player wishes to involve the police in an attempt to commence criminal proceedings, there is little that can be done to prevent him. The best course of action initially is to establish why the player feels that there is a need to prosecute the perpetrator. If it is because he is concerned that the player has not yet been adequately punished, then it will be advisable to postpone any action until after the sport's disciplinary process is complete[1]. From the perpetrator's point of view, an apology may be advisable.

1 See further para E6.70.

E6.11 If the victim still wishes to proceed, then the likely motivation is to secure compensation. However, various aspects of the criminal system – including the victim's lack of control over the process, as well as the more onerous evidential standard and more limited scope for compensation – mean that it would be far preferable to seek compensation from the perpetrator or his insurer by means of a negotiated settlement or a civil claim[1]. In these circumstances, the criminal justice route should be considered a last resort, for example where the perpetrator cannot be traced or is a 'man of straw' with no adequate insurance cover. Although there is no general duty to report the incident to the police, where the victim is seeking to secure compensation for the injuries caused, the incident must be reported to the police as soon as possible[2].

1 See generally Chapter E5.
2 See para E6.74.

B The offences

E6.12 The range of offences that may arise from incidents of participator violence is relatively small[1]. The most obvious charge would be common assault, for which no proof of actual resulting harm is required. However, consent by the victim to the 'assault' in question is an absolute defence to such a charge. This effectively precludes a charge of common assault in relation to an act committed during the course of a lawfully conducted sport or game, because the victim will be deemed to have consented to the non-injury-causing contact[2].

1 For an introduction to this area, see further, Gardiner *Sports Law* (2nd edn, 2001, Cavendish), ch 15 and Smith & Hogan *Criminal Law* (9th edn, 1999, Butterworths), ch 13.
2 *R v Coney* (1882) 8 QBD 534, especially per Stephen J at 549; *R v Brown* [1993] 2 WLR 556 at 592 per Lord Mustill. See Archbold *Criminal Pleading, Evidence and Practice* (2002, Sweet and Maxwell) (from hereon referred to as 'Archbold'), para 19-104. See further para E6.38 et seq.

E6.13 This leaves breach of the peace[1] and the offences of aggravated assault (ie where the victim suffers resulting harm) and homicide as the main potential charges. The most likely assault charges are those under the Offences Against the Person Act 1861 (OAPA 1861), particularly the s 47 offence of assault occasioning actual bodily harm[2] and the s 20 offence of assault inflicting grievous bodily harm[3], to which the defence of consent has only a limited application[4]. Where death follows the commission of one of these offences, a manslaughter charge may lie[5]. Some incidents might even amount, theoretically, to the offences of intentionally causing grievous bodily harm under s 18 of the OAPA 1861[6], and even (where death results) murder[7], but the onerous mens rea requirement to establish such offences makes them much less likely charges in the sporting context.

1 See para E6.15.
2 See para E6.16.
3 See para E6.21.
4 See para E6.38 et seq.
5 See para E6.28.
6 See para E6.25.
7 See para E6.32.

E6.14 The potential criminal liability of coaches, managers, trainers and even spectators, as accessories to assaults committed by the participants, must also be borne in mind[1].

1 See paras E6.33 to E6.35.

(a) Breach of the Peace

E6.15 The simplest charge arising from misconduct on the field of play is breach of the peace under s 115 of the Magistrates' Court Act 1980 and s 1361 of the Justices of the Peace Act. A breach of the peace is committed where the defendant causes a threat to another person or his property[1]. Such a charge will usually only be appropriate where the actions of the participants have caused or are likely to cause violence or disorder amongst the attendant spectators. For example, in the Scottish case of *Butcher v Jessop*[2], the applicant was a defender for Glasgow Rangers Football Club. In a match at their home ground against Glasgow Celtic Football Club, he and his goalkeeper got into a scuffle with the Celtic centre-forward. As the altercation had occurred in front of the Celtic fans in what was already a highly charged atmosphere, the court felt that the player's behaviour was likely to cause a breach of the peace in the guise of serious crowd disorder. Butcher was therefore bound over to keep the peace for two years.

1 *R v Howell* (1982) 73 Cr App Rep 31.
2 1989 SLT 593.

(b) Section 47 of the Offences Against the Person Act 1861: assault occasioning actual bodily harm

E6.16 Section 47 of the OAPA 1861 makes it a criminal offence to commit '[a]ny assault occasioning actual bodily harm'.

E6.17 First, the prosecution must prove that the defendant has committed an assault or battery upon the victim. Technically, an assault occurs where the victim has been caused to apprehend the immediate infliction of unlawful personal force, whereas battery is the actual infliction of unlawful personal force upon the victim[1].

1 *Fagan v Metropolitan Police Comr* [1969] 1 QB 439. The term assault is habitually used to cover both categories of conduct, although in sport it will usually be a battery that causes the harm.

E6.18 For the mens rea element of the offence, the prosecution has to show intention or recklessness, not as regards the causing of the harm, but rather as to the making of the contact[1]. This means that the prosecution must prove that the defendant intended to come into contact with the victim (or intended that the victim apprehend such contact). Intention means only that the perpetrator desired to bring about the prohibited outcome. Where participator violence is concerned, that will usually mean that the defendant intended to come into contact with the victim. Alternatively, the prosecution must prove that the defendant was subjectively reckless ie the defendant had foreseen the risk of coming into contact with the victim (or of making the victim apprehend such contact) but continued to perform the act regardless[2]. Again, where participator violence is concerned, that will mean any situation where the defendant realised that he might come into contact with the victim yet has gone on to perform the challenge that makes that contact.

1 *R v Savage; DPP v Parmenter* [1992] 1 AC 699. See also Archbold, para 19-190 et seq. These cases specifically hold that objective recklessness is not an acceptable form of mens rea for assault offences.
2 *R v Venna* [1976] QB 421.

E6.19 Finally, the prosecutor must prove that the assault or battery has caused actual bodily harm to the victim. Without this element, the prosecution is left with common assault, prosecution for which is barred by the victim's consent in playing the game in the first place[1]. Actual bodily harm has no formal definition. It must be such that it interferes with the health and comfort of the victim. It will include all forms of injury from bruising to fractures, including some serious fractures. Thus, for example, in *R v Davies*[2], during a football match the defendant hit the victim in the face because the victim had just fouled him. The blow fractured the victim's cheekbone. The defendant was convicted of assault occasioning actual bodily harm and sentenced to six months imprisonment.

1 See para E6.39.
2 [1991] Crim LR 70.

E6.20 As a general rule, the law does not recognise consent as a defence to the infliction of actual bodily harm. However, where the assault occasioning the harm occurs during the playing of sport, consent can be a defence to a charge under s 47 of the OAPA 1861 provided that the injury-causing act was a legitimate means of playing that sport. Punching an opponent, as in *R v Davies*, is not a legitimate means of playing football. Thus, in effect, all injury-causing acts are potentially criminal. Only those that fall within the scope of the defence of consent, which in general includes those that are within the rules and/or playing culture of the sport in question, will escape liability[1].

1 See para E6.40 et seq.

(c) Section 20 of the Offences Against the Person Act 1861: assault inflicting grievous bodily harm or wounding

E6.21 Section 20 of the OAPA 1861 provides that '[w]hosoever shall unlawfully and maliciously wound or inflict any grievous bodily harm upon any other person shall be guilty of an offence'. The most obvious difference from the OAPA 1861, s 47 offence is in the degree of injury involved: there must be a wound or grievous bodily harm. A wound has been specifically defined as any injury that breaks the skin[1]. Grievous bodily harm has no formal definition but will include injuries that constitute really serious bodily harm[2]. Additionally, however, the mens rea element is heightened: for the s 20 offence to be proved, the defendant must be shown to have foreseen not only the making of the contact, but also that such contact would cause some harm to the victim (although he does not necessarily have to foresee that it will cause grievous bodily harm)[3].

1 *Moriarty v Brookes* (1834) 6 C & P 684.
2 *R v Miller* [1954] 2 QB 282.
3 *R v Savage; DPP v Parmenter* [1992] 1 AC 699.

E6.22 For example, in *R v Billinghurst*[1], the defendant punched the victim off the ball following a lineout in a rugby union match, fracturing the victim's jaw in two places. The punch was an intentional contact and although the defendant might not have foreseen the actual degree of injury that resulted, he must have foreseen some harm, as some harm is inevitable when a punch is thrown. The degree of injury was sufficient to be regarded as grievous bodily harm and consequently the defendant was convicted under s 20 of the OAPA 1861.

1 [1978] Crim LR 553.

E6.23 As a general rule, the law does not recognise consent as a defence to the infliction of grievous bodily harm. However, where the assault occurs during the playing of sport, again consent can be a defence to a charge under s 20 of the OAPA 1861, provided that the injury-causing act was a legitimate means of playing that sport[1]. As punching is not a legitimate means of playing rugby union, consent could not operate as a defence in the *Billinghurst* case[2].

1 See para E6.40 et seq.
2 See para E6.41.

E6.24 Although the reported cases of aggravated assault charges in the on-field contest almost all involve off-the-ball incidents, such as fights, there is nothing to stop the law applying to on-the-ball acts, even those that are within the rules of the game. The rules of the game in question are not determinative of the criminality of the defendant's conduct as (again) '[n]othing can make lawful that which is unlawful by the law of the land'[1].

1 *R v Bradshaw* (1878) 14 Cox CC 83 at 84 per Bramwell LJ; and para E6.1.

(d) Section 18 of the Offences Against the Person Act 1861: assault intending to cause grievous bodily harm or wounding

E6.25 Section 18 of the OAPA 1861 provides that:

> [w]hosoever shall unlawfully and maliciously by any means whatsoever wound or cause grievous bodily harm to any person with intent to do some grievous bodily harm to any person shall be guilty of an offence.

Charges under s 18 of the OAPA 1861 are much rarer than those under ss 20 and 47 as they require proof not only that the initial contact was intentional but also that the perpetrator intended to wound or cause grievous bodily harm by that contact.

E6.26 If such proof exists, then defence arguments are severely limited: save for in the case of combat sports such as boxing and wrestling, the deliberate causing of such a high degree of personal injury to an opponent would be contrary not only to the rules of the game but also to the informal codes of conduct, or the 'playing culture', that participants in the sport adhere to, thereby precluding any argument based on consent[1]. Almost all such charges have occurred following incidents of off-the-ball violence, for example kicking[2], biting[3] or head-butting[4] an opponent whilst play has either stopped or is going on elsewhere. Consent will not apply to acts that have so little to do with the playing of sport.

1 See para E6.41.
2 *R v Calton* (1999) 2 Cr App Rep (S) 64.
3 *R v Johnson* (1986) 8 Cr App Rep (S) 343.
4 *R v Piff* (1994) 15 Cr App Rep (S) 737.

E6.27 The one reported case of prosecution for an OAPA 1861, s 18 offence arising out of an on-the-ball incident resulted in an acquittal, but its value as a precedent is questionable. In *R v Blissett*[1], the defendant's elbow came into contact with the face of the victim whilst they were both trying to head the ball during a professional football match. The victim suffered a fractured cheekbone and eye socket. He was unable later to resume his career as a professional footballer. The defendant was sent off by the referee for the challenge and was subsequently charged with causing grievous bodily harm with intent under s 18 of the OAPA 1861 but was acquitted at trial on the basis that this type of challenge occurred so regularly at this level of football that it was an integral part of the game and the victim should therefore be deemed to have consented to it. As the act was, in the eyes of the court, not criminal because it was consented to, the defendant could not be found guilty of any offence. The 'integral part of the game test' is the correct legal test in these circumstances[2]. However, its use in *Blissett* should be considered somewhat generous considering the dangers associated with the use of the elbow.

1 *R v Blissett* (1992) Independent, 4 December.
2 See para E6.47 et seq.

(e) Manslaughter

E6.28 Although rare in sport, where death results from an unlawful and dangerous act, a charge of constructive manslaughter may lie[1]. In contact sports, the unlawful act will usually be an assault under s 20 of the OAPA 1861. 'Dangerousness' is defined objectively for manslaughter. The prosecution must show that all sober and reasonable people would inevitably recognise that the injury-causing contact carried a risk of causing some harm[2]. If so, the defendant's lack of appreciation of this risk is irrelevant. Again, as with a charge under s 20 of the OAPA 1861, the foresight needs only to be of some harm, not of grievous bodily harm or death[3]. However, the defendant's assault must have in fact caused the victim's death[4].

1 *DPP v Newbury and Jones* [1977] AC 500 (where the defendants had dropped concrete blocks onto moving trains).
2 *R v Church* [1966] 1 QB 59.
3 *DPP v Newbury and Jones* [1977] AC 500.
4 See n 3.

E6.29 The nineteenth century football cases of *R v Bradshaw*[1] and *R v Moore*[2] illustrate the difficulties in bringing criminal charges in general and manslaughter charges in particular where participator violence is concerned. In *R v Bradshaw*, the defendant challenged the victim, who was dribbling the ball, by jumping at him. The force of the challenge ruptured the victim's intestines and he died the following day. In *R v Moore*, the victim had kicked the ball upfield and both he and the defendant were chasing after it. The goalkeeper got to the ball first and kicked it clear. At that instant, the defendant charged the victim, forcing his knees into the victim's back. This forced the victim to fall forwards onto the knees of the now crouching goalkeeper, causing serious internal injuries from which the victim died several days later.

1 (1878) 14 Cox CC 83.
2 (1898) 15 TLR 229.

E6.30 Both Bradshaw and Moore were charged with manslaughter. However, despite the similarity of the incidents, the respective juries reached different verdicts. Bradshaw was acquitted because he was performing an act that was an integral part of the playing of a physical sport such as football. The challenge was one that could be expected to be performed by participants in a game such as football, as it was played at that time. Although the judge did not say so expressly, he was in effect holding that where the act performed is an integral part of the game, then the consent of the victim will be implied and criminal liability will not attach to the act[1]. In contrast, Moore was convicted. His challenge was held to be beyond what was necessary for the successful playing of the game of football. Thus, the act could not be consented to by the victim as it was not an integral part of the playing of football. The lack of a judicial definition of what is an 'integral' part of the game and what is not is one of the ongoing reasons for the confusion in this area.

1 See further para E6.41 et seq.

E6.31 The foregoing cases involved 'constructive' manslaughter, ie where death results from the unlawful and objectively dangerous act of the defendant. An alternative charge would be manslaughter by gross negligence, as defined in the medical negligence case of *R v Adomako*[1], ie where the grossly negligent breach of a duty owed by the defendant to the victim leads to the death of the victim. To date there have been no cases of participator violence that have resulted in a charge of manslaughter by gross negligence. It is unlikely that such a charge would succeed because of the evidential difficulties in proving that the negligence of the sports participant was 'gross'. In the author's view, this particular charge should be considered inappropriate for cases of participator violence. The civil law of negligence is concerned more with the quality of the defendant's play. The criminal law is concerned more with whether the victim could be said to have consented to the challenge in issue. Thus, participator violence is better understood in terms of assault, consent and constructive manslaughter[2].

1 [1994] 3 All ER 79.
2 The liability of a governing body for either type of manslaughter (or other criminal offence) arising out of conduct on the field of play is extremely unlikely because of the requirement that the mens rea be supplied by one person. Mens rea cannot be aggregated, or spread around, the controlling members of a company: *Tesco Ltd v Nattrass* [1972] AC 153. Liability in tort, however, is less easy to rule out.

(f) Murder

E6.32 A murder charge requires proof beyond a reasonable doubt that the defendant intended to cause the death of another, and that the other was in fact killed as a result of the act, or that the defendant intends to cause grievous bodily harm to another and by his actions caused the other's death[1]. Charges of murder are likely to be even rarer than charges of intentionally causing grievous bodily harm under s 18 of the OAPA 1861, for the same reasons[2]. It is very difficult to conceive of such a charge arising from on-the-ball conduct. Such a change might be slightly more likely if death results from an off-the-ball incident such as a fight, but there is as yet no reported case along these lines.

1 *R v Moloney* [1985] AC 905.
2 See para E6.25.

(g) Liability as an accessory

E6.33 Persons other than the actual players on the field may theoretically be criminally responsible as accessories to the criminal acts committed by the participants. An accessory, or secondary party, is guilty of a crime if he aids, abets, counsels or procures the commission of a crime by the principal offender, in this context a criminal assault by a participant[1]. Each of the four terms has a separate meaning – aiding is providing assistance at the time of the commission of the crime; abetting is encouragement given at the time of the commission of the crime; counselling is encouragement given prior to commission of the crime; and procuring is the causing to happen of a crime[2] – but they are usually charged together. The mens rea is that the defendant intended to do acts knowing that they were capable of aiding the perpetrator of the crime, or that the defendant intentionally abetted, counselled or procured the offence.

1 Section 8 of the Accessories and Abettors Act 1861 for cases heard in the Crown Court and s 44 of the Magistrates' Court Act 1980 for cases heard in the magistrates' courts.
2 *A-G's Reference (No 1 of 1975)* [1975] 2 All ER 684.

E6.34 In *R v Coney*[1], the defendants were spectators at a prize fight. They were each held liable as accessories to a breach of the peace as their presence and encouragement had aided and abetted the fighters to cause a breach of the peace[2].

1 (1882) 8 QBD 534. See further para E6.78.
2 For a similar application in a non-sports context, see *Wilcox v Jeffery* [1951] 1 All ER 464.

E6.35 Another potential target of a charge of being an accessory to a criminal assault would be the coach or manager of a player who has committed an act of participator violence. For example, if a coach teaches a player how to injure an opponent without being caught or if a manager instructs a member of his team to injure his opposite number, then they could, theoretically, be guilty of aiding, abetting, counselling or procuring a criminal assault. Providing the court with the evidence that this has occurred will be difficult from a practical perspective as it will probably require members of the same club to give evidence against one another[1]. However, there is no theoretical bar to conviction of a coach or manager as an accessory in such circumstances.

1 See the problems associated with the civil assault case of *Rodgers v Bugden & Canterbury Bankstown* (1993) ATR 81–246, where the claim that a coach had encouraged his players to injure members of the opposition failed for lack of evidence.

C The defences

E6.36 The most common defence to charges arising from acts of participator violence is consent. Two further defences, self-defence and involuntary reflex, are mentioned briefly below, but they are of only marginal importance compared to consent. Provocation is only a defence to murder. It is not a defence to the assault offences or to manslaughter[1], but rather simply a mitigating factor upon sentencing after conviction of such crimes[2].

1 Section 3 of the Homicide Act 1957.
2 See para E6.69.

E6.37 There is some academic debate as to whether a lack of consent is an integral part of the assault offences and therefore that absence of consent has to be established by the prosecutor as part of his or her prima facie case; or alternatively whether the prosecutor can ignore the issue, establish his prima facie case without reference to consent, and leave the defendant to try to introduce evidence of the existence of consent as a defence to the charge[1]. However, from a practical point of view this argument has little impact. The defendant should be ready to submit evidence that all parties were participating in a lawful sport or game and the prosecution should be ready to establish lack of consent beyond reasonable doubt[2]. It should be noted that the link between a lack of mens rea in the defendant and the consent of the victim is very close and often blurred by both judges and commentators on the subject. The simplest way of considering the potential liability of a sports participant is firstly to establish that he or she has the requisite mens rea for an assault offence. If this is present, then secondly it should be analysed whether such an act is capable of being consented to by the victim. If it is, then there will likely be no criminal offence. If not, then a conviction is likely to follow.

1 See further, Smith & Hogan *Criminal Law* (9th edn, 1999, Butterworths), p 406.
2 *R v Brown* [1994] 1 AC 212.

(a) Consent to injury

E6.38 The basis of the defence of consent to an assault charge is that a defendant should not be prosecuted for an act to which the 'victim' consented. It removes the element of unlawfulness from the contact, thereby ousting the operation of the criminal law.

E6.39 The general rule, as explained in *R v Brown*, is that a person can consent to a common assault (ie one that does not cause any actual bodily harm)[1], but cannot lawfully consent to the application of force that causes him actual bodily harm or worse. However, there are several exceptions to this rule, including (because of the public interest in a healthy and vigorous populace) injuries that are inflicted during the course of participation in lawful sports and games:

> In some circumstances violence is not punishable under the criminal law. When no actual bodily harm is caused, the consent of the person affected precludes him from complaining. There can be no conviction for the summary offence of common assault if the victim has consented to the assault. *Even where violence is intentionally inflicted and results in actual bodily harm, wounding or serious bodily harm the accused is entitled to be acquitted if the injury was a foreseeable incident of a lawful activity in which the person injured was participating.* Surgery involves intentional violence resulting in actual or sometimes serious bodily harm but surgery is a lawful activity. Other activities carried on with consent by or on behalf of the injured person have been accepted as lawful notwithstanding that they involve actual bodily harm or may cause serious bodily harm. Ritual circumcision, tattooing, ear-piercing and violent sports including boxing are lawful activities[2].

1 *R v Brown* [1993] 2 WLR 556 per Lord Templeman.
2 *R v Brown* [1993] 2 WLR 556 per Lord Templeman (emphasis added.)

E6.40 Consent is only a defence to the aggravated assault charges under ss 47, 20 and 18 of the OAPA 1861 if the injury-causing act falls within the sports-specific exemption to the general rule on consent from *R v Brown*, ie if the injury was a foreseeable result of a lawful activity in which the victim was participating.

E6.41 What this means in practice is that consent is only a defence to an act of participator violence causing actual or greater bodily harm where the act was a necessary and integral part of the playing of the game, or part of the playing culture of the particular sport. A sports participant's consent is implied from the mere fact of his participation. By taking part in the game, each participant is deemed to consent to contacts that are a necessary part of the playing of the game, even if those contacts cause him harm. The implied consent will therefore extend to include all acts that are inherent within the game, such as tackling in both codes of rugby, and even to some commonly occurring incidents of foul play, such as pushing in football[1]. Consent will not extend to acts that are not an inherent part of the playing of the game, such as biting or punching an opponent, nor will it extend to acts that are intended to or that do in fact recklessly cause injury, for example a knee-high late tackle in football. Thus, participants are deemed to consent to force 'of a kind which could reasonably be expected to happen during a game', but 'there must obviously be cases which cross the line of that to which a player is deemed to consent'[2].

1 Williams 'Consent and Public Policy' [1962] Crim LR 74, particularly at p 80.
2 *R v Billinghurst* [1978] Crim LR 553. It is for this reason that the decision in *R v Blissett* (discussed above at para E6.27) should be treated with caution as the referee considered the act in question to amount to an intentional act of dangerous play by the defendant.

E6.42 Consent will therefore operate as a defence to the vast majority of injury-causing acts that occur during the course of sporting contests. But as the consent of the participant is implied from his taking part in the game (rather than from, say, a written consent form specifying the risks being accepted), the difficulty is then in defining the precise extent of that implied consent. When consent is at issue outside of the context of sport, it is defined subjectively from the perspective of the victim of the assault. The victim consents to a particular contact being made with him and thereby to the resultant injuries caused by that act. Thus, for example, a person who wishes to be tattooed consents to having a needle stuck into his or her skin repeatedly and ink rubbed into the wound to form an indelible pattern. In sport, however, it is not possible to assess the consent of each individual participant separately and subjectively. Team sports would be completely unplayable if each player was able to give an individual and differently defined version of which acts he consented to have happen to him during the game and which he did not. The playing of a sport is dependant upon a uniform acceptance of common standards and rules. Therefore, consent must be externally and uniformly implied on the part of all participants.

E6.43 However, the courts have found the parameters of acceptable conduct (to which consent should be inferred) difficult to identify. It is generally accepted that sport is different from other activities, that participation in sport is in the public interest, and that something other than the general rule from *R v Brown* must apply[1]. However, what this means in practice is difficult to define. Thus, it has been stated variously that sports participants do not intend to cause each other harm and that therefore no assault is committed[2], that consent does not extend to make lawful harm that was either intended or foreseen by the defendant[3], that consent extends to all injurious contacts except those that deliberately cause grievous bodily harm[4] and that sports participants consent only to the risk of harm being caused to them, not to the harm actually being caused to them[5].

1 See para E6.36 et seq.
2 *R v Coney* (1882) 8 QBD 534.
3 *R v Donovan* [1934] 2 KB 498.
4 Per Lord Mustill in *R v Brown* [1994] 1 AC 212, [1993] 2 All ER 75.
5 Law Com no 134, *Consent and Offences Against the Person* (1994) London: HMSO, para 10.17.

E6.44 The problem in sport is that most contacts are in fact intended and/or foreseen by the participants as being an integral part of the playing of the game. Such contacts are either encouraged or allowed by the rules of the game or are within the playing culture of the particular sport. Further, some degree of injury is foreseeable as a result of these contacts because of the context in which they occur, namely contact sports. Thus, technically all of the elements of the crime of assault will be present, but usually the contact will be deemed a necessary and integral part of the game and consent will operate as a defence.

E6.45 The rules of the game have a central role to play here. Where the 'assault' occurs as a legitimate means of playing the game, either because it is within the rules or is accepted as part of the way that the game is in fact played, then consent will usually operate as a defence. Only those assaults that are unconnected with the playing of the game will be found to be criminal.

E6.46 Thus, while playing within the rules of a game is not an automatic bar to prosecution[1], where the defendant has played the game within its rules it will be virtually impossible to prove that there was an absence of consent, or that there was either an intentional or reckless exceeding of the boundaries of such a consent. For example, a rugby player may intend to cause pain or injury to an opponent through the ferocity of a tackle. Where actual bodily harm or greater has been caused, technically all of the elements of a criminal offence will be present. However, given that consent to the contact (ie to the tackle itself not to the resultant injury) is a defence and that the tackle itself is a legitimate means of playing rugby, prosecution is simply not a viable option.

1 See para E6.1.

E6.47 In the author's view, it is important not to concentrate exclusively, in determining what is 'part of the game', on what is and is not allowed under the rules of a sport. Players actually consent to contacts that are either a necessary means of playing the game or are considered by those who play the game to be integral to the playing of that game. This can include not only any contacts that are within the strict application of the rules of the game but also some commonly occurring acts of foul play. This 'integral part of the game' or 'playing culture' test has not yet been formally accepted by English criminal courts. However, the judgments of the reported cases suggest that this is the test that the courts are at least tacitly applying. Injury-causing acts that cannot be said to be associated with the playing of the sport are therefore deemed to be criminal assaults. Those that have at least some connection with the playing of the game are generally left to be dealt with by a sport's internal disciplinary process.

E6.48 In Canada, a series of cases arising out of incidents in ice hockey matches has specifically addressed the issue of the nature of the consent of sports participants[1]. The test that has evolved is practical and pragmatic. It mirrors what is actually consented to by most sports participants and gives the necessary degree of uniformity that is required where a group of co-participants is concerned. The courts have identified a non-exclusive list of objectively defined criteria that describe the extent to which consent will extend to acts performed during contact sports, including the following.

1 See particularly *R v Cey* (1989) 48 CCC (3d) 480; and *R v Ciccarelli* (1989) 54 CCC (3d) 121.

E6.49 The nature of the game being played and its inherent contacts and rules must be examined. Some sports allow for a greater degree of contact than do others.

For example, 'light contact' sports such as basketball and netball allow only limited contract, whereas a greater degree of contact would be lawful in both codes of rugby.

E6.50 The conditions under which the sport was being played must also be examined. Was the sport being played informally, as in a game between friends in the park, or more formally, as within a league structure? A lesser degree of contact would be expected in the former case than in the latter.

E6.51 The nature of the injury-causing act and its surrounding circumstances must then be looked at to establish whether it was an integral part of the playing of the game or whether it was an assault unrelated to the aims of the game. Within this element, the extent of the force used and the degree of risk associated with performing the challenge in this particular manner can also be examined. If it is too dangerous, such as a spear tackle in either code of rugby, or an attack with the stick in hockey, then an assault will have been committed.

E6.52 The relative skill of the players should *not* be considered, as the same rules will apply to all participants in the same sport. A high, late football tackle that breaks an opponent's leg is an assault regardless of the level of play at which it occurs. The lack of skill of a particular player should not be capable of providing him or her with a defence to a criminal act. On the other hand, sports participants should not be punished for their lack of ability to play the game, but only for the dangerousness of their conduct in performing acts associated with the game.

E6.53 The rules *and* the playing culture of the game will determine the contacts to which participants consent. An act not in breach of the rules and not punished by the referee is less likely to be viewed as criminal as one that is in breach and was so punished. However, whether or not an act was in breach of the rules of the game and whether or not the act was penalised by the referee should not be conclusively determinative of criminal liability.

E6.54 Finally, the court looks to the mens rea of the defendant and what he was trying to do. Again, if the intention of the defendant was to perform a move associated with the playing of the sport, then the act is more likely to have been consented to, as opposed to an act that was simply intended to cause hurt or injury.

E6.55 Effectively, the criminal court will have to balance the expectations of the participants in a sport to be allowed to 'play the game' with the public interest in preventing acts of violence. The court must decide whether an act is a legitimate means of playing the sport in question and therefore lawful, or alternatively an unlawful assault unconnected with the playing of that sport. According to the Canadian approach, which the author hopes and expects will be followed by the English courts, participants will be held to consent to those acts that are an integral part of the playing culture of their sport but not to those outside of that playing culture.

E6.56 Such an approach does not allow sports participants to set their own limits on the acts to which consent can apply. In particular, outside of lawfully constituted combat sports[1], sports participants will not be able to consent to the intentional infliction of grievous bodily harm upon themselves. When cases of participator violence reach the courts, the judiciary has taken the stance that hard play can be tolerated but violent and dangerous conduct will not be[2]. In particular, off-the-ball violence will not be tolerated. In *R v Billinghurst*[3], despite a wealth of evidence from past and current rugby union players that punching was both expected and accepted by all participants, the judge held that consent could not apply to any punches thrown during the game. Punching may have been accepted by the participants but it was not accepted by the law. The defendant was convicted of an OAPA 1861, s 20 assault. Nor does consent apply to deliberately high or late tackles[4], or to any off-the-ball assault[5].

1 See para E6.77 et seq.
2 *R v Billinghurst* [1978] Crim LR 553; and para E6.41.
3 See n 2.
4 *R v Goodwin* (1995) 16 Cr App Rep (S) 885.
5 *R v Lloyd* (1989) 11 Cr App Rep (S) 36.

E6.57 The dearth of cases involving on-the-ball incidents demonstrates that as long as the injurious contact has something to do with the playing of the game, then the injured party will most likely be deemed to have consented to it. This will extend to some acts of foul play, such as pushing and tripping, even if this causes injury. However, where the injury-causing act is clearly outside of the playing culture of a sport, or carries too great a risk of causing injury, then consent should not operate as a defence even in an on-the-ball context. This test will, of necessity, be fluid and expert witnesses, such as current and/or former players, coaches and commentators, may well be called to give their opinion on the acceptability or otherwise of a particular challenge.

E6.58 The defence of consent will not be available to assaults that are committed after the end of the game or once a player has been withdrawn or sent off from the field of play. Any incident that occurs off the pitch or in the tunnel as the players leave the pitch is treated simply as a criminal assault. Two successful prosecutions clearly illustrate the point; in neither case could the victim be said to have consented in any way to the assault.

E6.59 R v Kamara In *R v Kamara*[1], the defendant, a professional football player, punched and broke the jaw of the victim, a member of the opposing team, after the final whistle of their match. The defendant was charged with assault inflicting grievous bodily harm under s 20 of the OAPA 1861 and claimed that he had suffered a high degree of racial abuse throughout the game. He pleaded guilty to the assault and apologised for his behaviour. It was also noted by the court that he had been fined and dropped by his club. He was fined £1,200 by the court and ordered to pay £250 in compensation to the victim.

1 (1988) Times, 15 April.

E6.60 R v Cantona In *R v Cantona*[1], the defendant had been sent off for a challenge that occurred during a professional football match. As he walked towards the players' tunnel, he was abused by a spectator. The defendant performed a flying kick at the spectator, catching him on the chest. The defendant was fined approximately £10,000 by both his club and the Football Association. On conviction for common assault, the defendant was sentenced to 120 hours of community service.

1 (1995) Times, 25 March.

E6.61 In Scotland the law operates in a broadly similar way[1]. In 1996, the Lord Advocate issued a series of instructions to Scottish Chief Constables outlining the circumstances in which incidents of participator violence should be brought before the courts. The Lord Advocate's main concern was that the police were not distracted from their main role as the primary source of control for the attendant spectators. The police should only become involved with participator violence where the incident went 'well beyond' that which would be expected during 'normal play'[2]. Although no definition is provided of either 'normal play' or that which goes 'well beyond' it, the sentiments clearly echo those of the Canadian courts[3]. Under this approach, consent will operate as a defence for the majority of cases where participator violence is concerned and only the most serious assaults, or those which have little or nothing to do with the playing of the game, should result in criminal action and ultimately conviction. However, no similar prosecution guidelines have been issued by the CPS for incidents that occur in England and Wales.

1 For more details on the Scottish approach to this issue, see Stewart *Sport and the Law: The Scots Perspective* (2000, Butterworths); Clark and Gane *A Casebook on Scottish Criminal Law* (2nd edn, 2001), ch 8.
2 See further Miller 'Criminal law and sport in Scotland: the Lord Advocate's Instructions of 10 July 1996 to Chief Constables' [1996] 4(2) SATLJ 40; and James and Gardiner 'Touchlines and Guidelines' [1997] Crim LR 38.
3 See para E6.48.

(b) Self-defence

E6.62 Very occasionally, self-defence may be an appropriate defence to a criminal charge arising from an incident of participator violence. Provided that the defendant is found to have honestly believed that he needed to use reasonable force either to repel or to prevent an attack on himself or another, and in fact only objectively reasonable force was used, then the defence will be available[1]. In the sporting context, this is likely to be applicable only where an off-the-ball incident has occurred, for example where a player is being attacked by another and takes action to protect himself. In *R v Hardy*[2], a case involving a group of rugby players, the defendant was acquitted of manslaughter after he killed an opponent with a single punch. His plea of self-defence was accepted as it was found that he was being attacked from behind and punched on the back of the head. His punch was a reasonable reaction in defence of himself to try and prevent further attacks.

1 *R v Williams* [1987] 3 All ER 411.
2 *R v Hardy* (1994) Guardian, 27 July.

(c) Involuntary reflex

E6.63 In America, a defendant charged with aggravated assault might seek to plead the defence of 'involuntary reflex', or 'instinctive reaction'. The availability of this defence under US criminal law may go some way to explaining why so few cases of participator violence have reached the criminal courts in the US. In *State v Forbes*[1], following an on-ice fight in a professional ice hockey match, the defendant and victim had both been sin-binned for seven minutes. On their return to the ice, the victim approached the defendant from behind and words were exchanged. The defendant hit out with the butt end of his stick and struck the victim in the face before hitting his head repeatedly on the ice. The victim suffered a fractured eye socket and required 25 stitches in his face. The defendant claimed that his conduct was an instinctive reaction based on how he had been taught to respond to such incidents ever since he had taken up hockey. Thus, there was no mens rea for the assault. This argument was sufficiently successful to force a hung jury and cause the prosecutor not to ask for a retrial.

1 *State v Forbes*, unreported (Case 63280 Minn Dist Ct 12 September 1975).

E6.64 The closest analogous defence in English law would be automatism. Automatism is a complete defence to a criminal charge where it can be shown that the defendant was acting without voluntary control of his actions[1]. The involuntary action must be produced by an external cause, such as concussion from a blow to the head, or post-traumatic stress disorder[2]. However, in the vast majority of cases, including most if not all cases of participator violence, the defendant will retain sufficient voluntary control over his actions for the defence to fail[3]. Further, the lack of a sufficiently external cause of the involuntary conduct would make this defence even harder to prove. The ongoing training regime of a club or sport is extremely unlikely to be accepted by courts in England as sufficient reason for committing an assault of this nature[4].

1 *Bratty v A-G for Northern Ireland* [1963] AC 386.
2 *R v T* [1990] Crim LR 256.
3 *A-G's Reference (No 2 of 1992)* [1994] QB 91.
4 Evidence that such a training regime was in place is more likely to give rise to a claim of vicarious liability on the part of a club where a tortious action has been brought by the victim. See for example, *Tomjanovich v California Sports Inc* [No H-78-243 (SD Tx 1979)].

D Sentencing for participator violence

(a) The sentences imposed

E6.65 In general, the custodial sentences received for committing a criminal assault whilst playing in a sports match appear to be about one third of the length of sentences passed for assaults committed in other contexts, despite the degree of injury that is often caused by the assault and the means by which it is caused[1]. For example, in *R v Lloyd*[2], the defendant had deliberately kicked a prone player during a rugby union match, fracturing his cheekbone. The defendant was charged with causing grievous bodily harm with intent under s 18 of the OAPA 1861. The court commented that sport is not a licence for thuggery, but imposed a sentence of only 18 months' imprisonment. In *R v Shervill*[3], after a similar incident in a football match, resulted in the laceration of the victim's face, requiring stitches, the defendant was convicted of unlawful wounding under s 20 of the OAPA 1861, but sentenced to only two months imprisonment. Where an off-the-ball head-butting incident shattered the victim's eye socket and cheekbone, following conviction under s 18 of the OAPA 1861 the defendant received a six-month custodial sentence[4]. Where the conviction is for assault occasioning actual bodily harm, the sentences are even shorter. In two separate cases, the defendant broke their victim's jaw with an off-the-ball punch in a football match. One received a sentence of six months imprisonment[5], the other 28 days[6].

1 For further detail, see Thomas *Current Sentencing Practice* (2001, Sweet & Maxwell), Vol 3, paras B2–23CO8 and B2–33A15; and para E6.68 et seq.
2 (1989) 11 Cr App Rep (S) 36.
3 (1989) 11 Cr App Rep (S) 284.
4 *R v Piff* (1994) 15 Cr App Rep (S) 737.
5 *R v Birkin* [1988] Crim LR 854.
6 *R v Lincoln* (1990) 12 Cr App Rep (S) 250.

E6.66 On the other hand, in the most recent reported case, *R v Moss*[1], the defendant was found to have punched an opponent off-the-ball in a game of rugby union, fracturing the victim's eye socket. He was convicted of inflicting grievous bodily harm under s 20 of the OAPA 1861, and imprisoned for eight months.

1 [2000] 1 Cr App Rep (S) 307.

E6.67 The above cases demonstrate that despite the similarity in the injuries caused and the ways that those injuries were inflicted, the actual sentence imposed can vary dramatically. The length of sentence imposed can vary from around one to 18 months in jail. The only constant factor is that compared to assaults that cause injuries of a similar nature committed outside the context of participation in sports, the sentences imposed are relatively short.

(b) *Arguments in support of mitigation of sentence*

E6.68 One explanation for the relatively minor punishments imposed on sports participants is the increasing number of arguments in support of pleas in mitigation that have been accepted by the courts. This mitigation is specific to sports cases and would not carry as much weight outside of sport as it does where participator violence is concerned.

E6.69 Thus, each of the following reasons have been used by the courts to explain why a comparatively short sentence has been imposed on the sports defendant. In *R v Birkin*[1], the seriousness of the injury was found to be neither expected nor intended. In *R v Lincoln*[2], the incident had occurred in the heat of the moment following a degree of provocation from the victim[3]. Finally in *R v Goodwin*[4], the victim had chipped the ball over the head of the defendant and then tried to run around him. The defendant elbowed him in the face, fracturing his cheekbone, jaw, palate and two molars. He was convicted of assault inflicting grievous bodily harm under s 20 of the OAPA 1861. However, the court took into consideration that the incident had taken place at about the time that one of the parties was playing the ball, and that the defendant had been banned by the governing body from playing rugby league for 14 months as a result of the incident, and therefore imposed only a four-month custodial sentence.

1 [1988] Crim LR 854.
2 (1990) 12 Cr App Rep (S) 250.
3 The 'provocation' was that the victim had stood, legitimately, just inside the touchline whilst the defendant took a throw in during a football match, thereby impeding his follow-through.
4 (1995) 16 Cr App Rep (S) 885.

E6.70 Despite their similarity of purpose, namely to punish those performing acts of participator violence in sports, the roles of the criminal courts and a sport's disciplinary process do not have as great an impact upon each other as might be expected. Where, as in *R v Goodwin*[1], the disciplinary tribunal sits in judgment on the defendant before the case has gone to trial, any ban imposed on the defendant may be taken into consideration by the court on sentencing. Similarly, the fines imposed on the defendants in *R v Kamara* and *R v Cantona* by their clubs and/or governing body would seem to have been taken into account by the courts in sentencing them for assault[2]. However, governing bodies have also been aware that to proceed to an internal disciplinary hearing whilst there is an ongoing criminal investigation may prejudice any eventual trial, and so have suspended their own proceedings pending completion of the criminal proceedings. For example, the Rugby Football Union's disciplinary tribunal did not hear the case against William Hardy until after the completion of the criminal process[3]. Theoretically, if a governing body does not stay the disciplinary process in deference to the criminal proceedings, an injunction may be granted to avoid prejudicing the defendant's case[4].

1 See para E6.69
2 See paras E6.59 and E6.60.
3 See para E6.62.
4 See, by way of analogy, *Conteh v Onslow-Fane* (1975) Times, 26 June.

E6.71 At present, although there is no authority on the issue, it is likely that a court would consider an assault against a referee to be more serious than an assault against another participant. As such an attack would be both against a figure of authority and unconnected with the playing of the game, a sentence towards the higher end of the scale should be expected. Pleas of the mitigation should be of little relevance, although a lengthy ban imposed by the relevant governing body may still lead to some form of reduction in the sentence imposed.

E Compensation through the criminal justice system

E6.72 One of the reasons for the increased use of the criminal law by victims of participator violence is to secure some form of compensation for their injuries where a civil action for damages is not a viable option[1]. To secure a Compensation Order from a defendant or to instigate a claim for compensation under the Criminal Injuries Compensation Scheme, a victim must report the incident to the police and co-operate with their investigation. If the victim does not take these steps as soon as is practicable after the injury has occurred, then both of the routes to compensation through the criminal justice system will be closed to him.

1 See para E6.7.

(a) Compensation orders

E6.73 Under s 130 of the Powers of Criminal Courts (Sentencing) Act 2000, the court can impose a compensation order on a convicted defendant for the benefit of the victim[1]. However, there are a number of limitations to this procedure. First, a conviction must be secured: a compensation order can only be imposed on the offender who is legally found to have caused the injuries. Secondly, the award is means-tested and must be capable of being paid within in a reasonable time, usually within two to three years[2]. Thirdly, the court will assess the amount of the claim by making reference to the tariff-based guidelines of the Criminal Injuries Compensation Scheme, which generally award a lesser amount of compensation than would be the case following a successful civil action[3]. Finally, where the trial proceeded in the magistrate's court, the maximum payable under a compensation order is £5,000 per conviction[4], which may be wholly inadequate in comparison to the victim's actual loss.

1 Section 130 of the Powers of Criminal Courts (Sentencing) Act 2000:
'(1)A court by or before which a person is convicted of an offence, instead of or in addition to dealing with him in any other way, may, on application or otherwise, make an order (in this Act referred to as 'compensation order') requiring him–

(a) to pay compensation for any personal injury, loss or damage resulting from that offence or any other offence which is taken into consideration by the court in determining sentence …

(4) Compensation under subsection (1) above shall be of such amount as the court feels appropriate, having regard to any evidence and to any representations that are made by or on behalf of the accused or the prosecutor.'

2 *R v Olliver and Olliver* (1989) 11 Cr App Rep (S) 10.

3 See para E6.74.

4 Section 131 of the Powers of Criminal Courts (Sentencing) Act 2000.

(b) The Criminal Injuries Compensation Scheme

E6.74 A potentially more effective source of damages would be to make a claim under the Criminal Injuries Compensation Scheme (CICS). The CICS is a state-run compensation scheme designed to compensate anyone who has been injured by a criminal act[1]. The injury can be physical, a recognised psychiatric illness, for example post-traumatic stress disorder, or the contraction of a disease, for example tetanus, but it must have been inflicted criminally. The first step that the victim must take is to report the incident to the police. A failure to do this will bar any potential claim. The victim must then apply to the CICS, describing the circumstances in which the injury occurred and the nature of the injury inflicted. The burden of proving these issues lies with the victim, but only to the civil standard, ie on the balance of probabilities.

1 Only the salient features of the scheme are outlined here. For more detail, see Goldrein *Butterworths Personal Injury Litigation Service* (2001, Butterworths), Pt XVI.

E6.75 Further, to be successful with a claim, the victim must co-operate with the police investigation into the incident, the claim must be brought within two years of the injury-causing act, and the value of the claim must exceed £1,000. Finally, the conduct of the victim is taken into account when establishing whether the value of the claim ought to be reduced or denied. Outside of the sports context, the CICS will look to the previous claims and convictions of the victim to try and establish whether he has brought the injury on himself. It is not clear what might be taken into account where the victim of participator violence is concerned; however, his previous disciplinary record may be relevant.

E6.76 The advantage of the CICS is that it pays out, if the foregoing conditions are satisfied, even without a conviction. Thus, for example, where the perpetrator cannot be found, or the CPS decides in its discretion not to prosecute him, the victim can still receive compensation. The disadvantages are that the tariff system used by the CICS is lower than the awards handed down by the courts in a tort action, a victim cannot claim for the first 28 weeks of lost earnings, and there must be complete cooperation with the police investigation, for which the victim might show a degree of reluctance[1].

1 See www.cics.gov.uk for a claim form and notes on the application process.

3 COMBAT SPORTS

E6.77 The legal status of combat sports poses particular problems. It requires that fighting that would in any other context be deemed to be unlawful be deemed lawful and in the public interest when performed in the name of sport. However, despite being considered an anomaly by the Law Commission[1], the fact remains that boxing and other lawfully constituted combat sports are exempted from the normal operation of the law of assault and consent.

1 Law Com no 134, *Criminal Law: Consent and Offences Against the Person*, (1994) London: HMSO, para 10.19 et seq.

E6.78 The difficulty faced by all combat sports, including boxing, is that there is no fully argued legal authority that explains how and why they are exempted from the normal operation of the criminal law. Indeed, no case has specifically ruled, as part of its ratio decidendi, that boxing is a lawful form of fighting and therefore exempted from the general rule on consent. Instead the exemption is implied from the decision of the House of Lords in *R v Coney*[1]. In that case, the court was discussing the legality of a prize fight, to determine whether the spectators could be criminally liable as accessories to the assaults occurring during the bout. The House of Lords ruled that prize fighting was unlawful because the protagonists intended to cause each other injury; their fists, through training, are analogous to dangerous weapons which they are not at liberty to use; prize fights give rise to disorderly crowds who cause breaches of the peace; and prize fighting is not fighting in the name of sport. In contrast, fighting in the guise of sparring was considered to be legally acceptable because of the increased precautions taken by and regulations imposed upon the fighters. There was also the adherence to the Marquis of Queensbury's Rules, the use of padded gloves as opposed to bare knuckle fighting, that the fight should last a predetermined number of rounds (as opposed to until one of the fighters could no longer continue) and that it was undertaken in private as a test of skill rather than in public for reward. From this, it has been inferred that modern boxing is also a lawful activity and exempted from the general rule on consent[2].

1 (1882) 8 QBD 534.
2 *R v Brown* [1993] 2 WLR 556 per Lord Templeman.

E6.79 Notwithstanding the weakness of this reasoning, it is extremely unlikely that boxing and other lawfully constituted combat sports would be held by the courts to be unlawful. It would instead require an Act of Parliament to declare that these sports should be illegal and that those who practise them be labelled as criminals. As Parliament has consistently refused to outlaw boxing over the past 40 years, its special status seems assured[1].

1 See further para A1.73; and Gardiner *Sports Law* (2nd edn, 2001, Cavendish) pp 685–692.

E6.80 Boxing is therefore a lawful sport and any injuries inflicted during the course of participation in boxing are deemed to be impliedly consented to by the victim and therefore are not criminal offences. As is the case with other contact sports, a criminal offence will only be committed where the injury is caused by a blow outside of the rules or playing culture of the sport[1]. For example, deliberate blows below the belt or 'rabbit punches' to the back of the head would be outside of the scope of the consent of the participants and therefore, theoretically, criminal assaults.

1 See para E6.41 et seq.

E6.81 *R v Coney* discussed wrestling in the same terms as sparring/boxing[1], and wrestling can therefore be considered to be a lawfully constituted combat sport, falling within the same exception to the general rule on consent. However, the status of other combat sports, particularly the various codes of martial arts and limited rules fighting, is less clear. The main difficulty here is the lack of any definition of a lawfully constituted combat sport or any mechanism outside of the court structure for deciding such an issue[2]. However, it is unlikely that a prosecution would be brought for any act performed as part of a sport that was recognised by UK Sport or one of the four regional sports councils. Such sports, for example judo, can draw close analogies with boxing and wrestling. They have a universally accepted, codified system of rules, administered by a competent governing body, overseen by qualified referees, with sufficient safeguards against injury in place and adequate post-fight medical provision available. The acceptance by the state and society of such sports, and their inclusion in the Olympic programme, would undoubtedly see them fall within the scope of the exemption granted to boxing.

1 (1882) 8 QBD 534 at 549 per Stephen J.
2 See further Law Com no 139, *Consent in the Criminal Law* (1995, HMSO), Pt XIII.

E6.82 Others of the more modern, hybrid forms of fighting, such as kick-boxing, or any of the various forms of 'limited rules' fighting, will have difficulty in fitting into the boxing exemption. They lack the necessary degree of organisation at governing body level, the consistency and coherency in their rules and adequate medical facilities at the fight itself. They bear a much closer resemblance to prize fighting than to boxing or wrestling. Until a means of recognition is established, these sports will continue to operate on the periphery of the law. Without the operation of the exception granted to boxing, all such fighting would be considered outside of the public interest and therefore illegal, being more analogous to street-fighting[1]. This would leave the combatants open to charges of assault and anyone else associated with the fight, such as the promoter, trainers and crowd, potentially liable as accessories to the unlawful assaults committed by the protagonists themselves[2]. However, without a complaint from an identifiable 'victim', a successful prosecution is unlikely. A number of such bouts have taken place in recent years with some attendant controversy but, as yet, without police involvement.

1 *A-G's Reference (No 6 of 1980)* [1981] QB 715. Fighting with single sticks or quarterstaffs is also mentioned in *R v Coney* as a lawfully constituted combat sport. However, it is unlikely that the exemption would still extend to this kind of combat. Its lack of regulation, in that there is no recognised governing body and no formal rules or competition structure, would place it outside of the exemption granted to boxing.
2 See para E6.33.

4 LAW REFORM

E6.83 In recent years, there has been a series of reports and recommendations about how the criminal law offences against the person and the law of consent should evolve in the future. The particular need for reform of the law of assault and consent has been clearly acknowledged[1].

1 Smith and Hogan *Criminal Law* (9th edn, 1999, Butterworths), p 497 and for details of the proposed new offences, p 429. For the full text and historical development of the proposals see Home Office Consultation Document *Violence: Reforming the Offences Against the Person Act 1861* (1998, HMSO).

E6.84 The Home Office Consultation Document *Violence: Reforming the Offences Against the Person Act 1861* of February 1998 acknowledged that:

> That Act was itself not a coherent statement of the law but a consolidation of much older law. It is therefore not surprising that the law has been widely criticised as archaic and unclear and that it is now in urgent need for reform.

Lord Ackner has agreed with blunter criticism that the Act 'is a rag-bag of offences brought together from a wide variety of sources with no attempt, as the draftsman frankly acknowledged, to introduce consistency or form'[1]. But, notwithstanding the admitted urgency, nothing more has been heard from the Home Office since February 1998, so lawyers and students must continue to grapple with archaic and unclear law. The present government has no immediate plans to enact the draft Bill appended to the Home Office's Consultation Document.

1 *R v Savage* [1991] 4 All ER 698 at 721

E6.85 Although the above criticism is directed specifically at the OAPA 1861, much the same can be said of the law of consent. Two Law Commission Consultation Papers were published in the 1990s specifically reviewing the law of consent[1]. In respect of sport, the Law Commission proposed that victim should be able to consent to a higher degree of injury (ie serious injury or grievous bodily harm) than is currently the case. However, such injuries could only be inflicted whilst playing or practising recognised sports in accordance with their rules[2]. This would mean that the law would regress to a more restrictive approach than has been developed through the common law. In the author's view, this is not the correct approach[3]. Again, despite the perceived urgent need for reform of the law, a third and final Consultation Paper is still awaited.

1 Law Com no 134, *Consent and Offences Against the Person* (1994) London: HMSO; and Law Com no 139, *Consent in the Criminal Law* (1995) London: HMSO (LCCP 139).
2 LCCP 139, para. 12.68. See LCCP 139, ch 13 for the proposed mechanism for recognising lawful sports.
3 See paras E6.41 and E6.47.

5 LIABILITY FOR MATCH FIXING

E6.86 The recent high-profile scandals in cricket, involving Hansie Cronje (who was found guilty), and in football, involving Bruce Grobelaar and Hans Segers (who were acquitted at their criminal trials), have brought to light a further area of potential criminal liability arising from the on-field conduct of participants in sports event, namely match fixing[1]. Match fixing occurs where the player accepts money from a third party to influence the outcome of a sports fixture. Most sports have regulations in place making such conduct a serious disciplinary offence[2]. However, theoretically at least, criminal charges may also lie.

1 See further, Gardiner et al *Sports Law* (2nd edn, 2001, Cavendish), p 358.
2 See further para A2.46. See for example, the International Cricket Council's Code of Conduct for Players and Team Officials which contains possibly the most developed regulations on betting, http://www.cricket.org/link_to_database/NATIONAL/ICC/RULES/CODE_OF_CONDUCT.pdf.

A Section 1 of the Prevention of Corruption Act 1906

E6.87 Grobelaar and Segers were both professional football goalkeepers accused of taking money to let in goals and thereby improperly influence the outcome of games. They were both charged with conspiracy to commit an offence under s 1 of the Prevention of Corruption Act 1906. Grobelaar was also charged individually under that section, which states that:

> [a]ny agent [who] corruptly accepts or obtains, or agrees to accept or attempts to obtain, from any person, for himself or for any other person, any gift or consideration as an inducement or reward for doing or forbearing to do, or for having done or forborne to do, any act in relation to his principal's affairs or business; or for showing or forbearing to show favour or disfavour to any person in relation to his principal's affairs or business

is guilty of an offence. In respect of match fixing, all that is required is that the player accepts money, or any other gift or reward, to influence corruptly the outcome of a match. Grobelaar and Segers were both acquitted[1].

1 See further the report of the subsequent libel trial, *Grobbelaar v News Group Newspapers Ltd* [2001] EWCA Civ 33, [2001] 2 All ER 437.

B Section 17 of the Gaming Act 1845

E6.88 A possible alternative charge would be under s 17 of the Gaming Act 1845, which states that:

> [e]very person who shall, by any fraud or unlawful device or ill practice in playing at or with cards, dice, tables, or other game, or in bearing a part in the stakes, wagers, or adventures, or in betting on the sides or hands of them that do play, or in wagering on the event of any game, sport, pastime, or exercise, win from any other person to himself, or any other or others, any sum of money or valuable thing

is guilty of an offence. Again, a match fixer who accepted money to influence the outcome of a game, or some aspect of it such as the number of corners conceded as part of a spread bet, could theoretically be guilty of this offence. However, the author is not aware of any prosecutions brought under this section in relation to match fixing.

C Conspiracy to defraud

E6.89 Finally, where either of the above offences is committed by two or more persons in agreement with each other, then a conspiracy to defraud may exist. Such a conspiracy may be charged as either statutory conspiracy, under s 1 of the Criminal Law Act 1977, or as the common law offence of conspiracy to defraud[1]. The important aspect of a conspiracy charge is that it is complete on agreement. Money need not change hands, or if it has, the match to be fixed need not have yet taken place. The agreement itself is the crime, not the performance of the agreed acts[2].

1 See further Smith and Hogan *Criminal Law* (9th edn, 1999, Butterworths), ch 13.
2 *R v Anderson* [1986] AC 27, [1985] 2 All ER 961.

CHAPTER E7

TAX AND FINANCIAL PLANNING FOR INDIVIDUALS

Richard Baldwin (Deloitte & Touche)

Contents

1 INTRODUCTION

E7.1 The affairs of sports people give rise to particular financial issues; often their working life is short and their income unpredictable. In many cases they start their career as a hobby and later success causes it to take off. Income may be low for years or stardom and recognition immediate. The working life span is uncertain since careers can end at an early age as a result of injury. Peak earnings are unlikely to continue for long and it is essential to plan for tax and to provide funds for ultimate retirement.

E7.2 Elite sports people are very visible. Their problems, particularly personal ones, can usually be found on the back pages of the press. They are often emotional and unpredictable as individuals and advising them requires great care.

E7.3 The tax authorities take a keen interest in sport. The Inland Revenue in particular will often build up significant information and knowledge about the individual's activities. As a result, those at the top of their sport attract a great deal of Inland Revenue attention. Unfortunately, however, financial information on sports people is often not particularly well kept. This makes it difficult to advise on financial and tax matters, particularly for those who are self-employed with many sources of income.

E7.4 Often their tax affairs are in arrears, returns and accounts not being submitted on time, even though the tax due is substantial. These cases are ripe for investigation and will often deliver substantial back tax. Even where tax reporting is up-to-date, it is not always accurate; the Inland Revenue gets a significant amount of information from other sources to check the accuracy of the income and expenses reported.

2 IMPORTANCE OF FINANCIAL PLANNING

A The availability of information

E7.5 The basics of financial planning for sports people are similar to those for other high earning individuals, ie income needs to be maximised and expenses controlled. However, sports people typically have additional considerations which must be borne in mind arising from their special circumstances. Financial planning involves ensuring that they:

- have sufficient disposable income to meet personal expenses;
- provide properly for the payment of taxes; and
- make adequate provision for funding in the long run in retirement.

E7.6 Personal objectives should be taken into account. It may be necessary to organise borrowing in the short term to meet financing requirements. For this, it will be essential to have reliable financial information.

B Potential problems

E7.7 Sports people have a history of failing to maintain adequate basic financial records, creating problems:

- If income receipts are not properly controlled, overdue or omitted income sources can go undetected temporarily or, in some cases, permanently.
- Inaccurate records can lead to overspending resulting in a lack of funds to meet future tax liabilities in respect of past earnings.
- Inaccurate and late tax returns and supporting records can render the taxpayer vulnerable to interest and penalties whether in respect of income tax or value added tax.
- Poor records can lead to inadequate tax reporting resulting in in-depth investigations by the tax authorities.

C Sources of income

E7.8 Many sports employees earn income outside their employment, and investment or promotional income should be properly recorded, together with related expenditure. The sources of income cover a whole range, from cash and consideration-in-kind through to prizes in the form of mementoes and trophies for permanent retention which would not ordinarily be regarded as income subject to tax. Details of all income should be recorded.

E7.9 The most common sources of income are:

- cash earnings, including bonuses;
- payments for the use of copyright;
- benefits in kind;
- competition prizes both in cash and in kind
- appearance money;
- a share in the pool of money or consideration in kind earned by team members, which is shared out;
- exhibition matches and competitions;
- sponsorship and endorsements;
- promotions and personal appearances;
- writing and broadcasting;
- image rights payments;
- video royalties.

D Contractual arrangements

E7.10 Contracts entered into will have an important impact on income, and equally importantly, when it is receivable or recognised in the accounts. Sometimes, however, contracts are poorly constructed, badly worded and are not clear on determining the basis for royalty entitlement or shares of profit. In the case of some sports, for example football, the governing body will determine the format of the playing contract to be followed. However, even in football, sportsmen will be entering into promotional contracts which are not in a standard form and require care and attention.

E7.11 Professional advice should be taken from a specialist with sports experience before contracts are executed to ensure that the contracts are complete and protect the position of the sports person. Certain specific points should be clearly dealt with:

- the services, rights or products covered;
- the length of the contract and provisions for termination;
- how any products are to be disposed of when the contract ends;
- entitlement to income arising after the contract expires but resulting from activities during the contract period;
- territories/locations in which the products or services are to be exploited;
- the basis for any royalties;
- the nature of any advances made and how they are to be recouped, if at all;
- provisions for the treatment of any withholding taxes;
- whether the amounts in the contract are inclusive or exclusive of VAT;
- how out-of-pocket expenses, eg for travelling, subsistence and professional fees, should be dealt with;
- agent's commission payment arrangements.

These are not exhaustive.

E Accounting for income and expenditure

E7.12 Financial planning objectives can only be achieved if records are kept in detail and updated regularly, ensuring that all income has been recognised and properly computed by the contractual due dates. This will ensure that income is not only received but also accurately reflected in accounts for the Inland Revenue. There will, no doubt, be areas for debate as to which period income will need to be reflected in, to comply with generally accepted accounting principles. Thus, for example, if advance royalties are paid, should they be treated as income on receipt or recognised as they are earned? Further, if the flow of payments under the contract is not even, how should this be reflected as income earned over the period of the contract?

E7.13 The benefits of accurately accounting for income are more than just satisfying the taxman:

- With accurate financial information, completeness of income tests may be performed and omissions identified.
- If actual receipts are compared with contractual entitlement, errors and omissions from royalty sources may be identified.
- Reviews of the financial information may enable the individual to decide whether the right to a royalty audit should be exercised.

E7.14 Control of expenditure is also important and generally is easier to exercise. If attention is paid to both sides of the equation, financial crises may be avoided. Particular areas of difficulty will be the identification of and distinction between personal and business expenditure. Detailed records will enable the sports person to save tax if he can justify the expenditure for business purposes.

F Budgeting

E7.15 Future tax and financial planning can only take place if there is adequate information on current profitability and estimates of future profitability can be made. For business planning, a proper strategy for commercial development also needs up-to-date accounting information on which to base forecasts. As matters proceed, income and expenditure budgets will be compared with actual figures so that corrective action can be taken. Clearly, financial information is only one aspect of financial control, but it is a very necessary one if maximum benefits are to be derived from current and future income.

G Planning

E7.16 Planning for the financial affairs of a sportsman must take into account the unpredictability and unevenness of income, including elements that are likely to be recurring as well as allowing for the unexpected contingency. Fluctuating earnings means "plan as you go" in accounting for tax on an arising basis if there is a non-recurring or uneven income pattern. Personal objectives and preferences are vital, since tax planning initiatives which involve disruption to personal life may be of little value if they are not consistent with personal circumstances. Objectives may be to maximise income for personal spending; or alternatively a more conservative lifestyle accumulating capital for the future. Sports people will need counselling on their approach to financial planning and in particular dealing with financial commitments. Adequate insurance may be important to protect the individual from injury if not covered by the employing club. Cover will vary from protection for specific events to longer term cover for loss of earnings. Finally, advisers should incorporate planning for retirement at the end of the sportsperson's active career, which will normally include investment through a pension arrangement and consideration of investment strategy.

H Investment strategy

E7.17 In establishing an investment strategy, basic investment criteria should be the cornerstone, with the taxation position always in mind. An orderly process of establishing investments should be undertaken, looking at the risks as well as the returns. Investment plans should be based on personal circumstances and the following major factors:

- the lifetime scale of the investment and liquidity;
- personal requirements and choices;
- the return on investments;
- levels of acceptable risk;
- relative risk and return;
- diversification.

E7.18 Tax should also be considered in any investment plan, including tax effective investments such as ISAs, the rate at which income is taxed and whether income tax is withheld at source and the taxation of any gains, including the availability of the annual exemption. For the high earner, a financial planning team needs to be built, including accountants, solicitors and financial advisers in order that the optimum overall solution can be found.

E7.19 In formulating any financial plan, all taxes need to be considered, including income tax, capital gains tax, value added tax and inheritance tax. Great care needs to be taken with the bite which the taxman can potentially take out of income, gains and wealth.

3 LIABILITY FOR INCOME TAX

A Scope

E7.20 Broadly, the UK income tax system seeks to charge tax on income arising in the UK regardless of where the recipient is resident and the worldwide income of persons resident in the UK. Residence is determined in relation to the UK income tax year which for individuals runs from 6 April to 5 April. Increasingly overseas sportsmen and sportswomen come to the UK to play; notwithstanding the fact that they may be nationals of another country, they may become resident here, subject to tax on their worldwide income.

E7.21 UK income tax laws divide streams of income into schedules; for sportsmen they are principally Schedule D for the self-employed and Schedule E for employees. These schedules are different in their application and can make a significant difference to the tax and social security bill. The UK resident sportsman will not only be subject to income tax on earnings but also on investment income and capital gains tax on any gains from the disposal of chargeable assets. There are no special tax reliefs for sports people; the general tax rules for taxpayers apply to determine taxability. Often this can prove difficult in practice. Special rules for non-domiciled individuals provide tax benefits to the foreign national taking up UK residence and coming to pursue a sports career in the UK. There are also special withholding tax rules for payments to non-resident sports people performing in the UK[1].

1 See further para D3.114 et seq.

B Residence

E7.22 The UK residence and domicile rules are primarily derived from case law rather than statute. The short-term visitor will be regarded as resident in the UK if:

(a) he is physically present for 183 days or more in the UK during a tax year; or
(b) he visits the UK regularly and after four years the visits during those years have averaged 91 days or more per tax year, in which case he will be treated as resident from the fifth year.

Normally, the days of arrival and departure are ignored in counting the days spent in the UK.

E7.23 A longer term visitor is regarded as UK resident if:

(a) he is physically present for 183 days or more in the UK during a tax year; or
(b) he owns or leases accommodation in the UK.

E7.24 Individuals coming to the UK intending to live here permanently or to remain in the country for three years (two years if coming for a purpose such as employment) or more are regarded as resident from the day of arrival.

E7.25 Most UK-based sportsmen pursuing their career in the UK will be treated as resident and ordinarily resident, paying tax on worldwide income and gains.

C Overseas aspects

E7.26 A person's domicile is where an individual 'belongs', rather than where he or she is resident at any time. Certain income of individuals resident but not domiciled in the UK will not be liable to UK tax unless remitted to the UK. There are rules which catch constructive remittances, eg back-to-back loans. The remittance basis which often benefits non-domiciled sportsmen applies to:

- investment income from assets situated outside the UK;
- capital gains from chargeable assets outside the UK;
- foreign emoluments, ie earnings during the course of an employment with an overseas employer where the duties are performed wholly outside the UK.

If income from these sources is not remitted to the UK, it is not taxed here.

E7.27 A non-resident is liable to tax on UK source income arising from activities as a sports person. This could occur if he or she is employed and part of the duties of the employment are carried on in the UK or, if self-employed, part of his or her profession is carried on here, eg by playing in a tournament or event. Prima facie, non-residents have a requirement to file UK income tax returns, although in practice UK tax obligations are usually fulfilled by tax being deducted from payments made under the special UK withholding tax requirements for non-resident sportsmen and entertainers.

E7.28 A resident sportsman earning income from abroad enjoys no special reliefs from UK tax, whether employed or self-employed. Indeed, he may have an exposure to tax overseas, since generally the double tax treaties, which the UK has negotiated with foreign countries, do not provide relief for sportsmen and entertainers.

D Taxable income

E7.29 The main sources of taxable income are likely to be:

- income from employment with the sports club;
- if not in employment, self-employed income (typically in non-team sports), or, alternatively, if in employment, any external income from sponsorship, merchandising and other related commercial activities will constitute self-employed income;
- investment income, including interest and dividends;
- income from property.

E7.30 The taxable income from each income source is computed according to the particular rules of the applicable tax schedule, which will proscribe what expenses, if any, are deductible. There are further reliefs and allowances which can be deducted from the aggregated taxable income to arrive at total income chargeable to tax. The main reliefs and allowances are:

- the basic personal allowance;
- interest relief on loans for the purchase of certain shares, ie those in a close company (which might be the sports person's personal service company) where certain conditions are fulfilled;
- payments to charity under the Gift Aid provisions.

E Tax rates

E7.31 The total income thus computed is chargeable to tax at graduated income tax rates, which for the year ended 2002/2003 are:

	Tax rate	Income
Lower rate band	10%	£1 – £1,920
Basic rate band	22%	£1,921 – £29,490
Higher rate band	40%	£29,901 plus

E7.32 Successful individuals will generally be chargeable at the top marginal rate of tax of 40%. However, special complex rules relate to dividend income, to which a lower marginal rate applies and which, after taking account of the associated tax credit, gives rise to an effective tax charge of 25% on any UK dividends received by a higher rate taxpayer.

E7.33 Gains from chargeable assets, eg shares and second properties, will be chargeable to capital gains tax which, for higher rate taxpayers, will be at the 40% rate after deducting reliefs and the annual exemption of £7,700 for 2002/03.

F Tax payment dates

E7.34 Income tax and the payment thereof is dealt with under a self-assessment system under which income tax for a year of assessment will be payable by means of two interim payments of equal amounts. These will be based normally on the liability of the previous year and due on 31 January in the year of assessment and 31 July following it. A final balancing payment will be due on 31 January following the end of the income tax year, together with any capital gains that may be due.

E7.35 These interim payments on account will not be required where:

- more than 80% of the income tax due for the tax year is met from tax paid at source, eg from employment income;
- where the tax due is less than £500 after any offsets.

E7.36 A claim can be made to reduce payments on account for a tax year if the liability is expected to be lower than in the current year. This may arise because income is expected to be lower or allowances and reliefs higher or because more of the income is taxed at source in the current year.

E7.37 Interest is charged on late payments on account from the date that the tax is due until it is paid. A surcharge of 5% is also payable if any tax is not due by 28 February following the end of the tax year, rising to 10% if it is still not paid by the following 31 July.

E7.38 If a tax return is submitted by 30 September following the end of the tax year and the tax owed is less than £2,000 in total, it can be settled by adjusting the tax code for the next tax year. This facility is not available to self-employed sportsmen.

G Annual tax returns

E7.39 Sports people will normally be required by the Inland Revenue to fill in annual tax returns which are usually issued on 6 April immediately after the end of the tax year. They are due by 30 September following the end of the tax year if the Inland Revenue is to calculate the tax liability or if the past year's tax is to be collected by an adjustment of the PAYE code number.

E7.40 In other cases, the deadline for filing the tax return is 31 January following the end of the tax year. If it is not filed by this date, penalties may arise.

E7.41 Adequate records must be kept to complete the self-assessment tax return. The Revenue has issued detailed guidance on what records will be sufficient for this purpose and there are penalties if adequate records are not kept.

E7.42 The Inland Revenue may decide to raise an inquiry into a tax return. The issue of an inquiry notice should not give rise to alarm and does not mean that the tax return is necessarily wrong. If full disclosure has been made, the Inland Revenue must issue an inquiry notice within twelve months of the filing deadline.

4 TAXATION OF EARNINGS

A Employed versus self-employed

E7.43 The measure of income and the taxability of expenditure are different for employees and the self-employed. The third way in which income might be taxed, which is again different, is via a personal service or management company[1].

1 See para E7.48.

E7.44 Particular sports rules may dictate the way in which the sportsman pays tax. Thus, in professional football in England, the rules of the Premier and Football Leagues and the Football Association specify a standard form of agreement for professionals that must be entered into by the sportsman. This contains terms relating to the expiry of contracts, earnings and out-of-pocket expenses. Football's rules effectively mean that professional footballers are treated as employees[1]. The rules prohibit the use of a service company to engage the sportsman for his performances for the football club. Often, other professional team sports have similar provisions. There will be other instances, however, where the distinction between employed and self-employed status is not so clear.

1 See paras E1.18 and E1.19.

E7.45 Generally, there has been a tightening in Inland Revenue attitudes on self-employment, with the Revenue seeking to characterise the relationship as an employment in order to collect tax earlier at source under PAYE, and to collect more NIC. An important case in this regard was *Hall v Lorimer*[1], where the taxpayer, a self-employed vision mixer, successfully argued that he was assessable under Sch D not Sch E. As a result, the following circumstances may sustain a self-employed argument:

- The engagement consists of numerous short-term engagements of one or two days.
- The individual has a professional skill.
- He is registered for VAT.
- The individual invoices for his services and bears the risk of bad debts.
- The individual markets his own services.
- There are no formal conditions of engagement.
- The individual has substantial costs of running his profession and has the potential to suffer real commercial risk in doing so.

Not all of these need be present but the greater the number of these tests which are met the more compelling the case is for treatment as self-employment.

1 [1994] STC 23.

B Individual versus team sports

E7.46 Self-employment requires the individual to be independent of the person engaging him. Typically, the status will apply to sports where the individual competes on his or her own and not as part of a team. This is generally accepted by the Inland Revenue but, as noted above[1], the situation may be determined under the contractual relationships specified under the sports governing body rules.

1 See para E7.44.

E7.47 Most sports people participating in team sports will be regarded as employees because of the element of control required by the team club. Where sports people have such employments also have external commercial income, their tax affairs are likely to be complex.

C Personal service companies

E7.48 There may be advantages in setting up a personal service company where the sports rules allow. In this case, the individual would normally be appointed a director drawing remuneration and paying tax under Sch E. The company itself will pay corporation tax on its profits after the payment of remuneration. Alternatively, income can be taken from the company in the form of dividends taxable as investment income in the sports person's hands[1].

1 See further para D3.85 et seq.

E7.49 Legislation was introduced from 6 April 2000 covering perceived tax avoidance involving the use of personal service companies. This will not apply to companies owned by sports people as long as they would be regarded as self-employed in the various engagements which the company enters into but for the existence of the personal service company[1].

1 See further para D3.106 et seq.

E7.50 The advantages and disadvantages of using a service or management company need to be evaluated, including commercial risk, the tax burden on the earnings and profits accruing, national insurance and the ability to fund pension contributions.

D Amateur versus professional

E7.51 Many sports people are of no interest to the tax authorities because they do not receive anything from participating other than reimbursement of out-of-pocket expenses. Often they start off life as amateur members of local sports clubs run for the benefit of the members rather than commercially. The Inland Revenue is interested in those working on a sporting activity on a professional basis, ie trying to make a profit. Thus, for example, it has in the past accepted that non-contract players play for many semi-professional clubs for the love of it. They do not have any oral or written contract and only receive a reimbursement of their actual expenses. Essentially there are two categories of sports people: those who do not make a profit and are not taxable and those that do.

E7.52 Whether an individual is described as an amateur by his sport's rules is not decisive in considering the tax position. Leading individuals in particular sports will be taxed on their earnings from those sports, but the many who participate as a leisure pursuit or hobby will often escape tax. The distinction between a hobby and a trade, profession or vocation subject to tax, is very much a question of fact and degree.

E7.53 A practical approach set out in its manual is adopted by the Inland Revenue in determining whether there is a taxable self-employed activity. Even the presence of an excess of earnings over expenses and the fact that the whole of the individual's time may be devoted substantially to sporting and associated activities is not decisive in determining whether a taxable activity exists. Inspectors need to ascertain the full facts before making their minds up, which will include:

- the nature and scale of the activities and the way in which they are organised;
- competitions and events entered into in the relevant period;
- the individual's final position in each event and any prizes received;
- any grants or similar receipts from sporting or other organisations and documentary support;
- attendance or performance fees, sponsorship and endorsement fees, again with copies of documentation;
- income from associated activities, including journalism, television appearances, etc;
- the terms of any agreement with an agent negotiating contracts on the individual's behalf;
- the cost and nature of expenses.

E7.54 Often, the sports person's activities will change from a leisure pursuit to operating on a professional and taxable basis. The timing of this will require careful consideration and agreement with the Inland Revenue as to when taxability arises. It may be that past losses can be brought forward to be offset against earnings as a professional. Allowances may be due on any equipment purchases for use as a professional.

5 SPECIAL TYPES OF INCOME AND EXPENDITURE

E7.55 Particular types of income received give rise to interesting tax treatments which are outlined below.

A Inducement payments

E7.56 Sports people sometimes receive payments to induce them to become registered with and subsequently employed by a particular club. Sometimes these are prohibited by sports rules; alternatively, the rules may specify the way in which they may be made. Historically, tax-free inducement payments and signing-on fees have been allowed under the rules of rugby league and football, and the courts have upheld tax-free treatment because of their capital nature. The sportsman's argument succeeded because he permanently gave up personal benefits, eg the ability to play amateur sport in return for the payment. The commercialisation of sport in recent years means that nowadays such an argument for tax-free status is unlikely to be available. Thus, in today's football industry, signing-on fees paid to professional footballers are made available under their contracts and fully taxable.

B Prizes

E7.57 Prizes and voluntary payments are normally subject to tax as earnings where the individual participates with the prize in mind. A pragmatic approach is, however, adopted by the Inland Revenue where occasional prizes are received, for example, in the form of trophies where the value is not substantial. In such cases, tax may be avoided. Prizes are not always taxed since an international footballer succeeded in justifying his claim not to be taxable on payments from the English Football Association and a third party following his performances in the 1966 World Cup[1].

1 *Moore v Griffiths* (1972) 48 TC 338.

C Termination payments

E7.58 Where a termination payment of £30,000 or less is made outside of any contractual provisions, it may be tax-free. In order to qualify, the sports person must not be entitled to the payment under the contract nor be promised the payment orally. A termination payment made for giving up an employment as a result of permanent injury may be tax-free without any limits applying. It is not, however, safe to assume that generally on the termination of an employment £30,000 can be paid tax-free; great care is required.

D Testimonials and benefits

E7.59 Football and cricket often provide benefits and testimonials for sportsmen, although they are more common in cricket than they are in football. Typically, a match will be organised on behalf of the sportsman so that the club supporters can show their appreciation. If the organisation of the match is independent of the club, being undertaken by a committee following certain well-established guidelines, the entire profit from the match can be given to the sportsman tax-free. In recent years, sportsmen have been awarded benefit or testimonial years during which a number of fund-raising events have been organised in addition to the match itself. These include dinners, golf days and other money-raising events. Whilst, in practice, the Inland Revenue has to date not sought to tax the proceeds from these events in the majority of cases, because of the increasing commercialisation of the sector it may only be a matter of time before the Inland Revenue argues that a taxable trade was being carried on.

E Share schemes

E7.60 In recent years, government has sought to encourage employees to purchase shares or to be given options over shares in their employer. Tax favoured share acquisition arrangements have been introduced into the tax legislation. Some of these schemes allow employees to acquire shares without any tax charge arising until they are sold. In addition, employees owning shares and holding them for two years will only pay an effective tax rate of 10% on any gain when they ultimately dispose of them. In the case of the Enterprise Management Incentive scheme, which involves the granting of options to the employee, the holding period starts when the option is granted not when the shares are acquired. Despite the advantages of Inland Revenue approved schemes, such as the EMI, there is little evidence that either approved or unapproved schemes are being made available to employed sports people on any scale.

F Expenses and benefits

E7.61 Sports people who are employed pay tax on cash earnings and expenses reimbursed and benefits provided subject to a claim for business expenses incurred wholly and exclusively and necessarily in the performance of their duties as employees.

E7.62 The measure of the tax charge on a benefit is normally the cost of providing it and typical benefits include:

- a company car;
- petrol for private mileage;
- the use of assets, for example, televisions and furniture;
- loans that are interest-free or at a lower than market rate;
- the provision of living accommodation;
- the payment of removal expenses.

E7.63 Deductible business expenses would include travel and subsistence, eg travel to competitions and away matches, and overseas trips and costs. Where a company car is not provided, reimbursement of business mileage in accordance with certain fixed rates set out by the Inland Revenue will not be taxable nor subject to NIC. The expenses test is very strict and would not prima facie include expenditure on smart clothing that the individual chooses to wear, for example, when attending the sports stadium.

G Sponsorship

E7.64 Sponsorship arrangements usually require the sports person to provide promotional services, for example, to sell a product. The arrangements can take many forms and payment can be in cash or in kind, sometimes its value depending upon sporting performance. Normally the arrangements will be evidenced in writing and will be taxable as part of the self-employed's total income from sport. If he or she is employed, then the sponsorship arrangement, which is unconnected with the employing club, could be treated as self-employed income. Some sponsorship income might be taxed as employment income under the contractual arrangements entered into, but this is unlikely to be common.

E7.65 In arriving at taxable sponsorship income, it is possible to deduct expenses incurred in earning it. If consideration is received in kind, the Inland Revenue is likely to argue that the measure of profit is the market value of what is received. However, tax relief may be available either by way of an expenses claim, in the case of sportswear, or by way of capital allowances if equipment is provided.

H Merchandising and image rights

E7.66 Fees or royalties received in relation to the use of image, name or logo, count as taxable income. Usually services are provided as well, in which event costs associated with their provision may be deducted in arriving at the profit from the sporting activity. In the case of an employed sports person carrying on self-employed activities outside the employment, care is required in connection with ownership of image rights, since the employer may argue that such rights in connection with duties for the club belong to it. However, with care image rights can be segregated from the employment relationship, exploited by the individual and taxed under the more favourable self-employed rules or through a personal service company[1].

1 See further para D3.78 et seq.

6 INVESTMENT INCOME AND GAINS

E7.67 The normal rules apply in relation to the taxation of investment income and gains. As with other taxpayers, financial planning should involve consideration of tax favoured investments whilst recognising that taxation is only one element in making the investment decision. These include:

- national savings products;
- individual savings accounts;
- pensions;

- principal private residence;
- furnished holiday lettings;
- the Enterprise Investment Scheme;
- life assurance policies;
- FURBS[1].

This list is not exhaustive and professional advice should be taken before investing.

1 See para E7.73.

7 RETIREMENT PLANNING

A Types of person

E7.68 Maximum opportunity should be taken to provide for retirement tax efficiently. Approved pension schemes fulfil an important role in this process providing a major opportunity to convert taxable income into tax-free funds. Full tax relief will normally be available for contributions to any pension scheme and the income and capital gains arising on the funds invested will accumulate tax free. Tax is, however, paid on the part of the funds paid out as a pension on retirement.

E7.69 A practical problem is the difficulty of persuading sports people, who are often young and earning substantial amounts of money, that part of their earnings should be invested for the future into a pension fund, which may not be available for direct use for a number of years.

E7.70 There are different types of pension plan for employed and self-employed sports people respectively. The self-employed will use a personal pension plan. The employed may be a member of an occupational scheme established by the employer club to which employer and employee will contribute. Where the employer does not make available an occupational scheme, an employed sports person can take out a personal pension plan to provide for retirement.

B Benefits of approved schemes

E7.71 The benefits of approved retirement schemes are:

- contributions are tax deductible (subject to certain limits); the sums invested can accumulate free of income and capital gains tax;
- a tax-free lump sum can be taken on retirement with the balance taken by way of a taxable pension;
- lower retirement ages have been agreed by the Inland Revenue in respect of many categories of sports persons;
- contributions made by the employer are free of national insurance charges;
- for the more adventurous, investments made by schemes can be tailored to the requirements of the sports person either by means of a self-invested personal pension scheme or a small self-administered pension scheme;
- a tax-free lump sum can be paid on death.

C Limits on contributions

E7.72 There is a limited ability to fund for retirement through approved pension schemes, because there are limits on the deductibility of contributions depending on the type of scheme entered into. With personal pension schemes, these limits apply to the contributions and start at 17·5% of net earnings. For occupational schemes, the limits are generally set by the amount of funds needed to provide a maximum pension of two-thirds of final salary on retirement. In order to maximise the tax and commercial benefits from these arrangements, professional advice is essential.

D Funded unapproved retirement benefit schemes (FURBS)

E7.73 The restricted level of contribution made to an approved scheme may make it beneficial to establish a funded unapproved retirement benefit scheme (FURBS) for employed sports people. FURBS provide retirement benefits which do not have approval and, unlike approved schemes, there is no limit on the level of the contribution which the employer can make. However, this contribution will be treated as taxable in the employees' hands. Once the contribution has been made, investment income and capital gains resulting from the investment are subject to lower rates. Income is taxed at 10% on dividends, 20% on income from savings deposit accounts etc, and 22% on other income, eg property. Furthermore, any capital gains realised by the FURB is taxable at a lower rate of 34%. On retirement, the entire fund can be paid out with no further tax liability occurring. As is the case with approved schemes, there is a lower retirement age for many categories of sports person.

8 OTHER TAXES

A Capital gains tax

E7.74 Capital gains tax (CGT) is a tax on profits arising from the sale of certain assets. Shareholdings, property, businesses and works of art are all examples of assets that can result in a capital gain. Some assets are exempt from capital gains tax, which include:

- the individual's only or main residence;
- life assurance policies;
- UK government securities and certain corporate bonds;
- private motor cars;
- betting and lottery winnings;
- chattels sold for less than £6,000;
- foreign currency bought for personal spending.

E7.75 Losses suffered on the sale of assets can be set off against capital gains in the same year or in later years. They cannot normally be set off against income subject to income tax.

E7.76 The net capital gain after deducting eligible losses and the annual exemption is taxed at the sports person's top income tax rate.

E7.77 There is an allowance for inflation for periods of ownership before 17 March 1998, and if the asset was acquired before 31 March 1982, the market value at that date may be substituted for the cost in computing the gain if this is worthwhile.

E7.78 In 1998 a taper was introduced for capital gains purposes under which part of the gain, depending on length of ownership, was deducted in arriving at the chargeable gain. The rate of taper depends upon whether the asset is a business asset or non-business asset. Its effect can reduce the effective rate of tax to as little as 10% for business assets (after two years) and 24% for non-business assets (after 10 years).

B Inheritance tax

E7.79 Inheritance tax (IHT) is a tax on certain lifetime gifts and on estates on death. The tax applies to worldwide assets if the sports person is domiciled in the UK, but only to UK assets if the sportsman is not. Inheritance tax on death is due in respect of all of the assets held at that time or gifted in the seven years before death. A charge may arise during lifetime on gifts in certain types of trust arrangement. There are a number of reliefs and exemptions potentially the most important for the sports person being shares in his own company and lifetime gifts where he or she survives seven years.

E7.80 The threshold is relatively low and the rate high, and estates in excess of £250,000 (from 6 April 2002) are subject to the full rate of 40%. Whilst IHT is not one of the taxes of prime concern to sports people who are typically reasonably young, it should form part of any financial planning exercise to ensure that wills are appropriately drafted and adequate insurance arrangements are in place.

9 NATIONAL INSURANCE CONTRIBUTION OBLIGATIONS AND PLANNING

E7.81 National Insurance Contributions (NIC) are generally payable by all sports people working in the United Kingdom. The liability and type of contribution depends on whether the individual is employed or self-employed. As with the income tax position, it is not always clear on which side of the line the individual falls, and status will depend on facts of the particular case. Collection of NIC is administered by the Inland Revenue.

E7.82 The self-employed are required to pay Class II and Class IV contributions, the former being at a flat rate per week and the latter at a percentage rate geared to the profits earned in the self-employment. Employees are required to pay Class I primary contributions which, again, are graduated as a percentage of earnings with a cap on the total earnings against which employees pay their appropriate percentage until 2003/04 when an additional 1% will be charged on earnings over the upper limit. Employers are also required to pay secondary Class I contributions which are, again, percentage based on earnings, but with no upper limit. Employers are also required to account for NIC on taxable benefits. Contributions are collected through the PAYE system.

E7.83 A sports person who is both employed and self-employed during the year may pay excess contributions, but can apply for a certificate of deferment in respect of Class II and Class IV liabilities. This can be done by submitting the appropriate form to the Inland Revenue.

E7.84 The relatively high rates of employers' contribution means that in the past it has been worth planning to reduce NIC. However, in recent years, the scope for planning has reduced since the authorities have progressively closed down loopholes. The principal area for planning is the basis on which any non-sports club earnings are treated: because of the lower levels of contributions for the self-employed, it may be worth using a self-employed rather than a service or management company structure.

10 VALUE ADDED TAX

E7.85 A sports person who operates as a self-employed individual or through a personal service company may need to consider VAT. If income in either of those capacities exceeds the registration limit of £55,000, registration may be necessary. In general terms, the considerations relating to registration, the types of supply and record keeping are the same as those for sports clubs, which are dealt with elsewhere in this work[1]. In particular, there are severe penalties and interest if registration is not effected.

1 See para C2.33 et seq.

E7.86 Particular issues may arise where the sports person works outside the UK, since there may be a requirement to register for VAT or the equivalent sales taxes. There are also special rules where royalties are paid from a transfer or assignment of a copyright or from the granting of a licence to use a copyright. Sponsorship can also be a difficult area and should be distinguished from true donations for VAT purposes. A sponsorship arrangement will usually be evidenced by a contract, and great care is required to ensure that the sports person does not lose out from a VAT perspective. There should always be appropriate VAT clauses in such contracts. It should be remembered that it is the individual's responsibility to charge VAT if he or she should be registered and is providing a taxable supply. Failure to charge VAT will mean that the cost will be picked up by the sports person not the customer or client.

INDEX

[all references are to paragraph number]